Fodor's 93 Germany

Fodor's Travel Publications, Inc.
New York • Toronto • London • Sydney • Auckland

ISBN 0-679-02295-3

Fodor's Germany

Editor: Christopher Billy
Editorial Contributors: Charles Barr, Hampton Binden, Sheila Brownlee, Hannah Clements, Michael Cresswell, Clive Freeman, Birgit Gericke, George Hamilton, Andrew Heritage, Liz Hulme, Michael Kallenbach, Helmut Koenig, Graham Lees, Tony Peisley, Anita Peltonen, Isabelle Pöhlman, Marcy Pritchard, Linda K. Schmidt, Michael Shea, Robert Tilley, Susan Williams
Creative Director: Fabrizio La Rocca
Cartographer: David Lindroth
Illustrator: Karl Tanner
Cover Photograph: Kevin Galvin

Design: Vignelli Associates

Special Sales

Fodor's Travel Publications are available at special discounts for bulk purchases (100 copies or more) for sales promotions or premiums. Special editions, including personalized covers, excerpts of existing guides, and corporate imprints, can be created in large quantities for special needs. For more information write to Special Marketing, Fodor's Travel Publications, 201 East 50th Street, New York, NY 10022. Inquiries from Canada should be sent to Random House of Canada, Ltd., Marketing Dept., 1265 Aerowood Dr., Mississauga, Ontario L4W 1B9. Inquiries from the United Kingdom should be sent to Fodor's Travel Publications, 20 Vauxhall Bridge Rd., London, England SW1V 2SA.

MANUFACTURED IN THE UNITED STATES OF AMERICA
10 9 8 7 6 5 4 3 2 1

Contents

Maps

Foreword

We would like to express our gratitude to the German National Tourist Board, German Information Center, Berlin Tourist Office, German Rail, Inc., Lufthansa German Airlines, LTU International Airways, and KD German Rhine Line for their help and support. Special thanks go to Hedy Wuerz, Helga Brenner-Khan, Birgit Fickert, Lucille Hoshabjian, Wolfgang Osinski, and Jan Myers.

While every care has been taken to assure the accuracy of the information in this guide, the passage of time will always bring change and, consequently, the publisher cannot accept responsibility for errors that may occur.

All prices and opening times quoted here are based on information supplied to us at press time. Hours and admission fees may change, however, and the prudent traveler will avoid inconvenience by calling ahead.

Fodor's wants to hear about your travel experiences, both pleasant and unpleasant. When a hotel or restaurant fails to live up to its billing, let us know and we will investigate the complaint and revise our entries where the facts warrant it.

Send your letters to the editors of Fodor's Travel Publications, 201 East 50th Street, New York, NY 10022.

Highlights '93 and Fodor's Choice

Highlights '93

This year should see the end of most of the reunification-related hurdles that have made life difficult for visitors since the Berlin Wall fell in 1989. Rail travelers who despaired at the inconvenience of getting to Berlin or any other of the cities deep in formerly Communist-run East Germany will be happy to hear that the old East German state railway, the Reichsbahn, is finally to be absorbed by the much more efficient Bundesbahn, the west German system. The multimillion-D-mark merger will lead to much better services nationwide. Berlin will be brought nearer other major German cities, although it will still be some time before the high-speed **InterCity Express** (ICE) trains penetrate as far as Germany's future capital. Traveling times between the cities that are served by the ICE lines will be progressively reduced in 1993 as more and more of the sleek red-and-silver trains come into service. Frankfurt and Munich, for example, are now just three hours apart by ICE—one hour less than in 1992. (With airport transfers factored in, it can actually take more time to fly between these two cities.) In 1993 stretches of newly laid track will link Hamburg, Bremen, Hanover, Frankfurt, Stuttgart, Mannheim, Würzburg, Augsburg, and Munich. The trains, capable of speeds of up to 266 kilometers per hour (165 miles per hour), have wider bodies, telephones in each car, and attendant call buttons; and each seat is equipped with earphones and a choice of music. First-class cars offer seats with video consoles, and every car provides updated electronic information fed onto a computer screen giving the time, the route, and speed of the train, and the name of the next stop. With the business traveler in mind, a special car has been stocked with office equipment, including electric typewriters, fax machines, a photocopier, and computer hookups.

Munich's new international airport opened in May 1992, replacing the old and cramped Reim Airport. The **Franz Josef Strauss Airport** (named after the late, long-serving Bavarian state premier), 10 years in the making, is the largest in southern Germany, capable of handling up to 14 million passengers a year. Located northeast of Munich, near the town of Freising, Strauss Airport offers direct S-bahn service to the inner city. It is, however, farther away from the city center than Riem: 28 kilometers (17 miles), compared with 10 kilometers (6 miles).

Two new luxury airport hotels have already opened and a third is scheduled to make its debut by the end of 1993. The **Arabella Airport** (166 rooms) and the **Mövenpick Cadett** (72 rooms), both in the expensive price category, are particularly good options for travelers who land late at night. The average traveling time by car between the airport and downtown Munich is about one hour, slightly less by metropolitan railway. The Arabella is five minutes away from the arrival and departure terminals by shuttle bus. The **Kempinski** hotel, due to open in late 1993, will also offer shuttle bus service.

Air travelers to Berlin, Leipzig, and Dresden will find airports in all three cities in an advanced state of expansion and reconstruction. Berlin's **Tegel Airport** is being expanded to accommodate the expected increase in traffic, while **Leipzig's** airport is being spruced up as that city moves to resume its status as an important east–west crossroads. Rail travelers arriving in Leipzig will find an already modernized railway station that bears no comparison to the down-at-the-heels structure of the Communist years.

Travel on the **Elbe River,** which winds through eastern Germany from Czechoslovakia to Hamburg, is expanding. A variety of five- and seven-day **luxury cruises** aboard specially designed flat-bottom power vessels are being offered by KD Rhine Line between Hamburg and Bad Schandau (near Dresden), Magdeburg and Bad Schandau, and Bad Schandau and Prague. Excursions take in a wealth of castles, stately former homes, and historic centers such as Dresden, Meissen, and Wittenberg, where Martin Luther launched the Reformation. This mode of travel doesn't come cheap, however—tour prices start at DM 1,050.

The dearth of accommodations in eastern Germany has led to a mushrooming of bed-and-breakfast establishments. B&B associations are still scarce, but tourist offices should have a list of local homes that have a *zimmer frei* (room to rent). The most novel solution to the hotel shortage can be found in Dresden, where a cruise ship—dubbed the **M.S. *Elbresidenz***—that's part of the KD Rhine Line has been enlisted as a hostelry. With the ship moored on the Elbe, close by the Brühlsche Terrasse, guests are not exactly roughing it; they're within a five-minute walk of the old city center, and they have a view Canaletto would envy.

These days, eastern Germany resembles a construction site, with public and private buildings being repaired and autobahns and streets being rebuilt. In Dresden the newly restored **Zwinger Palace** was reopened in 1992, and the renowned Sempergalerie collection, at press time on view at the Albertinum, will be returned to its home and displayed in its entirety. The **Belvedere** tower at the **Sanssouci** palace complex in Potsdam will reopen in 1993 after being restored.

Nowhere is this frantic building activity more evident than in Berlin, both east and west. Plans for the once-teeming **Potsdamerplatz,** a bombed-out shell of a square since World War II, include new office buildings for Sony and Daimler-Benz, and a cultural center consisting of several musical theaters, all linked by a glass-enclosed bridge over the *platz*. There's talk of rebuilding the famous **Hotel Adelon,** one of the great hotels of the city in the 1920s, at Pariserplatz, in front of the Brandenburger Tor. Another grand hotel of the same era, **Haus Cumberland,** on the Ku'damm, may reemerge when the federal department of finance, which now occupies the building, is moved to new offices.

The Tiergarten area of West Berlin has been the focus of much attention, as work continues on converting a former luxury hotel into a film center. The new **Filmhaus Esplanade** includes cinemas, film museums, a film and television academy, and several restaurants. At the Kulturforum, the celebrated **Philharmonie** concert hall reopened in spring 1992 after a major overhaul, and a new building housing the print and drawing collection formerly shown at Dahlem will open in 1993. This is the first step in a 20-year program to reunite the state art and ethnographic collections that were split during the war. To help pay for this monumental project, many formerly public museums in West Berlin are now charging admission, and admission prices for their East Berlin counterparts have gone up.

With reunification came a long-overdue opening of the archives in **Weimar** containing the papers and documents of the philosopher and poet Friedrich Nietzsche. They were kept behind locked doors for more than 40 years by East Germany's Communist rulers, who thought they had detected Fascist sentiments in Nietzsche's work. The archives are again open to the public.

Among new museums opened in Germany in 1992 were permanent exhibitions devoted to eatables: Europe's first asparagus museum, the **Europäisches Spargelmuseum,** in the heart of Germany's asparagus-growing region in Schrobenhausen, near Augsburg and the **Deutsches Brotmuseum** (bread museum) in Ulm. A cider museum—the **Frankfurter Apfelweinmuseum**—also opened in Frankfurt's Römer. Two new museums devoted to the history of the Jews in Germany are scheduled to open in the Nürnberg area in 1993—one in **Fürth** and the other in **Schnaittach.** The Fürth museum will be housed in the former city mansion of a Jewish family. In Schnaittach, the museum is installed in a 16th-century building that served as a synagogue and Talmud high school.

The opening of three museums in Bonn near the Chancellery should boost tourism—and spirits—in the Rhineland city that now has to share the honors as the nation's capital with distant Berlin. The **Municipal Art Museum** (opened in 1992) now displays its complete collection of German Expressionist and Neo-Expressionist paintings in a new building that increased exhibition space by 80%. Also opened in 1992, the **Exhibition Hall of the State of Germany** displays temporary exhibitions. A third institution, the **Museum for the History of the Federal Republic of Germany,** will open in 1993.

A unique museum charting one man's view and experience of the former Iron Curtain that divided Germany opened in 1992 in the village of Mödlareuth, near Hof in northern Bavaria. Mödlareuth was a community literally split in two by the political border of concrete and barbed-wire fences. The life of the divided village was recorded through the years in a collection of unique photographs taken by Arnt Schaffner. His efforts have been brought together in the **Deutsch-Deutsch Museum Mödlareuth.** The village is 16 kilometers (10 miles) north of Hof, beside Hirschberg. For more information, contact the Hof tourist office (Klosterstrasse 10, tel. 09281/815233).

Germany's **Romantik Hotels & Restaurants** association admits its first restaurant in the eastern part of the country in 1993—the Vincenz Richter restaurant in Meissen. Two new hotels join the group in 1993 as well: the **Romantik Hotel Gravenberg,** Solingen-Langenfeld, and **Die Krone,** Laudenbach, just off the Romantic Road, south of Würzburg.

Germany's castle hotel group, **Gast im Schloss,** added two new establishments to its list in 1992: **Schloss Neufahrn,** near Munich, and **Schloss Diepenbrock,** near Buchholz in northern Germany. Several new castle hotels are to be added to the chain in 1993.

Music lovers planning a visit to Munich during the annual **Opera Festival** should check first to see if the event is still on track. The city's opera house, the Nationaltheater, will be closed until at least the end of May 1993 while the stage hydraulic system is overhauled. At press time the festival was scheduled to take place in August, but the opera house's director, Wolfgang Sawallisch, has warned that the work could disrupt preparations and force him to cancel the festival entirely (the first time since the war).

Fodor's Choice

No two people will agree on what makes a perfect vacation, but it's fun and helpful to know what others think. We hope you'll have a chance to experience some of Fodor's Choices during your visit to Germany. For detailed information about each entry, refer to the appropriate chapters of the book.

Dining

Aubergine, Munich (*Very Expensive*)

Bado-La Poêle d'Or, Köln (*Very Expensive*)

Falkenstube, Freiburg (*Very Expensive*)

Säumerhof, Grafenau (*Very Expensive*)

Peter Lembcke, Hamburg (*Expensive*)

Weinhaus Brückenkeller, Frankfurt (*Expensive*)

Wullenwever, Lübeck (*Expensive*)

Zur Herrenmühle, Heidelberg (*Moderate–Expensive*)

Alte Schwede, Wismar (*Moderate*)

Ratskeller, Bremen (*Moderate*)

Ratsweinkeller, Hamburg (*Moderate*)

Straubinger Hof, Munich (*Inexpensive*)

Zum Roten Ochsen, Heidelberg (*Inexpensive*)

Lodging

Vier Jahreszeiten, Munich (*Very Expensive*)

Brenner's Park Hotel, Baden-Baden (*Very Expensive*)

Bristol Hotel Kempinski, Berlin (*Very Expensive*)

Dom-Hotel, Köln (*Very Expensive*)

Hotel Hirschgasse, Heidelberg (*Very Expensive*)

Steigenberger Frankfurter Hof, Frankfurt (*Very Expensive*)

Steigenberger Insel-Hotel, Konstanz (*Very Expensive*)

Garden Hotels, Hamburg (*Very Expensive*)

Alte Thorschenke, Cochem (*Expensive*)

Eisenhut, Rothenburg-ob-der-Tauber (*Expensive*)

Castles and Palaces

Altes Schloss, Meersburg

Burg Eltz, Mosel

Burg Katz, Rhine

Burg Trifels, Annweiler

Heidelberg Schloss

Neuschwanstein, Füssen

Schloss Sanssouci, Potsdam

Wartburg Castle, Eisenach

Museums

Alte Pinakothek, Munich

Deutsches Museum, Munich

Domschatzkammer, Aachen

Gemäldegalerie, Berlin

Gemäldegalerie Alte Meister, Dresden

Kunsthalle, Hamburg

Museum der Bildenden Kunste, Leipzig

Museum für Moderne Kunst, Frankfurt

Römisch-Germanisches Museum, Köln

Churches

Dom St. Bartholomäus, Frankfurt

Freiburg, Münster

Kölner Dom, Köln

Kaiserdom, Aachen

Kaiserdom, Speyer

Mainzer Dom, Mainz

Trier Dom, Trier

Vierzehnheiligen, Franconia

Wieskirche, Upper Bavaria

Towns Where Time Stands Still

Alsfeld

Bad Wimpfen

Bernkastel-Kues

Goslar

Hameln

Rothenburg-ob-der-Tauber

St. Martin

Wasserburg am Inn

Memorable Sights

Baden-Baden's casino

Brandenburger Tor and Wall remains, Berlin

The confluence of the Inn and Danube rivers at Passau

Hamburg's Reeperbahn

Munich's Oktoberfest

Opera night in Bayreuth

The Rhine in Flames fireworks

Scharlachrennen Festival, Nördlingen

Semper Opera House, Dresden

Wilhelmshöhe, Kassel

Unforgettable Excursions

A boat ride on Bavaria's Königsee

A Hamburg harbor cruise at night

A raft ride on the Isar River from Wolfratshausen to Munich

Cruises on the Rhine and Elbe

A round-trip ride from Freiburg on the Black Forest railway

A steam-train ride from Bad Doberan to the Baltic Sea

To the summit of Germany's highest mountain, the Zugspitze, by cable car . . . and to the depths of the country's largest salt mine, at Berchtesgaden

A torchlit sleigh ride through the Bavarian snow and a nighttime toboggan ride down an Alpine slope

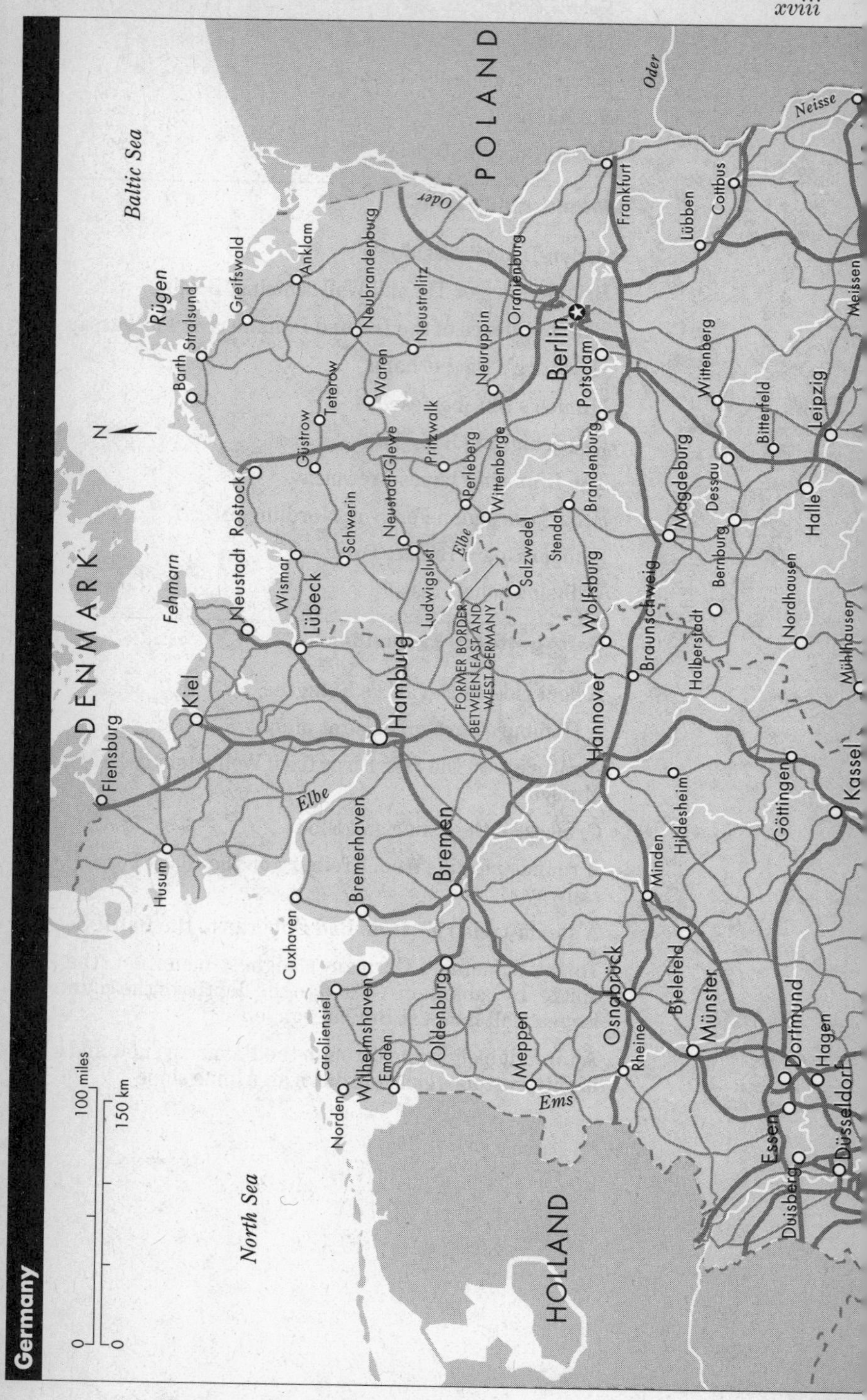

Germany

0 100 miles
0 150 km
DENMARK
N
Baltic Sea
Rügen
North Sea
Fehmarn
Flensburg
Husum
Kiel
Neustadt
Rostock
Barth
Stralsund
Greifswald
Anklam
Wismar
Lübeck
Cuxhaven
Elbe
Caroliensiel
Norden
Wilhelmshaven
Emden
Bremerhaven
Hamburg
Schwerin
Güstrow
Teterow
Waren
Neubrandenburg
Neustrelitz
Neustadt-Glewe
Ludwigslust
Pritzwalk
Oldenburg
Bremen
FORMER BORDER BETWEEN EAST AND WEST GERMANY
Elbe
Perleberg
Wittenberge
Neuruppin
Oranienburg
POLAND
Oder
Meppen
Ems
HOLLAND
Salzwedel
Stendal
Berlin
Potsdam
Brandenburg
Hannover
Wolfsburg
Osnabrück
Rheine
Minden
Braunschweig
Magdeburg
Frankfurt
Oder
Bielefeld
Hildesheim
Halberstadt
Bernburg
Dessau
Wittenberg
Lübben
Cottbus
Münster
Essen
Duisberg
Dortmund
Hagen
Düsseldorf
Göttingen
Kassel
Nordhausen
Mühlhausen
Bitterfeld
Halle
Leipzig
Meissen
Neisse

Köln
Siegen
Erfurt
Weimar
Gera
Chemnitz
Eisenach
Aachen
Bonn
Marburg
Bad Hersfeld
Saalfeld
Zwickau
Rhine
Alsfeld
Suhl
Giessen
Fulda
Meiningen
Plauen
BELGIUM
Koblenz
Hof
Coburg
Münchberg
Wiesbaden
Frankfurt-am-Main
Mainz
Mosel
Bingen
Bamberg
Bayreuth
CZECHOSLOVAKIA
Bad
Darmstadt
LUX.
Trier
Kreuznach
Main
Würzburg
Mannheim
Nürnberg
Rothenburg-o-d-Tauber
Fürth
Ludwigshafen
Heidelberg
Saarbrücken
Speyer
Heilbronn
Regensburg
Karlsruhe
Straubing
Deggendorf
Stuttgart
Baden-Baden
Passau
Tübingen
Danube
Isar
Danube
Offenburg
Ulm
Augsburg
Neu-Ulm
Rhein
Munich
Inn
FRANCE
Biberach
Memmingen
Freiburg
Tuttlingen
Ravensburg
Bad Reichenhall
Konstanz
Wangen
Rheinfelden
Berchtesgaden
Bodensee
Friedrichshafen
Garmisch-Partenkirchen
AUSTRIA
SWITZERLAND

Europe
Reykjavik
ICELAND
NORWAY
Bergen
SCOTLAND
NORTHERN IRELAND
Edinburgh
North Sea
Skagerrat
Belfast
IRELAND
Irish Sea
Dublin
GREAT BRITAIN
DENMARK
WALES
Hamburg
ENGLAND
Cardiff
HOLLAND
Amsterdam
The Hague
London
Rotterdam
ATLANTIC OCEAN
English Channel
Brussels
Bonn
BELGIUM
Frankfurt
Paris
LUXEMBOURG
FRANCE
Zürich
Munich
Bern
Salzburg
SWITZERLAND
Lyon
LIECHTENSTEIN
Milan
Nice
Marseille
Monaco
PORTUGAL
ANDORRA
Florence
Madrid
Lisbon
Barcelona
Corsica
SPAIN
Seville
Granada
Sardinia
Balearic Islands
Gibraltar
Mediterranean Sea
MOROCCO
ALGERIA
0
400 miles
TUNISIA
0
600 km

FINLAND
Gulf of Bothnia
Oslo
SWEDEN
Helsinki
Gulf of Finland
St. Petersburg
ESTONIA
Stockholm
Tartu
Kattegat
Gothenburg
Riga
Moscow
LATVIA
Copenhagen
LITHUANIA
Baltic Sea
Kaunas
RUSSIA
RUSSIA
Vilnius
Kaliningrad
Minsk
Berlin
POLAND
BELARUS
Warsaw
Cracow
Kiev
Prague
UKRAINE
CZECHOSLOVAKIA
MOLDOVA
Vienna
Budapest
Kishinev
AUSTRIA
HUNGARY
SLOVENIA
ROMANIA
Zagreb
CROATIA
Novi Sad
Bucharest
BOSNIA AND HERZEGOVINA
Belgrade
Black Sea
Sarajevo
SERBIA
Adriatic Sea
BULGARIA
MONTENEGRO
Priština
Rome
Sofia
Skopje
Titograd
ITALY
Istanbul
MACEDONIA
Tirane
Naples
Ankara
ALBANIA
TURKEY
Sea
GREECE
Aegean Sea
Ionian Sea
Sicily
Athens
CYPRUS
MALTA
Crete
Mediterranean Sea

World Time Zones

+11 +12 - -11 -10 -9 -8 -7 -6 -5 -4 -3 -2

Numbers below vertical bands relate each zone to Greenwich Mean Time (0 hrs.). Local times frequently differ from these general indications, as indicated by light-face numbers on map.

Algiers, **29**
Anchorage, **3**
Athens, **41**
Auckland, **1**
Baghdad, **46**
Bangkok, **50**
Beijing, **54**
Berlin, **34**
Bogotá, **19**
Budapest, **37**
Buenos Aires, **24**
Caracas, **22**
Chicago, **9**
Copenhagen, **33**
Dallas, **10**
Delhi, **48**
Denver, **8**
Djakarta, **53**
Dublin, **26**
Edmonton, **7**
Hong Kong, **56**
Honolulu, **2**
Istanbul, **40**
Jerusalem, **42**
Johannesburg, **44**
Lima, **20**
Lisbon, **28**
London (Greenwich), **27**
Los Angeles, **6**
Madrid, **38**
Manila, **57**

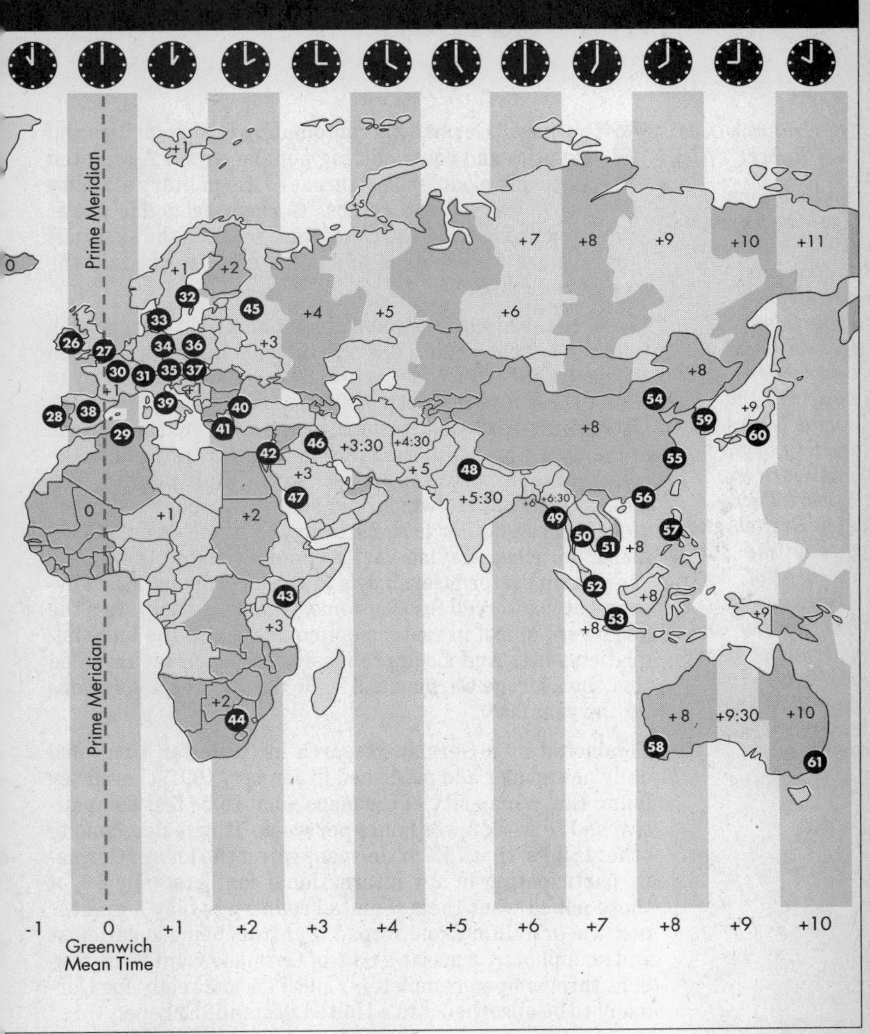

Mecca, **47**
Mexico City, **12**
Miami, **18**
Montréal, **15**
Moscow, **45**
Nairobi, **43**
New Orleans, **11**
New York City, **16**
Ottawa, **14**
Paris, **30**
Perth, **58**
Reykjavík, **25**
Rio de Janeiro, **23**
Rome, **39**
Saigon (Ho Chi Minh City), **51**
San Francisco, **5**
Santiago, **21**
Seoul, **59**
Shanghai, **55**
Singapore, **52**
Stockholm, **32**
Sydney, **61**
Tokyo, **60**
Toronto, **13**
Vancouver, **4**
Vienna, **35**
Warsaw, **36**
Washington, D.C., **17**
Yangon, **49**
Zürich, **31**

Introduction

By Graham Lees and Robert Tilley

British-born Graham Lees has lived in Germany for the past decade and reports on German and central European political and social issues for a variety of foreign publications. Robert Tilley, also British and a longtime resident of Munich, is a broadcaster and journalist whose work has appeared in German and British publications.

The "new" Germany is confounding foreign critics and skeptics and contradicting popular myth. A reunited Germany would pose a threat to the military stability of Europe, warned the critics. German economic power could steamroll across the Continent, moaned the skeptics. Germans are domineering and addicted to work, said the stereotype-makers.

Yet since the historic reunion of East and West Germany on October 3, 1990, after a political division lasting more than 40 years, the Germans seem to have gone out of their way to refute these dire predictions from abroad: Germany steadfastly stuck to its constitutional constraints limiting the use of its armed forces to the NATO arena and refused to become militarily involved in the Persian Gulf conflict. The federal government, which once showered money on the Soviet Union and other nations, seems to have run out of economic miracles. Having vastly underestimated the cost of shoring up eastern Germany's faltering economy, the government was forced to raise domestic taxes to help stem the downward spiral in eastern employment and the huge migration west. And a comprehensive social survey revealed that the average German had some unexpected aspirations for the year 2000.

Conducted by a German research institute for a national daily newspaper and published in January 1991, the survey found that a majority of Germans want to be less competitive and to work fewer hours per week. It revealed, among other things, that 75% of Germans reject the idea of Germany participating in any international conflicts; only 6% of those polled want their reunited country to play a greater political or military role abroad. Far from being isolationist and xenophobic, a massive 83% of Germans want their borders thrown open completely, and 71% are ready for Germany to be absorbed into a United States of Europe.

Perhaps partly as a legacy of Nazism, Germans are less likely than other Europeans to embrace their own national identity. A farmer in the Alps is a Bavarian first and a German only a distant second. This has generally been the case throughout centuries of German history, apart from the fateful last third of the last century and the first half of this one.

To outsiders, of course, Germans are Germans—whether they hail from Berchtesgaden or Berlin, Dortmund or Dresden. But in reality they are as different as Alaskans and Texans. The beer-swilling Bavarian in lederhosen and climbing boots can be seen in many an Alpine village, but the Berliner would disown him as a representative of the

German people. Then, too, the elegant Prussian who dominates the Berlin street scene would be regarded as an envoy from another nation when abroad in any town south of the Main River. Indeed, compared with the hearty animosity that separates the Bavarians and the "Prussians," the rivalry between the English and the Scots is schoolboy stuff.

Like the English-Scottish rivalry, it is rooted in a shared history scarred by internecine quarrels, although the most traumatic event occurred when Prussians and Bavarians were united in one of their many alliances against Austria. The Prussian commander reputedly manned the front line with untrained Bavarian peasants, many armed only with pitchforks. Thousands are said to have been slaughtered. My Munich taxi driver shares the opinion of many Bavarians on the subject. "It was a massacre," he sighed, tracing the roots of Prussian-Bavarian hostility to this single battle.

Certainly there are other causes, also rooted in history. The Bavarians are proud that their royal dynasty—the Wittelsbachs—is older than the Prussian house of Hohenzollern and, moreover, actually outlasted it. The fact that two of Bavaria's latter-day rulers were insane is smilingly dismissed as a slight deviation in the Wittelsbach line. Indeed, the much celebrated insanity of young King Ludwig II is welcomed as *Glück im Unglück* (a prevalent German expression meaning "fortune in misfortune"), for the eccentric king built a collection of castles that bankrupted the royal purse but now reap large sums of money in tourist revenues. Similarly, Ludwig's munificent patronage of Wagner cost the Bavarians dearly in terms of hard cash—but what an investment!

But there are other more visible differences that distinguish the Bavarian from his fellow German to the north or, for that matter, the Berliner from the Rhinelander, and both of these from the Saarlander. You've only got to join them at table to sort out one from another. This applies both to the food they eat and—above all—to their liquid refreshment.

The Berliner really does drink beer sweetened with fruit juice, and the Bavarian really does quaff what he calls his "hop-juice" from oversize liter mugs. Each regards the drinking habits of the other with amusement and some distaste. The Rhinelander, by contrast, is the country's wine connoisseur, and the humblest Rhineland home often holds a cellar full of the finest vintages.

Fine as Germany's wine indisputably is, beer is the country's drink and its emblem. The merging of the two Germanys has actually led to an increase in brewing for the first time in several years, mainly generated by eastern Germans' demand for the superior brews of the west that they had been denied for so long. The result: In 1991 Germany regained its world title as number one in the per capita consumption of beer. Germans down 144 liters (254 pints) a year, just ahead of closest rivals Czechoslovakia and Belgium and far surpassing Britain (197 pints) and the United States (165 pints). But the Bavarians take the gold medal: They drink a staggering 200 liters (352 pints) each.

Germany has more breweries than the rest of Europe put together, and the tiniest village is often dominated by a brewery that produces a beer that is world-class but consumed only by a small circle of lucky initiates who happen to live there. An English colleague of mine spends blissful vacations touring the country breweries of Bavaria on a bicycle. "I won't live long enough to sample them all," he says, recommending his tour to anyone who wants to get to know Germany and the Germans at close hand; which, in this case, means at eye level over the foaming rim of a full beer glass.

Beer gardens are the center of Bavarian life in the summer, which in a good year means the long, balmy span between Easter and the first cold snap of October. This is the time to visit Munich, when the velvety southern German nights draw families out, like moths to a candle, to the lantern-hung, throbbing beer gardens.

The Bavarians, of course, have no monopoly on outdoor delights such as these. In Frankfurt, on off-duty summer nights, the city's businessmen can be found in the cider pubs of Sachsenhausen; in Berlin, the pavement cafés are an extension of the German living room; while along the Rhine, the arrival of the first new wine after the grape harvest signals party time for all.

Indeed, the German is an outdoor person who shares an almost mystical empathy with nature. One need only look to the German folk song as a fascinating guide to this phenomenon. The close identification of the people with the beauty of their homeland is the chief characteristic of the German *Volkslied,* in which can be detected an atavistic fascination with the forests that cover a quarter of the land. Walking in the dense, dark forests that wrap themselves around most German cities is a national pastime, but the German forest is dying, with one-third of its trees probably irreversibly sick, victims of industrial pollution. It's significant that this pernicious threat to the German forest has mobilized the people like no other postwar force and given Germany's ecological political movement, the Greens, a big thrust forward. In fact, the Green philosophy has become so popular that it has been absorbed by the major political parties, and the Green Party itself, considered so radical when it was formed, has become almost superfluous.

More than three-quarters of the population believes that protecting the environment should become the highest priority of government and industry. It's an issue that has taken on a new sense of urgency now that broad swaths of eastern Germany have been found to be severely contaminated as a result of poor or nonexistent pollution control over the past four decades. Germans love their cars, but the country that has more automobiles per capita than anywhere else except the United States is apparently ready to give up its Mercedes, BMWs, Porsches, and Volkswagens. More than 50% of Germans say they want to see less road traffic by the year 2000. Reflecting this sentiment, the federal government has warned car manufacturers that it might impose a beer-bottle-style deposit surcharge on new cars, passed from owner to owner and eventually refunded by the manufacturer to the last owner when the vehicle is scrapped, the idea being to make the car industry more responsible for the millions of tons of nonrecyclable scrap created every year.

The problems that preoccupy most Germans, however, are those stemming from reunification. The euphoria has faded, and it's become apparent that Germany in many ways remains two countries. The physical divisions of the Berlin Wall and the Iron Curtain are gone, but "East" and "West" Germany somehow still exist, not least in the glaring differences in standards of living. The territory and people of former East Germany seem to bear the scars of Stalinist mismanagement more visibly than the neighboring countries of the old East Bloc. The infrastructure of eastern Germany is dilapidated and inadequate. One only has to drive eastward across the vanished Iron Curtain border to sense this—the roads immediately become bumpier.

Some laws, too, are not yet unified, leading to often bizarre, un-German confusion. In western Germany, a motorist can still have a couple of small beers and take to the road, but if he crosses into one of the five new eastern states he has automatically broken a long-standing communist law banning driving while under the influence of alcohol. There are still two rail networks: the west's superior Bundesbahn and the east's Reichsbahn (although the systems will eventually merge). And if you want to make a telephone call between the western and eastern halves (except calls within Berlin), you still have to dial the international code.

Economists and sociologists predict that it could take a generation to truly fuse the two halves of Germany. Today, Germans in the old western half refer disparagingly to their kinsfolk in the east as "Ossies," meaning easterners, implying that 40 years of communism has made them different. Certainly the eastern Germans are fighting for their economic lives; by summer 1991, 3 million of them—out of a work force of only 8.5 million—were either unemployed or working only part-time. Ironically, while thousands of disillusioned Germans apply to emigrate to Australia, New Zealand, or Canada, tens of thousands of people from the liberated East European countries are lining up to get into

Germany in search of a better life. Many come from the surviving pockets of ethnic German communities that were trapped after the political map of Europe changed in 1945, including the more than 2 million Volga Germans in the Soviet Union, persecuted by Stalin and exiled to Siberia from their centuries-old settlements along the Volga River.

The lingering differences between eastern and western Germany provide a fascinating and disturbing background for today's traveler. Although many historic buildings, indeed, whole towns, were found to be crumbling in eastern Germany because of lack of maintenance, the cash-strapped Communists did take some pride in Germany's architectural and cultural heritage. Weimar, for example, home to Goethe as well as Schiller, Herder, Liszt, Bach, and other literary and musical giants, is an eastern German showplace; and the restoration of Dresden continues apace.

Still, the traveler to eastern Germany cannot—not yet, anyway—expect to find the 1990s standards of comfort he or she may normally take for granted. Under the communist regime, the movements of foreign tourists were strictly controlled, as was the supply of services. As a result, there is an acute shortage of quality accommodations and restaurants, although improvements are steadily being introduced. For example, thousands of homeowners have become part-time businesspeople by providing travelers with a bed, plain cooking, and usually a little friendly guidance. A few nights in these bed and breakfasts is probably the best way of getting to know eastern Germany.

Another anomaly of reunification is the Bonn-versus-Berlin battle. Many people expected Berlin to automatically regain its prewar status as the nation's capital. This city of 3 million, for so many years the symbol of the Cold War, *was* designated the new federal capital and was the setting of the first unified parliamentary meeting after October 3, 1990. But Bonn remained the seat of government for almost nine months after reunification. The provincial city put up a strong fight to retain its prestigious position, and the public, government officials, and parliamentary representatives were almost evenly divided in their loyalties. Finally, on June 20, 1991, after a marathon debate lasting 12 hours, the Bundestag voted 337 to 320 in favor of moving the government to Berlin, allowing for a period of 12 years to make the transition. One study concluded that almost 100,000 people—one-third of Bonn's population, which consists mainly of civil servants, diplomats, and service-industry employees and their families—will be uprooted, resulting in a bill of more than $30 billion. The return of the capital to Berlin is just one facet of Germany's biggest challenge since postwar reconstruction: nothing short of restoring a nation.

1 Essential Information

Before You Go

Government Tourist Offices

Contact the German National Tourist Office at 122 E. 42nd St., New York, NY 10168, tel. 212/661–7200; or 444 South Flower Street, Suite 2230, Los Angeles, CA 90071, tel. 213/688–7332.

In Canada 175 Bloor Street East, North Tower, Suite 604, Toronto, Ontario M4 W3R8, tel. 416/968–1570.

In the U.K. Nightingale House, 65 Curzon Street, London W1Y 7PE, England, tel. 071/495–3990.

Tour Groups

Package tours are typically the most economical way to visit Germany. Thanks to the volume of passengers tour operators handle, they can negotiate significantly lower prices with airlines, hotels, and other travel suppliers than you can get on your own. There are, of course, potential drawbacks—you might find yourself dining with 20 people you don't particularly care for or being forced to march to the beat of someone else's drum. The key to a successful vacation is finding the tour that best suits your personal style, so ask a lot of questions. How many people are in the group? How much free time is there? Is there a special-interest tour I might find appealing?

The tours listed below should give you some idea of the wealth of programs available. Some are good introductory tours, some are more in-depth, others leave you to organize much of your own itinerary. For additional resources, contact your travel agent or the German National Tourist Office.

When considering a tour, be sure to find out (1) exactly what expenses are included, particularly tips, taxes, side trips, meals, and entertainment; (2) the ratings of all hotels on the itinerary and the facilities they offer; (3) the additional cost of single, rather than double, accommodations if you are traveling alone; and (4) the number of travelers in your group. Note whether the tour operator reserves the right to change hotels, routes, or even prices after you've booked, and check out the operator's policy regarding cancellations, complaints, and trip-interruption insurance. Many tour operators request that packages be booked through a travel agent; there is generally no additional charge for doing so.

General-interest Tours For a basic but good overview of the country, consider the 13-day "Best of Germany" from **Caravan Tours** (401 N. Michigan Ave., Suite 3325, Chicago, IL 60601, tel. 312/321–9800 or 800/227–2826). Caravan's "Gothic Splendor" is a little less hectic, featuring a four-day Rhine cruise. **Globus-Gateway** (95–25 Queens Blvd., Rego Park, NY 11374, tel. 718/268–7000 or 800/221–0090) runs a good, comprehensive tour, "Best of Germany," as well as a new United Germany trip. **Olson-Travelworld** (Box 10066, Manhattan Beach, CA 90226, tel. 310/546–8400) offers "Captivating Cities and Alpine Delights (16 days), which meanders through Germany, Austria, and Switzerland, and "Storybook Germany" (17 days), both strong on Old World charm. "Germany, Austria, and Eastern Europe" follows an intriguing itinerary that includes Berlin, Budapest, Vienna, and Prague. **American Express Vacations** (300 Pinnacle Way, Norcross, GA 30093, tel. 800/241–1700 or 800/421–5785 in GA) is a veritable supermarket of tours. You name it, they've either got it packaged or can customize a package for you. **Maupintour** (Box 807, Lawrence, KS 66044, tel. 913/843–1211 or 800/255–4266) has a comprehensive 16-day tour of eastern and western Germany that includes a Rhine cruise, as well as a leisurely two-week tour. **Taulk Tours** (Box 5027, Westport, CT 06881, tel. 800/468–2825 or 203/226–6911) has a 14-day tour that includes Berlin, Heidelburg, Munich, Bavaria, and a Rhine cruise. **Delta Air Lines** (tel. 800/338–2010) has a 13-day motorcoach tour that includes stops in Berlin, Heidelberg, Dresden, Köln, Hamburg, and Munich.

Special-interest Tours

Art/Architecture

Esplanade Tours (581 Boylston St., Boston, MA 02116, tel. 617/266–7465) offers several in-depth art and architecture tours led by noted lecturers.

Barge Cruising

Drift in leisure and luxury down the Rhine, Lahn, and Mosel rivers (crossing into France) with **Floating Through Europe** (271 Madison Ave., New York, NY 10016, tel. 212/685–5600).

Health/Fitness

DER Tours offers spa packages at five classic spas in the Black Forest and Bavaria.

Music

Dailey-Thorp Travel (315 W. 57th St., New York, NY 10019, tel. 212/307–1555) offers deluxe opera and music tours, including "Musical Heartland of Europe." The tour features operas in Berlin, Dresden, and Prague (Czechoslovakia). Itineraries vary according to available performances.

Wine/Cuisine

Travel Concepts (373 Commonwealth Ave., Suite 601, Boston, MA 02115–1815, tel. 617/266–8450) offers the "German Wine Academy." Usually based at Kloster Eberbach, a 12th-century monastery, the program includes tastings and visits to vineyards and wine cellars in 7 of Germany's 11 wine-producing regions. **DER Tours** (11933 Wilshire Blvd., Los Angeles, CA 90025, tel. 213/479–4140 or 800/421–4343) offers a tour called "Romantic Rhine and Wine."

Package Deals for Independent Travelers

DER Tours (11933 Wilshire Blvd., Los Angeles, CA 90025, tel. 310/479–4411 or 800/937–1234) specializes in independent packages. Travelers can choose from a variety of air, rail pass, car rental, and overnight options.

Delta Air Lines (tel. 800/872–7786, above) offers fly/drive and fly/rail packages, as well as three-night "city sprees," in Munich and Hamburg. All include round-trip airfare.

Europabus. The German railways section of this European-wide network offers several attractive German tours, including Romantic Germany and Eastern Germany (both seven days). Contact GermanRail in the United States or Deutsche Touring, Frankfurt (*see* Rail Passes, below).

Lufthansa German Airlines (680 Fifth Ave., New York, NY 10019, tel. 718/895–1277) offers air/hotel packages throughout the country, as does **TWA Getaway Vacations** (tel. 800/GET-AWAY).

Travel Bound (599 Broadway, Penthouse, New York, NY 10012, tel. 800/456–8656 or 212/334–1350) offers special rates at select hotels in Berlin, Heidelburg, Hamburg, and Munich, as well as sightseeing options and air transportation, when you fly round-trip on Pan Am and stay at the hotel for a minimum of three nights.

When to Go

The tourist season in Germany runs from May to late October, when the weather is at its best. In addition to many tourist events, this period has hundreds of folk festivals. The winter sports season in the Bavarian Alps runs from Christmas to mid-March. Prices everywhere are generally higher during the summer, so you may find considerable advantages in visiting out of season. Most resorts offer out-of-season (*Zwischensaison*) and "edge-of-season" (*Nebensaison*) rates, and tourist offices can provide lists of hotels that offer special low-price inclusive weekly packages (*Pauschalangebote*). Similarly, many winter ski resorts offer low rates for the periods between mid-January (after local school holidays) and Easter. The other advantage of out-of-season travel is that crowds are very much less in evidence. The disadvantages of visiting out of season, especially in winter, are that the weather, which is generally good in summer, is often cold and gloomy, and apart from ski resorts, some tourist attractions, especially in rural areas, are closed or have shorter hours.

Climate Germany's climate is temperate, although cold snaps can plunge the thermometer well below freezing, particularly in the Alps, the Harz region of Lower Saxony, and the higher regions of north Franconia. Summers are usually sunny and warm, though be prepared for a few cloudy and wet days. The south is normally always a few degrees warmer than the north. As you get nearer the Alps, however, the summers get shorter, often not beginning until the end of May. Fall is sometimes spectacular in the south: warm and soothing. The only real exception to the above is the strikingly variable weather in South Bavaria caused by the *Föhn*, an Alpine wind that gives rise to clear but very warm conditions. Föhn can occur in all seasons. Sudden atmospheric pressure changes associated with the Föhn give some people headaches.

The following are the average daily maximum and minimum temperatures for Munich.

Jan.	35F	1C	**May**	64F	18C	**Sept.**	67F	20C
	23	−5		45	7		48	9
Feb.	38F	3C	**June**	70F	21C	**Oct.**	56F	14C
	23	−5		51	11		40	4
Mar.	48F	9C	**July**	74F	23C	**Nov.**	44F	7C
	30	−1		55	13		33	0
Apr.	56F	14C	**Aug.**	73F	23C	**Dec.**	36F	2C
	38	3		54	12		26	−4

WeatherTrak provides information on more than 750 cities around the world at 900/370–8728 (cost: 95¢ per minute). The number plays a taped message that tells you to dial a three-digit access code for the destination in which you're interested. The code is either the area code (in the United States) or the first three letters of the foreign city. For a list of all access codes, send a self-addressed stamped envelope to Cities, 9B Terrace Way, Greensboro, NC 27403. For more information, call 800/247–3282.

Festivals and Seasonal Events

Top seasonal events in Germany include carnival festivities throughout the country in January and February, spring festivals (nationwide), Munich's Opera Festival in July, the July Richard Wagner Festival in Bayreuth, horse racing at Baden-Baden in August, wine festivals throughout the Rhineland in September, the Oktoberfest in Munich in late September, the Frankfurt Book Fair in October, and the December Christmas markets (nationwide). Contact the **German National Tourist Office** for exact dates and additional information.

January **New Year International Ski Jumping,** among other winter-sports competitions, at Garmisch-Partenkirchen.

Fasching season: Carnival events, including proclamations of carnival princes, street fairs, parades, masked balls, and more, take place in Munich, Köln, Bonn, Düsseldorf, Offenburg, and around the Black Forest. Festivities always run through February, finishing on *Fasching Dienstag* (Shrove Tuesday).

International Green Week Agricultural Fair is held in Berlin.

February **Internationale Filmfestspiele** is Germany's premier film festival.

International Toy Fair, with models, hobbies, and handicrafts, takes place in Nürnberg.

International Clock, Watch, Jewelry, Gems, and Silverware Trade Fair is held in Munich.

Frankfurt International Fair is a major consumer goods trade fair.

Black Forest Ski Marathon is a 60-kilometer (37-mile) ski race in Schonach-Hinterzarten.

March **Frankfurt Music Fair and Frankfurt Jazz Festival.**

Leipzig Trade Fair attracts businesspeople from throughout Europe.

Spring Fairs. In such towns as Münster, Hamburg, Nürnberg, Stuttgart, and Augsburg, festivities ring in the spring season.

Munich Fashion Week is a popular trade fair of the latest fashions.

International Easter Egg Fair takes place in Köln.

April **Stuttgart Jazz Festival.**

Munich Ballet Days.

German International Tennis Championships are held in Hamburg.

Mannheim May Fair is a traditional spring fair with flower floats and parades.

Walpurgis Festivals. Towns in the Harz Mountains celebrate this night before May Day.

May **International Mime Festival,** in Stuttgart, attracts some of the best in the world.

International May Festival brings a month of opera, ballet, and theater performances to Wiesbaden.

Mozart's Heritage in Dresden celebrates the composer with opera, symphony, and chamber music concerts.

Hamburg Summer is a whole season of festivals, concerts, plays, and exhibitions.

German Open Tennis Tournament takes place in Hamburg.
Folklore, Jazz, Rock, and Pop Music are featured on weekends of entertainment in Köln's Rheinpark.
Red Wine Festival is held at Assmannshausen in Rüdesheim.
"The Master Draught," a historical play about the Thirty Years War, is performed in Rothenburg.
Four Castles Illumination presents fireworks on the heights of Neckarsteinach.

Early June–Aug. **Frankfurt Summertime Festival** features outdoor activities throughout the city.
Franco-German Folk Festival is held in Berlin.
Castle Concerts and musical events are held in Munich's Residenz and Nymphenburg Palace.
Mosel Wine Week celebrations take place in Cochem.
Castle Illuminations, with spectacular fireworks, are presented in Heidelberg.
Frankfurt Craft Week.
Weilburg Castle Concerts.
Händel Festival is celebrated in Halle.
Music Days highlight Leipzig's cultural calendar.
Kiel Week is an international sailing regatta in Kiel.
Würzburg Mozart Festival is held in several Würzburg locations.
Nymphenburg Summer Festival, with concerts at Nymphenburg Palace, is held in Munich.
Munich Film Festival.
International Theater Festival takes place in Freiburg.
Kuntsfest Weimar is a month-long series of concerts held in Weimar.

July **Folk Festivals.** Outdoor festivities are held in Krov, Wald-Michelbach, Waldshut-Tiengen, Würzburg, Geisenheim, Speyer, Lübeck, Karlsruhe, Düsseldorf, Oestrich-Winkel, and Paderhorn.
Opera Festival is Munich's major operatic affair.
German-American Folk Festival is Berlin's celebration of two cultures.
Richard Wagner Festival is a major musical event in Bayreuth.
Old Town Festival includes castle illuminations in Neckarsteinach.
Kulmbach Beer Festival.
International Weissenhof Tennis Tournament for the Mercedes Cup is played in Stuttgart.

August **Castle Festival** features open-air theater presentations at the castle in Heidelberg.
Partenkirchen Festival Week is held in Garmisch-Partenkirchen.
Stuttgart European Music Festival.
Wine Festivals break out throughout the Rhineland.
Grand Baden-Baden Week highlights international horse racing at Iffezheim in Baden-Baden.

September **Oktoberfest** (last two weeks of Sept.) in Munich attracts millions of visitors from throughout Germany, Europe, and abroad.
Leipzig Trade Fair again draws commercial interests to that city.
Berlin Festival Weeks feature classical music concerts all month long.

October **Frankfurt Book Fair** is a famous annual literary event.
Berlin International Marathon.
Bremen Freimarkt is a centuries-old folk festival and procession in Bremen.

November **St. Martin's Festival,** with children's lantern processions, is celebrated throughout the Rhineland and Bavaria.
Antiques Fair is held in Berlin.

December **Six-Day Cycle Race** takes place in Munich.
Grand Slam Cup, in Munich, is the world's richest tennis tournament.
Christmas Markets are held in Augsburg, Munich, Heidelberg, Hamburg, Nürnberg, Lübeck, Freiburg, Berlin, Essen, and numerous smaller towns.

What to Pack

Pack light—luggage restrictions on international flights are tight. Airlines generally allow two pieces of check-in luggage and one carry-on piece per passenger. No piece of check-in luggage can exceed 62 inches (length + width + height) or weigh more than 70 pounds. The carry-on luggage cannot exceed 45 inches (length + width + height) and must fit under the seat or in the overhead luggage compartment. Passengers in first and business classes are also allowed to carry on one garment bag. It is always best, however, to check with your airline ahead of time to find out about its luggage restrictions.

What you pack depends more on the time of year than on any particular dress code. Winters can be bitterly cold; summers are warm but with days that suddenly turn cool and rainy. In the summer, take a warm jacket or heavy sweater for the Bavarian Alps, where the nights can be chilly even during the height of summer.

For the cities, pack as you would for an American city: dressy outfits for formal restaurants and nightclubs, casual clothes elsewhere. Jeans are as popular in Germany as anywhere else, and are perfectly acceptable for sightseeing and informal dining. In the evening, men will probably feel more comfortable wearing a jacket and tie in more expensive restaurants. Many German women are extremely fashion-conscious and wear stylish outfits to restaurants and the theater, especially in the larger cities.

If you plan to swim in a pool, take a bathing cap. They're obligatory in Germany, for both men and women. For stays in budget hotels, take your own soap. Many do not provide soap or provide only one small bar. You will need an electrical adapter for your hair dryer or other small appliances. The current is 220 volts, 50 cycles.

Taking Money Abroad

Traveler's checks and major U.S. credit cards, particularly Visa, are accepted in large cities and resorts. In smaller towns and rural areas, you'll need cash. Many small restaurants and shops in the cities also tend to operate on a cash basis. You won't get as good an exchange rate at home as abroad, but it's wise to exchange a small amount of money into German Deutschemarks before you go to avoid lines at airport currency-exchange booths. Most U.S. banks will exchange your money for Deutschemarks. If your local bank can't provide this service, you can exchange money through **Thomas Cook Currency Service.** To find the office nearest you, contact the service at 29 Broadway, New York, NY 10006, tel. 212/635–0515.

For safety and convenience, it's always best to take traveler's checks. The most recognized traveler's checks are **American Express, Barclay's, Thomas Cook,** and those issued through such major commercial banks as **Citibank** and **Bank of America.** Some banks will issue the checks free to established customers, but most charge a 1% commission fee. Buy part of the traveler's checks in small denominations to cash toward the end of your trip. This will save you from having to cash a large check and ending up with more foreign money than you need. You can also buy traveler's checks in Deutschemarks—a good idea if the dollar is falling and you want to lock into the current rate. Remember to take the addresses of offices where you can get refunds for lost or stolen traveler's checks. *The American Express Traveler's Companion,* a directory of offices to contact worldwide in case of loss or theft of American Express Traveler's checks, is available at most American Express travel offices. In Germany, to report lost American Express traveler's checks, call the Brighton, England, office toll-free at 0130 3100.

The best places to change money are banks and bank-operated currency-exchange booths in airports and railway stations. Hotels and privately run exchange firms will give you a significantly lower rate.

Getting Money from Home

There are at least three ways to get money from home: (1) Have it sent through a large commercial bank with a branch in the town where you're staying. The only drawback is that you must have an account with the bank; if not, you'll have to go through your own bank and the process will be slower and more expensive. (2) Have it sent through American Express. If you are a cardholder, you can cash a personal check or a counter check at an American Express office for up to $1,000; $200 will be in cash and $800 in traveler's checks. Goldcard holders can receive up to $5,000: $500 in cash and $4,500 in traveler's checks. There is a 1% commission on the traveler's checks. American Express also offers a service called **American Express MoneyGram,** which allows you to receive an unlimited amount of money. It works this way: You call home and ask someone to go to an American Express office or an American Express MoneyGram agent located in a retail outlet, and fill out an American Express MoneyGram. It can be paid for with cash or any major credit card. The person making the payment is given a reference number and telephones you with that number. The American Express MoneyGram agent calls an 800 number and authorizes the transfer of funds to an American Express office or participating agency in the town where you're staying. In most cases, the money is available immediately on a 24-hour basis. You pick it up by showing identification and giving the reference number. Fees vary according to the amount of money sent. For $1,000, the fee is $70; for $500, the fee is $45. For the American Express MoneyGram location nearest your home and to find out where the service is available overseas, call 800/543–4080. You do not have to be a cardholder to use this service. (3) Have it sent through **Western Union,** U.S. telephone number 800/325–6000. If you have a MasterCard or Visa, you can have money sent for any amount up to your credit limit. If not, have someone take cash or a certified cashier's check to a Western Union office. The money will be delivered within two business days to a post office in the city where you're staying. Fees vary with the amount of money sent. For $1,000 the fee is $59 if paying with cash; $64 if you use a credit card; for $500, the fee is $49 with cash; $54 with a credit card.

German Currency

The unit of currency in Germany is the Deutschemark (DM), divided into 100 pfennings (pf). Bills are DM 1,000, 500, 200, 100, 50, 20, 10, and the rarer 5. Coins are DM 5, 2, and 1, and 50, 10, 5, 2, and 1 pf. At press time (summer 1992), the mark stood at DM 1.56 to the U.S. dollar, DM 1.52 to the Canadian dollar, and DM 2.95 to the pound sterling.

The Deutschemark became the official currency of united Germany in July 1990. However, great discrepancies still exist in the standard of living between western and eastern Germany.

What It Will Cost

Western Germany has an admirably high standard of living—perhaps the highest in Europe—and eastern Germany's prices are rapidly rising, which inevitably makes it an expensive country to visit, particularly if you spend time in the cities. Many items—gas, food, hotels, and trains, to name but a few—are often more expensive than in the United States.

You can cut your budget by visiting less-known cities and towns and avoiding summer and winter resorts. All along the Main and Neckar rivers, for example, you will find small towns as charming as, but significantly less expensive than, the likes of Rothenburg and Heidelberg; similarly, Westphalia offers atmosphere but lower prices than the fabled towns and cities of the Rhine. Wine lovers should explore the Palatinate instead of the classical Rhine-Mosel tour. In north Germany, the East Frisian islands from Emden eastward are less crowded than their more expensive sisters along the North Frisian coast. Ski enthusiasts would do well to investigate the advantages of the Harz and Eifel mountains, most particularly Oberpfalz and Bayerischer Wald in East Bavaria. Known as the stepchild of German tourism, East Bavaria offers excellent quality at bargain rates.

The five new states (Saxony, Thuringia, Mecklenburg, Saxon-Anhalt, Brandenburg) of former communist East Germany still have a much lower standard of living than does old West Germany. Although prices are rising rapidly in some quarters—notably tourism—you will find such things as public transport and dining in moderate restaurants cheaper than they are in, say, the Black Forest or the Rhineland. Prices in leading hotels and restaurants in places such as Dresden have, however, already begun to match rates in Frankfurt and Munich. As the standard of living in the new states slowly rises, so too will the cost of living.

Passports and Visas

Americans To obtain a new passport, apply in person; renewals can be obtained in person or by mail. First-time applicants should apply to one of the 13 U.S. Passport Agency offices at least five weeks in advance of their departure date. In addition, local county courthouses, many state and probate courts, and some post offices accept passport applications. Necessary documents include: (1) a completed passport application (Form DSP-11); (2) proof of citizenship (certified birth certificate issued by the Hall of Records of your state of birth, or naturalization papers); (3) proof of identity (valid driver's license or state, military, or student ID card with your photograph and signature); (4) two recent, identical, two-inch-square photographs (black-and-white or color head shot with a white or off-white background); and (5) a $65 application fee for a 10-year passport (those under 18 pay $40 for a five-year passport). You may pay with a check, money order, or exact cash amount; no change is given. Passports are mailed to you in about 10–15 working days. To renew your passport by mail, you'll need to send a completed Form DSP-82, two recent, identical passport photographs, your current passport (if less than 12 years old and issued after your 16th birthday), and a check or money order for $55.

A tourist/business visa is not required for U.S. citizens staying up to three months in Germany, but longer stays generally require a visa. Check with the German Embassy, 4645 Reservoir Rd., NW, Washington, DC 20007, tel. 202/298–4000.

Canadians All Canadian citizens require a passport to enter Germany. Send your completed application (available at any post office or passport office) to the **Bureau of Passports,** Suite 215, West Tower, Guy Favreau Complex, 200 René Lévesque Blvd. West, Montreal, Quebec H2Z 1X4. Include $25, two photographs, a guarantor, and proof of Canadian citizenship. Applications can also be made in person at the regional passport offices in Edmonton, Halifax, Montreal, Toronto, Vancouver, or Winnipeg. Passports are valid for five years and are nonrenewable.

Visas are not required for Canadian citizens to enter Germany for stays of up to three months.

Britons All British citizens require a passport to enter Germany. Application forms are available from travel agencies and main post offices, or from the **Passport Office** (Clive House, 70 Petty France, London SW1H 9BR, tel. 071/279–3434). Send the completed form to a regional passport office or apply in person at a main post office. The application must be countersigned by your bank manager, or by a solicitor, barrister, doctor, clergyman, or justice of the peace who knows you personally. In addition, you'll need two photographs and a £15 fee. The occasional tourist might opt for a British Visitors' passport. It is valid for one year, costs £7.50, and is nonrenewable. You'll need two passport photographs and identification. Apply at your local post office.

Visas are not required for British citizens to enter Germany.

Customs and Duties

On Arrival From the beginning of 1993 and the start of a single, unrestricted market within the European Community (EC), there will no longer be restrictions for citizens of the 12 member countries traveling between EC countries. The following duty-free limitations apply to non-EC citizens and anyone entering Germany from outside the Community.

For goods obtained anywhere outside the EC or for goods purchased in a duty-free shop within an EC country, the allowances are: (1) 200 cigarettes or 100 cigarillos or 50 cigars or 250 grams of tobacco (these allowances are doubled if you live outside of Europe); (2) 2 liters of still table wine plus (3) 1 liter of spirits over 22% volume or 2 liters of spirits under 22% volume (fortified and sparkling wines) or 2 more liters of table wine; (4) 60 milliliters of perfume and 250 milliliters of toilet water; (5) other goods to the value of DM 115.

For goods obtained (duty- and tax-paid) within another EC country, the allowances are: (1) 300 cigarettes or 150 cigarillos or 75 cigars or 400 grams of tobacco; (2) 5 liters of still table wine plus (3) 1.5 liters of spirits over 22% volume or 3 liters of spirits under 22% volume (fortified or sparkling wines) or 3 more liters of table wine; (4) 90 milliliters of perfume and 375 milliliters of toilet water; (5) other goods to the value of DM 780.

Tobacco and alcohol allowances are for visitors aged 17 and over. Other items intended for personal use can be imported and exported freely. There are no restrictions on the import and export of German currency.

On Departure

U.S. Customs: If you are bringing any foreign-made equipment from home, such as cameras, it's wise to carry the original receipt with you or register it with U.S. customs before you leave (Form 4457). Otherwise you may end up paying duty on your return. U.S. residents may bring home duty-free up to $400 worth of foreign goods, as long as they have been out of the country for at least 48 hours and haven't made an international trip in 30 days. Each member of the family is entitled to the same exemption, regardless of age, and exemptions can be pooled. For the next $1,000 worth of goods, a flat 10% rate is assessed; above $1,400, duties vary with the merchandise. Included for travelers 21 or older are 1 liter of alcohol, 100 cigars (non-Cuban), and 200 cigarettes. Only one bottle of perfume trademarked in the United States may be imported. However, there is no duty on antiques or art over 100 years old. Anything exceeding these limits will be taxed at the port of entry, and may be taxed additionally in the traveler's home state. Gifts valued at under $50 may be mailed to friends or relatives at home duty-free, but not more than one package per day to any one addressee may be sent, and packages may not include perfumes costing more than $5, tobacco, or liquor.

Canadian Customs: Canadian residents have an exemption ranging from $20 to $300, depending on the length of stay out of the country. For the $300 exemption, you must have been out of the country for one week. For any given year, you are allowed one $300 exemption. You may also bring in duty-free up to 50 cigars, 200 cigarettes, 2.2 pounds of tobacco, and 40 ounces of liquor, provided these are declared in writing to customs on arrival and accompany the traveler in hand or in checked-through baggage. Personal gifts should be mailed as "Unsolicited Gift—Value under $40." Request the Canadian customs brochure "I Declare" for further details.

British Customs: Returning to the United Kingdom, there are two levels of duty-free allowances; tobacco and alcohol allowances are for travelers aged 17 and over.

For goods obtained anywhere outside the EC or for goods purchased in a duty-free shop within an EC country, the allowances are: (1) 200 cigarettes or 100 cigarillos or 50 cigars or 250 grams of tobacco (these allowances are doubled if you live outside of Europe); (2) 2 liters of still table wine plus (3) 1 liter of spirits over 22% volume or 2 liters of spirits under 22% volume (fortified and sparkling wines) or 2 more liters of table wine; (4) 60 milliliters of perfume and 250 milliliters of toilet water; (5) other goods to the value of £32.

For goods obtained (duty- and tax-paid) within another EC country, the allowances are: (1) 300 cigarettes or 150 cigarillos or 75 cigars or 400 grams of tobacco; (2) 5 liters of still table wine plus (3) 1.5 liters of spirits over 22% volume or 3 liters of spirits under 22% volume (fortified or sparkling wines) or 3 more liters of table wine; (4) 90 milliliters of perfume and 375 milliliters of toilet water; (5) other goods to the value of £420.

In addition, no animals or pets of any kind may be brought into the United Kingdom unless subjected to six months' quarantine. The penalties for doing so are severe and are strictly enforced.

Traveling with Film

If your camera is new, shoot and develop a few rolls of film before leaving home. Pack some lens tissue and an extra battery for your built-in light meter. Invest about $10 in a skylight filter and screw it onto the front of your lens. It will protect the lens and reduce haze.

Film doesn't like hot weather. If you're driving in summer, don't store film in the glove compartment or on the shelf under the rear window. Put it behind the front seat on the floor, on the side opposite the exhaust pipe.

On a plane trip, never pack unprocessed film in check-in luggage; if your bags get X-rayed, you can say goodbye to your pictures. Always carry undeveloped film with you through security and ask to have it inspected by hand. (It helps to isolate your film in a plastic bag, ready for quick inspection.) Inspectors at American airports are required by law to honor requests for hand inspection; abroad, you'll have to depend on the kindness of strangers.

The old airport scanning machines—still in use in some Third World countries—use heavy doses of radiation that can turn a family portrait into an early morning fog. The newer models—used in all U.S. and most German airports (those in the eastern part have less modern equipment)—are safe for anything from five to 500 scans, depending on the speed of your film. The effects are cumulative; you can put the same roll of film through several scans without worry. After five scans, however, you're asking for trouble.

If your film gets fogged and you want an explanation, send it to the **National Association of Photographic Manufacturers** (550 Mamaroneck Ave., Harrison, NY 10528). It will try to determine what went wrong. The service is free.

Language

The Germans are great linguists and you'll find that English is spoken in virtually all hotels, restaurants, airports, stations, museums, and other places of interest. However, English is not always widely spoken in rural areas; this is especially true of the eastern part of Germany.

Unless you speak fluent German, you may find some of the regional dialects hard to follow, particularly in Bavaria. While most Germans can speak "high," or standard, German, some older country people will only be able to speak in their dialect.

Staying Healthy

Sanitation and health standards in Germany are as high as those anywhere in the world, and there are no serious health risks associated with travel there. If you have a health problem that might require purchasing prescription drugs while in Germany, have your doctor write a prescription using the drug's generic name. Brand names vary widely from one country to another.

The **International Association for Medical Assistance to Travelers** (IAMAT) is a worldwide association that offers a list of approved physicians and clinics whose training meets British and American standards. For a list of German physicians and clinics that are part of this network, contact IAMAT (417 Center St., Lewiston, NY 14092, tel. 716/754–4883; in **Canada,** 40 Regal Rd., Guelph, Ontario N1K 1B5; in **Europe,** 57 Voirets, 1212 Grand-Lancy, Geneva, Switzerland). Membership is free.

Inoculations are not required for entry to Germany.

Insurance

Travelers may seek insurance coverage in four areas: health and accident, loss of luggage, flight, and trip cancellation. Your first step is to review your existing health and homeowner policies; some health-insurance plans cover health expenses incurred while traveling, some major-medical plans cover emergency transportation, and some homeowner policies cover the theft of luggage.

Health and Accident

Several companies offer coverage designed to supplement existing health insurance for travelers:

Carefree Travel Insurance (Box 310, 120 Mineola Blvd., Mineola, NY 11501, tel. 516/294–0220 or 800/323–3149) provides coverage for emergency medical evacuation and accidental death and dismemberment. It also offers 24-hour medical phone advice.

International SOS Assistance (Box 11568, Philadelphia, PA 19116, tel. 215/244–1500 or 800/523–8930), a medical assistance company, provides emergency evacuation services, worldwide medical referrals, and optional medical insurance.

Travel Guard International, underwritten by Transamerica Occidental Life Companies (1145 Clark St., Stevens Point, WI 54481, tel. 715/345–0505 or 800/782–5151), offers reimbursement for medical expenses with no deductibles or daily limits, as well as emergency-evacuation services.

Wallach and Company, Inc. (Box 480, Middleburg, VA 22117–

0480, tel. 703/687–3166 or 800/237–6615), offers comprehensive medical coverage, including emergency evacuation services worldwide.

Lost Luggage Luggage loss is usually covered as part of a comprehensive travel-insurance package that includes personal accident, trip cancellation, and sometimes default and bankruptcy insurance. Several companies offer comprehensive policies: **Access America, Inc.,** a subsidiary of Blue Cross–Blue Shield (Box 11188, Richmond, VA 23230, tel. 800/334–7525 or 800/284–8300); **Near Services,** (450 Prairie Ave., Suite 101, Calumet City, IL 60409, tel. 708/868–6700 or 800/654–6700); and **Travel Guard International** (*see* Health and Accident Insurance, above).

Trip-Cancellation and Flight Insurance Consider purchasing trip-cancellation insurance if you are traveling on a promotional or discounted ticket that does not allow changes or cancellations. You will then be covered if an emergency causes you to cancel or postpone your trip. Trip-cancellation insurance is usually included in combination travel insurance packages available from most tour operators, travel agents, and insurance agents.

Flight insurance, which covers passengers in the case of death or dismemberment, is often included in the price of a ticket when paid for with American Express, MasterCard, or other major credit cards.

Renting, Leasing, and Purchasing Cars

Renting If you're flying into a major German city you can save money by arranging to pick up and return your car at the airport. You'll have to weigh the added expense of renting a car from a major company with an airport office against the savings on a car from a budget company with offices in town. You could waste precious hours trying to locate the budget company in return for only a small financial savings. If you're arriving and departing from different airports, look for a one-way car rental with no return fees. If you're traveling to more than one country, make sure your rental contract permits you to take the car across borders and that the insurance policy covers you in every country you visit. Be prepared to pay more for a car with an automatic transmission. Since these cars aren't as readily available as those with manual transmission, you should reserve them in advance.

Rental rates vary widely, depending on size and model, number of days you use the car, insurance coverage, and whether special drop-off fees are imposed. In most cases, rates quoted include unlimited free mileage and standard liability protection. Not included are collision damage waiver (CDW), which eliminates your deductible payment should you have an accident; personal accident insurance; gasoline; and European value added taxes (VAT). The VAT is 14% throughout Germany.

Driver's licenses issued in the United States, Canada, and Britain are valid in Germany. You might also take out an international driving permit before you leave, to smooth out difficulties if you have an accident or as an additional identification. Permits are available for a small fee through local offices of the American Automobile Association (AAA) and the Canadian Automobile Association (CAA), or from their main offices

(**AAA,** 1000 AAA Dr., Heathrow, FL 32746, tel. 800/336–4357; **CAA,** 2 Carlton St., Toronto, Ontario M5B 1K4, tel. 416/964–3002).

It's best to arrange a car rental before you leave. You won't save money by waiting until you arrive in Germany, and you may find that the type of car you want is not available at the last minute. Rental companies usually charge according to the exchange rate of the dollar at the time the car is returned or when the credit-card payment is processed. Two companies with special programs to help you hedge against the falling dollar, by guaranteeing advertised rates if you pay in advance, are **Budget Rent-a-Car** (3350 Boyington St., Carrollton, TX 75006, tel. 800/527–0700) and **Connex Travel International** (23 N. Division St., Peekskill, NY 10566, tel. 800/333–3949).

Other budget rental companies serving Germany include **Europe by Car** (1 Rockefeller Plaza, New York, NY 10020, tel. 800/223–1516 or 800/252–9401 in CA), **Auto Europe** (Box 1097 Sharps Wharf, Camden, ME 04843, tel. 800/223–5555), **Foremost Euro-Car** (5430 Van Nuys Blvd., Suite 306, Van Nuys, CA 91401, tel. 800/272–3299), and **Kemwel** (106 Calvert St., Harrison, NY 10528, tel. 800/678–0678).

Other companies include **Avis** (tel. 800/331–1212); **Hertz** (tel. 800/654–3131); and **National** or **Europcar** (tel. 800/CAR–RENT).

Leasing For trips of 21 days or more, you may save money by leasing a car. Under a leasing arrangement, you are technically buying a car and then selling it back to the manufacturer after you've used it. You receive a factory-new car, tax-free, and with international registration and extensive insurance coverage. Rates vary with the make and model of car and length of time used. Car leasing programs are offered by Renault, Citroën, and Peugeot in France, and by Volkswagen, Ford, Audi, and Opel, among others, in Belgium. Delivery to Germany can be arranged for an additional fee. Before you go, compare long-term rental rates with leasing rates. Remember to add taxes and insurance costs to the car rentals, something you don't have to worry about with leasing. Companies that offer leasing arrangements include **Kemwel, Europe by Car,** and **Auto Europe,** all listed above.

GermanRail offers Rail and Drive packages, which combine a train Flexipass (*see* Rail Passes, below) with three days of unlimited-mileage car rental. Packages start at $185 (for a five-day Flexipass and three-day car rental over a month-long period).

Purchasing Given the weakness of the dollar, purchasing a car in Germany is less appealing today than it was a decade ago. The advantage is that you'll get what amounts to a free car rental during your stay in Europe. If you plan to purchase a car in Germany, be certain the prices quoted are for cars built to meet specifications set down by the U.S. Department of Transportation. You will also be subject to a U.S. customs duty. For more information, contact **Kemwel** or **Europe by Car,** both listed above, or ask your local car dealer to put you in touch with an importer.

Rail Passes

The **EurailPass,** valid for unlimited first-class train travel through 20 countries, including Germany, is an excellent value if you plan to travel around the Continent. The ticket is available for periods of 15 days ($430), 21 days ($550), one month ($680), two months ($920), and three months ($1,150). For those under 26, there is the **Eurail Youthpass,** for one or two months' unlimited second-class train travel at $470 and $640.

For travelers who like to spread out their train journeys, there is the **Eurail Flexipass.** With the 15-day pass ($280), travelers get five days of unlimited first-class train travel spread out over a 15-day period; a 21-day pass gives you nine days of travel ($450); and a one-month pass gives you 14 days ($610).

The EurailPass is available only if you live outside Europe or North Africa. The rates quoted above are for tickets purchased in the United States. Add 10% if you plan to buy your pass in Europe. Apply through your travel agent, or contact **GermanRail** (122 E. 42nd St., New York, NY 10168, tel. 212/922-1616).

The GermanRail (DB) Flexipass, now valid for the entire German rail network, is available to non-Germans. The "flexible" nature of the pass allows you to spread your days of train travel over a month-long period. A first-class pass costs $240 for five days, $360 for 10 days, and $450 for 15 days. A second-class pass costs $160 for five days, $240 for 10 days, and $300 for 15 days. A GermanRail Twin Pass gives a 10% discount on these rates for two people traveling together. A Youthpass (second-class only) for people aged 12–25 ranges from $110 to $180. All of these passes can be used on buses operated by the DB, as well as on tour routes along the Romantic and Castle roads served by Deutsche Touring (*see* Getting Around by Bus in Staying in Germany, below). Cruises on the Rhine, Main, and Mosel rivers operated by the Köln-Düsseldorfer (KD) Line are also included with the pass.

Student and Youth Travel

The **International Student Identity Card** (ISIC) entitles students to youth rail passes, special fares on local transportation, Intra-European student charter flights, and discounts at museums, theaters, sports events, and many other attractions. If purchased in the United States, the $14 cost of the ISIC also includes $3,000 in emergency medical insurance, $100 a day for up to 60 days of hospital coverage, and a collect phone number to call in case of emergencies. Apply to the **Council on International Student Exchange** (CIEE, 205 E. 42nd St., New York, NY 10017, tel. 212/661-1414). In Canada, the ISIC is available for CN$13 from **Travel Cuts** (187 College St., Toronto, Ont. M5T 1P7, tel. 416/979-2406).

The **Youth International Educational Exchange Card** (YIEE), issued by the **Federation of International Youth Travel Organizations** (FIYTO, 81 Islands Brugge, DK-2300 Copenhagen S, Denmark), provides similar services to nonstudents under the age of 26. In the United States, the card is available from CIEE (address above). In Canada, the YIEE is available from the **Canadian Hostelling Association** (CHA, 1600 James Naismith Drive, Suite 608, Gloucester, Ont. K1B 5N4, tel. 613/748-5638).

An **International Youth Hostel Federation** (IYHF) membership card is the key to inexpensive dormitory-style accommodations at more than 5,000 youth hostels in 70 countries around the world. Hostels provide separate sleeping quarters for men and women at rates ranging from $7 to $20 a night per person and are situated in a variety of facilities, including converted farmhouses, villas, and restored castles, as well as specially constructed modern buildings. IYHF membership is available in the United States through American Youth Hostels (AYH, Box 37613, Washington, DC 20013, tel. 202/783-6161) and in Canada through the **Canadian Hostelling Association** (address above). The cost for a first-year membership is $25 for adults 18–54. Renewal thereafter is $20 a year. For youths (17 and under), the rate is $10 a year, and for senior citizens (55 and older) the rate is $15 a year. Family membership is available for $35 a year.

Council Travel, a CIEE subsidiary, is the foremost U.S. student travel agency, specializing in low-cost charters and serving as the exclusive U.S. agent for many student airfare bargains and student tours. CIEE's 72-page *Student Travel Catalog* and "Council Charter" brochure are available free from any Council Travel office in the United States (enclose $1 postage if ordering by mail). Contact the CIEE headquarters (205 E. 42nd St., New York, NY 10017) for the branch office nearest you.

Students who would like to work abroad should contact CIEE's **Work Abroad Department** (205 E. 42nd St., New York, NY 10017, tel. 212/661-1414, ext. 1130). The council arranges various types of paid and voluntary work experiences overseas for up to six months. CIEE also sponsors study programs in Europe, Latin America, and Asia, and publishes many books of interest to the student traveler. These include *Work, Study, Travel Abroad: The Whole World Handbook* ($12.95 plus $1.50 book-rate postage or $3 first-class postage); and *Volunteer! The Comprehensive Guide to Voluntary Service in the U.S. and Abroad* ($8.95 plus $1.50 book-rate postage or $3 first-class postage).

The Information Center at the **Institute of International Education** (IIE) has reference books, foreign university catalogs, study-abroad brochures, and other materials, which may be consulted by students and nonstudents alike, free of charge.

The Information Center (809 UN Plaza, New York, NY 10017, tel. 212/883-8200) is open Monday–Friday 10–4. *It is not open on holidays.*

IIE administers a variety of grant and study programs offered by U.S. and foreign organizations, and publishes a well-known annual series of study-abroad guides, including *Academic Year Abroad, Vacation Study Abroad,* and *Study in the United Kingdom and Ireland.* The institute also publishes *Teaching Abroad,* a book of employment and study opportunities overseas for U.S. teachers. For a current list of IIE publications with prices and ordering information, write to Publications Service, Institute of International Education, 809 UN Plaza, New York, NY 10017. Books must be purchased by mail or in person; telephone orders are not accepted.

General information on IIE programs and services is available from its regional offices in Atlanta, Chicago, Denver, Houston, San Francisco, and Washington, DC.

Traveling with Children

Publications *Family Travel Times* is a newsletter published 10 times a year by **TWYCH** (Travel with Your Children, 45 W. 18th St., New York, NY 10011, tel. 212/206–0688). Subscription costs $35 and includes access to back issues and twice-weekly opportunities to call in for specific advice.

"Young People's Guide to Munich" is a free pamphlet available from the German National Tourist Office (747 Third Ave., New York, NY 10017, tel. 212/308–3300).

Hotels A likely choice for families is any one of the Schloss (castle) hotels in Germany; many have parklike grounds. U.S. representatives are **Europa Hotels and Tours** (14178 Woodinville-Duval Rd., Box 1278, Woodinville, WA 98072, tel. 800/523–9570, reservations only), and **DER Tours Inc.** (11933 Wilshire Blvd., Los Angeles, CA 90025, tel. 800/937–1239).

Home Exchange Exchanging homes is a surprisingly low-cost way to enjoy a vacation abroad, especially a long one. The largest home-exchange service, **Intervac U.S. International Home Exchange Service** (Box 590504, San Francisco, CA 94159, tel. 415/435–3497) publishes three directories a year. Membership, which costs $45, entitles you to one listing and all three directories. **Loan-a-Home** (2 Park La., 6E, Mount Vernon, NY 10552, tel. 914/664–7640) is popular with academics on sabbatical and businesspeople on temporary assignment. There's no annual membership fee or charge for listing your home, however one directory and a supplement costs $35. Loan-a-Home publishes two directories (in December and June) and two supplements (in March and September) each year. The set of four books costs $45 per year.

Getting There On international flights, children under two years not occupying a seat pay 10% of adult fare. Various discounts apply to children ages 2–12. Reserve a seat behind the bulkhead of the plane, which offers more legroom and can usually accommodate a bassinet (which some airlines will supply). At the same time, inquire about special children's meals or snacks, offered by most airlines. (See "TWYCH's Airline Guide," in the February 1990 and 1992 issues of *Family Travel Times*, for a rundown on children's services offered by 46 airlines.)

Regulations about infant travel on airplanes are in the process of being changed. Until they do, however, if you want to be sure your infant is secure, you should buy a separate ticket and bring your own infant car seat (but check with the airline in advance—some don't allow them). Some airlines allow babies to travel in their own car seats at no charge if there's a spare seat available; otherwise, safety seats will be stored and the child will have to be held by a parent. For the booklet *Child/Infant Safety Seats Acceptable for Use in Aircraft*, write to the **Federal Aviation Administration** (800 Independence Ave. SW, Washington, DC 20591, tel. 202/267–3479). If you opt to hold your baby on your lap, do so with the infant outside the seat belt so he or she won't be crushed in case of a sudden stop.

Baby-sitting Services First check with the hotel desk for recommended child-care arrangements. Also, most local tourist offices in Germany maintain updated lists of baby-sitters. The baby-sitters have all been screened. Expect to pay approximately DM 25 per hour. In Munich, for a tourist-office-approved service offering sitters who speak English, call 089/229–291. Also, contact the **Munich American High School** (Cincinnatistr. 61A, Munich, tel. 089/622–98354). The **American Women's Club of Frankfurt** (Abrams Bldg., Frankfurt, West Germany, APO, NY 09757) runs a child-care center at the military base near the Abrams Building (tel. 069/55–3129).

Hints for Disabled Travelers

The **Information Center for Individuals with Disabilities** (Fort Point Pl., 1st floor, 27–43 Wormwood St., Boston, MA 02210, tel. 617/727–5540) offers useful problem-solving assistance, including lists of travel agents that specialize in tours for the disabled.

Moss Rehabilitation Hospital Travel Information Service (1200 West Tabor Rd., Philadelphia, PA 19141–3099, tel. 215/456–9600; TDD 215/456–9602) provides (for a small fee) information on tourist sights, transportation, and accommodations in destinations around the world.

Mobility International USA (Box 3551, Eugene, OR 97403, tel. 503/343–1284), an internationally affiliated organization, coordinates exchange programs for disabled people around the world and offers information on accommodations and organized study programs. The annual fee is $20.

The **Society for the Advancement of Travel for the Handicapped** (347 Fifth Ave., Suite 610, New York, NY 10016, tel. 212/447–7284) offers access information. Annual membership costs $45, or $25 for senior travelers and students. Send a stamped, self-addressed envelope.

Travel Industry and Disabled Exchange (TIDE, 5435 Donna Ave., Tarzana, CA 91356, tel. 818/368–5648) provides (for a $15 per-person annual membership fee) a quarterly newsletter and a directory of travel agencies and tours to Europe, Canada, New Zealand, and Australia, all specializing in travel for the disabled.

The Itinerary (Box 2012, Bayonne, NJ 07002, tel. 201/858–3400) is a bimonthly travel magazine for the disabled. Subscriptions cost $10 for one year, $20 for two. ***Access to the World: A Travel Guide for the Handicapped,*** by Louise Weiss, offers tips on travel and accessibility around the world. It is available from Henry Holt & Co. for $12.95 (tel. 800/247–3912; the order number is 0805001417).

Hints for Older Travelers

The **American Association of Retired Persons** (AARP, 601 E St. NW, Washington, DC 20049, tel. 202/434–2277) has two programs for independent travelers: (1) the "Purchase Privilege Program," which offers discounts on hotels, airfare, car rentals, and sightseeing; and (2) the "AARP Motoring Plan," provided by Amoco, which offers emergency aid and trip-routing information for an annual fee of $33.95 per couple. The

AARP also arranges group tours, including apartment living in Europe, through **AARP Travel Experience from American Express** (400 Pinnacle Way, Suite 450, Norcross, GA 30071, tel. 800/927-0111). AARP members must be 50 or older. Annual dues are $5 per person or per couple.

When using an AARP or other identification card, ask for a reduced hotel rate at the time you make your reservation, not when you check out. At participating restaurants, show your card to the maitre d' before you're seated, since discounts may be limited to certain set menus, days, or hours. When renting a car, be sure to ask about special promotional rates, which may offer greater savings than the available discount.

Elderhostel (75 Federal St., 3rd floor, Boston, MA 02110-1941, tel. 617/426-7788) is an innovative, low-cost educational program for people 60 and older. Participants live in dorms on some 1,600 campuses around the world. Mornings are devoted to lectures and seminars; afternoons, to sightseeing and field trips. The all-inclusive fee for two- to three-week international trips, including room, board, tuition, and round-trip transportation, ranges from $1,800 to $4,500.

National Council of Senior Citizens (4331 F St. NW, Washington, DC 20004, tel. 202/347-8800) is a nonprofit advocacy group with some 5,000 local clubs across the country. Annual membership is $12 per person or per couple. Members receive a monthly newspaper with travel information and an ID card for reduced-rate hotels and car rentals.

Mature Outlook (6001 N. Clark St., Chicago, IL 60660, tel. 800/336-6330), a subsidiary of Sears Roebuck & Co., is a travel club for people over 50, with hotel and motel discounts and a bimonthly newsletter. Annual membership is $9.95 per couple. Instant membership is available at participating Holiday Inns.

Further Reading

Germany is the setting for many good spy novels, including *The Odessa File*, by Frederick Forsyth; John Le Carré's *A Small Town in Germany;* Alistair MacLean's *Where Eagles Dare;* Walter Winward's *The Midas Touch;* and *The Leader and the Damned*, by Colin Forbes.

If you like to travel with a historical novel, look for Christine Bruckner's *Flight of Cranes;* Timothy Findley's *Famous Last Words;* and Fred Uhlman's *Reunion*. Also, Silvia Tennenbaum's *Yesterday's Streets* covers three generations of a wealthy German family.

Other suggested titles include Günter Grass's *The Tin Drum;* Christa Wolf's *No Place on Earth;* and *Buddenbrooks*, by Thomas Mann. For a contemporary study of the Germans, read *Germany and the Germans* by British author John Ardagh.

For books about Berlin in the '20s, pick up Vicki Baum's *Grand Hotel*. Leon Uris's *Armageddon: A Novel of Berlin* is set at the end of World War II. Contemporary novels about Berlin include Len Deighton's *Berlin Game* and Peter Schneider's *The Wall Jumper*.

Arriving and Departing

From North America by Plane

Since the air routes between North America and Germany are heavily traveled, the passenger has a choice of many airlines and fares. But fares change with stunning rapidity, so consult your travel agent on what bargains are currently available.

Be certain to distinguish among (1) nonstop flights—no changes, no stops; (2) direct flights—no changes but one or more stops; and (3) connecting flights—two or more planes, one or more stops.

The Airlines The U.S. airlines that serve Germany are **Northwest Airlines** (tel. 800/447–4747), which flies to Frankfurt; **Delta** (tel. 800/241–4141), which flies to Frankfurt, Stuttgart, and Munich; **TWA** (tel. 800/892–4141), which flies to Frankfurt, Stuttgart, Munich, and Berlin; and **American Airlines** (tel. 800/433–7300), which flies to Frankfurt, Berlin, Hamburg, Munich, and Nürnberg. **Lufthansa** (tel. 800/645–3880), the German national airline, flies direct to Düsseldorf, Frankfurt, Köln/Bonn, Hamburg, Munich, and Stuttgart. Another German carrier, **LTU International Airways** (tel. 800/888–0200), flies from New York, Miami, Orlando, Atlanta, San Francisco, and Los Angeles to Frankfurt, Munich, and Düsseldorf.

Flying Time The flying time to Frankfurt from New York is 7.5 hours; from Chicago, 10 hours; from Los Angeles, 12 hours.

Enjoying the Flight If you're lucky enough to be able to sleep on a plane, it makes sense to fly at night. Many experienced travelers, however, prefer to take a morning flight to Europe and arrive in the evening, just in time for a good night's sleep. Since the air on a plane is dry, it helps to drink a lot of nonalcoholic liquids; drinking alcohol contributes to jet lag. Feet swell at high altitudes, so it's a good idea to remove your shoes while in flight. Sleepers usually prefer window seats to curl up against; those who like to move about the cabin should ask for aisle seats. Bulkhead seats (located in the front row of each cabin) have more legroom, but seat trays are attached to the arms of your seat rather than to the back of the seat in front of you. Bulkhead seats are generally reserved for the disabled, the elderly, and parents traveling with infants.

Discount Flights The major airlines offer a range of tickets that can increase the price of any given seat by more than 300%, depending on the day of purchase. As a rule, the further in advance you buy the ticket, the less expensive it is and the greater the penalty (up to 100%) for canceling. Check with airlines for details.

The best buy is not necessarily an APEX (advance purchase) ticket on one of the major airlines. APEX tickets carry certain restrictions: They must be bought in advance (usually 21 days); they restrict your travel, usually with a minimum stay of seven days and a maximum of 90; and they also penalize you for changes—voluntary or not—in your travel plans. But if you can work around these drawbacks, they are among the best-value fares available.

Charter flights offer the lowest fares but often depart only on certain days, and seldom on time. Though you may be able to arrive at one city and return from another, you may lose all or most of your money if you cancel your ticket. Don't sign up for a charter flight unless you've checked with a travel agency about the reputation of the packager. It's particularly important to know the packager's policy concerning refunds should a flight be canceled. One of the most popular charter operators to Europe is **Council Charter** (205 E. 42nd St., New York, NY 10017, tel. 800/800–8222 or 212/661–0311), a division of CIEE (Council on International Educational Exchange). Other companies advertise in the Sunday travel section of newspapers.

Somewhat more expensive—but up to 50% below the cost of APEX fares—are tickets purchased through companies known as consolidators, which buy blocks of tickets on scheduled airlines and sell them at wholesale prices. Here again, you may lose all or most of your money if you change plans, but at least you will be on a regularly scheduled flight with less risk of cancellation than on a charter. Once you've made your reservation, call the airline to make sure you're confirmed. Among the best-known consolidators are **UniTravel** (Box 12485, St. Louis, MO 63132, tel. 800/325–2222 or 314/569–2501) and **Access International** (101 W. 31st St., Suite 1104, New York, NY 10001, tel. 212/465–0707 or 800/825–3633). Others advertise in the Sunday travel sections of newspapers as well.

A third option is to join a travel club that offers special discounts to its members. Three such organizations are **Moment's Notice** (425 Madison Ave., New York, NY 10017, tel. 212/486–0500); **Discount Travel International** (114 Forrest Ave., Narberth, PA 19072, tel. 215/668–7184 or 800/334–9294); and **Worldwide Discount Travel Club** (1674 Meridian Ave., Suite 300, Miami Beach, FL 33139, tel. 305/534–2082). These cut-rate tickets should be compared with APEX tickets on the major airlines.

Smoking Regulations You can request a nonsmoking seat during check-in or when you book your ticket. If a U.S. airline tells you there are no seats available in the nonsmoking section, insist on one: Department of Transportation regulations require U.S. carriers to find seats for all nonsmokers on the day of the flight, provided they meet check-in time restrictions.

From North America by Ship

Although there are no ocean liners that make direct crossings from North America to Germany, several cruise ships use Hamburg as a port of call on their European cruises, which generally take place in the summer. These include ships of the Cunard Line and the Royal Viking Line. While the *QE2* is the only cruise ship that makes regular transatlantic crossings, other cruise ships that sail from European ports in the summer and North American ports in the winter make transatlantic repositioning crossings as one season ends and another begins. Some sail straight across, often at reduced rates to passengers. Others have several ports of call before heading for open sea. Arrangements can be made to cruise one way and fly one way. Since itineraries can change at the last minute, contact the cruise line for the latest information.

Cunard Line (555 Fifth Ave., New York, NY 10017, tel. 800/221–4770) operates four ships that make transatlantic crossings. The *QE2* makes regular crossings from July through December, between Southampton, England, or Cherbourg, France and New York City or sometimes Baltimore. Arrangements for the *QE2* can include one-way airfare. The *Sea Goddess I* sails to and from Madeira, Portugal, and St. Thomas, in the U.S. Virgin Islands, for their repositioning crossings. The *Vistafjord* sails to and from Naples, Italy, and Ft. Lauderdale, Florida, on its repositioning crossings. Cunard Line offers fly/cruise packages and pre- and post-land packages.

Royal Viking Line (95 Merrick Way, Coral Gables, FL 33134, tel. 800/634–8000) has two ships that cruise out of European ports. The *Royal Viking Queen* makes repositioning crossings from Barbados to Seville, Spain. The *Viking Sun* cruises from Ft. Lauderdale to Rome and from London to Montreal. Fly-cruise packages are available.

From the U.K. by Plane

British Airways and **Lufthansa** are the main airlines flying from London to Germany. Between them, they serve nine German destinations—10, including Münster, to which Lufthansa's subsidiary airline, **DLT**, flies.

The main gateways to Germany by air are Düsseldorf, Köln, Frankfurt, Munich, and Berlin. British Airways and Lufthansa each have up to two flights a day into Köln, with a flying time of 1¼ hours and a minimum round-trip fare of £90. British Airways has up to seven flights and Lufthansa six flights into Frankfurt from London, with a flying time of 1 hour and 25 minutes and a minimum fare of £95. Each airline has three flights into Munich, with a 1 hour and 40 minute flying time and a minimum fare of £135. British Airways has up to three nonstop and three one-stop flights into Berlin, with a nonstop flying time of 1 hour and 40 minutes and a minimum fare of £135. Lufthansa inaugurated flights into Berlin in late 1990.

Substantial discount fares can be obtained via travel agents instead of dealing directly with the airlines. Fixed-date (APEX) fares booked two weeks ahead and including at least one Saturday are also discounted.

The airlines also fly to Bremen, Hannover, and Stuttgart, and Lufthansa also has one flight a day into Nürnberg.

Commuter-style airline **Connectair** flies twice a day from Gatwick to Düsseldorf, with an £80 cheapest round-trip fare. **Air UK** flies weekdays from London's third airport, Stansted, to Frankfurt (1 hour and 55 minutes' flying time) and DLT's other Gatwick service also goes to Frankfurt.

Dan Air operates the cheapest regular charter flights from Gatwick four or more days a week to Berlin and Munich and two to Hamburg, Hannover, Frankfurt, Düsseldorf, and Stuttgart.

Increasing competition has brought fares down to lower levels than still exist on other European routes from the United Kingdom, and further improvement is expected now that British Midland, the U.K. independent airline, flies from Heathrow to Düsseldorf and Frankfurt.

For reservations: **British Airways** (tel. 081/897–4000); **Air UK** (tel. 0345/666777); **Lufthansa** (tel. 071/408–0442); **Connectair** (tel. 0293/862971); **Dan Air/GTF** (tel. 071/229–2474).

From the U.K. by Train

British Rail operates up to 10 services a day to Germany under its Rail Europe banner. Eight of the departures are from Victoria (via the Dover–Ostend ferry or jetfoil), with the other two from Liverpool Street (via Harwich–Hook of Holland).

The services, involving train changes (usually at Köln), include Köln, Koblenz, Frankfurt, Osnabruck, Hannover, Hamburg, Stuttgart, and Munich, with the journey time to Köln usually 9 hours via jetfoil, 12 hours via the Dover–Ostend ferry, and 13 hours via the Harwich–Hook route. To Munich, the times vary from 14 to 23 hours depending on the time of departure and route. The fastest train leaves Victoria at about 8 AM. Rail fares can be more expensive than plane fares; however, there are often discount offers. Ask British Rail for details.

Berlin is reached via Hannover in about 20 hours, with up to four departures a day—two from Victoria, two from Liverpool Street.

The cheapest round-trip fares to Köln and Munich are £77 and £154, with the ordinary fares set at £90 and £192. These apply to the Victoria departures; Liverpool Street services are more expensive.

A one-way fare to Berlin is £85; the round-trip fare is £169. Book through British Rail travel centers (tel. 071/834–2345).

From the U.K. by Bus

The fastest service is by **Europabus**, which has up to three departures a day from London's Victoria coach station. The buses cross the Channel on Sealink's Dover–Zeebrugge ferry service and then drive via the Netherlands and Belgium to Köln (14½ hours), Frankfurt (17½ hours), Mannheim (18¾ hours), Stuttgart/Nürnberg (20½ hours), and Munich (22¾ hours). One-way and round-trip fares are: Köln (£38/£62), Frankfurt (£40/£69), Mannheim (£43/£74), Stuttgart/Nürnberg (£51/£81), and Munich (£55/£91).

Bookings can also be made through **Transline** (tel. 0708/864911), which runs a service to 35 smaller towns in western Germany. There are up to four departures a week, also from Victoria, and the buses cross either via P&O European Ferries' Dover–Ostend or Sally Line's Ramsgate–Dunkerque services. Destinations include Hannover, Dortmund, Essen, and Düsseldorf as well as the smaller towns. Fares range from £32 to £36 one-way and £59 to £66 round-trip.

From the U.K. by Car

The choice of Channel crossing from the United Kingdom when driving to Germany, and not using the direct Harwich–Hamburg link, will depend on the final destination. If north Germany is the destination, then ports in the Netherlands are the most convenient. For central and southern Germany, the Belgian entry ports are best.

A sample of the mileages confirms this. For Berlin and Hanover, the Hook of Holland is considerably closer at 476 and 282 miles than Ostend at 520 and 387 miles respectively; for Munich, Ostend is 23 miles closer at 530. For Köln and Frankfurt, the two ports are almost equidistant. Both are considerably closer than the French ports.

For the Hook of Holland, ferries depart from Harwich—the east coast port reached from London via A-12 (about 2½ hours' drive). **Sealink** operates one ferry daily and one overnight; both sail year-round. It is an eight-hour crossing, and passengers' fares start at £27 (£9 supplement for first-class travel), car rates range from £32 to £63, and a two-berth cabin costs from £6 to £14.

Like Sealink, **Olau Line** operates newer, high-quality ships on its Netherlands route. There is one daily and one overnight departure from the north Kent port of Sheerness (two hours from London via A-2/M-2) to Vlissingen. The fare is £22; car rates start at £25.

P&O European Ferries operates services from Dover to both Zeebrugge (up to six a day) and Ostend, 19 miles southwest down the coast. Crossing time to Ostend is four hours, half an hour longer to Zeebrugge. Passengers' fares to both Belgian ports are £13, with car rates from £25 to £82.

All four ports mentioned are between one and two hours' drive of the German border. From the Hook, take A-12 to Arnhem and then A-1 toward Dortmund, Essen, and so on. From Vlissingen, take A-58 and then A-67 to Düsseldorf.

Both Zeebrugge and Ostend are a short drive from E-5, from which you can turn off onto E-3 at Ghent for Düsseldorf and Essen, or stay on and join A-61 for Bonn and, farther south, Koblenz, Wiesbaden, Frankfurt, and Mannheim.

P&O also operates a ferry service into Zeebrugge from Felixstowe (another English east coast port just north of Harwich); while **North Sea Ferries** operates from much farther north at Hull to Zeebrugge and Rotterdam Europoort, 3 kilometers (2 miles) south of the Hook.

There is a **Motorail** service from Paris to Munich. A distance of 575 miles, the journey takes 10 hours and there is one departure a day.

For ferry reservations: **Sealink,** tel. 071/834–8122; **P&O,** tel. 071/734–4431; **Olau,** tel. 0795/666666; **North Sea Ferries,** tel. 0482/795141; **French Motorail,** tel. 071/409–3518 (information only).

It is recommended that motorists acquire a green card from their insurance companies. This gives comprehensive insurance coverage for driving in Germany. The most comprehensive breakdown insurance and vehicle and personal security coverage is sold by the **Automobile Association** (AA) in its Five Star scheme.

Staying in Germany

Getting Around

By Plane Germany's internal air network is excellent, with frequent flights linking all major cities. Services are operated by **Lufthansa** and by Germany's other leading airline, **LTU**. Some internal flights are also offered by **British Airways.** In addition, three small airlines operate services between a limited number of northern cities and the East and North Frisian islands, though many of these flights operate only in the summer. Details of all internal services are available from travel agents; otherwise, contact Lufthansa at Frankfurt Airport (tel. 069/690–71222; 069/690–3050–9).

Lufthansa also runs an excellent train, the "Lufthansa Express," linking Düsseldorf, Köln, Bonn, and Frankfurt airports and acting as a supplement to existing air services. Only passengers holding air tickets may use the train, but there is no extra charge for it. Service is first class. Luggage is automatically transferred to your plane on arrival at the airport. German Railways operates a similar service called "Rail and Fly" (*see* below), and trains on the Köln-Munich line stop at Frankfurt airport instead of at Wiesbaden for connections with flights to and from Frankfurt.

By Train German Federal Railways—or **DB,** meaning Deutsche Bundesbahn, as it is usually referred to—operates one of the most comprehensive and fastest rail systems in Europe. DB runs trains in what was formerly West Germany, while train service in eastern Germany is still operated by the Reichsbahn. The two systems are expected to merge in the near future but in the meantime are increasingly integrating their networks. For instance, there are many more trains now linking the eastern cities of Leipzig, Dresden, Halle, Magdeburg, Potsdam, Rostock, and Schwerin—as well as Berlin—with western cities. DB offers a range of discounted fares and inclusive tickets, from family rovers to a Senior Citizen Card, but probably the best deal for the foreign visitor is the new Flexipass, which is valid for all German trains (*see* Rail Passes in Before You Go, above).

All major cities in western Germany are linked by fast Intercity (IC) hourly service. A DM 6 (DM 10 first class) surcharge is made regardless of distance on all Intercity journeys. (Holders of GermanRail Flexipasses pay no supplements.) IC provides excellent connections at the main nodal points—Hannover, Dortmund, Köln, Mannheim, Würzburg, Munich, and Frankfurt—and changing trains couldn't be easier. You only have to cross to the other side of the platform. Special train maps on platform notice boards give details of the layout of each IC train arriving on that line, showing where first- and second-class cars and the restaurant car are situated, as well as where they will stop along the length of the platform. If you have a reservation, it will give the number of the car with your seats; locate this car on the map so that you can stand on the platform exactly where your car will stop when the train pulls in. It is possible to check your baggage for Frankfurt Airport from any of 52 Intercity stations throughout Germany. Except on weekends, there is guaranteed overnight delivery.

Super high-speed Intercity Express (ICE) trains, capable of speeds of up to 165 miles per hour, were introduced in 1991 on the Hamburg–Munich and Hamburg–Frankfurt lines. Travel times have been cut by as much as 30% on these comfortable trains, allowing passengers to cross Germany from the north coast to Bavaria in six hours.

Although the eastern German Reichsbahn has train classifications similar to the DB, their trains remain much slower because of the poor condition of tracks and bridges. Many trains have first- and second-class cars, and longer-distance routes provide dining cars or buffet facilities. Since fewer people have cars in the east, trains are more heavily used and seat reservations are strongly advised for long journeys.

Rail passengers in possession of a valid round-trip air ticket can buy a heavily discounted "Rail and Fly" ticket for DB trains connecting with German airports: Hamburg, Bremen, Hannover, Düsseldorf, Köln/Bonn, Saarbrücken, Stuttgart, and Munich.

The IC network is complemented by fast regional trains (*Inter-Regio*), while E-trains provide slower local services. A DM 6 (DM 10 first class) surcharge is made regardless of distance on all IC trains, but seat reservations on IC services are free when tickets are bought 24 hours or more in advance. Bikes are not carried on IC or ICE trains.

Note that in high season you will frequently encounter lines at ticket offices for seat reservations. Unless you are prepared to board the train without a reserved seat, taking the chance of a seat being available, the only way to avoid these lines is to make an advance reservation by phone. Call the ticket office (*Fahrkarten Schalter*) of the rail station from which you plan to depart. Here again, you will probably have to make several attempts before you get through to the reservations section (*Reservierungen-Platzkarten*), but you will then be able to collect your seat ticket from a special counter without having to wait in line.

Tourist Rail Cards

Holders of British Rail Senior Citizens' Rail Cards can buy an "add-on" **European Senior Citizens' Rail Card** that permits half-price train travel in most European countries, including Germany. Senior citizens from other countries who intend to stay in Germany for some time should consider buying the DB **Senioren Pass.** This is available in two forms: the Senioren Pass "A" (which costs DM 75) allows half-price travel Monday through Thursday and Saturday, while Senioren B (DM 110) permits half-price travel any day of the week. Both are valid for a year and can be bought before going to Germany.

Travelers under 26 who have not invested in a **Eurail Youthpass,** or in any of the other rail passes, should inquire about discount travel fares under a Billet International Jeune (BIJ) scheme. The special one-trip tariff is offered by EuroTrain International, with offices in London, Dublin, Paris, Madrid, Lisbon, Rome, Zurich, Athens, Brussels, Budapest, Hannover, Leiden, Vienna, and Tangier. You can purchase a Eurotrain ticket at one of these offices or at travel-agent networks, mainline rail stations, and specialist youth-travel operators.

DB Regional Rail Rovers (**Tourenkarten**) cover some 73 areas, including all the main tourist regions. They are excellent value for the money. Valid for any 10 days within a 21-day vacation period, they cost around DM 50 for one person, DM 68 for two people traveling together, and DM 83 for a family (one or two parents, plus any number of unmarried children under 18 and grandparents). Unless you are going to Germany on a vacation run by the railways themselves, the Tourenkarten has to be bought when you arrive in Germany. However, there is one catch: To be eligible you must travel at least 250 kilometers (155 miles) on a German train to reach your vacation area and the same distance when you leave. So check distances carefully on your map—it may be worth making a slight detour to qualify.

For further information, contact **GermanRail** (747 Third Ave., New York, NY 10017, tel. 212/308–3106).

By Bus Germany has good local bus services, but no proper nationwide network like Greyhound. A large proportion of services are operated by the railways (**Bahnbus**) and are closely integrated with train services, while on less busy rail lines, services are run by buses in off-peak periods—normally midday and weekends. Rail tickets are valid on these services. The railways, in the guise of **Deutsche Touring,** also operate the German sections of the Europabus network. Contact them at Am Römerhof 17,6000-Frankfurt/Main 90, for details about a range of 2–7-day package tours.

One of the best services is provided by the Romantic Road bus between Würzburg (with connections to and from Frankfurt and Wiesbaden) and Füssen (with connections to and from Munich, Augsburg, and Garmisch-Partenkirchen). This is an all-reserved-seats bus with a stewardess, offering one- or two-day tours in each direction in summer, leaving in the morning and arriving in the evening. Details and reservations are available from Deutsche Touring (*see* above) or big city tourist offices.

All towns of any size operate their own local buses. For the most part, those link up with local trams (streetcars), electric railways services (S-bahn), and subways (U-bahn). Fares vary according to distance, but a ticket usually allows you to transfer freely between the various forms of transportation. Some cities issue 24-hour tickets at special rates.

By Bike Information on all aspects of cycling in Germany is available from the **Bund Deutscher Radfahrer,** the Association of German Cyclists (Otto-Fleck-Schneise 4,6000 Frankfurt 71). There are no formalities governing the importation of bikes into Germany, and no duty is required. Bikes can also be carried on trains—though *not* on IC or ICE trains—if you buy a *Fahrradkarte,* or bicycle ticket. These cost DM 6.50 per journey and can be bought at any train station. Those under 26 with a "Tramper Ticket"—a monthly rover that costs DM 234—can take bikes free of charge. Full details are given in the German railway's brochure *Fahrrad am Bahnhof.*

Bicycles are also available for rental at more than 270 train stations throughout the country, most of them in south Germany. The cost is DM 10–DM 12 per day, DM 6–DM 8 if you have a valid rail ticket. They can be returned at any other station.

By Boat River and lake trips are among the greatest delights of a vacation in Germany, especially along the Rhine, Germany's longest river. The Rhine may be viewed at a variety of paces: by fast hydrofoil, by express boat, by sedate motorship, or by romantic paddle steamer. For those in a hurry, there is a daily hydrofoil service from Düsseldorf right through to Mainz. It is advisable to book in advance for this. For gentler souls, there is a wide range of more leisurely cruises. German cruise ships also operate on the Upper Rhine as far as Basel, Switzerland; on the Main between Frankfurt and Mainz; on the Danube to Linz and on to Vienna; on the Europe Canal joining the Main and the Danube; on the Elbe and Weser and their estuaries; on the Inn and Ilz; and on the Ammersee, Chiemsee, Königsee, and Bodensee.

EurailPasses are valid on all services of the KD German Rhine Line and on the Mosel between Trier and Koblenz. (If you use the fast hydrofoil, a supplementary fee has to be paid.) DB Tourist Card holders are given a 50% reduction on KD ships. Regular rail tickets are also accepted, meaning that you can go one way by ship and return by train. All you have to do is pay a small surcharge to KD Rhine Line and get the ticket endorsed at one of the landing-stage offices. But note that you have to buy the rail ticket first and *then* get it changed.

KD Rhine Line also offers a program of luxury tours ranging from a five-day cruise along the Rhine from Amsterdam to Basel to a choice of seven 4–7-day trips along the River Elbe. Some Elbe trips connect with Hamburg and Prague, and Dresden is visited on all the Elbe tours. Prices start at DM 1,056 per person, including accommodations and all meals. The ships cruise slowly to give you time to appreciate the landscape. The tours can be booked either for the cruise only to fit in with your own program or as a complete vacation. One of the best and most attractive ways of seeing the glories of the Rhine and the Mosel is on one of the traditional KD old-time paddle steamers or on one of their large modern motor vessels. During the summer there are good services between Bonn and Koblenz and between Koblenz and Birgen; both trips take around five hours.

The cruises, especially for the newer Elbe routes, are in great demand, so reservations are necessary several months in advance.

KD has several budget deals, too; for example, on Sundays or holidays, children between 4 and 14 accompanied by adults pay only DM 5. Likewise, senior citizens pay only half price on Mondays. If it's your birthday, you travel free. For details of all KD services, contact the company in the United States at 170 Hamilton Avenue, White Plains, NY 10601–1788, tel. 914/948–3600, and at 323 Geary Street, San Francisco, CA 94102–1860, tel. 415/392–8817; in Germany contact Köln-Düsseldorfer Deutsche Rheinschiffahrt AG, Frankenwerft 15, 5000–Köln 1, tel. 0221/20880.

By Car

Entry formalities for motorists are few: All you need is proof of insurance, an international car-registration document, and an international driver's license. If you or your car are from an EC country, or from Austria, Norway, Switzerland, Sweden, or Portugal, all you need is your domestic license and proof of insurance. *All* foreign cars must have a country sticker.

Roads in the western part of the country are generally excellent, but many surfaces in eastern Germany, where an urgent improvement program is under way, are in poor condition.

There are three principal automobile clubs: **ADAC** (Allegmeiner Deutscher Automobil-Club, Am Westpark 8, 8000-Munich 70), **AvD** (Lyonerstr. 16, Frankfurt/Niederrad), and **DTC** (Amalienburgstr. 23, Munich 60).

ADAC and AvD operate tow trucks on all Autobahns; they also have emergency telephones every 1½ miles. On minor roads, go to the nearest call box and dial 19211. Ask, in English, for "road service assistance," if you have to use the service. Help is free, but all materials must be paid for.

Scenic Routes Germany boasts many specially designated tourist roads, all covering areas of particular scenic and/or historic interest. The longest is the **Deutsche Ferienstrasse,** the German Holiday Road, which runs from the Baltic to the Alps, a distance of around 1,070 miles. The most famous, however, and also the oldest, is the **Romantische Strasse,** the Romantic Road, which runs from Würzburg in Franconia to Füssen in the Alps, covering around 220 miles and passing some of the most historic cities and towns in Germany. (*See* Chapter 8 for full details.)

Among other notable touring routes—all with expressive and descriptive names—are the **Grüne Küstenstrasse** (Green Coast Road), running along the North Sea coast from Denmark to Emden; the **Burgenstrasse** (Castle Road), running from Mannheim to Nürnberg; the **Deutsche Weinstrasse** (German Wine Road), running through the heartland of German wine country; and the **Deutsche Alpenstrasse** (German Alpine Road), running the length of the country's south border. In addition, there are many other equally delightful, if less well-known, routes, such as the **Märchenstrasse** (the Fairy-tale Road); the **Schwarwald Hochstrasse** (the Black Forest Mountain Road); and the **Deutsche Edelsteinstrasse** (German Gem Road).

Regulations As elsewhere in Western Europe, in Germany you drive on the right, and road signs give distances in kilometers. Political reunification did not bring a consensus to the rules of the road, however. In the western part of Germany, unlimited speeds on the Autobahns continue, while in former East Germany—the five new states of Thüringia, Saxony, Saxony-Anhalt, Brandenburg, and Mecklenburg—a top limit of 100 kilometers per hour (60 miles per hour) remains in force (80 kilometers per hour on other country roads). Speed limits on non-autobahn country roads in western areas vary from 80 to 100 kilometers per hour.

An absolute ban on alcohol is strictly enforced for drivers in the east, but drivers in the west can still legally sit behind the wheel after drinking two small beers or wine. These inconsistencies are expected to be resolved soon.

Note that seat belts must be worn at all times by front- *and* back-seat passengers.

Fuel Gasoline (petrol) costs are between DM 1.35 and DM 1.60 per liter. As part of antipollution efforts, many German cars now run on lead-free fuel. All rental cars will run on leaded or unleaded gasoline. Some older vehicles cannot take unleaded fuel. German filling stations are highly competitive and bargains are often available if you shop around, but *not* at autobahn filling stations. Self-service, or *SB-Tanken*, stations are cheapest. Pumps marked *Bleifrei* contain unleaded gas.

Telephones

Apart from the more remote rural corners of eastern Germany, telephone links between western and eastern areas of the country were completely upgraded in 1992. When the system was improved, all area codes in the five new states acquired the prefix 03, replacing the previous 0037.

Local Calls Local public phones charge a minimum 30 pfennigs per call (for six minutes). All public phones take 10 pf, DM 1, and DM 5 coins. Most phone booths have instructions in English as well as German; if yours doesn't, simply lift the receiver, put the money in, and dial.

International Calls These can be made from public phones bearing the sign "Inlands and Auslandsgespräche." Using DM 5 coins is best for long-distance dialing; a four-minute call to the United States costs DM 15. To avoid weighing yourself down with coins, however, make international calls from post offices; even those in small country towns will have a special booth for international calls. You pay the clerk at the end of your call. Never make international calls from your hotel room; rates will be at least double the regular charge.

Operators and Information The German telephone system is fully automatic, and it's unlikely that you'll have to employ the services of an operator. If you do, dial 010, or 0010 for international calls. If the operator doesn't speak English (also unlikely), you'll be passed to one who does.

Mail

Postal Rates Airmail letters to the United States and Canada cost DM 1.40; postcards cost 80 pfennigs. All letters to the United Kingdom cost DM 1; postcards cost 60 pfennigs.

Receiving Mail You can arrange to have mail sent to you in care of any German post office; have the envelope marked "Postlagernd." This service is free. Alternatively, have mail sent to any American Express office in Germany. There's no charge to cardholders, holders of American Express traveler's checks, or anyone who has booked a vacation with American Express. Otherwise, you pay DM 2 per collection (not per item).

Tipping

The service charges on hotel bills suffice for most tips in your hotel, though you should tip bellhops and porters; DM 2 per bag or service is ample. Whether you tip the desk clerk depends on whether he or she has given you any special service.

Service charges are included in all restaurant bills (listed as *Bedienung*), as is tax (listed as *MWST*). Nonetheless, it is customary to round out the bill to the nearest mark or to leave about 5% (give it to the waiter or waitress as you pay the bill; don't leave it on the table).

In taxis, round out the fare to the nearest full mark as a tip. Only give more if you have particularly cumbersome or heavy luggage (though you will be charged 50 pfennigs for each piece of luggage anyway).

Opening and Closing Times

Banks Times vary from state to state and city to city, but banks are generally open weekdays from 8:30 or 9 to 3 or 4 (5 or 6 on Thursday). Branches at airports and main train stations open as early as 6:30 AM and close as late as 10:30 PM.

Museums Most museums are open from Tuesday to Sunday 9–6. Some close for an hour or more at lunch, and some are open on Monday. Many stay open late on Thursday.

Shops Times vary slightly, but generally shops are open 9 or 9:15–6:30 Monday through Friday and until 2 PM on Saturday, except for the first Saturday in the month, when the bigger stores stay open until 6 in winter and 4 in summer. Many shops also now remain open on Thursday evenings until 8:30.

National Holidays January 1; January 6 (Epiphany), April 4 (Easter Friday), April 12 (Easter Monday), May 1, May 20 (Ascension), May 31 (Easter Monday), June 10 (Corpus Christi), October 3 (German Unity Day), November 1 (All Saints' Day), November 17 (Repentance Day), Christmas, December 24–26 (Germany shuts down at midday on the 24th).

Sports and Outdoor Activities

The Germans are nothing if not sports-crazy, and there is practically no sport, however arcane, except perhaps cricket, that cannot easily be arranged almost anywhere in the country. A good number of sports packages—for sailboats, tennis, climbing, walking, horseback riding, to name only a few—are also available. Consult the German National Tourist Office or your travel agent for details. Below, we give details of some of the more popular participant sports. Details of important sporting events are also published every month by regional and local tourist offices.

Fishing Fishing is available at many locations in Germany, but a permit, valid for one year and costing from DM 10 to DM 20, available from local tourist offices, is required, as is a local permit to fish in a particular spot. These last are available from the owner of the stretch of water in which you plan to fish. Further details are available from local tourist offices or from **Verband der Deutschen Sportfischer** (Bahnhofstr. 35, 6050 Offenbach).

A number of hotels offer fishing for guests, but you will normally be expected to deliver your catch—if any—to the hotel.

Golf Golf in Germany is rapidly increasing in popularity, and there is a growing number of courses around the country. Clubs will usually allow nonmembers to play if they are not too busy; charges will be about DM 30 during the week and up to DM 60 on weekends and on public holidays. For information, write the **German Golf Association** (Leberberg 25, 6200 Wiesbaden).

Hiking and Mountaineering Germany's hill and mountain regions have thousands of miles of marked hiking and mountain-walking tracks. They are administered by regional hiking clubs and, where appropriate, mountaineering groups, all of which are affiliated with the **Verband Deutscher Gebirgs- und Wandervereine e.V.** (Reichs str. 4,6600 Saarbrücken 3). It can provide information on routes, hiking paths, overnight accommodations, and mountain huts in western Germany. The former East German state-run hiking organization has collapsed. Local tourist offices in eastern Germany can provide information about trails and regional hiking clubs.

For Alpine walking, contact the **Deutsche Alpenverein** (Praterinsel 5, D–8000 Munich 22). It administers more than 50 mountain huts and about 9,500 miles of Alpine paths. In addition, it can provide courses in mountaineering and touring suggestions for routes in both winter and summer. Foreign members are admitted.

There are also various mountaineering schools that offer week-long courses ranging from basic techniques for beginners to advanced mountaineering. Contact the **Verband Deutscher Ski- und Bergführer** (Lindenstr. 16, D–8980 Oberstdorf).

Local tourist offices and sports shops can usually supply details of mountain guides.

Horseback Riding Riding schools and clubs can be found throughout Germany. Rates are generally high, and most schools will insist on a minimum standard of competence before allowing novices to venture out. Alternatively, pony treks are available in many parts of the country. Contact the German National Tourist Office or local tourist offices.

Sailing A wide variety of sailing vacations and opportunities to rent sailboats is available throughout Germany. Most North Sea and Baltic resorts and harbors will have either sailing schools or sailboats of varying types to rent. Lake sailing is equally popular, particularly on the Chiemsee in Bavaria and on the Bodensee. For details, write **Verband Deutscher Segelschulen** (Graelstr. 45, 44 Münster).

Swimming Almost all larger towns and resorts have open-air and indoor pools, the former frequently heated, the latter often with wave or whirlpool machines. In addition, practically all coastal resorts have indoor seawater pools, as well as good, if bracing, beaches. Similarly, all German spas have thermal or mineral-water indoor pools. Finally, Bavaria's Alpine lakes and a large number of artificial lakes elsewhere have marked-off swimming and sunbathing areas.

Note that swimming in rivers, especially the larger ones, is not recommended and in some cases is positively forbidden—look for the "Baden Verboten" signs—either because of shipping or pollution, or both.

Bathing caps are obligatory at all indoor and outdoor pools; if you don't have your own, you can rent one. It's hard not to notice that the Germans are keen on nudism. Many pools will have special days for nude bathing only, and on certain beaches nude bathing is also allowed. Signs that read "FKK" mean nudity is allowed.

Tennis Courts are available practically everywhere, summer and winter. Local tourist offices will supply details of where to play, charges, and how to book, the latter being essential in most areas. Charges vary from DM 20 to DM 30 for outdoor courts and DM 25 to DM 35 for indoor courts.

Windsurfing This has become so popular, particularly on the Bavarian lakes, that it has had to be restricted on some beaches as a result of collisions between Windsurfers and swimmers. Nonetheless, there are still many places where you can windsurf and where Windsurfers can easily be rented. Lessons, at around DM 25 per hour, are also generally available. For further information, contact the German National Tourist Office or **VDWS** (Fasserstr. 30, 8120 Weilheim, Oberbayern).

Winter Sports South Bavaria is the big winter-sports region, with Garmisch-Partenkirchen the best-known center. There are also winter-sports resorts in the Black Forest, the Harz region, the Bavarian Forest, the Rhön Mountains, the Fichtelgebirge, the Sauerland, and the Swabian mountains. The season generally runs from the middle of December to the end of March, but at higher altitudes, such as the Zugspitze (near Garmisch), you can usually ski from as early as the end of November to as late as the middle of May. There's no need to bring skis with you—you can rent or buy them on the spot. Look for the special winter off-season rates (*Weisse Wochen*) offered by most winter sports-resorts for cross-country and downhill skiing vacations. Prices include seven days' bed and breakfast (or half-board) plus ski lessons.

For cross-country (or *Langlauf*) skiing, which is becoming increasingly popular—the equipment is considerably cheaper than downhill (or *Alpin*) equipment, and there is no waiting at ski lifts—there are stretches of prepared tracks (or *Loipen*) to be found in the valleys and foothills of most winter-sports centers, as well as in the suburbs of larger towns in south Bavaria.

Ski-bobbing is on the increase. There are runs and schools at Bayrischzell, Berchtesgaden, Garmisch-Partenkirchen, Füssen, and Oberstdorf in the Alps, as well as at Altglashütten, Bernau, and Felberg in the Black Forest. Ice rinks, many open all year, can be found everywhere.

Dining

The choice of eating places in Germany is extremely varied both in style and price. The most sophisticated spots—and the most expensive—are found principally in cities. Munich and Düsseldorf, for example, boast the only three-star restaurants in Germany, but Köln, Frankfurt, Hamburg, Aachen, Wiesbaden, and Berlin are close on their heels. At the opposite end of the scale, almost every street of the old West Germany has its *Gaststätte*, a sort of combination diner and pub, and every village its *Gasthof*, or inn. Such places, however, are harder to find in eastern Germany. The emphasis in the Gaststätte and Gasthof is on the characteristic German preference for *gut bürgerliche Küche*, or good home cooking, with simple food, wholesome rather than sophisticated, at reasonable prices. These are also places where people meet in the evening for a chat, a beer, and a game of cards, so you needn't feel compelled to leave as soon as you have eaten. They normally serve hot meals from 11:30 AM to 9 or 10 PM; many places stop serving hot meals between 2 and 6 PM, although you can still order cold dishes. Lunch rather than dinner is the main meal in Germany, a fact reflected in the almost universal appearance of a *Tageskarte*, or suggested menu, every lunchtime. And at a cost of DM 10 to DM 20, in either a Gaststätte or Gasthof, for soup, a main course, and simple dessert (though this is not always offered), it's excellent value. Coffee is generally available, although quality may vary, and it's perfectly acceptable to go into a Gastätte or country pub and order just a pot of coffee outside busy lunch periods. Some, though not all, expensive restaurants also offer a table d'hôte (suggested or special) daily menu. Prices will be much higher than in a Gaststätte or Gasthof, but considerably cheaper than à la carte.

Regional specialties are given in the Dining sections of individual chapters. For names of German foods and dishes, *see* the Menu Guide at the end of this book.

Budget Eating Tips

Foreign Restaurants Germany has a vast selection of moderately priced Italian, Greek, Chinese, and—largely as a result of the number of Yugoslav workers in Germany—Balkan restaurants. All are good value, though you may find the food in Balkan restaurants spicy. Italian restaurants are about the most popular of all specialty restaurants in Germany—the pizza-to-go is as much a part of the average German's diet as *Bratwurst* or a hamburger. You'll find that Chinese restaurants in particular offer special lunch menus.

Stand-up Snack Bars Often located in pedestrian zones, *Imbiss* stands can be found in almost every busy shopping street, in parking lots, train stations, and near markets. They serve *Würste* (sausages), grilled, roasted, or boiled, of every shape and size, and rolls filled with cheese, cold meat, or fish. Prices range from DM 3 to DM 6 per portion.

Department Stores For lunch, restaurants in local department stores (*Kaufhäuser*) are especially recommended for wholesome, appetizing, and inexpensive food. **Kaufhof, Karstadt, Horton,** and **Hertie** are names to note, as well as the enormous **KaDeWe** in Berlin.

Butcher Shops Known as *Metzgerei,* these often have a corner that serves warm snacks. The **Vinzenz-Murr** chain in Munich and Bavaria have particularly good-value food. Try *Warmer Leberkäs mit Kartoffelsalat,* a typical Bavarian specialty, which is a sort of baked meat loaf with sweet mustard and potato salad. In north Germany, try *Bouletten,* small hamburgers, or *Currywurst,* sausages in a piquant curry sauce.

Fast Food A number of fast-food chains exist all over the country. The best are **Wienerwald, McDonald's,** and **Burger King.** There are also **Nordsee** fish bars, serving hot and cold fish dishes.

Picnics Buy some wine or beer and some cold cuts and rolls (*Brötchen*) from a department store, supermarket, or delicatessen and turn lunchtimes into picnics. You'll not only save money, but you'll also be able to enjoy Germany's beautiful scenery. Or leave out the beer and take your picnic to a beer garden, sit down at one of the long wood tables, and order a *Mass* (liter) of beer.

Ratings The restaurants in our listings are divided by price into four categories: Very Expensive; Expensive; Moderate; and Inexpensive. *See* Dining in individual chapters for specific prices. Nearly all restaurants display their menus, with prices, outside; all prices shown will include tax and service charge. Prices for wine also include tax and service charge.

Lodging

The standard of German hotels—from sophisticated luxury spots (of which the country has more than its fair share) to the humblest country inn—is excellent. Rates vary enormously, though not disproportionately so in comparison with other north European countries. You can nearly always expect courteous and polite service and clean and comfortable rooms.

In addition to hotels proper, the country also has numerous Gasthöfe or *Gasthäuser,* which are country inns that serve food and also have rooms; pensions, or *Fremdenheime* (guest houses); and, at the lowest end of the scale, *Zimmer,* meaning simply "rooms," normally in private houses (look for the sign reading *Zimmer frei* or *zu vermieten* on a green background, meaning "to rent"; a red sign reading *besetzt* means that there are no vacancies).

Lists of German hotels are available from the German National Tourist Office and all regional and local tourist offices. (Most hotels have restaurants, but those listed as *Garni* will provide breakfast only.) Tourist offices will also make bookings for you at a nominal fee, but they may have difficulty doing so after 4 PM in high season and on weekends, so don't wait until too late in the day to begin looking for your accommodations. (If you do get stuck, ask someone who looks local—a postman, policeman, or waitress, for example—for a Zimmer zu vermieten or Gasthof; in rural areas especially you'll find that people are genuinely helpful). A hotel reservation service is also operated by **ADZ** (Corneliusstr. 34, W-6000 Frankfurt/Main, tel. 069/740767). It is able to make reservations in many hotels throughout the country for a small fee.

Many major American hotel chains—Hilton, Sheraton, Holiday Inn, Arabella, Canadian Pacific, Ramada, Preferred—have hotels in the larger German cities. Similarly, European chains are well represented.

Romantik Hotels Among the most delightful places to stay—and eat—in Germany are the aptly named Romantik Hotels and Restaurants. The Romantik group now has establishments throughout north Europe (and even a few in the United States), including around 60 in Germany itself. All are in atmospheric and historic buildings—an essential precondition of membership—and are personally run by the owners, with the emphasis on excellent food and service. Prices vary considerably from Very Expensive to Moderate (*see* Ratings, below), but in general represent good value, particularly the special-weekends and short-holiday rates. A three- or four-day stay, for example, with one main meal, is available at about DM 300 to DM 400 per person.

In addition, German Railways offers a special "Romantik Hotel Rail" program, which, in conjunction with a GermanRail Tourist Ticket, gives nine days' unlimited travel. You don't need to plan your route in advance—only your first night's accommodation needs to be reserved before you leave. The remaining nights can be reserved as you go. The package also includes sightseeing trips, a Rhine/Mosel cruise, bicycle rentals, and the like.

A detailed brochure listing all Romantik Hotels and Restaurants, which costs $7.50 (including mailing), and a free mini-guide are available from **Romantik Hotels Reservations** (Box 1278, Woodinville, WA 98072, tel. 206/486-9394; for reservations, tel. 800/826-0015).

Castle Hotels Of comparable interest and value are Germany's castle, or *Schloss*, hotels, all privately owned and run and all long on atmosphere. A number of the simpler ones may lack some amenities, but the majority combine four-star luxury with valuable antique furnishings, four-poster beds, stone passageways, and a baronial atmosphere. Some offer full resort facilities, too (tennis, swimming pools, horseback riding, hunting, and fishing). Nearly all are located away from cities and towns.

For a brochure listing 60 such castle hotels, write to **Gast im Schloss**, D-3526 Trendelburg 1, Germany. They, and your travel agent, can also advise on a number of packages available for castle hotels, including four- to six-night tours.

Spas Taking the waters in Germany, whether for curing the body or merely beautifying it, has been popular since Roman times. There are about 250 health resorts and mineral springs in the country—the word *Bad* before the name of a place usually means it's a spa—offering treatments, normally at fairly high prices. Beauty farms are normally found only in Very Expensive spa hotels. Although spas exist in eastern Germany, most are rundown and not highly recommended.

There are four main groups of spas and health resorts: (1) the mineral and moorland spas, where treatments are based on natural warm-water springs; (2) those by the sea on the Baltic and North Sea coasts; (3) hydropathic spas, which use an invigorating process developed in the 19th century; and (4) climatic health resorts, which depend on their climates—usually mountainous—for their health-giving properties.

The average cost for three weeks of treatment is from DM 900 to DM 2,500; for four weeks, DM 1,300 to DM 3,200. This includes board and lodging, doctor's fees, treatments, and tax. A complete list of spas, giving full details of their springs and treatments, is available from the German National Tourist Office, or from **Deutsche Bäderverband,** the German Health Resort and Spa Association (Schumannstr. 111, 5300 Bonn 1).

Rentals Bungalows or apartments (*Ferienwohungen* or *Ferienapartments*), usually accommodating two to eight people, can be rented throughout Germany. Rates are low, with reductions for longer stays. There is usually an extra charge for gas and electricity, and sometimes water. There is also normally a charge for linen, though you may also bring your own.

Details of rentals in all regions of the country are available from the regional and local tourist offices. In addition, the German Automobile Association issues listings of family holiday apartments; write **ADAC Reisen** (Am Westpark 8, 8000 Munich 70).

Farm Vacations *Urlaub auf dem Bauernhof,* or vacations down on the farm, have increased dramatically in popularity throughout Germany over the past five years, and almost every regional tourist office now produces a brochure listing farms in its area that offer bed-and-breakfasts, apartments, and entire farmhouses to rent. In addition, the German Agricultural Association (DLG) produces an illustrated brochure listing over 1,500 farms, all inspected and graded, from the Alps to the North Sea, that offer accommodations. It costs DM 7.50 (send an international reply coupon if writing from the United States) and is available from **DLG Reisedienst, Agratour** (Zimmerweg 16, D-6000 Frankfurt/Main 1) or the National Tourist Office.

Camping Campsites—some 2,000 in all—are scattered the length and breadth of Germany. The **DCC,** or German Camping Club (Mandlstr. 28, D-8000 Munich 40) produces an annual listing of 1,600 sites; it also details sites where trailers and mobile homes can be rented. Similarly, the German Automobile Association (*see* Rentals, above, for address) publishes a listing of all campsites located at autobahn exits. In addition, the German National Tourist Office publishes a comprehensive and graded listing of campsites.

Sites are generally open from May to September, though about 400 are open year-round for the very rugged. Most sites get crowded during high season, however. Prices range from around DM 10 to DM 15 for a car, trailer, and two adults; less for tents. If you want to camp elsewhere, you must get permission from the landowner beforehand; ask the police if you can't track him or her down. Drivers of mobile homes may park for one night only on roadsides and in autobahn parking-lot areas, but may not set up camping equipment there.

Youth Hostels Germany's youth hostels—*Jugendherbergen*—are probably the most efficient, up-to-date, and proportionally numerous of any country's in the world. There are about 600 in all, many located in castles that add a touch of romance to otherwise utilitarian accommodations. Since unification, many eastern German youth hostels have closed down. An effort is being made, however, to keep as many open as possible, and renovations are currently under way to bring eastern hostels up to the standards of their western counterparts.

Apart from Bavaria, where there is an age limit of 27, there are no restrictions on age, though those under 20 take preference when space is limited. You'll need an International Youth Hostel card, valid for one year, for reduced rates, usually about DM 12 to DM 18 for youth under 27 and DM 13.50 to DM 22 for adults (breakfast included). Cards are available from the **American Youth Hostels Association** (Box 37613, Washington, DC 20013), the **Canadian Hostelling Association** (333 River Rd., Ottawa, Ontario K1L 8H9), and in the United Kingdom, the **Youth Hostels Association,** 22 Southampton Street, London WC2. For listings of German youth hostels, contact the **Deutsches Jugendherbergswerk Hauptverband** (Bismarckstr. 8, D–4930 Detmold, tel. 05231/74010). Bookings for hostels in the new German states (former East Germany) of Saxony, Thüringia, Saxony-Anhalt, Brandenburg, and Mecklenburg can be made direct to Jugendtourist, Alexanderplatz 5, 1026 Berlin.

Ratings The hotels in our listings are divided by price into four categories: Very Expensive; Expensive; Moderate; and Inexpensive. *See* Lodging in individual chapters for specific prices. Note that there is no official grading system for hotels in Germany. Rates are by no means inflexible, and depend very much on supply and demand. Many resort hotels offer substantial reductions in winter, except in the Alps, where rates often rise in winter. Likewise, many Very Expensive and Expensive hotels in cities offer substantial reductions on weekends and when business is quiet. It's always worth checking to see if reductions are available; the savings can be considerable. You should be careful about trying to book late in the day at peak times. During trade fairs (most seem to be held in the spring and fall), rates in city hotels can rise appreciably. Breakfast is usually but not always included in room rates; be sure to check before you book. Check, too, to see if your room has a shower or a tub—some of the cheaper rooms have neither—as a room with a shower will be a little less expensive than a room with a tub. Finally, if you don't like the room you're offered, ask to see another.

Credit Cards

The following credit card abbreviations are used: AE, American Express; DC, Diners Club; MC, Mastercard; V, Visa.

Great Itineraries

The Castles of Ludwig II

Munich tour operators offer day trips to the four famous castles of Bavaria's flamboyant King Ludwig II, but for those who want to get to know them without distracting interruptions, there's no alternative but to strike out on your own. The castles are set in magnificent countryside that invites the visitor to linger and complete a stay with a walk or a hike undisturbed by the demands of a tour operator's timetable. If you're relying on public transportation, you'll have to return to Munich to visit the fourth castle, Herrenchiemsee, but arrange your itinerary so you can spend the night outside the city.

Length of Trip 6 to 7 days.

Getting Around **By Car:** From Munich, this is a 340 kilometer (210-mile) round-trip drive.

By Public Transportation: Füssen and the Chiemsee Lake are reached by fast trains from Munich, with local buses making connections. A train service links Munich with Oberammergau, but allow two hours.

The Main Route **Two Nights: Füssen.** Neuschwanstein and Hohenschwangau (Ludwig's childhood home) can both be reached on foot from Füssen. Alternatively, hire bikes from the local station. Allow at least a full day to appreciate Neuschwanstein.

Two Nights: Ettal. Buses run from the picturesque mountain village of Ettal to Linderhof (which some class as the finest product of Ludwig's imagination). Find time to visit the Ettal monastery. Oberammergau is a 10-minute bus ride away.

Two Nights: Chiemsee. The unfinished Herrenchiemsee palace stands on Herren Island in the Chiemsee. Passenger boats offer regular service to the island (and to the smaller, equally charming Fraueninsel) from the lakeside resorts of Prien and Gstadt. A mainline train service runs from Munich to Prien, and the Munich-Salzburg Autobahn runs alongside the south shore of the Chiemsee.

Further Information: *See* Excursions from Munich, in Chapter 3; Chapter 4; and Chapter 8.

Through Central Germany to the North Sea

The Germans have always waxed romantic about their rivers, and not just about the Rhine and the Danube. At the idyllic point where the rivers Werra and Fulda join to become the Weser there's a granite stone with an inscription in verse that, loosely translated, reads:

Where Werra and Fulda gently kiss
and thereby lose their right to be,
The stately Weser is born by this
Embrace and flows on to the far-off sea.

The Weser is truly stately, one of Germany's most beautiful rivers, bordered by sleepy towns with medieval streets of half-timbered houses running down to the water's edge, and spilling into the North Sea's great German Bight after donating its last services to the shipbuilders of Bremen and Bremerhaven. This is literally fairy-tale country, where the Grimm brothers lived and worked and soaked up the inspiration for their immortal stories. Our itinerary diverges from theirs, however, beginning on the banks of another great German river, the Main, at Aschaffenburg with its magnificent Renaissance palace, the former seat of the electors of Mainz. Behind Aschaffenburg rise the wild, wooded heights of the Spessart plateau, much of which is a protected national park. You'll leave the Spessart at the picturesque little town of Steinau an der Strasse, where the Grimm brothers spent their childhood, and then head into another wild area of central Germany, the Rhön Mountains. Here also you'll find the source of the Fulda River, the start of the main itinerary. From there, you continue on to Münden, where the Fulda "embraces" the Werra and travels onward as the Weser to the North Sea.

Length of Trip 7 to 10 days.

Getting Around **By Car:** From Frankfurt, take Autobahn A-3 (direction Würzburg and Munich) to Aschaffenburg, then follow the well-marked "Rhön- und Spessahrt" route through the Spessart and Rhön to Fulda. From Fulda, follow the Fulda River valley road to Bad Hersfeld, Rotenburg an der Fulda, and Kassel. From Kassel, follow the Wesertal road to Bremen and the sea.

By Public Transportation: All the main points on the route—Aschaffenburg, Fulda, Kassel and Bremen—can be reached by regular Intercity trains from Frankfurt. Bus services connect the smaller centers.

The Main Route **One Night: Aschaffenburg.** Spare a morning or an afternoon to tour the mighty Elector's Palace, the Renaissance-style Johannisburg.

Two Nights: Take your time traveling through the **Spessart,** pulling in to spend the night at bed-and-breakfast farmhouses along the way.

Two Nights: A similarly unhurried tour of the **Rhön** is recommended. Find time for an excursion to the Schwarzes Moor (Black Moor) on the edge of eastern Germany.

One Night: Fulda, with an evening stroll through its Baroque quarters.

One Night: Kassel. You'll need an entire day to appreciate fully the beauty of the Wilhelmshöhe park and palace.

Three Nights: You'll find three nights the minimum length of time to travel the **Wesertal** route to Bremen. If you're driving, reserve at least one night in one of the castle hotels in the Reinhardswald. For the rest of the trip, hunt out waterside hotels and guest houses along the banks of the Weser.

One Night: Bremen—and at least one day to sit back and take stock of the trip. Take a morning or afternoon excursion to the fishing-boat harbor of Bremerhaven.

Further Information: *See* Chapters 9 and 14.

The Castle Road

Just outside the city of Heilbronn, amid rich vineyards, are the romantic ruins of the castle of the "Faithful Women." The explanation of its strange name is as romantic as the castle's setting. The German King Konrad III laid siege to the castle in 1140, and in a moment of uncharacteristic weakness allowed the women living within its walls to leave with as many of their possessions as they could carry. He is said to have lost his regal cool when the women of the castle trooped out carrying their menfolk on their shoulders. But he kept his word—and the men of the castle were spared. It's a marvelous yarn, typical of the stories you'll hear throughout this "castle" trail. There are about 50 castles along the 180-mile route between Mannheim and Nürnberg, a greater concentration than in any other part of Germany. Time and other circumstances (some of the castles are in private hands or serve some municipal function and can't be visited) will prevent you from looking over them all. On the other hand, some are now hotels where you'll be tempted to linger at least for a meal, perhaps to stay the night.

Length of Trip 12 to 14 days.

Getting Around **By Car:** It's 291 kilometers (180 miles) from Mannheim to Nürnberg. Follow the Neckar Valley road, B-27, from Mannheim to Heilbronn, then take the Burgenstrasse (the Castle Road itself) to Rothenburg-ob-der-Tauber. From Rothenburg, head for Colmberg and Hessbach, joining B-13 for the final stretch to Ansbach and Nürnberg.

By Public Transportation: Mannheim, Heidelberg, Heilbronn, and Nürnberg are all connected by regular express train services, but you'll have to rely on country bus services to reach many of the remoter castles.

The Main Route **One Night: Mannheim.** Take part of the day to visit Mannheim's magnificent 18th-century Elector's Palace, one of the largest Baroque buildings in Europe, and the Reissinsel Park and its walks alongside the Rhine.

Two Nights: Heidelberg. Spend a full day exploring Heidelberg itself, then make an excursion to the Heiligenberg, into the Odenwald Forest or to the castles of Schadeck, Hornberg, Hirschorn (all of them hotels, with excellent restaurants), or to Zwingenberg and Minneburg.

Three Nights: Heilbronn. Plan excursions to the remains of the imperial palace of Bad Wimpfen and to the castles of Horneck, Guttenberg (with its aviary of birds of prey, including some fine eagles), Bad Rappenau, Ehrenberg, Weinsberg (the castle of "Faithful Women"), Neuenstein, and perhaps to the museum of bicycle and motorcycle technology at Neckarsulm.

Two Nights: Rothenburg an der Tauber. You'll want to spend at least a full day exploring Rothenburg, Europe's best-preserved medieval town. After that, make excursions along the Tauber River valley and to the castles of Langenburg, Bartenstein, and Colmberg.

Two Nights: Ansbach. Visit the margraves' palace and the 12th-century monastery church of Heilsbronn.

Two Nights: Nürnberg.

Further Information: *See* Chapter 8, Chapter 9, and Chapter 11.

Rivers of Wine

The Rhine and Mosel need no introduction, but who knows the attractions of their tributaries—the rivers Saar and Nahe? Or the remote villages scattered across the Hunsrück range of hills, which is bordered by all four rivers? A tour of the four "rivers of wine" will take you from the crowds and crush of the Rhine of picture-postcard fame to the less dramatic but much more peaceful valley of the Saar. The Hunsrück high road leads you back at your own pace to the point where the well-trodden tourist trail picks up again on the Nahe River. In little more than a week, you'll have skirted (and perhaps visited) Germany's most famous vineyards—and you should have tasted some of the country's finest wines.

Length of Trip 10 to 12 days.

Getting Around **By Car:** It's a 454-kilometer (280-mile) round-trip drive from Wiesbaden.

By Public Transportation: The rail journey along the Rhine between Bingen and Koblenz is Germany's most spectacular train ride. Riverboats also make the journey, and you can stop off at any point on the way. From Koblenz, the rail line hugs the contours of the Mosel River to Trier; alternatively, you can again choose to travel the river by boat. A combination of train and bus will complete the itinerary along the Saar and across the Hunsrück to the Nahe River. Bus tours are offered by travel agencies in Wiesbaden, Bingen, Koblenz, and Trier.

The Main Route **Two Nights:** The **Rheingau** region, between Eltville and Rüdesheim. Visit the vineyards of the Rheingau (they produce Germany's finest wine), and Bingen, at the mouth of the Nahe River.

Four Nights: Along the **Rhine** between Rüdesheim and Koblenz. See the vineyards of Bacharach, Boppard, Brey, Kaub, Lorch, Oberwesel, Spay, and St. Goar, and the castles (or what remains of them) of Ehrenfels, Katz, Reichenstein, Rheinstein, Schönburg, and Sooneck.

Four Nights: Along the **Mosel** between Koblenz and Trier. Take excursions to the Deutsche Eck (where the Mosel and Rhine meet) and to the vineyards of Alken, Bernkastel-Kues, Bremm (Europe's steepest vineyard), Ediger, Kobern-Gondorf, Kröv, Nehren, Neumagen (Germany's oldest wine town, praised by the 4th-century Roman poet Ausonius in his work *Mosella*), Piesport, Traben-Trarbach, Winningen (its August wine festival is one of Germany's oldest), Zell, and to the castles of Cochem, Ehrenburg, Eltz (a medieval picture-book castle so treasured by the Germans that they've engraved its image on their DM 500 bank notes), and Thurant.

Two Nights: Trier. Explore Trier and follow the Saar River to Saarburg, Mettlach, and as far as the great, "Saar Bend," a spectacular point where the river nearly doubles back on itself.

Two Nights: Idar-Oberstein. Venture into the Hunsrück hills and along the Nahe River to Bad Kreuznach. Take a day tour of the *Edelsteinstrasse* or "Precious Stones Route," a well-marked 48-kilometer (30-mile) itinerary, starting and ending in Idar Oberstein, where precious stones are still mined and polished.

Further Information: *See* Chapter 13.

Through the Black Forest

Many first-time visitors to the Black Forest literally can't see the forest for the trees. There are so many contrasting attractions that the basic, enduring beauty of the area passes them by. So in your tour of the forest, take time to stray from the tourist path and inhale the cool, mysterious air of its darker recesses. Walk or ride through its shadowy corridors or across its open upland; row a canoe and tackle the wild water of the Nagold and Wolf rivers. Then take time out to relax in any of the many spas, order a Baden wine enlivened by a dash of local mineral water, seek out the nearest restaurant that confesses to its food being influenced by the cuisine of neighboring France. And, if you have money to spare at the end of your tour, return to Baden-Baden, try your luck on the gaming tables, and celebrate your good fortune or forget ill fate at the bar of the casino's "Equipage" nightclub.

Length of Trip 12 to 14 days.

Getting Around **By Car:** It's a 405-kilometer (250-mile) round-trip drive from Stuttgart.

By Public Transportation: Stuttgart, Baden-Baden, and Freiburg are all on Intercity train routes, and local trains and buses link them with most towns and spas of the Black Forest. Bus tours of the Black Forest are offered by travel agencies in Baden-Baden and Freiburg.

The Main Route **Two Nights: Freudenstadt.** Take excursions to the Schwarzwald Museum at Lossburg, the Freilicht Museum Vogtsbauernhof near Wolfach, the Alpirsbach brewery, and the Glasswald lake near Schapbach.

One Night: Triberg area. See the Triberg waterfall and the clock museums of Triberg and Furtwangen.

Two Nights: Hinterzarten or **Titisee.** Visit the Feldberg, the Black Forest's highest mountain, and the Titisee and Schluchsee.

Two Nights: Freiburg. Explore Freiburg, the Schauinsland Mountain, the Dr. Faustus town of Staufen, and the vineyards on the slopes of the Kaiserstuhl.

One Night: Offenburg. Visit the surrounding vineyards.

Two Nights: Baden-Baden. Enjoy the sights in and around Baden-Baden and travel to the summit of nearby Merkur Mountain, to Schloss Favorite, and to Windeck Castle.

One Night: Bad Liebenzell. See Chapter 7.

Further Information: See Chapter 7.

Toward East Bavaria

There's a corner of Germany that's on the doorstep of the country's most popular tourist area and yet can seem a thousand miles from it. It stretches eastward from Munich to the Austrian border, its south edge marked by the Salzburg-bound autobahn, which propels most visitors and tourists to the greater attractions of the Bavarian Alps looming in the hazy distance. It's a gentle, pastoral region of rolling farmland, forgotten villages asserting their presence with hilltop, onion-domed Baroque churches, of reed-fringed lakes and willow-bordered rivers. And what rivers! You'll meet the Inn as it meanders northward in search of the Danube, Salzburg's Salzach River, then the mighty Danube itself as it surges into Austria, and finally the Isar, ice-green and—just as the poet promised—still "rolling rapidly" from its mountain source.

Length of Trip 7 to 8 days.

Getting Around **By Car:** It's a 405-kilometer (250-mile) round-trip drive from Munich.

By Public Transportation: The route can be covered entirely by train, beginning with the main-line route from Munich to Wasserburg and then using local services between the remaining towns.

The Main Route **One Night: Wasserburg.** Visit the medieval Amerang Castle (in summer, scene of chamber-music concerts) and the farmhouse museum at Amerang.

One Night: Laufen, on the Austrian border. Take excursions to the Waginger See, Germany's warmest lake, and across the Salzach River to the Austrian town of Oberndorf, where the Christmas carol "Silent Night" was composed.

One Night: Burghausen. In Altötting, see the 14th-century "Black Madonna" in an 8th-century chapel chosen by the Wittelsbachs to be the repository of silver urns containing the hearts of the Bavarian rulers.

Two Nights: Passau. Venture north into the Bavarian Forest and perhaps across the border into Czechoslovakia.

One Night: Straubing. Travel to the Danube towns Deggendorf and Bogen.

Further Information: *See* Chapter 6.

The Baltic Coast

Between the former East-West border town of Lübeck and the Polish frontier, Germany's "other" coastline is now wide open to the foreign visitor. As eastern Germany's window on the sea, the area was isolated from much of the rest of the world until the end of 1989. As a result, miles of sandy coastline, peppered with chalk cliffs and charming little coves, have largely escaped the attention of developers. But there is much more to this region than simply fresh sea breezes and sand: A wealth of architectural delights awaits inspection, from the well-preserved medieval town squares to the simple whitewashed seaside cottages with their roofs of reed thatch. The tour weaves a route through several of the old ports of the former Hanseatic League, the powerful merchants' organization that dominated trade on the Baltic in the Middle Ages and whose wealth financed so many of the fine buildings still standing today.

Length of Trip 7 to 10 days.

Getting Around **By Car:** The route runs 478 kilometers (298 miles) from Lübeck to Ahlbeck, on the island of Usedom along the Polish border.

By Public Transportation: There is regular train service from Lübeck through to Sassnitz. Two side trips can be taken aboard 19th-century steam trains. Bus services connect to most outlying areas.

The Main Route

One Night: Lübeck. A walk through the old town gates of the famous Holstentor, pictured on every DM 50 bank note, is highly recommended, as well as a stroll around the colonnaded market square, one of the prettiest in Europe.

One Night: Schwerin. The capital of the region is well worth the 64-kilometer (40-mile) detour, if only to marvel at the opulence of the lake-island palace of the Mecklenburg princes. A boat trip on the 18-kilometer (11-mile)-long Schwerinsee Lake is a relaxing diversion. Be sure to explore Wismar en route to or from Schwerin and inspect the ornate pump house built in 1602 on the town square.

Two Nights: Bad Doberan-Rostock. Make Rostock your base for several excursions to the coast, but allow time to explore this shipbuilding port's old town. Don't miss a ride on Molli, a 106-year-old steam train that chugs through the streets of Bad Doberan to the seaside resort of Kühlungsborn.

One Night: Stralsund. This bustling, centuries-old port, whose center still retains a medieval air, is the gateway to the picturesque island of Rügen. Accommodations are scarce, so you might seek out a bed-and-breakfast lodging; the local tourist office has listings.

Two Nights: Rügen. You could easily spend two or more days on this enchanting island, relaxing on one of the many sandy beaches or perhaps discovering your own secret cove.

One Night: Usedom Island. From Rügen, you can complete the tour in a day, ending up on Usedom Island. Try reserving a room at one of the seaside hotels in Ahlbeck or Heringsdorf, or hunt out a bed-and-breakfast guest house through the local tourist office.

Further Information: *See* Chapter 18.

2 Portraits of Germany

Germany at a Glance: A Chronology

c 5000 BC Primitive tribes settle in the Rhine and Danube valleys

c 2000–800 BC Distinctive German Bronze Age culture emerges, with settlements ranging from coastal farms to lakeside villages

c 450–50 BC Salzkammergut people, whose prosperity is based on abundant salt deposits (in the area of upper Austria), trade with Greeks and Etruscans; they spread as far as Belgium and have first contact with the Romans

9 BC–AD 9 Roman attempts to conquer the "Germans"—the tribes of the Cibri, the Franks, the Goths, and the Vandals—are only partly successful; the Rhine becomes the northeastern border of the Roman Empire (and remains so for 300 years)

212 Roman citizenship is granted to all free inhabitants of the Empire

c 400 Pressed forward by Huns from Asia, German tribes such as the Franks, the Vandals, and the Lombards migrate to Gaul (France), Spain, Italy, and North Africa, scattering the Empire's populace and eventually leading to the disintegration of central Roman authority

486 The Frankish kingdom is founded by Clovis; his court is in Paris

497 The Franks convert to Christianity

---

776 Charlemagne becomes king of the Franks

800 Charlemagne is declared Holy Roman Emperor; he makes Aachen capital of his realm, which stretches from the Bay of Biscay to the Adriatic and from the Mediterranean to the Baltic. Under his enlightened patronage, there is an upsurge in art and architecture—the Carolingian renaissance

843 The Treaty of Verdun divides Charlemagne's empire among his three sons: West Francia becomes France; Lotharingia becomes Lorraine (territory to be disputed by France and Germany into the 20th century); and East Francia takes on, roughly, the shape of modern Germany

911 Five powerful German dukes (of Bavaria, Lorraine, Franconia, Saxony, and Swabia) establish the first German monarchy by electing King Conrad I

962 Otto I is crowned Holy Roman Emperor by the Pope; he establishes Austria—the East Mark. The Ottonian renaissance is marked especially by the development of Romanesque architecture

1024–1125 The Salian Dynasty is characterized by a struggle between emperors and Church that leaves the empire weak and disorganized; the great Romanesque cathedrals of Speyer, Trier, Mainz, and Worms are built

1138–1254 Frederick Barbarossa leads the Hohenstaufen Dynasty; there is temporary recentralization of power, underpinned by strong trade and Church relations

1158 Munich, capital of Bavaria, is founded by Duke Henry the Lion; Henry is deposed by Emperor Barbarossa, and Munich is presented to the House of Wittelsbach, which rules it until 1918

1241 The Hanseatic League is founded to protect trade; Bremen, Hamburg, Köln, and Lübeck are early members. Agencies soon extend to London, Antwerp, Venice, and the Baltic and North seas; a complex banking and finance system results

mid-1200s The Gothic style, exemplified by the grand Köln Cathedral, flourishes

---

1456 Johannes Gutenberg (1397–1468) prints first book in Europe

1471 The painter Albrecht Dürer (dies 1528) is born during the Renaissance. The Dutch-born philosopher Erasmus (1466–1536), and the painters Hans Holbein the Younger (1497–1543), Lucas Cranach the Elder (1472–1553), and Albrecht Altdorfer (1480–1538) help disseminate the new view of the world. Increasing wealth among the merchant classes leads to strong patronage of the revived arts

1517 The Protestant Reformation begins in Germany when Martin Luther (1483–1546) nails his "Ninety-Five Theses" to a church door in Wittenberg, contending that the Roman Church has forfeited divine authority through the corrupt sale of indulgences. Though Luther is outlawed, his revolutionary doctrine splits the church; much of north Germany embraces Protestantism

1524–25 The (Catholic) Hapsburgs rise to power; their empire spreads throughout Europe (and as far as North Africa, the Americas, and the Philippines). In 1530, Charles V (a Hapsburg) is crowned Holy Roman Emperor; he brutally crushes the Peasants' War, one in a series of populist uprisings in Europe

1545 The Council of Trent marks the beginning of the Counter-Reformation. Through diplomacy and coercion, most Austrians, Bavarians, and Bohemians are won back to Catholicism, but the majority of Germany remains Lutheran; persecution of religious minorities grows

1618–48 Germany is the main theater for combat in the Thirty Years' War. The powerful Catholic Hapsburgs are defeated by Protestant forces, swelled by disgruntled Hapsburg subjects and the armies of King Gustav Adolphus of Sweden. The bloody conflict ends with the Peace of Westphalia (1648); Hapsburg and papal authority are severely diminished

---

1689 Louis XIV of France invades the Rhineland Palatinate and sacks Heidelberg. Elsewhere at the end of the 17th century, Germany consolidates its role as a center of scientific thought

1708 Johann Sebastian Bach (1685–1750) becomes court organist at Weimar and launches his career; he and Georg Friederic Händel (1685–1759) fortify the great tradition of German music. Baroque and, later, Rococo art and architecture flourish

1740–86 Reign of Frederick the Great of Prussia; his rule sees both the expansion of Prussia (it becomes the dominant military force in Germany) and the growth of Englightenment thought

c 1790 The great age of European orchestral music is raised to new heights in the works of Joseph Haydn (1732–1809), Wolfgang Amadeus Mozart (1756–1791), and Ludwig van Beethoven (1770–1827)

---

early 1800s Johann Wolfgang von Goethe (1749–1832) helps initiate Romanticism. Other German Romantics include the writers Friedrich Schiller (1759–1805) and Heinrich von Kleist (1777–1811); the composers Robert Schumann (1810–1856), Hungarian-born Franz Liszt (1811–1886), Richard Wagner (1813–1883), and Johannes Brahms (1833–1897); and the painter Casper David Friedrich (1774–1840). In architecture, the severe lines of neoclassicism become popular

1806 Napoléon's armies invade Prussia; it briefly becomes part of the French Empire

1807 The Prussian prime minister Baron vom und zum Stein frees the serfs, creating a new spirit of patriotism; the Prussian army is rebuilt

1813 The Prussians defeat Napoléon at Leipzig

1815 Britain and Prussia defeat Napoléon at Waterloo. At the Congress of Vienna, the German Confederation is created as a loose union of 39 independent states, reduced from more than 300 principalities. The *Bundestag* (national assembly) is established at Frankfurt. Already powerful Prussia increases, gaining the Rhineland, Westphalia, and most of Saxony

1848 The "Year of the Revolutions" is marked by uprisings across the fragmented German Confederation; Prussia uses the opportunity for further expansion. A national parliament is elected, taking the power of the Bundestag to prepare a constitution for a united Germany

1862 Otto von Bismarck (1815–1898) becomes prime minister of Prussia; he is determined to wrest German-populated provinces from Austro-Hungarian (Hapsburg) control

1866 Austria-Hungary is defeated by the Prussians at Sadowa; Bismarck sets up the Northern German Confederation in 1867. A key figure in Bismarck's plans is Ludwig II of Bavaria (the Dream King). Ludwig—a political simpleton—lacks successors, making it easy for Prussia to seize his lands

1867 Karl Marx (1818–1883) publishes *Das Kapital*

1870–71 The Franco-Prussian War: Prussia lays siege to Paris. Victorious Prussia seizes Alsace-Lorraine but eventually withdraws from all other occupied French territories

1871 The four south German states agree to join the Northern Confederation; Wilhelm I is proclaimed first Kaiser of the united Empire

1882 Triple Alliance is forged between Germany, Austria-Hungary, and Italy. Germany's industrial revolution blossoms, enabling it to catch up with the other great powers of Europe. Germany establishes colonies in Africa and the Pacific

c 1885 Daimler and Benz pioneer the automobile

1890 Kaiser Wilhelm II (rules 1888–1918) dismisses Bismarck and begins a new, more aggressive course of foreign policy; he oversees the expansion of the Navy

1890s A new school of writers, including Rainer Maria Rilke (1875–1926), emerges. Rilke's *Sonnets to Orpheus* gives German poetry new lyricism

1905 Albert Einstein (1879–1955) announces his theory of relativity

1906 Painter Ernst Ludwig Kirchner (1880–1938) helps organize *Die Brücke,* a group of artists who along with *Der Blaue Reiter* forge the avant-garde art movement Expressionism

1907 Great Britain, Russia, and France form the Triple Entente, which, set against the Triple Alliance, divides Europe into two armed camps

1914–18 Austrian Archduke Franz-Ferdinand is assassinated in Serbia. The attempted German invasion of France sparks World War I; Italy and Russia join the Allies, and four years of pitched battle ensue. By 1918, the Central Powers are encircled and must capitulate

---

1918 Germany is compelled by the Versailles Treaty to give up its overseas colonies and much European territory (including Alsace-Lorraine to France) and to pay huge reparations to the Allies; the tough terms leave the new democracy (the Weimar Republic) shaky

1919 The Bauhaus school of art and design, the brainchild of Walter Gropius (1883–1969), is born. Thomas Mann (1875–1955) and Hermann Hesse (1877–1962) forge a new style of visionary intellectual writing—until quashed by Nazism

---

1923 Germany suffers runaway inflation. Adolf Hitler's "Beer Hall Putsch," a rightist revolt, fails; leftist revolts are frequent

1925 Hitler publishes *Mein Kampf* ("My Struggle")

1932 The Nazi Party gains the majority in the Bundestag

1933 Hitler becomes chancellor; the Nazi "revolution" begins

1934 President Paul von Hindenburg dies; Hitler declares himself *Führer* (leader) of the Third Reich (empire). Nazification of all German social institutions begins, spreading a policy that is virulently racist and anti-Communist. Germany recovers industrial might and rearms

1936 Germany signs anti-Communist agreements with Italy and Japan, forming the Axis; Hitler reoccupies the Rhineland

1938 The *Anschluss* (annexation): Hitler occupies Austria; Germany occupies the Sudetenland in Czechoslovakia

1939–40 In August, Hitler signs a pact with the Soviet Union; in September he invades Poland; war is declared by the Allies. Over the next three years, there are Nazi invasions of Denmark, Norway, the Low Countries, France, Yugoslavia, and Greece. Alliances form between Germany and the Baltic states

1941–45 Hitler launches his anti-Communist crusade against the Soviet Union, reaching Leningrad in the north and Stalingrad and the Caucasus in the south. In 1944, the Allies land in France; their combined might brings the Axis to its knees. In addition to the millions killed in the fighting, over 6 million die in Hitler's concentration camps. Germany is again in ruins. Hitler kills himself. Berlin (and what becomes East Germany) is occupied by the Soviet Union

1945 At the Yalta Conference, France, the United States, Britain, and the Soviet Union divide Germany into four zones; each country occupies a sector of Berlin. The Potsdam Agreement expresses the determination to rebuild Germany as a democracy

1948 The Soviet Union tears up the Potsdam Agreement and attempts, by blockade, to exclude the three other Allies from their agreed zones in Berlin. Stalin is frustrated by a massive airlift of supplies to West Berlin

1949 The three Western zones are combined to form the Federal Republic of Germany (DDR); the new West German parliament elects Konrad Adenauer as chancellor (a post held until his retirement in 1963). Soviet-held East Germany becomes the Communist German Democratic Republic

1950s West Germany, aided by the financial impetus provided by the Marshall Plan, rebuilds its devastated cities and economy—the *Wirtschaftswunder* (economic miracle) gathers pace

1957 The Treaty of Rome heralds the formation of the European Economic Community (EEC); Germany is a founder member

1961 Communists build the Berlin Wall to stem the outward tide of refugees. The writers Heinrich Böll and Günter Grass emerge

1969–1974 The vigorous chancellorship of Willy Brandt pursues Ostpolitik, improving relations with Eastern Europe, the Soviet Union, and recognizing East Germany's sovereignty

mid-1980s The powerful German Green Party emerges as the leading environmentalist voice in Europe

1989 Discontent in East Germany leads to a flood of refugees westward and to mass demonstrations; Communist power collapses across Eastern Europe; the Berlin Wall falls

1990 Political instability ushers in the year. In March the first free elections in East Germany bring a center-right government to power. The Communists, faced with corruption scandals, suffer a big defeat, but are represented in the new, democratic parliament. The World War II victors hold talks with the two German governments and the Soviet Union gives its support for reunification. Economic union takes place on July 1, with full political unity on October 3. Five new states are created out of the former German Democratic Republic. In December, in the first democratic national German elections for 58 years, Chancellor Helmut Kohl's three-party coalition is reelected. Support for the Green Party wanes, and the Communists—renamed the Democratic Socialists—win 17 seats in the new parliament

1991 Nine months of emotional debate about the future capital of the reunited country finally ends on June 20, when parliamentary representatives vote in favor of quitting Bonn—seat of the West German government since 1949—and moving to Berlin, which was the capital until the end of World War II

Seeing Is Believing

By Christopher Hope

South African–born novelist Christopher Hope happened to be visiting West Berlin when the Wall fell; his eyewitness account appeared in The New Republic *one month later, in December 1989. His new novel,* Serenity House, *was published in 1992, as was a collection of short stories,* Swirsky Aloft.

You know that things are serious when the TV news stations start flying in their anchor men and women. Chattering groups of them thronged Berlin Airport when I arrived on November 12, father figures and mother confessors from the news desks of the American networks, the British Broadcasting Corp., Japanese TV, and the European pop and sports satellite channels. They were eager to present the news in situ, beside the Berlin Wall, in front of the Brandenburg Gate. They were attended by baggage bearers, drones, and soldiers who formed a kind of protective scrimmage, easing their costly charges through passport control, incredulous that mere officials should obstruct the faces welcomed into millions of homes each night.

Berliners have always displayed disrespect when faced with power or privilege. And household names become very parochial the moment they leave the house. The famous faces, it must be said, are paler than expected, the eyes flutter restlessly as if searching for makeup and the auto-cue. As the Berliners well knew, these were people who a few weeks ago could not have picked out their divided city on a map. Berlin flickered in the memory, if at all, mixed with images of Liza Minnelli belting out her stuff in *Cabaret.* Indeed, for most people Berlin was an improbable oasis in the East German wilderness, cut in two by the Wall, surrounded by Russian troops, a stump of a city crowded with allied soldiers, spiked with missiles, lined with steak houses.

Berlin was last in the news in a big way during the Berlin airlift, and during the building of the Wall in 1961. It was featured vividly when President Kennedy gazed out across the Wall and proclaimed: "I am a Berliner." But thereafter it was simply a schizophrenic city. A remnant of a vanished metropolis, occupied by its conquerors—in the West a prosperous fortress of 2 million people; in the East a prison house its masters called paradise, a place of outer darkness. Berlin was not a place—it was an issue. It never quite seemed to be part of modern Germany. When people thought of West Germany they tended to think of Bonn, the apologetic federal capital, of Mercedes and BMW, and of the strength of the deutsche mark. It was devoutly to be hoped that the two Germanys would one day be reunited, but outside the circles of the devout, no one was putting any money on it.

Since the erection of the Wall 30 years ago, Berlin has become a kind of distant theater of the cold war. A fine place for spy stories, the scene of memorable exchanges of secret agents; daring escapes by hugely brave men and women hidden in the cunning compartments of trucks and automobiles; flights by hot air balloon; midnight dashes through the sewers beneath the city. And of abortive escapes that ended in gunfire and bleeding bodies. Along the length of the Wall small tabernacles remember with a name or a photograph those who did not get away.

Then suddenly the world was stood on its head. The night of Friday, November 10, the East Germans began smashing through the Wall. By November 14 there were 22 new crossing points, with promises of more to come. And through these gaps poured the grateful tens of thousands. The invasion so long predicted was coming true. Even the direction was right—the invaders came from the East. But they carried not rifles but shopping bags, and they arrived not in tanks but on foot, or in tiny two-stroke motocars called Trabants, belching fumes, their fiberglass frames shivering on their uncertain chassis. To watch the tiny Trabant cross the Wall and go chugging along the broad West Berlin boulevards, impatiently followed by a gas-guzzling, absurdly fast turbo triumph of German automotive engineering, is to be present at a motorized street theater. The way into the future might be summed up by a single stage direction: "Exit a Trabant, pursued by a Porsche."

West Berliners, usually so laconic, acerbic, irreverent, melted in the face of this invasion. The Opera House offered free performances of Mozart's *Magic Flute*. The city fathers allowed free travel on the subway, the U-Bahn. They gave each new arrival 100 marks to spend. The department stores hung out welcome signs and exchanged the visitors' dud currency at the rate of ten East German marks for one West German mark. Around the square at the top of the Kufürstendamm, beside the ruins of the Kaiser Wilhelm Memorial Church commemorating the destruction of Berlin, sausage stalls appeared, trestle tables, beakers of beer, mobile toilets, street musicians, and unbounded conviviality. The visitors were quickly dubbed the *"Ossies"* to distinguish them from the West Berliners, who became, naturally, the *"Wessies."* When *Ossies* met *Wessies*, there took place in West Berlin the biggest damn family reunion Europe has seen since the War.

True, there were also a few party poopers about. Taxi drivers worried aloud about the cost of it all. After all, there were at least 1.2 million East Berliners (or were the last time any had been brave enough or foolhardy enough to count them), and at 100 marks a head, the overall subsidy for this invasion, in every sense, was not small beer. Similarly, guest workers employed to do the work that West Berliners disdain took a rather dim view. "What will happen to me?" the Turkish cleaning attendant of a block of flats asked her employer, "when the *Ossies* undercut me?"

Her employer appeared happily unconcerned. "I know, I've had three offers already."

And what of the thousands of troops that the Western allies and the Russians have kept massed along this crucial border? More worrying still, to the Poles and others—with sad memories of the last united Germany—where were the borders of Germany itself? Why had the West German chancelor, on a visit to Poland, declined to state that the postwar boundaries were immovable? And what on earth was one to make of a German people who, it seemed, were no longer preparing for the war but mounting shopping expeditions instead?

It was all very confusing and very euphoric and vaguely troubling all at once. Anyone who imagined that things would settle down did not, as they say in Berlin, have all his cups in the cupboard. Such people also mistook the significance of symbols. A Wall had once stood between East and West, built of stone and stained with blood. One night, without warning, it fell down. And only the rich bird life, thriving along its empty, eerie length, would mourn its passing. No one was surprised by the news that three Communist mayors from the East had committed suicide. It was the opinion of otherwise pacific matrons taking coffee in the Kempinski Eck, the famous plush, glass-fronted observatory on the Kurfürstedamm, that the disgraced former leader of East Germany, Erich Honecker, should "do the decent thing" and follow suit.

West Berliners have always detested the Wall, but they learned to live with it. They have jogged along its length and have daubed it with graffiti from end to end, but except on rare occasions when it thrust itself into view with a spectacular escape, or some important politician came to call and made a speech, they forgot about it. What West Berlin has never allowed anybody to forget is the War itself. Bullet holes are still to be seen, spattering the sides of buildings. Fragments of the portals of the old Berlin synagogue are cemented into the porch of the Jewish Community Center in Fasanenstrasse. West Berlin is a city loud with ghosts.

The area around the Wall added to the sense of war-torn desolation. Once it was the site of the Potsdamer Platz, among the busiest intersections in Europe, the very heart of Berlin. Since the War ended it has been a muddy, disconsolate slum. Taxi drivers assured visitors with laconic understatement that it was not "a development area." The deserted embassies look like the victims of some belowstairs revolt by the lower vegetable orders. Creepers spread across their facades and reach through open windows into empty rooms.

Reminders of the cataclysms are everywhere: the Hitler bunker; the site of the Gestapo torture chambers in Wilhelmstrasse; the fragmentary remains of the old Anhalter station, a crumbling facade and a few headless statues on a roof out of which trees have sprouted. Before the War the Anhalter dispatched 60 trains a day to Dresden, Rome, Vienna. Nearby is Friedrichstrasse, now a gray shadow of its prewar, tinselly self. It sputters out in a pizzeria and a rash of bars, ending abruptly when it runs up against Checkpoint Charlie. The graffiti on the Wall reveals the genial derision in which West Berliners hold the foreigner's tender fascination with this monstrous monument: "What are you staring at? Have you never seen a wall before?"

There has always been something inconsolably sad in the air of West Berlin. East Berlin, by contrast, has always pretended otherwise. East Berliners never spoke of their city as "East Berlin," but always and only as Berlin, the capital of the only legitimate Germany. They preferred to ignore the existence of the imposter stuck away in the middle of 110 miles of East German territory. East German soldiers were to be seen regularly changing the guard on Unter Den Linden, still doing the goose step, wearing helmets like soup plates.

Naturally I crossed the Wall into the East for the simple pleasure of witnessing East Germans moving the other way. They waited patiently in long lines, helped by the border guards to fill in their travel forms. It must be strange to ask directions from a man who a week earlier would have shot you for trying to leave the country. It must have been even stranger for the guards themselves, trained to snarl, shoot, and inspect the undersides of tourist buses with giant dentist mirrors. Overnight they had become part of the courtesy staff, obliging, efficient, seemingly delighted that most of the population planned a trip abroad.

I traveled to the East with a British novelist who had never made the crossing before. She had a theory that you could tell you were getting older when the popes started looking younger. But in Berlin, that test seemed really to apply to border guards. They appeared to have shed years overnight. "Please step this way to exchange your money," a smiling fellow invited toothily, holding the door. Only those used to making this dreary crossing would understand the novelty of his demeanor. I exchanged good West German marks for bad, an obligatory transfer, a tax on curiosity. One day East German banknotes will, like the Wall itself, become collectors' items. On the face of the 20-mark note Goethe stares back quietly, as if disturbed to find himself so framed.

There has never been much to see in the streets of East Berlin, or in the shops. A smart new coffeehouse adorns the corner of Friedrichstrasse, in its continuation on the other side of the Wall. It is always packed to capacity. Most of the customers appear to have taken up their seats soon after the building was completed and show no signs of leaving. In a nearby supermarket, food is more plentiful than it is, say, in Moscow. But a German economy, *any* German economy, must be in deep trouble if it cannot make even bottles of sauerkraut look attractive. But what lightens everything in a lovely, astonishing fashion are the chattering crowds of East Berliners at the crossing points, waiting to leave as if it were the most natural thing in the world. Most are going for the day, complete with bags, babies, and beaming smiles, heading for the bright lights of West Berlin.

And for citizens of a regime known for its prim moralizing, its political piety, and it claims to be untainted by the lures of Western junk, the *Ossies* show themselves to be endearingly human. They crowd the nonstop strip shows on Kant Strasse. The unexpected connection between vice and philosophy is a feature of West Berlin. After all, the crown (if that is the word) of Martin Luther Strasse happens to be an emporium known as Big Sexy Land. The clip joints reduced their entry fee and offered two free beers to our "Eastern guests" and reported that the crowds were "good-humored."

And so they were. They were also "different," a word that kept cropping up among West Berliners who observed the visitors closely. The *Ossies* manifest that special sort of raging docility that distinguishes Eastern European crowds, people accustomed to standing in line and monitoring their expectations every wish of the way. The *Wessies* looked upon the *Ossies* with a benign complexity attended by gentle satisfaction. They were, quite simply, as pleased as punch to see them in West Berlin—though not quite sure what to do with them.

And thus it was with a certain relief that the *Wessies* sought refuge in their bars, restaurants, and watering holes where the *Ossies* could not follow and sat talking excitedly over meals that only they could afford. And the *Ossies* would press their noses to the windows of the Paris Bar like gentle ghosts. Yet there was no discernible resentment in their stares. *Ossies* were to be seen striding through the most distant suburbs, stopping to stare at children playing in the park, or a man washing his car, or gathering in great crowds outside the windows of the BMW showrooms. After all, what qualitative difference is there among the objects of your fascination when you are seeing it all for the first time? It is all very natural, and not a little sad.

At the entrance to a large department store I watched a family of East Berliners, freshly arrived, wide-eyed and eerily silent. Father, mother, and a boy of about six were passing the chocolate counter. Suddenly the little boy stopped dead. He had seen the chocolates, homemade and gleaming darkly under the lights, perfection behind the glass, a costly pyramid, profligate, tempting, untouchable.

His adoration passed like an electric current into his mother and father and rooted them to the spot. No one spoke. After a while, like sleepers awakening, they shook themselves and went on their way. Seeing is believing. It's not the same as having, but it will do, for a while at least.

Germany and Beer

By Graham Lees

British-born Graham Lees has lived in Munich since the early '80s and has traveled throughout Germany in search of its beers. He is a member of the British Guild of Beer Writers and a founder member of Britain's Campaign for Real Ale.

No country is more closely associated with beer than Germany. And rightly so, for no other country has so many breweries or so much reverence for the heady brew. The Germans don't just produce *a* beverage called beer, they brew more than 5,000 varieties in a range of tastes and colors to tempt the palates of almost everyone. You'll find beer served up black, strong, and sweet, or pale, frothy, and bitter. If you're in Berlin, don't be surprised if it's tinged red or green and is served in what looks like a fruit bowl (that's Berliner Weisse).

The new, unified Germany has about 1,300 breweries, 40% of the world's total. Beer is brewed in farmhouse cellars by grandmothers, in backyards by retired soldiers, in push-button factories by young technicians, in monasteries and convents by monks and nuns. Beer is drunk for breakfast (usually Weizenbier, or wheat beer), lunch, and supper. It's drunk on Alpine peaks, in boisterous beer halls, in chic cafés, and during intermission at the opera. It's even dispensed in maternity wards. And in Bavaria, it is legal to sip beer in the office because the drink is officially recognized as a food: "liquid bread."

The quintessential hallmark of Germany's dedication to beer is the purity law, *das Reinheitsgebot*, which guards the quality of every last quaffable drop. (Many of the 100 or so breweries of former East Germany did not adhere to the purity law, but since reunification they are also adopting the code.) The oldest food-protection law in the world, it has remained unchanged since Duke Wilhelm IV introduced it in Bavaria in 1516. The law decrees that only malted barley, hops, yeast, and water may be used to make beer, except for specialty wheat beers (Weizenbier or, in north Germany, Weisse). In many other countries, it is common practice to substitute cheaper fermentables, such as rice grits, maize, or potato flakes, for barley. The Reinheitsgebot prevents the use of any such substitutes, as well as the addition of shelf-life-enhancing adjuncts, which are commonly used elsewhere.

Asking for a "beer" in most German hostelries is like going into a cheese shop and asking for cheese. Even the simplest country inn will more than likely have a choice of beers, and in many pubs there may be several different draft beers in addition to the standard selection of bottled beers. To take just one example from hundreds, there's a pub in the Weihenstephan brewery at Freising, in south Bavaria, that sells up to 11 different in-house brews. (The brewery itself, incidentally, claims to be the oldest in the world, with a history reaching back to the year 1040.)

The type of beer available varies from one part of the country to another. In areas of south Germany, the choice can also depend on the time of year. Some beers are brewed for a particular season or an event in the religious calendar. For instance, Munich's *Starkbierzeit* (strong-beer season) celebrates spring; the dark, malty, double-strength beers produced for the occasion have their origins in a 17th-century monastery where the monks reputedly fortified themselves with a nourishing but potent ale during the long days of Lent.

In north Germany, the most popular standard beers are export lagers or the paler, more pungent pilsners. There are countless varieties of pilsner, which takes its name from the Bohemian town of Pilsen (now Plzen) in Czechoslovakia, where this bitter, hops-fragrant beer originated in the last century. Popular German varieties of pilsner, now widely available, include Bitburger and Warsteiner, brewed in the north, and Löwenbräu and Fürstenberg in the south.

Should you wander into a watering hole in Köln or Düsseldorf, you will be offered something altogether different. The breweries of these two cities on the Rhine produce "old-fashioned" beers similar to English ales. In Köln, the light, soft-flavored tipple is called Kölsch. It's served flatter and warmer than most Continental beers. In nearby Düsseldorf, the darker Alt (old) beer has a creamy, mild taste. It is served straight from wooden barrels in small, narrow glasses, which a liter-swilling Bavarian would liken to thimbles.

Germany's biggest breweries are in the northern city of Dortmund, which feeds the industrial Ruhr region. But Bavaria is where the majority of the country's breweries—and beer traditions—are found. Indeed, while Germany as a whole is at the head of the international beer-drinking table, the Bavarians and the Saarlanders to the southwest consume more beer per person than does any other group in the country.

Many Bavarian breweries are tiny businesses catering, alongside the local butcher and baker, to just one village's needs. A large percentage of the state's 825 breweries are concentrated in the north of the state, where any attempt at sober-minded research is nearly impossible. Some northern Bavarian towns, which are really no more than large villages, maintain three or four breweries each; the beautifully preserved medieval town of Bamberg boasts 10. In that city, you can sample many of the brewing styles of the Franconia region, including what's probably the best example of smoked beer (Rauchbier), which is flavored with the aroma of beechwood smoke. Drink it in the black-beamed Schlenkerla tavern, where sturdy waitresses in black-and-white uniforms serve it from oak casks. Also in Bamberg, the Mahrs brewery tavern will refuse to serve you its delicious pils before 5 PM, when the day's barrel is tapped for homeward-bound workers. It would be sacrilege, they say, to open the barrel earlier, since it loses its freshness if it's not imbibed quickly.

Other, more quaint customs of the pub endure in this region. If someone walks into a room and raps his or her knuckles on each table before taking a seat, don't think you've stumbled across some secret rite: The person is simply using a traditional way to say hello or goodbye. There is one special table in nearly all pubs where strangers should never sit unless specifically invited to. This is the *Stammtisch,* where the most frequent customers gather to drink and exchange gossip. It's usually indicated by a sign.

There's no single word to signify the traditional German pub where you can enjoy a beer, a coffee, or something to eat at most times of the day and evening. It can be described by a variety of prefixes, however, including *Gasthof, Wirtschaft, Gaststätte*. The terms *Kneipe* and *Stube* often apply to small bars where the lights are low and the music is loud or seductive. Pubs are often named after an old craft, a creature, or a local landmark, hence: *Gaststätte Hammerschmied*—"The Hammersmith"; *Gasthof Hechten*—"The Pike." Old coach inns always have the word *post* in their names, and always offer accommodations at reasonable prices.

You will inevitably encounter the *Ruhetag,* the day in the week when a pub closes so that the landlord and staff can go fishing or enjoy a quiet beer or two on their own. The Ruhetag system is usually worked so at least one pub in a village or district stays open each day. It can be frustrating, though, to arrive in a village on the Ruhetag to find only one pub open.

Bavaria holds beer in such reverence that it remains one of the few places in Europe where brewing continues in religious foundations. It is mainly monks who keep up the tradition, but at Mallersdorf, a village 75 miles northeast of Munich, an order of Franciscan nuns produces its own delightful liquid bread. The convent ladies drink much of their tiny brewery's output themselves but, like all religious orders, are happy to share. They run a pub on the convent grounds.

Ultimately, all beer routes must lead the traveler to the world's beer-drinking capital: Munich. This is where you'll find the biggest beer halls, the largest beer gardens, the most famous breweries, the biggest and most indulgent beer festival, and the widest selection of brews; even the beer glasses are bigger. It's a measure of how seriously the Germans take their beer that they see no conflict in the fact that one of the most cosmopolitan cities in the country—a place with great art galleries and museums, an opulent opera house, and chic lifestyles—is internationally recognized as the most beer-drenched city on earth. Postcards are framed with the message "Munich, the Beer City."

First-time visitors to Munich invariably feel they haven't paid their respects to Gambrinus—the patron saint of brewers—unless they go to what has become the most famous of beer halls, the Hofbräuhaus. The fact is, however, that the Hofbräuhaus caters to tourists as much as to locals. A far more earthy watering hole is the Mathäser beer hall (near the main train station), which can accommodate more than 5,000 people. Up to 16,000 pints are downed here on a thirsty day.

In beer halls and beer gardens throughout Munich you will be served beer in liter-size (2-pint) glasses, which are called *Mass*. In Bavaria, the standard everyday pale beer is known as *Helles*, a term not used elsewhere; a dark beer is a *Dunkles*.

The appetite for beer in Munich is so great that four new breweries have been opened in the city since 1988. They are pint-size in comparison to the six brewing giants that slake most of Munich's thirst, but they have unusual attractions. One of them is in a converted train station (Grosshesselohe, on the S-7 line of the S-bahn), where customers can drink their favorite tipple while they watch through a window as the next batch is brewed. Another, in Luitpold Park, Schwabing, is run by a prince whose ancestors ruled Bavaria and invented the world's greatest beer festival, the Oktoberfest.

Bavarians are sometimes regarded with disdain by their less-indulgent Prussian brothers to the north. But not even the widest-girthed southerners can be held wholly responsible for the staggering consumption of beer and food at the annual Oktoberfest, which starts in September. Typically, 10 million pints of beer, as well as 750,000 roasted chickens and 650,000 sausages, are put away by revelers. Clearly, visitors must be helping a little.

German Beer: Coming to Terms

The Beers The alcohol content of German beers varies considerably. At the weaker end of the scale is the light Munich *Helles* (3.7% alcohol by volume) through *Pilsner* (around 5%) to *Doppelbock* (more than 7%).

Alt: literally, "old," referring to beer made according to an old formula. Especially associated with the copper-colored, top-fermented beer peculiar to Düsseldorf

Bock: strong beer, which can be light or dark, sweet or dry. One of the best is the pale *Maibock*, served up when the beer gardens reopen in spring and early summer

Doppelbock: stronger than *Bock*, usually dark, and not to be trifled with. The most famous version of this Munich specialty, available in March, is *Salvator*

Dunkles: dark beer, often slightly sweeter or maltier than pale (light) beers
Export: usually a pale (light-colored) beer of medium strength
Feierabend: called out when a drinking establishment is closing for the day
Halbe: half a *Mass*, the standard beer measure in Bavaria (*see* below). Note that in northern Germany, beer glasses are much smaller
Hefe: yeast. *Hefeweissbier* is a wheat beer with yeast particles
Helles: light beer. The term is more common in southern Bavaria and Munich
Klar, Kristall: wheat beer with the yeast removed
Kleines: a small glass of beer (in Bavaria)
Krug: an earthware drinking vessel, often referred to in English as a stein
Lager: German word meaning "store," adopted by the rest of the world to describe bottom-fermented beers as opposed to British-style, top-fermented ale. In Germany, the term refers to that stage of the brewing process during which beer matures in the brewery
Leichtbier: beer with low alcohol and calorie content, usually pale in color
Mass: a 1-liter–size (almost 2-pint) glass or earthenware mug
Naturtrüb: a new term for unfiltered beer, implying that the yeast has not been removed
Obergarig: top-fermented. This brewing style has been practiced for centuries and still is used to make Germany's wheat, *Alt*, and *Kölsch* beers
O' zapftis!: "Barrel is tapped!" Cry that announces the opening of the Munich Oktoberfest
Pils, Pilsner: A golden colored, dry, bitter-flavored beer named after Pilsen, the town in western Czechoslovakia where in the 19th century the style was first developed
Polizei Stunde: literally, "police hour"—closing time. Midnight or 1 AM in some big cities, usually earlier in small towns and villages
Prost: German for "cheers," a drinking toast, usually accompanied by the clinking of glasses
Radler: lemonade and beer mixed, known in Great Britain as a shandy
Rauchbier: smoked beer. Usually a dark brew with a smoky flavor that comes from infusing the malted barley with beechwood smoke
Untergarig: bottom-fermented. The lager-style method of brewing developed in the mid-19th century
Weissbier, Weizenbier: wheat beer. A highly carbonated, sharp and sour brew, often with floating yeast particles. Very refreshing on hot summer days

3 Munich

Introduction

Munich—München to the Germans—third-largest city in the Federal Republic and capital of the Free State of Bavaria, is the single most popular tourist destination in Germany. This simple statistic speaks volumes about the enduring appeal of what by any standard is a supremely likable city. Munich is kitsch and class, vulgarity and elegance. It's a city of ravishing Rococo and smoky beer cellars, of soaring Gothic and sparkling shops, of pale stucco buildings and space-age factories, of millionaires and lederhosen-clad farmers.

Germany's favorite city is a place with extraordinary ambience and a vibrant lifestyle all its own, in a splendid setting within view of the towering Alps.

Munich belongs to the relaxed and sunny south. Call it Germany with a southern exposure—although it may be an exaggeration to claim, as some Bavarians do, that Munich is the only Italian city north of the Alps.

Still, there's no mistaking the carefree spirit that infuses the place, a positively un-Teutonic joie de vivre that the Bavarians refer to as *Gemütlichkeit,* which could be loosely translated as conviviality, along with an easygoing approach to life, liberty, and the pursuit of happiness, Bavarian style.

It may be all too easy to point to the abundance of beer that flows through the city and its numerous beer restaurants, beer cellars, and beer gardens as the most obvious manifestation of this take-life-as-it-comes attitude. Certainly it's hard not to feel something approaching awe at the realization that Munich University has a beer faculty.

What makes Munich so special? How can its secret be explained? Is it that Munich, despite a population in excess of 1.3 million, retains something of a small-town, almost villagelike atmosphere? Is it in the variety of buildings that dot its center, giving the city, on the one hand, a Baroque grandeur, on the other the semblance of a toy town?

One explanation is that the flair for the fanciful is deeply rooted in Bavarian culture. And no historical figure better personifies this tradition than Ludwig II, one of the last of the Wittelsbachs, the royal dynasty that for almost 750 years ruled over Munich and southern Germany, until the monarchy was forced to abdicate in 1918.

For while Bismarck was striving from his Berlin power base to create a modern unified Germany, "Mad" Ludwig—also nicknamed the "Dream King"—was almost bankrupting the state's treasury by building a succession of fairy-tale castles and remote summer retreats in the mountains and countryside.

Munich bills itself as *Die Weltstadt mit Herz* (the cosmopolitan city with heart), which it most assuredly is. A survey suggests that, given the choice, most Germans would prefer to live in Munich rather than where they currently reside, even though it is probably the most expensive place in reunited Germany.

This is not to suggest that all Germans subscribe to the "I Love Munich" concept. Certain buttoned-up types in Hamburg or Düsseldorf, for example, might look down their imperious noses at Munich as being just a mite crass and somewhat tacky, and the Bavarians as only a few rungs up the ladder from the barbarians. So be it.

Munich is obviously Germany's "good-time city," its image indelibly tied to a series of splashy celebrations that have spread the city's fame far and wide. Mention of Munich invariably triggers thoughts of the colorful carnival season that goes by the name *Fasching*, and the equally gaudy spectacle of the 16-day beer festival known as *Oktoberfest*. The city has become synonymous with beer, *Wurst* (sausage), and Gemütlichkeit. This triad comes close to the essence of the Munich experience.

The stock image is the cavernous beer hall (such as the world-famous Hofbräuhaus) filled with the deafening echo of a brass oompah band and rows of swaying burly Bavarians in lederhosen being served by frumpy Fraus in flairing dirndl dresses. There really is a Munich like this. Every day of the week, in different parts of the city, you'll find scenes like this. But there are also many Müncheners who never step inside a beer hall, who never go near the Oktoberfest. They belong to the *other* Munich—a city of charm, refinement, and sophistication, represented by two of the world's most important art galleries and a noted opera house, a city of expensive elegance, where high-fashion shops seem to compete to put the highest price tags on their wares, a city of five-star nouvelle cuisine.

Endowed with vast tracts of greenery in the form of parks, gardens, and forests; grand boulevards set with remarkable edifices; fountains and statuary; and a river spanned by graceful bridges, Munich is easily Germany's most beautiful and interesting city. If the traveler were to visit only one city in Germany, this would be it. No question about it.

Add the fact that the city has changed dramatically over the past decade or so, and for the traveler who has not been here for a number of years, one might say that a whole new Munich has evolved in the interim. For, quietly and without fanfare, Munich has taken its place as the high-tech capital of Germany, developing into the number-one industrial center in the country and one of the most important in Europe. The concentration of electronics and computer firms—Siemens, IBM, Apple, and such—in and around the city has turned the area into the Silicon Valley of Germany.

All this has turned Munich into one of Europe's wealthiest cities. And it shows. Here everything is extremely upscale and up-to-date; this is the Yuppie capital of the Federal Republic.

At times the aura of affluence may become all but overpowering. But that's what Munich is all about these days and nights: a new city superimposed on the old; conspicuous consumption on a scale we can hardly imagine as a way of life; a fresh patina of glitter along with the traditional rustic charms. Such are the dynamics and duality of this fascinating metropolis that remains a joy to explore and get to know.

Essential Information

Important Addresses and Numbers

Tourist Information The **Fremdenverkehrsamt** (central tourist office) is located in the heart of the city (corner of Rindermarkt and Pettenbeckstr., tel. 089/239–1272), just around the corner from Marienplatz. This office can help with room reservations; if you arrive after hours, call for a recorded message detailing hotel vacancies. (Open Mon.–Fri. 9:30–6.) Longer hours are kept by the city tourist office at the **Hauptsbahnhof** train station (at the entrance on Bayerstr., tel. 089/239–1256; open 8 AM–11 PM). There is also a tourist office at Munich's new airport.

For information on the Bavarian mountain region south of Munich, contact the **Fremdenverkehrsverband München-Oberbayern** (Upper Bavarian Regional Tourist Office) on Sonnenstrasse 10 (tel. 089/597–347).

An official monthly listing of upcoming events, the *Monatsprogramm*, is available at most hotels and newsstands and all tourist offices for DM 2. Information in English about museums and galleries can be obtained round-the-clock by dialing 089/239–162, and about castles and city sights by dialing 089/239–172.

Consulates **U.S. Consulate General,** Königinstrasse 5, tel. 089/[illegible]–6280. **British Consulate General,** Amalienstrasse 62, tel. 089/28881. **Canadian Consulate,** Tal 29, tel. 089/222–661.

Emergencies **Police:** tel. 089/110. **Fire department:** tel. 089/112. **Ambulance:** tel. 089/19222. **Medical emergencies:** tel. 089/558–661. **Pharmacy emergency service:** tel. 089/594–475. **Internationale Ludwigs-Apotheke** (Neuhauserstr. 8, tel. 089/[illegible]60–3021; open Mon.–Fri. 8 AM–6 PM, Sat. 8 AM–1 PM) and **Europa-Apotheke** (Schützenstr. 12, near the Hauptbahnhof, tel. 089/595–423) stock a large variety of over-the-counter medications and personal-hygiene products.

English-language Bookstores The **Anglia English Bookshop** (Schellingstr. 3, tel. 089/283–642) has the largest selection of English-language books in Munich. Other selections can be found at the **Internationale Presse** store at the main train station, or at **Hugendubel** bookshop, 2nd floor, at Marienplatz.

Travel Agencies **American Express,** Promenadeplatz 6, tel. 089/21990. **ABR,** the official Bavarian travel agency, has outlets all over Munich; call 089/12040 for information.

Lost and Found **Fundstelle der Stadtverwaltung** (city lost-property office), Ruppertstrasse 19, tel. 089/2331. **Fundstelle der Bundesbahn,** (railway lost-property office), Hauptbahnhof, Bahnhofplatz 2, tel. 089/128–6664.

Car Rental **Avis:** Nymphenburgerstrasse 61, tel. 089/1260–0020; Balanstrasse 74, tel. 089/497–301.
Europcar: Schwanthalerstrasse 10A, tel. 089/5947–2325.
Hertz: Nymphenburgerstrasse 81, tel. 089/129–5001.
Sixt-Budget: Seitzstrasse 9, tel. 089/223–333.

Arriving and Departing by Plane

Munich's new **Franz Josef Strauss (FJS) Airport**—named after the late Bavarian former state premier—opened in May 1992. It is 28 kilometers (18 miles) northeast of the city center, between the small towns of Freising and Erding. One of the biggest and most modern airports in Europe, FJS is capable of handling 14 million passengers a year. Under construction for 10 years, this new facility has replaced the old Riem Airport, which is now being turned into a trade fair center.

Between FJS Airport and Downtown A fast train service links **FJS Airport** with Munich's Hauptbahnhof (the main train station). The S-8 line operates from a terminal directly beneath the airport's arrival and departure halls. Trains leave every 20 minutes, and the journey takes 38 minutes. Several intermediate stops are made, including Ostbahnhof (convenient for lodgings east of the River Isar), as well as city-center stations such as Marienplatz. A one-way ticket costs DM 10, DM 8 if you purchase a multiple-use strip ticket (*see* Getting Around, below). A family of up to five (two adults and three children) can make the trip for DM 16 by buying a *Tageskarte* ticket. An express airport bus service also links the airport with the Hauptbahnhof; the trip takes about 40 minutes, depending on traffic, and a one-way fare is DM 7. (Buses to the airport depart every 15 minutes from the north side of Arnulfstrasse, opposite the Eden Hotel Wolff.) An airport-city taxi fare costs between DM 70 and DM 80. During rush hour (7 AM–10 AM and 4 PM–7 PM), you need to allow up to one hour traveling time. If you're driving from the airport to the city, take route A–9 and follow the signs for München Stadtmitte. If you're driving to FJS from the city center, head north through Schwabing, join the A–9 Autobahn at the Frankfurter Ring intersection, and follow the signs for the airport ("Flughafen").

Arriving and Departing by Train, Bus, and Car

By Train All long-distance rail services arrive at and depart from the main train station; trains to and from destinations in Bavaria use the adjoining Starnbergerbahnhof. The new high-speed Intercity Express (ICE) trains connect Munich, Frankfurt, and Hamburg on one line; Munich, Würzburg, and Hamburg on another. For information on train schedules, call 089/592–991; most railroad information staff speak English. For tickets and travel information, go to the station information office or try the ABR travel agency, right by the station on Bahnhofplatz.

By Bus Long-distance buses arrive at and depart from the north side of the main train station. A taxi stand is located right next to it.

By Car From the north (Nürnberg and Frankfurt), leave the Autobahn at the Schwabing exit. From Stuttgart and the west, the Autobahn ends at Obermenzing. The Autobahns from Salzburg and the east, Garmisch and the south, and Lindau and the southwest all join the Mittlerer Ring (city beltway). When leaving any Autobahn, follow the Stadtmitte signs for downtown Munich.

Getting Around

On Foot Downtown Munich is only a mile square and is easily explored on foot. Almost all of the major sights in the city center are on the interlinking web of pedestrian streets that run from Karlsplatz by the main train station to Marienplatz and the Viktualienmarkt and extend north around the Frauenkirche and up to Odeonsplatz. The central tourist office issues a free map with suggested walking tours. For sights and attractions away from the city center, make use of the excellent public transportation system.

By Public Transportation Munich has an efficient and well-integrated public transportation system consisting of the **U-bahn** (subway), the **S-bahn** (suburban railway), the **Strassenbahn** (streetcars), and **buses.**

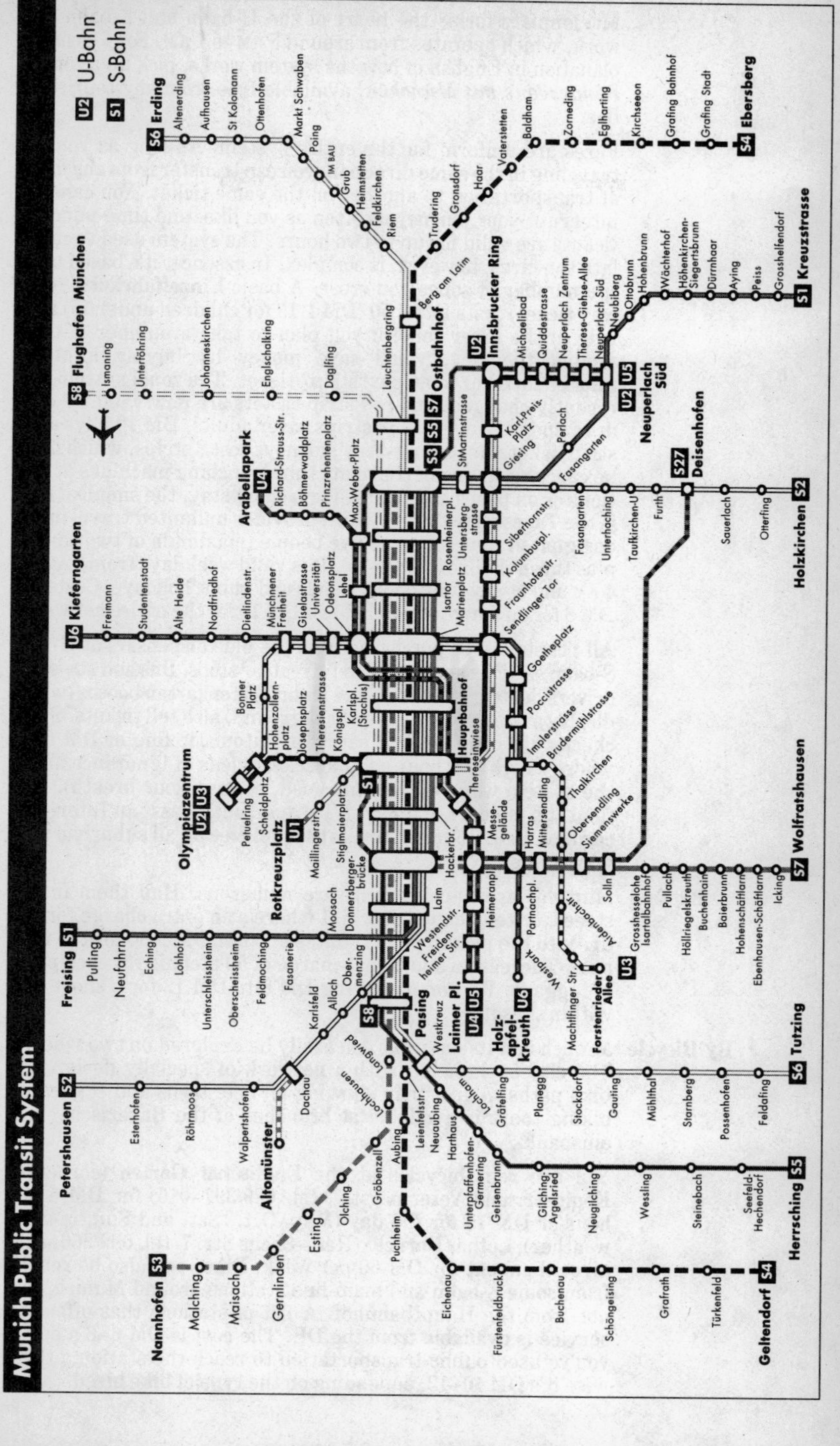

Munich Public Transit System

U2 U-Bahn
S1 S-Bahn

Petershausen S2
Esterhofen
Röhrmoos
Walpertshofen
Dachau
Karlsfeld
Allach
Obermenzing

Freising S1
Pulling
Neufahrn
Eching
Lohhof
Unterschleissheim
Oberscheissheim
Feldmoching
Fasanerie
Moosach

Nannhofen S3
Malching
Maisach
Gernlinden
Esting
Olching
Gröbenzell
Lochhausen
Langwied

Altomünster

Geltendorf S4
Türkenfeld
Grafrath
Schöngeising
Buchenau
Fürstenfeldbruck
Eichenau
Puchheim
Aubing
Leienfelsstr.

Herrsching S5
Seefeld-Hechendorf
Steinebach
Wessling
Neugilching
Gilching-Argelsried
Geisenbrunn
Unterpfaffenhofen-Germering
Harthaus
Neuaubing
Westkreuz

S6 Tutzing
Feldafing
Possenhofen
Starnberg
Mühlthal
Gauting
Stockdorf
Planegg
Gräfelfing
Lochham

S8 Pasing
Laim
Donnersbergerbrücke
Hackerbr.
Hauptbahnhof
Karlspl. (Stachus)
Isartor
Marienplatz
Rosenheimerpl.
Ostbahnhof
Leuchtenbergring

Olympiazentrum U2 U3
Petuelring
Scheidplatz
Bonner Platz
Hohenzollernplatz
Josephsplatz
Theresienstrasse
Königspl.

Rotkreuzplatz U1
Maillingerstr.
Stiglmaierplatz

U6 Kieferngarten
Freimann
Studentenstadt
Alte Heide
Nordfriedhof
Dietlindenstr.
Münchner Freiheit
Giselastrasse
Universität
Odeonsplatz
Lehel
Max-Weber-Platz

Arabellapark U4
Richard-Strauss-Str.
Böhmerwaldplatz
Prinzregentenplatz

S8 Flughafen München
Ismaning
Unterföhring
Johanneskirchen
Englschalking
Daglfing

S6 Erding
Altenerding
Aufhausen
St Kolomann
Ottenhofen
Markt Schwaben
Poing
IM BAU
Grub
Heimstetten
Feldkirchen
Riem

S3 S5 S7 Ostbahnhof
Berg am Laim
Trudering
Gronsdorf
Haar
Vaterstetten
Baldham
Zorneding
Eglharting
Kirchseeon
Grafing Bahnhof
Grafing Stadt
S4 Ebersberg

Laimer Pl.
U4 U5
Westendstr.
Friedenheimer Str.
Heimeranpl.
Messegelände
Theresienwiese
Sendlinger Tor
Fraunhoferstr.
Kolumbuspl.
Silberhornstr.
Untersbergstrasse
StMartinstrasse
Giesing
Karl-Preis-Platz
U2 Innsbrucker Ring
Michaelibad
Quiddestrasse
Neuperlach Zentrum
Therese-Giehse-Allee
Neuperlach Süd
U2 U5
Neuperlach Süd
Perlach
Fasangarten

Holzapfelkreuth U6
Westpark
Partnachpl.
Harras
Mittersendling
Implerstrasse
Poccistrasse
Goetheplatz
Brudermühlstrasse
Thalkirchen
Obersendling
Siemenswerke
Aidenbachstr.
Machtlfinger Str.
Forstenrieder Allee
U3

Solln
Grosshesselohe Isartalbahnhof
Pullach
Höllriegelskreuth
Buchenhain
Baierbrunn
Hohenschäftlarn
Ebenhausen-Schäftlarn
Icking
S7 Wolfratshausen

Fasangarten
Unterhaching
Taufkirchen-U
Furth
S27 Deisenhofen
Sauerlach
Otterfing
Holzkirchen S2

Neubiberg
Ottobrunn
Hohenbrunn
Wächterhof
Höhenkirchen-Siegertsbrunn
Dürrnhaar
Aying
Peiss
Grosshelfendorf
S1 Kreuzstrasse

Marienplatz forms the heart of the U-bahn and S-bahn network, which operates from around 5 AM to 1 AM. For a clear explanation in English of how the system works, pick up a copy of *Rendezvous mit München,* available free from any tourist office.

Fares are uniform for the entire system. As long as you are traveling in the same direction, you can transfer from one mode of transportation to another on the same ticket. You can also interrupt your journey as often as you like, and time-punched tickets are valid for up to two hours. The system used to calculate the fares, however, is complex. In essence, it's based upon the number of zones you cross. A basic **Einzelfahrkarte** (one-way ticket) costs DM 2.50 (DM 1.10 for children under 15) for a ride in the inner zone; if you plan to take a number of trips around the city, you'll save money by buying a **Mehrfahrtenkarte,** or multiple "strip" ticket. The zonal system was recently changed, and red strip tickets are now valid for children under 15 only. Blue strips cover adults. DM 10 buys a 10-strip ticket. Most inner-area journeys cost 2 strips, which must be canceled at one of the many time-punching machines at stations or on buses and trams. For a short stay, the simplest idea is the **Tageskarte** ticket, which provides unlimited travel in the designated zone for up to five people (maximum of two adults, plus three children under 15). It is valid weekdays from 9 AM till 4 AM and at any time on weekends and public holidays. Costs are DM 8 for an inner-zone ticket and DM 16 for the entire network.

All tickets can be purchased from the blue dispensers at U- and S-bahn stations and at bus and streetcar stops. Bus and streetcar drivers, all tourist offices, and Mehrfahrtenkarten booths (which display a white *K* on a green background) also sell tickets. Spot-checks are common and carry an automatic fine of DM 60 if you're caught without a valid ticket (pleas of ignorance about the system won't do you any good, so save your breath). One final tip: Holders of a Eurail Pass, a Youth Pass, an Inter-Rail card, or a DB Tourist Card can travel free on all suburban railway trains.

By Taxi Munich's cream-color taxis are numerous. Hail them in the street, or telephone 089/21611 (there's an extra charge for the drive to the pickup point). Rates start at DM 2.90 for the first mile. There is an additional charge of 50 pfennig for each piece of luggage. Reckon on paying DM 8 to DM 12 for a short trip within the city.

By Bicycle Munich and its environs can easily be explored on two wheels. The city is threaded with a network of specially designated bike paths. A free map showing all bike trails and suggested biking tours is available at branches of the Bayerische Vereinsbank.

You can rent bicycles at the **Englischer Garten** (corner of Königstr. and Veterinärstr., tel. 089/397–016) for DM 5 per hour or DM 15 for the day (May–Oct., Sat. and Sun. in good weather); **Lothar Borucki** (Hans-Sachs Str. 7, tel. 089/266–506) hires them out for DM 60 per week. Bikes can also be rented from some S-bahn and main-line stations around Munich, but not from the Hauptbahnhof. A list of stations that offer the service is available from the DB. The cost is DM 6–8 a day if you've used public transportation to reach the station; otherwise it's DM 10–12, depending on the type of bike hired.

Guided Tours

Orientation Tours A variety of city bus tours is offered by **Münchner Stadt-Rundfahrten** (Arnulfstr. 8, tel. 089/120–4248). The blue buses operate year-round, departing from in front of the Hertie department store on Bahnhofplatz (across from the main entrance to the train station). The Kleine Rundfahrt, a one-hour city tour, leaves daily at 10 AM and 2:30 PM, plus 11:30 AM in midsummer. The cost is DM 13. The Olympiagelände-Tour, which lasts about 2½ hours, explores the Olympia Tower and grounds; it departs daily at 10 AM and 2:30 PM, and the cost is DM 20. The Grosse Rundfahrt, or extended city tour, comes in two varieties; each lasts around 2½ hours and costs DM 23. The morning tour includes visits to the Frauenkirche and Alte Pinakothek; the afternoon tour visits Schloss Nymphenburg. They run Tuesday–Sunday, leaving at 10 and 2:30, respectively. The München bei Nacht tour provides five hours of Munich by night and includes dinner and visits to three night spots. It departs Wednesday–Saturday at 7:30 PM; the cost is DM 100.

Walking and Bicycling Tours The Munich tourist office (*see* Important Addresses and Numbers, above) organizes guided walking tours for groups or individuals; no advance booking is necessary. The meeting place is the **Fischbrunnen** (Fish Fountain) on Marienplatz (Mon., Tues., and Thurs. at 10 AM; cost: DM 6 per person). **City Hopper Touren** (tel. 089/272–1131) offers daily escorted bike tours March–Oct. Advance bookings only, and starting times are negotiable.

Excursions Bus excursions to the Alps, to Austria, to the royal palaces and castles of Bavaria, or along the Romantic Road can be booked through **ABR** (Hauptbahnhof, tel. 089/591–315 or 089/59041). **PanoramaTours** (Arnulfstr. 8, next to the Hauptbahnhof, tel. 089/591–504) operates numerous trips, including the Royal Castles Tour (Schlösserfahrt) of "Mad" King Ludwig's dream palaces (cost: DM 65 per person). Bookings can also be made through all major hotels in the city. The tours depart from in front of the Hauptbahnhof outside the Hertie department store.

The Upper Bavarian Regional Tourist Office (*see* Important Addresses and Numbers, above) provides information and brochures for excursions and accommodations outside Munich.

The **S-bahn** can quickly take you to some of the most beautiful places in the countryside around Munich. Line S-6, for example, will whisk you lakeside to Starnberger See in half an hour; line S-4 runs to the depths of the Ebersberger Forest. You can bring along a bicycle on S-bahn trains.

Exploring Munich

Highlights for First-time Visitors

Frauenkirche
Marienplatz
Viktualienmarkt
Asamkirche
Residenztheater
Englischer Garten
Alte Pinakotek

Schloss Nymphenburg
Deutsches Museum
Tierpark Hellabrunn (zoo)

Downtown Munich

Numbers in the margin correspond to points of interest on the Munich map.

1 Begin your tour of the city at the **Hauptbahnhof,** the main train station and site of the city tourist office, which is located on the corner of Bayerstrasse. Pick up a detailed city map here. Cross Bahnhofplatz, the square in front of the station, and walk toward Schützenstrasse. During the summer you'll see a blue-and-white maypole here—unless, that is, it's been stolen. A vigorous local custom, one that you'll find throughout Bavaria, holds that a neighboring town or city's maypole is fair game, and it will be returned only on payment of a suitable ransom, generally several barrels of beer. Notice the patterns painted on the pole; they represent the trades carried on in the city.

Schützenstrasse marks the start of Munich's pedestrian shopping mall, the Fussgängerzone, 1½ miles of traffic-free streets. Running virtually the length of Schützenstrasse is Munich's
2 largest department store, **Hertie.** At the end of the street you descend via the pedestrian underpass into another shopping empire, a vast underground complex of boutiques and cafés.
3 Above you is the busy traffic intersection, **Karlsplatz,** known locally as *Stachus*. You'll emerge at one of Munich's most popular fountains, a circle of water jets that act as a magnet on hot summer days for city shoppers and office workers seeking a cool corner. The semicircle of yellow-fronted buildings that back the fountain, with their high windows and delicate cast-iron balconies, gives the area a southern, almost Mediterranean, air.

Ahead stands one of the city's oldest gates, the **Karlstor,** first mentioned in local records in 1302. Beyond it lies Munich's main shopping thoroughfare, Neuhauserstrasse and its extension, Kaufingerstrasse. On your left as you enter Neuhauserstrasse is another attractive Munich fountain, a jovial, late-19th-century figure of Bacchus. Neuhauserstrasse and Kaufingerstrasse are a jumble of ancient and modern buildings. This part of town was bombed almost to extinction in World War II and has been extensively rebuilt. Great efforts were made to ensure that these new buildings harmonized with the rest of the old city, though some of the newer structures are little more than functional. Still, even though this may not be one of the architectural high points of the city, there are at least some redeeming
4 features. **Haus Oberpollinger,** a department store hiding behind an imposing 19th-century facade, is one. Notice the weather vanes of old merchant ships on its high-gabled roof.

Shopping, however, is not the only attraction on these streets. Worldly department stores rub shoulders with two remarkable churches: Michaelskirche and the Bürgersaal. You come first to
5 the **Bürgersaal,** built in 1710. Beneath its modest roof are two contrasting levels. The upper level—the church proper—consists of a richly decorated Baroque oratory. Its elaborate stucco foliage and paintings of Bavarian places of pilgrimage project a distinctly different ambience from that of the lower level, reached by descending a double staircase. This gloomy,

cryptlike chamber contains the tomb of Rupert Mayer, a famous Jesuit priest, renowned for his energetic and outspoken opposition to the Nazis.

A few steps farther is the restrained Renaissance facade of the
6 16th-century **Michaelskirche.** It was built by Duke Wilhelm V. Seven years after the start of construction the principal tower collapsed. The duke regarded the disaster as a sign from heaven that the church wasn't big enough, so he ordered a change in the plans—this time without a tower. Seven years later the church was completed, the first Renaissance church of this size in southern Germany. The duke is buried in the crypt, along with 40 members of Bavaria's famous Wittelsbach family (the ruling dynasty for seven centuries), including eccentric King Ludwig II. A severe neoclassical monument in the north transept contains the tomb of Napoléon's stepson, Eugene de Beauharnais, who married one of the daughters of Bavaria's King Maximilian I and died in Munich in 1824. You'll find the plain white stucco interior of the church and its slightly barnlike atmosphere soothingly simple after the lavish decoration of the Bürgersaal.

Time Out Across the road beckons the *Jugendstil* (German Art Nouveau) facade of the **Augustiner Gaststätte.** Within its late-19th-century interior a delicious nut-flavored beer is served. Even if you don't stay for a beer, take a look inside for more stunning examples of Bavarian Jugendstil.

The massive building next to Michaelskirche was once one of Munich's oldest churches, built in the late 13th century for Benedictine monks. It was secularized in the early 19th century, served as a warehouse for some years, and today houses the
7 **Deutsches Jagd- und Fischereimuseum** (German Museum of Hunting and Fishing). Lovers of the thrill of the chase will find it a fascinating place. It also contains the world's largest collection of fishhooks. *Neuhauserstr. 53. Admission: DM 4 adults, DM 2 children and senior citizens. Open Tues., Wed., Fri.–Sun. 9:30–5; Mon. and Thurs. 9:30–9.*

Turn left on Augustinerstrasse and you will soon arrive in Frauenplatz, a quiet square with a shallow sunken fountain.
8 Towering over it is **Frauenkirche** (Church of Our Lady), Munich's cathedral. It's a distinctive late-Gothic brick structure with two enormous towers. Each is more than 300 feet high, and both are capped by very un-Gothic, onion-shape domes. The towers have become the symbol of Munich's skyline, some say because they look like overflowing beer mugs. Unfortunately, the cathedral is closed through 1993 for major repair work. It is due to reopen early in 1994 in time for celebrations marking the 500th anniversary of its consecration. The main body of the cathedral was completed in 20 years—a record time in those days. The towers were added, almost as an afterthought, between 1524 and 1525. Jörg von Polling, the Frauenkirche's original architect, is buried within the walls of the cathedral. The building suffered severe damage during the Allied bombing of Munich and was lovingly restored from 1947 to 1957. Inside, the church combines most of von Polling's original features with a stark, clean modernity and simplicity of line, emphasized by slender white octagonal pillars that sweep up through the nave to the yellow-traced ceiling far above. As you enter the church, look on the stone floor for the dark im-

Alte Pinakothek, **25**
Alter Botanischer Garten, **32**
Alter Hof, **15**
Altes Rathaus, **11**
Antikensammlungen, **30**
Asamkirche, **13**
Bürgersaal, **5**
Deutches Jagd-und Fishereimuseum, **7**
Englischer Garten, **24**
Feldherrnhalle, **21**
Frauenkirche, **8**
Glyptothek, **29**
Hauptbahnhof, **1**
Haus Oberpollinger, **4**
Hertie, **2**
Hofgarten, **20**
Hotel Vier Jahreszeiten, **17**
Karlsplatz, **3**
Karolinenplatz, **27**
Königsplatz, **28**
Marienplatz, **9**
Maximilianstrasse, **16**
Michaelskirche, **6**
Nationaltheater, **18**
Neue Pinakothek, **26**
Neues Rathaus, **10**
Palace of Justice, **33**
Peterskirche, **14**
Residenz, **19**
Siegestor, **22**
Theatinerkirche, **23**
Viktualienmarkt, **12**
Wittelsbacher Fountain, **31**

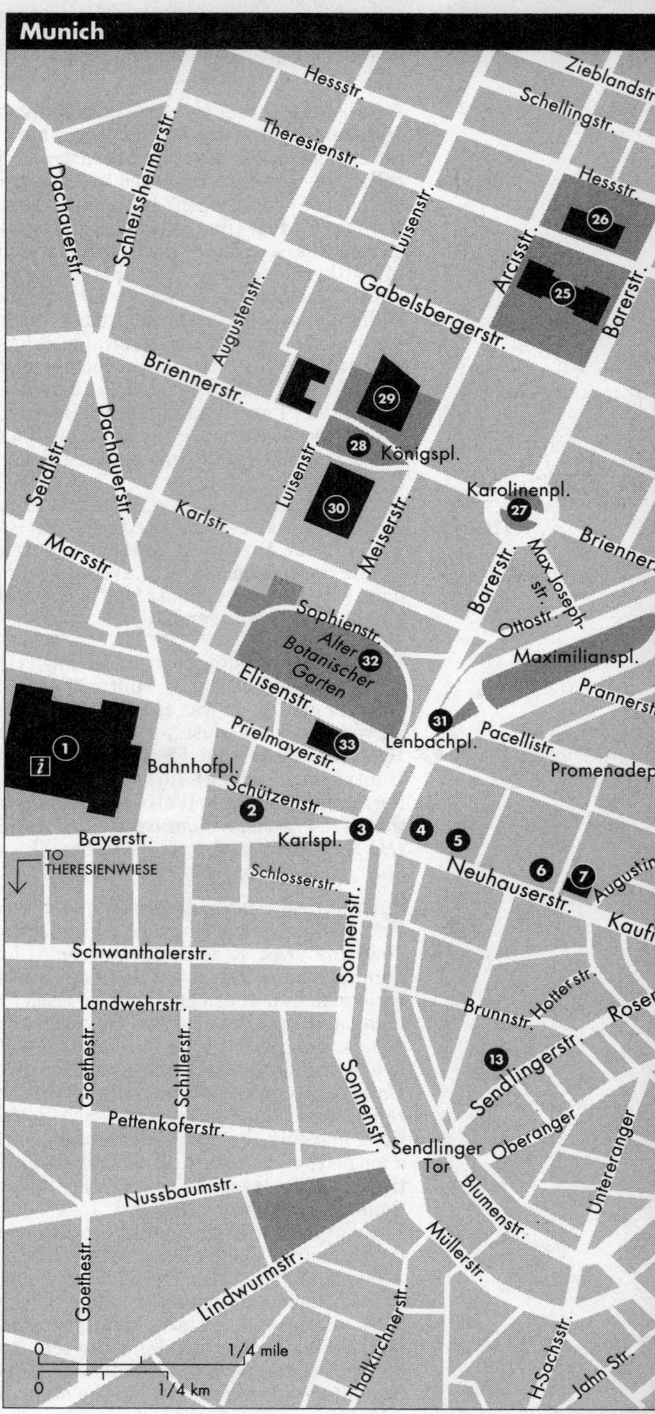

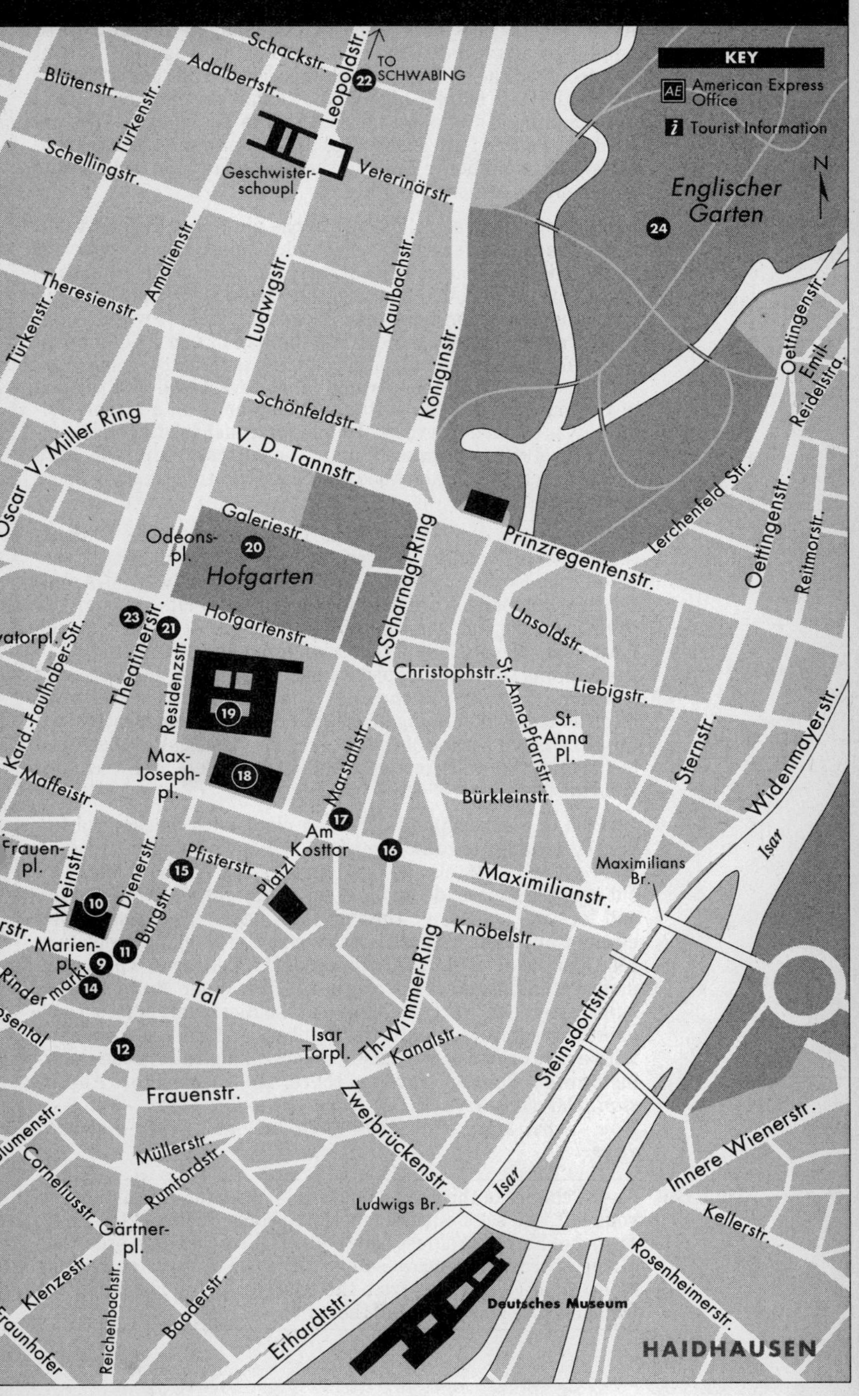
KEY
AE American Express Office
i Tourist Information
N
TO SCHWABING
Englischer Garten
Hofgarten
Schackstr.
Adalbertstr.
Blütenstr.
Türkenstr.
Leopoldstr.
Schellingstr.
Geschwister-schoupl.
Veterinärstr.
Amalienstr.
Theresienstr.
Ludwigstr.
Kaulbachstr.
Königinstr.
Schönfeldstr.
Oscar V. Miller Ring
V. D. Tannstr.
Galeriestr.
Odeons-pl.
Prinzregentenstr.
Lerchenfeld Str.
Oettingenstr.
Emil-Reidelstra.
Reitmorstr.
K-Scharnagl-Ring
Hofgartenstr.
Theatinerstr.
Residenzstr.
Kard.-Faulhaber-Str.
Unsoldstr.
Christophstr.
St.-Anna-Pfarrstr.
Liebigstr.
St. Anna Pl.
Sternstr.
Widenmayerstr.
Max-Joseph-pl.
Maffeistr.
Marstallstr.
Bürkleinstr.
Am Kosttor
Frauen-pl.
Weinstr.
Dienerstr.
Pfisterstr.
Platzl
Maximilianstr.
Maximilians Br.
Isar
Burgstr.
Knöbelstr.
Marien-pl.
Rindermarkt
Tal
Th-Wimmer-Ring
Steinsdorfstr.
Isar Torpl.
Kanalstr.
Frauenstr.
Zweibrückenstr.
Innere Wienerstr.
Müllerstr.
Rumfordstr.
Corneliusstr.
Gärtner-pl.
Ludwigs Br.
Kellerstr.
Rosenheimerstr.
Klenzestr.
Reichenbachstr.
Baaderstr.
Erhardtstr.
Deutsches Museum
Fraunhofer
HAIDHAUSEN
22
24
20
23
21
19
18
17
16
15
10
11
9
14
12

print of a large footstep—the *Teufelstritt* (Devil's footprint). According to local lore, the Devil challenged von Polling to build a nave without windows. Von Polling wagered his soul and accepted the challenge, building a cathedral that is flooded with light from 66-foot-high windows that are invisible to anyone standing at the point marked by the Teufelstritt. The cathedral houses an elaborate, 15th-century black-marble memorial to Emperor Ludwig the Bavarian, guarded by four 16th-century armored knights.

From the cathedral, follow any of the alleys heading east and
9 you'll reach the very heart of Munich, **Marienplatz,** which is surrounded by shops, restaurants, and cafés. The square is named after the gilded statue of the Virgin Mary that has been watching over it for more than three centuries. It was erected in 1638 at the behest of elector Maximilian I as an act of thanksgiving for the survival of the city during the Thirty Years' War, the cataclysmic religious struggle that devastated vast regions of Germany. When the statue, which stands on a marble column, was taken down to be cleaned for a eucharistic world congress in 1960, workmen found a small casket in the base containing a splinter of wood that was said to have come from the cross of Christ.

10 Marienplatz is dominated by the 19th-century **Neues Rathaus** (new town hall), built between 1867 and 1908 in the fussy, turreted, neo-Gothic style so beloved by King Ludwig II. Architectural historians are divided over its merits, though its dramatic scale and lavish detailing are impressive. Perhaps the most serious criticism is that the Dutch and Flemish style of the building seems out of place amid the Baroque and Rococo of
11 so much of the rest of the city. The **Altes Rathaus** (old town hall), a medieval building of assured charm, sits modestly, as if forgotten, in a corner of the square. Its great hall—destroyed in 1944 but now fully restored—was the work of architect Jörg von Halspach.

In 1904, a glockenspiel (a chiming clock with mechanical figures) was added to the tower of the new town hall; it plays daily at 11 AM and 9 PM (also at 5 PM June–Sept.). As the chimes peal out over the square, doors flip open and brightly colored dancers and jousting knights go through their paces. They act out two events from Munich's past: a tournament held on Marienplatz in 1568 and the *Schäfflertanz* (Dance of the Coopers), which commemorated the end of the plague of 1517. When Munich was in ruins after the war, an American soldier contributed some paint to restore the battered figures, and he was rewarded with a ride on one of the jousters' horses, high above the cheering crowds. You can travel up there, too, by elevator. *Admission: DM 2 adults, DM 1 children. May–Oct., Mon.–Fri. 9–4; Nov.–Apr., Mon.–Fri. 9:30–4; closed Sat., Sun., and holidays.*

Time Out As the chimes of the glockenspiel fade, duck into the arcades to your left and seek out the smoky welcome of **Donisl** (Weinstr. 1), one of Munich's oldest beer halls. If it's a cold day, order one of the sturdy homemade soups. Otherwise, try a refreshing wheat beer (Weissbier) from the barrel. During Fasching, the Donisl is often open most of the night.

If you're thinking of lunch after the glockenspiel performance, cross the square, head through the old town-hall arcade, turn right, and join the crowds doing their day's shopping at the 12 **Viktualienmarkt,** the city's open-air food market (*Viktualien* is an old German word for food). You'll find a wide range of produce available. German and international food, Bavarian beer, and French wines make the market a feast for the eyes as well as for the stomach. It is also the realm of the garrulous, sturdy market women, dressed in traditional country costume, who run the stalls with dictatorial authority; one of them was reprimanded recently by Munich's leading newspaper for rudely warning an American tourist not to touch the fruit!

Somewhere beneath the tough exterior of the typical Munich market woman a sentimental heart must beat, for each morning fresh flowers are placed in the extended hand of a statue that stands in the market. The statue is of Munich's famous comedian Karl Valentin and is one of some half-dozen memorial fountains with statues of legendary Bavarian music-hall stars, singers, and comedians from the past that grace the market square.

In summer, take a chair at one of the tables of a lively beer garden set up beneath great chestnut trees and enjoy an alfresco lunch of Bavarian sausages and sauerkraut.

Various *Metzgereien* (butcher shops) in and around the market dispense different types of sausages and will make up sandwiches either to go or to be eaten on the premises. For *Thüringer Rostbratwurstl*—a slightly spicy, long thin sausage—or *Nürnberger Bratwurstl,* head for the Schlemmermeyer Brotzeit Standl stall.

The market even sports a champagne bar where high-tone tidbits go along with the bubbly served by the glass.

From the market, follow Rosental into Sendlingerstrasse, one of the city's most interesting shopping streets, and head left toward Sendlinger Tor, a finely restored medieval brick gate. On your right as you head down Sendlingerstrasse is the remarkable 18th-century church of St. Johann Nepomuk, known as the 13 **Asamkirche** because of the two Asam brothers, Cosmas Damian and Egid Quirin, who built it. The exterior fits so snugly into the housefronts of the street (the Asam brothers lived next door) that you might easily overlook the church as you pass; yet the raw rock foundation of the facade, with its gigantic pilasters, announces the presence of something really unusual. Before you go in, have a look above the doorway at the statue of St. Nepomuk, a 14th-century Bohemian monk who drowned in the Danube; you'll see that angels are conducting him to heaven from a rocky riverbank. Inside you'll discover a prime example of true southern German, late Baroque architecture. Red stucco and rosy marble cover the walls; there is an explosion of frescoes, statuary, and gilding. The little church overwhelms with its opulence and lavish detailing—take a look at the gilt skeletons in the little atrium—and creates a powerfully mystical atmosphere. This is a vision of paradise on earth that those who are more accustomed to the gaunt Gothic cathedrals of northern Europe may find disconcerting. It is a fine example, though, of the Bavarian taste for ornament and, possibly, overkill. Is it vulgar or a great work of architecture? You'll want to decide for yourself.

Return down Sendlingerstrasse toward the city center and
turn right into the Rindermarkt (the former cattle market),
14 and you'll be beneath the soaring tower of **Peterskirche,** or Alter Peter (Old Peter), as Munich's oldest and smallest parish
church is affectionately known. The church traces its origins to
the 11th century and over the years has been restored in a variety of architectural styles. Today you'll find a rich Baroque interior with a magnificent late-Gothic high altar and aisle pillars
decorated with exquisite 18th-century figures of the apostles.
From the top of its 300-foot tower there's a fine view of the city
and, in clear weather, the Alps. A notice at the entrance to the
tower tells you whether the Alps can be seen, and it's worth the
long climb to the top. *Admission to the tower: DM 2 adults, 50
pf children. Open daily in summer 9–7; in winter Mon.–Sat.
9–6; Sun. and holidays 10–6.*

From Peterskirche, cross the busy street called Tal (it means
"valley," and was an early route into the old city) and step into
15 Burgstrasse. You'll soon find yourself in the quiet, airy **Alter
Hof,** the inner courtyard of the original palace of the Wittelsbach rulers of Bavaria. They held court here starting in
1253, and something of the medieval flavor of those times has
survived in this quiet corner of the otherwise busy downtown
area. Don't pass through without turning to admire the medieval oriel (bay window) that hides modestly on the south wall,
just around the corner as you enter the courtyard.

Time Out After all this sightseeing, take an opportunity to rest your legs and quench your thirst while at the same time continuing your tour of central Munich. On the little square called Am Platzl is Munich's most famous beer hall, the **Hofbräuhaus.** *Hofbräu* means "royal brew," a term that aptly describes the golden beer that is served here in king-size liter mugs. Duke Wilhelm V founded the brewery in 1589, and although it still boasts royal patronage in its title, it's now state-owned. If the downstairs hall is too noisy for you, there's a quiet restaurant upstairs. And if there are too many tourists, return on a Saturday night to join the locals at the weekly hop in the upstairs ballroom.

16 From the Hofbräuhaus, head north into **Maximilianstrasse,**
Munich's most elegant shopping street, named after King Maximilian II, whose statue you'll see far down on the right. The
king wanted to break away from the Greek-influenced classical
style of city architecture favored by his father, Ludwig I, so he
ingenuously asked his cabinet whether he could be allowed to
create something original. Maximilianstrasse was the result.
This broad boulevard, its central stretch lined with majestic
buildings (now museums and government offices), culminates
on a rise beyond the Isar River in the stately outlines of the
Maximilianeum, a 19th-century palace now housing the Bavarian *Landtag* (parliament). Across Maximilianstrasse as you enter from the Hofbräuhaus stands another handsome city
17 palace: the **Hotel Vier Jahreszeiten,** a historic watering hole for
princes, millionaires, and the expense-account jet set.

Turn left down Maximilianstrasse, away from the Maximilianeum, and you'll enter the square called Max-Joseph-Platz,
18 dominated by the pillared portico of the 19th-century **Nationaltheater,** home of the Bavarian State Opera Company. The
statue in the center of the square is of Bavaria's first king, Max
Joseph. Along the north side of this untidily arranged square

(marred by the entrance to an underground parking lot) is the
19 lofty and austere south wall of the **Residenz,** the royal palace of Wittelsbach rulers for more than six centuries. It began as a small castle, to which the Wittelsbach dukes moved in the 14th century, when the Alter Hof became surrounded by the teeming tenements of an expanding Munich. In succeeding centuries, the royal residence developed parallel to the importance, requirements, and interests of its occupants. As the complex expanded, it came to include the **Königsbau** (on Max-Josef-Platz) and then (clockwise) the **Alte Residenz;** the **Festsaal** (Banquet Hall); the **Altes Residenztheater** (Cuvilliés Theater); **Allerheiligenhofkirche** (All Soul's Church, now ruined); the **Residenztheater;** and the **Nationaltheater.** Building began in 1385 with the Neuveste (New Fortress), which comprised the northeast section; it burned to the ground in 1750, but one of its finest rooms survived: the 16th-century **Antiquarium,** which was built for Duke Albrecht V's collection of antique statues (today it's used chiefly for state receptions). The throne room of King Ludwig I, the **Neuer Herkulessaal,** is now a concert hall. The accumulated treasures of the Wittelsbachs can be seen in the **Schatzkammer,** or Treasury (one rich centerpiece is a small Renaissance statue of St. George, studded with 2,291 diamonds, 209 pearls, and 406 rubies), and a representative collection of paintings and tapestries is housed in the **Residenzmuseum.** Antique coins and Egyptian works of art are located in the two other museums of this vast palace. In the center of the complex, entered through an inner courtyard where chamber-music concerts are given in summer, is a small Rococo theater, built by François Cuvilliés from 1751 to 1755. The French-born Cuvilliés was a dwarf who was admitted to the Bavarian court as a decorative "bauble." Prince Max Emanuel recognized his latent artistic ability and had him trained as an architect. The prince's eye for talent gave Germany some of its richest Rococo treasures. *Admission to Treasury and Residenzmuseum: DM 3.50 adults, children free. Open Tues.–Sun. 10–4:30. Admission to Staatliche Münzsammlung (coin collection): DM 2.50 adults, DM 1 children, free Sun. and holidays. Open Tues.–Sun. 10–4:30; in winter Sun. 10–1. Admission to Staatliche Sammlung Ägyptischer Kunst (Egyptian art): DM 3 adults, DM 1 children, free Sun. and holidays. Open Tues.–Sun. 10–5. Admission to Cuvilliés Theater: DM 1.50 adults, DM 1 children. Open Mon.– Sat. 2–5, Sun. 10–5.*

Directly north of the Residenz on Hofgartenstrasse lies the for-
20 mer royal garden, the **Hofgarten.** Two sides of the pretty, formal garden are bordered by arcades designed in the 19th century by the royal architect Leo von Klenze. On the east side of the garden stands the new State Chancellery, built around the ruins of the 19th-century Army Museum. Its most prominent feature is its large copper dome. Bombed during World War II air raids, the museum stood untouched for almost 40 years as a grim reminder of the war.

In front of the Chancellery stands one of Europe's most unusual—some say most effective—war memorials. Instead of looking up at the monument you are led down to it: It is a sunken crypt, covered by a massive granite block. In the crypt lies a German soldier from World War I.

Time Out Munich's oldest café, the **Annast,** is located where the Hofgarten is bordered by busy Odeonsplatz. In summer, tables under the trees of the Hofgarten offer a delightful retreat from the hum of city traffic only 100 yards away.

You can be forgiven for any confusion about your whereabouts ("Can this really be Germany?") when you step from the Hofgarten onto Odeonsplatz. To your left is the 19th-century
21 **Feldherrnhalle,** a local hall of fame modeled on the 14th-century Loggia dei Lanzi in Florence. In the '30s and '40s it was the site of a key Nazi shrine, marking the place where Hitler's abortive rising, or *Putsch,* took place in 1923. All who passed it had to give the Nazi salute.

Looking north up Ludwigstrasse, the arrow-straight avenue
22 that ends at the Feldherrnhalle, you'll see the **Siegestor,** or victory arch, which marks the beginning of Ludwigstrasse. The Siegestor also boasts Italian origins; it was modeled on the Arch of Constantine in Rome. It was built to honor the achievements of the Bavarian army during the Wars of Liberation (1813–1815).

Completing this impressively Italianate panorama is the great yellow bulk of the former royal church of St. Kajetan, the
23 **Theatinerkirche,** a sturdily imposing Baroque building. Its lofty towers frame a restrained facade, capped by a massive dome. The church owes its Italian appearance to its founder, the Princess Henriette Adelaide, who commissioned it as an act of thanksgiving for the birth of her son and heir, Max Emanuel, in 1663. A native of Turin, the princess distrusted Bavarian architects and builders and thus summoned a master builder from Bologna, Agostino Barelli, to construct her church. He took as his model the Roman mother church of the newly formed Theatine order of Catholicism. Barelli worked on the building for 11 years but was dismissed before the project was completed. It was not for another 100 years that the Theatinerkirche was finished. Step inside to admire its austere, stucco interior.

Now head north up Ludwigstrasse. The first stretch of the street was designed by court architect Leo von Klenze. Much as Baron Haussmann was later to demolish many of the old streets and buildings in Paris, replacing them with stately boulevards, so von Klenze swept aside the small dwellings and alleys that stood here to build his great avenue. His high-windowed and formal buildings have never quite been accepted by Müncheners, and indeed there's still a sense that Ludwigstrasse is an intruder. Most visitors either love it or hate it. Von Klenze's buildings end just before Ludwigstrasse becomes Leopoldstrasse, and it is easy to see where he handed construction over to another leading architect, Friedrich von Gärtner. The severe neoclassical buildings that line southern Ludwigstrasse—including the Bayerische Staatsbibliothek (Bavarian State Library) and the Universität (University)—fragment into the lighter styles of Leopoldstrasse. The more delicate structures are echoed by the busy street life you'll find here in summer. Once the hub of the legendary artists' district of **Schwabing,** Leopoldstrasse still throbs with life from spring to fall, exuding the atmosphere of a Mediterranean boulevard, with cafés, wine terraces, and artists' stalls. In comparison, Ludwigstrasse is inhabited by the ghosts of the past.

At the south end of Leopoldstrasse, beyond the Siegestor, lies the great open quadrangle of the university, Geschwister-

Scholl-Platz, named after brother and sister Hans and Sophie Scholl, who were executed in 1943 for leading the short-lived anti-Nazi resistance movement known as the Weisse Rose (White Rose). At its north end, Leopoldstrasse leads into Schwabing itself, once Munich's Bohemian quarter but now distinctly upscale. Explore the streets of old Schwabing around Wedekindplatz to get the feel of the place. (Those in search of the Bohemian mood that once animated Schwabing should make for Haidhausen, on the other side of the Isar.)

24 Bordering the east side of Schwabing is the **Englischer Garten.** Three miles long and more than a mile wide, it's Germany's largest city park, stretching from the central avenue of Prinzregentenstrasse to the city's northern boundary. It was designed for the Bavarian Prince Karl Theodor by a refugee from the American War of Independence, Count Rumford. While Count Rumford was of English descent, it was the open, informal nature of the park—reminiscent of the rolling parklands with which the English aristocracy of the 18th century liked to surround their country homes—that determined its name. It has an appealing boating lake, four beer gardens, and a series of curious decorative and monumental constructions, including a Greek temple, the Monopteros, designed by von Klenze for King Ludwig I and built on an artificial hill in the southern section of the park. In the center of one of the park's most popular beer gardens is a Chinese pagoda, erected in 1789, destroyed during the war, and then reconstructed. The Chinese Tower beer garden is world-famous, but the park has prettier places in which to down a beer: the Aumeister, for example, along the northern perimeter. The Aumeister's restaurant is in an early 19th-century hunting lodge.

The Englischer Garten is a paradise for joggers, cyclists, and, in winter, cross-country skiers. The Munich Cricket Club grounds are in the southern section—proof, perhaps, that even that most British of games is not invulnerable to the single-minded Germans—and spectators are welcome. The park also has specially designated areas for nude sunbathing—the Germans have a positively pagan attitude toward the sun—so don't be surprised to see naked bodies bordering the flower beds and paths.

On the southern fringe of Schwabing are Munich's two leading art galleries, the Alte Pinakothek and the Neue Pinakothek, located next to each other on Barerstrasse. They are as complementary as their buildings are contrasting. The Alte Pinakothek (old picture gallery) was built by von Klenze between 1826 and 1836 to exhibit the collection of old masters begun by Duke Wilhelm IV in the 16th century, while the Neue Pinakothek (new picture gallery), a low brick structure, was opened in 1981 to house the royal collection of modern art left homeless when its former building was destroyed in the war.

25 The **Alte Pinakothek** is among the great picture galleries of the world. For many, a visit here will serve as the highlight of a Munich stay. The bulk of the works is northern European, though Italians and Spaniards—notably Giotto—are reasonably well represented. Nevertheless, the works of such painters as Van Eyck, Cranach the Elder, Dürer, Rembrandt, and Rubens constitute the star attractions. Among the richly filled rooms, seek out Altdorfer's *Alexanderschlacht,* centerpiece of the duke's original collection. The writer and critic Friedrich von Schle-

gel (1772–1829), seeing the painting, declared: "If Munich has any other paintings of this quality, then artists should make pilgrimages there as well as to Rome or Paris." Munich has many such paintings . . . and many such pilgrims. *Barerstr. 27. Admission: DM 4 adults, 50 pf children; free Sun. and holidays. Admission to both the Alte Pinakothek and Neue Pinakothek: DM 7 adults, DM 1 children. Open Tues.–Sun. 9–4:30, also Tues. and Thurs. 7 PM–9 PM.*

26 Across a sculpture-studded stretch of lawn is the **Neue Pinakothek.** It's a low brick building that combines high-tech and Italianate influences in equal measure. From outside, the museum does not seem to measure up to the standards set by so many of Munich's other great public buildings. On the other hand, the interior offers a magnificent environment for picture gazing, not the least as a result of the superb natural light flooding in from the skylights. The highlights of the collection are probably the Impressionist and other French 19th-century works—Monet, Degas, and Manet are all well represented. But there's also a substantial collection of 19th-century German and Scandinavian paintings—misty landscapes predominate—that are only now coming to be recognized as admirable and worthy products of their time. *Barerstr. 29. Admission: DM 4 adults, 50 pf children, free Sun. and holidays. Open Tues.–Sun. 9–4:30, also Tues. 7 PM–9 PM.*

Back on Barerstrasse, walk south toward the city center (turn
right from the old gallery or left from the new gallery). Before
27 you stretches the circular **Karolinenplatz,** with its central obelisk; it's a memorial, unveiled in 1812, to those Bavarians killed
fighting Napoléon. Turn right onto Briennerstrasse. Opening
28 up ahead is the massive **Königsplatz,** lined on three sides with
the monumental Grecian-style buildings by von Klenze that
gave Munich the nickname "Athens on the Isar." In the '30s the
great parklike square was laid with granite slabs, which re-
sounded with the thud of jackboots as the Nazis commandeered
the area for their rallies. Only recently were the slabs torn up;
since then the square has returned to something like the green
and peaceful appearance originally intended by Ludwig I. The
two templelike buildings he had constructed there are muse-
29 ums: The **Glyptothek** features a permanent exhibition of Greek
30 and Roman sculptures; and the **Antikensammlungen** (Antiquities Collection) has a fine group of smaller sculptures, Etrus-
can art, Greek vases, gold, and glass. *Glyptothek: Königspl. 3.
Admission: DM 3.50 adults, 50 pf children, free Sun. and holidays. Open Tues., Wed., and Fri.–Sun. 10–4:30, Thurs. noon–
8:30. Antiquities Collection: Königspl. 1. Admission: DM 3.50
adults, 50 pf children, free Sun. and holidays. Open Tues. and
Thurs.–Sun. 10–4:30, Wed. noon–8:30. A combined ticket to
both museums costs DM 6.*

Return to Karolinenplatz and head south along Barerstrasse. You'll come to Lenbachplatz, a busy square scarred by road intersections and tramlines, and lined by a series of handsome turn-of-the-century buildings. At the point where Lenbachplatz meets Maximiliansplatz you'll see one of Munich's most impressive fountains: the monumental late-19th-century
31 **Wittelsbacher Fountain.**

At the southwest corner of Lenbachplatz is the arched entrance
32 to the park that was once the city's botanical garden, the **Alter
Botanischer Garten.** A huge glass palace was built here in 1853

for Germany's first industrial exhibition. In 1931 the immense structure burned down; six years later the garden was redesigned as a public park. Two features from the '30s remain: a small, square exhibition hall, still used for art shows; and the 1933 Neptune Fountain, an enormous work in the heavy, monumental style of the prewar years. At the international electricity exhibition of 1882, the world's first high-tension electricity cable was run from the park to a Bavarian village 48 kilometers (30 miles) away.

Time Out Tucked away on the north edge of the Alter Botanischer Garten is one of the city's most central beer gardens. It's part of the **Park Café,** which at night becomes a fashionable disco serving magnums of champagne for DM 1,450 apiece. Prices in the beer garden are more realistic.

Opposite the southern exit of the park loom the ornate contours
33 of the 1897 law courts, the **Palace of Justice.** Just around the corner is the **Hauptbahnhof** (main railway station)—and the end of our tour.

Outside the Center

The site of Munich's annual beer festival—the renowned Oktoberfest—is only a 10-minute walk from the main train station; alternatively, take the U-4 or U-5 subway one stop. The festival site is Munich's enormous exhibition ground, the **Theresienwiese,** named after a young woman whose engagement party gave rise to the Oktoberfest. In 1810 the party celebrated the betrothal of Princess Therese von Sachsen-Hildburghausen to the Bavarian crown prince Ludwig, later Ludwig I. It was such a success, attended by nearly the entire population of Munich, that it became an annual affair. Beer was served then as now, but what began as a night out for the locals has become a 16-day international bonanza, attracting more than 6 million people. In enormous wooden pavilions that heave and pulsate to the combined racket of brass bands, drinking songs, and thousands of dry throats demanding more, they knock back around 5 million liters of beer. Like most of life's questionable pleasures, it has to be experienced once. Only the brave return for more.

The site is overlooked by a 19th-century hall of fame—one of the last works of Ludwig I—and a monumental bronze statue of the maiden **Bavaria,** more than 100 feet high. The statue is hollow, and 130 steps take you up into the braided head for a view of Munich through Bavaria's eyes.

The major attraction away from the downtown area is **Schloss Nymphenburg,** a glorious Baroque and Rococo palace that was a summer home to five generations of Bavarian royalty. It's located in the northwest suburb. To reach it, take the U-1 subway from the Hauptbahnhof to Rotkreuzplatz, then pick up streetcar number 12 heading for Amalienburg. Nymphenburg is the largest palace of its kind in Germany, stretching more than half a mile from one wing to the other. The palace grew in size and scope over a period of more than 200 years, beginning as a summer residence built on land given by Prince Ferdinand Maria to his beloved wife, Henriette Adelaide, on the birth of their son and heir, Max Emanuel, in 1663. As mentioned earlier, she had the Theatinerkirche built as a personal expression of thanks for the birth. The Italian architect Agostino Barelli, brought from Bologna for that project, was instructed to build the palace. It was completed in 1675 by his successor, Enrico Zuccalli. Within that original building, now the central axis of the palace complex, is a magnificent hall, the Steinerner Saal, extending over two floors and richly decorated with stucco and swirling frescoes. In the summer, chamber-music concerts are given here. The decoration of the Steinerner Saal spills over into the surrounding royal chambers, in one of which is the famous **Schönheitengalerie** (Gallery of Beauties). The walls are hung from floor to ceiling with portraits of women who caught the roving eye of Ludwig I, among them a butcher's daughter and an English duchess. The most famous portrait is of Lola Montez, a sultry beauty and high-class courtesan who, after a time as mistress of Franz Liszt and later Alexandre Dumas, captivated Ludwig I to such an extent that he gave up his throne for her.

The palace is set in a fine park, laid out in formal French style, with low hedges and gravel walks, extending into woodland. Tucked away among the ancient trees are three fascinating structures built as Nymphenburg expanded and changed occupants. Don't miss the **Amalienburg** hunting lodge. It's a Rococo gem, built by François Cuvilliés, architect of the Residenztheater. The silver-and-blue stucco of the little Amalienburg creates an atmosphere of courtly high life that makes it clear that the pleasures of the chase here did not always take place out-of-doors. In the lavishly appointed kennels you'll see that even the dogs lived in luxury. For royal tea parties, another building was constructed, the **Pagodenburg.** It has an elegant French exterior that disguises a suitably Oriental interior in which exotic teas from India and China were served. Swimming parties were held in the **Badenburg,** Europe's first post-Roman heated pool.

Nymphenburg contains so much of interest that a day hardly provides enough time for it all. Don't leave without visiting the former royal stables, the **Marstallmuseum,** or Museum of Royal Carriages. It houses a fleet of vehicles, including an elaborately decorated sleigh in which King Ludwig II once glided through the Bavarian twilight, postilion torches lighting the way. On the floor above are fine examples of Nymphenburg porcelain, produced here between 1747 and the 1920s. *Admission to the entire Schloss Nymphenburg complex: DM 6 (ask for a* Gesamtkarte, *or combined ticket). A ticket for just the palace, Schönheitengalerie, Amalienburg lodge, and Marstallmuseum costs DM 4.50. Children under 15 free. Open Apr.–Sept. 9–12:30 and 1:30–5; Oct.–Mar. 10–12:30 and 1:30–4. All except Amalienburg and gardens closed Mon. (Munich's botanic garden with its interesting tree collection and tropical greenhouses is adjacent to the palace grounds.)*

Beyond Nymphenburg, on the northwest edge of Munich, lies medieval **Schloss Blutenburg,** now the home of an international collection of children's books. Take a suburban line S-2 train to Obermenzing, then the number 73 or 76 bus to reach Blutenburg. The castle chapel, built in 1488 by Duke Sigismund, has some fine 15th-century stained glass. Sigismund loved the peace and quiet of Blutenburg (now disturbed by the roar of traffic on the nearby autobahn) and spent most of his time here rather than at the royal residence in Munich.

In 1597, Duke Wilhelm V also decided to look for a peaceful retreat outside Munich and found what he wanted at **Schloss Schleissheim,** then far beyond the city walls but now only a short ride on the suburban S-1 line (to Oberschleissheim station) and then bus number 292 (which doesn't run on weekends). A later ruler, Prince Max Emanuel, extended the palace and added a second, smaller one, the Lustheim. Separated from the main palace by a formal garden and a decorative canal, the Lustheim houses Germany's largest collection of Meissen porcelain. *Admission: combined ticket for the palaces and the porcelain collection, DM 5; children under 15 with adults free. Open Tues.–Sun. 10–12:30 and 1:30–4 (Apr.–Sept. until 5).*

The undulating circus-tentlike roofs that cover the stadia built for the 1972 Olympic Games are unobtrusively tucked away in what is now known as the **Olympiapark.** The roofs are made of translucent tiles that glisten in the midday sun and act as amplifiers for visiting rock bands like the Rolling Stones. Tours of the park on a Disneyland-style train run throughout the day from March through November. Take the elevator up the 960-foot Olympia Tower for a view of the city and the Alps; there's also a revolving restaurant near the top. *Admission to main stadium: DM 1 adults, 50 pf children. Open daily 8:30–6. Combined ticket for park tour and a ride up the tower: DM 7 adults, DM 4 children. Tower open daily 8 PM–midnight. Restaurant open daily 11–5:30 and 6:30 PM–10:30 PM; tel. 089/308–1039 for reservations.*

Munich for Free

All **city-run museums** are free on Sunday (though you still have to pay to see temporary exhibits). One of the best free evenings you'll ever have in Munich is a stroll along **Maximilianstrasse,** site of many of the best private art galleries. On the first Thursday of every month, when many of the galleries open their new exhibits, you can wander in and out of them all, attending the first-night parties and picking up as much free liquor as you can hold.

Free **music** and **concerts** are a regular feature of the city. There are free brass-band concerts at the **Chinese Tower** beer garden in the Englischer Garten on Wednesday and weekend afternoons in summer. On Sunday mornings the **Waldwirtschaft** beer garden, by the Isar River in the Grosshesselohe district (Georg-Kalb-Str. 3), has free jazz concerts (mostly of traditional jazz). Similarly, some of the bigger bars in **Schwabing** have jazz bands Sunday mornings (known locally as Frühschoppen—when the beer is also often sold at a special low price). At least one Munich church will have a full-sung **high mass** on Sunday mornings, often with an orchestra as well as a choir. The standards are remarkably high. But these events are not widely advertised in advance. See the tourist office's monthly **Monatsprogramm** for details.

In high summer during the school holidays, free entertainment and artistic "workshops" are organized for children in the main parks; one of the most popular locales for these events is the area between the Chinesischer Turm and the Kleinhesseloher Lake in the Englischer Garten.

Throughout the year, street entertainers ranging from magicians to student string quartets draw crowds in the traffic-free city center. Finally, schedule one day of your visit to catch the **glockenspiel** on the Neues Rathaus. The show is given daily at 11 AM and 9 PM (also 5 PM May–Sept.).

What to See and Do with Children

Take your children to the **zoo** (Tierpark Hellabrun). There are special areas where children can touch the animals and feed them and go for pony rides. It's a hands-on sort of place, just a 20-minute ride from downtown, too (*see* Parks and Gardens in Sightseeing Checklists, below).

The **Deutsches Museum** (*see* Museums and Galleries in Sightseeing Checklists, below) rates as the city's number-one museum for children. Budding scientists and young dreamers alike will be delighted by its extensive collections and its many activities that provide buttons to push and cranks to turn. It's on the Museuminsel (Museum Island) in the Isar River, a 10-minute walk from downtown. The tower of the Gothic **Altes Rathaus** (old town hall) provides a satisfyingly atmospheric setting for a little toy museum. It includes several exhibits from the United States. *Marienpl. Admission: DM 4 adults, DM 1 children; family ticket (2 adults plus children), DM 8. Open daily 10–5.*

Munich has several theaters for children, and with pantomime such a strong part of the repertoire, the language problem disappears. The best of them is the **Münchner Theater für Kinder** (Dachauerstr. 46, tel. 089/595–454 or 089/593–858). Two puppet theaters offer regular performances for children; the **Münchner Marionettentheater** (Blumenstr. 29a, tel. 089/265–712) and **Otto Bille's Marionettenbühne** (Breiterangerstr. 15, tel. 089/150–2168 or 089/310–1278). Munich is the winter quarters of the **Circus Krone,** which has its own permanent building (Marsstr. 43, tel. 089/558–166). The circus performs there from Christmas until the end of March.

In summer, seek out the 100-year-old **carousel** at the edge of the Englischer Garten beer garden, a beer-mug's throw from the famous Chinese Pagoda.

For young roller skaters, Munich has a roller disco, the **Roll Palast,** in the western suburb of Pasing (Stockackerstr. 5); take the suburban rail line S-5 or S-6 to Westkreuz. Roller skates can be rented. Just east of Munich is **No-Name City** (Gruberstr. 60a), a mock-up western town, with saloons, corral, live country music, and daily duels (with blank ammunition) in the cowboy-populated streets. Take suburban line S-6 to Poing; from there it's only 200 yards. *Admission: DM 10.50 adults, DM 7 children. Open Tues.–Sun. 9:30–6.*

Munich is Germany's leading **movie-making** center, and in the summer the studios at Geiselgasteig, on the southern outskirts of the city, open their doors to visitors. A "Filmexpress" transports you on a 1½-hour tour of the sets of *The Boat, Enemy Mine, The Never Ending Story,* and other productions. Take the number 25 streetcar to Bavariafilmplatz. *Admission: DM 10 adults, DM 6 children. Open Mar.–Oct., daily 9–4.*

Off the Beaten Track

For the cheapest sightseeing tour of the city center on wheels, board a **number 19 streetcar** outside the main train station (on Bahnhofpl.) and make the 15-minute journey to Max Weber Platz. Explore the streets around the square, part of the picturesque old residential area of Haidhausen, and then return by a different route on the **number 18 streetcar** to Karlsplatz. On a fine day, join the **chess players** at their open-air board at Schwabing's forumlike Münchner Freiheit Platz. On a rainy day, pack your swimming things and splash around in the art nouveau setting of the **Müllersches Volksbad,** Ludwigsbrücke opposite the Deutsches Museum. On a sunny day, join the locals in an ice cream and a stroll along the River Isar, where the more daring sunbathe nude on pebble islands. Alternatively, walk up the hill from the Volksbad and see what art exhibition or avant-garde film (often in English) is showing at the modern, redbrick **Gasteig Culture Center.**

Also in this area is a museum-piece cemetery, the **Südfriedhof,** where you'll find many famous names but few tourists. Four hundred years ago it was a graveyard beyond the city walls for plague victims and paupers. In the 19th century it was refashioned into an upscale last resting place by the city architect von Gärtner. Royal architect Leo von Klenze designed some of the headstones, and both he and Friedrich von Gärtner are among the famous names you'll find there. The last burial here took place more than 40 years ago. The Südfriedhof is on the Thalkirchnerstrasse, a short walk from the Sendlinger-Tor-Platz U-bahn station.

Sightseeing Checklists

Many of the points of interest listed here are discussed in greater detail in Exploring Munich, above.

Historical Buildings and Sites

Alter Hof (Old Palace). The first of the Wittelsbach royal residences in Munich, the palace serves today as local government offices.

Altes Rathaus (old town hall). This was Munich's first city hall, built in 1474, and restored after wartime bomb damage.

Bavaria. This monumental statue, Munich's Statue of Liberty, overlooks the Theresienwiese, site of the Oktoberfest.

Feldherrnhalle. Modeled on Florence's Loggia dei Lanzi, this arcade dominates the south end of Odeonsplatz.

Friedensengel (Angel of Peace). This striking gilded angel crowns a marble column in a small park overlooking the Isar River. It marks one end of Prinzregentenstrasse, the broad, arrow-straight boulevard laid out by Prince Regent Luitpold at the end of the 19th century.

Königsplatz. This enormous city square, laid out by Ludwig I, is flanked on three sides by Grecian temple–style exhibition halls and a massive neoclassical arch.

Marienplatz. This substantial square rates as the historic heart of Munich, invariably animated by visitors and locals alike.

Maximilianeum (Maximilianstr.). The Bavarian State Government meets in this lavish mid-19th-century arcaded palace. Built for Maximilian II as part of an ambitious city-planning scheme. Today only the terrace can be visited.

Münze (Pfisterstr. 4). Originally the royal stables, the Münze (mint) was created by court architect Wilhelm Egkl between

1563 and 1567. A stern neoclassical facade was added in 1809; the courtyard retains its Renaissance look.

Nationaltheater. The sturdy neoclassical bulk of the premier theater in Munich, home of the Bavarian State Opera Company, dominates the north side of Max-Joseph-Platz.

Neues Rathaus. The city's New Town Hall has a famed glockenspiel, the largest musical clock in Germany.

Residenz. This massive palace complex of the Wittelsbach rulers of Bavaria was remodeled numerous times over the centuries, much of it open to the public (*see also* Museums and Galleries, below).

Schloss Blutenburg. The well-preserved walled and moated castle was the hunting retreat of Duke Albrecht III. The castle's 15th-century chapel and Baroque hall can be visited.

Schloss Nymphenburg. The summer residence of the Wittelsbachs, this is Germany's largest Baroque palace (*see also* Museums and Galleries *and* Parks and Gardens, below).

Viktualienmarkt. Munich's open-air food market is among the most colorful and diverting sights in the city.

Museums and Galleries

Alte Pinakothek. This museum possesses one of the world's leading collections of old master paintings (*see* Downtown Munich in Exploring Munich, above).

Bayerisches Nationalmuseum. The Bavarian National Museum contains an extensive collection of Bavarian and other German art and artifacts. The highlight for some will be the medieval and Renaissance wood carvings, with many works by the great Renaissance sculptor Tilman Riemenschneider. Fine tapestries, arms and armor, a unique collection of Christmas crèches (the Krippenschau), Bavarian arts and crafts, and folk artifacts compete for your attention. *Prinzregentenstr. 3. Admission: DM 3 adults, 50 pf children, free Sun. and holidays. Open Tues.–Sun. 9:30–5.*

BMW Museum. Munich is where BMWs are made, and the museum, adjoining the factory next to Olympiapark, contains a dazzling collection of BMWs old and new. *Petuelring 130 (U-bahn No. 2 or 3 to Olympiazentrum station). Admission: DM 4.50 adults, DM 2 children, and DM 10 family ticket. Open daily 9--5.*

Deutches Jagd- und Fischereimuseum (German Museum of Hunting and Fishing). The world's largest collection of fishhooks and 500 stuffed animals make up just part of the attraction of one of Munich's most popular museums (*see* Downtown Munich in Exploring Munich, above).

Deutsches Museum (German Museum of Science and Technology). Founded in 1903 and housed in its present monumental building since 1925, this is one of the most stimulating and innovative science museums in Europe. Twelve miles of corridors, six floors of exhibits, and 30 departments make up the immense collections. Set aside a full day if you plan to do justice to the entire museum (*see* What to See and Do with Children, above). *Museumsinsel 1. Admission: DM 8 adults, DM 2.50 children. Open daily 9–5.*

Münchner Stadtmuseum (City Museum). Munich's history is illustrated by means of puppets, musical instruments, and photographs, as well as an exhibition that features old brewing artifacts. *Jakobspl. 1. Admission: DM 5 adults, DM 2.50 children, DM 7.50 family ticket; free Sun. and holidays. Open Tues.–Sun. 10–5, Wed. until 8:30.*

Neue Pinakothek. Late-18th- and 19th-century paintings, with strong French collections, make this one of the most compelling art galleries in Europe (*see* Downtown Munich in Exploring Munich, above).

Prähistorische Staatssammlung (State Prehistoric Collection). This is Bavaria's principal record of its prehistoric, Roman, and Celtic past. The perfectly preserved body of a young girl who was ritually sacrificed, recovered from a Bavarian peat moor, is among its more spine-chilling exhibits. Head down to the basement to see the fine Roman mosaic floor. *Lerchenfeldstr. 2. Admission: DM 2.50 adults, DM 1 children. Open Tues., Wed., and Fri.–Sun. 9–4, Thurs. 9–8.*

Paläontologisches Museum. The 10-million-year-old skeleton of a mammoth is the centerpiece of this paleontological and geological collection. *Richard-Wagner-Str. 10. Admission free. Open Mon.–Thurs. 8–4, Fri. 8–3.*

Residenzmuseum. This is the former royal palace of the Wittelsbachs, with priceless collections of state treasures (*see* Historical Buildings and Sites *and* Downtown Munich in Exploring Munich, above).

Schack-Galerie. Those with a taste for florid and romantic 19th-century German paintings will appreciate the collections of the Schack-Galerie, originally the private collection of one Count Schack. Others may find the gallery dull, filled with plodding and repetitive works by painters who now repose in well-deserved obscurity. *Prinzregentenstr. 9. Admission: DM 2.50 adults, 50 pf children; free Sun. and holidays. Open Wed.–Mon. 9–4:30.*

Staatliche Antikensammlungen und Glyptothek (State Collection of Antiquities and Sculpture). Ancient Greek and Roman collections are housed in two appropriately neoclassical buildings on the vast Königsplatz (*see* Downtown Munich in Exploring Munich, above).

Staatliche Graphische Sammlung (State Collection of Graphic Arts). A comprehensive collection of drawings and prints from the late Gothic period to the present day is housed here. *Meiserstr. 10. Admission free. Open weekdays 10–1 and 2–4:30.*

Staatliches Museum für Völkerkunde (State Museum of Ethnology). Arts and crafts from around the world are displayed in this extensive museum. There are also regular ethnological exhibits. *Maximilianstr. 42. Admission: DM 3.50 adults, 50 pf children; free Sun. and holidays. Open Tues.–Sun. 9:30–4:30.*

Staatliche Sammlung Ägyptischer Kunst (State Collection of Egyptian Art). This is just part of the remarkable collection housed in the Residenz, the former royal palace (*see* Historical Buildings and Sites *and* Downtown Munich in Exploring Munich, above).

Staatsgalerie Moderner Kunst (State Gallery of Modern Art). The gallery is in the west wing of the Hitler-era Haus der Kunst, a monumental pillared building at the south end of the Englischer Garten (the east wing has regular temporary exhibits). It features one of the finest collections of 20th-century paintings and sculptures in the world. *Prinzregentenstr. 1. Admission: DM 3.50 adults, 50 pf children; free Sun. and holidays. Open Tues.–Sun. 9–4:30, also Thurs. 7 PM–9 PM.*

Städtische Galerie im Lenbachhaus. This internationally renowned picture collection is housed in a delightful late-19th-century Florentine-style villa, former home and studio of the artist Franz von Lenbach. It contains a rich collection of works from the Gothic period to the present day, including an exciting assemblage of art from the early 20th-century *Blauer Reiter*, or Blue Rider, group: Kandinsky, Klee, Jawlensky, Macke, Marc, and Münter. *Luisenstr. 33. Admission: DM 5 adults, DM 2 children; free Sun. and holidays. Open Tues.–Sun. 10–6, Thurs. until 8.*

Stuck Villa. Like the Lenbach Gallery, this museum is the former home of one of Munich's leading turn-of-the-century artists, Franz von Stuck. His work covers the walls of the haunting rooms of the neoclassical villa, which is also used for regular art exhibits. *Prinzregentenstr. 60. Admission: varies from DM 2 upward according to exhibits. Open Tues., Wed., and Fri.–Sun. 10–5, Thurs. 10–9.*

Parks and Gardens

Alter Botanischer Garten. The city's former botanical garden is now a quiet downtown park (*see* Downtown Munich in Exploring Munich, above).

Englischer Garten. This is the largest city park in Germany, laid out at the end of the 18th century. Lakes, gravel paths, beer gardens, a Chinese pagoda, and a series of small, eye-catching temples number among its attractions (*see* Downtown Munich in Exploring Munich, above).

Botanischer Garten (Botanical Garden). A collection of 14,000 plants, including orchids, cacti, cyads, alpine flowers, and rhododendrons, makes up one of the most extensive botanical gardens in Europe. The park is located at the eastern edge of the Nymphenburg Palace park. *Menzingerstr. 63. Admission: DM 1.50 adults, children free. Open daily 9–5; hothouses open daily 9–noon and 1–4.*

Hirschgarten. A former deer park, the Hirschgarten still has wild buck and roe deer in enclosures. There are children's playgrounds and an attractive beer garden. It's located in the suburb of Nymphenburg; take any of the westbound S-bahn train lines to Laim.

Hofgarten. This is the former royal palace garden, located just to the north of the Residenz (*see* Downtown Munich in Exploring Munich, above).

Isar Valley. Munich's Isar River is no built-up waterway—north and south of the city center there are green, unspoiled banks, ideal territory for cyclists, joggers, and walkers. Nude sunbathing is tolerated on the banks and islands, although the river isn't recommended for swimming.

Luitpold Park (Karl-Theodor-Str.). This is Schwabing's city park, which includes a tobogganing hill made from the rubble of World War II air raids. Try the beer brewed in the cellar of Bambergerhaus, a café-restaurant owned by Prince Luitpold.

Olympiapark. Site of the 1972 Olympic Games, this is still very much the sporting center of the city (*see* Sports and Fitness, below, *and* Outside the Center in Exploring Munich, above).

Schloss Nymphenburg. The 500 acres of Schloss Nymphenburg's park are popular with walkers and joggers. In winter, marked trails beckon cross-country skiers (*see* Historical Buildings and Sites, Museums and Galleries, *and* Outside the Center in Exploring Munich, above).

Tierpark Hellabrun. This is the city zoo, among the finest in the world and one in which the animals are arranged according to geographical origin. Cages are kept to a minimum, with preference being given to enclosures wherever possible. The zoo's 170 acres include restaurants and children's areas. Take the number 52 bus from Marienplatz or the U-3 subway. *Admission: DM 6 adults, DM 3 children. Open daily 8–6.*

West Park. Laid out for the 1983 International Horticultural Exhibition, this has become one of the most popular of the city's parks. It was designed to resemble the landscape of Upper Bavaria, with gently undulating hills (popular among joggers and cross-country skiers) and lakes and valleys, the whole planted with regional and international flora. There are restaurants, cafés, beer gardens, children's play areas, an open-air theater, and a concert arena. Take U-bahn lines 3 or 6 to West Park.

Churches

Asamkirche. This is the most important and lavishly decorated late-Baroque church in the city, built by the brothers Asam. Don't miss it (*see* Downtown Munich in Exploring Munich, above).

Bürgersaal. The building is actually two churches in one, located in the heart of the city. The magnificently opulent Rococo upper church contrasts with the simple, cryptlike chapel below (*see* Downtown Munich in Exploring Munich, above).

Dreifaltigkeitskirche (Pacellistr.). This is the church of the Holy Trinity, built after a local woman prophesied doom for the city unless a new church was erected. It's a striking Baroque building, with heroic frescoes by Cosmas Damian Asam.

Franziskanerklosterkirche St. Anna im Lehel (St.-Anna-Str.). Though less opulently decorated than the Asamkirche, this small Franciscan monastery church, consecrated in 1737, impresses with its sense of movement and its heroic scale. It was largely rebuilt after wartime bomb damage. The ceiling fresco by Cosmas Damian Asam was removed before the war, and, after restoration, now glows in all its original vivid joyfulness. The ornate altar was also designed by the Asam brothers.

Frauenkirche (Church of Our Lady). Munich's soaring, brick Gothic cathedral, it has two lofty towers, capped by onion-shape domes, are enduring symbols of the city (*see* Downtown Munich in Exploring Munich, above).

Ludwigskirche (Ludwigstr. 22). Planted halfway along the severe, neoclassical Ludwigstrasse is this curious neo-Byzantine/early Renaissance-style church. It was built at the behest of Ludwig I to provide his newly completed suburb with a parish church. Though most will find the building a curiosity at best, it can be worth a stop to see the fresco of the *Last Judgment* in the choir. At 60 by 37 feet, it is one of the world's largest.

Michaelskirche. One of the most important and largest Renaissance churches in Germany, its construction began in 1583 (*see* Downtown Munich in Exploring Munich, above).

Peterskirche. Munich's oldest and smallest parish church was consecrated in 1368 on the site of four previous churches. Its tower, Alter Peter, is a local landmark (*see* Downtown Munich in Exploring Munich, above).

Salvatorkirche (Salvatorstr.). The bare brick exterior of this church points to the fact that it was almost certainly built by the same architect as the Frauenkirche. Today it's the principal Greek Orthodox church in Munich.

Theatinerkirche (St. Kajetan's). The dominating, ocher-yellow facade of the Theatinerkirche, framed by twin towers and a commanding dome, is one of the striking pieces of architecture in the downtown area (*see* Downtown Munich in Exploring Munich, above).

Shopping

Gift Ideas Munich is a city of beer, and beer mugs and coasters make obvious choices for souvenirs and gifts. There are several specialty shops downtown. The best is **Ludwig Mory,** in the city hall on Marienplatz. Munich is also the home of the famous **Nymphenburg porcelain** factory. There's a factory outlet on Odeonsplatz, just north of Marienplatz; otherwise you can buy direct from the factory, on the grounds of Schloss Nymphenburg (Nördliches Schlossrondell 8). Other German porcelain manufacturers also have outlets in the city. For Dresden and Meissen ware, go to **Kunstring Meissen** (Briennerstr. 4 and Karlspl. 5). For Bavarian arts and crafts, the **Bayerischer Kunstgewerberein** (Pacellistr. 7) is unbeatable. For wood carvings, pewter, painted glass, and molded candles, try **A. Kaiser** and **Sebastian Weseley** (Rindermarkt 1), or **Otto Kellnberger's Holzhandlung** and the neighboring **Geschenk Alm** (Heiliggeiststr. 7–8). All four are near the Viktualienmarkt. For the best chocolates, try **Confiserie Rottenhöfer** (Residenzstr. 26) or the **Café Schöne Münchnerin,** opposite the Haus der Kunst.

Antiques Bavarian antiques can be found in the many small shops around the Viktualienmarkt; Westenriederstrasse is lined with antiques shops. Also try the area north of the university; Türkenstrasse, Theresienstrasse, and Barerstrasse are all filled with stores selling antiques. Munich's biggest antiques outlet is the **Palais Bernheimer** (Ottostr. 4–8); the range of goods is immense and encompasses everything from simple and inexpensive pieces of pewter to old master paintings. If you're looking for a piece of Bavarian farmhouse furniture, check out **Friedrich's Bauern Möbel Markt** (Emil-Riedel-Str. 5). Fine examples of antique German clocks can be found at **Kunsthandlung Schaller** (Prannerstr. 5), or try **Romann's** on Blumen strasse (near the Viktualienmarkt). This is the area to explore if you're interested in upscale antiques. The **Carl Jagemann shop** (Residenzstr. 3), in the same neighborhood, has been in business for more than a century. **Kunsthandlung Hecht** (Herzogspitalstr. 7) is the place to go for country curios and religious antiquities.

Folk Costumes Those with a fancy to deck themselves out in lederhosen or a dirndl or to sport a green loden coat and little pointed hat with feathers should head for **Loden-Frey** (Maffestr. 7–9) or **Wallach** (Residenzstr. 3). The aptly named **Lederhosen Wagner** (Tal 77) is another good bet.

Shopping Districts Munich has an immense central shopping area, a mile and a half of pedestrian streets stretching from the train station to Marienplatz and north to Odeonsplatz. There's talk, too, of extending it still farther. The two main streets here are **Neuhauserstrasse** and **Kaufingerstrasse.** This is where most of the major department stores are located (*see* Department Stores, below). For upscale shopping, **Maximilianstrasse, Residenzstrasse,** and **Theatinerstrasse** are unbeatable and contain a glittering array of classy and tempting stores, the equal of any in Europe. Schwabing, located north of the university, boasts two of the city's most intriguing and offbeat shopping streets: **Schellingstrasse** and **Hohenzollernstrasse.** A delightful little open-air market is nearby at Elisabethplatz.

Department Stores **Hertie,** occupying an entire city block between the train station and Karlsplatz, is the largest and, some claim, the best department store in the city. **Ludwig Beck** (Marienpl. 11) is great anytime, but comes into its own as Christmas approaches. A series of booths, each delicately and lovingly decorated, contains craftsmen turning out traditional German toys. **Haus Oberpollinger** (Neuhauserstr.) and **Kaufhof** (Marienpl.) are two longtime favorites. **Karstadt** (Neuhauserstr.) has several floors offering a range of goods from silverware (including traditional Bavarian etched and lidded beer mugs) to the latest German electrical appliances. For the latest in fashion, try **K & L Ruppert** (Kaufingerstr.).

Food Markets Munich's **Viktualienmarkt** is *the* place. Located just south of Marienplatz, it's home to an array of colorful stands that sell everything from cheese to sausages, flowers to wine. A visit here is more than just an excuse to buy picnic makings: It's central to an understanding of the easy-come–easy-go nature of Müncheners. **Dallmayr** (Dienerstr.) is an elegant gourmet food store with delights ranging from the most exotic fruits to English jams. The store's famous specialty is coffee, with more than 50 varieties to blend as you wish. There's also an enormous range of breads, and a temperature-controlled cigar room.

Sports and Fitness

The **Olympiapark,** built for the 1972 Olympics, is the largest sports and recreation center in Europe. For general information about clubs, organizations, events, etc., contact the **Haus des Sports** (Briennerstr. 50, tel. 089/520–151) or the **Städtisches Sportamt** (Neuhauserstr. 26, tel. 089/233–6224).

Beaches and Water Sports There is sailing and windsurfing on Ammersee and Starnbergersee. Windsurfers should pay attention to restricted areas at bathing beaches. Information on sailing is available from **Bayrischer Segler-Verband** (Georg-Brauchle-Ring 93, tel. 089/157–02366). Information on windsurfing is available from **Verband der Deutschen Windsurfing Schulen** (Weilheim, tel. 0881/5267).

Golf **Munich Golf Club** has two courses that admit visitors, but not on weekends. Visitors must be members of a club at home. Its 18-hole course is at Strasslach in the suburb of Grünwald, south of the city (tel. 08170/450). Its nine-hole course is more centrally located, at Thalkirchen, on the Isar River (tel. 089/723–1304). The greens fee is DM 65 for either course.

Hotel Fitness Centers **Bayerischer Hof** (Promenadepl. 2–6, tel. 089/21200) has a rooftop pool, a sun terrace, a sauna, and tennis nearby.

Park Hilton International München (Am Tucherpark 7, tel. 089/38450), facing the Englischer Garten, has marked running trails, an indoor pool, a sauna, and massage and spa facilities.

München Sheraton (Arabellstr. 6, tel. 089/92640) has a large indoor pool that opens onto a garden. In the room with the pool are weights and some exercise equipment.

Vier Jahreszeiten Kempinski (Maximilianstr. 17, tel. 089/230–390) is proud of its rooftop swimming pool; it also has a gym with weights and exercise equipment, sauna, massage room, and solarium, and jogging maps in each room.

A. Kaiser, **13**
Barerstrasse, **36**
Bayerischer Kunstgewerberein, **4**
Café Schöne Münchnerin, **32**
Carl Jagemann, **24**
Confiserie Rottenhöfer, **28**
Dallmayr, **23**
Friedrich's Bauern Möbel Markt, **33**
Geschenk Alm, **19**
Haus Oberpollinger, **11**
Hertie, **1**
Hohenzollernstrasse, **38**
K&L Ruppert, **10**
Karstadt, **7**
Kaufhof, **12**
Kaufingerstrasse, **9**
Kunsthandlung Hecht, **8**
Kunsthandlung Schaller, **5**
Kunstring Meissen, **2, 31**
Lederhosen Wagner, **20**
Loden-Frey, **25**
Ludwig Beck, **21**
Ludwig Mory, **22**
Maximilianstrasse, **39**
Neuhauserstrasse, **6**
Nymphenburg Porcelain, **30**
Otto Kellnberger's Holzhandlung, **18**
Palais Bernheimer, **3**
Residenzstrasse, **27**
Romanus, **15**
Schellingstrasse, **37**
Sebastian Weseley, **14**
Theatinerstrasse, **26**
Theresienstrasse, **34**
Türkenstrasse, **35**
Viktualienmarkt, **16**
Wallach, **29**
Westenriederstrasse, **17**

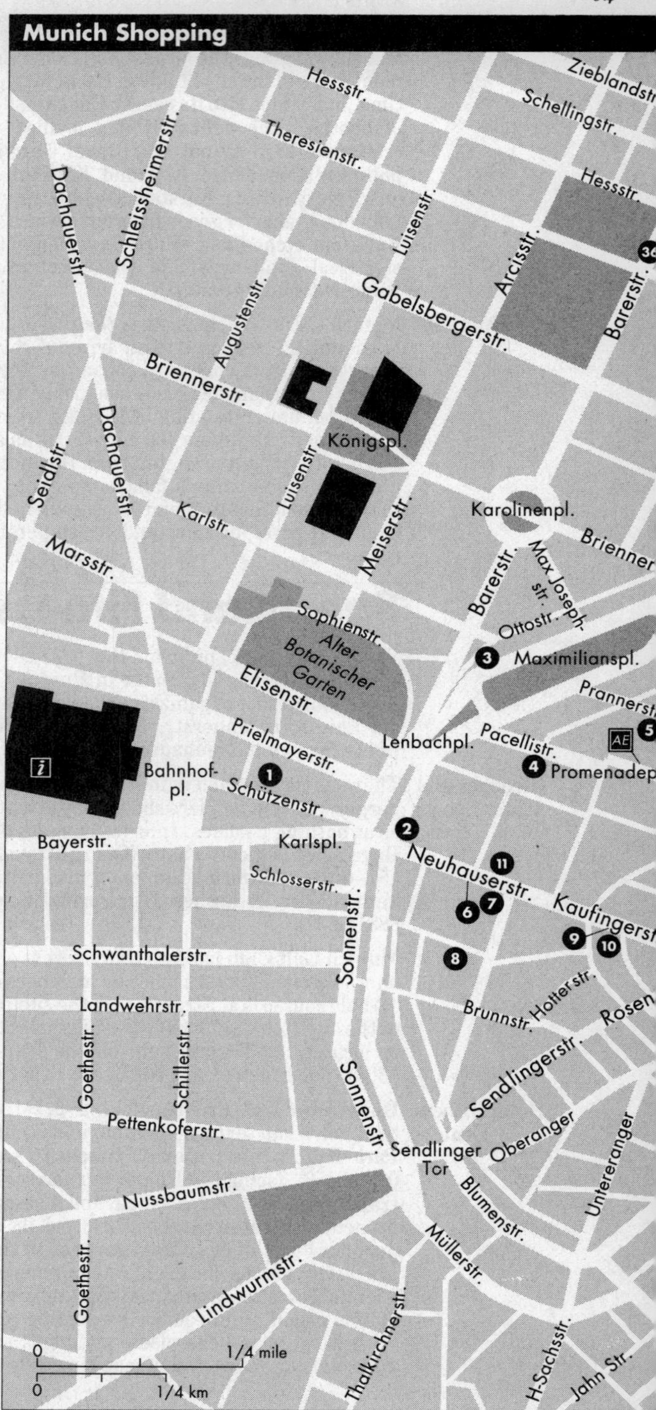

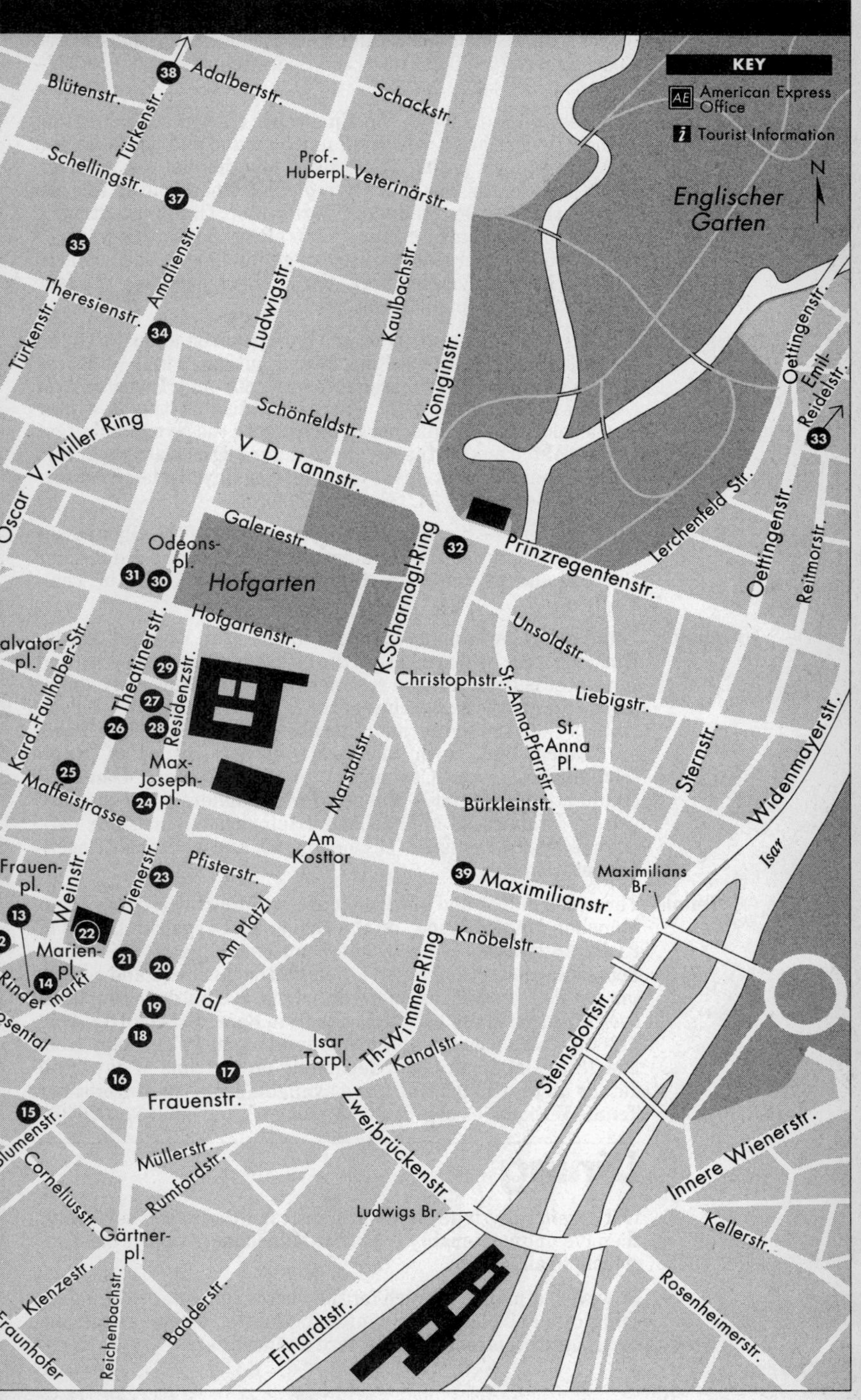
KEY
AE American Express Office
i Tourist Information
N
Englischer Garten
Blütenstr.
Adalbertstr.
Schackstr.
Türkenstr.
Schellingstr.
Prof.-Huberpl.
Veterinärstr.
Amalienstr.
Theresienstr.
Türkenstr.
Ludwigstr.
Kaulbachstr.
Königinstr.
Oettingenstr.
Emil-Reidelstr.
Schönfeldstr.
Oscar V. Miller Ring
V. D. Tannstr.
Lerchenfeld Str.
Oettingenstr.
Reitmorstr.
Galeriestr.
Odeons-pl.
K-Scharnagl-Ring
Prinzregentenstr.
Hofgarten
Hofgartenstr.
Unsoldstr.
Salvator-pl.
Kard.-Faulhaber-Str.
Theatinerstr.
Residenzstr.
Christophstr.
St.-Anna-Pfarrstr.
Liebigstr.
St. Anna Pl.
Sternstr.
Widenmayerstr.
Max-Joseph-pl.
Maffeistrasse
Marstallstr.
Bürkleinstr.
Am Kosttor
Isar
Frauen-pl.
Weinstr.
Dienerstr.
Pfisterstr.
Maximilianstr.
Maximilians Br.
Am Platzl
Knöbelstr.
Marien-pl.
Rindermarkt
Tal
Th.-Wimmer-Ring
Rosental
Isar Torpl.
Kanalstr.
Steinsdorfstr.
Frauenstr.
Zweibrückenstr.
Blumenstr.
Müllerstr.
Rumfordstr.
Corneliusstr.
Innere Wienerstr.
Gärtner-pl.
Ludwigs Br.
Kellerstr.
Klenzestr.
Reichenbachstr.
Baaderstr.
Erhardtstr.
Rosenheimerstr.
Fraunhofer
2
13
14
15
16
17
18
19
20
21
22
23
24
25
26
27
28
29
30
31
32
33
34
35
37
38
39

Hiking and Climbing Information is available from **Deutscher Alpeinverein** (Praterinsel, tel. 089/235–0900) and from the sporting-goods stores **Sport Scheck** (tel. 089/21660) and **Sport Schuster** (tel. 089/237–070).

Jogging The best place to jog is the **Englischer Garten** (U-bahn stop: Münchner-Freiheit), which is 7 miles around and has lakes and dirt and asphalt paths. The broken blue line on the main asphalt path marks the 1972 Olympic marathon route. You can also jog through **Olympiapark** (U-bahn stop: Olympiazentrum). A pleasant morning or evening jog is along the **Isar River,** a half mile from the Sheraton, or you can go for a jog in the 500-acre park of **Schloss Nymphenburg.** For a longer jog along the Isar River, take the S-bahn to Unterföhring.

Ice Skating There is an indoor ice rink at the **Eissportstadion** in Olympiapark (Spiridon-Louis-Ring 3) and outdoor rinks at **Prinzregenten Stadium** (Prinzregentenstr. 80) and **Eisbahn-West** (Agnes-Bernauer Str. 241). There is outdoor skating in winter on the lake in the **Englischer Garten** and on the **Nymphenburger Canal.** Watch out for the *Gefahr* (danger) signs warning of thin ice. Further information is available from **Bayerischer Eissportverband** (Betzenweg 34, tel. 089/81820).

Rowing Rowboats can be hired on the southern bank of the **Olympiasee** in Olympiapark, at the **Kleinhesseloher See** in the Englischer Garten, and on the **Hinterbruler See** near the zoo in Thalkirchen.

Swimming You can try swimming outdoors in the Isar River at Maria-Einsiedel, but be warned that the river flows from the Alps and the water is frigid even in summer. Warmer natural swimming can be found off the beaches of the lakes near Munich—for example, the **Ammersee** and **Starnbergersee.** There are pools at **Cosima Bad,** with man-made waves (corner of Englschalkingerstr. and Cosimastr., in Bogenhausen); **Dantebad** (Dantestr. 6); **Florian's Mühle** (Florianmühlerstr., in the suburb of Freimann); **Michaelibad** (Heinrich-Wielnad-Str. 24); **Olympia-Schwimmhalle** (Olympiapark); and **Volksbad** (Rosenheimerstr. 1).

Tennis There are indoor and outdoor courts at **Münchnerstrasse 15,** in München-Unterfohring; at the corner of **Drygalski-Allee** and **Kistlerhofstrasse,** in München-Fürstenried; and at **Rothof Sportanlage** (Denningerstr.), behind the Arabella and Sheraton hotels. In addition, there are about 200 outdoor courts all over Munich. Many can be booked via **Sport Scheck** (tel. 089/21660), which has installations around town. Prices vary from DM 18 to DM 25 an hour, depending on the time of day. Full details on tennis in Munich are available from the **Bayerischer Tennis Verband** (Georg-Brauchle-Ring 93, tel. 089/157–02640).

Dining

If it's generally true that Germans take their food seriously, then it's unquestionably true that Müncheners take it most seriously of all.

However, dining in Munich for the visitor turns out to be something of a split-level affair, offering haute cuisine on the one hand, unpretentious regional fare on the other.

With Munich rating as Germany's gourmet capital, it's no wonder that it is endowed with an inordinate number of Michelin-star restaurants for a non-French city, including two three-star establishments—real French-style operations—with chef-owners who honed their skills under such Gallic masters as Paul Bocuse.

For connoisseurs, wining and dining at Aubergine or the Königshof could well turn into the equivalent of a religious experience; culinary creations are accorded the status of works of art on a par with a Bach fugue or Dürer painting, with tabs worthy of a king's ransom.

Epicureans are convinced that one can dine as well in Munich as in any other city on the Continent, including Paris, Brussels, and Rome, and perhaps it's true. Certainly it is in a number of the top-rated restaurants listed below.

However, for many the true glory of Munich's kitchen artistry is to be experienced in those rustically decorated, traditional eating places that serve down-home Bavarian specialties in ample portions.

The city's renowned beer and wine restaurants offer great atmosphere, low prices, and as much wholesome German food as you'll ever want. They're open at just about any hour of the day or night—you can order your roast pork at 11 AM or 11 PM.

Snacking in Munich

Munich is home to a type of pre-McDonald's fast food that derives from a centuries-old tradition. A tempting array of delectables is available at most hours of the day and night under various Bavarian names.

The generic term for Munich snacks is *Schmankerl*. And Schmankerl are served at *Brotzeit*, literally "bread time." According to a saying, "*Brotzeit ist die schönste Zeit*" (Bread time is the best time).

Very much in this tradition is a Teutonic version of the British elevenses, a mid-morning snack that goes by the name *Pause* in the German-speaking world and reaches its apogee as a minor feast in Bavaria, especially Munich.

What one eats in the morning in Munich is *Weisswurst*, a tender minced-veal sausage, made fresh daily, steamed, and served with sweet mustard, a crisp roll or pretzel, and *Weissbier* (wheat beer).

Legend has it that this delicious white sausage was invented in 1857 by a butcher who had a hangover and mixed the wrong ingredients. A plaque on a wall in Marienplatz marks the spot where the "mistake" was made. The claim is that the genuine article is available only in and around Munich, served between midnight and noon and at no other time. A complex protocol is involved in the ordering and eating of Weisswurst, but it need not be of concern here. The point is to enjoy this delicacy to which restorative qualities are attributed (hence its popularity with late-night revelers).

Another favorite Bavarian specialty is *Leberkäs*, literally "liver cheese," although neither liver nor cheese is involved in its construction. It is a spicy meat loaf, baked to a crusty turn each morning and served in succulent slabs throughout the day. A *Leberkäs Semmel*—a wedge of the meat loaf between two halves of a crispy bread roll—is the favorite Munich on-the-hoof snack.

After that comes the repertoire of sausages indigenous to Bavaria, including types from Regensburg and Nürnberg.

More substantial repasts include *Tellerfleisch,* boiled beef with freshly grated horseradish and boiled potatoes on the side, served on wooden plates. (A similar dish is called *Tafelspitz.*)

Among roasts, *Sauerbraten* (beef) and *Schweinsbraten* (pork) are accompanied by dumplings and red cabbage.

Haxn refers to ham hocks roasted over a beech fire for hours, until they're crisp on the outside, juicy on the inside. They are served with sauerkraut and potato purée.

You'll also find soups, salads, fish and fowl, cutlets, game in season, casseroles, hearty stews, desserts, and what may well be the greatest variety and highest quality of baked goods in Europe, including pretzels. No one need ever go hungry or thirsty in Munich.

Old Munich restaurants, called *Gaststätten,* feature what's referred to as *gutbürgerliche Küche,* loosely translated as good regional fare, and include brewery restaurants, beer halls, beer gardens, rustic cellar establishments, and *Weinstuben* (wine houses). More than a hundred such places brighten the scene.

Highly recommended restaurants in each price category are indicated by a star ★.

Category	**Cost***
Very Expensive	over DM 95
Expensive	DM 65–DM 95
Moderate	DM 45–DM 65
Inexpensive	DM 30–DM 45

**per person for a three-course meal, excluding drinks*

Very Expensive

★ **Aubergine.** German gourmets swear by the upscale nouvelle cuisine of Eckhart Witzigmann, chef and owner of the most sophisticated, if not exactly the most elegant, restaurant in town. The decor is streamlined modern—white and glittery. The service is appropriately polished. If you want a gastronomic experience on the grand scale, try the pigeon cutlets in lentils, or the elaborately prepared devilfish, and the semolina soufflé with pears in cinnamon. *Maximilianspl. 5, tel. 089/598–171. Reservations required. Jacket and tie required. DC, MC, V. Closed Sun., Mon., 2 weeks in Dec.*

Boettner's. This is the oldest of Munich's classy restaurants, in business since 1905 and still going strong. There's a time-honored and quiet quality to its gracious bar and the dark, wood-paneled dining room. They provide a welcome contrast to the bustle of the city center outside. Seafood dominates the menu; try the lobster pot or the pike soufflé. *Theatinerstr. 2, tel. 089/221–210. Reservations required. Jacket and tie required. AE, DC, MC, V. Closed Sat. evening, Sun., and holidays.*

Gasthof Böswirth. This former farmhouse on the northwest outskirts of the city (take the S-3 tram to Lochhausen, or the

A-8 Autobahn) is named after the young couple who run it. Chef Werner Böswirth produces regional favorites with nouveau accents—try the veal medallions filled with mozzarella—while Frau Böswirth caters to visitors' needs in the bright dining room furnished in pale pine. *Waidachanger Str. 9, tel. 089/811–9763. Reservations advised. Dress: casual but neat. AE, DC, MC. Closed for lunch; closed Sun., Mon., and 2 weeks at Easter.*

Königshof. Ask for a panoramic window table overlooking Karlsplatz, in what is probably Munich's most exquisitely decorated restaurant, with service to match. French nouvelle cuisine dominates. *Karlsplatz 25, tel. 089/551–360. Reservations required. Jacket and tie required. AE, DC, MC, V.*

Sabitzer's. Further evidence of upscale Munich's love affair with nouvelle cuisine, though with Bavarian influences, is provided by the classy offerings at Sabitzer's. Within its elegant gold-and-white 19th-century interior, you'll dine on such specialties as wild salmon with stuffed goose livers and lamb with venison. *Reitmorstr. 21, tel. 089/298–584. Reservations required. Jacket and tie required. AE, DC, MC. Closed Sun.*

Expensive

★ **Austernkeller.** This elegant and softly lit vaulted-cellar restaurant concentrates on delicate seafood specialties. Oysters—*Austern* in German—dominate the menu, but a wide range of other shellfish is featured, too. *Dinner only. Stollbergstr. 11, tel. 089/298–787. Reservations advised. Jacket and tie required. AE, DC, MC, V. Closed Mon. and Christmas.*

Käferschanke. Fresh fish, imported daily from the south of France, is the attraction here. Try the grilled prawns in a sweet-sour sauce. The rustic decor, complemented by some fine antiques, is a delight. The restaurant is located in the upscale Bogenhausen suburb, a 10-minute taxi ride from downtown. *Schumannstr. 1, tel. 089/41681. Reservations advised. Jacket and tie required. AE, DC, MC. Closed Sun. and holidays.*

★ **Preysing Keller.** Devotees of all that's best in modern German food—food that's light and sophisticated but with recognizably Teutonic touches—will love the Preysing Keller. It's in a 16th-century cellar, though it has been so overrestored that there's practically no indication of its age or original character. Never mind; it's the food, the extensive wine list, and the perfect service that make this special. Try the fixed-price seven-course menu—a bargain at DM 100 per person—for best value and a fine sampling of the most underrated restaurant in Munich. *Innere-Wiener-Str. 6, tel. 089/481–015. Reservations required. Jacket and tie required. No credit cards. Closed Sun. and Dec. 23–Jan. 7.*

Moderate

Bistro Terrine. The name may make you think that this is no more than a humble, neighborhood French-style restaurant. In fact, excellent classic French dishes are served within its appealing Art Nouveau interior. Order from the fixed-price menu to keep the check low; à la carte dishes are appreciably more expensive. *Amalienstr. 89, tel. 089/281–780. Reservations advised. Jacket and tie required. AE, MC. Closed Mon., Sat. lunch, and Sun.*

Franziskaner. Vaulted archways, cavernous rooms interspersed with intimate dining areas, bold blue frescoes, long wood tables, and a sort of spic-and-span medieval atmosphere—the look without the dirt—set the mood. This is the

Aubergine, **7**
Austernkeller, **19**
Bistro Terrine, **26**
Boettner's, **10**
Donisl, **9**
Franziskaner, **13**
Gasthof Böswirth, **29**
Glockenbach, **1**
Goldene Stadt, **2**
Grigoris, **28**
Halali, **25**
Haxnbauer, **17**
Hofbräuhaus, **18**
Hundskugel, **3**
Käferschanke, **23**
Königshof, **5**
Le Gourmet, **6**
Max Emanuel Bräuerei, **27**
Nürnberger Bratwurstglöckl, **8**
Pfälzer Weinprobierstube, **11**
Piroschka Csarda, **24**
Preysing Keller, **21**
Ratskeller, **14**
Sabitzer's, **22**
Schloss-Hotel Grünwald, **20**
Spatenhaus, **12**
Spöckmeier, **15**
Straubinger Hof, **16**
Weinhaus Neuner, **40**

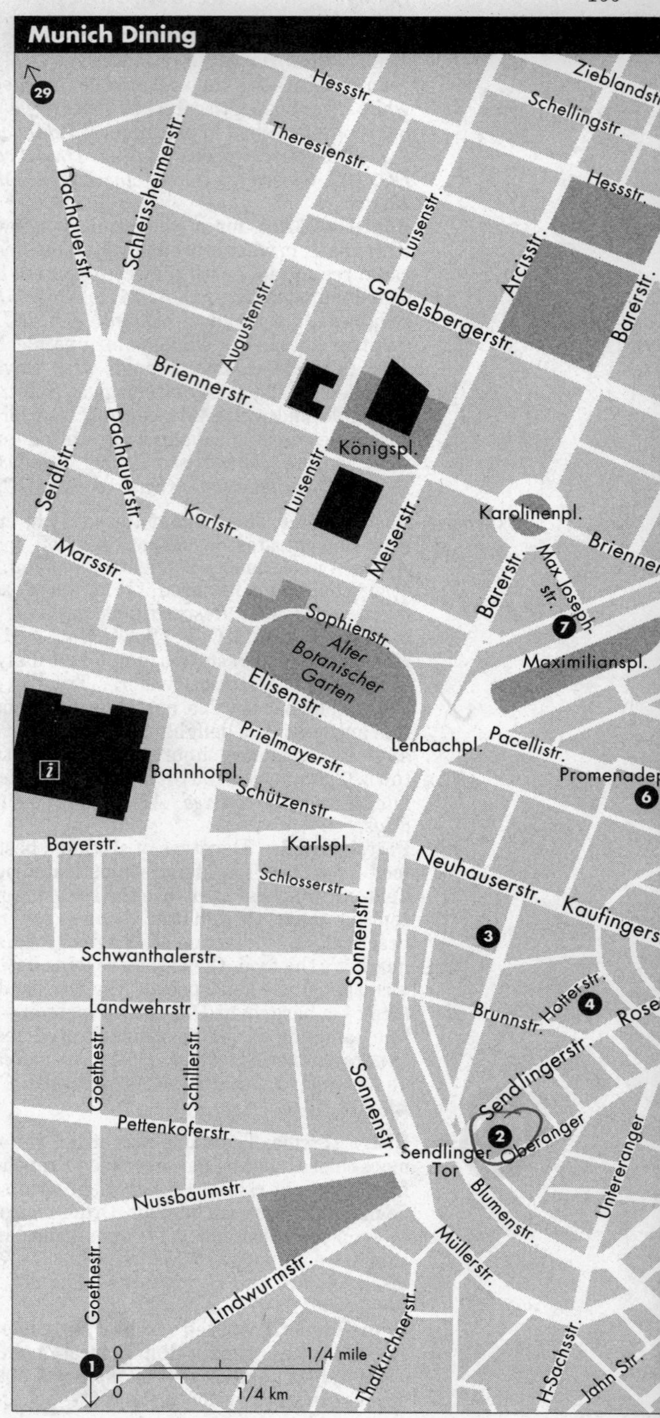

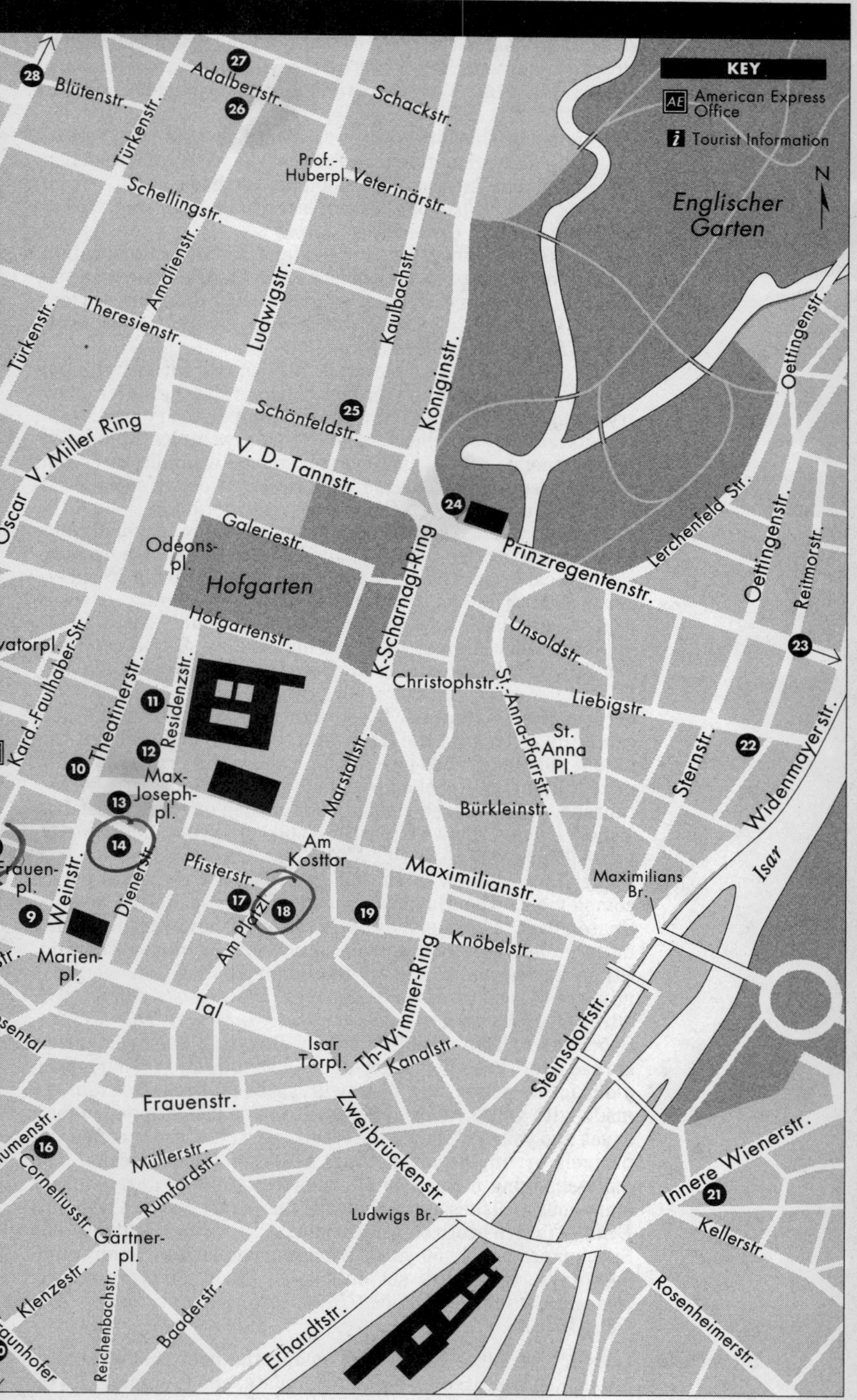
KEY
American Express Office
Tourist Information
N
Englischer Garten
Blütenstr.
Adalbertstr.
Schackstr.
Türkenstr.
Prof.-Huberpl.
Veterinärstr.
Schellingstr.
Amalienstr.
Ludwigstr.
Kaulbachstr.
Theresienstr.
Türkenstr.
Oettingenstr.
Schönfeldstr.
Königinstr.
Oscar V. Miller Ring
V. D. Tannstr.
Lerchenfeld Str.
Galeriestr.
Odeons-pl.
Hofgarten
K.-Scharnagl-Ring
Prinzregentenstr.
Oettingenstr.
Reitmorstr.
Hofgartenstr.
Unsoldstr.
Kard.-Faulhaber-Str.
Theatinerstr.
Residenzstr.
Christophstr.
St.-Anna-Pfarrstr.
Liebigstr.
St. Anna Pl.
Sternstr.
Widenmayerstr.
Max-Joseph-pl.
Marstallstr.
Bürkleinstr.
Am Kosttor
Maximilianstr.
Isar
Frauen-pl.
Weinstr.
Dienerstr.
Pfisterstr.
Maximilians Br.
Am Platzl
Knöbelstr.
Marien-pl.
Th.-Wimmer-Ring
Tal
Steinsdorfstr.
Isar Torpl.
Kanalstr.
Frauenstr.
Zweibrückenstr.
Müllerstr.
Rumfordstr.
Corneliusstr.
Innere Wienerstr.
Gärtner-pl.
Ludwigs Br.
Kellerstr.
Klenzestr.
Reichenbachstr.
Baaderstr.
Erhardtstr.
Rosenheimerstr.

place for an early morning Weisswurst and a beer; Bavarians swear it will banish all trace of that morning-after feeling. The Franziskaner is located right by the State Opera. *Peruastr. 5, tel. 089/231–8120. No reservations. Dress: informal. No credit cards.*

Glockenbach. This former beer tavern turned gourmet restaurant has a daily-changing menu that always features fresh fish. It's small and increasingly popular, so book early. *Kapuzinerstr. 29, tel. 089/534–043. Reservations required. Dress: informal. MC, V. Closed Sun., Mon.*

Goldene Stadt. Named for the "Golden City" of Prague, capital of Czechoslovakia, this is the place for authentic Bohemian specialties. Try the roast duck or goose with dumplings. *Oberanger 44, tel. 089/264–382. Reservations advised. Dress: informal. AE, DC, MC. Closed Sun.*

Halali. The Halali is an old-style Munich restaurant with polished wood paneling and antlers on the walls that offers new-style regional cooking. Venison in juniper-berry sauce and marinated beef on a bean salad are two examples from its inventive menu. Save room for the homemade vanilla ice cream. *Schönfeldstr. 22, tel. 089/285–909. Reservations advised. Jacket and tie required. MC. Closed Sun. and holidays.*

Ratskeller. Munich's Ratskeller is one of the few city-hall cellar restaurants to offer vegetarian dishes alongside the normal array of hearty and filling traditional fare. If turnip in cheese sauce is on the menu, you won't need to be a vegetarian to appreciate it. The decor is much as you would expect, with vaulted stone ceilings and flickering candles. *Marienpl. 8, tel. 089/220–313. Reservations advised. Dress: informal. AE, MC, V.*

Schloss-Hotel Grünwald. If you want a breather from the city, catch the 25 tram to the Grünwald terminus and seek out this quaint old inn perched on cliffs high above the Isar River. Dine on traditional fare cooked with flair in the antiques-strewn restaurant, or in the tree-shaded beer garden offering great Isar Valley views. Grünwald Castle stands adjacent. *Zeillerstr. 1, tel. 089/641–7935. AE, DC, MC. Closed Jan. 1–14.*

★ **Spatenhaus.** A view of the opera house and the royal palace complements the Bavarian mood of wood-paneled, beamed Spatenhaus. The menu is international, however, featuring more or less everything from artichokes to *zuppa Romana.* Strike a compromise and try the Bavarian Plate, an enormous mixture of local meats and sausages. *Residenzstr. 12, tel. 089/227–841. Reservations advised. Dress: informal. DC, MC, V.*

Spöckmeier. This rambling solidly Bavarian beer restaurant spread over three floors, including a snug *Keller* (cellar), is famous for its homemade Weisswurst, the fat breakfast sausage made with white veal and herbs. If you've just stopped in for a snack and you don't fancy the Weisswurst, just order coffee and pretzels or, in the afternoons, a wedge of cheesecake. The daily-changing menu also offers more than two dozen hearty main-course dishes and a choice of four draft beers. The house *Eintopf* (a rich broth of noodles and pork) is a meal in itself. The Spöckmeier is only 50 yards from Marienplatz; on sunny summer days, tables are set outside in the traffic-free street. *Rosenstr. 9, tel. 089/268–088. Reservations not necessary. AE, DC, MC, V.*

Inexpensive

Donisl. This place ranks high among the beer restaurants of Munich. It's located just off Marienplatz, and in summer its tables spill out onto the sidewalk. But the real action is inside. The large central hall, with painted and carved booths and garlands of dried flowers, is animated night and day by locals and visitors alike. The atmosphere, like the food, is rough-and-ready. The beer flows freely. *Weinstr. 1, tel. 089/220–184. No reservations. Dress: informal. AE, DC, MC, V.*

Grigoris. Traditional and off-beat Greek dishes are served in this very friendly, small Schwabing venue run by owner Grigoris and his wife, Johanna—whose recipes are available in a book on sale at the restaurant. Lamb is served daily with a changing range of sauces. Vegetarians can choose from five different dishes. *Tengstr. 31, tel. 089/271–5625. Reservations advised. Dress: informal. AE, DC, V. Closed Mon.*

Haxnbauer. This is one of Munich's more sophisticated beer restaurants. There's the usual series of interlinking rooms—some large, some small—and the usual sturdy/pretty Bavarian decoration. But here there is much greater emphasis on the food than in other similar places. Try the *Leberkäs* (meat loaf made with pork and beef) or *Schweineshaxn* (pork shanks). *Munzstr. 2, tel. 089/221–922. Reservations advised. Dress: informal. MC, V.*

Hofbräuhaus. The heavy stone vaults of the Hofbräuhaus contain the most famous of the city's beer restaurants. Crowds of singing, shouting, swaying beer drinkers—make no mistake; this is a place where beer takes precedence over food—fill the atmospheric and smoky rooms. Picking their way past the tables are hefty waitresses in traditional garb bearing frothing mugs. Some people love it. Others deplore the rampant commercialization and the fact that the place is now so obviously aimed at the tourist trade. It's just north of Marienplatz. *Am Platzl, tel. 089/221–676. No reservations. Dress: informal. No credit cards.*

Hundskugel. This is Munich's oldest tavern, dating back to 1440; history positively drips from its crooked walls. The food is surprisingly good. If *Spanferkel*—roast suckling pig—is on the menu, make a point of ordering it. This is simple Bavarian fare at its best. *Hotterstr. 18, tel. 089/264–272. Reservations advised. Dress: informal. No credit cards.*

Max Emanuel Bräuerei. Folk music and theater are featured in this time-honored Munich institution, located next to the university. The clientele is predominantly young, and the atmosphere is always lively. In summer you can eat in the delightful little beer garden. The food is wholesomely Bavarian, with some Greek and French touches. *Adalbertstr. 33, tel. 089/271–5158. Dress: informal. DC, MC.*

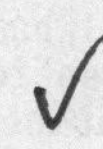

★ **Nürnberger Bratwurstglöckl.** This is about the most authentic old-time Bavarian sausage restaurant in Munich, and it's always crowded. Wobbly chairs, pitch-black wood paneling, tin plates, and, downstairs, some seriously Teutonic-looking characters establish an unbeatable mood. The menu is limited, with *Nürnberger Bratwurstl mit Kraut*—finger-size Nürnberg sausages—taking pride of place. The beer, never in short supply, is served straight from wooden barrels. The restaurant is right by the Frauenkirche—the entrance is set back from the street and can be hard to spot—and makes an ideal lunchtime stop. *Frauenpl. 9, tel. 089/220–385. Reservations advised. Dress: informal. No credit cards. Closed Sun.*

Pfälzer Weinprobierstube. A warren of stone-vaulted rooms of various sizes, wood tables, flickering candles, dirndl-clad waitresses, and a vast range of wines add up to an experience as close to everyone's image of timeless Germany as you're likely to get. The food is reliable rather than spectacular. Local specialties predominate. *Residenzstr. 1, tel. 089/225–628. No reservations. Dress: informal. No credit cards.*

★ **Piroschka Csarda.** This big, colorful venue is decorated Hungarian gypsy-style and tucked into a corner of the Haus der Kunst art gallery. The excellent-value menu features classics such as Hungarian fish soup and *Fiaker* (coachman) goulash. Gypsy violin music complements. *Prinzregentenstr. 1, tel. 089/295–425. Dress: informal. AE, DC, MC, V. Open evenings only, until 1:30 AM. Closed Sun.*

★ **Straubinger Hof.** Call early if you want a table at this famous old establishment. The Weisswurst is served fresh from 9 AM onward, and business is brisk, with stall holders from the Viktualienmarkt across the road jostling for the first out of the pan. In summer, the little beer garden outside is the place to be. *Blumenstr. 5, tel. 089/260–8444. No reservations. Dress: informal. No credit cards. Closed Sat. evenings, Sun., and Aug. 25–Sept. 10.*

Weinhaus Neuner. Munich's oldest wine tavern serves good food as well as superior wines in its three varied nooks and crannies: the wood-paneled restaurant, the wine tavern *(Weinstübl)*, and small bistro. The choice of food is remarkable, from nouvelle German to old-fashioned country fare. Specialties include home-smoked beef and salmon. *Herzogspitalstr. 8, tel. 089/260–3954. Reservations advised. Dress: informal. AE, DC, MC. Closed Sat. lunch, Sun.*

Lodging

Make reservations well in advance, and be prepared for higher-than-average rates. Though Munich has a vast number of hotels in all price ranges, many of the most popular are full year-round; this is a major trade and convention city as well as a prime tourist destination. If you plan to visit during the *Mode Wochen* (fashion weeks) in March and September or during the Oktoberfest at the end of September, make reservations at least four months in advance.

Some of the large Very Expensive hotels that cater to expense-account business travelers offer very attractive weekend discount rates—sometimes as much as 50% below normal prices. Conversely, regular rates can go up during big trade fairs. Check well in advance either through your travel agent or directly with the hotel.

The tourist office at Rindermarkt 1, 8000 Munich 1, has a reservations department, but note that it will not accept telephone reservations. There's also a reservations office at the airport. The best bet for finding a room if you arrive without a reservation is the tourist office in the main train station, on the south side abutting Bayerstrasse (open daily 8 AM–10 PM, no telephone bookings). You'll be charged a small fee, but the operation is supremely well organized.

The closer to the city center you stay, the higher the price. Consider staying in a suburban hotel and taking the U-bahn or S-bahn into town. Rates are much more reasonable, and a 15-minute train ride is no obstacle to serious sightseeing. Check out the city tourist office "Key to Munich" packages. These include reduced-rate hotel reservations, sightseeing tours, theater visits, and low-cost travel on the U- and S-bahn. Write to the Sendlingerstrasse tourist office.

Highly recommended lodgings in each price category are indicated by a star ★.

Category	Cost*
Very Expensive	over DM 250
Expensive	DM 180–DM 250
Moderate	DM 120–DM 180
Inexpensive	under DM 120

**All prices are for two people in a double room, including tax and service charge.*

Very Expensive

Bayerischer Hof. This is one of Munich's most traditional luxury hotels. It's set on a ritzy shopping street, with a series of exclusive shops right outside the imposing marble entrance. Public rooms are decorated with antiques, fine paintings, marble, and painted wood. Old-fashioned comfort and class abound in the older rooms; some of the newer rooms are more functional. *Promenadenpl. 2–6, tel. 089/21200. 440 rooms with bath. Facilities: 3 restaurants, nightclub, rooftop pool, garage, sauna, masseur, hairdresser. AE, DC, MC, V.*

City Hilton. Newest of the two Munich Hiltons, this hotel is just a two-minute walk from the Gasteig cultural center, home of the city's Philharmonic and the biggest concert hall in Germany. *Rosenheimerstr. 15, tel. 089/48040. 483 rooms with bath. Facilities: 2 restaurants, piano bar, conference rooms. AE, DC, MC, V.*

Park Hilton. The hotel is big on the outside, intimate on the inside, with as cheerful and accommodating a staff as you're likely to encounter in any European hotel, the glitziness of the lobby and reception area notwithstanding. The hotel is located beside the vast Englischer Garten, away from the city center, but a downtown-bound tram stops nearby—or you can take the hotel's own courtesy minibus, which runs a return service for guests. A fast-flowing stream with a beer garden beside it runs throughout the grounds. *Am Tucherpark 7, tel. 089/38450. 477 rooms with bath. Facilities: 3 restaurants, swimming pool, fitness center, sauna, massage, nearby tennis courts, golf packages. AE, DC, MC, V.*

Platzl. This recently restored hotel stands in the historic heart of Munich. It's opposite the famous Hofbräuhaus beer Keller and a couple of minutes' walk from Marienplatz and many other landmarks. The country brewery owners have fitted rooms out in rustic Bavarian style. Adjoining the hotel is Platzl Bühne, a famous Bavarian folk theater where you may not understand the thigh-slapping humor, but you're sure to have fun. *Platzl 1, tel. 089/470–5091. 170 soundproofed rooms with bath. Facilities: restaurant, bar, rooftop fitness center, sauna, steam bath, underground garage. AE, DC, MC, V.*

Rafael. Close to Marienplatz, this elegant hotel opened only in late 1989, in a beautifully renovated neo-Renaissance building, which in the late 19th century was a high-society ballroom. Today it tries to recapture some of that bygone era with 24-hour service, including personalized services such as in-house butlers. Rooms have many extras, including fax machines.

Adria, **23**
An der Oper, **10**
Arabella Airport, **22**
Bauer, **20**
Bayerischer Hof, **8**
Brack, **7**
City Hilton, **18**
Eden Hotel Wolff, **4**
Fürst, **9**
Gästehaus am Englischen Garten, **26**
Gröbner, **14**
Intercity, **5**
Königin Elizabeth, **1**
Kriemhild, **2**
Mayer, **6**
Monopteros, **25**
Park Hilton, **24**
Pension Beck, **17**
Platzl, **11**
Rafael, **12**
Regent, **3**
Schloss-Hotel Grünwald, **19**
Sheraton, **21**
Splendid, **16**
Torbräu, **13**
Vier Jahreszeiten Kempinski, **15**

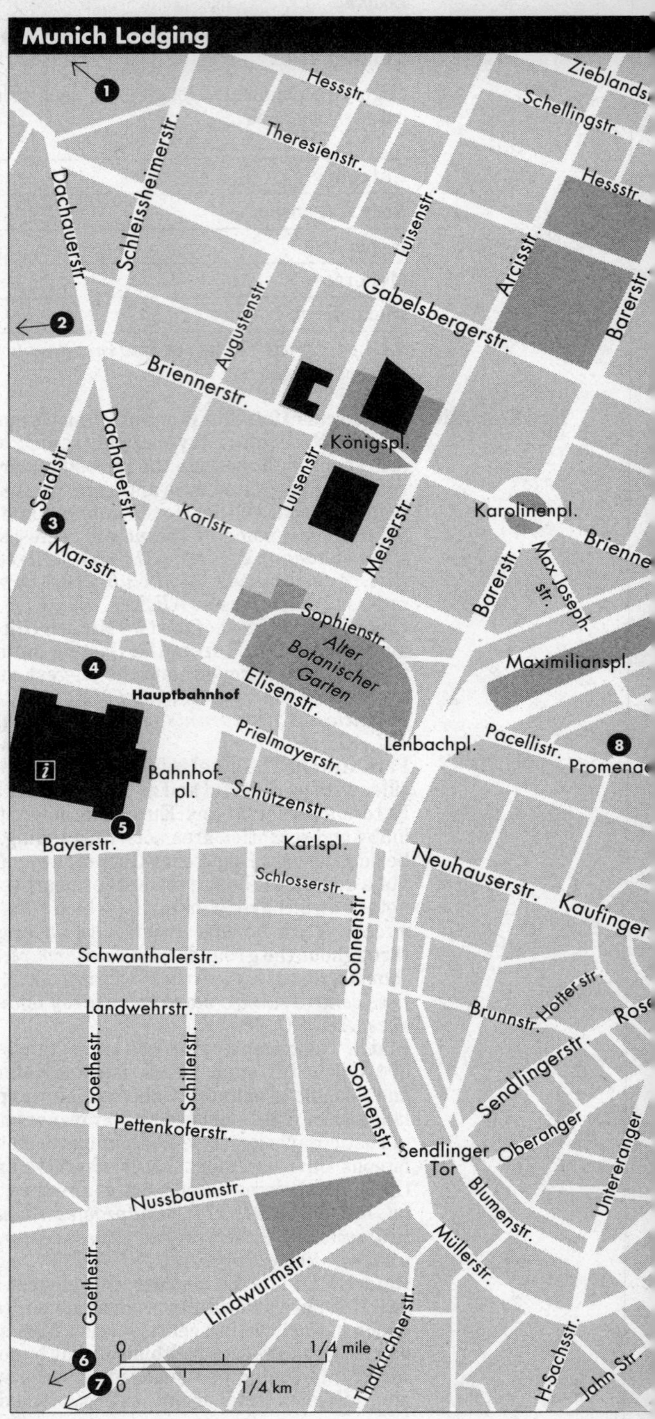

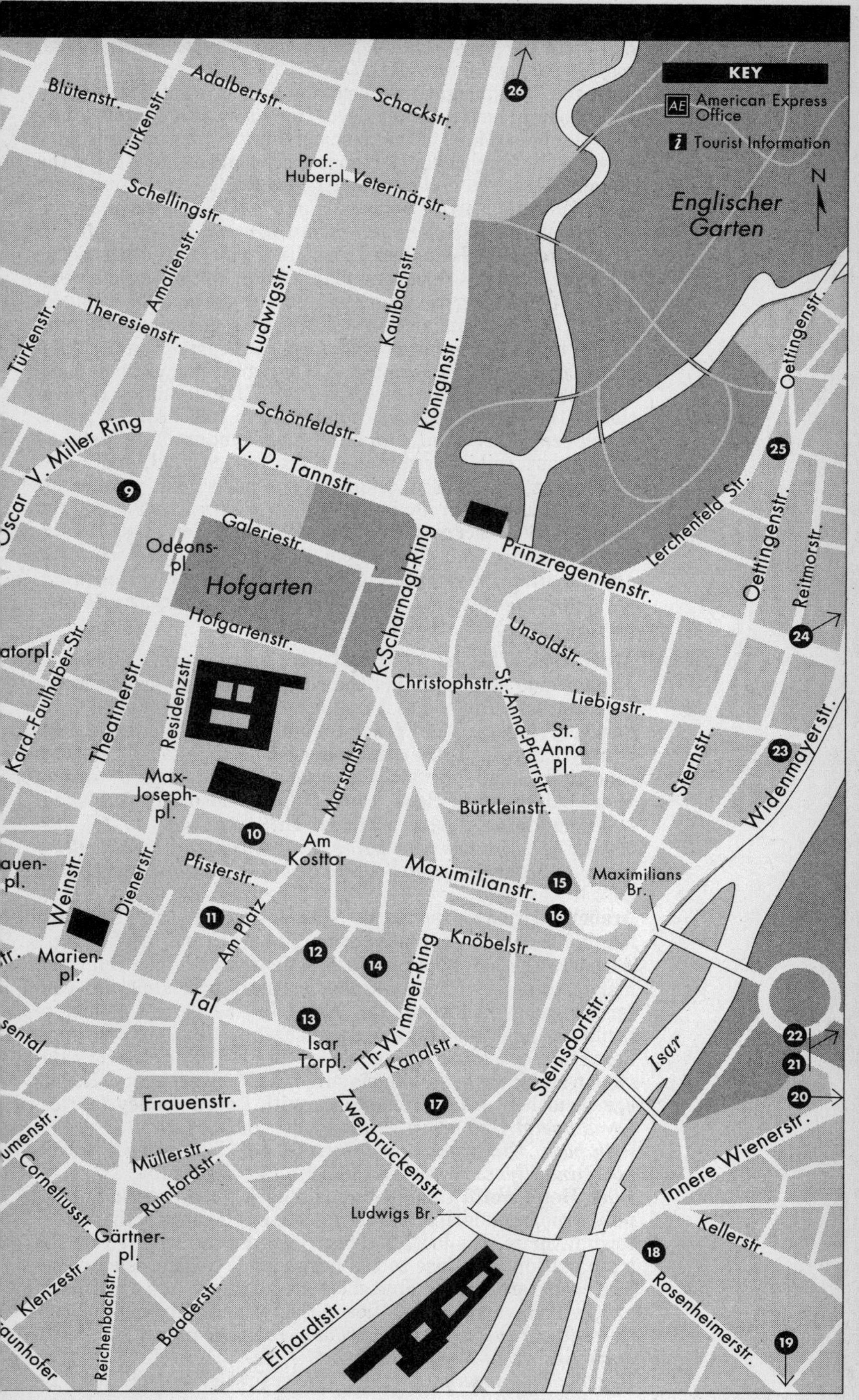
KEY
American Express Office
Tourist Information
N
Englischer Garten
Blütenstr.
Adalbertstr.
Schackstr.
Türkenstr.
Prof.-Huberpl.
Veterinärstr.
Schellingstr.
Amalienstr.
Ludwigstr.
Kaulbachstr.
Theresienstr.
Türkenstr.
Königinstr.
Oettingenstr.
Schönfeldstr.
Oscar V. Miller Ring
V. D. Tannstr.
Lerchenfeld Str.
Galeriestr.
Odeons-pl.
Hofgarten
K-Scharnagl-Ring
Prinzregentenstr.
Oettingenstr.
Reitmorstr.
Hofgartenstr.
Unsoldstr.
atorpl.
Kard.-Faulhaber-Str.
Theatinerstr.
Residenzstr.
Christophstr.
St.-Anna-Pfarrstr.
Liebigstr.
St. Anna Pl.
Sternstr.
Widenmayerstr.
Marstallstr.
Max-Joseph-pl.
Bürkleinstr.
Am Kosttor
Maximilianstr.
Maximilians Br.
auen-pl.
Weinstr.
Dienerstr.
Pfisterstr.
Am Platz
Knöbelstr.
Marien-pl.
Th.-Wimmer-Ring
Tal
Steinsdorfstr.
Isar
sental
Isar Torpl.
Kanalstr.
Frauenstr.
Zweibrückenstr.
Innere Wienerstr.
Müllerstr.
Rumfordstr.
Corneliusstr.
Ludwigs Br.
Kellerstr.
Gärtner-pl.
Klenzestr.
Reichenbachstr.
Baaderstr.
Erhardtstr.
Rosenheimerstr.
aunhofer

Neuturmstr. 1, tel. 089/290–980. 67 rooms and 7 suites (up to DM 1,150 per night) with bath. Facilities: restaurant, 2 bars, rooftop pool, solarium. AE, DC, MC, V.

Sheraton. This bright, modern, and spacious hotel is surprisingly homey (Laura Ashley decor) for such a large international-style chain. Many of the rooms in this 22-story building have views of the Englischer Garten and city, and on clear days, the distant Alps. *Arabellastr. 6. tel. 089/92640. 650 rooms with bath. Facilities: 4 restaurants, nightclub, beer garden, swimming pool, fitness center, sauna, hairdresser. AE, DC, MC, V.*

★ **Vier Jahreszeiten Kempinski.** The Vier Jahreszeiten—it means the Four Seasons—has been playing host to the world's wealthy and titled for more than a century. It has an unbeatable location, on Maximilianstrasse, Munich's premier shopping street, only a few minutes' walk from the heart of the city. Elegance and luxury set the tone throughout; many rooms have handsome antique pieces. A five-year, DM 30-million renovation of the entire hotel was completed in 1989. All the rooms have been refurbished, new baths and soundproofing installed throughout, public areas rebuilt and redecorated, and a new restaurant, Bistro Eck, added on the main floor, joining the Theater bar-restaurant in the cellar. *Maximilianstr. 17, tel. 089/230–390; reservations in the U.S. from Kempinski Reservation Service, tel. 516/794–2670. 341 rooms with bath; 25 apartments; Presidential Suite. Facilities: 3 restaurants, nightclub, rooftop pool, garage, sauna, car rental, Lufthansa check-in desk. AE, DC, MC, V.*

Expensive

An der Oper. This gem of a small hotel is on a narrow, quiet, and elegant side street around the corner from the swank Maximilianstrasse. Big names from the opera stay here: conductors, dancers, singers. The French restaurant Bouillabaisse is a celebrity haunt, as is the atmospheric Opera Cellar. The rooms tend to be small and fairly spartan and offer little by way of view, but they are clean, comfortable, and nicely furnished, with soundproof double windows. *Falkenturmstr. 10, tel. 089/290–0270. 55 rooms with bath. Run on bed-and-breakfast basis, with two restaurants loosely tied to the establishment. AE, DC, MC.*

Arabella Airport. Opened in November 1991, this first-class lodging is only five minutes from the new Franz Josef Strauss Airport. The hotel operates a courtesy shuttle bus. Built primarily to cater to businesspeople (there are numerous conference-room facilities), the Arabella has plenty of leisure facilities and is ideal for any traveler who has an early morning departure or a late evening arrival flight. The three-story Bavarian rustic-style building is surrounded by greenery. Rooms are furnished in light pinewood, with Laura Ashley fabrics. *Freisingerstr. 80, 8059 Schwaig, tel. 08122/8480. 166 rooms with bath. Facilities: 2 restaurants, bar, indoor pool, whirlpool, and fitness room. AE, DC, MC, V. Expensive.*

Eden Hotel Wolff. Chandeliers and dark wood paneling in the public rooms underline the old-fashioned elegance of this downtown favorite. It's located directly across the street from the train station and close to the fairgrounds of Theresienwiese. The rooms are comfortable; most are spacious. You can dine on excellent Bavarian specialties in the intimate Zirbelstube restaurant. *Arnulfstr. 4, tel. 089/551–150. 210 rooms with bath. Facilities: restaurant. AE, DC, MC, V.*

Regent. This new hotel (1987) offers first-class facilities—including a notable gourmet restaurant—without hurting the wallet. It's in a busy part of town near the main train station, but the modern guest rooms have been soundproofed. *Seidlstr. 2, tel. 089/551–590. 172 rooms with bath. Facilities: restaurant, nightclub, bar, sauna, solarium, whirlpool. AE.*

Schloss-Hotel Grünwald. On the southern edge of the city, this rustic lodging offers quiet, eclectically designed rooms (from Bavarian farmhouse motifs to Laura Ashley) with clifftop views of the Isar River valley stretching toward the Alps. Next door is a castle with a local history museum. Nearby is the terminus of the number 25 tram, which will take you into the city. *Zeillerstr. 1, tel. 089/641–7935. 13 rooms and 3 suites with bath. Facilities: restaurant, wine bar, beer garden, sun terrace. AE, DC, MC. Closed Jan. 1–14.*

★ **Splendid.** Chandelier-hung public rooms, complete with antiques and Oriental rugs, give this small hotel something of the atmosphere of a spaciously grand 19th-century inn. The service is attentive and polished. Have breakfast in the small courtyard in summer. There's no restaurant, but the bar serves snacks as well as drinks. The chic shops of the Maximilianstrasse are a five-minute stroll in one direction; an equally brief walk in the other brings you to the Isar River. *Maximilianstr. 54, tel. 089/296–606. 37 rooms and 4 apartments. Facilities: bar. AE, MC, V.*

Torbräu. You'll sleep under the shadow of one of Munich's ancient city gates—the 14th-century Isartor—if you stay here. Newly renovated, this snug hotel offers comfortable, Scandinavian-modern rooms and an excellent location midway between the Marienplatz and the Deutsches Museum (and around the corner from the Hofbräuhaus). The Torbräu has a moderately priced Italian restaurant, the Firenze, and a good café tucked away in a corner of the arcaded facade. *Tal 37, tel. 089/225–016. 82 rooms with bath. Facilities: restaurant, café, bowling alley. AE, MC, V.*

Moderate

Adria. A modern and comfortable hotel, the Adria is located on the edge of Munich's museum quarter, in the attractive Lehel district, a short walk from the Isar River and the Englischer Garten. There's no restaurant, but there is a large and bright breakfast room. *Liebigstr. 8, tel. 089/293–081. 51 rooms with bath. AE, DC, MC, V. Closed Dec. 24–Jan. 6.*

Bauer. Head here for good-value Bavarian-rustic inn that provides country comforts (painted wardrobes, raw light pine, lots of blue-and-white-check patterns), yet is within easy reach of the city. The family-run Bauer, 10 kilometers (6 miles) from the city center, is best for those traveling by car, although the S-bahn train line S-3 is nearby. *Münchnerstr. 6, Feldkirchen, tel. 089/90980. 119 rooms and 1 suite with bath. Facilities: restaurant, terrace café, indoor pool, sauna. AE, DC, MC, V.*

Brack. This modest but comfortable hotel on one of Munich's prettiest tree-lined streets is just south of the center and opposite the Poccistrasse subway station. The Brack has no restaurant but provides a good buffet breakfast to set you up for the day. *Lindwurmstr. 153, tel. 089/771–052. 50 rooms with bath. AE, DC, MC, V.*

★ **Gästehaus am Englischen Garten.** Reserve well in advance for a room at this popular converted 200-year-old water mill adjoining the Englischer Garten park. The hotel, complete with ivy-clad walls and shutter-framed windows, is only a five-minute walk from the bars and shops of Schwabing. There's no restaurant, but who needs one with Schwabing's numerous eating possibilities so close? Be sure to ask for a room in the main building; the modern annex down the road is cheaper but lacks charm. In summer, breakfast is served on the terrace. *Liebergesellstr. 8, tel. 089/392–034. 27 rooms, most with bath or shower. No credit cards.*

Intercity. Despite a location near the train station, double-glazing of all the windows ensures peace in this longtime downtown favorite. Try for one of the Bavarian-style rooms; the others are basic and little more than adequate. There's an excellent restaurant offering good-value Bavarian specialties. *Bahnhofpl. 2, tel. 089/558–571. 208 rooms and 4 apartments with bath. Facilities: restaurant, bar, skittle alley. DC, MC, V.*

Königin Elizabeth. A bright, modern interior, with the emphasis on pink, lies behind the protected neoclassical facade of this three-year-old hotel, a 15-minute tram ride northwest of the center. Children under 12 stay free in their parents' room. *Leonrodstr. 79, tel. 089/126–860. 80 rooms. Facilities: restaurant, bar, beer garden, fitness center with whirlpool, sauna, and steambath. AE, DC, MC, V.*

Mayer. If you appreciate good value above convenient location, head for this family-run hotel 25 minutes by suburban train from the Hauptbahnhof. The Mayer offers first-class comforts and facilities at prices less than half those charged by similar lodgings in town. Built in the 1970s, the Mayer is furnished in Bavarian country "rustic" style—lots of pine and solid green, red, and check fabrics. Chef (and hotel owner) Rainer Radach was a student of two of Germany's most respected master chefs. The Mayer is a 10-minute walk, or short taxi ride, from Germering station, on the S-5 suburban line, eight stops west of the Hauptbahnhof. *Augsburgerstr. 45, 8034 Germering, tel. 089/840–1515. 56 rooms with bath. Facilities: restaurant, indoor pool. AE, MC.*

Inexpensive

★ **Fürst.** Centrally located in a quiet street just off Odeonsplatz on the edge of the university quarter, this very basic, clean guest house is constantly busy. Book early. *Kardinal-Döpfner-str., tel. 089/281–043. 18 rooms, 4 with bath. No credit cards.*

Gröbner. You'll stay here because you appreciate not only the terrific central location—the Hofbräuhaus is just around the corner—but also the appeal of a friendly, family-run hotel. American guests are especially welcome. The rooms are basically furnished but clean. Try for one on the second floor; they are especially large and airy. *Herrnstr. 44, tel. 089/293–939. 30 rooms, some with bath. No credit cards.*

Kriemhild. If you're traveling with children, you'll appreciate the low rates of this welcoming, family-run pension in the western suburb of Nymphenburg. It's a 10-minute walk from the palace itself and around the corner from the Hirschgarten park, site of one of the city's best beer gardens. It's a 30-minute tram ride (No. 12) from downtown. There's no restaurant, but there is a small bar. An extensive breakfast buffet is included in the room rate. *20 rooms, some with bath. Guntherstr. 16, tel. 089/170–077. Facilities: bar. MC, V.*

★ **Monopteros.** There are few better deals in Munich than this little hotel. It's located just south of the Englischer Garten, with a tram stop (No. 20) for the 10-minute ride to downtown right by the door. The rooms may be basic, but the excellent service and warm welcome, added to the great location, more than compensate. There's no restaurant. *Oettingenstr. 35, tel. 089/292–348. 11 rooms, 3 with shower. No credit cards.*

Pension Beck. Frau Beck and her daughter run this rambling, friendly little pension with an authoritative but personal touch. It sprawls over several floors of a handsome Art Nouveau building in Lehel, within easy walking distance of downtown. Frau Beck aims to provide two essentials: "A comfortable bed and a good cup of coffee." If you share her priorities, this is a place you'll love. *Thierschstr. 36, tel. 089/225–768. 50 rooms, most with bath. No credit cards.*

The Arts and Nightlife

The Arts

Details of concerts and theater performances are listed in *Vorschau* and *Monatsprogramm*, booklets available at most hotel reception desks, newsstands, and tourist offices. Some hotels will make ticket reservations; otherwise use one of the ticket agencies in the city center, such as **A-Z Schalterhalle** (Sendlingerstr. 79, tel. 089/267–024), **Residenz Bücherstube** (concert tickets only; Theatinerstr., tel. 089/220–868), or **Hieber Max** (Liebefrauenstr. 1, tel. 089/226–571).

Theater Munich has scores of theaters and variety-show haunts, although most productions will be largely impenetrable if your German is shaky. (An English-speaking company, the **Company,** presents about four productions a year; tel. 089/343–827). Listed here are all the better-known theaters, as well as some of the smaller and more progressive spots. A visit to one or more will underline just why the Bavarian capital has such an enviable reputation as an artistic hot spot. Note that most theaters are closed during July and August.

Bayerisches Staatsschauspiel/Neues Residenztheater (Bavarian State Theater/New Residence Theater) (Max-Joseph-Pl. The box office is at Maximilianstr. 11, tel. 089/221–316). Open Mon.–Fri. 10–1 and 3:30–5:30, Sat. 10–12:30, and one hour before the performance.

Cuvilliés-Theater/Altes Residenztheater (Old Residence Theater) (Max-Joseph-Pl.; entrance on Residenzstr.). The box office, at Maximilianstrasse 11 (tel. 089/221–1316), is open Mon.–Fri. 10–1 and 3:30–5:30, Sat. 10–12:30, and one hour before the performance.

Deutsches Theater (Schwanthalerstr. 13, tel. 089/593–427). The box office is open Mon.–Fri. noon–6, Sat. 10–1:30.

Gasteig (Rosenheimerstr. 5, tel. 089/4809–8614). This modern cultural complex includes two theaters—the Carl-Orff Saal and the Black Box—where plays in English are occasionally performed. The box office is open Mon.–Fri. 10:30–2 and 3–6, Sat. 10:30–2.

Kleine Komödie (Bayerischer Hof Hotel, Promenadepl., tel. 089/292–810; Max-II-Denkmal, Maximilianstr., tel. 089/221–859). The box office at Bayerischer Hof is open Mon.–Sat. 11–8, Sun. and holidays 3–8. The box office at Max-II-Denkmal is open Tues.–Sat. 11–8, Mon. 11–7, Sun. and holidays 3–8.

Marionettentheater (Blumenstr. 29A, tel. 089/265–712). The box office is open Tues.–Sun. 10–noon.

Münchner Kammerspiele-Schauspielhaus (Maximilianstr. 26, tel. 089/237–21328). The box office is open Mon.–Fri. 10–6, Sat., Sun., and holidays 10–1.

Platzl am Platzl (Munzstr. 8–9, tel. 089/237–03711). Daily show (except Sunday) with typical Bavarian humor, yodeling, and *Schuhplattler* (the slapping of Bavarian leather shorts in time to the oompah music).

Prinzregententheater (Prinzregentenpl. 12, tel. 089/225–754). The box office is open Mon.–Fri. 10–1 and 3:30–5:30, Sat. 10–12:30, and one hour before the performance.

Theater Kleine Freiheit (Maximilianstr. 31, tel. 089/221–123). The box office is open Mon.–Sat. from 11, Sun. from 2.

Concerts Munich and music go together. Paradoxically, however, it's only since 1984 that the city has had a world-class concert hall: the Gasteig center, a lavish brick complex standing high above the Isar River, east of downtown. It's the permanent home of the Munich Philharmonic Orchestra, which regularly performs in its Philharmonic Hall. In addition to the Philharmonic, the city has three other orchestras: the Bavarian State Orchestra, based at the National Theater; the Bavarian Radio Orchestra, which gives Sunday concerts at the Gasteig; and the Kurt Graunke Symphony Orchestra, which generally puts on operettas at the Gärtnerplatz theater. The leading choral ensembles are the Munich Bach Choir, the Munich Motettenchor, and Musica Viva, the latter specializing in contemporary music. (*See* above for information on where to buy tickets.)

Bayerischer Rundfunk (Rundfunkpl. 1, tel. 089/558–080). The box office is open Monday–Friday 9–noon and 1–5.

Galerie im Lenbachhaus (Luisenstr. 33, tel. 089/521–041). Though this is primarily an art gallery, chamber-music concerts are sometimes held here.

Herkulessaal in der Residenz (Hofgarten, tel. 089/224–641). The box office opens one hour before performances.

Hochscule für Musik (Arcisstr. 12, tel. 089/559–101). Concerts featuring music students are given free of charge.

Kongressaal des Deutscher Museums (Museumsinsel 1, tel. 089/221–790). The box office opens one hour before performances.

Olympiahalle (tel. 089/306–13577). The box office is open Mon.–Thurs. 8–5, Fri. 8–2. For pop concerts.

Nightlife

Munich's nighttime attractions vary with the seasons. The year starts with the abandon of *Fasching*, the Bavarian carnival time, when every night is party night. No sooner has Lent brought the sackcloth curtain down on Fasching than the local weather office is being asked to predict when the spring sunshine will be warm enough to allow the city's 100 beer gardens to open. From then until late fall the beer garden dictates the style and pace of Munich's nightlife. When it rains, the indoor beer halls and taverns absorb the thirsty like blotting paper.

The beer gardens and beer halls close at midnight, but there's no need to go home to bed then: Some bars and nightclubs are open until 3 AM, and a few have all-night licenses. A word of caution about some of those bars, however: Most are run honestly and prices are only slightly higher than normal, but a few may be unscrupulous. The seedier are near the main train station. Stick to beer or wine if you can, and pay as you go. And if you feel you're being duped, call the cops—the customer is usually, if not always, right.

For a city with such a free-and-easy reputation, Munich lacks the raunchy, no-holds-barred forthrightness of Hamburg's Reeperbahn. There are no live sex shows, and prostitution, though not illegal, is purveyed discreetly. For striptease shows, explore the region south of the main railway station (Schillerstrasse, for example) or the neighborhood of the famous Hofbräuhaus (am Platzl).

Clubs **Intermezzo** (Maximilianpl. 34). It's said to have the prettiest strippers and most exotic dancers in town. Tall claim, but worth checking out. Closed Sun.

Lola Montez (Am Platzl 1). Named after the gal who cost Ludwig I his crown, this cabaret and striptease night spot is also heading for a chapter in local history. Expensive, but no rip-off.

Maxim (Farbergraben 33). This club is tucked away behind the pedestrian shopping precinct, but, fetching though they might be, these women are not for sale (a rule that applies throughout the central city zone, by the way).

Discos Schwabing is discoland. There are three in a 50-yard stretch of Occamstrasse: **Albatros, California New,** and **Valentino. Peaches,** on the neighboring Feilitzstrasse, and **Sunset** (Leopoldstr. 69) are also young and fun. Across town, **East Side** (Rosenheimerstr. 30) has an older clientele (well, not too old) and lots of plush and class. **PI** (on the east side of the Haus der Kunst) and the **Park-Café** (Sophienstr. 7) are the most fashionable discos in town, but you'll have to talk yourself past the doorman to join the chic crowds inside. The **Lenbach Palast** (Lenbachpl. 3) is less choosy and, frankly, more fun, with live bands nightly. The noisiest disco in town is **Crash** (Lindwurmstr. 88). The youngsters love it, despite the risk of ruptured eardrums. Closed Sun.

Bars and Singles Every Munich bar is singles territory. Try **Schumann's** (Maximilianstr. 36) anytime after the curtain comes down at the nearby opera house (and watch the barmen shake those cocktails; closed Sat.), but wait till after midnight before venturing into the **Alter Simpl** (Turkenstr. 57) for a sparkling crowd despite the gloomy surroundings. **Harry's New York Bar** (Falkenturmstr. 9) offers escape from the German bar scene, and it serves genuine Irish Guinness. **Humphrey's Bogärtchen** (Isartal 26, tel. 089/761–144) is a candlelit piano bar where you're bound to hear "As Time Goes By " at some point in the evening. Different again is the **Paulaner Bräuhaus** (Kapuzinerpl. 5), an ornate 19th-century pub with a minibrewery of gleaming copper behind the bar. One of the most popular gay bars is **Henderson's** (Rumfordstr. 2).

Jazz Munich likes to think it's Germany's jazz capital, and to reinforce the claim, some beer gardens have taken to replacing their brass bands with funky combos. Purists don't like it, but jazz enthusiasts are happy. The combination certainly works at **Waldwirtshaft Grosshesselohe** (Georg Kalb-Str. 3), in the southern suburb of Grosshesselohe. Sundays are set aside for jazz, and if it's a fine day the excursion is much recommended. Some city pubs also set aside Sunday midday for jazz: Try **Doktor Flotte** (Occamstr. 8). The best of the jazz clubs are **Allotria** (Oskar-von-Miller-Ring 3); **Nachtcafé** (Maximilianpl. 5, open until 5 AM); **Schwabinger Podium** (Wagnerstr. 1); **Unterfahrt** (Kirchenstr. 96); and **Jenny's Place in the Blue Note,** Moosacherstr. 24, near the Olympiazentrum (tel. 089/351–0520), new live-jazz venue of a vivacious English actress and singer who has a great voice and a warm welcome for visitors from the United States and Britain.

Excursions

The excursions covered here are by no means the only ones you can make from Munich. Practically all the attractions in the Alps, for example, or those at the south end of the Romantic Road—the resort town of Garmisch-Partenkirchen and Ludwig II's palaces and castles preeminently—make ideal destinations for one- or two-day trips out of town. For full details of these and many other destinations around Munich, *see* Chapters 4 and 8.

Tour 1: Ammersee and Andechs

The Ammersee is the country cousin of the better-known, more cosmopolitan Starnbergersee, and many Bavarians (and tourists, too) like it all the more as a result. Fashionable Munich of centuries past thought it too far for an excursion, not to mention too rustic for its sophisticated tastes. So the shores remained relatively free of the villas and parks that ring the Starnbergersee, and even though the upscale holiday homes of Munich's moneyed classes today claim some stretches of the eastern shore, the Ammersee still offers more open areas for bathing and boating than the bigger lake to the west. Bicyclists can circle the 12-mile-long lake (it's nearly 4 miles across at its widest point) on a path that rarely loses sight of the water. Hikers can spin out the tour for two or three days, staying overnight in any of the comfortable inns that crop up along the way. Dinghy sailors and windsurfers can zip across in minutes with the help of the Alpine winds that swoop down from the mountains. A ferry boat cruises the lake at regular intervals during summer, dropping and picking up passengers at several pier head stops. Join it at Herrsching.

Getting There

By Car

Take Autobahn 96—follow the signs to Lindau—and just before it ends, 20 kilometers (12 miles) west of Munich, take the exit for Herrsching, the lake's principal town. Herrsching is 40 kilometers (25 miles) from Munich.

By Train

Herrsching, on the east bank of the lake, is the end of the S-5 suburban line, a half-hour ride from Munich's central Marienplatz. From Herrsching station, the number 952 bus runs north along the lake, and the number 956 runs south.

Exploring

In Herrsching, head for the lake and the delightful promenade, part of which winds through the resort's park. The 100-year-old villa that sits so comfortably in the park, overlooking the lake and the Alps beyond, seems almost as though it might have been built by Ludwig II, such is its romantic and fanciful mixture of medieval turrets and Renaissance-style facades. It was built for the artist Ludwig Scheuermann and is now a municipal cultural center and the scene of chamber-music concerts on some summer weekends.

Three miles south of Herrsching—you can reach it on the number 956 bus—is one of southern Bavaria's most famous places of pilgrimage, the Benedictine monastery of **Andechs.** The crowds of pilgrims are drawn not only by the beauty of the hilltop monastery and its 15th-century pilgrimage church, decked out with glorious Rococo decoration in the mid-18th century and a repository of religious relics said to have been brought from the Holy Land 1,000 years ago, but also by the beer brewed there. The monastery makes its own cheese as well, and it's an excellent accompaniment to the rich, almost black beer. You can enjoy both at large wood tables in the monastery tavern or on the terrace outside.

Follow the lake to its southwest corner and you'll find the little town of **Diessen,** with its magnificent Baroque abbey-church. Stop in to admire its opulent stucco decoration and sumptuous gilt and marble altar. Leonard Bernstein conducted the Mozart Requiem here in 1988. Visit the church in late afternoon, when the light falls sharply on its crisp gray, white, and gold facade, etching the pencillike tower and spire against the darkening sky over the lake. Don't go without at least peeping into neighboring St. Stephen's courtyard, its cloisters smothered in wild roses. There's a delightful tearoom, too, that serves the excellent local beer.

Dining In Herrsching, the **Gasthof zur Post** (Andechstr. 1) is everything a Bavarian tavern should be. The weekday lunch menu is an unbeatable value, and the locally brewed dark beer is unbeatable, period. Along the lakeside promenade you'll find several idyllic terrace restaurants; the **Alba-Seehotel** is the best. For the best *tirami su* outside Italy, stroll to the end of the promenade and call in at the **Restaurante da Mario.** In Diessen, make for the central Carl-Orff-Platz and pause to admire the rustic exterior of the **Gasthaus Unterbräu Gotsfried,** then venture inside for another indelible culinary impression (or, in summer, find a table outside in the leafy beer garden). The nearby **Hotel-Gasthof-Seefelder Hof** also has a delightful beer garden.

Tour 2: Dachau

The first Nazi concentration camp was built just outside this town. Dachau preserves the memory of the camp and the horrors perpetrated there with deep contrition while trying, with commendable discretion, to signal that it also has other things to offer visitors. It's an older place than nearby Munich, for example, with local records going back to the time of Charlemagne in the 9th century. And it's a handsome town, too, built on a hilltop with fine views of Munich and the Alps.

Getting There
By Car Dachau is 20 kilometers (12 miles) northwest of Munich. Take the B-12 country road, or the Stuttgart autobahn to the Dachau exit.

By Train Dachau is on the S-2 suburban railway line, a 20-minute ride from Munich's Marienplatz.

Exploring Make for the town center and climb the hill to the **castle.** What you'll see is the one remaining wing of a palace built by the Munich architect Josef Effner for the Wittelsbach ruler Max Emanuel in 1715, a replacement for the original castle built in the 15th century. In the Napoleonic Wars at the beginning of the 19th century the palace served as a field hospital, treating French and Russian casualties from the Battle of Austerlitz (1805). The wars made a casualty, too, of the palace, and three of the four wings were demolished by order of King Max I Joseph. What's left now was the ballroom, and, on weekends in summer, it's still used for concerts. There's a 16th-century carved ceiling, with painted panels representing characters from ancient mythology. There's also a 250-year-old Schlossbrauerei (castle brewery), which hosts the town's own beer and music festival each year during the first half of August.

Downtown you'll find the parish church of **St. Jacob,** a towering 16th-century building that dominates the adjacent square, the former haymarket.

Dachau served as a lively artists' colony in the 19th century, and the tradition lives on: There are art shops wherever you look. The **Dachauer Gemäldegalerie** in Konrad-Adenauer-Strasse is a good place to try.

To reach the **Dachau Concentration Camp Memorial** (Alte Römerstr. 75) by car, leave the center of the town along Schleissheimerstrasse and turn left into Alte Römerstrasse; the site is on the left. By public transport, take the number 722 bus from the Dachau S-bahn train station to Robert-Bosch-strasse and walk along Alte Römerstrasse for 100 yards. Photographs, contemporary documents, the few remaining cell blocks, and the grim crematorium create a somber and moving picture of the camp, where more than 200,000 people lost their lives. *Admission free. Open Tues.–Sun. 9–5. A documentary film (in English) is shown at 11:30 and 3:30.*

Dining The **Bräustüberl,** 50 yards from the castle, has a shady beer garden for summer lunches. In the town center, the **Helferwirt** has a secluded garden and a cozy restaurant serving Bavarian fare. Next to the ivy-covered town hall, on Freisingerstrasse, is the solid, historic **Zieglerbräu,** once a 17th-century brewer's home, now a wood-paneled restaurant.

Tour 3: Landshut

If fortune had placed Landshut 64 kilometers (40 miles) south of Munich, in the protective folds of the Alpine foothills, instead of the same distance north, in the dull flatlands of Lower Bavaria, this delightful, historic town would have been overrun by visitors long ago. Landshut's geographical misfortune is the discerning visitor's good luck, for the town is never overcrowded, with the possible exception of the three summer weeks every four years (next in 1993) when the Landshuter Hochzeit is celebrated. The festival commemorates the marriage in 1475 of Prince George of Bayern-Landshut, son of the expressively named Ludwig the Rich, to Princess Hedwig, daughter of the king of Poland. The whole town gets swept away in a colorful reconstruction of the event that increased its already regal importance and helped to give it the majestic air you'll still find within its ancient walls.

Getting There

By Car Landshut is a 45-minute drive northwest from Munich on either Autobahn 92—follow the signs to Deggendorf—or the B-11 highway.

By Train Landshut is on the Plattling–Regensburg–Passau line, a 40-minute ride by express train from Munich.

Exploring A 10-minute bus ride will take you from the train station to the heart of the old town. There are parking lots right outside it, too. Landshut has not just one magnificent, cobbled market street but two: The one in **Altstadt** (Old Town) is considered by many to be the most beautiful city street in Germany; the one in **Neustadt** (New Town) projects its own special appeal. The two streets run parallel to each other, tracing a course between the Isar River and the heights overlooking the town. A steep path from Altstadt takes you up to **Burg Trausnitz,** sitting commandingly on the heights. This castle was begun in 1204 and accommodated the Wittelsbach dukes of Bayern-Landshut until 1503. *Admission, including guided tour: DM 2.50 adults, children free. Open daily 9–noon and 1–5.*

In the 16th century, the Wittelsbachs moved into a new palace (the *Stadtresidenz)* on **Altstadt,** the first Italian Renaissance building of its kind north of the Alps. The Renaissance facade of the palace forms an almost modest part of the architectural splendor and integrity of Altstadt, where even the ubiquitous McDonald's has to serve its hamburgers behind a baroque facade. *Admission: DM 2 adults, children free. Open daily 9–noon and 1–5.*

Soaring over the street scene is the 436-foot tower and bristling spire of **St. Martin's** church, the tallest brick church tower in the world. The church contains some magnificent Gothic treasures and a 16th-century carved Madonna. Moreover, it is surely the only church anywhere in the world to contain an image of Hitler, albeit in devilish pose. The Führer and other Nazi leaders are portrayed as executioners in a 1946 stained-glass window showing the martyrdom of St. Kastulus. In the nave of the church is a clear and helpful description of its history and its treasures, an aid to English-speaking visitors that could profitably be copied by other churches and historical sites in Germany.

Dining There are several attractive Bavarian-style restaurants in Altstadt and Neustadt, most of them with charming beer gardens. The best are **Brauereigasthof Ainmiller** (Altstadt 195), **Gasthaus Schwabl** (Neustadt 500), **Zum Hofreiter** (Neustadt 505), and the **Hotel Goldene Sonne** (Neustadt 520). The **Klausenberg Panorama-Restaurant** (Klausenberg 17) has a terrace with a fine view of the town and the surrounding country. For an inexpensive but satisfactory lunch, the **Buddha** (Apothekergasse) serves a good, fixed-price Chinese meal for around DM 12 per person. If you're looking for an authentic Bavarian dining experience, make your way to the old episcopal town of Freising, halfway between Landshut and Munich. It's the site of the world's oldest brewery (AD 1040), the **Bayerische Staatsbrauerei Weihenstephan;** where you can select from a beer menu that lists 11 different brews. Freising is the final stop on the S-1 suburban railway line from Munich, and one stop from Landshut by express train.

Lodging Landshut has four principal hotels, besides a handful of reasonably priced and comfortable inns. The hotels are: **Hotel Kaiserhof** (Papiererstr. 2, tel. 0871/6870; Expensive), an attractive 18th-century–style riverside building; **Romantik Hotel Fürstenhof** (Stethaimerstr. 3, tel. 0871/82025; Moderate), a tastefully modernized Art Nouveau villa; **Hotel Goldene Sonne** (Neustadt 520, tel. 0871/23087; Moderate), a historic inn in the Old Town; and **Hotel Luitpold** (Luitpoldstr. 43, tel. 0871/61538; Inexpensive), a modern hotel between the train station and town.

Tour 4: Starnbergersee

The Starnbergersee was one of Europe's first pleasure grounds. Royal coaches trundled out from Munich to its wooded banks in the Baroque years of the 17th century; in 1663 Elector Ferdinand Maria threw a huge shipboard party at which 500 guests wined and dined as 100 oarsmen propelled them around the lake. Today pleasure steamers perform the same task for visitors of less than noble rank. The lake is still lined with the Baroque palaces of Bavaria's aristocracy, but their owners now have to share the lakeside with public parks, beaches, and boat yards. The Starnbergersee is one of Bavaria's largest lakes—12 miles long and 3 miles across at its widest point—so there's plenty of room for swimmers, sailors, and windsurfers. On its west shore is one of Germany's finest golf courses, but it's about as difficult for the casual visitor to play a game there as it was for a Munich commoner to win an invitation to one of Prince Ferdinand's boating parties. Those on the trail of Ludwig II should note that it was on the Starnbergersee (beside the village of Berg) that the doomed monarch met his watery death under circumstances that remain a mystery.

Getting There
By Car The north end of the lake, where the resort of Starnberg sits in stately beauty, is a 30-minute drive from Munich on Autobahn 95. Follow the signs to Garmisch and take the Starnberg exit. Country roads then skirt the west and east banks of the lake.

By Train The S-6 suburban line runs from Munich's central Marienplatz to Starnberg and three other towns on the lake's west bank: Possenhofen, Feldafing, and Tutzing. The journey from Marienplatz to Starnberg takes 35 minutes. The east bank of the lake can be reached by bus from the town of Wolfratshausen, the end of the S-7 suburban line.

Exploring From Starnberg train station, take a stroll along the lakeside promenade for an overall impression of the shimmering beauty of this fascinating stretch of water, with the hazy hint of mountains at its southern rim. Rent bicycles at the station and pedal around the top of the lake to Percha, where a well-marked path will lead you south 3 kilometers (2 miles) to Berg. Leave the bicycles outside the castle park and stroll the half mile through thick woods to the **King Ludwig II Memorial Chapel,** built near the point in the lake where the king's body was found on June 13, 1886. He had been confined in nearby Berg Castle after the Bavarian government took action against his withdrawal from reality and into expensive castle-building fantasy. A mile across the lake is the castle of **Possenhofen,** home of Ludwig's favorite cousin, Sissi. Local lore says they used to send affectionate messages across the lake to each other. Sissi married the Austrian emperor Franz Joseph I but returned frequently to the Starnbergersee, to spend more than 20 consecutive summers in the lakeside castle (which has now been converted into luxury apartments). Just offshore is the tiny **Roseninsel** (Rose Island), where King Maximilian II built a summer villa. You can swim to its tree-fringed shores or sail across in a dinghy or on a Windsurfer (Possenhofen's boat yard is one of the lake's many rental points).

Dining The most elegant dining in Starnberg is at the **Maximilian** (Ostwaldstr. 16), where Bavarian fare with chic nouvelle touches is offered. For an airy tavern, try the **Gasthof in der Au**

(Josef-Jager-Huber-Str. 15). If you fancy a view of the lake, make for the **Seerestaurant Undosa,** where the atmosphere is always boisterous. Farther down the lake, on the outskirts of Possenhofen, is the **Forsthaus am See** (Am See 1, Pocking-Possenhofen), where you dine beneath a carved panel ceiling imported from Austria's South Tyrol. The restaurant has a lakeside beer garden and its own pier for guests who arrive by boat. From Tutzing, at the end of the S-6 suburban line, a short walk up into the hills leads to the **Forsthaus Ilka-Höhe,** a rustic lodge with a fine view of the lake and excellent Bavarian food (closed Tues. Oct.–Mar.). On the other side of the lake, near the Berg Castle grounds and the King Ludwig II Memorial Chapel, try the **Dorint Seehotel Leoni** (Assenbucherstr. 44, Berg-Leoni), where you can also rent bicycles (tel. 08151/5060), or the **Strandhotel Schloss Berg** (Seestr. 17), which has a lakeside dining terrace.

Tour 5: Wasserburg am Inn

Wasserburg floats like a faded ship of state in a benevolent, lazy loop of the Inn River, which comes within a few yards of cutting the ancient town off from the wooded slopes of the encroaching countryside. The river caresses the southern limits of the ancient town center, embraces its eastern boundary with rocky banks 200 feet high, returns westward as if looking for a way out of this geographical puzzle, and then heads north in search of its final destination, the Danube. Wasserburg sleeps on in its watery cradle, a perfectly preserved, beautifully set medieval town, once a vitally important trading post, later thankfully ignored by the industrialization that gripped Germany in the 19th century. Only one bridge connects the ancient town center with the newer suburbs across the river—a bridge that regularly collapses under winter assaults by ice floes.

Getting There

By Car Take the B-304 highway from Munich, which leads directly to Wasserburg. It's a 45-minute drive.

By Train Take either the suburban line S-4 to Ebersberg and change to a local train to Wasserburg, or the Salzburg express, changing at Grafing Bahnhof to the local line. Both trips take 90 minutes.

Exploring You're never more than 100 yards or so from the river in Wasserburg's old town center. There are two large parking lots on the north and east banks, and it's only a few minutes' walk to the central Marienplatz. There you'll find Wasserburg's late-Gothic brick **town hall.** *Admission: DM 1 adults, 50 pf children. Guided tours Tues.–Fri. at 10, 11, 2, 3, and 4; Sat.–Sun. at 10 and 11.*

Marienplatz is also the site of the town's oldest church, the 14th-century **Frauenkirche,** which incorporates an ancient watchtower. Head up the hill to the imposing 15th-century parish church of **St. Jakob** to view its intricate Baroque pulpit, carved in 1640. Head south toward the river again; in two minutes you'll be at the walls of the **castle** that originally gave Wasserburg (Water Castle) its name. Take the river path back toward the town center, cross the bridge, and look back at the collection of Gothic and Renaissance buildings along the shore. It has a southern, almost Italian look, typical of many Inn River towns. At the end of the bridge, next to the 14th-century town gate, is one of Germany's most unusual museums, the **Erstes Imaginäres Museum,** a collection of more than 400 world-famous paintings. There isn't an original among them: Every single one is a precise copy. *Admission: DM 3 adults, DM 1.50 children. Open May–Sept., Tues.–Sun. 11–5; Oct.–Apr., Tues.–Sun. 1–5.*

Wasserburg is a convenient base for enticing walks along the banks of the Inn River and into the surrounding countryside. A half-hour walk south leads to the village of **Attel.** Another half hour into the Attel River valley and one reaches the enchanting castle-restaurant of **Schloss Hart** (tel. 08039/1774).

Dining You'll find the most compelling atmosphere for dining in Wasserburg at the **Herrenhaus** (Herrengasse 17, tel. 08071/2800; Moderate); it has a centuries-old vaulted wine cellar. For simple and traditional Bavarian fare, make for the **Gasthaus Zum Löwen** (Marienpl. 10, tel. 08071/7400; Inexpensive), a wood-paneled restaurant whose tables spill out onto the sidewalk in summer.

Lodging For solid comfort along with antiques in some of the rooms, good, hearty food, and a beer garden, try the **Hotel Fletzinger** (Fletzingergasse 1, tel. 08071/8010; Moderate). **The Pichlmayr** (Anton-Wogerstr. 2, tel. 08071/40021; Moderate) on the edge of town has 25 brightly painted pastel-colored rooms with bath. Modern facilities include a fitness center with sauna, and there's also a Bavarian-style restaurant.

4 The Bavarian Alps

Including Garmisch, Oberammergau, and Berchtesgaden

Introduction

Oberbayern, or Upper Bavaria, is Germany's favorite year-round vacationland, for visitors and Germans alike.

This part of Bavaria, fanning south from Munich to the Austrian border, is arguably the most attractive area in the country. Scenically, it comes closest to what most of us think of when we see or hear the name Germany. In fact, upon initial exposure, the area may appear as something of a cliché. Stock images from tourist office posters—the fairy-tale castles you've seen in countless ads, those picturebook villages of too-good-to-be-true wood homes with brightly frescoed facades and window boxes filled with flowers in summer, sloping roofs heavy with snow in winter—are brought to life here. To complete the picture, onion-dome church spires rise out of the mist against the backdrop of the mighty Alps. Even the people sometimes appear to be actors completing a carefully staged scene.

The entire area, from close to the Bodensee (Lake Constance) in the west, to Berchtesgaden in the east, is laced with possibilities for delightful excursions. Here, too, you will find a wide range of resorts at which to spend a weekend or week, to use either as bases for further explorations or as places to relax and take advantage of sporting opportunities.

Coming south from Munich, you will soon find yourself on a gently rolling plain leading to a lovely land of lakes fed by Alpine rivers and streams, surrounded by ancient forests. In time, the plain merges into foothills, which suddenly give way to a jagged line of Alpine peaks. In places such as Tegernsee, snowcapped mountains seem to rise straight up from the gem-like lakes.

If you continue south you will encounter cheerful villages with richly frescoed houses, some of the finest Baroque churches in Germany, and any number of minor spas where you can stay on to "take the waters" and tune up the system.

Accommodations run the gamut from luxury hotels in such sophisticated Alpine resort areas as Garmisch-Partenkirchen and Berchtesgaden, to cozy—and much less expensive—inns in simple villages. In addition, all through the region private homes offer Germany's own version of bed-and-breakfasts, indicated by signs of *Zimmer Frei* (rooms available).

Sports possibilities are legion: downhill and cross-country skiing and ice-skating in winter; tennis, swimming, sailing, golf, and, above all, hiking in summer. Marked hiking trails lead from the glorious countryside, along rivers and lakes, through woods, and high into the Alps.

For those who enjoy driving, the Deutsche Alpenstrasse (German Alpine Road), makes for a spectacular journey by car. The entire route between Lindau, on Lake Constance, and Berchtesgaden adds up to about 485 kilometers (300 miles). The dramatic stretch between Garmisch-Partenkirchen and Berchtesgaden runs about 300 kilometers (185 miles) and affords wonderful views.

This tour of the Alps takes you east from Garmisch-Partenkirchen to Berchtesgaden. Oberammergau, the magnificent 18th-century abbey of Ettal, and Ludwig II's Versailles-style château at Herrenchiemsee are all covered, along with numerous villages, lakes, and other Alpine attractions. (Note that Neuschwanstein, the most famous of Ludwig's castles, is covered in our Romantic Road chapter. It's located just outside Füssen and makes an ideal day trip from Garmisch-Partenkirchen.)

Essential Information

Important Addresses and Numbers

Tourist Information The Bavarian regional tourist office in Munich, **FVV München Oberbayern** (Sonnenstr. 10, 8000 Munich 2, tel. 089/597–347), provides general information about Upper Bavaria and the Bavarian Alps. There are local tourist information offices in the following towns:

Bad Reichenhall: Kur-und-Verkehrsverein, im Kurgastzentrum, Wittelsbadcherstr. 15, 8230 Bad Reichenhall, tel. 08651/3003.

Bad Tölz: Kurverwaltung, Ludwigstrasse 11, 8170 Bad Tölz, tel. 08041/70071.

Bayerischzell: Kuramt, Kirchplatz 2, 8163 Bayerischzell, tel. 08023/648.

Berchtesgaden: Kurdirektion, Königseerstrasse 2, 8240 Berchtesgaden, tel. 08652/5011.

Garmisch-Partenkirchen: Verkehrsamt der Kurverwaltung, Bahnhofstrasse 34, 8100 Garmisch-Partenkirchen, tel. 08821/18022.

Mittenwald: Kurverwaltung, Dammkarstrasse 3, 8102 Mittenwald, tel. 08823/33981.

Oberammergau: Verkehrsamt, Eugen-Papst-Strasse 9a, 8103 Oberammergau, tel. 08822/1021.

Prien am Chiemsee: Kurverwaltung, Alter Rathausstr. 11, 8210 Prien, tel. 08051/69050.

Reit im Winkl: Verkehrsamt, Rathausplatz 1, 8216 Reit im Winkl, tel. 08640/80020.

Rottach-Egern: Kuramt, Nördliche Hauptstrasse 9, 8183 Rottach-Egern, tel. 08022/671–341.

Car Rental **Avis:** Hindenburgstrasse 35, tel. 08821/55066, **Garmisch-Partenkirchen;** Nymphenburgerstr. 61, tel. 089/126–0020, **Munich.**

Europcar: Hirtenstr. 14, tel. 089/557–145, **Munich.**

Hertz: Zugspitzstrasse 81, tel. 08821/18787, **Garmisch-Partenkirchen;** Nymphenburger-Strasse 81, tel. 089/129–5001, **Munich.**

Sixt-Budget: Seitzstrasse 9, tel. 089/223–333, **Munich.**

Arriving and Departing by Plane

Munich, 95 kilometers (60 miles) northwest of Garmisch-Partenkirchen, is the main airport for the Bavarian Alps. There is easy access from Munich to the Autobahns that lead to the Alps (*see* Arriving and Departing by Car, below). If you're staying in Berchtesgaden at the east end of the Alps, the airport at Salzburg in Austria is closer but has fewer international flights.

Arriving and Departing by Car, Train, and Bus

By Car Three Autobahns reach deep into the Bavarian Alps: A-7 from Ulm to Füssen at the west end of the Alps; A-95 from Munich to Garmisch; and A-8 from Munich to Salzburg and Innsbruck. All provide speedy access to the Alpine foothills, where they connect with a comprehensive network of well-paved country roads that penetrate high into the mountains. (Germany's highest road runs through Berchtesgaden at more than 5,000 feet.)

By Train Garmisch-Partenkirchen and Mittenwald are on the Intercity network, which has regular direct service to all regions of the country. (Klais, just outside Garmisch, is Germany's highest Intercity train station.) Bad Reichenhall and Berchtesgaden are linked directly to north German cities by the FD (Fern-Express) express service.

By Bus The Alpine region is not well served by long-distance bus services: Stick to trains if you plan to travel extensively. The south section of the Europabus route, along the Romantische Strasse (Romantic Road), connects Frankfurt, Wiesbaden, Würzburg, Munich, and Augsburg with the resorts of Schongau and Füssen (*see* Chapter TK). Seat reservations, which are obligatory, can be made through **Deutsche Touring GmbH** (Am Römerhof 17. 6000 Frankfurt/Main 90, tel. 069/790–3240.) Many travel agents—ABR in Bavaria, for instance—can also make reservations.

Getting Around

By Car The Deutsche Alpenstrasse, not a continuous highway but a series of roads, runs from Lindau in the west to the Austrian border beyond Berchtesgaden in the east, skirting the northern edge of the Alps for most of the way before heading deep into the mountains on the final stretch between Inzell and Berchtesgaden. Another route, the so-called Blaue Route (Blue Route), follows the valleys of the Inn and Salzach rivers along the German-Austrian border above Salzburg. This off-the-beaten-track territory includes three quiet lakes: the Tachingersee, the Wagingersee, and the Abstdorfersee. They are the warmest bodies of water in Upper Bavaria, ideal for family vacations. At Wasserburg, on the Inn River, you can join the final section of the Deutsche Ferienstrasse (German Holiday Road), another combination of roads that run on to Traunstein, east of Chiemsee, and then into the Alps. The Chiemsee and two other popular lakes, the Starnbergersee and the Ammersee, are within easy reach of Munich by Autobahn.

By Train Most Alpine resorts are connected with Munich by regular express and slower service. Munich's S-bahn (suburban service) extends as far as two lakes, the Starnbergersee and the Ammersee, where the Alpine foothills really begin.

By Bus Villages not served by train are connected by post bus. This is a fun and inexpensive way to get around, but service is slow and irregular. Larger resorts operate buses to outlying areas.

By Boat Passenger boats operate on all the major Bavarian lakes. They're mostly excursion boats and many run only in summer. However, there's an important year-round service on the Chiemsee that links the mainland with the islands of Herreninsel and Fraueninsel. Four boats on the Starnbergersee and four on the Ammersee (including a fine old paddle steamer) make round-trips of the lake several times a day, leaving from Starnberg and Stegen/Inning. Eight boats operate year-round on the Tegernsee, connecting Tegernsee town, Rottach-Egern, and Bad Wiessee. A fleet of 21 silent, electrically driven boats glides through the waters of the Königsee near Berchtesgaden to the most remote of Bavaria's lakes, the Obersee.

Guided Tours

Bus tours to King Ludwig II's castles at Neuschwanstein and Linderhof and to the Ettal monastery near Oberammergau are offered by the **ABR** travel agencies in Garmisch-Partenkirchen (tel. 08821/55125) and Oberammergau (tel. 08822/4921). Tours to Neuschwanstein, Linderhof, Ettal, and into the neighboring Austrian Tyrol are also offered by a number of other Garmisch travel agencies: **Biersack** (tel. 08821/4920), **Frankl** (tel. 08821/51700), **Karrasch** (tel. 08821/2111), **Kümmerle** (tel. 08821/4955), **Roser** (tel. 08821/2926), **Teixeira** (tel. 08821/58580), and **Weiss-Blau** (tel. 08821/3766). The Garmisch mountain railway company, the **Bayerische Zugspitzbahn** (tel. 08821/58058) offers special excursions to the top of the Zugspitze, Germany's highest mountain, by cog rail and/or cable car (*see* Tour 1 in Exploring the Alps, below). **German Federal Railways** (tel. 089/598–484 or 0821/96600) offers special excursion fares from Munich and Augsburg to the top of the Zugspitze. In Berchtesgaden, the **Schwaiger** bus company (tel. 08652/2525) offers bus tours of the area and over the Austrian border as far as Salzburg.

Exploring the Alps

Highlights for First-time Visitors

Zugspitze
Kloster Ettal
Schloss Linderhof
Oberammergau
Tegernsee
Tatzelwurm gorge and waterfall
Kehlsteinhaus
Boat excursion on the Königsee in Berchtesgaden National Park

Tour 1: Garmisch-Partenkirchen

Numbers in the margin correspond to points of interest on the Bavarian Alps map.

1 **Garmisch-Partenkirchen,** or Garmisch, as it's more commonly known, is the undisputed Alpine capital of Bavaria. This bustling, year-round resort and spa area is an ideal center from which to explore the Bavarian Alps. Once two separate communities, Garmisch and Partenkirchen were fused in 1936 to accommodate the winter Olympics. Today, with a population of 27,000, the area is large enough to offer every facility expected from a major Alpine resort but is still small enough not to overwhelm.

Although it seems an essentially modern town—few of its buildings predate World War I—Garmisch-Partenkirchen has

The Bavarian Alps

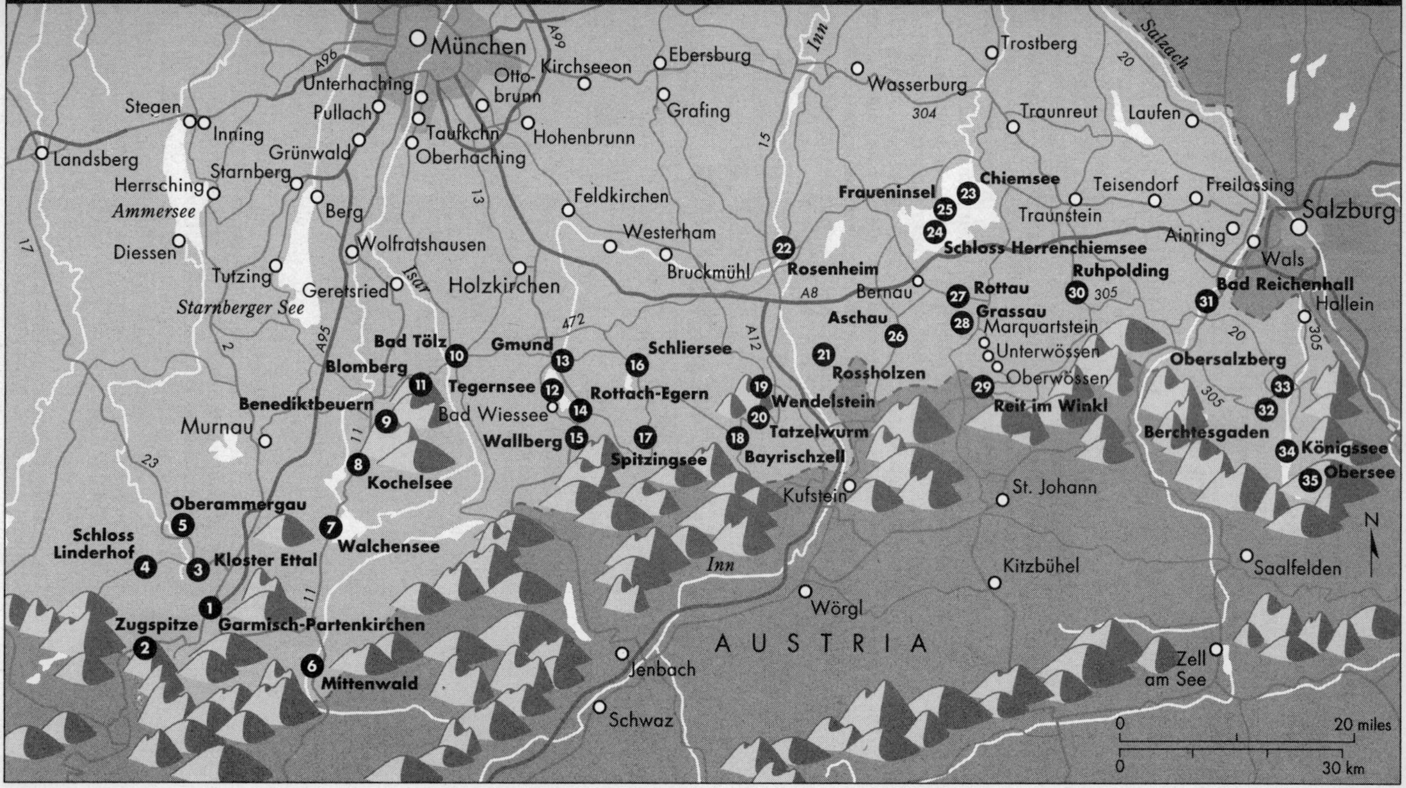

a long history. Partenkirchen, the older half, was founded by the Romans. The road the Romans built between Partenkirchen and neighboring Mittenwald can still be followed. It was a major route well into the 17th century, a piece of the principal road between Rome and Germany. Much of the astounding wealth of the Fugger family in Augsburg (*see* Chapter TK) resulted from trade between the south of Germany and Venice, which were connected by the Roman route.

Partenkirchen was economically devastated in the first half of the 17th century by the Thirty Years' War. The town was spared physical destruction but went into a decline and became little more than a backwater. By the early 18th century, it was rejuvenated by the discovery of iron ore. Today, of course, tourism keeps Garmisch-Partenkirchen thriving.

Winter sports rank high on the agenda here. There are more than 62 miles of downhill ski runs, 40 ski lifts and cable cars, and 93 miles of cross-country ski tracks (called *Loipen*). One of the principal stops on the international winter sports circuit, the area hosts a week of international races every January. You can usually count on good skiing from December to April, or into May on the Zugspitze.

2 The number-one attraction in Garmisch is the **Zugspitze,** the highest mountain (9,731 feet) in Germany. For those who want to make a night of it, there's a comfortable hotel at the top, the Schneefernhaus. There are two ways up the mountain: a leisurely 75-minute ride on a cog railway, or a 10-minute hoist by cable car. The railway journey starts from the train station in the center of town; the cable car begins its giddy ascent from the Eibsee, just outside town on the road to Austria. You can buy a round-trip combination ticket, which allows you to mix your mode of travel up and down the mountains; this fare also includes a separate cable ride for the final 1,037 feet from the hotel to just below the peak. The cost of this ticket is DM 55 adults, DM 33 children aged 4–16 (free for children under 4); one-way fare is DM 33 for train or cable car.

You can also take a cable car to one of the lesser peaks. The round-trip fare to the top of the **Alpspitze,** some 2,000 feet lower than the Zugspitze, is DM 27 adults, DM 16 children aged 4–16; to the top of the **Wank** and back costs DM 19 (you ride in four-seat cable cars). Both mountains can be tackled on foot, providing you're properly shod and physically fit. For details on other mountain hikes and on staying in mountain huts, contact Deutscher Alpenverein (German Alpine Association, Praterinsel 5, 8000 Munich, tel. 089/235–0900).

There are innumerable less arduous but hardly less spectacular walks (186 miles of marked trails) through the pine woods and upland meadows that cover the lower slopes of the mountains. If you have the time and stout walking shoes, try one of the two that lead to striking gorges. The **Höllentalklamm** route starts at the Zugspitze Mountain railway terminal in town and ends at the top of the mountain (you'll want to turn back before reaching the summit unless you have mountaineering experience). The **Partnachklamm** route is even more challenging; if you attempt all of it, you'll have to stay overnight in one of the mountain huts along the way. It starts at the Olympic ice stadium in town and takes you through a spectacular tunneled water gorge, past a pretty little mountain lake, and far up the

Zugspitze. An easier way to tackle this route is to ride part of the way up in the Eckbauer cable car that sets out from the Olympic ice stadium. There's a handy inn at the top where you can gather strength for the hour-long walk back down to the cable-car station. Horse-drawn carriages also cover the first section of the route in summer; in winter you can skim along it in a sleigh (tel. 08821/55917 for information).

Garmisch-Partenkirchen isn't all skiing, skating, and hiking, however. In addition to the two Olympic stadiums in the Partenkirchen side of the city, there are some other attractions worth seeing. In Garmisch, the 18th-century parish church of St. Martin, off the Marienplatz, contains some significant stucco work by the Wessobrunn artists Schmuzer, Schmidt, and Bader. Across the Loisach River on Pfarerhausweg stands another, older St. Martin's, whose Gothic wall paintings include a larger-than-life-size figure of St. Christopher. Nearby, on Frühlingstrasse, are some beautiful examples of Upper Bavarian houses; at the end of Zöppritzstrasse lies the villa of composer Richard Strauss, who lived there until his death in 1949.

Not a culture-vulture? Then it might interest you to know that après-ski festivities begin as early as 4 PM, and the town boasts an active nightlife.

Excursions from Garmisch

Garmisch-Partenkirchen is an excellent center from which to tour the magnificent surrounding Alpine region. For many, a visit to the little village of Oberammergau, combined with a side trip to the monastery of Ettal and Ludwig II's jewel-like Linderhof château, is a highlight of their stay in Germany. This trip can be extended by visits to Ludwig II's most famous royal castle, Neuschwanstein, and the exquisite Rococo Wieskirche (*see* Chapter 8). Oberammergau is 20 kilometers (12 miles) north of Garmisch. To reach it, you must first pass the massive
3 walls of **Kloster Ettal**, the great monastery founded in 1330 by Holy Roman Emperor Ludwig der Bayer (Ludwig the Bavarian) for a group of knights and a community of Benedictine monks. The abbey was replaced with new buildings in the 18th century and now serves as a school. However, the original 10-sided church was brilliantly redecorated in 1744–1753, becoming one of the foremost examples of Bavarian Rococo. It is open to visitors. The church's chief treasure is its enormous dome fresco (83 feet wide), painted by Jacob Zeiller, circa 1751–52. The mass of swirling clouds and the pink-and-blue vision of heaven is typical of the Rococo fondness for elaborate and luminous illusionistic ceiling painting.

A liqueur with legendary health-giving properties, made from a centuries-old recipe, is still distilled at the monastery by the monks. It's made with more than 70 mountain herbs. You can't get the recipe, but you can buy bottles of the libation (DM 19 each) from the small stall outside the monastery.

Time Out Across the road, the **Hotel Ludwig der Bayer** (Kaiser-Ludwig Pl. 10, tel. 08822/6601) named after the monastery's founder, serves excellent coffee and monastery-brewed beer. For more solid refreshment, the menu runs the full gamut of Bavarian fare.

Some 10 kilometers (6 miles) west from Ettal, along a narrow
4 mountain valley road, is **Schloss Linderhof,** the only one of Ludwig II's royal residences to have been completed during the monarch's short life, and the only one in which he spent much time. It was built on the grounds of his father's hunting lodge between 1874 and 1878.

For a proper appreciation of Linderhof and the other royal castles associated with Ludwig's name, it helps to understand the troubled king for whom they were created.

"Mad" King Ludwig II is the haunting presence indelibly associated with Alpine Bavaria. He was one of the line of dukes, electors, and kings of the Wittelsbach dynasty who ruled Bavaria from 1180 to 1918. The Wittelsbachs are credited with having fashioned the grandiose look of Munich that exists today. This art-loving family started the city's great art collections, promoted the fine arts and music (Ludwig II was a patron of Richard Wagner), and set up a building program that ran for centuries.

Ludwig II concentrated on building monumental edifices for himself rather than for the people, and devoted a good part of his time and energies (along with an inordinate percentage of the royal purse) to this endeavor.

Grandest of his extravagant projects is Neuschwanstein, the monumental structure to the king's monumental ego that came close to breaking the Wittelsbach bank. It was built over a 17-year period starting in 1869, and today, ironically, is one of Germany's top tourist attractions. (*See* Chapter 8.)

Towering Neuschwanstein offered highly visible proof that the eccentric king had taken leave of his senses and was bleeding the treasury dry. In 1886, the government officially relieved Ludwig of his royal duties for reasons of insanity and had him confined in the small Schloss Berg on the shore of his beloved Starnbergersee, where he had spent summers in his youth.

On day two of the king's stay at the Schloss, he drowned under mysterious circumstances. A cross in the lake in front of the castle marks the place where it happened.

Linderhof was the smallest of this ill-starred king's castles, and yet, ironically, his favorite country retreat. Set in grandiose sylvan seclusion, between a reflecting pool and the green slopes of a gentle mountain, this charming French-style Rococo confection is said to have been inspired by the Petit Trianon of Versailles. From an architectural standpoint, it could well be considered a disaster, a mish-mash of conflicting styles, lavish on the outside, vulgarly overdecorated on the inside. Ludwig's bedroom is filled with brilliantly colored and gilded ornaments; the Hall of Mirrors is a shimmering dreamworld; and the dining room boasts a fine piece of 19th-century engineering—a table that rises and descends from and to the kitchens below. The formal gardens contain further touches of Ludwig's love of fantasy: There's a Moorish Pavilion—bought wholesale from the 1867 Paris Universal Exposition—and a grotto, said to have been modeled on Capri's Blue Grotto but with a rock that slides back at the touch of a button. The gilded Neptune fountain in the lake in front of the palace shoots a jet of water 105 feet into the air, higher than the roof of the building.

According to stories, while staying at Linderhof the eccentric king would dress up as Lohengrin to be rowed in a swan boat on the grotto pond; in winter, he took off on midnight sleigh rides behind six plumed horses and a platoon of outriders holding flaring torches. *Admission: DM 8 adults, DM 3 children. Open Apr.–Sept., 9–12:15 and 12:45–5:30, Oct.–Mar., 10–12:15 and 12:45–4.*

5 The renowned wood-carver's village of **Oberammergau** is magnificently situated above an Alpine valley, 11 kilometers (7 miles) northeast of Linderhof. Its main streets are lined with beautifully frescoed houses, occupied for the most part by families whose men are engaged in the highly skilled wood-carving craft, which has flourished here for nearly four centuries. Wood carving was Oberammergau's route to economic recovery after the depredations of the Thirty Years' War, and the art still flourishes here.

However, Oberammergau is best known not for its wood carving but for its Passion Play, which is performed, in faithful accordance to a solemn vow, once every decade in years ending with zero. The play started as an offering of thanks, commemorating the fact that in 1633 the Black Plague stopped just short of the village.

The Passion Play was first performed in 1634 and has been presented every 10 years since 1680, with an additional 350th anniversary performance in 1984.

The 16-act, 5½-hour play depicts the final days of Christ, from the Last Supper through the Crucifixion and Resurrection. It is presented on a partly open-air stage against a mountain backdrop every day from late May to late September each Passion Play Year (the next will be held in the year 2000).

A visit to Oberammergau during a play year may be considered something of a mixed blessing, in view of the crowds attracted to this small village and the difficulty of obtaining tickets (most are available only through package tours).

Locals count on seeing a half million visitors or more in summers when the Passion Play is presented. The entire village is swept up by the play, with some 1,500 residents directly involved in its preparation and presentation. Men grow beards in hopes of capturing key roles; young women put off marriage in hopes of securing the role of Mary—which until the 1990 performances went only to unmarried girls. In that year, however, the tradition was broken amid much local controversy when a 31-year-old mother of two was given the part.

If you visit Oberammergau in a nonplay year you can still visit the theater, the Oberammergau Passionsspielhaus, and explore backstage. Tours of the huge building, with its 5,200-seat auditorium, and vast stage open to the mountain air, are given by guides who will demonstrate the remarkable acoustics by reciting Shakespearean soliloquies. *Passionsweise. Admission with guided tour: DM 4 adults, DM 2.50 children. Open daily 10–noon and 1:30–4:30. Festival information: Verkehrsbüro, Oberammergau, tel. 08822/4921.*

The preoccupation of villagers with the Passion Play doesn't totally push aside the wood-carvers. You can still find many at work even during play years. Oberammergau's shop windows are crammed with their creations. From June through September, a workshop is open free to the public at the Pilatushaus (Verlegergasse); potters and traditional painters can also be seen at work. You can even sign up for a week-long course in wood carving (classes are in German), at a cost of between DM 460 and DM 650, bed and breakfast included.

Historic examples of the skill of Oberammergau craftsmen are on view at the Heimatmuseum, which also includes one of Germany's finest collections of Christmas crèches, dating from the mid-18th century. *Dorfstr. 8. Admission: DM 2.50 adults, 50 pf children. Open May 10–Oct. 10, Tues.–Sat. afternoons only.*

Many of the exteriors of Oberammergau's homes, such as the 1784 Pilatushaus on Ludwig-Thoma-Strasse, are decorated with stunning frescoes. In summer, geraniums pour from every window box, and the village explodes with color.

Oberammergau's 18th-century **St. Peter and St. Paul church** is regarded as the finest work of Rococo architect Josef Schmuzer and has striking frescoes by Matthäus Günther.

Along the Alps

A range of attractions line the Alps between Garmisch and Berchtesgaden to the east. Many of them lie on the Deutsche Alpenstrasse, the German Alpine Road, the most scenic of the west–east Alpine routes. All can be visited on day trips from Garmisch-Partenkirchen and/or Berchtesgaden. This tour
6 goes first to **Mittenwald,** 20 kilometers (12 miles) southeast of Garmisch and snugly set beneath the towering peaks of the Karwendel range, which separates Bavaria from Austria.

Many regard Mittenwald as the most beautiful town in the Bavarian Alps. It is situated on the spine of an important north–south trade route dating from Roman times. In the Middle Ages, Mittenwald became the staging point for goods shipped up from Verona by way of the Brenner Pass and Innsbruck. From there, goods were transferred to rafts, which carried them down the Isar to Munich. As might be expected, Mittenwald grew rich on this traffic; its early prosperity is reflected to this day in the splendidly decorated houses with ornately carved gables and brilliantly painted facades that line its main street. In the mid-17th century, however, the international trade route was moved to a different pass, and the fortunes of Mittenwald went into swift decline.

Prosperity returned to Mittenwald in 1684, when a farmer's son, Matthias Klotz, returned from a 20-year stay in Cremona as a master violin maker. In Cremona, Klotz had studied with Nicolo Amati, who gave the violin its present form. Klotz brought his master's pioneering ideas back to Mittenwald. He taught the art to his brothers and friends; before long, half the men in the village were making violins. With the ideal woods for violins coming from neighboring forests, the trade flourished. Mittenwald soon became known as "The Village of a Thousand Violins," and stringed instruments—violins, violas, and cellos—made in Mittenwald were shipped around the world. Klotz's craft is still carried on in Mittenwald, and the town has a fascinating museum, the **Geigenbau und Heimatmuseum,** devoted to it. *Obermarkt 4, tel. 08823/8561. Admission: DM 2 adults, 50 pf children. Open weekdays 10–11:45 and 2–4:45, weekends and public holidays 10–noon.*

Ask the curator of the museum to direct you to the nearest of the several violin makers who are still active in Mittenwald. One of these craftsmen lives close to the museum and is happy to demonstrate the skills handed down to him by the successors of Klotz. The museum itself is next to Mittenwald's 18th-century **St. Peter and St. Paul church.** Check the back of the altar and you'll find Klotz's name, carved there by the violin maker himself. In front of the church is a monument to Klotz. The church itself, with its elaborate and joyful stucco work, which coils and curls its way around the interior, is one of the most important Rococo structures in Bavaria. Note its Gothic choirloft, incorporated into the church in the 18th century. The bold frescoes on its exterior are characteristic of *Lüftlmalerei,* an art form that reached its height in Mittenwald. You can see other fine examples of it on the facades of three famous houses: the Goethehaus, the Pilgerhaus, and the Pichlerhaus.

Time Out Just down the street from the museum and the church is the 17th-century **Hotel Post** (Obermarkt 9). Ask for their *Apfelkuchen* (apple cake) with coffee. If you need something more substantial, the lunch menu will give you the strength for an afternoon hike in the surrounding mountains.

The road north from Mittenwald, B-11, runs between the
7 8 **Walchensee** and the **Kochelsee,** two of the most popular Bavarian Alpine lakes. They are longtime favorites for summer getaways, and offer good swimming, water sports, and mountain walks (the 5,400-foot-high Benediktenwand, east of Kochel, is a challenge for mountaineers; the 5,300-foot-high Herzogstand, above the Walchensee, is more suitable for the less adventurous—the summit can be reached by chair lift, DM 10 round-trip). On the shores of the Kochelsee is one of the most extensive swimming lidos in Bavaria, with a collection of indoor and outdoor pools, water slides, and enough other games to keep a family amused the whole day long. *Trimini, Kochel. Admission: 3-hour ticket DM 8 adults, DM 4 children; all-day family ticket DM 25. Open daily 9–8:30.*

The attractive little lakeside town of Kochel boasts a local hero, the Schmied von Kochel or Blacksmith of Kochel. His fame stems from his role—and eventual death—in the 1705 peasants' uprising at Sendling, just outside Munich. You can see his statue in the town center.

Some 10 kilometers (6 miles) north of Kochel on B-11 lies the Benediktenwand, a mountain that takes its name from the ancient Benedictine monastery at its foot. Founded in the mid-8th
9 century, the monastery of **Benediktbeuern** is thought to be the oldest Benedictine institution north of the Alps. It was a flourishing cultural center in the Middle Ages; paradoxically, it also gave birth to one of the most profane musical works of those times, the *Carmina Burana.* The 1937 orchestration of the work by Bavarian composer Carl Orff is regularly performed in the monastery courtyard, the place where the original piece was first heard in the 12th century. The father of the Asam brothers, whose church-building and artistic decoration made them famous far beyond the borders of 18th-century Bavaria, painted the frescoes of the 17th-century monastery church. Cosmas Damian Asam, the eldest son, was born at Benediktbeuren.

Sixteen kilometers (10 miles) northeast of Benediktbeuren on
10 B-472 lies the old market town of **Bad Tölz.** Visit, if you can, on a Wednesday morning—market day—when the main street is lined with stalls that stretch to the Isar River, the dividing line between the Old and New towns. The New Town sprang up with the discovery in the mid-19th century of iodine-laden springs, which promoted Tölz into the ranks of German spas and allowed the locals to call their town *Bad* (bath or spa) Tölz. You can take the waters, enjoy a full course of health treatment at any of the many specially equipped hotels, or just splash around in Bad Tölz's large lido, the **Alpamare,** where one of its indoor pools is disguised as a South Sea beach, complete with surf. *Ludwigstr. 13. Admission: 3-hour ticket DM 19 (weekends DM 22) adults, DM 14 children. Open daily 8AM–9PM.*

Bad Tölz clings to its ancient customs and traditions more tightly than does any other Bavarian community. Folk costumes, for example, are not only preserved but are worn regularly. The town is also famous for its painted furniture, particularly farmhouse cupboards and chests. You can admire samples of painted furniture, as well as folk costumes and other historic crafts, in the **Heimatmuseum,** housed in the Altes Rathaus (Old Town Hall). *Marktpl. Admission free. Open Tues.–Sat. 10–noon and 2–4, Thurs. 10–noon and 2–6, Sun. 10–1.*

If you're in Bad Tölz on November 6, you'll witness one of the most colorful traditions of the Bavarian Alpine area: the Leonhardi-Ritt equestrian procession, which marks the feast day of St. Leonhard, the patron saint of horses. The procession ends north of the town at an 18th-century chapel on the Kalvarienberg, above the Isar River.

Drive 3 kilometers (2 miles) west of Bad Tölz along B-472 and you'll reach the base of the town's local mountain, the
11 **Blomberg.** It's an easy walk to the top, but you can also take a chair lift, which makes the journey in 12 minutes. If you're in a hurry to get down, rent a wheeled toboggan and try your luck on the dry run that snakes and curves its way down the mountain. It's great fun for kids, but it can be expensive unless you ration the number of runs. *Admission: DM 6 a ride adults, DM 4.50 children. Open Apr.–Oct., daily 9–5.*

About 17 kilometers (10 miles) east of Bad Tölz on B-472 is one
12 of the loveliest of the Alpine lakes, the **Tegernsee,** which is dotted with sails in summer and ice skaters in winter. Its wooded shores are lined with flowers in late spring; in fall, its trees provide a colorful contrast to the dark, snowcapped mountains. Elbowing each other for room on the banks of this heavenly stretch of water are expensive health clinics, hotels, and a former **Benedictine monastery.** The monastery, set in parklike grounds on the southeast shore of the lake, was founded in the 8th century. In the Middle Ages it was one of the most productive cultural centers in southern Germany; the musician and poet Minnesänger Walther von der Vogelweide (1170–1230) was one of its welcomed guests in the 12th century. Not so welcome were Hungarian invaders who had laid the monastery to waste in the 10th century. Fire caused further damage in following centuries, and secularization sealed the monastery's fate at the beginning of the 19th century, when a Bavarian king, Maximilian I, bought the surviving buildings for use as a summer retreat. Now the site houses a school, a church, a brewery, a restaurant, and a beer tavern.

Time Out Follow King Max's footsteps into the vaulted rooms in which busy waitresses bustle around where Benedictine monks once meditated. The monastery's dark beer is very strong; the food is basic Bavarian.

The late-Gothic monastery **church** was refurbished in Italian Baroque style in the 18th century. Opinions remain divided as to the success of the remodeling, which was the work of a little-known Italian architect named Antonio Riva. Whatever you think of his designs, you'll admire the frescoes by Hans Georg Asam, whose work you saw at the monastery of Benediktbeuren. If you like what you've seen, you may also want to visit
13 the parish church of **Gmund,** at the north end of the lake, and
14 the church of St. Laurentius at **Rottach-Egern,** on the south
shore. In both places you'll find further evidence of Asam's talents.

Rottach-Egern is a fashionable and upscale resort. Its classy shops, chic restaurants, and clutch of boutiques are as well-stocked and interesting as many in Munich. Also, its leading hotels are world-class. If you want to visit in style, Bachmair's, on the water's edge (Seestr. 47, tel. 08022/2720), is the place to stay; the flashy nightclub and casino at Bad Wiessee, on the west shore of the lake, can help you spend your money (*see* The Arts and Nightlife, below).

The mountain slopes above Bad Wiessee offer fine views, but
15 for the best vista of all climb the 5,700-foot **Wallberg,** at the
south end of the Tegernsee. It's a hard, four-hour hike, though anyone in good shape should be able to make it since it involves no rock climbing. If you don't wish to climb, ride the cable car, which makes the ascent in 15 minutes and costs DM 9 each way. At the summit there's a hotel, the Berggasthof Sonnenbichel (tel. 08022/81365), with a restaurant and sun terrace. Several mountain trails set out from the summit; in winter the skiing is excellent.

From the town of Tegernsee on the eastern shore you can follow an upland footpath 9 kilometers (6 miles) east to the next lake—
16 the quieter, less fashionable **Schliersee.** Or you can drive the 27
kilometers (18 miles) there. The difference between the two lakes is made clear in the names local people have long given them: the Tegernsee is called the Herrensee (or Master's Lake), while the Schliersee is known as the Bauernsee (or Peasant's Lake). There are fine walking and ski trails on the mountain slopes that ring the Schliersee.

Like the Tegernsee, the Schliersee was the site of a monastery, built in the 8th century by a group of noblemen. It subsequently became a choral academy, which was eventually moved to Munich. Today only the restored 17th-century **abbey church** recalls this piece of the Schliersee's history. The church has some fine frescoes and stucco work by Johann Baptist Zimmermann.

A spectacular 10-kilometer (6-mile) drive south from Schlier-
17 see takes you around hairpin bends to the tiny **Spitzingsee,** cra-
dled 3,500 feet up between the Taubenstein, Rosskopf, and Stumpfling peaks. The walking in this area is breathtaking in every sense. There's skiing, too.

18 **Bayrischzell,** 10 kilometers (6 miles) east, is the next stop. To
reach it, you pass one of the highest mountains of the area, the
19 6,000-foot **Wendelstein.** At its summit is a tiny stone-and-slate-

roof chapel that's much in demand as an off-beat place to marry. The cross above the entrance was carried up the mountain by Max Kleiber, who designed the 19th-century church. Today there are two easier ways up: a cable car (which sets out from beside the train station at Osterhofen and costs DM 22 round-trip for adults, with reductions for families) and a historic old cog railway (catch it at Brannenburg, on the north side of the mountain).

While the slopes of the Wendelstein attract expert skiers, those above Bayrischzell beckon the rest. The town is in an attractive family resort area, where many a Bavarian first learns to ski. The wide-open slopes of the Sudelfeld Mountain are ideal for those who enjoy undemanding skiing; in the summer and fall they offer innumerable upland walking trails.

A mile or two east of Bayrischzell on the Sudelfeld Road is the
20 **Tatzelwurm** gorge and waterfall, named after a winged dragon that supposedly inhabits these parts. This can be an eerie place to drive through at dusk. From the gorge, the road drops sharply to the valley of the Inn River and leads to another busy ski resort, Oberaudorf.

The Inn River valley, one of Europe's most ancient trade routes, carries the most important road link between Germany and Italy. The wide, green Inn flows rapidly here, and in the
21 parish church of St. Bartholomew at **Rossholzen,** 16 kilometers (10 miles) north of Oberaudorf, you can see memorials to the local people who have lost their lives in its chilly waters. The church has a fine late-Gothic altar.

22 Rossholzen is 10 kilometers (6 miles) south of **Rosenheim,** a medieval market town that has kept much of its character despite the onslaught of industrial development. The arcaded streets of low-eaved houses are characteristic of Inn valley towns.

Rosenheim is a good center from which to explore the Chiemgau region, an area of mountainous lakes dominated by the wide Chiemsee, Bavaria's largest stretch of water. Between Rosenheim and the Chiemsee are a number of smaller lakes, set amid rich, rolling farmland and largely forgotten by the crowds
23 who make for the nearby Alps. The **Chiemsee,** which has long been popular, retains something of the quiet charm and strange melancholy that attracted Ludwig II in the last century. It was here on one of three islands that he built the most sumptuous of
24 his palaces, **Schloss Herrenchiemsee.** It was based on Louis XIV's great palace at Versailles. But this was the result of more than simple admiration of Versailles on Ludwig's part: With his name being the German for Louis, he was keen to establish that he, too, possessed the absolute authority of his namesake, the Sun King. As with most of Ludwig's projects, the building was never completed, and Ludwig was never able to stay in its state rooms. Nonetheless, what remains is impressive—and ostentatious. There are regular ferries out to the island from Stock, on the shore. If you want to make the journey in style, take the 100-year-old steam train—which glories in the name of Feuriger Elias, or Fiery Elias—from the neighboring town of Prien to Stock. A horse-drawn carriage takes you to the palace itself. The single most spectacular attraction in the palace is the Hall of Mirrors, a dazzling gallery (modeled on that at Versailles) where candle-lit concerts are held in the

summer. Also of interest are the ornate bedroom Ludwig planned and the stately formal gardens. The south wing houses a museum containing Ludwig's christening robe and death mask, as well as other artifacts of his life. *Palace and museum admission: DM 5 adults, DM 2.50 children. Open Apr.–Sept., daily 9–5; Oct.–Mar., daily 10–4. Guided tours offered May–Sept.*

25 The smaller **Fraueninsel** (Ladies' Island) is a charming retreat. A Benedictine convent founded here 1,200 years ago now serves as a school. One of its earliest abbesses, Irmengard, daughter of King Ludwig der Deutscher, died here in the 9th century. Her grave was discovered in 1961. In the same year, early frescoes in the convent chapel were brought to light.

Just south of the Chiemsee, in a small, flat valley of the Chi-
26 emgauer Alps, is the enchanting village of **Aschau,** site of
Schloss Hohenaschau, one of the few medieval castles in southern Germany to have been restored in the 17th century in Baroque style. The renovation gave its stately rooms a new elegance. Chamber-music concerts are presented regularly in the Rittersaal (Knights Hall) during the summer. *Tel. 08052/392. Admission: DM 3 adults, children free. Open May–Sept., Tues. and Fri. 9–5.*

At Aschau you'll join the most scenic section of the Alpine Road, route B-305. It snakes through a series of towns and villages before ending at the Austrian border, just beyond Berchtesgaden. Rosenheim, Bad Reichenhall, and Berchtesgaden—all with good road connections to the rest of Germany—are ideal centers from which to explore this part of the Alps.

From Aschau the Alpine Road heads into the mountains, passing through a string of villages—Bernau, Rottau, Grassau,
Marquartstein, and Oberwössen—pretty enough to make you
27 want to linger. In summer, the farmhouses of **Rottau** virtually
disappear behind facades of flowers, which have won the village
28 several awards. The houses of **Grassau** shrink beside the bulk of
the 15th-century church of the Ascension, worth visiting for its rich 17th-century stucco work. The 11th-century castle above Marquartstein is in private hands and can't be visited, so press on to the villages of Unter-, Hinter-, and Oberwössen.

Time Out The **Hotel zur Post** at Unterwössen (Hauptstr. 51, tel. 08641/8736) beckons the traveler at any time of day with strong coffee, delicious homemade pastries, locally brewed beer, and Bavarian specialties. Closed Mon.

Eight kilometers (5 miles) farther, not much more than a snowball's throw from the Tyrolean border, lies the mountain resort
29 of **Reit im Winkl,** famous for the clarity of its light in summer
and the depth of its snowfalls in winter. The Winklmoosalm Mountain, towering above Reit im Winkl, can be reached by bus or chair lift and is a popular ski area in winter and a great place for bracing upland walks in summer and fall.

The next stretch of the Alpine Road takes you past three shimmering mountain lakes—the Weitsee, the Mittersee, and the
30 Lödensee—before dropping down to busy **Ruhpolding,** once a
quiet Alpine village and now a leading resort. This is where the Bavarian tourist boom began back in the '30s. Back then, tourists were welcomed at the train station by a brass band. The

welcome isn't quite so extravagant these days, but it's still warm. In the 16th century, the Bavarian rulers journeyed out to Ruhpolding to hunt, and the Renaissance-style hunting lodge of Prince Wilhelm V still stands (it's now used as the offices of the local forestry service). The hillside 18th-century **Pfarrkirche St. Georg** (parish church of St. George) is one of the finest churches in the Bavarian Alps. In one of its side altars stands a rare 13th-century carved Madonna, the Ruhpoldinger Madonna. Note also the atmospheric crypt chapel in the quiet churchyard.

East of Ruhpolding lies a small portion of Bavaria that fits like a pocket into the fabric of Austrian territory that surrounds it on three sides. This southeast corner of Germany is dominated by two resorts of international fame: Bad Reichenhall and
31 Berchtesgaden. Although Berchtesgaden is more famous, **Bad Reichenhall** is older and claims a more interesting history, thanks to the saline springs that made the town rich. The springs, which form Europe's largest saline source, were first tapped in pre-Christian times; the salt they provided in the Middle Ages supported the economies of cities as far away as Munich and Passau. In the early 19th century King Ludwig I built an elaborate salt works and spa house here—the **Alte Saline** and **Quellenhaus**—in vaulted, pseudomedieval style. Their pump installations are astonishing examples of 19th-century engineering. *Admission: DM 3 adults, DM 1.50 children. Open daily 10–11:30 and 2–4.*

Bad Reichenhall even possesses a 19th-century "saline" chapel, part of the spa's facilities and built in exotic Byzantine style at the behest of Ludwig I. Salt is so much a part of the town that you can practically taste it in the air. Not surprisingly, most of the more expensive hotels offer special spa treatments based on the health-giving properties of the saline springs. The waters can also be taken in the attractive spa gardens throughout the year (open Mon.–Sat. 8–12:15 and 3–5, Sun., and holidays 10–12:15). Bad Reichenhall's own symphony orchestra performs five days a week during the summer season and four days a week in winter. Like most resorts in the area, this one also has a casino. (*See* The Arts and Nightlife, below.)

It's ironic that Bad Reichenhall, which flourishes on the riches of its underground springs, has a 12th-century basilica dedicated to **St. Zeno,** patron saint of those imperiled by floods and the dangers of the deep. Much of this ancient church was remodeled in the 16th and 17th centuries, but some of the original cloisters remain.

32 **Berchtesgaden,** 18 kilometers (11 miles) south of Bad Reichenhall, is an ancient market town set in the noblest section of the Bavarian Alps. While as a high-altitude ski station it may not have quite the charm or cachet of Garmisch-Partenkirchen, in summer it serves as one of the region's most popular (and crowded) resorts, with top-rated attractions in a heavenly setting.

Berchtesgaden has an image problem: Its name is indelibly linked to that of Adolf Hitler—it was "Der Führer's" favorite mountain retreat. High on the slopes of Obersalzberg he built a luxurious headquarters hideaway, where many top-level Nazi staff meetings were held during World War II.

But Berchtesgaden had been a resort long before Hitler's time. Members of the ruling Wittelsbach dynasty started coming here in 1810. Their ornate palace stands today and is one of the town's major attractions, along with the former Nazi complex and a working salt mine.

Salt—or "white gold," as it was known in medieval times—was the basis of Berchtesgaden's wealth. In the 12th century Emperor Barbarossa gave mining rights to a Benedictine abbey that had been founded here a century earlier. The abbey was secularized early in the 19th century, when it was taken over by the Wittelsbach rulers. The last royal resident, Crown Prince Rupprecht, who died here in 1955, furnished it with rare family treasures that now form the basis of a permanent collection.

Königliches Schloss Berchtesgaden now serves as a museum. Fine Renaissance rooms provide the principal exhibition spaces for the prince's collection of sacred art, which is particularly rich in wood sculptures by such great late-Gothic artists as Tilman Riemanschneider and Veit Stoss. You can also visit the abbey's original, cavernous 13th-century dormitory and cool cloisters, which still convey something of the quiet and orderly life led by medieval monks. *Admission: DM 5 adults, DM 2.50 children under 16. Open Easter–Sept., Sun.–Fri. 10–1 and 2–5; Oct.–Easter, Mon.–Fri. 10–1 and 2–5. No admission after 4 PM, when last tour starts.*

The skill of wood carving in Berchtesgaden dates back to long before the time when Oberammergau established itself as the premier wood-carving center of the Alps. Examples of Berchtesgaden wood carvings and other local crafts are on display at one of the most interesting museums of its kind in the Alps, the Heimatmuseum. *Schroffenbergerallee 6. Admission: DM 3 adults, DM 1 children. Open Mon.–Fri. 9–12 and 2–5, Sat. 9–1; guided tours 10 AM and 3 PM Mon.–Fri. only.*

For many travelers, the pièce de résistance of a Berchtesgaden stay might well be a visit to its salt mine, the **Salzbergwerk.** In the days when the mine was owned by Berchtesgaden's princely rulers, only selected guests were allowed to see how the source of the city's wealth was won from the earth. Today DM 12.50 will buy anyone a tour of the installation. Dressed in traditional miner's clothing, visitors sit astride a miniature train that transports them nearly half a mile into the mountain to an enormous chamber where the salt is mined. A couple of rides down wooden chutes used by the miners to get from one level to another, and a boat ride on an underground saline lake the size of a football field are included in the 1½-hour tour. *1 mi from Berchtesgaden on the B–305 Salzburg Rd. Admission: DM 13.50 adults, DM 7 children under 11. Open May–mid-Oct., daily 8:30–5; mid-Oct.–Apr., Mon.–Sat. 12:30–3:30.*

For an experience of a different kind, in summer a bus takes
33 visitors up to **Obersalzberg,** site of Hitler's luxurious mountain retreat on the north slope of the Hoher Goll. (Most of the Nazi complex was destroyed in 1945, as was Hitler's chalet; only a few basement walls remain.) The hairpin bends of Germany's highest road lead to the base of the 6,000-foot peak on which sat the so-called Adlerhorst or Eagle's Nest, the **Kehlsteinhaus.** Hitler had the road built in 1937–39. It climbs more than 2,000 feet in less than 4 miles and comes to an end at a lot that clings

to the mountain about 500 feet below the Kehlsteinhaus. A tunnel in the mountain brings you to an elevator that whisks you up to the Kehlsteinhaus—and what appears to be the top of the world. There are refreshment rooms and a restaurant where you can steel yourself for the giddy descent to Berchtesgaden. The round-trip (Berchtesgaden post office to Eagle's Nest and back) costs DM 24 per person (there is no family ticket per se, though each family group is only required to pay fares for two children). By car you can travel only as far as the Obersalzberg bus station. The return fare from there is DM 18. Open mid-May–mid-Oct.

The view from the Kehlsteinhaus is stunning: The jagged Watzmann slumbers above Berchtesgaden and, when the light and the mood are right, it's quite possible to believe the atavistic myth that surrounds the mountain. According to an ancient saga, the Watzmann range of nine distinct peaks is actually a royal family turned to stone by an angry god; their blood forms the two mountain lakes, the Obersee and the Königsee.

Both lakes lie within the Berchtesgaden National Park, 210 square kilometers (82 square miles) of wild mountain country where flora and fauna have been left to develop as nature intended. The park is modeled on the United States' Yellowstone National Park; no roads penetrate the area, and even the mountain paths are difficult to follow. The park administration organizes guided tours of the area from June till September (contact the Nationale Parkverwaltung, Doktorberg 6, 8240 Berchtesgaden, tel. 08652/61068).

One less strenuous way into the National Park is by boat. A
fleet of 21 excursion boats, electrically driven so that no noise
34 disturbs the peace of the lake, operates on the **Königsee.** Only
the skipper of the boat is allowed to shatter the silence with a
trumpet fanfare to demonstrate the lake's remarkable echo.
The notes from the trumpet bounce back and forth from the almost vertical cliffs that plunge into the dark, green water. A cross on a rocky promontory marks the spot where a boatload of pilgrims hit the cliffs 100 years ago and sank. The voyagers, most of whom drowned, were on their way to the tiny, twin-towered Baroque chapel of St. Bartholomä, built in the 17th century on a peninsula where an early Gothic church once stood. The princely rulers of Berchtesgaden built a hunting lodge at the side of the chapel; its rooms now serve as a tavern and a restaurant.

35 Another lake, the much smaller **Obersee,** can be reached by a 15-minute walk from the second stop on the boat tour. The Obersee rivals the larger lake for sheer beauty. Its backdrop of jagged mountains and precipitous cliffs is broken by a waterfall, the Rothbachfall, that plunges more than 1,000 feet to the valley floor. *Boat service on the Königsee runs year-round (except when the lake freezes over). Round-trips can be interrupted at St. Bartholomä and Salletalm, the landing stage for the Obersee. The round-trip lasts almost 2 hours, without stops, and costs DM 17.50 per person (no reductions for children).*

What to See and Do with Children

If it's winter, **rent skis or a sled** from any resort sports shop and make for the slopes. Bayerischzell, Lengries, Neuhaus am

Schliersee, and Oberammergau have excellent facilities for young beginners. Wishing you could take a **sleigh ride** through the snow? Call Harold Zischk at Bad Wiessee (tel. 08022/81096). His two-hour tour high above the Tegernsee costs DM 27 for adults and DM 15 for children; in Berchtesgaden, call 08651/3453.

If it's summer, head for any of the lakes or, if the water's not warm enough for **swimming,** try one of the numerous lidos. The finest are at Garmisch, Oberammergau, Kochel, Bad Tölz, and Penzberg. Also in summer, the **Blomberg Mountain** outside Bad Tölz has one of Europe's longest dry toboggan runs. You hurtle at great speed for nearly a mile down the mountain on a wheeled toboggan.

In winter, children can accompany foresters to **feed deer** at several points in the Alps. For Garmisch, tel. 08821/2038 or 08821/2135; Oberammergau, tel. 08822/515 or 08824/422; Schliersee, tel. 08026/356 or 08026/392; Ruhpolding, tel. 08663/1227.

A 90-year-old **steam train** (tel. 08022/75438), with original cars, puffs along a 10-mile stretch of private track in and out of Tegernsee. *Full round-trip fare: DM 8.50 adults, DM 4.50 children.*

For the very young, there's a charming **fairy-tale park** (Märchenwald) and big adventure playground at Wolfratshausen, about 20 kilometers (12 miles) north of Bad Tölz on the B-11. Mechanical tableaux tell 24 favorite fairy tales in German and English. *Admission: DM 5 adults, DM 4 children. Open daily 9–5.*

Off the Beaten Track

On weekends year-round, Bavarian Alps resorts can be uncomfortably crowded. But there are still valleys and peaks where you can find solitude. Avoid anyplace with a cable car or funicular railway. Travel by water whenever possible. Board a boat at **Königsee,** for instance, and glide silently between the cliffs that plunge into the lake; then leave your fellow passengers behind at one of the two stopping points and strike out into **Berchtesgaden National Park.** No roads penetrate it, and the few hiking trails are refreshingly uncrowded. The Königsee itself is crowded at the resort end, but there are other lakes in the region where you can get away from it all. Try the **Wagingersee,** Germany's warmest lake.

Looking to trace your German roots? The **Deutsches Wappenmuseum** (Jennerbahnstr. 30, Königsee) has 4,000 German coats of arms and heraldic emblems, and can assist in ancestor tracing. There are no fixed opening hours, so call (tel. 08652/61910) to arrange an appointment.

In the village of Hasslberg near Ruhpolding you can visit a 300-year-old **bell foundry,** now a fascinating museum of the ancient craft of the foundryman and blacksmith. *Admission: DM 4.50 adults, DM 2 children. Open Mon.–Sat. 10–noon and 2–4.*

Shopping

Berchtesgaden and Oberammergau have centuries-old **woodcarving** traditions. In both towns and in surrounding villages you'll find shops crammed with the work of local craftsmen. In Berchtesgaden, there's a central selling point at **Schloss Adelsheim** (Schroffenbergallee). Berchtesgaden is famous for its *Spanschachtel*, delicate, finely constructed wood boxes made to contain everything from pins and needles to top hats. You'll find modern versions in every souvenir shop and, if you're lucky, you might even come across a 100-year-old example in one of the town's antiques shops. In Oberammergau, you can buy wood carvings directly from craftsmen who demonstrate their skills from April to June and September to November in a "living workshop" at the **Pilatushaus** (Verlegergasse).

Some of the **flowers** and **herbs** that grow in the Bavarian Alps have healing properties, and some long-established "apothecaries" put together herbal mixtures that are redolent of the elixir of life. **Josef Mack KG** (Innsbruckerstr. 37, Bad Reichenhall) has been in this business since 1856; **Dricoolo KG** (Ludwigstr. 27, Bad Reichenhall) is another established herb vendor. In Ruhpolding, there's an herb garden at **Gasthaus Jürgant** (Branderstr. 23a), where visitors can pick the basic ingredients of the preparations on sale, which include a potent herbal liqueur.

It's not the kind of gift every visitor wants to take home, but just in case you'd like a violin, cello, or even a double bass from a town that has been making these instruments for centuries—Mittenwald—the place to try is **Walther Georg** (Isarauenstr. 17). For traditional Bavarian costumes—dirndls, embroidered shirts and blouses, and lederhosen—try the **Trachtenstub'n** (Obermarkt 35, Mittenwald) or any of the **Dollinger** shops throughout southern Bavaria. In Ruhpolding the **Handweberei Fegg** (Seehauserstr. 33) turns out Bavarian-style tablecloths and furniture coverings directly from the loom.

Sports and Fitness

Bicycling Most local rail stations rent bikes for about DM 10 a day (DM 6 if you have a valid train ticket). Many local sports shops also have bikes for rent: **Sport Eich** (Fendtgasse 5, Oberammergau, tel. 08822/6148) and **Sport Bittner** (Andreas-Fendt-Ring 1, Bischofswiesen, near Berchtesgaden, tel. 08652/7511) are two. Rates are around DM 20 per day and up to DM 85 per week. Mountain bike tours are arranged from Berchtesgaden. Call the **Outdoor Club** (Bahnhofstr. 11, tel. 08652/66066). The Chiemsee area is a popular (and flat) area for cycling. For details of tours lasting from three hours to three days, contact Chieming Tourist Office, 8224 Chieming, tel. 08664/245.

Bowling Many resort hotels have their own bowling alleys (usually for English-style skittles; rarely tenpin). The **Hotel Bayerischer Hof** in Bad Reichenhall (tel. 08651/6090) organizes skittle weeks from March to June. The DM 580 cost includes half-pension, unlimited skittling, and two competitions with prizes.

Gliding See the Alps from above. If hang gliding's your thing, Oberammergau's your place (tel. 08822/520 or 08822/4470). For plane gliding, try the Alpine Gliding School in Unterwössen (tel. 08641/8205).

Golf There are American-run golf courses at **Gmund,** on the Tegernsee, and at **Obersalzberg** (tel. 08652/2100) in Berchtesgaden. The latter has nine holes, set 3,300 feet up, and a distracting view of the Watzmann range. It is open for play from May through October. A spectacular 18-hole course is located at **Bad Wiessee,** high above the Tegernsee (tel. 08022/8769).

Hiking The Bavarian Alps are veined with networks of marked paths. You can set off from just about any resort and find a number of scenic routes to follow. Mountain guides are available for the Berchtesgaden area; for details, call Roland Bannert (tel. 08652/7615). Oberammergau is an ideal starting point for hiking tours into the surrounding mountains. There are a variety of paths to choose from. Each year, on August 24, visitors can take part in an organized Mountain Hiking Day *(Gibirgswandertag)* called "In King Ludwig's Footsteps" in memory of Bavaria's "Dream King." At dusk, huge bonfires are set ablaze on surrounding mountains.

Mountain Climbing The Zugspitze climbing school in Garmisch-Partenkirchen (tel. 08824/344) organizes courses in rock climbing, ski touring, and deep-snow skiing, and provides guides for walking, skiing, or climbing tours of one day or longer. For information on this service in the Berchtesgaden area, call 08652/5371 or 08652/66066.

Skiing The Bavarian Alps are Germany's winter playground. All you have to do is choose your resort and everything is laid out: ski rentals, ski school, lifts, and transportation. Vacations can be enjoyed for as little as DM 300. Contact local tourist offices for details. If you're a Nordic skier, match your speed against Bavaria's best in Oberammergau's annual "King Ludwig Race," held the first weekend in February. Oberammergau also hosts events over distances of 6 kilometers (4 miles) and 15 kilometers (9 miles) every Wednesday during the winter season.

Swimming The lakes are warm enough in summer for swimming, often topping 70F, but Bavaria has fine beach resorts for year-round fun in the water. The best are in Garmisch-Partenkirchen, Oberammergau, Kochel, Penzberg, and Bad Tölz (*see* Along the Alps in Exploring the Alps, above).

Water Sports **Sailing** schools can be found everywhere on Bavaria's lakes. **Captain Glas** (tel. 08157/8100) at Possenhofen on the west shore of the Starnbergersee has one of the largest fleets and can fix you up with anything from a small sailboat to a cabin cruiser. Surfboards can be hired for DM 15 an hour from the boat yard at **Seeshaupt** at the south end of the lake, and for a similar fee at other lakes, especially in Urfeld, at the northern end of the Walchensee.

Dining and Lodging

Dining

Specialties here are much the same as in the rest of Bavaria, but local dishes to try are *Forelle* (trout), *Lachsforelle,* and

Bachsaibing (freshwater salmon trout). If you visit Chiemsee or Walchensee, look out for *Renke*, a meaty white lake fish.

Highly recommended restaurants are indicated by a star ★.

Category	Cost*
Very Expensive	over DM 90
Expensive	DM 55–DM 90
Moderate	DM 35–DM 55
Inexpensive	under DM 35

**per person for a three-course meal, including service but not drinks*

Lodging

With few exceptions, all hotels and Gasthäuser in the Bavarian Alps and lower Alpine regions are traditionally styled, low-roofed chalets with wood balconies and multicolored masses of flowers in summer. Standards are high, even in simpler lodgings. The choice is wide—from superluxurious, world-class hotels to basic Gasthofs. Garmisch-Partenkirchen and Berchtesgaden are bountifully supplied with accommodations in all price ranges. Check out the special seven-day packages. Away from the main tourist centers you may sometimes be able to find bed-and-breakfast lodgings for under DM 20 per person. As a general rule, the farther from the popular Alpine resorts you stay, the lower the rates will be.

Highly recommended hotels are indicated by a star ★.

Category	Cost*
Very Expensive	over DM 180
Expensive	DM 120–DM 180
Moderate	DM 80–DM 120
Inexpensive	under DM 80

**All prices are for two people in a double room, including tax and service charge.*

Bad Reichenhall
Lodging

Steigenberger-Hotel Axelmannstein. Situated in a spacious, manicured park in the town center, this hotel with the air of a Bavarian palace commands prices encountered in top hotels in the most expensive cities in Germany. In exchange, you'll reside in luxurious comfort, in rooms ranging in style from Bavarian rustic to Laura Ashley demure. *Sakzburgerstr. 2, tel. 08651/4001. 143 rooms with bath. Facilities: indoor pool, sauna, fitness room, tennis court, playroom with child-care service, beauty salon, 2 restaurants, bar. AE, DC, MC, V. Very Expensive.*

Hotel Bayerischer Hof. Centrally located (a short walk from the train station), this is a quiet, modern hotel with style and the expected Alpine atmosphere. *Bahnhofpl. 14, tel. 08651/6090. 64 rooms with bath or shower. Facilities: indoor pool, sauna, solarium, hairdresser, resident doctor, bowling alley, 3 res-*

taurants, nightclub. AE, DC, MC, V. Closed Jan. 5–Feb. 8. Expensive.

Alpenhotel Fuchs. Beautifully located outside the town amid Alpine meadows, with the mountain range at its back, the family-run Fuchs assures guests they can sit out on its southern terrace and soak up the sun even in midwinter. Inside, they can soak up the Bavarian style of the public rooms. *Nonn 50, tel. 08651/61048 or 08651/61049. 37 rooms, 35 with bath. Facilities: fitness room, children's playroom, horseback riding, restaurant. AE, DC, MC, V. Closed Nov. 1–Dec. 22. Moderate.*

Bad Tölz
Lodging
★

Hotel Jodquellenhof. *Jodquellen* are the iodine springs that have made Bad Tölz wealthy. You can take advantage of these revitalizing waters at this luxurious spa hotel, where the emphasis is on fitness. The imposing 19th-century building adjoining the Alpamare lido contains comfortable and stylish rooms. *Ludwigstr. 15, tel. 08041/5090. 81 rooms with bath. Facilities: outdoor pool, indoor thermal baths, sauna, solarium, restaurant. AE, DC, MC, V. Very Expensive.*

Hotel Am Wald. This modern but traditional lodging is set in its own spacious grounds in the "new" half of town, a 10-minute stroll from Bad Tölz's ancient quarter. Rooms are decorated and furnished country style. *Austr. 39, tel. 08041/9014. 20 rooms with bath. Facilities: restaurant, indoor pool, fitness room, sauna, solarium. AE, DC, MC, V. Closed Nov. 7–Dec. 20. Moderate.*

Bad Wiessee
Dining
★

Freihaus Brenner. Proprietor Josef Brenner has brought a taste of nouvelle cuisine to the shores of the Tegernsee, where his attractive restaurant sits, commanding fine views. Try any of his suggested dishes—they range from wild rabbit in elderberry sauce to fresh lake fish. *Freihausstr. 4, tel. 08022/82004. Reservations advised. Jacket and tie optional. MC. Moderate.*

Lodging

Hotel Rex. Standing high above the Tegernsee and backed by mountains, the Hotel Rex is ideal for those who value solitude and solid comfort. Fine Bavarian antiques give the hotel a special flair. *Münchnerstr. 25, tel. 08022/82091. 56 rooms and 2 suites with bath or shower. Facilities: solarium, restaurant (for guests only). No credit cards. Closed Nov. 1–Apr. 15. Expensive.*

Berchtesgaden
Dining
★

Hotel-Restaurant Geiger. Dine at this paneled, Bavarian-style restaurant under the baleful eyes of hunting trophies in the cozy Bauernstube, or enjoy the more elegant, antique-furnished Biedermeier Salon. The Geiger, a 15-minute bus ride from the center of town, specializes in mountain trout and local game. *Berchtesgadenerstr. 103, Stanggass, tel. 08652/5055. Reservations advised. Jacket and tie optional. AE, DC, V. Closed Nov. 15–Dec. 15. Expensive.*

Alpenhotel Denninglehen. Nonsmokers will appreciate the special dining room set aside just for them in this mountain hotel's restaurant. The restaurant is 3,000 feet up in the resort area of Oberau, just outside Berchtesgaden, and its terrace offers magnificent views. *Am Priesterstein 7, 8240 Berchtesgaden-Oberau, tel. 08652/5085. Reservations advised. Dress: informal. MC. Closed Dec. 1–20. Moderate.*

Hotel Post. This is a centrally located and solidly reliable hostelry with a well-presented international menu. If fish from the nearby Königssee is offered, order it. In summer you can eat in the beer garden. The Casablanca bar is ideal for a premeal aperitif. *Maximilianstr. 2, tel. 08652/5067. Reservations advised. Jacket and tie optional. AE, DC, MC, V. Moderate.*

Fischer. You can pop into this farmhouse-style eatery for *Apfelstrudel* and coffee or for something more substantial from a frequently changing international and local menu. It's a short walk across the bridge from the railway station. *Königsseerstr. 51, tel. 08652/4044. Reservations advised in July and August. Dress: informal. AE. Closed Nov. 1–Dec. 18. Inexpensive.*

Lodging

Hotel Geiger. Early Victorian antiques and Bavarian peasant pieces mix well in the luxurious interior of this former farmhouse set in spacious grounds on the outskirts of town. *Stanggass, tel. 08652/5055. 52 rooms with bath. Facilities: indoor and outdoor pools, sauna, solarium, fitness room, restaurant. AE, DC, V. Closed Nov. 15–Dec. 15. Very Expensive.*

Stoll's Hotel Alpina. Set above the Königssee in the delightful little village of Schönau, the Alpina offers rural solitude and easy access to Berchtesgaden. Families are catered to: There are special family-size apartments and a playroom. *Ulmenweg 14, tel. 08652/5091. 48 rooms with bath. Facilities: indoor and outdoor pools, sauna, solarium, sun terrace, resident doctor, restaurant. AE, DC, MC, V. Closed Nov. 4–Dec. 17. Expensive.*

★ **Vier Jahreszeiten Hotel.** This centrally located, comfortably solid old hotel has been owned by the same family since 1876. Antique furniture and an understated Bavarian accent make it a favorite. *Maximilianstr. 20, tel. 08652/5026. 62 rooms and 3 apartments with bath or shower. Facilities: indoor pool, sauna, solarium, fitness room, restaurant. AE, DC, MC, V. Expensive.*

Hotel Grünberger. This is an older-style residence whose cozy rooms have farmhouse-style furnishings and some original antiques. Only a few strides from the train station in the town center, the Grünberger overlooks the River Ache, beside which you can relax on a private sun terrace. *Hansererweg 1, tel. 08652/4560. 65 rooms with bath. Facilities: restaurant. No credit cards. Moderate.*

Hotel Krone. It may not be that pretty to look at, but the Krone has spectacular views of the town and the Alps from all of its balconied rooms. (When you book, make sure you ask for a room with a balcony.) This modern, family-run lodging is a 10-minute walk from the town center. *Am Rad 5, tel. 08652/62051. 22 rooms with bath. Facilities: restaurant, sun terrace, bar. No credit cards. Moderate.*

Hotel Watzmann. The USAAF Director of Operations in Berchtesgaden awarded the Hotel Watzmann a special certificate of appreciation for its hospitality to American servicemen. They, in turn, appreciate its cozy Bavarian style and good restaurant. *Franziskanerpl., tel. 08652/2055. 37 rooms, half with shower. Facilities: heated garden-terrace, restaurant. AE, MC, V. Closed Nov. 3–Dec. 18. Inexpensive.*

Hotel zum Türken. The 10-minute journey from Berchtesgaden is worth it for the view. Confiscated by the Nazis, it's located at the foot of the road up to Hitler's mountaintop retreat. Remains of their wartime bunkers adjoin the hotel. *8240 Obersalzberg-Berchtesgaden, tel. 08652/2428. 17 rooms, half with bath or shower. AE, DC, MC, V. Closed Nov. 1–Dec. 20. Inexpensive.*

Bergen *Lodging* ★ **Hotel Säulner Hof.** A cheery wood-burning fire in the open fireplace, a cozy bar, and the enveloping comfort of thick rugs and brightly painted Bavarian antiques welcome the winter visitor to the Säulner Hof. In summer it also has attractions, not least of which is its ample terrace, with views of the mountains. *Säulnerweg 1, tel. 08662/8655. 15 rooms with bath or shower. Facilities: restaurant, bar. MC. Closed Nov. and most of Jan. Inexpensive.*

Chiemsee *Lodging* **Pension Jägerhof.** This comfortable, well-appointed pension is only 100 yards from the Chiemsee, in the village of Gstadt. *Breitbrunnerstr. 5, tel. 08054/242. 30 rooms, 11 with bath or shower. Facilities: sauna, solarium, fitness room. AE, DC, MC, V. Closed Nov. 1–Easter. Moderate.*

Unterwirt zu Chieming. You can catch the boat to the islands of the Chiemsee right outside this small pension in the village of Chieming. It's located practically on the water's edge. *Hauptstr. 32, tel. 08664/551. 20 rooms, 8 with bath. No credit cards. Closed Mon., Tues., and first 3 weeks of Nov. Inexpensive.*

Ettal *Dining* **Bayerische Stube.** Fresh mountain trout—*Forelle*—is the specialty of the Hotel Benediktenhof's traditional Bavarian restaurant. Try the venison when it's in season. *Zieglerstr. 1, tel. 08822/4637. Reservations advised. Dress: informal. No credit cards. Closed Nov. 1–Dec. 22. Moderate.*

★ **Hotel Ludwig der Bayer.** If the hotel's Bräustuberl is full, try its neighboring Klosterstube. There should be a pillared, paneled corner where you can enjoy a plate of pork knuckle, Bavarian dumplings, and a mug of monastery brewed beer. Wash it down with the locally distilled liqueur. *Kaiser Ludwig Pl. 10, tel. 08822/6601. Reservations advised. Dress: informal. No credit cards. Closed Nov. 9–Dec. 22. Moderate.*

Poststüberl, Hotel Zur Post. Fish and game are the specialties in this stylish country inn. If you miss lunch, and it's too early for dinner, try the homemade cakes. Few meals cost more than DM 25, and the monastery beer is particularly tasty. *Kaiser Ludwig Pl. 18, tel. 08822/596. No reservations. Dress: informal. AE, DC, MC, V. Closed Nov. 20–Dec. 20. Inexpensive.*

Lodging **Benediktenhof.** The open beams and colorfully painted walls are part of this former farmstead's 250-year history. Bedrooms are furnished in Bavarian Baroque or peasant style, with brightly decorated cupboards and bedsteads. *Zieglerstr. 1, tel. 08822/4637. 16 rooms and 1 apartment with bath or shower. Facilities: sun terrace, restaurant. No credit cards. Closed Nov. 1–Dec. 22. Moderate.*

★ **Hotel Ludwig der Bayer.** This large, comfortable hotel is run by the Benedictine order from the monastery across the road. There's nothing monastic about the furnishings, however, except for the carved religious figures that share the space with some fine antiques. *Kaiser Ludwig Pl. 10, tel. 08822/6601. 65 rooms with bath or shower. Facilities: indoor pool, sauna, solarium, tennis court, bowling alleys, sun terrace, fitness room, bike rental, restaurant. No credit cards. Moderate.*

Hotel-Gasthof Zur Post. The Post is a child-friendly, old-world Gasthof located in the center of Ettal. *Kaiser Ludwig Pl. 18, tel. 08822/596. 18 rooms and 4 apartments, most with bath or shower. Facilities: restaurant (with children's menu), gardens, children's playground. AE, DC, MC, V. Closed Nov. 20–Dec. 20. Inexpensive.*

Garmisch-Partenkirchen
Dining

★ **Alpenhof.** This high-class venue is in the town's casino, but there's no gambling with your money at the dining tables. Classic dishes such as duck with orange-pepper sauce and grilled scampi with Provençale sauce are sure bets. *Bahnhofstr. 74, tel. 08821/59055. Reservations advised. Jacket and tie required. DC, MC, V. Expensive.*

Posthotel Partenkirchen. Wood paneling encloses you in the rustic elegance of a 500-year-old vaulted cellar setting. Traditional Bavarian dishes share the menu with Swiss, French, and vegetarian specialties. *Ludwigstr. 49, tel. 08821/51067. Reservations advised. Jacket and tie optional. AE, DC, MC, V. Expensive.*

Fraundorfer. This traditional Bavarian inn has been in operation since 1820. Live country music and yodeling are a regular dinner accompaniment, and folk dances are held from time to time. Guest rooms are also available. *Ludwigstr. 24, tel. 08821/2176. No reservations. Dress: informal. MC, V. Closed Tues. and Nov. 6–Dec. 6. Inexpensive.*

Riessersee. Situated on the shores of a tranquil, small, green lake a 3-kilometer (2-mile) walk from town, this café-restaurant is an ideal spot for lunch or afternoon tea (on weekends there's live zither music 3–5 PM). House specialties are fresh trout and local game. The Riessersee also has rooms. *Riess 6, tel. 08821/50181. Reservations not necessary. Dress: informal. No credit cards. Inexpensive.*

Lodging

★ **Clausings Posthotel.** This is one of the Romantik group—and romantic it certainly is, from the enveloping luxury of its rooms to its pastel pink Baroque facade, which faces Garmisch's central Marienplatz. The range of rare antiques in the public rooms is remarkable. *Marienpl. 12, tel. 08821/7090. 31 rooms, most with bath or shower. Facilities: dance orchestra, beer garden, 3 restaurants. AE, DC, MC, V. Very Expensive.*

Grand Hotel Sonnenbichl. This elegant and old established lodging on the outskirts of Garmish offers panoramic views of the Wetterstein Mountains and the Zugspitze, but only from its front rooms—the rear rooms face a wall of rock. *Burgstr. 97, tel. 08821/7020. 90 rooms and 4 suites with bath. Facilities: indoor pool, solarium, sauna, fitness room, sun terrace, 3 restaurants, bar. AE, DC, MC, V. Very Expensive.*

Staudacherhof. An onion-dome–topped turret is the focal point of this attractive hotel with Bavarian country-style rooms. It's near to the town center, but in a spacious location with a mountain backdrop. *Höllentalstr. 48, tel. 08821/55155. 38 rooms with bath. Facilities: heated outdoor pool, indoor pool, sauna, solarium, resident ski instructor in winter, restaurant, beer tavern. AE. Very Expensive.*

★ **Wittelsbach.** Dramatic mountain vistas from bedroom balconies and a spacious garden terrace make this small modern hotel especially attractive. Public rooms are rustic, and the bedrooms are rather plain. Ask for a room facing south for Zugspitze views. *Von-Brugstr. 24, tel. 08821/53096. 60 rooms. Facilities: indoor pool, sauna, restaurant. AE, DC, MC, V. Closed Oct. 20–Dec. 20. Expensive.*

Edelweiss. Named after the famous white Alpine flower, this small hotel garni positively oozes mountain charm. The place is inlaid with warm pinewood, with Bavarian furnishings and primary colors to match. In summer, the edelweiss—located on a quiet street in the town—is festooned with that other favorite Bavarian flower—the geranium. *Martinswinkelstr. 17, tel.*

08821/2458. 13 rooms with bath. No restaurant, but there's a buffet breakfast. No credit cards. Moderate.

Hotel Garmischer Hof. Situated in the town center, within easy reach of the train and cable-car stations, the swimming pool, and the spa park, the Garmischer Hof is a comfortable, traditional hotel, with an appealing garden and fine views. There's no restaurant. *Bahnhofstr. 53, tel. 08821/51091. 43 rooms with bath or shower. AE, DC, MC, V. Moderate.*

Gästehaus Kornmüller. American visitors are particularly fond of the Kornmüller, a traditional Bavarian guest house on the outskirts of town. *Höllentalstr. 36, tel. 08821/3557. 32 rooms and 8 apartments. AE, MC, V. Inexpensive.*

Grainau
Lodging
★

Hotel Post. Overshadowed by Germany's highest mountain, the mighty Zugspitze, the Post is set in some of the finest Bavarian countryside; two small, pretty lakes are only a short walk away. Bedrooms are large and airy; public rooms are comfortably furnished in the style of a country house. *Postgasse 10, Ober Grainau, tel. 08821/8853. 33 rooms and 7 apartments with bath or shower. Facilities: restaurant (for hotel guests only). AE, DC, MC, V. Closed Nov.–Dec. 20 and Jan. 10–Feb. 10. Moderate.*

Grassau
Dining

Sperrer. You'll have to tear yourself away from the magnificent mountain views here in order to study the menu. Solid Bavarian fare dominates it. Try the roast pork at any time; in summer, have it served in the Sperrer's pretty garden. *Ortenburgerstr. 5, tel. 08641/5011. Reservations advised. Dress: informal. No credit cards. Closed Mon. and Nov. Moderate.*

Hirschegg
Lodging
★

Hotel Walserhof. Hirschegg is actually in Austria, in the dead-end Kleinwalsertal Valley, jointly administered with Germany. The legal tender is DM. The Walserhof looks one way toward Austria, the other way toward Germany. It's a four-star establishment—extremely comfortable—and has homey touches that make it special. *D-8985 Hirschegg/Kleinwalsertal, tel. 08329/5684. 28 rooms, 4 apartments, and 4 suites with bath. Facilities: indoor pool, sauna, solarium, fitness center, tennis court, restaurant. No credit cards. Closed Nov. 5–Dec. 18. Very Expensive.*

Kochel
Lodging

Alpenhotel Schmied von Kochel. The Schmied von Kochel (Blacksmith of Kochel) was a local folk hero, and the use of his name is one of several traditional touches that distinguish this 100-year-old Alpine-style hotel. A zither player can be heard most summer evenings in the restaurant. *Schlehdorferstr. 6, tel. 08851/216. 34 rooms with bath or shower. Facilities: solarium, sauna, bowling alley, restaurant. MC, V. Expensive.*

Mittenwald
Dining
★

Alpenrose. Drop in during the fall for the best venison you'll taste in these parts: The entire month of October is devoted to venison dishes. Hearty Bavarian fare is offered year-round. *Obermarkt 1. tel. 08823/5055. Reservations advised. Dress: informal. Moderate.*

Post Hotel. Pause at the cozy bar for an aperitif and to make the difficult choice between the Post's wine tavern and its rustic Poststüberl. In summer, the charming terrace is the best spot. The menu offers mostly traditional Bavarian fare. *Obermarkt 9, tel. 08823/1094. Reservations advised. Dress: informal. No credit cards. Moderate.*

Lodging

Hotel Rieger. A rustic Bavarian hotel of great charm, the Rieger boasts modern health/cure facilities and deep-pile comfort. *Dekan-Karl-Pl. 28, tel. 08823/5071. 46 rooms with bath or shower. Facilities: indoor pool, sauna, solarium, whirlpool, games room, restaurant. AE, DC, MC, V. Closed mid-Oct.–Dec. 19. Expensive.*

Post Hotel. The 17th-century Post is the oldest and most attractive hotel in town. *Obermarkt 9, tel. 08823/1094. 97 rooms, most with bath. Facilities: indoor pool, sauna, solarium, therapeutic baths, resident doctor, games room, sun terrace, restaurant. No credit cards. Closed Nov. 26–Dec. 10. Expensive.*

Murnau
Lodging

Regina Hotel. From your balcony at the Regina you'll have a sweeping view of the Alps. The hotel is located on the edge of a park, within easy driving distance of the mountains and several lakes. *Seidlpark 2, tel. 08841/2011. 60 rooms and 2 suites with bath or shower. Facilities: indoor swimming pool, sauna, solarium, fitness room, bowling alley, restaurant. AE, DC, MC. Very Expensive.*

Oberammergau
Dining

Ammergauer Stubn. A homey beer tavern, the Stubn, located in the Wittelsbach hotel, offers a comprehensive menu that combines Bavarian specialties with international dishes. *Dorfstr. 21, tel. 08822/1011. Reservations advised. Dress: informal. AE, DC, MC. Closed Tues. and Nov. 7–Dec. 10. Moderate.*

Hotel Wolf. The restaurant of the Wolf hotel serves regional dishes in a traditional Bavarian ambience. Try the venison when it's in season, or the fat mountain trout at any time of the year. *Dorfstr. 1, tel. 08822/6971. Reservations advised. Dress: informal. AE, DC, MC. Moderate.*

Alte Post. You can enjoy carefully prepared local cuisine on the original pine tables in this 350-year-old inn. There's a special children's menu, and in summer, meals are also served in the beer garden. *Dorfstr. 19, tel. 08822/1091. Dress: informal. AE, MC, V. Inexpensive.*

Lodging

★ **Hotel Wolf.** Americans in particular value this attractive old hotel—about 30% of guests are from the United States. Blue shutters punctuate its white walls; the steeply gabled upper stories bloom with flowers. *Dorfstr. 1, tel. 08822/6971. 31 rooms with bath. Facilities: outdoor pool, sauna, solarium, beer tavern, sun terrace, restaurant. AE, DC, MC, V. Expensive.*

Parkhotel Sonnenhof. Away from the sometimes crowded town center, the modern Sonnenhof offers a quiet corner where you can sun yourself on your bedroom balcony (every room has one), as well as soak up the Alpine view. *König-Ludwigstr. 12, tel. 08822/1071. 72 rooms with bath. Facilities: indoor pool, sauna, solarium, children's playroom, bowling alley, restaurant, bar. AE, DC, MC, V. Expensive.*

Hotel Turm Wirt. Rich wood paneling reaches from floor to ceiling in this popular and historic old hotel, located in the shadow of Oberammergau's mountain, the Kofel. The hotel's own band presents regular Bavarian folk evenings. *Ettalerstr. 2, tel. 08822/3091. 22 rooms with bath. Facilities: children's playroom, games room, restaurant. AE, DC, MC, V. Closed most of Jan. and Nov.–mid-Dec. Moderate.*

Wittelsbach. A traditional old hotel in the town center, the Wittelsbach has been fully renovated to provide soundproof rooms, all styled to match the fairy-tale atmosphere that pervades Oberammergau. *Dorfstr. 21, tel. 08822/1011. 50 rooms* *with bath. AE, DC, MC, V. Facilities: restaurant, English-speaking hairdresser. Closed Nov.–mid-Dec. Moderate.*

Reit im Winkl
Dining

Kupferkanne. Outside, a garden surrounds the building; inside, you could be in an Alpine farmstead. The food is good country fare enhanced by some interesting Austrian specialties. Try the *Salzburger Brez'n* (spicy hard rolls) soup. *Weitseestr. 18, tel. 08640/1450. Reservations advised. Dress: informal. DC, MC. Closed Mon. and Nov. Moderate.*

Rosenheim
Dining
★

Rossetti. An Italian restaurant in Bavaria? There are plenty, of course, in Munich, but the Rossetti in out-of-the-way Rosenheim bears comparison with the best. Elegant without pretensions, it's attractively set in a turn-of-the-century villa. If you fancy pasta other than Swabian noodles, this is the place. *Münchenerstr. 66, tel. 08031/33388. Reservations advised. Jacket and tie optional. DC, MC, V. Closed Mon. Moderate.*

Ruhpolding
Dining

Zur Post. Look for the Zur Post sign in any Bavarian town or village and you can be confident of good local fare. Ruhpolding's Zur Post is no exception. In business for more than 650 years, it has been in the hands of the same family for 150 years. It is also possible to obtain lodging here; call beforehand for room reservations. *Hauptstr. 35, tel. 08663/1035. No reservations. Dress: informal. MC. Closed Mon. Moderate.*

Schliersee
Dining and Lodging

Schlierseer Hof. You can eat and sleep in this modern, traditional-style, lakeside hostelry with many facilities. The restaurant concentrates on local fish (ask for *Renke*, a delicate white fish from the lake) and game (if it's being offered, try the braised venison in the rich house sauce). Rooms are fashioned with pinewood and bright check fabrics. *Seestr. 21, tel. 08026/4071. 42 rooms with bath. Facilities: outdoor pool, sauna, restaurant, wine bar, sail boats. AE, DC, MC, V. Moderate–Expensive.*

Seeon-Seebruck
Dining

Lambachhof. This fine old Bavarian homestead stands right on the banks of the Chiemsee, so fresh lake fish figures prominently on the menu. The Lambachhof also rears its own lambs, using only natural fodder; its roast lamb is exceptional. Camping and overnight lodging are also available. *Lambach 8–10, tel. 08667/427. Reservations advised. Dress: informal. No credit cards. Closed Tues. May–Oct. and Dec.–Jan. Moderate.*

Tegernsee
Dining

Der Leeberghof. This gentrified country restaurant offers traditional Bavarian cooking with flair and panoramic views. Try chef Michael Hamburger's jellied duck with plums, or fish fillets with pickled cabbage and forest berries. An alternative to dessert might be goat cheese and coriander bread. *Ellingerstr. 10, tel. 08022/3966. Reservations advised. Jacket optional. MC. Expensive.*

Seehotel Zur Post. This is another lakeside hotel-restaurant, with a fine winter garden and terrace. Fresh lake fish is recommended, but chef Hartmut Münchof would also like you to try some of his special creations, such as avocado salad. *Seestr. 3, tel. 08022/3951. Reservations advised. Dress: informal. DC, MC, V. Closed early Jan.–Feb. 15. Moderate.*

★ **Herzogliches Bräustuberl.** Once a monastery, then a royal retreat, the Bräustuberl is now a beer hall popular with locals. Only snacks are served in this often crowded and atmospheric place, but hearty Bavarian meals are served in the adjoining Keller. The beer is brewed on the premises. In summer, quaff it beneath the huge chestnuts and admire the lake and mountains over the rim of your glass. *Schlosspl. 1, tel. 08022/4141. No reservations. Dress: informal. No credit cards. Inexpensive.*

Urfeld
Dining

Post Hotel. Traditional local fare becomes memorable when sampled in this old coach inn on the banks of the Walchensee. On warm days you can dine outside and watch the Windsurfers glide by. Specialties include Renke. Moderately priced rooms are available, as are lakeside apartments in a modern annex. *8111 Urfeld, tel. 08851/249. Dress: informal. No credit cards. May be closed end of Nov.–early Dec. Inexpensive.*

Waging am See
Dining
★

Kurhausstüberl. This southeastern corner of Bavaria, around its warmest lake, the Wagingersee, was a quiet backwater before the Kurhausstüberl's fame spread. Yet the country-style restaurant's reticence is unchanged. Award-winning chef Alfons Schubeck bases his nouvelle cuisine on solid Bavarian foundations, rediscovering the possibilities of a tiny lake fish that anglers usually throw back, and making soups from cress and side dishes from wild asparagus. Look out for the leg of venison, too. *Am See, tel. 08681/4666. Reservations required. Jacket and tie optional. AE, DC, MC, V. Dinner only. Closed Mon., Tues., Jan., and 2 weeks in Oct. Very Expensive.*

The Arts and Nightlife

The Arts

Concerts

Every summer, **Schloss Hohenaschau,** regarded as one of the finest castles of southern Germany, hosts a series of chamber concerts in its courtyard, its chapel, and its impressive banquet hall. Contact the Kurverwaltung (8213 Aschau im Chiemgau, tel. 08052/392) for program details and reservations. King Ludwig's fantastic **Schloss Neuschwanstein** is the scene every September of a short season of chamber-music concerts, presented in the richly decorated minstrels' hall. (It was here that Ludwig hoped to stage concerts of music by his life-long hero, Richard Wagner, an ambition that, like so many of the doomed monarch's aims, remained unfulfilled.) Contact the Schlossverwaltung Neuschwanstein (8959 Hohenschwangau, tel. 08362/7077) for details and tickets. Bavarian folk music and dancing are performed on Saturday evenings during the summer in the **Bayernhalle** (Brauhausstr. 19, Garmisch-Partenkirchen). Concerts of classical and popular music are presented Saturday through Thursday, mid-May through September, in the resort park bandstand in Garmisch, and on Fridays in the Partenkirchen resort park.

Theater

Both **Berchtesgaden** and **Garmisch-Partenkirchen** have entertaining *Bauerntheaters* (folklore theaters). A working knowledge of German helps if you plan a visit. Berchtesgaden's theater company (Franziskanerpl., tel. 08652/2858) has daily performances in summer and performs Thursday through Sunday in winter (except from November to Christmas). The Garmisch-Partenkirchen company (Rassensaal, Ludwigstr. 45) performs less frequently. Program details are available from the tourist office (tel. 08821/18022) or any hotel.

Nightlife

There are **casinos** in Garmisch-Partenkirchen (tel. 08821/-53099), Bad Reichenhall (tel. 08651/4091), and Bad Wiessee (tel. 08022/82028). They are state-run, and the same regulations apply to all of them. You'll need your passport to get in, and you must be respectably dressed (jacket and tie). These establishments are open daily from 3 PM to 3 AM.

5 The Bodensee

Introduction

The Bodensee (Lake Constance) is the largest lake in the German-speaking world—424 kilometers square, 339 kilometers around (163 miles square, 210 miles around)—and is bordered by Germany, Switzerland, and Austria. It's called a lake, but actually it's a vast swelling of the Rhine, gouged out by a massive glacier in the Ice Age and flooded by the river as the ice receded. The Rhine flows into its southeast corner, where Switzerland and Austria meet, and leaves at its west end.

Visitors should be grateful: These immense natural forces have created one of the most ravishing corners of Germany, a natural summer playground, ringed with little towns and busy resorts. Gentle, vineyard-clad hills slope down to the lakeshore. To the south, the Alps provide a jagged and dramatic backdrop. It's one of the warmest areas of the country, too, the result not just of its geographic location—it's almost the southernmost region of Germany—but of the warming influence of the lake, which gathers heat in the summer and releases it in the winter like a massive radiator. There are corners of the Bodensee that enjoy a near-tropical climate, where lemons, bougainvillea, and hibiscus flourish and vines grow in abundance. The lake itself practically never freezes (it has done so only once this century and twice in the last).

R&R may provide the major reason for visiting the Bodensee, but it's by no means the only one. The natural attractions of the lake, not least its abundance of fresh fish and its fertile soil, were as potent several thousand years ago as they are today. This is one of the oldest continually inhabited areas of Germany, and you'll want to pay your respects to at least part of this heritage. Highlights include the medieval island town of Lindau; Friedrichshafen, birthplace of the zeppelin; the Rococo abbey church of Birnau; and the town of Konstanz on the Swiss-German border. It would be a shame, too, once you're at the Bodensee, not to take advantage of the area's proximity to Austria and Switzerland (and to little Lichtenstein). A day trip to one or more is easy to make, and formalities are few.

Essential Information

Important Addresses and Numbers

Tourist Information Information on the entire Bodensee region is available from the **Internationaler Bodensee-Verkehrsverein-Fremdenverkehrsamt** (8990 Lindau, tel. 08382/26000). For information on Upper Swabia, contact the **Fremdenverkehrsverband Bodensee-Oberschwaben** (Schützenstr. 8, Konstanz, tel. 07531/22232). There are local tourist information offices in the following towns:

Friedrichshafen: Tourist-Information, Friedrichstrasse 18, 7990 Friedrichshafen, tel. 07541/21729.
Konstanz: Tourist-Information Konstanz, Bahnhofplatz 13, 7750 Konstanz, tel. 07531/284–376.
Lindau: am Hauptbahnhof, 8990 Lindau, tel. 08382/26000.
Meersburg: Kur- und Verkehrsverwaltung, Kirchstrasse 4, 7758 Meersburg, tel. 07532/82383.
Radolfzell: Städtisches Verkehrsamt, Rathaus, Marktplatz 2, 7760 Radolfzell, tel. 07732/3800.

Ravensburg: Städtisches Verkehrsamt, Marienplatz 54, 7980 Ravensburg, tel. 0751/82324.

Tuttlingen: Städtisches Verkehrsamt, Rathaus, 7200 Tuttlingen, tel. 07461/99203.

Überlingen: Verkehrsamt Überlingen, 7770 Überlingen, tel. 07551/4041.

Car Rental **Avis:** Siemenstrasse 3, **Friedrichshafen,** tel. 07541/56091; Zaehringer Platz 33–35, **Konstanz,** tel. 07531/57857.

Europcar: Eckenerstrasse 50, **Friedrichshafen,** tel. 07541/21841. Macaivestrasse 10, **Konstanz,** tel. 07531/62052.

Hertz: Loewentalerstrasse 49, **Friedrichshafen,** tel. 07541/31233.

Arriving and Departing by Plane

The closest international airport to the Bodensee is Zurich, in Switzerland, 60 kilometers (40 miles) from Konstanz. Munich airport is 240 kilometers (150 miles) from Konstanz; Frankfurt airport is 375 kilometers (230 miles) from Konstanz. The little airport at Friedrichshafen, on the north shore of the lake, has flights from all three airports.

Arriving and Departing by Car and Train

By Car The A-96 Autobahn runs virtually all the way from Munich to Lindau, but for a less hurried, more scenic route take the B-12 via Landsberg and Kempten. If you want to take a more scenic but slower route from Frankfurt, take the B-311 at Ulm and follow the Oberschwäbische Barockstrasse (the Upper Swabian Baroque Road) to Friedrichshafen. An alternative, no less scenic route to Lindau, at the east end of the lake, is on the Deutsche Alpenstrasse (the German Alpine Road). It runs east–west from Salzburg to Lindau, passing Garmisch-Partenkirchen and Füssen along the way.

By Train There are Intercity trains to Lindau from Frankfurt (via Stuttgart and Ulm) and from Munich. There are also frequent and fast train services from Zurich and Basel in Switzerland.

Getting Around

By Car Lakeside roads in the Bodensee area are good, if crowded in summer; all offer scenic diversions to compensate for the occasional slow going in heavier traffic. You may want to drive around the entire lake, crossing into Switzerland and Austria; formalities at border crossing points are few. However, in addition to your passport, you'll need insurance and registration papers for your car. If you're taking a rental car, check with the rental company to make sure it imposes no restrictions on crossing these frontiers. Car ferries link Romanshorn in Switzerland on the south side of the lake with Friedrichshafen on the north side next to Lindau, and Konstanz with Meersburg. Taking either saves substantial mileage while driving around the lake.

By Train Local trains encircle the Bodensee, stopping at most towns and villages.

By Bus Railway and post buses serve most smaller communities that have no train links. Service is less than frequent, however; use local buses only if time is no object.

By Boat The German-Swiss-Austrian **Weisse Flotte** (White Fleet) line has been ferrying passengers around the lake for more than 120 years. Boats link most of the larger towns and resorts; numerous excursions are also available (*see* Guided Tours, below). If you plan to use the ferries extensively, buy a **Bodensee Pass.** It gives 15 days' unlimited travel on all ferries, as well as on many trains, buses, and some local mountain railways. Cost is DM 70 (DM 35 for children 6 to 16). Contact **Bodensee-Schiffsbetriebe der Deutschen Bundesbahn** (Hafenstr. 6, 7750 Konstanz, tel. 07531/281–398). There are also offices in Friedrichshafen (tel. 07541/201–389) and Lindau (tel. 08382/6099).

Guided Tours

City Tours Most of the larger tourist centers have regular tours with English-speaking guides. In **Friedrichshafen,** there are tours from May through September on Tuesdays at 9:30, leaving from the tourist office (Friedrichstr. 18). There are tours of **Konstanz** from May through September daily from the tourist office (Bahnhofpl. 13). **Lindau** offers tours, also starting from the tourist office (Am Hauptbahnhof), from April through October on Tuesdays and Fridays at 9:30 and 11. Meersburg tourist office (Kirchstr. 4) offers guided tours that include a visit to the wine museum; tours are held from April through October on Wednesdays at 10. The **Radolfzell** tourist office (Marktpl. 2) arranges tours from May through September on Saturdays at 10 for groups of 10 or more.

Boat Tours There are numerous excursions around the lake organized by the Weisse Flotte lasting from one hour to a full day. Many cross to Austria and Switzerland; some head west along the Rhine to the Schaffhausen Falls, the largest waterfall in Europe. (*See* Getting Around by Boat, above, for addresses.) Information on excursions on the lake is also available from all local tourist offices and travel agencies.

Excursions Bus trips to destinations in and around the Bodensee can be booked from tour operators in all the larger towns. Typical tours include visits to cheese-makers in the Allgäu, the rolling Alpine foothills east of the Bodensee; tours around the Black Forest; tours to Baroque churches and castles around the lake; and tours to the ancient town of St. Gallen across the border in Switzerland. Operators include **Seehas-Reisen** (Hussenstr. 46, Konstanz, tel. 07531/26016), **Autoreisen Bregenz** (Seepromenade 15, Überlingen, tel. 07551/4047), and **Reisebüro Kast** (Münsterstr. 31–33, Überlingen, tel. 07551/63628).

Special-interest Tours Flights around the Bodensee are offered by **Konair** (Flugpl., Konstanz, tel. 07531/61110). A 20-minute flight over Konstanz itself costs DM 80 per person. A 30-minute flight around the lake costs DM 100, a 45-minute flight costs DM 120. For DM 170, you can have the plane for an hour, easily time enough to fly south over parts of the Alps. Sightseeing flights also operate from the Lindau-Wildberg airstrip (tel. 08389/271).

Wine-tasting tours are also available. In Überlingen, tastings are held in the atmospheric Spitalweingut zum Heiligen Geist on Thursdays at 7 PM; contact the tourist office. In Konstanz, wine tasting is offered Tuesdays at 5 PM in the half-timbered Spitalkellerei (Brückengasse 12, tel. 07531/28842). In Meersburg, tastings are held Tuesdays and Fridays at 6 PM; contact the tourist office or Georg Hack (tel. 07532/9097).

Exploring the Bodensee

Highlights for First-time Visitors

Altes Schloss, Meersburg
Meersburg, from the lake
The gardens at Mainau
The Nikolausmünster, Überlingen
The Romanesque churches of Reichenau
The Rococo Wallsfahrtskirche at Birnau
The Zeppelin Museum at Friedrichshafen
At least one ride on the lake

Tour 1: Lindau and Environs

Numbers in the margin correspond to points of interest on the Bodensee map.

1 The showpiece of the Bodensee, and starting point of the tour, is **Lindau,** located at the southeast corner of the lake just a mile or two from the Austrian border. Lindau is an island town, tethered to the shore by a 210-yard causeway. Stand at the water's edge in its newer, mainland section, the so-called Gartenstadt (Garden Town—the name comes from its abundance of flowers and shrubs), on a hazy summer's day and the walls and roofs of old Lindau seem to float on the shimmering water, an illusion intensified by the miragelike backdrop of the Alps.

Lindau was originally three islands, on one of which the Romans built a military base. Under the Romans, the islands developed first as a fishing settlement, then as a trading center, a stage on the route connecting the rich lands of Swabia to the north with Italy. (It was a role that continued for hundreds of years: One of the most important stagecoach services between Germany and Italy in the 18th and 19th centuries was based here, the Lindauer Bote—Goethe traveled on it on his first visit to Italy in 1786.) Commercial importance brought political power, and in 1275 little Lindau was made a Free Imperial City within the Holy Roman Empire. As the Empire crumbled toward the end of the 18th century, battered by Napoléon's revolutionary armies, so Lindau fell victim to competing political groups. It was ruled (briefly) by the Austrian Empire before passing into Bavarian rule in 1805.

The proud symbol of Bavaria, a **seated lion,** is one of the most striking landmarks you'll see in Lindau. The lion in question, 20 feet high and carved from Bavarian marble, stares out across the lake from a massive plinth at the end of one of the harbor walls. At the end of the facing wall there's a lighthouse, the **Neuer Leuchtturm.** You can climb up to its viewing platform for a look out over the waters. On a clear day you'll see the Three Sisters, three peaks in Lichtenstein. *Admission: DM 1 adults, 40 pf children. Open daily 9:30–6.*

The **Alter Leuchtturm,** or old lighthouse, stands at the edge of the inner harbor on the weathered remains of the original 13th-century city walls.

From the harbor, plunge into the maze of ancient streets that make up the Altstadt (the Old Town). Eventually they all lead to the **Altes Rathaus** (Old Town Hall), the finest of Lindau's

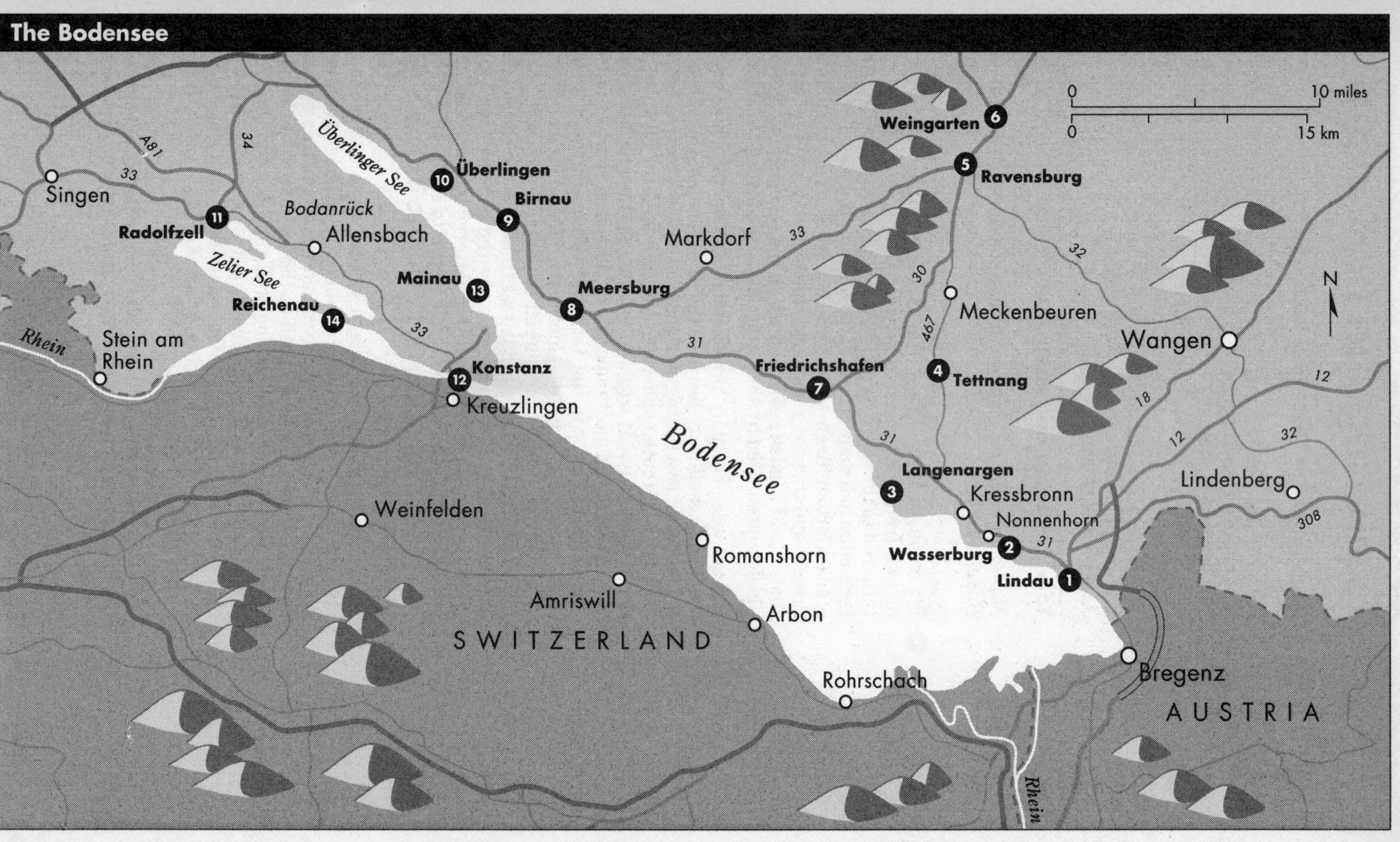
The Bodensee
0
10 miles
0
15 km
N
Überlinger See
10 Überlingen
9 Birnau
6 Weingarten
5 Ravensburg
Singen
11 Radolfzell
Bodanrück
Allensbach
Zelier See
Markdorf
13 Mainau
8 Meersburg
14 Reichenau
Meckenbeuren
Wangen
Stein am Rhein
Rhein
12 Konstanz
Kreuzlingen
7 Friedrichshafen
4 Tettnang
Bodensee
3 Langenargen
Kressbronn
Nonnenhorn
2 Wasserburg
1 Lindau
Lindenberg
Weinfelden
Romanshorn
Amriswill
Arbon
SWITZERLAND
Rohrschach
Bregenz
AUSTRIA
Rhein
A81
34
33
33
33
31
31
31
30
467
32
32
12
12
18
308

handsome historical buildings. It was constructed between 1422 and 1436 in the midst of what was then a vineyard (now a busy thoroughfare) and given a Renaissance face-lift 150 years later, though the original stepped gables were retained. The emperor Maximilian I held an imperial council here in 1496; a fresco on the south facade depicts a scene from this high point of local history. The building was not always used for such noble purposes: Part of it served as the town prison. An ancient inscription, enjoining the townsfolk "to turn aside from evil and learn to do good," identifies it.

Face away from the town hall and walk down to the **Barfüsserkirche,** the Church of the Barefoot Pilgrims. Built from 1241 to 1270, it has for many years been Lindau's principal theater. The Gothic choir is a memorable location for concerts, especially of church music. The tourist office on Bahnhofplatz can provide details of performances.

Continue along Ludwigstrasse to Fischergasse, where you'll find a watchtower, once part of the original city walls. Pause in the little park behind it, the **Stadtgarten.** If it's early evening, you'll see the first gamblers of the night making for the neighboring casino.

Lindau's market square, Marktplatz, is just around the corner. A series of sturdily attractive old buildings line it, among them the 18th-century **Haus zum Cavazzen,** richly decorated with stucco and frescoes. Today it's the municipal art gallery and local history museum. *Am Marktpl. Admission: DM 3 adults, DM 1 children. Open Tues.–Sun., 10–noon and 2–5.*

Two contrasting churches also stand on Marktplatz: the simple, sparely decorated Gothic Stephanskirche and the more elaborate, Baroque Marienkirche. Both have charm—the Stephanskirche for its simplicity, the Marienkirche for its Baroque exuberance.

From Marktplatz, walk along pedestrians-only **Maximilianstrasse,** the main street of the old town, distinguished by half-timbered and gabled old houses.

Time Out The **Weinstube Frey** is a 16th-century wine tavern. Try fresh lake fish and a crisp white Bodensee wine for an excellent lunch. Smoked ham from the Black Forest is also a specialty. *Maximilianstr. 15.*

Turn right off Maximilianstrasse down cobbled Schafsgasse to reach the **Peterskirche** on Schrannenplatz. It's a solid Romanesque building, constructed in the 10th century and reputedly the oldest church in the Bodensee region. Step inside to see the frescoes by Hans Holbein the Elder (1465–1524). A number depict scenes from the life of St. Peter, the patron saint of fishermen and thus an important figure to the inhabitants of Lindau.

From Lindau, head west along the lake. The first attraction
2 you'll reach is **Wasserburg,** 6 kilometers (4 miles) away. It's a sort of Lindau in miniature, another jewel of a town that's actually *in* the lake, at the end of a narrow causeway. Wasserburg means "water castle," and that's exactly what this enchanting town once was, a fortress built on the site of a Roman watchtower. The original owners, the counts of Montfort zu Tettnang, sold it to the wealthy Fugger family of Augsburg to pay

off mounting debts. When, in the 18th century, the Fuggers fell on hard times, too, the castle passed into the hands of the Hapsburgs. In 1805 it was taken over by the Bavarian government.

The Fuggers, when they bought Wasserburg, were among the richest families in Europe. During the final days of their ownership, they were so impoverished that they couldn't even afford to pay for the upkeep of the drawbridge that connected the castle with the shore. Instead they built a causeway, linking the little castle permanently with the shore. Cars aren't allowed into Wasserburg these days, and one of the pleasures of a visit here is to wander undisturbed through its tangle of ancient streets. The castle itself is now a hotel, the Schloss Hotel Wasserburg (Hauptstr. 5, tel. 08382/5692; closed Jan.–Mar. 15), offering surprisingly reasonably priced accommodations.

The most unusual castle in the region stands at the water's
3 edge in **Langenargen,** 8 kilometers (5 miles) west. **Montfort Castle**—it was named after its original owners, the counts of Montfort-Werdenberg—was a conventional enough medieval fortification until it was rebuilt in the 19th century in pseudo-Moorish style by its new owner, King Wilhelm I of Württemberg. If you can, see it from the lake from a steamer: The castle is especially memorable in the early morning or late afternoon, when the softened, watery light gives additional mystery to its Oriental outline. These days, very unromantically, the castle is a municipal tourist center, with a café, a restaurant, and a disco. *Admission free. Open, May–Sept. daily.*

Langenargen is worth visiting to see its central market square, Marktplatz, site of a Baroque parish church and the town museum. The museum contains a series of paintings by German painter Hans Purrmann (1880–1966), an admirer of the French painter Henri Matisse and cofounder of the Academie Matisse in Paris in 1908. The academy faltered soon after it was founded, and, between 1915 and 1935 (at which point Purrmann's work was outlawed by the Nazis), he lived in Langenargen. The museum may appeal only to those with an advanced taste for lesser-known 20th-century painting. *Marktpl. 20. Admission: DM 2.50. Open Apr.–Oct., Tues.–Sun. 10–noon and 3–5. Closed Mon.*

Tour 2: Tettnang, Ravensburg, and Weingarten

Leave the lake now, and head north 12 kilometers (8 miles) on
4 B-467 to the little town of **Tettnang,** former ancestral home of the counts of Montfort zu Tettnang. By 1780 the dynasty had fallen on such hard times that it sold the entire town to the Hapsburgs. Twenty-five years later it passed to the Bavarian ruling dynasty, the Wittelsbachs. You'll want to visit principally to see what remains of the family's extravagant Baroque palace, the Neues Schloss. It was built in the early 18th century, burned down in 1753, and then partially rebuilt before the family's finances ran dry. Enough remains, however, to give some idea of the Montfort's former wealth and ostentatious lifestyle. *Admission: DM 1 adults, 50 pf children. Open Wed. and Sat. 2–4, Sun. 10–noon.*

Time Out The last of the Montfort line, Count Anton IV, spent his declining years in a modest house in the town, now the **Gasthof Krone.**

The inn has its own brewery, and you can try its excellent beer in the parlor where Count Anton dreamed of former glories. If you visit in the late spring, order up one of the asparagus dishes: Tettnang is one of Germany's leading asparagus-growing centers. *Bärenpl.*

---

5 Thirteen kilometers (8 miles) north of Tettnang on B-467, then B-30, is **Ravensburg,** an attractive city that once competed with Augsburg and Nürnberg for economic supremacy in southern Germany. It proved an uneven contest. The Thirty Years' War of the mid-17th century finally put an end to Ravensburg's remaining hopes of economic leadership; after the war, the city was reduced to little more than a medieval backwater. The city's loss proved fortuitous only in that many of its original medieval features have remained much as they were when built. Fourteen of the town gates and towers have survived, for example, while the Altstadt (the Old Town) is among the best preserved in Germany. Leave your car at the Untertor gate and explore the city on foot—cars have been banned from the Old Town. Head down Bachstrasse and you'll come to one of Ravensburg's most interesting churches, the former **Karmelitenklosterkirche,** once part of a 14th-century monastery and now a Protestant church. Ecclesiastical and commercial life were never entirely separate in medieval towns such as Ravensburg. The stairs on the west side of the chancel in the church, for example, lead to the former meeting room of the Ravensburger Gesellschaft (the Ravensburg Society), an organization of linen merchants established in 1400 to direct trade in the product that was largely responsible for the town's rapid economic growth.

The adjacent Marienplatz square has many old buildings that recall Ravensburg's wealthy years: the late-Gothic **Rathaus** (Town Hall), with a picturesque Renaissance bay window; the 14th-century **Kornhaus,** once the corn exchange for the whole of Upper Swabia; the 15th-century **Waaghaus,** the town's weighing station and central warehouse, incorporating a tower where the watchman had his lookout; and the colorfully frescoed **Lederhaus,** once the headquarters of the leather workers.

Time Out Among the historic facades of Marienplatz, you'll see the welcoming door of the **Posthotel Lamm.** Step inside for a taste of true Bodensee cooking in a traditional interior. Ask for a wine from any of the Bodensee vineyards or for the Ravensburg-brewed beer. *Marienpl.*

One of the city's defensive towers is visible from Marienplatz, the **Grüner Turm** (Green Tower), so called because of its green tiles; many are the 14th-century originals. Walk past the Grüner Turm and the neighboring Frauenturm to the **Liebfrauenkirche** (Church of Our Lady). It, too, is a 14th-century structure, elegantly simple on the outside but almost entirely rebuilt inside. Some of the original stained glass remains, however, as does the heavily gilded altar. Seek out the *Ravensburger Schutzmantelmadonna*, a copy of the 15th-century original that's now in Berlin's Dahlem Museum.

A short walk southeast of the Liebfrauenkirche is the massive **Obertor,** the oldest gate in the city walls. This was once one of Ravensburg's most secure defensive positions. From it, you can see another of the city's towers, the **Mehlsack,** or Flour Sack tower, 170 feet high and standing on the highest point of the city. If you can stand the 240-step climb, head up to the summit for the view south to the Bodensee and the Alps. *Admission free. Open mid-Mar.–mid-Oct., 1st and 3rd Sun. of the month only, 10–noon.*

Five kilometers (3 miles) north of Ravensburg on B-30 is the
6 pilgrimage town of **Weingarten,** site of the largest Baroque church in Germany, 220 feet high and over 300 feet long. It's the church of one of the oldest and most venerable convents in the country, founded in 1056 by the wife of Guelph II. (The Guelph dynasty ruled large areas of Upper Swabia; the family Guelph-Wittens is historically linked to a branch of Britain's monarchy, as is another ancient blue-blood German family, the Saxe-Coburg of northern Bavaria. Saxe-Coburg remained the British royal family name until World War I necessitated a patriotic change to Windsor in 1917.) Generations of Guelphs lie buried in the Weingarten basilica. Of greater significance, indeed the reason that the majestic basilica was built, is the little vial it possesses, said to contain drops of Christ's blood. First mentioned by Charlemagne, the vial passed to the convent in 1094, at a stroke making Weingarten one of Germany's foremost places of pilgrimage. On the Friday after Ascension (May 28 in 1993), the anniversary of the day the relic was entrusted to the convent, a huge procession of pilgrims, headed by 2,000 horsemen (many local farmers breed horses just for this procession) wends its way to the basilica. It was decorated by some of the leading German and Austrian artists of the early 18th century, with stucco by Franz Schmuzer, ceiling frescoes by Cosmas Damian Asam, and an altar—itself among the most breathtakingly ornate in Europe; the towers on either side are nearly 80 feet high—by Donato Frisoni. The organ, installed between 1737 and 1750, is among the largest in the country.

Weingarten achieved additional recognition in the '50s, when archaeologists discovered hundreds of Alemann graves from the 6th, 7th, and 8th centuries just outside the town. If you want to learn about these early Germans, visit the **Alemannenmuseum** in the Kornhaus, at one time a granary. *Karlstr. 28. Admission free. Open Wed. and weekends 3–5. Closed Feb. and Nov.*

Tour 3: Friedrichshafen and Meersburg

7 The road back to the lake, B-30, takes you to **Friedrichshafen,** named after its founder, King Friedrich I of Württemberg. It's a young town, founded by Friedrich in 1811, and almost wiped off the map by wartime air raids on its munitions factories. Curious though it may seem in an area otherwise given over to resort towns and agriculture, Friedrichshafen played a central role in Germany's aeronautic tradition, a tradition that saw the development of the zeppelin airship before World War I and the Dornier flying boat in the '20s and '30s. In both cases, it was the broad, smooth waters of the lake that made Friedrichshafen attractive to the pioneer airmen: The zeppelins were built in enormous floating hangars on the lake; the Dorniers were tested on its calm surface. The story of the zeppelins is fascinating. If you're interested, make for the **Zeppelin-und-Bodensee-museum,** where the whole unlikely tale is told in detail, complete with models—one 26 feet long—plans, photographs, and documents. *Adenauerpl. 1. Admission: DM 3. Open May–*

Oct., Thurs.–Tues. 10–5, Wed. 10–7; Nov.–Apr., Tues.–Sun. 10–noon and 2–5.

From the museum, it's a short walk along the lakeside promenade to Friedrichshafen's **Schloss Hofen,** a small palace that served as the summer residence of the kings of Württemberg until 1918. The palace was formerly a priory—its foundations date to the 11th century—and the adjoining priory church is a splendid example of local Baroque architecture. The swirling white stucco of the interior was executed by the Wessobrun Schmuzer family, whose master craftsman, Franz, was responsible for much of the finest work in the basilica of Weingarten. Franz Schmuzer also created the priory church's magnificent marble altar.

Your next stop, 18 kilometers (11 miles) west along the lake, is
8 the historic old town of **Meersburg.** The most romantic way to approach Meersburg is from the lake. Seen from the water on a summer afternoon, with the sun slanting low across the water, the steeply terraced town can seem floodlit, like some elaborate stage setting. (There's little denying that Meersburg is well aware of its too-good-to-be-true charm—some may find the gusto with which it has embraced tourism crass; indeed, the town can at times get unpleasantly crowded.) Assuming your visit is by boat, you'll step ashore in the Unterstadt, the lower town, which clings to the lakeshore about 150 feet below the Oberstadt, or upper town. The climb between the two halves is not arduous, but there's a bus if you can't face the hike.

Meersburg is said to have been founded in 628 by Dagobert, king of the Franks, the man who, it's claimed, laid the first stone of the **Altes Schloss** (Old Castle), which watches majestically over the town and the lake far below. It's Germany's oldest inhabited castle, and one of the most impressive. The massive central tower, named after Dagobert, has walls 10 feet thick. In 1526, the Catholic bishop of Konstanz set himself up in the castle after Konstanz had embraced Protestantism and thrown him out. The castle remained the home of the bishops until the middle of the 18th century, when they had, as they saw it, a more suitable residence built, the Baroque Neues Schloss. Plans to tear down the Altes Schloss in the early 19th century were shelved when the castle was taken over by one Baron Joseph von Lassberg, a man much taken by its medieval romance. He turned it into a home for like-minded poets and artists, among them his sister-in-law, Annette von Droste-Hülshoff (1797–1848), generally considered one of Germany's finest poets. Her small-scale, carefully crafted poems are drenched in impressions gained from the lake and the mountains laid out before the castle. The Altes Schloss is still private property, but much of it can be visited, including the richly furnished rooms where Annette von Droste-Hülshoff lived, as well as the imposing knights' hall, the minstrels' gallery, and the sinister dungeons. The **castle museum** contains a unique collection of medieval jousting equipment. *Schlosspl. Admission: DM 6 adults, DM 4 children. Open Mar.–Oct., daily 9–6; Nov.–Feb., daily 10:30–5.*

The spacious and elegant **Neues Schloss** is located directly across from the castle. It was built partly by Balthasar Neumann, the leading German architect of the 18th century, and partly by an Italian, Franz Anton Bagnato. Neumann's work is most obvious in the stately sweep of the grand double staircase, with its intricate grillwork and heroic statues. The other standout of the interior is the glittering Speigelsaal, the hall of mirrors, now the site of an international music festival held in the summer (*see* The Arts and Nightlife, below). In an unlikely combination of 18th-century grace and 20th-century technology, the top floor of the palace houses the **Dornier Museum.** It traces the history of the German aircraft and aerospace industries. *Schlosspl. Admission: DM 3 adults, DM 1.50 children. Open Apr.–Oct., daily 10–1 and 2–6. Guided tours in English can be arranged by advance booking (tel. 07532/82383).*

Sun-bathed, south-facing Meersburg has been a center of the Bodensee wine trade for centuries. You can pay your respects to the noble trade in the **Weinbau Museum,** one of the most comprehensive wine museums in Germany. A massive barrel, capable of holding 50,000 liters, and an immense wine press dating from 1607 are highlights of the collection. The museum has another claim to fame: It's located in the house where Dr. Frank Anton Mesmer (1734–1815), pioneer of hypnotism—"mesmerism"—lived in the early 19th century. *Vorburggasse 11. Admission: DM 1 adults, children free. Open Apr.–Sept., Tues., Fri., and Sun. 2–5.*

From the museum, it's only a short walk to Meersburg's picturesque market square, **Marktplatz,** surrounded by pretty, half-timbered houses, among them the medieval Rathaus, the town hall.

Time Out The **Weinkeller in Truben** continues the wine theme—its front door is one end of a huge wine barrel. Inside, wine racks stretch from the floor to the whitewashed, vaulted ceiling. Order a bottle of local wine and try one of the cheese-based dishes. *Steigstr.*

East of the Obertor, the town gate at the north end of the town, is an idyllic retreat almost hidden among the vineyards, the **Fürstenhausen,** built in 1640 by a local vintner and later used as a holiday home by poet Annette von Droste-Hülshoff. It's now a museum containing many of her personal items and giving a vivid sense of Meersburg in her time. *Stettnerstr. 9. Admission: DM 3 adults, DM 1.50 children. Open Easter–mid-Oct., Mon.–Sat. 10–noon and 2–6, Sun. and holidays 2–6.*

Tour 4: Birnau, Überlingen, and Radolfzell

If you have any interest in the Rococo, you won't want to miss
9 **Birnau,** 10 kilometers (6 miles) along the lake. It's the site of the **Wallsfahrtskirche** pilgrimage church, the Rococo masterpiece of architect Peter Thumb. Built between 1746 and 1750, the church has a simple exterior, with plain gray-and-white plaster and a tapering clocktower spire over the main entrance; the interior, by contrast, is overwhelmingly rich, a Rococo gem, full of movement, light, and color. It's hard to single out highlights from such a profusion of ornament, but seek out the *Honigschlecker* (the Honey Sucker), a gold-and-white cherub beside the altar dedicated to St. Bernard of Clairvaux, "whose words are sweet as honey" (it's the last altar on the right as you face the high altar). The cherub is sucking honey from his finger, which he's just pulled out of a beehive. If this sort of dainty punning strikes you as misplaced in a place of worship, you'll probably find the small squares of glass set into the pink screen

that rises high above the main altar; the gilt dripping from the walls; the swaying, swooning statues; and the swooping figures on the ceiling equally tasteless. If, like many, you are entranced by the plump cherub, odds are the rest of the building will be very much to your taste.

Birnau stands 3 kilometers (2 miles) or so along the lake from
10 **Überlingen,** the German Nice, as the tourist office likes to call it. It's located midway along the north shore of the Überlingersee, a narrow branch of the Bodensee that projects northwest out of the main body of the lake. Überlingen is an ancient city, a Free Imperial City since the 13th century, with no less than seven of its original city gates and towers left, as well as substantial portions of the old city walls. (What was once the moat is now a delightfully grassy place in which to walk, with the walls of the old town towering over you on one side and the Stadtpark—city park—stretching away on the other.) The heart of the city is the Münsterplatz, site of the Altes Rathaus (Old Town Hall) and the **Nikolausmünster** itself, the church of St. Nicholas. It's a huge church for such a small town, built between 1512 and 1563 on the site of at least two previous churches. The interior is all Gothic solemnity and massiveness, with a lofty stone-vaulted ceiling and high, pointed arches lining the nave. The single most remarkable feature is not Gothic at all, however, but opulently Renaissance—the massive high altar, fully four stories high, carved from white painted wood that looks almost like ivory. Statues, curlicues, and columns jostle for space on it.

Left of the church is the intricate, late-Gothic **Town Hall.** Go inside to see the **Ratsaal,** the council chamber, a high point of Gothic decoration. Its most striking feature amid the riot of carving is the series of figures representing the states of the Holy Roman Empire. There's a naiveté to the figures—their beautifully carved heads are all just a little too large, their legs a little too spindly—that makes them easy to love. *Münsterpl. Admission free. Open weekdays 9–noon and 2:30–5.*

From Überlingen, you can either drive the 10 kilometers (6 miles) back to Meersburg and take the ferry over to Konstanz or continue around the end of the Überlingersee, drive across the neck of the Bodanrück Peninsula—which juts into the west end of the Bodensee to Radolfzell—and continue from there to Konstanz. If you take the latter route, it's 23 kilometers (14 miles) from Überlingen to Radolfzell, and another 16 kilometers (10 miles) to Konstanz.

11 It's worth the extra mileage to see **Radolfzell,** an old lakeside town that wears its history with some style (aside from the ugly high rises surrounding it). It was an Austrian outpost for much of its existence, Austrian property from 1267 to 1415 and again from 1455 to the early 19th century. There are those same half-timbered buildings and sinewy old streets that you'll find in other historic Bodensee towns, that same elegant lakeside promenade and those same chic shops. But the tourist hype is less obtrusive—there's not the sense that Radolfzell has decided that it might as well give up being a real town and turn itself over entirely to the tourist trade. There are no outstanding sights here, it's true, but it's an appealing place for a night or two. And if you must have some culture, go and see the 14th-century **Liebfrauenmünster,** a sturdy Gothic church right on the lakeshore.

Tour 5: Konstanz

12 And so to **Konstanz,** the largest and most famous city on the Bodensee, the only Germany city on the south shore, a German enclave almost in Switzerland (parts of the town actually *are* in Switzerland; the border runs across the southern half of Konstanz—crossing it is easy, with formalities reduced to a minimum). Because it's practically in Switzerland, Konstanz (or Kreuzlingen, as the Swiss call their part) suffered no wartime bombing—the Allies were unwilling to risk inadvertent bombing of neutral Switzerland—with the result that Konstanz is among the best-preserved major medieval towns in Germany. Its proximity to Switzerland also made this one of the most tense borders in the war. There's a famous story of a German Jew who, having crossed the border, was stopped by a Swiss policeman in Kreuzlingen. Having no papers, the German could do little more than pretend that he was Swiss, out for a stroll and a beer. The policeman looked him up and down, and said *"Ja, Schweizerisches Bier ist gut."* (Yes, Swiss beer is good.") Then he walked slowly away.

It's claimed that Konstanz was founded in the 3rd century by the emperor Constantine Chlorus, father of Constantine the Great. The story is probably untrue, though it's certain that there was a Roman garrison here. By the 6th century, Konstanz had become a bishopric; in 1192, it was made a Free Imperial City. But what really put Konstanz on the map was the Council of Konstanz, held between 1414 and 1417 and probably one of the most remarkable gatherings of the medieval world. Upwards of 100,000 people are said to have descended on the city during the great council. It was an assembly that was to have profound consequences, consequences that are still felt today. The council was not principally a political gathering so much as a religious one, though the point at which the politics stopped and the religion began was not always easy to identify: To enjoy either religious supremacy or political power in medieval Europe was, to a large extent, to enjoy both.

What was the council? It was convened to settle the Great Schism, the rift in the church brought about in the 14th century when the papacy moved from Rome to Avignon in the south of France. With the move, a rival pope declared himself in Rome. Whatever else it may not have done, the council did at least resolve the problem of the pope: In 1417, it elected Martin V as the true, and only, pope. What it failed to do, however, was to solve the underlying problems about the nature of the church that, in part at least, had caused the schism in the first place. At stake was the primacy of the German Holy Roman Emperor in electing the pope (and thus in extending his, the emperor's, power) and the primacy of the pope in determining church affairs (and thus in extending the power of the Holy Roman Emperor still further).

Leading the rebel camp was Jan Hus (1372–1415), a theologian from Prague in Bohemia (part of modern Czechoslovakia), opposed both to the political power of the Holy Roman Emperor and to the religious primacy of the pope. He was, in effect, a church reformer 100 years before his time, a man calling for a fundamental reinterpretation of Christian dogma and for the cleansing of the Church's corrupt practices.

What happened at Konstanz? Hus attended the council, having been promised safe-conduct by the emperor Sigismund on condition that he would not say mass or preach. The emperor, however, needed a deal with the church, one that would restore his role in electing the pope. The church agreed, on condition that Hus be done away with. (Sigismund, too, had much to gain from Hus's death; with Hus out of the way, he hoped to restore his control of Bohemia.) So, safe-conduct notwithstanding, Hus was accused of having broken his side of the agreement—the emperor was seen to blush as the charges were read—and condemned to be burned at the stake, as indeed he duly was, in July 1415.

Neither the emperor nor the papacy gained much in the long run. Hus's death sparked violent uprisings in Bohemia that took until 1436 to suppress. Likewise, his reforming doctrines were the direct inspiration, a century later, of Martin Luther, a man whose actions caused a far greater schism than anything the Council of Konstanz had had to deal with—the Reformation itself, and the permanent division of the church between Catholics and Protestants. (Konstanz itself became a Protestant city in the Reformation, a revenge of sorts for the brutal treatment of Hus.)

Hus remains a key figure to Konstanz: There's a Hussenstrasse (Hus Street); the spot where he was killed is marked by a stone slab—the Hussenstein—and, appropriately, the square it's in is now the Lutherplatz; and the magnificent Konzilgebäude (Council Hall)—so called because it's claimed that the council of cardinals met here to choose the new pope, Martin V, in 1415 (they didn't; they met in the cathedral)—has a statue of Hus outside it. The Dominican monastery where Hus was held before his execution is still here, too, doing duty as a luxurious hotel, the Steigenberger Insel-Hotel (*see* Dining and Lodging, below).

But for most visitors, Konstanz, for all its vivid history, is a town to be enjoyed for its more worldly pleasures—its elegant Alstadt (Old Town), trips on the lake, walks along the promenade, the classy shops, the restaurants, the views. The heart of the city is the **Gondelhafen,** the harbor, with the simple bulk of the Konzilgebäude looming behind it. Put up in 1388 as a warehouse, the building is now a concert hall. Alongside the Hus statue is one of a more recent figure from the city's history, Graf Zeppelin, born in Konstanz in 1837.

Walk around the council building and take the street called Marktstatte. It leads to the **Rosgarten Museum,** the museum of local history. If you want to learn more about the Council of Konstanz, step inside. *Rosgartenstr. 3–5. Admission: DM 2.50 adults, children free. Open Tues.–Sun. 10–5.*

Continue up Marktstatte to the **Altes Rathaus** (Old Town Hall), built in the Renaissance and painted with boldly vivid frescoes—swags of flowers and fruits, shields, architectural details, sturdy knights wielding immense swords. Walk into the courtyard to admire its Renaissance restraint.

To see the spot where Hus was killed, continue past the Town Hall along Paradiesstrasse to Lutherplatz. Alternatively, turn right down Wessenbergstrasse, the main street of the old town. It leads to **St. Stephanskirche,** an austere, late Gothic church with a very un-Gothic Rococo chancel. It stands in a little square surrounded by fine half-timbered houses. Look at the **Haus zur Katz** (on the right as you walk into the square). It was the headquarters of one of the city's trade guilds in the Middle Ages; now it houses the city archives.

Now walk through to the **Münster** (the cathedral), built on the site of the original Roman fortress. Building on the cathedral continued from the 10th century through the 19th, resulting in today's oddly contrasting structure. The twin-towered facade, for example, is sturdily Romanesque, blunt and heavy-looking; the elegant and airy chapels along the aisles are full-blown 15th-century Gothic; the complex nave vaulting is Renaissance; the choir is severely neoclassical. Make a point of seeing the Holy Sepulchre tomb in the Mauritius Chapel at the far end of the church behind the altar. It's a richly worked 13th-century Gothic structure, 12 feet high, still with some of its original, vivid coloring and gilding, and studded with statues of the Apostles and figures from the childhood of Jesus.

Finally, you should walk up to the Rhine, through the **Niederburg,** the oldest part of Konstanz, a tangle of old, twisting streets. Once at the river, take a look at the two city towers here, the **Rheintor**—it's the one nearer the lake—and the aptly named **Pulverturm** (Powder Tower), the former city arsenal.

There are two easy island excursions you can make from Kon-
13 stanz. The first is to **Mainau,** "the island of flowers," 7 kilometers (4½ miles) north of Konstanz and easily reached by car (though cars aren't allowed on the island) and by boat. One of the most unusual sites in Europe, Mainau is a tiny island given over to the cultivation of rare plants. Not many people visit Germany expecting to find banana plantations, let alone such exotic flora as bougainvillea and hibiscus. But on Mainau these (and hundreds of more commonplace species) flourish, nurtured by the freakishly warm and moist climate. Visit in the spring and you'll find over a million tulips, hyacinths, and narcissi in bloom; rhododendrons and roses flower in May and June; dahlias dominate the late-summer display. The island was originally the property of the Teutonic Knights, who settled here in the 13th century. In the 19th century, Mainau passed to Grand Duke Friedrich I of Baden, a man with a passion for botany. He laid out most of the gardens and introduced many of the island's more exotic specimens. His daughter, Victoria, later queen of Sweden, gave the island to her son, Prince Wilhelm, and it has remained Swedish ever since. Today it's owned by Prince Wilhelm's son, Count Lennart Bernadette (who lives in the castle on the island, which can't be visited). There is a children's zoo to help keep younger visitors amused. Its wandering groups of tiny pot-bellied pigs are a hit with all visitors. *Admission: DM 8 adults, DM 6 senior citizens, DM 3 children 6–16, children under 6 free. Open Apr.–Oct., daily 9 AM–dusk.*

There's something of the same profusion of plant life to be seen
14 on the other excursion from Konstanz, **Reichenau,** though in this case it's vegetables that dominate rather than flowers. In fact, Reichenau is the single most important vegetable-growing area in Germany, with fully 15% of its area covered by greenhouses and practically the entire remainder of the island growing something or other. Though it seems unlikely, amid the cabbages and the cauliflowers and the lettuces and the carrots and the potatoes, there are three of the most important

and—for some, anyway—beautiful Romanesque churches in Europe on the island. Little Reichenau, 3 miles long and 1 mile wide, connected to the Bodanrück Peninsula by just a narrow causeway, was one of the great monastic centers of the early Middle Ages. Secure from marauding tribesmen on its fertile island, the monastic community blossomed from the 8th to the 12th century, in the process developing into a major center of learning and the arts.

There are three villages on the island—Oberzell, Mittelzell, and Unterzell. Each is the site of one of the churches, with Mittelzell the site of the monastery itself. The first church you'll reach is the **Stiftskirche St. Georg** (the collegiate church of St. George), in Oberzell, built around 900. Cabbages grow in serried ranks up to its rough plaster walls. Small round-headed windows, a simple tower, and russet-color tiles provide the only exterior decoration. Inside, look for the wall paintings along the nave; they date from around 1000 and show the miracles of Christ. Their simple colors and unsteady outlines have an innocent, almost childlike charm. The striped backgrounds are typical of Romanesque frescoes.

The next church, begun in 816, is the largest and most important of the trio. It's the **Münster of St. Maria and St. Markus,** the monastery church itself. The monastery was founded in 725 by St. Pirmin; under the abbots Waldo (786–806) and Hatto I (806–23), it became one of the most important cultural centers of the Carolingian empire. It reached its zenith around 1000 under the rule of Abbot Hermanus Contractus, "the miracle of the century," when 700 monks lived here. It was then probably the most important center of book illumination in Germany. Though it's larger than St. Georg, the church here has much the same simplicity. It's by no means crude (though it can't be called technically sophisticated), just marvelously simple, a building that's utterly at one with the fertile soil in which it stands. Visit the **Schatzkammer** to see some of the more important treasures that are still here. They include a 5th-century ivory goblet with two carefully incised scenes of Christ's miracles and some priceless stained glass that is almost 1,000 years old. *Admission: DM 1 adults, 50 pf children. Open May–Sept., daily 11–noon and 3–5.*

The third church, the **Stiftskirche St. Peter and St. Paul,** at Unterzell, is a less perfect expression of the Romanesque, in part because it contains a number of later additions, most of them 15th century, and some Baroque stucco and frescoes. But it's worth a look anyway, if only to see the Romanesque frescoes in the apse, uncovered in 1990 during restoration work.

What to See and Do with Children

If your children are tired of swimming and smashing balls around the miniature golf courses, take them to the zoo at **Affenburg** to feed the apes. It's about 8 kilometers (5 miles) north of Überlingen, in a forest. There are 200 Barbary apes here. Your admission price includes food you can give the apes. *Admission: DM 6 adults, DM 3 children. Open mid-Mar.–Oct., daily 9–noon and 1–6.*

There's another **zoo** halfway between Konstanz and Radolfzell. It features wild animals from all over Europe: bears, wolves, bison, and boars. It also has a petting zoo, with miniature goats, donkeys, and deer. *Allensbach. Admission: DM 4 adults, DM 2 children 4–16, children under 4 free. Open Mar.–Sept., daily 9–6; Oct.–Feb., daily 10–5.*

In Lindau there's a large **model railway** located in the Luitpold Kaserne (camp) behind the train station. *Hintere Inselstr., tel. 08382/26000. Admission DM 3 adults, DM 1.50 children. Open Apr.–end of Oct.; hours vary, advisable to call ahead.*

For a day trip to Switzerland with the kids, try **Conny-Land,** just south of Konstanz on the road to Zurich. It's Europe's biggest dolphin aquarium, and it also features go-carts, a minitrain, pony rides, a monorail, remote-controlled boats, and a petting zoo. The admission price allows unlimited use of all rides and facilities. Have lunch in the restaurant: huge glass panels allow a look into the dolphin pool. *Admission: 9 Swiss francs adults, Sfrs. 6 children. Open daily 9–6; dolphin and sea lion shows at 1:30 and 4:30.*

In Überlingen, at the **Heimatmuseum,** a vast collection of dolls' houses can be seen. *Admission: DM 2.50 adults, DM 1 children. Open Apr.–Oct., Tues.–Sat. 9–12:30 and 2–5, Sun. 10–3.*

Or, down the Rhine at Stein am Rhein is Switzerland's largest doll collection in the **Puppenmuseum.** *Schwarzhorngasse 136. Admission: 3 Sfrs. adults, 1.50 Sfrs children. Open mid-Mar.–Oct., Tues.–Sun. 10–5.*

Off the Beaten Track

Head for the **Hat Museum** at Lindenberg, 16 kilometers (10 miles) northeast of Lindau in the Allgäu. It charts two centuries of hat-making. (Open Wed. 3–5:30 and Sun. 10–noon.) Or contemplate the achievements of the crusade for world peace as documented in Europe's first **Peace Museum.** It's in Bad Schachen, just outside Lindau. *Lindenhofweg 25. Admission free. Open mid-Apr.–Sept., Tues.–Sat. 10–noon and 2:30–5, Sun. 10–noon.*

If you're in Friedrichshafen you can make a nostalgic return to school with a visit to the **School Museum;** it's in the Schnetzenhausen suburb. There are convincing reconstructions of schoolrooms from 1830, 1880, and 1930—and not a pocket calculator in sight. *Tel. 07541/21729. Admission free. Open May–Oct., daily 10–5., Nov.–Apr., Tues.–Sun. 2–5.*

Just north of Konstanz on the Bodanrück Peninsula is the 1,000-acre **Wollmatinger Ried,** an area of moorland that's now a bird sanctuary. There are three-hour guided tours of the moor on Wednesdays and Saturdays, April through mid-October, at 4 PM, and two-hour tours June through mid-September on Tuesdays, Thursdays, and Fridays at 9 AM. Most of the birds you'll see are waterbirds, naturally; there are also remains of prehistoric stilt houses. Bring sturdy, comfortable shoes and mosquito repellent (if you can). Binoculars can be rented. Contact **DBV Naturschutzzentrum Wollmatinger Ried** (FritzArnold-Str. 2e, Konstanz, tel. 07531/78870).

Shopping

The Bodensee is artists' territory, and shopping here means combing the many small galleries and artists' shops in lakeside towns and resorts for watercolors, engravings, and prints. Two reliable addresses are **Hans Müsken's** shop in Konstanz (Zollernstr. 3) and **Michael Zeller's** two shops in Lindau (Maximilianstr. and Cramergasse). Zeller organizes the celebrated, twice-yearly **Internationale Bodensee-Kunstauktion** (art auction); it's held in the spring and fall.

There's some fine local antiques and jewelry to hunt out, too. Two prominent craftsmen are **Christoph Rose** in Singen/Hohentwiel, just outside Radolfzell (Engestr. 1), and **Michael Zobel** in Konstanz (Augustinerstr. 4).

Pottery is a craft that's practiced in many places around the lake. You can find fine examples at **Angelika Ochsenreiter's** shop in Lindau (Ludwigstr. 29).

Sports and Fitness

Bicycling Bikes can be rented from the train stations at Friedrichshafen, Konstanz, Lindau, and Überlingen for DM 12 a day (DM6 with a valid train ticket) and from some sports shops (inquire at tourist offices). In Konstanz, **Velotours** (Mainaustr. 34, tel. 07531/52085) organizes lakeside package tours of four to nine days, April through October. Bikes can be taken on all lake ferries.

Boating There are more than 30 boatyards and sailing schools where you can rent boats; most will ask to see some kind of document (a proficiency certificate, for example, from a sailing school) to show you know how to handle a vessel under sail. Motorboats and rowboats can be rented in every resort without any such formalities. Windsurfers will also have no trouble finding boards to rent from any of the 35 rental points around the lake. Canoes can be rented from the **Huber** sports shop in Konstanz (Gottlieberstr. 32). Water-skiers are catered to on the lake, although the fun isn't inexpensive. The Bodensee is fine cruising water, too, and yachts can be chartered from the **Bodensee-Segelschule Wallhausen** (Zum Witmoos 10, 7750 Konstanz 19, tel. 07533/780) or the **Bodensee Yachtschule** in Lindau (Christoph Eychmüller Schiffswerfte 2, tel. 08382/5140) and Radolfzell (Zeppelinstr. 23, tel. 07732/54390).

Bowling Every resort has at least one hotel with a bowling alley. Konstanz has two bowling centers, each with eight alleys—the **Kegelzentrum Oberlohn** (Maybachstr. 18) and the **Kegel-und Freizeit-Center** (Markgrafenstr), which also has firing ranges, billiard tables, and dart boards.

Fishing Anglers agree that the Bodensee is one of the biggest challenges Germany has to offer, with some fine sport in its mountain-fed waters. You'll need a license to fish; they are available, usually for a nominal fee, through the tourist office of the resort where you intend to fish. Information about fishing vacations can be obtained from the tourist office in the town hall (Rathaus at Moos, near Radolfzell, tel. 07732/2544).

Golf Lindau has an 18-hole course on the grounds of a castle, **Schloss Schönbühl.** Guests are welcome. Contact the **Golf-Club Lindau-**

Bad Schachen (Kemptenerstr. 125, 8990 Lindau, tel. 08382/78090). Konstanz also has an 18-hole course that welcomes foreign visitors provided they are members of clubs in their own countries. Contact the **Golf-Club Konstanz** (Langenrain, Hofgut Kargegg, 7753 Allensbach 3, tel. 07533/5124).

Horseback Riding There are riding stables in most Bodensee resorts, and some fine lakeside bridle paths, including a 12-mile trail from Konstanz to Radolfzell. You can rent horses from the **Reitschule Braunschweig** (Mainaustr. 78a, 7750 Konstanz, tel. 07531/61604).

Swimming The resorts of the Bodensee tell Germans they don't have to travel as far as the Mediterranean—the lake has comparable beaches and cleaner water. The beach's boast is debatable, but the water certainly sparkles. Open-air pools and lidos abound—at last count, there were 150 around the lake. Lindau's **Eichwald** lido has a lake beach a ½ mile long and one acre of sunbathing lawns (Eichwaldstr. 16, Reutin district). The **Jakob** lido in Konstanz has a lakeside leisure area and heated pools.

Tennis Every resort has its tennis club, and you should have no difficulty getting onto a court. The biggest court complexes are at **Lindau** (Sutzenbergstr. 15, tel. 08382/28998) and **Ravensburg** (St. Christinastr. 1, tel. 0751/64640).

Dining and Lodging

Dining

Fish specialties predominate around the Bodensee. There are 35 different types of fish in the lake, with *Renke* and *Felchen* the most highly prized. Felchen belongs to the salmon family and is best eaten *blau* (poached) in rosemary sauce or baked in almonds (*Müllerin*). Wash it down with a top-quality Meersburg white wine. If you venture north to Upper Swabia, you'll find that *Pfannkuchen* and *Spätzle* are the most common specialties. Both are flour-and-egg dishes. Pfannkuchen, or pancakes, are generally filled with meat, cheese, jam, or sultanas, or chopped into fine strips and scattered in a clear consommé soup known as *Flädlesuppe*. Spätzle, tiny golden-roasted and dumplinglike noodles, are the usual accompaniment for the Swabian Sunday roast-beef lunch of *Rinderbraten*. One of the best-known Swabian dishes is *Maultaschen,* a kind of ravioli, usually served floating in a broth strewn with chives.

Highly recommended restaurants are indicated by a star ★.

Category	Cost*
Very Expensive	over DM 90
Expensive	DM 55–DM 90
Moderate	DM 35–DM 55
Inexpensive	under DM 35

**per person for a three-course meal, including tax and tip but not wine*

Lodging

There's a wide range of hotels in all the towns and resorts around the lake, from venerable, wedding-cake-style Edwardian palaces to more modest and modern *Gasthöfe* (inns). If you're visiting in July and August, make reservations well in advance and expect higher-than-average prices. For lower rates and a more rural atmosphere, consider staying away from the lake in Upper Swabia or the Allgäu.

Highly recommended hotels are indicated by a star ★.

Category	Cost*
Very Expensive	over DM 180
Expensive	DM 120–DM 180
Moderate	DM 80–DM 120
Inexpensive	under DM 80

**All prices are for a standard double room for two, including tax and service charge.*

Friedrichshafen
Dining and Lodging

Buchhorner Hof. This traditional lakeside, hotel has been run by the same family since it opened in 1870. Hunting trophies on the walls, leather armchairs, and Turkish rugs decorate the public areas; bedrooms are large and comfortable. The restaurant is plush and subdued, with delicately carved chairs and mahogany-paneled walls. It offers a choice of menus that feature such dishes as pork medallions, perch fillet, and lamb chops. *Friedrichstr. 33, tel. 07541/2050. 65 rooms with bath. Facilities: restaurant, bar, sauna, solarium. AE, DC, MC, V. Closed Dec. 20–Jan. 10. Very Expensive.*

Krone. This hotel with Bavarian modern rustic decor—not to be confused with the City-Krone—is in the district of Schnetzenhausen in quiet, semirural suroundings. The restaurant specializes in game dishes and fish from the nearby Bodensee. *Untere Mühlbachstr. 1, tel. 07541/4080. 92 rooms with bath and balcony. Facilities: heated outdoor pool, indoor pool, sauna, solarium, outdoor and indoor tennis courts, children's playroom, sun terrace, restaurant. AE, DC, MC, V. Closed Dec. 10–25. Expensive.*

Konstanz
Dining

Engstler's. Informal and friendly, Engstler's is a noisy, popular restaurant across the street from the Council Building. The food is distinctly red-blooded, with game dishes heavily featured. Venison goulash and roast boar are favorites; whitefish fillet numbers among the fish dishes. Special children's menus are also available. In summer, eat in the beer garden. *Fischmarkt 1, tel. 07531/23126. Reservations not required. Dress: informal. AE, DC, V. Closed Jan. and Feb. Inexpensive.*

Dining and Lodging
★

Seehotel Siber. The most elegant dining in the region is offered at the Seehotel Siber. Though it's a little hotel—in a turn-of-the-century villa—the adjoining restaurant is the major attraction. The food, prepared by Bertold Siber, one of Germany's leading chefs, is classical with regional touches. Try his lobster salad, bouillabaisse with local lake fish, or glazed pigeon breasts with mushrooms and truffle sauce. The restaurant is divided into three rooms: One is done up like a library, with massive bookcases; the center room is airy and spacious, with a white ceiling and bold modern paintings; the third has mint-color walls and a deep green carpet. In summer you can eat on a terrace overlooking the lake. Bedrooms numbers 3 and 7 have balconies affording similar views. *Seestr. 25, tel. 07531/63044. 11 rooms with bath. Facilities: restaurant (reservations essential, jacket and tie required). AE, DC. Hotel and restaurant closed in Feb. Very Expensive.*

★ **Steigenberger Insel-Hotel.** If the Seehotel offers the best dining in town, then this must be the best hotel, or at least the most luxurious. It's a former 13th-century monastery—the original cloisters are still here—where Jan Hus was held before his execution and, much later, Graf Zeppelin was born. Bedrooms are spacious and stylish, more like those in a private home than in a hotel, and many have lake views. The restaurant is rather imposing, with some fine arches and great views over the lake. The Dominikaner Stube has regional specialties, and there's the clubby, relaxed Zeppelin Bar. Gardens bright with flowers surround the hotel, keeping the bustle of Konstanz at bay. *Auf der Insel 1, tel. 07531/25011. 95 rooms with bath, 6 suites. Facilities: beach, outdoor pool, games room, childcare, 2 restaurants, bar. AE, DC, MC, V. Very Expensive.*

Lodging

Waldhaus Jakob. Located in a quiet corner of town, this new hotel (opened 1990) is in a lovingly restored 19th-century house with a neo-Gothic facade. The decor of the guest rooms is tastefully modern. *Eichhornstr. 84, tel. 07531/81000. 40 rooms with bath. Facilities: restaurant, bike rental. AE, DC, V. Moderate.*

Lindau

Dining

★ **Restaurant Hoyerberg Schlössle.** A location offering a commanding view across the lake to Bregenz and the Alps combines with elegant nouvelle cuisine to make this about the best dining experience in Lindau. The specialties are fish and game, changing seasonally. There are fixed-price menus of six and eight courses; one offers lobster, noodles with white truffles and goose liver, and roast breast of squab. The decor features brick-trimmed arched windows, fresh flowers, and elegant, high-back chairs. Dine on the terrace for the terrific view. *Hoyerbergstr. 64, tel. 08382/25295. Reservations essential. Jacket and tie required. AE, DC, MC, V. Closed Jan. 10–Feb. and Mon. Very Expensive.*

Gasthaus zum Sünfzen. Located in the heart of the Old Town, the Gasthaus zum Sünfzen is an appealing old inn with little leaded windows and a simple, wood-paneled interior. The food features such regional specialties as venison and lake fish, and sausages from the restaurant's own butcher shop. Try either the spinach Spätzle or the Felchen fillet. The menu changes daily and seasonally. *Maximilianstr. 1, tel. 08382/5865. Reservations advised. Dress: informal. AE, DC, MC, V. Closed Feb. Inexpensive.*

★ **Historische Bräugaststätte zum Schlechterbräu.** This is where the locals come for *Frühschoppen*, a Sunday brunch—and a vigorous tradition in this part of the country—of two fat sausages with sauerkraut and a tall glass of beer. The interior is authentically Teutonic, with oak booths and colorful stained-glass lamps. The food is every bit as robust, with Bavarian specialties predominating. Try the juicy *Schweinshaxen* (grilled pork knuckle). In summer, you can eat in the beer garden. The restaurant is located in the Old Town, on the island, near the Peterskirche. *In der Grub 28, tel. 08382/5842. Reservations not required. Dress: informal. No credit cards. Closed late Feb. and mid-Nov. Inexpensive.*

Lodging **Bayerischer Hof.** Spanning a large section of Lindau's harbor promenade, the 19th-century "Hof" is one of the most commanding buildings in town. Many of the exquisitely refurbished rooms adorned with classic furnishings and Laura Ashley fabrics look out over the lake. Its terraced café is a favorite rendezvous. *Seepromenade, 8990 Lindau, tel. 08382/5055. 105 rooms with bath. Facilities: bar, café, outdoor pool, masseur, games room, boat and bike rental. DC, MC, V. Closed Dec.–Easter. Very Expensive.*

Schachen-Schlössle. A turreted 15th-century manor house set amid peaceful gardens compensates for not being on Lindau island, but you are still very close to the waterfront in the Bad Schachen district of the mainland town. This is a remarkably good value, with rooms decorated in authentic rustic style. Book well in advance. *Enzisweilerstr. 5, tel. 08383/5069. 8 rooms, plus suites in adjoining building. Facilities: restaurant, bar. AE, DC, MC, V. Closed Jan.–Mar. Moderate.*

Meersburg
Dining **Winzertrinkstube.** The Winzertrinkstube is located down the steep hill from the Altes Schloss. The dining room is centered around an 18th-century wine press, now doing duty as a vast, geranium-filled flower pot. The food is heartily Swabian: Try *Käsespätzle* (cheese Spätzle) or Maultaschen. The terrace is a perfect spot for people-watching. *Steigstr. 33, tel. 07532/6484. Reservations advised. Dress: informal. No credit cards. Closed Dec.–Feb. Inexpensive.*

Lodging **Strandhotel Wilder Mann.** This 18th-century nobleman's home on the lake's edge has its own 750-foot stretch of shoreline. Modern, deep-pile comforts are to be found in the antiques-filled guest rooms, with dark pine furniture and tapestries predominating. The restaurant's pastries are first-rate, as is the wine cellar. *Bismarckplatz 2, tel. 07532/9011. 33 rooms with bath, 2 suites. Facilities: outdoor pool, solarium, sun terrace, restaurant. No credit cards. Closed mid-Dec.–Feb. Very Expensive.*

Zum Bären. Built in 1605, the Zum Bären will be the choice of those who value atmosphere over modern convenience. Creaking staircases and wood ceilings ensure maximum Old World charm, though colorful wallpapers and bright bedspreads lighten the mood. Service is excellent, the result perhaps of the fact that the hotel has been owned and run by the same family since the mid-19th century. *Marktpl. 11, tel. 07532/6044. 16 rooms with bath. Facilities: restaurant/wine bar. No credit cards. Restaurant closed Dec.–Mar. 15 and Mon. Moderate.*

Überlingen
Dining and Lodging
★ **Parkhotel St. Leonard.** Located about a mile from the lake on a vineyard-covered hillside, the modern St. Leonard offers elegance and style. All rooms have balconies, but try for one with a view of the lake. The restaurant is sleekly contemporary and has a French chef. Local lake fish are a specialty. In summer, you dine on a canopied terrace. Try the fresh trout with almond-butter sauce. Four- and six-course fixed-price menus are also offered. *Obere St. Leonardstr. 83, tel. 07551/808–100. 150 rooms with bath. Facilities: restaurant, bar, indoor pool, sauna, solarium, indoor and outdoor tennis, billiards. AE, MC. Very Expensive.*

★ **Romantik Hotel Hecht.** The little Hecht offers discreetly chic Old World comforts and superb food. It's a former Weinstube, built in 1762 and easy to spot with a magnificent sign (a gold fish clutching a bunch of grapes in its jaws). The restaurant is rustically decorated, with old plates and serving dishes ranged around the walls and a splendid grandfather clock. Fish is the main offering—try it either blau or Müllerin. If your tastes run to more exotic fare, Thai menus are also available—call a day or so ahead. *Münsterstr. 8, tel. 07551/63333. 10 rooms with bath. Facilities: restaurant (reservations advised). AE, DC. Closed mid-Feb. Restaurant closed Mon. Expensive.*

The Arts and Nightlife

The Arts

Music The region has its own orchestra, the **Bodensee Symphony Orchestra,** founded in 1932 and based in **Konstanz,** and with a season running from October through April. Program details and bookings are available from **Bodensee Symphonie Orchester** (Spanierstr. 3, 7750 Konstanz, tel. 07531/52855). Konstanz has an annual summer music festival, from mid-June to mid-July, with a program of international events, including celebrated organ concerts in the cathedral. For program details and bookings, contact the Konstanz tourist office (tel. 07531/284–376). Performances are held in the Council Building. **Überlingen** also has an international music festival, with concerts every Tuesday from May to September in the lakeside Kursaal. For program details and bookings, contact the **Städtische Verwaltung** (Landungspl. 7, 7770 Überlingen, tel. 07551/4041 and 07551/87291). **Meersburg** has an annual international chamber music festival in the magnificent Hall of Mirrors (Spiegelsaal) of the Neues Schloss. The concerts are held every Saturday from June to September. For program details and bookings, contact the **Städtische Kur und Verkehrsverwaltung** (Kircst. 4, 7758 Meersburg, tel. 07532/82382). Several other castles and churches in the region are the scene of regular chamber music concerts and recitals, particularly in summer. For program details, contact the regional tourist office: the **Internationaler Bodenseeverkehrsverein und Fremdenverkehrsverband Bodensee-Oberschwaben** (Schützenstr. 8, 7750 Konstanz, tel. 07531/22232).

Theater **Konstanz** claims Germany's oldest active theater. Its **Stadttheater** (Konzilstr.) was originally a Jesuit college, where plays were staged as early as 1609. The theater has an annual repertory program of up to a dozen productions, and, apart from its main auditorium with seating for 400, it has a small workshop theater. For program details and bookings, contact the **Stadttheater Konstanz** (Konzilstr. 11, 7750 Konstanz, tel. 07531/200–750). **Lindau** and **Ravensburg** both have city theaters where touring productions are regularly staged.

Nightlife

Most of the towns and resorts of the Bodensee have regular evenings of entertainment for visitors, ranging from traditional folk music and dancing to more modern fare such as jazz and pop concerts. Local tourist offices have programs. Many resort hotels also organize regular *Heimatabende* (folk-music evenings) or *Gästeabende* (guests' evenings); in some, Saturday night really is dance night.

In summer you can dance on the water—on one of the evening cruises organized by the Bodensee **Weisse Flotte** operators. The boats pick up dancers and revelers every Saturday night from May to September in Konstanz, Lindau, Meersburg, Rorschach, and Überlingen. For further details and bookings, contact the **Bodensee-Schiffsbetriebe der Deutschen Bundesbahn** (Hafenstr. 6, 7750 Konstanz, tel. 07531/281–398).

The **disco** scene is concentrated in Konstanz. **Flair** (Reichenauerstr. 212) is one of the biggest and best. Meersburg claims to have the most romantic disco—**Barcarole,** candlelit and overlooking the lake (Fährhaus Meersburg, Fährepl.).

Konstanz and Lindau have **casinos,** called Spielbank. They open 3 PM–3 AM daily. But the Las Vegas of the lake is at **Bregenz,** just across the Austrian border, on the southeast shore. Perhaps the secret of its success lies in the generous practice of handing visitors their entrance money back in chips. You'll need a passport not only for the Bregenz casino but for the German ones, too.

6 The Bavarian Forest

Including Passau

Introduction

For years, this picturesque region of southeast Germany was one of the most isolated parts of Western Europe, its eastern boundary having been flanked by the Iron Curtain from World War II until 1989. It has retained its rural charm partly because of its isolation, but also because of a vast tract of protected forest—one of the largest in Europe—peppered with pretty, ancient villages of jumbled red roofs and onion-domed churches.

But the Bayerischer Wald (Bavarian Forest) has long been a well-kept secret with vacationing Germans in search of relaxing holidays at mountainside lodges or country inns linked by well-marked hiking and biking trails. Farming and forestry remain the chief activities of the locals, but tourism is growing as the region opens up in the wake of the collapse of communism in neighboring Czechoslovakia. Old contacts between Germans and Bohemian Czechs are also being revived rapidly, and no visit to the Bavarian Forest would be complete without at least a day trip across the border; bus trips into Bohemia are organized by every local German tourist office.

The region's flavor is also vastly different from the stock concept of the Bavaria of Munich and the Alpine region, a world supposedly populated by jolly peasants—men in lederhosen and funny green hats with feathers and buxom women decked out in flowing dirndls—who spend their time singing along with oompah bands and knocking back great mugs of beer. The people of the Bavarian Forest are reserved, less effusive; even their accent is gentler than that of their southern countrymen.

This is a region for those in search of peace and quiet: hikers, nature lovers, anglers, horseback riders, skiers looking for uncrowded slopes, and golfers distressed by the steep greens fees of more fashionable courses. It's also a low-cost destination offering good-quality dining and lodging at budget prices.

The Bavarian Forest can be a welcome alternative to the tourist hype and crowds in places like Munich and Rothenburg. If the low-key and understated is your style, then you are sure to find this area very much to your taste.

Essential Information

Important Addresses and Numbers

Tourist Information There are local tourist information offices in the following towns:

Bayerisch-Eisenstein: Verkehrsamt Bayerisch-Eisenstein, Schulbergstrasse, 8371 Bayerisch-Eisenstein, tel. 09925/327.
Bodenmais: Verkehrsverein Bodenmais, Bahnhofstrasse 55, 8373 Bodenmais, tel. 09924/77835.
Cham: Verkehrsverein Cham, Propsteistrasse 46, 8490 Cham, tel. 09971/4933.
Deggendorf: Verkehrsverein Deggendorf, Oberer Stadtplatz 4, 8360 Deggendorf, tel. 0991/380169.
Freyung: Verkehrsamt Freyung, Rathausweg 1, 8393 Freyung, tel. 08551/4455.
Furth im Wald: Verkehrsverein Furth im Wald, Schlossplatz 1, 8492 Furth im Wald, tel. 09973/3813.

Grafenau: Verkehrsamt Grafenau, Am Rathaus, 8352 Grafenau, tel. 08552/2085.

Passau: Fremdenverkehrsverein Passau, Am Rathausplatz, 8390 Passau, tel. 0851/33421.

Regen: Verkehrsamt Haus des Gastes, 8370 Regen, tel. 09921/2929.

St. Englmar: Verkehrsamt St. Englmar, Rathausstrasse 6, 8449 St. Englmar, tel. 09965/221.

Straubing: Städtisches Verkehrsamt Straubing, Rathaus, Theresienplatz, 8440 Straubing, tel. 09421/16307.

Tittling: Verkehrsamt Tittling, Marktplatz 10, 8391 Tittling, tel. 08504/2666.

Viechtach: Städtisches Kur- und Verkehrsamt, Rathaus, 8374 Viechtach, tel. 09942/1622.

Waldkirchen: Fremdenverkehrsamt Waldkirchen, Ringmauerstrasse 14, 8392 Waldkirchen, tel. 08581/20250.

Zwiesel: Verkehrsamt Zwiesel, Im Rathaus, 8372 Zwiesel, tel. 09922/1308.

Car Rental **Budget:** Stelzlhof 7, 8390 Passau, tel. 0851/603–839. **Europcar:** Neuburgerstrasse 93, Passau, tel. 0851/6033.

Arriving and Departing by Plane

The nearest airports are at Munich and Nürnberg. Each is about 160 kilometers (100 miles) from the western edge of the Bavarian Forest.

Arriving and Departing by Car

The principal road links with the Bavarian Forest are the A-3 Autobahn from Nürnberg and the A-92 Autobahn from Munich. Nürnberg is 104 kilometers (65 miles) from Regensburg and 229 kilometers (140 miles) from Passau. Munich is 120 kilometers (75 miles) from Regensburg and 179 kilometers (110 miles) from Passau. Traffic on both roads is relatively light, even at peak periods.

Getting Around

By Car The small country highways and side roads within this region are less traveled, making the whole area something of a paradise for those who have experienced only the high-speed mayhem of most other German roads. B-85 runs the length of the Bavarian Forest from Passau to Cham, and its designation as a route of special scenic interest (the Ostmarkstrasse) extends northward to Bayreuth.

By Train Two main rail lines cross the region: One runs west to east via Nürnberg, Regensburg, Passau, and Vienna; the other runs south to north via Munich, Landshut, and Straubing. This latter route slices right through the heart of the Bavarian Forest on its way to Czechoslovakia (if you fancy overnighting in Prague, this is the train route to take). Plattling, just south of Deggendorf, and Cham are the main rail junctions for the area. Passau is the principal rail gateway on the border between southeast Germany and Austria.

By Bus Villages not on the railway line are well served by post bus. Passau has a municipal bus service that reaches into the hinterland.

By Boat The Danube, an important means of transport through eastern Bavaria, links the whole area with the rest of Germany and Eastern Europe. The Danube shipping company of **Ludwig Wurm** (Donaustr. 71, 8444 Irlbach, tel. 09424/1341) operates a passenger service in the summer between Regensburg and Passau. The company's comfortable motor ship *Agnes Bernauer* travels the Regensburg–Passau stretch on Sundays and the Deggendorf–Passau stretch on Tuesdays, Wednesdays, and Thursdays from July through September (Wednesdays and Thursdays only in June). The Passau shipping company of **Wurm & Köck** (Höllgasse 26, 8390 Passau, tel. 0851/2065) operates a service between Passau and Linz in Austria. Ships of the **Erste Donau-Dampfschiffahrts-Gesellschaft,** or DDSG for short (DDSG Schiffstation, Im Ort 14a, 8390 Passau, tel. 0851/33035), sail between Passau and Vienna. Wurm & Köck also operates short cruises on the Danube, the Inn, and the Ilz rivers (*see* Guided Tours, below).

Guided Tours

The tourist offices at Freyung, Grafenau, and Tittling organize bus tours of the region and excursions into Czechoslovakia. The Freyung tourist office (tel. 08551/4455) has weekly half-day trips to the Bavarian National Park and to the Dreisessel Mountain for DM 8. The **Wolff** bus company in Furth im Wald (tel. 09973/2061) offers one- and two-day excursions to Prague in Czechoslovakia twice a week between May and October, plus trips to the former royal spa town of Karlsbad (now Karlovy Vary) in Bohemia, as do the tourist offices of Grafenau (tel. 08552/2085) and Tittling (tel. 08504/2666). In Tittling, the **Hötl** bus company (tel. 08504/2092) has daily excursions into the Bavarian Forest in summer. The **Furth im Wald** tourist office (tel. 09973/3813) publishes a sightseeing guide to border areas of Czechoslovakia, including the historic town of Domažlice.

Guided tours of Passau are organized from April through October by the city tourist office (tel. 0851/33421). There are two tours (at 10:30 and 2:30) from Monday to Friday, and one (at 2:30) on Saturdays and Sundays. Tours start at King Max Joseph monument in the Domplatz (the cathedral square) and last one hour. The cost is DM 3 per person. Tours of the Dom take place weekdays from May to November at 12:30 PM, starting from the right-hand aisle inside the cathedral (cost: DM 1).

Cruises on Passau's three rivers begin and end at the Danube jetties on Fritz-Schäffer Promenade. Forty-five–minute trips on the Danube, Inn, and Ilz are run year-round by **Wurm & Köck** (Höllgasse 26, 8390 Passau, tel. 0851/2065). The cost is DM 7 adults, DM 3 children. Wurm & Köck also has regular cruises on the Austrian section of the Danube that reach as far as Linz. A cruise to Linz, with an overnight stay in a four-star hotel and a return trip by train, costs DM 99. Longer cruises, to Vienna, for example, cost between DM 165 and DM 325 per person. On Saturdays from April through October, evening cruises with music are offered. Duty-free cigarettes and alcohol can be bought during cruises to the Austrian sections of the Danube and Inn; a liter of Austrian rum costs just DM 20 at the ship's bar.

On the Inn River, an Austrian shipping operator, **M. Schaurecker** (A.-Stifterstr. 581, A-4780 Schärding, tel. 0043/771–

23231), runs a daily service Tuesday through Sunday, mid-March through October, between Passau and the enchanting Austrian river town of Schärding. The round-trip fare is DM 12.

Exploring the Bavarian Forest

Highlights for First-time Visitors

Heilige Grabkirche, Deggendorf
Metten Abbey library
Bavarian Forest National Park
Passau Cathedral organ
Neue Residenz, Passau
View from the Mariahilfberg, Passau

From Cham to Dreiburgenland

Numbers in the margin correspond to points of interest on the Bavarian Forest map.

The gateway to the Bavarian Forest—and a key point on the
1 Ostmarkstrasse scenic route—is the little town of **Cham.** Located on the Regen River, Cham is distinguished by intact sections of original 14th-century town walls, including a massive tower, the Straubinger Turm. It also possesses a 15th-century town hall and an even older town wall gate, the Biertor.

Heading southeast from Cham on B-85, look for the ruins of a
2 medieval castle perched on the 2,500-foot-high **Haidstein** peak. Around the year 1200, it was home to the German poet Wolfram von Eschenbach. On the slopes is a 1,000-year-old linden tree known as Wolframslinde (Wolfram's linden tree). With a circumference of more than 50 feet, its hollow trunk could easily shelter 50 people.

As you head south on B-85 you'll pass sunny villages with trim streets and gardens and see two sinuous lakes created by the dammed Regen River. From here the Weisser (white) Regen soon becomes the Schwarzer (black) Regen.

Between the village of Prackenbach and the little town of
3 Viechtach you'll see a dramatic section of the **Pfahl,** one of Europe's most extraordinary geological phenomena. The ridge of glistening white quartz juts dramatically out of the ground in an arrow-straight spur that extends more than 100 kilometers (60 miles) through the Bavarian Forest. Here the quartz rises in folds to heights of 100 feet or more.

4 Stop in **Viechtach** to see its spectacularly decorated Rococo church and to visit the **Kristall Museum,** which houses a glittering display of semiprecious stones and crystals from all over the world. *Bahnhofstr., tel. 09942/8107. Admission: DM 3 adults, DM 1 children. Open daily 10–5 except public holidays.*

Ten kilometers (6 miles) beyond Viechtach is Patersdorf. Here you can turn right (south) onto B-11 toward the historic Danube town of Deggendorf, 21 kilometers (13 miles) away, and the

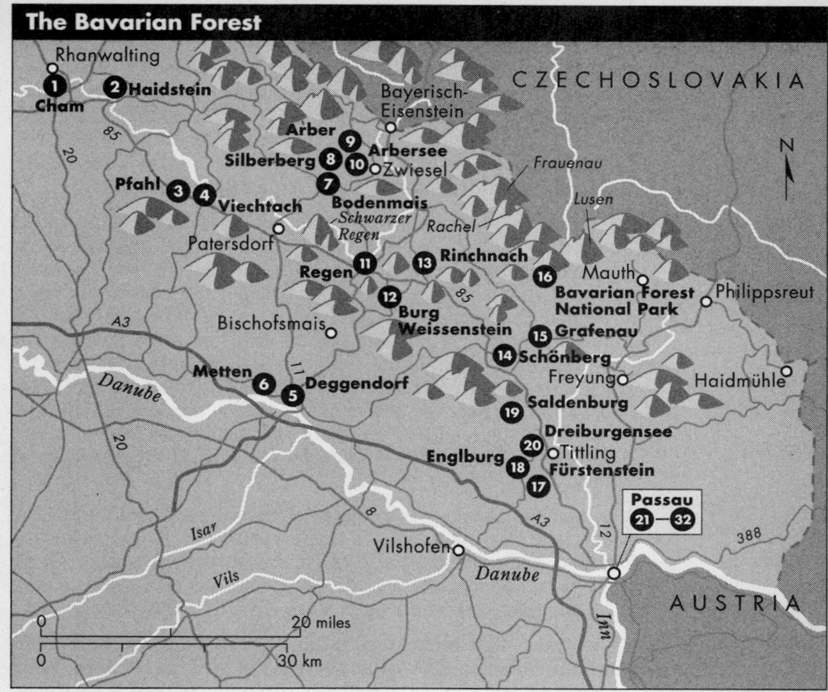

monastery of Metten, or turn left to visit the little spa of Bodenmais.

5 **Deggendorf** nestles between the Danube and the forested hills that rise in tiers to the Czech border. The town was once a settlement on the banks of the Danube, but repeated flooding forced its inhabitants to move to higher ground in the 13th century. A 30-yard stretch of the original town wall remains from those early years; there are other points of interest from later centuries, including a 16th-century **Rathaus** (Town Hall) located in the center of the wide main street, the Marktstrasse. *Tel. 0991/4004. Tower open weekdays 10–noon and 2–4, Sat. 10–noon. Admission: DM 1.50 adults and children.*

At one end of the Marktstrasse stands the **Heilige Grabkirche,** which was originally built as a Gothic basilica in the 14th century. Its lofty tower—regarded as the finest Baroque church tower in southern Germany—was added 400 years later by the Munich master builder Johann Michael Fischer. *Admission free. Open daily 9–sunset.*

Behind the church is the **Stadtmuseum** (City Museum), with exhibits tracing the history of the Danube people. *Admission free. Open Tues.–Sun. 10–4, Thurs. 10–8.*

Lovers of the Baroque may want to make a 7-kilometer (4-mile) side trip northwest of Deggendorf to the ancient Benedictine
6 abbey of **Metten,** founded in the 9th century by Charlemagne. Within its white walls and quiet cloisters is one of Germany's outstanding 18th-century libraries, with a collection of 160,000 books whose gilded leather spines are complemented by the he-

roic splendor of their surroundings: Herculean figures support the frescoed, vaulted ceiling, and allegorical paintings and fine stucco work identify different categories of books. In the monastery church is Cosmas Damian Asam's altar painting of *Lucifer Destroyed by St. Michael,* created in about 1720. Its vivid coloring and swirling composition are typical of the love of drama and movement in Baroque art. *Admission free (donations welcome). Guided tours daily at 10 and 3, except Easter.*

7 **Bodenmais,** 14 kilometers (9 miles) northeast of Patersdorf, is a
health resort tucked into a valley below the Bavarian Forest's
highest mountain, the 4,800-foot-high Arber. A nearby silver
mine helped Bodenmais gain prosperity before tourism
reached this isolated part of the country. The 700-year-old
mine was closed in 1962, but you can still view its workings near
8 the summit of the 3,000-foot-high **Silberberg** (Silver Mountain).
You can take the chair lift from the Arber Road, about 3 kilometers (2 miles) north of Bodenmais, or enjoy the easy, 25-minute
walk from the road to the entrance of the mine. *Admission, including guided tour: DM 5 adults, DM 3 children. Open daily
10–4.*

Bodenmais also boasts a long tradition of glass making. Glass foundries have been busy in the Bavarian Forest for centuries; indeed, some Germans still call it the Glass Forest. Two glassworks can be visited in Bodenmais: the **Austen Glashütte** and the **Waldglashütte** (both open Mon.–Fri. 9–6, Sat. 9–2).

9 The **Arber**—the highest mountain of both the Bavarian Forest
and the Bohemian Forest on the other side of the border—is located 13 kilometers (8 miles) north of Bodenmais. A bus service
runs from Bodenmais to the base of the mountain, where a
chair lift makes the 10-minute trip to the summit. A short walk
10 from the bottom of the lift leads to the **Arbersee lake,** surrounded by thick forest.

Time Out You can quench your thirst or fortify yourself for a hike up the Arber at the friendly **Gasthof Schareben** on the shores of the lake.

From Bodenmais, you'll join the Ostmarkstrasse again at
11 **Regen** (20 kilometers/12 miles south), a busy market town with
fine 16th-century houses around its large central square. On
the last weekend in July the town celebrates an event that made
culinary history: the creation in the 17th century of *Pichel-
steiner Eintopf* (pork and vegetable stew), a filling dish that
has become a staple throughout Germany. The celebrations include sports events on the Regen River, so pack a swimsuit if
you fancy joining in.

Regen has another claim to fame: a Christmas crèche created by Frau Maria-Elisabeth Pscheidl, who has been making the items for more than 30 years. Today her collection is claimed to be the biggest—and (according to the local tourist office) best—of its kind in the world—even the Vatican has given it a seal of approval. Many of her creations are displayed in the **Pscheidl Bayerwald-Krippe Museum,** run by the town council in Frau Pscheidl's home. The collection grows from week to week. "I'll be adding to it as long as God allows me to," says Frau Pscheidl. *Ludwigsbrücke 3. Admission: DM 2 adults, DM 1.50 children. Open whenever Frau Pscheidl is at home.*

Just south of Regen, on the heights of Weissenstein, are the
12 ruins of **Burg Weissenstein.** The far, square tower rising from the surrounding rubble is all that remains of the original 11th-century castle, which was largely destroyed in the War of the Austrian Succession during the 18th century.

Eight kilometers (5 miles) east of Regen, still on the Ost-
13 markstrasse, lies the village of **Rinchnach.** Once the administrative center of church lands that extended deep into the Bavarian Forest, it is now a sleepy resort. Its importance began with the arrival in the 11th century of a monk who had left his monastery in search of greater solitude. Over the centuries, this once-lonely retreat grew (with royal Bavarian patronage) into an important monastery. The **monastery church** you see today was built in the 15th century. In 1727, Johann Michael Fischer was summoned from Munich to extend and renovate it in Baroque style. Visit its expansive and lordly interior to see his masterful wrought-iron work and some typically heroic frescoes.

Drive 17 kilometers (10 miles) south and turn left off the
14 Ostmarkstrasse to the village of **Schönberg,** set snugly within the encroaching forest. Linger in its Marktplatz (market square), where arcaded shops and houses present an almost Italian air. As you head farther south down the Inn Valley, this Italian influence—the so-called Inn-Valley style—becomes more pronounced.

Time Out Drop in anytime of day at the **Gasthof zur Post,** where you can eat well and inexpensively from a menu that reads like a guide to the cuisine of the Bavarian Forest. The local beer is thought by many to be the best in the region.

Three miles east of Schönberg, deep in the Bavarian Forest, is
15 **Grafenau,** a typical little resort distinguished (for some people, anyway) as the favorite retreat of former West German Chancellor Willy Brandt.

Some 10 kilometers (6 miles) north of Grafenau is the main en-
16 trance to the **Bavarian Forest National Park,** a 32,000-acre stretch of protected dense forest. Bears, wolves, and lynx roamed wild in these parts until well into the 19th century. Substantial efforts have been made to reintroduce these and other animals to the park, though today the animals are restricted to large enclosures. Well-marked paths lead to points where the animals can best be seen. Bracing walks also take you through the thickly wooded terrain to the two highest peaks of the park, the 4,350-foot **Rachel** and the 4,116-foot **Lusen.** Specially marked educational trails trace the geological and botanical history of the area, and picnic spots and playgrounds abound. In winter, park wardens will lead you through the snow to where wild deer from the mountains feed. A visitor center—**The National Park-Haus**—is located at the main entrance to the park. Slide shows and English-language brochures provide introductions to the area.

South of Grafenau lies the **Dreiburgenland,** (the Land of the Three Castles). Its name comes from three famous castles:
17 18 19 **Fürstenstein, Englburg,** and **Saldenburg.** The little village of Fürstenstein likes to call itself the "Pearl of the Dreiburgenland." From the walls of its castle you can get a fine view of the Danube plain to the south and the mountains of the Bavari-

20 an Forest to the north. On the shores of the **Dreiburgensee** in Tittling, you'll find the **Freilichtmuseum** (Open-Air Museum), which boasts 50 reconstructed Bavarian Forest houses. You can sit on the benches of a 17th-century schoolhouse, drink schnapps in an 18th-century tavern, or see how grain was ground in a 15th-century mill. *Museum-Dorf Bayerische Wald, by Hotel Dreiburgensee, Tittling tel. 08504/8482. Admission: DM 3. Open daily 9–5.*

Passau

Twenty kilometers (12 miles) south on the Ostmarkstrasse, at the eastern limit of lower Bavaria and the Bavarian Forest, lies
21 the ancient city of **Passau,** a remote yet important embarcation point for the traffic that has plied its way along the Danube River for centuries, traveling between Germany, central Europe, and the Black Sea. Two other rivers meet at Passau: the Inn and the much smaller Ilz. The town's strategic location at the confluence of these three rivers has inevitably given rise to comparison with other cities built on water, including Venice.

While Passau is no "Venice of the North," it does share with that Italian city a certain quality of light that painters throughout the centuries have been attracted to and tried to capture in their work. The typical Inn Valley buildings along its old streets, with their low, graceful arcades, give the city something of a Mediterranean air. It should come as no surprise that many of the architects who worked in Passau were Italian.

Settled first by the Celts, then by the Romans, Passau soon passed into the possession of prince-bishops, whose power once stretched beyond Vienna into present-day Hungary. The influence they wielded over nearly six centuries has left its traces in the town's Residenz (bishop's palace), Sommerschloss Freudenhain (the bishops' summer castle), and magnificent Dom (cathedral).

Passau is situated on a narrow point of land where the Inn and Danube meet, with wooded heights rising on the far sides of both rivers. Fine old homes line the waterfront, and streets of varying levels rise to a hill in the center of the old city. Picturesque archways join one house to another, adding to the harmoniously proportioned appearance of this delightful small city. Little wonder that the 18th-century traveler Alexander von Humboldt included Passau in his list of the seven most beautifully situated cities in the world.

For 45 years, Passau was a backwater because of its location in a "lost" corner of Germany abutting the Iron Curtain. But recent political changes have placed the old city back in the limelight, and despite its years of isolation, you will find it elegant and dignified; its grande-dame atmosphere has far more in common with the stately demeanor of Vienna or Prague than with the brash approach of some cities in the Federal Republic.

Numbers in the margin correspond to points of interest on the Passau map.

Start your tour at a city square—the Kleiner Exerzierplatz—where progress has pushed aside a more gracious past. What was once a Benedictine monastery garden now houses a park-
22 ing lot and the **Nibelungenhalle,** a Nazi-era hall that seats 8,000. The name is taken from the *Nibelungenlied*, an epic

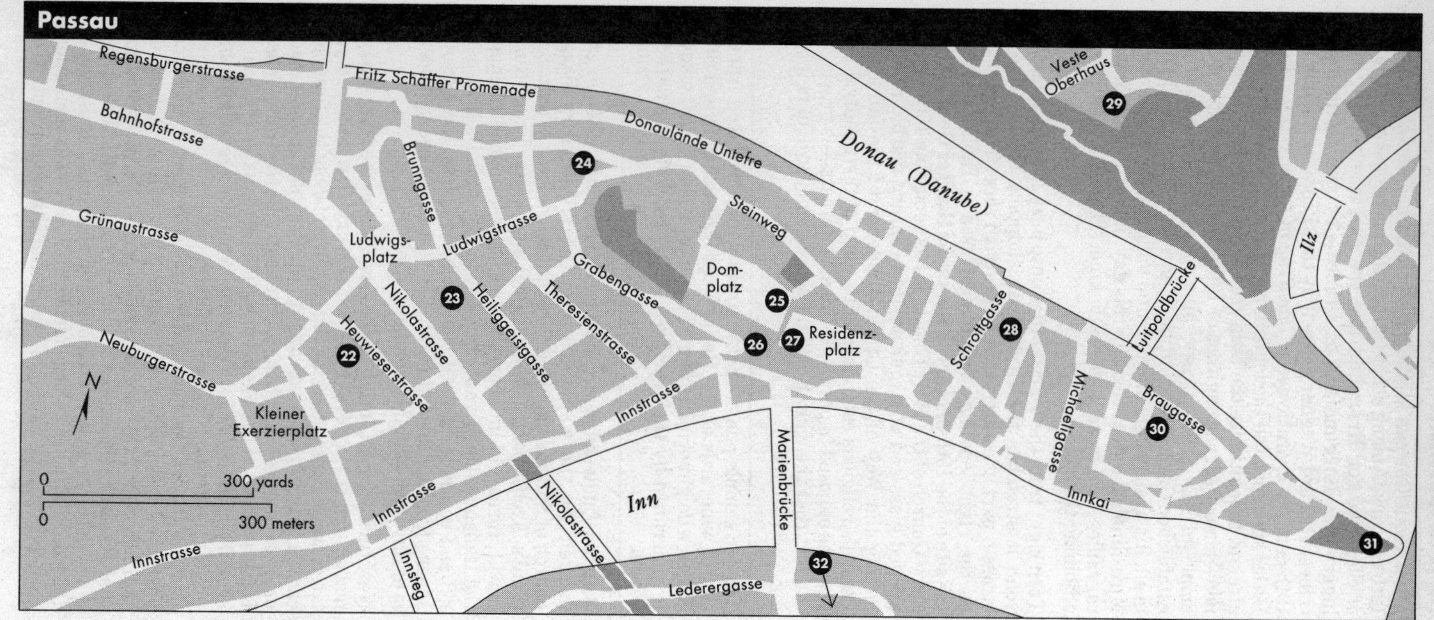

Alte Residenz, **26**
Dom, **25**
Dreiflusseck, **31**
Mariahilfberg, **32**
Neue Residenz, **27**
Nibelungenhalle, **22**
Niederburg Abbey, **30**
Rathaus, **28**
Rindermarkt, **24**
Spitalkirche Heiliger Geist, **23**
Veste Oberhaus, **29**

poem about German mythology written in Passau during the 12th century. Among other things, the poem describes the love of Siegfried for Kriemhild and the overthrow of the Nibelungs—the Burgundians of France—by the German Hun tribes. Richard Wagner chose it as the theme for his immense 19th-century operatic cycle, *The Ring of the Nibelung*. Later, Hitler appropriated the legend, recasting it in Nazi dress in an attempt to legitimize the Nazi creed. His obsession with Wagner—almost surpassing that of Ludwig IIs—was another example of his desire to see himself as an extension of an established Germanic tradition. Hence the name of the hall. All in all, it's a fairly ugly monumental building, the kind for which Mussolini had a weakness. To this day, it is still used for political rallies, of a more democratic kind. There's a tourist office adjoining the hall.

Turn right from the tourist office onto busy Ludwigsplatz. Beyond it stretches the city's main shopping street, Ludwigstrasse, part of an attractive pedestrian zone. The first street on the right leading off Ludwigstrasse is Heiliggeistgasse,
23 the site of the 15th-century **Spitalkirche Heiliger Geist,** or Infirmary Church of the Holy Ghost. It has some fine 16th-century stained glass and an exquisite 15th-century marble relief depicting the Way of the Cross. Evidence of the influence of Passau's religious establishments—and of their central European, as opposed to purely Germanic interests—is provided by the fact that the church still possesses vineyards in neighboring Austria.

Time Out You can sample one of the Austrian wines produced from the church vineyards at the **Heilig Geist Stift-Schenke und Stifts-Keller,** a neighboring tavern. The union of church and vineyard is underlined by the crucifixes that hang from the darkened beams.

---

24 Back on Ludwigstrasse, walk to **Rindermarkt,** the old cattle market. On the way you'll pass the 17th-century Baroque **church of St. Paul** and walk through the medieval **Paulusbogen** (Paul's Arch), part of the original city walls. From Rindermarkt, turn right into narrow Luragogasse (named after one of the Italian builders who were busy in Passau in the 18th century) and continue on until you reach **Domplatz,** the expansive square fronting the cathedral. The statue you see in its center is of Bavarian King Maximilian Joseph I.

25 Now turn your attention to the **Dom,** the cathedral. A baptismal church stood here in the 6th century. Two hundred years later, when Passau became the seat of a bishop, the first basilica was built. It was dedicated to St. Stephan and became the original mother church of St. Stephan's Cathedral in Vienna. Little was left of the medieval basilica after a fire reduced it to smoking ruins in the 17th century. What you see today is an impressively heroic Baroque building, complete with dome and flanking towers. As you wander around its marble- and stucco-encrusted interior, you may feel as if you're in an Italian cathedral. There's little here to remind you of Germany and much that proclaims the exuberance of Rome. Beneath the octagonal dome is the largest church organ in the world. Built between 1924 and 1928, and enlarged from 1979 to 1980, it claims no less than 17,388 pipes and 231 stops. Lunchtime concerts (DM 3

adults, DM 1 children) are given on the monstrous instrument from May through October at noon weekdays and on Thursdays (DM 6 adults, DM 3 children) at 7:30 PM.

Bordering Domplatz are a number of sturdy 17th- and 18th-cen-
26 tury buildings, including the **Alte Residenz,** the former bishop's
27 palace. Today it's a courthouse. The **Neue** (New) **Residenz** is next door, though its main entrance faces Residenzplatz, one of the most gracious and quiet corners of the town. Step through the stately Baroque entrance of the palace to see the dazzling staircase, a scintillating study in marble, fresco, and stucco.

Outside again, turn into Schrottgasse and head toward the Danube. You'll soon find yourself staring at the bright Gothic
28 facade of Passau's 13th-century **Rathaus** (town hall). Originally the home of a successful merchant, it was taken over after an uprising in 1298 and declared the seat of city government. Two assembly rooms of the Rathaus contain wall paintings depicting scenes from local history and lore, including the (fictional) arrival in the city of Siegfried's fair Kriemhild. The Rathaus can be visited only on guided tours arranged by the tourist office (*see* Guided Tours in Essential Information, above).

Outside the Rathaus, face the Danube, cross the bridge on your
29 right—the Luitpoldbrücke—and climb up to the **Veste Oberhaus,** the powerful fortress commissioned by Bishop Ulrich II in 1219. Today the Veste Oberhaus is Passau's most important museum, containing exhibits that illustrate the 2,000-year history of the city. It also commands a magnificent view of Passau and the three rivers that converge on it. *Museum admission: DM 3 adults, DM 1.50 children. Open Tues.–Sun. 9–5. A bus service operates from Rathausplatz Mar. 23–Oct. 13, Tues.–Sun. 12:30–4:30; June 1–Oct. 13, also 10:30–11:30. Closed Feb.*

Walk back across the Luitpoldbrücke and turn left to
30 **Niederburg Abbey.** Founded in the 8th century as a convent, it was destroyed by fire and rebuilt in the last century in a clumsy Romanesque style. Today it's a girls' school. In its church you can see the 11th-century tomb of a queen who was once abbess here—Gisela, sister of the emperor Heinrich II and widow of Hungary's first and subsequently sainted king, Stephan, who became the patron of the Passau cathedral.

Head now to Passau's other major river, the Inn, just a few steps away. Follow the river to the point where the Danube,
31 Ilz, and Inn meet—the **Dreiflusseck** (Corner of the Three Rivers). It's the end of the journey for the Inn—which flows here from the mountains of Switzerland and through Austria—and the much shorter Ilz, which rises in the Bavarian Forest; from here their waters are carried by the Danube to the Black Sea. The Inn's green water, the typical color of a mountain river, gives way slowly to the darker hues of the Danube, and the brownish Ilz adds its small contribution to this colorful natural phenomenon.

Another place to take in the meeting of the three rivers is the
32 **Mariahilfberg,** site of a 17th-century monastery pilgrimage church. It is located on the other side of the Inn, in the so-called Innstadt, or Inn City. It was here that in 1974 archaeologists uncovered the site of the Roman citadel of Boiotro, a stout fortress with five defense towers and walls more than 12 feet thick. A Roman well was also found, its water still plentiful and fresh. A 15th-century merchant's home has been converted

into a museum to house the items brought to light by the continuing excavations. *Römermuseum Kastell Boiotro, Am Severinstor. Admission: DM 2 adults, DM 1 children. Open Mar.–Nov., Tues.–Sun. 10–noon and 2–4 (June–Aug. from 1 PM). A guided tour is given the 1st and 3rd Wed. of the month at 5 PM.*

What to See and Do with Children

Passau has a fascinating **toy museum,** which includes many exhibits from the United States. There is a good collection of dolls, as well as many ancient model steam engines and locomotives. *Residenzplatz. Admission: DM 3 adults, family ticket DM 5. Open Mar.–Oct., daily 9:30–5:30; Nov.–Mar., weekends only.*

At Ortenburg, 22 kilometers (14 miles) west of Passau, there's an extensive **deer park,** where children can feed the animals. (Admission: DM 4 adults, DM 2 children. Open daily 8–6.) In winter, children can accompany wardens into the **Bavarian Forest National Park** to feed the wild deer. Contact the Nationale Parkverwaltung Bayerischer Wald (8352 Grafenau, tel. 08552/1300).

In the hamlet of Irgenöd, just outside Ortenburg, is the biggest **aviary** in eastern Bavaria. *Admission: DM 5 adults, DM 2.50 children. Open Apr.–Oct., 10–6.*

Beside the Grosse Arbersee Lake children can wander through the **Märchenwald** (Fairytale Wood), which features a collection of colorful model scenes from famous stories. *Entrance opposite Hotel Arberseehaus; open Easter–mid-Oct., daily 9–5.* In Loifling, near Cham, the **Churpfalz Park** offers hours of fun—from a puppet theater to miniature trains and a water carousel—while parents can wander 'round the extensive gardens. *Admission: DM 7.50, DM 4.50 children. Open Apr.–mid-Oct., daily 9–6.*

Off the Beaten Track

Anywhere in the Bavarian Forest is off the beaten track, but if you're looking for something more than isolated forest walks and glades, seek out two extraordinary private collections. The world's largest **snuffbox collection** is to be found on the third floor of Weissenstein castle near Regen. The 1,300 snuffboxes on display were collected over a period of 46 years by Regen's former mayor, Alois Reitbauer. His reward was an entry in the *Guinness Book of Records. Open late May–mid-Sept., daily 10–noon and 1–5.*

At Rhanwalting, near Cham, you'll find one of Germany's most unusual collections of **clocks** and time-measuring machines. It's in the back room of a country inn, the Uhren Wirt (literally, Clock Inn). Landlord Gerhard Babl has spent 30 years building up his collection of more than 400 timepieces. When he's not serving beers, he's happy to show you around between 10 AM and 5 PM.

An unusual reminder of the border that cuts through this forested region—and until recently divided two opposing political systems—is visible in **Bayerisch Eisenstein.** Here, at the foot of the Arber, the border runs through the middle of the sleepy town's train station. You might still see traces of Iron Curtain fortifications, though most were removed during 1990. The frontier gets confusing around the summit of Mt. Dreisessel, west of Altreichenau, and it's possible to walk in and out of a virtually forgotten corner of Czechoslovakia—a feat that was possible even during the years when the border was guarded everywhere else by heavily armed soldiers.

Dreisessel means "three armchairs," an apt description of the summit and its boulders, which are shaped like the furniture of a giant's castle. If you're driving to the Dreisessel, take B-12 to Philippsreut, just before the frontier, then follow the well-marked country road. The mountain is about 67 kilometers (40 miles) from Passau.

Shopping

In virtually every resort of the Bavarian Forest you'll find shops selling **glassware,** local **pottery,** and **wood carving** as well. In Passau, make for the **Ludwigstrasse** pedestrian zone. In Deggendorf, the small streets of the old quarter around the Rathaus are prime territory for shoppers.

The Bavarian Forest is famous for its **glassware,** which has been made in tiny workshops here for the past 500 years. Today more than 100 family glassware-making firms survive. At some you can watch the glass shapes being blown by craftsmen; nearly all have on-site exhibits and shops. The largest direct-sales outlet is the **Joska** foundry in Bodenmais next to the post office (open Mon.–Fri. 9–6; free tours 9–11:45 and 1–3:45, Sat. 9–12). The **Eisch** family in Frauenau, on the edge of the Bavarian Forest National Park, has been making glass since 1680 and their winged elephant trademark is internationally recognized as a mark of quality. Their glass foundry in Frauenau is open to visitors Monday through Friday 9–3 and Saturday 9:30–noon. You can buy directly from the showroom.

Sports and Fitness

Bicycling You can bicycle along the Danube from its source at Donaueschingen in southwest Germany to Passau on the Austrian border, a route that skirts the foothills of the Bavarian Forest for much of its final stretch. Excursion boats that ply the Danube between Regensburg and Passau carry bikes, enabling you to cycle one stage of the journey and let the Danube float you back. Bikes can be rented at most rail stations (DM 10–12 a day; DM 6–8 if you have a valid ticket) and at many resorts. **Sport Weinberger** (Jahnstr. 20, tel. 09924/397) in Bodenmais has a big selection.

Fishing The Weisser and Schwarzer Regen rivers are a challenge for anglers; there's also good fishing in the Danube, Inn, and Ilz rivers. Local tourist offices can supply permits. In Passau, call the local fishing club (tel. 0851/52407).

Golf Golfers can enjoy at least two advantages in the Bavarian Forest: lower greens fees (sometimes a fraction of what's charged in Upper Bavaria) and clubs that welcome visitors. There's a challenging course at **Schaufling,** high above Deggendorf, that offers fine views of the Bavarian Forest and the Danube plain.

Furth im Wald has a nine-hole course (tel. 09973/2089); at **Lam** there is an 18-holer (tel. 09943/1081).

Hiking The Bavarian Forest is prime hiking country, crisscrossed with trails of great variety and varied challenge. The longest, the **Pandurensteig,** runs nearly 167 kilometers (100 miles) from Waldmünchen in the northwest to Passau in the southeast, crossing the heights of the Bavarian Forest National Park. The trail can be covered in stages with the aid of a special tourist program that transfers hikers' luggage from one overnight stop to the other. Get details from **Fremdenverkehrsverband Ostbayern** (Landshuterstr. 13, 8400 Regensburg, tel. 0941/57186). Three resorts—Kellberg, Hauzenberg, and Buchelberg—have joined in a hiking-holiday scheme called **Wandern mit Tapetenwechsel** (Hiking with Change of Scene). The package consists of 14 days' hiking, bed-and-breakfast accommodations, tour assistance, and luggage transportation, all for around DM 450. For details, contact the **Verkehrsamt Kellberg** (8391 Thyrnau, tel. 08501/320).

Skiing Alpine skiers make for the World Cup slopes of the **Grosser Arber** (the summit is reached by chair lifts from Bayerisch-Eisenstein and from just outside Bodenmais). Other ski areas in the Bavarian Forest are not as demanding, and many resorts are ideal for family skiing vacations. St. Englmar, Frauenau, Furth im Wald, Waldmünchen, and the villages around the Brotjackelriegel, near Deggendorf, are the best. Cross-country trails are found everywhere in the Bavarian Forest; a map of 22 of the finest can be obtained free of charge from the **Fremdenverkehrsverband Ostbayern** (*see* Hiking, above). The pretty resort of Thurmansbang has a trail that stops at all of the best bargain inns of the area. For DM 230, Thurmansbang offers a week's bed-and-breakfast accommodations, cross-country ski instructions, and equipment rentals. Contact the **Verkehrsamt Thurmansbang** (tel. 08504/1642).

Swimming There are multipool lidos throughout the Bavarian Forest. The best are at Deggendorf, Passau, Vilshofen, Viechtach, and Waldkirchen. In summer, the forest lakes beckon swimmers, but avoid the Danube—it's doubly dangerous: There's a fast current, and the water is badly polluted.

Water Sports Sailboats and surfboards can be rented at most lakes; the Rannasee, the Perlsee, and the Egingersee are three of the prettiest. The Regen and the Inn rivers are perfect for canoeists. Canoes can be rented from **J. Denk** (Schmiedgasse 18, Passau, tel. 0851/31450) or through the tourist office in Roding, on the banks of the Regen (tel. 09461/1066).

Dining and Lodging

Dining

Food in the Bavarian Forest tends toward the wholesome and the hearty; large portions are very much the norm. Specialties include *Regensburger* (short, thick spicy sausages, rather like the *Bratwurst* of Nürnberg). Another sausage served here is *Bauernseufzer* (farmer's sigh). Dumplings, made out of virtually anything and everything, appear on practically every menu. Try *Deggendorfer Knödel* if you fancy something really local. The Danube provides a number of excellent types of fish, particularly *Donauwaller* (Danube catfish), from Passau. This is served *blau* (boiled) or *gebacken* (breaded and fried). The town of Tirschenreuth in the north of the region is the home of the equally delicious *Karpfen* (carp). Radishes are a specialty, especially *Weichser Rettiche*, and are a good accompaniment to the many local beers. Passau alone has four breweries—visit the Hacklberg brewery, one of the most photogenic in all Germany, and try "zwickel" beer.

Highly recommended restaurants are indicated by a star ★.

Category	Cost*
Very Expensive	over DM 90
Expensive	DM 55–DM 90
Moderate	DM 35–DM 55
Inexpensive	under DM 35

**per person for a three-course meal, including tax and tip but not drinks*

Lodging

Prices here are among the lowest in Germany. You'll find everything from humble bed-and-breakfasts and farmhouses charging barely DM 20 per person to first-class hotels. Many hotels offer special 14-day packages for the price of a 10-day stay, and 10-day packages for the price of a 7-day stay. There are also numerous packages available for riding, fishing, biking, tennis, hiking, and skiing vacations, with accommodations at low rates. All local tourist offices can supply lists of accommodations; most can help with reservations.

Highly recommended hotels are indicated by a star ★.

Category	Cost*
Very Expensive	over DM 180
Expensive	DM 120–DM 180
Moderate	DM 80–120
Inexpensive	under DM 80

**All prices are for a standard double room for two, including tax and service charge.*

Bayerisch-Eisenstein
Dining

Restaurant Waldspitze. On Tuesday and Friday nights the floor is cleared for dancing; on weekends there's a zither player. The mood, like the food, is very Bavarian, with excellent Austrian strudel representing just about the only foreign influence. *Hauptstr. 4, tel. 09925/714. Reservations advised. Dress: informal. No credit cards. Moderate.*

Lodging

★ **Sporthotel Brennes.** Ask for a room with a view of the Grosser Arber, the highest mountain of the Bavarian and Bohemian forests. The ski run begins virtually at the front door. *Brennes 14, tel. 09925/256. 33 rooms with bath. Facilities: solarium, restaurant. AE, DC, MC, V. Closed Nov.–mid-Dec. and Mar.–Apr. Expensive.*

Waldspitze. This is a large, comfortable, and well-appointed hotel, with a variety of sports facilities and a sauna and steam bath for relaxing tired muscles. *Hauptstr. 4, tel. 09925/308. 50 rooms and 100 suites with bath. Facilities: indoor pool, table tennis, billiards, sauna, solarium, steam bath, restaurant. No credit cards. Moderate.*

Pension Sonneneck. A traditional Bavarian guest house on the edge of forest hiking trails, the Sonneneck offers Alpine and cross-country skiing in winter. Lessons are conducted by the hotel's certified proprietor. *Am Buchenacker 18, tel. 09925/467/8. 23 rooms, most with bath. Facilities: sauna, fitness room, games room, sun terrace, lodgers-only restaurant. No credit cards. Inexpensive.*

Bischofsmais
Lodging

Hotel Wastlsäge. Rolling, forested countryside surrounds this extensive resort hotel. The cross-country skiing is great, and the walking trails are endless. *Lina-Müller–Weg 3, tel. 09920/170. 86 rooms and 5 apartments with bath or shower. Facilities: indoor pool, sauna, solarium, masseur, tennis courts, bowling alleys, table tennis, billiards, hairdressing salon, restaurant. AE, MC, V. Closed Nov.–mid-Dec. Moderate.*

Bodenmais
Lodging

Bodenmaiser Hof. In a holiday town with lots of choices, the Hof's quality and reputation bring German visitors back year after year. Guest rooms paneled in pale pine are a cut above the average, with ample facilities. The geranium-bedecked Hof even has its own bakery and butcher shop, which ensures the freshness and quality of the food prepared for guests. *Risslochweg 4, 8373 Bodenmais, tel. 09924/1841. 13 rooms with bath. Facilities: restaurant, sauna, solarium, fitness room, sun terrace. No credit cards. Moderate.*

Cham
Dining

Bürgerstuben. The Stuben is in Cham's central Stadthalle (city hall). Tasty local dishes and an appealingly simple atmosphere add up to an authentic Bavarian experience. *Fürtherstr. 11, tel. 09971/1707. Reservations advised on weekends. Dress: informal. DC. Inexpensive.*

Lodging

Randsbergerhof. At this rambling old hotel with beamed ceilings and ornate, hand-painted walls, owner Fritz Wittmann and his family sponsor public evenings of folk music and dancing. *Randsbergerhofstr. 15, tel. 09971/1266. 85 rooms with bath. Facilities: sauna, solarium, bowling alley, squash courts, cinema, restaurant. AE. Moderate.*

Gästeheim am Stadtpark. The most expensive single room in this friendly guest house costs all of DM 35. The place is unbeatable for value and basic comfort. *Tilsiterstr. 3, tel. 09971/2253. 11 rooms with shower. MC. Inexpensive.*

Deggendorf
Dining

Charivari. Richard Kerscher's flower-bedecked restaurant offers a complete change from the typical fare of the region. Classic French specialties include duck in orange sauce, but try the *Pickelsteiner Eintopf*, a fish-and-vegetable hotpot, often with salmon. *Bahnhofstr. 26, tel. 0991/7770. Reservations advised. Jacket and tie advised. AE, MC. Closed Sun., Mon. and Sat. lunch. Expensive.*

Ratskeller. If you eat here, beneath the vaulted ceilings of the Rathaus (town hall), you could easily find yourself sharing a table with a town councillor, perhaps even the mayor. The menu is strictly Bavarian; the beer flows freely. *Oberer Stadpl. 1, tel. 0991/6737. No reservations. Dress: informal. MC. Closed Fri. Moderate.*

Zum Grafenwirt. In winter, ask the host for a place near the fine old tiled stove that sits in the dining room. Try such filling dishes as roast pork and Bavarian dumplings. In summer, watch for the appearance of Danube fish on the menu. *Bahnhofstr. 7, tel. 0991/8729. Reservations advised on weekends. Dress: informal. Closed Tues. and June 2–18. AE, DC, MC. Moderate.*

Lodging ★ **Schlosshotel Egg.** The "Egg" of this castle-hotel's name isn't a reference to what you can expect in its excellent restaurant; it comes from Thiemo de Ekke, the original owner of the castle back in the 12th century. Today the hotel is an atmospheric and memorable place in which to lay your head, but try for a room in the castle itself rather than in the adjoining guest house—all are large, and some have four-poster beds. The hotel is located 13 miles outside Deggendorf. *8351 Schloss Egg, tel. 09905/289. 19 rooms with bath. Facilities: restaurant. AE, DC, MC, V. Expensive.*

Berggasthof Rusel. This mountainside inn, high above Deggendorf and a 15-minute drive from the town center, is an ideal retreat for walkers, golfers, and skiers. A golf course is near at hand; mountain trails start at the front door; and the inn has its own ski lift, which is floodlit six nights a week. *8351 Schaufling (on B-11 north), tel. 09920/316. 35 rooms, 20 with bath. Facilities: restaurant. AE, DC, MC, V. Closed Nov. Inexpensive.*

Grafenau
Dining ★ **Säumerhof.** The Bavarian Forest isn't known for haute cuisine but here, in one of its prettiest resorts, is a restaurant that bears comparison with Germany's best. It's part of a small country hotel (with 10 moderately priced and homey rooms if you want to stay the night) run by the Endl family. The kitchen is Gebhard Endl's territory, where he produces original, nouvelle-inspired dishes using mainly local produce. Try the pheasant on champagne cabbage, or the roast rabbit in herb-cream sauce. *Steinberg 32, tel. 08552/2401. Reservations advised. Jacket and tie optional. No credit cards. Very Expensive.*

Lodging **Parkhotel.** The modern exterior of this hotel disguises a cozy, traditional interior, with exposed wood beams and dark paneling. A large open fire in the lounge continues the rustic theme. *Freyungerstr. 51, tel. 08552/2444. 50 rooms with bath. Facilities: indoor pool, sauna, solarium, restaurant, bicycle rentals. AE, DC, MC, V. Closed Nov. 18–Dec. 16. Very Expensive.*

Steigenberger-Hotel Sonnenhof. If you have children, this is the hotel for you: The staff includes a *Spieltante* (playtime auntie) who keeps youngsters amused. It's a gracious, modern hotel, set on extensive grounds with many sports activities, plus horse-drawn sleigh rides in winter. *Sonnenstr. 12, tel. 08552/2033. 196 rooms with bath. Facilities: indoor pool, indoor and outdoor tennis courts, minigolf, sauna, solarium, shooting gallery, bowling alley, fitness center, beauty salon, nightclub, 2 restaurants, bar. AE, DC, MC, V. Expensive.*

Haidmühle
Dining **Adalbert Stifter.** Named after a popular 19th-century Bavarian Forest poet, this friendly country hotel-restaurant at the foot of the Dreisessel Mountain is at its best turning out the sort of time-honored dishes Stifter knew. Try one of the Bohemian-style roasts, for instance, served with fresh dumplings. *Frauenberg 32, tel. 08556/355. Reservations advised. Dress: informal. Closed Nov.–Dec. 20. MC. Moderate.*

Mauth
Dining

Barnriegel. This family-run restaurant is on the edge of the Bavarian Forest National Park and caters to appetites sharpened by a day's walking. If sauerbraten is on the menu, order it. Local lake fish is also a specialty. *Hauptstr. 2, Finsterau, tel. 08557/701. Reservations advised. Dress: informal. No credit cards. Closed Mon. Apr.–June. Moderate.*

Passau
Dining

★ **Passauer Wolf.** This riverside hotel-restaurant has big-city flair and a cuisine hard to match in this part of Germany. No Bavarian Gemütlichkeit here; instead, the elegance of starched linen and fine porcelain. Prices can be high, but quality is tops. Try any of the Danube fish dishes. *Rindermarkt 6–8, tel. 0851/34046. Reservations required. Jacket and tie required. AE, DC, MC, V. Closed Sun. evening. Expensive.*

★ **Heilig-Geist-Stiftsschenke.** For atmospheric dining, this onetime monastery-turned-wine-cellar, dating from the 14th century, is a must. In summer you eat beneath chestnut trees; in winter, seek out the warmth of the vaulted dining rooms. The wines are excellent and suit all seasons. *Heiliggeistgasse 4, tel. 0851/2607. Reservations advised. Dress: informal. AE, DC, MC. Closed Wed. and Jan 10–Feb. 2. Moderate.*

★ **Gasthof Andorfer.** One of the finest wheat beers in lower Bavaria is brewed and served here, and you can drink it on a lime-tree-shaded terrace overlooking the grain fields. The brewery tavern is in Passau-Ries, a couple of miles north of the city center, near the Veste Oberhaus fortress. The menu is basic, but the beer and the surroundings are what count. There are a few rooms if you fancy spending the night. *Rennweg 2, tel. 0851/51372. No reservations. Dress: informal. No credit cards. Closed weekends. Inexpensive.*

Peschl Terrasse. The beer you sip on the high sun terrace overlooking the Danube is brought fresh from the old town brewery below, which, along with this traditional Bavarian restaurant, has been in the same family since 1855. *Rossstränke 4, tel. 0851/2489. No reservations. Dress: informal. No credit cards. Closed Mon. Inexpensive.*

Ratskeller. The arched rooms of Passau's time-honored Ratskeller are a short walk from the Danube. Fish figures prominently on the menu; there are also imaginative meat dishes. Wash down whatever you order with a glass of beer. *Rathauspl., tel. 0851/2630. No reservations. Dress: informal. No credit cards. Inexpensive.*

Lodging

Hotel König. Though built only in 1984, the König blends successfully with the graceful Italian-style buildings alongside its elegant waterfront setting on the Danube. Rooms are large and airy; most have a fine view of the river. *Untere Donaulände 1, tel. 0851/35028. 40 rooms with bath. Facilities: sauna, solarium. AE, DC, MC, V. Expensive.*

Weisser Hase. More than four centuries of tradition lie within the stout walls of the centrally located Weisser Hase (White Rabbit), but the rooms are plain. *Ludwigstr. 23, tel. 0851/34066. 117 rooms, 95 with bath. Facilities: wine bar and restaurant. AE, DC, MC, V. Expensive.*

★ **Wilder Mann.** Sleep beneath chandeliers and richly stuccoed ceilings in beds of carved oak or with ornate 19th-century decoration. The pool is memorably located in the 11th-century vaulted cellars of this onetime merchant's house. Class and comfort abound. *Am Rathauspl., tel. 0851/35071. 60 rooms and 5 suites with bath. Facilities: indoor pool, roof terrace, restaurant, café. AE, DC, MC. Expensive.*

★ **Schloss Ort.** Those with a yen to stay in a 13th-century castle that's been modernized with taste will appreciate not only the atmospheric surroundings of the Schloss Ort but its great location at the Dreiflusseck, meeting point of the Danube, Ilz, and Inn. *Ort 11 (am Dreiflusseck), tel. 0851/34072. 38 rooms, most with bath or shower. Facilities: riverside terrace and garden, restaurant. AE, DC, MC, V. Closed mid-Jan.–Feb. Moderate.*

Regen
Lodging

Burggasthof Weissenstein. The ruins of the medieval Weissenstein castle loom over you as you breakfast on the sunny terrace of the Burggasthof, which overlooks the old town. Ask for a room with a view of either. *Weissenstein 32, tel. 09921/2259. 15 rooms with bath. Facilities: restaurant. No credit cards. Closed Nov. Inexpensive.*

Gasthof-Pension Wieshof. A former farmhouse, the Wieshof retains a rural air while offering modern comfort. Wood paneling, beams, and antiques add to the rustic atmosphere. *Poschetsriederstr. 2, tel. 09921/4312. 15 rooms with bath. Facilities: bowling alley. No credit cards. Inexpensive.*

Schönberg
Dining and Lodging
★

Hotel Antonios Hof. The wood balconies of this chalet-style hotel, located on the edge of the Bavarian Forest National Park, provide a colorful contrast to its comfortably traditional interior. Wood is everywhere, from the low beams of the snug tavern to the carved pillars of the restaurant. Try the fish if you eat here: it comes directly from the hotel's own pond. *Unterer Marktpl. 12, tel. 08554/575. 40 rooms with bath. Facilities: indoor pool, sauna, solarium, bowling alleys, restaurant. No credit cards. Moderate.*

Viechtach
Dining and Lodging

Kur-und-Sporthotel Schmaus. This place is for the energetic with a big appetite. All-weather sports facilities at the Schmaus range from tennis to swimming. The kitchen of the hotel—run by the same family for generations—turns out meals on the assumption that every guest has just finished a 25-mile hike through the forest. In summer, dine in the grill garden. Ask for a room in the older part—some of the modern rooms are plain. *Stadtplatz 5, tel. 09942/1627. 42 rooms with bath. Facilities: restaurant, wine bar, pool, sauna, solarium, tennis hall, sun terrace. AE, DC, MC, V. Moderate.*

Vilshofen
Lodging

Bayerischer Hof. Vilshofen's Bayerischer Hof may be stars short of Munich's famous hotel of the same name, but it offers comfortable accommodations in a pleasant, parklike setting. *8358 Vilshofen, tel. 08541/5065. 31 rooms, half with bath or shower. Facilities: beer garden, restaurant (closed Sat. in winter). MC. Closed Dec. 27–Jan 10. Moderate.*

Zwiesel
Dining

Bräustüberl. Sample the beers of one of the oldest—and, some say, best—breweries in the Bavarian Forest, the Erste Dampfbierbrauerei. The brewery is next door; visitors are welcome. There's a basic menu of Bavarian fare. *Regenerstr. 9, tel. 09922/1409. No reservations. Dress: informal. No credit cards. Inexpensive.*

Gasthof Deutscher Rhein. Bohemian cuisine is the specialty at this traditional forest-country tavern, which also has guest rooms and a brewery (producing eight different brews), all under one roof. There's live Bavarian zither music most summer evenings. *Am Stadtpl., tel. 09922/1651. Reservations advised. Dress: informal. AE, DC, MC, V. Closed Sun. evening, Mon. Inexpensive.*

Lodging **Hotel zur Waldbahn.** The great-grandfather of the current owner, assisted by 13 children, built the Hotel zur Waldbahn more than 100 years ago to accommodate travelers on the trains connecting Czechoslovakia with all points south. Today the emphasis is still put on making the traveler feel at home within the hotel's historic, wood-paneled walls. *Bahnhofpl. 2, tel. 09922/3001. 28 rooms with bath or shower. Facilities: restaurant, sauna, whirlpool, fitness room. No credit cards. Closed Nov. Moderate.*

Kurhotel Sonnenberg. Located high above Zwiesel, the Sonnenberg offers fine views of the forest and quick access to mountain walks and ski runs. It's a sporty hotel, with numerous fitness facilities. *Augustinerstr. 9, tel. 09922/2031. 31 rooms, 1 apartment, 1 suite; all double rooms with bath or shower. Facilities: indoor pool, sauna, solarium, fitness room, beauty salon, restaurant. No credit cards. Moderate.*

The Arts

Passau is the cultural center of Lower Bavaria and its Europäische Wochen (European Weeks) festival—featuring everything from opera to pantomine—is now a major event on the European music calendar. The festival runs from June to early August. For program details and reservations, write the **Kartenzentrale der Europäischen Wochen Passau** (Nibelungenhalle, 8390 Passau tel. 0851/7966).

Passau also has a thriving theater company, the **Stadttheater,** which has its home in the beautiful little Baroque opera house of Passau's prince-bishops. Program details and reservations from **Stadttheater Passau** (Gottfried-Schäffer-Str. 8390 Passau). The city's cabaret company, the **Theater im Scharfrichter-Haus** (Milchgasse 2, tel. 0851/35900) is nationally famous and hosts a German cabaret festival every fall (Oct.–Dec.). Fall is also the time for Passau's annual Kirmes (fair), followed in December by a **Christkindlmarkt** in the Nibelungenhalle (Dec. 1–20). A Christmas market is also held in Cham.

At **Furth im Wald** (north of Cham), August sees Germany's oldest street **folk festival,** dating from medieval times. Dressed in period costume, townsfolk take part in the ritual slaying of a fire-breathing "dragon" that stalks the main street.

The Stiftung Worlen Museum Moderner Kunst (Braugasse 17, tel. 0851/34091), a new modern-art gallery, opened in Passau in 1990.

Jazz fans make for nearby Vilshofen every June for the annual international jazz festival, staged in a special tent on the banks of the Danube. For program details and reservations, call 08541/2080.

7 The Black Forest

Including Freiburg

Introduction

The Black Forest—*Schwarzwald* in German—is a name that conjures up images of a wild, isolated place where time passes so slowly it can be measured by the number of rings on the trunks of felled trees. And this southwest corner of Germany is indeed a rural region where dense woodland stretches away to the horizon; but it is neither inaccessible nor a backwater. The first recorded holidaymakers checked in here 19 centuries ago, when the Roman emperor Caracalla and his army rested and soothed their battle wounds in the natural-spring waters of what later became Baden-Baden.

Celebrated names have long been associated with the Black Forest. In 1770 the 15-year-old daughter of the empress Maria Theresa, traveling between Vienna and Paris with an entourage of 250 officials and servants in some 50 horse-drawn carriages, made her way along the coach road through the Höllental (Hell Valley) to spend the night at Hinterzarten, where the future Queen Marie Antoinette checked into a renowned coach inn that had been in business since 1446; now called the Park Hotel Adler, it's still number one in that prestigious resort town *(see* Dining and Lodging, below).

In the 19th century, just about everyone who mattered in Europe gravitated to Baden-Baden: kings, queens, emperors, princes and princesses, members of Napoléon's family, and the Russian nobility, along with actors, actresses, writers, and composers. Turgenev, Dostoevsky, and Tolstoy were among the Russian contingent. Victor Hugo was a frequent visitor. Brahms composed lilting melodies in this calm setting. Queen Victoria spent her vacations here. This is still a favorite vacation setting for millionaires, movie stars, and the new corporate royalty.

Mark Twain could be said to have put the Black Forest on the tourist map for Americans. In his 1880 book *A Tramp Abroad*, he waxed poetic on the beauties of this forest.

Today you can come here for rest and relaxation and to "take the waters," as the Romans first did, at thermal resorts large or small. The Black Forest offers a wide range of sporting activities, catering particularly to the German enthusiasm for hiking with its virtually limitless trails wending their way in and out of the woods. In winter these same trails serve as tracks for cross-country skiing on some of the most ideally suited terrain in all of Europe for this popular sport.

The Black Forest's enviable sporting scene is blessed by dependable snow in winter and warming sun in summer. Freudenstadt, at the center of the Black Forest, claims the greatest number of annual hours of sunshine of any town in Germany. Most resorts offer tennis, swimming, and bicycle riding, and some boast golf courses of international standards.

The Black Forest is Germany's southernmost wine region and home to some of the country's finest traditional food. Black Forest smoked ham and Black Forest cake are both world-famous, and that's only the beginning.

The Black Forest also happens to be the home of the cuckoo clock, despite Orson Welles's claim in *The Third Man* that all Switzerland managed to create in 500 years of peace and prosperity was this trivial timepiece. Cuckoo clocks are still made (and sold) here, as they have been since more or less time immemorial, along with hand-carved wood artifacts and exquisite examples of glassblowing *(see* Shopping, below).

For all its fame, the Black Forest still offers great value. It's possible to stay at a modest, family-run country inn or farmhouse where you'll start the day with an enormous breakfast to keep you going for the better part of the day—all for not much more than the price of a meal in a German city restaurant.

Essential Information

Important Addresses and Numbers

Tourist Information Information for the entire Black Forest is available from **Fremdenverkehrsverband,** Bertoldstrasse 45, 7800 Freiburg, tel. 0761/31317. There are local tourist information offices in the following towns:

Baden-Baden. Kurverwaltung, Augustaplatz 8, 7570 Baden-Baden, tel. 07221/275–200.
Badenweiler. Kurverwaltung, Ernst-Eisenlohr-Strasse 4, 7847 Badenweiler, tel. 07632/72110.
Bad Herrenalb. Kurverwaltung, 7506 Bad Herrenalb, tel. 07083/7933.
Bad Liebenzell. Kurverwaltung, Kurhausdamm 4, 7263 Bad Liebenzell, tel. 07052/408–100.
Feldberg. Kurverwaltung im Ortsteil Altglashütten, Kirchgasse, 1, 7821 Feldberg, tel. 07655/8019.
Freiburg. Verkehrsamt, Rotteckring 14, 7800 Freiburg im Breisgau, tel. 0761/368–9090.
Freudenstadt. Kurverwaltung, Promenadenplatz 1, 7290 Freudenstadt, tel. 07441/8640.
Pforzheim. Stadtinformation, Rathaus, Marktplatz 1, 7530 Pforzheim, tel. 07231/392–190.
Schluchsee. Kurverwaltung, Fischbacherstrasse, 7826 Schluchsee, tel. 07656/7732.
Titisee-Neustadt. Kurverwaltung, in Kurhaus, 7820 Titisee-Neustadt, tel. 07651/810104.
Triberg. Kurverwaltung im Kurhaus, Luisenstrasse 10, 7740 Triberg, tel. 07722/8123–0231.
Wildbad. Verkehrsamt, König-Karl-Strasse 7, 7547 Wildbad, tel. 07081/10280.

Car Rental **Avis:** in **Baden-Baden,** Langestrasse 93, tel. 07221/31717; in **Freiburg,** St.-Georgenerstrasse 7, tel. 0761/42288.
Europcar: in **Baden-Baden,** Rheinstrasse 29, tel. 07221/64031; in **Freiburg,** Wilhelmstrasse 1A, tel. 0761/31066.
Hertz: in **Baden-Baden,** Lichtenalerstrasse 39, tel. 07221/22471; in **Freiburg,** Eschholzstrasse 42, tel. 0761/272–020.

Arriving and Departing by Plane

The closest international airports are at Stuttgart and the Swiss border city of Basel, the latter just 70 kilometers (40 miles) from the largest city in the Black Forest, Freiburg.

Arriving and Departing by Train and Car

By Train The main rail route through the Black Forest runs north–south, following the Rhine Valley. There are fast and frequent trains to Freiburg and Baden-Baden from most major German cities.

By Car The Rhine Valley Autobahn, A-5, runs the length of the Black Forest, connecting with the rest of the Autobahn system at Karlsruhe, north of the Black Forest.

Freiburg, the region's major city, is 410 kilometers (260 miles) from Munich and 275 kilometers (170 miles) from Frankfurt.

Getting Around

By Train Local lines connect most of the smaller towns. Two east–west routes—the Black Forest Railway and the Höllental Railway—are among the most spectacular in the country. Details are available from **Deutsche Bundesbahn** (German Railroads) in Freiburg (tel. 0761/36440).

By Car Good two-lane highways crisscross the entire region, making driving here easy and fast. The region's tourist office *(see* Important Addresses and Numbers, above) has established a series of specially designated tourist driving routes: the High Road, the Low Road, the Spa Road, the Wine Road, and the Clock Road. Though intended primarily for drivers, most points along them can also be reached by train or bus.

Guided Tours

Bus tours of the Black Forest are available in **Freiburg** and **Baden-Baden.** The Freiburg tourist information office offers one-day tours of the Black Forest and parts of neighboring Switzerland. Tours start from DM 40 for adults and DM 29 for children. In Baden-Baden, contact the **Deutsches Reisebüro** (Sofienstr. 16, tel. 07221/24666). Half-day tours to the French city of Strasbourg are also available.

Exploring the Black Forest

Highlights for First-time Visitors

Pforzheim Schmuckmuseum
Erzgrube Lake
Die Wolfacher Glashütte (glassblowing factory), Wolfach
Freiburg Münster
Baden-Baden

Pforzheim to Freiburg

Numbers in the margin correspond to points of interest on the Black Forest map.

1 Our tour begins at **Pforzheim,** an ancient city founded by the Romans and standing on a hilly site at the meeting place of three rivers, the most important of which is the Würm. The city is located on the A-8 Autobahn, the main Munich–Karlsruhe route. Pforzheim was almost totally destroyed in World War II, but painstaking reconstruction has restored much of the city to

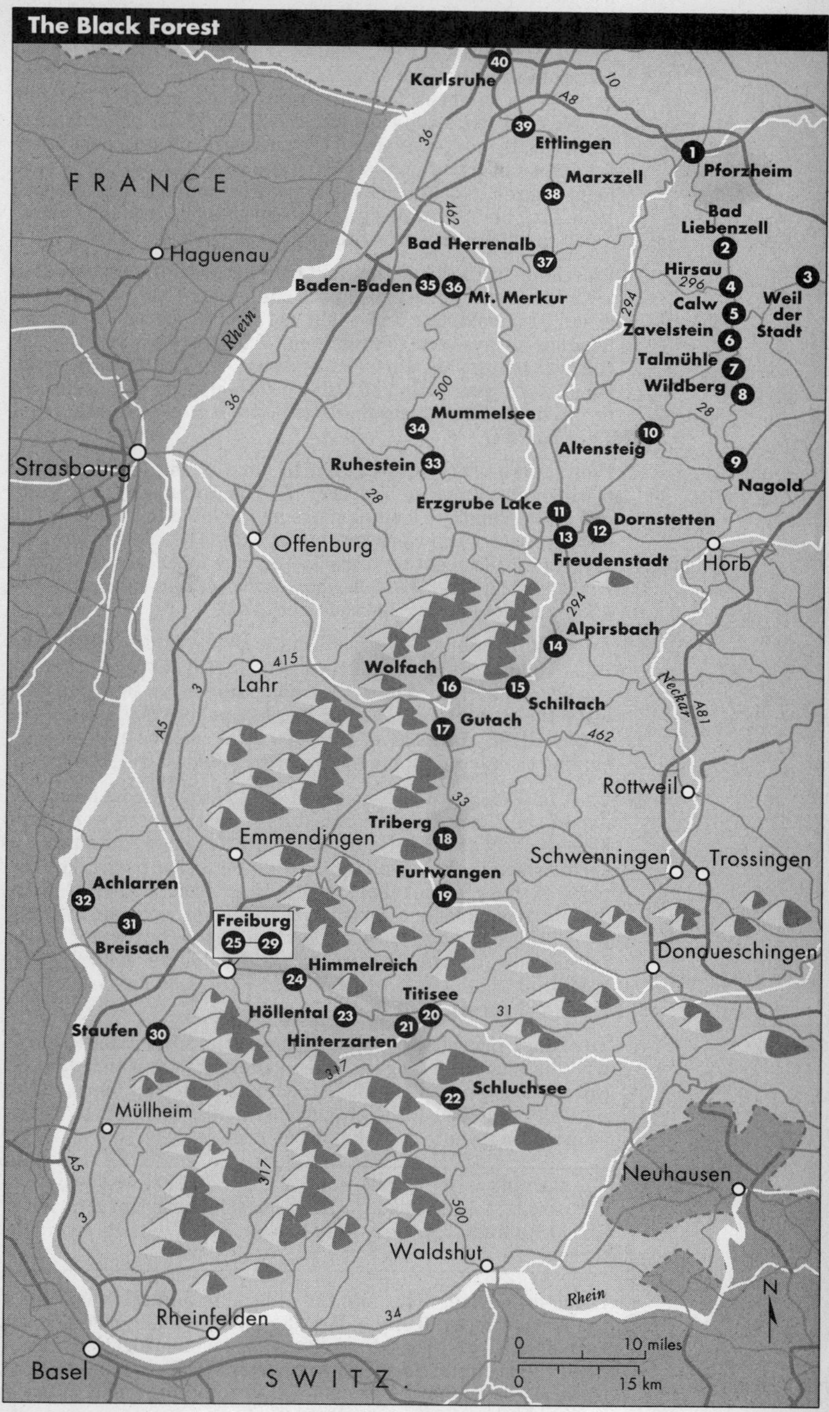

The Black Forest
FRANCE
SWITZ.
40 Karlsruhe
39 Ettlingen
1 Pforzheim
38 Marxzell
2 Bad Liebenzell
37 Bad Herrenalb
3 Weil der Stadt
4 Hirsau
5 Calw
6 Zavelstein
7 Talmühle
8 Wildberg
9 Nagold
10 Altensteig
35 36 Baden-Baden
Mt. Merkur
34 Mummelsee
33 Ruhestein
11 Erzgrube Lake
12 Dornstetten
13 Freudenstadt
14 Alpirsbach
15 Schiltach
16 Wolfach
17 Gutach
18 Triberg
19 Furtwangen
20 Titisee
21 Hinterzarten
22 Schluchsee
23 Höllental
24 Himmelreich
Freiburg 25 29
30 Staufen
31 Breisach
32 Achlarren
Haguenau
Strasbourg
Offenburg
Lahr
Emmendingen
Horb
Rottweil
Schwenningen
Trossingen
Donaueschingen
Neuhausen
Müllheim
Waldshut
Rheinfelden
Basel
Rhein
Neckar
A8
10
36
462
296
294
500
28
415
3
A5
A81
33
31
317
34
0 10 miles
0 15 km
N

its former elegance. For an example of the thoroughness of this postwar restoration work, visit the church of **St. Michael** in the center of the city. The original mixture of 13th- and 15th-century styles has been faithfully reproduced; contrast the airy Gothic choir with the church's sturdy Romanesque entrance. However, by no means are all the postwar buildings here faithful echoes of traditional styles. Take a look at another Pforzheim church, **St. Matthew's,** a tentlike construction built in 1953, long before the designers of the similarly styled Olympic stadium in Munich were at their drawing boards.

Pforzheim is known as the Gold City because of its association with the jewelry trade. Explore the jewelry shops on streets around Leopoldplatz and you'll see how important that business has always been to Pforzheim. The Reuchlinhaus, the city cultural center, has a jewelry museum, the **Schmuckmuseum.** Its glittering collection of 17th- to 20th-century jewelry is one of the finest in the world. *Jahnstr. 42. Admission free. Open Tues.–Sun. 10–5.*

Pforzheim's other major claim to fame is as a center of the German clock-making industry. In the **Technisches Museum,** one of the country's leading museums devoted to the craft, you can see watch- and clock-makers at work; there's also a reconstructed 18th-century clock factory. *Admission free. Bleichstr. 81. Open Wed. 9–noon and 3–6, and every 2nd and 4th Sun. of the month 10–noon and 2–7.*

Leave Pforzheim on the road south, B-463, which follows the twists and turns of the pretty little Nagold River. Gardeners should look for the signs to the **Alpine Garden** (on the left as you leave the city limits). The garden, located on the banks of the Würm River, stocks more than 100,000 varieties of plants, including the rarest Alpine flowers. *Open Apr.–Sept., daily 9–7.*

2 Back on B-463, you'll soon reach picturesque **Bad Liebenzell,** one of the Black Forest's oldest spas. Bathhouses were built here as early as 1403. Nearly six centuries later, the same hot springs feed the more modern installations that have taken the place of these medieval originals. Apart from medicinal baths (highly recommended for the treatment of circulatory problems), there is a lido with outdoor and indoor hot-water pools. *Paracelsus Baths. Admission: DM 11 for 2½ hours. Open Wed.–Sat. 8:30 AM–8 PM, Mon. and Tues. 8:30 AM–5 PM, Sun. 8:30 AM–7 PM.*

The other principal pastime in and around Bad Liebenzell is walking along the Nagold River valley. Winding through the thick woods around the little town is a path that leads to the partially restored 13th-century castle of **Liebenzell,** today an international youth center and youth hostel.

Time Out For morning coffee or afternoon tea, the **Café Schweigert** is ideally situated in the town center, overlooking the river. For lunch or dinner, try the nearby **Kronen Hotel,** with its riverside terrace.

If you have time, drive into the hills behind Bad Liebenzell to
3 the former imperial city of **Weil der Stadt,** a small, sleepy town with only its well-preserved city walls and fortifications to remind the visitor of its onetime importance. The astronomer Johannes Kepler, born here in 1571, was the first man to track

and accurately explain the orbits of the planets; the **Kepler Museum** in the town center is devoted to his discoveries. *Keplergasse 2. Admission: DM 1. Open Apr.–Sept., daily 9–5; Oct.–Mar, 1st and 3rd Sun. of the month 9–5.*

4 **Hirsau,** 5 kilometers (3 miles) southwest on B-463, is the site of the ruins of a 9th-century monastery, now the setting for open-air theater performances in the summer.

5 **Calw,** 3 kilometers (2 miles) farther south, is one of the prettiest towns of the Black Forest. The novelist Hermann Hesse (1877–1962) was born here.Pause on the town's 15th-century bridge over the Nagold River; if you're lucky you'll see a local tanner spreading hides on the river wall to dry, as his ancestors did for centuries. The town's market square, with its two sparkling fountains, is an ideal spot for relaxing, picnicking, or people-watching, surrounded by 18th-century half-timbered houses whose sharp gables stab at the sky.

6 On the road south again, watch for a sign to **Zavelstein,** 5 kilometers (3 miles) out of Calw. The short detour up a side valley to this tiny town is well worth taking, particularly in spring, when surrounding meadows are carpeted with wild crocuses.

Back on the main road going south, you'll come next to the vil-
7 lage of **Talmühle.** Here a side road leads to one of the oldest and, until it closed in 1924, most productive silver mines of the Black Forest, the **Neublach** mine. Since then a new use has been found for the mine's extensive workings. Doctors discovered that the dust-free interior of the mine helped in the treatment of asthma patients. Today, rather incongruously, a therapy center is located in the mine. The ancient shafts can also be visited. *Admission: DM 4 adults, DM 3 children. Open Apr.–Nov., Mon–Fri. 10–4, Sun. 10–4.*

8 Arrive in **Wildberg,** 8 kilometers (5 miles) farther south, on the third Sunday of July in an even-numbered year and you'll witness one of Germany's most picturesque contests, the **Schäferlauf,** in which Black Forest shepherds demonstrate their skills and speed in managing their flocks. Those unable to time their arrival quite so precisely will find that the appealing little fortified town nonetheless has much to command attention, including a 15th-century wooden town hall and the remains of a medieval castle.

Time Out In the town of **Nagold,** 10 kilometers (7 miles) farther south, drop in at the half-timbered **Alte Post** inn on the main street. Kings and queens have taken refreshment here on journeys through the Black Forest. Order a glass of the local beer and a plate of Black Forest smoked ham, or a pot of strong coffee and a slice of the famous Black Forest cake.

---

9 Leaving **Nagold,** head west toward Freudenstadt on local high-way B-28, a road that skirts another jewel of the Black Forest,
10 the ancient town of **Altensteig,** on a sunny terracelike slope above the Nagold River. Climb up the hill and you will discover the peace and beauty of the medieval town square below the fine Gothic castle.

11 In summer, pause at **Erzgrube Lake,** 9 kilometers (6 miles) farther along B-28, for a swim or a picnic. Boats and sailboards can be rented. The Black Forest is at its thickest here, with 200-year-old trees towering to heights of 150 feet or more.

B-28 skirts the oldest town of the northern Black Forest,
12 **Dornstetten.** If you fancy another dip into the past, stop to see the 17th-century town hall, flanked by equally venerable old buildings, their low, red-roofed eaves framing magnificent half-timbered facades. The fountain dates from the 16th century.

13 The road snakes through lush farmland to **Freudenstadt,** another war-torn city rebuilt with painstaking care. It's a young city by German standards, founded in 1599 to house workers from the nearby silver mines and refugees from religious persecution in what is now the Austrian province of Carinthia (*Freudenstadt* means City of Joy). You'll find the streets still laid out in the checkerboard formation decreed by the original planners, the vast central square still waiting for the palace that was intended to stand there. It was to have been built for the city's founder, Prince Frederick I of Württemberg; he, unfortunately, died before work could begin. Don't miss Freudenstadt's Protestant parish church, just off the square. Its lofty nave is L-shaped, a rare architectural liberty in the early 17th century, when this imposing church was built. Freudenstadt claims to enjoy more annual hours of sunshine than any other German resort, so sit in the sunbathed Renaissance arcades of the fine main square and bask in the warmth of the rays.

Time Out Sixteen kilometers (10 miles) farther, take a break for a glass of beer at any of the small taverns in the village of **Alpirsbach.** The unusually soft water gives the village-brewed beer a flavor that is widely acclaimed. The brewery was once part of a monastic settlement and visitors are welcome to look around. In summer, concerts are held regularly in Alpirsbach's fine 11th-century parish church.

---

14 15 South of **Alpirsbach,** stop at **Schiltach,** 10 kilometers (6 miles) along, to admire the frescoes on the 16th-century town hall. They tell the town's history more vividly than any local chronicle could. Look for the figure of the Devil, who was blamed for burning down the town on more than one occasion.

Leaving Schiltach, follow the B-294 highway 14 kilometers (9
16 miles) to **Wolfach.** It's the site of **Die Wolfacher Glashütte,** the only remaining Black Forest factory where glass is blown using the centuries-old techniques that were once common throughout the region. *Admission: DM 2.50 adults, DM 1.50 children. Open daily 9–3:30.*

Just outside Wolfach is one of the most diverting museums in the Black Forest, the **Vogtsbauernhof Freilichtmuseum** (Open-Air Museum). Farmhouses and other rural buildings from all parts of the region have been transported here from their original locations and reassembled, complete with traditional furniture, to create a living museum of Black Forest building types through the centuries. *Admission: DM 5 adults, DM 3 children. Open Apr.–Nov., daily 8:30–6.*

The road south from Wolfach follows the **Gutachtal,** a valley famous for the traditional costume worn by its women on feast days and holidays. If you're curious about why some women wear black pom-poms on their hats and others wear red, the answer's simple: Married women wear black pom-poms; unmar-
17 ried wear red. The village of **Gutach** is one of the best spots in

the Black Forest to see traditional thatched roofs. Escalating costs caused by a decline in thatching skills, in addition to the ever-present risk of fire, mean that there are already substantially fewer thatched roofs in Gutach than there were 20 years ago. But you'll still find more here than in just about any other town in the region.

At the head of the valley, 13 kilometers (9 miles) south, lies the
18 town of **Triberg,** site of Germany's highest waterfall, where the Gutach River plunges nearly 500 feet over seven huge granite steps. The pleasant 30-minute walk from the center of Triberg to the top of the spectacular falls is well signposted.

For some, however, the most compelling reason for visiting Triberg is to see the **Heimatmuseum** (Wallfahrtstr. 4), the local history museum. This is cuckoo-clock country, and the museum has an impressive collection of clocks. The oldest dates from 1640; its simple wooden mechanism is said to have been carved with a bread knife. Die-hard clock enthusiasts will want to con-
19 tinue on to the **Uhrenmuseum** in **Furtwangen,** 16 kilometers (10 miles) south. It's another clock museum, the largest in Germany, and charts the development of Black Forest clocks, the cuckoo clock taking pride of place. Its massive centerpiece is a 25-hundredweight astronomical clock built by a local master. *Admission: DM 3 adults, DM 1 children. Open Apr.–Oct., daily 9–5.*

From Furtwangen, you're only 21 kilometers (13 miles) from
20 the Black Forest's lakeland, with the **Titisee,** a rare jewel among lakes, as star attraction. Set in a mighty forest, the 1½-mile-long lake is invariably crowded in summer with boats and Windsurfers. Boats and boards can be rented at several points along the shore.

From Titisee it's 5 kilometers (3 miles) to the lovely 800-year-
21 old town of **Hinterzarten,** the most important resort in the southern Black Forest. Some buildings date from the 12th century, among them **St. Oswald's** church, built in 1146. Hinterzarten's oldest inn, **Weisses Rossle,** has been in business since 1347. The **Park Hotel Adler,** established in 1446, has been under the same family management for 14 generations, although the original building was burned down during the Thirty Years' War and the inn where Marie Antoinette and her retinue put up in 1770 has been considerably altered since her visit.

Hinterzarten is situated at the highest point along the Freiburg–Donaueschingen road, and from it a network of far-ranging hiking trails fans out into the surrounding forest. In winter Hinterzarten is one of Germany's most popular centers for *Langlauf* (cross-country skiing).

From Hinterzarten, it's 25 kilometers (16 miles) to the moun-
22 tain-enclosed **Schluchsee,** the biggest of the Black Forest lakes. Take highway B-317 along the lower slopes of the 4,500-foot Feldberg, the Black Forest's highest mountain, then pick up B-500. Schluchsee is a diverse resort, offering swimming, windsurfing, fishing, and, in winter, skiing. For details, contact the local tourist office (tel. 07650/7732).

From Schluchsee head toward the largest city in the southern Black Forest, Freiburg. To get there by the shortest route
23 you'll have to brave the satanically named **Höllental** (Hell Val-

ley). The first stop at the end of the valley is a little village
24 called, appropriately enough, **Himmelreich,** or Kingdom of Heaven. The village is said to have been given its name in the 19th century by railroad engineers, who were grateful that they had finally laid a line through Hell Valley. At the entrance to Höllental is a deep gorge, the **Ravennaschlucht.** It's worth scrambling through to reach the tiny 12th-century chapel of **St. Oswald,** the oldest parish church in the Black Forest.

Back on B-31, watch for the appearance of a bronze statue of a deer high on a roadside cliff, 5 kilometers (3 miles) farther. It commemorates the local legend of a deer that amazed hunters by leaping the deep gorge at this point. Another 16 kilometers (10 miles) will bring you to Freiburg.

25 **Freiburg,** or Freiburg im Breisgau, to give the town its full name, was founded in the 12th century. Despite extensive wartime bomb damage, skillful restoration has helped re-create the original and compelling medieval atmosphere of one of the most appealing historic towns in Germany. Freiburg has had its share of misadventures through the years, especially in the 17th and 18th centuries. In 1632 and 1638 Protestant Swedish troops in the Thirty Years' War captured the city; in 1644 it was taken by Catholic Bavarian troops; and in 1677, 1713, and 1744 French troops captured it. For Americans, Freiburg has particular significance: The 16th-century geographer Martin Waldseemüller, who first put the name America on a map in 1507, was born here.

Numbers in the margin correspond to points of interest on the Freiburg map.

Towering over the rebuilt medieval streets of the city is its most
26 famous landmark, the **Münster,** Freiburg's cathedral. The pioneering 19th-century Swiss art historian Jacob Burckhardt described its delicately perforated 370-foot spire as the finest in Europe. If you've seen the spire of the Salisbury cathedral in England, you'll want to decide for yourself whether Burckhardt was right. The cathedral took three centuries to build, from around 1200 to 1515. You can easily trace the progress of generations of builders through the changing architectural styles, from the fat columns and solid, rounded arches of the Romanesque period to the lofty Gothic windows and airy interior of the choir, the last parts of the building to be completed. Of particular interest are the luminous 13th-century stained-glass windows; a 16th-century triptych (three-panel painting) by Hans Baldung-Grien; and paintings by Holbein the Younger and Lucas Cranach the Elder. If you can summon the energy, climb the tower; the reward is a magnificent view of the city and the Black Forest beyond. Go on a Friday and you'll see the colorfully striped awnings of the market stalls spread out below, a fitting accompaniment to the 16th-century market house, the
27 **Kaufhaus.** The four statues you see on the fine facade beneath its steeply pitched roof are of Hapsburg monarchs.

Time Out Stroll to Oberlinden square and visit Germany's most ancient inn, **Zum Roten Bären,** the Red Bear. Order a *Viertel*—a quarter-liter glass—of the local wine and perhaps a plate of locally smoked ham. The inn is also a small hotel.

---

28 The city's other main square is **Rathaus Platz,** where Frei-
29 burg's famous **Rathaus** (Town Hall) stands, constructed from

Kaufhaus, **27**
Münster, **26**
Rathaus, **29**
Rathaus Platz, **28**

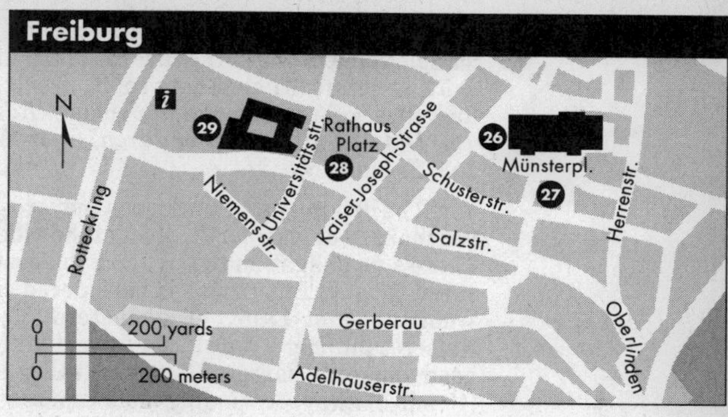

two 16th-century patrician houses joined together. Among its attractive Renaissance features is an oriel, or bay window, clinging to a corner and bearing a bas-relief of the romantic medieval legend of the Maiden and the Unicorn.

Numbers in the margin correspond to points of interest on the Black Forest map.

Having braved Hell Valley to get to Freiburg, a visit to the
30 nearby town of **Staufen,** where Dr. Faustus is reputed to have made his pact with the Devil, should hold no horrors. It's 20 kilometers (12 miles) south of Freiburg via B-31. The legend of Faustus is remembered today chiefly because of Goethe's drama of the same name, written in the early 19th century. The play depicts the doctor as a man driven by fear of death to make a pact with the Devil; in return for immortality, Faustus sells his soul. In fact, the original Faustus was an alchemist, an early scientist, in the 16th century. He made a pact not with the Devil but with a local baron who was convinced Faustus could make his fortune by discovering the secret of how to make gold from base metals. In his attempts Dr. Faustus died in an explosion that produced such noise and sulfurous stink that the townspeople were convinced the Devil had carried him off. You can visit the ancient inn, the **Gasthaus Löwen,** on the market square, Marktplatz, where Faustus lived and died. The frescoes on its walls tell his story in vivid detail.

North to Baden-Baden and Karlsruhe

Staufen is on the Wine Road, the **Weinstrasse,** another of the routes drawn up by the tourist authorities of the Black Forest. It's also the southernmost point of this Black Forest tour. From here the tour makes its way north through the southernmost vineyards of Germany, source of the prized Baden wine, to Baden-Baden.

Twenty kilometers (12 miles) northwest of Freiburg on B-31 is
31 the town of **Breisach.** It stands by the Rhine River; everything you see to the west on the opposite bank is in France. Towering high above the town and the surrounding vineyards is the **Stephansmünster,** the cathedral of St. Stephen, built between 1200 and 1500 (and almost entirely rebuilt after World War II). As at Freiburg, the transition from sturdy Romanesque styles to airy and vertical Gothic styles is easy to see. North of the town rises the **Kaiserstuhl,** or Emperor's Chair, a volcanic out-

crop clothed in vineyards that produce high-quality wines.
32 Sample some in one of the taverns of the village of **Achlarren,** 2 or 5 kilometers (3 miles) north of Breisach; you can also visit the fine little **wine museum** in the village. *Admission to the museum: DM 2 adults, DM 1 children. Open Apr.–Oct., Mon–Fri. 2–5, Sat. and Sun. 11–4.*

You'll be driving past numerous vineyards and wine villages as you make your way north. Most of the vineyards offer tastings. There's no obligation to buy, and you certainly won't be pressured into it. But praise is considered polite. You leave the Weinstrasse at **Lahr,** 40 kilometers (25 miles) north of the Kaiserstuhl. Here you should turn right (east) onto B-415 and head along the narrow **Shuttertal Valley** to **Zell,** 15 kilometers (10 miles) away. A winding mountain road takes you the 21 kilometers (13 miles) to the A-28 highway. Turn right to **Freudenstadt,** then left for B-500 and Baden-Baden.

You're back on the Black Forest High Road now, the Schwarzwald Hochstrasse, in the land of myth and fable. At the village
33 of **Ruhestein,** the side road on the left leads to the **Allerheiligen** monastery ruins. This 12th-century monastery was secularized in 1803, at which point plans were drawn up to turn it into a prison. Two days later, lightning started a fire that burned the monastery to the ground. To this day the locals claim it was divine intervention.

Five kilometers (3 miles) north of Ruhestein you'll reach anoth-
34 er potent source of local myth. This is the **Mummelsee,** a small, almost circular lake that has fascinated local people and visitors alike for centuries. Because of the lake's high mineral content, there are no fish in it. According to legend, however, sprites and other spirits of the deep find it to their liking. The Romantic lyric poet Mörike (1804–1875) immortalized the lake in his ballad *The Spirits of the Mummelsee.* The lake is a popular destination in the summer; if you can, visit during the mist-laden days of spring and fall victim to its full mysterious appeal.

From the Mummelsee, it's downhill all the way to the famous
35 and fashionable spa of **Baden-Baden,** set in a wooded valley of the northern Black Forest and sitting atop the extensive underground hot springs that gave the city its name. The Roman legions of the emperor Caracalla discovered the springs when they settled here in the 1st century and named the place Aquae. The leisure classes of the 19th century rediscovered the bubbling waters, establishing Baden-Baden as the unofficial summer residence of many of Europe's royal families, who left their imprint on the city in the palatial homes and stately villas that still grace its tree-lined avenues.

The small, neat city, so harmoniously set within the surrounding forest, has a flair and style all its own. As Germany's ultimate high-fashion resort, it lives unashamedly on leisure and pleasure. Here the splendor of the Belle Epoch lives on to a remarkable extent. Some claim that one out of five residents is a millionaire. In the evening, Baden-Baden is a soft-music-and-champagne-in-a-silver-bucket kind of place, and in the daytime, it follows the horseback-riding-along-the-bridle-paths tradition. It features a crowded season of ballet performances, theater, concerts, and recitals, along with exciting horse racing and high-stakes action at its renowned casino.

Baden-Baden claims that the casino, Germany's first, is the most beautiful in the world, a boast that not even the French can challenge, for it was a Parisian, Jacques Bénazet, who persuaded the sleepy little Black Forest spa to build gambling rooms to enliven its evenings. In 1853, his son Edouard Bénazet commissioned Charles Séchan, a stage designer associated with the Paris opera house, to come up with a design along the lines of the greatest French imperial palaces. The result was a series of richly decorated gaming rooms in which even an emperor could feel at home—and did. Kaiser Wilhelm I was a regular visitor, as was his chancellor, Bismarck. Visitors as disparate as the Russian novelist Dostoevsky, the Aga Khan, and Marlene Dietrich were all patrons.

Few people visit Baden-Baden to go sightseeing (though those who feel the urge might want to see the **Neues Schloss,** or New Castle, a 19th-century fortress that was rebuilt in the Renaissance style for the grand dukes of Baden; today it's a museum of local history). If you come here to take the waters, still have a flutter in the casino *(see* The Arts and Nightlife, below), and perhaps swim in the positively palatial **Caracalla Baths,** a vast complex with no fewer than seven pools, opened in 1985 *(see* Sports and Fitness, below). Above all, you'll want to stroll around this supremely elegant resort and sample the gracious, Old World atmosphere of a place that, more than almost anywhere else in Europe, retains the feeling of a more unhurried, leisured age.

Time Out Step into the warm elegance of the **Café König.** Order a pot of coffee and a wedge of Black Forest cake and listen to the hum of money and leisure from the spa crowd, who have made this quiet corner their haunt.

Leaving Baden-Baden, take the road to **Gernsbach,** a couple of miles to the east. The road skirts Baden-Baden's own mountain

36 peak, the 2,000-foot-high **Merkur.** You can take the cable car to the summit. *Cost round-trip: DM 5 adults, DM 3 children. Open daily 10–6.*

37 Drive the 15 kilometers (10 miles) to **Bad Herrenalb,** another popular Black Forest spa, set amid the wooded folds of the Alb River valley. Railway enthusiasts will admire the train station here; it's actually Baden-Baden's original 19th-century station. It was saved from destruction during the modernization of the Baden-Baden station when it was transported here and put up in all its former glory.

Eight kilometers (5 miles) north on the road to Karlsruhe, the

38 final point of the tour, lies the village of **Marxzell.** A group of ancient locomotives and other old machines at the side of the road announces the presence of the **Fahrzeugmuseum,** a wonderland for the technically minded. Every kind of early engine is represented in this museum dedicated to the German automobile pioneer Karl Benz (1844–1929), the man who the Germans claim built the first practical automobile in 1888, a claim hotly disputed by the French. *Karlsruhestr. 2. Admission: DM 5 adults, DM 3 children. Open daily 2–5.*

39 From Marxzell, head for **Ettlingen,** a 1,200-year-old town that's now practically a suburb of its newer and much larger neighbor, **Karlsruhe.** Ettlingen, bordered by the Alb River, is a jewel of a town, its ancient center a maze of traffic-free cobbled streets.

Visit in summer for the annual Schlossberg theater and music festival in the beautiful **Baroque Schloss** (palace) *(see* The Arts and Nightlife, below). The palace was built in the mid-18th century, and its striking domed chapel, today a concert hall, was designed by Cosmas Damian Asam, a leading figure of south German Baroque. Its ornate, swirling ceiling fresco is typical of the heroic, large-scale, illusionistic decoration of the period.

40 **Karlsruhe,** founded at the beginning of the 18th century, is a young upstart compared with ancient Ettlingen. But what it lacks in years, it makes up for in industrial and administrative importance, sitting, as it does, astride a vital Autobahn and railroad crossroads. Its major attraction for the visitor is the former palace of the Margrave Karl Wilhelm, today the **Badische Landesmuseum,** the museum of local history. The town quite literally grew up around the palace, which was begun in 1715; 32 avenues radiate out from it, 23 leading into the extensive grounds, the remaining nine forming the grid of the old town. It's said that the margrave fell asleep under a great oak while searching for a fan lost by his wife and dreamed that his new city should be laid out in the shape of a fan. True or false, the fact is that the city is built on a fan pattern, and all the principal streets, with one exception, lead directly to the palace. The exception is the Kaiserstrasse, constructed in 1800, which runs parallel to the palace.

Despite wartime bomb damage, faithful restoration has ensured that much of the old town retains its original and elegant 18th-century appearance. Walk to the **Marktplatz,** the central square, to see the austere stone pyramid that marks the margrave's tomb and the severe neoclassical **Stephanskirche,** the church of St. Stephen, modeled on the Pantheon in Rome and built around 1810. The interior, rebuilt after the war, is incongruously modern.

What to See and Do with Children

Take a slide down the **dry toboggan run** at **Poppeltal,** located on the Schwarzwald-Baderstrasse, 20 kilometers (12 miles) south of Wildbad. The narrow, twisting run descends more than half a mile through the forest. In Baden-Baden there's a toy museum, **Stadtspiegelzeugmuseum,** featuring dolls' houses, some 200 years old (Gernsbacherstr. 48, tel. 07221/32511. Open Tues.–Fri. 3–6, Sun. 2–6. Admission DM 3.50).

Stargazers will love Freiburg's **planetarium** (Friedrichstr. 51). Performances are at 7:30 PM Tuesday and Friday, 3 PM on Wednesday (Admission: DM 3 adults, DM 2 children).

Tour the disused silver mines at **Neublach,** at Talmühle *(see* Exploring the Black Forest, above). Ride the **Black Forest Railway** through "Hell Valley" from Freiburg to the mountain resort of Hinterzarten, or the **steam trains** along the Wutach River valley departing from Blumberg, 55 kilometers (34 miles) southeast of Titisee. Spend a few hours, or even the day, at the Black Forest's own Disneyland, **Europa Park,** at Ettenheim, 40 kilometers (25 miles) north of Freiburg on the Karlsruhe-Basel Autobahn. It's open from April to the third Sunday of October. In Steinen-Hofen, 20 kilometers (12 miles) north of Rheinfelden, **Vogelpark Wiesental** has 300 species of exotic birds on display, many of them housed in a giant building with a tropical ecosystem. (Admission: DM 5 adults, DM 2.50 children. Open Mar. 15–Nov. 15, 9–5.)

Off the Beaten Track

At **Schapbach,** in the enchanting Wolf River valley, head up into the hills to **Glaswald Lake** and you should have this tree-fringed stretch of water all to yourself. Parts of the neighboring Poppel Valley are so wild that carnivorous flowers number among the rare plants that carpet the countryside. Visit the valley's **Hohloh Lake** nature reserve, near Enzklösterle, in July and August and you'll find the bug-eating *Sonnentau* in full bloom. Farther north, just off B-500 near **Hornisgrinde Mountain,** a path to the remote and romantic **Wildsee** passes through an experimental area of forest where the trees are left untended.

Shopping

Shopping in the Black Forest means cuckoo clocks. For the widest range in the entire area, try **Hansen** (Münsterpl. 6) in Freiburg. The staff speaks English and will ship goods to the United States and Canada; they can also arrange tax refunds.

Wood carvings, glass, and pottery are all good buys in the Black Forest. **Gaisser** (Langestr.), located in Baden-Baden's attractive pedestrian shopping zone, stocks glass and porcelain from all over Germany, with many specialties from the Black Forest.

Buy a Black Forest smoked ham as an aromatic souvenir. It's a specialty that's prized all over Germany. You can buy one at any butcher shop in the region, but it's more rewarding to visit a *Schinkenräucherei* (smokehouse), where the ham is cured. **Hermann Wein's Schinkenräucherei** in Freudenstadt sells smoked hams, and the staff is glad to show people around. You'll need to call in advance (tel. 07443/8041).

The region's wines, especially the dry Baden whites and delicate reds, are highly prized in Germany. Buy them directly from any vintner on the Wine Road. In Baden-Baden, visit the 400-year-old **Nägelsförster Hof** wine tavern and shop at Yburg, where you can also enjoy panoramic views of the town. Wine tastings are featured daily (tel. 07221/24053).

Sports and Fitness

Bicycling Bicycles can be rented at nearly all the train stations in the Black Forest. The cost is DM 10 a day (DM 6 if you have a railway ticket). Several regional tourist offices offer tours on which the biker's luggage is transported separately from one overnight stop to the next. Six- to 10-day tours are available for as little as DM 174 per person, including bed-and-breakfast and bike rental. Contact the **Fremdenverkehrsverband Schwarzwald** in Freiburg (for full details *see* Important Addresses and Numbers, above). For the superfit, Titisee-Neustadt organizes a tour through 12 of the Black Forest's mountain passes. Contact **Kurverwaltung** (7820 Titisee-Neustadt, tel. 07651/20668) for details.

Fishing The Black Forest, with its innumerable mountain rivers and streams, is a fisherman's paradise. Fishing without a license is forbidden, and fines are automatically levied on anyone caught doing so. Licenses cost DM 8 a day and are available from most local tourist offices, which can usually also provide maps and rental equipment. Contact the **Fremdenverkehrsverband Schwarzwald** (Bertodstr. 45, Freiburg, tel. 0761/31317) for details.

Golf There are courses at Baden-Baden, Bad Herrenalb, Badenweiler, Donaueschingen, Freiburg, and Freudenstadt. The 18-hole Baden-Baden course is considered one of Europe's finest. Contact the **Golf Club** (Fremersbergstr. 127, Baden-Baden, tel. 07221/23579).

Horseback Riding Farms throughout the Black Forest offer riding holidays; addresses are available from local tourist offices and the **Fremdenverkehrsverband Schwarzwald** in Freiburg. Many of the larger towns have riding clubs and stables where visitors can rent horses, including **Baden-Baden** (Gunzenbachstr. 4a, tel. 07221/31876). The resort of **Wehr** offers a 14-day stay in a bed-and-breakfast and 10 hours of riding for DM 115; similar vacation packages are offered throughout the region.

Swimming Most of the larger resorts and towns in the Black Forest have pools, either indoor or outdoor. You can also swim in any of the region's lakes, if you can stand the cold. The most lavish swimming pool in the region is the **Caracalla** complex in Baden-Baden. Opened in 1985, it has five indoor pools and two outdoor pools, a sauna, a solarium, and Jacuzzis, plus thermal water-therapy treatment courses. *Römerpl. 11, tel. 07221/275–940. Admission: DM 18 for 2 hours. Open Tues., Wed., Fri., Sat. 8 AM–10 PM.*

The **Friedrichsbad** swimming pool in Baden-Baden offers mixed nude bathing. *Römerpl. 1, tel. 07221/275–920. Admission: DM 38; children under 16 not admitted. Open Mon.–Sat. 9 AM–10 PM.*

Winter Sports Despite Swiss claims to the contrary, the Black Forest is the true home of downhill skiing. In 1891 a French diplomat was sighted sliding down the slopes of the **Feldberg,** the Black Forest's highest mountain, on what are thought to be the world's first downhill skis. The idea caught on among the locals, and a few months later Germany's first ski club was formed. In 1907, the world's first ski lift was opened at Schollach. There are now more than 200 ski lifts in the Black Forest. The slopes of the Feldberg are still the top ski area. Five days' skiing lessons in Hinterzarten cost from DM 130, with ski passes from DM 70 for a full week. Accommodations can be had for about DM 150 a week. (Call the **Verkehrsamt,** Hintergarten, tel. 07652/1501, for details.) Cross-country ski instruction is given in every resort, and tours of two days and more are offered by many tourist offices. Schonach's three-day trip includes a party in a mountain hut and two nights in bed-and-breakfasts for DM 265. (Call the **Kurverwaltung, Schonach im Schwarzwald,** tel. 07722/6033, for details.) The Black Forest is ideal country for walkers. The three principal trails are well marked and cross the region from north to south, the longest stretching from Pforzheim to the Swiss city of Basel, 280 kilometers (175 miles) away. Walks vary in length from a few hours to a full weekend. The **Clock-carriers' Road,** following the path of early Black Forest clock dealers, is a perennial favorite. Three nights' lodging in bed-and-breakfasts plus transport of your luggage is available for DM 175 and up. Contact the **Fremdenverkehrsverband** in Freiburg (*see* Important Addresses and Numbers in Essential Information, above).

Dining and Lodging

Dining

Restaurants in the Black Forest range from the well-upholstered luxury of Baden-Baden's chic eating spots to simple country inns. Some specialties here betray the influence of neighboring France, but if you really want to go native, try *z'Nuni*, the local farmers' second breakfast, generally eaten around 9 AM. It consists of smoked bacon, called *Schwarzwaldgeräuchertes*—the most authentic is smoked over fir cones—a hunk of bread, and a glass of chilled white wine. No visitor to the Black Forest will want to pass up the chance to try *Schwarzwälder Kirschtorte,* Black Forest cherry cake. *Kirschwasser*, locally called *Chriesewässerle* (from the French *cerise*, meaning cherry), is cherry brandy, the most famous of the region's excellent *schnapps.*

Ratings Highly recommended restaurants in each price category are indicated by a star ★.

Category	Cost*
Very Expensive	over DM 90
Expensive	DM 55–DM 90
Moderate	DM 35–DM 55
Inexpensive	DM 25–DM 35

**per person for a three-course meal, excluding drinks, service charge, and tax*

Lodging

Accommodations in the Black Forest are varied and numerous, from simple rooms in farmhouses to five-star luxury. *Gasthofs* (inns), all offering as much local color as you'll ever want and low prices, abound. In summer, Schluchsee and Titisee are crowded, so make reservations well in advance. Some spa hotels close for the winter.

Ratings Highly recommended lodgings in each price category are indicated by a star ★.

Category	Cost*
Very Expensive	over DM 180
Expensive	DM 120–DM 180
Moderate	DM 80–DM 120
Inexpensive	under DM 80

**All prices are for two people in a double room, excluding service charge.*

Baden-Baden
Dining
★

Pospisil's Merkurius. The owner-chef here is Czech-born Pavel Pospisil, and his classic cooking has Bohemian touches. The comfortable, homey restaurant, complete with fireplace, is part of a small country-house hotel 8 kilometers (5 miles) south of Baden-Baden in Varnhalt. Typical dishes include wild hare or lobster in delicate sauces. *Klosterberg 2, tel. 07223/5474. Reservations required. Jacket and tie required. AE, DC, MC. Closed Mon. and Tues. Very Expensive.*

Zum Alde Gott. The draw here is the classy combination of upscale rustic appeal with distinctive nouvelle German cooking; figs in beer pastry make for a memorable dessert. With only 12 tables, the mood is intimate and sophisticated. The restaurant is located in the suburb of Neuweier. *Weinstr. 10, tel. 07223/5513. Reservations advised. Dress: informal. DC, MC, V. Closed Fri. lunch, Thurs. Very Expensive.*

Allee. This large restaurant in the noble Europäischer Hof hotel mixes international and regional dishes, with the emphasis on classic French cooking. The buffet lunch is a particularly good value. *Kaiserallee 2, tel. 07223/23561. Reservations advised. Jacket and tie required. AE, DC, MC, V. Expensive.*

La Terrazza. Tucked away at the end of the elegant Augusta arcade is this glass-enclosed oasis of peace and good Italian food. In the summer, look for a table on the charming, fountain-cooled inner courtyard. *Augusta-Arkaden, Lichtentalerstr. Reservations advised. Dress: neat but casual. AE, DC, MC, V. Moderate.*

Löwenbräukeller. This Bavarian-style restaurant with a small, tree-shaded beer garden serves only one beer—Munich's famous Löwenbräu—along with a wide selection of Baden wines. The food is simple and filling, with regional specialties predominating. *Gernsbacherstr. 9, tel. 07221/22311. No reservations. Dress: informal. No credit cards. Inexpensive.*

Waldhorn. Set in a villagelike suburb (Oberbeuern) on the edge of the forest, this old inn offers garden charcoal grills every evening in summer—regional dishes prepared with flair. *Beuernerstr. 54, tel. 07221/72288. No reservations. Dress: informal. AE, DC, MC, V. Closed Mon., 1st week of Mar. Inexpensive.*

Lodging
★

Brenner's Park Hotel. This hotel claims, with some justification, to be one of the best in the world. It's a stately mansion off Baden-Baden's leafy Lichtentaler Allee, set on spacious private grounds. Luxury abounds, and all the rooms and suites (the latter costing up to DM 1,400 a day) are luxuriously furnished and appointed. *An der Lichtentaler Allee, tel. 07221/3530. 68 rooms and 20 suites with bath. Facilities: sauna, indoor pool, in-house spa, resident doctor, beauty salon, games room, bar, 2 restaurants. AE, DC, MC. Very Expensive.*

Krämers Quisisana. In this elegant turn-of-the-century hotel set in its own spacious park, you might want to lock yourself away from the outside world for days. Most of the guest rooms, decorated in the style of an English country house, have balconies, and the hotel's spa facilities are extensive. *Bismarck-str. 21, tel. 07221/3446. 56 rooms and 9 suites with bath. Facilities: therapeutic baths, resident doctor, masseur, indoor pool, sauna, solarium, beauty salon, 2 restaurants, bar. MC, V. Very Expensive.*

★ **Romantik-Hotel Der Kleine Prinz.** This is a beautifully modernized, small, 19th-century mansion for romantics. Each of its rooms is decorated in a different style, ranging from art nouveau to Manhattan modern. The tower room has a spiral staircase; two rooms have fireplaces; a number have Jacuzzis. The restaurant (closed Jan.) is small and sophisticated, and offers German nouvelle food. *Lichtentalerstr. 36, tel. 07221/3464. 33 rooms and 9 suites with bath. Facilities: restaurant. AE, DC, MC, V. Very Expensive.*

Hotel Bischoff. The Friedrichsbad Roman baths are right across the street, and most other attractions in Baden-Baden are only a short walk away from this solidly comfortable, fin de siècle villa-hotel. The bedrooms are basically but adequately furnished; there's a cozy breakfast room, but no restaurant. *Römerpl. 2, tel. 07221/22378. 21 rooms with shower. AE, DC, MC, V. Closed Dec. and Jan. Moderate.*

★ **Laterne.** This is one of Baden-Baden's oldest hotels (it dates from the late 17th century), as well as one of its smallest. The public rooms, the restaurant, and some of the bedrooms have original beams and woodwork and antique Black Forest furnishings. It's centrally but quietly located in a pedestrian zone. *Gernsbacherstr. 10, tel. 07221/29999. 10 rooms with bath or shower. Facilities: restaurant. AE, DC, MC, V. Moderate.*

Am Markt. This is a 250-year-old building located in the quiet, traffic-free zone and close to such major attractions as the Roman baths; it's been run by the Bogner family for more than three decades. *Marktpl. 17–18, tel. 07221/22747. 28 rooms, 14 with bath. Facilities: restaurant. AE, DC, MC, V. Inexpensive.*

Hotel Löhr. Flower boxes spill scarlet geraniums down the plain front of this squat, city-villa hotel in summer and autumn. Rooms are small but quiet, and each has a television and a minibar, unusual luxuries for this price range. The Kurhaus and casino are a minute's walk away. There's no restaurant, but the immediate area has an abundance. *Adlerstr. 2, tel. 07221/26204. 30 rooms, 26 with bath. MC. Inexpensive.*

Bad Herrenalb
Lodging

Mönchs Posthotel. An enchanting 19th-century building with ornate turrets, situated in beautiful gardens, the Mönchs Posthotel has a restaurant noted for its French cuisine. *Dobelstr. 2, tel. 07083/7440. 28 rooms, 11 suites, and 3 apartments with bath. Facilities: heated outdoor pool, solarium, beauty salon, masseur, restaurant. AE, DC, MC. Expensive.*

Bad Liebenzell
Lodging

Thermen-Hotel. Idyllically located between the spa park and the forest, this striking 16th-century half-timbered mansion opened as a luxury hotel in 1988. *Am Kurpark, tel. 07052/408–300. 22 rooms with bath. Facilities: indoor pool, hot springs, café-terrace. AE, DC, V. Expensive.*

Baiersbronn
Dining

Bareiss. This is one of the most elegant and sophisticated restaurants in Germany, one that has been winning plaudits for many years. It's in the Mitteltal hotel—itself a substantial luxury hotel—and offers magnificent French nouvelle cuisine prepared under the direction of leading chef Manfred Schwarz. The fixed-price *gastronomique* menu, at DM 110 per person, represents surprisingly good value, too. *Kurhotel Mitteltal, Gärtenbühlweg 14, tel. 07442/470. Reservations required. Jacket and tie required. AE, DC. Closed Mon., Tues., June 5–July 6, and Nov. 26–Dec. 24. Very Expensive.*

★ **Schwarzwaldstube.** This is an award-winning French restaurant (not to be confused with the nearby Hotel Schwarzwald) in the Sporthotel Traube Tonbach. You dine at antique tables beneath a ceiling of gnarled beams and straw thatch. Try for a table by the large window overlooking the Tonbach Valley. *Tonbachstsr. 237, tel. 07442/492–665. Reservations required. Jacket and tie required. AE, DC, MC, V. Closed Mon., Tues., and July 10–28. Expensive.*

Bühl
Dining
★ **Wehlauer's.** This four-star restaurant in the small Badischer Hof Hotel mixes classic French cuisine and delicate variations on regional dishes. Look for halibut with egg sauce and sweetbreads in *salfordiere* sauce, a Vosges specialty. *Hauptstr. 36, 07223/23063. Reservations required. Jacket and tie required. AE, DC, MC. Closed Jan. 1–18. Expensive.*

Lodging
Schlosshotel Bühlerhöhe. This new "castle hotel" has rapidly established itself as one of the leading luxury hotels of the entire Black Forest. It stands majestically in its own extensive grounds high above Baden-Baden on the scenic route that snakes across the heights of the Black Forest. The views are spectacular, and beautiful woodland trails start virtually at the hotel door. *Schwarzwaldhochstr. 1, tel. 07226/55100. 90 rooms with bath. Facilities: 2 restaurants, bar, indoor pool, sauna, fitness center. AE, DC, MC, V. Very Expensive.*

★ **Plättig.** You can enjoy views across the Rhine into France at this excellent-value traditional hotel. The facilities and comforts here are many, not least the summer terrace, where you can feast on homemade Black Forest cake. *Schwarzwaldhochstr., tel. 07226/55300. 49 rooms and 9 suites with bath. Facilities: indoor pool, resident doctor, fitness room, games room, restaurant, wine bar. AE, DC, MC, V. Expensive.*

Cafe-Pension Jägersteig. Magnificent views of the wide Rhine Valley as far as the French Vosges Mountains are included in the reasonable room rate at this spectacularly located mountain pension, high above the town of Bühl and its surrounding vineyards. *Kappelwindeckstr. 95a, tel. 07223/24125. 12 rooms, 9 with bath or shower. No credit cards. Closed Jan. 10–Feb. 20. Moderate.*

Ettlingen
Dining
Ratsstuben. Dine in a 16th-century cellar by the fast-flowing Als River; it was originally used to store salt. The food is heartily Teutonic. *Am Markt/Kirchgasse 1–3, tel. 07243/14754. Reservations advised. Dress: informal. DC, MC, V. Moderate.*

Lodging
★ **Hotel-Restaurant Erbprinz.** This is one of the most historic hotels in Ettlingen, one that even has its own trolley-car stop. For many, the real reason for staying here is the top-rated restaurant, which offers magnificent nouvelle German specialties. In the summer, dine in the charming garden, hidden away behind the hotel's green and gilt fencing. *Rheinstr. 1, tel. 07243/3220. 50 rooms with bath or shower. Facilities: restaurant. AE, DC, MC, V. Very Expensive.*

Freiburg
Dining
★ **Falkenstube.** The Colombi Hotel's restaurant has collected high praise from notoriously finicky French restaurant critics. The gracious atmosphere is set by softly lit oak paneling; the food is distinctive French nouvelle. The veal with foie gras and truffles makes for a memorable meal. For best value, try the 10-course "gourmet menu." *Rotteckring 16, tel. 0761/31415. Reservations required. Jacket and tie required. AE, DC, MC, V. Closed Sun. Very Expensive.*

Alte Weinstube zur Traube. The fruit of the vine is not the only item on the menu at this cozy, old wine tavern, which offers a rich and varied selection of classic French and Swabian dishes. *Zander* (pike) roulade with crab sauce and braised pork with lentils are especially recommended. *Schusterstr. 17, tel. 0761/32190. Reservations advised on weekends and in Aug. Dress: informal. AE, DC, MC, V. Closed Sun., Mon. lunch, and July 15–30. Expensive.*

Enoteca. The newly opened Enoteca offers its customers three dining possibilities—a bright and cheerful bistro, a smart restaurant, and, for late-night eating (until 1:30 AM), a bar. The bar menu is limited, but the bistro and restaurant call equally on a kitchen that is rapidly building a reputation for Italian dishes of skill and imagination. Try the lamb osso buco, the rolled lamb with Gorgonzola filling, or any of the ravioli. As the name of the restaurant suggests, the wine list is extensive. *Schwabentorplatz, tel. 0761/30751. Reservations advised for restaurant. Dress: informal. AE, DC, MC, V. Moderate.*

Kühler Krug. Venison dominates the proceedings at this restaurant, which has even given its name to a distinctive saddle-of-venison dish. Those who prefer fish can choose from the imaginative range of freshwater varieties available. *Torpl. 1, tel. 0761/29103. Reservations advised. Dress: informal. AE, MC. Closed Thurs. and 3 weeks in June. Moderate.*

Oberkirchs Weinstuben. The landlord of this Old Town tavern in a small hotel personally bags some of the game that ends up in the kitchen. Fresh trout is another specialty. In summer, the dark oak dining tables spill onto a garden terrace. *Münsterplatz 22, tel. 0761/31011. Dress: informal. V. Closed Sun., public holidays, and Christmas Eve–Jan. 22. Moderate.*

Ratskeller. For typical Black Forest ambience, make for the Ratskeller, nestling in the shadow of the cathedral on Münsterplatz. The dark interior, with wood paneling and exposed beams, is complemented by the time-honored dishes, with roast meats and rich sauces predominating. *Münsterplatz 11, tel. 0761/37530. Reservations advised. Dress: informal. Closed Sun. evening and Mon. Moderate.*

★ **Zum Roten Bären.** The Red Bear has a history dating from 1120 and is said to have been an inn since 1311, making it the oldest in Germany. True or not, it's the archetypal German history-book inn; it also offers lodging. Prices are surprisingly low given the high quality, with fixed-price meals starting at DM 25 per person. The best deals are on the *Tageskarte* (menu of the day). Many seasonal specialties, including game, are served, and *Spätzle* comes with most dishes. *Oberlinden 12, tel. 0761/36913. Reservations advised. Dress: informal. AE, DC, MC, V. Moderate.*

Lodging

Park Hotel Post. A hotel since the turn of the century, with good old-fashioned service to match, the Park Hotel Post is right next to the train station. The Jugendstil facade with stone balconies and central copper-dome tower has earned the building protected status. *Eisenbahnstr. 35, tel. 0761/31683. 41 rooms, most with bath. AE, DC, MC, V. Expensive.*

Rappen. Located in the heart of the pedestrian-only Old Town, this hotel features brightly painted farmhouse-style rooms. The appealing rustic theme extends to the excellent restaurant. Wine lovers will appreciate the wide choice—more than 200—of regional vintages. *Münsterpl. 13, tel. 0761/31353. 20 rooms with bath. Facilities: restaurant with garden terrace. AE, DC, MC, V. Moderate.*

Hotel Adler. The Adler (German for "eagle") is 8 kilometers (5 miles) as the crow flies from the center of Freiburg, but there is a good bus service. The rural location guarantees peace and quiet, and although it's a modern structure, the hotel—with its steep eaves, balconies, and profusion of flower boxes—has the atmosphere of a country inn. *Im Schülerdobel 1, tel. 0761/65413. 12 rooms, most with bath. Facilities: restaurant, parking. No credit cards. Inexpensive.*

Freudenstadt
Dining

Bären. Fish—local trout is a specialty—and traditional, simple Swabian dishes are the main attractions of this robustly Teutonic restaurant. If you want to eat as the locals do, try *Maultaschen,* a delicious ravioli dish that Swabians swear by. For best value, try one of the specials from the Tageskarte. *Langestr. 33, tel. 07441/2729. Reservations advised. Dress: informal. DC, V. Closed Mon. and Jan. Moderate.*

★ **Ratskeller.** Ask for a table near the *Kachelofen* if it's cold outside; that's a large, traditional tiled heating stove, and a central feature of this atmospheric haunt on picturesque Marktplatz. Swabian dishes and venison are featured prominently on the menu, but try the homemade trout roulade with crab sauce if it's available. The fixed-price menu, starting from DM 15, offers the best value. *Marktpl. 8, tel. 07441/2693. Reservations advised. Dress: informal. AE, DC, MC, V. Closed Tues. and Feb. Moderate.*

Lodging

★ **Schwarzwaldhotel Birkenhof.** If you need to recharge tired batteries, there are few better places in which to do so than this superbly equipped hotel. Old-fashioned comfort and a woodland setting complement a wide range of sports facilities. The two restaurants offer a choice between classic French cuisine and sturdy Black Forest fare. *Wildbaderstr. 95, tel. 07441/4074. 60 rooms with bath. Facilities: indoor pool, sauna, solarium, Jacuzzi, massage room, squash, table tennis, bowling alley, 2 restaurants, terrace café, bar. AE, DC, MC, V. Expensive.*

Gut Lauterbad. This tastefully renovated 18th-century house turned hotel is an excellent value, peppered with antiques, such as ornate carved wardrobes and Meissen porcelain. Nestled in its own tranquil park, complete with trout-fishing ponds, the hotel is located on the edge of the forest, south of the town center. *Dietrichstr. 5, tel. 07741/7496. 21 rooms with bath. Facilities: indoor pool, sauna, solarium, fitness room, restaurant, terrace café, bar. AE, DC, MC, V. Closed Nov. 20–Dec. 18 and Jan. 10–31. Moderate.*

Schwanen. Owned and run by the Bukenberger family since 1900, the centrally located Schwanen, only a two-minute walk from the train station, offers good-value lodging and eating and above-average comfort. *Forststr. 6, tel. 07441/2267. 17 rooms with bath or shower. Facilities: restaurant. V. Inexpensive.*

Gutach im Elztal
Dining and Lodging

★ **Romantik Hotel Stollen.** The flower-strewn balconies and low roofs of this hotel disguise a distinctive and luxurious interior. Run by the same family for 140 years, it combines understated comfort—some rooms have four-poster beds—with attentive service: You are treated as if you were staying in a family home rather than a hotel. The restaurant—which comes complete with a roaring log fire—offers regional food with nouvelle touches. The hotel is located 21 kilometers (15 miles) northeast of Freiburg. *7809 Gutach im Elztal, tel. 07685/207. 12 rooms with bath. Facilities: restaurant. AE, MC, V. Closed Jan. 10–20; restaurant closed Tues. Expensive.*

Hinterzarten
Lodging

Park Hotel Adler. The Riesterer family has owned this historic property since 1446. It's one of Germany's finest hotels, standing on nearly 2 acres of grounds that are ringed by the Black Forest. Marie Antoinette once ate here, and the highest standards are kept up in the French restaurant and a paneled 17th-century dining room. An orchestra accompanies dinner and later moves to the bar to play for dancing. All rooms are sumptuously appointed. *Adlerpl., tel. 07652/1270. 42 rooms and 32 suites with bath. Facilities: indoor pool, sauna, solarium, indoor and outdoor tennis, table tennis, golf range, 2 restaurants, bar. AE, DC, MC, V. Very Expensive.*

★ **Kesslermühle.** The Mühle, or mill, was first mentioned in local records in the 12th century. In the 15th century it passed from the Kessler family to the Birkenbergers, whose descendants still run the hotel that the original mill became. Extensive modernization has produced a snug place to lay your head. The wood-paneled restaurant is atmospheric. *Erlenbruckerstr. 45, tel. 07652/1290. 31 rooms with bath. Facilities: indoor pool, sauna, gym, table tennis, billiards, restaurant, café, bar. MC. Closed Nov. 5–Dec. 18. Expensive.*

Sassenhof. Traditional Black Forest styles reign supreme here. The rooms are furnished with rustic pieces, brightly painted and decoratively carved. There's no restaurant, but guests are welcome to use the kitchen. *Adlerweg 17, tel. 07652/1515. 15 rooms and 6 suites with bath. Facilities: indoor pool, solarium, sauna. No credit cards. Closed mid-Nov.–mid-Dec. Expensive.*

Nagold
Dining

★ **Romantik Restaurant Alte Post.** This 17th-century half-timbered inn has the kind of ambience lesser establishments believe can be built in with false beams. The menu ranges from traditional Swabian dishes to classic (and expensive) French offerings. For best value try the local food; the veal in mushroom sauce and venison (in season) are reliable favorites. *Bahnhofsstr. 2, tel. 07452/4221. Reservations advised. Jacket and tie required. AE, DC, MC, V. Closed Sat. lunch, 2 weeks in Jan., and 2 weeks in July–Aug. Expensive.*

Lodging

Hotel Post Gasthaus. Run by the former proprietors of the neighboring Alte Post restaurant, this hotel is part of a historic and charming old coach inn. Parts of the ivy-clad building are modern, but the same standards of comfort are offered throughout. *Bahnhofstr. 3, tel. 07452/4048. 24 rooms with bath. AE, DC, MC, V. Expensive.*

Pforzheim
Dining

★ **Silberburg.** Nouvelle cuisine with a Swiss touch, emphasizing poultry, fish, and fresh vegetables, is the policy of this cozy restaurant. Try the duck in one of chef Gilbert Noesser's exquisite sauces. *Dietlingerstr. 27, tel. 07231/41159. Reservations advised. Dress: informal. No credit cards. Closed Mon., Tues. lunch, and 3 weeks in Aug. Expensive.*

★ **Pic-Pic.** People in the know come here for imaginative dishes at low prices. There are about 40 of them on the vast menu; none costs more than DM 36. *Zerrennerstr. 6, tel. 07231/101–939. Reservations advised. Dress: informal. No credit cards. Closed lunch. Moderate.*

Lodging

Ruf. When it opened at the beginning of the century, this hotel was described by a visiting English journalist as "a house that is aware of its importance for the numerous German and foreign visitors . . . to Pforzheim." Whether or not it is still "aware of its importance," it still aims to offer the same degree of reliable comfort—the hotel is nothing fancy, but it is dependably efficient and welcoming. The excellent restaurant is decorated with intricate wrought iron and stained glass. *Bahnhofplatz 5, tel. 07231/16011. 51 rooms with bath. Facilities: restaurant. AE, DC, MC, V. Expensive.*

Titisee
Dining and Lodging

Romantik Hotel Adler Post. Located in the Neustadt district of Titisee, about 5 kilometers (3 miles) from the lake, this solid old building has been owned and run by the Ketterer family for 140 years. All the rooms are comfortably and traditionally furnished. The restaurant, the Rotisserie zum Postillon, offers excellent local specialties. *Hauptstr. 16, tel. 07651/5066. 32 rooms with bath. Facilities: indoor pool, sauna, solarium, restaurant. AE, DC, MC, V. Closed last week of Mar. Expensive.*

The Arts and Nightlife

The Arts

Music Freiburg's annual **Zeltmusik** festival is a musical jamboree held June and July in tents—*Zelt* is German for "tents"—that sprout on the city outskirts. The accent is on jazz, but most types of music are featured, including classical. The city also has a Philharmonic orchestra; it gives concerts year-round in the city theater. Chamber-music concerts are presented in the summer in the courtyard of the ancient Kufhaus, opposite the Münster. The Münster itself is the scene of an annual summer program of organ recitals. For program details and tickets for all the above, contact **Freiburg Verkehrsamt** (Rotteckring 14, tel. 0761/216–3289). For jazz, make for the **Jazz Haus** (Schnewlinstr. 1), where live music is featured nightly. Baden-Baden's orchestra performs regularly at the **Kurhaus** (Werderstr.) and also presents an annual two-week summer festival, the **Musikalischer Sommer.** For program details and tickets, call 07221/275–2500.

Theater Freiburg has an annual summer theater festival. Performances are given in the city's theater complex and spill out onto the streets and squares as well. Street theater is also featured in the annual **Schlossberg** festival, held in August, a popular and informal carnival-like event centering on the castle. Baden-Baden's **Theater am Goetheplatz** presents a regular program of drama, opera, and ballet. Call 07221/275–268 for program details and tickets.

Movies English-language movies are shown at Freiburg's **German-American Institute** (Kaiser-Joseph-Str. 266, tel. 0761/31645).

Nightlife

Black Forest nightlife means Baden-Baden's elegant **casino,** first and foremost. There's a DM 5 admission charge; bring your passport as ID. You'll have to sign a form guaranteeing that you can meet any debts you run up (minimum stake is DM 5—maximum DM 20,000). If your tastes run to the less formal, the city's leading disco, the **Club Taverne** (closed Mon. and Tues.), is located in the same building. For a more muted evening, try the **Oleander Bar** in Baden-Baden's top hotel, Brenner's Park-Hotel (Lichtentaler Allee); a piano offers a soothing accompaniment to the tinkle of ice in your glass.

Nightlife in Freiburg revolves around the city's wine bars and wine cellars. **Oberkirch's Weinstuben** and **Die Zwiebel,** both located on Münsterplatz, are typically atmospheric; you can also look for night spots on any of the streets around the cathedral. The top discos are **Far Out** (Universitätstr. 3), **Le Caveau** (Oberlinden 8), and **Sound** (Nussmannstr. 9). Students gather at **EL.PL** (Schiffstr. 16).

8 The Romantic Road

Including Würzburg, Rothenburg-ob-der-Tauber, and Augsburg

Introduction

Of all the specially designated tourist routes that crisscross Germany, none rivals the aptly named Romantische Strasse, or Romantic Road. It's not so much the road itself that is the big attraction, for the scenery to be encountered along the way (with a few exceptions) is more domestic and rural than spectacular. What makes the Romantic Road so memorable are the medieval towns, villages, castles, and churches that stud its 420-kilometer (260-mile) length. Many of these are tucked away beyond low hills, their spires and towers poking up through the greenery.

Within the massive gates of formerly fortified settlements, half-timbered houses lean against each other along narrow cobbled lanes. Ancient squares are adorned with fountains and flowers, and formidable walls are punctuated by watchtowers built to keep a lookout for marauding enemies. The sights of the Romantic Road add up to a pageant of marvels of history, art, and architecture, providing a concentrated essence of Germany at its most picturesque and romantic.

The road runs south from Würzburg in the north of Bavaria to Füssen on the border with Austria. You can, of course, follow it in the opposite direction, as a number of bus tours do. Either way, among the major sights, you'll see one of Europe's most scintillating Rococo palaces, in Würzburg. Rothenburgob-der-Tauber may well be the best-preserved medieval town on the Continent. Then there's the handsome Renaissance city of Augsburg. Finally, for most visitors, the highlight will be Ludwig II's captivating fantasy castle of Neuschwanstein.

The concept of the Romantic Road could be considered something of a marketing ploy. At a time when West Germany was trying to rebuild its tourist industry in the wake of the devastation of World War II, an enterprising public-relations type dreamed up the name to apply to this historic passage through several regions of southern Germany that could be advertised as a single package with a catchy title. And that was how, in 1950, the Romantic Road was born, soon to evolve into one of Europe's most heavily traveled tourist trails.

The name itself refers not so much to the kind of romance lovers engage in as to a variation of the word meaning wonderful, fabulous, imaginative. And, of course, the Romantic Road started as a road on which the Romans traveled. By any name, this passage can make for a memorable journey.

On its way the road crosses former battlefields where armies fought for control of the region and the towns that dot it. Paradoxically, it was the most cataclysmic of these conflicts, the Thirty Years' War of the early 17th century, that by destroying their economic base, assured the survival of the most historic of the Romantic Road towns.

As you travel the Romantic Road, two names crop up again and again: Walther von der Vogelweide and Tilman Riemenschneider. It might be helpful to know a little about these masters of the Middle Ages.

Walther von der Vogelweide, who died in Würzburg in 1230, was the most famous of the German *Minnesänger*, the poet-musicians who wrote and sang of courtly love in the age of chivalry, when knights and other nobles hired them for their artistic services to help win the favors of fair ladies. Von der Vogelweide broke with this tradition by writing love songs to maidens of less-than-noble rank; he also accepted commissions of a political nature, producing what amounted to medieval political manifestos. His work was romantic, lyrical, witty, and filled with a sighing wistfulness and philosophical questioning.

Tilman Riemenschneider, Germany's master of late-Gothic sculpture, lived an extraordinary life. His skill with wood and stone was recognized at an early age. His success became so great that he soon presided over a major Würzburg workshop, with a team of assistants. Riemenschneider worked alone, however, on the life-size figures that dominate his sculptures. His characteristic grace and harmony of line can be identified in such features as the folds of a robe.

At the height of his career, Riemenschneider was appointed city councillor; later he became mayor of Würzburg. In 1523, however, he made the fateful error of siding with the revolutionaries in the Peasants' Revolt. He was arrested and held for eight weeks in the dungeons of the Marienburg fortress above Würzburg, where he was frequently tortured. Most of his wealth was confiscated, and he returned home a broken man, with little will to continue his work.

Riemenschneider died six years after his fall from favor, in 1531. For nearly three centuries he and his sculptures were ignored and all but forgotten. Only in 1822, when ditchdiggers uncovered the site of his grave, did Riemenschneider once again come to be included among Germany's greatest artists. He was enthusiastically championed by the Romantics of the 19th century. His works were sought out, catalogued, and guarded with zealous admiration. Today Riemenschneider is recognized as the towering giant of German sculpture. The richest collection of his works is in Würzburg, although other masterpieces are on view in churches and museums in other cities along the Romantic Road as well as in other parts of Germany; for example, the renowned Windsheim Altar of the Twelve Apostles is found in the Palatine Museum in Heidelberg.

Essential Information

Important Addresses and Numbers

Tourist Information

Two regional tourist information offices cover the towns along the Romantic Road. These are: **Fremdenverkehrsverband Allgäu Bayerisch-Schwaben,** Fuggerstrasse 9, 8900 Augsburg, tel. 0821/33335; and **Fremdenverkehrsverein Bodensee-Oberschwaben,** Schützenstrasse 8, 7750 Konstanz, tel. 07531/22232. For information on the Romantic Road itself, *see* Getting Around by Car, below. Local tourist offices include:

Amorbach: Rathaus, 8762 Amorbach, tel. 09373/778.
Aschaffenburg: Dalbergstrasse 6, 8750 Aschaffenburg, tel. 06021/30426.
Augsburg: Verkehrsverein, Bahnhofstrasse 7, tel. 0821/502-070.
Dinkelsbühl: Tourist-Information, Marktplatz, tel. 09851/90240.

Donauwörth: Städtisches Verkehrsamt, Rathausgasse 1, tel. 0906/789–145.

Feuchtwangen: Fremdenverkehrsamt, Marktplatz 1, tel. 09852/90444.

Füssen: Kurverwaltung, Augsburger Strasse 2, tel. 08362/7077.

Harburg: Fremdenverkehrsverein, Schlossstrasse 1, tel. 09003/1011.

Landsberg am Lech: Fremdenverkehrsamt, Hauptplatz 1, tel. 08191/128–246.

Mespelbrunn: Hauptstrasse 173, 8751 Mespelbrunn, tel. 06092–319.

Nördlingen: Städtisches Verkehrsamt, Marktplatz 2, tel. 09081/4380.

Rothenburg-ob-der-Tauber: Tourist-Information, Rathaus, Marktplatz 2, tel. 09861/40492.

Schongau: Verkehrsverein, Bahnhofstrasse 44, tel. 08861/7216.

Schwangau: Kurverwaltung, Rathaus, Münchenerstrasse 2, tel. 08362/81051.

Wertheim: Am Spitzen Turm, 6980 Wertheim, tel. 09342/301–230.

Würzburg: Fremdenverkehrsamt, Haus zum Falken, Marktplatz, tel. 0931/37398.

Car Rental

Avis: Klinkerberg 31, tel. 0821/38241, **Augsburg;** Nürnberger Strasse 107, tel. 0931/200–3939, **Würzburg.**

Europcar: Pilgerhausstrasse 24, tel. 0821/312–033, **Augsburg;** Friedenstrasse 15, tel. 0931/88150, **Würzburg.**

Hertz: Eberlestrasse 67, tel. 0821/541–800, **Augsburg;** Hoechbergerstrasse 10, tel. 0931/415–221 or 414–145, **Würzburg.**

Arriving and Departing

By Plane The major international airports serving the Romantic Road are Frankfurt, at its north end, and Munich, at its south end. Regional airports include Nürnberg, Stuttgart, and Augsburg, home base of the private airline Interot.

By Car The northernmost city of the Romantic Road—and the natural starting point for a tour—is Würzburg on the Frankfurt–Nürnberg Autobahn. It's 115 kilometers (72 miles) from Frankfurt and 280 kilometers (175 miles) from Munich. Augsburg, the largest city on the Romantic Road, is 70 kilometers (44 miles) from Munich and 365 kilometers (228 miles) from Frankfurt. Full information on the Romantic Road is available from **Tourist Information Land an der Romantischen Strasse** (Kreisverkehrsamt, Crailsheimerstrasse 1, 8800 Ansbach, tel. 0981/4680) or from **Arbeitsgemeinschaft Romantische Strasse** (Marktplatz, 8804 Dinkelsbühl, tel. 09851/90271).

By Train Both Würzburg and Augsburg are on the Intercity network and have fast, frequent service to and from Frankfurt, Munich, and Stuttgart. The new high-speed Intercity Express connects Würzburg with Hamburg and Munich. Less frequent trains link most of the other major towns of the Romantic Road.

By Bus From mid-March until the end of October, daily bus service covers the northern stretch of the Romantic Road, leaving Frankfurt at 8:15 AM and arriving in Munich at 6:55 PM. From early May until early October, a second bus covers the section of the route between Würzburg and Füssen: Buses leave Würzburg daily at 9 AM and arrive in Füssen at 7:45 PM. In the other direction, from early May until early October, buses leave Füssen at 8:15 AM daily, arriving in Würzburg at 7:20 PM. From mid-March until the end of October, buses leave Munich at 9 AM and arrive at Frankfurt at 7:55 PM. All buses stop at the major sights along the road. Reservations are essential; contact **Deutsche Touring GmbH** (Am Römerhof 17, 6000 Frankfurt/Main 90, tel. 069/790–3240). Local buses cover much of the route but are infrequent and slow.

Getting Around

By Car The Romantic Road is most easily traveled by car, starting from Frankfurt or Würzburg as outlined below and following the B-27 country highway south to meet roads B-290, B-19, B-292, and along the Wörnitz River on B-25.

Guided Tours

City Tours All the cities and towns on the Romantic Road offer guided tours, either on foot or by bus. Details are available from the local tourist information offices. Following is a sample of the more typical tours.

In **Würzburg,** guided walking tours (in German) start at the tourist office at 10:30 AM Monday to Friday from April 15 to November 9. Tours in English are given Tuesday to Saturday at 11 AM from May through October. **Augsburg** has self-guided walking tours, with routes of varying lengths posted on color-coded signs throughout the downtown area May through October. A twice-daily bus tour—"2,000 Years in Two Hours"—takes in all the main sights. Tours start from the Rathaus; the cost is DM 12 adults, DM 6 children.

Rothenburg-ob-der-Tauber's night watchman, dressed in traditional garb, conducts visitors on a nightly tour of the town, leading the way with a lantern. Tours begin at 9 PM and cost DM 3. The night watchman in **Dinkensbühl** also does a nightly round, and though he doesn't give official tours he is always happy to answer questions from inquisitive visitors. Daily guided tours of Dinkensbühl in horse-drawn carriages are a fun way to see the little town.

Bus Tours From mid-March to the beginning of November, the **Deutsche Touring** company *(see* Arriving and Departing by Bus, above) operates a variety of tours of one to three days' duration to Rothenburg and sections of the Romantic Road. The one-day tour to Rothenburg has an English-speaking guide, and the DM 109 fare (DM 89 children) includes lunch, a guided tour of Rothenburg, and admission charges to various museums.

Train Tours **Deutsche Bundesbahn** (German Railways) offers special weekend excursion rates covering travel from most German railroad stations to Würzburg and hotel accommodations for up to four nights. Details are available at any train station.

Boat Trips Three shipping companies offer excursions on the Main River from Würzburg. The **Fränkische Personenschiffahrt** (Kranenkai 1, tel. 0931/51722) and the **Würzburger Personenschiffahrt Kurth & Schiebe** (Am Alten Kranen, tel. 0931/58573) operate excursions to the vineyards in and around Würzburg; wine tasting is included in the price. Fränkische Personenschiffahrt

(FPS for short) also offers cruises of up to two weeks on the Main, Neckar, and Danube rivers, and on the Main–Danube canal. **Kurth & Schiebe** and **Veitschöchheimer Personenschiffahrt** (Am Alten Kranen, tel. 0931/55633) offer daily service to Veitschöchheim, site of the palace that was once the summer residence of the bishops of Augsburg.

Exploring the Romantic Road

Highlights for First-time Visitors

Würzburg Residenz
Rothenburg-ob-der-Tauber
Dinkelsbühl
Augsburg Cathedral
Wieskirche
Schloss Neuschwanstein

Aschaffenburg to Würzburg

Numbers in the margin correspond to points of interest on the Romantic Road map.

If you're approaching the Romantic Road from Frankfurt, the
1 first town you'll reach is **Aschaffenburg,** on the Main River, gateway to Franconia (*see* Chapter 9) and the streams and woods of the Spessart Hills. It's a small town, which, despite the ring of factories encircling it—Aschaffenburg is a major textile-producing center—has retained its quiet, market-town atmosphere. The historic center has been carefully preserved, with much of it now an elegant pedestrian mall.

Begin your visit at **Schloss Johannisburg.** This imposing Renaissance castle, built between 1605 and 1615, was the residence of the prince-electors of Mainz, hereditary rulers of Aschaffenburg. The exterior of the doughty sandstone castle harks back to the Middle Ages. Four massive corner towers guard the inner courtyard. The interior contains two small museums. The **Schloss Museum** (Castle Museum) charts the history of the town and contains a representative collection of German glass. The **Staatsgalerie** (City Art Gallery) has a small section devoted to Lucas Cranach the Elder (1472–1553), a leading painter of the German Renaissance, including typical enigmatic nudes and haunting landscapes. The palace grounds contain a striking copy of the temple of Castor and Pollux in Pompeii, constructed for Ludwig I of Bavaria in 1840. If you've admired the lavish neoclassical buildings Ludwig put up in Munich, this powerful structure will be appealing. *Admission to castle and museums: DM 3 adults, DM 1.50 children.Open Apr.–Sept., Tues.–Sun. 10–noon and 1–5; Oct.–Mar., Tues.–Sun. 10–noon and 1–4.*

Time Out For an ideal introduction to Franconian wines and regional specialties, stop at the **Schlossweinstuben** (tel. 06021/12440), a wine cellar/restaurant in the castle. From the terrace, there's a fine view over the Main Valley.

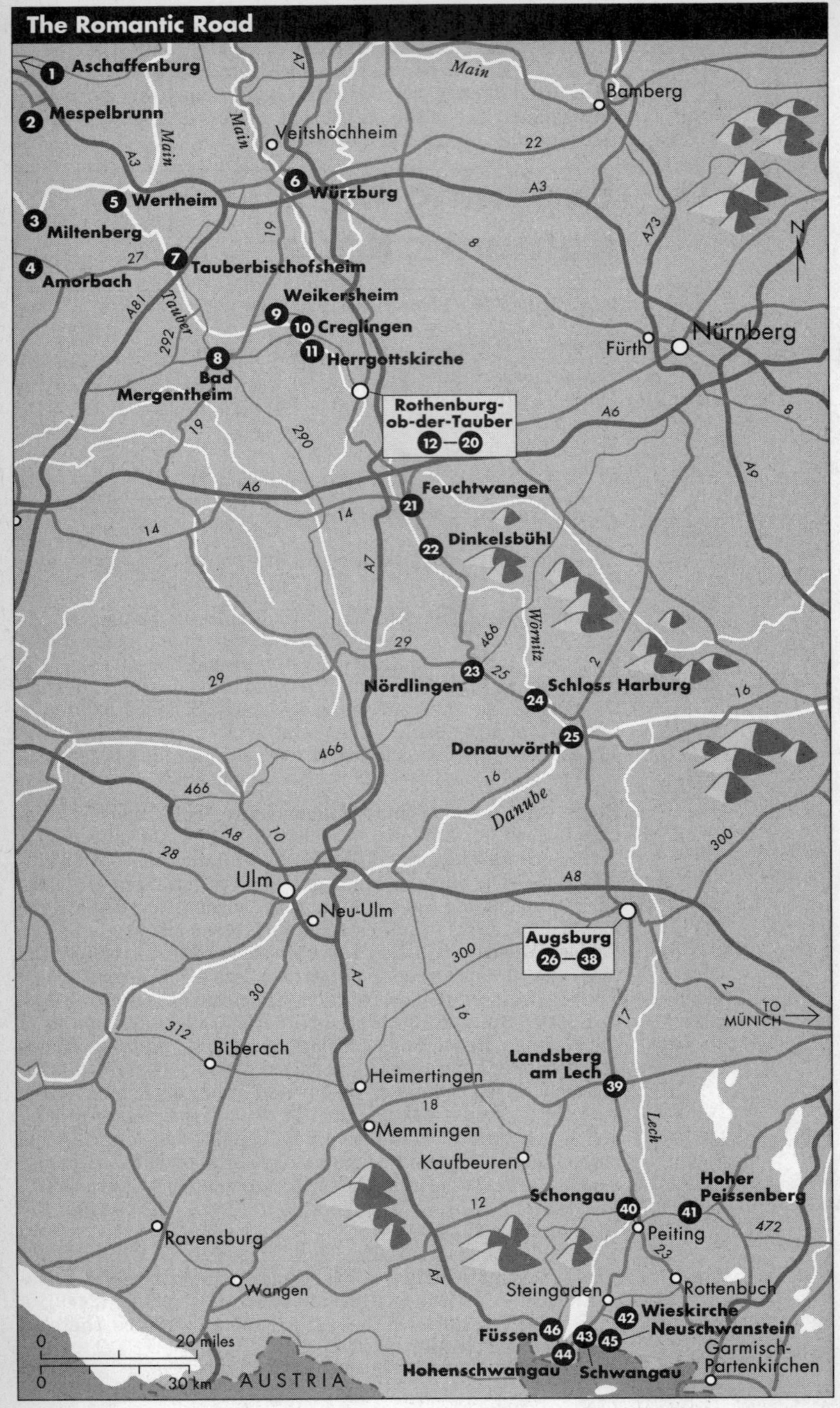
The Romantic Road
1 Aschaffenburg
2 Mespelbrunn
3 Miltenberg
4 Amorbach
5 Wertheim
6 Würzburg
7 Tauberbischofsheim
8 Bad Mergentheim
9 Weikersheim
10 Creglingen
11 Herrgottskirche
Rothenburg-ob-der-Tauber 12—20
21 Feuchtwangen
22 Dinkelsbühl
23 Nördlingen
24 Schloss Harburg
25 Donauwörth
Augsburg 26—38
39 Landsberg am Lech
40 Schongau
41 Hoher Peissenberg
42 Wieskirche
43 Neuschwanstein
44 Hohenschwangau
45 Schwangau
46 Füssen
Main
Bamberg
Veitshöchheim
Tauber
Nürnberg
Fürth
Wörnitz
Danube
Ulm
Neu-Ulm
Biberach
Heimertingen
Memmingen
Kaufbeuren
Lech
Peiting
Rottenbuch
Steingaden
Ravensburg
Wangen
Garmisch-Partenkirchen
TO MÜNICH
AUSTRIA
0 20 miles
0 30 km

To reach the center of Aschaffenburg, start on Karlsstrasse and continue along Fürstengasse, which leads to Landlingstrasse and the **Stiftskirche** (Collegiate Church) of Sts. Peter and Alexander, on a small hill. Little remains of the original Romanesque building here save the cloisters; most of what you see dates from the 16th and 17th centuries. Pause before you go in to admire the tapering green spire and the imposing, slightly out-of-kilter facade. Inside, the *Lamentation of Christ*, a gaunt and haunting painting by Matthias Grünewald (c. 1475–1528), is the most notable of a number of paintings on view. It was part of a much larger and now lost altarpiece. See how, in spite of the lessons of Italian Renaissance painting, naturalism and perspective still produce an essentially Gothic image, attenuated and otherworldly.

Castle lovers may enjoy a 17-kilometer (10-mile) excursion southeast from Aschaffenburg on B-8 to the small, romantic
2 castle of **Mespelbrunn.** This lies in the still sparsely populated forest area of the Spessart, the former hunting grounds of the archbishops of Mainz.

The castle of Mespelbrunn is surrounded by a moat and dominated by a massive round tower dating from the mid-16th century. The **Rittersaal** (Knight's Room) on the first floor displays Teutonic suits of armor, assorted weapons, and massive, dark furniture. A more delicate note is struck by the 18th-century **Chinesische Salon** (Chinese Room) upstairs. From the castle, hiking paths lead into the forested surroundings, for Spessart is a walker's paradise. *Admission: DM 3 adults, DM 1.50 children. Open Apr.–Sept., Mon.–Sat. 9–noon and 1–5, Sun. 9–5.*

From Aschaffenburg you can take the A-3 Autobahn 63 kilometers (40 miles) direct to Würzburg, the official starting point of the Romantic Road (*see* below), or first head south on route B-469, along the banks of the Main, to Miltenberg. From Miltenberg you can take a more leisurely drive east past a succession of riverside towns on the way to Würzburg.

3 The little town of **Miltenberg** stands amid the hills and forests of the Odenwald. (If you've seen Rothenburg-ob-der-Tauber and loved it but hated the crowds, Miltenberg will provide the antidote.) For most, the Marktplatz, the steeply sloping town square, is the standout. A 16th-century fountain, bordered by geraniums, splashes in its center; all around, tall half-timbered houses, some six stories high, their crooked windows bright with yet more flowers, stand guard. To see more of these appealing buildings, stroll down Hauptstrasse, site of the Rathaus (Town Hall) and the 15th-century Haus zum Riesen (House of the Giant). The town takes its name from its castle, whose entrance is on the Marktplatz. You can peek into the courtyard (open in the summer only) to see the standing stone in it. Though the stone's origins and meaning are obscure, most scholars agree that it's probably Roman and is connected with a fertility rite (there's no denying its phallic qualities).

Time Out The **Haus zum Riesen** (Hauptstr.), built in 1590, is one of the oldest inns in Germany. Stop in for a glass of beer or wine and to admire its gnarled and ancient timbers.

4 From Miltenberg, you can take a side trip to **Amorbach,** 8 kilometers (5 miles) south on B-469. The town itself is not the attraction; rather, it's the massive onetime Benedictine abbey

church of **St. Maria** that will claim your attention. The building is interesting chiefly as an example of the continuity of German architectural traditions, the superimposition of one style on another. You'll see examples of works here from the 8th century through the 18th. The facade of the church, for all that it seems a run-of-the-mill example of Baroque work, with twin domed towers flanking a lively and well-proportioned central section, is in fact a rare example of the Baroque grafted directly onto a Romanesque building. Look closely and you'll notice the characteristic round arches of the Romanesque marching up the muscular towers. It's the onion-shape domes at their summits and the colored stucco applied in the 18th century that make them seem Baroque. There are no such stylistic confusions in the interior, however: All is Baroque power and ornamentation. *Admission: DM 3 adults, DM 2 children. Tours of the church and former monastery buildings are given Apr.–Sept., Mon.–Sat. 9–noon and 1–6, Sun. 11–6; Mar. and Oct., Mon.–Sat. 9–noon and 1:30–5:20, Sun. 11–6; Nov.–Feb., Mon.–Fri. 11 and 2:15, Sat. 11 and 2–4, Sun. 2–4.*

From Amorbach, backtrack to Miltenberg and follow B-469 for 70 kilometers (43 miles) to Würzburg. For most of the drive, you'll be sticking close to the Main River. A succession of riverside towns remind you that this is among the most appealingly
5 unspoiled regions of Germany. The largest town is **Wertheim,** 30 kilometers (18 miles) from Miltenberg, located where the Main and Tauber rivers meet. It was founded in 1306 and proclaims its medieval origins through a jumble of half-timbered houses with jutting gables. Those in the central Marktplatz are the most attractive. The principal sight is the ruined **Kurmainzisches Schloss** (castle), built for the counts of Wertheim in the 11th century. The ruins are convincingly romantic; the view from them over the Main Valley is memorable. Now drive the remaining 40 kilometers (24 miles) to Würzburg.

Würzburg

6 The basically Baroque city of **Würzburg,** the pearl of the Romantic Road, is a heady example of what happens when great genius teams up with great wealth. Situated at the confluence of two age-old trade routes, Würzburg has been a prosperous city since more or less time immemorial. And it still shows. Starting in the 10th century, Würzburg was ruled by the powerful (and rich) prince-bishops who created the city with all the glittering attributes that you see today.

Set on the banks of the Main River as it passes through a calm valley backed by vineyard-covered hills, this glorious old city is overlooked by a fortified castle on dominating high ground on the far side of the river. This is Festung Marienberg, constructed between 1200 and 1600, and for 450 years residence of the prince-bishops.

From the start, you should be advised that present-day Würzburg is by no means 100% original. In fact, the city you will visit turns out to be largely restored. It happened this way: At the very end of World War II, for reasons that remain unclear, Würzburg was all but obliterated in an Allied saturation bombing raid. The date was March 16, 1945—seven weeks before Germany capitulated. Although the bombing lasted no more than 20 minutes, 87% of Würzburg was wiped off the map, with some 4,000 buildings destroyed and at least that many people killed.

Painstaking reconstruction has returned most of the city's famous sights to their former splendor, in many cases using original stones from the bombed-out structures. In fact, those who knew prewar Würzburg insist that the heart of the city is now every bit as impressive as it was prior to 1945 and, except for a new pedestrian zone, remains a largely authentic restoration.

High on the list of compelling reasons for visiting Würzburg is the **Residenz**, the glorious Baroque palace where the line of prince-bishops lived after coming down from their hilltop fortress, Festung Marienberg.

Pleasure-loving Prince-Bishop Johann Phillip Franz von Schönborn financed the venture. Construction started in 1719 under the brilliant direction of Balthasar Neumann, the German architectural genius of his age. Most of the interior decoration was entrusted to the Italian stuccoist Antonio Bossi and the Venetian painter Giovanni Battista Tiepolo. But the man whose spirit infuses the Residenz is von Schönborn, who unfortunately did not live to see the completion of what has come to be considered the most beautiful palace of Germany's Baroque era and one of Europe's most sumptuous buildings, frequently referred to as the "Palace of Palaces." This dazzling structure is located a 10-minute walk from the railway station, along Kaiserstrasse and then Theaterstrasse.

Anyone harboring doubts as to whether the prince-bishops of 18th-century Würzburg were bishops first and princes only incidentally will have them swept aside in a hurry. The Residenz is irrefutable evidence of the worldly power of these glamorous rulers and men of God.

From the moment you enter the building, the splendor of the Residenz is evident, as the largest Baroque staircase in the country, the **Treppenhaus,** stretches away from you into the heights. Halfway to the second floor, the stairway splits and peels away at 180 degrees to the left and right.

Dominating the upper reaches of this vast space is Tiepolo's giant fresco of **The Four Continents,** a gorgeous exercise in blue and pink with allegorical figures at the corners representing the continents (only four were known of at the time).

Next, make your way to the **Weissersaal** (the White Room) and then beyond to the grandest of the state rooms, the **Kaisersaal** (Throne Room). The Baroque/Rococo ideal of *Gesamtkunstwerk*—the fusion of the arts—is illustrated to perfection here. Architecture melts into stucco, stucco invades the frescoes, the frescoes extend the real space of the room into their fantasy world. Nothing is quite what it seems, and no expense was spared to make it so. Tiepolo's frescoes show the visit of the emperor Frederick Barbarossa to Würzburg in the 12th century to claim his bride. The fact that the characters all wear 16th-century Venetian dress hardly seems to matter. Few interiors anywhere use such startling opulence to similar effect. The room is airy, magical, intoxicating. You'll find more of this same expansive spirit in the **Hofkirche,** the chapel, which offers further proof that the prince-bishops experienced little or no conflict between their love of ostentation and their service to God. Among the lavish marbles, rich gilding, and delicate stuccowork, note the Tiepolo altarpieces, ethereal visions of *The Fall of the Angels* and *The Assumption of the Virgin*. Finally, tour the palace garden, the **Hofgarten;** the entrance is next to the chapel. This 18th-century formal garden, with its stately gushing fountains and trim, ankle-high shrubs outlining geometrical flower beds and gravel walks, is the equal of any in the country. *Admission, including guided tour: DM 4.50 adults, DM 3.50 students over 14 and senior citizens, DM 1.50 children. Open Apr.–Sept., Tues.–Sun. 9–5; Oct.–Mar., Tues.–Sun. 10–4.*

Time Out Sample your first Würzburg wine either in the extensive cellars of the Residenz, where you'll find a cozy **tavern,** or by making for one of two famous institutions in the immediate area. The nearest is the **Bürgerspital:** From the square fronting the Residenz, take the first street on the right, Theaterstrasse; the Bürgerspital is about halfway down the street on the right. Originally this was a medieval hospice established by wealthy burghers for Würzburg's poor and old. Not only did they get a roof over their heads, they received a daily allowance of one liter of wine (two on Sundays). Today there's no free wine, but buying a quarter liter of good Franconian white wine from the Bürgerspital's own vineyards won't make a dent in anyone's budget. Ask for a tour of the wine cellar: Its barrels are the size of a Volkswagen. Just down the road, on Juliuspromenade, is another of these charitable institutions, the **Juliusspital** (Julius Hospice), established in 1576 by a Würzburg bishop.

To the left is Würzburg's attractive pedestrian shopping area, Schönbornstrasse, named after the bishop who commissioned Neumann to build the Residenz. On the left as you enter the street is another example of Neumann's work, the distinctive Baroque **Augustinerkirche** (Church of St. Augustine). The church was a 13th-century Dominican chapel; Neumann's additions date from the early 18th century. At the end of Schönbornstrasse is Würzburg's Romanesque cathedral, the **Dom,** begun in 1045. Step inside and you'll find yourself, somewhat disconcertingly, in a shimmering Rococo treasure house. This is, perhaps, only fitting: Prince-Bishop von Schönborn, who came up with the concept of the Residenz, is buried here, and it's hard to imagine him slumbering amid the dour weightiness of a Romanesque edifice.

Alongside the cathedral is the **Neumünster,** built above the grave of the early Irish martyr St. Kilian, who brought Christianity to Würzburg and, with two companions, was put to death here in 689. Their missionary zeal bore fruit, however, for 17 years after their death, a church was consecrated in their memory. By 742, Würzburg had become a diocese; over the following centuries 39 churches flourished throughout the city. Once an abbey church, the Neumünster's former cloistered churchyard contains the grave of Walther von der Vogelweide, the most famous minstrel in German history.

Across the pedestrian zone toward the river lies Würzburg's market square, the **Markt,** with shady trees and a framework of historic old facades. At one end, flanked by a Rococo mansion, are the soaring late-Gothic windows of the 14th- to 15th-century **Marienkapelle** (St. Mary's Chapel), where architect Balthasar Neumann lies buried. Pause beneath its finely carved portal and inspect the striking figures of Adam and

Eve; you shouldn't have great difficulty recognizing the style of Tilman Riemenschneider. The original statues are in Würzburg's museum, the Mainfränkische Museum, on the Marienberg, across the river; the ones in the portal of the Marienkapelle are copies.

On your explorations along the edge of the pedestrian zone and market square note the exquisite "house Madonnas," small statues of the Virgin set into corner niches on the second level of many old homes. So many of these lovely representations of the city's patron saint can be seen that Würzburg is frequently referred to as "the town of Madonnas."

On the way to the **Marienburg Fortress,** you'll cross the Old Main Bridge, already standing before Columbus sighted America. Among the city's glories are the twin rows of infinitely graceful statues of saints that line the bridge. Note particularly the *Patronna Franconiae* (more commonly known as the Weeping Madonna). There's also a great view of the fortress from the bridge—statues in the foreground, Marienburg and its surrounding vineyards as the focal point—which makes the perfect photograph to treasure as a souvenir of this historic city.

To reach the Marienburg, you can make the fairly stiff climb on foot or take the bus from the Old Main Bridge. It runs every half hour starting at 9:45 AM.

The Marienburg was the original home of the prince-bishops, beginning in the 13th century. The oldest buildings—note especially the **Marienkirche,** the core of the complex—date from even earlier, around 700. In addition to the rough-hewn medieval fortifications, there are a number of fine Renaissance and Baroque apartments. The highlight of a visit to the Marienburg is the **Mainfränkisches Museum** (the Main-Franconian Museum). The rich and varied history of Würzburg is brought alive by this remarkable collection of art treasures. The standout is the gallery devoted to Würzburg-born Renaissance sculptor Tilman Riemenschneider, including the originals of the great Adam and Eve statues, copies of which adorn the portal of the Marienkapelle. You'll also be exposed to fine paintings by Tiepolo and Cranach the Elder, and to exhibits of porcelain, firearms, antique toys, and ancient Greek and Roman art. Wine lovers won't want to miss the old winepresses, some of which are enormous. Other exhibits chart the history of Franconian wine. *Admission to Marienburg Fortress is free. Open Apr.–Sept., Tues.–Sun. 9–noon and 1–5; Oct.–Mar., Tues.–Sun. 10–noon and 1–5. Admission to Mainfränkische Museum: DM 3 adults, DM 1 children. Open Apr.–Oct., Tues.–Sun. 10–5; Nov.–Mar., Tues.–Sun. 10–4.*

To see the original summer palace of the prince-bishops, you have to go a little north of Würzburg, to Veitshöchheim. Though it has little of the glamorous appeal of the Residenz, the sturdy Baroque building provides further evidence of the great wealth of the worldly rulers of Würzburg. *Admission, including guided tour: DM 2.50 adults, DM 1.50 students over 14, senior citizens, and children. Open Apr.–Sept., Tues.–Sun. 9–noon and 1–5.*

The Tauber Valley

The Romantic Road heads south from Würzburg, following the B-27 country highway, to the lovely valley of the Tauber at the
7 small town of **Tauberbischofsheim,** 36 kilometers (22 miles) southwest. There are no major sights here. What you'll want to do is linger in its shady pedestrian mall; stroll down to the sleepy Tauber River; and visit the parish church, site of a side altar richly carved by a follower of Tilman Riemenschneider.

8 Follow B-290 16 kilometers (10 miles) south to **Bad Mergentheim,** the premier resort of this region. Between 1525 and 1809, Bad Mergentheim was the home of the Teutonic Knights, one of the most successful of the medieval orders of chivalry. Their greatest glories came in the 15th century, when they had established themselves as one of the dominant powers of the Baltic, ruling large areas of present-day eastern Germany, Poland, and Lithuania. The following centuries saw a steady decline in the order's commercial success. In 1809, Napoléon expelled the Teutonic Knights from Bad Mergentheim. The French emperor had little time for what he considered the medieval superstition of orders such as this and felt no compunction for disbanding them as he marched east through Germany in the opening stages of his ultimately disastrous Russian campaign. The expulsion of the order seemed to be the death knell of the little town. But in 1826 a shepherd discovered mineral springs on the north bank of the river. They proved to be the strongest sodium sulfate and bitter-salt waters in Europe, with health-giving properties that ensured the little town's future prosperity. Excavations subsequently showed that the springs had been known in the Iron and Bronze ages before becoming choked with silt. A museum tracing the history of the Order was recently opened in the Knights' former castle—the **Deutschordensschloss**—at the eastern end of the town. *Deutschordensmuseum. Admission free. Open Mar.–Oct., Tues.–Fri. 2:30–5:30. Sat., Sun., and public holidays 10–noon and 2:30–5:30.*

Eleven kilometers (7 miles) southeast of Bad Mergentheim stands the village of **Stuppach,** whose chapel guards one of the great Renaissance German paintings, the so-called *Stuppacher Madonna* by Matthias Grünewald (c. 1475–1528). The painting is believed to have been produced for a church in nearby Aschaffenburg; no one seems clear on how it found its way here in 1812. It was only in 1908 that experts finally recognized it as the work of Grünewald; repainting in the 17th century had turned it into a flat and unexceptional work. Grünewald was one of the leading painters of the early Renaissance in Germany. Though he was familiar with the developments in perspective and natural lighting of Italian Renaissance painting, his work remained resolutely anti-Renaissance in spirit: tortured, emotional, dark. You'll want to compare it with that of Dürer, his contemporary, if you visit Munich's Alte Pinakothek museum. Whereas Dürer used the lessons of Italian painting to reproduce its clarity and rationalism, Grünewald used them for expressionistic purposes to heighten his essentially Gothic imagery.

B-19 leads you 12 kilometers (8 miles) to the little town of
9 **Weikersheim,** which provides another excuse to linger on the long road south. The town is dominated by the castle of the

counts of Hohenlohe. The great hall of the castle is the scene each summer of an international youth music festival, and the Rittersaal (Knight's Hall) contains life-size stucco wall sculptures of animals, reflecting the counts' love of hunting. In the cellars you can drink a glass of cool wine drawn from the huge casks that seem to prop up the building. Outside again, stroll through the enchanting gardens and enjoy the view of the Tauber and its leafy valley.

Follow the Tauber Valley 20 kilometers (12 miles) farther to
10 **Creglingen.** Here you can detour up a side valley, the Herrgottstal (Valley of the Lord). The valley has been an important place of pilgrimage since the 14th century, when a farmer had a vision of a heavenly host plowing his field. A chapel, the
11 **Herrgottskirche** (Chapel of Our Lord), was built by the counts of Hohenlohe. In the early 16th century, Tilman Riemenschneider was commissioned to carve an altarpiece for it. This is the reason you come here. This enormous work, 33 feet high, depicts in minute detail the life and ascension of the Virgin Mary. Riemenschneider entrusted much of the background detail to the craftsmen of his Würzburg workshop, but he allowed no one but himself to attempt the life-size figures of this masterpiece. Its intricate detail and attenuated figures are a high point of late-Gothic sculpture.

Now drive the remaining 20 kilometers (12 miles) to Rothenburg-ob-der-Tauber, for most people the quintessential town of the Romantic Road.

Rothenburg-ob-der-Tauber

12 **Rothenburg-ob-der-Tauber** (literally, "the red castle on the Tauber") is the kind of gemlike medieval town that even Walt Disney might have thought too good to be true, with gingerbread architecture galore and a wealth of fountains and flowers against a backdrop of towers and turrets. The reason for its survival is simple. Rothenburg was a small but thriving 17th-century town that had grown up around the ruins of two 12th-century churches that had been destroyed by an earthquake. Then it was laid low economically by the havoc of the Thirty Years' War, the cataclysmic religious struggle that all but destroyed Germany in the 17th century. The town's economic base was devastated, and it slumbered until modern tourism rediscovered it. And here it is, milking its "best-preserved-medieval-town-in-Europe" image to the full, undoubtedly something of a tourist trap, but genuine enough for all that. There really is no place else quite like it. Whether Rothenburg is at its most appealing in the summer, when the balconies of its ancient houses are festooned with flowers, or in the winter, when snow lies on its steep gables and narrow streets, is a matter of taste. Few people are likely to find this extraordinary little survivor from another age anything short of remarkable.

Numbers in the margin correspond to points of interest on the Rothenburg-ob-der-Tauber map.

13 Begin your visit by walking around the **city walls,** more than a mile long. Stairs every 200 or 300 yards provide ready access. There are great views of the tangle of pointed and tiled roofs,
14 and of the rolling country beyond. Then make for the **Rathaus** (Town Hall), the logical place to begin an exploration of Rothenburg itself. Half the building is Gothic, begun in 1240,

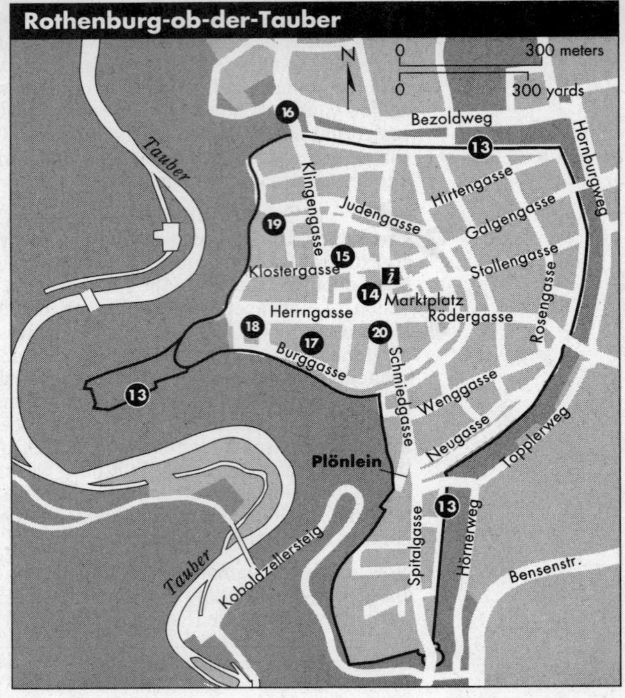

the other half classical, begun in 1572. A fire in 1501 destroyed part of the structure, hence the newer, Renaissance section, which faces the main square. Go inside to see the **Historiengewölbe,** a museum housed in the vaults below the building that charts Rothenburg's role in the Thirty Years' War. Great prominence is given to the Meistertrunk (Master Drink). This event will follow you around Rothenburg. It came about when the Protestant town was captured by Catholic forces. During the victory celebrations, so the story goes, the conquering general was embarrassed to find himself unable to drink a great tankard of wine in one go, as his manhood demanded. He volunteered to spare the town further destruction if any of the city councillors could drain the mighty draught. The mayor, a man by the name of Nusch, took up the challenge and succeeded, and Rothenburg was preserved. The tankard itself is on display at the Reichsstadtmuseum (*see* below). As it holds six pints, the wonder is not so much that the conquering general was unable to knock it back but that he would ever have tried it in the first place. On the north side of the main square is a mechanical figure that acts out the epic Master Drink daily at 11 AM and 3 PM; and the town holds an annual pageant celebrating the feat, with townsfolk parading the streets dressed in 17th-century garb. The festival begins in the courtroom of the town hall, where the event is said to have occurred. *Rathauspl. Admission: DM 2 adults, DM 1 children. Open mid-Mar.–Oct., daily 9–6.*

15 Just north of the town hall is the **Stadtpfarrkirche St. Jakob** (parish church of St. James), the repository of further works by Tilman Riemenschneider, including the famous Heiliges Blut

(Holy Blood) altar. Above the altar a crystal capsule is said to contain drops of Christ's blood. The church has other items of interest, including three fine stained-glass windows in the choir dating from the 14th and 15th centuries and the famous Herlin-Altar, with its 15th-century painted panels. *Open Easter–Oct., daily 9–5; Nov.–Easter, daily 10–noon and 2–4.*

16 Another of Rothenburg's churches, **St. Wolfgang's,** is built into the defenses of the town. From within the town it looks like a peaceful parish church; from outside it blends into the forbidding city wall. Through an underground passage you can reach the sentry walk above and follow the wall for almost its entire length.

17 Two museums you won't want to miss are the **Mittelalterliches**
18 **Kriminalmuseum** and the **Puppen und Spielzeugmuseum.** The former sets out to document the history of German legal processes in the Middle Ages and contains an impressive array of instruments of torture. The latter is an enchanting doll and toy museum housed in a 15th-century building near the Rathaus. There are 300 dolls, the oldest dating from 1780, the newest from 1940. *Mittelalterliches Kriminalmuseum: Burggasse 3. Admission: DM 3.50 adults, DM 2 children. Open Apr.–Oct., daily 9:30–6; Nov.–Mar., daily 2–4. Puppen und Spielzeugmuseum: Hofronnengasse 13. Admission: DM 3.50 adults, DM 1.50 children. Open Mar.–Dec., daily 9:30–6; Jan.–Feb., daily 11–5.*

19 The **Reichsstadtmuseum** (Imperial City Museum) turns out to be two attractions in one. It's the city museum, and it contains artifacts that illustrate Rothenburg and its history. Among them is the great tankard, or *Pokal,* of the Meistertrunk. The setting of the museum is the other attraction; it's a former convent, the oldest parts of which date from the 13th century. Tour the building to see the cloister, the kitchens, and the dormitory, then see the collections. *Hofronnengasse 13. Admission: DM 3.50 adults, DM 1.50 children. Open Apr.–Oct., daily 10–5; Nov.–Mar., daily 1–4.*

Cobbled Hofronnengasse runs into the Marktplatz (Market Square), site of an ornate Renaissance fountain, the
20 **Herterlichbrunnen.** To celebrate some momentous event—the end of a war, say, or the passing of an epidemic—the *Schäfertanz* (Shepherds' Dance) was performed around the fountain. The dance is still done, though for the benefit of tourists rather than to commemorate the end of a threat to Rothenburg. It takes place in front of the Rathaus several times a year, chiefly at Easter, in late May, and throughout June and July.

Feuchtwangen, Dinkelsbühl, and Nördlingen

Numbers in the margin correspond to points of interest on the Romantic Road map.

Our next main stop on the Romantic Road is the captivating little town of Dinkelsbühl, within a ring of tower-capped ramparts and a moat. However, if you're driving there from
21 Rothenburg, stop first at **Feuchtwangen,** the town just before it. Its central market square, with a splashing fountain and an ideal setting of half-timbered houses, rivals even the attractions of Rothenburg and Dinkelsbühl. Summer is the time to

go, when open-air theater productions are staged in the low, graceful cloisters next to the **Stiftskirche,** the collegiate church, from mid-June to the beginning of August. Inside the church is a 15th-century altar carved by Albrecht Dürer's teacher, Michael Wohlgemut. Don't miss the **Heimatmuseum** (local history museum), with its excellent collection of folk arts and crafts. *Open Tues.–Sat. 9–12 and 2–5. Admission: DM 1.50.*

22 **Dinkelsbühl** is only 12 kilometers (8 miles) farther south. Within its mellow walls the rush of traffic seems an eternity away. There's less to see here than in Rothenburg, but the mood is much less tourist-oriented, less precious. It's thought that the town originated in the 6th century as the court of a Franconian king. Like Rothenburg, Dinkelsbühl was caught up in the Thirty Years' War, and, again like Rothenburg, it preserves a fanciful episode from those bloody times. Local lore says that when Dinkelsbühl was under siege by Swedish forces and in imminent danger of destruction, a young girl led the children of the town to the enemy commander and implored him in their name for mercy. The commander of the Swedish army, Colonel Klaus Dietrich von Sperreuth, is said to have been moved almost to tears, and he spared the town. Whether or not it's true, the story is a charming one, and it is retold every year in a pageant by the children of Dinkelsbühl during a 10-day festival in July.

Touring Dinkelsbühl is not so much a matter of taking in specific sights—museums, palaces, parks, and churches, say—as of simply wandering around the historic area, pausing to admire a facade, a shop window, or the juxtaposition of architectural styles—from Gothic through Baroque—that makes this little town memorable. Altrathausplatz, Seringerstrasse, Bahnhofstrasse, Marktplatz, and Turrngasse will all reward lovers of quaint, picture-postcard Teutonic townscapes. The one standout sight for many is the **Stadtpfarrkirche St. Georg** on the Marktplatz. Big enough, at 235 feet long, to be a cathedral, St. Georg's is among the best examples in Bavaria of the late-Gothic style. Note especially the complex fan vaulting that spreads sinuously across the ceiling. If you can face the climb, head up the 200-foot tower for amazing views over the jumble of Dinkelsbühl's rooftops.

The cry of *So G'sell so*—"All's well"—still rings out every night
23 across the ancient walls and turrets of **Nördlingen,** the next stop along the Romantic Road. The town employs sentries to sound out the traditional message from the 300-foot-high tower of the central parish church of St. Georg at half-hour intervals between 10 PM and midnight. The tradition goes back to an incident during the Thirty Years' War when an enemy attempt to slip into the town was detected by an alert townswoman. From the church tower—known locally as the Daniel (open 8 AM–dusk)—you'll get an unsurpassed view of the town and the surrounding countryside, including, on clear days, all of 99 villages. However, the climb is only for the fit: The tower has 365 steps, one for each day of the year. The ground plan of the town is two concentric circles, like the rings of a tree. The inner circle of streets, whose central point is St. Georg's, marks the earliest boundary of the medieval town. A few hundred yards beyond it is the outer boundary, a wall built to accommodate the expanding town. Fortified with 11 towers and punctuated by five massive gates, it's one of

the best-preserved town walls in Germany. You can stroll along it for about 2 miles of its length.

For an even more spectacular view of Nördlingen, contact the local flying club, the **Rieser Flugsportverein** (tel. 09081/4099), and take to the sky in a light aircraft. The sight of Nördlingen nestling in the trim, green Swabian (southwestern Germany) landscape is well worth the cost. You'll notice another phenomenon from the air: the basinlike formation of the **Ries,** a 15-mile-wide crater caused by a huge meteorite nearly 15 million years ago. Until the beginning of this century, it was believed that the crater was the remains of an extinct volcano. In 1960, it was proven that the Ries was caused by a meteorite at least ½ mile in diameter that hit the ground at more than 100,000 miles per hour. The impact had the destructive energy of 250,000 atomic bombs of the size that obliterated Hiroshima. It also turned the surface rock and subsoil upside down, hurling debris as far as Czechoslovakia and wiping out all plant and animal life within a radius of 300 miles. The compressed rock, or *suevit,* formed by the explosive impact of the meteorite was used to construct many of the town's buildings, including St. Georg's tower.

The next stop on the Romantic Road is where the little Wörnitz River breaks through the Franconian Juran Mountains, 20 kilometers (12 miles) south. Here you'll find one of southern Ger-
24 many's best-preserved medieval castles. **Schloss Harburg** was already old when it passed into the possession of the counts of Oettingen in 1295; before that time it had belonged to the Hohenstaufen emperors. The ancient and noble house of Oettingen still owns the castle, and treasures collected by the family through the centuries can be seen in it. The collection includes some works by Tilman Riemenschneider, along with illuminated manuscripts dating as far back as the 8th century and an exquisite 12th-century ivory crucifix. *Admission, including guided tour: DM 8 adults, DM 2 children. Open mid-Mar.–Oct., daily 9–11:30 and 1:30–5:30.*

Eleven kilometers (7 miles) south, the Wörnitz River meets the
25 Danube at the old walled town of **Donauwörth.** If you're driving, pull off into the clearly marked lot on B-25, just north of town. Below you sprawls a striking natural relief map of Donauwörth and its two rivers. The oldest part of town is on an island in the river, connected to the rest of town by a wood bridge and greeted on the north bank by the single surviving town gate, the Riederstor. North of the gate is one of the finest avenues of the Romantic Road: Reichsstrasse (Empire Street), so named because it was once a vital link in the Road of the Holy Roman Empire between Nürnberg and Augsburg. The broad street—known by the locals as the Gute Stube (front room) of their town—is lined by solid, centuries-old houses and shops that tell their own tales of Donauwörth's prosperous past. The Fuggers, a famous family of traders and bankers from Augsburg, acquired a palatial home here in the 16th century; its fine Renaissance-style facade under a steeply gabled roof stands proudly at the upper end of Reichsstrasse.

Augsburg

26 **Augsburg,** 50 kilometers (30 miles) south, is the next stop on the Romantic Road. Home of the Fuggers, who led the city into the Renaissance, Augsburg is Bavaria's third-largest city, after

Munich and Nürnberg. Augsburg's history dates to 15 years before the birth of Christ, when one Drusus, son of the Roman Emperor Augustus, set up a military camp here on the banks of the Lech River. The settlement that grew up around it was known as Augusta, a name Italian visitors to the city still give it. It was granted city rights in 1156, and 200 years later, first mention can be found in municipal records of the Fugger family, who were to Augsburg what the Medicis were to Florence. On your tour of the city you will encounter traces of that extraordinary family at almost every turn.

Numbers in the margin correspond to points of interest on the Augsburg map.

Begin at the Verkehrsverein (city tourist office), on Bahnhofstrasse, the street running into the city center from the Hauptbahnhof (train station). The maps and information you can pick up include a pamphlet listing three tours that are signposted in three different colors. Follow the blue route first
27 to one of Augsburg's many historic churches, **St. Annakirche.** This former Carmelite monastery dates from the 14th century. Visitors can wander through its quiet cloisters and view the chapel used by the Fugger family until the Reformation. In 1318, Martin Luther stayed in the monastery during his meetings with Cardinal Cajetanus, the papal legate sent from Rome to persuade the reformist to renounce his heretical views. Luther refused, and the place where he publicly declared his rejection of papal pressure is marked with a plaque on Augsburg's main street, the Maximilianstrasse.

Outside St. Annakirche, follow the green route southward,
28 along Martin-Luther-Platz, past the **Maximilian-Museum,** a permanent exhibition of Augsburg arts and crafts. *Phillipine-Welser-Str. 24. Admission free. Open Tues.–Sun. 10–4.*

At the end of the square in front of you is Maximilianstrasse; here you'll notice one of the three monumental and elaborate fountains that splash amid the buzz of traffic on this historic old
29 street. The **Mercury fountain,** 1599, by the Dutch master Adrian de Vries (after a Florentine sculpture by Giovanni da Bologna) shows winged Mercury in his classic pose. Farther up Maximilianstrasse is another de Vries fountain: a bronze Hercules struggling to defeat the many-headed Hydra. The lantern-lined street was once the scene of a wine market; today the high-gabled, pastel facades of the 16th-century merchant houses assert themselves against encroaching postwar shops. On the right, as you walk up the slight incline of the street, stands the former home and business quarters of the Fuggers. The 16th-century building now houses a restaurant in its cellar and offices on the upper floors. In the ground-floor entrance are busts of two of Augsburg's most industrious Fuggers, Raymund and Anton, tributes from a grateful city to the wealth these merchants brought to the community. Beyond a modern glass door is a quiet courtyard with colonnades, originally reserved for the Fugger womenfolk.

Another wealthy family, the von Liebenhofens, built a rival palace only a few paces up the street. The 18th-century palace now bears the name of a baron who married into the banking family, von Schaezler. The von Liebenhofens wanted to outdo the Fuggers—but not at any price. Thus, to save money in an age when property was taxed according to the size of the street

Deutsche Barockgalerie, **30**
Dom St. Maria, **36**
Fuggerei, **34**
Maximilian-Museum, **28**
Mercury Fountain, **29**
Mozarthaus, **37**
Oblatter Wall, **38**
Rathaus, **35**
Rotes Tor, **32**
St. Annakirche, **27**
Sts. Ulrich and Afra, **31**
Vogeltor, **33**

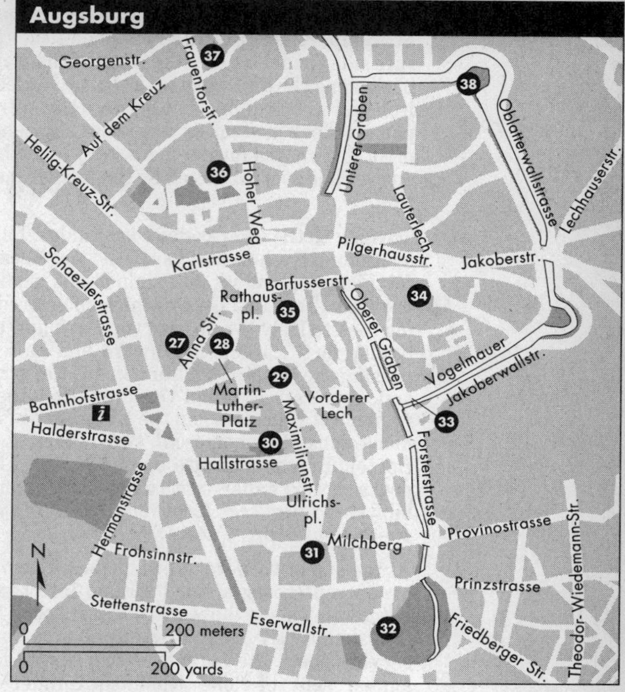

frontage, they constructed a long, narrow building running far back from Maximilianstrasse. The palace is composed of a series of interconnecting rooms that lead into a green-and-white Rococo ballroom: an extravagant, two-story hall heavily decorated with mirrors, chandeliers, and wall sconces. Marie Antoinette, on her way from Vienna to Paris to marry Louis XVI, was guest of honor at the inauguration ball in 1770.

Descendants of the von Liebenhofens bequeathed the palace to the city of Augsburg after the war; today its rooms contain the
30 **Deutsche Barockgalerie** (German Baroque Gallery), a major art collection that features works of the 17th and 18th centuries. The palace adjoins the former church of a Dominican monastery. A steel door behind the banquet hall of the palace leads into another world of high-vaulted ceilings, where the Bavarian State Collection highlights an exhibition of early Swabian old master paintings. Among them is a Dürer portrait of one of the Fuggers. *Maximilianstr. 46. Admission free, but donations are encouraged. Open May–Sept., Tues.–Sun. 10–5; Oct.–Apr., Tues.–Sun. 10–4.*

At the top of Maximilianstrasse on Ulrichsplatz, at the highest
31 point of the city, is the former monastery church of **Sts. Ulrich and Afra,** two churches built on the site of a Roman cemetery where St. Afra was martyred in AD 304. The original, Catholic building was begun as a late-Gothic construction in 1467; a Baroque-style preaching hall was added in 1710 as the Protestant church of St. Ulrich. St. Afra is buried in the crypt, near the tomb of St. Ulrich, a 10th-century bishop credited with helping to stop a Hungarian army at the doors of Augsburg in the battle

of the Lech River. The remains of a third patron of the church, St. Simpert, are preserved in one of the church's most elaborate side chapels. From the steps of the magnificent altar, look back along the high nave to the finely carved Baroque wrought-iron and wood railing that borders the entrance. As you leave, pause to look into the separate but adjacent Protestant church of St. Ulrich, the former monastery assembly hall that was taken over and reconstructed by the Lutherans after the Reformation.

Turning to the color-coded tour guides, follow the green route south for a few hundred yards and you'll reach the city's ancient fortifications and its most important medieval entrance gate,
32 the **Rotes Tor** (Red Gate), which once straddled the main trading road to Italy. From here you can follow the traces of the early city fortifications northward and back to the city center,
33 passing the Gothic **Vogeltor** (Bird Gate) astride Oberer Graben and, on the street called Vorderer Lech, the rebuilt 16th-century home of Hans Holbein the Elder, one of Augsburg's most famous sons (the homes of two others, Leopold Mozart and Bertolt Brecht, are also on our route). The Holbein house is now a city art gallery with a regularly changing program of exhibitions. *Vorderer Lech 20. Open May–Oct., Tues.–Sun. 10–5; Nov.–Apr., Tues.–Sun. 10–4.*

At the end of Vorderer Lech, make a sharp right and follow the green route over a small stream into the tranquillity of the
34 **Fuggerei.** This is the world's oldest social housing scheme, established by the Fugger family to accommodate the city's deserving poor. The 147 homes still serve the same purpose; the annual rent of "one Rheinish Guilder" (DM 1.72) hasn't changed, either. Understandably, there's quite a demand to take up residence in this peaceful, leafy estate. There are four requirements: Residents must be Augsburg citizens, Catholic, and destitute through no fault of their own, and they must pray daily for their original benefactors, the Fugger family.

From the Fuggerei, follow the green route back into the city center, stopping at the **Brecht** family home, a modest artisan's house. Here the renowned playwright Bertolt Brecht, author of *The Threepenny Opera,* was born and lived until he moved on, first to Munich and then, during Hitler's reign, to Scandinavia and later the United States. After the war he settled in East Berlin, to direct the Berliner Ensemble. Today the house serves as a memorial center dedicated to Brecht's life and work. *Auf dem Rain 7. Admission: DM 2 adults, DM 1 children. Open May–Oct., Tues.–Sun. 10–5; Nov.–Apr., Tues.–Sun. 10–4.*

Two left turns will bring you to Rathausplatz, the center of Augsburg, dominated by the 258-foot-high **Perlachturm** (open
35 Apr.–Sept., daily 10–6) and the adjacent massive, square **Rathaus** (Town Hall). The great building, Germany's largest city hall when it was built in the early 17th century, is one of the finest Renaissance structures north of the Alps. (The Rathaus can be visited between 10 and 6 on days when no official functions are taking place.)

Time Out Behind the Rathaus, down the street called Hunoldsgraben, is one of Augsburg's oldest wine taverns, the **Augsburger Schmuckkastchen.** It used to belong to a 14th-century monastery; now it's the realm of Bacchus. Beer, light meals, and coffee are served, but wine is what you're expected to order. *Closed Mon.*

From the great square in front of the Rathaus (its 16th-century fountain commemorates the 1,600th anniversary of the founding of Augsburg), turn north again along the shopping streets
36 of Karolinenstrasse and Hoher Weg to the **Dom St. Maria** (Cathedral of the Virgin Mary); its square Gothic towers will signal the way. An Episcopal church stood here in the 9th century, and a 10th-century Romanesque crypt, built in the time of Bishop Ulrich, remains from those early years. The heavy bronze doors on the south portal date from the 11th century; 11th-century windows on the south side of the nave depict the prophets Jonah, Daniel, Hosea, Moses, and David, to form the oldest cycle of stained glass in central Europe. Five altarpieces by Hans Holbein the Elder are among the cathedral's other treasures.

A short walk from the cathedral, still following the green route, will take you to the quiet courtyards and small raised garden of the former Episcopal residence, a series of fine 18th-century buildings in Baroque and Rococo styles that now serve as the offices of the Swabian regional government. Although less than 64 kilometers (40 miles) from the capital of Bavaria, we're now firmly in Swabia, once such a powerful dukedom under the Hohenstaufens that its territory covered virtually all of present-day Switzerland. Today Swabia has become an administrative district of Bavaria, and Augsburg has yielded the position it once held to the younger city of Munich.

37 Head north again, along Frauentorstrasse, to the **Mozarthaus,** birthplace of Leopold Mozart, father of Wolfgang Amadeus Mozart and an accomplished composer and musician in his own right. A comfortable 17th-century home, it now serves as a Mozart memorial and museum, with some fascinating contemporary documents on the Mozart family. The last Augsburg family connection died just a few years ago. *Frauentorstr. 30. Admission free. Open Mon., Wed., Thurs. 10–noon and 2–5; Fri. 10–noon and 2–4; Sat. and Sun. 10–noon.*

Retrace your steps to the city center. If you have time and energy, you can continue your tour with a walk along the remains of the city's ancient north and east defenses. For part of the way a pleasant walk follows the moat, which was once part of the for-
38 tifications. At the **Oblatter Wall** you can rent a boat and row between the green, leafy banks—a welcome break and a fine way to say farewell to Augsburg.

Toward the Alps

Numbers in the margin correspond to points of interest on the Romantic Road map.

Leaving Augsburg southward on B-17—the southern stretch of the Romantic Road—you'll drive across the Lech battlefield, where the Hungarian invaders were stopped in 955. Rich Bavarian pastures extend as far as the Lech River, which follows the country road for much of its way. About 32 kilometers (20
39 miles) south is the historic old town of **Landsberg am Lech,** in whose prison Adolf Hitler wrote much of *Mein Kampf.* The town was founded by the Bavarian ruler Heinrich der Löwe (Henry the Lion) in the 12th century and grew wealthy from the salt trade. You'll see impressive evidence of Landsberg's

early wealth among the solid old houses packed within its turreted walls; the early 18th-century Altes Rathaus (Old Town Hall) is one of the finest of the region.

The German artist Sir Hubert von Herkomer was born in a small village just outside Landsberg. Within the town walls is an unusual monument—not to Sir Hubert (he was knighted in England in 1907) but to his mother, Josefine. It's a romantic, medieval-style tower, bristling with turrets and galleries, built by Sir Hubert himself. He called it his Mutterturm, or "mother tower." The young Hubert was taken by his parents to the United States and later, when they couldn't settle in America happily, to England. He died in Devon in 1914. The 100th anniversary of the completion of the Mutterturm was in 1988, and an exhibition on the life and work of this remarkable man was held within its rough-stone walls.

Beyond Landsberg, the Bavarian Alps rise along the southern horizon, signaling the end of the Romantic Road. Some 30 ki-
40 lometers (18 miles) south is another old walled town, **Schongau,** founded at about the same time as Landsberg, with virtually intact wall fortifications, together with towers and gates. In medieval and Renaissance times, the town was an important trading post on the route from Italy to Augsburg. The steeply gabled, 16th-century Ballenhaus was a warehouse before it was elevated to the rank of Rathaus (Town Hall).

If you're driving, leave the Romantic Road just beyond Schongau, at the village of **Peiting,** and take B-472 to the nearby sum-
41 mit of the 3,000-foot-high **Hoher Peissenberg,** the first real peak of the Alpine chain. A pilgrimage chapel was consecrated on the mountain in the 16th century; a century later a larger church was added, with a fine ceiling fresco and delicate carvings by local Bavarian masters.

After returning to Peiting, take B-23 to **Rottenbuch,** where the Augustinian order built an impressive monastery on the Ammer River in the 11th century. The Gothic basilica was redecorated in Rococo style during the 18th century. The lavish interior of cream, gold, and rose stucco work and statuary is stunning.

Rottenbuch is a worthy preparation for the next—and most glorious—example of German Rococo architecture, the
42 **Wieskirche** (Church of the Meadow). It stands in an alpine meadow just off the Romantic Road near Steingaden, its yellow and white walls and steep red roof set off by the dark backdrop of the Trauchgauer Mountains. The architect Dominicus Zimmermann (former mayor of Landsberg and creator of much of that town's Rococo architecture) was commissioned in 1745 to build the church on this spot, where, six years earlier, a local woman claimed to have seen tears running down the face of a picture of Christ. Although the church was dedicated as the Pilgrimage Church of the Scourged Christ, it is now known as the Wieskirche. Visit it on a fine day, when alpine light streaming through its high windows displays the full glory of the glittering interior. This is Bavarian Rococo at its scintillating best. Together with the pilgrimage church of Vierzehnheiligen in north Bavaria, the Wieskirche represents the culmination of German Rococo ecclesiastical architecture. As at Vierzehnheiligen, the simple exterior gives little hint of the ravishing interior. A complex oval plan is animated by a series of brilliantly

colored stuccos, statues, and gilt. A luminous ceiling fresco completes the decoration. Note the beautifully detailed choir and organ loft. Concerts are presented in the church in the summer. Contact the Städtische Musikschule Schongau (tel. 08861/7216) for details. Zimmermann, the architect of the church, is buried in the 12th-century former abbey church of Steingaden. Although his work was the antithesis of Romanesque architecture, he was laid to rest in a dour, late-Romanesque side chapel.

From Steingaden, the road runs beneath the Ammergau range
43 22 kilometers (13 miles) to **Schwangau,** a lakeside resort town and an ideal center from which to explore the surrounding mountains. Schwangau is where you encounter the heritage of Bavaria's famous 19th-century king, Ludwig II. Both his childhood home and the most spectacular of his exotic castles are at the town's doorstep. Ludwig spent much of his youth at Schloss Hohenschwangau; it is said that its neo-Gothic atmosphere provided the primary influences that shaped the construction of the wildly romantic Schloss Neuschwanstein, the fairy-tale castle Ludwig built across the valley after he became king.

44 **Hohenschwangau** palace was built by the knights of Schwangau in the 12th century. Later it was remodeled by Ludwig's father, the Bavarian crown prince (and later king) Maximilian, between 1832 and 1836. It was here that the young Ludwig met the composer Richard Wagner. Their friendship shaped and deepened the future king's interest in theater, music, and German mythology—the mythology upon which Wagner drew for his "Ring" cycle of operas. Wagner saw the impressionable Ludwig principally as a potential source of financing for his extravagant operas rather than as a kindred spirit. For all his lofty idealism, the composer was hardly a man to let scruples interfere with his self-aggrandizement.

Ludwig's love of the theater and fantasy ran so deep that when
45 he came to build **Neuschwanstein,** he employed a set designer instead of an architect. The castle soars from its mountainside like a stage creation—it should hardly come as a surprise that Walt Disney took it as the model for his castle in the movie *Sleeping Beauty* and later for the Disneyland castle itself.

The life of the proprietor of this spectacular castle reads like one of the great Gothic mysteries of the 19th century. Here was a king, a member of the Wittelsbach dynasty that had ruled Bavaria since 1180, who devoted his time and energies to creating architectural flights of fancy that came close to bankrupting the Bavarian government. Finally, in 1886, before Neuschwanstein was finished, members of the government became convinced that Ludwig had taken leave of his senses. A medical commission set out to prove that the king was insane and forced him to give up his throne. Ludwig was incarcerated in the much more modest lakeside castle of Berg on the Starnbergersee. Then, on the evening of June 13, 1886, the king and the doctor attending him disappeared. Late that night their bodies were pulled from the lake. The circumstances of their deaths remain a mystery to this day.

The interior of Ludwig's fantasy castle is a fitting setting for this grim tale. His bedroom is tomblike, dominated by a great Gothic-style bed. The throne room is without a throne; Ludwig died before one could be installed. Corridors are outfitted as a ghostly grotto, reminiscent of Wagner's *Tannhäuser*. During the 17 years from the start of construction until his death, the king spent only 102 days in this country residence. Chamber concerts are held at the beginning of September in the gaily decorated minstrels' hall, one room at least that was completed as Ludwig conceived it. (Program details are available from the Verkehrsamt, Schwangau, tel. 08362/81051.) There are some spectacular walks around the castle. Make for the **Marienbrücke** (Mary's Bridge), spun like a medieval maiden's hair across a deep, narrow gorge. From this vantage point, there are giddy views of the castle and the great Upper Bavarian plain beyond. *Admission to Schloss Hohenschwangau, including a guided tour: DM 8 adults, DM 4 children under 14 and senior citizens. Open Apr.–Sept., daily 8:30–5:30; Oct.–Mar., daily 10–4. Admission to Schloss Neuschwanstein, including a guided tour: DM 8 adults, DM 4 children under 14. Open Apr.–Sept., daily 8:30–5:30; Oct.–Mar., daily 10–4. The two castles are ½ mi from each other and about 1 mi from the center of Schwangau. Cars and buses are barred from the approach roads, but the 1-mi journey to Neuschwanstein can be made by horse-drawn carriages, which stop in the village of Hohenschwangau. A bus from the village takes a back route to the Aussichtspunkt Jugend; from there, it's only a 10-minute walk to the castle. The Schloss Hohenschwangau is a 15-minute walk from the village.*

If you plan to visit Hohenschwangau or Neuschwanstein, bear in mind that more than 1 million people pass through the two castles every year. Authorities estimate that on some summer weekends the number of people who tour Neuschwanstein is matched by the number who give up at the prospect of standing in line for up to two hours. If you visit in the summer, get there early. The best time to see either castle without waiting in a long line is a weekday in January, February, or early March. The prettiest time, however, is in the fall.

The castles are only 5 kilometers (3 miles) from the official end
46 of the Romantic Road, the border town of **Füssen,** set at the foot of the mountains that separate Bavaria from the Austrian Tyrol. Füssen also has a notable castle, the Hohes Schloss, one of the best-preserved late-Gothic castles in Germany. It was built on the site of the Roman fortress that once guarded this Alpine section of the Via Claudia, the trading route from Rome to the Danube. The castle was the seat of Bavarian rulers before Emperor Heinrich VII mortgaged it and the rest of the town to the bishop of Augsburg for 400 pieces of silver. The mortgage was never redeemed, and Füssen remained the property of the Augsburg episcopate until secularization in the early 19th century. The castle was put to good use by the bishops of Augsburg as their summer Alpine residence. It has a spectacular 16th-century Rittersaal (Knights' Hall) with a fine carved ceiling, and a princes' chamber with a Gothic tiled heating oven. *Magnuspl. 10. Admission: DM 4 adults, DM 2 children. Open daily 2–4.*

The presence, at least in summer, of the bishops of Augsburg ensured that Füssen received an impressive number of Baroque and Rococo churches. A Benedictine abbey was built in the 9th century at the site of the grave of St. Magnus, who spent most of his life ministering in Füssen and the surrounding countryside. A Romanesque crypt beneath the Baroque abbey church has a partially preserved 10th-century fresco, the oldest in Bavaria.

The abbey was secularized and never reclaimed by the Catholic church, and today it serves as Füssen's Rathaus (Town Hall). In summer, chamber concerts are held in the high-ceilinged, Baroque splendor of the abbey's Fürstensaal (Princes' Hall). *Program details are available from the Füssen tourist office, Augsburger Torplatz 1, tel. 08362/7077.*

Complete your tour of the Romantic Road with a stroll down a street that—like Augsburg's Maximilianstrasse—was once part of the Roman Via Claudia. Now it's Füssen's main shopping street—a cobblestone pedestrian walkway, lined by high-gabled medieval houses and backed by the bulwarks of the castle and the easternmost buttresses of the Allgäu Alps. The Lech River, which has accompanied you for much of the final section of the Romantic Road, rises in those mountains and embraces the town as it rushes northward. One of several lakes in the area, the Forggensee is formed from a broadening of the river. *A pleasure boat makes 1½-hour cruises on the lake from the beginning of June through September. Fare is DM 10 adults, DM 5 children.*

What to See and Do with Children

In **Würzburg,** take a boat trip on the Main River (*see* Guided Tours in Essential Information, above). In **Rothenburg-ob-der-Tauber,** young imaginations soar while roaming through the dungeons beneath the Rathaus and the grisly exhibits in the **Mittelalterliches Kriminalmuseum** (Medieval Criminal Museum). A rack, thumbscrews, and various other torture devices will keep parents busy answering questions. The town also has the enchanting **Puppen und Spielzeugmuseum** (Doll and Toy Museum), with enough dolls to keep youngsters amused for hours (*see* Rothenburg-ob-der-Tauber, above). You might also seek out the adventure playground in the dry moat in front of the **Würzburger Tor,** where, on a fine day, you can sun yourself while the children play in the shadow of Rothenburg's ancient walls.

Augsburg has an excellent **puppet theater** (Spitalgasse 15, next to the Rotes Tor) and a **zoo** with more than 1,900 animals. *Admission: DM 6 adults, DM 3.50 children. Open Apr.–Sept., daily 8:30–6; Oct.–Mar., daily 8:30–dusk or 5 (whichever is earlier).*

Young cowboys will feel at home in **"Western City,"** in the village of Dasing, just outside of Augsburg. *Admission: DM 6 adults, DM 5 children. Open Palm Sunday–Nov., Tues.–Sun. 9–6.*

At **Königsbrunn,** just outside Augsburg, is a **lido** with five heated pools, complete with water cannons, chutes, and geysers. *Admission for 2 hours: DM 14 adults, DM 8 children. Open daily 10:30–7:30.*

A mile outside **Schongau,** suitably set in a wood, is one of the popular **Märchenwälder** (fairy-tale forests) that dot the German landscape, complete with mechanical models of fairy-tale scenes, deer enclosures, and an old-time miniature railway. *Schongau Märchenwald, Diessenstr. 6. Admission: DM 4 adults, DM 2 children. Open Easter–Oct., daily 9–7.*

If you're in Schongau during the winter, take a **sleigh ride** into the mountains to feed the wild deer. Josef Kotz sets off daily from the Karbrücke bridge at 2:30 (tel. 08362/8581).

Off the Beaten Track

Getting off the beaten track in one of Germany's most popular tourist areas is not as hard as you might think. Even in Rothenburg-ob-der-Tauber there are corners that the world passes by. Pull on the bell at the **Staudthof** in Herrngasse, hand over DM 1, and you'll gain admittance to the town's oldest patrician home, a 450-year-old haven of peace that's belonged to the von Staudt family for three centuries. The yew trees in the quiet courtyard have been there that long, too; some are thought to be 1,000 years old. The shutters are painted in the yellow and black of the Hapsburgs as tribute to the fact that it was the Hapsburgs who raised two members of the von Staudt family to the nobility. Linger at the low wall along Rothenburg's **Burggasse** as dusk falls on the valley below. Watch the sun set from the west defense walls of the lovely little hilltop town of **Schillingsfurst,** halfway between Feuchtwangen and Rothenburg.

Visit Bavarian forester Siegfried Niestroj's **butterfly farm** in Dinkelsbühl (open daily 9–6). It's next to the town's Rothenburger Tor.

One of Germany's most unusual museums, the **Fingerhutmuseum,** can be found opposite the Herrgottskirche outside Creglingen. *Fingerhut* is German for "thimble," and the museum has thousands of them, some dating from Roman times. *Open Apr.–Oct., daily 9–6; Nov.–Mar., daily 1–4.*

Shopping

Hummel **porcelain** figures are a perennial favorite among visitors to this area of Germany. Prices vary dramatically, so be sure to shop around. You'll find a wide selection at competitive prices at **Otto Wolf** (Marktpl.) in Nördlingen. Hummel figures and other German porcelain and glassware can be found in Dinkelsbühl at **Weschcke and Ries** (Segringerstr.) and, in Rothenburg, at **Unger's** (Herrngasse) and the **Kunstwerke Friese** (Grüner Markt, near the Rathaus). The Kunstwerke Friese also stocks a selection of the beautifully crafted porcelain birds made by the Hummel manufacturers, the Goebel Porzellanfabrik.

Locally made **pottery** is enjoying a renaissance in some of the Romantic Road towns. **Jürgen Pleinkies** (Segringerstr.) in Dinkelsbühl is energetically trying to restore his town's former reputation for fine earthenware; he also offers courses at the potter's wheel. Local artists don't lack for inspiration in these beautiful Romantic Road towns; a large selection of their work can be found at the **Reichstadt** gallery (Segringerstr.).

Children will love **Käthe Wohlfahrt's** shop (Herringasse) in Rothenburg. Her **Weihnachtsdorf** (Christmas village) is a wonderland of locally made toys and decorations; even in summer there are Christmas trees hung with brightly painted wood baubles. In Rothenburg, the centuries-old onetime home of **Georg Nusch** (Burggasse)—the councillor who saved the town by accepting General Tilly's wine-drinking challenge—is a shop stacked high with local glassware and other handicrafts.

In Augsburg the place to shop is the broad **Maximilianstrasse,** once the city's wine market. The Romantic Road's true **wine** center is Würzburg. Visit any of the vineyards that rise from the Main River and choose a *Bocksbeutel,* the distinctive green, flagon-shape wine bottles of Franconia. It's claimed that the shape came about because wine-guzzling monks found it the easiest to hide under their robes. In Würzburg itself, you'll want to linger on traffic-free **Schönbornstrasse** and the adjacent marketplace. Wine and the familiar goblets in which it is served in this part of the world are sold in many of the shops here. You can buy directly from two ancient city institutions: the **Bürgerspital** (Theaterstr.) and the **Juliusspital** (Juliuspromenade). Both sell wine from their own vineyards, as well as the glasses from which to drink it.

Sports and Fitness

Bicycling Bikes can be rented at all train stations on the Romantic Road. Rental is DM 12 a day (DM 6 if you have a valid rail ticket). Some tourist offices—Dinkelsbühl is one—have a limited number of bikes for rent. You'll need ID, such as a passport, as a deposit against the safe return of the bike.

Canoeing The Lech River, which follows the southern stretch of the Romantic Road for much of its way, offers excellent canoeing. There's good sport, too, to be had on the Tauber and Wörnitz rivers. Contact the **DON canoe club** at Donauwörth (tel. 0906/5962).

Golf **Augsburg Golf Club** (tel. 08234/5621) welcomes visiting members of overseas golf clubs. For scenery and a mild challenge, try the nine-hole course at **Schloss Colberg** (tel. 0981/5617). It's 20 kilometers (12 miles) east of Rothenburg.

Hang Gliding Although there are eagles in those mountains, the winged forms you see in the skies above Füssen and Schongau are more likely to be hang gliders. This is a leading center of the sport. For information, contact the **Allgäu Drachenflugschule** (tel. 08362/107).

Mountain Climbing and Walking The mountains above Füssen and Schwangau beckon climbers and walkers. Contact the **Bergschule Ostallgäu** in Schwangau (tel. 08362/81463) for guides, maps, and other information.

Sailing and Windsurfing The lakes around Füssen offer excellent sailing and windsurfing. **Lutz Selbach** has several boathouses, two of which, Hopfensee and Weissensee (tel. 08362/5429), rent sailing dinghies and Windsurfers. For boats and Windsurfers on the larger Forggensee, **Egon Ganahl** (tel. 08362/471) is the man to contact.

Skiing Füssen, Schwangau, and surrounding villages are popular ski resorts. All have sports shops offering lessons and equipment. Schwangau also has its own ski school (tel. 08362/8455).

Dining and Lodging

Dining

The best Franconian and Swabian food combines hearty regional specialties with nouvelle elements. Various forms of pasta are common. Try *Pfannkuchen* (pancakes) and *Spätzle* (small tagliatelle-like ribbons of rolled dough), the latter often served with roast beef, or *Rinderbraten*, the traditional Sunday lunchtime dish. One of the best regional dishes is *Maultaschen*, a Swabian version of ravioli, usually served floating in broth strewn with chives. Würzburg is one of the leading wine-producing areas of Germany, and beer lovers will want to try the many Franconian beers, whose brands and flavors change from town to town.

All the historic cities and towns along the Romantic Road have a wide selection of good-value restaurants. This being such an important tourist area and the heartland of picture-postcard Germany, a great many are firmly in the heavy-beamed, open-fireplace mold. If it's classy, international-style restaurants you want, you may be disappointed.

Ratings Highly recommended restaurants in each price category are indicated by a star ★.

Category	Cost*
Very Expensive	over DM 90
Expensive	DM 55–DM 90
Moderate	DM 35–DM 55
Inexpensive	DM 20–DM 35

**per person for a three-course meal, including tax and excluding drinks*

Lodging

With a few exceptions, the Romantic Road features mostly quiet and rustic hotels rather than slick, modern purpose-built city lodgings. You'll find high standards of comfort and cleanliness throughout the region. Make reservations as far in advance as possible if you plan to visit in the summer. Hotels in Würzburg, Rothenburg, and Füssen in particular are often full year-round. Augsburg hotels are now in big demand because of accommodation shortages in nearby Munich. Tourist information offices can sometimes help with accommodations, even in high season, especially if you arrive early in the day.

Ratings Highly recommended hotels in each price category are indicated by a star ★.

Category	Cost*
Very Expensive	over DM 180
Expensive	DM 120–DM 180

Moderate	DM 80–DM 120
Inexpensive	under DM 80

**All prices are for two people in a double room, excluding service charges.*

Aschaffenburg
Dining and Lodging
★ **Romantik Hotel Post.** This is the number-one choice in town for both dining and lodging. Despite extensive wartime damage, the restored Post exudes class and that inimitable German coziness. All rooms are individually furnished. Eating here can be an experience not just for the excellent local specialites but because there's an original 19th-century mail coach in the rustic-looking restaurant. *Goldbachstr. 19–21, tel. 0621/21333. 71 rooms with bath. Facilities: sauna, indoor pool, restaurant, parking. AE, DC, MC, V. Expensive.*

Aschaffenburger Hof. This modern hotel offers high standards of comfort and service. Try for one of the rooms facing the courtyard. The restaurant provides better-than-average local specialties, plus vegetarian main dishes. *Frohsinnstr. 11, tel. 06021/21441. 65 rooms with bath. Facilities: restaurant, parking. AE, DC, MC, V. Expensive.*

Zum Ochsen. Located just around the corner from Schloss Johannisburg, this cozy old hotel-tavern serves hearty Franconian fare at very reasonable prices. *Karlstr. 16, tel. 06021/23132. 34 rooms. AE, DC, MC, V. Closed 3 weeks in Aug. and 1 week in Jan. Moderate.*

Augsburg
Dining
★ **Cheval Blanc.** Located on the southeast outskirts of Augsburg, 4 miles from downtown, this first-class restaurant in the Hotel Gregor has big-city flair, thanks to the skill and imagination of its Austrian chef, Franz Fuchs. Try the shrimp ravioli on a bed of fresh spinach, or tenderloin of rabbit with lightly sautéed vegetables. *Landsbergerstr. 62, Haunstetten, tel. 0821/80050. Reservations required. Jacket and tie required. AE, DC, MC, V. Dinner only. Closed Sun., Mon., and Aug. 3–24. Expensive.*

Zum alten Fischertor. This is one of the culinary high points along the Romantic Road, offering a mix of regional specialties and French haute cusine. Try the Swabian dumplings, for instance, with cuttlefish filling. The Augsburg-style herb soup is also delicious. *Pfärrle 14, tel. 0821/518–662. Reservations advised. Jacket and tie required. DC, MC, V. Closed Sun., Mon., Aug. 1–19, and Dec. 24–30. Expensive.*

Fuggerkeller. The vaulted cellars of the former Fugger home on Augsburg's historic Maximilianstrasse are now a bright and comfortable restaurant, owned and run by the luxurious Drei Mohren Hotel above it. The midday specials are a particularly good value; try the Swabian-style stuffed cabbage rolls in a spiced meat sauce. Prices for dinner are higher. *Maximilianstr. 38, tel. 0821/516–260. Reservations advised. Dress: informal. AE, DC, MC, V. Closed Sun. dinner and first 3 weeks in Aug. Moderate.*

★ **Welser Kuche.** You can practically hear the great oak tables groan under the eight-course menus of Swabian specialties offered here. You'll need to give a day's notice if you want the eight-course menu, however. Be sure to try Spätzle, the Swabian version of pasta. *Maximilianstr. 83, tel. 0821/33930. Reservations advised. Dress: informal. Open evenings only. Moderate.*

Lodging ★ **Steigenberger Drei Mohren Hotel.** Kings, princes, even Napoléon slept here; so did the British commander who defeated him at Waterloo, the duke of Wellington. The historic hotel, however, takes its name from three very early guests of less renown: three Abyssinian bishops who sought shelter in this worldly German city. *Maximilianstr. 40, tel. 0821/510–031. 100 rooms and 5 suites with bath. Facilities: parking, garden terrace, hairdresser, restaurant, bar. AE, DC, MC, V. Very Expensive.*

Alpenhof Ringhotel. Located on the outskirts of Augsburg, the Alpenhof nevertheless allows easy access to the city center. Modern and well appointed, the hotel has a restaurant decorated in quintessential Romantic Road style—you'll dine amid carved pillars and lots of wrought iron. *Donauwörtherstr. 233, tel. 0821/413051. 136 rooms with bath or shower. Facilities: indoor pool, sauna, solarium, fitness room, billiards, table tennis, casino, children's playground. AE, DC, MC, V. Expensive.*

Dom Hotel. Just across the street from Augsburg's cathedral, this is a snug, comfortable establishment with a personal touch. Ask for one of the attic rooms, where you'll sleep under beam ceilings and wake to a rooftop view of the city. *Frauentorstr. 8, tel. 0821/153–031. 43 rooms with bath or shower. MC, V. Moderate–Expensive.*

Hotel Post. Centrally located on a tree-lined avenue, this hotel offers modern, comfortable accommodations in friendly, well-run surroundings. The breakfast room, decked out in crisp blue-and-white checks, makes for a good start to the day. *Fuggerstr. 5/7 (Am Konigspl.), tel. 0821/36044. 50 rooms, most with bath or shower. AE, DC, MC, V. Closed Christmas and New Year's Day. Moderate–Expensive.*

Augsburger Hof. A preservation order protects the beautiful Renaissance facade of this charming old Augsburg mansion, the interior of which was completely reconstructed to create a comfortable and up-to-date hotel. The cathedral is around the corner, the town center a five-minute stroll away. *Auf dem Kreuz 2, tel. 0821/314083. 40 rooms with bath. Facilities: restaurant, garden, sauna. AE, MC, V. Moderate.*

Bad Mergentheim
Dining ★

Victoria. This is one of the area's finest spa hotels, combining cosmopolitan flair with rural peace and quiet. Rooms are large, luxurious, and furnished in the style of a country mansion, with king-size beds, well-cushioned armchairs, subdued lighting, and fine prints on the textile-hung walls. The lounge is scarcely less opulent, with an open fireplace and a library. The excellent restaurant, with a magnificent tiled oven taking pride of place, draws a clientele from far afield. *Poststr. 2–4, tel. 07931/5930. 73 rooms with bath. Facilities: tavern, wine bar, hairdressing salon, beauty parlor, sauna, solarium, parking. AE, DC, MC, V. Very Expensive.*

Kettler's Altfränkische Weinstube. You'll want to come here to try the Nürnberger Bratwürste—finger-size spicy sausages—and to enjoy the atmosphere of a snug 180-year-old Franconian tavern. The wine list is enormous. *Krumme Gasse 12, tel. 07931/7308. Reservations advised. Dress: informal. No credit cards. Closed Dec. 23–Jan. 15. Inexpensive.*

Dinkelsbühl
Lodging

Deutsches Haus. This picture-postcard medieval inn with a facade of half-timbered gables and flower boxes has many rooms fitted with antique furniture. *Weinmarkt 3, tel. 09851/2346. 14* *rooms and 1 suite with bath. Facilities: sauna, solarium, restaurant. AE, DC, MC, V. Closed Dec. 24–Jan. 6. Expensive.*

Blauer Hecht. A brewery-tavern in the 18th century (they still brew in the backyard), this hotel has lately been renovated to a high standard of comfort. It's central but quiet. *Schweinemarkt 1, tel. 09851/811. 44 rooms, 1 apartment, 1 suite, all with bath or shower. Facilities: indoor pool, sauna. AE, DC, MC, V. Closed Jan. Moderate.*

Donauwörth
Dining

Traube. This restaurant recently celebrated its 300th anniversary, although it began life under a different name. Within its old walls you'll be offered home-style Swabian-Bavarian fare at low prices. *Kapellstr. 14, tel. 0906/6096. Reservations advised. Dress: informal. AE, DC, MC, V. Inexpensive–Moderate.*

Lodging
★

Parkhotel. A new group has been formed in Germany to bring together hotels that have one feature in common: an idyllic location. This one qualifies because of its fine site high above Donauwörth. *Sternschanzenstr. 1, tel. 0906/6037. 35 rooms with bath or shower. Facilities: wine tavern, bowling alleys, public swimming pool next door. AE, DC, MC, V. Moderate.*

Feuchtwangen
Dining

Greifen-Stube. You'll dine here within walls decorated with frescoes of Feuchtwangen's past; the pictures will tell you that the emperor Maximilian and the dancer Lola Montez were also guests. Dine as they must have done—on such local Franconian dishes as lambs' kidneys in a mustard sauce or tender breast of partridge. *Marktpl. 8, tel. 09852/2002. Reservations required. Jacket and tie required. AE, DC, MC, V. Closed Jan.–mid-Feb. Moderate.*

Lodging
★

Romantik Hotel Greifen Post. The solid, market-square exterior of this hotel gives little hint of the luxuries within. Ask for the room with the four-poster or, if that's taken, settle for one of the other so-called "romantic" rooms. If you've got two days to spare, try one of the "Romantic Weekend" packages for the best value. *Marktpl. 8, tel. 09852/2002. 41 rooms, 2 apartments, 1 suite, all but one with bath. Facilities: indoor pool, sauna, solarium, restaurant. AE, DC, MC, V. Expensive.*

Füssen
Dining

Alpen-Schlössle. A *Schlössle* is a small castle, and although this comfortable, rustic restaurant isn't one, it is located on a mountain site, just outside Füssen, that King Ludwig might well have chosen for one of his homes. If wild duck is on the menu, don't leave without tasting it. *Alatseestr. 28, tel. 08362/4017. Reservations advised. Dress: informal. No credit cards. Closed Tues. and Nov.–mid-Dec. Rooms available. Moderate.*

Gasthaus zum Schwanen. This modest, cozy establishment offers good regional cooking with no frills, at low prices. The Swabian *Maultaschen*—a kind of local ravioli—are made on the premises and are excellent. *Brotmarkt 4, tel. 08362/6174. Dress: informal. No credit cards. Closed Sun. evening, Mon., and Nov. Inexpensive.*

Lodging

Hotel Sonne. *Sonne* means "sun," and this is an appropriately bright, cheerful, and modern hotel in Bavarian style with traditional furnishings. *Reichenstr. 37, tel. 08362/6061. 32 rooms with bath or shower. Facilities: café (but no restaurant), disco/nightclub. AE, DC, MC, V. Moderate.*

Kurhotel Berger. This is perhaps the best place to end up after a foot-sore tour of the Romantic Road: The hotel specializes in soothing aches and pains with medical baths in the local spa water. Views of the Alps in the quiet Bad Faulenbach district, about a mile from the town center, add to the restful atmosphere. *Alatseestr. 26, tel. 08362/6031. 36 rooms with bath. Facilities: indoor pool, sauna, resident doctor, terrace, restaurant, café. No credit cards. Closed Nov.–Dec. 20. Moderate.*

Miltenberg
Dining and Lodging
★ **Zum Riesen.** You won't find a more atmospheric place than this little half-timbered, family-run inn, which claims to be Germany's oldest established lodging, in business since the 12th century (though much of the present structure dates from the 16th century). The considerable promise of the fairy-tale exterior is matched by the interior, though modern necessities have been thoughtfully and unobtrusively provided. The service has just that touch of informality that makes the difference between a good and a memorable hotel. The adjoining restaurant continues the Old World theme. *Hauptstr. 97, tel. 09371/3644. 14 rooms with bath. Facilities: restaurant, parking. DC, MC. Closed Dec.–mid-Mar. Moderate–Expensive.*

Nördlingen
Dining
Meyers-Keller. An unassuming exterior belies the cozy, rustic interior of this unassuming restaurant, a short walk from Nördlingen's Altstadt. The menu is anything but simple Bavarian; try any of the fish dishes, all prepared with flair. *Marienhöhe 8, tel. 09081/4493. Reservations advised. Dress: informal. AE, MC. Closed Mon. Expensive.*

Lodging
Hotel Schützenhof. This small, comfortable hotel in traditional style, on the outskirts of town, is known for its excellent restaurant, which specializes in fresh fish from the surrounding lakes and rivers. *Kaiserwiese 2, tel. 09081/3940. 15 rooms with bath. Facilities: bowling alley. AE, DC, MC, V. Closed first 2 weeks in Aug. and 2 weeks in Jan. Moderate.*

★ **Hotel Sonne.** The great German poet Goethe stayed here and was only one in a long line of distinguished guests, headed by Emperor Friedrich III in 1487. The vaulted cellar wine-tavern is a reminder of those days. Today the historic old hotel is in the loving hands of an Englishwoman and her Anglophile husband. *Marktpl. 3, tel. 09081/5067. 40 rooms, all with bath or shower. Facilities: wine tavern. AE, MC. Closed Dec. 26–mid-Jan. Moderate.*

Rothenburg-ob-der-Tauber
Dining
★ **Die Blaue Terrasse.** The view of the Tauber Valley from the windows of the Hotel Goldener Hirsch's restaurant almost rivals their nouvelle cuisine, prepared with regional touches. Snails and asparagus (in season) are perennial favorites. *Untere Schmiedgasse 16/25, tel. 09861/7080. Reservations advised. Jacket and tie required. AE, DC, MC, V. Closed mid-Dec.–Jan. Expensive.*

★ **Baumeisterhaus.** In summer, you can dine in one of Rothenburg's loveliest courtyards, a half-timbered oasis of peace that's part of a magnificent Renaissance house. If the weather's cooler, move inside to the paneled dining room. The menu, changed daily, features Bavarian and Franconian specialties. *Obere Schmiedgasse 3, tel. 09861/3404. Reservations advised. Dress: informal. AE, DC, MC, V. Moderate.*

Reichs-Küchenmeister. Master chefs in the service of the Holy Roman Emperor were the inspiration for the name of this hotel-restaurant. Test the skills of the present chef by ordering any of the game dishes. *Kirchpl. 8, tel. 09861/2046. Reservations advised. Dress: informal. AE, DC, MC, V. Closed Tues. Nov.–Mar. Moderate.*

Lodging ★ **Hotel Eisenhut.** It's appropriate that the prettiest small town in Germany should have one of the prettiest small hotels in the country. It stands in the center of town and is located in what were originally four separate town houses, the oldest dating from the 12th century, the newest from the 16th. Inside there are enough oil paintings, antiques, and heavy beams to make any Teutonic knight feel at home. The hotel has a fine restaurant. *Herrngasse 3, tel. 09861/7050. 82 rooms, 3 suites, all with bath or shower. Facilities: restaurant. AE, DC, MC, V. Very Expensive.*

Hotel Goldener Hirsch. This lantern-hung, green-shuttered 15th-century patrician house is an inextricable part of Rothenburg's history: It was here that the Meistertrunk play was first performed. Baroque antiques are everywhere, from the lobby to the uppermost, bay-windowed bedroom. *Untere Schmiedgasse 16, tel. 09861/7080. 80 rooms, most with bath or shower. AE, DC, MC, V. Closed mid-Dec.–Jan. Very Expensive.*

★ **Romantik Hotel Markusturm.** This hotel belongs to the Romantik group, and romantic it certainly is: a 13th-century (but fully modernized) sharp-eaved house that is practically embraced by the ancient Markus tower and gate. If you stay at the height of the season, you'll hear the night watchman making his rounds. *Rödergasse 1, tel. 09861/2370. 26 rooms, most with bath. Facilities: restaurant, riding stables nearby, solarium, sauna. AE, DC, MC. Closed Jan. Very Expensive.*

Klosterstüble. Nestling in the shadow of a church and dating from the 16th century, this attractive historic house was renovated recently to include late-20th-century comforts. *Heringsbronnengasse 5, tel. 09861/6774. 14 rooms with bath. Facilities: restaurant. DC, MC, V. Moderate.*

Zum Rappen. Close to one of the town's gates, the Würzburger Tor, this long-established tavern offers modest comforts but central location at reasonable prices. *Würzburger Tor 6, tel. 09861/6071. 70 rooms, some with shower. Facilities: restaurant, beer garden, wine bar. AE, DC, MC, V. Closed Jan. Moderate.*

Gasthof Klingentor. This sturdy old staging post is outside the city walls but still within a 10-minute walk of Rothenburg's old town center. Rooms have recently been redecorated and furnished to a high standard of comfort. A well-marked cycle and hiking path starts outside the front door. *Mergentheimer Str. 14, tel. 09861/3468. Facilities: restaurant, garden, parking. MC. Inexpensive.*

Schillingfurst
Lodging

Hotel Zapf "An der Wornitzquelle." The River Wornitz rises practically in the back garden of this enchanting country hotel (hence the name: "source of the Wornitz"). Although this inn has a striking stepped-gable Renaissance facade, most rooms are in the less lovely modern extension; they are nevertheless comfortable and well-furnished, with balconies offering views of the fortified town of Schillingfurst and the surrounding countryside. *Dombuhler Strasse 7–9, tel. 09868/5020. 26 rooms with bath/shower. Facilities: restaurant, beer garden, terrace-garden, solarium, table tennis, bicycles, parking. MC. Inexpensive.*

Schongau
Dining

Hotel Holl. Hotelier Alexander Holl takes full advantage of the local lakes and rivers to stock the menu with fresh and imaginative fish dishes. The restaurant is on the outskirts of town, but it's worth the stroll. There is a small hotel attached. *Altenstadterstr. 39, tel. 08861/4051. Dress: informal. AE, DC, MC, V. Closed Sat., Jan. 1–15, and Aug. 1–15. Moderate.*

Schwangau
Dining

König Ludwig. The restaurant (and hotel) carries the name of the king so closely associated with the Schongau area, and the kitchen can be relied upon to produce some dishes bordering on the regal, particularly when game is in season. *Kreuzweg 11, tel. 08362/81081. Reservations advised. Dress: informal. AE. Closed Nov. 5–Dec. 15. Moderate.*

Coloman. The regional nature of many of the dishes and the country-house style of this paneled, wood-beamed restaurant tell you you're in the Allgäu area of Bavaria. In summer, the outdoor beer garden is a shady delight. *Kroeb 2, tel. 08362/8288. Dress: informal. No credit cards. Closed Nov. 3–Dec. 11. Inexpensive.*

Weikersheim
Lodging

Laurentius. This traditional old hotel on Weikersheim's market square is an ideal stopover on a tour of the Romantic Road. You can avoid the crowds and the relatively high prices of nearby Rothenburg and still be within an hour's car ride of most of the sights of the northern part of the route. Rooms are very comfortable and individually furnished, some with fine old German antiques. The vaulted ground floor has a cozy wine-tavern and a very good restaurant named (like the hotel) after the patron saint of cooks. *Marktplatz 5, tel. 07934/7007. 12 rooms with bath. Facilities: parking. DC, MC, V. Moderate.*

Würzburg
Dining

Juliusspital Weinstuben. The wine you drink here is from the tavern's own vineyard; the food—predominantly hearty Franconian specialties—takes second billing to the excellent local wines. *Juliuspromenade 19, tel. 0931/54080. Reservations advised. Dress: informal. No credit cards. Closed Wed. and Feb. Moderate.*

★ **Ratskeller.** The vaulted cellars of Würzburg's Rathaus shelter one of the city's most popular restaurants. Beer is served, but Franconian wine is what the regulars drink. The food is staunch Franconian fare. *Beim Grafeneckart, Langgasse 1, tel. 0931/13021. No reservations. Dress: informal. AE, DC, MC, V. Closed Tues. Nov.–Mar. and mid-Jan.–early Feb. Moderate.*

Backofele. More than 400 years of tradition are sustained by this historic old tavern. You can dine well and inexpensively on such dishes as oxtail in Burgundy sauce and homemade rissoles in wild mushroom sauce. *Ursulinergasse 2, tel. 0931/59059. Reservations advised. Dress: informal. No credit cards. Inexpensive.*

Stadt Mainz. Recipes from the original proprietor's own cookbook, dated 1850, form the basis of the imaginative fish-dominated menu of the Stadt Mainz hotel's restaurant. Eel from the Main River, prepared in a dill sauce, and locally caught carp and pike are good bets. *Semmelstr. 39, tel. 0931/53155. Reservations advised on weekends. Dress: informal. No credit cards. Closed Sun. dinner and Mon., and Dec. 20–Jan. 20. Inexpensive.*

Zum Stachel. On a warm spring or summer day, take a bench in the ancient Mediterranean-like courtyard of the Stachel, which is shaded by a canopy of vine leaves and girded by high walls of mellow, creeper-hung stone. The food is satisfying Franconian fare, from lightly baked onion cake to hearty roast pork, but the reason to stop here is to sample the wine, which is made from grapes grown in the tavern's own vineyard. *Gressengasse 1, tel. 0931/52770. No reservations necessary. No credit cards. Inexpensive.*

Lodging ★ **Hotel Rebstock.** Centuries of hospitality are contained behind this hotel's Rococo facade. The spacious lobby, with its open fireplace and beckoning bar, sets the tone. If you fancy opulent living, ask for one of the two luxury suites (at least DM 400). All rooms are individually decorated. *Neubaustr. 7, tel. 0931/30930. 81 rooms, 2 suites, all with bath or shower. Facilities: restaurant, bar. AE, DC, MC, V. Closed first 2 weeks in Jan. Very Expensive.*

Hotel Walfisch. You'll breakfast on the banks of the Main in a dining room that commands views of the river valley and the vineyard-covered Marienberg above Würzburg. For lunch and dinner, try the hotel's cozy Walfischstube restaurant. *Am Pleidenturm 5, tel. 0931/50055. 41 rooms, most with shower. Facilities: restaurant. AE, DC, MC, V. Very Expensive.*

Hotel Greifenstein. The Greifenstein, recently modernized with care and taste, offers comfortable, individually furnished rooms in a quiet corner of the city just off the market square. The cheaper doubles are small but lack no comforts or facilities. *Häfnergasse 1, tel. 0931/51665. 40 rooms with bath. Facilities: restaurant. AE, DC, MC, V. Expensive.*

Franziskaner. This comfortable and friendly family-run hotel is centrally located; it's only a two-minute walk from the city's pedestrian shopping area. *Franziskanerpl. 2, tel. 0931/15001. 47 rooms, most with bath or shower. AE, DC, MC, V. Moderate–Expensive.*

Stadt Mainz. This traditional Franconian inn dates from the 15th century. Its bedrooms are simply but comfortably furnished. *Semmelstr. 39, tel. 0931/53[illegible]55. 21 rooms. No credit cards. Closed Dec. 20–Jan. 20. Moderate.*

Strauss. Close to the river and the pedestrian-only center, this lodging has been run by the same family for more than 100 years. The emphasis is on clean, simple comforts. The restaurant specializes in Franconian cuisine. *Juliuspromenade 5, tel. 0931/30570. 77 rooms, many with shower. Facilities: restaurant. AE, DC, MC, V. Closed Dec. 20–Feb. 1. Moderate.*

The Arts

Most of the towns on the Romantic Road have annual arts festivals. Local tourist information offices can supply details of programs and make ticket reservations. The leading festivals are Würzburg's Mozart Festival, held in the Residenz in June; Augsburg's Mozart Festival, in September; Rothenburg's Meistertrunk drama festival, in June; and Dinkelsbühl's Kinderzeche festival, in July. Those in Rothenburg and Dinkelsbühl celebrate historical events when the towns were saved from conquest and destruction, and combine plays, concerts, and carnival-like attractions. Every other year—1994 is the next—Nördlingen and nearby villages host the Rieser Cultural Season.

Music Augsburg has chamber and symphony orchestras, as well as a ballet and opera companies. Performances are given September through July in the Kongresshalle (Göggingerstr. 10, tel. 0821/324–2348). Würzburg has a highly regarded Philharmonic orchestra, directed by Britain's Jonathan Seers. For information, call 0931/58686. Chamber-music concerts are given year-round at Oettingen Castle (tel. 09082/20000) and at Neuschwanstein Castle (tel. 08362/81051).

Theater Augsburg and Würzburg both have city theater companies that offer a regular repertoire of German classics, modern drama, and comedy. Good knowledge of German is required if you plan a visit. Augsburg also has an annual open-air drama season, with the old city walls as a backdrop, in June and July; it moves to the romantic setting of the inner courtyard of the Fugger Palace in July and August (for details, call 0821/36604). Dinkelsbühl has an open-air theater season from late June to mid-August.

9 Franconia

Including Nürnberg, Bamberg, Regensburg, and Bayreuth

Introduction

The ancient kingdom of the Franks is known today as Franconia or, in German, Franken. Although mainly rural, its castles and its architecturally rich towns provide a solid reminder of the region's past importance in the Holy Roman Empire. It was only in the early 19th century, following Napoléon's conquest of what is now southern Germany, that the area was incorporated into northern Bavaria. Modern Franconia stretches from the Bohemian Forest on the Czechoslovak border in the east to the outskirts of Frankfurt in the west. But its heart—and the focal point of this tour—is an area known as the Fränkisches Schweiz (the Franconian Switzerland), bounded by Nürnberg on the south, Bamberg on the west, and the cultural center of Bayreuth on the east.

Despite its beauty and history, Franconia is not a mainstream tourist destination; many Germans simply drive straight through on their way south. But the region rates high with epicures in search of authentic German regional cuisine. It is also noted for its liquid refreshments, from both the grape and the grain. Franconian white wine, often sold in distinctive stubby bottles called *Bocksbeutel*, is renowned as one of the driest in Germany. And the region has the biggest concentration of village breweries in the world, producing a wide range of styles, the most distinctive of which is *Rauchbier*, a dark and heady smoked brew.

Our coverage of Franconia begins at Coburg in the north and ends at Regensburg, on the Danube River, in the south. En route, it covers the historic cities of Bayreuth, Bamberg, and Nürnberg, as well as such memorable sights as the magnificent Baroque abbey of Weltenburg and the Rococo pilgrimage church of Vierzehnheiligen. The unspoiled hills and valleys of the Frankenwald (Franconian Forest) provide bucolic relief from the competing urban attractions of Franconia. (For information on Würzburg, perhaps the most celebrated of all the historic cities of Franconia and the starting point of the Romantic Road, *see* Chapter 8.)

Essential Information

Important Addresses and Numbers

Tourist Information The principal regional tourist office for Franconia is **Fremdenverkehrsverband Franken,** Am Plärrer 14, 8500 Nürnberg 81, tel. 0911/264–202. There are local tourist information offices in the following towns:

Ansbach. Rathaus, Martin-Luther-Platz 1, 8800 Ansbach, tel. 0981/51243.
Bamberg. Geyerswörthstrasse 3, 8600 Bamberg, tel. 0951/871–161.
Bayreuth. Luitpoldplatz 7–9, 8580 Bayreuth, tel. 0921/88588.
Ingolstadt. Hallstrasse 5, 8070 Ingolstadt, tel. 0841/305–415.
Coburg. Herrngasse 4, 8630 Coburg, tel. 09561/74180.
Kloster Banz and **Vierzehnheiligen.** Alte Darre am Stadtturm, 8623 Staffelstein, tel. 09573/4192.
Kronach. Marktplatz, 8640 Kronach, tel. 09261/97236.

Kulmbach. Stadthalle, Sutte 2, 8650 Kulmbach, tel. 09221/802-216.
Lichtenfels. Am Marktplatz 1, 8620 Lichtenfels, tel. 09571/795-221.
Nürnberg. Frauentorgraben 3, 8500 Nürnberg 70, tel. 0911/23360.
Regensburg. Altes Rathaus, 8400 Regensburg, tel. 0941/507-2145.
Weissenburg. Martin-Luther-Platz 3, 8832 Weissenburg, tel. 09141/907-124.

Travel Agencies **American Express,** Alderstrasse 2, Nürnberg, tel. 0911/232-397.

Car Rental **Avis:** Markgrafenallee 6, tel. 0921/26151, **Bayreuth;** Mainzer Landstrasse 170, tel. 069/230-101, **Frankfurt;** Allersbergerstrasse 139, tel. 0911/49696, **Nürnberg;** Friedenstrasse 8, tel. 0941/97001, **Regensburg.**
Europcar: Mainzer Landstrasse 160, tel. 069/234-002, **Frankfurt;** Nürnberg airport, tel. 0911/528-484, **Nürnberg;** Ziegelsdorferstrasse 118, tel. 0941/35085, **Regensburg;** Friendenstrasse 15, tel. 0931/881-150, **Würzburg.**
Herz: Mainzer Landstrasse 139, tel. 069/233-151, **Frankfurt;** Nürnberg airport, tel. 0911/527-710, **Nürnberg;** Ladehofstrasse 4, tel. 0941/22151, **Regensburg.**
Sixt-Budget: Frankfurt airport, tel. 069/690-5237, **Frankfurt;** Scharrerstr. 5, tel. 0911/495-63, **Nürnberg;** Im Gewerbepark 6, tel. 0941/401-035, **Regensburg.**

Arriving and Departing by Plane

The major international airports for Franconia, with regular flights from the United States, are at Frankfurt and Munich. The most important regional airports are at Nürnberg and Bayreuth. There are frequent flights between Frankfurt and Nürnberg.

Arriving and Departing by Car and Train

By Car Franconia is served by five main Autobahns: A-7 from Hamburg; A-3 from Köln and Frankfurt; A-81 from Stuttgart; A-6 from Heilbronn; and A-9 from Munich. Nürnberg is 167 kilometers (104 miles) from Munich and 222 kilometers (139 miles) from Frankfurt. Regensburg is 120 kilometers (75 miles) from Munich and 332 kilometers (207 miles) from Frankfurt.

By Train Fast Intercity trains run hourly between Frankfurt and Munich, with stops at Würzburg and Nürnberg. The trip takes about four hours. There are also hourly trains from Munich to Regensburg and from Regensburg to Nürnberg.

Getting Around

By Car The most famous scenic route in Franconia is the Romantic Road (*see* Chapter 8), but almost as interesting are the east section of the Burgenstrasse, the Castle Road, which runs west to east from Heidelberg to Nürnberg; and the Bocksbeutel Strasse, the Franconian Wine Road, which follows the course of the Main River from Zeil am Main along the wine-growing slopes of the valley to Aschaffenburg.

By Train If you start in Frankfurt and plan to visit the wine towns along the Main River, there are good local trains to Aschaffenburg, Miltenberg, and other small river towns (*see* Chapter 8). There are no direct train links to either Bayreuth or Bamberg. To explore southern Franconia, use the local trains from Nürnberg to Treuchtlingen, Ansbach, and Ingolstadt.

By Bus The bus service between major centers in Franconia is poor; it's better to drive or ride the train. Other than the buses along the Romantic Road, the only major service is from Rothenburg-ob-der-Tauber to Nürnberg. However, local buses run from most train stations to smaller towns and villages, though the service isn't frequent. Buses for the Fichtelgebirge in northern Franconia leave from Bayreuth's post office near the train station.

By Bicycle Renting bicycles is popular in Franconia, and the tourist authorities have made great efforts to attract cyclists. The terrain of the Altmühltal Valley is particularly suitable for biking, and the tourist office in Eichstätt (Domplatz 18, 8078 Eichstätt, tel. 08421/7977) issues leaflets on suggested cycling tours and lists of outlets where you can rent bikes. Bicycles can also be rented from most major train stations (the cost is DM 10 per day, DM 6 if you have a rail ticket). Other tourist offices can supply details of special cycling routes in their regions.

By Boat A total of 15 different lines operate cruises through the region from April to October. Contact the **Fremdenverkehrsverband Franken** (Am Plärrer 14, Nürnberg, tel. 0911/264–202) and ask for details of their "Weisse Flotte" cruises. Or contact a travel agent in advance.

Guided Tours

The most popular excursions are boat trips on the Danube from Regensburg to Ludwig I's imposing Greek-style Doric temple of Walhalla, and one to the monastery at Weltenburg. There are daily sailings to Walhalla from Easter through October. The round-trip fare to Walhalla is DM 11 adults, DM 6 children under 14. The round-trip takes three hours. Weltenburg can be reached from Regensburg by changing boats at Kelheim, or you can pick up a shorter cruise from Kelheim. The Regensburg–Kelheim boat ride takes 2½ hours. Kelheim to Weltenburg takes only 30 minutes. Daylong upstream cruises from Regensburg that take in Weltenburg via the Altmühltal (a scenic wooded gorge) are also possible. For information on departures from Regensburg, call 0941/55359. For information on Kelheim departures, call 09441/3402 or 09441/8290.

There are also regular trips in the summer along the Main River from Aschaffenburg to Würzburg and from Würzburg to Bamberg. These are scenic routes worth considering for those with the time to do so. For information, contact **Fränkische Personen-Schiffahrt,** Kranenkai 1, Würzburg, tel. 0931/55356 and 0931/51722, or the Würzburg tourist office, Marktplatz, 8700 Würzburg, tel. 0931/37398.

For boat tours around Bamberg, contact **Fritz Kropf,** Kapuzinerstrasse 5, tel. 0951/26679. Tours leave daily at 2:30 and 4; the cost is DM 5.50 adults, DM 4 children.

Exploring Franconia

Highlights for First-time Visitors

The *Bamberg Rider* statue, Bamberg
Altes Rathaus, Bamberg
Dürer's House, Nürnberg
The Markgräfliche's Opera House, Bayreuth
Regensburg Cathedral
The Stone Bridge, Regensburg
Vierzehnheiligen Pilgrimage Church
Walhalla
Weltenburg Abbey Church

Coburg, Bayreuth, and Bamberg

Numbers in the margin correspond to points of interest on the Franconia map.

1 **Coburg,** reached from Würzburg on B-19 and B-303, is a historic town on the Itz River, just a few miles from the former East German border. Whether glittering under the summer sky or frosted white with the snows of winter, Coburg is a jewel, and surprisingly little known. It was founded in the 11th century and remained in the possession of the dukes of Saxe-Coburg-Gotha until 1918; the present duke still lives there. In fact, it's as the home of the Saxe-Coburgs, as they are generally known, that the town is most famous. They were a remarkable family. Superficially just one among dozens of German ruling families, they established themselves as something of a royal stud farm, providing a seemingly inexhaustible supply of blue-blooded marriage partners to ruling houses the length and breadth of Europe. The most famous of these royal mates was Prince Albert, husband of Queen Victoria. Their numerous children, married off among more of Europe's kings, queens, and emperors, helped to spread the tried-and-tested Saxe-Coburg stock even farther afield. There's a statue of the high-minded consort in the Marktplatz, the main square. (Queen Victoria has a further, special claim to fame in the annals of Coburg: Legend has it that on a visit to her new husband's hometown, she had the first flush toilet in Germany installed.)

The Marktplatz, ringed with gracious Renaissance and Baroque buildings, is the place to start your tour. The **Rathaus** (Town Hall), begun in 1500, is the most imposing structure. A forest of ornate gables and spires projects from its well-proportioned facade. Look at the statue of the **Bratwurstmännla** on the building; the staff he carries is claimed to be the official length against which the town's famous bratwurst sausages are measured.

Time Out If you think this is the sort of story that appears only in guidebooks, console yourself by trying a bratwurst from one of the stands in the square that sell them.

Just off the square, on Schlossplatz, you'll find **Schloss Ehrenburg,** the ducal palace. Built in the mid-16th century, it has been greatly altered over the years, principally following a fire in the early 19th century. The then duke took this opportunity to rebuild the palace in a heavy Gothic style. It was in this dark

Franconia

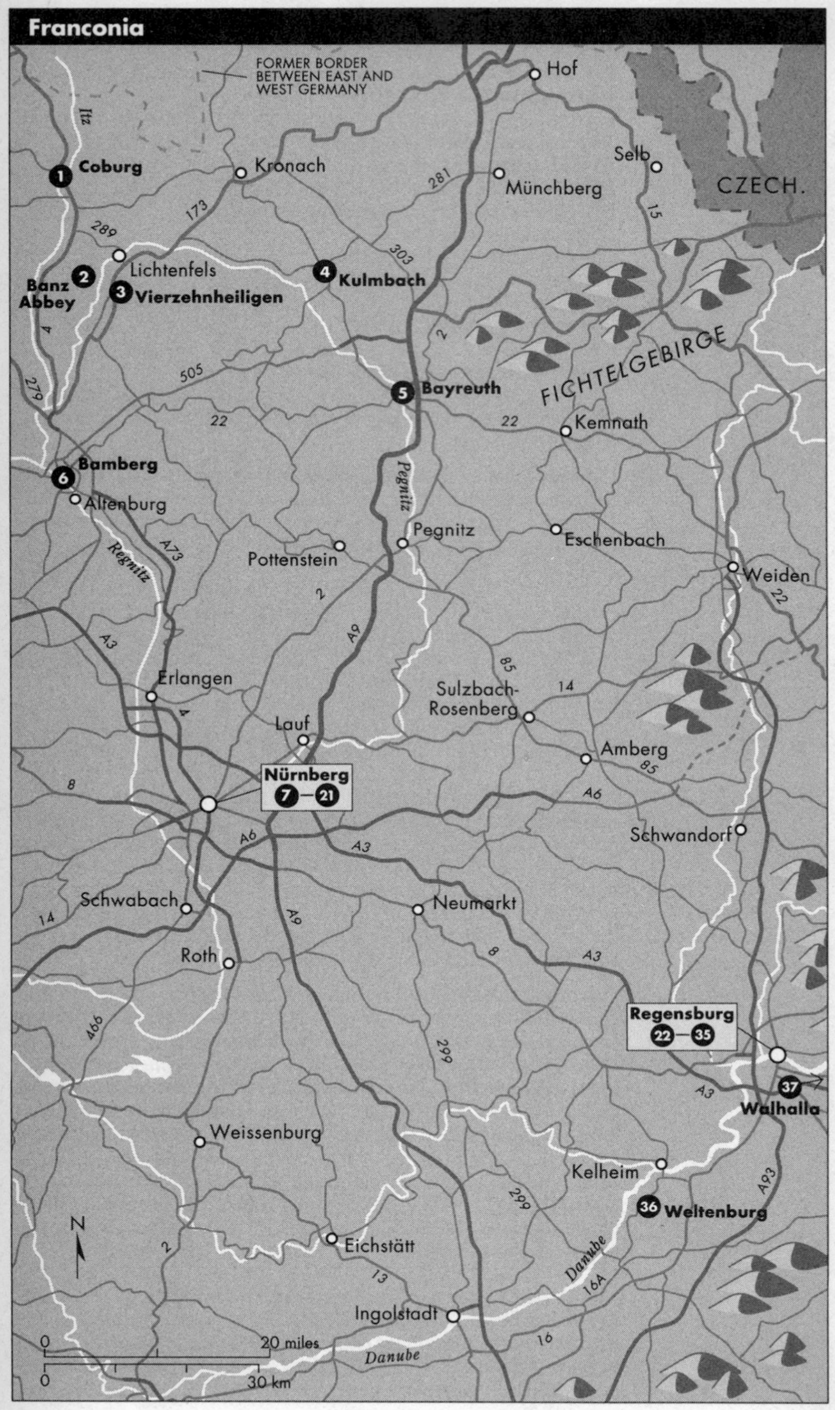
FORMER BORDER BETWEEN EAST AND WEST GERMANY
Hof
Selb
CZECH.
Itz
1 Coburg
Kronach
Münchberg
281
173
289
303
15
Lichtenfels
2 Banz Abbey
3 Vierzehnheiligen
4 Kulmbach
FICHTELGEBIRGE
505
279
5 Bayreuth
22
Kemnath
6 Bamberg
Altenburg
Pegnitz
Pottenstein
Eschenbach
Regnitz
A73
Weiden
A3
A9
Erlangen
Sulzbach-Rosenberg
85
14
Lauf
Amberg
Nürnberg 7—21
8
A6
Schwandorf
Schwabach
Neumarkt
Roth
A3
466
299
Regensburg 22—35
37 Walhalla
Weissenburg
Kelheim
36 Weltenburg
A93
N
Eichstätt
Danube
16A
13
Ingolstadt
16
0
20 miles
30 km

and imposing heap that Prince Albert spent much of his childhood. The throne room; the Hall of Giants, named for its larger-than-life frescoes; and the Baroque-style chapel can all be visited. *Schlosspl. Admission: DM 4 adults, children (with parents) free. Tours Apr.–Sept., daily at 10, 11, 1:30, 2:30, 3:30, and 4:30; and Oct.–Mar., daily at 10, 11, 1:30, and 2:30.*

The major attraction in Coburg, however, is the **Veste Coburg** (the fortress), one of the largest and most impressive in the country. To reach it, you pass through the **Hofgarten** (Palace Gardens), today the site of the **Naturwissenschaftliches Museum** (Natural History Museum). It's the country's leading museum of its kind, with more than 8,000 exhibits of flora and fauna, as well as geological, ethnological, and mineralogical specimens. *Admission: DM 2. Open Apr.–Sept., daily 9–6; Oct.–Mar., daily 9–5.*

The brooding bulk of the castle lies beyond the garden on a small hill above the town. The first buildings were constructed around 1055, but with progressive rebuilding and remodeling through the centuries, today's predominantly late-Gothic/early Renaissance edifice bears little resemblance to the original rude fortress. It contains a number of museums (all open the same hours as the castle). See the **Fürstenbau,** or Palace of the Princes, where Martin Luther was sheltered for six months in 1530. Among the main treasures are paintings by Cranach. Dürer, Rembrandt, and Cranach (again) are all represented at the **Kunstsammlungen,** the art museum in the fortress, as are many examples of German silver, porcelain, arms and armor, and furniture. Finally, there's the **Herzoginbau,** the duchess's building, a sort of 18th-century transportation museum, with carriages and ornate sledges for speeding in style through the winter snows. *Admission to Fürstenbau and Herzoginbau: DM 3.50 adults, DM 1.50 children. Open Apr.–Oct., Tues.–Sun. 9:30–noon and 2–4; Nov.–Mar., 10–noon and 2–3:30. Admission to Kunstsammlungen: DM 3 adults, DM 1 children. Open Apr.–Oct., Tues.–Sun. 9:30–1 and 2–5; Nov.–Mar., Tues.–Sun. 2–5.*

Time Out For a taste of old Coburg, step into the 18th-century **Loreley** tavern (Herrengasse 14, tel. 09561/92470) opposite Schloss Ehrenburg. A warren of dark paneled rooms, the Loreley oozes history, and serves up excellent local dishes. Ask for *Coburger Klösse* (dumplings).

From Coburg, take B-4 south for a mile or so, then turn left (southwest) onto B-289 and follow the signs to Lichtenfels, 9 kilometers (5 miles) away. Lovers of Baroque and Rococo church architecture should make a right here to see Banz Abbey and Vierzehnheiligen, probably the two most remarkable churches in Franconia. They stand on opposite sides of the Main River valley, about 5 kilometers (3 miles) southwest of Lichtenfels.
2 The larger, though in some ways the less impressive, is **Banz Abbey,** standing high above the Main on what some call the "holy mountain of Bavaria." There had been a monastery here since 1069, but the present buildings—now home to a lucky group of senior citizens—dates from the end of the 17th century. The highlight of the complex is the **Klosterkirche** (Abbey Church), the work of architect and stuccoist Johann Dientzenhofer. Two massive onion-dome towers soar above the restrained yellow sandstone facade. Note the animated statues

of saints set in niches, a typical Baroque device. Inside, the church shimmers and glows with lustrous Rococo decoration. *Open Apr.–Sept., daily 8:30–11:30 and 1–5:30; Oct.–Mar., Mon.–Sat. 8:30–11:30 and 1–4:30.*

From the terrace there's a striking view over the Main to
3 **Vierzehnheiligen.** What you're seeing is probably the single most ornate Rococo church in Europe, although you might not know it just from looking at the exterior. There are those same onion-dome towers, the same lively curving facade, but little to suggest the almost explosive array of paintings, stucco, gilt, statuary, and rich rosy marble inside. The church was built by Balthasar Neumann (architect of the Residenz at Würzburg; *see* Chapter 8) between 1743 and 1772 to commemorate a vision of Christ and 14 saints—*Vierzehnheiligen* means "14 saints"—that appeared to a shepherd in 1445. Your first impression will be of the richness of the decoration and the brilliance of the coloring, the whole more like some fantastic pleasure palace than a place of worship. Notice the way the entire building seems to be in motion—almost all the walls are curved—and how the walls and ceiling are alive with delicate stucco. In much the same way the builders of Gothic cathedrals aimed to overwhelm through scale and verticality Neumann wanted to startle worshipers through light, color, and movement. Anyone who has seen the gaunt Romanesque cathedrals of Protestant north Germany will have little difficulty understanding why the Reformation was never able to gain more than a toehold in Catholic southern Germany. There are few more uplifting buildings in Europe.

If it was beer that brought you to Germany, you'll want to drive the 32 kilometers (20 miles) east from Lichtenfels along B-289
4 to **Kulmbach.** In a country in which the brewing and drinking of beer breaks all records, this town produces more per capita than anywhere else in Germany: 9,000 pints per man, woman, and child. A quarter of the work force in Kulmbach earns a living directly or indirectly from beer. One of Kulmbach's five breweries also produces the strongest beer in the world—the *Doppelbock* Kulminator 28—which takes nine months to brew and has an alcohol content of more than 11%. Tours of the Erste Kulmbacher Union brewery (EKU-str. 1, tel. 09221/820), where Kulminator 28 is made, are given Monday through Thursday, but on a reservation-only basis. Another special local brew is *Eisbock*, which is frozen as part of the brewing process to make it stronger. The locals claim it's the sparklingly clear spring water from the nearby Fichtelgebirge hills that makes their beer so special. Kulmbach celebrates its beer every year in a nine-day festival that starts on the last Saturday in July. The main festival site, a mammoth tent, is called the Festspulhaus, or, literally, "festival swallowing house," a none-too-subtle dig at nearby Bayreuth and its Festspielhaus, where Wagner's operas are performed.

Time Out The **EKU Inn** (Klostergasse 7) serves some of Kulmbach's less potent brews on draft, plus a good selection of local dishes. Buy a bottle of Kulminator 28 as a souvenir.

It would be unfair to pretend that Kulmbach is nothing but beer, beer, and more beer. The old town, for example, contains a warren of narrow streets that merit exploration. Likewise, no visitor here will want to miss the **Plassenburg,** symbol of the town and the most important Renaissance castle in the country. It's located a 20-minute hike from the old town on a rise overlooking Kulmbach. The first building here, begun in the mid-12th century, was torched by marauding Bavarians, who were anxious to put a stop to the ambitions of Duke Albrecht Alcibiades, a man who seems to have had few scruples when it came to self-advancement and who spent several years murdering, plundering, and pillaging his way through Franconia. His successors built today's castle starting in about 1560. Externally, there's little to suggest the graceful Renaissance interior, but as you enter the main courtyard the scene changes abruptly. The tiered space of the courtyard is covered with precisely carved figures, medallions, and other intricate ornaments, the whole comprising one of the most remarkable and delicate architectural ensembles in Europe. Inside, you may want to see the **Deutsches Zinnfigurenmuseum** (Tin Figures Museum), with more than 300,000 ministatuettes, the largest collection of its kind in the world. *Admission: DM 2 adults, DM 1 children. Open Apr.–Sept., daily 10–4:30; Oct.–Mar., Tues.–Sun. 10–3:30.*

Twenty-two kilometers (14 miles) south of Kulmbach on route
5 303, then route 2, is **Bayreuth,** pronounced "By-roit." Bayreuth means Wagner. This small Franconian town was where 19th-century composer and man of myth Richard Wagner finally settled after a lifetime of rootless shifting through Europe, and here he built his great theater, the Festspielhaus, as a suitable setting for his grandiose and heroic operas. The annual Wagner festival, first held in 1876, regularly brings the town to a halt as hordes of Wagner lovers descend on Bayreuth, pushing prices sky-high, filling hotels to bursting, and earning themselves much-sought-after social kudos in the process (to some, it's one of *the* places to be seen). The festival is usually held in July, so unless you plan to visit the town specifically for it, this is the time to stay away (*see* The Arts, below). Likewise, those whose tastes do not include opera and the theater will find little here to divert them. Bayreuth has no picture-postcard setting, and there is little here that is not connected in some way with music, specifically Wagner's.

As it's Wagner who brings most visitors to Bayreuth, it's only fitting to start a tour of the town with a visit to the house he built here, the only house he ever owned, in fact: **Wahnfried.** It's a simple, austere neoclassical building, constructed in 1874, just south of the town center. Today it's a museum celebrating the life of this maddening and compelling man, though, after wartime bomb damage, all that remains of the original construction is the facade. Here Wagner and his wife, Cosima, daughter of composer Franz Liszt, lived; and here, too, they are buried. Hitler, whose admiration for Wagner knew few limits, stayed here during visits to the Wagner festival, the guest of the by then near-senile Cosima. The other great figure with whom Wagner is associated, King Ludwig II of Bavaria, the young and impressionable "dream king" who provided much of the financial backing for Wagner's vaultingly ambitious works, is remembered, too; there's a bust of him in front of the entrance to the house. Though the house is something of a shrine to Wagner, even those who have little interest in the composer will find it intriguing and educational. Standout exhibits include the original scores for a number of his operas, including *Parsifal, Tristan und Isolde, Lohengrin, Der fliegende Ho-*

lländer, and *Die Götterdämmerung*. You can also see designs, many of them original, for productions of his operas, as well as his piano and huge library. At 10, noon, and 2, excerpts from his operas are played in the living room. *Richard-Wagner-Str. 48. Admission: DM 2.50 adults (DM 3.50 in July and Aug.), DM 1 children. Open daily 9–5.*

From the museum, you will be close to the **Neues Schloss** (New Palace). If Wagner is the man most closely associated with Bayreuth, then it's well to remember that had it not been for the woman who built this glamorous 18th-century palace, he would never have come here in the first place. She was the Margravina Wilhelmina, sister of Frederick the Great of Prussia and wife of the margrave (marquis) of Brandenburg. While the margrave was an altogether unremarkable man, his wife was a woman of enormous energy and decided tastes. She devoured books; wrote plays and operas (which she directed and, of course, acted in); and built, transforming much of the town and bringing it near bankruptcy. Her distinctive touch is much in evidence at the New Palace, built when a mysterious fire conveniently destroyed parts of the original palace. Anyone with a taste for the wilder flights of Rococo decoration will love it. The **Staatsgalerie** (State Art Gallery), containing a representative collection of mainly 19th-century Bavarian paintings, is also housed in the palace. *Ludwigstr. 21. Admission: DM 3 adults, DM 1.50 children. Open Apr.–Sept., daily 10–noon and 1:30–4:30; Oct.–Mar., daily 1:30–3:30.*

Wilhelmina's other great architectural legacy is the **Markgräfliches Opernhaus** (Margrave Opera House), just a step or two from the New Palace. Built between 1745 and 1748, it is a Rococo jewel, sumptuously decorated in red, gold, and blue. Apollo and the nine Muses cavort across the frescoed ceiling. It was this delicate 500-seat theater that originally drew Wagner to Bayreuth, since he felt that it might prove a suitable setting for his own operas. In fact, while it may be a perfect place to hear Mozart, it's hard to imagine a less suitable setting for Wagner's epic works. Catch a performance here if you can *(see* The Arts, below); otherwise, take a tour of the ravishing interior. *Admission: DM 2 adults, DM 1.50 children. Open Apr.–Sept., daily 9–11:30 and 1:30–4:30; Oct.–Mar., daily 10–11:30 and 1:30–3.*

Now you'll want to head up to the **Festspielhaus;** it's located a mile or so north of the downtown area at the head of Bürgerreutherstrasse. This plain, almost intimidating building is the high temple of the cult of Wagner. The building was conceived, planned, and financed by the great man specifically as a setting for his monumental operas. Today it is very much the focus of the annual Wagner festival, still masterminded by descendants of the composer. The spartan look is partly explained by Wagner's near-permanent financial crises and partly by his desire to achieve perfect acoustics. For this reason, the wood seats have no upholstering, and the walls are bare of all ornament. The stage is enormous, capable of holding the huge casts required for Wagner's largest operas. *Auf dem Grünen Hügel. Admission: DM 2 adults, DM 1.50 children. Open Jan.–mid-June, Sept., Oct., and Dec., Tues.–Sun. 10–11:30 and 1:30–3. Closed mid-June–Aug. and Nov.*

The **Altes Schloss Eremitage** (Old Castle and Hermitage), 5 kilometers (3 miles) north of Bayreuth, makes an appealing change from the sonorous and austere Wagnerian mood of much of the town. It's an early-18th-century palace, built as a summer palace and remodeled in 1740 by the Margravina Wilhelmina. While her taste is not much in evidence in the drab exterior, the interior, alive with light and color, displays her guiding hand in every elegant line. The standout is the extraordinary **Japanese room,** filled with Oriental treasures and chinoiserie furniture. The park and gardens, partly formal, partly natural, are enjoyable for idle strolling in summer. *Admission to the Schloss (guided tours only): DM 2 adults, DM 1.50 children. Tours given Apr.–Sept., daily at 9, 11:30, 1, and 4:30; Oct.–Mar., daily at 10, 11:30, 1, and 2:30.*

Time Out For simple regional specialties and a wide choice of beers, try the restaurant of the **Weihenstephan** hotel (Bahnhofstr. 5, tel. 0921/20203), located close by the train station. You can sit on the terrace in summer.

6 **Bamberg,** the next major city on the tour, is 60 kilometers (37 miles) west of Bayreuth on B-22. Bamberg is one of the great historic cities of Germany, filled with buildings and monuments that recall its glorious days as the seat of one of the most powerful ruling families in the country. Though founded as early as the 2nd century AD, Bamberg rose to prominence only in the 11th century, under the irresistible impetus provided by its most famous son, Holy Roman Emperor Heinrich II. His imperial cathedral still dominates the historic area.

The city lies on the Regnitz River, about 80 kilometers (50 miles) north of Nürnberg. The historic center is a small island in the river; to the west is the so-called Bishops' Town, to the east the so-called Burghers' Town. Connecting them is a bridge on which stands the **Altes Rathaus** (Old Town Hall), a highly colorful rickety Gothic building dresssed extravagantly in Rococo. It's best seen from the adjacent bridge upstream, where it appears to be practically in danger of being swept off by the river. The preeminent pleasure of a visit is to stroll through the narrow, sinuous streets of old Bamberg, past half-timbered and gabled houses and formal 18th-century mansions. Peek into cobbled, flower-filled courtyards or take time out in a waterside café, watching the little steamers as they chug past the colorful row of fishermen's houses that make up Klein Venedig (Little Venice).

Start your tour at the **Dom,** the imperial cathedral, on Domplatz, heart of Bishops' Town. It's one of the most important of Germany's cathedrals, a building that tells not only Bamberg's story but that of much of Germany as well. The first building here was begun by Heinrich II in 1003, and it was in this partially completed cathedral that he was crowned Holy Roman Emperor in 1012. In 1237 it was mostly destroyed by fire, and the present late-Romanesque/early Gothic building was begun. From the outside, the dominant features are the massive towers at each corner. Heading into the dark interior, you'll find one of the most striking collections of monuments and art treasures of any European church. The most famous is the *Bamberger Reiter* (Bamberger Rider), an equestrian statue, carved—no one knows by whom—around 1230 and thought to be an allegory of knightly virtue. The larger-than-life-size figure is an extraordinarily realistic work for the period, more like a Renaissance statue than a Gothic piece. Compare it with the mass of carved figures huddled in the tympana, the semicircular spaces above the doorways of the church; while these are stylized and obviously Gothic, the *Bamberg Rider* is poised and calm. In the center of the nave you'll find another great sculptural work, the massive tomb of Heinrich and his wife, Kunigunde. It's the work of Tilman Riemenschneider, Germany's greatest Renaissance sculptor. Pope Clement II is also buried in the cathedral, in an imposing tomb under the high altar; he is the only pope to be buried north of the Alps.

After you've toured the cathedral, go next door to see the **Diözesanmuseum** (Cathedral Museum). In addition to a rich collection of silver and other ecclesiastical objects, the museum contains a splinter of wood and the *heilige Nagel*, or "holy nail," both reputedly from the cross of Jesus. A more macabre exhibit is Heinrich's and Kunigunde's skulls, mounted in elaborate metal supports. The building itself was designed by Balthasar Neumann, the architect of Vierzehnheiligen Church, and constructed between 1730 and 1733. *Dompl. 5. Admission: DM 2.50 adults, 50 pf. children. Open Apr.–Sept., daily 9–noon and 1:30–5; Oct.–Mar., daily 9–noon and 1:30–4.*

Keep your ticket for the cathedral museum to visit the adjoining **Neue Residenz** (Dompl. 8; open same hours). This immense Baroque palace was the home of the prince-electors. Their wealth and prestige can easily be imagined as you tour the glittering interior. Most memorable is the **Kaisersaal** (Throne Room), complete with impressive ceiling frescoes and elaborate stuccowork. You'll also be able to visit the rose garden in back of the building, which offers a fine view of the Benedictine abbey church of St. Michael.

The palace also houses the **Staatsbibliothek** (State Library). Among the thousands of books and illuminated manuscripts are the original prayer books belonging to Heinrich and his wife, a 5th-century manuscript by the Roman historian Livy, and handwritten manuscripts by the 16th-century painters Dürer and Cranach. *Admission free. Open Mon.–Fri. 9–5, Sat. 9–noon.*

End your tour of Domplatz with a visit to the **Alte Hofaltung,** the former imperial and episcopal palace. It's a sturdy and weather-worn half-timbered Gothic building with a graceful Renaissance courtyard. Today it contains the **Historisches Museum,** with a collection of documents and maps charting Bamberg's history that will appeal most to avid history buffs and/or those who read German well. *Dompl. 7. Admission: DM 2 adults, 50 pf children. Open Dec.–Apr., Tues.–Fri. 9–1, Sat. and Sun. 9–4:30; May–Oct., Tues.–Sun. 9–5. Closed Nov.*

From Domplatz, walk down the hill to the **Altes Rathaus,** 200 or so yards away, one of the most bizarrely situated municipal buildings in Europe. It is perched on a little island in the Regnitz River, a stone bridge connecting it to the onetime rival halves of Bamberg. Half the building is Gothic, half is Renaissance; between them is an ornate Baroque gateway topped by an elegantly tapering spire. While here you'll get just about the best view of the fishermen's houses of Klein Venedig (Little Venice).

From the bridge you can walk over to the **Hoffmann-Haus** on Schillerplatz. Ernst Theodor Hoffmann, a Romantic writer, composer, and illustrator lived in this little house between 1809 and 1813. Hoffmann is probably best remembered not for one of his own works but for an opera written *about* him and his stories, by composer Jacques Offenbach, *The Tales of Hoffmann.* The house has been preserved much as it was when Hoffmann lived here—complete with the hole in the floor of his upstairs study through which he talked to his wife below. *Schillerpl. 26. Admission: DM 1 adults, 50 pf children. Open May–Oct., Tues.–Fri. 9:30–5:30, weekends 9:30–1.*

Time Out The **Brauereiausschank Schlenkerla** (Dominikanerstr. 6, tel. 0951/56060), is a centuries-old monastery turned beer tavern. The black furniture, wall paneling, and dresses of the waitresses match the beer—Rauchbier—a strong malty brew with a smoky aftertaste. The unusual flavor comes from a beechwood-smoke brewing process. There are also excellent Franconian specialties at reasonable prices. Try the *Rauchschinken* (smoked ham) or the *Bierbrauervesper*—composed of smoked meat, sour-milk cheese, and black bread and butter, all served on a wood platter. *Prost!* (Closed Tues.)

Nürnberg to Regensburg

7 **Nürnberg** is the principal city of Franconia, and second in size and significance in Bavaria only to Munich. Its origins date from at least 1040. It's among the most historic and visitable of Germany's cities; the core of the old town, through which the Pegnitz River flows, is still surrounded by its original medieval walls. Nürnberg has always taken a leading role in German affairs. It was here, for example, that the first "diet," or meeting of rulers, of every Holy Roman Emperor was held. And it was here, too, that Hitler staged the greatest and most grandiose Nazi rallies and the Allies held the war trials. Wartime bombing destroyed much of medieval and Renaissance Nürnberg, though faithful reconstruction has largely re-created the city's prewar atmosphere.

The city grew because of its location at the meeting point of a number of medieval trade routes. With prosperity came a great flowering of the arts and sciences. Albrecht Dürer, the first indisputable genius of the Renaissance in Germany, was born here in 1471, and he returned in 1509 to spend the rest of his life here. (His house is one of the most popular tourist shrines in the city.) Other leading Nürnberg artists of the Renaissance include woodcarver Michael Wolgemut and sculptors Adam Kraft and Peter Vischer. Earlier the minnesingers, medieval poets and musicians, chief among them Tannhäuser, had made the city a focal point in the development of German music. In the 15th and 16th centuries their traditions were continued by the Meistersingers. Both groups were celebrated much later by Wagner. Among a great host of inventions associated with Nürnberg, the most significant were the pocket watch, gun casting, the clarinet, and the geographical globe (the first of which was made before Columbus discovered the Americas).

Nürnberg is rich in special events and celebrations. By far the most famous is the Christkindlmarkt, an enormous pre-Christmas market that runs from November 27 to Christmas Eve. The highlight is the December 10 candle procession, in which thousands of children march through the city streets. There are few sights in Europe to compare with the flickering of their tiny lights in the cold night air, the entire scene played out against the backdrop of centuries-old buildings.

Numbers in the margin correspond to points of interest on the Nürnberg map.

The historic heart of Nürnberg is compact; all principal sights are within easy walking distance. To get a sense of the city, begin your tour by walking around all or part of the **city walls.** Finished in 1452, they come complete with moats, sturdy gateways, and watchtowers. Year-round floodlighting adds to their
8 brooding romance. Stop at the **Königstor** (Royal Gate), by the Hauptbahnhof (main train station), to see the **Handwerkerhof,** a "medieval mall" with craftsmen busy pretending it's still the Middle Ages. They turn out puppets, baskets, pewter mugs and plates, glassware, and the city's famous *Lebkuchen* (gingerbread cookies).

Time Out The **Bratwurstglöcklein** (Am Königstor, tel. 227–625), located in the Handwerkerhof, offers some of the best bratwurst in Nürnberg. Sauerkraut and potato salad are the traditional accompaniments. Wash it all down with a glass of beer. *Closed Sun., holidays, and Dec. 25–Mar. 1.*

---

9 From the Königstor, head up Königstrasse to **St. Lorenz Kirche.** Opinions are divided as to the most beautiful church in the city, but many think St. Lorenz Kirche deserves the honor. If you visit it and St. Sebaldus Kirche *(see* below), you can make up your own mind. St. Lorenz was begun around 1220 and completed in about 1475. It's a sizable church; two towers flank the main entrance, which is covered with a forest of carvings. In the lofty interior, note the works by sculptors Adam Kraft and Veit Stoss: Kraft's great stone tabernacle to the left of the altar and Stoss's *Annunciation* at the east end of the nave are considered their finest works. There are many other carvings throughout the building, a fitting testimonial to the artistic richness of late-medieval Nürnberg.

From the church, walk up to the Hauptmarkt, crossing the little museum bridge over the Pegnitz River. To your right, set on
10 graceful arcades over the river, is the **Helig-Geist-Spital** (Holy Ghost Hospital), begun in 1381. It's worth looking into the courtyard to admire its elegant wood balconies and spacious arcades. Continue the few paces to the **Hauptmarkt** (Main Market). Like Munich's Viktualienmarkt, Nürnberg's market is more than just a place to do the shopping. Its colorful stands, piled high with produce and shaded by striped awnings, are a central part of the city. The red-armed market women, whose acid wit and earthy homespun philosophy you'll have to take on trust unless your command of German extends to an in-depth familiarity with the Nürnberg dialect, are a formidable-looking bunch, dispensing flowers, fruit, and abuse in about equal measure. It's here that the Christkindlmarkt is held.

There are two principal sights in the market. One is the
11 **Schöner Brunnen** (Beautiful Fountain). It's an elegant, 60-foot-high Gothic fountain carved around the year 1400, looking for all the world as though it should be on the summit of some lofty Gothic cathedral. Thirty figures arranged in tiers stand sentinel on it. They include prophets, saints, local noblemen, sundry electors of the Holy Roman Empire, and one or two strays, such as Julius Caesar and Alexander the Great. A gold ring is

Albrecht-Dürer-Haus, **18**
Alt-Stadt-Museum, **16**
Altes Rathaus, **14**
Die Kaiserburg, **17**
Frauenkirche, **12**
Gänsemännchenbrunnen, **15**
Germanisches Nationalmuseum, **20**
Helig-Geist-Spital, **10**
Königstor, **8**
St. Lorenz Kirche, **9**
St. Sebaldus Kirche, **13**
Schöner Brunnen, **11**
Spielzeugmuseum, **19**
Verkehrsmuseum, **21**

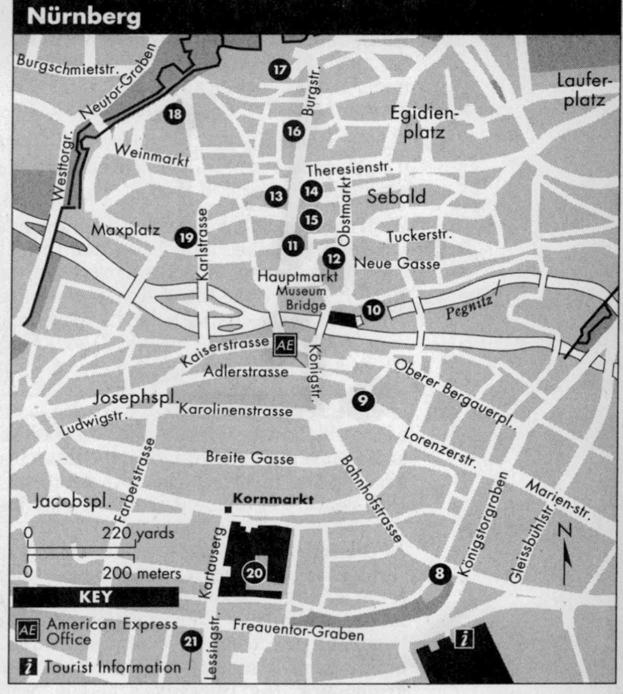

set into the railing surrounding the fountain, reputedly placed there by an apprentice carver. Stroking it is said to bring good luck. Cynics will enjoy the sight of Germans and tourists alike examining the railing for the ring and surreptitiously rubbing it.

12 The other major attraction is the **Frauenkirche** (Church of Our Lady), which was built, with the approval of Holy Roman emperor Charles IV, in 1350 on the site of a synagogue that burned down in a pogrom in 1349. (The area covered by the Hauptmarkt was once the Jewish quarter of the city.) These days, most visitors are drawn not so much by the church itself as by the **Männleinlaufen,** a clock dating from 1500 that's set in its facade. It's one of those colorful mechanical marvels at which the Germans have long excelled—a perfect match between love of punctuality and ingenuity. Every day at noon the electors of the Holy Roman Empire glide out of the clock to bow to the emperor Charles IV before sliding back under cover. It's worth scheduling your morning to catch the display.

From the Hauptmarkt, continue the short distance north to
13 the 13th-century **St. Sebaldus Kirche,** on Sebaldkircheplatz. Though the church lacks the number of art treasures boasted by rival St. Lorenz, its lofty nave and choir are among the purest examples of Gothic ecclesiastical architecture in Germany: elegant, tall, and airy. Veit Stoss carved the crucifixion group at the east end of the nave, while the elaborate bronze shrine, containing the remains of St. Sebaldus himself, was cast by Peter Vischer and his five sons around 1520.

14 Abutting the rear of the church is the **Altes Rathaus** (Old Town Hall), built in 1332, destroyed in World War II, and subsequently painstakingly restored. Visit its dungeons, hacked from the underground rock. *Rathauspl. Admission: DM 2. Open May–Sept., Mon.–Fri. 10–4, Sat. and Sun. 10–1.*

15 Facing the town hall is the bronze **Gänsemännchenbrunnen** (Gooseman's Fountain). It's an elegant work of great technical sophistication, cast in 1550.

Walk north from the Altes Rathaus along Burgstrasse. On your
16 left you'll pass the Fembohaus, now the **Alt-Stadt-Museum** (Old City Museum). A dignified, patrician dwelling completed in 1598, it's one of the finest Renaissance mansions in Nürnberg. The story of the city is told in its museum. *Burgstr. 14. Admission: DM 3. Open year-round, Tues.–Fri. and Sun. 10–5, Sat. 10–1.*

Time Out In a medieval courtyard off Burgstrasse 19, under the shadow of the castle, the **Hausbrauerei Altstadthof** offers food, drink, and a working cottage industry. Reactivating brewing rights granted the tavern in the 16th century, the new owners use 19th-century equipment ordinarily confined to a museum.

At the end of Burgstrasse you'll reach Nürnberg's number-one
17 sight, **Die Kaiserburg** (the Imperial Castle). This immense cluster of buildings, standing just inside the city walls, was the residence of the Holy Roman Emperors. Impressive rather than beautiful, the complex comprises three separate groups of buildings. The oldest, dating from around 1050, is the **Burggrafenburg,** the Burgrave's Castle, with a craggy, ruined seven-sided tower and bailiff's house. It stands in the center of the complex. To the east is the **Kaiserstallung** (Imperial Stables). These were built in the 15th century as a granary, then converted into a youth hostel after the war. The real interest, however, centers on the Imperial Castle itself, the westernmost part of the fortress. The standout feature here is the Renaissance **Doppelkappelle** (Double Chapel). The lower part of the chapel was used by the castle minions and is accordingly austere, befitting their lowly status. The adjoining upper part, correspondingly richer, larger, and more ornate, was where the emperor and his family worshiped. Also visit the **Rittersaal** (Knight's Hall) and the **Kaisersaal** (Throne Room). Their heavy oak beams, painted ceilings, and sparse interiors have changed little since they were built in the 15th century.

Descending from the west part of the castle, walk across the
18 cobbled square to the **Albrecht-Dürer-Haus,** located opposite the Tiergärtner gate. This was the home of the great German painter from 1509 to his death in 1528. It is also about the best-preserved late-medieval house in the city, typical of the prosperous merchants' homes that once filled Nürnberg. Admire the half-timbering of the upper stories and the tapering gable before stepping inside. Dürer was the German Leonardo, the Renaissance man incarnate, bursting with curiosity. A great painter, Dürer excelled equally in print making; he raised the woodcut, a notoriously difficult medium, to new heights of technical sophistication, combining great skill with a haunting, immensely detailed drawing style and complex allegorical subject matter. A number of original prints adorn the walls. The house also offers a convincing sense of what life was like in ear-

ly 16th-century Germany. *Albrecht-Dürer-Str. 39. Admission: DM 3.50 adults, DM 2 children and senior citizens. Open Mar.–Oct. and Christkindlmarkt, Tues. and Thurs.–Sun. 10–5, Wed. 10–9; Nov.–Feb., Tues., Thurs., and Fri. 10–5, Wed. 10–9.*

19 The **Spielzeugmuseum** (Toy Museum) is located on Sigmundstrasse. To reach it, walk down the street that runs past Dürer's house. There are few places where a toy museum seems more appropriate. Nürnberg likes to call itself the toy capital of the world, and this museum does its best to prove why. One or two exhibits date from the Renaissance; most, however, are from the 19th century. Simple dolls vie with mechanical toys of extraordinary complexity. There's even a little Ferris wheel. *Sigmundstr. 220. Admission: DM 3 adults, 50 pf. children. Open Tues. and Thurs.–Sun. 10–5, Wed. 10–9.*

A final sight in the historic area for those with interest in
20 German cultural achievements is the **Germanisches Nationalmuseum** (Germanic National Museum), located close by the Hauptbahnhof. You could spend an entire day visiting this vast and fascinating museum. It is the largest of its kind in Germany, and about the best-arranged. The setting gets everything off to a flying start; the museum is located in what was once a Carthusian monastery, complete with cloisters and monastic outbuildings. Few aspects of German culture, from the Stone Age to the 19th century, are not covered here, and quantity and quality are evenly matched. For some, the highlight may be the superb collection of Renaissance German painting (with Dürer, Cranach, and Altdorfer well represented). Others may prefer the exquisite medieval ecclesiastical exhibits—manuscripts, altarpieces, statuary, stained glass, jewel-encrusted reliquaries—or the collections of arms and armor, or the scientific instruments, or the toys. Few will be disappointed. *Kornmarkt. Admission free. Open Tues.–Sun. 9–5.*

21 Children love the **Verkehrsmuseum** (Transportation Museum), located just south of the National Museum outside the city walls. December 7, 1835, saw the first-ever train trip in Germany, from Nürnberg to nearby Fürth. A model of the epochal train is here at the museum, along with a series of original 19th- and early 20th-century trains and stagecoaches. Stamp lovers will also want to check out some of the 40,000-odd stamps in the extensive exhibits on the German postage system. *Lessingstr. 6. Admission: DM 4 adults, DM 2 children. Open daily 9:30–5.*

22 **Regensburg,** 90 kilometers (56 miles) southeast of Nürnberg, is one of the best-preserved cities in Germany. Everything here is original, since the city suffered no major damage in World War II. It is also one of Germany's most historic cities. The mystery, then, would appear to be: Why is Regensburg not better known? Few visitors to Bavaria (or even Franconia) venture this far off the well-trod tourist trails. Even Germans are astonished that such a remarkable city should exist in comparative obscurity.

The key to Regensburg is the Danube. The city marks the northernmost navigable point of the great river, and it was this simple geographical fact that allowed Regensburg to control trade along the Danube between Germany and central Europe. The great river was a highway for more than commerce, however: It was a conduit of ideas as well. It was from Regensburg, for example, in the 7th and 8th centuries that Christianity was spread across much of central Europe. By the Middle Ages, Regensburg had become a political, economic, and intellectual center of European significance. Today the city may long since have given way to Munich in political clout and sheer size, but for many centuries it was the most important city in southeast Germany, eclipsed by Munich only when Napoléon ordered the dismemberment of the Holy Roman Empire in the early years of the 19th century. That he presided over its decline from Regensburg, a Free Imperial City since the 13th century and meeting place of the Imperial Diet (parliament) since the 17th, was an irony he appreciated.

Regensburg's story begins with the Celts in around 500 BC. They called their little settlement Radasbona. In AD 179, as an original marble inscription in the Museum der Stadt Regensburg proclaims, it became a Roman military post called Castra Regina. Little remains of the Roman occupation save a fortified gate, the Porta Praetoria, in the old town. When Bavarian tribes migrated to the area in the 6th century, they occupied what remained of the Roman town and, apparently on the basis of its Latin name, called it Regensburg. Irish missionaries led by St. Boniface in 739 made the town a bishopric before heading down the Danube to convert the heathen in lands even more far-flung. Charlemagne, first of the Holy Roman Emperors, arrived at the end of the 8th century, incorporating Regensburg into his burgeoning lands. And so, in one form or another, prospering all the while and growing into a glorious medieval and, later, Renaissance city, Regensburg remained until Napoléon turned up.

Any serious tour of Regensburg—not for nothing is it known as "the city of churches"—involves visiting an unusually large number of places of worship. If your spirits wilt at the thought of inspecting them all, you should see at least the Dom (cathedral), famous for its boys' choir, the Domspatzen (Cathedral Sparrows), and then go on to the remaining attractions.

Numbers in the margin correspond to points of interest on the Regensburg map.

23 Begin your tour at the **Steinerne Brücke** (Stone Bridge). It leads south over the Danube to the almost-too-good-to-be-true
24 **Brückturm** (Bridge Tower): all tiny windows, weathered tiles, and pink plaster. (The brooding building with a massive roof to the left of the tower is an old salt warehouse.) The bridge is a central part of Regensburg history. Built in 1141, it was rightfully considered a miraculous piece of engineering at the time—and, as the only crossing point over the Danube for miles, effectively cemented Regensburg's control of trade in the region.

25 From the bridge, look up at the commanding towers of the **Dom St. Peter.** The cathedral, modeled on the airy, vertical lines of French Gothic architecture, is something of a rarity this far south in Germany. It wouldn't look out of place in Köln or Bonn. Begun in the 13th century, it stands on the site of a much earlier Carolingian church. Construction dragged on for almost 600 years, and it was finally finished when Ludwig I of Bavaria, then the ruler of Regensburg, had the towers built. (These were replaced in the mid-1950s after their original soft limestone was found to be badly eroded.)

Alte Kapelle, **28**
Altes Rathaus, **33**
Brückturm, **24**
Dom St. Peter, **25**
Karmelitenkirche, **29**
Museum der Stadt Regensburg, **32**
Neupfarrkirche, **26**
Niedermünster, **30**
Porta Praetoria, **31**
St. Emmeramus, **35**
St. Kassian, **27**
Schloss Thurn-und-Taxis, **34**
Steinerne Brücke, **23**

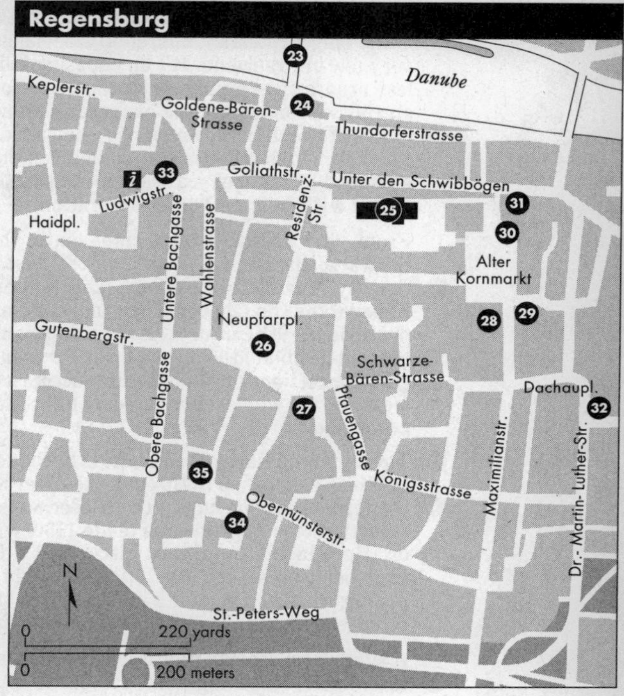

Walk under the Bridge Tower to Domplatz, the cathedral square. Before heading into the building, admire its intricate and frothy facade, embellished with delicate and skillful carving. A remarkable feature of the cathedral is its size, able to accommodate 7,000 people, three times the population of Regensburg when construction began. Standouts of the austere interior are the glowing 14th-century stained glass in the choir and the exquisitely detailed statues of the Archangel Gabriel and the Virgin in the crossing (the meeting point of nave and choir). The **Domschatzmuseum** (Cathedral Museum) contains more valuable treasures. The entrance is in the nave. *Admission: DM 2.50. Open Apr.–Oct., Tues.–Sat. 10–5, Sun. 11:30–4; Dec.–Mar., Fri. and Sat. 10–4, Sun. 11:30–4; closed Nov.*

Complete your tour of the cathedral with a visit to the **cloisters,** reached via the garden. These contain a small octagonal chapel, the **Allerheiligenkapelle** (All Saints' Chapel), a typically solid Romanesque building, all sturdy grace and massive walls. You can barely make out the faded remains of stylized 11th-century frescoes on its ancient walls. The equally ancient shell of St. Stephan's church, the **Alter Dom** (Old Cathedral), can also be visited. *Admission: DM 2.50. The cloisters, chapel, and Alter Dom can be seen only on guided tours: mid-May–Oct., daily at 10, 11, and 2; Oct.–Mar., daily at 11 and noon; Apr.–mid-May, daily at 11 and 2.*

To the south of the cathedral are the Neupfarrkirche and the church of St. Kassian. To the east lie the Niedermünster church, the Karmelitenkirche, and the Alte Kapelle. The

26 **Neupfarrkirche** (Neupfarrplatz), built between 1519 and 1540,
is the only Protestant church in Regensburg, indeed one of a
very few in Franconia. It's an imposing building, substantially
less ornate than any other in the city. Some may find its restraint welcome after the exuberance of so many of the other
27 places of worship. **St. Kassian** is a much older building, the oldest church in the city, in fact, founded in the 8th century. Don't
be fooled by its dour exterior; inside, the church has been endowed with delicate Rococo decoration.

From St. Kassian, turn right onto the pedestrians-only
Schwarze-Bären-Strasse, one of the best shopping streets in
28 the city. Turn left at the end. This will bring you to the **Alte**
Kapelle, the Old Chapel. This, too, is a Carolingian structure,
put up in the 9th century. As at St. Kassian, the dowdy exterior
gives little hint of the joyous Rococo treasures within, extravagant concoctions of sinuous gilt stucco, rich marble, and giddy
frescoes, the whole illuminated by light pouring in from the upper windows.

29 The adjoining **Karmelitenkirche** is Baroque from crypt to cupo-
la. Finally, head north through the Alter Kornmarkt square to
30 the former parish church, the **Niedermünster,** another ancient
structure (construction started in 1150) with a Baroque interi-
or. Here in 1982 workmen discovered a Roman altar, dating
from between AD 180 and 190, dedicated to the emperor Com-
modus; a little stone plinth indicates that the altar was used for
incense offerings. The site is open to the public.

A substantial Roman relic is located just round the corner from
31 the church (turn right as you leave it). This is the **Porta**
Praetoria, one of the original city gates, a rough-hewn and
blocky structure. Look through the grille on its east side to see
a section of the original Roman street, located about 10 feet below today's street.

Time Out For a taste of old Regensburg, head to the **Historische Wurstküche** (literally, "sausage kitchen"); it's located just by the Stone Bridge. It's the oldest and most authentic sausage restaurant in Regensburg. This is the place to try *Schweinebratwurst über Buchenholzkohle gebraten,* finger-size pork sausages grilled over beech-wood charcoal; they are easier to eat than to pronounce. Sit on the terrace for the view over the Danube while enjoying these tidbits. Prices are low. *Thundorferstr. 3. Open daily 8–7.*

From the Porta Praetoria, you can either backtrack through
32 Kornmarkt to the **Museum der Stadt Regensburg** or continue
along Goldene-Bären-Strasse to the Fischmarkt and Altes Rathaus (Old Town Hall). For many, the museum is one of the highlights of a visit to the city, both for its unusual and beautiful
setting—a former Gothic monastery—and for its wide-ranging
collections, from Roman artifacts to Renaissance tapestries, all
helping to tell the story of Regensburg. The most significant
exhibits are the paintings by Albrecht Altdorfer (1480–1538), a
native of Regensburg and, along with Cranach, Grünewald,
and Dürer, one of the leading painters of the German Renaissance. His work has the same sense of slight distortion—of
heightened reality—you find in that of his contemporaries, in
which the lessons of Italian painting are used to produce an
emotional rather than a rational effect. What's really signifi-

cant about Altdorfer is his interest in landscape not merely as the background of a painting but as its subject. Figures in many of his works are simply incidentals. What's even more intriguing is that Altdorfer's obviously emotional response to landscape would not have seemed out of place in the 19th century. Far from seeing the world around him as essentially hostile, or at least alien, like the Romantics of the 19th century he saw it as something intrinsically beautiful, to be admired for its own sake, whether wild or domesticated. *Dachaupl. 2–4. Admission: DM 3 adults, DM 1 children. Open Tues.–Sat. 10–4, Sun. and holidays 10–1.*

33 The **Altes Rathaus,** a picture-book complex of medieval buildings with half-timbering, windows large and small, and flowers in tubs, is among the best-preserved of its kind in the country, as well as one of the most historically important. It was here, in the imposing Gothic **Reichssaal** (Imperial Hall), that the "everlasting Imperial Diet" met from 1663 to 1805. This could be considered a forerunner of the German parliament, where representatives from every part of the Holy Roman Empire—plus the emperor and the prince-electors—assembled to discuss and determine the affairs of the far-reaching German lands. The hall is sumptuously appointed with tapestries, flags, and heraldic designs. Note especially the wood ceiling, built in 1408. If you have kids in tow, they'll want to see the adjoining torture chamber, the **Fragstatt,** and execution room, the **Armesünderstübchen.** Medieval notions of justice can be gauged by the fact that any prisoner who withstood three days of "questioning" here without confessing was released. *Rathauspl. Admission: DM 5 adults, DM 2.50 children under 18. Open daily 9–4. Tours in English daily, except Sun. (times vary according to season).*

34 There's one more major sight in the downtown area, the **Schloss Thurn-und-Taxis.** To reach it from the Rathaus, head down Bachgasse for 500 yards. Members of the Thurn-und-Taxis family still live in this enormous structure, originally the Benedictine monastery of St. Emmeram. The Thurn-und-Taxis were not only the leading family of Regensburg from around 1600 onward but one of the most influential families in Germany; their fortune came from running the German postal system, a monopoly they enjoyed until 1867. The former abbey cloisters are probably the architectural treasure of the palace itself, with their elegant and attenuated late-Gothic carving. As for the rest of the building, much of which was extensively rebuilt at the end of the 19th century, opinions remain divided. Some consider it the most vulgar and ponderously overdecorated specimen of its kind in Germany. Others admire its Victorian bombast and confidence. You can also visit the **Marstallmuseum** (Transport Museum) in the palace if you have a weakness for 18th- and 19th-century carriages and sleighs. *Admission to palace and cloisters: DM 3. Open for guided tours only, Mon.–Fri. at 2:15 and 3:30, Sun. and holidays at 10:15 and 11:30. Admission to Marstallmuseum: DM 3.50. Open for guided tours only, Mon.–Fri. at 2, 2:40, and 3:15, Sun. at 10, 10:40, and 11:15.*

35 Next to the palace there's one more church to be visited, **St. Emmeramus.** It's the work of the Asam brothers and is decorated in their customary and full-blown late-Baroque manner.

Numbers in the margin correspond to points of interest on the Franconia map.

There are two noteworthy sights in the environs of Regensburg (either one makes a good day trip). The first is the great abbey church of St. George and St. Martin, by the banks of the Dan-
36 ube at **Weltenburg.** The most dramatic approach to the abbey is by boat from Kelheim, 10 kilometers (6 miles) downstream *(see* Guided Tours in Essential Information, above). On the stunning ride, the boat winds between towering limestone cliffs that rise straight up from the tree-lined riverside. The abbey church, constructed between 1716 and 1718, is commonly regarded as the masterpiece of the brothers Cosmas Damian and Egid Quirin Asam, two leading Baroque architects and decorators of Bavaria (Cosmas Damian was the architect, Egid Quirin was the painter, sculptor, and stuccoworker). If you've seen their little church of St. John Nepomuk in Munich, you'll know what pyrotechnics to expect here, albeit on a substantially larger scale. To some, this kind of frothy confection, with painted figures whirling on the ceiling, lavish and brilliantly polished marble, highly wrought statuary, and stucco dancing rhythmic arabesques across the curving walls, is more high kitsch than high art. To others, the exuberance, drama, and sheer technical sophistication of this concentrated style may appear to be like Mozart's music in stone. Whichever view you take, it's hard not to be impressed by the bronze equestrian statue of St. George over the high altar, reaching down imperiously with his flamelike, twisted gilt sword to dispatch the winged dragon at his feet.

Time Out The abbey monks brew their own delicious dark beer, which you can sample on draft while sitting under ancient chestnut trees in the courtyard. Meals are also served. *Open daily until 6.*

Another excursion from Regensburg you won't want to miss (especially if you have an interest in the wilder expressions of 19th-century German nationalism) is by Danube riverboat *(see* Guided Tours in Essential Information, above) to the incongru-
37 ous Greek-style Doric temple of **Walhalla,** 11 kilometers (7 miles) east of the city. To get to the temple from the river, you'll have to climb 358 marble steps; this is not a tour to take if you're not in good shape. (There is, however, a parking lot near the top.) Walhalla—a name resonant with Nordic mythology—was where the god Odin received the souls of dead heroes. This monumental temple on a commanding site high above the Danube was erected to honor German heroes through the ages, in the prevailing neoclassical style of the 19th century. Walhalla, built in 1840 for Ludwig I, turns out to be a copy of the Parthenon in Athens. Even if you consider the building more a monument to kitsch than a tribute to the great men of Germany, you will at least be able to muse on the fact that it is a supremely well-built structure, its great, smooth-fitting stones and expanses of costly marble evidence of both the financial resources and the craftsmanship that were Ludwig's to command.

What to See and Do with Children

The number-one attraction for children is the **Spielzeug Museum** (Toy Museum) in Nürnberg *(see* Nürnburg to Regensburg,

Guided Tours, above). Nürnberg also has a **zoo;** children love its dolphinarium. *Am Tiergarten 30, tel. 0911/571-346. Admission: DM 6 adults, DM 3 children. Open daily 9-sunset.*

If you're in Franconia during the four weeks prior to Christmas, by all means consider taking your children to Nürnberg's **Christkindlmarkt,** the most lavish and spectacular Christmas market in Germany. The highlight is the December 10 candle procession.

In Regensburg, visit the **Figurentheater,** or Puppet Theater (Dr.-Johann-Maier-Str. 3, tel. 0941/28328). There are performances from May through September, Saturday and Sunday at 3. And the torture chamber at the **Altes Rathaus** can be a great place for kids to unlock their imagination.

Children may not be too struck by the Abbey Church at Weltenburg or by Ludwig I's grandiose Walhalla, but they'll appreciate the **boat rides** to them on the Danube *(see* Guided Tours, above). For trips on the Main River between Aschaffenburg and Würzburg, call 0931/91553.

Neustadt, north of Coburg, is a center of toy and doll making. The **Museum der Deutschen Spielzeugindustrie** shows how toys were made throughout the centuries, providing a fascinating diversion for a rainy afternoon. *Hindenburgpl. 1, tel. 09568/5600. Admission: DM 2. Open Tues.-Sun. 10-5.*

Coburg also has a doll museum, **Coburger Puppenmuseum.** *Steingasse, just off the town square, tel. 09561/74047. Admission: DM 1.50 adults, 50 pf children. Open Tues.-Sun. 10-5.*

Coburg's **Naturwissenschaftliches Museum** (Natural History Museum) can provide a diverting hour or two *(see* above).

Finally, all children can appreciate the sense of medieval and Renaissance life in the narrow, atmospheric streets of Nürnberg and Regensburg. Let the past come alive for them.

Off the Beaten Track

The area between Aschaffenburg and Würzburg is wine country. Though many of the local wineries offer tours, few beat the one at Miltenburg's **St. Kilian Kellerei** offered by wine master Bernard Lorenz. Call two days in advance to be sure of getting his services (tel. 09371/2120). In addition to giving you the full story of how the wines are made, he'll take you to the wine cellars set in the cliffs along the river, time permitting.

Though the whole of Franconia offers many delightful small medieval towns, few tourists visit **Kronach,** east of Coburg. It was here that Renaissance master painter Lucas Cranach the Elder was born at the end of the 15th century; you can visit his house at Marktplatz 1. A cluster of half-timbered buildings and a fine Renaissance town hall complete the appeal of this flower-strewn square. Outside the town, see the **Rosenberg fortress.** *Admission: DM 3 adults, DM 1.50 children. Open Apr.-Dec., daily 10-5.*

Fans of the British monarchy may want to visit the 550-year-old castle in which Prince Albert was born in 1819. Located in an English-style park beside the Itz River near the village of Rödental, 9 kilometers (6 miles) north of Coburg, **Schloss Rosenau** was restored in 1990 and opened to the public. A mix of architectural styles ranging from Renaissance to neo-Gothic, the castle features furniture made especially for the Saxe-Coburg family by noted Viennese craftsmen, and other pieces from the period of Albert's youth. One room houses exhibits devoted to Victoria and Albert. *Admission: DM 2 adults, DM 1.50 children and students. Open Tues.–Sun. 10–noon and 1–4:30.*

If you fancy a hike to a Disney-style castle, visit **Altenburg,** 2 miles outside Bamberg (or take the No. 10 bus). It's a "medieval" castle built on the site of a much older castle in the 19th century, during the full flood of Romantic enthusiasm for the days of chivalry and courtly love. *Admission free. Open Apr.–Oct., daily 9–5.*

For a change of pace after Franconia's castles, palaces, and churches, take a look at the **Teufelhöhle** (Devil's Cave) at Pottenstein, midway between Bayreuth and Nürnberg. It contains some spectacular stalagmites and stalactites. (Tours Apr.–Oct., daily 8–6.) There's another cave 5 kilometers (3 miles) outside Kelheim, near Regensburg. This is the **Schulerloch** (Schoolboy's Cave). It was inhabited by Neanderthal man. (Tours Easter–Oct.)

At Neustadt, 18 kilometers (11 miles) northeast of Coburg, inspect the world's only "stone beer" brewery, **Rauchenfelser Steinbier** (Am Brunn 1, tel. 09261/52051). Entrepreneur Gerd Borges has revived a preindustrial-age method of brewing using special, heated stones. The result is a uniquely flavored brew. Call ahead to arrange a tour.

Northwest of Coburg, at **Rodach,** you can rest your travel-weary muscles at the therapeutic thermal baths. *Admission: DM 9. Open Mon. and Fri.–Sun. 9–7, Tues.–Thurs. 9–9. Children under 10 must have a doctor's certificate.*

Neustadt and Rodach are on the former east-west German border. A drive across the now-vanished dividing line to nearby Sonneberg or Hildburghausen, respectively, still offers a stark visual reminder of the yawning gulf in standards of living and development that existed between the two Germanys for 40 years.

Shopping

Specialties in **Coburg** include some delicious foods (not all of which you'll be permitted to bring home with you; check to see that you're not infringing customs regulations). For bratwurst, smoked ham, *Schmätzchen* (gingerbread), and *Elizenkuchen* (almond cake), try **Grossman's** (Ketchinggasse 20–24). For other traditional German goods, take a look at **Franz Denk's** shop (Kirchhof 4); his stoneware is expensive but exceptional. Off the market square, you'll find **Kaufmann's** (Judengasse). Run by a husband-and-wife team, it has fine hand-blown glass and homemade jewelry.

Lichtenfels, southeast of Coburg, is the place for baskets; there's even a state-run basket-weaving school here. The best selection is at **Es Körbla** (Stadtknechtgasse), just off the market square.

If you've enjoyed a visit to **Kulmbach's** Plassenburg museum, the world's largest collection of tin figures, visit **Wanderer und**

Ranning (Obere Stadt 34) and buy some to take home. The shop boasts more than 1,000 tin figures in all shapes and sizes. Traditional *Trachtenschmuck* silver jewelry is sold in three shops in town: **Brückner** and **Juwelier Hubschmann** (both on Langgasse), and **Giorgio Canola** (Kressinsteinerstr. 11).

Bayreuth's main shopping streets are Maximilianstrasse and Richard-Wagner-Strasse, both with department stores and sophisticated boutiques. The Hofgarten Passage, an arcade off Richard-Wagner-Strasse, has several fine shops, including **Piccola Tazza,** which sells puppets, and **Laurenstein,** with chocolates from Germany, Belgium, and Switzerland. **C. V. Brocke** (Operastr. 18) has painted-glass pictures and pewter figurines. **Döring's** (corner of Kammererstr. and Kirchgasse) sells stoneware and figurines.

Bamberg's main shopping area runs along Hauptwachstrasse. Across from the tourist information center is **Pappenberg's,** a shop selling communion, wedding, and baptism candles, all of which can be engraved. It also features beeswax candles, pewter, and wood carvings. An excellent place to shop for pottery is **Der Topferladen** (Untere Brücke 1), near the Altes Rathaus. The shop sells decorative plates, mugs, and bowls from more than 70 potters. If you want a small gift, around the corner is **Renate's Allerlei** (Untere Brücke 7). It has stuffed animals, porcelain, nutcrackers, and linen tablecloths. **Zensinger's** (Katzenberg 4) has unusual decorative glass and a large assortment of polished-stone necklaces and crystals. **Pierron Goldsmith** (Hauptwachstr. 6) has polished-stone necklaces, garnets, and the ornate silver jewelry worn with traditional costumes. On Saturday mornings there's a small **flea market** on the Untere Brücke.

Across from the main train station in **Nürnberg** is the famous **Handwerkerhof** (Handicraft Court). It has many shops where engravers, glassblowers, silversmiths, goldsmiths, and other artisans make their wares. You can watch them work and buy examples of their art. (The market is closed Christmas–Feb.) The historic area has numerous quality shops, especially on Königstrasse and Karolinenstrasse. Children will love the **Spielwaren Virnich** toy store (corner of Königstr. and Luitpoldstr.) For a wide range of souvenirs, try **Elsässer** (Königstr.). If you don't find what you're looking for there, try **Ostermayr** (Königstr. 33–37), or turn down Karolinenstrasse, where there are three more large stores selling souvenirs. Department stores and bakeries sell Nürnberg's famous *Lebkuchen* (gingerbread cookies). During the month before Christmas, you can shop at the **Christkindlmarkt** for tree decorations, toys, polished stones, socks, mittens, spices, and much more.

Regensburg is famous for its crafts. **Gewürz-Eckerl** (Unter d. Schwibbögen) sells attractive handmade puppets, glass ornaments, and fine jewelry. **Wiedemann Zinn und Keramik** (Brückstr. 4) offers a wide selection of pewter and pottery. If you fancy yourself in a dirndl or sporting a pair of lederhosen, try **Emess Moden** (Wahlenstr. 12).

Sports and Fitness

Bicycling Bikes can be rented at train stations for DM 12 per day (DM 6 if you have a valid rail ticket). Local tourist offices can suggest other places to rent bikes. (*See* Getting Around in Essential Information, above, for further information on biking in Franconia.)

Fishing Various areas along the Main River have good fishing. The Miltenburg tourist office offers a seven-day fishing vacation, with reduced prices for board and lodging; call 09371/400–119 for details. The fishing around Coburg is good, with up to 13 different kinds of fish to catch. Contact the local tourist office (tel. 09561/741–80), which can also give information on fishing in Lake Wüstenahorn. Note that you'll need a license to fish anywhere in Germany. Contact any tourist office for one; the cost is DM 10 for one year. In addition, expect to pay daily charges of between DM 8 and DM 15; reduced weekly rates are also available.

Golf Coburg has a nine-hole course (tel. 09561/1277) across from Schloss Tambach on B-303. There's an 18-hole course at Bayreuth-Thurnau (tel. 09228/319).

Hang Gliding and Gliding Hang-gliding enthusiasts can take part in a 14-day training course at Stadtsteinach in the Frankenwald. Contact the tourist office (Badstr. 5, 8652 Stadtsteinach, tel. 09225/774). The air currents of the Rhön and Spessart regions are ideal for gliding, and you can take part in round-trip flights by contacting the tourist offices at Aschaffenburg *(see* Important Addresses and Numbers in Essential Information, above) and Miltenburg. Alternatively, write the Spessart regional tourist office (Promenadenweg 11, 8776 Heigenbrücken).

Hiking The vast stretches of forest and numerous nature parks in much of northern Franconia make this an ideal destination for hiking vacations, a fact that the Germans have not been slow to exploit. There are more than 25,000 miles of hiking trails, the greatest concentration in the Altmühltal Nature Park—Germany's largest—and in the Frankenwald. There are also marked trails in the Fichtelgebirge Mountains, in Swiss Franconia, and in and around Coburg, including the romantic valleys of the Upper Main and Rodach, bordering the foothills of the vast Thüringer Forest.

Dining and Lodging

Dining

Franconia offers a wide range of dining experiences, though with a preponderance of *Gasthaüser*, inns offering simple but good local specialties. Most offer inexpensive lunch menus. Traditional dishes you'll want to try include *Sauerbraten* (marinated slices of beef), *Schweinshaxe* (pig's knuckle), and the ever-present *Knödel* (dumplings). The region has hundreds of small breweries (Bamberg alone has 10; Bayreuth 7), so always ask for the local brew wherever you're staying. In the Main Valley towns, you should try the delightfully dry wines produced there; they are served in the familiar bulbous green bottles known as *Bocksbeutel*.

Highly recommended restaurants in each price category are indicated by a star ★.

Category	Cost*
Very Expensive	over DM 90
Expensive	DM 55–90
Moderate	DM 35–55
Inexpensive	under DM 35

**per person for a three-course meal, including sales tax and excluding drinks and service charge*

Lodging

Make reservations well in advance for hotels in all the larger towns and cities if you plan to visit anytime between June and September. If you're visiting Bayreuth during the annual Wagner festival in July, consider making reservations up to a year in advance. And remember, too, that during the festival prices can be double the normal rates. Standards of comfort and cleanliness are high throughout the region, whether you stay in a simple pension or in a modern, international chain hotel.

Highly recommended hotels in each price category are indicated by a star ★.

Category	Cost*
Very Expensive	over DM 180
Expensive	DM 120–DM 180
Moderate	DM 80–DM 120
Inexpensive	under DM 80

**All prices are for two people in a double room.*

Bamberg
Dining
★

Bottingerhaus. Dine on classy nouvelle specialties in the upscale Baroque surroundings of the most sophisticated restaurant in Bamberg, or pay a visit to the simpler wine cellar in the bowels of the building. In summer, try for a table on the terrace overlooking the garden. *Judengasse 14, tel. 0951/54074. Reservations advised. Jacket and tie required (informal dress in wine cellar). AE, DC, MC, V. Closed Christmas. Expensive (Moderate in wine cellar).*

Würzburger Weinstuben. This should be your choice for unmistakably German, half-timbered Old World atmosphere and good-value local specialties. A wide range of wines are available, and there's a garden for romantic summer dining. *Zinkenwörth 6, tel. 0951/22667. Reservations advised. Dress: informal. AE, DC, MC, V. Closed end of Aug.–mid-Sept., Tues. for dinner, and Wed. Moderate.*

Brauerei Spezial. Unpretentious Franconian fare fills the menu in this traditional beer restaurant, one of 10 pubs in Bamberg that brew their own beer. The dining style is communal, with everybody sitting at gnarled and scrub-topped wooden benches. Order *fränkische Klöße*, the local herb-filled version of a Bavarian dumpling, with any cut of pork. A natural accompaniment is the delicately flavored smoked house beer. Rooms are also available. *Obere Königstr. 10, tel. 0951/24304. No credit cards. Closed Sat. afternoon and dinner. Inexpensive.*

Dining and Lodging ★ **Romantik Hotel Weinhaus Messerschmitt.** Built in 1422 and owned and run by the same family since 1832, this will be the choice of anyone who values small, one-of-a-kind hotels. The 18th-century exterior is opulent; the dark paneled interior is tasteful and soothing. The restaurant is exceptional. Look for the chestnut soup and Franconian duck; for a culinary adventure, try the eels in dill sauce. *Langestr. 41, tel. 0951/27866. 12 rooms with bath. Facilities: restaurant. AE, DC, MC, V. Expensive.*

Brudermühle. A 14th-century inn upgraded to a modern hotel in 1980, the Brudermühle sits among the jumble of ancient tiled red roofs of the old town. Rooms are ornately furnished; the restaurant serves a mix of local Franconian specialties and international cuisines. In summer, you can dine—or simply stop for coffee and cake—on the sheltered sun terrace and watch Bamberg go about its business. *Schranne 1, tel. 0951/54091. 16 rooms with bath. Restaurant reservations advised. Dress: informal. DC, MC, V. Moderate.*

Gasthof Weierich. Located alongside the walls of the towering cathedral, the Weierich boasts three charmingly decorated restaurants, each offering game (in season), fish, and other Franconian specialties. Lodging is also available in 23 moderately priced rooms. *Lugbank 5, tel. 0951/54004. Reservations advised. Dress: informal. No credit cards. Moderate.*

Lodging ★ **Barock Hotel am Dom.** Standing close by the cathedral in the heart of the old town, this hotel offers a stylish combination of Old World elegance and discreet modern luxury. No restaurant. *Vorderer Bach 4, tel. 0951/54031. 19 rooms. AE, DC, MC. Closed Jan. 6–31. Moderate.*

Cafe am Dom. If you blink you'll miss it, because this tiny place is tucked away in one of Bamberg's narrow medieval streets, a favorite retreat for older women in hats who know where to find the best cakes in town. The smell of home baking greets you when you wake in one of the simple but cozy and sparkling rooms above the café, that offer a truly spellbinding view across the ancient red-tiled rooftops of Bamberg. *Ringleingasse 2, tel. 0951/56852. 10 rooms, none with bath. No credit cards. Inexpensive.*

Bayreuth

Dining ★ **Schloss Hotel Thiergarten.** Located 6½ kilometers (4 miles) from Bayreuth in the Thiergarten suburb, this small, onetime hunting lodge, now beautifully converted into a hotel *(see* below) and two stunning restaurants, provides one of the most elegant dining experiences in Franconia. The intimate Kaminhalle (the name means fireplace, a reference to the lavishly ornate one here) and the Venezianischer Salon, dominated by a glittering 300-year-old Venetian chandelier, both offer sophisticated and memorable regional and nouvelle specialties. *Tel. 09209/1314. Reservations required. Jacket and tie required. DC, MC, V. Closed Feb. 15–Mar. 15, Sun. for dinner, and Mon. Very Expensive.*

Cuvee. Within just a couple of years, owner Wolfgang Hauenstein has elevated the status of this elegant restaurant into the don't-miss category, with his mixture of nouvelle cuisine and traditional regional specialties featuring a modern twist. The cellar includes 14 varieties of champagne. *Markgrafenallee 15, tel. 0921/23422. Reservations advised.*

Jacket and tie required. DC, MC, V. Closed Sun. and last 2 weeks in Sept. Expensive.

Weihenstephan. Long wood tables, fulsome regional specialties, and beer straight from the barrel (from the oldest brewery in Germany) make this a perennial favorite with tourists and locals alike. In summer, the flower-strewn and crowded terrace is the place to be. *Bahnhofstr. 5, tel. 0921/82288. No reservations. Dress: informal. No credit cards. Moderate.*

Wolffenzacher. The rowdy, wood-paneled atmosphere and the good-value local specialties—this is a great place to try *Schweinshaxe*—make this traditional haunt a good, low-cost bet. The city-center location is a plus. *Badstr. 1, tel. 0921/64522. Reservations advised. Dress: informal. MC. Inexpensive.*

Lodging

★ **Schloss Hotel Thiergarten.** If you plan to stay in this near-regal little hotel, be sure to make reservations well in advance. Some may find the furnishings a trifle faded, but there's no denying the class of this baronial spot. Staying here is like staying with your favorite elderly millionaire aunt. *(See* above for details of the two restaurants.) *Tel. 09209/1314. 10 rooms with bath. Facilities: sauna, terrace, 2 restaurants. DC, MC, V. Closed Feb. 15–Mar. 15. Very Expensive.*

★ **Goldener Anker.** No question about it: If you've booked far enough in advance, this is *the* place to stay in Bayreuth. The hotel is located right by the Markgräfliche's Opernhaus and has been entertaining composers, singers, conductors, and players for more than 100 years, as the signed photographs in the lobby and the signatures in the guest book make clear. Rooms are small but individually decorated; many have antique pieces. The restaurant is justly popular. *Opernstr. 6, tel. 0921/65051. 28 rooms with bath. Facilities: parking, restaurant. No credit cards. Closed Dec. 20–Jan. 10. Expensive.*

Am Hofgarten. This delightful small establishment is more like a private home than a hotel. All rooms are individually decorated and have many personal touches. There's an appealingly rustic bar and a small garden out back (but no restaurant). Composer Franz Liszt lived in the house opposite. *Lisztstr. 6, tel. 0921/69006. 18 rooms, 9 with bath. Facilities: bar. AE, DC, MC. Closed mid-Dec.–mid-Jan. Moderate.*

Gasthof Vogel. This is probably the best low-cost bet in town. It's centrally located (near the Stadthalle) and offers basic, well-run comfort. There's a noisy beer restaurant and a tree-shaded courtyard. *Friedrichstr. 13, tel. 0921/68268. 8 rooms, with bath. Facilities: beer restaurant. No credit cards. Inexpensive.*

Coburg

Dining

★ **Coburger-Tor Restaurant Schaller.** Located just south of the city center, this hotel-restaurant provides surprisingly upscale dining in a softly lit and distinctly well-upholstered ambience. The food is sophisticated nouvelle, an especially good value if you order one of the fixed-price menus. The desserts are luscious. *Ketschendorfer-Str. 22, tel. 09561/25074. Reservations required. Jacket and tie required. No credit cards. Closed Fri. and Sat. lunch. Very Expensive.*

Ratskeller. An entirely different experience is offered in the stone vaults of this establishment, the sort of emphatically Teutonic place where local specialties always taste better. Try the sauerbraten, along with a large glass of frothy beer. *Markt 1, tel. 09561/92400. Reservations advised. Dress: informal. No credit cards. Moderate. Closed Sun.*

★ **Goldenes Kreuz.** In business since 1477, this restaurant boasts all the rustic decor you'll ever want and large portions of Franconian food. Goose with dumplings provides an authentically hearty experience. Not for lovers of nouvelle cuisine. *Herrngasse 1, tel. 09561/90473. Reservations advised. Dress: informal. No credit cards. Inexpensive.*

Lodging

★ **Blankenburg.** Located north of the town center, this excellent-value modern hotel has a stylish restaurant that has become noted for its gourmet fare. Families are encouraged with the offer of free lodging for children up to 15 years old sharing their parents' room. Admission to an adjoining indoor swimming and wave pool is free to guests. *Rosenauerstr. 30, tel. 09561/75005. 34 rooms and 2 suites with bath. Facilities: terrace in herb garden, restaurant, parking. AE, DC, MC, V. Expensive.*

Goldene Traube. High levels of comfort plus an excellent central location are provided by this sturdy favorite. Some of the cheaper rooms are plain, however. *Am Viktoriabrunnen 2, tel. 09561/9833. Facilities: sauna, restaurant, parking. AE, DC, MC, V. Moderate–Expensive.*

Nürnberg

Dining

★ **Goldenes Posthorn.** Though rebuilt after the war, the authentic heart of old Nürnberg still beats in this ancient restaurant by the cathedral. In their day, both Dürer and Hans Sachs ate here. The food is nouvelle Franconian; try the pigeon terrine or quail stuffed with walnuts and goose livers. The wine list is extensive. *An der Sebalduskirche, tel. 0911/225–153. Reservations required. Jacket and tie required. DC, MC. Closed Sun. Very Expensive.*

★ **Essigbrätlein.** Some rank this as the top restaurant in the city, indeed one of the best in Germany. As the oldest restaurant in Nürnberg, built in 1550, it is unquestionably one of the most atmospheric, having been used originally as a meeting place for wine merchants. Today its elegant period interior is *the* place to eat *Essigbrätlein* (roast loin of beef). Other dishes blend Franconian and nouvelle recipes. *Weinmarkt 3, tel. 0911/225–131. Reservations required. Jacket and tie required. AE, DC, V. Closed Sat., Sun. lunch, Mon., first week in Jan., and 1 week in June. Expensive.*

★ **Romantik-Restaurant Rottner.** Located in the Grossreuth-Schweinau suburb, southwest of the city center, the gingerbread-house exterior is a foretaste of the delights to be brought to your table in this family-run inn. The nouvelle style prevails here, even in regional dishes. In summer, your pheasant breasts in Franconian wine sauce can be sampled on the garden terrace. *Winterstr. 15, tel. 0911/612032. Dress: informal. MC. Closed Sat. lunch, Sun., and Dec. 27–Jan. 30. Expensive.*

Nassauer Keller. The exposed-beam-and-plaster decor complements the resolutely traditional cooking. Try the duck and the apple strudel. The restaurant has a memorable location in the cellar of a 12th-century tower by the church of St. Lorenz. *Karolinenstr. 2–4, tel. 0911/225–967. Reservations advised. Jacket and tie required. AE, DC, MC. Moderate.*

Bratwurst Haüsle. There are few better places to try Nürnberg's famous grilled sausages—roasted over an open fire and served on heavy pewter plates with horseradish and sauerkraut—than this dark, wood-paneled old inn. The mood is noisy and cheerful. *Rathauspl. 1, tel. 0911/227–695. Dress: informal. No credit cards. Closed Sun. Inexpensive.*

★ **Helig-Geist-Spital.** Heavy wood furnishings and a choice of more than 100 wines make this authentic and picturesque wine tavern a popular spot for visitors. It may be touristy, but it's the real thing for all that. *Spitalgasse 16, tel. 0911/221–761. Dress: informal. AE, DC, MC, V. Inexpensive.*

Lodging

Altea Hotel Carlton. This stylish old hotel, sturdy in a grande-dame way, is quietly efficient and offers thick-carpeted, old-fashioned luxury. The restaurant is plushly expensive and a pleasure in the summer, when you can sit out on the shaded terrace. It's located on a quiet side street close to the train station. *Eilgutstr. 13, tel. 0911/20030. 115 rooms and 5 suites with bath. Facilities: restaurant, bar, sauna. AE, DC, MC, V. Very Expensive.*

Maritim. If you value modern convenience over Old World charm, consider staying in this luxuriously modern hotel, opened in 1986. You won't find so much as a hint of the medieval glories of old Nürnberg here, but the service is impeccable, the spacious rooms are tastefully (if blandly) furnished, and the public areas are elegantly well-heeled. It's located just south of the historic area. *Frauentorgraben 11, tel. 0911/23630. 316 rooms with bath. Facilities: 2 restaurants, bar, sauna, indoor pool, solarium, parking. AE, DC, MC, V. Very Expensive.*

Am Josephplatz. This 150-year-old lodging in the heart of the city's old center was completely renovated in 1987 and now belongs to the Romantik Hotels chain. The neo-Gothic facade is today a protected monument, but the rooms behind it are decorated in a contemporary style. There's no restaurant, but a solid buffet breakfast is served to guests. *Josephplatz 30, tel. 0911/241–156. 30 rooms with bath. Facilities: bar, sauna. AE, DC, MC. Closed Christmas–New Year's Day. Expensive.*

Burg-Hotel Grosses Haus, Burg-Hotel Kleines Haus. Two hotels, one name. Both are in the old town a few blocks from each other, and stand under the castle's gaze; both provide private-home comforts and facilities such as indoor pools and saunas. Their chief difference is in the price: The bigger hotel, Grosses Haus, offers smarter rooms bedecked with Laura Ashley fabrics, and better views (it's next to Dürer's house), and subsequently is costlier than its smaller sister. Neither has a restaurant. *Grosses Haus: Lammsgasse 3, tel. 0911/204414. 42 rooms and 4 suites with bath. AE, DC, MC, V. Expensive. Kleines Haus: Schildgasse 16, tel. 0911/203040. 22 rooms with bath. AE, DC, MC, V. Moderate.*

Regensburg

Dining

★ **Bischofshof am Dom.** A gourmet oasis amid the simplicity and heft of the regional fare, this restaurant rates high among prestigious European food critics. Try the lobster soup and duck in honey sauce if they're on the menu. *Krauterermarkt 3, tel. 0941/59086. Reservations advised. Dress: informal. AE, DC, MC, V. Expensive.*

Alter Simpl. Next to the town hall (Rathaus) in the old town center, this hostelry exudes history. Sit in one of the cozy nooks and crannies and try one of chef Harry Flashar's fresh beef steaks, a specialty of the house. *Fischgassl 4, tel. 0941/999–395. Reservations not necessary. Dress: informal. No credit cards. Closed Sun. Moderate.*

Reissbierbrauer. The atmosphere in this former church is pure Bavarian, down to the checked blue-and-white tablecloths. The menu features pork, sausages, and dumplings. *Am*

Schwanenpl., tel. 0941/55581. Reservations advised. Dress: informal. No credit cards. Moderate.

Lodging ★ **Parkhotel Maximilian.** A handsome 18th-century building in the old town with memorably exotic public areas, this is the most elegant and sophisticated hotel in Regensburg. Bedrooms are less opulent, but all are intelligently and comfortably decorated. If you're feeling homesick, there's an American-style steakhouse. *Maximilianstr. 28, tel. 0941/51042. 53 rooms with bath. Facilities: 3 restaurants, café, parking. AE, DC, MC, V. Very Expensive.*

Kaiserhof am Dom. Stay here for the great view of the cathedral. The building itself oozes 18th-century charm, with exposed beams, stone walls, and rough plaster; however, some rooms are dull. Try to get one with a view. *Kramgasse 10, tel. 0941/54027. 31 rooms with bath. Facilities: restaurant. AE, MC. Closed Dec. 23–Jan. 6. Moderate.*

Roter Hahn. This small, modernized inn takes its name from the quiet narrow medieval street on which it's situated, wedged in the old town center close to the famous Stone Bridge over the Danube. Rooms are plain but comfortable and well serviced. *Rote Hahnengasse 10, tel. 0941/560–907. 27 rooms, some with shower. Facilities: restaurant. No credit cards. Inexpensive.*

The Arts

Opera Opera lovers cheerfully admit that there are few more intense operatic experiences than that offered by the annual **Wagner festival** in Bayreuth. The festival is held in July. If you want tickets, write to **Theaterkasse** (Luitpoldpl. 9, 8580 Bayreuth), but be warned: The waiting list is years long! You have only a slim chance of obtaining tickets unless you plan your visit a couple of years in advance. Rooms can be nearly impossible to find during the festival, too. If you don't get tickets, you can console yourself with visits to the exquisite 18th-century **Markgräfliches Opernhaus;** performances are given most nights in July and August. Check with the tourist office for details. A wide repertoire of opera is also offered at the **Landestheater** in Coburg, October through mid-July. Call 09561/95021 for tickets.

Concerts Ansbach hosts a **Bach Week** in odd-numbered years in early August. Contact **Geschäftsstelle im Rathaus** (Postfach 1741, 8800 Ansbach, tel. 0981/51243) for tickets. Bamberg is a city of music. The **Bamberg Symphony Orchestra** gives regular concerts; those in the cathedral, normally given with the Bamberg Choir, can be memorable. Call 0951/25256 for tickets. Organ concerts are given in the cathedral at noon every Saturday, May through October. You can catch opera and operetta at the **Hoffmann Theater** (Schillerpl. 5, tel. 0951/87498), September through July. In June and July, open-air performances are also given at the **Alte Hofhaltung.** Call 0951/25256 for tickets. Regensburg offers a range of musical experiences, though none so moving as a performance by the famous boys' choir **Domspatzen** (Cathedral Sparrows). The best-sung mass is held on Sunday at 9 AM. It can be a remarkable experience, and it's worth scheduling your visit to the city to hear the choir.

Theater The best theaters in Franconia are in Nürnberg and Regensburg. In Nürnberg, call 0911/22988 for tickets for all theaters. The leading theater in Regensburg is the **Stadttheater** (Bismarckpl. 7, tel. 0941/59156).

10 Rhineland Palatinate

Including Mainz and Worms

Introduction

For most travelers—even seasoned ones—the Rhineland means the spectacular stretch between Bingen (where the river leaves the Rheingau region and swings north) and the ancient city of Koblenz (at the mouth of the Mosel). But there's another part of the Rhineland where vineyards climb slopes crowned by ancient castles. This is the Rhineland Palatinate (Rheinland-Pfalz in German). It lacks the spectacular grandeur of the river above Bingen, the elegance of the resorts of Boppard and Koblenz, and the cachet of the wines of the Rheingau. But for that reason the crowds are smaller, the prices lower, and the pace slower. And there are attractions here you won't find in the more popular stretch of the river farther north, including the warmest climate in Germany. The south-facing folds of the Palatinate hills shelter communities where lemons, figs, and sweet chestnuts grow alongside vines. It's a region where few Autobahns penetrate and where most other roads lead to truly off-the-beaten-track territory. One of these roads is Germany's first specially designated Weinstrasse (Wine Road), a winding, often narrow route with temptations—vineyards and farmsteads that beckon the traveler to sample the current vintage. If you're covering the route by car, take along a nondrinker as co-driver, or split the driving between you. And take your time.

Where the Wine Road ends, three of Germany's oldest cities beckon: Speyer, Worms, and Mainz. They are among the Rhineland's great imperial centers, where emperors and princes met and where the three greatest Romanesque cathedrals in Europe stand. After covering the Wine Road, this chapter explores these cities. From the most northerly, Mainz, you are poised to explore the remainder of the Rhineland. (For full details, *see* Chapter 13.)

Essential Information

Important Addresses and Numbers

Tourist Information

Information on the Wine Road can be obtained from the **Weinstrasse Zentrale für Tourismus,** Postfach 2124, 6740 Landau; **Fremdenverkehrsverband,** Bezirksstelle Pfalz, Hindenburgstrasse 12, 6730 Neustadt an der Weinstrasse; and **Mittelhaardt-Deutsche Weinstrasse,** Weinstrasse 32, 6705 Deidesheim an der Weinstrasse. There are local tourist information offices in the following towns:

Bad Dürkheim. Verkehrsamt, Mannheimerstrasse 24, 6702 Bad Dürkheim, tel. 06322/793–276.
Deidesheim. Verkehrsamt Stadthalle, Bahnhofster., 6705 Deidesheim, tel. 06326/5021.
Landau. Verkehrsamt, Marktstrasse 50, 6740 Landau, tel. 06341/13180.
Neustadt an der Weinstrasse. Verkehrsamt, Exterstrasse 4, 6730 Neustadt an der Weinstrasse, tel. 06321/855–329.
Mainz. Verkehrsverein Mainz, Bahnhofstrasse 15, 6500 Mainz, tel. 06131/233–741.
Speyer. Verkehrsamt der Stadt Speyer, Maximilianstrasse 11, 6720 Speyer, tel. 06232/14395.

Worms. Verkehrsverein der Stadt Worms, Neumarkt 14, 6520 Worms, tel. 06241/853–560.

Car Rental **Avis:** Mainzer Landstrasse 170, tel. 069/23010, **Frankfurt;** Wormser Landstrasse 22, tel. 06232/32068, **Speyer;** Alzeyer Strasse 44, tel. 06241/591–081, **Worms.**
Europcar: Stephanstrasse 15, tel. 069/291028, **Frankfurt;** Rheinallee 107, tel. 06131/677073, **Mainz.**
Hertz: Hanauer Landstrasse 106–108, tel. 069/449–090, **Frankfurt;** Bensheimerstrasse 1, tel. 06241/43790, **Worms.**

Arriving and Departing by Plane

Frankfurt is the closest major international airport for the entire Rhineland, with regular flights from the United States. Autobahn access to Mainz, the northernmost point of the itinerary, is fast and easy. Stuttgart Airport serves the southern half of the region. Take Autobahn 8 to Karlsruhe and then drive the 36 kilometers (22 miles) to the southern point of the wine route.

Getting Around

By Car Most roads in the region are narrow and winding, a far cry from the highways of much of the rest of Germany. Autobahn 6 runs northeast/southwest across much of the southern part of the region, from Saarbrücken on the French border to the Rhine, reaching it just above Mannheim. Halfway along, a spur—Autobahn 61/63—branches north to Mainz. Driving conditions are good everywhere, with all roads well surfaced.

By Train Mainz is the only major city in the region with regular Intercity services; there are hourly connections to and from major German cities. To reach the southern part of the region, travel through Karlsruhe and Landau. Railroad buses service those towns not on the rail network.

By Bus Buses crisscross the region, with most services running to and from Mainz. Post buses connect smaller towns and villages. For information, timetables, and reservations, contact **Deutsche Touring GmBH** (Am Römerhof 17, 6000 Frankfurt/Main 90, tel. 069/79030).

Guided Tours

A number of the smaller towns and villages offer sightseeing tours in the summer, some including visits to neighboring vineyards. At Annweiler, for example, tours of the town are given on Wednesdays, beginning at the Rathaus at 10 AM, where you are given a glass of wine. The tourist office also organizes tours to Trifels Castle. Details of this and all other tours in the region are available from local tourist information offices. There are city tours of Speyer, Mainz, and Worms. Mainz also offers a walking tour of the old town on Saturdays starting at 10 AM. For details of all Rhine River tours, contact **Köln-Düsseldorfer Deutsche Rheinschiffahrt** (Frankenwerft 15, 5000 Köln 1, tel. 0221/208–8288).

Exploring the Rhineland Palatinate

Highlights for First-time Visitors

The Romanesque cathedrals of Speyer, Worms, and Mainz
Dörrenbach Village
Burg Trifels
Village of St. Martin
Gutenberg Museum, Mainz
Synagogue, Worms

Along the Wine Road

Numbers in the margin correspond to points of interest on the Rhineland Palatinate map.

Although the north end of the Wine Road is a favored starting point for many visitors because of its proximity to Mainz and Frankfurt, the logical place to begin your tour is at its south point, at the town in which the Wine Road itself began,
1 **Schweigen-Rechtenbach** on the French border. It was in this little wine village, in July 1935, that a group of vintners hit on the idea of establishing a tourist route through the vineyards of the region. To get the road off to a suitable start they put up a massive stone arch, the **Deutsches Weintor** (German Wine Gate). There's an open gallery halfway up the arch that offers a fine view of the vineyards that crowd the countryside between the Vosges Mountains, over the French border, and the Rhine, away to the east. Some of Schweigen's best wine comes from the vineyards on the French side of the border; you can walk across the frontier—it's only 200 yards from the arch—with no formalities and compare vintages. For a further investigation of the region's wines, follow the **Weinlehrpfad**, the "wine inspection path." It begins in Schweigen and ambles for about a mile through the vineyards of the nearby Sonnenberg. It was the first of scores of such walking routes that you'll find in wine-producing areas throughout Germany. The path is well marked and easy to follow.

Drive north on B-38 to Bad Bergzabern, 10 kilometers (6 miles) away. A mile before you reach the town, turn left to see the vil-
2 lage of **Dörrenbach.** It's an enchanting place, tucked snugly in a protective fold of the Palatinate hills. The Renaissance **Rathaus** (Town Hall) has a flower-hung facade, crisscrossed with so much timber there's hardly room for the tiny-paned windows.

Time Out The little spa town of **Bad Bergzabern** rivals any in Germany for harmonious Renaissance streets of half-timbered old houses. One of the most appealing—it has a distinctive painted bay window—houses the **Zum Engel** tavern. Its ancient interior makes an excellent layover for a cup of coffee, a beer, a glass of wine, and/or a bite to eat. *Königstr. 45, tel. 06343/4933. Closed Tues.*

3 Drive north, following the signs to **Klingenmünster,** 8 kilometers (5 miles) away. The village has the ruins of a 7th-century Benedictine monastery, with a still-intact Baroque chapel. If

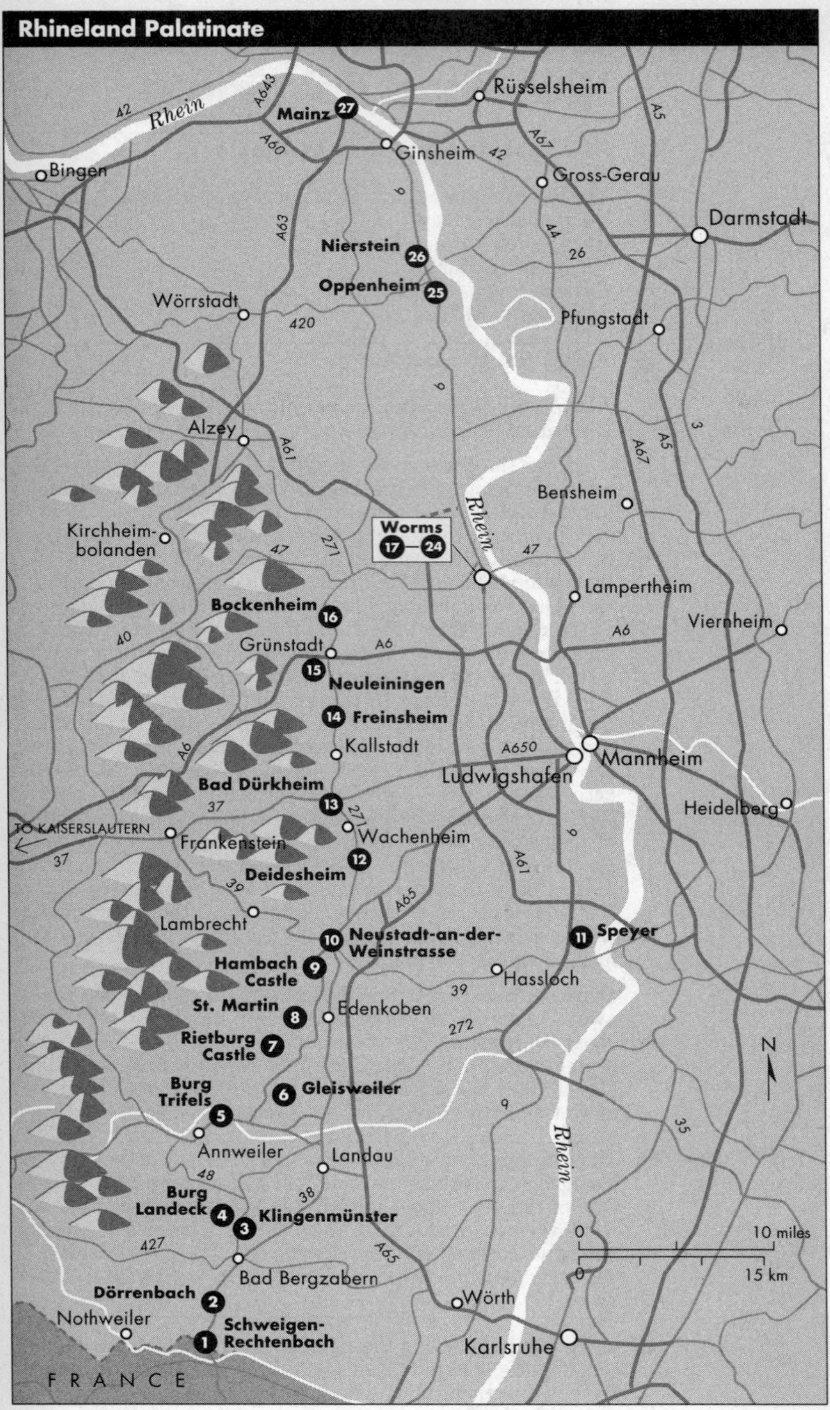
Rhineland Palatinate
Rhein
Mainz 27
Rüsselsheim
Ginsheim
Bingen
Gross-Gerau
Darmstadt
Nierstein 26
Oppenheim 25
Wörrstadt
Pfungstadt
Alzey
Bensheim
Kirchheim-bolanden
Worms 17—24
Lampertheim
Viernheim
Bockenheim 16
Grünstadt
15 Neuleiningen
14 Freinsheim
Kallstadt
Mannheim
Ludwigshafen
Bad Dürkheim
13
Heidelberg
TO KAISERSLAUTERN
Frankenstein
Wachenheim
12
Deidesheim
Lambrecht
10 Neustadt-an-der-Weinstrasse
11 Speyer
Hambach Castle 9
Hassloch
St. Martin 8
Edenkoben
Rietburg Castle 7
N
6 Gleisweiler
Burg Trifels 5
Annweiler
Landau
Burg Landeck 4
3 Klingenmünster
0
10 miles
15 km
Bad Bergzabern
Dörrenbach 2
Wörth
Nothweiler
1 Schweigen-Rechtenbach
Karlsruhe
FRANCE

castles are your thing, you can walk from the monastery to the
4 ruins of **Burg Landeck.** The walk, through silent woods of chestnut trees, takes about half an hour. Your reward will be a magnificent view from the castle over the Rhine Valley and south as far as the Black Forest.

There's a more spectacular, and more famous, castle another 8 kilometers (5 miles) north, outside the village of Annweiler.
5 This is **Burg Trifels,** one of the most romantic buildings in the country, its drama only slightly spoiled by the fact that what you see today is a rather free reconstruction of the original Romanesque castle, rebuilt in 1937 (a period when a lot of Germans were keen on reestablishing what they saw as the glories of their "race"). The original castle was constructed in the mid-12th century by the emperor Barbarossa, who once wrote: "Whoever has Trifels possesses the empire." In 1193, English King Richard the Lion-Hearted, captured by Barbarossa on one of Richard's endless forays across Europe, was held for ransom here (the English grudgingly paid the immense sum). Of more lasting significance was the fact that from 1126 to 1273 Burg Trifels housed the imperial crown jewels. That's what's said to have led to the legend that Burg Trifels was the site of the Holy Grail, the bowl used by Christ at the Last Supper. In the Middle Ages, the Holy Grail was the object of numerous knightly quests, the purpose of which was not so much to find the Grail as to prove one's steadfastness and Christian virtue by embarking on an impossible task. Replicas of the imperial crown jewels are on display in the castle museum. *Admission: DM 3 adults, DM 1.50 children under 14. Open Apr.–Sept., Tues.–Sun. 9–1 and 2–6; Oct.–Mar., Tues.–Sun. 9–1 and 2–5.*

If you visit Burg Trifels, you'll pass the ruins of two neighboring castles as you head up the hill. These are the castles of **Scharfenberg** and **Anebos.** Their craggy, overgrown silhouettes add greatly to the romance of a visit to Burg Trifels.

Head back to the Wine Road and follow the signs to **Edenkoben.** A drive of 12 kilometers (8 miles) will bring you to the little
6 town of **Gleisweiler,** reputedly the warmest spot in Germany. A flourishing subtropical park supports the claim. Further proof of the mild climate hereabouts is supplied by the fig trees that grow in abundance on many south-facing walls. This is also about the only area in Germany in which lemons are grown. The sun-drenched charms of the region attracted Bavaria's King Ludwig I in the middle of the 19th century. He called it "a garden of God" and compared its light to that of Italy. In the 1850s he built himself a summerhouse in the hills above the town; Edenkoben responded by putting up a statue of its royal guest in the main square. You can pay your respects to the Bavarian monarch by visiting his handsome neoclassical villa. Today it houses paintings by the German Impressionist Max Slevogt (1868–1932). The paintings have a certain dreamy charm, but many visitors will find the grandiose setting more diverting. *Villa Ludwigshohë. Admission: DM 3. Open Apr.–Sept., Tues.–Sun. 9–1 and 2–6; Oct.–Mar., Tues.–Sun. 9–1 and 2–5.*

On the opposite (north) side of the valley, facing the Villa
7 Ludwigshohë, are the ruins of **Rietburg Castle.** The only chair lift in the Rhineland Palatinate will whisk you up to them if you feel like checking out the terrific view.

Time Out The other reason for visiting Rietburg Castle is to have lunch on the terrace of the **café** here. Drink in the view as you eat.

Back on the Wine Road, a mile or two will bring you to the vil-
8 lage of **St. Martin.** It's said to be the most beautiful in the area, a reputation it nurtures by encouraging the surrounding vineyards to encroach on its narrow streets. You'll find vines clinging everywhere, linking the ancient houses with curling green garlands. Visit the little 15th-century church to see the imposing Renaissance tomb of the Dalberg family. Their castle, now romantically ruined, stands guard over the village.

There's another castle hereabouts you can visit, especially if your blood is stirred by tales of German nationalism and the
9 overthrow of tyranny. It's **Hambach Castle,** standing about a half mile outside the village of Hambach, itself about 8 kilometers (5 miles) north of St. Martin. It's not the castle, built in the 11th century and largely ruined in the 17th, that's the attraction. Rather, you'll visit to honor an event that happened here in May 1832. Fired by the revolutionary turmoil that was sweeping across Europe and groaning under the repressive yoke, as they saw it, of a distant and aristocratic government, 30,000 stalwart Germans assembled at the castle demanding democracy, the overthrow of the Bavarian ruling house of Wittelsbach, and a united Germany. The symbol of their heroic demands was a flag, striped red, black, and yellow, which they flew from the castle. The old order proved rather more robust than these proto-democrats had reckoned on; the crowd was rapidly dispersed with some loss of life. The new flag was banned. It was not until 1919 that the monarchy was ousted and a united Germany became fully democratic. Fittingly, the flag flown from Hambach nearly 90 years earlier was adopted as that of the new German nation. (It was a short-lived triumph: Hitler did away with both democracy and the flag when he came to power in 1932, and it was not until 1949, with the creation of the Federal Republic of Germany, that both were restored.) The castle remains a focus of the democratic aspirations of the Germans. Exhibits chart the progress of democracy in Germany. *Admission: DM 4 adults, DM 2.50 children. Open Mar.–Nov., daily 9–5.*

A mile or two north of Hambach, high rises announce the presence of the biggest town on the Wine Road and the most
10 important wine-producing center in the region, **Neustadt-an-der-Weinstrasse.** It's a bustling town, the narrow streets of its old center still following the medieval street plan. It's wine that makes Neustadt tick, and practically every shop seems linked with the wine trade. A remarkable 5,000 acres of vineyards lie within the official town limits. If you need to get your sightseeing fix, make for central Marktplatz to see the Gothic **Stiftskirche** (Collegiate Church). It's an austere Gothic building, constructed in the 14th century for the elector of the Rhineland Palatinate. Inside, a wall divides the church in two, a striking reminder of former religious strife. The church, indeed the whole region, became Protestant in the Reformation during the 16th century. At the beginning of the 18th century, the Catholic population of the town petitioned successfully to be allowed a share of the church. The choir (the area around the altar) was accordingly designated the Catholic half of the church, while the nave, the main body of the church, was reserved for the Protestants. To keep the squabbling communi-

ties apart, the wall was built inside the church. Is it an instance of religious tolerance or intolerance? And who got the better deal? As you wander around the church—be sure to look at the intricate 15th-century choir stalls and the little figures, monkeys, and vine leaves carved into the capitals of the nave columns—you can ponder these matters.

Time Out Duck into the ancient confines of the **Herberge aus der Zunftzeit** (Mittelgasse), a 14th-century tavern offering excellent local wines and specialties. Try a slice of *Zwiebelkuchen* (onion tart) and a glass of Kirchberg wine. *Closed Mon.*

---

11 If you have time, make the side trip to **Speyer,** 29 kilometers (18 miles) east of Neustadt on the west bank of the Rhine. Speyer was one of the great cities of the Holy Roman Empire, founded probably in Celtic times, taken over by the Romans, and expanded in the 11th century by the Ottonian Holy Roman Emperors. Between 1294 and 1570, no fewer than 50 full diets (meetings of the rulers of the Holy Roman Empire) were convened here. The focus of your visit will be the imperial cathedral, the **Kaiserdom,** one of the largest medieval churches in Europe, certainly one of the finest Romanesque cathedrals and a building that more than any other in Germany conveys the pomp and majesty of the early Holy Roman emperors. It was built in only 30 years, between 1030 and 1060, by the emperors Konrad II, Heinrich III, and Heinrich IV. A four-year restoration program in the 1950s returned the building to almost exactly its condition when first completed. If you have any interest in the achievements of the early Middle Ages, this is not a building to miss. Speyer Cathedral, thanks chiefly to the fact that later ages never saw fit to rebuild it, and partly to the intelligent restorations of the '50s, embodies all that is best in Romanesque architecture.

There's an understandable tendency to dismiss most Romanesque architecture as little more than a cruder version of Gothic, the style that followed it and that many consider the supreme architectural achievement of the Middle Ages. Where the Gothic is seen as delicate, soaring, and noble, the Romanesque by contrast seems lumpy and earthbound, more fortress-like than divine. It's true that even the most successful Romanesque buildings are ponderously massive, but they possess a severe confidence and potency that can be overwhelming. What's more, look carefully at the decorative details and you'll see vivid and often delicate craftsmanship.

See as much of the building from the outside as you can before you venture inside. You can walk most of the way around it, and there's a fine view of the east end from the park by the Rhine. If you've seen Köln Cathedral, the finest Gothic cathedral in Germany, you'll be struck at once by how much more massive Speyer Cathedral is in comparison. The few windows are small, as if crushed by the surrounding masonry. Notice, too, their round tops, a key characteristic of the style. The position of the space-rocket-like towers, four in all (two at either end), and the immense, smoothly sloping dome at the east end give the building a distinctive, animated profile; it has a barely suppressed energy and dynamism. Notice, too, how much of a piece it is; having been built all in one go, the church remains faithful to a single vision. Inside, the cathedral is dimly mysterious, stretching to the high altar in the distance. In contrast to Gothic cathedrals, whose walls are supported externally by flying buttresses, allowing the interior the minimum of masonry and the maximum of light, at Speyer the columns supporting the roof are massive. Their bulk naturally disguises the side aisles, drawing your eye to the altar. Look up at the roof; it's a shallow stone vault, the earliest such vaulted roof in Europe. Look, too, at the richly carved capitals of the columns, filled with naturalistic details—foliage, dogs, birds, faces.

No fewer than eight Holy Roman emperors are buried in the cathedral, including, fittingly enough, the three who built it. They lie in the crypt. This, too, should be visited to see its simple beauty, uninterrupted by anything save the barest minimum of decorative detail. The entrance is in the south aisle. *Kaiserdom. Open Mon.–Sat. 9–6, Sun. 2–6. For information about guided tours, call 06232/102–259.*

Treasures from the cathedral and the imperial tombs are kept in the city's excellent museum, the **Historisches Museum der Pfalz,** on nearby Grosses Pfaffengasse. In 1992 the museum staged a highly successful exhibition on the history of the Salier dynasty, and there were plans to extend the event into 1993. While the exhibition is on, the museum's permanent displays are closed to the public, as is the wine museum that is part of the complex. Both are scheduled to be open sometime in 1993. Check with the tourist office for details.

North to Worms

12 Back on the Wine Road, the wine town of **Deidesheim,** 6 kilometers (4 miles) from Neustadt, is the next stop north. It was here that the bishops of Speyer, among the most powerful clerics in Germany during the Middle Ages, had their administrative headquarters. Their former palace is now mostly a ruin, its moat a green and shady park. Make sure you see the town square, Marktplatz. It's bordered on three sides by flower-smothered, half-timbered houses, the whole forming one of the most picturesque ensembles in the Rhineland Palatinate. Climb the impressive stairway to the Rathaus (Town Hall); the entrance is through a curious porch crowned by a helmetlike roof and spire. Ask to view the fine wood-paneled assembly hall where councillors and envoys of successive bishops of Speyer haggled over church finances.

Time Out Look for the golden lion sign of the **Deidesheimer Hof** (Marktpl.) on the right side of the three-cornered market square. At the St. Urban wine tavern, in the cool interior of this ancient inn, you'll eat and drink in quiet comfort. Look, too, for the names Gerümpel and Goldbächel on the wine list: They are the very best the area has to offer.

Don't leave Deidesheim without strolling down the street called Feigengasse. It's named after the fig trees (*Feigen*) that grow in front of practically every house.

Eight kilometers (5 miles) and two charming wine villages (Forst and Wachenheim) farther, you'll reach another bustling
13 little Wine Road town: **Bad Dürkheim.** Bad Dürkheim has a boast that's hard to beat: a wine cask so big it contains a restaurant with seating for 420 (the Bad Dürkheimer Riesenfass, am Wurstmarktgelände). On weekends it reverberates to the mu-

sic of a brass band. In mid-September, it's the focal point of what the locals claim is the world's biggest wine festival, a week of revelry and partying during which the wine flows freely.

The **Pfälzerwald** nature park begins just beyond Bad Dürkheim's town limits. It's Germany's largest uninterrupted area of forest and a favorite stretch for hiking. If you don't fancy a full-fledged walking tour, at least give yourself an hour or two to experience its lonely, rugged grandeur.

Head north from Bad Dürkheim a couple of miles to Kallstadt.
14 Turn right to see **Freinsheim,** 4 kilometers (2½ miles) away. The little town is one of the best-preserved in the region, a winning combination of winding medieval streets and high-gabled, half-timbered buildings. A counterpoint to this toy-town charm is provided by the stately Baroque Rathaus (Town Hall), an elegantly classical building with an unusual covered staircase leading up to the imposing main entrance. Take a look, too, at the original medieval walls that still encircle the old town; conical-roofed towers punctuate them at rhythmic intervals.

More too-good-to-be-true charm is provided by the town of
15 **Neuleiningen,** 10 kilometers (6 miles) north of Kallstadt. Until quite recently, this was among the most backward and impoverished areas of the country. The people were called *Geesbocke,* or "billy goats," a mocking reference to the fact that these were the only animals they could afford to keep. The name lives on today in the village's most historic inn, Zum Geesbock. Stop in to sample a glass or two of local wine and to admire the Renais-
16 sance interior. The Wine Road ends at **Bockenheim,** 10 kilometers (6 miles) north of Neuleiningen.

Worms to Mainz

From Bockenheim, you can continue north along B-271 to Mainz and the Rheingau or make the detour to the ancient
17 imperial city of **Worms** (pronounced "Vawrms"). Why visit Worms? First, to see the great, gaunt Romanesque cathedral; it presents a less perfect expression of the Romanesque spirit than does Speyer Cathedral but exudes much of the same craggy magnificence. Second, because Worms, though devastated in World War II, is among the most ancient cities in Germany, founded as far back perhaps as 6,000 years ago, settled by the Romans, and later one of the major centers of the Holy Roman Empire. More than 100 diets of the empire were held here, including the one in 1521 before which Martin Luther came to plead his "heretical" case. Third, because Worms is one of the most important wine centers in Germany; anyone who has fallen under the spell of the Rhineland Palatinate's golden wines will want to sample more here. There's some industry on the outskirts of the city, but the rebuilt old town is compact and easy to explore.

It was the Romans who made Worms important, but it was a Burgundian tribe, established in Worms from the 5th century, that gave the city its most compelling legend—the Nibelungen. The story, written probably in the 12th century and considerably elaborated throughout the years, is complex and sprawling, telling of love, betrayal, greed, war, and death. It ends when the Nibelungen—the Burgundians—are defeated by Attila the Hun, their court destroyed, their treasure lost, their heroes dead. (One of the most famous incidents tells how Hagen, treacherous and scheming, hurls the court riches into the Rhine; by the Nibelungen bridge there's a bronze statue of him, caught in the act.)

The Nibelungen may be legend, but the story is based on historical fact. For instance, it's known that a Burgundian tribe was defeated, in present-day Hungary, by Attila the Hun in 437. Not until Charlemagne resettled Worms almost 400 years later, making it one of the major cities of his empire, did the city prosper again. Worms wasn't just an administrative and commercial center but a great ecclesiastical city as well. The first expression of this religious importance was the original cathedral, consecrated in 1018. In 1171 a new cathedral was started. This is the one you come to Worms to see.

Numbers in the margin correspond to points of interest on the Worms map.

If you've seen Speyer Cathedral, you'll quickly realize that
18 **Worms Cathedral,** by contrast, contains many Gothic elements. In part this is simply a matter of chronology. Speyer Cathedral was completed more than 100 years before the one at Worms was even begun, long before the lighter, more vertical lines of the Gothic style were developed. But there's another reason. Once built, Speyer Cathedral was left largely untouched in later periods; at Worms, the cathedral was remodeled frequently as new styles in architecture and new values developed. Nonetheless, as you walk around the building, you'll find that same muscular confidence, that same blocky massiveness as at Speyer. The ground plan of the church is similar, too, with two towers at each end, a prominent apse at the east end, and short transepts (the "arms" of the church). The Gothic influence is most obvious inside, especially in the great rose window at the west end (over the main entrance). It could almost be in a French church and presents a striking contrast to the tiny, round-headed windows high up in the nave. Notice, too, how a number of the main arches in the nave are pointed, a key characteristic of the Gothic style. It wasn't only in the Gothic period that the cathedral was altered, however. As you near the main altar you'll see the lavish Baroque screen of columns supporting an opulent gold crown that towers above the altar. This is the Baroque at its most potent. The choir stalls, installed in 1760, are equally opposed in spirit to the body of the church. Intricately carved and gilded, they proclaim the courtly and sophisticated glamour of the Rococo. *Open Apr.–Oct., daily 8–6; Nov.–Mar., daily 9–5.*

Outside the cathedral, cross the square to see the simple
19 **Dreifaltigkeit Church** (Church of the Holy Trinity). Remodeling of the church in the 19th century produced today's austere building (the facade and tower are still joyfully Baroque). It's a Lutheran church, and as good a place as any in the city to recall Luther's appearance in 1521 before the Holy Roman Emperor and massed ranks of Catholic theologians to defend his heretical beliefs. Luther ended his impassioned plea against the corruption of the church and for its reform (hence Reformation) with the ringing declaration, "Here I stand, I can do no different. God help me. Amen!" He was duly excommunicated. *Open Apr.–Oct., daily 8–6; Nov.–Mar., daily 9–5. Tours of the tower: second Sun. of the month at 2 and 4.*

Cathedral, **18**
Dreifaltigkeit Church, **19**
Judenfriedhof, **22**
Liebfrauenkirche, **24**
Lutherdenkmal, **20**
Städtisches Museum, **23**
Synagogue, **21**

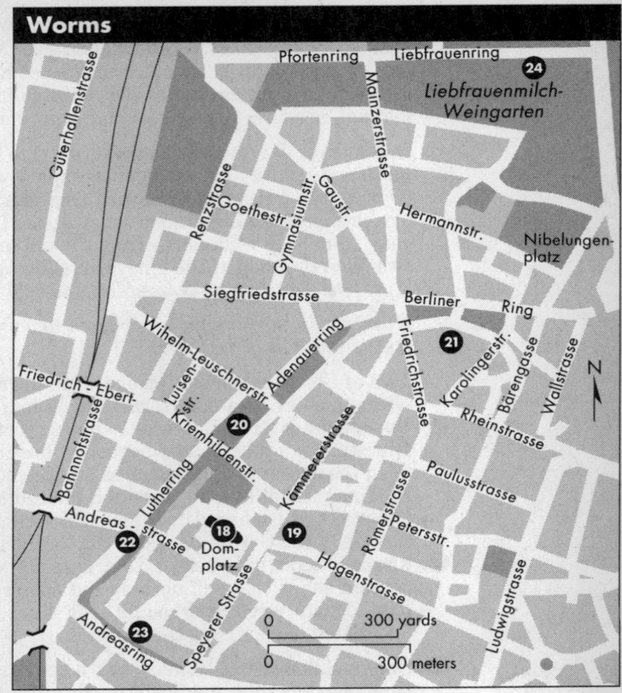

From the church, walk back past the cathedral to see the
20 **Lutherdenkmal,** a 19th-century group of statues of Luther and other figures from the Reformation. It's on the little area of grass next to the street called, appropriately enough, Lutherring.

Worms was also one of the most important Jewish cities in Germany, a role that came to a brutal end with the rise of the Nazis. From the Luther monument you can walk along
21 Lutherring to see the rebuilt **synagogue,** the oldest in the country. It was founded in the 11th century; in 1938, it was entirely destroyed. In 1961, the synagogue was rebuilt, using as much of the original masonry as had survived. Next to the synagogue, in a former Jewish family home, is the **Judaica Museum,** which documents the history of the Jewish community in Worms. The exhibits include artifacts from as far back as the 11th century. *Raschi-Haus, Judengasse. Admission: DM 2 adults, DM 1 children. Open Tues.–Sun. 10–noon and 2–5.*

22 The ancient Jewish cemetery, the **Judenfriedhof,** west of Domplatz off the Lutherring, can also be visited. *Admission free. Open daily 10–noon and 2–4.*

23 To bone up on the history of the city, visit the **Städtisches Museum** (Municipal Museum). It's housed in the cloisters of a former Romanesque church. *Weckerlingpl. Admission: DM 2 adults, DM 1 children. Open Tues.–Sun. 10–noon and 2–5.*

If you visit the city in late August or early September, you'll find it embroiled in its carnival, the improbably named Backfischfest, or Baked Fish Festival. The highlight is the **Fischer-**

stechen, a kind of water-borne jousting in which contestants spar with long poles while balancing on the wobbly decks of flat-bottom boats. The winner is crowned King of the River; the losers get a dunking. Baked fish is the culinary highlight of the festival, of course. The wine is never in short supply.

Don't leave Worms without visiting the vineyard that gave
birth to Germany's most famous export wine, Liebfraumilch
(Our Lady's Milk). The vineyard encircles the Gothic pilgrim-
24 age church of the **Liebfrauen** convent, the **Liebfrauenkirche,** an
easy 20-minute walk north from the old town. Buy a bottle or
two from the shop at the vineyard. *Church and vineyard open Apr.–Oct., daily 9–6; Nov.–Mar., daily 9–5.*

Numbers in the margin correspond to points of interest on the Rhineland Palatinate map.

Two of Germany's most famous wine towns—Oppenheim and
Nierstein—lie between Worms and Mainz, the end of this tour.
25 **Oppenheim** is 26 kilometers (16 miles) north of Worms on B-9;
Nierstein is a mile or two beyond. Oppenheim is said to have
been the center of Charlemagne's wine estates. Take a look at
the fine market square, fussily bordered on all sides by time-
honored half-timbered buildings. Then climb the steep stepped
streets to the Gothic church of St. Catherine, the **Katharinen-**
26 **kirche. Nierstein** is a town that lives for wine; entire streets
contain shops that sell nothing but the precious liquid. Many
have ornate wood or wrought-iron signs, brilliantly painted
and gilded, advertising their wares.

27 Sixteen kilometers (10 miles) north lies the city of **Mainz,** a bustling, businesslike but friendly Rhine-side city, with a brilliantly planned central pedestrian zone that makes touring on foot a breeze. All streets lead to the spacious market square, flattened in the war but since rebuilt with its medieval flavor intact. Watching over the square with the dignity of age is the sturdy, turreted **cathedral,** the third of the great Romanesque cathedrals of the Rhine. Step inside and silence falls about you like a cloak. One thousand years of history accompany you through the aisles and chapels. The first cathedral here—dedicated to Sts. Martin and Stephan—was built at the end of the 10th century. In 1002, Heinrich I, the last Saxon emperor of the Holy Roman Empire, was crowned in the still-far-from-complete building. In 1009, on the very day of its consecration, the cathedral burned to the ground. Rebuilding began almost immediately. The cathedral you see today was largely finished at the end of the 11th century. Substantial sections were rebuilt at the end of World War II. Before that, in the 18th century, an imposing Baroque spire was constructed; similarly, in the Gothic period, rebuilding and remodeling did much to alter the Romanesque purity of the original. With all these additions and modifications, can the cathedral really be considered Romanesque? The answer has to be yes, if only because its ground plan links it so firmly to the cathedrals at Speyer and Mainz. Notice the towers at each end and the spires that rise between them; one may be Baroque, but its positioning and something of its bold impact produce an effect that is nothing if not Romanesque. Inside, though pointed arches proliferate, the walls have the same grim, fortresslike massiveness of Speyer. True, there's more stained glass, but the weight of masonry is full-fledged Romanesque. The **Dom und Diözesan Museum** (Cathedral Treasury and Museum) contains a series of rich ecclesiasti-

cal objects that will appeal to anyone with a taste for the intricate skills of medieval and Renaissance craftsmen. *Admission free. Open Mon.–Sat. 9–noon and 2–5. Closed Thurs. and Sat. afternoons.*

Opposite the east end of the cathedral on Liebfrauenplatz is one of the most popular attractions in the Rhineland, the **Gutenberg Museum.** It charts the life and times of Mainz's most famous—and unquestionably most influential—son, Johannes Gutenberg (1390–1468). It was in Mainz, in 1456, that Gutenberg built the first machine that could print from movable type. The significance of his invention was immense, leading to an explosion in the availability of information. This wasn't actually the building in which Gutenberg worked; that's long since disappeared, but a vivid sense of his original workshop is conveyed. There's a fine reconstruction of his printing machine, as well as exhibits charting the development of printing and bookbinding. But the highlight must be the copy of the Gutenberg Bible, one of only 47 extant, not only one of the most historically significant books in the world but surely one of the most beautiful. Gutenberg played such a central role in the history and life of Mainz that he has his own festival, *Johannisnacht,* in mid-June. *Liebfrauenpl. 5. Admission free. Open Tues.–Sat. 10–5, Sun. 10–1.*

From the Gutenberg Museum, return to the 20th century by crossing Rheinstrasse to the **Rathaus** (Town Hall). This is no ancient structure but an unashamedly modern glass-and-concrete building put up in the 1970s. Opinions have been divided over its merits for as long as the building's been here.

For another example of modern Mainz, take a look at the church of **St. Stephan.** It's on Willigisplatz, ½ mile south of the Rathaus. You'll walk through the rebuilt old town on your way there, an example of sensitive reconstruction following near-total destruction in the war. The church itself is one of the oldest single-nave Gothic buildings in this part of the Rhineland. But look at the stained glass in the choir; it was designed by Russian-born painter Marc Chagall in the 1970s. Its vivid coloring is a strangely beautiful complement to the austere Gothic design of the rest of the church.

Mainz claims to put on the wildest pre-Lent carnival in Germany. Be here in early February if you want to put that boast to the test. The city erupts in a Rhineland riot of revelry, the high point of which is the procession through the old town.

What to See and Do with Children

On the Wine Road you'll find what is claimed to be one of Europe's biggest leisure parks, the **Hassloch Holidaypark.** It's at Hassloch, on B-39 between Neustadt and Speyer. A circus, a dolphinarium, a replica of the Lilliputians' town from the book *Gulliver's Travels,* an adventure playground, and an elaborate medieval mock-up, the "Robber Knights of Falkenstein Mountain," number among the attractions. *6733 Hassloch-Pfalz, tel. 06324/599–3900. Admission: DM 18 adults, DM 12 children. Open mid-Mar.–Oct., daily 9–6.*

There's another, smaller park, the **Kurpfalz Park,** close by at Wachenheim, between Deidesheim and Bad Dürkheim. It has all the fun of the fair, plus a wildlife park. *Tel. 06325/2077. Ad-*

mission: DM 12 adults, DM 8 children. Open Easter–Oct., daily 9–6. The wildlife park is open year-round.

Nierstein has two museums, both in the Altes Rathaus on Marktplatz, that seem to fascinate youngsters. One is the **Palaeontological Museum,** considerably more interesting than it sounds, with a 265-million-year-old fly among the exhibits. *Admission free. Open Sun. only 10–1.*

The other is the **Schiffartmuseum,** the Shipping Museum, which charts in graphic form the history of shipping on the Rhine. *Admission free. Open Sun. only 10–noon.*

If **zoos** are your thing, there's a little one at Landau. *Hinderburgstr. 12. Admission: DM 3.50 adults, DM 1.50 children under 14. Open daily 9–6.*

Neustadt has a **railway museum,** packed with old-timers from the age of steam. *Neustadt railway station, Schillerstr. entrance, tel. 06231/30390. Admission: DM 4 adults, DM 2 children. Open Sat. 9–4, Sun. 10–9:30.*

There's a marvelous display of more than 15,000 **toy soldiers,** calculated to make every schoolboy's heart beat faster, in a private museum housed in the vaulted basement of the **Wilms book shop** in Bad Bergzaubern. *Weinstr. 153, tel. 06321/35254. Admission free. Open Mon.–Fri. 9–6, Sat. 9–noon.*

There's a charming wildlife park with an adventure playground at Silz, the **Wildpark Südliche Weinstrasse.** Every second Sunday, May through October, there is a children's fest. *Admission: DM 4 adults, DM 2 children. Open 8:30–dusk.*

Children can scramble up the artificial sand dunes at **Freizeitbad Moby Dick,** a water sports–oriented leisure center in Rülzheim, south of Landau. *Tel. 07272/8337. Admission: DM 18.50 adults, DM 10 children. Open Tues.–Sun. 10 AM–10 PM, Mon. 1PM–10 PM.*

Off the Beaten Track

Climb through the woods above the town of **Frankenstein** on A-37, between Kaiserslautern and Mannheim, to the ruins of the medieval castle that watches over the ugly, brooding town. Whether it's the castle that helped inspire Mary Shelley, author of *Frankenstein,* no one knows, but it's easy to imagine how a romantic soul might be stirred by the ruins.

Stroll through the groves of sweet **chestnut trees** in the hills above Bad Dürkheim. They're among the few remaining in Germany, the descendants of saplings planted by the Romans 2,000 years ago.

The click and whir of roulette balls may not suggest an off-the-beaten-track activity, but Bad Dürkheim's little **casino** is definitely a change from the high rollers of Baden-Baden and Mainz. If you fancy a quiet flutter, try your luck here. *Men must wear a jacket and tie. Open daily 2 PM–2 AM. Admission DM 5.*

If plants are your passion, seek out the unusual **Kakteenland Bisnaga** at Steinfeld, just north of the French border. This is cactus country, with more than 1,000 different spiny and spiky species. *Wengelspfad 1. Admission free. Open weekdays 8–5.*

In nearby Nothweiler there's an ancient iron mine, the **St. Anna Ironworks,** that's now open to visitors. The mine is said to date from Celtic times, before the birth of Christ. *Open Apr.–Oct., Mon.–Sat. 2–6, Sun. noon–5.*

Shopping

Shopping in the Rhineland Palatinate means **wine.** This is a region that's given over to wine, and you'll find entire streets in many towns and villages dominated by shops devoted to the product of the grape. Likewise, vineyards along the roadside invite you in to pass judgment on the year's vintage. **Karl Sauter** in Neustadt-an-der-Weinstrasse (118 Hampstr.) is a walking encyclopedia of knowledge, and his shop is one of the best places to pick up a gift box of the area's best. The **Winzergenossenschaft Vier Jahreszeiten-Kloster Limburg** is a group of vintners who won a federal gold medal of honor in 1986 for their wine promotion; you're in very good hands with any of its members. The organization has its headquarters and cellars at Limburgerstrasse 8, Bad Dürkheim. It's open Monday through Friday 8–noon and 1–5, Saturday 8:30–12:30. One of its leading members, **Heinz Kroning,** opens his extensive cellars for visitors on Tuesday.

Wineglasses, bottle openers (some of them elaborately carved from local wood), and **wine coolers** are among other gift ideas. Worms' tourist office (Neumarkt 14) sells the most original wine cooler, a terra-cotta replica of a Roman example unearthed by archaeologists.

Also try the **Winzergenossenschaft** at Edenkoben (Weinstr. 130, open daily). In the same town, **Studio Rhodt** (Theresienstr. 111) has an interesting selection of handmade ceramics for sale.

Antiques hunters report that it's worthwhile digging through two shops in Worms: **Antik-Markt** (Hochheimerstr. 76) and **Antik Schimmel** (Kammererstr. 48). The city also has a **flea market;** it's held Saturdays in March, June, September, and December in the city's main parking lot, near the Rhine. Mainz has a famous **flea market,** the Krempelmarkt, held along the banks of the Rhine every third Saturday of the month (except Apr. and Oct.).

Pirmasens, on the edge of the Palatinate forest, the Pfälzerwald, is Germany's shoe center; it can be worth a detour from the Wine Road to stock up on a pair or two. While in the area, why not make the trip 32 kilometers (20 miles) northwest to Homberg, on the Saarbrucken–Kaiserslautern road, for a homberg from the town that gave the famous hat its name?

Sports and Fitness

Bicycling The vineyard-lined country roads on either side of the Wine Road are a cyclist's dream. You can rent bikes at any of the main train stations for DM 12 a day (DM 6 if you have a valid train ticket). Many of the towns and villages along the Wine Road also have shops where you can rent a bike. In Annweiler, try the **Fahrradgeschäft Seel** (Gerbergasse 27); in Bad Dürkheim, **Fahrradverleih Thyssen** (Schlossgartenstr. 3); and in Neustadt, the **Firma Rottmayer** (Remigiusstr. 13).

Climbing The sandstone cliffs of the Palatinate forest, the Pfälzerwald, are fun and relatively safe to tackle. The tourist office in **Annweiler am Trifels** (tel. 06346/2200) will tell you where the best climbing can be found.

Golf The Palatinate has its own golf club, the **Golf Club Pfalz e.V.,** with an 18-hole course at Geinsheim, near Neustadt an der Weinstrasse (tel. 06327/2973). Visitors are welcome. There's also a club at Bad Kreuznach (tel. 06708/2145).

Hiking You can cover the entire Wine Road on foot, along a clearly marked trail that winds its way between the vineyards covering the slopes of the Palatinate forest. Maps and information can be obtained from the **Fremdenverkehrsverband** (Bezirkstelle Pfalz, Exterstr. 4, 6730 Neustadt an der Weinstrasse). The **Wasgau nature park** on the edge of the Palatinate forest is also fine walking country, and the tourist office at Dahn offers a vacation package that includes not only overnight stops but a walking stick and a bottle of locally made schnapps to help you cover the distance between them. Contact the **Fremdenverkehrsbüro Dahn** (Schulstr. 29, 6783 Dahn, tel. 06391/5811).

Horseback Riding There is ample opportunity in this fine riding country. Recommended stables include **Gerd Helbig's Reiterhof** at Silz (tel. 06346/5927); the **Gut Hohenberg** (tel. 06346/2592); and the **Ferien und Reiterhof Münz** (tel. 06346/5272). All are near Annweiler am Trifels.

Swimming There are open-air and indoor pools in many parts of the Rhineland Palatinate. One of the biggest swimming complexes in Germany is in **Wörth** (on Autobahn 65, between Landau and Karlsruhe). The **Wörth Badepark** (Bad-Allee) has 10 pools, a wave machine, and two water slides, each more than 80 yards long. **Speyer's** lido (Geibstr. 4) also has a spectacular water slide. There are thermal baths at **Bad Bergzabern** and **Bad Dürkheim;** here you can splash around in warm pools overlooking the sun-drenched vineyards that clothe the hills around the town.

Tennis Tennis players will find courts in most towns and villages. Those at **Bad Dürkheim** are so beautifully located that you might have difficulty concentrating on the game; make reservations at the **Papillon Cafe** (tel. 06322/793–275). Speyer has a tennis club that accepts visitors: the **Tennisclub Weiss-Rot** (Holzstr., tel. 06232/67979).

Dining and Lodging

Dining

Though Mainz can offer more elegant dining, in most of the towns and villages of the Rhineland Palatinate you'll eat local specialties in local inns. Sausages are more popular here than in almost any other area of the country, with the herb-flavored *Pfälzer* a favorite. *Hase im Topf,* a highly flavored rabbit pâté made with port, Madeira, brandy, and red wine, is another specialty to look for. The Rhineland Palatinate, though not geographically the largest wine-producing area in the country, nonetheless produces more wine than does any other region in Germany, and all restaurants will have a range of wines to offer.

Highly recommended restaurants in each price category are indicated by a star ★.

Category	Cost*
Very Expensive	over DM 90
Expensive	DM 55–90
Moderate	DM 35–55
Inexpensive	under DM 35

**per person for a three-course meal, not including drinks*

Lodging

Accommodations are plentiful, with those along the Wine Road mostly simple and inexpensive inns. The region has many bed-and-breakfasts; keep an eye open for signs reading *Zimmer Frei,* meaning "rooms available." If you plan to visit during any of the wine festivals in the late summer and fall, make reservations well in advance—and expect higher prices.

Highly recommended hotels in each price category are indicated by a star ★.

Category	Cost*
Very Expensive	over DM 180
Expensive	DM 120–DM 180
Moderate	DM 80–DM 120
Inexpensive	under DM 80

**All prices are for two people in a double room.*

Annweiler
Dining

Burg-Restaurant Trifels. Eat in the shadows of Burg Trifels, where Richard the Lion-Hearted once stayed in less happy circumstances. In summer, try for a table on the terrace; the view is terrific. Palatinate specialties—including delicious dumplings—are featured on the menu. *Auf den Schlossackern, tel. 06346/8479. Dress: informal. MC, V. Moderate.*

Lodging

Pension Bergterrasse. The Michel family runs this quiet country pension like a real home-away-from-home and are ready with holiday help, ranging from the best wines to try to the most picturesque forest paths to walk. They'll even lend you a bike. *Trifelsstr. 8, tel. 06346/7219. 25 rooms with bath. Facilities: restaurant, wine bar, garden. No credit cards. Inexpensive.*

Zum Goldenen Lamm. At this half-timbered country inn at Ramberg, 7 kilometers (4.5 miles) north of Annweiler, the Lergenmüller family carries on an old rural tradition of supplying beer, wine, and meat to the neighborhood—there's a butcher shop in the inn! *6741 Ramberg, tel. 06345/8286. 26 rooms with bath. Facilities: restaurant. No credit cards. Restaurant closed Tues. Inexpensive.*

Bad Dürkheim
Dining
★

Bad Dürkheimer Riesenfass. This must be Germany's most unusual restaurant, located in the biggest wine barrel in the world, with room for 420 people inside and an additional 230 on the terrace. The food, like the wine, is robustly local. It's touristy but fun. *Am Wurstmarktgelände, tel. 06322/2143. Reservations advised. Dress: informal. No credit cards. Moderate.*

Restaurant-Weinstube Käsbüro. Despite the name—it means "cheese office"—this historic old tavern specializes in fish and game dishes. It's located about a mile from the center of Bad Dürkheim, in Seebach, and is well worth hunting out. *Dorfpl., Seebach, tel. 06322/8694. Reservations advised. Dress: informal. MC, V. Moderate.*

Lodging

Kurparkhotel. Ask for a room overlooking the little spa park; on summer evenings you'll be serenaded by the orchestra that plays on its bandstand. Rooms are large and airy, and some have views of the vineyards above the town. Temptation lurks in the lobby—the hotel has direct access to the spa's casino. *Schlosspl. 1–4, tel. 06322/7970. 110 rooms with bath. Facilities: restaurant, bar, terrace, garden, sauna, solarium, indoor thermal pool, spa, beauty salon. AE, DC, MC, V. Very Expensive.*

Garten-Hotel Heusser. The Garten Hotel-Heusser describes itself as an "oasis of peace"—and it's not much of an exaggeration. There are vineyards all around, and most rooms have fine views of the rolling Palatinate countryside. One disadvantage: This vineyard oasis is a thirsty 20-minute walk from the town center. *Seebacherstr. 50–52, tel. 06322/2066. 76 rooms with bath. Facilities: restaurant, outdoor and indoor pools, sauna, solarium. AE, DC, MC, V. Expensive.*

Landhaus Fluch. In this recently built, tastefully decorated hotel in the Seebach district, every room has a flower-decked balcony with forest views. You'll greet the day with a copious buffet breakfast. *Seebacherstr. 95, tel. 06322/2488. 24 rooms with bath. Facilities: gardens, parking. No credit cards. Closed Dec. 20–Jan. 15. Moderate.*

Deidesheim
Dining

★ **Zur Kanne.** Seasoned Wine Road travelers know that this place is worth making time for. The historic walls of what claims to be the oldest inn in the Rhineland Palatinate contain a small restaurant whose fame has spread throughout the region. Try any of the local specialties; they're prepared with flair and imagination. *Brennessel* (nettle) soup is a reliable favorite. *Weinstr. 31, tel. 06326/396. Reservations advised. Jacket and tie required. DC, MC, V. Closed Tues. Expensive.*

Lodging

★ **Deidesheimer Hof.** This is the showpiece hotel of the Deidesheim-based Hahnhof group, a country-wide chain of wine restaurants. It's a traditional old Deidesheimer house, immaculately clean and comfortable, and run with slick but friendly efficiency. *Am Marktpl., tel. 06326/1811. 26 rooms, most with bath. Facilities: restaurant, wine tavern. AE, DC, MC, V. Moderate–Expensive.*

Grünstadt
Lodging

Pfalzhotel Asselheim. This fine old country hotel stands on the outskirts of Grünstadt, a town near the north end of the Wine Road. Surrounded by vineyards, the Pfalzhotel is situated near the edge of the Pfälzerwald nature park. Low beams, fine wood paneling, rustic antiques, and huge tiled ovens combine harmoniously in the restaurant and public areas—even the indoor swimming pool has half-timbered walls. The bedrooms aren't quite so atmospheric, but they are modern and comfortable. *Holzweg 6, Grünstadt-Asselheim, tel. 06359/800399. 30 rooms with bath or shower. Facilities: restaurant, wine tavern, wine garden, indoor pool, sauna, bowling, table tennis, bike rental. AE, DC, MC, V. Moderate.*

Mainz
Dining
★ **Gourmet Restaurant Rheingrill.** This is the restaurant of the Hilton. Ask for a table overlooking the Rhine. The food is distinctly upscale and nouvelle. If lobster with black noodles is on the menu, be sure to try it. The game dishes are also good. *Rheinstr. 68, tel. 06131/245–129. Reservations advised. Jacket and tie required. AE, DC, MC, V. Closed Mon. Expensive.*

Kartäuser Hof. If the weather is warm, try for a table in the walled courtyard, a pretty sun trap smothered in flowers in the summer. There's a warm welcome at any time of year, however, in this pleasant restaurant that often features locally caught fish. There's also an impressive wine list, dominated by local vineyards. *Kartäuser Str. 14, tel. 06131/222956. Dress: informal. Reservations advised. AE, DC, MC, V. Moderate.*

★ **Rats- und Zunftstuben Heilig Geist.** The most atmospheric dining in Mainz is offered here. Parts of the building date from Roman times, but most of it is Gothic, with vaulted ceilings and stone floors. The menu features Bavarian specialties with nouvelle touches. *Rentengasse 2, tel. 06131/225–757. Reservations advised. Dress: informal. AE, DC, MC. Closed Sun. dinner and Mon. Inexpensive.*

Weinhaus Schreiner. Mainz's oldest wine tavern has been in the hands of the Schreiner family since the mid-18th century and has won many awards from the local Vintner's Association. The menu is shorter than the wine list, but it's full of robust Palatinate fare. If marinated beef Rhineland style is on when you visit, it's your lucky day. *Rheinstr. 38, tel. 06131/225720. Reservations not necessary. Dress: casual. No credit cards. Inexpensive.*

Lodging
★ **Hilton International.** A terrific location right by the Rhine, allied with the reliable standards of comfort and service expected of the chain, make the Hilton the number-one choice in Mainz. Don't expect to find much in the way of old German atmosphere. The Rheingrill restaurant is exceptional (*see* above). *Rheinstr. 68, tel. 06131/2450. 435 rooms and 14 suites, all with bath. Facilities: 2 restaurants, hair salon, shopping mall, gym, sauna, solarium, casino. AE, DC, MC, V. Very Expensive.*

Hotel-Restaurant Am Lerchenberg. The location isn't ideal—some 6½ kilometers (4 miles) from the city center—but this family-run hotel is friendly, comfortable, and peaceful, and there's a bus stop right outside the door. This could be a very good choice, though, if you're interested in biking and hiking—open countryside is only a few steps away. *Hindemithstr. 5, tel. 06131/73001. 53 rooms with shower. Facilities: restaurant, sun terrace, garden, sauna, solarium, fitness room. AE, DC, MC, V. Expensive–Moderate.*

Hotel Pfeil-Continental. This centrally located hotel shares the building with the tourist office, so advice and information are close at hand. The Pfeil faces a busy street, so try for a room at the back. There's no restaurant, but the immediate vicinity has a wide choice of eating places. The guest rooms are simply furnished and clean. *Bahnhofstr. 15, tel. 06131/232179. 31 rooms, 22 with bath/shower. MC. Moderate–Inexpensive.*

Zum Schildknecht. In this picturesque medieval house—one of the oldest in Mainz—you climb steep stairs to reach cozy bedrooms tucked under the steep-eaved roof. There's a wine tavern on the ground floor (serving wine from its own vineyard), so expect some noise at night. *Heiliggrabgasse 6, tel. 06131/*

225755. 11 rooms, 8 with bath/shower. No credit cards. Inexpensive.

Neustadt-an-der-Weinstrasse
Dining

Ratsherrenstuben. On Mondays in the quiet courtyard of the half-timbered building that houses the Ratsherrenstuben, you'll find a corner where a fraternity of Neustadt vintners have met for centuries to discuss business. Afterward, they adjourn to the restaurant. Join them in sampling the local wines and full-bodied local specialties. *Marktpl. 10–12, tel. 06321/2070. Reservations advised. Dress: informal. DC, MC, V. Closed Wed. Moderate.*

Zur Festwiese. You'll find above-average local and regional cuisine in this hotel restaurant in a pleasant town-center location. See if the popular *Pfälzer* sausage is on the day's menu *Festplatzstr. 6, tel. 06321/32506. Dress: informal. AE, DC, MC, V. Closed Sun. dinner. Moderate.*

Weinstube Eselsburg. A consummate artist is in charge here. The tavern's jovial landlord finds time between serving creative Palatinate dishes to sketch and paint. He sings, too—the evenings can lengthen into quite a party. The tavern is in the Musbach area of Neustadt, a 10-minute drive from the town center. *Kurpfalzstr. 62, Neustadt-Mussbach, tel. 06321/66984. Dress: informal. No credit cards. Inexpensive.*

Lodging

Burckshof. Its conical turrets and high gables make the Burckshof easy to spot among the vineyards beyond Neustadt. And this elegant little palace of a hotel is well worth finding (it's between the villages of Gimmeldingen and Königsbach). Sample a local wine on the balustraded terrace or in the hotel's charming garden. *6730 Neustadt 15, tel. 06321/66016. 21 rooms, most with bath. No credit cards. Moderate.*

Pfalzgraf. Centrally located in the pedestrian zone, no more than a minute's walk from the train station, this hotel is in a tastefully modernized turn-of-the-century building. Ask for a mansard room; they're small but cozy. *Friedrichstr. 2, tel. 06321/2185. 31 rooms, most with bath. Facilities: restaurant, café. AE, DC, MC, V. Moderate.*

Speyer
Dining
★

Wirtschaft zum Alten Engel. Regional dishes from the Palatinate and the French Alsace region dominate the menu in this historic cellar tavern in the heart of the city. Try the mushroom gratinée. *Mühlturmstr. 1a, tel. 06232/76732. Reservations advised. Dress: informal. AE, DC, MC. Closed lunch, Sat. and Aug. Moderate.*

Lodging

Goldener Engel. The "Golden Angel" has been in business since 1701 and offers simple, time-honored atmosphere allied with appealing modern comfort. There's no restaurant, but it adjoins the Wirtschaft zum Alten Engel (*see* above). *Mühlturmstr. 27, tel. 06232/76732. 41 rooms and 2 suites with bath. AE, DC, MC, V. Expensive.*

Hotel Kurpfalz. This is a turn-of-the-century villa, fully renovated and given a convincing Old World atmosphere. It's family-run and small. There's no restaurant. *Mühlturmstr. 5, tel. 06232/24168. 10 rooms and 1 suite, all with bath. AE, DC, MC. Moderate.*

Worms
Dining
★

Rotisserie Dubs. Make the trek to Wolfgang Dubs's sleekly appointed restaurant to eat his excellent steak in snail sauce, a substantially more appetizing dish than it sounds. The restaurant is located in the suburb of Rheindürkheim, a 10-minute ride from downtown. *Kirchstr. 6, tel. 06242/2023. Reservations* *required. Jacket and tie required. MC. Closed Sat. lunch, Tues., and 2 weeks in July. Expensive.*

Bacchus. The name here is apt: This is the place if you want to drink some of the best wine in the region. The food is ample, with local specialties predominating. *Obermarkt 10, tel. 06241/6913. Reservations advised. Jacket and tie required. AE, DC, MC, V. Moderate.*

Lodging **Central.** Although a few miles southwest of Worms, in Frankenthal, this well-equipped hotel makes a good base. *Karolinenstr. 6, tel. 06233/8780. 80 rooms with bath. Facilities: indoor pool, sauna, squash courts, bowling alley, hairdresser, 2 restaurants, bar. AE, DC, MC, V. Expensive.*

Dom Hotel. This is the best hotel in Worms, modern and centrally located, though offering little more than functional comfort. The Bacchus restaurant (*see* above) compensates, however. *Obermarkt 10, tel. 06241/6913. 60 rooms with bath. Facilities: restaurant. AE, DC, MC, V. Moderate.*

The Arts and Nightlife

The Arts

Music Regular organ- and chamber-music concerts are given in the three great Romanesque cathedrals of the area—in **Mainz, Speyer,** and **Worms.** Mainz also has an annual **cathedral-music festival** that lasts through the summer. Organ recitals are given in the cathedral every Saturday at noon from mid-August to mid-September. Classical-music concerts are also given regularly at the **Kurfürstliches Schloss** (Diether-von-Isenburg-Str., tel. 06131/228–729). Speyer is developing a taste for music since its musical celebrations in 1990 marking the town's 2,000th anniversary. Concerts are scheduled for early fall. Contact the local tourist office for details.

Theater The area's theatrical activity is concentrated in Mainz. The city's resident company, the **Theater der Landeshauptstadt Mainz,** performs regularly in the Grosses Haus, Gutenbergerplatz, and at two other smaller venues; call 06131/123–365 or 06131/123–366 for program details and tickets. The Palatinate has its own repertory theater company, the **Pfalz Theater** in Kaiserslautern (Fruchthallstr. 24, tel. 0631/80020). In the summer it tours the region, giving performances in local theaters and in many of the area's ruined castles. Worms has a city theater, the **Städtisches Spiel und Festhaus,** where concerts and drama productions are staged. For program details and tickets, contact the box office on Rathenaustrasse or call 06241/22525. In Speyer, the city's theater is the **Stadthalle** (Obere Langgasse); contact the local tourist office, the Verkehrsamt (Maximilianstr. 11), for program details and tickets.

Nightlife

Mainz and Bad Dürkheim both have **casinos,** with adjacent bars for celebrating a lucky evening or drowning losers' sorrows. Bad Dürkheim's nightlife is otherwise crammed into Friday and Saturday nights at the Dorint Hotel's **Cotton Club** dance bar. In **Mainz,** night owls make for the Altstadt, the old town. The central Marktplatz is the scene of a nightly program of open-air pop music, jazz, and street cabaret from May through

September. Worms has a square-dance club, **The Crackers,** which welcomes guests. Call 06241/23400 if you'd like to join in. The discotheques and bars of **Worms** are concentrated around Judengasse. If you tire of the wine taverns of the Wine Road, try the exotic **Bahama Club** (Landauerstr. 65) in Neustadt-an-der-Weinstrasse. Neustadt has surprisingly upbeat nightlife; **Madison** (am Kartoffelmarkt 2) is the "in" place.

Wine Festivals

The wine festivals of the towns and villages of the Wine Road are numerous enough to take up several vacations. From late May through October, the entire area seems to be caught up in one long celebration. The most important festivals are the **Dürkheimer Wurstmarkt** (Germany's biggest wine festival), in mid-September; the **Weinlesefest,** in Neustadt-an-der-Weinstrasse (with the coronation of the local Wine Queen), in the first week of October; Schweigen-Rechtenbach's **Rebenblütenfest,** in the first week of July; Bad Bergzabern's **Böhammerfest,** in early July; Landau's **Herbstmarkt,** in mid-September; Edenkoben's **Südliches Weinstrasse Grosses Weinfest,** in late September; and the **Mainzer Weinmarkt** in Mainz's Volkspark, the last weekend of August and the first weekend of September.

11 Heidelberg and the Neckar Valley

Including Stuttgart

Introduction

It may lack the dramatic beauty and historic resonance of the Rhine, but the Neckar River has attractions enough to make a tour along its banks a memorable vacation. This chapter covers its most distinctive stretch, from Mannheim, where the Neckar empties into the Rhine, just 80 kilometers (55 miles) south of Frankfurt, to Heilbronn, and from there continues on to Stuttgart. For much of the route, you'll be driving along the Burgenstrasse, the Castle Road (this section of the Neckar has proportionately more castles than any comparable stretch of the Rhine). From Mannheim, whose industrial suburbs enclose a city of surprising charm, the route runs southeast to the ancient university town of Heidelberg, for many the apotheosis of romantic Germany. With the exception of a detour south to the town of Schwetzingen (glorying in the name "Germany's asparagus capital"), the route next snakes its scenic way east, then south, between the river and the wooded slopes of the Odenwald Forest, before hitting the rolling, vine-covered countryside around Heilbronn. After that, it's a 49-kilometer (30-mile) drive, partly along the Neckar, to Stuttgart.

It's a busy road—this is not off-the-beaten-track territory—but there are plenty of opportunities along the way to escape into quiet side valleys and to visit little towns that sleep in leafy peace. You'll find just as much to charm you here as along the Romantic Road, but little of the tourist hype. Scarcely one of these towns is without its guardian castle, standing in stern splendor above medieval streets. This is a region that can delight—and sometimes surprise—even the most hardened traveler.

Essential Information

Important Addresses and Numbers

Tourist Information

For information on the entire Burgenstrasse, contact **Arbeitsgemeinschaft Burgenstrasse,** Rathaus, Marktplatz, 7100 Heilbronn, tel. 07131/562–271. There are local tourist information offices in the following towns and cities:

Bad Wimpfen: Verkehrsamt, Marktplatz 1, 7107 Bad Wimpfen, tel. 07063/7052.
Heidelberg: Verkehrsverein Heidelberg, Friedrich-Ebert-Anlage 2, 6900 Heidelberg, tel. 06221/21341.
Heilbronn: Verkehrsverein Heilbronn, Rathaus, Marktplatz, 7100 Heilbronn, tel. 07131/562–270.
Mannheim: Tourist-Information, Bahnhofplatz 1, 6800 Mannheim 1, tel. 0621/101–011.
Mosbach: Städtisches Verkehrsamt, Rathaus, 6950 Mosbach, tel. 06261/82236.
Stuttgart: Verkehrsamt der Stadt Stuttgart, Lautenschlagerstrasse 3, 700 Stuttgart 1, tel. 0711/22280.

Car Rental

Avis: Karlsruherstrasse 43, tel. 06221/22215, **Heidelberg;** Salzstrasse 112, tel. 07131/72077, **Heilbronn;** Augartenstrasse 112–114, tel. 0621/442091, **Mannheim;** Katharinenstrasse 18, tel. 0711/241441, **Stuttgart.**
Europcar: Bergheimerstrasse 159, tel. 06221/20845, **Heidelberg;** Neckarauerstrasse 50–52, tel. 0621/852055, **Mannheim;**

Hertz: Kurfürstenanlage 1, tel. 06221/23434, **Heidelberg;** Karl-Wüst-Strasse 30, tel. 07131/76061, **Heilbronn;** Friedrichsring 36, tel. 0621/22997, **Mannheim;** Leitzstrasse 51, tel. 0711/817233, **Stuttgart.**

Arriving and Departing by Plane

The nearest airports to the Neckar Valley are at Frankfurt and Stuttgart. There's fast and easy access by car and train to all major centers along the Neckar from both.

Getting Around

By Car Mannheim is a major junction of the Autobahn system, easily reached from all parts of the country. Heidelberg and Heilbronn are also served by Autobahn. A 15-minute drive on A-656 speeds you from Mannheim to Heidelberg; Heilbronn stands beside the east–west A-6 and the north–south A-81. The route followed in this chapter, the Burgenstrasse, also unromantically designated A-37, follows the north bank of the Neckar from Heidelberg to Mosbach, from which it runs down to Heilbronn as A-27. It's a busy road, and a fast one. If you need a change of pace, cross the river at Mosbach to Obrigheim and continue south on the slower B–39.

By Train Mannheim is West Germany's most important rail junction. Along with nearby Heidelberg, there are hourly Intercity trains to it from all major German cities. Mannheim is also a major stop for the new super-high-speed ICE service, which reaches 250 kilometers (155 miles) per hour on the Mannheim–Stuttgart stretch. There are express trains to Heilbronn from Heidelberg and Stuttgart. Local services link many of the smaller towns along the Neckar.

By Bus Europabus 189 runs the length of the Burgenstrasse daily from June through September. There are stops at towns and villages all along the Neckar. For information, timetables, and reservations, contact **Deutsche Touring GmBH** (Am Römerhof 17, 6000 Frankfurt/Main 90, tel. 069/79030). Local buses run from Mannheim, Heidelberg, Heilbronn, and Stuttgart to most places along the river; post buses connect the rest.

Guided Tours

City Tours There are guided tours of **Heidelberg** at 10 and 2 daily from May through October (Saturdays only, at 2, November through March, and 2 daily in April) from the train station and Bismarckplatz. Contact **Heidelberg Service** (tel. 06221/29641) or the tourist office (tel. 06221/21341) for details. The tours cost DM 16 (DM 11 for children).

In **Heilbronn,** the tourist office offers a **"Viertel nach Sechs"** tour, meaning "quarter after six," which is just when the tour begins (that's 6 PM!). The tours are given every Tuesday from early May through September; the cost is DM 6, and all tours end with a free glass of wine. On the first Wednesday in June, July, August, and September, tours are offered in a 1927 Paris city bus. The cost of DM 19.50 (DM 12.50 for children) includes a welcome-aboard drink. Contact the tourist office for details (tel. 07131/562270). Ten times a year (contact the tourist office for 1993 schedules), a "Heilbronn by Night" tour is offered. The DM 66 cost gives entry to no less than eight wine taverns and restaurants, with drinks and snacks in each; the tour ends at a strip club. There are daily bus tours of Mannheim, May through September, at 10. Tours leave from the Wasserturm and cost DM 12 (DM 9 for children).

The tourist office in **Stuttgart** offers daily two- and three-hour sightseeing tours of the city (weekends only November through March) as well as "Stuttgart by Night" tours in summer. For details, go to the tourist board "*i-Punkt*" (tel. 0711/2228240) in the underground Klett-Passage at the main train station.

Boat Tours The **Rhein-Neckar-Fahrgastschiffahrt** (RNF) company (tel. 06221/20181) offers boat rides from Heidelberg along the Neckar and down the Rhine to Speyer and Worms. From Easter through October, there are regular trips on the Neckar from Heilbronn. Contact **Personenschiffahrt Stumpf** (tel. 07131/85430) or the tourist office (tel. 07131/562–270) for details.

Exploring Heidelberg and the Neckar Valley

Highlights for First-time Visitors

Apothekenmuseum, Heidelberg
Hotel zum Ritter, Heidelberg
Klostergasse, Bad Wimpfen
Twelve Apostles Altar-Piece, Kurpfälzisches Museum, Heidelberg
The Renaissance Clock, Heilbronn Rathaus
The Quadratstadt, Mannheim
The views from the Philosophenweg and the Königstuhl, Heidelberg
Staatsgalerie, Stuttgart

Mannheim

Numbers in the margin correspond to points of interest on the Neckar Valley map.

The tour begins where the Neckar and the Rhine meet—at
1 **Mannheim,** a major industrial center and the second-largest river port in Europe. Inside its industrial sprawl lurks an elegant old town, carefully rebuilt after wartime bomb damage. Mannheim is unusual among the cities of the Rhine for having been founded only in 1606, but it's even more unusual for having been laid out on a grid pattern. It was the forward-looking Palatinate Elector Friedrich IV who built the city, imposing on it the rigid street plan that forms the heart of the old town, or Quadratstadt (literally, "squared town"). Streets running northeast–southwest—from one river to the other—are labeled A through U; those running northwest–southeast are numbered 1 through 7. So if you're looking for the central Marktplatz, it's G-1 on your map; if you're looking for the best restaurant in town—Da Gianni—it's R-7. Rationalism rules. The only exception to this system is Kurpfalzstrasse, which cuts through the heart of the town, leading southwest from the

Götz von Berlichingen (1480–1562). Von Berlichingen was a remarkable fellow. When he lost his right arm fighting in a petty dynastic squabble, the Landshut War of Succession, in 1504, he had a blacksmith fashion an iron one for him. The original designs for this fearsome artificial limb are on view in the castle, as is a suit of armor that belonged to him. Scenes from his life are also represented. For most Germans, the rambunctious knight is best remembered for a remark he delivered to the Palatinate elector and that was faithfully reproduced by Goethe in his play about von Berlichingen (called, simply, *Götz von Berlichingen).* Responding to a reprimand from the elector, von Berlichingen told him, more or less, to "kiss my ass" (the original German is substantially more earthy). To this day, the polite version of this insult is known as a "Götz von Berlichingen"; practice it on the Autobahn when a BMW screeches on its brakes, headlights flashing, inches from your rear bumper. *Admission: DM 2.50 adults, DM 1 children. Open Apr.–Nov., daily 9–5.*

During the Peasants' War (1525), Götz von Berlichingen and his
28 troops destroyed the fine medieval castle of **Horneck,** 5 kilometers (3 miles) upriver. It was subsequently rebuilt and stands in all its medieval glory. Once it was owned by the Teutonic Order of Knights; today it has a more mundane role as the retirement home of a German charity.

29 30 Two spas now await the tired traveler: **Bad Rappenau** and **Bad Wimpfen.** Bad Rappenau's brine baths are said to ease not just aching limbs but asthma, rheumatism, and circulatory problems, too. It's an attractive little town, with a picturesque Rathaus (Town Hall) that was once a moated castle. However, Bad Wimpfen, 10 kilometers (6 miles) farther, is of greater interest, a town rich in history and beauty. The Romans founded it, building a fortress here and a bridge across the Neckar in the 1st century AD. By the early Middle Ages, Bad Wimpfen had become an imperial center; the 12th-century Emperor Barbarossa built his largest palace here. Much of what remains of it can be visited, including the imperial living quarters with their stately pillared windows, from which the royal inhabitants enjoyed fine views of the river below. *Kaiserpl. Admission: DM 2. Open Apr.–Sept., Tues.–Sun. 9–noon and 2–5.*

After you've seen the fortress you'll want to explore the small, winding streets of the historic center, a picture-postcard jumble of Gothic and Renaissance buildings. **Klostergasse,** a stage set of a street, is the standout. If you want to see the town in more detail, follow the marked walking tour; it begins at the Rathaus and is marked by signs bearing the town arms, an eagle with a key in its beak. Highlights of the tour are two churches: the early Gothic Ritterstiftskirche (Knights' Church) of **Sts. Peter and Paul;** and the **parish church** on the market square, Marktplatz. Sts. Peter and Paul stands on a charming square, shaded by gnarled chestnut trees. The rough-hewn Romanesque facade is the oldest part of the church, left standing when the town ran out of money after rebuilding the remainder of the church in Gothic style during the 13th century. The outline of the walls of this original building are clearly visible on the floor inside. The cloisters are delightful, an example of German Gothic at its purest and most uncluttered. In the parish church, be sure to see the 13th-century stained glass; it's among the oldest in the country.

31 Motorbike fans won't want to miss the town of **Neckarsulm,** 10 kilometers (6 miles) up the valley. It's a busy little industrial center, home of the German automobile manufacturer Audi and site of the **Deutsches Zweirad Museum** (German Motorcycle Museum). It's located close by the NSU factory, where motorbikes were first manufactured in Germany. Among its 180 exhibits is the world's first mass-produced machine (the Hildebrand and Wolfmüller), a number of famous racing machines, and a rare Daimler machine, the first one made by that legendary name. The museum also has an exhibit of old bicycles, the oldest dating from 1817, and early automobiles. All are arranged over four floors in a handsome 400-year-old building that belonged to the Teutonic Order of Knights until 1806. *Urbanstr. 11. Admission: DM 5 adults, DM 3 children, DM 10 for a family ticket. Open daily 9–noon and 1:30–5.*

32 It's 6 kilometers (4 miles) now to the city of **Heilbronn.** The city owes its name to a "holy well," or Heiligen Brunnen, a little fountain that bubbles up out of the ground by the church of St. Kilian; it owes its fame to the Romantic German classic *Das Käthchen von Heilbronn,* by early 19th-century writer Heinrich von Kleist. The virtuous, put-upon Käthchen was modeled by von Kleist on the daughter of Heilbronn's lord mayor, and the family home still stands on the west side of the central square, Marktplatz. Its ornate oriel window, decorated with figures of four of the prophets, makes it easy to spot.

Most of the leading sights in Heilbronn are grouped in and around Marktplatz, dominated by the sturdy **Rathaus,** built in the Gothic style in 1417 and remodeled in the Renaissance. Set into its clean-lined Renaissance facade beneath the steeply eaved red roof is a magnificently ornate 16th-century **clock.** It's divided into four distinct parts. The lowest is an astronomical clock, showing the day of the week, the month, and the year. Above it is the main clock; note how its hour hand is larger than the minute hand, a convention common in the 16th century. Above this there's a smaller dial that shows the phases of the sun and the moon. Then, at the topmost level, suspended from a delicate stone surround, there's a bell, struck alternately by the two angels that stand on either side of it. Be here at noon, when the whole elaborate mechanism swings into action. As the hour strikes, an angel at the base of the clock sounds a trumpet; another turns an hour glass and counts the hours with a scepter. Simultaneously, the twin golden rams between them charge each other and lock horns while a cockerel spreads its wings and crows.

Time Out Heilbronn is one of the largest wine-producing cities in Germany, with more than 1,000 acres of vineyards within the city limits. Try any of the local wines in the historic tavern **Schwarzer Kater,** a short walk from the market square. *Lammgasse 2.*

Behind the market square is Heilbronn's most famous church, the **Kilianskirche** (Church of St. Kilian), dedicated to the Irish monk who brought Christianity to the Rhineland in the Dark Ages and lies buried in Würzburg. Its lofty Gothic tower was capped in the early 16th century with a fussy, lanternlike structure that ranks as the first major Renaissance work north of the Alps. At its summit there's a soldier carrying a banner decorated with the city arms. Walk around the church to the south side (the side opposite the main entrance) to see the well that gave the city its name.

Stuttgart

From Heilbronn it's a 49-kilometer (30-mile) drive south on B-
33 27 to **Stuttgart.** While the road follows along the Neckar only for a short distance, Stuttgart is located right on the river and can be considered as a logical extension of our tour of the Neckar Valley.

Stuttgart is a place of fairly extreme contradictions. It has been called, among other things, "Germany's biggest small town" and "the city where work is a pleasure." For centuries, Stuttgart, whose name derives from Stutengarten, or stud farm, remained a pastoral backwater along the Neckar. Then the Industrial Revolution propelled the city into the machine age, only to be leveled in World War II. Since then, Stuttgart has regained its position as one of Germany's top industrial centers.

Here, *schaffen*—"to do, make, produce"—is all. This is Germany's "can do" city, whose native sons have turned out Mercedes-Benz and Porsche cars, Bosch electrical equipment, and a host of other products exported worldwide. It is only fitting that one end of the main street, Königstrasse, is emblazoned with a neon sign proclaiming "Bosch" on a high rise, and the other end shines with the Mercedes star.

Yet Stuttgart is also a city of culture and the arts, with world-class museums and a famous ballet company. The city is also the domain of fine local wines; the vineyards actually approach the city center in a rim of green hills. In fact, forests, vineyards, meadows, fields, and orchards comprise more than half of the city, which is enclosed on three sides by seemingly endless woods.

An ideal introduction to the contrasts of Stuttgart is a guided city bus tour (*see* Guided Tours in Essential Information, above), including a visit to the needle-nosed TV tower, high on a mountaintop above the city, affording stupendous views. The tower, built in 1956, was the first of its kind in the world.

On your own, any exploration of Stuttgart would start at the Hauptbahnhof (main train station) end of Königstrasse, a pedestrian shopping street, continuing on to the **Schlossplatz** (Castle or Royal Square), a huge square enclosed by reconstructed royal palaces, with elegant arcades branching off to other stately plazas. The magnificent Baroque **Neues Schloss,** now occupied by the Baden-Württemberg state government offices, dominates the square.

Across the street is **Altes Schloss** (Old Castle), the former residence of the counts and dukes of Württemberg. Built as a moated castle around 1320, with wings added in the mid-15th century to turn this into a Renaissance palace, the Altes Schloss was considerably rebuilt between 1948 and 1970 to repair wartime damage. The palace now houses the **Württemberggisches Landesmuseum** (Württemberg State Museum), with imaginative exhibits tracing the development of the area from the Stone Age to modern times. The medieval displays are especially noteworthy. *Admission free. Open Tues.–Sun. 10–5, Wed. 10–7.*

Look into the neighboring **Stiftskirche** (Collegiate Church), on Schillerplatz, a late-Gothic church built in 1433–1531, before strolling through the Schlossgarten, on the other side of the Schlossplatz. If you continue in the park across Schillerstrasse, you'll come to the Park Wilhelma, with a zoo and botanical gardens. Here you can walk along the banks of the Neckar River.

For lovers of modern art and architecture the high point of a visit to Stuttgart is likely to be the **Staatsgalerie** (State Gallery), reached from the Oberer Schlossgarten by crossing Konrad-Adenauer-Strasse. The old part of the complex, dating from 1843, contains paintings from the Middle Ages through the 19th century, including works by Cranach, Holbein, Hals, Memling, Rubens, Rembrandt, Cézanne, Courbet, and Manet. Connected to the original building is the New State Gallery, designed by British architect James Stirling in 1984 as a melding of classical and modern, sometimes jarring, elements (such as chartreuse window mullions!). It's considered to be one of the most successful Post-Modern buildings, and now attracts more visitors than any other German museum. The building houses 20th-century art, with artists such as Braque, Chagall, de Chirico, Dali, Kandinsky, Klee, Mondrian, and Picasso represented. Look for Otto Dix's *Grossstadt (Big City)* tryptych, which distills the essence of 1920s Germany on canvas. *Konrad-Adenauer-Str. 30–32, tel. 071/2125050. Admission free. Open Wed. and Fri.–Sun. 10–5, Tues. and Thurs. 10–8.*

Time Out **Café Königsbau** (Königstr. 28, tel. 0711/290787) is a local institution, at once the city's most elegant and most popular café, ideally situated overlooking the Schlossplatz. Stop here for a coffee and a wedge of homemade Swabian apple cake, or a bottle of the locally brewed Dinkelacker beer.

Auto enthusiasts will want to venture somewhat out of town to visit the **Mercedes-Benz Museum,** at the oldest car factory in the world, to view the collection of historic racing and luxury cars on display, as well as pioneering engines for ships and planes. *Mercedesstrasse 136, Stuttgart-Untertürkheim. Admission free. Open Tues.–Sun. 9–5. Closed on public holidays.*

At the **Gottlieb Daimler Memorial Workshop,** where the first successful internal combustion engine was perfected, in 1883, you can see the tools, blueprints, and models of early cars that helped to pave the way for the Mercedes line. *Taubenheimstrasse 13, Stuttgart-Bad Cannstatt, tel. 071/1755588. Admission free. Open Apr.–Oct., daily 11–4.*

Perhaps only true auto aficionados will venture as far as the **Porsche Museum,** at the Porsche factory in the northern suburb of Zuffenhausen, to view a small but significant collection of legendary Porsche racing cars. Still, for those who care, it's worth the trip. *Porschestrasse 42, Stuttgart-Zuffenhausen, tel. 071/8275685. Admission free. Open Mon.–Fri. 9–12 and 1:30–4.*

What to See and Do with Children

The **Heidelberg** tourist office issues a special publication, *Heidelberg fur Kinder* ("Heidelberg for Children"), that lists activities and attractions. Pick it up free from any of the city's three tourist offices. The city has a **zoo** on the banks of the Neckar on

Tiergartenstrasse. *Admission: DM 6 adults, DM 3 children, DM 4 senior citizens and students. Open Apr.–Sept., Mon.–Thurs. and Sat. 9–7, Fri. 9–9, Sun. 10–6; Oct.–Mar., Mon.–Sat. 9–5.*

On the Königstuhl heights above the city there's a children's park and small fairground, the **Märchenparadies,** with fairy-tale tableaux, rides, a miniature railroad, and more. (Admission: DM 7 adults, DM 2 children. Open mid-Mar.–mid-Oct., daily 10–6.) Children love the ride up the mountain on the funicular, too (*see* Heidelberg, above).

The **Auto and Technik Museum** at Sinsheim, 20 kilometers (12 miles) south of Neckargemünd, offers 1,000 exhibits, encompassing the complete history of mechanized transportation. *Admission: DM 13 adults, DM 8 children. Open daily 9–6.*

There is more for auto fans 32 kilometers (20 miles) east of Heilbronn on the Burgstrasse at Langenburg. The **Deutsches Automuseum** (tel. 07905/1041) has a big collection of veteran cars and vintage racing vehicles. *Open Easter–Oct., daily 8:30–noon and 1:30–6.*

Twenty kilometers (12 miles) south of Heilbronn, on B–27, you'll find one of southern Germany's best fun parks, the **Freizeitpark Tripsdrill,** located at Cleebronn/Tripsdill. (Admission: DM 14 adults, DM 12 children. Open Easter–Nov., daily 9–6.) North of Heilbronn on the same road are some intriguing caves, the **Eberstädter Höhlen** (open daily 10–4).

Youngsters under age six are sure to be thrilled by the star show put on at the **Carl Zeiss Planetarium** in Stuttgart's Mittlerer Schlossgarten (younger children aren't allowed inside; it's feared they would disturb the cosmic hush of the presentations). *Admission: DM 6 adults, DM 3 children. Shows: Tues. and Thurs. 10 and 3; Wed. and Fri. 10, 3, and 8; weekends 2, 4, and 6.*

Off the Beaten Track

In **Heidelberg,** escape the crowds by crossing the Theodor Heuss Bridge to the north bank of the Neckar and climbing the heights above the river along the path called **Philosophenweg.**

Along the Neckar Valley road (B–27), all the small valleys—the locals call them "Klingen"—that cut north into the Odenwald are off-the-beaten-track territory. The most atmospheric of them all is the **Wolfsschlucht,** which starts below the castle at Zwingenberg. The dank, shadowy little gorge features in Carl Maria von Weber's opera *Der Freischütz.* If you see a vulture circling overhead, don't be alarmed. It's likely to be from Claus Fentzloff's unusual **aviary** at Guttenberg castle, farther along the Neckar Valley. He keeps vultures, eagles, and rare breeds of owls, showing them daily at 11 and 3, March through November.

For unusual musuems in Neckarland, try the **Lucky-Charm Museum** in Bad Wimpfen (Kronengässchen 2. Open Fri. 4–8, Sat.–Sun. 11–8) and the **Bonsai** museum of miniature trees in Heidelberg (Mannheimerstr. 401. Open Mon.–Fri. 10–6, Sat.–Sun. 10–4).

In Stuttgart, architecture buffs will want to seek out the **Weissenhofsiedlung** (Weissenhof Colony), a minicity created for a 1927 exhibition of the "New Home." Using a zoning plan designed by Mies van der Rohe, 16 leading architects from five countries—among them Mies, Le Corbusier, and Walter Gropius—were invited to create residences offering optimal living conditions at affordable prices. The still-functioning colony, which had a significant influence on the development of 20th-century housing, is situated on a hillside overlooking Friedrich-Ebert-Strasse. To get there from the city center, take the number 10 tram, in the direction of Killesberg, to the Kunstakadamie stop. The Stuttgart tourist office issues a brochure indicating which architects designed the various homes.

Shopping

Wine is the chief product of the Neckar region, and Heilbronn is the place to buy it. The city has an internationally renowned wine festival in the second week of September, the "Weindorf," where more than 200 wines from the Heilbronn region alone are offered. Outside festival time, you'll find numerous shops stocking wine in Heilbronn's central shopping zone, and you can also buy directly from vineyards. A good one to try is the **Amalienhof** (Lukas-Cranach-Weg 5).

There are numerous vineyards along the Neckar Valley road (B-27) between Heidelberg and Heilbronn. Those around **Gundelsheim** are judged to be the best, but for sheer historical worth you can't beat a bottle from the **Hornberg Castle** estate, which once stocked the table of the knight Götz von Berlichingen (*see* Along the Burgenstrasse in Exploring Heidelberg and the Neckar Valley, above).

The Neckar Valley is also famous for its **glass** and **crystal.** You can buy directly from the factory at Neckarzimmern or from Heidelberg shops such as **Crystal** (Hauptstr. 135) and **König** (Universitätspl.). Both are in Heidelberg's excellent pedestrian shopping zone, which stretches for more than ½ mile through the ancient heart of the city. Heilbronn also has an extensive central pedestrian shopping mall. In both cities, you can find interesting and often reasonably priced German **antiques.** In Heidelberg try **Spiess & Walther** (Friedrich-Ebert-Anlage 23a); in Heilbronn, take time to comb **Monika Finkbeiner's** well-stocked shop (Allee 38). Heidelberg has a **flea market** in the Dehner suburb every second Saturday.

Heidelberg has two tempting **markets.** On Wednesday and Sunday mornings, make for the central market square, Marktplatz; on Tuesday and Friday mornings, make for Friedrich-Ebert-Platz. Sunday's is a flea market; the others are a mixture of flea and green markets.

Mannheim is the city to head for to find German **fashions** at their best. A top selection is stocked by the **CC-Boutique** at number 17 Q-7 Street. Or comb the **Ova-Passage,** a stylish city shopping mall at number 6 on P-7 Street. **Stuttgart** is the home base of two of Germany's top men's fashion designers. You'll find them well represented at **Holy's** (Königstr 54). Designer jewelry is the specialty of Günter Krauss's glittering shop (Kronprinzenstr. 21); the design of the shop itself—walls of white Italian marble with gilded fixtures and mirrors—has won many awards.

Sports and Fitness

Bowling You can scatter the pins at Heidelberg's **Euro-Bowling Center** (Bergheimerstr. and Mittermaierstr., tel. 06221/23233).

Golf Visiting golfers can tee off with no problem at two Heidelberg clubs, the **Golfclub Heidelberg** in the neighboring village of Lobbach-Lobenfeld (tel. 06226/40490) and the **Hohenhardter Hof Club** (Wiesloch 4, tel. 06222/72081). In Heilbronn you can play at the **Golfclub Heilbronn-Hohenlohe,** in the village of Friedrichsruhe (tel. 07132/3680).

Hiking Stuttgart has a 53-kilometer (33-mile) network of marked hiking trails in the surrounding hills; follow the signs with the city's emblem, a horse, set in a yellow ring.

Horseback Riding In Heidelberg there are stables at the city **zoo** (tel. 06221/42728) and at Pleikartsforstenhof 5 (tel. 06221/32059). Heilbronn has a riding club where you can hire horses and also take lessons, the **Reiterverein Heilbronn** (Im Sternberg 5, tel. 07131/78469).

Roller-skating Wednesday night is disco night at the roller-skating rink at Heilbronn's **Europaplatz.** It's great fun. The rink is open daily from 9 to 9.

Swimming You'll find open-air and indoor swimming pools in all towns and most villages along your way. Heidelberg has a pool fed by thermal water at Vangerowstrasse 4, and pools at the extensive **Tiergartenschwimmbad** next to the zoo. Heilbronn's favorite lido, the **Freibad Neckarhalde,** has a view of the river. It's not advisable to swim in the Neckar River.

Tennis Most towns and villages along the Neckar have local tennis clubs that accept visitors. In Heidelberg, you can play at the **Kirchheimerweg** courts (tel. 06221/12106). In Heilbronn, the tennis schools at Böckingerstrasse 170 (tel. 07131/46166) and Viehweide 91 (tel. 07131/42905) can arrange lessons and partners.

Dining and Lodging

Dining

Heidelberg, Mannheim, and Stuttgart offer the most elegant dining in the region, though in Heidelberg you'll be dining with tradition at your table: There are few restaurants in the city that don't have decor to match the stage-set atmosphere of the town. Elsewhere, you'll find atmospheric and frequently excellent food in the restaurants of the castle hotels along the Neckar. In smaller towns along the valley, simple inns, dark and timbered, are the norm. Outside Heidelberg, Mannheim, and Stuttgart, prices can be low. Specialties in the Neckar Valley are much the same as those along the Wine Road, with sausages and local wines figuring prominently. Stuttgart's more modest restaurants feature one of Germany's truly great authentic regional cuisines, based on age-old Swabian recipes.

Highly recommended restaurants are indicated by a star ★.

Category	Cost*
Very Expensive	over DM 90
Expensive	DM 55–DM 90
Moderate	DM 35–DM 55
Inexpensive	under DM 35

**per person for a three-course meal including tax but not drinks*

Lodging

If you plan to visit Heidelberg in summer, make reservations well in advance and expect to pay top rates. To get away from the crowds, consider staying out of town—at Neckargemünd, say—and driving or taking the bus into the city. Staying in a castle hotel can be fun. This area is second only to the Rhine for baronial-style castle hotels studding the hilltops. Most have terrific views as well as stone-passageways-and-four-poster-bed atmosphere. Stuttgart's hotels cater, on the one hand, to the expense-account business traveler, along with jet-setters from around the world who come here to pick up their new Mercedes or Porsche at the source, and, on the other, to German families on holiday. Thus, Stuttgart boasts several luxury hotels as well as a wide range of family-style hotels at a relatively modest cost.

Highly recommended hotels are indicated by a star ★.

Category	Cost*
Very Expensive	over DM 180
Expensive	DM 120–DM 180
Moderate	DM 80–DM 120
Inexpensive	under DM 80

**Prices are for two people in a double room.*

Heidelberg
Dining

★ **Le Gourmet.** Elegant rusticity, complete with high-class nouvelle cuisine, obligatory exposed beams, stone walls, and wood ceilings, sums up the restaurant of the Hirschgasse Hotel. Herbs from the hotel's own garden are used extensively. *Hirschgasse 3, tel. 06221/403–2160. Reservations advised. Jacket and tie required. AE, DC, MC, V. Dinner only. Closed Sun., public holidays, and Dec. 23–Jan. 7. Very Expensive.*

Giardino. An Italian restaurant in Heidelberg? A paradox perhaps, but also quite an experience. Il Giardino is the elegant and smoothly run restaurant of the Prinzhotel, offering classic Italian cuisine. For best value, try the gourmet menu (the first course is a salad of fish and black truffles) at DM 118 per person. *Neuenheimer Landstr. 5, tel. 06221/40320. Reservations advised. Jacket and tie required. AE, DC, MC, V. Dinner only. Closed Tues. Expensive.*

★ **Zur Herrenmühle.** You'll sample delicately prepared classic French cuisine from pewter plates at rough-hewn tables at this atmospheric 17th-century tavern in the old town. Fish is the specialty here, and the desserts are noteworthy. In summer, diners can eat in a peaceful inner courtyard *Hauptstr. 237, tel.*

06221/12909. Reservations advised. Dress: informal. AE, DC, MC. Closed lunch. Moderate–Expensive.

Merian Stuben. Ornate 19th-century decor, high ceilings, and deferential uniformed waiters combine to give an unmistakably Victorian air to this restaurant. The large menu, ranging from local specialties to international dishes, is very correct, too. There are several rooms, but the most atmospheric one is on the ground floor. The Merian adjoins the Stadthalle beside the river, and in summer several tables are placed on a balustraded terrace, but a busy road disturbs the setting. *Neckarstaden 24, tel. 06221/27381. Reservations unnecessary. Dress: informal. AE, DC, MC, V. Closed Mon. and Jan. Moderate.*

★ **Romantik-Restaurant zum Ritter St. Georg.** The venison you eat here—dine in either the Knight's Tavern or the Alderman's Hall—comes from the restaurant's own hunting grounds outside Heidelberg. This is the restaurant of the most emphatically Teutonic hotel in town, and it offers a full-bodied taste of old-time Germany. *Hauptstr. 178, tel. 24272. Reservations advised. Dress: informal. AE, DC, MC, V. Moderate.*

Perkeo. Ask for a table in the atmospheric Schlosstube, and, if suckling pig is on the menu, ask for that, too. You'll then be dining in the style for which this historic old restaurant has been known for close to three centuries. *Hauptstr. 75, tel. 06221/160613. Reservations advised. Dress: informal. AE, DC, MC, V. Inexpensive.*

Schnookelooch. This picturesque and lively old tavern dates from 1407 and is inextricably linked with Heidelberg's history and its university. Most evenings a piano player joins the fun. *Haspelgasse 8, tel. 06221/22733. Reservations required. Dress: informal. No credit cards. Inexpensive.*

★ **Zum Roten Ochsen.** This is about the most famous and time-honored of Heidelberg's old taverns. Bismarck and Mark Twain ate here; so, too, many years later, did John Foster Dulles. It's been run by the Spengel family for more than a century, and they jealously guard the rough-hewn, half-timbered atmosphere. Many of the oak tables have initials carved into them, legacy of thousands of former visitors. The mood is festive and noisy, with rowdy singing most nights. *Hauptstr. 217, tel. 06221/20977. Reservations required. Dress: informal. No credit cards. Closed Sun., public holidays, and mid-Dec.–mid-Jan. Inexpensive.*

Lodging

★ **Europäischer Hof.** This is the classiest and most luxurious of Heidelberg's hotels, handy for about everything in town and with a wide range of facilities. Public rooms are sumptuously furnished, while bedrooms are spacious and tasteful. If you fancy a splurge, go for one of the suites; the best have Jacuzzis. *Friedrich-Ebert-Anlage 1, tel. 06221/5150. 137 rooms and 13 suites with bath. Facilities: shops, 6 whirlpools, beauty salon, restaurant, bar, courtyard gardens. AE, DC, MC, V. Very Expensive.*

★ **Hotel Hirschgasse.** Located across the river on the edge of town (which you may find inconvenient if you want to go back and forth more than once a day), the Hirschgasse is one of the oldest buildings in the area, with a 500-year-old history. First a farmhouse, later a tavern where university students indulged their fencing duels, the Hirschgasse is named in Mark Twain's *A Tramp Abroad.* Only Laura Ashley–style suites are available. The restaurant is exceptional. *Hirschgasse 3, tel. 06221/*

403–2160. 22 suites with bath. Facilities: restaurant. AE, DC, MC, V. Closed Dec. 23–Jan. 7. Very Expensive.

Prinzhotel. This is the elegant sister hotel of the Hirschgasse, but it is of late-19th-century origin. It's located across the river from the old town; fight for a room with a view of the river. *Neuenheimer Landstr. 5, tel. 06221/40320. 47 rooms and 3 suites, all with bath. Facilities: restaurant, whirlpool, sauna, steam bath, solarium. AE, DC, MC, V. Very Expensive.*

Holländer Hof. The yellow-and-white painted facade of this ornate 19th-century building beside a centuries-old pack-horse bridge stands out on the old-town waterfront of the Neckar River. Many of its timelessly furnished rooms overlook the busy waterway and the forested hillside above the opposite shore. *Neckarstaden 66, tel. 06221/12091. 38 rooms and 1 suite with bath. Facilities: restaurant, bar, baby-sitting service, sun terrace. AE, DC, MC, V. Expensive.*

★ **Romantik Hotel zum Ritter St. Georg.** If this is your first visit to Germany, stay here. It's the only Renaissance building in Heidelberg, and it offers atmosphere by the barrel-load. The Red Baron would feel right at home in the dining room, complete with suit of armor, rough plaster walls, arched doorways, and exposed beams. Bedrooms are clean and comfortable, some traditional, some more modern. *Hauptstr. 178, tel. 06221/24272. 31 rooms with bath. Facilities: restaurant. AE, DC, MC, V. Expensive.*

Central. This establishment provides simple overnight comforts only, but in an expensive town these are good-value lodgings on the castle side of the Neckar River, beneath the Königstuhl. Bed and breakfast only. *Kaiserstr. 75, tel. 06221/20672. 51 rooms with bath. AE, MC, V. Moderate.*

Gutsschänke Grenzhof. This small hotel on the rural fringes of Heidelberg in the district of Grenzhof has maintained some of the atmosphere of its former role as farmhouse. The hotel is set in expansive gardens, and walking trails skirt the front door. *Grenzhof No. 9, tel. 06202/3604. 10 rooms with bath. Facilities: restaurant (dinner only), café, beer garden. AE, MC. Moderate.*

Heilbronn

Dining

★ **Wirtshaus am Götzenturm.** This is no ordinary *Wirtshaus* (inn), but a charming and classy restaurant furnished with country antiques. Try one of the four-course, fixed-price menus; the wines are of equally good value. *Allerheiligenstr. 1, tel. 07131/80534. Reservations required. Jacket and tie required. No credit cards. Closed lunch and all day Sun. Expensive.*

Festhalle Harmonie. Eat on the terrace in summer to enjoy the view of the city park. Inside, the decor fuses traditional and modern styles. For best value, try one of the fixed-price menus. *Friedrich-Weber-Allee 28, tel. 07131/86890. Reservations required. Jacket and tie required. No credit cards. Closed most of Aug. Moderate.*

★ **Ratskeller.** For sturdy and dependable regional specialties—try Swabian *Maultaschen*, a kind of local ravioli—and as much Teutonic atmosphere as you'll ever want, you won't go wrong in this, the basement restaurant of the town hall. *Marktpl. 7, tel. 07131/84628. Reservations advised. Dress: informal. No credit cards. Closed Sun. dinner. Moderate.*

Lodging

Insel-Hotel. You'll sleep in the middle of the Neckar River and yet be within walking distance of Heilbronn's old-town center. *Insel* means "island," and that's where the luxurious Insel-Hotel is located, on a river island tethered to the city by the busy

Friedrich-Ebert Bridge. A family-run establishment, the Insel combines a personal touch with the sleek service and facilities expected of a large chain. Ask for a room overlooking the tree-fringed river—you'll have a view of its green banks and of the city spires beyond. *Friedrich-Ebert-Brücke, tel. 07131/6300, 120 rooms with bath. Facilities: restaurant, wine tavern, bar, terrace café, pool, sauna, solarium, parking. AE, DC, MC, V. Very Expensive.*

Hotel Zur Post. This sturdy hotel is run by the Mangler family, who offer their guests comfort and friendly service at a very reasonable price. Personal touches include bright prints on the pastel walls and fresh flowers. The Zur Post doesn't have a restaurant, but there's no shortage of places to eat in the neighborhood. The Mangler family also runs the nearby Hotel Allee-Post; ask for rooms there if the Zur Post is full. *Bismarckstr. 5, tel. 07131/627040. 20 rooms with shower. (Hotel Allee-Post, Titotstr. 12, tel. 07131/81656.) No credit cards. Moderate–Inexpensive.*

Hirschhorn
Dining and Lodging

Schlosshotel Hirschhorn. Not so much a castle hotel as a pleasant if undistinguished modern hotel in a castle, the Hirschhorn is perched on a hilltop overlooking the medieval village and the Neckar River, 22 kilometers (14 miles) east of Heidelberg. Hallways have that rough-plaster medieval look, lest you forget you're in a castle; rooms are furnished in approved Student Prince style. The views are terrific, and the restaurant much better than average. *6932 Hirschhorn/Neckar, tel. 06272/1373. 23 rooms and 2 suites with bath. Facilities: garden, restaurant, café. V. Closed Dec.–Jan. Expensive.*

Leimen

Hotel Seipel. Leimen, a pleasant wine village 6½ kilometers (4 miles) south of Heidelberg, is tennis star Boris Becker's hometown. The Seipel offers a viable alternative to more expensive accommodations in the larger cities of the Neckar Valley. It's a clean, modern hotel on the edge of a sports park and woodland. The rooms are furnished in dark red wood with dove-gray drapes and upholstery. *Am Sportpark, tel. 06224/7040. 30 rooms with bath. Facilities: reading room, fitness room, steam bath, solarium, parking. AE, DC, MC, V. Moderate.*

Mannheim
Dining

★ **Da Gianni.** Sophisticated Italian dishes, with a distinctly nouvelle accent, are served in this classy haunt in the Quadratstadt. Try the pigeon with artichoke or the homemade egg noodles with duck. *R–7 34, tel. 0621/20326. Reservations required. Jacket and tie required. AE, MC. Closed Mon. and 3 weeks in July. Very Expensive.*

★ **L'Epi d'Or.** French nouvelle cuisine and sophisticated local specialties are the hallmark of Norbert Dobler's city-center restaurant. The warm lobster salad is a classic; or try the saddle of lamb. *H–7 3, tel. 0621/14397. Reservations required. Jacket and tie required. AE, DC, MC, V. Closed Sun. and 2 weeks in June. Expensive.*

Alte Munz. For old German atmosphere, local specialties, and a wide range of beers, the Alte Munz is hard to beat. Try the suckling pig if it's available. *P–7 1, tel. 0621/28262. Reservations advised. Dress: informal. AE, MC, V. Moderate.*

Lodging

★ **Maritim Parkhotel.** It may be part of a chain, but the turn-of-the-century Parkhotel is the number-one choice in town, offering opulent comforts very much in the grand manner. The pillared, chandelier-hung lobby sets the mood; rooms are spaciously elegant. *Friedrichspl. 2, tel. 0621/45071. 187 rooms* *and 3 suites, all with bath. Facilities: restaurant, bar, indoor pool, sauna, steam bath, solarium, beauty salon, fitness room. AE, DC, MC, V. Very Expensive.*

Löwen-Seckenheim. This modest but comfortable modern hotel in the Seckenheim district has a popular tavern-style restaurant and in summer a beer garden. *Hauptrasse 159, tel. 0621/48080. 65 rooms, most with bath. Facilities: restaurant, bar. AE, MC. Closed Dec. 23–Jan. 7. Moderate.*

Page-Hotel. The Mannheim "Page" opened recently in a central location, offering a surprisingly high level of comfort for the moderate rates. Guest rooms are comfortably furnished in warm cherry wood. *Bismarckstr. L12, tel. 0621/10037. 62 rooms with bath. Facilities: restaurant, bar. AE, DC, MC, V. Moderate.*

Neckargemünd
Dining

Waibel's Gasthaus Neckartal. If the weather's fine, choose a table on the terrace, which commands a fine view of the river. But even if the river is obscured by fog, you'll still be glad you came, because Waibel's offers some of the best traditional specialties—in the fall, try the locally famous venison stew. *Ortsstr. 9, Rainbach, tel. 06223/2455. No reservations. Dress: informal. AE, MC. Closed Mon., Tues., and Jan. Inexpensive.*

Lodging

Hotel zum Ritter. Built in the 16th century, the half-timbered zum Ritter is an appealingly historic hotel overlooking the River Neckar, with exposed beams, and creaking passages. Ask for a room with a view. *Neckarstr. 40, tel. 06223/7035. 40 rooms with bath. AE, MC, V. Moderate–Expensive.*

Dining and Lodging

Zum Röss'l. The Röss'l has been catering to Neckar Valley travelers for nearly 350 years. You'll dine in a wood-paneled restaurant, choosing from a menu stocked from the Röss'l's own butcher shop or the nearby river. The Röss'l even has its own distillery, which produces an excellent brandy. Above the restaurant are 13 small but comfortably furnished rooms (a double is less than DM 90), six with bath. *Heidelberger Strasse 15, tel. 06223/2665. MC. Moderate.*

Neckarsulm
Lodging

Astron Hotel. Ask for a mansarde room at the newly built Astron—the rooms under the steep eaves are very cozy, decorated in harmonious pastel tones. Fresh flowers are a welcome touch. *Sulmstr. 2, tel. 07132/3880. 84 rooms with bath. Facilities: restaurant, bar, terrace, sauna, solarium, beauty salon, parking. AE, DC, MC, V. Expensive.*

Neckarzimmern
Dining and Lodging
★

Burg Hornberg. Midway between Heidelberg and Heilbronn stands the ancient castle where knight Götz von Berlichingen, immortalized by Goethe, spent his declining years. Some complain that it hasn't much panache for an 11th-century castle, but rooms are comfortable and some have great views over the hotel's own vineyards to the river. The restaurant features venison (in season) and fresh fish. *Neckarzimmern 6951, tel. 06261/4064. 27 rooms and 1 suite with bath. Facilities: garden, sun terrace, minigolf, wine bar, restaurant. MC, V. Expensive.*

Obrigheim
Dining and Lodging

Hotel Schloss Neuburg. This centuries-old sentinel castle stands high above the Neckar and the Odenwald. Sensitive modernization has ensured that many original features have been retained while many essential comforts have been added. Many bedrooms have oak beams. *Obrigheim 6952, tel. 06261/7001. 13 rooms with bath. Facilities: terrace restaurant. AE, DC, MC. Closed first 3 weeks in Jan. Moderate.*

Schwetzingen
Dining

Löwe. The "Lion" has been a favorite staging post for travelers for two centuries. The attractive old house, with its steeply eaved, dormer-windowed red roof, was originally a butcher shop and wine tavern. Now it's a very comfortable hotel and an excellent restaurant, although the wine tavern is still in place, basically unchanged. The restaurant serves imaginatively prepared Palatinate specialties (the marinated beef is a must), and the famous Schwetzingen asparagus dominates the menu throughout the summer. *Schlossstr. 4–6, tel. 06202/26066. AE, DC, MC, V. Moderate.*

Lodging

Hotel am Theater. Schwetzingen's delightful Rococo theater is just a few steps away from this newly built and stylish hotel—hence the name. Many of the comfortable, individually furnished rooms have views of the nearby palace park; for the best outlook and the coziest accommodation, ask for a room under the hotel's steep, dormered roof. *Hebelstr. 15, tel. 06202/10028. 19 rooms and 4 apartments, all with bath. Facilities: restaurant, terrace café, parking. AE, DC, MC, V. Moderate–Expensive.*

Stuttgart
Dining

Zeppelin-Stüble. Hearty down-home Swabian dishes are the specialties at this cozy restaurant in the fairly buttoned-up Steigenberger-Hotel Graf Zeppelin. At the top the list are *Maultaschen*, somewhat similar to Italian ravioli, served in a delicate broth, and *Spätzle*, the tiny dumplings that take the place of potatoes in this part of Germany. *Lautenschlagerstrasse 2, tel. 0711/224013. Reservations advised. Dress: informal. AE, DC, MC, V. Moderate–Expensive.*

Lodging

Am Schlossgarten. This modern eight-story glass and concrete luxury hotel is set in spacious gardens in the heart of the city, a stone's throw from the Staatstheater, the state parliament, and several other landmarks. The hotel's Schlossgarten Restaurant offers a mixture of international and regional dishes. Try the calves' tail soup with goose liver, and the turbot with leeks and lobster cream sauce. *Schillerstr. 23, tel. 0711–20260. 123 beds with bath. Facilities: 2 restaurants, garden café, sun terrace, bar. AE, DC, MC, V. Very Expensive.*

Zur Weinsteige. Hand-carved German oak bedsteads and cupboards furnish the more expensive rooms of this very comfortable, family-run hotel located south of the city's palace park. Settle for more conventional furnishings and the room rate drops considerably. Typical Baden-Württemberg style also dominates in the rustic restaurant and wine tavern, both of which are decorated with lots of carved wood, wrought iron, and colored glass. *Hohenheimer Str. 30, tel. 0711/245396. 23 rooms with bath. Facilities: parking. AE, DC, MC, V. Expensive–Moderate.*

The Arts and Nightlife

Information on all upcoming events in **Heidelberg** is listed in the monthly *Ketchup* magazine (which costs DM 3); the monthly *Konzerte im Heidelberger Stern* (available free—pick it up at the tourist office); and *Heidelberg Aktuell* (also free and available from the tourist office). The **Heilbronn** tourist office publishes a similar monthly listings magazine, *Heilbronn Today & Tomorrow;* it, too, is available free. Tickets for theaters in Heidelberg are available from **Theaterkasse** (Theaterstr. 4, tel. 06221/20519). In Heilbronn, you can buy tickets from the tourist office (07131/562–270). In addition to the English-language *Stuttgart's Theatres-Museums* booklet, with detailed information on the city's theaters and museums, the **Stuttgart** tourist office issues a monthly *Monatsspiegel* (DM 2 a copy) that lists all cultural, artistic, and sporting events scheduled for that period.

The Arts

Theater and Music Heidelberg has a thriving theater scene. The **Theater der Stadt** (Friedrichstr. 5) is the best-known theater in town; others include the **Zimmer Theater** (Hauptstr. 118, tel. 06221/21069) and the **Theater in Augustinum** (Jasperstr. 2, tel. 06221/3881). For information on performances at the castle during the annual Schloss-Spiele festival, call 06221/58976. Heilbronn's **Stadttheater** (Berliner Pl. 1, tel. 07131/563–001) is the leading venue in the city. In summer, **classical concerts** are given in the gardens behind the Festhalle; contact the tourist office for details of performances and tickets.

Stuttgart's internationally renowned ballet company performs regularly at the **Staatstheater** (Oberer Schlossgarten, tel. 0711/221795). Directed by former Stuttgart Ballet prima ballerina Marcia Haydée, the repertoire includes the great ballets of her predecessor, choreographer John Cranko. The ballet season runs from September through June. For program details contact the Stuttgart tourist office (*see* Important Addresses and Numbers in Essential Information, above). The box office is open Monday through Friday 9–1 and 2–5. The Staatstheater also serves as home for the State Opera, along with both classic and avant-garde plays.

Nightlife

Heidelberg's nightlife is concentrated around the Heiliggeistkirche (Church of the Holy Ghost), in the old town. For a fun night out, try the **Hard Rock Café** (Hauptstr.); it's not exactly Student Prince territory, but it's a good place for videos and burgers. For blues, jazz, and funk, try **Hookemann** (Fischmarkt 3); admission is free. Germany's oldest jazz cellar is **Cave 54** (Krämergasse 2). The **Goldener Reichsapfel** nearby is always crowded after 10 PM; the mood is smoky and loud. **Club 1900** (Hauptstr.) is a well-established disco. The fanciest bars, along with many trendy cafés, are along the main pedestrian street, Haupstrasse. For most, however, nightlife in Heidelberg means a visit to one of the student taverns to drink wine and beer, lock arms, and sing. There are no better places to try than **Zum Roten Ochsen** and **Schnookelooch,** both in business for several centuries.

Heilbronn has one of the biggest and liveliest wine festivals in the Neckar Valley—the **Weindorf,** held in mid-September in the streets and squares around the city hall. But it's not all tradition in Heilbronn. The city has a colorful nightlife—for discos, try the **BOSS-Club** (Mosbacherstr. 8) or **Le Freak** (Albert-Schäffler-Str. 8).

Stuttgart's most vibrant nightlife is likely to be encountered in the numerous popular wine taverns, where just about everyone orders a *Viertelesglas*, local wine served in the typically Swabian quarter-liter glass mug with a handle. Between November and February, join the crowds in the *Besenwirtschaften* (broom inns), which are private wine inns serving the owner's new wine of the season.

12 Frankfurt

Introduction

Frankfurt, home of the second-biggest airport in Europe (after London's Heathrow), is the gateway to Germany for most air travelers. Although it's only the sixth-largest German city, its post–World War II role as the country's financial capital has given it an ultramodern, metropolitan atmosphere. A Hamburg banker described it this way: "It's more aggressive and competitive than other German cities, but also more open and hospitable. Frankfurt is more American in temperament than the average German city." It's certainly gone all-out to give itself a late-20th-century face. While bigger cities, such as Munich, have attempted with considerable success to reclaim the physical character of their past, Frankfurt has developed a New York–style skyline. Not for nothing is this city of 625,000 people nicknamed "Mainhattan"—after the River Main on which it stands.

So why come to Frankfurt? Partly because it's a deeply historic city, one of the joint capitals of Charlemagne's empire, the city where no fewer than 30 Holy Roman Emperors were elected and crowned, the city where Gutenberg set up his print shop, the city where Goethe was born, the city where the first German parliament met. There may be only faint shadows of this original Frankfurt for you to see today, but they are here nonetheless and, this being Germany, beautifully cared for, too.

Frankfurt's commercial clout has its historic side as well. The city was a major trading center as early as the 12th century. Its first international Autumn Fair was held in 1240; in 1330 its Spring Fair was inaugurated. Both are still going strong today. The stock exchange, one of the half dozen most important in the world, was established in 1595. The Rothschilds opened their first bank here in 1798.

And while Frankfurt may be a city of balance sheets and share prices, it still possesses something of the glitzy panache and high living that are such conspicuous features of today's German cities. It's more than just a question of expense-account restaurants and sleek cars. Rather, there's the feeling that you are in the heart of a powerful, sophisticated, and cosmopolitan nation. There may not be much here to remind you of the Old World, but there's a great deal that explains Germany's astonishing success story.

Essential Information

Important Addresses and Numbers

Tourist Information For advance information, write to the **Verkehrsamt Frankfurt/Main** (Kaiserstr. 52, tel. 069/2123–8800). The main tourist office is at Römerberg 27 (tel. 069/2123–8708) in the heart of the old town. It's open Monday through Friday from 9 AM to 7 PM (Nov.–Mar. 9–6) and Saturday through Sunday from 9:30 AM to 6 PM. A secondary information office is at the main train station (Hauptbahnhof) opposite track 23 (tel. 069/2123–8849). This location is open Monday through Saturday from 8 AM to 10 PM (Nov.–Mar. 8 AM–9 PM) and Sunday from 9:30 AM to 8 PM. Both offices can help you find accommodations.

Two information offices at the airport can also help with accommodations: The **FAG Flughafen-Information,** on the first floor of arrivals hall B (open daily 6:45 AM–10:15 PM) and the **DER Deutsches Reisebüro,** in arrivals hall B-6 (open daily 8 AM–9 PM).

Consulates **U.S. Consulate General,** Seismayerstrasse 21, tel. 069/75350.

British Consulate General, Bockenheimer Landstrasse 42, tel. 069/170–0020.

Emergencies **Police:** tel. 110. **Fire:** tel. 112. **Medical Emergencies:** tel. 069/660–7271.

Pharmacies: tel. 069/11500. **Dental Emergencies:** tel. 069/660–7271.

English-language Bookstores **British Bookshop,** Börsenstrasse 17, tel. 069/280–492.
American Book Center (ABC), Jahnstr. 36, tel. 069/552816.
America Haus (library, newspapers, cultural events), Staufenstrasse 1, tel. 069/722–860.

Travel Agencies **American Express International,** Steinweg 5, tel. 069/210–548.
Thomas Cook, Kaiserstrasse 11, tel. 069/13470.
D.E.R. Deutsches Reisebüro, Eschersheimer Landstrasse 25–27, tel. 069/156–6289.
Hapag-Lloyd Reisebüro, Rossmarkt 21, tel. 069/216–2286.

Lost and Found **Fundbüro Stadt,** Mainzer Landstrasse 323, tel. 069/750–02403; **Fundbüro Bahn,** at the train station, tel. 069/265–5831; **Fundbüro Flughafen,** at the airport, tel. 069/960–2413.

Car Rental **Avis,** Mainzer Landstrasse 170, tel. 069/230–101.
Europcar, Stephanstrasse 15, tel. 069/291–028.
Hertz, Hanauer Landstrasse 106–108, tel. 069/449–090.

Arriving and Departing by Plane

Frankfurt airport is the biggest on the Continent, being second only to London's Heathrow. There are direct flights to Frankfurt from many U.S. cities and from all major European cities. It's located 10 kilometers (6 miles) southwest of the downtown area, by the Köln–Munich Autobahn.

Between the Airport and Downtown Getting into Frankfurt from the airport is easy. There are two S-Bahn lines (suburban trains) that run from the airport to downtown Frankfurt. One line, S-14, goes to Hauptwache square in the heart of Frankfurt. Trains run every 20 minutes; the trip takes about 15 minutes. The other line, S-15, goes to the Hauptbahnhof (main train station), just west of the downtown area. Trains run every 10 minutes; the trip takes 11 minutes. One-way fare for both services is DM 3.70 (DM 4.60 during rush hours). Intercity express trains to and from most major West German cities also stop at the airport. There are hourly services to Köln, Hamburg, and Munich, for example. City bus number 61 also serves the airport, running between it and the Südbahnhof train station in Sachsenhausen, south of the downtown area. The trip takes about 30 minutes; the fare is DM 3.70 (DM 4.60 during rush hours). A taxi from the airport into the city center normally takes around 20 minutes; allow double that in rush hours. The fare is around DM 35. If you're picking up a rental car at the airport, getting into Frankfurt will be easy. Take the main road out of the airport and follow the signs for Stadtmitte (downtown).

Arriving and Departing by Train, Bus, and Car

By Train Euro-city and Intercity trains connect Frankfurt with all German cities and many major European cities. The new Intercity Express line links Frankfurt with Hamburg, Munich, and a number of other major German cities. All long-distance trains arrive at and depart from the Hauptbahnhof. For information, call **Deutsche Bundesbahn** (German Railways), tel. 069/19419, or ask at the information office in the station.

By Bus More than 200 European cities—including all major West German cities—have bus links with Frankfurt. Buses arrive and depart from the south side of the Hauptbahnhof. For information and tickets, contact **Deutsche Touring,** Am Römerhof 17, tel. 069/79030.

By Car Frankfurt is located at the meeting point of a number of major Autobahns, of which the most important are A-3, running south from Köln and then on to Würzburg, Nürnberg, and Munich; and A-5, running south from Giessen and then on to Mannheim, Heidelberg, Karlsruhe, and the Swiss-German border at Basel. A complex series of beltways surround the city. If you're driving to Frankfurt on A-5 from either north or south, exit at Nordwestkreuz and follow A-66 to the Nordend district, just north of downtown. Driving south on A-3, exit onto A-66 and follow the signs to Frankfurt-Höchst and then the Nordend district. Driving north on A-3, exit at Offenbach onto A-661 and follow the signs for Frankfurt-Stadtmitte.

Getting Around

On Foot Downtown Frankfurt is compact and easily explored on foot. There are fewer pedestrians-only streets in the downtown area than in some other major German cities; the most important radiate from Hauptwache square. The Römer complex, south of Hauptwache, is also pedestrianized. From here, you can easily cross the river on the Eisener Steg (Iron Bridge) to Sachsenhausen, most of whose tangle of small streets are best explored on foot. For sights and attractions away from the downtown area, make use of the excellent public transportation system.

By Public Transportation Frankfurt lays claim to a smooth-running, well-integrated public transportation system, consisting of the U-bahn (subway), S-bahn (suburban railway), and Strassenbahn (streetcars). Fares for the entire system are uniform, though based on a complex zone system that can be hard to figure out. A basic one-way ticket for a ride in the inner zone costs DM 1.90 (DM 2.60 during rush hours). For rides of just a stop or two, buy a **Kurzstrecken Karte;** cost is DM 1.30. The best buy of all is a day ticket. It costs DM 5 and allows unlimited travel in the inner zone for the day on which it is bought. For information and assistance, call 269–462.

By Taxi Fares start at DM 3.60 and increase by DM 1.80 per kilometer. There is an extra charge of 50 pfennigs per piece of baggage. You can hail taxis in the street or call them at 069/250–001, 069/230–033, or 069/545–011. Note that there's an extra charge to have the driver come to the pickup point.

By Bike In summer, you can rent bikes at the **Goetheturm** (Goethe Tower) at the edge of the Frankfurt Stadtwald (tel. 069/49111).

Guided Tours

Orientation Tours Two-and-a-half-hour bus tours taking in all the main sights with English-speaking guides are offered by the tourist office throughout the year. Tours, which operate twice daily, from March through October, leave at 10 AM from the airport, stopping at 10:30 AM at the train station tourist office (opposite Track 23), and at 2:15 PM from Römerberg 27. From November to February there is only one daily tour, leaving at 10 AM from the airport and 10:30 AM from the train station. The cost is DM 28 adults, DM 14 children.

Special-interest Tours The city transit authority (tel. 069/136–82425) runs a brightly painted old-time streetcar—the **Ebbelwei Express** (Cider Express)—on Saturdays and Sundays every 35 minutes between 1:30 and 6:30. Departures are from the Ostbahnhof (east train station) and the fare—it includes a free glass of cider (or apple juice) and a pretzel—is DM 3 (DM 2 children). All the major attractions in the city are covered as the streetcar trundles along. The ride lasts just over 30 minutes. The **Historische Eisenbahn Frankfurt** (Eschborner Landstr. 140, tel. 069/539–147) runs a vintage steam train along the banks of the Main River on occasional weekends January through mid-May and every weekend mid-May through September. The train runs from the Eisener Steg west to Frankfurt-Griesham and east to Frankfurt-Mainkur. The fare is DM 5 one-way, DM 9 round-trip.

Walking Tours The tourist office arranges walking tours on demand (tel. 069/212–38849). Tours are tailored to suit individual requirements, and costs vary accordingly.

Excursions **CTI Tours** (Wiesenhüttenplatz 39, tel. 069/231091) and **Deutsche Touring** (Am Römerhof 17, tel. 069/79030) offer a variety of tours into the areas immediately around Frankfurt as well as farther afield. Destinations include the Rhine Valley, with steamship cruises and wine-tasting and day trips to the historic towns of Heidelberg and Rothenburg-ob-der-Tauber. Deutsche Touring also offers an afternoon bus tour of Frankfurt daily from the end of April through October. The 2½-hour tour costs DM 34 (DM 24 children). Full information is available from both organizations. A **Casino Bus** service operates daily to the casino at Bad Homburg in the Taunus. It leaves every hour between 2:15 and 11:15 PM (the last bus back to Frankfurt leaves Bad Homburg at 3 AM) from Baslerplatz. The fare of DM 9.50 includes entry to the casino.

Boat Trips There are a variety of round-trips and excursions on the Main River. The **Köln-Dusseldorfer** line (tel. 069/2088–288) offers the most trips; they leave from the Frankfurt Mainkai am Eisernen Steg, just south of the Römer complex. The **Fahrgastschiff Wikinger** company (tel. 069/293960) and the **Frankfurter Personenschiffahrt Anton Nauheimer Company** (tel. 069/281–884) also offer trips along the Main and excursions to the Rhine. Combined boat and wine-tasting trips are offered by **Deutsche Touring** (tel. 069/79030). Pleasure boats of the **Primus Line** cruise the Main and Rhine rivers from Frankfurt, sailing as far as the Loreley and back in a day. For details and reservations, contact Frankfurter Personenschiffahrt, Mainkai 36, tel. 069/281884.

Exploring Frankfurt

Highlights for First-time Visitors

Hauptwache
Römerberg Square
Goethehaus und Goethemuseum
Sachsenhausen
Städelsches Kunstinstitut und Städtische Galerie

The Old Town

Numbers in the margin correspond to points of interest on the Frankfurt map.

Start your tour of Frankfurt in the reconstructed old town, at
1 the square called **Hauptwache,** hub of the city transportation
network. The Hauptwache is a handsome 18th-century building a single story high under a steeply sloping roof. It was built as the city's guardhouse and prison; today it serves as a café. An underground shopping mall stretches below the square.

2 To the south of the square is the **Katharinenkirche** (Church of St. Katherine), the most important Protestant church in the city. What you see today is a simplified version of the second church on the site, put up after the war. It was in the original church here that the first Protestant sermon was preached in Frankfurt, in 1522. Goethe was baptized here. Step inside to see the simple, postwar stained glass. *Open daily 10–5.*

Head south from the church along Berlinerstrasse to the circu-
3 lar bulk of the **Paulskirche** (Church of St. Paul's), a handsome,
mostly 18th-century building that, church or not, is more interesting for its political than for its religious significance. It was here that the short-lived German parliament met for the first time in May 1848. The parliament was hardly a success—it was disbanded within a year, having achieved little more than offering the Prussian king the crown of Germany, but it remains a focus for the democratic aspirations of the German people. The building you see today, modeled loosely on the original, was rebuilt after the war in the expectation that it would become the home of the new German parliament. The German Book Dealers' annual Peace Prize is awarded in the hall, as is the Goethe Prize. *Paulsplatz. Open daily 10–3.*

Walk along the pedestrian street called Neue Krame and over Braubachstrasse. On your left you'll pass the Gothic turrets and crenellations of the **Steinernes Haus** (Stone House), originally built in 1464, destroyed in World War II, and rebuilt from 1957 to 1960 with an altered interior. Today it is the home of the Frankfurt Kunstverein (Arts Association), which regularly mounts special exhibits (for details, call 069/285–339). *Markt 44. Admission: DM 6. Open Tues.–Sat. 11–6.*

You are now entering the historic heart of Frankfurt, the an-
4 cient **Römerberg Square,** which has been the center of civic life
for centuries. Immediately on your right and occupying most of
5 the square is the city hall, called the **Römer.** It's a modest-look-
ing building compared with many of Germany's city halls, though it has undeniable charm. Its gabled Gothic facade with ornate balcony is widely known as the city's official emblem.

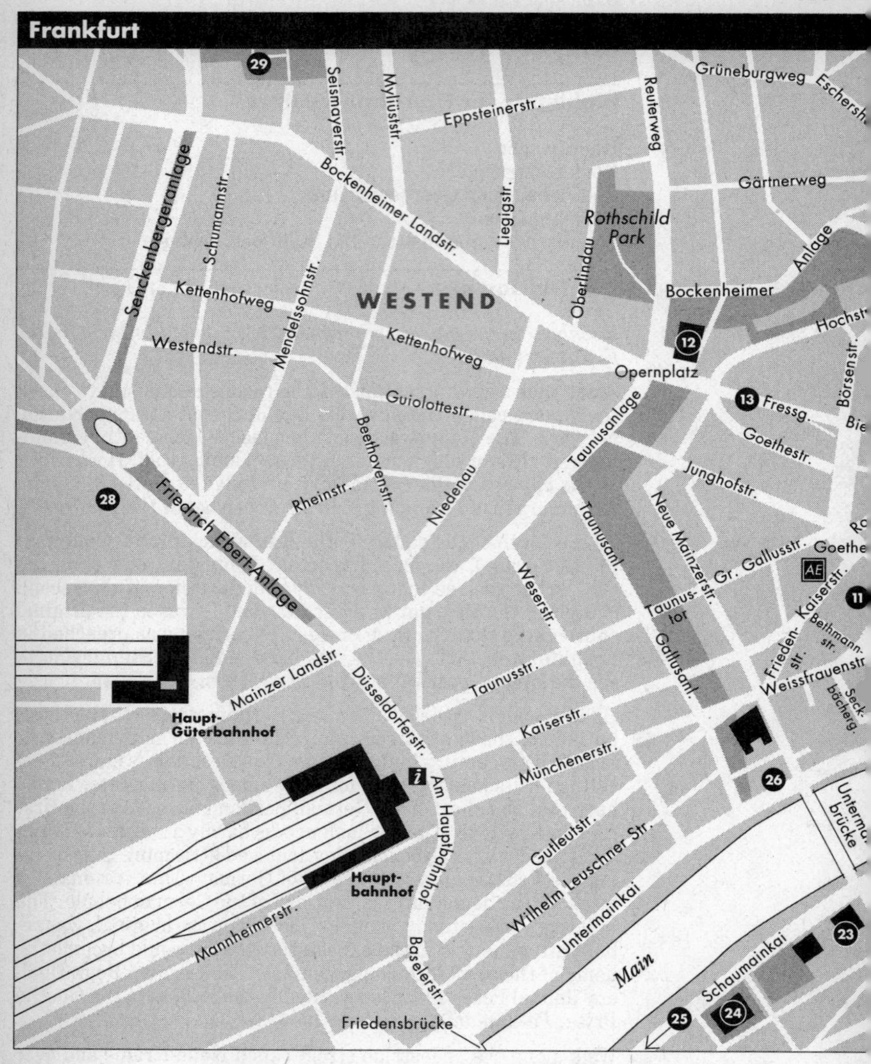
Frankfurt
Grüneburgweg
Eschersh
Reuterweg
Seismayerstr.
Mylíusstr.
Eppsteinerstr.
Senckenberganlage
Schumannstr.
Bockenheimer Landstr.
Liebigstr.
Gärtnerweg
Rothschild Park
Oberlindau
Anlage
Bockenheimer
Mendelssohnstr.
Kettenhofweg
WESTEND
Hochstr.
Westendstr.
Kettenhofweg
Opernplatz
Börsenstr.
Guiolettestr.
Fressg.
Goethestr.
Taunusanlage
Beethovenstr.
Junghofstr.
Niedenau
Rheinstr.
Friedrich Ebert-Anlage
Taunusanl.
Neue Mainzerstr.
Gr. Gallusstr.
Goethe
Weserstr.
Taunustor
Kaiserstr.
Bethmannstr.
Frieden-str.
Gallusanl.
Weissfrauenstr.
Mainzer Landstr.
Düsseldorferstr.
Taunusstr.
Haupt-Güterbahnhof
Kaiserstr.
Seckbächerg.
Münchenerstr.
Am Hauptbahnhof
Untermainbrücke
Gutleutstr.
Wilhelm Leuschner Str.
Haupt-bahnhof
Untermainkai
Mannheimerstr.
Main
Baselerstr.
Schaumainkai
Friedensbrücke

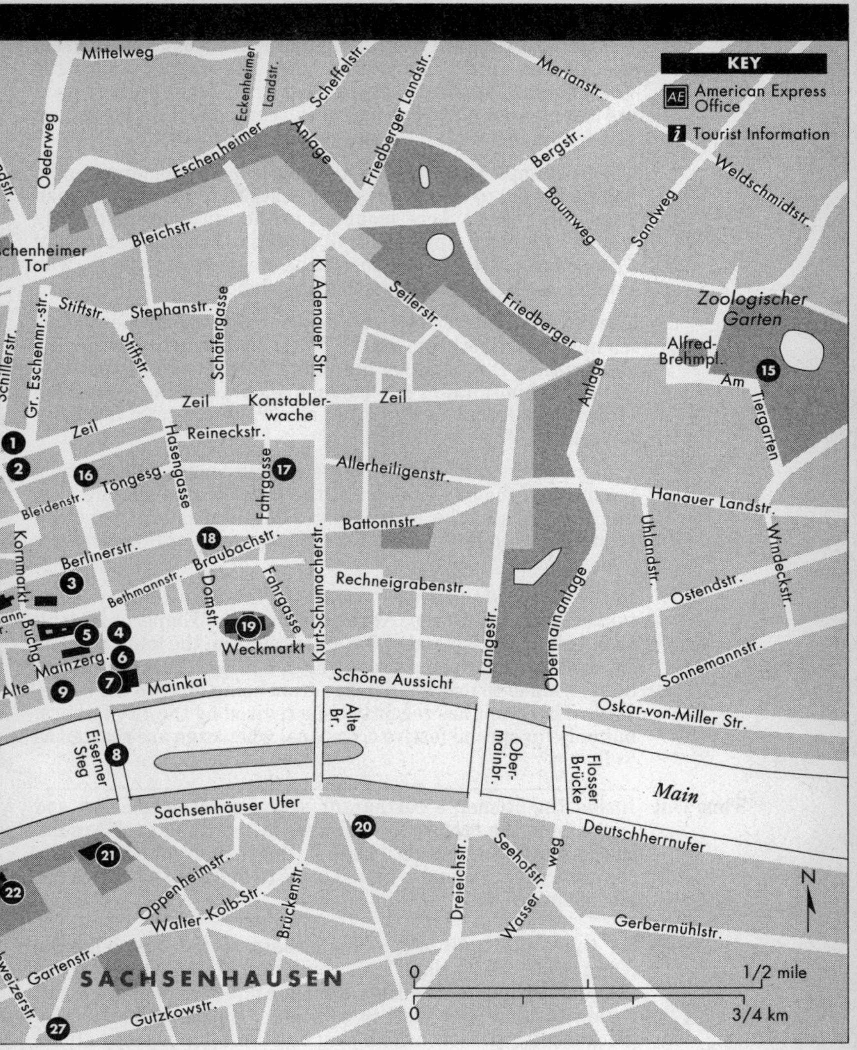
KEY
American Express Office
Tourist Information
Mittelweg
Eckenheimer
Landstr.
Scheffelstr.
Friedberger Landstr.
Merianstr.
Oederweg
Eschenheimer
Anlage
Bergstr.
Weldschmidtstr.
Bleichstr.
Baumweg
Sandweg
Eschenheimer Tor
Stiftstr.
Stephanstr.
Schäfergasse
K. Adenauer Str.
Seilerstr.
Friedberger
Zoologischer Garten
Alfred-Brehmpl.
Am
Tiergarten
Schillerstr.
Gr. Eschenmr.-str.
Zeil
Konstabler-wache
Anlage
Reineckstr.
Hasengasse
Töngesg.
Fahrgasse
Allerheiligenstr.
Hanauer Landstr.
Bleidenstr.
Battonnstr.
Uhlandstr.
Windeckstr.
Kornmarkt
Berlinerstr.
Braubachstr.
Recheneigrabenstr.
Ostendstr.
Bethmannstr.
Domstr.
Kurt-Schumacherstr.
Langestr.
Obermainanlage
Buchg.
Mainzerg.
Weckmarkt
Sonnemannstr.
Alte
Mainkai
Schöne Aussicht
Oskar-von-Miller Str.
Alte Br.
Eiserner Steg
Ober-mainbr.
Flosser Brücke
Main
Sachsenhäuser Ufer
Deutschherrnufer
Seehofstr.
Wasserweg
Oppenheimstr.
Walter-Kolb-Str.
Brückenstr.
Dreieichstr.
Gerbermühlstr.
N
Gartenstr.
SACHSENHAUSEN
Gutzkowstr.
0
1/2 mile
3/4 km

Three individual patrician buildings make up the Römer. From left to right they are the Alt-Limpurg, the Zum Römer (from which the entire structure takes its name), and the Löwenstein. The mercantile-minded Frankfurt burghers used the complex not only for political and ceremonial purposes, but also for trade fairs and other commercial ventures.

The most important events to take place in the Römer were the banquets held to celebrate the coronations of the Holy Roman Emperors. These were mounted in the glittering and aptly named **Kaisersaal** (Imperial Hall), starting in 1562, last used in 1792 to celebrate the election of the emperor Francis II, who would later be forced by Napoléon to abdicate.

The most vivid description of the ceremony was by Germany's leading poet, Goethe, in his "Dichtung und Wahrheit" ("Poetry and Truth"). It is said that the young Goethe, as a 16-year-old, smuggled himself into the banquet celebrating the coronation of Emperor Joseph II by posing as a waiter to get a firsthand impression of the festivities.

Today visitors can see the impressive full-length 19th-century portraits of the 52 emperors of the Holy Roman Empire that line the walls of the banqueting hall. *Admission free. Open Mon.–Sat. 9–6, Sun. 10–4. Closed when official functions are taking place.*

In the center of the square stands the fine 16th-century **Fountain of Justitia** (Justice). At the coronation of Emperor Matthias in 1612, wine instead of water flowed from the fountain. The crush of thirsty citizens was so great, however, that they had to be restrained to prevent damage from being done to the stonework. This event has recently been revived by the city fathers, but only for special festive occasions, when oxen are roasted as well.

Time Out Inside the Römer a restaurant serves local specialties and wines from the municipal vineyards in the Rheingau. Around the corner at Limpurger Gasse 2, the restaurant's shop sells the same products and is a good place to buy a bottle of Hock or Hochheimer wine.

---

6 On the south side of the Römerberg is the **Nikolaikirche** (Church of St. Nicholas). It was built in the late 13th century as the court chapel for the Holy Roman Emperors, and it's worth trying to time your visit to coincide with the chimes of the glockenspiel carillon, which ring out three times a day. It's a wonderful sound. *Carillon chimes daily at 9 AM, noon and 5 PM. Nikolaikirche open Mon.–Sat. 10–5.*

7 Beside the Nikolaikirche is the **Historisches Museum** (Historical Museum), where you can see a perfect scale model of the old town, complete with every street, house, and church. There is also an astonishing display of silver, exhibits covering all aspects of the city's life from the 16th to the 20th century, and a children's museum. *Saalgasse 19. Admission free. Open Tues. and Thurs.–Sun. 10–5, Wed. 10–8. Children's museum 1–5.*

Behind the church, on the east side of the square, is a row of painstakingly restored half-timbered houses, dating from the 15th and 16th centuries. They are an excellent example of how the people of Frankfurt have begun, albeit belatedly, to take seriously the reconstruction of their historic buildings.

Leaving the square, walk the short distance to the Main River. At Mainkai, the busy street that runs parallel to the tree-lined river, you will see on your left the **Rententurm,** one of the city's medieval gates, with its pinnacled towers at the base of the main spire extending out over the walls. To your right and in
8 front is the **Eiserner Steg,** an iron bridge built as a pedestrian walkway to connect central Frankfurt with the old district of Sachsenhausen. From here river trips and boat excursions start, as well as the old steam train. (For details, *see* Tours and Excursions, above.)

9 Stroll along Mainkai, past the Eiserner Steg, to **Leonhardskirche** (St. Leonard's Church), which is a magnificently preserved 15th- and 16th-century building, with a fine 13th-century porch. Its main treasure is the beautifully carved Bavarian altar, circa 1500.

Continue a short way along Mainkai, then turn right into the
10 narrow Karmeliter Gasse, which will take you to the **Karmeliterkirche** (Carmelite Church and Monastery). Within its quiet cloisters is the largest religious fresco north of the Alps, a 16th-century representation of the birth and death of Christ. Jörg Ratgeb, the creator of this 262-foot-long fresco, was one of the most important artists of his time, but it did not prevent his brutal death by quartering in 1526 for his part in the Peasants' Rebellion. The church and monastery buildings were secularized in 1803 and now house the city archives and the Early and Prehistory Museum. *Münzgasse 4. Admission free. Cloisters open weekdays 8–4.*

Time Out Pop into **Wacker's Kaffeegeschäft** (Kornmarkt, off Berlinerstr.) an ancient café where you can choose a pot of coffee from 20 varieties of fresh-roasted beans.

11 From here it's a short way to the **Goethehaus und Goethemuseum** (Goethe's House and Museum). Coming out of the Karmeliterkirche into Münzgasse, turn left and go to the junction of Bethmannstrasse and Berliner Strasse. Use the pedestrian walkway and cross over to the north side of Berliner Strasse, then turn left again onto Grosser Hirschgraben. Outside No. 23 there will probably be a small crowd of visitors entering and leaving. This is where Johann Wolfgang von Goethe was born in 1749. Although the original house was destroyed by Allied bombing, it has been carefully rebuilt and restored in every detail as the young Goethe would have known it. The room in which Goethe was born has been turned into a memorial, and the one in which he wrote is set up as it used to be. In Goethe Senior's study, look for the little window that was installed so he could keep an eye on the street outside and, in particular, on young Johann, who was well known to wander afield. The adjoining museum contains a permanent collection of manuscripts, paintings, and memorabilia documenting the life and times of Germany's outstanding poet. *Grosser Hirschgraben 23, tel. 069/282–824. Admission: DM 3 adults, DM 2 children. Open Apr.–Sept., Mon.–Sat. 9–6, Sun. 10–1; Oct.–Mar., Mon.–Sat. 9–4, Sun. 10–1. Guided tours Mon.–Sat. 10:30 and 2, Sun. 10:30.*

On leaving the Goethehaus turn left, and at the end of Grosser Hirschgraben bear left again and retrace your steps up Rossmarkt. Cross over to the Gutenberg Memorial and contin-

ue along the pedestrian zone to Rathenau-Platz. From here take a window-shopping stroll past the elegant shops and boutiques of Goethestrasse, which ends at Opernplatz and Frank-
12 furt's reconstructed opera house, the **Alte Oper.** Wealthy Frankfurt businessmen gave generously for its original construction in the 1870s, provided they were given priority for the best seats. Kaiser Wilhelm II traveled all the way from Berlin for the gala opening in 1880. Destroyed by incendiary bombs in 1944, the opera house remained in ruins for many years while controversy raged over its reconstruction. The new building, in the classical proportions and style of the original, was finally opened in 1981, and now houses modern facilities for opera, ballet, concerts, and conferences.

The steps of the opera house, or the Rothschild Park opposite, are a good spot from which to take in the impressive sight of Frankfurt's modern architecture. In this part of the new town you are close to the financial center (the West End), and if you look down Taunusanlage and Mainzer Landstrasse, the view both to the right and left is dominated by gleaming skyscrapers that house the headquarters of West Germany's biggest and richest banks. More than 350 international banks also have offices here, confirming Frankfurt's position as the country's financial capital. If you have a camera, take a photo, especially in the early evening, when the setting sun is mirrored in the glass and metal facades.

Return to the beginning of the pedestrian zone. This is the site of Bockenheimer Tor, one of the gateways in the old walled city. Wander at leisure down Grosse Bockenheimer Strasse,
13 known locally as **Fressgasse** (Food Street). It's a gourmet shopper's paradise and one of Frankfurt's liveliest streets.

Time Out Stop at any of the attractive cafés, restaurants, or delicatessens that line Fressgasse; the selection is enormous, and you're certain to find something to your taste. In the summer you can sit at tables on the sidewalk and dine alfresco. *Prost!*

Next, cross over onto Biebergasse, a continuation of the main
14 shopping center. Just around the corner is the Frankfurt **Börse** (Stock Exchange), Germany's leading stock exchange and financial powerhouse. The Borse was founded by Frankfurt merchants in 1558 to establish some order in their often chaotic dealings, but the present building dates from the 1870s. In the past, the trading on the dealers' floor was hectic. These days, computerized networks and international telephone systems have removed some of the drama, but it is still an exciting scene to watch. There is a visitors' gallery. *Admission free. Open weekdays 11:30–1:30.*

From here there is a choice of two routes. You can continue along Biebergasse, past the Hauptwache, and walk east along the **Zeil,** the city's largest pedestrian zone and main shopping street. It is lined with department stores selling every conceivable type of consumer goods and can get very crowded. The far end of the Zeil brings you to Alfred-Brehm Platz and the en-
15 trance to the **Zoologischer Garten** (Zoological Garden). This is one of Frankfurt's chief attractions, ranking among the best zoos in Europe. Its remarkable collection includes some 5,000 animals of 600 different species, a Bears' Castle, an Exotarium (aquarium plus reptiles), and an aviary, reputedly the largest

in Europe. Many of the birds can be seen in a natural setting. The zoo is an ideal place for a family outing, as it also has a restaurant and a café, along with afternoon concerts in summer. *Zoo admission: DM 7 adults, DM 3 children. Exotarium admission: DM 3.50 adults, DM 1.50 children. Combined ticket price: DM 8.50 adults, DM 4 children. Open mid-Mar.–Sept., daily 8–7; mid-Oct.–mid-Feb., daily 8–5; between seasons open daily 8–6.*

Alternatively, if you don't want to go all the way down the Zeil, just after the Hauptwache turn right down Liebfrauenstrasse. Here, in more peaceful surroundings, you will come to the
16 **Liebfrauenkirche** (Church of Our Lady), a late-Gothic church dating from the end of the 14th century. Among its few surviving features of interest are the fine tympanum relief over the south door, the ornate Rococo furnishings, the 16th-century choir, and the frieze work around the pointed arches. Outside, there is also a delightful Rococo fountain.

Turn off onto Töngesgasse and walk to Fahrgasse. Follow the
17 signs to the **Staufenmauer,** which is one of the few surviving stretches of the old city wall. The Staufenmauer and the Saalhofkapelle (Chapel) (near the Eiserner Steg bridge) are the two oldest parts of the medieval city in evidence today. *Admission free. Saalhofkapelle. Open Tues. and Thurs.–Sat. 10–5, Wed. 10–8, Sun. 10–5.*

On the corner of Berlinerstrasse and Domstrasse you'll see the
18 striking fanlike outline of Frankfurt's new **Museum für Moderne Kunst** (Museum of Modern Art). Opened in June 1991, this museum houses a spectacular collection of contemporary works by artists such as Siah Armajani, Joseph Beuss, and Andy Warhol. *Domstr. 10. Admission free. Open Tues.–Sun. 8 AM–10 PM.*

Time Out Even if you don't have much time to spend in the museum, you can take a break from sightseeing in its bright and airy restaurant and café. Prices are low and the quality of the coffee is very high.

Cross Berliner Strasse at a convenient point, bear left along Braubachstrasse for a few yards, and then turn right onto
19 Domstrasse. You are now at the **Dom St. Bartholomäus** (Cathedral of St. Bartholomew) or Kaiserdom (Imperial Cathedral), as it is more popularly known. This grand Gothic structure dates from 1290 and was used primarily for imperial coronations, hence the name. It was built to replace an earlier church established by Charlemagne's son, Ludwig the Pious, on the present site of the Römerberg. The cathedral suffered little damage during World War II and still contains most of its original treasures, including a life-size crucifixion group and a fine 15th-century altar. Its most impressive exterior feature is its tall, red sandstone tower (almost 300 feet high), which was added between 1415 and 1514. Excavations in front of the main entrance in 1953 revealed the remains of a Roman settlement and the foundations of a Carolingian imperial palace. *Admission free. Open Mar.–Oct., daily 9–noon and 3–6; Nov.–Feb., daily 9–noon and 3–5.*

Walk on now, down the lane called Zum Pfarrturm, and head toward the river. On the Mainkai, cross to **Sachsenhausen** over the Alte Brücke. Formerly a village separate from Frankfurt,

Sachsenhausen is said to have been established by Charlemagne, who arrived here with a group of Saxon families in the 8th century and formed a settlement on the banks of the Main. It was an important bridgehead for the crusader Knights of the Teutonic Order and, in 1318, officially became part of Frankfurt. After crossing the bridge, look along the bank to your left
20 and you'll see the 15th-century **Kuhhirtenturm** (Shepherd's Tower), the only remaining part of Sachsenhausen's original fortifications. The composer Paul Hindemith lived in the tower from 1923 to 1927 while working at the Frankfurt Opera.

Sachsenhausen is now largely residential but is also renowned for its collection of museums, most of which are threaded along the riverbank. The district has a distinctly medieval air, with narrow back alleys, quaint little inns, and quiet squares that have escaped the destructive tread of the modern developer. There is much of authentic historical interest here. For Frankfurters and visitors alike, it is where you'll also find the best city nightlife—from clubs and discos to traditional taverns and restaurants, tucked in among the half-timbered houses.

Time Out Sachsenhausen is the home of the famous *Ebbelwei* (apple-wine or cider) taverns. Look for a green pine wreath over the entrance to tell passersby that a freshly pressed—and alcoholic—apple juice is on tap. You can eat well in these small inns, too, though the menu might need some explanation. For example, *Handkas mit Musik* does not promise music at your table. The *Musik* means that the cheese, or *Kas* (from Käse) will be served with raw onions, oil, vinegar, and bread and butter. Most traditional apple-wine taverns serve this specialty without a fork, and those who ask for one give themselves away as strangers. There are about 15 of these taverns; two of the best-known are **Zum Gemalten Haus** (Schweizerstr. 67), and **Lorsbacher Tal** (Grosse Rittergasse 49).

No fewer than seven top-ranking museums line the Sachsenhausen side of the Main, on Schaumainkai, known locally as the Museumsufer (Museum Riverbank). These range from exhibitions of art, crafts, and architecture to the German Film Museum.

21 One of Frankfurt's newest museums is the **Museum für Kunsthandwerk** (Museum of Decorative Arts), which was opened in 1985. This award-winning building, designed by the American architect Richard Meier, contains a vast collection of European and Asian handicrafts, including furniture, glassware, and porcelain. *Schaumainkai 17. Admission free. Open Tues. and Thurs.–Sun. 10–5, Wed. 10–8.*

22 A little farther along is the **Deutsches Architekturmuseum** (German Architectural Museum), currently Frankfurt's most popular museum. Created by German architect Oswald Mathias Ungers, it is housed within a period villa, though the interior is entirely modern. There are five floors of drawings, models, and audiovisual displays that chart the progress of German architecture through the ages, as well as many special exhibits. *Schaumainkai 43. Admission free. Open Tues. and Thurs.–Sun. 10–5, Wed. 10–8.*

Next door is Germany's first museum devoted exclusively to the
23 cinema, **Deutsches Filmmuseum** (German Film Museum). The exhibits include an imaginative collection of film artifacts. The

It's easy to recognize a good place when you see one.

American Express Cardmembers have been doing it for years.

The secret? Instead of just relying on what they see in the window, they look at the door. If there's an American Express Blue Box on it, they know they've found an establishment that cares about high standards.

Whether it's a place to eat, to sleep, to shop, or simply meet, they know they will be warmly welcomed.

So much so, they're rarely taken in by anything else.

Always a good sign.

museum has its own movie theater. *Schaumainkai 41. Admission free. Open Tues. and Thurs.–Sun. 10–5, Wed. 10–8.*

24 Farther on you will come to the **Städelsches Kunstinstitut und Städtische Galerie** (Städel Art Institute and Municipal Gallery). This building houses one of the most significant art collections in Germany, with fine examples of Flemish, Dutch, German, and Italian old masters, plus a sprinkling of French Impressionists. *Schaumainkai 63. Admission: DM 3 adults, DM 2 children. Open Tues. and Thurs.–Sun. 10–5, Wed. 10–8.*

25 Finally, it's worth stopping at the **Städtische Galerie Liebieghaus** (Liebieg Municipal Museum of Sculpture). Here, in this charming 17th-century villa, is housed the city's internationally famous collection of classical, medieval, and Renaissance sculpture. Some pieces are exhibited in the lovely gardens surrounding the house. *Schaumainkai 71. Admission free. Open Tues. and Thurs.–Sun. 10–5, Wed. 10–8.*

From there you can backtrack along the Schaumainkai to the Untermain Brücke, cross the bridge to the other side of the river, turn left into Untermainkai, and at number 14–15 come to
26 the **Jüdisches Museum** (Jewish Museum), housed in the former Rothschild Palais. Designed by the architect Ante von Kostelac, the museum focuses on Frankfurt's centuries-old Jewish community, the second largest in Germany after Berlin prior to the Hitler years. The museum contains extensive archives of Jewish history and culture, including a library of 5,000 books, a large photographic collection, and a documentation center. *Untermainkai 14–15. Admission free. Open Tues.–Sun. 10–5, Wed. 10–8.*

If you have time and energy, there is more to explore in Sachsenhausen. It's very much the up-and-coming district—take a
27 short detour down to **Schweizer Platz;** you'll find it full of new shops, boutiques, cafés, and bars thronging with people and activity.

Retrace your steps back to Schaumainkai and return to the north bank of the river by way of the Friedensbrücke bridge, which will take you, via Baseler Strasse, to the main train station, in Frankfurt's West End.

From here, three avenues lead to the center of town: Kaiserstrasse, Münchenerstrasse, and Taunusstrasse. They are lined with fast-food joints, shops, strip clubs, cinemas, and restaurants, and at night, with neon lights flashing and rock music blaring, have a rather seedy atmosphere.

Continue past the main train station and wander north along
28 Friedrich-Ebert-Anlage to the **Messe,** a vast complex of exhibition halls where some of the world's greatest trade fairs are held annually. In addition to the two major fairs in spring and fall, among the more important smaller ones are the Automobile Show in March, the Fur Fair at Easter, and the International Book Fair in early fall.

Farther north still, along Senckenbergeranlage, is the delight-
29 ful **Palmengarten und Botanischer Garten** (Tropical Garden and Botanical Garden). The large greenhouses enclose a variety of lush tropical and subtropical flora, including 800 species of cactus, while the surrounding park offers numerous leisure facilities. During most of the year there are flower shows and exhibitions; in summer, concerts are held in an outdoor band-

shell. Situated between the Palmengarten and the adjoining Grüneburgpark, the botanical gardens contain a wide assortment of wild, ornamental, and rare plants from around the world. *Entrance at Siesmayerstr. 61. Admission: DM 4.50 adults, DM 1.50 children. Open Apr.–Sept., daily 9–6; Oct.–Mar., daily 9–dusk.*

Frankfurt for Free

Finding something for nothing in Frankfurt, a town of high finance and commerce, is a bit of a challenge. With some imagination and planning, though, you can enjoy much of what Frankfurt has to offer without spending too much. For example, it won't cost you anything to get a glimpse of what makes Frankfurt tick—there's no charge to enter the visitors' gallery of the Börse, or Stock Exchange (*see* Exploring Frankfurt, above).

You can spend hours roaming through the **city-run museums** and not have to spend a cent—they don't charge admission except for special exhibitions. *Strandgut* magazine is your best bet for finding out about free or low-cost events in Frankfurt. This free magazine, available in many of Frankfurt's *Kneipen* (pubs) and at most movie theaters, will let you know what's happening around town. Movie and theater programs, as well as live music and other events, are listed here. Look for *Eintritt Frei* (admission free) alongside the listings, and you'll know you've found one of Frankfurt's freebies.

Live jazz concerts are held every Sunday morning in the **Historic Museum on Römerberg.** These concerts are very popular and tend to get rather crowded, but the atmosphere is always lively and friendly and the music enjoyable—a fine way to spend a relaxing Sunday morning, especially if you were out on the town Saturday night.

Check out the **Kleinmarkthalle** close to Liebfrauenberg for a taste of a real old Frankfurt institution. This covered market hall is a feast for the eyes as well as the stomach, with everything from fresh fruits and vegetables and butchers selling homemade Hessian sausages to brilliantly colored flowers. The gallery upstairs is reserved for more exotic products from such foreign countries as Turkey and Lebanon. It's open from 8 AM to 6 PM on weekdays, Saturday from 8 AM to 1 PM. Weekends are flea-market time in Frankfurt. On Saturdays, sift through the jumble at the **Frankfurter Flohmarkt** on Schaumainkai below the Eiserner Steg (from 9 AM). On Sunday mornings, wander through the Sachsenhausen flea market at the **Schlachthof** (abbatoir) on Seehoferstrasse, where antiques and artworks can be found among the secondhand offerings.

All you'll need to invest is energy when you climb the **Goetheturm** (Goethe Tower) on the Sachsenhäuser Berg hill. Climbing the many steps up to the top of the 463-foot tower yields a sweeping view of all of Frankfurt and its environs, and on a clear day, as far as the Taunus.

What to See and Do with Children

Your children can see birds and animals up close at the Frankfurt **Zoologischer Garten.** Of special interest is the **Exotarium,** where special climatic conditions are created, and the special nocturnal section, where children can see nighttime creatures moving about. In association with the zoo is the **Natural History Museum of Senckenberg,** where exhibitions on prehistoric animals have been designed partly with children in mind. The displays will take your children back to dinosaur times and get their imaginations going (*see* Sightseeing Checklists, below).

For outdoor activity and a chance to run and play, Frankfurt's parks offer ample room. The **Palmengarten** has wide, open lawns landscaped with shrubs, flower borders, and trees. There is a little lake where you can rent rowboats, a play area for kids, and a wading pool. Concerts take place in the music pavilion, and there is much to see in the Palm House itself (*see* Sightseeing Checklists, below).

Excursions on the **vintage streetcar,** the **steam train** along the river, or a **boat** will be fun and exciting for the kids and provide a chance for you to sit and enjoy the scenery (*see* Guided Tours in Essential Information, above).

Off the Beaten Track

The old quarter of **Höchst** is Frankfurt's most western suburb. Located on the Main River, during the Middle Ages it was a town in its own right, governed by Mainz until it was engulfed by the spread of Frankfurt. Unlike Frankfurt, however, Höchst was not devastated by wartime bombing and still possesses many of its original historic buildings. It's worth taking the time to explore the picturesque Altstadt (Old Town), with its attractive market and half-timbered houses.

Höchst was once a porcelain manufacturing town to rival Dresden and Vienna. Production ceased in the late 18th century, but was revived by an enterprising businessman in 1965. Today you can tour the factory of **Höchster Porzellan Manufaktur** (Bolongarostr. 186, tel. 069/300–9020). You must call to arrange for a guided tour of the works. You can also see a fine exhibit of porcelain at the **Bolongaropalast** (Bolongaro Palace), a magnificent residence facing the river. It was built in the late 18th century by an Italian snuff manufacturer. Its facade—almost the size of a football field—is nothing to sneeze at. Also on Bolongaro Strasse is the **Höchster Schloss.** Built in 1360, this castle was originally the seat and customs house of the archbishop of Mainz. Destroyed and rebuilt several times, it now houses the **local history museum.** Höchst can be reached via the S-1 and S-2 suburban trains from the main train station, or Konstablerwache station. *Admission free. Open daily 10–4.*

Of greater interest is the **Justiniuskirche,** Frankfurt's oldest church, located at the corner of Justiniusplatz and Bolongaro Strasse. Dating from the 7th century, the church is part early Romanesque, part 15th-century Gothic. The view from the top of the hill is well worth the walk.

For the best view of Frankfurt take the lift to the viewing platform of the 1,090-foot television tower, the **Europaturm,** the highest in Western Europe. At the 730-foot level there's a spectacular son-et-lumière show; one floor below that is a classy restaurant, Windows. *Wilhelm-Epstein-Str. 20.*

The major attraction to the southwest of the city is the **Stadtwald** (City Forest), which is threaded with lovely paths and trails, as well as containing one of Germany's most impressive sports stadiums. Of particular interest is the Waldehrpfad—a trail leading past a series of rare trees, each identified by a small sign. The Stadtwald was the first place in Europe where trees were planted from seed (they were oaks, sown in 1398), and there are still many extremely old trees in evidence. In addition to bird sanctuaries and wild-animal enclosures, the forest also boasts a number of good restaurants and is a pleasant place in which to eat and linger. *Take bus No. 36 from Konstablerwache to Hainer Weg.*

North of Frankfurt is the district of Seckbach. The 590-foot Lohrberg hill is a favorite among Frankfurters, as the climb yields a fabulous view of the town and the Taunus, Spessart, and Odenwald hills. Along the way you'll also see the last remaining vineyard within Frankfurt, the **Seckbach Vineyard.** *Take the U-4 subway to Seckbacher Landstr., then bus No. 43 or 38.*

Still within Frankfurt but definitely off the beaten track is scenic **Holzhausen Park.** This small park is quiet and peaceful, complete with willow trees and a little moated palace, the **Holzhausen Schlösschen.** *Take the subway to Holzhausenstr.*

Also within Frankfurt, visit the **old Jewish quarter** near Börneplatz. The **Alter Jüdischer Friedhof** (Old Jewish Cemetery) is located on the east side of the square. Partly vandalized in the Nazi era, it is nearly all that remains of prewar Jewish life in Frankfurt. The cemetery can be visited by prior arrangement only. *Corner of Kurt-Schumacher-Str. and Battonstr., tel. 069/740–2125.*

During excavation, a Jewish **ritual bath,** or *Mikwe,* was uncovered. Citizens' groups went to work to make sure that it was preserved, and it remains, incorporated into the office block, dwarfed by modern buildings. *Eckenheimer Landstr.*

Sightseeing Checklists

Historic Buildings and Sites

All of the historic buildings and sites listed below appear in the Exploring Frankfurt section of this chapter unless otherwise noted.

Alte Oper (Old Opera House). Built between 1873 and 1880 and destroyed during World War II, Frankfurt's old opera house has been beautifully reconstructed in the style of the original.

Bolongaropalast (Bolongaro Palace). A grand and aristocratic residence built by a family of Italian snuff manufacturers in the 1770s. (*See* Off the Beaten Track, above.)

Börneplatz. This is the historic center of Frankfurt's Jewish community. (*See* Off the Beaten Track, above.)

Börse (Stock Exchange). For those interested in international finance, this is the center of West Germany's stock and money market.

Deutschordenshaus (House of the Teutonic Order). A Baroque building, it once belonged to the Knights of the Teutonic Order. It was built in 1709 above a Gothic cellar. Next door is a church that dates to 1309. *Brueckenstr. 3–7. The church can be visited by prior arrangement only (tel. 069/609–10830).*

Eiserner Steg (Iron Bridge). A pedestrian walkway, the bridge connects the center of Frankfurt with Sachsenhausen.

Eschenheimer Turm (Eschenheimer Tower). Built in the early

15th century, this tower remains the finest example of the city's original 42 towers. *Eschenheimer Tor.*

Europaturm (Telecommunications Tower). At 332 meters (1,090 feet), this is the highest tower in Western Europe and the fourth-highest in the world. (*See* Off the Beaten Track, above).

Fressgasse (Food Street). The street's proper name is Grosse Bockenheimer Strasse, but Frankfurters have given it this sobriquet because of the amazing choice of delicatessens, wine merchants, cafés, and restaurants to be found here.

Goetheturm (Goethe's Tower). Located at the edge of the Stadtwald on the Sachsenhauser Berg, this is Germany's highest wood tower.

Hauptwache (Guardhouse). An attractive Baroque building, it was originally constructed as a municipal guardhouse in 1729. Today it houses a café and a tourist information office.

Höchster Schloss (Höchst Castle). This 14th-century castle, destroyed and rebuilt several times, now houses the Höchst city museum and the Hoechst AG company museum. (*See* Off the Beaten Track, above.)

Kuhhirtenturm (Shepherd's Tower). This is the last of nine towers, built in the 15th century, that formed part of Sachsenhausen's fortifications.

Messe (Exhibition Halls). This huge complex of buildings holds some of the most important trade fairs in the world.

Rententurm (Renten Tower). Another of the city's fortifications, the Rententurm was built in 1456 along the Main River.

Römer (City Hall). With its gabled Gothic facade, the Römer is the traditional symbol of Frankfurt and has been the center of civic life here for 500 years.

Römerberg. This square, lovingly restored after wartime bomb damage, is the historical focal point of the city.

Sachsenhausen. The old quarter of Sachsenhausen, on the south bank of the Main River, is of great historical interest, sensitively preserved and very popular with residents and tourists alike.

Steinernes Haus (Stone House). This Gothic-style patrician house has also served as a trading post. Today it's an art gallery.

Zeil. This pedestrian shopping street ranks among Germany's busiest and best. (*See* Shopping, below.)

Churches and Cathedrals

Dom St. Bartholomäus (Cathedral of St. Bartholomew). Also known as the Kaiserdom (Imperial Cathedral), the Dom was built largely between the 13th and 15th centuries and survived the bombs of World War II with most of its original treasures intact.

Justiniuskirche (Church of St. Justinius). Situated in the old quarter of Höchst, this church dates from the days of the Carolingians and is older than anything that remains in Frankfurt proper. (*See* Off the Beaten Track, above.)

Karmeliterkirche (Carmelite Church and Monastery). The cloisters of this former monastery contain one of the most significant religious frescoes north of the Alps.

Katharinenkirche (Church of St. Catherine). This church was originally built in 1678–1681, the first independent Protestant church in the Gothic style.

Leonhardskirche (St. Leonard's Church). This beautifully preserved 13th-century building with five naves boasts some fine old stained glass.

Liebfrauenkirche (Church of Our Lady). Dating from the 14th century, this late-Gothic church still possesses a few of its original treasures.

Nikolaikirche (Church of St. Nicholas). The glockenspiel rings out three times a day at this small red sandstone church, which dates from the late 13th century.

Paulskirche (Church of St. Paul). Site of the first all-German parliament in 1848–1849, the church is now used mainly for formal ceremonial occasions.

Saalhofkapelle (Saalhof Chapel). Near the Eiserner Steg-bridge and behind the Rententurm, this small 12th-century chapel is one of the oldest buildings in the city. *Saalgasse 31.*

Museums and Galleries

Bundespost Museum (Postal Museum). On display are the various means of transporting mail through the ages—from the mail coach to the airplane. There's also an exhibition of stamps and stamp-printing machines, as well as a reconstructed 19th-century post office. *Schaumainkai 53. Admission free. Open Tues. and Thurs.–Sun. 10–5; Wed. 10–8. Reopened in Sept. 1990 after renovation.*

Deutsches Architekturmuseum (German Architecture Museum). The museum houses an impressive collection of drawings, models, and audiovisual displays tracing the development of German architecture.

Deutsches Filmmuseum (German Film Museum). Germany's first museum of cinematography houses an exciting collection of film artifacts.

Goethehaus und Goethemuseum (Goethe's House and Museum). The birthplace of Germany's most famous poet has been faithfully restored and is furnished with many original pieces that belonged to his family. The museum next door contains a comprehensive collection of Goethe memorabilia.

Historisches Museum (History Museum). This fascinating museum encompasses all aspects of the city's history over the past eight centuries.

Jüdisches Museum (Jewish Museum). Housed in the former Rothschild Palais, this museum tells the story of Frankfurt's Jewish quarter.

Kaisersaal (Imperial Hall). Inside the Römer, this former banquet hall now holds a gallery of portraits of the 52 emperors of the Holy Roman Empire.

Museum für Kunsthandwerk (Museum of Applied Arts). Here more than 30,000 objects, representing European and Asian handicrafts, are exhibited in displays with changing themes.

Museum für Moderne Kunst (Museum of Modern Art). Housed in a distinctive triangular building designed by Austrian architect Hans Hollein, this newly opened collection features American Pop art and works by such German artists as Gerhard Richter and Joseph Beuys. *Domstr. 10. Admission free. Open Tues. and Thurs.–Sun. 10–5, Wed. 10–8.*

Museum für Völkerkunde (Ethnological Museum). The exhibits depict the lifestyles and customs of primitive societies from different parts of the world. The collection includes masks, cult objects, and jewelry. *Schaumainkai 29. Admission free. Open Tues. and Thurs.–Sun. 10–5, Wed. 10–8.*

Naturkundermuseum Senckenberg (Natural History Museum). This is the largest natural-history museum in Germany, with Europe's most impressive collection of dinosaurs, whales, and other large mammals. Fossils, animals, plants, and geological exhibits are all displayed in an exciting, hands-on environment.

The most important single exhibit is the diplodocus, imported from New York and the only complete specimen of its kind in Europe. *Senckenberganlage 25. Admission: DM 5 adults, DM 2 children. Open Mon., Tues., Thurs., and Fri. 9–5; Wed. 9–8; weekends 9–6. Free guided tour Wed. at 6 PM and Sun. and public holidays at 10:30 AM.*

Schirn Kunsthalle (Schirn Art Gallery). One of Frankfurt's most modern museums houses a fine collection of 20th-century art. Located opposite the cathedral. *Am Römerberg 6a. Admission: DM 3–DM 6, depending on current exhibition. Open Tues.–Fri. 10–9, weekends 10–7.*

Städelsches Kunstinstitut and Städtische Galerie (Städel Art Institute and Municipal Gallery). One of West Germany's most important art collections, with paintings by Dürer, Vermeer, Rembrandt, Rubens, Monet, Renoir, and other great masters.

Städtische Galerie Liebieghaus (Liebieg Municipal Museum of Sculpture). The sculpture collection from different civilizations and epochs here is considered one of the most important in Europe. *Graphic collection open to view Tues. and Thurs.–Sun. 10–5, Wed. 10–8.*

Struwwelpeter-Museum. This museum contains a collection of letters, sketches, and manuscripts by Dr. Heinrich Hoffmann, physician and creator of the children's-book hero Struwwelpeter, the character you see as a puppet or doll in Frankfurt's shops. *Hochstr. 45–47. Admission: DM 1 adults and children over 13, 50 pf children under 13. Open Tues. and Thurs.–Sun. 11–5, Wed. 11–8.*

Parks and Gardens

Anlagenring. When the fortification wall surrounding Frankfurt was demolished in the 19th century, the open space on both sides of the structure was turned into a park. A 3-mile ring of green now encircles the city center, north of the Main. It's an ideal circuit for joggers and fitness enthusiasts.

Nizza. On the north bank of the Main, directly opposite the museums on Schaumainkai, is this pretty promenade bordered by a wide variety of Mediterranean trees and shrubs. There are footpaths and benches, too.

Palmengarten und Botanischer Garten (Tropical Garden and Botanical Gardens). A splendid cluster of tropical and semitropical greenhouses contains a wide variety of flora, including cacti, orchids, and palms. The surrounding park has many recreational facilities. The botanical gardens feature a number of special collections, including a 2½-acre rock garden as well as rose and rhododendron gardens.

Stadtwald (City Forest). With its innumerable paths and trails, bird sanctuaries, and sports facilities, the Stadtwald is used by citizens and visitors alike for recreation and relaxation. (*See* Off the Beaten Track, above.)

Volkspark Niddertal. This park was the site of the 1989 *Bundesgartenschau* (Bu'ga'schau), the annual federal garden show, which takes place in a different German city each year. The fairgrounds become a public park area after the exhibition.

Zoologischer Garten (zoo). Founded in 1858, this is one of the most important and attractive zoos in Europe, with many of the animals and birds living in a natural environment.

Shopping

Gift Ideas Frankfurt, the financial capital of Germany, is not best known for gifts and souvenirs. It is, however, the home of the largest selection of **Meissen porcelain** outside Meissen itself found, improbably, in the Japanese department store **Mitsukoshi** (Kaiserstr.). More typical Frankfurt specialties include **Apfelwein,** or apple wine; it can be purchased in most supermarkets and in the taverns in Sachsenhausen, south of the river. Look, too, for **Bethmännchen und Brenten** (marzipan cookies) and **Frankfurter Kranz** (a sort of creamy cake) in local bakeries and sweetshops. **Jewelry** designed and made by local craftsmen is an unusual gift to take home. **La Galleria** (Berlinerstr.) and **Luise Schloze** (Kaiserstr.) both have good selections. A **Struwwelpeter** puppet or doll, named after the character in the famous children's book by Heinrich Hoffmann, also makes a good gift to take home. If you want to stock up on wine, stop in at **Limpurger Gasse 2,** next to the Römer, where wine produced in the municipal vineyards of the Rheingau is sold.

Shopping Districts The heart of Frankfurt's shopping district is the ritzy pedestrian street called **Zeil,** running east from Hauptwache square. City officials claim it's the country's busiest shopping street, with an unrivaled annual turnover of more than 1 billion deutsche marks. Some call the Zeil the "shopping mile," others the "golden mile." The two-story mall under the **Hauptwache** is hardly less classy and busy.

The streets running off Zeil and the Hauptwache are home to a series of upscale fashion shops. Try **Goethestrasse** and **Steinweg** for designer clothing, shoes, and leather goods; **Rossmarkt** and **Kaiserstrasse** for jewelry and watches; **Schillerstrasse** for glass and porcelain; **Braubachstrasse, Fahrgasse,** and **Weckmarkt** for art and antiques; and **Düsseldorfer Strasse** for furs.

There's another elegant shopping mall, extending over three stories, in the **BfG building** on the corner of Theaterplatz and Neue-Mainzer-Strasse.

Extending west from the Hauptwache is **Grosse Bockenheimer Strasse** (or Fressgasse to the locals). Cafés, restaurants, and, above all, food shops are the draw here. This is the place for fish—fresh or smoked—cheeses, and a wide range of local specialties, including frankfurters.

Sachsenhausen over the river boasts a multitude of ever-more-chic stores. Check out what is probably the most classy butcher shop in Germany, the **Metzgerei Meyer** on Schweizer Strasse. With its stark green-and-black Italian tiles and subtle spotlighting, it's more like a jewelry store than a place that sells sausages. Sachsenhausen also has a wealth of antiques shops.

In **Niederrad,** also just over the river adjacent to Sachsenhausen, visit Steinmetzbetrieb Ferdinand Stang (Hahnstr. 18) for an amazing selection of art objects made from all types of stone.

Flea Markets Frankfurt has two weekend flea markets: on Saturdays, from 9 to 2, on Schaumainkai below the Eiserner Steg, and on Sundays from 8 to 2 at the Schlachthof (abbatoir) on Seehoferstrasse in Sachsenhausen. Whichever you choose to visit, get there early if you're looking for bargains. There's a wide range of goods on display, a lot of it pretty junky, though you can sometimes find better-quality goods, too. In any event, both markets are colorful and vivid places to explore.

Sports and Fitness

For information on all sports in Frankfurt, call the city sports office (tel. 069/212–33565).

Bicycling Opportunities for biking in the city are limited, but get away from the downtown area and Frankfurt's parks and forests offer terrific places for biking. In summer, you can rent bikes at the **Goetheturm** on the northern edge of the Stadtwald (tel. 069/49111).

Hotel Fitness Centers **Steigenberger Airporthotel** (Unterschweinsteige 16, tel. 069/69851), about 1 mile from the Frankfurt airport, has an indoor pool, sauna, and solarium and jogging paths in the nearby woods.

Intercontinental (Wilhelm-Leuschner-Str. 43, tel. 069/26050) overlooks the Main River, along whose banks you can jog. The hotel has an indoor pool, health club, gym, and sauna.

Hotel Gravenbruch Kempinski (Neu-Isenburg 2, tel. 06102/5050) is about 15 minutes by car outside of Frankfurt. It's located in a 37-acre park, with tennis courts, two Olympic-size pools, and jogging paths through the woods.

Frankfurter Hof (Kaiserpl. 17, tel. 069/21502) is a venerable hotel without fitness facilities; however, it can arrange for guests to use the **Judokan Sport und Fitness Center,** a 10-minute walk away. An hourly fee is charged.

Jogging A good place to jog morning or evening is along the Main River. You can stick to one side or do a loop, crossing a bridge, going down the other bank, and crossing back over another bridge. **Grüneberg Park,** in the city center, is part of the old Rothschild estate. It's 1 mile around, with a Trimm Dich ("get fit") exercise facility in the northeast corner. For a vigorous forest run, take the Strassenbahn (streetcar) to **Hohemark** (a 30-minute ride). For jogging, swimming, and tennis, take the Strassenbahn to the **Stadtwald,** a 4,000-acre forest park south of the city.

Skating The new **Eissporthalle** (Am Bornheimer Hang 4, Ratsweg, tel. 069/41–9141) has two rinks, one outdoor, the other indoor. It's open in winter 9 AM–10:30 PM.

Swimming The **Rebstockbad** (August-Euler-Str. 7, tel. 069/708–078) has an indoor pool, a pool with a wave machine and palm-fringed beach, and an outdoor pool with giant water chutes. There's also a solarium, a Japanese sauna, a gym, billiard tables, and a restaurant, where you can fortify yourself after your workout (open Fri.–Mon. and Wed. 9 AM–10 PM, Tues. and Thurs. 9 AM–8 PM). A similar center is the **Stationbad** (Morfelder Landstr. 362, tel. 069/678–040), which has an outdoor pool, solarium, and exercise lawns. The **Brentanobad** (Rödelheimer Parkweg, tel. 069/783–695) has an outdoor pool surrounded by lawns and old trees; it's often crowded in summer.

Tennis Courts are available at the **Nidda Park** sports center. Next to the **Stationbad** (*see* above) you'll find 20 courts (cost: DM 14 per hour). Call 069/67840 for reservations.

Dining

Dining in Frankfurt—the expense-account city par excellence—can be expensive. You'll need to make reservations well in advance, too, if you plan to eat in any of the fancier restaurants: With business in the city a year-round affair, there are few moments when most restaurants are not booked solid. The good news is that the range and quality of the city's dining experience are terrific. You can find everything from the most sophisticated French haute cuisine to earthy local dishes in neighborhood beer restaurants, known as *Gasthofs*.

Highly recommended restaurants in each price category are indicated by a star ★.

Category	Cost*
Very Expensive	Over DM 95
Expensive	DM 65–DM 95
Moderate	DM 45–DM 65
Inexpensive	DM 25–DM 45

**per person for a three-course meal, excluding drinks*

Very Expensive

★ **Erno's Bistro.** Erno's (prop. Erno W. Schmitt) is something of a Frankfurt institution. It's small and chic—and *very* popular with visiting power brokers—and offers classy nouvelle specialties (or "cuisine *formidable*," as Erno prefers to call them). Fish dishes predominate—all the fish is flown in daily, most of it from Paris—with specialties varying according to what's available in the markets that day. This is also one of those rare restaurants where you can sit back with confidence and let the staff—all the waiters speak English—choose your meal for you. You won't regret it. *Liebigstr. 15, tel. 069/721–997. Reservations required. Jacket and tie required. AE, DC, MC, V. Closed Sat., Sun., 1 week at Easter, and mid-June–mid-July.*

Humperdinck. Those in search of affluent and oh-so-tasteful Frankfurt need look no farther than the soothingly chic Humperdinck (named after the 19th-century composer Engelbert Humperdinck—not the crooner—whose house this was). The food fuses nouvelle and classic French elements; choose one of the fixed-price menus for the best value. The restaurant is located just south of Grüneburg Park. *Grüneburgweg 95, tel. 069/722–122. Reservations required. Jacket and tie required. AE, DC, MC, V. Closed Sat. lunch and Sun.*

Papillon. Although it's part of the airport Sheraton, the Papillon has won over the country's most respected food critics, who agree that this is Germany's best airport restaurant. No whisper of a jet engine can be heard, and there's no rush or bustle in the velvety, luxurious interior dining room. Kitchen manager Klaus Bohler concentrates on a small but vividly imaginative daily-changing menu, on which you'll find such delicacies as lobster medallions in hazelnut oil or breast of pigeon and white cabbage. *Sheraton Hotel, Frankfurt airport (Terminal Mitte), tel. 069/697–70. Reservations advised. Jacket and tie required. AE, DC, MC, V.*

★ **Restaurant Français.** The green-and-gold surroundings of this restaurant of the incomparably luxurious Steigenberger Hotel Frankfurter Hof, with crystal chandeliers and tapestries on the walls, provide an appropriately sumptuous setting for some of the finest food in Frankfurt. The food is French (of course), traditional rather than nouvelle, and served with the sort of panache you might expect in one of the best restaurants in Paris. For a memorable gastronomic treat, try the stuffed quail in truffle-butter sauce. *Am Kaiserpl. 17, tel. 069/20251. Reservations required. Jacket and tie required. AE, DC, MC, V. Closed Sun. and 4 weeks in July or Aug.*

Expensive

Jacques Offenbach. Dine in this gourmet restaurant in the bowels of the lavishly restored Opera House. The mood is low-key but classy, with subdued lighting and pale walls. The food is mostly French, featuring traditional and nouvelle dishes in equal measure. This is *the* place to eat after a performance at the Opera House; it takes orders up to midnight. *Opernpl. 1, tel. 069/134–0380. Reservations advised. Jacket and tie required. Closed lunch and July.*

La Femme. At this increasingly popular bistro, the quality of the turn-of-the-century Art Nouveau decor matches the standard of chef Rudolf Kruse's culinary creations. These include lobster in Riesling wine, lamb with aubergines, and mussels with salmon. *Am Weingarten 5, tel. 069/7071606. Reservations necessary. Dress: informal. AE, DC, MC, V. Closed lunch and Sun.*

★ **Weinhaus Brückenkeller.** Sophisticated dining in Frankfurt isn't just a matter of refined French food in expense-account restaurants. This establishment offers magnificent German specialties in the sort of time-honored, arched cellar that would have brought a lump to Bismarck's throat. What's more, though the food may be unmistakably Teutonic, it's light and delicate—for example, cream of cucumber soup, or veal on tomato vinaigrette. In addition to the terrific antique-strewn surroundings and the classy food, there's a phenomenal range of wines to choose from: The cellars—don't be shy about asking to see them—hold around 85,000 bottles. *Schutzenstr. 6, tel. 069/284–238. Reservations advised. Jacket and tie required. AE, DC, MC, V. Closed lunch, Sun., and 3 weeks in July.*

Moderate

★ **Börsenkeller.** The dark, rather masculine atmosphere of this restaurant reflects its favored status among businessmen from the nearby stock exchange. Soft lighting, heavy arches, and high-backed booths establish the mood. The food is traditional and substantial, though always prepared with some style. See if venison stew is on the day's menu. *Schillerstr. 11, tel. 069/281–115. Reservations advised. Jacket and tie required. AE, DC, MC, V. Closed Sun.*

Charlot. The French cuisine of this very popular restaurant has acquired an Italian touch since the arrival of chef Mario, but it has survived the transition well. The Opera House is just across the street, so after the curtain falls you'll be fighting with the music buffs for a place in the French bistro–style dining rooms, spread over two floors. But you might also be sharing a table with Luciano Pavarotti. *Opernplatz 10, tel. 069/287–007. Reservations advised. Dress: informal. AE, DC, MC.*

Die Gans. The name of this restaurant means goose, which is one of the many game dishes on chef Uwe Stolzenberger's menu. Other offerings include venison, rabbit, and lobster. A house specialty called *Die Gans* is a sampling of all of these, plus other delicacies. *Schweizerstr. 76, tel. 069/615075. Reservations advised. Dress: informal. AE, DC, MC, V. Closed lunch.*

Börsenkeller, **8**
Cafe GegenwART, **10**
Charlot, **5**
Die Gans, **16**
Erno's Bistro, **4**
Gildestuben, **9**
Humperdinck, **3**
Jacques Offenbach, **6**
La Femme, **1**
Lunico, **7**
Papillon, **17**
Pelikan, **2**
Restaurant Français, **14**
Steinernes Haus, **13**
Weinhaus Brückenkeller, **11**
Zum Gemalten Haus, **15**
Zur Eulenberg, **11**

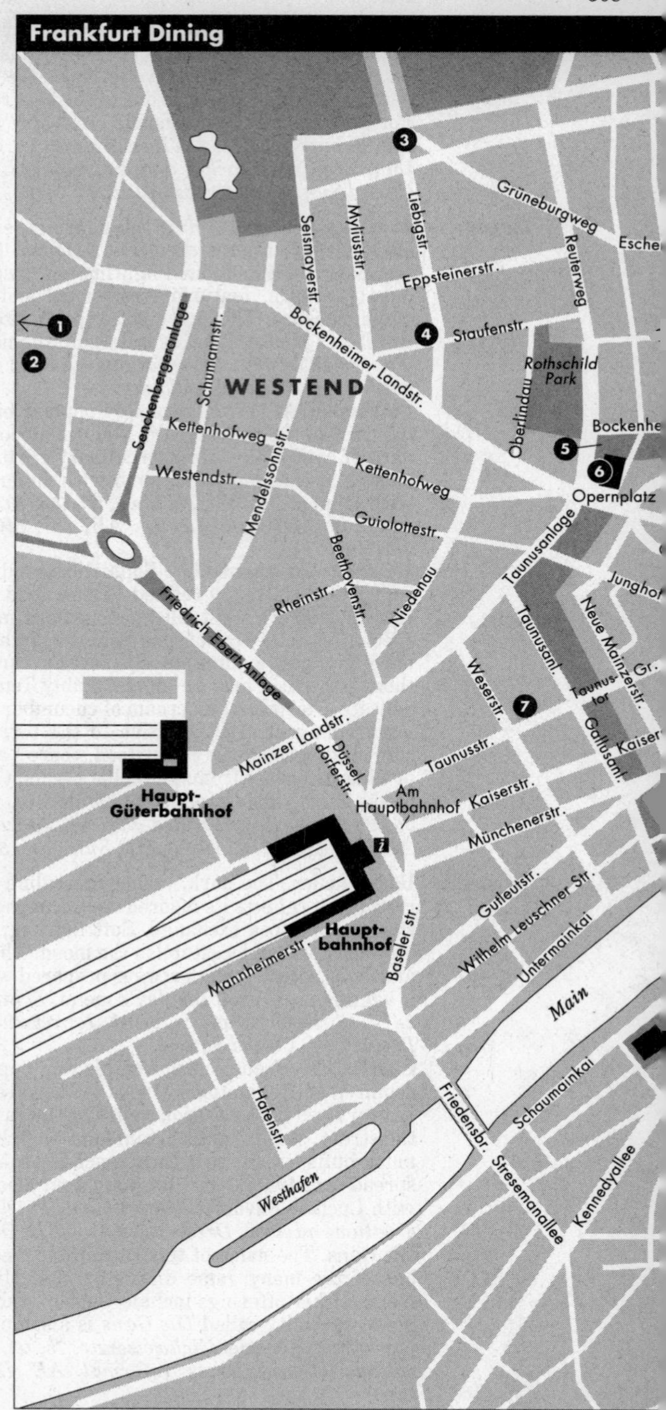

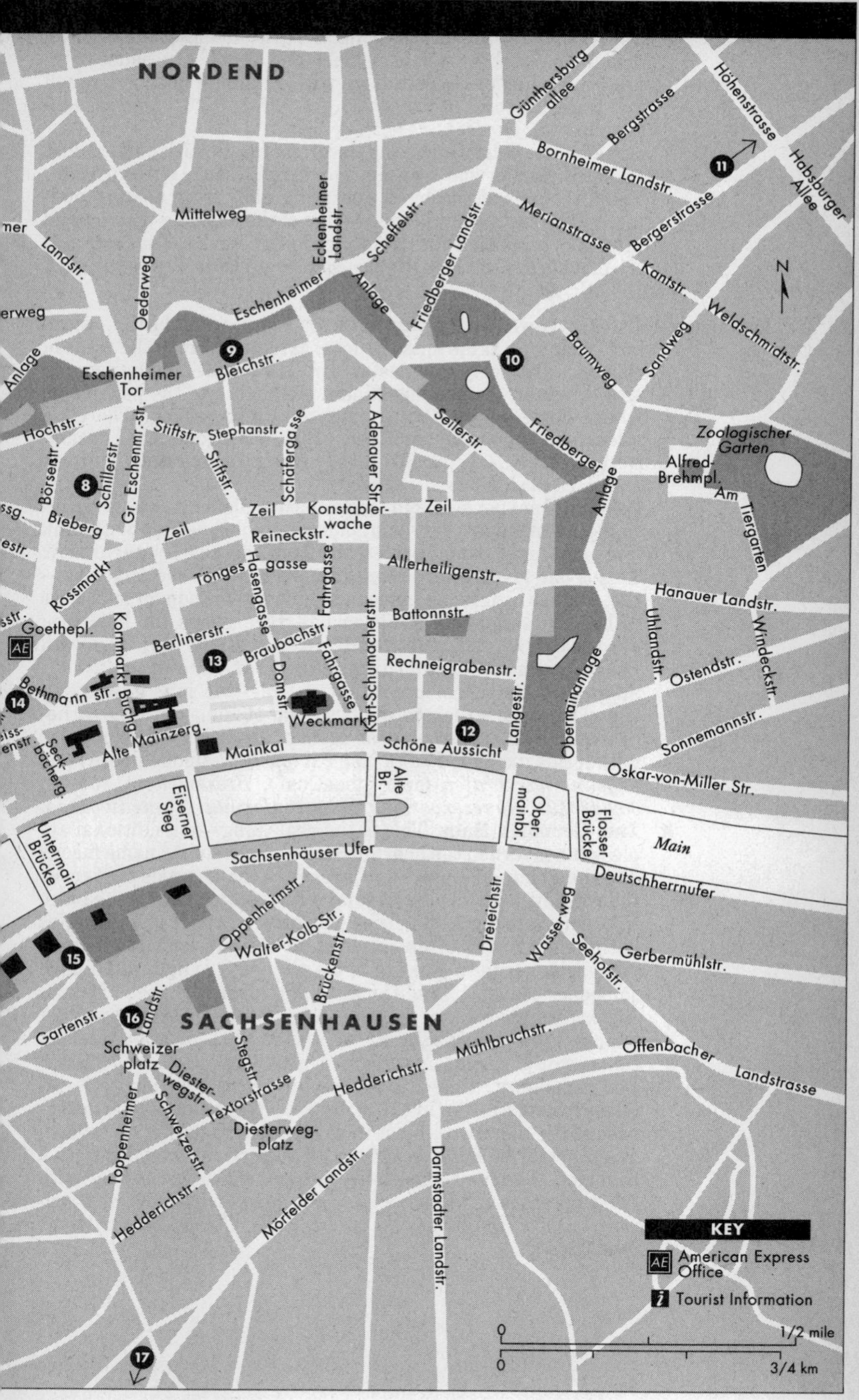
NORDEND
SACHSENHAUSEN
Main
Mittelweg
Oederweg
Eschenheimer Landstr.
Eschenheimer Anlage
Scheffelstr.
Friedberger Landstr.
Günthersburg allee
Bergstrasse
Höhenstrasse
Bornheimer Landstr.
Habsburger Allee
Merianstrasse
Bergerstrasse
Kantstr.
Weldschmidtstr.
Sandweg
Baumweg
Friedberger Anlage
Seilerstr.
Zoologischer Garten
Alfred-Brehmpl.
Am Tiergarten
Eschenheimer Tor
Bleichstr.
Hochstr.
Stiftstr.
Stephanstr.
Schäfergasse
K. Adenauer Str.
Börsenstr.
Schillerstr.
Gr. Eschenmr.-str.
Bieberg
Zeil
Konstablerwache
Reineckstr.
Tönges gasse
Hasengasse
Fahrgasse
Allerheiligenstr.
Rossmarkt
Goethepl.
Kornmarkt
Berlinerstr.
Braubachstr.
Battonnstr.
Hanauer Landstr.
Uhlandstr.
Windeckstr.
Ostendstr.
Recheneigrabenstr.
Kurt-Schumacherstr.
Domstr.
Weckmarkt
Bethmann str.
Buchg.
Alte Mainzerg.
Seckbächerg.
Mainkai
Schöne Aussicht
Langestr.
Obermainanlage
Sonnemannstr.
Oskar-von-Miller Str.
Eiserner Steg
Alte Br.
Obermainbr.
Flosser Brücke
Untermain Brücke
Sachsenhäuser Ufer
Deutschherrnufer
Dreieichstr.
Wasserweg
Seehofstr.
Gerbermühlstr.
Oppenheimstr.
Walter-Kolb-Str.
Brückenstr.
Gartenstr.
Landstr.
Schweizer platz
Diesterwegstr.
Stegstr.
Textorstrasse
Hedderichstr.
Mühlbruchstr.
Offenbacher Landstrasse
Diesterwegplatz
Toppenheimer
Schweizerstr.
Mörfelder Landstr.
Darmstadter Landstr.
KEY
AE American Express Office
Tourist Information
0 1/2 mile
0 3/4 km
N
8
9
10
11
12
13
14
15
16
17

Gildestuben. This is a lusty Bohemian beer tavern with a spacious beer garden overlooking a park. Sample such Czech dishes as *Svickova* (smoked beef and cranberry sauce with juicy dumplings). Wash it down with genuine Pilsener Urquell and Budvar beers. *Bleichstr. 38, tel. 069/283–228. Dress: casual. No credit cards.*

Lunico. The delicate-looking decor contrasts with such robust Italian dishes as veal in cream and Marsala sauce with rigatoni. The kitchen is also robust, operating daily from noon to midnight. The restaurant is on the edge of the business district and thus is open until 4 AM during trade-fair weeks. *Taunsstr. 47, tel. 069/251010. Reservations necessary. Dress: informal. AE, DC, MC, V.*

Inexpensive

Cafe GegenwART. The accent on *art* is quite deliberate—regularly changing exhibitions by local artists decorate the walls of this friendly, noisy café-restaurant. It's frequented by a young crowd, and in the summer diners spill out onto the pavement, where Riviera-style tables brighten up the scene. There's a French accent on the menu, too—the tomato fondue is a dream. *Berger Str. 6, tel. 069/497–0544. Reservations not required. Dress: casual. No credit cards.*

Pelikan. Inexpensive but imaginative dishes from a daily-changing menu are served up here on tables decked with pink linen to students and professors from the nearby university. This is one place where vegetarians are not in the minority—the Pelikan offers an unusually good selection of meatless dishes. In summer a boulevard terrace opens for business. *Jordanstr. 19, tel. 069/701287. Reservations not required. Dress: casual. No credit cards. Closed Sat. lunch and Sun.*

Steinernes Haus. An unpretentious historic inn, it was salvaged from the wreckage of World War II along with the cathedral and town hall around the corner. Traditional fare popular with locals includes *Frankfurter Rippchen* (smoked pork) and *Zigeunerhackbraten* (spicy meatloaf). *Braubachstr. 35, tel. 069/283491. No reservations. Dress: informal. No credit cards.*

★ **Zum Gemalten Haus.** This is the real thing—a traditional apple-wine tavern in the heart of Sachsenhausen. Its name means "At the Painted House," a reference to the frescoes that cover the walls inside and out. In summer, the courtyard is the place to be; in winter, you sit in the noisy tavern proper at long tables with benches. It's often crowded, so if there isn't room when you arrive, order a glass of apple wine and hang around until someone leaves. Traditional cider-tavern dishes include *Rippchen* (smoked pork), but come here for *Rinderselcher* (smoked beef). *Schweizerstr. 67, tel. 069/614–559. No reservations. Dress: casual. No credit cards. Closed Mon. and Tues.*

Zur Eulenburg. Take the subway or a streetcar out to Seckbacher Landstrasse, in the district of Bornheim, a mile northeast of the old town, to eat in this popular apple-wine tavern. You'd better be hungry, though: The portions would satisfy a caveman. The house speciality is home-cured roast beef with fried potatoes. *Eulengasse 46, tel. 069/451–203. No reservations. Dress: informal. No credit cards. Closed lunch, Mon., and Tues.*

Lodging

With a host of businesspeople descending on Frankfurt year-round, most hotels in the city are expensive (though many also offer significant reductions on weekends, an option worth checking out) and are frequently booked up well in advance. The majority of the larger hotels are located around the main train station, close to the business district and the trade-fair center and a 15- to 20-minute walk from the old town. Lower prices and—for some, anyway—more atmosphere are offered by smaller hotels and pensions in the suburbs; the efficient public transportation network makes them easy to reach. Many hotels add up to a 50% surcharge during trade-fair weeks. Fifteen major fairs are planned for 1993. The dates to avoid (unless you intend to visit one of the fairs in question) are: January 30–February 3 (The Premiere); August 21–25 (International Autumn Fair); September 9–19 (IAA motor show); and October 6–11 (Frankfurt Book Fair). These dates may change, so it's best to confirm them with the German-American Chamber of Commerce (tel. 212/974–8830; in London, tel. 071/734–0543).

Highly recommended hotels in each price category are indicated by a star ★.

Category	Cost*
Very Expensive	over DM 250
Expensive	DM 180–DM 250
Moderate	DM 120–DM 180
Inexpensive	under DM 120

**All prices are for two people in a double room, including tax and service.*

Very Expensive

Arabella Grand Hotel. The emphasis at this new addition to Frankfurt's list of luxury hotels is on the "grand." Everything is large-scale, from the palatial public rooms to the vast double bedrooms. The center-city location means that the views from many of the rooms are onto backyards and car parks, but pull the heavy drapes and it's another world, one of understated luxury. *Konrad-Adenauer-Str. 7, tel. 069/28910. 367 rooms and 11 suites with bath. Facilities: 2 restaurants, bar, pool, sauna, solarium, fitness center, beauty parlor, boutiques, parking. AE, DC, MC, V.*

★ **Hessischer Hof.** This is the choice of many businesspeople, not just because of its location opposite the trade-fair building but for the air of class and style that pervades its handsome and imposing interior (the exterior is nondescript). The public rooms are subdued and traditional; bedrooms are elegantly chic, and many of them are furnished with antiques. The restaurant features excellent nouvelle cuisine; it also has a fine display of Sevres porcelain ranged around the walls. *Friedrich-Ebert-Anlage 40, tel. 069/75400. 106 rooms and 14 suites with bath. Facilities: restaurant, 2 bars. AE, DC, MC, V.*

★ **Hotel Gravenbruch Kempinski.** Located a 15-minute drive south of the downtown area in its own leafy grounds, this hotel offers elegance and sophistication. It's built around a 16th-century manor house and combines substantial modern luxury with Old World charm. All the rooms are spacious and classy;

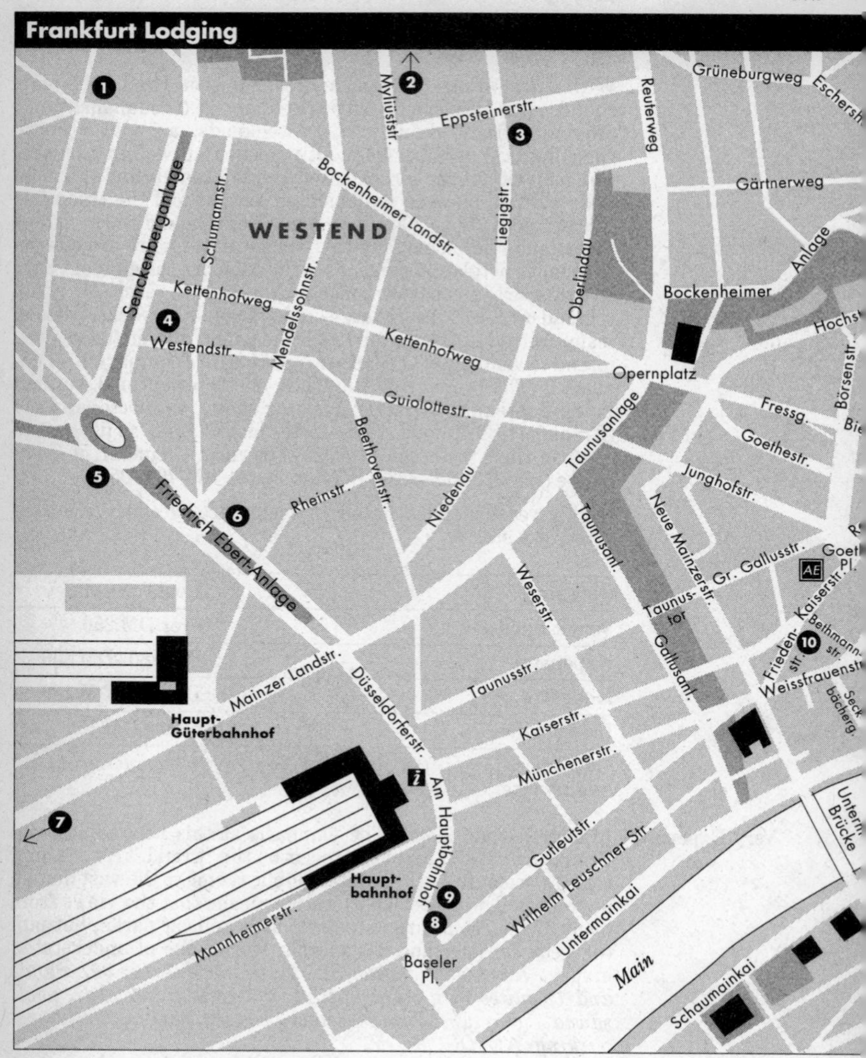

Am Zoo, **13**
An der Messe, **4**
Arabella Grand Hotel, **11**
Attache, **5**
Harheimer Hof, **12**
Hessischer Hof, **6**
Hotel Gravenbruch Kempinski, **16**
Hotel National, **8**
Hotel-Pension West, **1**
Hotel Post, **7**
Liebig, **3**
Maingau, **14**
Motel Frankfurt, **15**
Parkhotel, **9**
Pension Uebe, **2**
Steigenberger Frankfurter Hof, **10**
Waldhotel Hensel's Felsenkeller, **17**

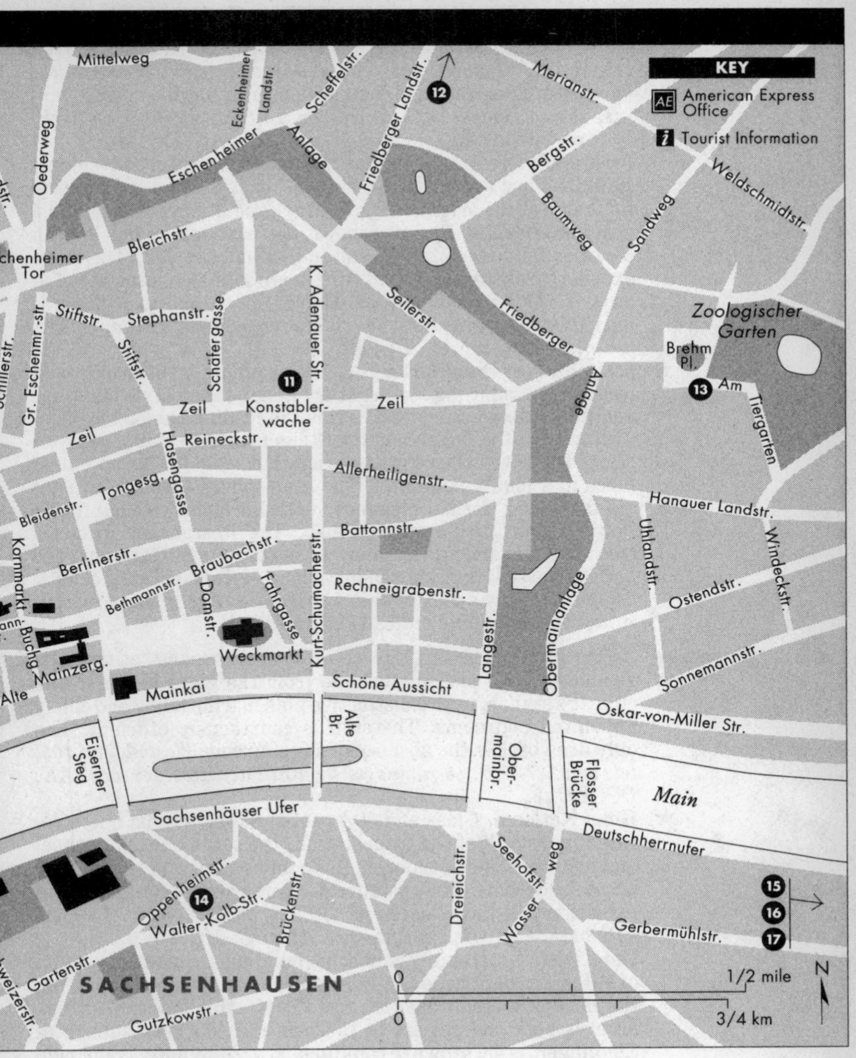
KEY
American Express Office
Tourist Information
Mittelweg
Eckenheimer Landstr.
Scheffelstr.
Friedberger Landstr.
Merianstr.
Oederweg
Eschenheimer Anlage
Bergstr.
Weldschmidtstr.
Baumweg
Sandweg
Bleichstr.
Eschenheimer Tor
Seilerstr.
Friedberger Anlage
Zoologischer Garten
Brehm Pl.
Am Tiergarten
Stiftstr.
Stephanstr.
Schäfergasse
K. Adenauer Str.
Schillerstr.
Gr. Eschenmr.-str.
Zeil
Konstablerwache
Reineckstr.
Hasengasse
Allerheiligenstr.
Hanauer Landstr.
Tongesg.
Bleidenstr.
Battonnstr.
Uhlandstr.
Windeckstr.
Kornmarkt
Berlinerstr.
Braubachstr.
Fahrgasse
Recheneigrabenstr.
Kurt-Schumacherstr.
Obermainanlage
Ostendstr.
Bethmannstr.
Domstr.
Weckmarkt
Langestr.
Buchg.
Mainzerg.
Sonnemannstr.
Alte
Mainkai
Schöne Aussicht
Oskar-von-Miller Str.
Eiserner Steg
Alte Br.
Obermainbr.
Flosser Brücke
Main
Sachsenhäuser Ufer
Deutschherrnufer
Seehofstr.
Wasserweg
Dreieichstr.
Oppenheimstr.
Walter-Kolb-Str.
Brückenstr.
Gerbermühlstr.
Gartenstr.
SACHSENHAUSEN
Gutzkowstr.
0
1/2 mile
3/4 km
N

those in the newer annexes have views of the lake. Of the three restaurants, the Gourmet is the most formal. *6078 Neu Isenberg 2, tel. 06102/5050. 268 rooms and 30 suites with bath. Facilities: 3 restaurants, bar, indoor and outdoor pools, tennis, sauna, masseur, hairdresser, Lufthansa check-in desk, limo service to and from airport and city. AE, DC, MC, V.*

Parkhotel. This is another businessman's favorite, conveniently located just south of the train station. The hotel is a successful fusion of the original 19th-century red-stone building and a postwar addition. Recent renovations have left rooms in both parts equally comfortable and individually styled. The more expensive restaurant—La Truffe—is one of the classiest in the city. *Wiesenhüttenpl. 28, tel. 069/26970. 310 rooms with bath. Facilities: 2 restaurants, bar, wine restaurant, sauna, solarium, fitness room. AE, DC, MC, V.*

★ **Steigenberger Frankfurter Hof.** The combination of an old-town location, an imposing 19th-century Renaissance-style building, and full-bodied luxury makes this the leading choice for many visitors. It's the flagship of the Steigenberger chain, though it offers the sort of personal service that wouldn't seem out of place in a family-run hotel. The atmosphere throughout is of old-fashioned, formal elegance, with burnished woods, fresh flowers, and thick-carpeted hush. The Restaurant Français (*see* above) is among the gourmet high spots of Germany; the bar is a classy late-night rendezvous. *Am Kaiserpl. 17, tel. 069/21502. 330 rooms and 30 suites with bath. Facilities: 4 restaurants, bar, shopping mall. AE, DC, MC, V.*

Expensive

★ **An der Messe.** This little place—the name means "at the fairgrounds"—is a pleasing change from the giant hotels of the city. It's stylish, with a distinctive pink marble lobby and chicly appointed bedrooms. The staff is courteously efficient. The only drawback is the absence of a restaurant. *Westendstr. 104, tel. 069/747–979. 46 rooms with bath. Facilities: terrace. AE, DC, MC, V.*

★ **Hotel National.** Class and style set the tone at this hotel, located just south of the train station. It's set in a former school and has some fine antiques in the public rooms and some of the larger bedrooms. The restaurant offers excellent local and international dishes. *Baselerstr. 50, tel. 069/273–940. 71 rooms with bath. Facilities: restaurant. AE, DC, MC, V.*

Hotel Post. A strikingly handsome building—a modern version of a Hessen country house, with graceful slate gables following the lines of a traditional thatched roof—this modern, stylish hotel is near the airport in the peaceful southern suburb of Sindlingen. Downtown Frankfurt is a 20-minute train ride away. That's the hotel's only real drawback, however. Otherwise, it offers facilities on a par with more expensive establishments in the city center. Some of the smaller rooms fit into the moderate price range. *Bahnstr. 12, Sindlingen, tel. 069/37010. 105 rooms with bath. Facilities: restaurant, beer tavern, wine bar, pool, sauna, solarium, parking. AE, DC, MC, V.*

Moderate

Am Zoo. As the name suggests, this hotel is close to the zoo, which is handy if you have children. It offers above-average lodging for the price. The kitchen makes its own cakes for the coffeeshop; the restaurant's ornate windows will keep you preoccupied while you wait for dinner. *Alfred-Brehm Platz 6, tel. 069/490–771. 85 rooms with bath. AE, DC, MC, V. Closed Dec. 20–Jan. 5.*

Harheimer Hof. Modern and comfortable but in the suburbs, this is reasonably priced hotel packed with good facilities. It may be a few miles north of the center, in Harheim, but don't try reserving a room at the last minute. *Alt Harheim 11, tel. 06101/4050. 46 rooms with bath. Facilities: restaurant, café, bar, solarium, fitness equipment, bowling alley, beauty salon. AE, DC, MC, V.*

Liebig. A comfortable, family-run hotel, this establishment has spacious, high-ceilinged rooms and a friendly feel. Ask for a room at the back—it's much quieter. Try the Weinstube restaurant for excellent Hessen wine. *Liebigstr. 45, tel. 069/727–551. 20 rooms with bath. Facilities: restaurant. MC, DC, V.*

Maingau. This excellent-value hotel is within easy reach of the downtown area, close to the lively Sachsenhausen quarter, with its cheery apple-wine taverns. Rooms are basic but clean and comfortable, some with TVs. Families with children are welcome. *Schifferstr. 38–40, tel. 069/617–001. 100 rooms with bath. Facilities: restaurant. AE, MC.*

Motel Frankfurt. You don't have to arrive by car to stay at the Frankfurt Motel, one of Germany's most comfortable. It's set in sylvan surroundings away from the motorway grid that surrounds the city. Even so, it's only 15 minutes away by fast public transport. The guest rooms are modern, comfortable, and quiet, and most of them have parkland views. *Eschersheimer Landstr. 204, Eschersheim, tel. 069/568–011. 121 rooms with bath. Facilities: restaurant, bar, parking. AE, DC, MC, V.*

Inexpensive

Attache. This simple but comfortable downtown hotel has no restaurant, but a buffet breakfast provides a hearty start to the day. *Kölnerstr. 10, tel. 069/730282. Facilities: bar. AE, DC.*

★ **Hotel-Pension West.** For home comforts, a handy location (close to the university), and good value, try this family-run pension. It's in an older building and scores highly for old-fashioned appeal. The rooms are hardly luxurious but are more than adequate for a night or two. *Gräfstr. 81, tel. 069/778–011. 20 rooms with bath. MC. Closed Christmas.*

Pension Uebe. Try for one of the mansard rooms in this friendly, centrally located pension—they are very snug and furnished in Hessen farmhouse style, with rocking chairs and basketwork handicraft. Chandeliers lend a touch of luxury to some of the larger rooms on the lower floors. *Grüneburgweg 3, tel. 069/591–209. 19 rooms, 17 with bath. Facilities: parking. AE, DC, MC, V.*

Waldhotel Hensels Felsenkeller. Helmut Braun's traditional old hotel backs onto the woods that ring Frankfurt, yet the city center is just a 15-minute train ride away (the nearest stop is a three-minute walk). Rooms are quite basic, but there are plans to modernize them and add more amenities. *Buchrainerstr. 95, tel. 069/652–086. 14 rooms, 7 with bath. Facilities: restaurant, parking. MC.*

The Arts and Nightlife

The Arts

The arts get top billing in Frankfurt—the city has the largest budget for cultural expenditure of any city in the country. The **Städtische Bühnen**—the municipal theaters—are the leading venues, but Frankfurt also has about the most lavish opera house in the country, the **Alte Oper** (Old Opera House), a magnificently ornate heap that was rebuilt and reopened in 1981 after near-total destruction in the war; paradoxically, however, only light operettas are performed there today.

Tickets for theaters can be purchased from the tourist office at Römerberg 27 and from all theaters. Alternatively, try the **Ludwig Schäfer** agency in Sachsenhausen (Schweizer-Str. 28a, tel. 069/623–779), the ticket office in the **Hertie** department store (Zeil 90, tel. 069/294–848), or **Kartenkiosk Sandrock** (Hauptwache Passage, tel. 069/20115). For information about concerts, call 069/11517. Pick up a copy of the twice-monthly listings magazine *Frankfurter Wochenschau* from any tourist office.

Theater The **Kammerspiele Theater** (Hofstr. 2, tel. 069/236–061) and the municipally owned **Schauspiel Theater** (Theaterpl. tel. 069/236–061) present highbrow German drama, old and new. Productions at **Die Komödie** theater (Neue Mainzerstr. 18, tel. 069/284–580) are less earnest but no less impenetrable if your German is poor. For a more zany theatrical experience, try **Die Schmiere** (Seckbächer Gasse 2, tel. 069/281–066), which offers trenchant satire and also disarmingly calls itself "the worst theater in the world." If you're looking for English-language productions, try either the **Café-Theater** (Hamburger Allee 45, tel. 069/777–466), the **American Playhouse** (Hansaallee 150, tel. 069/151–8326), or the **English Theater** (Kaiserstr. 52, tel. 069/242–3160).

Concerts and Opera The most glamorous venue for classical-music concerts is the **Alte Oper** (Old Opera) (Opernpl. tel. 069/134–0400). The main hall, a restrained, elegant auditorium, seats 2,500. The rear of the auditorium can be sealed off to form a 500-seat theater. Below, there's another auditorium, Hindemith Hall, with seating for 340. Even if you don't take in a performance, it's worth having a look at the ponderous and ornate lobby, an example of 19th-century classicism at its most self-confident. Both the city's respected opera company and the highly regarded Frankfurt Ballet perform at the **Städtische Bühnen** (Theaterpl., tel. 069/256–2434).

The **Festhalle** (tel. 069/75750) at the trade-fair building is the scene for many rock concerts and other large-scale spectaculars. Frankfurt's new cultural center, the **Künstlerhaus Mouson Turm** (Waldschmidtstr. 4, tel. 069/405–8950) hosts a regular series of concerts of all kinds, as well as plays and exhibits.

Nightlife

Frankfurt, for all its unabashed internationalism and sophisticated expense-account living, is unlikely to win many votes as Germany's premier after-hours town. True, there's a red-light district, centered on the tawdry streets around the train station, especially **Kaiserstrasse** and **Münchnerstrasse,** though it's hardly in the same league as Hamburg's Reeperbahn. Most of the larger hotels also have bars, discos, and nightclubs. There's little to distinguish them from thousands of similar haunts the world over, but they're tried and tested.

For more genuinely local nightlife, head over the river to **Sachsenhausen,** Frankfurt's "Left Bank." It's hardly the quaint old Bohemian quarter it likes to bill itself as, but for bars, discos, clubs, and beer and wine restaurants this is about the best place to try. If you're in search of a rowdy night out, check out the **Apfelwein** (cider) taverns—they're touristy but fun. A green wreath over the door identifies them. If the area doesn't agree with you, try the ever-more-fashionable district of **Bornheim,** northeast of downtown. It has an almost equal number of bars, clubs, and the like, but the atmosphere is less forced, more authentic.

Frankfurt does have one trump card, however—**jazz.** Many German cities like to call themselves the jazz capital of the country, but Frankfurt probably has a better claim to the title than most. Fittingly, it's here, in the fall, that the German Jazz Festival is held. There are hundreds of jazz venues, from smoky back-street cafés all the way to the Old Opera House. But **Der Jazzkeller** has been the most noted venue for German jazz fans for decades (*see* below).

Bars and Nightclubs

Cooky's (Am Salzhaus 4) is one of the most popular local haunts for listening to rock music; live bands perform on Monday nights. You can also dance and have a meal. It's open nightly until 4 AM. If you're seeking something altogether more soothing, try the **Casablanca Bar** (Parkhotel, Wiesenhüttenplatz 28) for piano music and a little crooning (open Mon.–Sat. 8 PM–2 AM). **Jimmy's Bar** (Friedrich-Ebert-Anlage 40), in the Hessischer Hof Hotel, is distinctly more classy—and expensive. It's a favorite with high-flying executives and other big spenders. **John's Place** (Steinweg 7) is intimate and relaxed, taking its cue from genial owner John Paris. He offers good food and a mellow atmosphere. **St. John's Inn** (Grosser Hirschgraben 20) offers an English-style scene and more than 300 different whiskeys from which to choose, and the restaurant stays open until 2 AM. For a beer tour of Germany, visit the Frankfurter Bierhaus for a choice of 44 different brews served in vaulted cellars with regional tidbits (Schutzenstr. 10).

Discos

Bizarre though it may seem, about the best disco in the city is at the airport. It's **Dorian Gray,** easily reached by S-bahn and located in section C, level 0. It attracts a surprisingly upscale crowd and has loud music and soft lights. **Plastik** (Seilerstr. 34) is more obviously trendy, the sort of place where the Frankfurt beau monde flocks to see and be seen. South of the river in Sachsenhausen, try the **Evergreen** disco (Paradiesgasse 23).

Jazz

Der Frankfurter Jazzkeller (Kleine Bockenheimer Str. 18a) is the oldest jazz cellar in Germany, founded by legendary trumpeter Carlo Bohländer. It offers hot, modern, free jazz. **Jazz Kneipe** (Berlinstr. 70) is a reliable bet for swing jazz and is open until 4 AM. **Schlachthof** (Deutschherrnufer 36) is the place for Dixieland jazz, beer by the barrelfull, and apple wine; the mood is rowdy and fun. **Sinkkasten** (Brönnerstr. 9) features jazz, rock, pop, and African music; it's sometimes hard to get into but worth the effort for serious fans (open weekends 8 PM–1 AM, 8 PM–2 AM).

Excursions

Frankfurt is so centrally located in Germany that the list of possible excursions—day trips and longer treks—is nearly endless. It is a gateway to the Rhineland in the west, the Neckar Valley in the south, and Franconia in the southeast, and the ideal starting point for journeys into all of these regions. Thus, the list of excursions here is merely a selection of destinations that are not covered in other chapters. For full details of other excursions from Frankfurt, *see* chapters 8, 9, 11, and 13.

Tour 1: Bad Homburg

Just a few miles north of Frankfurt, Bad Homburg lies at the foot of the **Taunus** hills. The Taunus, with their rich forests, medieval castles, and picturesque towns, are regarded by many Frankfurters as their territory. On weekends you can see them enjoying "their" playground: hiking through the hills; climbing the **Grosse Feldberg;** taking the waters at a health-giving mineral spring; or just lazing in the sun. The Bad Homburg spa was first known to the Romans but was rediscovered and made famous in the 19th century. Illustrious visitors included the Prince of Wales, the son of Queen Victoria, and Czar Nicholas II. And here in 1841, the world's first casino was founded. Today the sights in Bad Homburg include a 17th-century castle and the picturesque Altstadt (Old Town), but perhaps the most captivating sight is the enchanting Kurpark.

Getting There
By Car Less than 45 minutes of driving on the A-5 Autobahn (Frankfurt–Dortmund) will take you to Bad Homburg.

By Train or Bus Bad Homburg has its own station. Take the S-bahn from Frankfurt at Konstable Wache (S-5 line). Buses and streetcars can also get you there.

Exploring The first stop you'll want to make in Bad Homburg is at the **tourist bureau** downtown. There you'll find local maps, advice, and assistance in booking accommodations, if necessary. You can also get information about and tickets to various local events. *Verkehrsamt. Louisenstr. 58–60, tel. 06172/121–310. Open weekdays 8:30–6, Sat. 8–1.*

The most historically noteworthy sight in the city itself is the 17th-century **Schloss.** The 172-foot **Weisser Turm** (White Tower) is all that remains of the medieval castle that once stood here. The Schloss that stands here today was built between 1680 and 1685 by Friedrich II of Hesse-Homburg, and a few alterations were made during the 19th century. The state apartments are exquisitely furnished, and the Spiegelkabinett (Hall of Mirrors) is especially worth a visit. In the surrounding park, look for two venerable trees from Lebanon, now almost 150 years old. *Schlosspl. Admission: DM 3 adults, DM 1.50 children. Open Tues.–Sun. 10–5.*

Also within the town, and certainly its greatest attraction over the centuries, is the **Kurpark,** with its more than 31 fountains. In the park you'll find not only the popular, highly saline Elisabethenbrunnen spring but also a Siamese temple and a Russian chapel, mementos left by two distinguished guests—King Chulalongkorn of Siam and Czar Nicholas II.

Only 6½ kilometers (4 miles) from Bad Homburg, and accessible by direct bus service, is the **Saalburg Limes** fort, the best-preserved Roman fort in Germany. Built in AD 120, the fort could accommodate a cohort (500 men) and was part of the fortifications along the 342-mile-long Limes Wall. The fort has been rebuilt as the Romans originally left it, with wells, armories, parade grounds, and catapults, as well as shops, houses, baths, and temples.

About a 30-minute walk from the fort is a fine open-air museum at **Hessenpark,** near Neu Anspach. The museum consists of 135 acres of rebuilt villages with houses, schools, and farms typical of the 18th and 19th centuries. A visit here yields a clear, concrete picture of the world in which the 18th- and 19th-century Hessians lived. *Admission: DM 4 adults, DM 1.50 children. Open Mar. 21–Oct. 1, Sun.–Tues. 9–6; Oct. 1–mid-Nov., Sun–Tues. 9–5; mid-Nov.–Mar. 20, weekends only 9–5.*

Just a short, convenient bus ride from Bad Homburg is the highest mountain in the Taunus, the 2,850-foot **Feldberg.** After a hike in the mountains, there are easy bus connections to the towns of Königstein and Kronberg. **Königstein** is a health-resort town with the ruins of a 13th-century castle and a noteworthy **Rathaus** (Town Hall). Many painters have chosen the nearby town of **Kronberg** as their setting. This picturesque old town, with its half-timbered houses and winding streets, was the home of the Kronberger School, an important contributor to 19th-century German art. Visit the 15th-century **Johaniskirche** with its late-Gothic murals.

Dining

Most of the well-known spas in Bad Homburg have restaurants, but they tend to be very expensive. For an inexpensive and enjoyable meal, try one of the numerous Italian or Greek restaurants located throughout the city.

Galerie-Restaurant Schildkröte. Many of the Schildkröte's regular customers make the journey from Frankfurt to enjoy chef Ansgar Mauritz's excellent cuisine. The accent is French, although the rustic, half-timbered setting, complete with enormous granite fireplace, is definitely German. *Mussbachstr. 19, tel. 06172/23307. Reservations advised. Jacket and tie required. AE, DC, MC, V. Open evenings only, closed Tues. Expensive.*

Zum Adler. This simple restaurant serves traditional Hessian fare. It's a good break after a tour of the open-air museum at Hessenpark. *Neu Anspach. Dress: casual. AE, DC, MC, V. Moderate.*

Lodging

Hardtwald Hotel. Located in a quiet spot in the forest but within easy access of the town center, this modern hotel is quite comfortable and offers pleasantly and intelligently furnished rooms. *Philosophenweg 31, tel. 06172/25016. 39 rooms with bath. Facilities: restaurant, terrace café. AE, DC, MC, V. Closed Dec. 20–Jan. 20. Moderate.*

Haus Fischer Garni. This family-operated pension is simple and clean. It is located near a park and is convenient to the old town. *Landgrafenstr. 12, tel. 06172/24927. 11 rooms with bath. No credit cards. Inexpensive.*

Tour 2: Limburg

The imposing seven-spired cathedral at **Limburg** will greet you upon arrival, seeming to grow out of the cliff that holds it. Modern Limburg grew around its old town—a city that developed because it was at the crossroads of the Köln–Frankfurt and Hessen–Koblenz highways in the 9th century. The old town still boasts a number of beautiful patrician and merchant houses, evidence of the city's importance in the Middle Ages.

Getting There
By Car
The Frankfurt–Köln Autobahn (A-3) has two Limburg exits. Take either. The drive should take you less than an hour from Frankfurt.

By Train or Bus
Limburg has its own railway station as well as regular bus service from Frankfurt, Koblenz, Wiesbaden, and the Frankfurt airport.

Exploring
Upon arriving in the center of Limburg, visit the **Verkehrsamt** (tourist office) to receive city maps, help with accommodations if necessary, and general information. *Hospitalstr. 2, tel. 06431/203–222. Open Apr.–Oct., weekdays 8–12:30 and 1:30–5, Sat. 10–noon; Nov.–Mar., closed Fri. afternoons and Sat.*

The first sight to take in is the **Stifts-und Pfarrkirche St. Georg und Nikolaus,** the cathedral that you'll see towering above the Lahn River. Construction of the cathedral began in 1220, and evident in the building is the transition from Romanesque to Gothic style; each side presents a new perspective. Extensive restoration recently uncovered the original medieval coloring and bright frescoes from the 13th century.

Treasures from the cathedral are on display in the **Diözesanmuseum** in the **Schloss,** next door to the cathedral. It houses ecclesiastical art treasures from the bishopric of Limburg. Be sure to see the Byzantine cross reliquary that was stolen from the palace church in Constantinople in 1204 and the Patri-Stab (Peter's Staff), set with precious stones and adorned with gold.

The **Schloss** adjacent to the cathedral dates from the 7th or 8th century, although the castle's current building only goes back to the 13th century. The group of residences, the chapel, and other buildings added in the 14th to 16th centuries serve as an architectural counterbalance to the cathedral. The castle is closed to visitors, although the museum is open from mid-March to mid-November. *Admission: DM 2 adults, DM 1 children. Open mid-Mar.–mid-Nov., Tues.–Sat. 9:30–12:30 and 2–5, Sun. 11–5.*

Only 6 kilometers (4 miles) from Limburg is the small town of **Runkel,** with an impressive 12th-century fortress. The fortress tower provides a panoramic view over the Taunus and the Westerwald.

About 20 kilometers (12 miles) south of Limburg is the state-recognized spa resort of **Bad Camberg,** a historic town located in the western foothills of the **Hochtaunus** (Taunus highlands). This city offers numerous half-timbered houses, remains of the city's gate and fortifications, and an attractive ensemble of buildings in the center of town, including the **Hohenfeldsche Kapelle** (chapel) of 1650. They stand in striking contrast to the modern **Kurhaus** across the street.

Dining **St. Georgs-Stuben.** In the Stadthalle, only a few minutes' walk from the center of Limburg, this pleasant restaurant serves local and international dishes. Try the house specialty, the St. Georgsteller, a filling pork-steak meal. *Hospitalstr. 4, tel. 06431/26027. Dress: casual. AE, DC, MC, V. Moderate.*

Lodging **Zimmerman.** Recent renovation has left some of the rooms of this pleasant hotel decorated in an elegant "English" style. The service is attentive and the breakfasts hearty. The restaurant is for hotel guests only. *Blumenroderstr. 1, tel. 06431/4611. 30 rooms, most with bath, and 6 suites with bath. Facilities: restaurant. AE, DC, MC, V. Moderate–Expensive.*

Dom Hotel. Centrally located and ideal for a brief visit to see the old town, this old established hotel offers standard comforts backed by friendly service. *Grabenstr. 57, tel. 06431/24077. 57 rooms and 2 suites with bath. Facilities: restaurant. AE, DC, MC, V. Moderate.*

13 The Rhineland

Including Bonn, Düsseldorf, Koblenz, Köln, and Trier

Introduction

The importance of the Rhine can hardly be overestimated. Throughout recorded history—at least for the past 2,000 years—the Rhine has served as Europe's leading waterway. While by no means the longest river in Europe (the Danube is more than twice its length), it has long been the main river-trade artery between the heart of the Continent and the North Sea.

The Rhine runs for 1,355 kilometers (840 miles), from Lake Constance to Basel in Switzerland, then north through Germany, and then west through the Netherlands to Rotterdam. It forms a natural frontier between Germany and France for part of its length and was once Europe's major highway between Basel and the Atlantic, before the advent of overland transportation.

Great cities—such as Basel, Strasbourg, Mainz, Köln, and Düsseldorf—grew up along the Rhine's banks. No wonder Germans refer to their favorite river as *Vater Rhein*, or Father Rhine, the way Americans call the Mississippi Old Man River.

One section of the Rhine became Germany's top tourist site all of 200 years ago. Around 1790 a spearhead of adventurous travelers from various parts of Europe arrived by horse-drawn carriages to explore the sector of the river between Bingen and Koblenz, now known as the Middle Rhine Valley. Needless to say, they were all but overwhelmed by the dramatic and romantic scenery, which exists nowhere else on the Continent. It didn't take long for the word to spread.

Other travelers followed in their coach tracks, and soon thereafter the first sightseeing cruises went into operation.

Poets, painters, and other artists were attracted by this magnet: Goethe, Germany's greatest poet, was enthralled; Heinrich Heine wrote a poem tied to the Lorelei legend that was eventually set to music and made the unofficial theme of the landmark; and William Turner captured misty Rhine sunsets on canvas. In 1834, the first-ever Baedeker guidebook detailed the attractions of this stretch of the river in meticulous detail. At about the same time, the advent of the railroad opened up the region to an early form of mass tourism. By the mid-19th century, the Rhine Valley was known throughout Europe; in 1878, Mark Twain's "A Tramp Abroad" spread the word to potential travelers in the United States.

Today the passage through the Rhine Valley still makes for one of Europe's most memorable journeys. Ideally, the way to go is by car—up one side and down the other—with time out for a cruise. But even the train route between Wiesbaden and Koblenz offers thrilling views—the landmarks may flash by at top speed, a little like a home movie running out of control, but you still gain exposure to the essential aspects of the Rhine's beauty: hilltop castles silhouetted against the sky, ravishing river sights, and glimpses of pretty-as-a-picture wine villages.

The Mittel Rhein (Middle Rhine) could be considered an obligatory day trip out of Frankfurt—it's quite possibly Germany's number-one, not-to-be-missed excursion. But there's far more to the Rhine as it wends its way north to Köln and Düsseldorf.

This chapter divides the Rhineland into four tours. The first covers the Middle Rhine, the 129-kilometer (80-mile) stretch from Mainz (40 kilometers; 25 miles, west of Frankfurt, the natural starting point for any visit to the Rhineland) to Koblenz. Of all the many and varied regions of the river, no other has the same array of scenery, history, architecture, and natural beauty as this magical stretch. Mention the Rhineland to most visitors, and this is the area they'll assume you mean. It is a land of steep and thickly wooded hills, of terraced vineyards rising step by step above the riverbanks, of massive hilltop castles, and of tiny wine villages hugging river shores. It is also a land of legend and myth. For example, the Lorelei, a steep mountain of rock jutting out of the river, was once believed to be the home of a beautiful and bewitching maiden who lured boatmen to a watery end in the swift currents. It was the home, too, of the Nibelungs, a Burgundian race said to have lived on the riverbanks who serve as subjects for no less than four of Wagner's epic operas, *Der Ring des Nibelungen*.

The most famous tributary of the Rhine is the Mosel, which flows into the river at Koblenz. The second tour covers its snaking passage through another great wine-producing area, with scenery almost as striking as that found along the Rhine. At its west end, almost on the French border, is Trier, once one of the greatest cities in the Roman Empire.

The third tour covers Bonn, a sleepy university town that unexpectedly became the capital of West Germany, and Köln (Cologne), the greatest of the Rhine cities, a vibrant and bustling metropolis boasting the largest and most dramatic Gothic cathedral in the country.

The fourth tour is a side trip to Aachen, capital of Charlemagne's Holy Roman Empire in the 9th century and site of the most important Carolingian (pre-Romanesque) cathedral in Europe. Today this elegant spa town on the Belgian and Dutch borders has a quiet, civilized charm.

The fifth and final tour returns to the Rhine, to the elegant city of Düsseldorf, located 40 kilometers (25 miles) north of Köln.

If you plan to make any trip through the Rhineland, remember that this is one of Germany's major tourist areas, drawing visitors from around the world. As a result, prices here in summer are high, often substantially above those found elsewhere in the country. Make reservations well in advance, and don't expect to have the place to yourself.

Essential Information

Important Addresses and Numbers

Tourist Information The Rhineland regional tourist office, **Fremdenverkehrsverband Rheinland Pfalz** (Postfach 1420, 5400 Koblenz, tel. 0261/31079), provides general information on the entire region. There are also local tourist information offices in the following towns and cities:

Aachen: Verkehrsverein Bad Aachen, Haus Löwenstein, Am Markt 39, 5100 Aachen, tel. 0241/180–29.
Bernkastel-Kues: Stadt. Verkehrsbüro, Am Gestade 5, 5550 Bernkastel-Kues, tel. 06531/4023.

Bonn: Tourist Information Cassius-Bastei, Münsterstrasse 20, 5300 Bonn, tel. 0228/773466.

Cochem: Verkehrsamt, Endertplatz, 5590 Cochem, tel. 02671/3971.

Düsseldorf: Verkehrsverein, Konrad Adenauer Platz 12, tel. 02111/350505.

Köln: Verkehrsamt der Stadt Köln, Untere Fettenhenen 19, 5000 Köln 1, tel. 0221/2213345.

Koblenz: Fremdenverkehrsamt der Stadt Koblenz, Verkehrspavillon, 5400 Koblenz, tel. 0261/31304.

Rüdesheim: Städtisches Verkehrsamt, Rheinstrasse 16, 6200 Rüdesheim, tel. 06722/2962.

St. Goarshausen: Verkehrsamt, Bahnhofstrasse 5422 St. Goarshausen, tel. 06771/427.

Trier: Tourist Information, an der Porta Nigra, Postfach 3830, 5500 Trier, tel. 0651/978080.

Wiesbaden: Verkehrsbüro, Rheinstrasse 15, Ecke Wilhelmstrasse, 6200 Wiesbaden, tel. 0611/1729780.

Embassies

United States, Deichmanns Aue 29, 5300 Bonn, tel. 0228/3391.

Great Britain, Friedrich-Ebert-Allee 77, 5300 Bonn, tel. 0228/234–061.

Canada, Friedrich-Wilhelmstrasse 18, 5300 Bonn, tel. 0228/231061.

Travel Agencies

American Express: Burgmauer 14, 5000 **Köln,** tel. 0221/235–613; Kaiserstrasse 8, Postfach 100146, 6000 **Frankfurt,** tel. 069/21051; Webergasse 8, Postfach 1245, 6200 **Wiesbaden,** tel. 0611/39144. Heinrich Heine Allee 14, 4000 **Düsseldorf,** tel. 0211/80222.

Car Rental

Avis: Bahnhofplatz 7, **Aachen,** tel. 0241/24025; Adenauerallee 4–6, **Bonn,** tel. 0228/223–047; Clemensstrasse 29, **Köln,** tel. 0221/23433; Berlinerallee 32, tel. 0211/329050, **Düsseldorf;** Mainzer Vandstrasse 170, **Frankfurt,** tel. 069/230–101; Friedrich-Ebert-Ring 50, **Koblenz,** tel. 0261/300120; Herzogenbuscherstrasse 31, **Trier,** tel. 0651/12722.

Europcar: Renterstrasse 124, **Bonn,** tel. 0228/221–075; Burgunderstrasse 40, tel. 0211/5047041, **Düsseldorf;** Schlossstrasse 32, **Frankfurt,** tel. 069/775033; Köln-Bonn Airport, **Köln,** tel. 02203/53088.

Hertz: Juelicherstrasse 250, **Aachen,** tel. 0241/162–686; Adenauerallee 216, **Bonn,** tel. 0228/217–041; Immermannstrasse 65, tel. 0211/357025, **Düsseldorf;** Köln-Bonn Airport, **Köln,** tel. 02203/61085; Gutleutstrasse 87, **Frankfurt,** tel. 069/2425–2627.

Sixt-Budget: Am Wehrhahn 77, tel. 0211/360401, Düsseldorf; Mombacherstr. 33, tel. 06131/31003, **Mainz;** Eurenerstrasse 5, **Trier,** tel. 0651/820821.

Arriving and Departing by Plane

The Rhineland is served by three international airports: Frankfurt, Düsseldorf, and Köln-Bonn. There are direct flights from the United States and Canada to Frankfurt, Düsseldorf, and Köln/Bonn. All three airports are part of a comprehensive network of air services throughout Europe. Bus and rail lines connect each airport with its respective downtown area and provide rapid access to the rest of each region.

Getting Around

By Car The Autobahns and other highways of the Rhineland are busy, so allow plenty of time to complete any trip you make. Frankfurt is 126 kilometers (79 miles) from Koblenz, 175 kilometers (110 miles) from Bonn, 190 kilometers (119 miles) from Köln, and 230 kilometers (143 miles) from Düsseldorf. The most spectacular stretch of the Rhineland is along the Middle Rhine, between Mainz and Koblenz. Highways (though not Autobahns) hug the river on each bank, and car ferries crisscross the Rhine at many points. Road conditions throughout the region are excellent.

By Train Intercity and Eurocity expresses connect all the cities and towns of the area. Hourly Intercity routes run between Düsseldorf, Köln, Bonn, and Mainz, with most services extending as far south as Munich and as far north as Hamburg. The Mainz–Bonn route runs beside the Rhine, between the river and the vine-covered heights, offering spectacular views all the way.

By Bus There are two Europabus routes running across the Rhineland: one originates in Britain and terminates in Munich, crossing the Rhineland between Köln and Frankfurt; the other runs between Frankfurt and Trier, stopping at the Frankfurt airport, Wiesbaden, Mainz, Bingen, and several towns along the Mosel River. All Europabuses are comfortable and fast. For details on services and reservations, contact **Deutsche Touring** (am Römerhof 17, Postfach 900244, 6000 Frankfurt/Main 90, tel. 069/79030). Local bus services connect most smaller towns and villages throughout the Rhineland.

By Boat No visit to the Rhineland is complete without at least one river trip. Fortunately, there are many cruise options from which to choose (*see* Guided Tours, below).

Guided Tours

Boat Trips Trips along the Rhine and Mosel range from a few hours to days or even a week or more in length. The major operator, with a fleet of 25 boats, is the **Köln-Düsseldorfer Deutsche Rheinschiffahrt** (Frankenwerft 15, 5000 Köln 1, tel. 0221/208–8288), known as the K-D Rhine line. It offers daily services on the Rhine, Mosel, and Main rivers from April through October, as well as a year-round program of excursions, principally along the Rhine. For the best values, check out the K-D's combined river-rail tickets, which allow you to break your river trip at any place the boats stop and continue by train. For further sailings along the Rhine, contact the Koblenz–Rüdesheim **Hebel** line (tel. 06742/2420), which operates from March through December; for trips along the Mosel, contact **Mosel-Personenschiffahrt Bernkastel-Kues** (Goldbachstr. 52, Bernkastel-Kues, tel. 06531/8222).

If you want to combine the Rhine with wine, the K-D line has a week-long "floating wine seminar," aboard the pride of its fleet, the motor-ship *Helvetia*, which makes stops at vineyards on both the Mosel and Rhine rivers on a wine-tasting route that ends in Basel, Switzerland. The K-D Rhine line also organizes three- and four-day cruises along the Mosel that stop at most of the wine villages between Koblenz and Trier.

Two shipping companies in Koblenz organize short "castle cruises" from Easter through September. Two boats, the *Undine* and the *Marksburg,* ply the Rhine between Koblenz and Boppard, passing 10 castles during the 75-minute, one-way voyage. Details and reservations are available from **Personenschiffahrt Merkelbach** (Emserstr. 87, 5400 Koblenz-Pfaffendorf, tel. 0261/76810); and **Personenschiffahrt Wolfgang Vomfell** (Koblenzerstr. 64, 5401 Spay/Rhein, tel. 02628/2431). Another Koblenz operator, **Rhein und Moselschiffahrt Gerhard Collee-Holzenbein** (Rheinzollstr. 4, tel. 0261/37744), runs day cruises as far as Rüdesheim on the Rhine and Cochem on the Mosel.

From Köln, three shipping companies operate boat tours on the Rhine: The **Köln-Düsseldorfer** line (Frankenwerft 15, tel. 0221/2088288) has hourly trips starting at 9:30, daily, April through September; the **Rhein-Mosel Schiffahrt** (Konrad Adenauer-Ufer, tel. 0221/121714) has daily departures every 45 minutes starting at 10, April through September; and the **Dampfschiffahrt Colonia** (Lintgasse 18, tel. 0221/211325) has daily departures every 45 minutes beginning at 10, April through October. All tours leave from the landing stages near the Hohenzollern Brücke, a short walk from the cathedral.

Bus Tours

Limousine Travel Service (Wiesenhüttenpl. 39, tel. 069/230492) has a daily bus trip from Frankfurt along the "Riesling Route" that encompasses the vineyards of the Rhineland between Frankfurt and Rüdesheim. The tour includes a wine tasting and a trip along the Rhine to the wine village of St. Goar. The cost is DM 105.

Bus trips into the countryside around Köln (to the Eifel Hills, the Ahr Valley, and the Westerwald) are organized by several city travel agencies. Three leading tour operators are **Globus Reisen** (Hohenzollernring 86, tel. 0221/160260), **Univers-Reisen** (am Rinkenpfuhl 57, tel. 0221/209020), and **Küppers-Reiseburo-Etrav** (Longericher-Strasse 183, tel. 0221/210966).

City Tours

Bus tours of Köln leave from outside the tourist office (opposite the main entrance to the cathedral) at 10, 11, 1, 2, and 3 PM, May through October, and at 11 and 2 PM November through April. The tour lasts two hours and costs DM 20 adults, DM 8 children; English-speaking guides are available. **"Köln by Night"** bus tours are offered Fridays and Saturdays in July and August. These trips leave the tourist office at 8 PM and feature a tour of the city, a boat ride on the Rhine, a cold supper, and visits to a wine tavern and the Köln TV tower; the cost is DM 45. A two-hour **walking tour** of the city is also available (in German only). Tours leave from outside the tourist office daily at 4:30, May through September; the cost is DM 7. Most central hotels offer a special tourist package, the **"Kölner Knüller,"** which includes a sightseeing tour voucher, a pass for all the city's museums, and other reductions. The package costs DM 20. City tours of Düsseldorf leave from bus quay 10, Friedrich-Ebert-Strasse (across from the Hauptbahnhof) daily at 10, noon, and 3, April to mid-October and Saturday at 2:30 mid-October to March. The 2½-hour tour includes a boat trip on the Rhine and a visit to the top of the 700-foot-high Rhine television tower. The cost is DM 21 adults, DM 15 children.

Exploring the Rhineland

Highlights for First-time Visitors

Aachen Cathedral
Beethovenhaus, Bonn
Burg Eltz
Königsallee, Düsseldorf
Köln Cathedral
Porta Nigra, Trier
Römische Palastula, Trier
Trier Cathedral
View from Siebenburgenblick
Wilhelmstrasse, Wiesbaden

The Mittel Rhein

Numbers in the margin correspond to points of interest on the Rhineland map.

If you're flying into Frankfurt, you'll begin your tour of the Rhine 40 kilometers (25 miles) west of the city at the point
1 where the Main River joins the mighty Rhine, at **Wiesbaden.** It's located on the east bank of the Rhine, almost opposite the town of Mainz (*see* Chapter 10), and marks the start of the most famous stretch of the Rhine, the **Rheingau,** home of Germany's finest wines and some of its most enchanting (and crowded) wine villages.

Wiesbaden, one of the oldest cities in Germany, was founded 2,000 years ago by Roman legions attracted by its hot springs. Its elegant 19th-century face, however, is what captures one's attention today. The compact city gained prominence in the mid-19th century when Europe's leisure classes rediscovered the hot springs. The English, in particular, had a weakness for Wiesbaden—witness the church of **St. Augustine of Canterbury,** built between 1863 and 1865 for the city's many English visitors—but the Germans, too, were enticed.

By 1900, Wiesbaden boasted the largest number of millionaires of any German city, Berlin included. To get a taste of its 19th-century opulence, wander along **Wilhelmstrasse,** whose mint-condition fin-de-siècle buildings and expensive stores provide eloquent proof of the city's continuing affluence. Wiesbaden hasn't always prospered in this century, however. The outbreak of World War I in 1914 halted the social whirl, and in the war's aftermath, the city was occupied by French and British troops.

The 19th-century residence of the dukes of Nassau, onetime rulers of Wiesbaden, is perhaps symbolic of Wiesbaden's fall from the social heights. Today the classical facade of the former palace houses the mundane offices of the provincial government of Hessen.

Time Out Soak up Wiesbaden's 19th-century charm in the wood-paneled warmth of the centrally located **Café Maldaner** (Marktstr. 34). Don't be surprised if you think you're in Vienna—the café was opened in 1859 as a Viennese coffeehouse catering to the city's Austrian visitors.

Having paid homage to Wiesbaden, you'll want to set off down the Rhine to explore the Rheingau, whose vine-covered slopes rise up from the river between Wiesbaden and Bingen, 25 kilometers (15 miles) to the west. There, the Rhine abruptly turns north. Technically, the Rheingau begins just east of Wiesbaden, at Hochheim (the town that gave its name to Hock wine), but it's the sunny, southern stretch you're about to explore that people generally think of when they hear a reference to the Rheingau. For the most scenic route, take the river-hugging B-42.

2 The first town you'll reach on the road west is **Eltville.** It's the geographic heart of the Rheingau, though Rüdesheim, 15 kilometers (9 miles) west, enjoys greater fame. Eltville's half-timbered buildings crowd narrow streets that date from Roman times. Though the Romans imported wine to Germany, they never made it here. It was Charlemagne, so the story goes, who in the 9th century first realized that the sunny slopes of the Rheingau could be used to produce wines. Eltville's vineyards may not go that far back, but some, including **Hanach** and **Rheinberg,** have been in use since the 12th century. Today the town is best known for the production of Sekt, sparkling German wine (champagne by any other name, though the French ensured that it could not legally be called that by including a stipulation in the Treaty of Versailles in 1919). Sekt cellars rest coolly beneath the town's winding streets. Those of the **Matheus Muller Company** are several miles long and hold up to 15 million bottles. While the cellars are not open to the public, you can amble through the courtyards of some formidable old vineyard buildings, including the white-walled, slate-roofed **Eltzerhof,** one of the more beautiful. Eltville also has its own **castle,** commissioned by the archbishop of Trier in 1330. The prince-archbishop of Mainz admitted Johannes Gutenberg, father of the modern printing press, to the court in Eltville, thereby saving the inventor from financial ruin.

In Eltville, the Gothic parish church of **Sts. Peter and Paul** has some fine 14th-century stained glass and ceiling frescoes; its walls are lined with the tombstones and monuments of noble families who rose to prominence on the prestige of the local wine.

To see one of Germany's oldest church organs, dating from
3 around 1500, drive inland a mile or so to the village of **Kiedrich.** The west entrance to the church is richly carved.

4 The drive from Kiedrich back to the river at **Oestrich-Winkel** takes you past the largest vineyard in the Rheingau. Oestrich-Winkel is the site of the oldest stone dwelling in the country, the **Graues Haus** (Gray House). It dates from the 9th century and is now open as a very good restaurant.

5 Continue on to **Geisenheim,** a name inextricably linked with Rheingau wines at their finest. "Rhineland is wineland" is a saying in this part of the world, and indeed, you'll see a checkerboard of terraced vineyards stretching from the Rhine's riverside villages all the way back to a protective line of forests at the base of the Taunus Mountains. Geisenheim has some of the most renowned vineyards in the area, with grapes that create wines on a par with those from the Loire Valley and Burgundy.

From the vintner's point of view, this part of Germany has the ideal conditions for the cultivation of the noble Riesling grapes:

The Rhineland

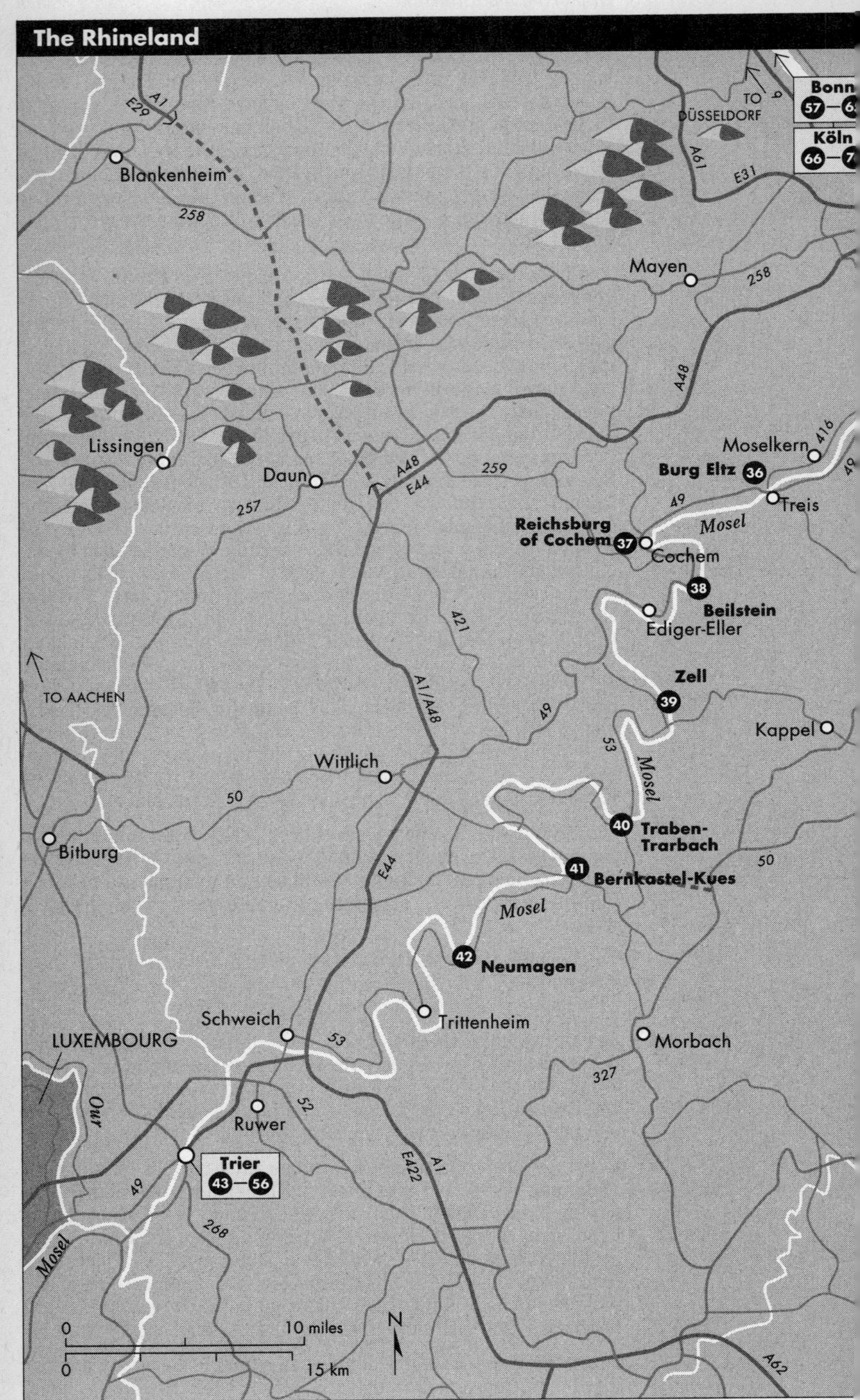

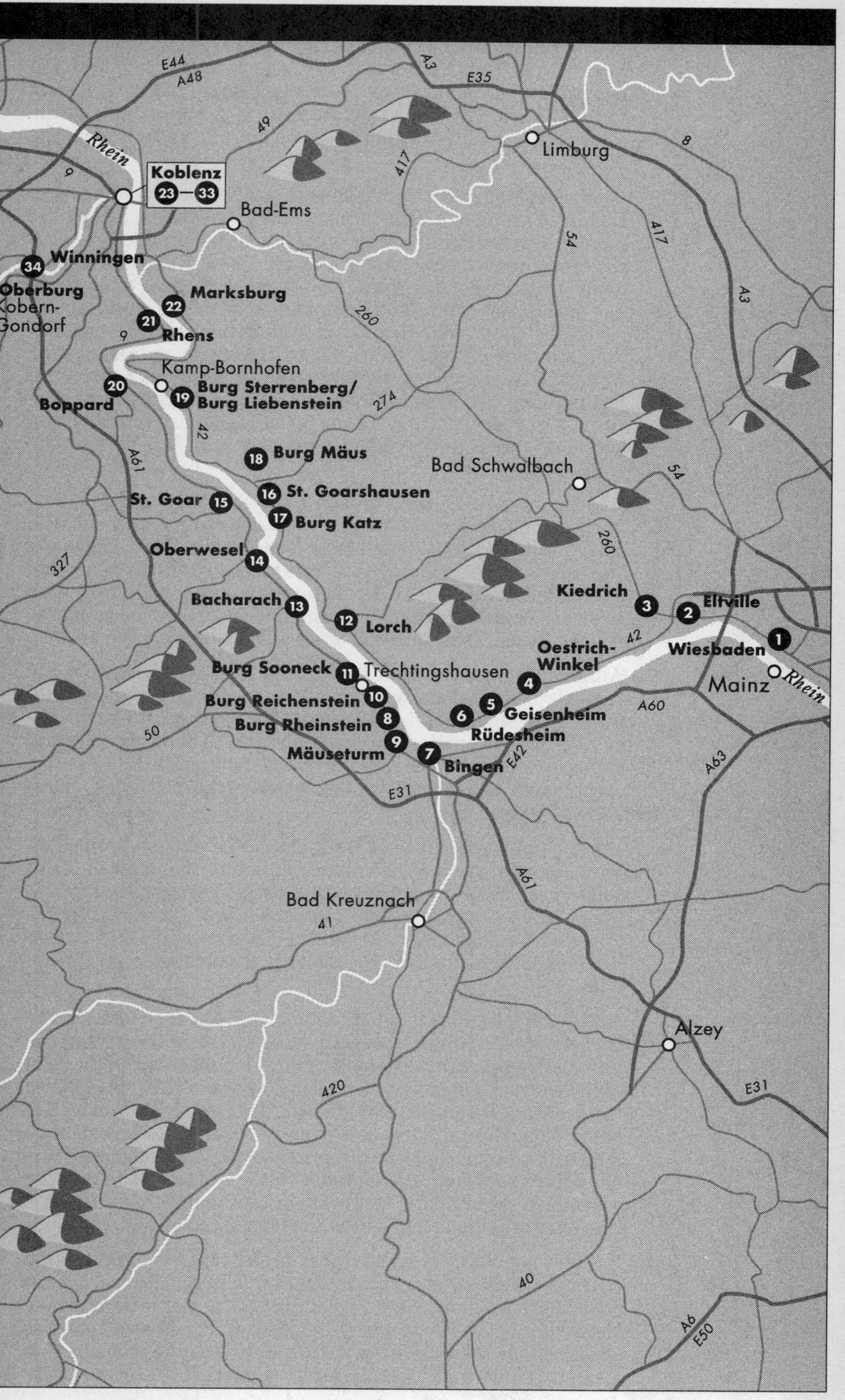

Koblenz
23—33
Rhein
Limburg
Bad-Ems
Winningen
34
Oberburg
Kobern-
Gondorf
Marksburg
22
21
Rhens
Kamp-Bornhofen
20
Boppard
19
Burg Sterrenberg/
Burg Liebenstein
18
Burg Mäus
Bad Schwalbach
St. Goar
15
16
St. Goarshausen
17
Burg Katz
Oberwesel
14
Kiedrich
3
2
Eltville
Bacharach
13
12
Lorch
1
Wiesbaden
Oestrich-
Winkel
4
Mainz
Rhein
Burg Sooneck
11
Trechtingshausen
10
Burg Reichenstein
8
Burg Rheinstein
9
Mäuseturm
7
Bingen
6
5
Geisenheim
Rüdesheim
Bad Kreuznach
Alzey
E44
A48
A3
E35
49
417
8
9
54
417
A3
260
9
274
42
A61
54
260
327
42
A60
50
E42
A63
E31
A61
41
420
E31
40
A6
E50

a perfect southern exposure; shelter from cold north winds; slopes with the proper pitch for drainage; soil containing slate and quartz to reflect the sun and hold heat through the night and moisture in the morning; and long sunny days from early spring until late fall. (Although the Rheingau is at approximately the same latitude as Newfoundland, you'd never know it from the weather.)

In Geisenheim, visit the 18th-century **Schloss Johannisberg,** built on the site of a 12th-century abbey and still owned by the von Metternich family. Schloss Johannisberg produces what is generally regarded as one of the very best Rheingau wines, along with a renowned Sekt. On the castle terrace you can order the elegant estate-bottled golden wine by the glass. As you savor the cool, rich, clear-as-crystal drink, you can contemplate all that makes this corner of Europe so special. Views down across the vineyards take in the river at its calmest. If you're lucky, the Rhine will be enveloped in a pastel mood worthy of a Turner painting. As you leave the castle, you can buy a bottle or two of the excellent wine at a shop just outside the walls.

Rüdesheim and Bingen beckon now, 8 kilometers (5 miles)
6 north, along the banks of the Rhine. **Rüdesheim** is arguably the Rhine Valley's prettiest and most popular wine town. Set along the river's edge, it is a picturesque place of half-timbered and gabled medieval houses. Everything here is somehow related to either wine or tourists or both. You can visit wine cellars to inspect great casks with elaborate and lovingly carved heads.

Angling up from the river toward the romantic old town is the region's most famous Weingasse (wine alley), the extraordinary Drosselgasse (Thrush Lane). This narrow, 200-yard-long cobbled lane is lined with cozy wine taverns and rustic restaurants. At night, voices raised in song and brass bands create a cacophony, shattering whatever peace the town may have known by day.

Rüdesheim turns out to be very much of a plus-and-minus affair. You can love it in the morning, before the day's quota of tour buses start disgorging their passengers, and hate it at night, when an aura of exploitation takes over and it gets far too crowded for comfort. It is definitely worth a visit, though—how long of a visit may depend on the circumstances or time of day.

Above Rüdesheim, at an elevation of 1,000 feet, stands the **Niederwald-Denkmal,** a colossal stone statue of Germania, the heroically proportioned woman who symbolizes the unification of the German Empire in 1871. Built between 1876 and 1883 on the orders of Bismarck, this giant figure came within an inch of being blown to smithereens during the dedication ceremonies. At the unveiling, held in the presence of the kaiser and Bismarck, an anarchist attempted to blow up the statue and the assembled dignitaries. However, in true comic-opera style, a rain shower put out the fuse on the bomb, and all survived.

Niederwald can be reached by car or chair lift, or you can climb to the statue's steep perch. Whichever way you choose, the ascent offers splendid views, including one of the little island in the middle of the Rhine where the Mäuseturm (Mouse Tower) is situated (*see* below). The chair-lift station to the monument is located a short walk from the Drosselgasse. It operates continual every day from late March to early November; round-trip fare is DM 8 adults, DM 4 children.

Wine buffs and those who enjoy wandering through old castles won't want to miss Rüdesheim's **Schloss Brömserburg,** one of the oldest castles on the Rhine, built more than 1,000 years ago by the Knights of Rüdesheim on the site of a Roman fortress. Inside its stout walls are wine presses, drinking vessels, and collections related to viticulture from prehistoric times to the present. *Weinmuseum in der Brömserburg, Rheinstr. 2. Admission: DM 3 adults, DM 2 children. Open Apr.–Oct., daily 9–6.*

7 The town of **Bingen,** on the opposite riverbank, celebrates the festival of St. Rochus every year in mid-August. In **St. Rochus chapel,** built in 1666 in memory of Bingen's plague victims, you'll see a portrait of Goethe, the 18th-century man of letters and prophet of Romanticism, posing improbably as the saint. To get to Bingen, take the short ferry ride from the Adlerturm jetty in Rüdesheim (DM 1.50 adults, 75 pf children).

The number-one excursion from Bingen is the boat ride to the romantic **Castle of Burg Rheinstein.** It was Prince Friedrich von Preussen, a cousin of Emperor Wilhelm I, who acquired the original medieval castle in 1825 and transformed it into the picture-book castle you see high above the Rhine today. The prince is buried in the castle's fanciful Gothic chapel.

8 The ride to **Burg Rheinstein** takes you past one of the most fa-
9 mous sights on the Rhine, the **Mäuseturm** (Mouse Tower), a 13th-century edifice clinging to a rock in the river. According to legend, it was constructed by an avaricious bishop as a customs post to exact taxes from passing river traffic. The story suggests that the greedy bishop grew so unpopular that he was forced to hole up in the tower, where he was eventually devoured by mice.

Beyond the Mäuseturm there are two other medieval castles
10 you can visit: **Burg Reichenstein,** which towers high above the
11 picturesque wine town of **Trechtingshausen;** and **Burg Sooneck,** which in the 12th century was the most feared stronghold in the Rhineland. Reichenstein castle is now a luxurious hotel where you can enjoy lunch in an excellent restaurant with a sensational view. Sooneck, towering above the Rhine on a rocky outcrop, was destroyed several times during its colorful history and rebuilt in its present form in 1840 by the Prussian King Friedrich Wilhelm IV. From the castle you can follow a path through vineyards to one of the most spectacular vantage points of the entire Rhineland: the **Siebenburgenblick** (Seven-Castle View).

Three kilometers (2 miles) north of Burg Sooneck, at the village of **Niederheimbach,** take the ferry back across the Rhine to
12 the historic little wine town of **Lorch,** whose ancient walls mark the northernmost limit of the Rhinegau. Its parish church of **St. Martin** has a Gothic high altar and 13th-century carved choir stalls.

Northward from Lorch, both banks of the river offer competing attractions. The only way anyone could get to see them all would be to zigzag back and forth across the river by ferry. Fortunately, at most points between here and Koblenz, crossing the Rhine is easy via small ferries that run frequently.

13 Downstream from Lorch, on the west bank, lies busy **Bacharach,** whose long association with wine is indicated by its name, which comes from the Latin "*Bacchi ara,*" meaning "altar of Bacchus," the Roman god of wine. The town was a thriving center of Rhine wine trade in the Middle Ages. Something of its medieval atmosphere can still be found in the narrow streets within its 14th-century defensive walls and towers.

Time Out Stop by the old marketplace and look for the gold painted sign of the **Wein Haus Altes Haus.** Wine has been served in this half-timbered tavern for four centuries. Ask for any Bacharach Riesling and you won't be disappointed. *Marktpl.*

---

14 **Oberwesel,** 8 kilometers (5 miles) north of Bacharach, also retains its medieval look. Sixteen of the original 21 towers that studded the town walls still stand; one does double duty as the bell tower of the 14th-century church of **St. Martin.** Towering above the town are the remains of the 1,000-year-old **Burg Schönburg,** whose massive walls, nearly 20 feet thick in places, were not strong enough to prevent its destruction by rampaging French troops in 1689. Part of the castle has been restored and today houses a comfortable hotel.

The ruins of another medieval castle, **Burg Rheinfels,** stand at
15 the outskirts of the next stop along the road, the town of **St.
Goar,** named after an early missionary who became the patron
saint of Rhine boatmen and tavern keepers. The Rhine here
narrows dramatically, funneling its waters into a treacherous
maelstrom of fast-flowing currents and eddies. These rushing
torrents are what gave rise to the legend of the Lorelei, a grim,
400-foot-high rock that protrudes from the river just outside
16 **St. Goarshausen.** So many boats were wrecked on it that people
began to say a bewitching water nymph with golden tresses inhabited the rock and lured sailors to watery graves by her
beauty and strange songs.

These days, in season, the Lorelei's siren song can serve as a trap for tourists rather than sailors. Excursion boats leave regularly from Koblenz and Bingen on Lorelei cruises, and as these overcrowded vessels pass within sight of the famed cliffs, each and every one plays a taped version of the Lorelei song (a Heinrich Heine poem set to music), blasting the creation above the roar of the river.

You can see a statue of the Lorelei in St. Goarshausen. To get there, take the ferry from St. Goar.

North and south of St. Goarshausen are two castles whose
14th-century owners feuded so unrelentingly that the for-
17 tresses came to be known as Katz (cat) and Maus (mouse). **Burg
Katz,** just north of St. Goarshausen, was built in 1371 by Count
Wilhelm II von Katzenelnbogen (literally, "cat's elbow"). It
was he who dubbed the rival castle south of St. Goarshausen
18 **Burg Mäus.** The rivalry, however, was a serious matter. There
was constant competition between many of the castle-bound
nobles of the Rhine to establish who would extract tolls from
passing river traffic, a lucrative and vicious business. Napoléon, not one to respect medieval traditions, put an end to the
fighting in 1806 when he destroyed Burg Katz. It was later reconstructed using the original medieval plans. Neither of the
castles is open to the public.

If you visit this area in September, stay for the Rhein in Flammen (Rhine in Flames) festival, a pyrotechnic orgy of rockets and flares that light up the towns of St. Goar and St. Goarshausen and their surrounding vineyards.

Rivalry between neighboring castles was common even when
the keepers were members of the same family. At **Kamp-**
19 **Bornhofen,** 12 kilometers (8 miles) north of St. Goar, are **Burg**
Sterrenberg and **Burg Liebenstein,** once owned by two brothers. When their relations deteriorated over a river-toll feud, they built a wall between them. Today the castles keep the rivalry going by running competing wine taverns.

Across from Kamp-Bornhofen is the mile-long promenade of el-
20 egant **Boppard,** usually lined with excursion and pleasure
boats. Luxurious hotels, restaurants, and spa facilities are Boppard's hallmarks. There are also wine taverns of every caliber. The old quarter is part of a walking tour marked by signs from the 14th-century **Carmelite church** on Karlmeliterstrasse. (Inside the church, grotesque carved figures peer from the choir stalls.) There are substantial ruins from a 4th-century Roman fort in Boppard. Take the chair lift up **Gedeonseck** to view this stretch of the Rhine from on high.

21 At Boppard, the river swings east and then north to **Rhens,** a town that traces its origins back some 1,300 years. A vital center of the Holy Roman Empire, Rhens was where German kings and emperors were elected and then presented to the people. The monumental site where the ceremonies took place, the **Königstuhl,** is on a hilltop just outside Rhens, on the road to Waldesch. It was here, in 1388, that the rift between the Holy Roman Empire and the papacy (to which the emperor was nominally subject) proved final. The six German prince-electors who nominated the emperor declared that henceforward their decisions were final and need no longer be given papal sanction.

22 **Marksburg,** the final castle on this fortress-studded stretch of the Rhine, is located on the opposite bank of the river, 500 feet above the town of **Braubach.** Marksburg was built in the 12th century to protect silver and lead mines in the area; so successfully were its medieval builders that the castle proved impregnable—it is the only one in the entire Middle Rhine Valley to have survived the centuries intact. Within its massive walls is a collection of weapons and manuscripts, a medieval botanical garden, and a restaurant.

Koblenz

23 The ancient city of **Koblenz** now looms ahead. Located at a geographical nexus known as the **Deutsches Eck** (corner of Germany), Koblenz is the heart of the Middle Rhine region. Rivers and mountains converge here, where the Mosel flows into the Rhine on one side and the Lahn flows in on the other. Three mountain ridges intersect at Koblenz as well.

Koblenz serves as the cultural, administrative, and business center of the Middle Rhine. Its position at the confluence of two rivers bustling with steamers, barges, tugs, and every other kind of river boat makes it one of the most important traffic points on the Rhine.

The heart of historic Koblenz is close to the point where the Rhine and Mosel meet. Koblenz was founded by the Romans in

AD 9. Its Roman name, Castrum and Confluentes (the camp at the confluence), was later corrupted to Koblenz. It became a powerful city in the Middle Ages, when it controlled trade on both rivers. The city suffered severe bomb damage from air raids during the last world war (85% of its buildings were destroyed), but extensive restoration has done much to re-create the atmosphere of old Koblenz. An English-speaking guide leads a walking tour of the old town every Saturday at 2:30, June–October.

Numbers in the margin correspond to points of interest on the Koblenz map.

Koblenz is centered on the west bank of the Rhine, but begin
24 your tour on the opposite side, at **Festung Ehrenbreitstein,** Europe's largest fortress. Set 400 feet above the river, it offers a commanding view of the old town (the view alone justifies a visit). Ride the cable car (the Sesselbahn) up if the walk is too daunting. The earliest buildings date from about 1100, but the bulk of the fortress was constructed in the 16th century. In 1801, Napoléon's forces partially destroyed Festung Ehrenbreitstein; the French then occupied Koblenz for 18 years, a fact that some claim accounts for the Gallic joie de vivre of the city. More concrete evidence of French occupation can be seen in the shape of the fortress's 16th-century **Vogel Greif cannon.** The French absconded with it after they first penetrated the city in 1794; the Germans took it back in 1940; and the French commandeered it again in 1945. The 15-ton cannon was peaceably returned in 1984 by French President François Mitterrand. It is on view at the **Staatliche Sammlung Technischer Kulturdenkmäler Museum,** one of several museums in the fortress. The others include the **Rheinmuseum,** which charts the history of the Rhineland, and the **Museum für Vorgeschichte und Volkskunde,** the museum of prehistory and ethnography. If you can schedule your visit to Koblenz for August, you'll catch one of the most spectacular fireworks displays in Europe at the fortress on the second Saturday of the month. *Fortress and museum: Admission free. Open Easter–Oct., daily 9–5.*

25 The place to begin a tour of the **old town** is the **Pfaffendorfer Brücke.** Three competing attractions stand at its west end. The
26 most conspicuous is the gracious **Residenzschloss,** the prince-elector's palace. It was built in 1786 by Prince-Elector Clemens Wenzeslaus as an elegant replacement for the grim Ehrenbreitstein fortress. The popular prince, who also built the city's still-thriving theater, cemented his popularity by throwing a three-day party when he moved in. He lived there for only three years, however; in 1791 he was forced to flee to Augsburg when the French stormed the city. Today the palace is home to the city government. To the left of the palace is the
27 **Weindorf,** a self-contained wine "village," constructed for a mammoth exhibition of German wine in 1925. It is now one of the city's prime tourist attractions.

Time Out If the weather's good, there are few more enjoyable ways to spend time in Koblenz than over a glass of wine at one of the tables covered in checked cloth in the **Weindorf's** leafy gardens. On weekends at some taverns jazz bands spice up the scene for the traditional **Frühschoppen,** which is a brunch accompanied by wine.

Deutsches Eck, **29**
Festung Ehrenbreitstein, **24**
Liebfrauenkirche, **32**
Moselanlangen, **31**
Pfaffendorfer Brücke, **25**
Residenzschloss, **26**
Rheinanlagen, **28**
St. Kastor Kirche, **30**
Schängelbrunnen, **33**
Weindorf, **27**

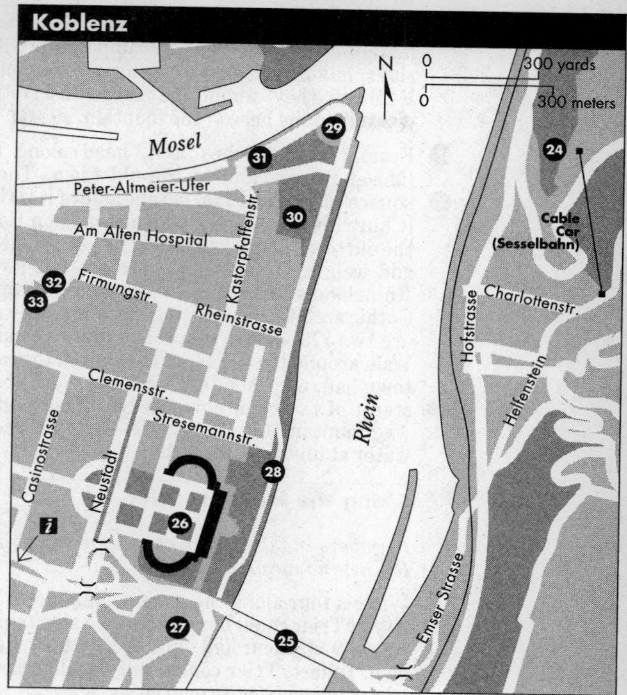

28 The third attraction here is the 10 kilometer-long (6-mile) riverside promenade, the **Rheinanlagen,** one of the longest in the Rhineland. If you want to cover it all, rent a bike. When the weather's good, it can be fun to while away an hour or so pedaling along the Rhine.

29 From the bridge, you can either head straight into the old town or stroll along to the **Deutsches Eck.** You'll have seen this curious structure from the fortress; if you have a taste for the more unusual manifestations of Germany's nationalism, it's worth a closer look. The sharply pointed piece of land juts into the river like the prow of some early ironclad warship. It's a historic site, first settled and named by the German Order of Knights in 1216. In 1897 a statue of Kaiser Wilhelm I, the first emperor of the newly united Germany, was erected on the Deutsches Eck. It was destroyed at the end of World War II, however, and replaced by the ponderous altarlike monument to German unity you see today. The monument was again in the spotlight recently amid the excitement over German reunification.

30 Standing just behind the Deutsches Eck is **St. Kastor Kirche,** a sturdy Romanesque basilica consecrated in 836 and remodeled through the centuries. It was here in 843 that the Treaty of Verdun was signed, formalizing the division of Charlemagne's great empire and leading to the creation of Germany and France as separate states. Inside, compare the squat columns in the nave, typical of the muscular architecture of the Romanesque style with the complex and decorative fan vaulting of the Gothic sections. The **St. Kastor fountain** outside the church is an intriguing piece of historical oneupmanship. It was built by

the occupying French to mark the beginning of Napoléon's ultimately disastrous Russian campaign of 1812. When the Russians, having inflicted a crushing defeat on Napoléon, reached Koblenz, they added the ironic inscription "Seen and approved" to the base of the fountain.

31 From the Deutsches Eck, head along the **Moselanlangen**
(Mosel Promenade) to the old town. The focus is the little
32 square called **Am Plan.** On one side of it is the **Liebfrauenkirche**
(Church of Our Lady), which stands on Roman foundations at
the old town's highest point. The bulk of the church is of austere
and weighty Romanesque design, but its choir is one of the
Rhineland's finest and most ornate examples of 15th-century
Gothic architecture. Rising incongruously above the west front
are two 17th-century Baroque towers topped by onion domes.
Walk around to the rear of the church to reach the 17th-century
town hall, a former Jesuit college. You'll be drawn to the little
33 statue of a street urchin, the **Schängelbrunnen** (literally "scalawag fountain") in the square—every three minutes he spouts
water at unwary passersby.

Along the Mosel to Trier

Numbers in the margin correspond to points of interest on the Rhineland map.

While a tour along the meandering Mosel River to the historic city of Trier could be considered a side trip from the Rhine, it's actually an excursion endowed with a magic and charm all its own. In fact, Trier could easily qualify as the best-kept secret when it comes to German cities.

You don't have to travel far up the Mosel Valley to be reminded that wine plays every bit as important a role here as it does along the Rhine. The river's zigzag course passes between steep, terraced slopes where grapes have been grown since Roman times.

The Mosel is one of the most hauntingly beautiful river valleys
on earth: turreted castles look down from its leafy perches, its
hilltops are crowned with bell towers, and throughout its expanse, skinny church spires stand against the sky. For more
than 100 miles, the silvery Mosel River meanders past a string
of storybook medieval wine villages, each more attractive than
34 the other. The first village you'll reach, **Winningen,** 15 kilometers (10 miles) from Koblenz, is the center of the valley's largest
vineyards. Stop off to admire Germany's oldest half-timbered
house in **Kirchenstrasse** (No. 1); it was built in 1320. On the
slopes above Winningen's narrow medieval streets is a mile-
long path reached by driving up Fährstrasse to Am Rosenhang.
Once there, high above the Mosel, you'll get a bird's-eye view of
the **Uhlen, Röttgen, Bruckstück, Hamm,** and **Domgarten** vineyards.

For an even finer view of the river and its rich valley, follow the
road for 8 kilometers (5 miles) to **Kobern-Gondorf,** on the north
bank of the river, and turn off into the idyllic little Mühlental
Valley. Here you can climb up through the steep vineyards to
35 the remains of **Oberburg** castle, built in the 12th century by the
powerful Knights of Leyen. On the way, you'll pass a 13th-cen-
tury Romanesque chapel, **St. Matthew's.**

The Mosel bristles with almost as many castles as the Rhine. Among them is what many deem the most impressive in the
36 country, **Burg Eltz.** It's located above the village of Moselkern, 15 kilometers (10 miles) from Koben-Gondorf. The best way to reach the castle from Moselkern is to walk 3 kilometers (2 miles) along a gentle footpath that winds through the wild valley. A small shuttle bus, operating from the car parking lot, will carry those not inclined to walk (DM 2 per person). It's worth the trek to see what may well be the most perfectly proportioned medieval castle in Germany. Perched on the spine of an isolated, rocky outcrop, bristling with towers and pinnacles, it at first looks unreal—like an image suspended in time and space. Upon closer exposure, Burg Eltz turns out to be the apotheosis of all one expects of a medieval castle: In its own special way, it's easily as impressive as "Mad" King Ludwig's fantasy creation, Neuschwanstein. But Burg Eltz is the real thing: an 800-year-old castle, with modifications from the 16th century. It's a mystery why Burg Eltz is not better known, or more visited. There are few sites in Germany that offer a more vivid sense of the centuries unfolding. The magic continues in the interior, which is decorated with heavy Gothic furnishings. There is also an interesting collection of old weapons. *Admission: DM 5.50 adults, DM 3.50 children. Open Apr.–Oct., Mon.–Sat. 9–5:30, Sun. 10–5:30.*

Destruction was the fate suffered by the next castle along the
37 valley, the famous **Reichsburg** (Imperial Fortress) **of Cochem,** 15 kilometers (10 miles) from Berg Eltz. The 900-year-old castle was rebuilt in the 19th century after Louis XIV stormed it in 1689. Today it stands majestically over Cochem. *Admission: DM 3.50 adults, DM 1.50 children. Open daily 9–6.*

Cochem itself is one of the most attractive towns of the Mosel Valley, with a riverside promenade to rival any along the Rhine. If you're traveling by train, just south of Cochem you'll be plunged into Germany's longest railway tunnel, the Kaiser-Wilhelm, an astonishing 2½-mile-long example of 19th-century engineering that saves travelers a 21-kilometer (13-mile) detour along one of the Mosel's great loops.

By car, follow the loop of the river for 8 kilometers (5 miles)
38 past Cochem and you'll reach the little town of **Beilstein.** It has a mixture of all the picture-pretty features of a German river and wine town in this romantic area of the country. Take a look at the marketplace carved into the rocky slope.

Time Out At the village of **Ediger-Eller,** 10 kilometers (6 miles) from Beilstein, stop by the roadside vineyard of **Freiherr von Landenberg** (Moselstr. 60). Sample a glass of wine from the Baron's vines and visit his private viticulture museum.

---

39 **Zell,** 12 kilometers (8 miles) upriver, on another great loop, is a typical Mosel River town, much like Cochem. Located about midway between Koblenz and Trier, this small, historic town is made up of picturesque red-roofed homes and age-old fortifications falling into ruin. A scenic backdrop is provided by the vineyards that produce the famous Schwarze Katz (Black Cat) wine, which is rated as one of Germany's very best whites. Stroll the town's medieval arc along the river. On your way you'll notice a small, twin-towered castle, Schloss Zell, dating from the 14th century. After considerable restoration, the cas-

tle evolved into an elegant hotel furnished with exquisite antiques. Its restaurant serves regional cuisine and wine from the owner's own Black Cat vineyards.

Straddling the Mosel 18 kilometers (11 miles) farther along is
40 **Traben-Trarbach,** a two-town combination that serves as headquarters of the regional wine trade and offers a popular wine festival in summer. Visit the ruins of **Mont Royal** high above Traben on the east bank. This enormous fortress was built around 1687 by Louis XIV of France, only to be dismantled 10 years later under the terms of the Treaty of Rijswijk. Partially restored by the Nazis, the fortress retains some of its original forbidding mass.

41 **Bernkastel-Kues** is 27 kilometers (17 miles) away by road, but if you're in the mood for some exercise, you can reach it on foot from Traben-Trarbach in about an hour by taking the path that cuts across the tongue of land formed by the exaggerated loop of the river. The road, following the river, practically doubles back on itself as it winds leisurely along. Bernkastel, on the north bank of the river, and Kues, on the south, were officially linked early this century. **Marktplatz,** the heart of Bernkastel, meets all the requirements for the ideal small-town German market square. Most of the buildings are late-Gothic/early Renaissance, with facades covered with intricate carvings and sharp gables stabbing the sky. In the center of the square is **Michaelsbrunnen** (Michael's fountain), a graceful 17th-century work. Wine used to flow from it on special occasions in bygone years. Today, although wine flows freely in the town—especially during the local wine festival in the first week of September—only water ever comes from the fountain. There's a fortress here, too: **Burg Landshut,** a 13th-century castle glowering above the town. Visit it for some amazing views of the river either from its ramparts or from the terrace of the restaurant within its old walls, and to wander around its flower-strewn remains. In summer, a bus makes the trip up to the castle every hour from the parking lot by the river. The town's most famous wine is known as Bernkasteler Doktor. According to a story, the wine got its unusual name when it saved the life of the prince-bishop of Trier, who lay dying in the castle. After all other medicinal treatment had failed to cure him, he was offered a glass of the local wine—which miraculously put him back on his feet. Try a glass of it yourself at the castle (or buy a bottle from the vineyard bordering the street called Hinterm Graben).

The town's remaining attraction owes its existence to Cardinal Nikolaus Cusanus, a 15th-century philosopher and pioneer of German humanist thought. He founded a religious and charitable institution, complete with a vineyard, on the riverbank in Kues. The vineyard is still going strong, and tastings are held daily at 3 in the St. Niklaus-Hospital (Cusanusstr. 2). The buildings here comprise the largest Gothic ensemble on the Mosel. Among them is the Mosel-Weinmuseum. *Admission: DM 2 adults, DM 1 children. Open May–Oct., daily 10–5; Nov.–Apr., daily 2–5.*

From Bernkastel-Kues to Trier is a further 66 kilometers (41 miles) of twisting river road. Endless vineyards and little river towns punctuate the snaking path of the Mosel. Among them is
42 **Neumagen,** settled by the Romans in the 4th century. In its main square, there's a modern copy of the famous carved relief

of a Roman wine ship plying a choppy-looking Mosel. If you continue on to Trier, you can see the original in the Landesmuseum.

43 **Trier's** claim to fame is not only that it's the oldest town in Germany but that it's also the first civilized settlement in Europe. It dates from 2,000 BC, when Prince Trebeta, son of an Assyrian queen, arrived here and set up residence on the banks of the Mosel; he named the place Treberis, after himself. An inscription on a historic old house on Trier's marketplace states: "*Ante Romam Treveris stetit annis mille trecentis*" ("1,300 years before Rome stood Trier").

Eventually the legions of Julius Caesar set up camp at this strategic point of the river, and Augusta Treverorum (the town of Emperor Augustus in the land of the Treveri) was founded in 16 BC. It was described as "*urbs opulentissima*"—as beautiful a city as existed beyond Rome itself.

Around AD 275, an Alemannic tribe stormed Augusta Treverorum and reduced it to rubble. But it was rebuilt in even grander style and renamed Treveris. Eventually it evolved into one of the leading cities of the empire and was promoted to *Roma Secunda*, "a second Rome" north of the Alps. As a powerful administrative capital, it was adorned with all the noble civic buildings of a major Roman settlement, plus public baths, palaces, barracks, an ampitheater, and temples. Roman emperors such as Diocletian (who made it one of the four joint capitals of the empire) and Constantine lived in Trier for years at a time.

Trier survived the collapse of Rome and became an important center of Christianity; it was later one of the most powerful archbishoprics in the Holy Roman Empire. The city thrived throughout the Renaissance and Baroque periods, taking full advantage of its location at the meeting point of major east–west and north–south trade routes, and growing fat on the commerce that passed through. It also became one of Germany's most important wine-exporting centers. A later claim to fame is as the birthplace of Karl Marx. To do justice to the city, consider staying for at least two full days. A ticket good for all the Roman sights in Trier costs DM 6 adults, DM 3 children. Between May and October, there are walking tours of the city conducted by the local tourist board in English. The walking tour leaves from the gate at 2. The cost is DM 8 adults, DM 4 children.

Numbers in the margin correspond to points of interest on the Trier map.

44 Begin your tour at the **Porta Nigra** (the Black Gate), located by the city's tourist office. This is by far the best-preserved Roman structure in Trier and one of the grandest Roman buildings in northern Europe. It's a city gate, built in the 4th century. Its name is misleading, however: The sandstone gate is not actually black but dark gray. Those with an interest in Roman construction techniques should look for the holes left by the original iron clamps that held the entire structure together. This city gate also served as part of Trier's defenses and was proof of the sophistication of Roman military might and ruthlessness. Attackers were often lured into the two innocent-looking arches of the Porta Nigra only to find themselves enclosed in a courtyard—and at the mercy of the defending

Amphitheater, **54**
Barbarathermen, **53**
Bischöfliches Museum, **49**
Dom, **48**
Hauptmarkt, **46**
Kaiserthermen, **52**
Karl-Marx-Haus, **55**
Liebfrauenkirche, **47**
Porta Nigra, **44**
Rheinisches Landesmuseum, **51**
Römische Palastaula, **50**
Städtisches Museum Simeonstift, **45**
Weininformation Mosel-Saar-Ruwer, **56**

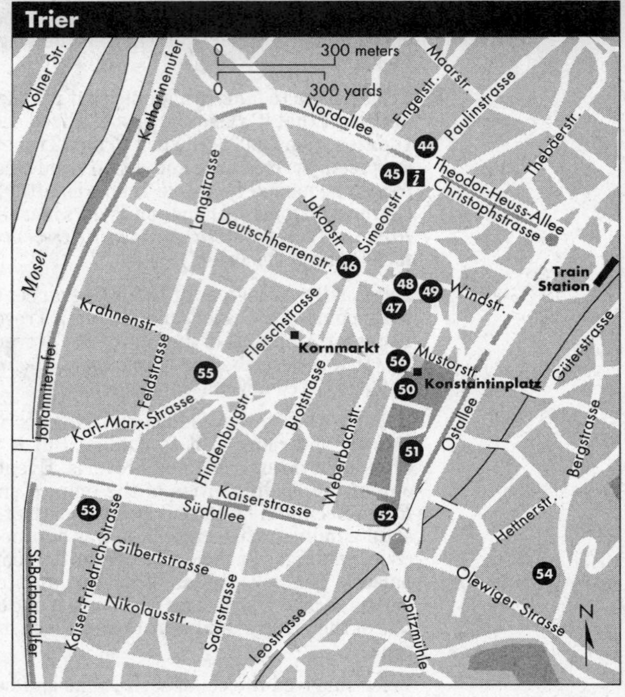

forces. *Admission: DM 2 adults, DM 1 children and senior citizens. Open Apr.–Oct., daily 9–1 and 2–5; Nov. and Dec., daily 10–4; Jan.–Mar., Tues.–Sun. 9–1 and 2–5.*

To the side are the remains of the Romanesque Simeonskirche,
45 today the **Städtisches Museum Simeonstift** (open Tues.–Fri. 9–5, Sat. and Sun. 10–1). The church was built in the 11th century by Archbishop Poppo in honor of the early medieval hermit Simeon, who for seven years shut himself up in the east tower of the Porta Nigra. Collections of art and artifacts produced in Trier from the Middle Ages to the present now commemorate Simeon's feat. Simeon also has one of Trier's main streets named after him: Simeonstrasse. It leads directly to
46 **Hauptmarkt**, the main square of old Trier. A 1,000-year-old market cross and a richly ornate 16th-century fountain stand in the square.

From Hauptmarkt, turn left (east) down Stirnstrasse to see Trier's great **Dom** (cathedral). Before you go in, take a look at
47 the adjoining 13th-century **Liebfrauenkirche** (Church of Our Lady). It's one of the oldest purely Gothic churches in the country. The interior is elegantly attenuated.

48 If you want a condensed history of Trier, visit the **Dom:** There is almost no period of the city's past that is not represented here. It stands on the site of the Palace of Helen of Constantine, mother of the emperor Constantine, who knocked the palace down in AD 326 and put up a large church in its place. The church burned down in 336 and a second, even larger one was built. Parts of the foundations of this third building can be seen

in the east end of the current structure (begun in about 1035). The cathedral you see today is a weighty and sturdy edifice with small, round-headed windows, rough stonework, and asymmetrical towers, as much a fortress as a church. Inside, Gothic styles predominate—the result of remodeling in the 13th century—though there are also many Baroque tombs, altars, and confessionals. This architectural jumble of Romanesque, Gothic, and Baroque styles gives the place the air of a vast antiques shop. Make sure you visit the Baroque **Domschatzmuseum** in the treasury, site of two extraordinary objects. One is the 10th-century **Andreas Tragalter** (St. Andrews's Portable Altar), made of gold by local craftsmen. It is smaller than the Dom's main altar, but it is no lightweight. The other treasure is the **Holy Robe,** the garment supposedly worn by Christ at the time of his trial before Pontius Pilate and gambled for by Roman soldiers. The story goes that it was brought to Trier by Helen of Constantine, a tireless collector of holy relics. It is so delicate and old that it is displayed only every 30 years (you'll have to come back in 2019 if you want to see it); the rest of the time it lies under a faded piece of 9th-century Byzantine silk. *Domschatzmuseum admission: DM 1 adults, 50 pf children. Open Mon.–Sat. 10–12 and 2–5, Sun. 2–4.*

Excavations around the cathedral have unearthed a series of
49 antiquities, most of which are housed in the **Bischöfliches Museum** (Episcopal Museum) in Windstrasse, just behind the cathedral. The exhibits include a 4th-century ceiling painting believed to have adorned the emperor Constantine's palace. *Windstr. 6–8. Admission: DM 1 adults, 50 pf children. Open Mon.–Sat. 9–1 and 2–5, Sun. 1–5.*

Time Out There's a time-honored welcome at the **Steipe Ratskeller** in the cellars beneath the Rathaus (Town Hall), where you can tuck into the hearty local fare or just order a coffee, beer, or glass of Mosel wine. *Hauptmarkt 14.*

Just south of the cathedral complex—take Konstantinstrasse—is another impressive reminder of Trier's Roman
50 past: the **Römische Palastaula** (Roman Basilica). Today this is the major protestant church of Trier. When first built by the emperor Constantine around AD 300, it was the Imperial Throne Room of the palace. At 239 feet long, 93 feet wide, and 108 feet high, it demonstrates the astounding ambition of its Roman builders and the sophistication of their building techniques. It is the second-largest Roman interior in existence—only the Pantheon in Rome is larger. Look up at the deeply coffered ceiling: More than any other part of the building, it conveys the opulence of the original structure. *Konstantinstr. Open Apr.–Oct., Mon.–Sat. 9–1 and 2–6, Sun. 11–1 and 2–6; Nov.–Mar., Tues.–Sat. 11–noon and 3–4, Sun. 11–noon.*

From the Palastaula, turn south. To your left, facing the
51 grounds of the prince-elector's palace, is the **Rheinisches Landesmuseum** (Rhineland Archaeological Museum), which houses the largest collection of Roman antiquities in Germany. Pride of place goes to the 3rd-century stone relief of a Roman ship transporting immense barrels of wine up the river. If you stopped off in Neumagen on the way to Trier, you probably saw the copy of it in the town square. *Ostallee 44. Admission free. Open Mon.–Fri. 9:30–4, Sat. 9:30–1, Sun. 9–1.*

52 From the museum, walk down to the ruins of the **Kaiserthermen** (imperial baths), just 200 yards away. Begun by Constantine in the 4th century, these were once the third-largest public baths in the Roman Empire, exceeded only by Diocletian's baths in Yugoslavia and the baths of Caracalla in Rome. They covered an area 270 yards long and 164 yards wide. Today only the weed-strewn fragments of the **Calderium** (hot baths) are left, but they are enough to give a fair idea of the original splendor and size of the complex. When the Romans pulled out, the baths were turned into a fortress (one window of the huge complex served as a city gate for much of the Middle
Ages), then a church, and then a fortress again. Don't confuse
53 them with the much smaller **Barbarathermen** (open same
hours) in Kaiser-Friedrich-Str. *Admission: DM 2 adults, DM 1 children. Open Jan.–Mar. and Nov., Tues.–Sun. 9–1 and 2–5; Apr.–Sept., daily 9–1 and 2–6; Oct., daily 9–1 and 2–5; closed Dec.*

54 Just east of the Kaiserthermen are the remains of the **Amphitheater** built around AD 100, the oldest Roman building in Trier. In its heyday it seated 20,000 people. You can climb down to the cellars beneath the arena to see the machines that were used to change the scenery and the cells where lions and other wild animals were kept before being unleashed to devour maidens and do battle with gladiators. *Olewigerstr. See Porta Nigra for hours and admission.*

After this profusion of antiquities, you may want to shift gears
55 and see the **Karl-Marx-Haus** on Karl-Marx-Strasse, south of
Kornmarkt in the old town. It was here that Marx was born in 1818. Serious social historians will feel at home in the little house, which has been converted into a museum charting Marx's life and the development of socialism around the world. A signed first edition of *Das Kapital*, the tome in which Marx sought to prove the inevitable decline of capitalism, may prove a highlight for some. *Admission: DM 3 adults, DM 2 children. Open Apr.–Oct., Tues.–Sun. 10–6, Mon. 1–6; Nov.–Mar., Tues.–Sun. 10–1 and 3–6, Mon. 3–6.*

Trier is, of course, also a city of wine, and beneath its streets are cellars capable of storing nearly 8 million gallons. To get to
know the wines of the region, drop in at the tavern run by the
56 **Weininformation Mosel-Saar-Ruwer** (Konstantinpl. 11, tel.
0651/73690). The city also has a wine trail, a picturesque 1½-mile walk studded with information plaques that lead to the wine-growing suburb of **Olewig.**

Bonn and Köln

Numbers in the margin correspond to points of interest on the Rhineland and Bonn maps.

57 **Bonn,** the quiet university town on the Rhine, is now the interim seat of reunited Germany's federal government and parliament, but in a parliamentary vote on June 20, 1991, it lost out to Berlin as the permanent capital city of the country. In reality, Bonn will continue to share the responsibility of governing Germany with Berlin. The upper house of parliament—the **Bundesrat**—will remain in Bonn, as will nearly half the ministries and two-thirds of the civil servants. Moving the rest of the government to Berlin is expected to take 12 years and will be costly—as much as $30 billion.

Alter Friedhof, **62**
Beethovenhaus, **64**
Government Buildings, **65**
Kurfürstliches Schloss, **59**
Münster, **58**
Poppelsdorfer Schloss, **60**
Rathaus, **63**
Rheinisches Landesmuseum, **61**

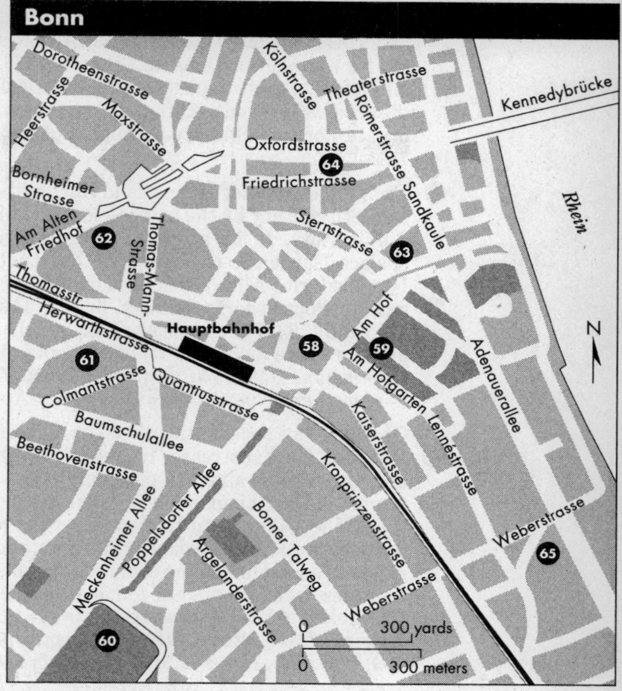

The choice, in 1949, of Bonn as capital of the newly created Federal Republic was never meant to be permanent. At the time, few Germans thought the division of their country would prove anything other than temporary, and they were certain that Berlin would again become the capital before long. Popular legend now has it that Bonn, aptly described in the title of John Le Carré's spy novel *A Small Town in Germany* was chosen as a stopgap measure to prevent weightier contenders such as Frankfurt from becoming the capital, a move that would have lessened Berlin's chances of regaining its former status.

Germans tend to deride their postwar capital for its lack of character. Some suggest that Bonn's greatest asset is its surrounding countryside: the legendary **Siebengebirge** (Seven Hills) and the **Kölner Bucht Valley.** In the capital's streets, old markets, stores, pedestrian malls, parks, and the handsome Südstadt residential area, life is unhurried and unsophisticated by larger city standards. Guided tours of Bonn start from the tourist office (Münsterstr. 20) *May–Oct., Mon.–Sat. at 10 and 2; Sun. and Apr. at 10; Nov.–Mar., Sat. at 2. The 2-hour tour costs DM 16 adults, DM 8 children.*

Bonn's status may be new, but its roots are ancient. The Romans settled this part of the Rhineland 2,000 years ago, calling
58 it Castra Bonnensia. Bonn's cathedral, the **Münster,** stands where two Roman soldiers were executed in AD 253 for holding Christian beliefs. **Münsterplatz,** site of the cathedral and a short walk from the tourist office in Münsterstrasse 20, is the logical place to begin your tour. The 900-year-old cathedral is

vintage late Romanesque, with a massive octagonal main tower and a soaring spire. It was chosen by two Holy Roman Emperors for their coronations (in 1314 and 1346), and was one of the Rhineland's most important ecclesiastical centers in the Middle Ages. The bronze 17th-century figure of St. Helen and the ornate Rococo pulpit are highlights of the interior. *Open daily 7AM–7PM.*

59 Facing the Münster is the grand **Kurfürstliches Schloss,** built in the 18th century by the prince-electors of Köln; today it houses a university. If it's a fine day, stroll through the Hofgarten (Palace Gardens), or follow the chestnut-tree avenue called Poppelsdorfer Allee southward to another electors' palace, the
60 smaller **Poppelsdorfer Schloss,** built in Baroque style between 1715 and 1753. The palace has a beautiful botanical garden with an impressive display of tropical plants. *Meckenheimer Allee. Admission: DM 1, children free. Open May–Sept., weekdays 9–6, weekends and holidays 9–1; Oct.–Apr., weekdays 9–6.*

On your way back to the old town, take Meckenheimer Allee
61 and then Colmanstrasse, to see the **Rheinisches Landesmuseum** (the walk is about ¼-mile long). The museum, one of the largest in the Rhineland, charts the history, art, and culture of the Rhine Valley from Roman times to the present. The main draw is the skull of a Neanderthal man, regarded by anthropologists as a vital link in the evolutionary chain. The skull was put together from fragments found in the Neander Valley near Düsseldorf in 1856. *Colmantstrasse 14–16, tel. 0228/72941. Admission: DM 4 adults, DM 2 children. Open Tues. and Thurs. 9–5, Wed. 9–8, Fri. 9–4, and weekends 11–5.*

At the end of Colmantstrasse, take the underpass below the
62 railroad line and follow Thomastrasse for 300 yards to the **Alter Friedhof** (the Old Cemetery). This ornate graveyard is the resting place of many of the country's most celebrated sons and daughters. Look for the tomb of composer Robert Schumann and his wife Clara. *Am Alten Friedhof. Open Mar.–Aug., daily 7 AM–8 PM; Sept.–Feb., daily 8–6. Guided tours May–Sept. at 3 on Tues. and Thurs.*

From the Alter Friedhof, follow Sternstrasse into the old town center and proceed to the **Markt** (market), where you'll find an
63 18th-century **Rathaus** (Town Hall) that looks like a pink doll's house.

64 Just north of the town hall are Bonngasse and the **Beethovenhaus.** The latter has been imaginatively converted into a museum celebrating the life of the great composer. Here you'll find scores, paintings, a grand piano (his last, in fact), and an ear trumpet or two. Perhaps the most impressive exhibit is the room in which Beethoven was born—empty save for a bust of the composer. *Bonngasse 20, tel. 0228/632500. Admission: DM 5 adults, DM 1.50 children. Open Apr.–Sept., Mon.–Sat. 9–1, 2–5, Sun. 10–1; Oct.–Mar., Mon.–Sat. 10:30–4, Sun. 10–1.*

A tour of Bonn would not be complete without some mention of the government buildings, which will continue as such until the government's move to Berlin is completed, and which are located in a complex about a mile south of downtown. Strung along the Rhine, in spacious, leafy grounds between Adenauer-
65 allee and the river, are the offices of the **Federal President,** the high-tech **Chancellery,** and the **Federal Parliament;** the '60s high rise you see contains the offices of members of parliament.

Time Out On your way back to town, turn left off Adenauerallee at its intersection with Weberstrasse, cross the railway line, and make for the **Mierscheid** bar-restaurant (Weberstrasse 43), long a hangout of Bonn politicians.

Numbers in the margin correspond to points of interest on the Rhineland and Köln maps.

66 **Köln** (Cologne), 27 kilometers (17 miles) north of Bonn, is the largest city on the Rhine (the fourth largest in Germany) and one of the most interesting. While not as old as Trier, it has been a dominant power in the Rhineland since Roman times. Known throughout the world for its scented toilet water, eau de cologne (first produced here in 1705 from an Italian formula), the city is today a major commercial, intellectual, and ecclesiastical center. Many business travelers are attracted to its numerous trade fairs, held in the two massive convention centers located on the Deutzer side of the Rhine.

Köln is a vibrant, bustling city, with something of the same sparkling spirit that makes Munich so memorable. It claims to have more bars than any other German city and a host of excellent eating places. It also puts on a wild carnival every February, with three days of orgiastic revelry, bands, parades, and parties that last all night. Bus tours of Köln take place daily, May–October 15, at 10, 11, 1, 2, and 3; October 16–April at 11 and 2. The two-hour tour costs DM 20 adults, DM 8 children. Walking tours are conducted daily May–September at 4:30 on Friday and Saturday. In July and August, Friday- and Saturday-night tours take in traditional Köln pubs as well as a boat ride on the Rhine. All tours begin outside the tourist office (Fettenhennen 19, opposite the cathedral).

Köln was first settled by the Romans in 38 BC. For nearly a century it grew slowly, in the shadow of imperial Trier, until a locally born noblewoman, Julia Agrippina, daughter of the Roman general Germanicus, married the Roman emperor Claudius. Her hometown was elevated to the rank of a Roman city and given the name Colonia Claudia Ara Agrippinensium. For the next 300 years, Colonia (hence Cologne, or Köln) flourished. Proof of the richness of the Roman city is provided today by the **Römisch-Germanisches Museum** (Roman-German Museum)—one place you won't want to miss if you have any interest in Roman heritage. When the Romans left, Köln was ruled first by the Franks, then by the Merovingians. In the 9th century, Charlemagne, the towering figure who united the sprawling German lands (and ruled much of present-day France) and was the first Holy Roman Emperor, restored Köln's fortunes and elevated it to its preeminent role in the Rhineland. Charlemagne also appointed the first archbishop of Köln. The ecclesiastical heritage of Köln forms one of the most striking characteristics of the city, which has no fewer than 12 Romanesque churches. Its Gothic cathedral is the largest and the finest in Germany.

Köln eventually became the largest city north of the Alps and, in time, evolved into a place of pilgrimage second only to Rome. In the Middle Ages, it was a member of the powerful Hanseatic League, occupying a position of greater importance in European commerce than did either London or Paris.

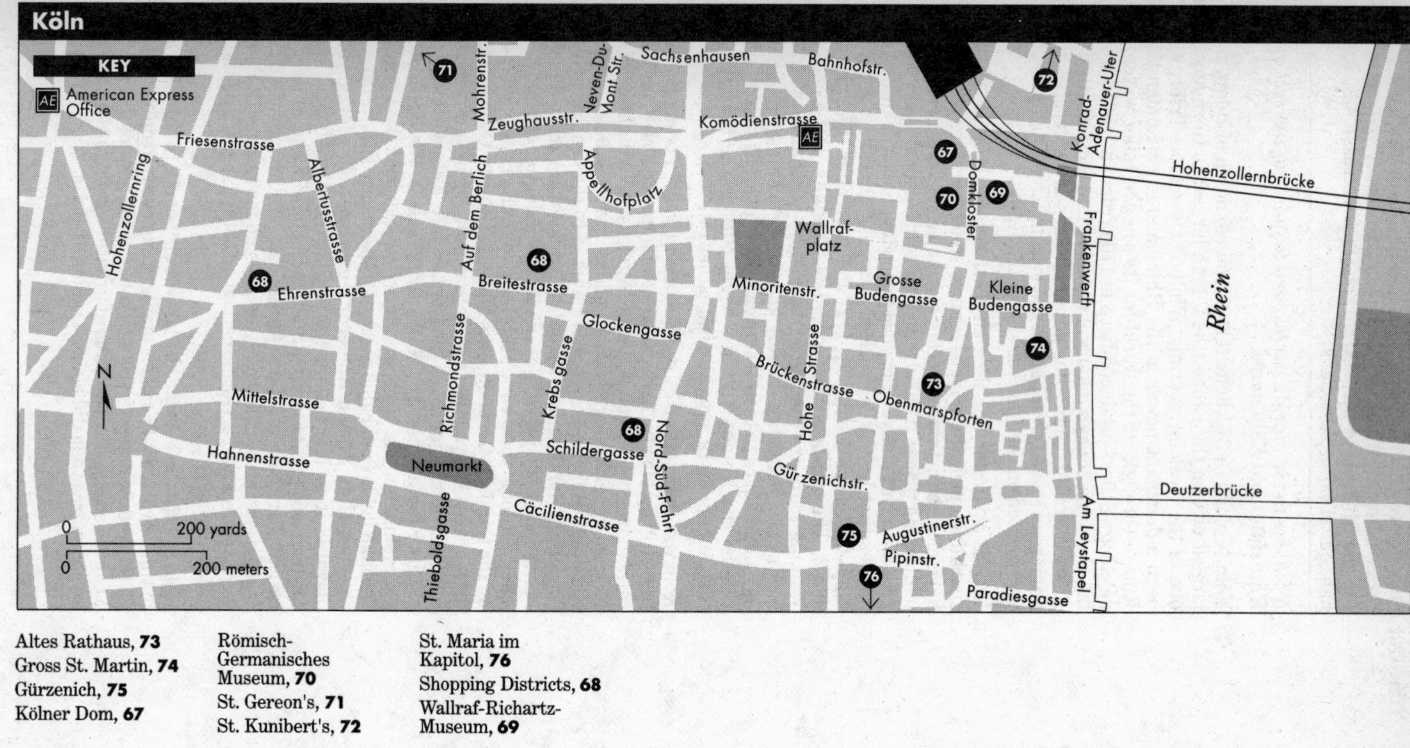

Altes Rathaus, **73**
Gross St. Martin, **74**
Gürzenich, **75**
Kölner Dom, **67**
Römisch-Germanisches Museum, **70**
St. Gereon's, **71**
St. Kunibert's, **72**
St. Maria im Kapitol, **76**
Shopping Districts, **68**
Wallraf-Richartz-Museum, **69**

Köln entered modern times as the number-one city of the Rhineland. Then, in World War II, bombings destroyed 90% of it. Only the cathedral remained relatively unscathed. Almost everything else had to be rebuilt more or less from the ground up, including all of the glorious Romanesque churches.

Early reconstruction was accomplished in a big rush—and in what might seem something of a slapdash manner. A good part of the former old town along the Hohe Strasse (old Roman High Road) was turned into a pedestrian shopping mall, one of the first in Germany. Though the mall won accolades in the press when it opened, it is pretty much without charm or grace.

The same could be said for the totally re-created facades of the old-town dwellings facing the river—they emerged looking like Disneyland kitsch, nothing to be taken seriously. Add the fact that six-lane expressways wind their way along the rim of the city center—barely yards from the cathedral—and the heart of Köln turns out to be something of a mishmash of bad and beautiful, a mixed blessing.

On the plus side, much of the Altstadt (Old Town), ringed by streets that follow the line of medieval city walls, is closed to traffic. Most major sights are within this orbit, easily reached on foot. Here, too, you'll find the best shops.

67 Towering over the old town is the extraordinary Gothic cathedral, the **Kölner Dom,** dedicated to Sts. Peter and Mary. It's comparable to the best French cathedrals; a visit to it may prove a highlight of your trip to Germany. What you'll see is one of the purest expressions of the Gothic spirit in Europe. Here, the desire to pay homage to God took the form of building as large and as lavish a church as possible, a tangible expression of God's kingdom on earth. Its spires soar heavenward and its immense interior is illuminated by light filtering through acres of stained glass. Spend some time admiring the outside of the building (you can walk almost all the way around it). Notice how there are practically no major horizontal lines—all the accents of the building are vertical. It may come as a disappointment to learn that the cathedral, begun in 1248, was not completed until 1880. Console yourself with the knowledge that it was still built to original plans. At 515 feet high, the two west towers of the cathedral were by far the tallest structures in the world when they were finished (they are still the tallest in a church). The length of the building is 470 feet; the width of the nave is 147 feet; and the highest part of the interior is 140 feet.

The cathedral was built to house what was believed to be the relics of the Magi, the three kings or wise men who paid homage to the infant Jesus (the trade in holy mementos was big business in the Middle Ages, and not always too scrupulous). Since Köln was by then a major commercial and political center, it was felt that someplace special had to be constructed to house the relics. Anxious to surpass the great cathedrals then being built in France, the masons set to work. The size of the building was not simply an example of self-aggrandizement on the part of the people of Köln, however; it was a response to the vast numbers of pilgrims who arrived to see the relics. The ambulatory, the passage that curves around the back of the altar, is unusually large, allowing cathedral authorities to funnel large numbers of visitors up to the crossing (where the nave and transepts meet, and where the relics were originally displayed), around the back of the altar, and out again. Today the relics are kept just behind the altar, in the same enormous gold-and-silver **reliquary** in which they were originally displayed. The other great treasure of the cathedral is the **Gero Cross,** a monumental oak crucifixion dating from 975. Impressive for its simple grace, it's in the last chapel on the left as you face the altar.

Other highlights to admire are the stained-glass windows, some of which date from the 13th century; the 15th-century altar painting; and the early 14th-century high altar with its surrounding arcades of glistening white figures and its intricate choir screens. The choir stalls, carved from oak around 1310, are the largest in Germany, seating 104 people. There are more treasures to be seen in the **Dom Schatzkammer,** the cathedral treasury, including the silver shrine of Archbishop Engelbert, who was stabbed to death in 1225. *Admission: DM 2 adults, DM 1 children. Open Mon.–Sat. 9–5:30, Sun. 12:30–4:30.*

Back down at street level, you'll have the choice of either more
68 culture or commerce. Köln's **shopping district** begins at nearby **Wallrafplatz,** and a recommended shopping tour will take you down Hohe Strasse, Schildergasse, Neumarkt, Mittelstrasse, Hohenzollernring, Ehrenstrasse, Breite Strasse, Tunisstrasse, Minoritenstrasse, and then back to Wallrafplatz.

Grouped around the cathedral is a collection of superb muse-
69 ums. If your priority is painting, try the ultramodern **Wallraf-Richartz-Museum** and Museum Ludwig complex (which includes the Philharmonic concert hall beneath its vast roof). Together, they form the largest art collection in the Rhineland. The Wallraf-Richartz-Museum contains pictures spanning the years 1300 to 1900, with Dutch and Flemish schools particularly well represented (Rubens, who spent his youth in Köln, has a place of honor, but there are also outstanding works by Rembrandt, Van Dyck, and Frans Hals). Of the other old masters, Tiepolo, Canaletto, and Boucher are all well represented. Renoir, Bonnard, Monet, Sisley, Pissarro, and Cézanne number among the more modern painters. The **Museum Ludwig** is devoted exclusively to 20th-century art; its Picasso collection is outstanding. *Bischofsgartenstr. 1, tel. 0221/221–2379. Admission: DM 8 adults, DM 5 children. Open Tues.–Sun. 10–5, Thurs. 10–8.*

70 Opposite the cathedral is the **Römisch-Germanisches Museum,** built from 1970 to 1974 around the famous Dionysus mosaic that was uncovered at the site during the construction of an air-raid shelter in 1941. The huge mosaic, more than 100 yards square, once covered the dining-room floor of a wealthy Roman trader's villa. Its millions of tiny earthenware and glass tiles depict some of the adventures of Dionysius, the Greek god of wine and, to the Romans, the object of a widespread and sinister religious cult. The pillared 1st-century tomb of Lucius Publicius, a prominent Roman officer, some stone Roman coffins, and a series of memorial tablets are among the museum's other exhibits. Bordering the museum on the south is a restored 90-yard stretch of the old Roman harbor road. *Roncallipl. 4, tel. 0221/221–4438. Admission: DM 5 adults, DM 1.50 children. Open Tues.–Fri. and weekends 10–5, Wed. and Thurs. 10–8.*

Six blocks west of the train station, on the site of an old Roman burial ground, stands one of the most exquisite of the city's

71 many Romanesque churches: **St. Gereon's** (Gereonshof 4). Experts regard St. Gereon's as one of the most noteworthy medieval structures still in existence, ranking it with St. Sophia in Istanbul and the Florence Cathedral. An enormous dome rests on walls that were once clad in gold mosaics. Roman masonry still forms part of the structure, which is believed to have been built over the grave of its namesake, the 4th-century martyr and patron saint of Köln.

Another notable Romanesque church on this side of the city is
72 **St. Kunibert's** (Kunibertkloster 6), which stands along the Rhine, just three blocks north of the train station. St. Kunibert's is the most lavish of the churches from the late Romanesque period. Dedicated in 1247, the church contains an unusual room, concealed under the altar, which gives access to a pre-Christian well; the well was believed to promote fertility in women.

73 Now head south to the nearby **Alter Markt** and its **Altes Rathaus,** the oldest town hall in Germany (if you don't count the fact that the building was entirely rebuilt after the war). The square has a handsome assembly of buildings—the oldest dating from 1135—in a range of styles. There was a seat of local government here in Roman times, and directly below the current Rathaus are the remains of the Roman city governor's headquarters, the Praetorium. Go inside to see the 14th-century **Hansa Saal,** whose tall Gothic windows and barrel-vaulted wood ceiling are potent expressions of medieval civic pride. The figures of the prophets, standing on pedestals at one end, are all from the early 15th century. Ranging along the south wall are nine additional statues, the so-called *Nine Good Heroes,* carved in 1360. Charlemagne and King Arthur are among them. *Altes Rathaus, Alter Markt. Admission: DM 2 adults, DM 1 children. Open weekdays 8:30–4:45, Sat. 10–2. Praetorium. Open Tues.–Sun. 10–5.*

Now head across Unter Käster toward the river and one of the
74 most outstanding of Köln's 12 Romanesque churches, the **Gross St. Martin.** Its massive 13th-century tower, with distinctive corner turrets and an imposing central spire, is another landmark of Köln. The church was built on the riverside site of a Roman granary.

Gross St. Martin is the parish church of Köln's colorful old city, the **Martinsviertel,** an attractive combination of reconstructed, high-gabled medieval buildings, winding alleys, and tastefully designed modern apartments and business quarters. Head here at night—the place comes to vibrant life at sunset.

At the south end of the district, in Gürzenichstrasse, you'll find one of Germany's most attractive cultural centers, the
75 **Gürzenich.** This Gothic structure, all but demolished in the war but carefully reconstructed, takes its name from a medieval knight (von Gürzenich), from whom the city acquired a quantity of valuable real estate in 1437. The official reception and festival hall built on the site has played a central role in the city's civic live through the centuries. A concert here can be a memorable experience. Part of the complex consists of the remains of the 10th-century Gothic church of **St. Alban,** left ruined after the war as a memorial to the city's war victims. On what's left of the church's floor (made of slate from the nearby Eifel Hills and Rhine cobblestones), you can see a sculpture of a couple

kneeling in prayer. It's an oddly moving work, a fitting memorial to the ravages of war.

Directly south of the Gürzenich, across Pipinstrasse, is the Ro-
76 manesque church of **St. Maria im Kapitol** (Kasinostr. 6). Built in the 11th and 12th centuries on the site of a Roman temple, St. Maria's is best known for its two beautifully carved 16-foot-high doors and its enormous crypt, the second-largest in Germany (after the one in Speyer Cathedral). Another memorial sculpture to the many citizens of Köln who died during World War II, the *Mourning Woman*, stands in the adjacent cloister.

Aachen

It's not in the Rhineland proper, but **Aachen,** 70 kilometers (45 miles) from Köln, less than an hour away by car or train, is an essential excursion for anyone staying in Köln. It's an essential excursion, too, if you have any interest in German history, for like the city of Charlemagne, Aachen bears the stamp of this most famous Holy Roman Emperor as no other place in Germany does. Aachen is also known by two other names: Bad Aachen, because of the hot springs that give it health-resort status; and Aix-la-Chapelle, because of the eight-sided chapel built by Charlemagne in the late 8th century that now serves as the core of the city's imposing cathedral.

Charlemagne's father, Pepin the Short, had settled in Aachen because of the healthy sulfur springs emanating from the nearby Eifel Mountains (Roman legions earlier pitched camp here because of these same healing waters). After his coronation in Rome in 800, Charlemagne spent more and more time in Aachen, building his spectacular palace and ruling his vast empire from within its walls.

The **Dom** (cathedral) remains the single greatest storehouse of Carolingian architecture in Europe. Built over the course of 1,000 years, it features a mixture of styles ranging from the imperial chapel at its heart to its 19th-century bell tower. In the cathedral's cool, august interior, you'll find Charlemagne's sturdy marble throne, a battered but still impressive monument. It's just one of many extraordinary treasures here: The **Domschatzkammer** (cathedral treasury) is about the richest in Europe. Though Charlemagne had to journey all the way to Rome for his coronation, the next 32 Holy Roman Emperors were crowned here in Aachen. The coronations were almost invariably accompanied by the presentation of a lavish gift to the cathedral. In the 12th century, Barbarossa gave the great chandelier you'll find hanging in the center of the imperial chapel; his grandson, Emperor Friedrich II, donated the glistening, richly ornamented golden shrine in which the remains of Charlemagne are kept. Emperor Karl IV, son of the king of Bohemia, journeyed from Prague in the late 14th century with the sole purpose of commissioning a bust of Charlemagne for the cathedral. The bust, on view in the treasury, contains a piece of bone from Charlemagne's skull. The Ottonian emperor Otto III gave the cathedral its fine 10th-century altar painting, while the 11th-century emperor Heinrich II donated its fine copper pulpit. *Dom open 7–7. Domschatzkammer admission: DM 3 adults, DM 2 children and senior citizens. Open Apr.–Sept., Mon. 10–2, Tues., Wed., Fri., Sat. 10–6, Thurs. 10–8,*

Sun. 10:30–5; Oct.–Mar., Tues.–Sat. 10–5, Sun. 10:30–5, Mon. 10–2.

Opposite the cathedral, across Katschhof Square, is the **Rathaus** (Town Hall). It was built starting in the early 14th century on the site of the Aula, or great hall, of Charlemagne's palace. Its first major official function was the coronation banquet of the Emperor Karl IV in 1349, held in the great Gothic hall you'll find there today. The austere, vaulted hall, with its archways decorated with lightly drawn emblems and its rough stone walls bearing the 20th-century equivalent of medieval torches, was largely rebuilt after the war. On the north wall of the building are statues of 50 Holy Roman Emperors. The greatest of the mall, Charlemagne, stands in bronze atop a graceful fountain, the Kaiserbrunnen, in the center of the square. *Rathaus. Admission: DM 2 adults, DM 1 children. Open weekdays 8–1 and 2–5, weekends 10–1 and 2–5.*

Time Out If you need a rest after these cultural calls, stop off in the little street near the cathedral known as Büchel and seek out the **Alte Aachener Kaffeestuben,** a delightful old coffee shop.

The hot springs that drew the Romans and Charlemagne's father to Aachen can still be enjoyed by visitors. Just south of the cathedral is the arcaded, neoclassical **Elisenbrunnen.** Experts agree that the spa waters here—the hottest north of the Alps—are effective in helping to cure a wide range of ailments. Drinking the sulfurous water in the approved manner, however, can be an unpleasant business. Still, if you want to emulate the great and the good who have, through the centuries, dutifully swallowed their medicine—Dürer, Frederick the Great, and Charlemagne himself, among them—hold your nose as you drink it. There are three pools in the city where you can sit in the waters, too. In Dürer's time, the baths were enjoyed for more than their health-giving properties, and there were regular crackdowns on the orgylike goings-on. Today modesty reigns in the hot pools of Aachen.

Like all German spas, Aachen also has its **Spielbank** (casino). It's housed in the porticoed former **Kurhaus,** on the parklike grounds fronting Monheimsallee (facing the Kurbad Quellenhof). *Open Mon.–Thurs. 3 PM–2 AM, Fri. and Sat. 3 PM–3 AM.*

Düsseldorf

The fifth and final tour returns to the Rhine, to elegant **Düsseldorf,** located 40 kilometers (25 miles) north of Köln. At first glance Düsseldorf may present little of the drama of Köln, with its remarkable skyline. However, in close-up, Düsseldorf turns out to be unique among German cities, with more than enough charm and beauty to justify including it on a Rhineland itinerary.

Düsseldorf has gained the reputation of being the richest city in Germany, with an extravagant lifestyle created by the postwar "economic miracle"—in other words, the essence of the "new" Germany (before reunification, of course). As home to the highest concentration of top moneymakers in the country, Düsseldorf is a glittering showcase for all the good things the deutsche mark can buy. And yet Düsseldorf, so close to all this industry, manages to present an image of calm beauty.

Although 80% of prewar Düsseldorf was destroyed in World War II, the city has since been more or less rebuilt from the ground up—in part re-creating landmarks of long ago, restoring a medieval riverside quarter, but in the main initiating what may well be the most successful updating of a major German city.

It may be difficult to believe that this dynamic city could have started life as a small fishing village at the confluence of the Rivers Rhine and Düssel. The name means "village" (*Dorf*) on the Düssel. Obviously this *Dorf* is a village no more.

Raised expressways speed traffic past towering glass-and-steel structures. Underground pedestrian passageways crisscross major intersections. Glass-enclosed shopping malls showcase the fanciest outfits, fabulous furs, jewelry, and leather goods, all sporting prestigious designer names and the highest price tags, only fitting for Germany's top fashion center.

Nowhere is that more evident than on the **Königsallee,** known as the "Kö," a wide double boulevard, divided by a pretty ornamental waterway, running between Corneliusplatz and Graf-Adolf Platz. Beyond the Triton Fountain, situated at the street's north end, begins a series of parks and gardens. Rows of chestnut trees line the waterway and boulevard, affording shade for the string of sidewalk cafés that are the pride and joy of Düsseldorfers. Here one senses a *joie de vivre* hardly expected in a city of devoted to big business and overachieving.

Time Out While on the Kö, stop at **Café Bittner** (Königsallee 18) for a coffee and pastry or a snack. This is the classic Düsseldorf café, and a longtime favorite of residents. Café Bittner, by the way, is reputed to have the best chocolates in Düsseldorf.

Head north to Corneliusplatz and walk into the lovely **Hofgarten** park, once the garden of the Elector's Palace. Laid out in 1770 and completed 30 years later, today the Hofgarten serves as an oasis of greenery at the heart of downtown, and as a focal point for Düsseldorf culture.

Here you will reach Düsseldorf's impressive 19th-century **opera house,** home of the Deutsche Oper am Rhein, along with the Baroque **Schloss Jägerhof,** more a combination town house and country lodge than a castle. It houses the Goethe Museum, featuring original manuscripts, first editions, personal correspondence, and other memorabilia of one of Germany's greatest writers. *Jacobistrasse 2, tel. 0211/8996262. Admission: DM 3 adults, DM 1 children. Open Tues.–Sun. 10–5.*

The **North Rhineland-Westphalia Art Collection** (Grabbeplatz 5), removed some time ago from the Schloss Jägerhof, is now on display in a spacious new building along the western rim of the Hofgarten. Here you will encounter a dazzling array of modern paintings from France and the United States, including examples by Bonnard, Braque, Matisse, Léger, Johns, and Pollock. If you are wondering why there are so many Paul Klees, the Swiss painter lived in Düsseldorf for a time and taught at the National Academy of Art. *Admission: DM 5. Open Tues.–Sun. 10–6.*

At the northern extremity of the Hofgarten, close to the Rhine, the **Kunstmuseum** (Museum of Fine Arts), features a collection of paintings by old masters and German Expressionists, running the gamut from Rubens, Goya, Tintoretto, and Cranach the Elder to the romantic Düsseldorf School and such modern German painters as Beckmann, Kirchner, Nolde, Macke, and Kandinsky. *Ehrenhof 5, tel. 0211/8992460. Admission: DM 10 adults, DM 5 children. Open Tues.–Sun. 10–5, Wed. 10–8.*

Walk back to Corneliusplatz and the Kö, then head to the right for the restored **Altstadt** (Old Town), facing the Rhine. Narrow alleys thread their way to some 200 restaurants and taverns, many serving local specialties, crowded into the one-square-kilometer area between the Rhine and Heine Allee. Look for the *Radschläger*, the young boys who demonstrate their cartwheeling abilities, a Düsseldorf tradition, for the admiration (and tips) of visitors.

A plaque at Bolkerstrasse 53 indicates where Heinrich Heine was born in 1797, but it is at the **Heinrich Heine Haus**, at Bolker-strasse 14, that the Heine Institute maintains an archive of significant manuscripts of this early 19th-century poet. Part of this complex is a former residence of composer Robert Schumann. *Tel. 0211/8995571. Admission DM 3 adults, DM 1.50 children. Open Tues.–Sun. 11–5.*

Time Out Among beer buffs, Düsseldorf is famous for its Altbier, so called because of the old-fashioned brewing method still used. The mellow and malty copper-colored brew is produced by eight breweries in the town. The most atmospheric place to drink it is **Zum Uerige** (*Bergerstr. 1*). Here the beer is poured straight out of polished oak barrels and dished out by bustling waiters in long green aprons.

The cobbled, traffic-free streets of the old town lead to Burgplatz, with its 13th-century **Schlossturm** (Castle Tower), all that remains of the castle built by the de Berg family, who founded Düsseldorf. The tower also houses the **Schiffahrt Museum,** which charts 2,000 years of Rhine boat building and river history. *Burgplatz 30, tel. 0211/8994195. Admission: DM 3 adults, DM 1 children. Open Tues.–Sun. 10–5.*

While on the Burgplatz see if you can spot the crooked spire of the Gothic **St. Lambertus Church** on nearby Stiftsplatz. The spire became distorted because unseasoned wood was used in its construction. The Vatican elevated the 14th-century brick church to a Basilica Minor (small cathedral) in 1974 in recognition of its role in church history. Built in the 13th century, with additions from 1394, St. Lambertus contains the tomb of William the Rich and a graceful late-Gothic tabernacle.

From Burgplatz or Stiftsplatz you can stroll south along the riverside promenade, watching the ships ply the Rhine and looking across to the "new" Düsseldorf developed on the opposite shore.

What to See and Do with Children

There are few parts of Germany that offer more for children than the Rhineland, with its castles, legends, and easily accessible rivers. In the wooded hills above the Rhine and Mosel are several **wild animal parks.** The one near the village of **Rheinböllen** (follow the signs from Bacharach) has bears and bison, as well as the usual fallow deer. (Open daily Mar.–Sept.) There's another well-stocked animal park just outside the Mosel wine village of **Klötten.** (Open year-round, daily.) **Königswinter,** near Bonn, has a **crocodile and snake farm,** the only one of its kind in Germany. (Open year-round, daily.)

You'll find **fairy-tale parks** in several parts of the Rhineland—Wiesbaden's **Taunus Wonderland** has an Indian village and a miniature Wild West railway. (Open year-round, daily.) In Dötzheim, just outside Wiesbaden, there's a miniature **Grimm fairy-tale landscape,** with scaled-down hamlets complete with tiny houses and streets. Bonn has a young people's theater, the **Theater der Jugend** (Hermannstr. 50, tel. 0228/463–672), and a fascinating natural-history museum, the **Museum Alexander König** (Adenauerallee 150–164, tel. 0228/211026).

Düsseldorf's **Aqua-Zoo** (Kaiserwertherstr. 380, tel. 0211/8996150) in the Nordpark offers a unique exhibition of aquatic creatures in their natural habitats. Among the highlights are the tropical park with crocodiles and the penguin habitat. All tanks can be viewed from above and through glass walls.

Köln's **zoo,** founded in 1860, is West Germany's third-oldest and one of the most interesting. Local children love it, perhaps because of its large monkey population and jungle house. *Riehlerstr. 73. Admission: DM 6 adults, DM 2.50 children. Open Apr.–Sept., daily 9–6; Oct.–Mar., daily 9–dusk.*

Köln also has a **puppet theater** (Rösratherstr. 133, tel. 02208/2408) and a **children's theater** (Bürgerzentrum Alte Feuerwache, Melchiorstr. 3, tel. 0221/739–1073). For possibly the most popular outing of all in Köln, take your children to the **Gebrüder Grimm** (Brothers Grimm) book and toy shop on Mauritiussteinweg 110. The **Düsseldorfer Marionettentheater** is at Bolkerstrasse 7 (tel. 0211/328432).

Shopping

Wine is more or less synonymous with the Rhine. If you haven't room for a bottle or two in your carry-on luggage, settle for one of the next best things: a couple of boxed glasses, or a locally carved corkscrew, or a basketwork wine server. If it's wine you want, bear in mind that there are few bargains to be found in Germany's duty-free airport shops, so buy before you fly.

Every Rhine and Mosel village has several wine shops, as well as cellars where you can sample before you buy. Many cellars offer tours with English-speaking guides. One of the best is the **Weingut Wilhelm Wasum** (Mainzerstr. 20–23, Bacharach). Another reliable Bacharach cellar is the **Weingut Wolfgang Eberhard** (Borbacherstr. 6–7); it's been in the same family for more than 250 years.

For wine glasses and Westerwald ceramics, seek out the **Phil Jost** shop in Bacharach (Rosenstr. 16). It offers some real bargains on "seconds." Along the Mosel, the **J. Köll** company (Ravenestr. 35, Cochem) encourages callers to try the local wines in its cask-lined cellars. For fine Mosel wine glasses in Cochem, head for **Karl Hürter** (Herrenstr. 20). On the same street, **Faber's** and **Die Vitrine** have large selections of locally made handicrafts, as well as fine linens, glassware, and pewter.

In **Wiesbaden,** you'll find one of Germany's most elegant shopping streets: the broad, tree-lined **Wilhelmstrasse.** At the end of June, when the **Wilhelmstrassenfest** is held, it's partytime along Wilhelmstrasse—Rheingau wine and Sekt flow in abundance. Wine corks pop again in mid-August for Wiesbaden's **Rheingauer Weinfest,** Germany's largest wine festival. Wiesbaden is a German **antiques** center, too; you'll find the best selections along **Taunusstrasse.**

The international comings and goings in **Bonn** keep antiques dealers busy there. Two to visit are **Paul Schweitzer** (Muffendorfer Hauptstr. 37) and **Ehlers Antiquitäten** (Berliner Freiheit 28). Bonn is a city of **markets,** with two open daily: the **Wochenmarkt** on Marktplatz and the **Blumenmarkt,** a flower market, on Remigiusplatz. There's a huge **flea market** from April through October on the third Saturday of each month at **Rheinaue** (Ludwig-Erhard-Str.). If you're in the Bonn area on the second weekend of September, don't miss the **Pützchens Markt,** a huge country fair.

Koblenz has two flea markets held each Saturday in summer at **Peter-Almeier-Ufer** and at **Florinsmarkt.** For antiques and handicrafts, prowl the old city around the cathedral or make for the **Weindorf** (wine village), where more than just wine is offered.

Trier boasts high-class shops along the pedestrian streets in the **old town:** Simeonstrasse, Fleischstrasse, Nagelstrasse, Palatstrasse, and Hauptmarkt. For local handicrafts, glassware, ceramics, and fabrics, make for **Kunsthandwerkerhof** (Simeonstiftpl.).

In **Düsseldorf,** the east side of the **Königsallee** is lined with some of Germany's trendiest boutiques, grandest jewelers, and most extravagant furriers. The most famous names in fashion are all represented here.

The center of **Köln,** south of the cathedral, is one huge pedestrian shopping zone. It'll take you about half an hour to stroll through it all. From the cathedral, head south along Hohe Strasse to Schildergasse, then to Neumarkt, Mittelstrasse, Hohenzollernring, Ehrenstrasse, Breitestrasse, Tunisstrasse, Minoritenstrasse, and back to the starting point, Wallrafplatz. Between Mittelstrasse and Ehrenstrasse is a glass-roofed bazaar where dozens of shops share space. **Mittelstrasse** and **Hohestrasse** are best for German fashions and luxury goods (**Offermann's** on Hohestrasse has a large selection of fine leather items and beautifully finished travel accessories). Hohestrasse is also the best place to look for Köln's most celebrated product: **eau de cologne.** In nearby Glockengasse (No. 4711, of course) you can visit the house where the 18th-century Italian chemist Giovanni-Maria Farina first concocted it. Köln is also known for delicious **Ludwig chocolate.** You'll have no difficulty finding it in any of the delicatessens along the route. **Lintgasse** is the place for antiques; flea markets are held every third Saturday at the **Alter Markt** in the old town, and every fourth Sunday at **Nippes** (Wilhelmpl.). The best department stores are **Kaufhof** (Hohestr.), **Hertie** (Neumarkt), and **Karstadt** (Breitestr.).

Sports and Fitness

Bicycling Most local train stations have bikes to rent for DM 10 a day (DM 6 if you have a valid train ticket). Listings of additional outlets for rental bikes are available from train stations.

Boating Rowboats and canoes can be hired at most Rhine and Mosel river resorts. For a motorboat, try the **Lahr Charter Boot** (Grenzerstr. 29, Koblenz, tel. 02603/6541).

Jogging For jogging, running, or walking in Düsseldorf, the Rheinpark in Golzheim, by the river just north of the Altstadt, serves as an idyllic setting.

Swimming Even though West Germany's environmental minister swam the Rhine in 1988 to prove that the river was no longer polluted, only the brave and/or foolhardy are likely to follow his example in either the Rhine or the Mosel. The Rhineland has a substantial number of pools, indoor and outdoor, where the swimming is much safer. Trier's **Stadtbad,** with five heated pools, and Wiesbaden's **Opelbad,** located high above the city on the Neroberg, are among the best. Köln has more than 20 outdoor pools; the one at **Müngersdorfer Stadium** (Aachenerstr.) is heated. There are also two lido-type complexes in Köln: **Deutz-Kalker Bad,** on the street of the same name, and **Kombibad Hohenberg** (Schwarzburgerstr. 91). Bonn's diplomats plunge in at the Kurfürstendad—it's in the Bad Godesberg park.

Tennis The **Freizheit Park** (tel. 02603/81095) in Koblenz's Industriekreisel has eight indoor tennis courts, plus a swimming pool and a sauna for postmatch relaxation. Wiesbaden's **Henkell ice stadium** (Höllerbornstr.) becomes a tennis court during the summer months. The **Ferienpark Hochwald** (tel. 06589/1011) at Kell, near Trier, is one of the leading tennis complexes in Germany. In Köln, try **City Sport** (Rhondroferstr. 10, tel. 0221/411-092), or **Squashpark** (Neusserstr. 718a, tel. 0221/740-8866). Düsseldorf's **Rhine Stadium** has 18 public courts.

Dining and Lodging

Dining

If you come to the Rhine hoping to eat fish, you'll be disappointed: The polluted waters of the river have destroyed all but a few of the fish that once thrived. Practically the only fish dishes in the region feature seafood flown in from France; prices are correspondingly high. However, there are numerous local specialties that are hearty rather than sophisticated: *Himmel und Erde,* a mixture of potatoes, onions, and apples; *Hämmchen,* or pork knuckle; *Hunsrücker Festessen,* sauerkraut with potatoes, horseradish, and ham. There are many small inns and restaurants offering these and other regional dishes. At the other end of the scale, Düsseldorf, Köln, and Wiesbaden boast some of the most sophisticated restaurants in Europe, many offering delectable nouvelle cuisine. The Rhineland is wine country, and every restaurant and café offers a large selection of wines.

Highly recommended restaurants are indicated by a star ★.

Category	Cost*
Very Expensive	over DM 90
Expensive	DM 55–DM 90
Moderate	DM 35–DM 55
Inexpensive	under DM 35

**per person for a three-course meal, including tax but not alcohol*

Lodging

There's a vast selection of places to lay your head. The most romantic are the old, riverside inns and hotels and the castle-hotels, some of which are enormously luxurious. In the cities of the Rhineland, there's a similarly large choice. Some of the most expensive hotels are among the finest in Europe. Modern high rises are common. A great many hotels close for the winter; most are also booked well in advance, especially for the wine festivals in the fall and during important trade fairs, as in Düsseldorf. Whenever possible, make reservations long before you visit.

Highly recommended hotels are indicated by a star ★.

Category	Cost*
Very Expensive	over DM 180
Expensive	DM 120–DM 180
Moderate	DM 80–DM 120
Inexpensive	under DM 80

**Prices are for two people in a double room, excluding service charges.*

Aachen
Dining
★ **Gala.** For the most elegant dining in Aachen, make for the Gala restaurant, adjoining the casino. The mood is discreetly classy, with dark paneled walls and original oil paintings; the food is regional, with nouvelle touches. *Monheimsallee, 44, tel. 0241/153–013. Reservations required. Jacket and tie required. AE, DC, MC, V. Dinner only. Closed Mon. Very Expensive.*

La Becasse. Sophisticated French nouvelle cuisine is offered in this upscale modern restaurant, located just outside the old town by the Westpark. Try the distinctively light calves' liver. *Hanbrucherstr. 1, tel. 0241/74444. Reservations required. Jacket and tie required. AE, DC, MC, V. Closed Sat. for dinner, Sun. and Mon. for lunch. Expensive.*

Zum Schiffgen. This is a traditional inn where the pot roasts and stews are justly voted tops by the locals. Dishes change with the seasons. See if venison stew is on the menu, which is remarkably low-priced. *Hühnermarkt 21, tel. 0241/33529. No reservations. Dress: informal. AE, DC, MC, V. Closed Sun.–Wed. dinner. Inexpensive.*

Lodging
★ **Steigenberger Hotel Quellenhof.** The Quellenhof offers the sort of pampered luxury that often appeals to older guests. Built during World War I as a country home for the kaiser, it's very much one of Europe's grande dames: spacious, elegant, and formal. The flower-filled Parkrestaurant, one of the best restau-

rants in northern Germany, serves haute cuisine in the grand manner. The hotel is located near the Kurpark and the casino, and guests have direct access by lift to the thermal baths. *Monheimsallee 52, tel. 0241/152–081. 200 rooms with bath. Facilities: pool, thermal treatments, house doctor, restaurant, parking. AE, DC, MC, V. Very Expensive.*

Krott. In the heart of the city, but positioned in the traffic-free pedestrian zone, this family-run hotel offers not only convenience but also considerable comfort. It's a short walk from virtually all the major attractions. *Wirichsbongardstr. 16, tel. 0241/48373. 20 rooms with bath. Facilities: restaurant, sauna, solarium. AE, DC, MC, V. Expensive.*

Benelux. For low-cost accommodations, the centrally located Benelux offers one of the best deals in town. Small and family-run, it has comfortable modern rooms and a smattering of antiques in the public areas. *Franzstr. 21, tel. 0241/22343. 33 rooms with bath. Facilities: parking. AE, DC, MC, V. Moderate.*

Bacharach
Dining and Lodging

Altkölnischer Hof. Tucked in a quiet square in medieval Bacharach, the Altkölnischer is a small, half-timbered hotel built at the turn of the century. Vivid geraniums are planted under the small windows; rooms are simply but attractively furnished in country style; and the rustic restaurant offers typical local dishes and some excellent wines. *Blücherstr. 2, tel. 06743/1339. 20 rooms with bath. Facilities: restaurant, parking. AE, DC, V. Closed Oct.–Apr. Moderate.*

Bernkastel-Kues
Dining and Lodging

Hotel Römischer Kaiser. A riverside location directly on the promenade offers fine views of either the waterway or the surrounding vineyards. All the rooms have balconies. The hotel's restaurant is noted for its good, reasonably priced regional wines. *Marktstr. 29, tel. 06531/3038. 35 rooms, all with bath. AE, DC, MC, V. Closed Jan.–Feb. Moderate.*

Zur Post. Picture-book Germany is alive and well at the appealing, early-19th-century Zur Post. Behind its colorful, flower-laden facade lurk the obligatory exposed wood beams, a dark paneled restaurant (with over 100 wines), and tastefully decorated bedrooms. *Gestade 17, tel. 06531/2022. 42 rooms with bath. Facilities: solarium, sauna, restaurant, parking. AE, DC, MC, V. Closed Jan. Moderate.*

Bingen
Lodging

Rheinhotel Starkenburger Hof. In business since the middle of the 19th century, the Starkenburger Hof, decorated throughout in warm shades of brown and gold, is the number-one choice in Bingen. It overlooks the Rhine, so don't settle for a room without a view. There's no restaurant. *Am Rheinkai, 1, tel. 06721/14341. 30 rooms, 25 with bath. AE, DC. Closed Jan.–Feb. Moderate.*

Bonn
Dining
★

Schaarschmidt. This popular and highly acclaimed stalwart of the Bonn restaurant scene moved its premises across the Rhine to suburban Bevel, but nothing else has changed. The menu still offers the best asparagus to be found (in season) in Bonn; the lamb dishes are a delight; and the wine list is virtually endless. *Siegfried Leopold-Str. 66, tel. 0228/460–056. Reservations recommended. Dress: informal, DC, MC. Closed Mon. Expensive.*

Das Haus Daufenbach. The stark white exterior of the Daufenbach, located by the church of St. Remigius, disguises one of the most distinctive restaurants in Bonn. The mood is rustic, with simple wood furniture and antlers on the walls.

Specialties include *Spanferkel* (suckling pig) and a range of imaginative salads. Wash them down with wines from the restaurant's own vineyards. *Brüderfasse 6, tel. 0228/637–9944. Reservations recommended. Dress: informal. AE, DC, MC, V. Closed Sun. dinner. Moderate.*

Em Hottche. Travelers have been given sustenance at this tavern since the late 14th century, and today it offers one of the best-value lunches in town. The interior is rustic, the food stout and hearty. *Markt 4, tel. 0228/658596. No reservations. Dress: informal. AE, DC, MC, V. Closed last 2 weeks in Dec. Inexpensive.*

Lodging

★ **Bristol.** The Bristol could be in Dallas for all the German atmosphere it has, but for modern elegance and a terrific central location, it's an established favorite. *Prinz-Albert-Str. 2, tel. 0228/26980. 120 rooms with bath. Facilities: indoor pool, sauna, solarium, bowling alley, restaurant. AE, DC, MC, V. Very Expensive.*

Domicil. A group of buildings around a quiet, central courtyard has been stylishly converted into a new hotel of great charm and comfort. The rooms are individually furnished and decorated—in styles from fin-de-siècle romantic to Italian modern. Lots of glass gives the public rooms a friendly airiness. *Thomas-Mann-Str. 24–26, tel. 0228/729–090. 40 rooms, all with bath. Facilities: sauna, whirlpool, games room, boutique, hairdressing salon and beauty parlor, restaurant, coffee bar. AE, DC, MC, V. Closed Christmas to New Year's Day. Very Expensive.*

Rheinland Bonn. This modest lodging has the advantage of being a short walk from the center of the old town. Rooms are comfortable, and although there is no restaurant, a good buffet breakfast greets the day. *Berliner Freiheit 11, tel. 0228/658096. 31 rooms with bath. AE. Moderate.*

Sternhotel. For good value, solid comfort, and a central location, the family-run Stern is tops. Rooms can be small, but all are pleasantly furnished. There's no restaurant, but snacks are available at the bar. *Markt 8, tel. 0228/654–455. 70 rooms with bath. AE, DC, MC, V. Moderate.*

Boppard
Dining and Lodging

★ **Hotel Klostergut Jakobsberg.** Stay here for the amazing location on the north bank of the Rhine (the hotel's about 12 kilometers, or 8 miles, north of Boppard), the array of sports facilities, the excellent food, and the sumptuous furnishings. The hotel is housed in a castle (make sure you see its gem of a chapel) and boasts a sophisticated baronial atmosphere. The place has an extensive collection of hunting trophies and rifles, and a considerable assembly of paintings and prints, not to mention imposing tapestries. This is real *Prisoner of Zenda* stuff. The hotel raises its own cattle and cultivates Japanese *shiitake* mushrooms. Both are put to good use in its restaurant. The veal medallions in goose-liver sauce are superb. *5407 Boppard-Rhein, tel. 06742/3061. 104 rooms and 6 suites with bath. Facilities: indoor pool, indoor and outdoor tennis courts, sauna, solarium, squash, bowling alley, golf course, skeet and trap shooting, horseback riding, heliport, restaurant. AE, DC, MC, V. Very Expensive.*

Cochem
Dining and Lodging

★ **Alte Thorschenke.** There are few more authentic or atmospheric old inns in the Rhineland than this ancient and picturesque spot in the heart of Cochem. Creaking staircases, four-poster beds, river views, and exposed beams combine to produce an effect that's almost too good to be true. The restaurant boasts an extensive selection of local wines. Avoid the modern annex if you want to experience the full charm of this romantic haunt. *Brückenstr. 3, tel. 02671/7059. 51 rooms with bath. Facilities: restaurant. AE, DC, MC, V. Closed Jan.–mid-Mar. Expensive.*

★ **Weissmühle.** You'll want to stay—or eat—here as much to see the picture-book village of Endertal, just outside of Cochem, as to lay your head on the hotel's ample pillows. The place is decorated in that inimitable German gingerbread style, with carved beams and lace curtains galore. Try the trout or the spit-roasted kebabs. *Endertal, tel. 02671/8955. 36 rooms with bath. Facilities: bowling alley, sun terrace, restaurant. DC, MC, V. Moderate–Expensive.*

Brixiade. Despite its modern-looking facade, the Brixiade has been welcoming guests—Kaiser Wilhelm II among them—for more than 100 years. Ask for a room with a view over the town and the river. The restaurant offers a fixed-price menu and magnificent local wines. Dine on the terrace in summer. *Uferstr. 13, tel. 02671/3015. 38 rooms with bath. Facilities: restaurant. AE, V. Moderate.*

Düsseldorf
Dining

★ **Grill Royal.** The name says it all. You get the royal treatment here for more or less a king's ransom (not atypical in Düsseldorf). The setting in this main restaurant of Hotel Breidenbacher Hof (*see* below) is dark woodwork, candlelight, and glistening silver. The menu features the "new" German cuisine, light, delicate, and ravishing when it all works, as it does here. This is truffle territory, dishes that even Brillat-Savarin might have approved of. *Heinrich Heine Allee 36, tel. 0211/13030. Reservations required. Jacket and tie required. AE, DC, MC, V. Dinner only Sat.–Sun. Very Expensive.*

Orangerie. To dine here lets you know why Düsseldorf is also known as "Dazzeldorf." In a glittering setting, with the clientele dressed to the nines, every meal turns into a glamorous production. While you can order à la carte, the idea here is to let the chef devise a multicourse "surprise" meal highlighted with the finest delicacies. *Bolkerstrasse 30, tel. 0211/131828. Reservations required. Jacket and tie required. AE, DC. Closed Sun. Very Expensive.*

★ **Rôtisserie.** The decor is subdued and the atmosphere hushed, but the food sparkles at this gourmet restaurant in the Steigenberger Parkhotel (*see* Lodging, *below*). Chef Alfred Schreiber serves classic French cuisine prepared with imagination and a light touch (although butter and cream have not been altogether banned). Superb starters might include whipped sorrel-chervil soup and a gossamer parfait of quail with raisins and green pepper, followed by such entrées as shellfish lasagna layered with asparagus, wild mushrooms, and lobster sauce, and medallions of lamb with a shallot-mustard crust. Some German classics are always on the menu; the restaurant's rendition of *Rote Grütze* (fruit-flavor pudding) with vanilla sauce is especially admirable. *Corneliusplatz 1, tel. 0211/13810, fax 0211/131679. Reservations recommended. Jacket and tie required. AE, DC, MC, V. Very Expensive.*

Zum Schiffchen. This is probably the most colorful of all the old riverside brewery taverns in the Altstadt, in business since 1628. Napoleon ate here in 1811. Today, as then, one sits at long scrubbed wooden tables and dines community-style on down-to-earth fare. Beer comes straight from the barrel, including the local *Altbier*. The day's specials invariably include grilled pork chops that come to the table sizzling; eels are another good bet. During the asparagus season (May), that is exactly what to order, along with cold ham—a classic dish in the Rhineland. *Hafenstrasse 5, tel. 0211/132422. Reservations unnecessary. Dress: informal. AE, DC, MC. Closed Sun. and holidays. Moderate.*

Lodging

★ **Hotel Breidenbacher Hof.** Rated among the two or three top choices in Germany, this superluxurious hotel offers understated elegance with superb white-glove service. The location is as central as you can get. The palatial lobby is studded with 17th- and 18th-century antiques, with the theme continuing in the beautifully appointed rooms. *Heinrich Heine Allee 36, tel. 0211/13030. 132 rooms with bath. Facilities: 2 restaurants, bar. AE, DC, MC, V. Very Expensive.*

★ **Steigenberger Parkhotel.** Miraculously quiet despite its central location on the edge of the Hofgarten and at the beginning of the Königsallee, this 91-year-old hotel is anything but stodgy. The city's chic congregate in the lobby's Etoile Lounge, where weekly jazz performances and English teas keep things lively. The soaring ceilings add to the spaciousness of the guest rooms, each individually decorated in a restrained, elegant style, many with Directorie touches. Dressing rooms with multiple entrances and phones, and extra-powerful portable blowdryers in rare-marble-clad bathrooms are some of the more luxurious appointments. The pampering continues at the breakfast buffet, served in the Rôtisserie (*see* Dining, above), where champagne and smoked salmon are appropriate starters for a shopping expedition on the Kö. *Corneliusplatz 1, tel. 0211/13810, fax 0211/131679. 160 rooms with bath. Facilities: restaurant, 2 bars, open-air terrace café, valet parking. AE, DC, MC, V. Very Expensive.*

Hotel Esplanade. This is a small, modern hotel in an exceptionally quiet, leafy location, but still close to where the action is. From the inviting lobby to attractive decor in the rooms, the sense here is one of intimacy. *Fürstenplatz 17, tel. 0211/375010. 80 rooms with bath. Facilities: 2 restaurants, bar, fitness room, heated pool. AE, DC, MC, V. Expensive.*

Koblenz

Dining

Weinhaus Hubertus. This is about the most atmospheric restaurant in Koblenz. The flower-laden, half-timbered 17th-century exterior gives a good idea of the country-style mood inside. Antiques and dark wood predominate. The food is ample and cooked with gusto. *Florinsmarkt. 54, tel. 0261/31177. Reservations advised. Dress: informal. No credit cards. Closed lunch. Moderate.*

Fährhaus am Stausee. The garden terrace where you can dine on warm sunny days extends to the banks of the Mosel. The restaurant's name comes from the ancient river-ferry crossing point that existed here until a bridge was built. A range of dishes, predominantly fish, fill the menu of this old established restaurant. *An der Fähre 3, Metternich, tel. 0261/2093. Reservations unnecessary. MC. Inexpensive–Moderate.*

Lodging

Scandic Crown. The elegantly modern Scandic Crown is full of style and class. It may be short on old-German atmosphere, but it's long on polished service, well-upholstered comfort, and terrific views. The rooms are elegantly understated. *Julius-Wegeler-Str. 2, tel. 0261/1360. 167 rooms with bath. Facilities:*

sauna, Jacuzzi, 2 restaurants, bar. AE, DC, MC, V. Expensive.

Kleiner Riesen. The riverside location and simple comforts of the Kleiner Riesen single it out as the sort of well-run, straightforward hotel that's not always easy to find. It's an older hotel, offering basic, no-nonsense value for the money. There's no restaurant. *Kaiserin-Augusta-Anlagen 18, tel. 0261/32077. 27 rooms with bath. Facilities: parking. AE, DC, MC, V. Moderate.*

Köln
Dining and Lodging

★ **Dom-Hotel.** The Dom is in a class of its own. Old-fashioned, formal, and gracious, with a stunning location right by the cathedral, it offers the sort of Old World elegance and discreetly efficient service few hotels aspire to these days. The antique-filled bedrooms, generally in Louis XV or Louis XVI style, are subdued in color, high-ceilinged, and spacious. The view of the cathedral is something to treasure; enjoy it from the glass-enclosed Atelier am Dom, where you can dine informally on anything from wild boar served with chanterelle ragout to tofu piccata with ratatouille and curried rice. The weekend package of DM 230 per night for a double room is a bargain, including champagne on arrival, a sightseeing tour of the city, and reduced museum entrance fees. *Domkloster 2A, tel. 0221/20240. 125 rooms with bath. Facilities: restaurant, terrace café, bar, parking. AE, DC, MC, V. Very Expensive.*

★ **Excelsior Hotel Ernst.** The Empire-style lobby in sumptuous royal blue, bright yellow, and gold is striking, and a similar boldly conceived grandeur extends to the remaining public rooms in this hotel founded in 1863, just down the street from the main train station and across from the cathedral. Old master paintings (including a Van Dyke) are everywhere; you'll be served breakfast in a room named after the Gobelins tapestries that hang there. Guest rooms are appropriately more intimate in scale, with spectacular marble bathrooms and designer fixtures. Ultimately, though, it's the genuine warmth and helpfulness of the staff that make this a truly great hotel. The Hansestube, which attracts a local business crowd with gourmet lunch specials, has a more hushed ambience in the evening. Looking like anything but a *Stube* (barrack), the lacquered-wood–paneled restaurant with rust-colored velvet banquettes and peach-hued napery serves French haute cuisine with an occasional nod to the health-conscious. Mushroom lovers will want to try the veal medallions in a rich cream sauce with a huge mound of morels. The wine cellar is famous for its French Burgundies and Bordeaux. *Domplatz, tel. 0221/2701, fax 0221/135150. 160 rooms with bath. Facilities: restaurant, bar, beauty salon, masseuse, shop, fitness room. AE, DC, MC, V. Very Expensive.*

★ **Bado-La Poêle d'Or.** At first glance, the heavy furnishings and hushed atmosphere of the Poêle d'Or make it seem like the last place you'd find light and sophisticated nouvelle cuisine in Germany. But for some years, those in the know have been claiming this as one of the finest dining establishments in Europe. Even such apparently simple dishes as onion soup have been winning plaudits. Order salmon with lemon-ginger sauce if you want to sample the full glory of the place. *Komödienstr. 50–52, tel. 0221/134–100. Reservations required. Dress: casual chic. AE, DC, MC, V. Closed Sun., Mon. for lunch, 3 weeks in mid-summer. Very Expensive.*

★ **Chez Alex.** For upscale nouvelle cuisine with a strong French accent, check out the delicate offerings here. The decor is very classy, with antiques, fine paintings, and deep leather chairs. The lamb fillet Provençale with Roquefort sauce is memorable. *Mühlengasse 1–3, tel. 0221/230–560. Reservations required. Jacket and tie required. AE, DC, MC. Closed Sat. dinner and Sun. Expensive.*

Die Tomato. If you don't like tomatoes, stay away from this popular little restaurant. The red fruit—to be seen growing at the door in summer—is featured in a menu that changes daily and concentrates on fish dishes. *Aachenerstr. 11, tel. 0221/252962. Reservations unnecessary. Dress: informal. AE, DC, MC. Closed Sun. lunch. Moderate.*

Gaststätte Früh am Dom. For real down-home German food, there are few places to compare with this time-honored former brewery. Bold frescoes on the vaulted ceilings establish the mood. Such dishes as Hämmchen provide an authentically Teutonic experience. The beer garden is delightful for summer dining. *Am Hof 12–14, tel. 0221/236–618. Reservations advised. Dress: informal. No credit cards. Moderate.*

★ **Weinhaus im Waldfisch.** The black-and-white gabled facade of this 400-year-old restaurant signals that here, too, you'll come face-to-face with no-holds-barred traditional specialties in a time-honored atmosphere. Try Himmel und Erde, and any of the wide range of wines. The restaurant is tucked away between the Heumarkt (Haymarket) and the river. *Salzgasse 13, tel. 0221/219–575. Reservations advised. Dress: informal. DC, MC. Closed Mon., weekends, and holidays. Moderate.*

Lodging

Hotel im Wasserturm. What used to be Europe's tallest water tower is now a 12-story luxury hotel-in-the-round, opened at the end of 1989 after a four-year, DM $70 million conversion. The neoclassic look of the brick exterior was retained by order of Cologne conservationists. The ultramodern interior was the work of the French designer Andrée Putman, renowned in the United States for her work on Morgan's Hotel, New York. *Kaygasse 2, tel. 0221/20080. 36 rooms and 37 suites and maisonettes with bath. Facilities: 24-hour room service, sauna, limousine. AE, DC, MC, V. Very Expensive.*

★ **Altstadt.** Located close by the river in the old town, this is the place for charm and low rates. All the rooms are individually decorated, and the service is impeccable—both welcoming and efficient. There's no restaurant. *Salzgasse 7, tel. 0221/234–187. 28 rooms with bath. Facilities: sauna. AE, DC, MC, V. Closed Christmas. Moderate.*

Rüdesheim
Dining and Lodging

Hotel Jagdschloss Niederwald. This is not so much a place to overnight as a luxury resort hotel where you might want to spend your entire vacation. It's set in the hills 5 kilometers (3 miles) out of Rüdesheim, with predictably good views over the Rhine and the Rheingau. The former hunting lodge of the dukes of Hesse, it has a lavish, baronial atmosphere. The restaurant can be magnificent. Families will appreciate the wide range of activities offered. *Auf dem Niederwald 1, tel. 06722/1004. 49 rooms with bath. Facilities: restaurant, bar, indoor pool, sauna, gym, tennis courts, horseback riding. DC, MC, V. Restaurant closed Jan. 1–Feb. 14. Very Expensive–Expensive.*

★ **Romantik Hotel Schwan.** This must be one of the most "romantic" of the Romantik chain. A Renaissance half-timbered building with green shutters, tubs of flowers, high gables, and sloping roofs, it sits in the village of Oestrich, about 8 kilometers (5 miles) east of Rüdesheim, right on the Rhine. The restaurant offers fine local specialties and an extensive wine list; wine-tasting sessions are held among the oak casks in the ancient cellars. *Rheinallee 5–7, Oestrich, tel. 06723/3001. 62 rooms with bath. Facilities: restaurant, terrace, parking. AE, DC, MC, V. Closed Nov.–mid-Mar. Expensive.*

Rüdesheimer Hof. For a taste of Rheingau hospitality, try this typical inn. There's a terrace for summer dining on excellent local specialties, which you can enjoy along with any of the many wines offered. *Geisenheimerstr. 1, tel. 06722/2011. 42 rooms with bath. Facilities: restaurant, terrace, parking. AE, DC, MC, V. Closed mid-Nov.–mid-Feb. Moderate.*

St. Goar/ St. Goarshausen
Dining and Lodging

Schlosshotel auf Berg Rheinfels. Located directly opposite Burg Maus, this castle-hotel breathes a regal air. Its ponderously grand interior is furnished with intricate French and Spanish antiques. Ask for a room with a view. The restaurant offers hearty regional specialties. Medieval-style banquets *(Spektakulum)*, complete with minstrels, serving wenches, and oxen on spits, are offered in summer. *Schlossberg 47, tel. 06741/8020. 44 rooms with bath. Facilities: indoor and outdoor (heated) pools, miniature golf, fishing, restaurant, bar. AE, DC, MC, V. Expensive.*

Herrmannsmühle. This is an Alpine chalet-style hotel with heavy pine furnishings decorated with floral patterns. It stands just outside town by its own vineyards and offers good value at low prices. *5422 St. Goarshausen, Rhein-Loreley-stadt, tel. 06771/7317. 10 rooms with bath. Facilities: restaurant. No credit cards. Closed mid-Nov.–Feb. Inexpensive.*

Trier
Dining

★ **Pfeffermühle.** The stately Pfeffermühle stands alongside the Mosel, by the cable-car station. This former fisherman's home is now considered to be the best restaurant in town. The food is nouvelle French. The rabbit in sherry sauce is outstanding, as is the lobster in champagne gelée with asparagus tips. The wine list features vintage Mosels. *Zurlaubener Ufer 76, tel. 0651/26133. Reservations required. Dress: casual chic. MC. Closed Sun. and July 10–31. Expensive.*

★ **Zum Domstein.** The centrally located, bustling Domstein is built above a Roman cellar, and it takes its history seriously—not only keeping its wines well stored within its ancient walls, as the Romans did, but serving authentic Roman dishes in the restaurant above. Many of them are the staples of today's Italian cuisine (the sauces are so rich they could have contributed to the downfall of the Roman Empire). *Hauptmarkt 5, tel. 0651/74490. No reservations. Dress: informal. AE, DC, V. Closed Christmas. Moderate.*

Ratskeller zur Steipe. Buried in the vaults beneath the town hall, the Ratskeller offers Teutonic mood and fare. Try *Steipenteller*, the house specialty, a massive tray of mixed meats. In summer, you can move upstairs and eat on the terrace. *Hauptmarkt 14, tel. 0651/75052. Reservations advised. Dress: informal. AE, DC, V. Closed Mon. and Jan.–Easter. Inexpensive.*

Lodging

Hotel-Cafe Astoria. This beautifully renovated 19th-century city villa is ideally located between the Mosel river and the old town. Ask for a room on the first floor: they are larger, although all rooms are cozy and comfortably furnished. *Bruch-*

hausenstr. 4, tel. 0651/73890. 25 rooms with shower. Facilities: bar, café, courtyard terrace. AE, MC, V. Moderate.

★ **Petrisberg.** This will be the choice of anyone who values classic modern design and a location away from the downtown area. The building is unimposing externally, but inside features striking antiques and rooms with superb views over vineyards, forests, and parklands. For all that, it's no more than a 10-minute walk from the old town. There's a moody *weinstube* (wine bar) in the basement, but no restaurant. *Sickingenstr. 11, tel. 0651/41181. 30 rooms and 3 suites with bath. Facilities; bar, weinstube, parking. No credit cards. Moderate.*

Wiesbaden
Dining

★ **Die Ente vom Lehel.** The formal and elegant restaurant of the Nassauer Hof (*see* below) provides one of the most memorable dining experiences in Germany. Nouvelle cuisine is king here. For a dessert you'll never forget, try *Dialog der Früchte* (dialogue of fruits), a startling combination of vivid pureed fruits that swirl around your plate. *Kaiser-Friedrich-Pl. 3, tel. 0611/133–666. Reservations required. Jacket and tie required. AE, DC, MC, V. Closed Sun., Mon., and July–early Aug. Very Expensive.*

Weihenstephan. Bavarian specialties are offered in this Alpine-style restaurant 5 kilometers (3 miles) south of the city center in suburban Biebrich. Even Bavarian beer is available, despite this being the most famous wine-producing area of the country. The mood is as hearty as the cooking. *Armenruhstr. 6, tel. 0611/61134. Reservations advised. Dress: informal. AE. Closed Sat. Moderate.*

Lodging

★ **Nassauer Hof.** Located opposite the Kurpark, the Nassauer Hof epitomizes elegance and style. Set in a turn-of-the-century building, it combines the best of Old World graciousness with German efficiency and comfort. Rooms are large and classy; the bar is a chic place for a rendezvous. *Kaiser-Friedrich-Pl. 3–4, tel. 0611/1330. 183 rooms and 22 suites with bath. Facilities: indoor pool, sauna, massage, restaurant, bar, parking. AE, DC, MC, V. Very Expensive.*

★ **Schwarzer Bock.** For period charm, there are few hotels to beat the stylish Schwarzer Bock. The building dates from 1486, though most of what you see today is from the 19th century. The lavish public rooms are filled with antiques, flowers, and paintings; the opulent bedrooms are individually decorated in styles ranging from Baroque to modern. The thermal swimming pool will soothe away the pain of paying the bill. *Kranzpl. 12, tel. 0611/1550. 140 rooms and 20 suites with bath. Facilities: indoor pool, sauna, massage, beauty farm, roof garden, restaurant, bar, parking. AE, DC, MC, V. Expensive–Very Expensive.*

The Arts and Nightlife

The Arts

Music

Aachen has a municipal orchestra that gives regular concerts in the **Kongresszentrum Eurogress,** Monheimsallee. **Bonn** means Beethoven, and every three years the city hosts a **Beethoven Festival.** The next one takes place in 1992, from September 11 to October 4. Contact the Bonn tourist office (tel. 0228/773466) for programs and ticket information. The Bonn **Symphony Orchestra** opens its winter season in grand style every September with a concert on the market square, in front of city hall. Otherwise, concerts are given in the Beethovenhalle (they're free on Sunday mornings). From May through October, the **Bonner Sommer** festival offers a colorful program of folklore, music, and street theater, much of it outdoors and most of it free. Chamber-music concerts are given regularly at the **Schumannhaus** (tel. 0228/773–6666). In May and June, concerts are held on Sunday evenings in the **Bad Godesberg Redoute;** admission is free. In July and August, **organ recitals** are given Wednesday evenings at 8 in the **Church of the Holy Cross** (Kaiserpl.). Contemporary composers edge out Beethoven and the classics in a summer **"Festival of New Music."**

Düsseldorf, home to Mendelssohn, Schumann, and Brahms, boasts the finest concert hall in Germany after Berlin's Philharmonie: the **Rheintonhalle** (Ehrenhof 1, tel. 0211/8995540), a former planetarium on the edge of the Hofgarten. It's the home of the **Düsseldorfer Symphoniker,** which plays from September to mid-June. Düsseldorf's highly regarded opera company and renowned ballet perform at **Deutsche Oper am Rhein** (Heinrich Heine Allle 16a, tel. 0211/133949).

In **Koblenz,** the **Rheinische Philharmonie** orchestra plays regularly in the **Rhein-Mosel-Halle,** (Julius-Wegeler-Str). **Organ recitals** are frequently given in two fine churches: the **Christuskirche,** and the **Florinskirche.**

Köln's Westdeutsche Rundfunk Orchestra performs regularly in the city's excellent concert hall, the **Philharmonie** (Bischofsgarten 1, tel. 0221/2801). The smaller **Gürzenich Orchestra** also gives regular concerts in the Philharmonie, but the natural setting for its music is the restored **Gürzenich,** medieval Köln's official reception mansion. Year-round **organ recitals** in Köln's cathedral are supplemented from June to August with a summer season of organ music. Organ recitals and chamber concerts are also presented in the churches of St. Maria Himmelfahrt (Marzellenstr. 26), St. Aposteln (Neumarkt 30), and Trinitätskirche (Filzengraben 4). For details on all church concerts, tel. 0221/534–856.

Trier's cathedral is the magnificent setting for much of the sacred music to be heard in the city; there are **organ recital festivals** in May, June, August, and September.

Wiesbaden's Symphony Orchestra gives concerts in the **Staatstheater's Grosses Haus** and in the equally impressive **Kurhaus.** Organ recitals are given every Saturday at 11:30 in the Gothic **Marktkirche** (Marktpl.).

Theater

Bonn is a city of theaters. The newly restored **Pantheon** (Bundeskanzlerplatz, tel. 0228/212–521) is now the center of the city's theater scene.

Koblenz has a theatrical tradition dating back to the 18th-century rule of the Prince-Elector Clemens Wenzeslaus. The gracious neoclassical theater he built in 1787 is still in regular use; tel. 0261/34629 for program details and tickets.

Köln's two principal theaters are the **Schauspielhaus** (Offenbachpl. 1) and the smaller **Kammerspiele** (Ubierring 45). Telephone 0221/2218400 for program details and tickets for both. Of the 20 or so private theaters in the city, **Der Keller** (Kleingedankstr. 6, tel. 0221/318–059) is the best-known venue for contemporary drama.

The **Hessisches Staatstheater** is based in Wiesbaden's fine late-19th-century theater on Christian-Zais-Strasse (opposite the Kurhaus and casino). Classical drama, opera, ballet, and musicals are presented in the **Grosses Haus** (tel. 06121/132–325); less ambitious productions are given in the **Kleines Haus** (tel. 06121/132–327). The Grosses Haus is also the scene in early summer of Wiesbaden's annual **International May Arts Festival,** West Germany's second oldest. **Bonn** hosts a famous dance festival, the **International Dance Workshop,** in July and August. For program details and tickets, call 0228/11517. Opera, ballet, and musicals are also staged regularly at the **Oper der Stadt Bonn** (Am Böselagerhof 1, tel. 0228/773–666), which is popularly known as "La Scala of the Rhineland."

Köln's opera company, the **Oper der Stadt Köln** (Schauspielhaus, Offenbachpl. 1) is known for exciting classical and contemporary productions. The city's small ballet company, the **Kölner Tanzforum,** hosts an international festival, the **Internationale Sommerakademie des Tanzes,** every July.

Nightlife

Nightlife in Bonn? There's the story of the visitor who asked where he could find some action in Bonn. "She's taken the night off to visit her aunt in Köln," was the reply. Things have changed, considering the number of bars and taverns in the Altstadt. Try a Budweiser or Pilsener Urquell in the **Lampe** (Breitestr. 35); after midnight, move on to the **Locke** (Prinz-Albertstr. 20). The **Marktschänke** (Eifelstr. 2) is popular with the dawn chorus of taxi drivers, market traders, and all-nighters. No wonder: It *opens* at 5 AM. Singles could try a bar called **Die Falle** (Belderberg 15). The **Cave Club '77** (Bertha von Süttnerpl. 25) and the **CD Nightclub** (Rheingasse 14) have music and some adult spice. The **Jazz Galerie** (Oxfordstr. 24) has live jazz and rock Friday and Saturday beginning at 8 PM. The **Pinte** (Breitestr. 46) is smaller, smokier, and fun. Discogoers head for Bad-Godesburg, where the suburb's resident diplomats let their hair down at **Sky** (Bonnerstr. 48). If that's too far, settle for **La Grange,** in downtown Weselstrasse 5.

Bonn's gamblers make for nearby Bad Neuenahr, where the casino is open daily 2 PM–3 AM.

Singles in **Koblenz** make for the **Tanzcafé Besselink** (opposite the main train station)—it's open until 3 AM. Disco fans favor the **Apropos** (Schulgasse 9) and the **Metro Club** in Koblenz-Hochheim (Alte Heerstr. 130). The nightclub scene is dominated by the **Mocambo** (Poststr. 2a) and the **Petit Fleur** (Rheinstr. 30).

Wiesbaden's nightlife tends to center on the **casino** and **Kurhaus** complex. You'll find a mix of casino winners and losers celebrating or drowning their sorrows in the **Pavillon Bar** of the Kurhaus.

Köln's nightlife is found in three distinct areas: around the **Friesenplatz** S-bahn (suburban railway) station in **Zulpicherstrasse** and between the **AlterMarkt** and **Neumarkt** in the old city. While this is not Hamburg, virtually all tastes are catered to. Singles head for **Big Ben** (Im Klapperhof 48) and the **Intermezzo** (Unter Kaester 5). The **Moulin-Rouge Tingle-Tangle Club** (Maastrichterstr. 68) probably has the best striptease in town. This is discoland, too. **Bierdorf, Clou, Das Ding, Disco 42,** and **Zorba the Buddha** (yes, the Buddha) are all "in." For the last word in disco experience, make for the **Alter Wartesaal** in the Hauptbahnhof on Friday or Saturday night. The old waiting room has been turned into a concert hall and disco, enabling Köln's boppers to get down on ancient polished parquet and check their style in original mahogany-framed mirrors. Many streets off the Hohenzollernring and Hohenstaufenring, particularly Roonstrasse, provide a broad range of nightlife. For good classic jazz try **Papa Joe's Biersalon** (Alter Markt 50). Two other worthwhile jazz clubs are the **Subway** (Aachnerstr. 82) and the **Stadtgarten** (Venloerstr. 40), both of which sometimes feature international musicians.

Düsseldorf nightlife is pretty much concentrated in the **Altstadt,** a landscape of pubs, discotheques, ancient restored brewery houses, and jazz clubs in the vicinity of the Marktplatz and along cobbled streets named Bolker, Kurze, Flinger, and Mühlen. Just follow the crowds to the ones with the greatest appeal. A more sophisticated mood is set in the modern part of the city. **Bei Tony** (Lorettostr. 12) and **Front Page** (Mannesman Ufer) are fashionable upscale bars; **Sam's West** on the Kö and **Ratinger Hof** in the Altstadt are number-one discos.

14 The Fairy-tale Road

Including Bremen

Introduction

The majority of holiday visitors to West Germany who arrive via the international airport at Frankfurt head west to the Rhineland or south into the Black Forest or Bavaria. Some may find their way into the Taunus Mountains on Frankfurt's doorstep. Relatively few, however, venture north to follow a fascinating trail that leads deep into the heart of Germany, not only into the land itself but into the German character as well.

This is the Fairy-tale Road, or Märchenstrasse. It starts just a 20-minute rail or car journey east of Frankfurt in the town of Hanau and from there wends its way north some 600 kilometers (about 370 miles) through parts of Germany that shaped the lives and imagination of the two most famous chroniclers of German folk history and tradition, the brothers Grimm. (Note that though the route is best explored by car, many of the attractions along its meandering path can also be reached by train.)

The Fairy-tale Road is the most recent of Germany's special tourist routes. It doesn't have the glamour of the Romantic Road, but in its own way it is, perhaps, a route more in tune with romantics. It certainly doesn't suffer from the commercialism of the Wine Road.

Following this course from stem to stern—in other words, from Frankfurt all the way to Bremen—can make for a fairly long and tiring journey. However, you can pick up the route anywhere along its length to take in the highlights and still come remarkably close to the spirit and essence of fairy-tale Germany as recorded by these two master storytellers.

The zigzag course detailed here follows the spine of the Fairy-tale Road and includes a number of side trips and detours to nearby destinations worthy of a visitor's attention.

Fairy tales come to life in forgotten villages where black cats snooze in the windows of half-timbered houses; in ancient forests where wild boar snort at timid deer; in misty valleys where the silence of centuries is broken only by the splash of a ferryman's oar.

In a way, this could be considered a dual trip, going forward geographically and at the same time back into the reaches of childhood, imagination, and German folk consciousness, to visit Old World settings steeped in legend and fantasy. The Grimms set it all down for posterity.

From early childhood they were enthralled by tales of enchantment, of kings and queens, of golden-haired princesses saved from disaster by stalwart princes—folk tales, myths, epics, and legends that dealt with magic and wicked witches, predatory stepmothers, along with supporting casts of goblins and wizards.

However, the Grimms did not invent these tales, which were in the public domain long before they started to collect them. In time the brothers gathered some 200 of their favorite stories to create a book that would become known and loved in every part of the world and in many languages.

The Grimms' devotion to fairy tales could be considered merely a sideline to their main careers. Jacob was a grammarian who formulated Grimm's Law, a theory of linguistics relating Greek and Latin to German. Wilhelm was a literary scholar and critic. Together they spent most of their energies compiling a massive dictionary of the German language.

But it is as the authors of *Kinder und Hausmärchen (Children's and Household Tales)*, a work that has been called the best-known book after the Bible, that they are remembered. In 1812, the Grimms introduced the world to a cast of characters that included Cinderella, Hansel and Gretel, Little Red Riding Hood, Rapunzel, Rumpelstiltskin, Sleeping Beauty, Snow White, and other unforgettable stars of the world of make-believe.

The Fairy-tale Road leads through parts of Germany in which the brothers lived and gathered and situated their tales; through the states of Hesse and Lower Saxony, to follow along the Fulda and Weser rivers via a string of highways and byways that lead through a countryside as beguiling as any in Europe.

Essential Information

Important Addresses and Numbers

Tourist Information Information on the Fairy-tale Road can be obtained from the **Deutsche Märchenstrasse** (Postfach 102660, 3500 Kassel, tel. 0561/100–3288). There are local tourist information offices in the following towns:

Alsfeld. Verkehrsbüro, Rittergasse 5, 6320 Alsfeld, tel. 06631/182165.
Bad Pyrmont. Kur-und-Verkehrsverein, Arkaden 14, 3280 Bad Pyrmont, tel. 05281/4627.
Bodenwerder. Städtische Verkehrsamt, Bruckenstrasse 7, 3452 Bodenwerder, tel. 05533/40541.
Bremen. Verkehrsverein, Hillmannpl. 6, 2800 Bremen, tel. 0421/308–000.
Fulda. Städtische Verkehrsbüro im Stadtschloss, 6400 Fulda, tel. 0661/102–345.
Göttingen. Fremdenverkehrsverein, Altes Rathaus, 3400 Göttingen, tel. 0551/54000.
Hanau. Verkehrsbüro, Altstädter Markt 1, 6450 Hanau, tel. 06181/252–400.
Hameln. Verkehrsverein, Deisterallee (am Bürgergarten), 3250 Hameln, tel. 05151/202–617.
Kassel. Tourist Information, Obere Königsstrasse 8, 3500 Kassel, tel. 0561/787–8002.
Münden. Verkehrsbüro, Rathaus am Markt, 3510 Münden, tel. 05541/75313.
Steinau an der Strasse. Verkehrsamt Am Kumpen 1–3, 6497 Steinau an der Strasse, tel. 06663/5655.

Travel Agencies **American Express,** Am Wall 138, **Bremen,** tel. 0421/14171.

Car Rental **Avis:** Kirchbachstrasse 200, tel. 0421/211–077, **Bremen;** Mainzer Landstrasse 170, tel. 069/230–101, **Frankfurt;** Drehbahn 15–25, tel. 040/341–651, **Hamburg.**
Sixt-Budget: Duckwitzstrasse 55, tel. 0421/511–616, **Bremen;** Am Römerhof, tel. 069/705018, and Frankfurt Airport, tel.

069/690–5237, **Frankfurt;** Leipzigerstrasse 56, tel. 0561/54093, **Kassel.**

Hertz: Neuenland Airport, tel. 0421/555–350, **Bremen;** Gutleutstrasse 87, tel. 069/2425–2627, **Frankfurt;** Kirchenallee 34–36, tel. 040/280–1201, **Hamburg.**

Arriving and Departing by Plane

Frankfurt, Hannover, and Hamburg are the closest international airports to the area. Each is within an hour's drive or rail journey from one or more of the Fairy-tale Road's major centers. Frankfurt, for instance, is less than half an hour from Hanau, the start of the route. Hamburg is less than an hour from Bremen, the end of it.

Arriving and Departing by Bus

Long-distance Europabus services from Scandinavia through Germany to the Balkans call at Bremen, Kassel, and Göttingen. For information, timetables, and reservations, contact **Deutsche Touring GmbH.** (Am Römerhof 17, 6000 Frankfurt/Main 90, tel. 069/79030).

Getting Around

By Car Germany's Autobahn network penetrates deep into the area. Hanau, Fulda, Kassel, Göttingen, and Bremen are all served directly by Autobahns. The Fairy-tale Road itself incorporates for part of its length one of Germany's loveliest scenic drives, the Wesertalstrasse, or Weser Valley Road, from Münden in the south to Hameln in the north.

By Train Fulda, Kassel, and Göttingen are served by Germany's ultramodern InterCity Express line, which reduces traveling time between Frankfurt and Hamburg to three hours and 45 minutes. All other centers and most of the smaller towns are connected by rail, supplemented by railroad buses.

By Bus Frankfurt, Kassel, Göttingen, and Bremen all have city bus services that extend into the countryside along the Fairy-tale Road.

By Boat From May through September two companies—**Oberweser-Dampfschiffahrt** and **Weisse Flotte Warnecke**—each with a fleet of six ships—operate daily services on the Weser River between Hameln, Bodenwerder, and Bad Karlshafen. On Monday, Wednesday, Friday, and Saturday, the Oberweser-Dampfschiffahrt boats sail as far as Münden, and on Tuesday, Thursday, Saturday, and Sunday, from Münden to Hameln. On the days when there is no service between Bad Karlshafen and Münden, a bus service ferries boat passengers between the two towns. For further information and bookings, contact **Oberweser-Dampfschiffahrt** (Inselstr. 3, 3250 Hameln, tel. 05151/22016) or **Weisse Flotte Warnecke** (Hauptstr. 39, 3250 Hameln, tel. 05151/3975, and on Weserstr., Bodenwerder, tel. 05533/4864).

Guided Tours

By Bus Erwin Radke's bus company in Oldendorf operates regular tours throughout the region from April through November.

For details, contact **Erwin Radke** (Hesslingen 143, 3253 Hess. Oldendorf 19, tel. 05152/2172). Excursions are also offered by a Hameln company, **Rattenfänger-Reisen** (Bahnhofstr. 18/20, tel. 05151/108–491). Some local authorities—Bad Karlshafen, for example—also organize bus tours. Contact individual tourist offices for details.

By Boat The Oberweser-Dampfschiffahrt Company and Warnecke's Weisse Flotte (White Fleet) operate summer services on the Weser River between Hameln and Münden. Both companies will give you advice on how to combine a boat trip with a tour by bike, bus, or train. The Oberweser-Dampfschiffahrt Company also has a daily excursion from Hameln to the nearby Ohrberg Park and pleasure gardens: On Sunday afternoons it offers a 2½-hour "Kaffeereise" (coffee trip) on the river. From April through October, an excursion boat makes a four-hour trip daily up the Fulda River from Kassel. It leaves the Altmarkt pier at 2 and returns at 6. The trip costs DM 16 adults, DM 9 children.

Exploring the Fairy-tale Road

Highlights for First-time Visitors

Steinau Castle and Amtshaus
Alsfeld's Altes Rathaus
Kassel's Staatliche Kunstsammlungen
Münden
The Sababurg
Hameln (Hamlin)

Hanau

Numbers in the margin correspond to points of interest on the Fairy-tale Road map.

The Fairy-tale Road begins in "once upon a time" fashion at a point you can reach only on foot—the brothers Grimm memorial in the Neustädter Marktplatz of
1 **Hanau,** the little town in which the brothers were born, Jacob in 1785, Wilhelm a year later.

The bronze memorial, erected in 1898, is a larger-than-life-size statue of the brothers, one seated, the other leaning on his chair, the two of them deep in conversation, in a fitting pose for these scholars who unearthed so many medieval myths and legends, earning their reputation as the fathers of the fairy tale.

The degree to which the brothers have influenced the world's concept of fairy tales—those of *The Arabian Nights* excepted—is remarkable. But it would be a mistake to imagine them as kindly, bewhiskered old gents telling stories in their rose-clad cottage for the pleasure of village children. As already mentioned, they were serious and successful academics, with interests ranging far beyond what we may think of as children's light amusements. Their stories probe deep into the German psyche and deal with far more complex emotions than is suggested by the occasional "happily ever after" endings; witness

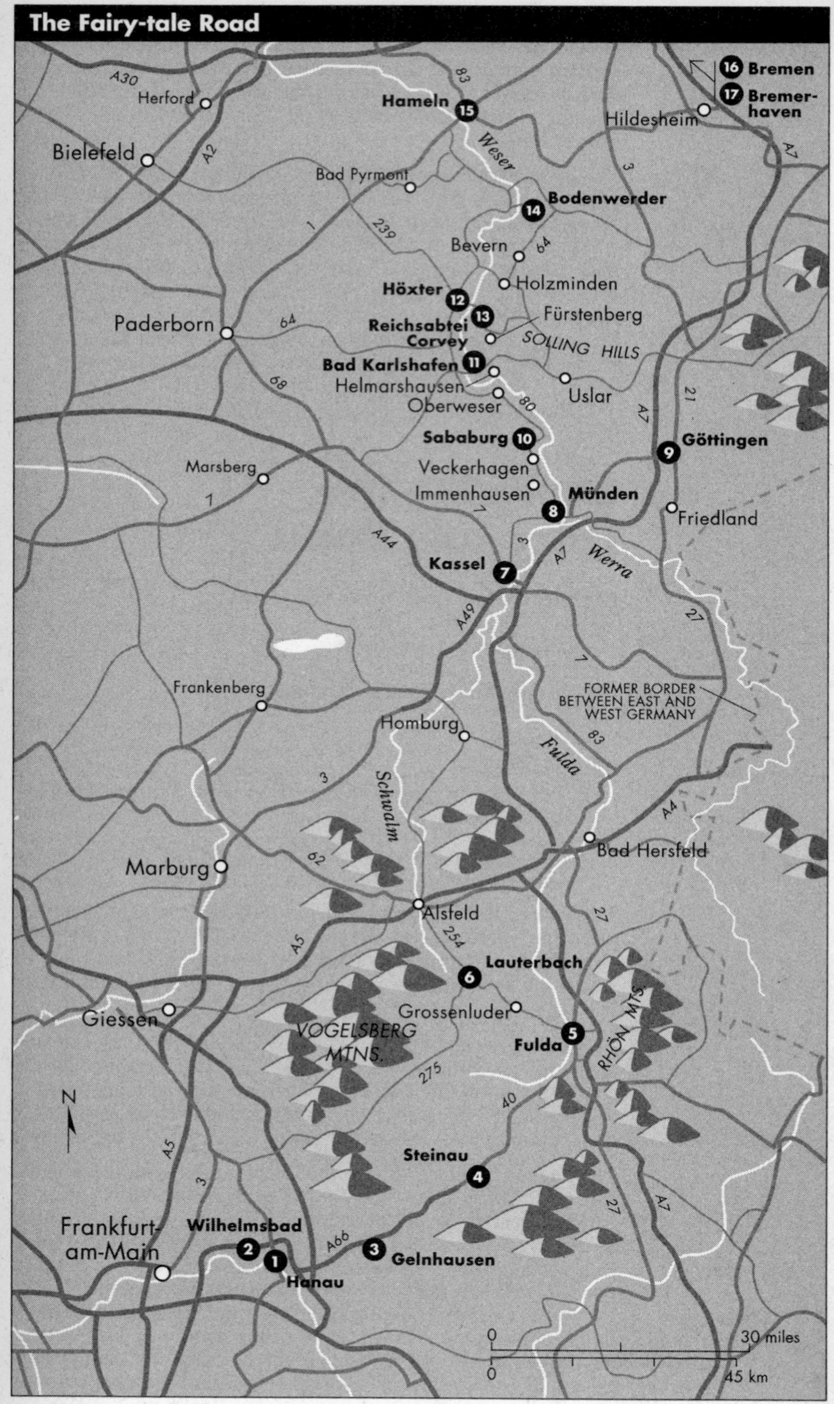
The Fairy-tale Road
16 Bremen
17 Bremerhaven
Hildesheim
A30
Herford
Hameln 15
Weser
Bielefeld
A2
Bad Pyrmont
Bodenwerder 14
Bevern
Holzminden
Höxter 12
Reichsabtei Corvey 13
Fürstenberg
Paderborn
SOLLING HILLS
Bad Karlshafen 11
Helmarshausen
Oberweser
Uslar
Sababurg 10
Göttingen 9
Veckerhagen
Marsberg
Immenhausen
Münden 8
Friedland
A44
Kassel 7
A7
Werra
A49
Frankenberg
FORMER BORDER BETWEEN EAST AND WEST GERMANY
Homburg
Fulda
Schwalm
A4
Bad Hersfeld
Marburg
Alsfeld
A5
Lauterbach 6
Grossenluder
Giessen
VOGELSBERG MTNS.
Fulda 5
RHÖN MTS.
N
Steinau 4
Frankfurt-am-Main
Wilhelmsbad 2
1 Hanau
A66
3 Gelnhausen
0
30 miles
0
45 km

the Stephen Sondheim–James Lapine musical *Into the Woods*, based to a large extent on the Grimm's works.

Behind the statue is the solid bulk of Hanau's 18th-century **Rathaus** (Town Hall). Every day at noon its bells play a tribute to another of the city's famous sons, the composer Paul Hindemith (1895–1963), by chiming out one of his canons. At 10 AM the carillon plays a choral composition; at 2 PM a minuet; and at 4 a piece entitled *Guten Abend* (Good Evening) rings out for the crowds hurrying across the Marktplatz to complete their shopping before returning home.

Hanau was almost completely obliterated by wartime bombing raids, and there's little of the Altstadt (Old Town) that the Grimm brothers would recognize now. Behind the Rathaus, however, is a corner that has been faithfully reconstructed. It's dominated by the **Altes Rathaus** (Old Town Hall), a handsome 16th-century Renaissance building, its two half-timbered upper stories weighted down by a steep slate roof. Today it's the home of the German goldsmiths' craft. Known as the **Deutsches Goldschmiedehaus** (German Goldsmiths' House), it contains a permanent exhibit and regular national and international displays of goldsmiths' and silversmiths' crafts. *Altstädter Markt 6. Admission charge depends on exhibit. Open Tues.–Sun. 10–noon and 2–5.*

You'll find various memorials and museums devoted to the brothers Grimm all along the Fairy-tale Road. For the first memorial, however, you have to head in another direction—to **Schloss Philippsruhe,** a palace on the banks of the Main River in the suburb of Kesselstadt (a No. 1 or No. 10 bus will take you there in 10 minutes). Schloss Philippsruhe has much more than Grimm exhibits to offer: It's the oldest French-style Baroque palace east of the Rhine. Philippsruhe may remind you of Versailles, although its French-trained architect, Julius Ludwig Rothweil, planned it along the lines of another palace in the Paris area, the much smaller Clagny Palace. Philippsruhe—as its name, "Philipp's Rest," suggests—was built for Count Philipp Reinhard von Hanau. He didn't enjoy its riverside peace for long, however: He died less than three months after moving in. After the French builder Jacques Girard completed work on the palace, creating its very French appearance, the invading French confiscated it in 1803. Later Napoléon gave it as a present to his sister Pauline Borghese, who then put it up for sale. American forces took over Philippsruhe as a military quarters for a time in 1945, and until the postwar reconstruction of Hanau was complete it served as the town hall. Every year on the first weekend of September, the palace grounds are invaded again—this time by the people of Hanau, for a great party to commemorate the rebuilding of their war-ravaged town. *Schloss Philippsruhe, Kesselstadt. Admission free. Open Tues.–Sun. 10–5.*

In the early 19th century, following the withdrawal of the French from Hanau, the original formal gardens were replanned as an informal, English-style park. You'll find the contrast between formal palace and informal wooded grounds striking. As you leave or enter, pause to study the entrance gate; the 19th-century gilding, made by Parisian masters, is real gold.

Time Out If the weather's fine, seek out a place beneath the white canvas sunshades on the palace terrace, now a café with a view over the Main River that was once enjoyed by Count Philipp Reinhard. In inclement weather head for the palace's bistro, with its open fire and hot, strong coffee.

Just north of Philippsruhe and a short bus ride from the center of Hanau is the city spa of **Wilhelmsbad.** It was built at the end of the 18th century by Crown Prince Wilhelm von Hessen-Kassel at the site where two peasant women, out gathering herbs, had discovered mineral springs. For a few decades Wilhelmsbad rivaled Baden-Baden as Germany's premier spa and fashionable playground. Then, about 100 years ago the springs dried up, the casino closed, and Europe's wealthy and titled looked for other amusements. But this is still Grimm fairy-tale land, and Wilhelmsbad, the sleeping-beauty spa, awoke from its slumber in the '60s to become a rejuvenated resort. The fine Baroque buildings and bathhouses were restored, parkland cleared and relaid in informal English style, riding stables opened, and one of Germany's loveliest golf courses laid out where the leisure classes once hunted pheasants.

2

Return to Hanau to rejoin the Grimm Fairy-tale Road, following B-43 about 20 kilometers (12 miles) northeast to **Gelnhausen.** Here on an island in the sleepy little Kinzig River are the remains of a castle that might well have stimulated the imagination of the Grimm brothers in their travels in this area. Emperor Friedrich I—known as Barbarossa, or Red Beard—built the castle in this idyllic spot during the 12th century; in 1180 it was the scene of the first all-German Imperial Diet. Located on an island, the castle was hardly designed as a defensive bastion and was accordingly sacked in the Thirty Years' War. Today only parts of the russet walls and colonnaded entrance remain. Still, stroll beneath the castle's ruined ramparts on its watery site and you'll get a tangible impression of the medieval importance of the court of Barbarossa. *Follow the signs to Burg Barbarossa. Admission: DM 1 adults, 50 pf children under 14. Castle open Mar.–Oct., Tues.–Sun. 10–1 and 2–5:30; Nov.–Feb., Tues.–Sun. 10–1 and 2–4:30.*

3

For clear evidence of the formative influence on the brothers Grimm, you need only travel another 20 kilometers (12 miles) along the Fairy-tale Road, to the little town of **Steinau**—full name Steinau an der Strasse (Steinau "on the road," referring to an old trade route between Frankfurt and Leipzig). Here father Grimm served as local magistrate and the Grimm brothers spent much of their childhood.

4

Steinau dates from the 13th century and is typical of villages in the region. Marvelously preserved half-timbered houses are set along cobblestone streets; imposing castles bristle with towers and turrets. In its woodsy surroundings one can well imagine encountering Little Red Riding Hood, Snow White, or Hansel and Gretel.

The main street is named after the brothers; the building where paterfamilias was employed is now known as the "fairy-tale house." At the top of the town stands a castle straight out of a Grimm fairy tale. Originally an early medieval fortress, it was rebuilt in Renaissance style between 1525 and 1558 and used by the counts of Hanau as their summer residence and later to guard the increasingly important trade route between Frankfurt and Leipzig. It's not difficult to imagine the young Grimm boys playing in the shadow of its great gray walls, perhaps venturing into the encircling dry moat.

The fine, half-timbered, turreted house where the family resided is only a few hundred yards from the castle. Officially called the **Amthaus,** it now contains the tourist office and a museum of exhibits from the childhood of the brothers Grimm. *Open Mon.–Fri. 8–noon and 1–5. There's another, larger Grimm museum in the castle itself, the Grimm Museum im Schloss. Admission: DM 2 adults, DM 1 children. Open Mar.–Oct., Tues.–Sun. 10–11:30 and 1–4:30; Nov.–Feb., Tues.–Sun. 10–11 and 1–3.*

In front of the castle, in Steinau's ancient market square, Am Kumpen, is the Gothic church of **St. Catherine,** where the Grimm brothers' grandfather, Friedrich, was parson. Across the square, in the former stables of the castle, is a small puppet theater, **Die Holzkuppe,** where presentations of the Grimm fairy tales are staged. *Die Holzkuppe Marionettentheater. Call 06663/245 for program details.*

In the center of the square is a **Grimm memorial fountain.** It was built only in 1985, but its timeless design blends perfectly with the background provided by Steinau's 16th-century **Rathaus** (Town Hall). The six bronze figures you see on the white stucco facade of the Rathaus represent a cross section of 16th-century Steinau's population—from the builder who helped construct the town to the mother and child who continue its traditions.

With the Rhön Mountains on your right, head north now on B-40 and leave the Fairy-tale Road for a detour to the ancient
5 episcopal city of **Fulda,** a treasure trove of Baroque architecture. Its grandest example is the immense **bishops' palace,** on Schlossstrasse, crowning the heights of the city. The great collection of buildings began as a Renaissance palace in the early 17th century and was transformed into its present Baroque splendor a century later by Johann Dientzenhofer. Much of the palace is now used as municipal offices, but you can visit several of the former public rooms. The Fürstensaal (Princes' Hall) on the second floor provides a breathtaking display of Baroque decorative artistry, with ceiling paintings by the 18th-century Bavarian artist Melchior Steidl. Concerts are regularly held within its fabric-clad walls (contact the city tourist office in the palace for program details; tel. 0661/102–345). The palace also has permanent displays of the faience ceramics for which Fulda was once famous, as well as some fine local glassware. *Schlossstr. Admission: DM 3 adults, DM 1.50 children. Open Sat.–Thurs. 10–6, Fri. 2–6.*

Pause at the windows of the great Fürstensaal to take in the view across the palace park to the **Orangery.** If you have time after your palace tour, stroll over for a visit. There's a pleasant café on the first floor.

Across the broad boulevard that borders the park you'll see the tall twin spires of the **Dom,** Fulda's 18th-century cathedral. The Dom was built by Dientzenhofer on the site of an 8th-century basilica, which at the time was the largest church north of the Alps. The basilica had to be big enough to accommodate the ever-growing number of pilgrims from all parts of Europe who converged on Fulda to pray at the grave of the martyred St. Boniface, the "Apostle of the Germans." A black alabaster bas-relief depicting his death marks the martyr's grave in the crypt. The cathedral museum contains a document bearing his writing, along with several other treasures, including a fine 16th-century painting by Lucas Cranach the Elder of Christ and the adulteress (who looks very comely in her velvet Renaissance costume). *Dom Museum, Dompl. Admission: DM 3 adults, DM 1.50 children. Open Apr.–Oct., weekdays 10–5:30, Sat. 10–2, Sun. and holidays 12:30–5:30; Nov.–Mar., weekdays 10–12:30 and 1:30–4:30, Sat. 10–2, Sun. and holidays 12:30–4. Closed Jan.*

On one side of the cathedral you'll see one of Germany's oldest churches, the **Michaelskirche,** or Church of St. Michael, built in the 9th century along the lines of the Church of the Holy Sepulchre in Jerusalem. It has a harmony and dignity that match the majesty of the Baroque facade of the neighboring Dom.

From the Dom, head into the center of town, passing on your right the former guardhouse of the bishops' palace and on your left the 18th-century city parish church. Your goal is the Rathaus, about the finest Renaissance half-timbered town hall in this part of the country. The half-timbering, separating the arcaded first floor from the steep roof and its incongruous but charming battery of small steeples, is particularly delicate.

Kassel is the next major stop on the road north. If you're in a hurry, the quickest route is via Autobahn 7. But the Fairy-tale Road gives Autobahns a wide berth, so take B-254 into the Vogelsberg Mountains via Grossenluder to Lauterbach, some
6 25 kilometers (15 miles) northeast of Fulda. **Lauterbach,** a resort town of many medieval half-timbered houses, has not just one castle but two—the Riedesel and the Eisenbach. The town is the setting of one of the Grimm's fairy tales, the one in which the Little Scalawag loses his sock. Lauterbach's other claim to fame is its garden gnomes, turned out here by the thousands and exported all over the world. These ornaments are made in all shapes and sizes, from three inches to three feet tall, by the firm of Heissner Keramik. Several shops in Lauterbach sell the gnomes if you'd like to take one home with you.

The Fairy-tale Road continues north to **Alsfeld,** notable for its medieval town center of beautifully preserved half-timbered houses that in places lean out to almost touch one another across narrow, winding cobbled streets. Seek out Kirchplatz, a small square behind the late-Gothic Walpurgiskirche off the main square, and No. 12, whose rightward lurch seems to defy gravity. So, too, does the jewel of Alsfeld—and one of Germany's showpieces—the Altes Rathaus (Old Town Hall), built in 1512. Its facade, combining a stone-colonnade ground floor, half-timbered upper reaches, and dizzily steep, top-heavy slate roof punctured by two pointed towers shaped like witches' hats, would look right at home in Disneyworld. If you want to get an unobstructed view of this remarkable building (which is not open to the public) for your photo album, avoid the Marktplatz on Tuesday and Friday, when market stalls clutter the square.

From there the routing follows the little Schwalm River through a picturesque region so inextricably linked with the Grimm fairy tales that it's known as Rotkäppchenland (Little

Red Riding Hood country). On a side road, **Neustadt** is the home of the 13th-century circular tower from which Rapunzel supposedly let down her golden tresses. About 10 kilometers (6 miles) north is **Schwalmstadt,** the capital of the area. If you happen to be here on one of the town's many festival days, you'll see local people decked out in the traditional folk costumes that are still treasured in these parts.

Of passing interest is the fact that some 40 kilometers (25 miles) southwest, on the Route 3 Kassel highway, is **Marburg,** where the Grimm brothers attended the university and began their folktale research.

Time Out At Homberg, 19 kilometers (12 miles) north of Schwalmstadt, stop at the 15th-century **Krone inn** (tel. 05681/2407), on the market square; it's the oldest guest house in Germany. Within its half-timbered walls you can eat and drink and dream of centuries past.

Some 40 kilometers (24 miles) north of Homberg you'll arrive at
7 the ancient city of **Kassel.**

Here the brothers Grimm worked as librarians at the court of the king of Westphalia, who was Jerome Bonaparte, Napoléon's youngest brother. The Grimms continued to collect stories and legends. Many French tales were recounted to them by Dorothea Viehmann, "the Fairy-tale Lady," who lived in the neighboring village of Baunatal.

In the center of Kassel, the **Brüder Grimm Museum** occupies five rooms of the Palais Bellevue, where the brothers once lived and worked. Exhibits include furniture, memorabilia, letters, manuscripts, and editions of their books, as well as paintings, aquarelles, etchings, and drawings by Ludwig Emil Grimm, a third brother and a graphic artist of note. *Palais Bellevue, Schöne Aussicht 2. Admission free. Open daily 10–5.*

Although seldom included on tourist itineraries in the past, Kassel turns out to be one of the unexpectedly delightful cities of western Germany, full of contrasts and surprises. Much of its center was destroyed in World War II, and Kassel subsequently became the first German city to construct a traffic-free pedestrian downtown. The city has an unusually spacious and airy feel, due in large part to the expansive parks and gardens along the banks of the Fulda River. Today it is a major cultural center, with a vibrant theater and an internationally known art festival, Dokumenta, held once every five years.

Kassel's leading art gallery, the **Staatliche Kunstsammlungen** (State Art Collection), is one of Germany's best. It houses 17 Rembrandts, along with outstanding works by Rubens, Hals, Jordaens, Van Dyck, Dürer, Altdorfer, Cranach, and Baldung Grien. *Schloss Wilhelmshöhe. Admission free. Open Tues.–Sun. 10–5.*

The art gallery is located in part of the 18th-century **Wilhelmshöhe Palace,** which served as a royal residence from 1807 to 1813, when Jerome, Napoléon's brother, was king of Westphalia. Later it became the summer residence of the German emperor Wilhelm II. The great palace stands at the end of the 3-mile-long Wilhelmshöher Allee, an avenue that runs straight as an arrow from one side of the city to the other. Beyond the palace, the Wilhelmshöhe heights are crowned by an astonishing monument, a red-stone octagon bearing a giant statue of **Hercules,** built at the beginning of the 18th century. You can climb inside the octagon to the base of the Hercules statue. *Admission: DM 2 adults, DM 1 children. Open mid-Mar. to mid-Nov., Tues.–Sun. 10–4*

From there, the view of Kassel spreads below you, bisected by the straight line of the Wilhelmshöher Allee. But that's only for starters: At 3:30 PM on Sundays and Wednesdays from mid-May through September, water gushes from a fountain beneath the Hercules statue, rushes down a series of cascades to the foot of the hill, and ends its precipitous journey on a 175-foot-high jet of water. It's a natural phenomenon, with no pumps. It takes so long to accumulate enough water that the sight can be experienced only on those two special days, on holidays, and, during the summer, on the first Saturday of each month, when the cascades are also floodlit. The number 1 bus runs from the city to the Wilhelmshöhe. The number 23 climbs the heights to the octagon and the Hercules statue. A café lies a short walk from the statue, and there are several restaurants in the area.

The Wilhelmshöhe was laid out as a Baroque park, its elegant lawns separating the city from the thick woods of the Habichtswald (Hawk Forest). It comes as something of a surprise to see the turrets of a romantic medieval castle, the **Löwenburg** (Lion Fortress), breaking the harmony. There are more surprises, for this is no true medieval castle but a fanciful, stylized copy of a Scottish castle, built 70 years after the Hercules statue that towers above it. The architect was a Kassel ruler who displayed an early touch of the mania later seen in the castle-building excesses of Bavaria's eccentric Ludwig II. The Löwenburg contains a collection of medieval armor and weapons, tapestries, and furniture. *Admission, including guided tour: DM 2 adults, DM 1 children. Open Tues.–Sun. 10–4.*

One other museum has to be included in this tour of Kassel. It's the **Deutsches Tapeten Museum,** the world's most comprehensive museum of tapestry, with more than 600 exhibits tracing the history of the art through the centuries. *Brüder-Grimm-Pl. 5. Admission free. Open Tues.–Fri. 10–5, weekends 10–1.*

Leaving Kassel, follow B-3 16 kilometers (10 miles) north to
8 **Münden;** its official name is Hannoversch-Münden, but it is usually referred to by the contraction. Back in the 18th century the German scientist and explorer Alexander von Humboldt included Münden in his short list of the world's most beautiful towns (Passau, in eastern Bavaria, was another choice). You just may agree with him when you get here.

A 650-year-old bridge crosses the Weser River to lead into this old walled settlement that appears untouched by recent history—frozen in the dim and distant past, you might think. You'll have to travel a long way through Germany to find a grouping of half-timbered houses as harmonious as that in this beautiful old town, surrounded by forests and the Fulda and Werra rivers, which join and flow as the Weser River to Bremen and the North Sea.

Take your camera with you on a stroll down Langenstrasse; No. 34 is where the famous Dr. Eisenbarth died, in November 1727. The extraordinary doctor won a place for himself in German folk history as a result of his success both as a physician and as a marketplace orator; a quack who delivered what he promised!

A dramatization of his life is presented in the summer in front of the medieval Rathaus. (Contact the Verkehrsbüro Naturpark Münden, 3510 Münden, tel. 05541/75313, for details.)

From Münden, you'll have the choice of following the Fairy-tale Road northward along the Weser River or making a short detour to another of the cities so closely associated with the
9 brothers Grimm: **Göttingen,** where they served as professors and librarians at the ancient university from 1830 to 1837.

The university appears to dominate every aspect of life in Göttingen, and there's scarcely a house more than a century old that doesn't bear a plaque linking it with a famous person who once studied or taught here. In one of the towers of the city's old defense wall, Otto von Bismarck, the "Iron Chancellor" and founder of the 19th-century German Empire, pored over his books as a 17-year-old law student. It looks like a romantic student's den now (the tower is open to visitors), but Bismarck was a reluctant tenant—he was banned from living within the city center because of "riotous behavior" and his fondness for wine. The taverns where Bismarck and his cronies drank are still there, all of them associated with Göttingen luminaries. Even the defiantly 20th-century Irish Pub has established itself within the half-timbered walls of a historic old house that once belonged to an 18th-century professor.

The strong link between the students and their university city is symbolized by a statue in the central market square. There stands the **Gänseliesel,** the little Goose Girl of German folklore, carrying her geese and smiling shyly into the waters of a fountain. Above her pretty head is a charming wrought-iron *Jugendstil* (Art Nouveau) bower of entwined vines. The students of Göttingen contributed money toward the erection of the bronze statue and fountain in 1901, and they have given it a central role in a custom that has grown up around the university: Graduates who earn a doctorate traditionally give Gänseliesel a kiss of thanks. Göttingen says she's the most kissed girl in the world. There was a time, however, when the city fathers were none too pleased with this licentious boast, and in 1926 they banned the tradition. A student challenged the ban before a Berlin court but lost the case. Officially the ban still stands, although neither the city council nor the university takes any notice of it.

Directly behind the Gänseliesel is the Rathaus. It was begun in the 13th century but never completely finished. The result is the part-medieval, part-Renaissance building you see today. The bronze lion's-head knocker on the main door dates from early in the 13th century and is the oldest of its type in Germany. Step through the door, and in the lobby striking murals tell the city's story. The medieval council chamber served for centuries as the center of civic life. Within its painted walls and beneath its heavily beamed ceiling, the council met, courts sat in judgment, visiting dignitaries were officially received, receptions and festivities were held, and traveling theater groups performed.

In the streets around the town hall you'll find magnificent examples of Renaissance architecture. Many of these half-timbered, low-gabled buildings house businesses that have been there for centuries. The **Ratsapotheke** (pharmacy) across from the town hall is one; medicines have been doled out there since 1322.

A short stroll up the street on your left, Weenderstrasse, will bring you to the most appealing shop front you're likely to find in all Germany: the 16th-century Schrödersches Haus. On the way, you'll pass the ancient student tavern Zum Szültenbürger. Another tavern, Zum Altdeutschen, is around the corner on Prinzenstrasse (the street is named after three English princes, sons of King George III, who lived in a house here during their studies in Göttingen from 1786 to 1791). Don't be shy about stepping into either of these taverns, or any of the others that catch your eye: The food and drink are inexpensive, and the welcome invariably warm and friendly.

Back in Weenderstrasse, take note of the Sparkasse bank building. It was once the Hotel zur Krone, where King George V of Hannover had his headquarters in June 1866 before setting off for the fateful battle of Langensalza, where he lost his kingdom to Bismarck's warrior-state of Prussia, soon to preside aggressively over the newly united Germany.

Behind Weenderstrasse, on Ritterplan, is Göttingen's only noble home, a 16th-century palace that is now the **Städtisches Museum** (City Museum). It has an instructive exhibition charting the architectural styles you'll come across in this part of Germany, as well as a valuable collection of antique toys and a reconstructed apothecary's shop. *Ritterplan. Admission free. Open weekdays 10–5, weekends 10–1.*

Not far from the city, near Gleichen, outdoor performances of Grimm fairy tales are presented on a woodland stage at Bremke on certain summer weekends. Check with the local tourist office for dates.

To pick up the Fairy-tale Road where it joins the scenic Weser Valley Road, return to Münden and head north on B-64. Ten kilometers (6 miles) north of Münden in the village of Vecker-
10 hagen, take a left turn to the signposted **Sababurg.** You're now on the road to Dornröschen's, or Sleeping Beauty's castle. It stands just as the Grimm fairy tale tells us it did, in the depths of the densely wooded Reinhardswald, still inhabited by deer and wild boar. Sababurg was built as a 14th-century fortress by the archbishop of Mainz to protect a nearby pilgrimage chapel. Later it was destroyed and then rebuilt as a turreted hunting lodge for the counts of Hessen. Today it is a fairly luxurious hotel. Even if you don't stay the night, a drive to the castle (it has an excellent restaurant) will be a highlight of any stay in this region.

From the castle, follow another road back to the Weser Valley riverside village of Oberweser. Turn left and take B-80 north. This is one of Germany's most haunting river roads, where the fast-flowing Weser snakes between green banks that hardly show where land ends and water begins. After some 13 kilometers (8 miles), you'll come to the Weser harbor town and spa of
11 **Bad Karlshafen.** From its inland harbor German troops embarked to join the English Hannoverian forces in the American War of Independence. George III, the English king who presided over the loss of the American colonies, was a Hannoverian—his grandfather, George I, spoke only German when he became king of England in 1715—and it was only natural that the people of Hannover should rally to the English cause in

times of crisis. Flat barges took the troops down the Weser to Bremen, where they were shipped across the North Sea for the long voyage west. Many American families can trace their heritage to this small spa and the surrounding countryside.

Viewed from one of the benches overlooking the harbor, there's scarcely a building that's not in the imposing Baroque style. The grand Rathaus behind you is the best example. Bad Karlshafen stands out in solitary splendor amid its neighboring Weser Valley towns, whose half-timbered architecture has given rise to the expression "Weser Renaissance." You'll see examples of that style wherever you travel in this area, from Münden to Hameln (where it reaches a spectacular climax).

12 The Rathaus at **Höxter,** the next stop on the road north, is a picture-postcard-pretty example of the Weser Renaissance style, combining three half-timbered stories with a romantically crooked tower.

13 Across the river from Höxter lies **Reichsabtei Corvey** (the Imperial Abbey of Corvey), optimistically described by some as the "Rome of the North" and idyllically set between the wooded heights of the Solling region and the Weser. The 1,100-year history of the abbey is tightly bound up with the early development of German nationhood. It was chosen as the site of several sessions of the German Imperial Council in the 12th century, and in the 9th-century abbey church you can step into the lodge used by several Holy Roman Emperors. The composer of the German national anthem, Hoffmann von Fallersleben, worked for 14 years in the abbey's vast library, where, in the 16th century, the first six volumes of the annals of the Roman historian Tacitus were discovered. *Admission: DM 3.80 adults, DM 2 children. Open Apr.–Oct., daily 9–6.*

Follow the Weser River north another 33 kilometers (20 miles) and you'll reach a town that plays a central role in German pop-
14 ular literature, **Bodenwerder,** the birthplace of the Lügenbaron ("Lying Baron") von Münchhausen. Münchhausen used to entertain friends with a pipe of rich Bremen tobacco, a glass of good wine, and stories of his exploits as a captain in wars against the Turks and the Russians. They were preposterous, unbelievable stories, which one of his friends, on the run from the German authorities, had published in England. From England they found their way back to Germany, and the baron became a laughingstock—as well as a famous figure in German literary history. The imposing family home in which he grew up is now the Rathaus; one room has been turned into the **Münchhausen Museum,** crammed with mementos of the baron's adventurous life. Included is a cannonball on which the baron claimed to have ridden into orbit during the Russo-Turkish War of 1736, flying around the Earth to reach the moon, or so he insisted. In front of the house you'll see a statue of Münchhausen in a scene from one of his most outlandish stories. He's riding half a horse; the other half, said Münchhausen, was chopped off by a castle portcullis, but he rode on without noticing the accident.

15 It's back to the Grimm trail that we return now, to **Hameln** (or Hamlin, to give the city its English name), the German town of Pied Piper fame. The story of the Pied Piper of Hameln had its origins in an actual event. In the 13th century an inordinate number of young men in Hameln were being conscripted to

fight in an unpopular war in Bohemia and Moravia, so that citizens became convinced that they were being spirited away by the Devil playing his flute. In later stories the Devil was changed to a gaudily attired rat catcher who rid the town of rodents by playing seductive melodies on his flute so that the rodents followed him willingly, waltzing their way right into the Weser. However, when the town defaulted on its contract with the piper and refused to pay up, the piper settled the score by playing his merry tune to lead Hameln's children on the same route he had taken the rats. As the children reached the river, the Grimms wrote, "they disappeared forever."

This tale is included in the Grimms' other book, *German Legends*. A variation of the story appears on the plaque of a 17th-century house at 28 Osterstrasse, fixing the date of the event as June 26, 1284. In more recent times, the Pied Piper tale has been immortalized via an ultramodern sculpture group set above a reflecting pool in a pedestrian area of town. Today you'll find Hameln tied to its Pied Piper myth every bit as much, say, as the little Bavarian village of Oberammergau is dominated by its Passion Play. There are even rat-shaped pastries in the windows of Hameln's bakeries. The house that bears the Pied Piper plaque—a brilliant example of Weser Renaissance—is known as the Rattenfängerhaus, the rat catcher's house, despite the fact that it was built some time after the sorry story is said to have occurred. To this day, no music is played and no revelry of any kind takes place in the street that runs beside the house, the street along which the children of Hameln are said to have followed the piper.

The Rattenfängerhaus is one of several beautiful half-timbered houses on the central Osterstrasse. At one end is the Hochzeitshaus (Wedding House), now occupied by city government offices and a tourist information center. Every Sunday from mid-May to mid-September the story of the Pied Piper is played out at noon by actors and children of the town on the terrace in front of the building. The half-hour performance is free: Get there early to ensure a good place. The carillon of the Hochzeitshaus plays a "Pied Piper song" every day at 8:35 and 11:05, and mechanical figures enacting the story appear on the west gable of the building at 1:05, 3:35, and 5:35.

Time Out Just up the street is the historic old hostelry **Zur Krone.** If it's a sunny day, take a seat on the terrace in front of the hotel's half-timbered facade. If it's cool, there's a warm welcome inside.

Bremen

Although the influences that shaped the lives and the work of the Grimm brothers weaken north of Hameln, the Fairy-tale
16 Road continues as far as the great seaport of **Bremen,** a city that plays a central role in the delightful fable of the Bremer Stadtmusikanten, or Bremen Town Musicians, a rooster, cat, dog, and donkey quartet that came to Bremen to seek its fortune. You'll find statues of this group in various parts of the city, the most famous being a handsome bronze of the four, one perched on the back of another, to form a pyramid of sorts. This statue stands alongside the northwest corner of the Rathaus on one of Europe's most impressive market squares, bordered by the Rathaus, an imposing 900-year-old Gothic cathedral, a

16th-century guild hall, and a modern glass-and-steel state parliament building, with a high wall of gabled town houses as backdrop.

On the square stands the famous stone statue of the knight Roland, erected in 1400. Three times larger than life, the statue serves as Bremen's shrine, good-luck piece, and symbol of freedom and independence.

The ancient Rathaus is a structure of great interest, a Gothic building that acquired a Renaissance facade in the early 17th century. The two styles combine harmoniously in the magnificent, beamed banquet hall, where painted scenes from Bremen's 1,200-year history are complemented by model galleons and sailing ships that hang from the ceiling in vivid recollection of the place such vessels have in the story of the seafaring city. Bremen is Germany's oldest and second-largest port—only Hamburg is bigger—and it has close historical seafaring ties with North America. Forty-eight kilometers (30
17 miles) upriver, at **Bremerhaven,** is the country's largest and most fascinating maritime museum, the **Deutsches Schiffahrtsmuseum,** with a harbor containing seven genuine old trading ships. *Von-Renzelen-Str., tel. 0471/482070. Admission: DM 4 adults, DM 2 children. Open Apr.–Sept., Tues.–Sun. 10–6.*

Bremen, together with Lübeck and Hamburg, was an early member of the Hanseatic League, and its rivalry with the larger port on the Elbe is still tangible. Though Hamburg may still claim its historical title as Germany's "door to the world," Bremen likes to boast: "But we have the key."

Charlemagne established a diocese here in the 9th century, and a 15th-century statue of him, together with seven princes, adorns the Rathaus. In its massive vaulted cellars is further evidence of the riches accumulated by Bremen in its busiest years: barrels of fine, 17th-century Rhine wine. Other bounty from farther afield formed the foundation of one of the city's many fascinating museums, the **Übersee Museum,** a unique collection of items tracing the histories and cultures of the many peoples with whom the Bremen traders came into contact. One section is devoted to North America. *Bahnhofspl. 13. Admission: DM 2 adults, 50 pf children. Open Tues.–Sun. 10–6.*

Don't leave Bremen without strolling down Böttcherstrasse, a stretch of houses and shops reconstructed between 1924 and 1931 in historical exactitude at the initiative of a Bremen coffee millionaire, Ludwig Roselius. Walk, too, through the idyllic Schnoorviertel, a jumble of houses, taverns, and shops once occupied or frequented by fishermen and tradespeople.

Shopping

Grimm-related souvenirs are to be found everywhere in this region, ranging from the cheap and vulgar to finely designed porcelain figures. Among the most popular gift ideas are bound editions of the Grimm brothers' fairy tales. The incredible tales of Baron Münchhausen make equally popular buys.

Kassel, Fulda, Göttingen, and Hameln all have attractive central pedestrian areas where it's a pleasure to shop for all manner of gift items. In Bremen bargain-hunters should make for the idyllic Schnoorviertel.

Germany's oldest **porcelain** factory is at Fürstenberg, high above the Weser River, halfway between Kassel and Hameln. The crowned gothic letter *F* that serves as its trademark is world-famous. You'll find Fürstenberg porcelain in shops throughout the area, and in some of the towns (Bad Karlshafen and Höxter, for instance). By far the most satisfactory way of starting a Fürstenberg collection, or adding to it, is to make the journey up to the 18th-century castle where production first began in 1747 and buy directly from the manufacturer. Fürstenberg and most dealers will take care of shipping arrangements and any tax refunds.

A good selection of **garden gnomes** featuring Grimm fairy-tale characters is available at the Heissner Shop (Schlitzerstr. 24) in Lauterbach.

If you're interested in buying **regional costumes** such as Hessen *Trachten* dresses, try Berdux (Hirschberg 1) in Schwalmstadt, just north of Alsfeld.

There are some excellent small, privately run **potteries** and **glassworks** in the area. In Bad Karlshafen, you can watch the craftsmen and craftswomen at work in a studio in the Baroque Rathaus and buy goods directly from them. In the village of Immenhausen, just north of Kassel, you can visit a local glass foundry (the **Glashütte Süssmuth**) and watch glassblowers create fine works that are also for sale (shop hours: Mon.–Fri. 9–5, Sat. 9–1). The very finest, however, find their way into a neighboring museum (open Mon.–Fri. 9–5, Sat. 9–1, Sun. 10–5), where you'll get fascinating insight into the glassblower's craft.

Sports and Fitness

Bicycling Bicycles can be rented from most railway stations for DM 10 a day (DM 6 with a valid ticket) and from many tourist offices. The two Weser River excursion companies (*see* Guided Tours in Essential Information, above) take bikes aboard their boats and recommend routes that combine riverside cycle tours and boat trips.

Golf There are golf courses at Bad Orb, Bad Pyrmont, Fulda, Göttingen, Hanau, Kassel, and Polle-Holzminden; guests are welcome at all. There are particularly attractive courses at Hanau (on the former hunting grounds at Wilhelmsbad) and Kassel (high above the city on the edge of Wilhelmshöhe Park).

Hiking The hills and forests between Hanau and Hameln are a hiker's paradise. The valleys of the Fulda, Werra, and Weser rivers make enchanting walking country, with ancient waterside inns positioned along the way. Local tourist information offices of the area have established a hiking route from Münden in the south to Porta-Westfalica, where the Weser River breaks through the last range of north German hills and into the lower Saxony plain. Contact **Fremdenverkehrsverband Weserbergland-Mittelweser** (3250 Hameln, tel. 05151/202517) for information.

Horseback Riding This part of Germany is horse country, and most resorts have riding stables. There's a large and well-equipped equestrian center at Löwensen, near Bad Pyrmont (call 05281/10606 for information).

Water Sports Great canoeing can be enjoyed on both the Fulda and Weser rivers. For information on Fulda river trips and canoe rental, call 0561/22433. **Busch Bootstouristik** (3525 Oberweser, tel. 05574/818) rents canoes from April to October on the Fulda, Weser, and Werra and organizes trips of up to a week on all three rivers. Motorboats can be rented from **Weisse Flotte Warnecke** in Bodenwerder (tel. 05533/4864).

Dining and Lodging

Dining

If you are in the western area of the region, try Westphalian ham, famous for more than 2,000 years. The hams can weigh as much as 33 pounds and are considered particularly good for breakfast, when a huge slice is served on a wood board with rich, dark pumpernickel bread baked for some 20 hours. If you're keen to do as the locals do, you'll wash it down with a glass of strong, clear Steinhäger schnapps. A favorite main course is *Pfefferpothast*, a sort of heavily browned goulash with lots of pepper. The "hast" at the end of the name is from the old German word *Harst*, meaning "roasting pan." Rivers and streams filled with trout and eels are common around Hameln. Göttinger *Speckkuchen* is a heavy and filling onion tart. In Bremen, *Aalsuppe grün*, eel soup seasoned with dozens of herbs, is a must in summer.

Ratings Highly recommended restaurants in each price category are indicated by a star ★.

Category	Cost*
Very Expensive	over DM 90
Expensive	DM 55–DM 90
Moderate	DM 35–DM 55
Inexpensive	DM 20–DM 35

**per person for a three-course meal, including tax and excluding drinks and service charge*

Lodging

Make reservations well in advance if you plan to visit in the summer. Though it's one of the less-traveled tourist routes in Germany, the main points of the Fairy-tale Road are popular. Accommodations cover the spectrum from modern high rises to ancient and crooked half-timbered buildings.

Ratings Highly recommended hotels in each price category are indicated by a star ★.

Category	Cost*
Very Expensive	over DM 180
Expensive	DM 120–DM 180

Moderate	DM 80–DM 120
Inexpensive	under DM 80

**All prices are for two people in a double room, excluding service charges.*

Bad Karlshafen
Dining

Gaststätte-Hotel Weserdampfschiff. You can step right from the deck of a Weser pleasure boat into the welcoming garden of this popular riverside hotel-tavern. Fish from the river land right in the tavern's frying pan. *Weserstr. 25, tel. 05672/2425. Dress: informal. No credit cards. Inexpensive.*

Bad Oeynhausen
Lodging
★

Romantik Hotel Hahnenkamp. This attractive, homey, half-timbered country house is known throughout the region for the huge collection of miniature cockerel figures from which it takes its name. *Alte Reichstr. 4 (on the Minden Road), tel. 05731/5041. 24 rooms with bath or shower. Facilities: restaurant. AE, DC, MC, V. Closed Dec. 21–24. Expensive.*

Bevern
Dining

Enzianhütte. The Weser River winds lazily below this terraced restaurant. If it's too chilly to sit outside, there's a cozy room with an open fireplace. Some traditional dishes are cooked on the grill over the fire. *Am Ochsenbrink 2, tel. 05535/8710. Reservations advised. Dress: informal. AE, DC, MC. Closed Wed. Moderate.*

Bodenwerder
Dining

Restaurant Goldener Anker. You'll want to work up an appetite before tucking into the vast portions of regional specialties offered by the Golden Anchor. Sit on the terrace in the summer and enjoy the view over the Weser River. There are 15 inexpensive rooms, with shower or bath, if you fancy staying the night. *Weserstr. 13, tel. 05533/2135. Reservations advised. Dress: informal. No credit cards. Closed Nov.–Easter. Inexpensive.*

Lodging

Hotel Deutsches Haus. The fine half-timbered facade of this solidly comfortable country hotel vies for attention with the nearby former home of Baron Münchhausen, now Bodenwerder's town hall. The town park is outside the front door, and the Weser River is a short walk away. *Münchhausenpl. 4, tel. 05533/3925. 43 rooms with bath. Facilities: games room, restaurant. AE, DC, MC, V. Moderate.*

Bremen
Dining
★

Park Restaurant. Chef Bernhard Stumpf, formerly of the renowned Restaurant Français in Frankfurt, has transformed the Park into one of the finest dining establishments in Germany. Located in the Park Hotel Bremen (*see* Lodging, below), it is somewhat small for a hotel restaurant, but the floor-to-ceiling windows and lacquered ceiling open up the room. Stunning in yellow, black, and cream, the dining room is decorated with shimmering crystal chandeliers, classical molding, marble urns, and Louis XVI chairs, all of which add to the sense of occasion. Chef Stumpf adds a dash of fantasy to his classic French dishes, which may include broccoli flan with autumn vegetables atop a pine-nut and celery sauce, sautéed fillet of beef with ox-marrow ragout, and cottage-cheese soufflé in fig-honey sauce. The wine list is staggering, with 340 vintages from around the world. *Im Bürgerpark, tel. 0421/3408–555 or 3408–601. Reservations required. Dress: jacket and tie required. AE, DC, MC, V. Very Expensive.*

★ **Grashoff's Bistro.** Locals say this is Bremen's number-one bistro, serving regional dishes prepared with a lighter touch and high-quality wine at sensationally low prices. The menu changes daily. *Contrescarpe 80, tel. 0421/14740. Reservations advised. Dress: informal. DC. Closed Sun. and evenings. Moderate.*

★ **Ratskeller.** Said to be Germany's oldest and most renowned Ratskeller restaurant, this one specializes in solid, typical northern German fare, including the finest poultry and freshest seafood, prepared in ingenious ways. However, it's no place for beer drinkers. Shortly after the restaurant opened in 1408, the city fathers decreed that only wine could be served there, and the ban on beer still exists today. You'll dine in a cellar lined with wine casks, including an 18th-century barrel that could house a family of wine drinkers. Wine connoisseurs have 600 labels from which to choose. *Am Markt, tel. 0421/321676. Reservations advised. Dress: informal. DC, MC. Moderate.*

Friesenhof. This is the place if you want to try something local other than fish. Traditional meat dishes dominate the menu; portions are large. *Hinter dem Schütting 12–13, tel. 0421/337666. Reservations advised. Dress: informal. AE, DC, MC, V. Inexpensive.*

Lodging

★ **Park Hotel Bremen.** The service doesn't get any more gracious than at this grand hotel by a lake in the 800-acre Bürgerpark, close by the main train station. Aside from the impressive central dome, the architecture—'50s international style—is banal. What does shine is the ever-accommodating staff, who'll be glad to provide you with suitable jogging clothes for the 15-minute run to the historic center, or arrange a complimentary limousine into town if you'd rather motor. No one would blame you, however, if you wanted to stay put in such luxurious digs. You need look no farther than the Park Restaurant (*see* Dining, above) for a sumptuous dining experience. The guest rooms differ radically in decor—Moorish, Japanese, and Italian Modern are just some of the themes—and the bathrooms are lined with 12 different kinds of marble. The rooms in the wing, added in the '70s, are not as large as those in the main building. For the best view of the lake, ask for number 253, and take breakfast in the glass-enclosed terrace café. *Im Bürgerpark, tel. 0421/3408–555 or 3408–611, fax 0421/3408–602. 150 rooms with bath. Facilities: restaurant, bistro, terrace café, bar, beauty salon, masseuse, complimentary use of jogging clothes and bicycles, limousine service, indoor parking. AE, DC, MC, V. Very Expensive.*

Mercure Columbus. Elegantly renovated and now under French management, this hotel is conveniently adjacent to the train station and only a short stroll from the old-town attractions. The decor is modern and many of the rooms are spacious. *Bahnhofplatz 5, tel. 0421/14161. 147 rooms and 5 suites. Facilities: sauna, solarium, restaurant, bar. AE, DC, MC, V. Very Expensive–Expensive.*

★ **Hotel Landhaus Louisenthal.** American visitors particularly like this family-run country-house hotel on the outskirts of Bremen—30% of its guests are from the United States. The 150-year-old building boasts Old World charm and a caring management. *Leher Heerstr. 105, tel. 0421/232–076. 58 rooms and 2 apartments, all with bath or shower. Facilities: sauna, solarium, restaurant. AE, DC, MC, V. Moderate.*

Fulda

Dining

★ **Corniche de France.** Step off Fulda's central Kanalstrasse and into the cozy Corniche and you'll think you're in France instead of the hinterland of Hessen. Cast-iron pillars, glass canopies, and romantic lamps give the restaurant a Gallic intimacy. The menu, too, is mostly French, but with an imaginative German/Austrian touch—typified by the snails in light puff-pastry. *Kanalstrasse 3, tel. 0661/70200. Reservations advised. Dress: informal. AE, DC, MC, V. Closed Sun. and Mon. midday and 3 weeks in summer. Moderate.*

Lodging

Maritim Hotel am Schlossgarten. This is the luxurious showpiece of the Maritim chain, housed in a 17th-century Baroque building overlooking Fulda palace park. Try for a room with a view of the park. Chandeliers, oil paintings, and antiques establish an elegant air. *Pauluspromenade 2, tel. 0661/2820. 112 rooms and 2 suites with bath. Facilities: restaurant, café, bar, indoor pool, sauna, solarium, bowling alleys. AE, DC, MC, V. Very Expensive.*

★ **Romantik Hotel Goldener Karpfen.** Fulda is famous for its Baroque buildings, and this hotel is a short walk from the finest of them. The hotel, too, dates from the Baroque era but has a later facade. Inside, it has been renovated to a high standard of comfort. Afternoon coffee in the comfortable, tapestry-upholstered chairs of the hotel's lounge is one of Fulda's delights. *Simpliciuspl. 1, tel. 0661/70044. 50 rooms and 4 suites with bath or shower. Facilities: restaurant, sauna, fitness room. AE, DC, MC, V. Very Expensive–Expensive.*

Zum Kurfürsten. In the heart of the old town, this lodging is itself part of Fulda's Baroque face. But behind the venerable facade guests are assured of modern facilities. *Schloss-str. 2, tel. 0661/70001. 68 rooms with bath. Facilities: sauna, restaurant. AE, DC, MC, V. Expensive–Moderate.*

Gelnhausen
Lodging

Hotel Burg Mühle. *Mühle* means "mill," and this recently expanded and modernized hotel was once the tithe-mill of the neighboring castle. In the restaurant, the mill wheel churns away as you eat. *Burgstr. 2, tel. 06051/82050. 34 rooms with shower. Facilities: restaurant, sauna, solarium. AE, DC, MC, V. Expensive.*

Göttingen
Dining

Ratskeller. You dine here in the vaulted underground chambers of Göttingen's 15th-century city hall, choosing from a traditional menu with the friendly assistance of chef Michael Jansen. *Am Markt 9, tel. 0551/56433. Reservations advised. Dress: informal. AE, DC, MC, V. Moderate.*

★ **Zum Schwarzen Bären.** The "Black Bear" is one of Göttingen's oldest tavern-restaurants, a 16th-century half-timbered house that breathes history and hospitality. The specialty of the house is *Bärenpfanne*, a generous portion of local meats. *Kurzestr. 12, tel. 0551/58284. Reservations advised. Dress: informal. AE, DC, MC. Closed Mon. Inexpensive.*

Lodging

Gebhards Hotel. Though located just across a busy road from the train station, this hotel stands aloof and unflurried on its own grounds, a sensitively modernized 18th-century building that's something of a local landmark. *Goethe-Allee 22–23, tel. 0551/49680. 60 rooms, with bath or shower. Facilities: restaurant, indoor pool. AE, DC, MC, V. Very Expensive.*

Hotel Beckman Garni. The Beckman family runs this pleasant and homey hotel with friendly efficiency. The family takes particular pride in the hotel garden, a quiet and lush retreat in all seasons. The hotel is 5 kilometers (3 miles) out of town, with good bus links to downtown. *Ulrideshuser-Str. 44, Göttingen-Nikolausberg, tel. 0551/21055. 26 rooms, 18 with bath or shower. Facilities: neighboring rustic restaurant with bowling alley. AE, DC, MC, V. Inexpensive.*

Hameln
Dining
★

Rattenfängerhaus. This is Hameln's most famous building, reputedly the place where the Pied Piper stayed during his rat-removing assignment. Rats are all over the menu, from "Rat-remover cocktail" to a "Rat-tail dessert." But don't be put off: The traditional dishes are excellent, and the restaurant is guaranteed to be rodent-free. *Osterstr. 28, tel. 05151/3888. Reservations advised. Dress: informal. AE, DC, MC, V. Inexpensive.*

Lodging
★

Hotel zur Kröne. If you fancy a splurge, ask for the split-level suite. With prices starting at DM 380 a night, it's an expensive but delightful luxury. The building dates from 1645 and is a half-timbered marvel. Avoid the modern annex, however; it lacks all charm. *Osterstr. 30, tel. 05151/7411. 35 rooms, 1 apartment, all with bath or shower. Facilities: restaurant. AE, DC, MC, V. Very Expensive–Expensive.*

Christinenhof. This protected, half-timbered, 17th-century landmark was converted into a small hotel in 1989. It's tastefully decorated in dark cherry wood and marble. *Alte Markstr. 18, tel. 05151/7168. 18 rooms with bath. Facilities: sauna, indoor pool, bar. AE, MC, V. Moderate.*

Hotel zur Börse. A long-established, family-run property in the old town, this hotel offers comfortable accommodations and friendly service. Its attractive winter garden is a pleasant retreat. *Osterstr. 41 (entrance on Kopmanshof), tel. 05151/7080. 34 rooms with shower. Facilities: restaurant. AE, DC, V. Closed Christmas and New Year's Day. Moderate.*

Hanau
Lodging

Brüder Grimm Hotel. Located a few minutes' walk from the Brüder Grimm memorial in Hanau's central market square, the hotel that carries their name has a fairy-tale restaurant on the top floor. Accommodations are modern and comfortable. Try for the "Eckzimmer"; it's the largest and best-decorated room. *Kurt-Blaum-Pl. 6, tel. 06181/3060. 80 rooms and 15 apartments with bath or shower. Facilities: restaurant, sauna, whirlpool. AE, DC, MC, V. Expensive.*

Höxter
Dining
★

Schlossrestaurant Corvey. Three kilometers (2 miles) south of the charming town of Höxter lies Corvey Abbey, whose attractions include an excellent restaurant. You can dine outside under centuries-old trees in summer and inside before a blazing hearth in winter. The lunchtime menu is a particularly good value. *Reichsabtei Corvey, tel. 05271/8323. Weekend reservations advised. Dress: informal. AE, DC, MC, V. Closed Feb. Moderate.*

Kassel
Dining

Die Pfeffermühle. The "Peppermill" is in Kassel's Gude Hotel, but it's no conventional hotel restaurant. The menu is truly international: Indian and Russian dishes share space with traditional German fare. *Frankfurterstr. 299, tel. 0561/48050. Reservations advised. Dress: informal. AE, DC, MC, V. Closed Sun. evening. Moderate.*

Ratskeller. Here you'll eat within the embracing surroundings of cellar vaults. If you're lucky, you'll call when owner-chef Robert Kuhn is holding one of his "specialty" weeks. *Obere Konigstr. 8, tel. 0561/15928. Reservations advised. Dress: informal. AE, DC, MC, V. Inexpensive.*

Lodging

City-Hotel. This new hotel in the city center, just a few minutes from the Rathaus, is sympathetically designed to blend in with its ancient surroundings. Inside, rooms are stylishly decorated and furnished. *Wilhelms-höher Allee 40, tel. 0561/71871. 44* *rooms with bath. Facilities: beauty salon, therapeutic baths, sauna, solarium, restaurant, café, bar. AE, DC, MC, V. Expensive.*

Schlosshotel Wilhelmshöhe. Set in the beautiful Baroque Wilhelmshöhe Park, this is no ancient palace but a modern hotel with its own sports center. *Schlosspark 2, tel. 0561/30880. 100 rooms with bath. Facilities: restaurant, cafë, bar, indoor pool, whirlpool, sauna, solarium; tennis, golf, and riding stables all in immediate vicinity. AE, DC, MC, V. Expensive.*

Sababurg
Lodging
★

Burghotel Sababurg. A medieval fortress thought to have been the inspiration for the brothers Grimm's tale of *The Sleeping Beauty*, this is now a small luxury hotel snugly set in the castle walls and surrounded by the oaks of the Reinhardswald. You need a car to reach it, but even the drive is an experience to be remembered. *3520 Hofgeismar, tel. 05671/8080. 18 rooms with bath. Closed Jan.–Mar. Facilities: restaurant. AE, DC, MC, V. Expensive.*

Steinau
Lodging

Weisses Ross. This may be a simple inn, but you can sleep within its gnarled walls in the knowledge that the Grimm brothers overnighted here almost 200 years ago. *Brüder-Grimmstr. 48, tel. 06663/5804. 6 rooms, most with bath. Facilities: restaurant. No credit cards. Inexpensive.*

Uslar
Dining
★

Romantik Hotel Menzhausen. The half-timbered exterior of this 16th-century establishment is matched by the cozy interior of its comfortable, well-appointed restaurant. The 400-year-old wine cellar harbors outstanding vintages, served with reverence at excellent prices. The hotel itself has 38 well-appointed rooms, many with antiques. *Langestr. 12, tel. 05571/2051. Weekend reservations advised. Dress: informal. Facilities: restaurant, indoor pool, sauna. AE, DC, MC. Expensive.*

The Arts and Nightlife

The Arts

Music

Bremen has a Philharmonic orchestra of national stature. It plays regularly throughout the year at the city's concert hall; call 0421/36361 for program details and tickets. From September 26 to October 3, 1993, Bremen will host the 68th **Bach Music Festival.** For information and tickets, contact the Bremen Tourist Office (Hillmanplatz 6, tel. 0421/308–000). In **Fulda,** chamber-music concerts are given regularly from September through May in the chandelier-hung splendor of the bishops' palace; call 0661/102–326 for program details and tickets. **Göttingen's** symphony orchestra presents about 20 concerts a year. In addition, the city has a nationally known boys' choir and an annual Handel music festival in June. Call 0551/56700 for program details and tickets for all three. In **Kassel,** outdoor concerts are held in Wilhelmshöhe Park on Wednesday, Saturday, and Sunday afternoons from May through September. Classical-music concerts are also given by the city's municipal orchestra in the Stadttheater; call 0561/10940 for program details and tickets.

Theater

Bremen has three theaters that regularly stage classical and modern dramas, comedies, and musical comedies: the Schauspielhaus; the Concordia; and the Musiktheater. Call 0421/365–

3333 for program details and tickets. In **Fulda,** one wing of the magnificent bishops' palace is now the city's main theater; call 0661/102–326 for program details and tickets. **Göttingen's** two theater companies—the 100-year-old Deutsches Theater and the Junge Theater—are known throughout Germany; call 0551/496–911 for program details and tickets. **Hameln's** main theater, the Weserbergland Festhalle (Rathauspl. tel. 0515/3747), has a regular program of drama, concerts, opera, and ballet from September through June; call for program details and tickets. **Kassel** has no fewer than 35 theater companies. The principal venues are the Schauspielhaus, the Tif-Theater, the Stadthalle, and the Komödie. Call 0561/158–523 for program details and tickets for all.

Nightlife

Bremen may be Germany's oldest seaport, but it can't match Hamburg for racy nightlife. Nevertheless, the streets around the central Marktplatz and in the historic Schnoor district are filled with atmospheric taverns and bars of various kinds. In **Göttingen** the ancient student taverns that crowd the downtown area are the focus of local nightlife, but for something more sophisticated try the Malibu (Lange Geismar 33). **Kassel** is disco city. The Jet Set (Untere Königstr.) and Jenseits von Eden (Untere Königstr.) are two to try. Club 21 (Friedrich-Ebert-Str. 61a) is another favorite.

15 Hamburg

Introduction

Until not so very long ago Hamburg could have been considered Germany's best-kept secret, virtually ignored by the streams of foreign visitors to the Federal Republic whose itineraries invariably included the Rhine, the Romantic Road, and Munich.

Lately this has changed, and Hamburg is now neck-and-neck with Munich as Germany's second-favorite city among foreign visitors (Berlin still takes first place). And yet Hamburg still has something of an image problem. Mention of the city invariably triggers thoughts of the gaudy night world of the Reeperbahn, that sleazy strip of clip joints, sex shows, and wholesale prostitution. With reputedly the Continent's most wicked after-dark diversions, the Reeperbahn has helped make Hamburg Europe's "sin city" supreme. But to those who know Hamburg, the Reeperbahn's presence could be considered an indication of the city's prevailing live-and-let-live attitude, part and parcel of the dramatic diversity and apparently irreconcilable contradictions that make up this fascinating port.

Hamburg is both a city and a state. Its official title—the Free and Hanseatic City of Hamburg—refers to its status as an international trading post dating from the Middle Ages. For hundreds of years Hamburg ranked as Europe's leading port, yet it is situated 100 kilometers (62 miles) from the sea.

Hamburg gained world renown as the kingpin of the Hanseatic League, that medieval mafia of north German merchant cities that banded together to dominate shipping in the Baltic and the North Sea, with trading satellites set up in Bergen, Visby, Danzig, Riga, Novgorod, and other points of the compass.

Between the 12th and 16th centuries, Hamburg and her sister cities held a virtual monopoly on trade in this part of Europe. But it was only after the demise of the Hansa that Hamburg arrived at the crest of its power.

During the 19th century the largest shipping fleets on the seas, with some of the fastest ships afloat, were based here; tentacles of shipping lanes reached to the far corners of the earth. Ties to New York, Buenos Aires, and Rio de Janeiro were stronger than those to Berlin or Frankfurt. During the four decades leading up to World War I, Hamburg became one of the world's richest cities. Its aura of wealth and power was projected right up to the outbreak of World War II, and even today it shows.

The miracle of present-day Hamburg is that in spite of having been virtually wiped off the map by the 1940–1944 bombing raids, it now stands as a remarkably faithful replica of that glittering prewar city. In what surely must rank as the most successful reconstruction of any major German city, Hamburg is once again a place of enormous style, verve, and elegance.

Situated at the mouth of the Elbe, one of Europe's great rivers and the 97-kilometer (60-mile) umbilical cord that ties the harbor to the North Sea, Hamburg is still one of Europe's busiest ports. Each year some 15,000 ships sail up the lower Elbe carrying more than 50 million tons of cargo—from petroleum and locomotives to grain and bananas.

Hamburg, or "Hammaburg," was founded in 810 by Charlemagne. For centuries it was, of course, a walled city, its gigantic outer fortifications making for a tight little world that remained relatively impervious to outside influences. The Thirty Years' War passed it right by. Napoléon's domination of much of the Continent in the early 19th century hardly touched Hamburg. However, the Great Fire of 1842 all but obliterated the original city; a century later World War II bombing raids destroyed port facilities and leveled more than half of the city proper. So what you see today is the "new" Hamburg, with some Old World touches—and a handsome place it has become.

The distinguishing feature of downtown Hamburg is the Alster. Once an insignificant waterway, it was dammed during the 18th century to form an artificial lake. Divided at its south end, it is known as the Binnenalster (Inner Alster) and the Aussenalster (Outer Alster), the two separated by a pair of graceful bridges, the Lombard Brücke and the John F. Kennedy Brücke. The Inner Alster is lined with stately hotels, department stores, fine shops, and cafés; the Outer Alster is framed by the spacious greenery of parks and gardens against a backdrop of private mansions.

From late spring into fall, sailboats and board-surfers skim across the surface of the Outer Alster. White passenger steamers zip back and forth. The view from one of these vessels (or from the shore of the Outer Alster) is of the stunning skyline of six spiny spires (five churches and the Rathaus) that is Hamburg's identifying feature. It all makes for one of the most distinctive and appealing downtown areas of any European city.

Sometimes called a "Venice of the North," the city is threaded with countless canals and waterways, spanned by some 1,000 bridges, more even than you'll find in Venice. Swans glide on the canals. Arcaded passageways run along the waterways. In front of the Renaissance-style Rathaus is a square that resembles the Piazza San Marco. So the allusion to Venice is not totally frivolous.

But what truly distinguishes Hamburg from most other cities is the extent of greenery at its heart. Almost half of its area is devoted to either agriculture or parkland. This fondness for growing things has been a dominant treasure of Hamburg for centuries. In the 16th century anyone caught chopping down a tree was sentenced to death!

Hamburg is endowed with considerable architectural diversity. Of particular interest are the 14th-century houses of Deichstrasse—the oldest residential area in Hamburg—and the Kontorhausviertel (literally, "Business House Quarter").

The latter contains some unique clinker-brick buildings from the '20s. A variety of turn-of-the-century *Jugendstil* (Art Nouveau) buildings can also be found in various parts of the city. Of course, as in most German cities, high rises are much in evidence. A few project a certain grace and style, others are merely functional and undistinguished.

Anyone accustomed to the *Gemütlichkeit* (conviviality) and jolly camaraderie of Munich should be advised that Hamburg on initial exposure presents a more somber face.

Hamburgers are staunchly conservative in dress and demeanor and liberal in politics. Members of the merchant elite are extremely status-conscious, yet not inclined to put on airs. People here are reputed to be notoriously frugal on the one hand, generous hosts on the other, with a penchant for indulging their tastes for the most refined delicacies. In a city that vibrates with energy, the people work hard and play hard, and turn out to be friendlier than they may at first appear.

Essential Information

Important Addresses and Numbers

Tourist Information The main branch of the tourist office is the **Tourismus Zentrale Hamburg** (Burchardstr. 14, tel. 040/300–510). It's open Monday through Friday 7:30 AM–6 PM, Saturday 7:30 AM–3 PM. In addition to its comprehensive hotel guide, the tourist office also publishes a monthly program of events in the city, *Hamburg Vorschau,* available for DM 2.30, which details upcoming shows, plays, movies, and exhibits. The illustrated magazine *Hamburg Tips* is issued quarterly and details major seasonal events; it's free of charge.

Other tourist offices include **Tourist Information im Bieberhaus** (Hachmannplatz, tel. 040/3005–1245; open Mon.–Fri. 7:30 AM–6 PM, Sat. 8 AM–3 PM). It's located just outside the main train station. There's also a tourist office in the **station** (tel. 040/300–51230); it's open daily 7 AM–11 PM. The **airport tourist office** (tel. 040/300–51240) is open 8 AM–11 PM. At the harbor, there's an office at the **St. Pauli Landungsbrücken** (boat landings); it's open daily 9–6 (tel. 040/300–51200). There's also an office in the **Hanse Viertel** shopping mall, open weekdays 10–6:30 (Thurs. 10–9), Saturday 10–3 (10–6 on the first Sat. of the month), Sunday 11–3 (tel. 040/300–51220).

All offices can help with accommodations, and there's a central booking office for telephone callers (tel. 040/19412). A DM 5 fee is charged for every room reserved; the cost is then deducted when you pay the hotel.

Consulates **U.S. Consulate General,** Alsterufer 28, tel. 040/411710. **British Consulate General,** Harvestehuder Weg 8a, tel. 040/446–071.

Emergencies **Police:** tel. 110. **Ambulance** and **Fire Department:** tel. 112. **Medical Emergencies:** tel. 040/228–022. **Dentist:** tel. 040/468–3260 or 040/11500.

English-language Bookstore **Frensche** (Spitalerstrasse 26e, tel. 040/327–585) stocks books and newspapers.

Travel Agencies **American Express,** Rathausmarkt 5, tel. 040/331–141.

Car Rental **Avis,** Drehbahn 15–25, tel. 040/341–651. **Hertz,** Amsinckstrasse. 45, tel. 040/230–045.

Arriving and Departing by Plane

Hamburg's international airport, **Fuhlsbüttel** (tel. 040/50750) is 11 kilometers (7 miles) northwest of the city. All major U.S. airlines fly to Hamburg; there are also regular flights from Britain. There are frequent flights from other major German cities.

Between the Airport and Downtown An **Airport-City-Bus** runs between the airport and Hamburg's Hauptbahnhof (main train station) daily at 20-minute intervals. Along the way, buses stop at the hotels Reichshof, Atlantic, and Hamburg-Plaza, the central bus station at Adenauerallee 78, and at the fairgrounds. Buses run from 6:30 AM to 10:30 PM. Tickets are DM 8 per person, children under 4 free. The **Airport-Express** (bus No. 110) runs every 10 minutes between the airport and the Ohlsdorf U- and S-bahn station, a 17-minute ride from the main train station. The fare is DM 3.40 adults, DM 1.20 children. A taxi from the airport to the downtown area will cost about DM 25. If you're picking up a rental car at the airport, follow the signs to "Stadtmitte" (downtown).

Arriving and Departing by Train, Bus, and Car

By Train Euro-City and Intercity trains connect Hamburg with all German cities and many major European cities. Two new Intercity Express "super train" lines link Hamburg with Frankfurt and Munich, and Würzburg and Munich, respectively. There are two principal stations: the centrally located **Hauptbahnhof** and **Hamburg-Altona,** located west of the downtown area. For information, call 040/19419 for the main station, and 040/39182850 for Hamburg-Altona.

By Bus The ZOB, or **Zentral-Omnibus-Bahnhof,** Hamburg's bus station, is located right behind the Hauptbahnhof (Adenauerallee 78). For information call 040/247–575, or contact the **Deutsche Touring-Gesellschaft** in Frankfurt (Am Römerhof 17, tel. 069/7931).

By Car Hamburg is easier to handle by car than are many other German cities, and relatively uncongested by traffic. Incoming Autobahns connect with Hamburg's three beltways, which then take you easily to the downtown area. Follow the signs for "Stadtmitte."

Getting Around

On Foot The historic center of Hamburg can be easily explored on foot. The downtown area's Binnenalster and Jungfernstieg, many shopping streets and shopping galleries, and harbor are all close enough to make walking easy.

By Public Transportation The HVV, Hamburg's public transportation system, includes the **U-bahn** (subway), the **S-bahn** (suburban train), and **buses.** A one-way fare is DM 3.40 adults, DM 1.20 children, and tickets are available on all buses and at the automatic machines in all stations and at most bus stops. An **all-day ticket** (Tageskarte) valid from 9 AM to 1 AM costs DM 6.50 for unlimited rides on the HVV system. If you're traveling with family or friends, a **group or family ticket** (Gruppen- od. Familienkarte) is a good value; a group of up to four adults and three children can travel around for the entire day for only DM 11.50.

In the north of Hamburg, the HVV system connects with the **A-bahn** (Alsternordbahn), a suburban train system that extends into Schleswig-Holstein.

Night buses (Nos. 600–640) serve the downtown area all night, leaving the Rathausmarkt and Hauptbahnhof every hour.

Information on the HVV system can be obtained directly from the **Hamburg Passenger Transport Board** by calling 040/322-911 (open daily 7 AM–8 PM).

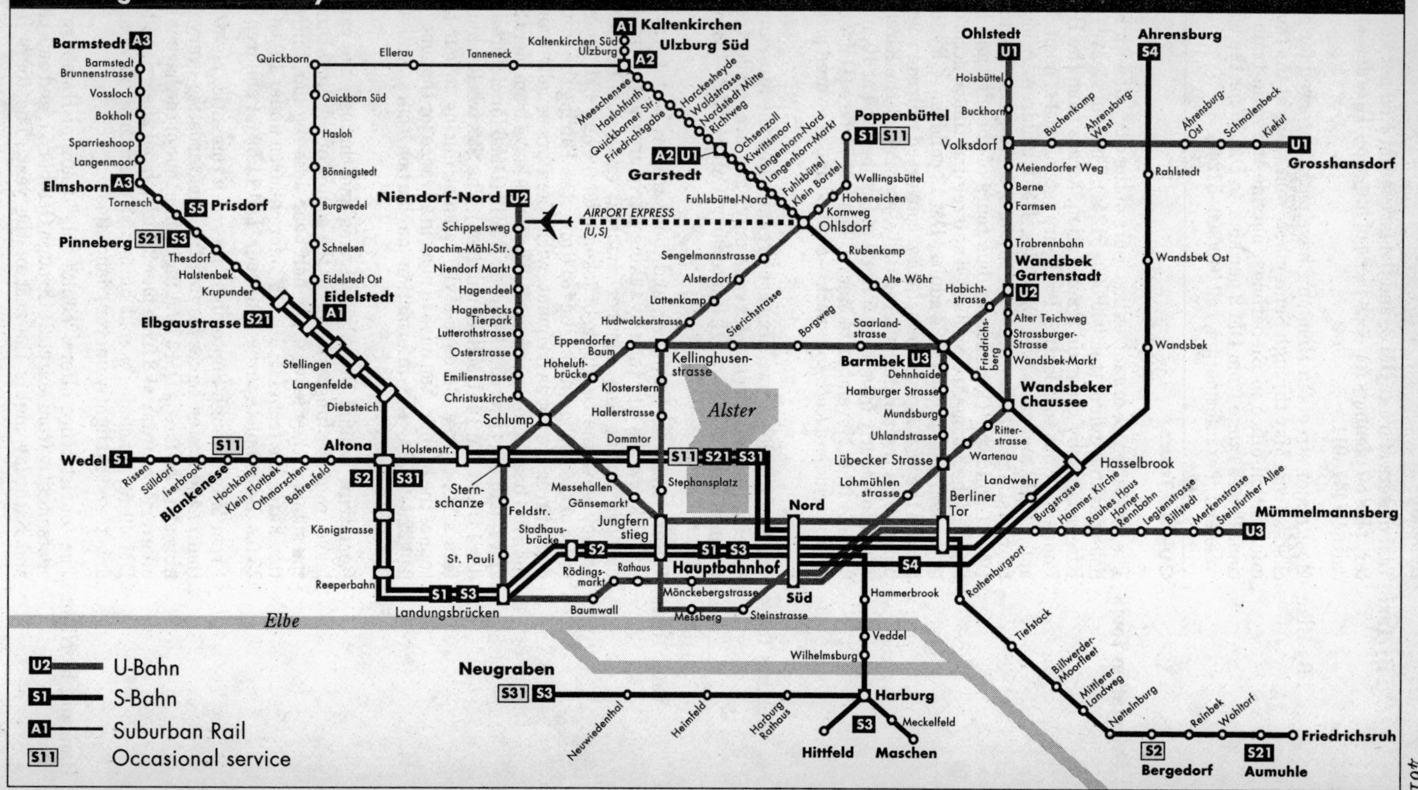
Hamburg Public Transit System
Barmstedt A3
Barmstedt Brunnenstrasse
Vossloch
Bokholt
Sparrieshoop
Langenmoor
Elmshorn A3
Tornesch
S5 Prisdorf
Pinneberg S21 S3
Thesdorf
Halstenbek
Krupunder
Elbgaustrasse S21
Quickborn
Quickborn Süd
Hasloh
Bönningstedt
Burgwedel
Schnelsen
Eidelstedt Ost
Eidelstedt A1
Ellerau
Tanneneck
A1 Kaltenkirchen
Kaltenkirchen Süd
Ulzburg
Ulzburg Süd
A2
Meeschensee
Haslohfurth
Quickborner Str.
Friedrichsgabe
Harckesheyde
Waldstrasse
Nordstedt Mitte
Richtweg
A2 U1 Garstedt
Ochsenzoll
Kiwittsmoor
Langenhorn-Nord
Langenhorn-Markt
Fuhlsbüttel
Klein Borstel
Fuhlsbüttel-Nord
Poppenbüttel S1 S11
Wellingsbüttel
Hoheneichen
Kornweg
Ohlsdorf
AIRPORT EXPRESS (U,S)
Niendorf-Nord U2
Schippelsweg
Joachim-Mähl-Str.
Niendorf Markt
Hagendeel
Hagenbecks Tierpark
Lutterothstrasse
Osterstrasse
Emilienstrasse
Christuskirche
Schlump
Stellingen
Langenfelde
Diebsteich
Altona
Holstenstr.
Wedel S1
Rissen
Sülldorf
Iserbrook
Blankenese
S11
Hochkamp
Klein Flottbek
Othmarschen
Bahrenfeld
S2 S31
Sternschanze
Feldstr.
Königstrasse
St. Pauli
Reeperbahn
Landungsbrücken
S1 - S3
Ohlstedt U1
Hoisbüttel
Buckhorn
Volksdorf
Buchenkamp
Ahrensburg-West
Ahrensburg-Ost
Schmalenbeck
Kiekut
U1 Grosshansdorf
Meiendorfer Weg
Berne
Farmsen
Trabrennbahn
Wandsbek Gartenstadt U2
Ahrensburg S4
Rahlstedt
Wandsbek Ost
Wandsbek
Sengelmannstrasse
Alsterdorf
Lattenkamp
Hudtwalckerstrasse
Sierichstrasse
Borgweg
Saarlandstrasse
Rubenkamp
Alte Wöhr
Habichtstrasse
Alter Teichweg
Strassburger-Strasse
Wandsbek-Markt
Friedrichsberg
Eppendorfer Baum
Hoheluftbrücke
Kellinghusenstrasse
Klosterstern
Hallerstrasse
Dammtor
Barmbek U3
Dehnhaide
Hamburger Strasse
Mundsburg
Uhlandstrasse
Lübecker Strasse
Lohmühlenstrasse
Berliner Tor
Wandsbeker Chaussee
Ritterstrasse
Wartenau
Landwehr
Hasselbrook
Alster
S11 - S21 - S31
Stephansplatz
Messehallen
Gänsemarkt
Jungfernstieg
Stadhausbrücke
S2
Rödingsmarkt
Rathaus
Baumwall
Nord
Hauptbahnhof
Süd
Mönckebergstrasse
Messberg
Steinstrasse
Burgstrasse
Hammer Kirche
Rauhes Haus
Horner Rennbahn
Legienstrasse
Billstedt
Merkenstrasse
Steinfurther Allee
Mümmelmannsberg U3
S4
Rothenburgsort
Hammerbrook
Elbe
Veddel
Wilhelmsburg
Neugraben S31 S3
Neuwiedenthal
Heimfeld
Harburg Rathaus
Harburg
S3
Meckelfeld
Hittfeld
Maschen
Tiefstack
Billwerder-Moorfleet
Mittlerer Landweg
Nettelnburg
S2 Bergedorf
Reinbek
Wohltorf
S21 Aumuhle
Friedrichsruh
U2 U-Bahn
S1 S-Bahn
A1 Suburban Rail
S11 Occasional service

By Taxi Taxi meters start at DM 3, and the fare is DM 1.60 per kilometer, plus 50 pfennigs for each piece of luggage. To order a taxi, call 040/441–011.

By Bike Most major streets in Hamburg have paths reserved for bicyclists. From May through September, rent bikes at the tourist information office in Bieberhaus, outside the main train station. Prices range from DM 2 per hour to DM 20 for the whole weekend. For information, call 040/300–51245.

Guided Tours

Orientation Tours The tourist office organizes bus tours of the city, all with English-speaking guides (tel. 040/300–51244). The tours leave from Kirchenallee by the main train station, across from the Hotel Phoenix. A bus tour lasting 1 ¾ hours sets off at 11, noon, 1, 3, and 4 daily and costs DM 18 adults, DM 9 children. A longer tour, lasting 2½ hours, starts at 10 and 2, costing DM 22 adults, DM 11 children. Combination bus tours of the city and boat tours of the harbor are conducted at irregular times, according to season. They cost DM 24 adults, DM 12 children. City tours aboard the nostalgic *Hummelbahn*, converted railroad wagons pulled by a tractor, are offered daily, starting at the Kirchenallee stop hourly from 10 to 5 April to October and at 10, noon, 2, and 4 from November to March. The DM 15 fare (DM 7 children) includes a *Rollmop* snack—a rolled and skewered pickled herring.

Walking Tours Tours of the downtown area are organized by the **Museum für Arbeit.** They are held weekends only, and are conducted in German only. May through September. Call 040/298–42364 for information.

Boat Tours Water dominates Hamburg, and there are few better ways to get to know the city than by taking a trip around the massive harbor. During the summer months, excursion boats and barges leave the Landungsbrücken (piers) every half hour for tours of the harbor lasting up to 90 minutes. During the winter, departures are not as frequent, with operators usually waiting for a full boat before setting off. The boats leave from piers 2, 3, and 7, and the trips cost between DM 12 (DM 6 for children under 14) and DM 16 (DM 8 for children). The **Störtebeker** line offers a six-course Baroque-style banquet during a four-hour tour of the harbor. You have to book in advance for that one (tel. 040/220–2552). For information on harbor tours, call 040/3117070 or 040/314–644.

Boat trips around the Alster Lakes and through the canals leave from the Jungfernstieg in the center of the city. During the summer they leave every half hour, less regularly in winter. Fares are from DM 10 (DM 5 for children under 14) to DM 23 for the complete three-hour tour (DM 11.50 for children).

From May through September, there's a romantic, nighttime tour of the Alster Lakes leaving the Jungfernstieg every evening at 8 (the fare is DM 17). A nighttime tour of the harbor sets off every Saturday at 8 from pier 2 with a band aboard, and the DM 49 fare includes a cold buffet, as much beer as you can drink, and a (slightly uneven) dance floor.

Hamburg by Night The tourist office offers "adults-only" tours of Hamburg hot spots nightly from March 24 through October 31, and on Friday and Saturday nights the rest of the year. The tours leave

Kirchenallee (opposite the Phonix Hotel) at 8 and take in a cross section of the city's night spots, including St. Pauli sex bars. The DM 99 fare includes drinks along the way. If you want a taste of Hamburg's no-holds-barred nightlife but don't want to head out on your own, this is a reasonable introduction.

Exploring Hamburg

Highlights for First-time Visitors

Alter Botanische Garten (Old Botanical Gardens)
Hauptbahnhof
Michaelis Kirche
Reeperbahn
Fischmarkt (Fish Market)
The harbor

Downtown Hamburg

Numbers in the margin correspond to points of interest on the Hamburg map.

1 Your tour begins at **Dammtor** train station, an elevated steel-and-glass Jugendstil structure built in 1903. Recently renovated, it is one of many Art Nouveau buildings you'll see during your stay in Hamburg. Pick up a detailed city map from the first-floor Booking Hall. Turn left out of the station and head toward the Congress Centrum Hamburg (CCH), a vast, modern conference-and-entertainment complex at the northeast
2 corner of **Planten un Blomen** park.

3 Planten un Blomen and the adjoining **Alter Botanischer Garten** (Old Botanical Gardens) lie within the remains of the 17th-century fortified wall that defended the city during the Thirty Years' War, the cataclysmic religious struggle that raged in Germany between 1618 and 1648. The remains of the old fortifications and moats have since been cleverly integrated into a huge, tranquil park on the edge of the city center.

The entire park area is known as **Wallringpark** and includes Planten un Blomen and the Alter Botanischer Garten, plus the Kleine and Grosse Wallanlagen parks to the south. You'll need to cover a lot of ground on foot to see everything Wallringpark has to offer, but a trip on the light railway—which crosses all four parks—will give you a taste of its many aspects. If you take the railway, aim to finish your journey at Stephansplatz.

The walking tour will take you through Planten un Blomen and the Alter Botanischer Garten. Past the Congress Centrum, bear left in a sweeping arc through the ornamental Planten un Blomen Park. This park, opened in 1935, is famous all over Germany for its well-kept plant, flower, and water gardens, and offers many places to rest and admire the flora. If you visit on a summer's evening, you'll see the **Wasserballet,** an illuminated fountain "dance" in the lake set to organ music. Make sure you get to the lake in good time for the show—it begins at 10 PM each evening during the summer (at 9 PM in September).

Follow the signs to the Alter Botanischer Garten, an equally green and open park that specializes in rare and exotic plants. Tropical and subtropical species are grown under glass in hot-

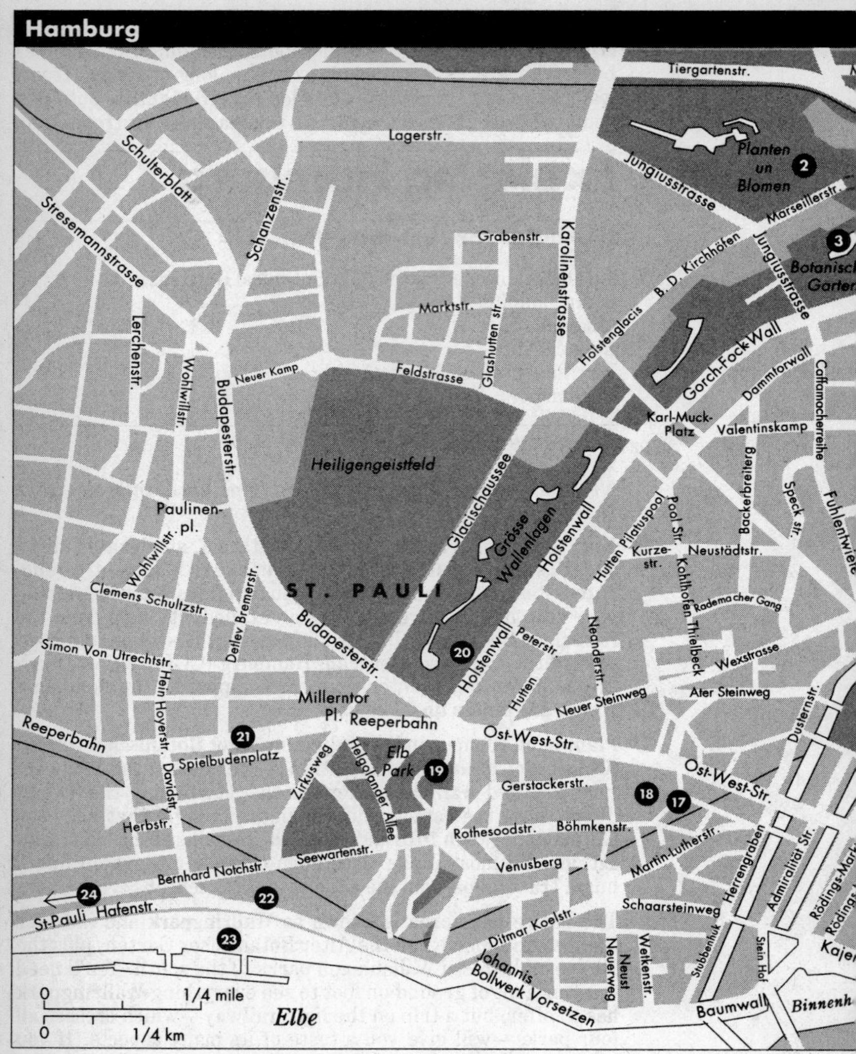

Alter Botanischer Garten, **3**
Bismarckdenkmal, **19**
Blankenese, **24**
Chilehaus, **12**
Dammtor, **1**
Deichstrasse, **15**
Fischmarkt, **22**
Hauptbahnhof, **7**
Jakobikirche, **10**
Jungfernstieg, **4**
Katherinenkirche, **13**
Kontorhausviertal, **11**
Krameramts-wohnungen, **17**
Kunsthalle, **8**
Landungsbrücken, **23**
Michaeliskirche, **18**
Mönckebergstrasse, **6**
Museum für Hamburgische Geschichte, **20**
Museum für Kunst und Gewerbe, **9**
Nikolaikirche, **16**
Planten un Blomen, **2**
Rathaus, **5**
Reeperbahn, **21**
Speicherstadt, **14**

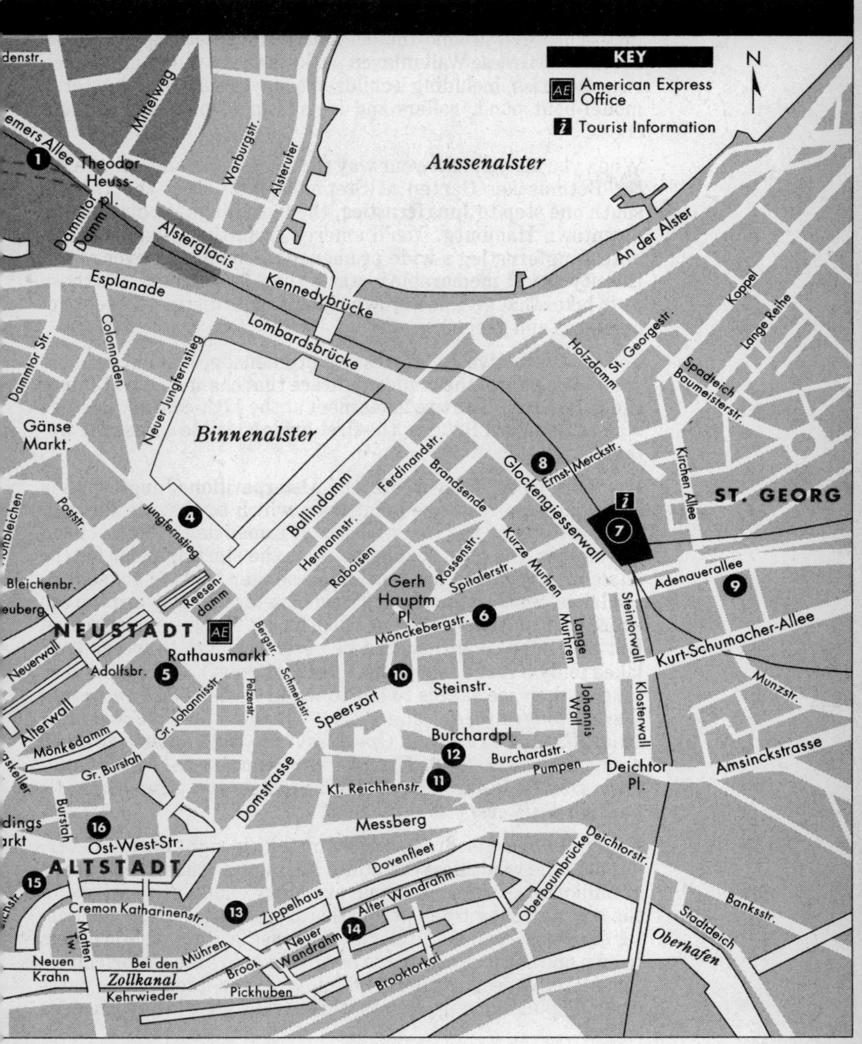
KEY
American Express Office
Tourist Information
N
Aussenalster
Binnenalster
ST. GEORG
NEUSTADT
ALTSTADT
Mittelweg
Warburgstr.
Alsterufer
Theodor Heuss-pl.
Dammtor Damm
Alsterglacis
Esplanade
Kennedybrücke
Lombardsbrücke
An der Alster
Dammtor Str.
Colonnaden
Neuer Jungfernstieg
Gänse Markt
Poststr.
Jungfernstieg
Ballindamm
Ferdinandstr.
Brandsende
Glockengiesserwall
Ernst-Merckstr.
Holzdamm
St. Georgstr.
Koppel
Lange Reihe
Spadteich
Baumeisterstr.
Kirchen Allee
Hermannstr.
Raboisen
Rossenstr.
Kurze Murhen
Spitalerstr.
Gerh Hauptm Pl.
Mönckebergstr.
Adenauerallee
Steintorwall
Lange Murhren
Kurt-Schumacher-Allee
Munzstr.
Bleichenbr.
Reesendamm
Rathausmarkt
Bergstr.
Schmiedestr.
Pelzerstr.
Gr. Johannisstr.
Adolfsbr.
Neuerwall
Alterwall
Mönkedamm
Gr. Burstah
Burstah
Speersort
Steinstr.
Johannis Wall
Klosterwall
Burchardpl.
Burchardstr.
Pumpen
Deichtor Pl.
Amsinckstrasse
Domstrasse
Kl. Reichhenstr.
Messberg
Ost-West-Str.
Dovenfleet
Deichtorstr.
Oberbaumbrücke
Cremon
Katharinenstr.
Zippelhaus
Alter Wandrahm
Neuer Wandrahm
Bei den Mühren
Brook
Brooktorkai
Matten Tw.
Neuen Krahn
Zollkanal
Kehrwieder
Pickhuben
Oberhafen
Stadtdeich
Banksstr.
1
2
4
5
6
7
8
9
10
11
12
13
14
15
16

houses, with specialty gardens—including herbal and medicinal—clustered around the old moat. The special appeal of the **Kleine** and **Grosse Wallanlagen** parks is their well-equipped leisure facilities, including a children's playground and theater, a model-boat pond, roller- and ice-skating rinks, and outdoor chess.

When you leave, make your way to the east entrance, to the Alter Botanischer Garten at Stephansplatz. Take the U-bahn
4 south one stop to **Jungfernstieg,** the most elegant boulevard in downtown Hamburg. You'll emerge from the U-bahn station onto Jungfernstieg's wide promenade, looking out over one of the city's most memorable vistas—the Alster Lakes. It's these twin lakes that give downtown Hamburg its distinctive sense of openness and greenery.

Today's attractive Jungfernstieg promenade, laid out in 1665, used to be part of the muddy millrace that channeled water into the Elbe River. The two lakes meet at the 17th-century defense wall at Lombard Brücke, the first bridge visible across the water.

Hamburg's best-known café, the **Alsterpavillon** (Jungfernstieg 54), is an ideal vantage point from which to observe the constant activity on the Inner Alster. It's open daily 10 AM–11 PM. In summer, the boat landing below is the starting point for the *Alsterdampfer*, the flat-bottom passenger boats that teem on the lakes. Small sailboats and rowboats hired from yards on the shores of the Alster are very much a part of the summer scene. But in winter conditions can be severe enough to freeze both lakes (only 8 feet deep at their deepest point), and commuters take to their ice skates to get to work. *Alster Lake and canal tours, Jungfernstieg, tel. 040/341–141. Fare for lake tour: DM 10 adults, DM 5 children. Operates Apr.–Oct., departing daily every half hour 10–6. Fare for combination lake and canal tour: DM 15 adults, DM 7 children. Operates Apr.–Oct., departing daily every 40 min. 10–6.*

Every Hamburger dreams of living within sight of the Alster, but only the wealthiest can afford it. Hamburg has its fair share of millionaires, some of whom are lucky enough to own one of the magnificent garden properties around the Alster's perimeter (the locals call it "Millionaire's Coast"). But you don't have to own one of these estates to be able to enjoy the waterfront—the Alster shoreline offers 4.6 miles of tree-lined public pathways. Popular among joggers, these trails are a lovely place for a stroll.

It's hardly surprising that the area around Jungfernstieg contains some of Hamburg's most exclusive shops. Even the unpredictable nature of the northern German weather isn't enough to deter Hamburgers from pursuing a favorite pastime: window-shopping. Hidden from view behind the sedate facade of Jungfernstieg is a network of nine covered arcades that together accounts for almost a mile of shops offering everything from cheap souvenirs to expensive haute couture. Many of the air-conditioned passages have sprung up in the past two decades (*see* Shopping, below), but some already existed in the 19th century (the first glass-covered arcade, called Sillem's Bazaar, was built in 1845).

Turn off the Jungfernstieg onto Reesendamm Street and make
5 your way to the next stop on your tour—the **Rathaus** (Town

Hall). To most Hamburgers this large building is the symbolic heart of the city. As a city-state—an independent city and simultaneously one of the 15 federal states of newly reunited Germany—Hamburg has a city council and a state government, both of which have their administrative headquarters in the Rathaus.

Both the Rathaus and the Rathausmarkt (Town Hall Market) lie on marshy land—a fact that everyone in Hamburg was reminded of in 1962 when the entire area was severely flooded. The large square, with its surrounding arcades, was laid out after Hamburg's Great Fire of 1842. The architects set out to create an Italian-style square, drawing on St. Mark's in Venice for inspiration. The rounded glass arcade bordered by trees was added in 1982.

Building on the Nordic Renaissance-style Rathaus began in 1866 when 4,000 wooden piles were sunk into the moist soil to provide stability for its mighty bulk. Building was completed in 1892, the year a cholera epidemic claimed the lives of 8,605 people in 71 days. A fountain and monument to that unhappy chapter in Hamburg's life can be found in a courtyard at the rear of the Rathaus.

No one is likely to claim that this immense building, with its 647 rooms and towering central clock tower, is the most graceful structure in the city, but for the sheer opulence of its interior, it's hard to beat. Although you get to see only the state rooms, the tapestries, huge staircases, glittering chandeliers, coffered ceilings, and grand portraits convey forcefully the wealth of the city in the last century and give insight into the bombastic municipal taste. The starting point for tours of the Rathaus interior is the ground-floor Rathausdiele, a vast pillared hall. *English-language tours: DM 1 adults, 50pf children. Hourly Mon.–Thurs. 10:15–3:15; Fri.–Sun., 10:15–1:15.*

Leave the Rathaus square by its east side, perhaps pausing to join other visitors to the city who are relaxing on the steps of the striking memorial to the poet Heinrich Heine, a real Ham-
6 burg fan. Beyond lies **Mönckebergstrasse,** a broad, bustling street of shops that ends at the Hauptbahnhof. Mönckebergstrasse is a relatively new street—it was laid out in 1908, when this part of the old town was redeveloped. Although the shops here are not quite as exclusive as those of Jungfernstieg, the department stores and shopping precincts on both sides of the street provide a wide selection of goods at more easily affordable prices. One word of warning to shoppers: If you want to go on a shopping spree on a Saturday, you will find that the shops close at 2 PM—unless it is the first Saturday of the month, when the shops are open from 9 to 6:30. This rather quirky rule applies to all of Hamburg's shopping centers and throughout most of Germany.

When you reach the end of Mönckebergstrasse, you'll meet the busy main road of Steintorwall, which was the easternmost link of the former defense wall encircling the old town in the 17th century. Rather than battling to cross against the fast-moving traffic,
7 take the pedestrian underpass to the **Hauptbahnhof.**

The Hauptbahnhof was opened in 1906 and completely renovated in 1991. Today it caters to a heavy volume of international, national, and suburban rail traffic. Despite the fact that it was badly damaged during the Second World War and has been modernized many times over, its architectural impact remains intact. This enormous 394-foot-long cast-iron-and-glass building is accentuated by a 460-foot-wide glazed roof that is supported only by pillars at each end. The largest structure of its kind in Europe, it is remarkably spacious and light inside.

Retrace your steps and leave the Hauptbahnhof the way you
entered. Turn right on Steintorwall, which continues as
8 Glockengiesserwall Strasse, until you come to the **Kunsthalle**
(Art Gallery) on the corner of Ernst-Merckstrasse.

The Kunsthalle houses one of the most important art collections in West Germany. It comprises two linked buildings: The one facing you is known as the Kunsthaus, exhibiting mainly contemporary works; adjoining it on your left is the Renaissance-style Kunsthalle, built in 1868. The entrance to both, which are known collectively as the Kunsthalle, is via the Kunsthaus building.

The Kunsthalle's 3,000 paintings, 400 sculptures, and coin and medal collection present a remarkably diverse picture of European artistic life from the 14th century to the present. Masterpieces in the gallery's possession include the oldest known representation of the murder of Thomas à Becket, the head of the English church in the 14th century. This painting, called *Thomas Altar,* was done by Meister Francke in 1424 and depicts Becket's death in Canterbury Cathedral.

One room of paintings shows works by local artists since the 16th century. There is also an outstanding collection of German Romantic paintings, including works by Runge, Friedrich, and Spitzweg. An exhibition of European art by such painters as Holbein, Rembrandt, Van Dyck, Tiepolo, and Canaletto is on display, as are examples of the late-19th-century Impressionist movement by artists from Leibl and Lieberman to Manet, Monet, and Renoir. *Glockengeisserwall 1, tel. 040/24862612. Admission: DM 3 adults, 70pf children. Open Tues.–Sun. 10–6.*

A quite different but equally fascinating perspective on art is
9 offered by the nearby **Museum für Kunst und Gewerbe** (Museum
of Arts and Crafts). To reach it, head in the direction from
which you came until you see the major crossroads with Kurt-Schumacher-Allee on your left. Turn down this street, and you'll find the museum on the first block on your left.

The Museum für Kunst und Gewerbe was built in 1876 as a museum and school combined. Its founder, Justus Brinckmann, intended it to be a stronghold of the applied arts to counter what he saw as a decline in taste due to industrial mass production. A keen collector, Herr Brinckmann amassed a wealth of unusual objects, including a fine collection of ceramics from all over the world. The museum houses a wide range of exhibits from a collection of 15th- to 18th-century scientific instruments (ground floor) to an Art Nouveau room setting, complete with ornaments and furniture, all either original or faithfully reproduced (first floor). *Steintorpl. 1, tel. 040/248–62630. Admission free. Open Tues.–Sun. 10–6.*

Time Out The museum has a small restaurant called **Destille** on the first floor, offering an extensive buffet that includes salads and desserts. Open Tues.–Sat. 10–4.

---

10 Return to the city center for a visit to the **Jakobikirche** (St. James's Church), just off the Mönckebergstrasse. Turn right out of the museum onto Kurt-Schumacher-Allee, cross over Steintorwall by the subway and continue west along Steinstrasse to the Jacobikirche on your right—you'll recognize it by its needle spire.

This 13th-century church was almost completely destroyed during the Second World War. Only the furnishings, put into storage until restoration of the building was completed in 1962, survived. The interior is not to be missed—it houses such treasures as the vast Baroque organ on which J. S. Bach played in 1720 and three Gothic altars from the 15th and 16th centuries. *Steinstr. Open weekdays 10–4, Sat. 10–1.*

Upon leaving the Jakobikirche, cross over Steinstrasse and
head down Mohlenhofstrasse, bearing left at the end onto
Burchardstrasse. This area, south of the Jakobikirche between
11 Steinstrasse and Messberg, is known as the **Kontorhausviertal**
(Business-House Quarter). Its fascination lies in a series of imaginative clinker-brick buildings designed in the New Objectivity style of 1920s civic architect Fritz Schumacher.

12 Of particular interest in this quarter is the **Chilehaus** at the corner of Burchardstrasse and Pumpen, a fantastical 10-story building that at first looks like a vast landlocked ship. The Chilehaus was commissioned by businessman Henry Sloman, who traded in saltpeter from Chile. This building is the most representative example of the northern German clinker-brick architecture of the '20s.

Next, your tour will take you south toward the Freihafen (Free
Port) to see the 19th-century warehouse city of **Speicherstadt,**
13 with a visit to the restored **Katherinenkirche** (St. Catherine's
Church) en route. From the Messberg end of Pumpen Street, cross the busy Ost-West-Strasse by Messberg station and continue down Dovenfleet, which runs alongside the Zoll Kanal (Customs Canal). Continue until Dovenfleet turns into Bei den Mühren, and you'll see the distinctive green copper spire of the Katherinenkirche.

The church is dedicated to St. Catherine, a princess of Alexandria martyred at the beginning of the 4th century. Both the exterior and interior of the church were severely damaged during World War II, but it has since been carefully reconstructed according to the Baroque design. Almost none of the original interior furnishings escaped destruction. Only two 17th-century epitaphs (to Moller and von der Feehte) remain. *Bei den Mühren. Open daily in the summer 9–6, in winter 9–4.*

Continue for about 220 yards along Bei den Mühren with the
14 looming bulk of the **Speicherstadt** warehouses in view across
the canal. Cross the first bridge you come to—it leads to the center of the warehouse district in the Free Port.

Hamburg's free-port status has existed since the 12th century, when Emperor Barbarossa, the Holy Roman Emperor Frederick I, granted the city special privileges, which included freedom from customs dues on the Elbe River. The original free port was situated at the point where the Alster meets the Elbe near Deichstrasse, but it was moved farther south as Hamburg's trade increased over the following centuries. The advent of steamships in the middle of the 19th century necessitated a total restructuring of the free port, and the Speicherstadt warehouses came into being.

The warehouses offer another aspect of Hamburg's extraordinary architectural diversity. A Gothic influence is apparent here, with a rich overlay of gables, turrets, and decorative outlines. These massive rust-brown warehouses are still used today to store and process every conceivable commodity, from coffee and spices to raw silks and handwoven Oriental carpets. Although you won't be able to go in, the nonstop comings and goings will give you a good sense of a port at work.

As you leave the Free Port over the bridge by which you entered, you'll pass through a customs control point, at which you may be required to make a customs declaration. Turn left after the bridge, where Bei den Mühren becomes Neuen Krahn.
15 Take your second right—onto **Deichstrasse,** which runs alongside Nikolaifleet, a former course of the Alster and one of Hamburg's oldest canals.

You are now in one of the oldest residential areas of the Old Town of Hamburg, which dates from the 14th century. Many of the original houses on Deichstrasse were destroyed in the Great Fire of 1842, which broke out in No. 42 and left some 20,000 people homeless. The houses you see today date mostly from the 17th to 19th centuries, but a few of the early dwellings escaped the ravages of the fire.

Number 27 Deichstrasse, for example, built in 1780 as a warehouse, is the oldest of its kind in Hamburg. And farther along at No. 39 is the Baroque facade of a house built in 1700. Today Deichstrasse is a protected area of great historical interest. All the buildings in the area have been painstakingly restored—thanks largely to the efforts of public-spirited individuals. You may wish to make a small detour down one of the narrow alleys between the houses (Fleetgänge) to see the fronts of the houses facing the Nikolaifleet. After exploring this lovely area, take the Cremon Bridge at the north end of Deichstrasse. This angled pedestrian bridge spans Ost-West-Strasse.

Time Out There are three good basement restaurants in this area if you are ready for a break. The **Alt Hamburger Aalspeicher** serves fresh fish dishes; the **Alt Hamburger Bürgerhaus** specializes in traditional Hamburg fare; and the **Nikolaikeller,** an upscale old Hamburg tavern, offers the biggest herring menu in Germany. All three are on Deichstrasse and Cremon.

The Cremon Bridge will take you to Hopfenmarkt square, just
16 a stone's throw from the ruins of the **Nikolaikirche** (St. Nicholas's Church). You won't need precise directions to find the church, with its 476-foot tower—the second-highest in Germany. Only the tower and outside walls of the 19th-century neo-Gothic church survived World War II. Unlike most of the other war-torn churches in Hamburg, the Nikolai was not rebuilt. Instead, the tower was declared a monument to those killed and persecuted during the war.

The Weinkeller unter St. Nikolai, a wine cellar and small wine museum located beneath the former church, is open for browsing and wine tasting as well as for the purchase of wine. *Ost-West-Str. between Hopfenmarkt and Neue Berg. Open weekdays 1–6, Sat. 9–1.*

Turn right onto Ost-West-Strasse and cross to the other side at the Rödingsmarkt U-bahn station. Continue along Ost-West-Strasse until you reach Krayenkamp, a side street to your left
17 that opens onto the historic **Krameramtswohnungen** (Shopkeepers-Guild Houses). The distance from the Nikolaikirche to Krayenkamp is about a ½ mile.

This tightly packed group of courtyard houses was built between 1620 and 1626 for the widows of members of the shopkeepers' guild. They were used as homes for the elderly after 1866, when the freedom to practice trades was granted. The half-timbered, two-story dwellings were restored in the 1970s and are now protected buildings. Their unusual twisted chimneys and decorative brick facades have drawn more than curious visitors—an artists' colony has taken firm root here.

One of the houses, marked "C," is open to the public. A visit inside the furnished setting gives one a sense of life in one of these 17th-century dwellings. Some of the houses have been converted to suit modern-day commercial purposes—you'll find a gallery, shops, and a bar-cum-restaurant in the style of Old Hamburg. *Historic House "C," Krayenkamp 10. Admission free. Open Tues.–Sun. 10–5.*

Time Out The restaurant **Galerie Stuben** (Krayenkamp 11, tel. 040/365–800) in the Krameramtswohnungen quarter is open daily from noon to midnight.

The Krameramtswohnungen lie in the shadow of Hamburg's
18 best-loved and most famous landmark, **Michaeliskirche** (St. Michael's Church), on the other side of Krayenkamp Road. Michaeliskirche, or "Michel," as it is called locally, is Hamburg's principal church and northern Germany's finest Baroque ecclesiastical building. Constructed on this site in the 17th century, it was razed when lightning struck almost a century later. It was rebuilt in the late 18th century in the decorative Nordic Baroque style, but fell victim in 1906 to a terrible fire that destroyed much of the church. A replica was erected in 1912, but it suffered yet more bad luck during the Second World War. By 1952, it had once again been restored.

The Michel has a distinctive 433-foot brick-and-iron tower bearing the largest tower clock in Germany, 26 feet in diameter. Just above the clock is the viewing platform (accessible by an elevator or stairs), which affords a magnificent panaroma of the city, the Elbe River, and the Alster Lakes. Twice a day, at 10 AM and 9 PM (on Sundays at noon only), a watchman plays a trumpet solo from the tower platform, and during festivals an entire wind ensemble crowds onto the platform to perform. Traffic permitting, the music can be heard at street level. *Michaeliskirche: open daily 9–5. St. Michael's Tower: open in the summer Mon.–Sat. 9–5:30, Sun. 11:30–5:30; in winter Mon., Tues., and Thurs.–Sat. 10–4, Sun. 11:30–4. Elevator fee: DM 3 adults, DM 1.80 children. Staircase fee (449 steps): DM 1.80.*

Time Out Just opposite the Michel is one of Hamburg's most traditional restaurants, the **Old Commercial Room** (Englische Planke 10, tel. 040/366–319). Try one of the local specialties here, such as *Labskaus* (a traditional sailors' dish) or *Aalsuppe* (eel soup). Open daily 11 AM–1 AM.

Return to the Krayenkamp entrance to the Michel and turn right. Stay on this road for about 220 yards, until you reach a
19 park, the enormous **Bismarckdenkmal** (Bismarck Monument) rising high above the greenery. Take the pathway leading to it, and as you climb you'll realize that part of its height is due to the sandy hill on which it stands. The colossal 111-foot granite monument, erected between 1903 and 1906, is a mounted statue of Chancellor Bismarck, the Prussian "Iron Chancellor" who was the force behind the unification of Germany. The plinth features bas-reliefs of various German tribes. Created by the sculptor Hugo Lederer, the statue symbolizes the German Reich's protection of Hamburg's international trade.

Leave the monument by the north exit onto Ost-West-Strasse. Cross it and continue straight ahead up the street called
20 Holstenwall to the **Museum für Hamburgische Geschichte** (Museum of Hamburg History). Because Holstenwall is a fast-flowing street, you may wish to cross by the St. Pauli U-bahn station on the traffic island.

A visit to this museum is highly recommended—it will give you an excellent overall perspective of the forces that have guided Hamburg's development over the centuries. The museum's vast and comprehensive collection of artifacts charts the history of Hamburg from its origins in the 9th century to the present. The Hamburg Historical Society began building the collection in 1839—three years before the Great Fire—and salvaged a number of items for display in the museum. More material was acquired in 1883 when several street blocks were torn down to make way for the expansion of the Free Port, and these provide an excellent record of life at the time.

Of particular interest to American visitors is the record of German immigrants to the United States between 1850 and 1914. The Historic Emigration Office's microfilm file lists the names of almost 5 million people who left the port of Hamburg for the promise of a better life in the New World. The first-floor office will research individual cases for visitors and provide information and documents. Allow an hour for this service, and expect to pay a fee of between $30 and $60.

Among the museum's many attractions are an exhibit that describes, through pictures and models, the development of the port and shipping between 1650 and 1860 and a 16th-century architectural model of Solomon's Temple measuring 11 feet square and made of five different types of wood.

Railway buffs will delight in the railway section and escape into past eras of train travel. The centerpiece of this section is a model layout of the Hamburg-to-Harburg rail link, complete with a puffing miniature steam locomotive. As a modern Intercity train is put through its paces, you may also see a 32:1 scale model of the legendary propeller-driven Reichsbahn *Zeppelin* of 1931 heading past in the opposite direction. Trains from every decade of the 20th century run strictly according to timetable on what is the largest model railway in Europe today. *Holstenwall 24, tel. 040/350–42360. Admission to the museum: DM 4 adults, DM 2 children. Open Tues.–Sun. 10–6. Historic Emigration Office: open Tues.–Sat. 10–1 and 2–5.*

Return along Holstenwall to the St. Pauli U-bahn station—you are now at the start of a long, neon-lit street stretching nearly a
21 ½ mile as far as the eye can see. This is the **Reeperbahn**. The

hottest spots in town are concentrated in St. Pauli Harbor area, on the Reeperbahn and on a little side street known as the Grosse Freiheit (or Great Freedom, and that's putting it mildly!). The shows are expensive and explicit, but to walk through this area is an experience in itself, and you can soak up the atmosphere without spending anything. It's *not* advisable, however, to travel through this part of the city alone at night.

St. Pauli is sometimes described as a "Babel of sin," but that's not entirely fair. It offers a broad menu of entertainment in addition to the striptease and sex shows. Among its other attractions are theaters, clubs, music pubs, discos, a bowling alley, and Panoptikum, the only waxworks museum in West Germany (located between the St. Pauli U-bahn and Davidstrasse). The Theater Schmidt on the Reeperbahn, a more recent arrival to the local scene, offers a repertoire of live music, vaudeville, chansons, and cabaret, while the St. Pauli Theater on Spielbudenplatz, a veteran of the age of velvet and plush, serves up a popular brand of lowbrow theater in Hamburger dialect.

It's no understatement to say that while some of the sex clubs may be relatively tame, a good many others are pornographic in the extreme. None gets going until about 10; all will accommodate you till the early hours. Order your own drinks rather than letting the hostess do it for you, pay for them as soon as they arrive, and be sure to check the price list again before handing over the money. If you order whiskey, for example, you can be sure you will not get an inexpensive brand.

Saturday night finds St. Pauli pulsating with people determined to have as much fun as possible. As the bright lights begin to fade sometime around daybreak, those who are made of
22 stern stuff continue their entertainment at the **Fischmarkt** (Fish Market).

The Altona Fischmarkt swings into action every Sunday morning at 5 in the summer and two hours later in the winter. It is by far the most celebrated of Hamburg's many markets and is worth getting out of bed early for. If you're coming from the Reeperbahn, return to the St. Pauli U-bahn station and travel one stop south to Landungsbrücken station. Turn right at the crossroads at the foot of the hill and walk beside the Elbe for about 220 yards, and you'll see the market stalls on the road to your left.

Sunday fish markets became a tradition in the 18th century, when fishermen used to sell their catch before church services began. Today freshly caught fish is only one of a compendium of wares on sale at the popular Fischmarkt in Altona. In fact, you can find almost anything—from live parrots and palm trees to armloads of flowers and bananas, valuable antiques to second-, third-, and fourth-hand junk. You'll find plenty of bars and restaurants in the area where you can breakfast on strong coffee or even raw herring, and live jazz is played in the auction hall, the Fischauktionshalle, at Sunday morning jam sessions (Grosse Elbestrasse 9). *Fischmarkt: between Grosse Elbstr. and St. Pauli Landungsbrücken. Open Sun. 5–10 AM in summer and 7–10 AM in winter.*

A visit to the port is not complete without a tour of one of the most modern and efficient harbors in the world. Hamburg is Germany's largest seaport, with 33 individual docks and 500 berths lying within its 78 square kilometers (30 square miles).

Short round-trips by ferry leave from the nearby landings at
23 **Landungsbrücken.** To find the booking hall and departure point, leave the Fischmarkt and return the way you came, but instead of turning left up the hill to the U-bahn station, bear right toward the long limestone building instantly recognizable by its two towers. This is Landungsbrücken, the main passenger terminal for a whole range of ferry and barge rides, both one-way and round-trip, along the waterways in, around, and outside Hamburg. In the first-floor booking hall is the main ticket office and information desk.

There's usually a fresh breeze, so do dress warmly enough for your trip, but don't expect rolling surf and salty air, as Hamburg's port is 56 nautical miles from the North Sea. The HADAG line and other companies organize round-trips in the port lasting about one hour and taking in several docks. *Harbor tours run year-round, with frequent starting times. Fare for 1-hour trip: DM 12 adults, DM 6 children. In summer, the tours start at half-hourly intervals from Pier No. 2 at Landungsbrücken. In winter, tours start whenever a boat is full.*

You can combine an evening trip around the harbor with a cold buffet dinner, as much beer as you can drink, and dancing on a "party ship." Book at the HADAG pavilion on Landungsbrücken (tel. 040/313–687). *Fare: DM 59. Departures May 3–Dec. 6 at 8 PM.*

One trip you should try to make is to the waterside village of
24 **Blankenese,** 14½ kilometers (9 miles) west of Hamburg. Take a ferry (14 kilometers) from Landungsbrücken to get there. But you'll need plenty of energy when you arrive to tackle the 58 flights of steep and narrow lanes crisscrossing the hills and valleys of the village.

Blankenese is another of Hamburg's surprises—a city suburb with the character of a quaint fishing village. Some Germans like to compare it to the French and Italian rivieras. Many of them consider it the most beautiful part of Hamburg. In the 14th century Blankenese was an important ferry point, but it wasn't until the late 18th and 19th centuries that it became a popular residential area.

Time Out A fine view and good food await you at **Sägebiel's Fährhaus** (Blankenese Hauptstr. 107, tel. 040/861–514), a former farmhouse where Kaiser Wilhelm once celebrated his birthday. The fish dishes are recommended.

You have a choice of transportation back to the city—by ferry, by S-bahn, or on foot. The celebrated Elbe River walk is long—about 8 miles (13 kilometers) from Blankenese to Landungsbrücken—but it's one of Hamburg's finest.

What to See and Do with Children

Harbor tours are obvious choices. Other watery options include rowboat rentals on the Stadtpark lake (*see* Sightseeing Checklists, below) and surrounding canals. Hamburg's zoo is a private one, Hagenbecks Tierpark, and is so popular that it has its own subway stop, on the U–2 line (*see* Sightseeing Checklists, below). There are 2,500 animals, most in more than 50 open-air enclosures. Kids love the enormous Kodiak bears. *Admission: DM 15 adults, DM 10 children. Admission to dolphinarium: DM 5.50 adults, DM 4 children. Open daily 8–sunset.*

Sightseeing Checklists

All sites listed below are discussed in the Exploring Hamburg section, above, unless noted otherwise.

Historical Buildings and Sites

Bismarckdenkmal (Bismarck Monument). Monument to Chancellor Bismarck, the "Iron Chancellor," who was the force behind the unification of Germany. *U-bahn: St. Pauli.*

Chilehaus (Chile House). An unconventional office building in the heart of the Kontorhausviertal district, built in the 1920s for a businessman who traded with Chile. *U-bahn: Messberg.*

Dammtorbahnhof (Dammtor Train Station). A fine example of turn-of-the-century Jugendstil (Art Nouveau) architecture.

Deichstrasse. This is the oldest residential area of the Old Town of Hamburg. *U-bahn: Rödingsmarkt.*

Fischmarkt (Fish Market). This colorful Sunday morning market starts at 5 AM in summer and 6 AM in winter and closes at 10 AM. *U-bahn: Landungsbrücken.*

Hamburger Hafen (Hamburg Harbor). There's a constant bustle around the port, the largest in West Germany. Choose one of the many boat excursions that leave regularly from the boat landings at Landungsbrücken. *U-bahn: Landungsbrücken.*

Hauptbahnhof (Main Train Station).

Krameramtswohnungen (Shopkeepers-Guild Houses). A tightly packed group of courtyard houses built in the late 17th century by the Merchants' Guild for the widows of its late members. *U-bahn: Rödingsmarkt.*

Rathaus (Town Hall). The late-19th-century Nordic Renaissance–style building is home to Hamburg's city council and state government. *U-bahn: Rathaus.*

Reeperbahn. This street cuts through Hamburg's lively St. Pauli entertainment quarter. *S-bahn: Reeperbahn, or U-bahn: St. Pauli.*

Speicherstadt. These imposing warehouses in the Free Port offer the world's largest continuous storage facility. *U-bahn: Baumwall, Rödingsmarkt, or Messberg.*

Churches

Jakobikirche (St. James's Church). This 13th-century church was rebuilt after severe damage during World War II, but some of its treasures remained intact, including a unique Baroque organ and three Gothic altars. *U-bahn: Mönckebergstr.*

Katherinenkirche (St. Catherine's Church). This restored Baroque church overlooking the harbor was dedicated to the martyred 4th-century Princess Catherine of Alexandria. *U-bahn: Messberg.*

Michaeliskirche (St. Michael's Church). Hamburg's most famous landmark and one of the most important late-Baroque churches in Germany. The viewing platform, accessible by stairs or elevator, affords a magnificent panorama of the city, encompassing the Elbe River and Alster Lakes. *U-bahn: Rödingsmarkt or St. Pauli.*

Nikolaikirche (St. Nicholas's Church). Only the tower and outside walls remain of this 19th-century neo-Gothic church destroyed in World War II. *U-bahn: Rödingsmarkt or Rathaus.*

Petrikirche (St. Peter's Church). Considered the oldest church in Hamburg, this early 13th-century building fell victim to the Great Fire of 1842 and was rebuilt shortly afterward. It has a tall copper-covered spire and contains a number of attractions, including a Gothic pulpit and various votive panels. *U-bahn: Rathaus.*

Museums and Galleries

Kunsthalle (Art Gallery). Hamburg's principal gallery houses one of the most important art collections in Germany, with paintings from the Middle Ages to the present. *U-bahn: Hauptbahnhof.*

Museum fur Hamburgische Geschichte (Museum of Hamburg History). The museum traces the history of Hamburg from its origins in the 9th century to the present. *U-bahn: St. Pauli.*

Museum für Kunst und Gewerbe (Museum of Arts and Crafts). This interesting little museum houses a wide variety of examples of the applied arts. *U-bahn: Hauptbahnhof.*

Museum für Völkerkunde (Museum of Ethnology). One of the largest museums of its kind in West Germany, it has particularly good displays on Africa and South America. *Rothenbaumchausee 64. Open Tues.–Sun. 10–6. U-bahn: Hallerstr.*

Oevelgönne Museumhafen (Oevelgönne Harbor Museum). The aim of this privately owned museum is to maintain and restore ships for occasional outings and public display. Most of the restored ships are seaworthy, and among the collection are steam tugs, wooden cutters, and fire-fighting ships. *Beim Anleger Neumühlen; take bus No. 183. Open Sat.–Sun. 11–8. Closed Jan. and Feb.*

Open Markets

Blankenese. A lively fruit and vegetable market in the heart of this suburb manages to preserve the charm of a small village. *Bahnhofstr. S-bahn: Blankenese train station. Open Tues. 8–2, Fri. 8–6, Sat. 8–1.*

Isemarkt. This market is considered by many Hamburgers to be the city's best, with more than 300 stalls offering everything from fresh produce to clothing and toys. The stalls are set up on a strip of land beneath the elevated railway between St. Pauli and Poppenbüttel. Some of the older houses on Isestrasse have particularly attractive Jugendstil facades. *Between the U-bahn stations of Hoheluftbrücke and Eppendorfer Baum. Tues. and Fri. 8:30–2.*

Fischmarkt (Fish Market). Fish of all shapes and sizes can be bought at this market, as well as a wide range of other goods, including flowers, fruit and vegetables, antiques, and secondhand junk. Its location by the harbor adds a further dimension to the attractiveness of this weekly market. *In summer, Sun. 5–10 AM; in winter, 7–10 AM. S- or U-bahn: Landungsbrücken.*

Parks and Gardens

Alsterpark. Lying on the northwest bank of the Alster is the 173-acre Alsterpark, a well-kept park of trees and gardens with a magnificent view of the city skyline. It is a popular destination for weekend strollers. *Harvestehuderweg.*

Hagenbecks Tierpark (Zoological Gardens). Opened in 1848, this privately owned zoo was the first in the world to use open-air animal enclosures. It has 62 acres of landscaped gardens and parkland, with some 2,500 animals separated from the public by invisible ditches. It also has a large dolphinarium and a well-equipped children's playground. *Hagenbeckallee at Hamburg-Stellingen. Admission: DM 15 adults, DM 10 children. Open daily 8–sunset. U-bahn: Hagenbecks Tierpark.*

Hirschpark (Deer Park). This is an attractively landscaped park with a game enclosure. Stop by the Hirschparkhaus for tea and homemade whole-grain breads at the nearby Witthüs Teestuben, a charming old thatched-roof cottage. *Main entrance: Mühlenberg. S-bahn: Blankenese.*

Stadtpark. This park, north of the city center, offers 445 acres of parkland and 19 miles of footpaths as well as recreational facilities, including open-air pools, sunbathing areas, and a planetarium. Plays are staged and rock concerts held here in the summer. *In Winterhude. U-bahn: Saarlandstr. or Borgweg.*

Wallringpark. This vast and well-kept park and garden area is just to the west of the city center and contains four parks: the ornamental Planten un Blomen flower garden; the herb and specialty gardens of the Alter Botanischer Garten, and the Kleine and Grosse Wallanlagen parks, which offer numerous leisure facilities. A miniature railway crosses all four parks. *Main entrance: Stephansplatz. Open Mar.–Oct., daily 7 AM–10 PM; Nov.–Feb., daily 7 AM–8 PM.*

Shopping

Gift Ideas As a great port, Hamburg offers goods from all over the world. You may find it bizarre, but this is one of the best places in Europe for buying tea, for example. Smoked salmon and caviar are also terrific buys here. But for those with salt in their veins, it's the city's maritime heritage that produces some of the most typical goods. The most famous must be a *Buddelschiffe*, a ship in a bottle. There are few better places to look for one, or for a blue-and-white striped sailor's shirt, a sea captain's hat, ship models, even ship's charts, than the little shops and stalls lining the landing stages at **St. Pauli Harbor. Binikowski** (Lokstedter Weg 68) is great for ships in bottles. **Gäth & Peine** (Mörkenstr. 12) is the place to look for flags from around the world. **Harry's Hamburger Hafenbasar** (Bernard-Nocht-Str. 63) is the best place of all for any of these specialty goods, a Hamburg institution and an experience not to be missed. The city has the distinction of being home to the largest caviar mail-order business in Europe, **Seifarth and Company** (Robert-Koch-Str. 17, tel. 040/524–0027); it offers lobsters, salmon, and exotic teas, too.

Antiques Check out the **Antik-Center** in the old market hall, close to the main train station at Klosterwall 9–21 (closed Mon.). It features a wide variety of pieces, large and small, valuable and not so valuable, from all periods. Alternatively, take a look at the shops in the **St. Georg** district, especially those between **Lange Reihe** and **Koppel.** You'll find a mixture of genuine antiques *(Antiquitäten* in German) and junk *(Trödel).* You won't find many bargains, however. **ABC-Strasse** is another happy hunting ground for antiques lovers.

Shopping Districts Hamburg's main shopping districts are among the most elegant on the Continent, and the city has Europe's largest area of covered shopping arcades, most of them packed with small, exclusive boutiques. The leading street is **Jungfernstieg,** just about the most upscale and expensive in the country. It's lined with classy jewelers—**Wempe, Brahmfeld & Guttruf,** and **Hintze** are the top names—and chic clothing boutiques such as **Linette** and **Ursula Aust.** Prices are high, but the quality is tops. The streets called **Grosse-Bleichen** and **Neuer Wall** that lead off Jungfernstieg continue the high-price-tag mood. They also lead to the city's three most important covered or indoor shopping malls: the marble-clad **Galleria; Hanse Viertel;** and **Kaufmannshaus.** The malls all connect, and hardened shoppers may want to spend several hours exploring them. The mood is busily elegant, and you'll understand why Hamburgers call it their "Quartier Satin"!

Spitalerstrasse, running from the main train station to Gerhard-Hauptmann-Platz, is a pedestrians-only shopping street that's lined with stores. Prices here are noticeably lower than those in Jungfernstieg. Parallel **Mönckebergstrasse** is also a premier shopping street and the site of the city's best-known chain department stores: **Kaufhof, Karstadt,** and **Hertie.**

Away from the downtown area in fashionable **Pöseldorf,** take a look at **Milchstrasse** and **Mittelweg.** Both are bright and classy, with small boutiques, restaurants, and cafés. The leading name is **Jill Sander** (Milchstr. 8), the city's best-known designer of women's clothing and accessories.

Department Stores Hamburg's most famous department store is the **Alsterhaus** on Jungfernstieg. Large and elegant, it's a favorite with locals and a must for visitors. Even Prince Charles and Princess Diana stopped in here during a visit to Hamburg. Don't miss its amazing food department. Reward yourself for having braved the crowds by ordering a glass of champagne; it's a surprisingly good value. Other leading chain stores are **Kaufhof, Karstadt,** and **Hertie** (*see* above), offering much the same goods at similar prices as in branches in other cities across the country.

Food and Flea Markets There are more than 50 markets in Hamburg each week; check with the tourist office for a full listing. The most famous is the **St. Pauli Fischmarkt,** held on Sundays between 5 AM (7 AM in winter) and 10 AM. Fish is the main offering, some of it sold directly from fishing boats, but you can also find fruits and vegetables and a miscellaneous selection of bric-a-brac. It's a terrific place for early morning browsing. The market's also a traditional setting for a last beer after a night on the town. In the heart of **Blankenese,** there's a lively fruit and vegetable market on Tuesdays (8 AM–2 PM), Fridays (8 AM–6 PM), and Saturdays (8 AM–1 PM) that offers real village charm. Take the S-bahn to Blankenese to reach it. The **Isemarkt,** near the Hoheluftbrücke, is considered the most beautiful market in the city; it boasts around 300 stalls selling produce, fish, clothing, and toys. The market is held Tuesdays and Fridays 8:30 AM–2 PM.

Sports and Fitness

Bicycling There are bike paths throughout downtown and many outlying areas. You can rent bikes from the tourist office (*see* Important Addresses and Numbers in Essential Information, above) for DM 2 per hour, April through September. A day's rental costs DM 10 (DM 20 for the weekend).

Golf There are two leading clubs: **Hamburger Golf-Club Falkenstein** (In de Bargen 59, tel. 040/812–177); and **Golf-Club auf der Wendlohe** (Oldesloerstr. 251, tel. 040/550–5014).

Jogging The best places for jogging are around the Planten un Blomen and Alt Botanischer Garten parks and along the leafy promenade around the Alster. The latter is about 4 miles long.

Sailing You can rent rowboats and sailboats on the Alster in the summer between 10 AM and 9 PM for around DM 12 an hour, plus DM 3 per additional person. For more advanced sailing, contact the **Yacht-Schule Bambauer** (Schöne Aussicht 20a, tel. 040/220–0030).

Swimming Don't even think about swimming in the Elbe or the Alster—they're health hazards. There are, however, pools, indoor and outdoor, throughout the city. A full listing is available from the tourist office. Two to try are **Alster Schwimmhalle** (Ifflandstr. 21) and **Blankenese** (Simrockstr. 45).

Tennis and Squash The **Hamburger Tennis Verband** (Hallerstr. 89, tel. 040/445–078) has full listings of the many indoor and outdoor courts in the city. Listings are also available from the tourist office. For squash, try the **Squash Center Marquardt** (Hagenbeckstr. 124a, tel. 040/546–074). It has 17 courts, a swimming pool, a sauna, and a solarium.

Dining

The city offers a wide range of dining experiences, from sophisticated nouvelle cuisine in sleekly upscale restaurants to robust local specialties in simple harborside taverns. Seafood naturally figures prominently. The most celebrated dish is probably *Aalsuppe*, eel soup, a tangy concoction not entirely unlike Marseilles's famous bouillabaisse. A must in summer is *Aalsuppe grün*, seasoned with dozens of herbs. Smoked eel, *Räucheraal*, is equally good. In fall, try *Bunte oder Gepflückte Finten*, a dish of green and white beans, carrots, and apples. Available anytime of year is *Küken ragout*, a concoction of sweetbreads, spring chicken, tiny veal meatballs, asparagus, clams, and fresh peas cooked in a white sauce. Other Hamburg specialties include *Stubenküken* (chicken), *Vierländer Mastente* (duck), *Birnen, Bohnen und Speck* (pears, beans, and bacon), and the sailors' favorite, *Labskaus*—a stew made from pickled meat, potatoes, and (sometimes) herring, and garnished with a fried egg, sour pickles, and lots of beets.

Highly recommended restaurants in each price category are indicated by a star ★.

Category	Cost*
Very Expensive	over DM 95
Expensive	DM 65–DM 95
Moderate	DM 45–DM 65
Inexpensive	DM 25–DM 45

**per person for a three-course meal, excluding drinks*

Very Expensive **Landhaus Dill.** Located in a former coach inn on the road to Blankenese, this restaurant offers a varied and imaginative menu, with nouvelle specialties predominating. In summer, try the lobster salad—it will be prepared right at your table. In fall, try the wild duck with port-wine sauce. Vegetarian meals are also available. *Elbchaussee 404, tel. 040/828–443. Reservations required. Jacket and tie required. AE, DC, MC, V. Closed Tues.–Fri. lunch and all day Mon.*

★ **Landhaus Scherrer.** Though this establishment is located only minutes from the downtown area in Altona, its parklike setting—the building was originally a brewery—seems worlds away from the high-rise bustle of the city. The mood is elegantly low-key, with wood-paneled walls and soft lighting. The food fuses sophisticated nouvelle specialties with more down-to-

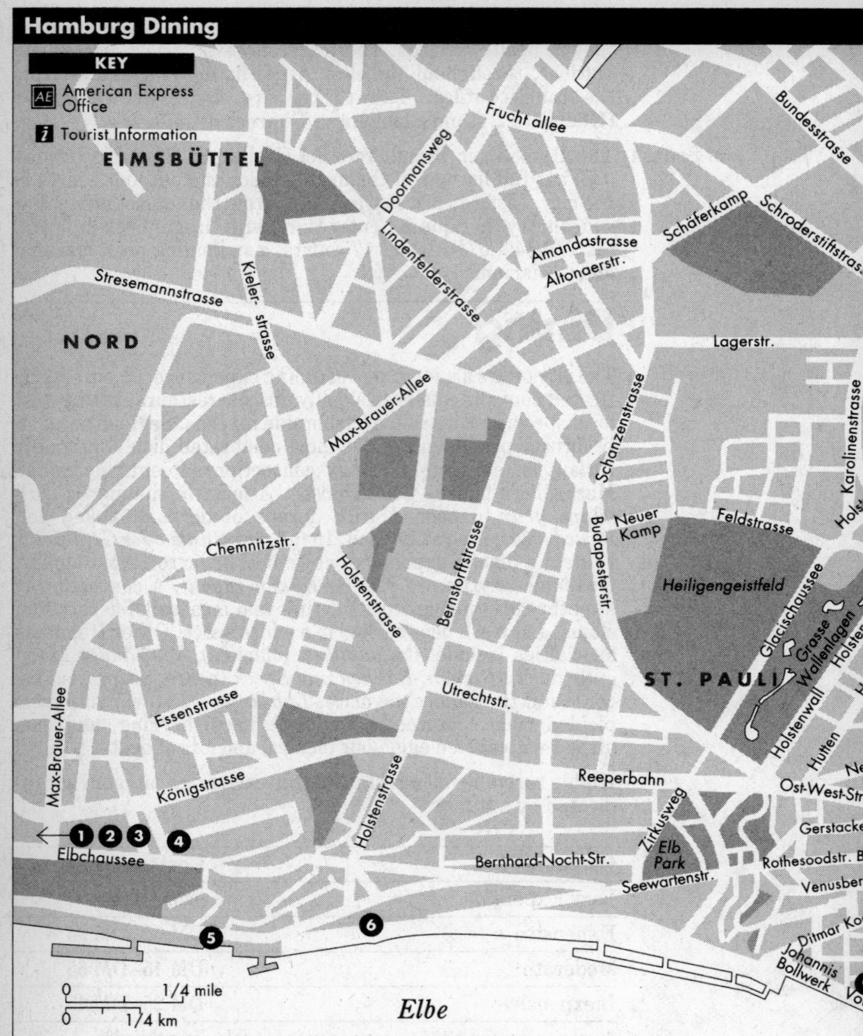

Ahrberg, **3**
At Nali, **7**
Bei Max, **10**
Fischereihafen-Restaurant Hamburg, **5**
Fischerhaus, **6**
Il Giardino, **11**
L'Auberge Française, **8**
La Mer, **15**
Landhaus Dill, **1**
Landhaus Scherrer, **2**
Le Canard, **4**
Le Château, **12**
Peter Lembcke, **14**
Ratsweinkeller, **13**
Sagres, **9**
Vico, **16**

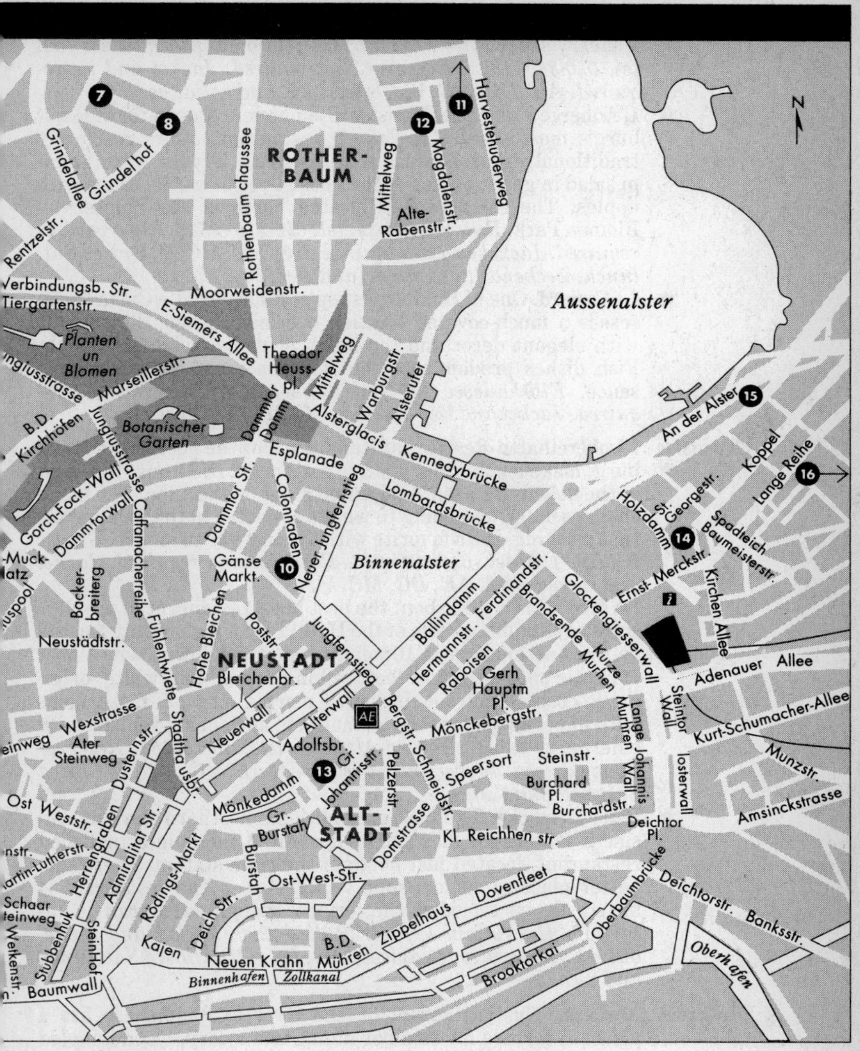
ROTHER-
BAUM
NEUSTADT
ALT-
STADT
Aussenalster
Binnenalster
Grindelallee
Grindel hof
Rentzelstr.
Verbindungsb. Str.
Tiergartenstr.
Moorweidenstr.
Rothenbaum chaussee
Mittelweg
Magdalenstr.
Alte-
Rabenstr.
Harvestehuderweg
E-Siemers Allee
Planten
un
Blomen
Theodor
Heuss-
pl.
Marseillerstr.
Jungiusstrasse
B.D.
Kirchhöfen
Botanischer
Garten
Dammtor
Damm
Warburgstr.
Alsterufer
Alsterglacis
Esplanade
Kennedybrücke
Lombardsbrücke
Gorch-Fock-Wall
Dammtorwall
Dammtor Str.
Colonnaden
Neuer Jungfernstieg
Gänse
Markt.
Caffamacherreihe
Backer-
breiterg
Neustädtstr.
Fuhlentwiete
Hohe Bleichen
Poststr.
Bleichenbr.
Jungfernstieg
Ballindamm
Hermannstr.
Ferdinandstr.
Brandsende
Glockengiesserwall
Kurze
Murhen
Raboisen
Gerh
Hauptm
Pl.
Mönckebergstr.
Bergstr.
Schmeidstr.
Alterwall
Neuerwall
Adolfsbr.
Gr.
Johannisstr.
Pelzerstr.
Wexstrasse
Ater
Steinweg
Dusternstr.
Stadtha usbr.
Mönkedamm
Gr.
Burstah
Speersort
Steinstr.
Burchard
Pl.
Burchardstr.
Lange
Murhren
Johannis
Wall
Steintor
Wall
Iosterwall
Deichtor
Pl.
Domstrasse
Kl. Reichhen str.
Ost Weststr.
Herrengraben
Admiralitat Str.
Rödings-Markt
Burstah
Ost-West-Str.
Deich Str.
Schaar
Steinweg
Stubbenhuk
SteinHof
Kajen
Neuen Krahn
B.D.
Mühren
Zippelhaus
Dovenfleet
Brooktorkai
Oberbaumbrücke
Deichtorstr.
Banksstr.
Oberhafen
Binnenhafen
Zollkanal
Baumwall
An der Alster
Koppel
Lange Reihe
Holzdamm
St. Georgestr.
Spadteich
Baumeisterstr.
Ernst-Merckstr.
Kirchen Allee
Adenauer Allee
Kurt-Schumacher-Allee
Munzstr.
Amsinckstrasse
AE
N
7
8
10
11
12
13
14
15
16

earth local dishes. Try the pickled calves' brains with lentils in a sherry sauce. The wine list is exceptional. *Elbchaussee 130, tel. 040/880–1325. Reservations required. Jacket and tie required. AE, DC, MC, V. Closed Sun. and holidays.*

★ **L'Auberge Française.** Monsieur Lemercier, proprietor of Hamburg's most successful French restaurant, offers resolutely traditional dishes. Seafood is his specialty. Try the warm scampi salad in garlic butter or the goose liver in truffle sauce with apples. The restaurant is located north of the Planten un Blomen Park. *Rutschbahn 34, tel. 040/410–2532. Reservations required. Jacket and tie required. AE, DC, MC, V. Closed Sat. lunch, weekends in summer, and Dec. 20–Jan. 10.*

★ **Le Canard.** One of Hamburg's top restaurants, Le Canard possesses a much-coveted location overlooking the Elbe River, with elegant decor and top-notch nouvelle cuisine to match. Fish dishes predominate, but try the roast lamb in thyme sauce. *Elbchaussee 139, tel 040/8805057. Reservations required. Jacket and tie required. DC, MC, V. Closed Sun.*

Expensive

★ **Fischereihafen-Restaurant Hamburg.** For the best fish in Hamburg, make for this big, upscale restaurant in Altona, just west of the downtown area and located right on the Elbe. The menu changes daily, according to what's available in the fish market that morning. It's a favorite with the city's beau monde. *Grosse Elbstr. 143, tel. 040/381–816. Reservations required. Jacket and tie required. AE, DC, MC, V.*

La Mer. This is just about the best hotel restaurant in the city, the elegant dining room of the Hotel Prem, memorably located on the Aussenalster, a 10-minute ride from downtown. A host of subtle specialties are featured in the gold-and-white, original Rococo restaurant, including marinated *inoki* mushrooms with imperial oysters and salmon roe, and spring venison with elderberry sauce. *An der Alster 9, tel. 040/245454. Reservations advised. Jacket and tie required. AE, DC, MC, V. Closed Sat. and Sun. lunch.*

★ **Peter Lembcke.** The best of traditional northern German cuisine is featured in this simply decorated and long-established restaurant, located just north of the train station. There's no better place to eat eel soup or Labskaus. The restaurant is nearly always crowded; the service, though warm, can be uncertain. *Holzdamm 49, tel. 040/243–290. Jacket and tie required. Reservations advised. AE, DC, MC. Closed Sat. lunch and Sun.*

Moderate

Ahrberg. This restaurant on the river in Blankenese has a pleasant terrace for summer dining and a cozy, wood-paneled dining room for colder days. The menu features a range of traditional German dishes and seafood specialties. Try the shrimp-and-potato soup or, in season, the fresh carp. *Strandweg 33, tel. 040/860–438. Reservations advised. Dress: informal. AE, DC, MC, V. Closed Sun.*

Il Giardino. The attractive courtyard garden here makes a delightful setting for low-key summer dining. The menu offers Italian and nouvelle specialties. The wine list is extensive. *Ulmenstr. 19, tel. 040/470–147. Reservations advised. Dress: informal. AE, MC, V. Closed lunch and Mon.*

★ **Le Château.** The elegant surroundings of a modernized 19th-century mansion in fashionable Pöseldorf are the scene of some of the classiest eating in the city. The food has a distinct French bias, with nouvelle specialties well to the fore. Fish "potpourri" with champagne and saffron is a longtime favorite. *Milch-*

str. 19, tel. 040/444–200. Reservations advised. Jacket and tie required. AE, DC, MC, V. Closed Sat. and Sun. lunch.

★ **Ratsweinkeller.** For atmosphere and robust local specialties, there are few more compelling restaurants in Germany than this cavernous, late-19th-century haunt under the town hall. High stone and brick arches, with ship models suspended from them, and simple wood tables set the mood. You can order a surprisingly fancy or no-nonsense meal; the fixed-price menus at lunch are a bargain. Fish specialties predominate, but there's a wide choice of other dishes, too. *Grosse-Johannisstr. 2, tel. 040/364–153. Reservations advised. Dress: informal. AE, DC, MC, V. Closed Sun. and holidays.*

Inexpensive

At Nali. This is one of Hamburg's oldest and most popular Turkish restaurants; it has the added advantage of staying open till 2 AM, handy for those hankering after a late-night kebab. Prices are low and the service is reliable and friendly. *Rutschbahn 11, tel. 040/410–3810. Reservations advised. Dress: informal. AE, DC, MC, V.*

Bei Max. This is one of Hamburg's liveliest beer taverns, serving excellent local brews and hot meals until 2 AM. You'll rub shoulders at the English-style bar with a cross section of Hamburg pleasure-seekers, from Yuppies to late-night theatergoers. For a meal, take a place at one of the heavy oak tables and tuck into such local fare as pickled herring or Hamburg-style potato soup (spiced with smoked pork). *Colonnaden 9, tel. 040/346–435. No reservations. No credit cards.*

★ **Fischerhaus.** Always busy (expect to share a table) and plainly decorated, this establishment offers time-honored Hamburg fish specialties. It's hardly haute cuisine, but the standards, like the service, are ultrareliable. This is a great place to try eel soup. The clientele matches the food. *Fischmarkt 14, tel. 040/314–053. No reservations. Dress: informal. No credit cards.*

Sagres. Portuguese and Spanish restaurants are part of the city's seafaring tradition, and this is one of the best. Fight your way through the Portuguese dockworkers to find a place at the bar, where you'll probably have to wait for a table. The mood is busy and cheerful, the decor simple. Try swordfish for an adventurous meal. *Vorsetzen 46, tel. 040/371–201. No reservations. Dress: informal. No credit cards.*

Vico. It will be love at first sight in one of Hamburg's better Greek restaurants. Authentic dishes at moderate prices are featured here, especially when you order the Aphrodite-Platte, which combines generous portions of gyros, souvlaki, bifteki, tzatziki, and french fries for an unbeatable DM 16.50. Scampi and octopus are only a couple of marks dearer. The decor is more German provincial than Greek, but at these prices one can't demand the Acropolis. *Lübeckerstr. 133, tel. 040/250–3614. No reservations. MC. Closed Mon.*

Lodging

Hamburg has a full range of hotels, from five-star, grande-dame luxury to simple pensions. The nearly year-round conference and convention business keeps most rooms booked well in advance. But it also means that many of the more expensive hotels offer lower weekend rates, when all those businesspeople have gone home. The tourist office can help with reservations if you arrive with nowhere to stay (*see* Important Addresses and Numbers in Essential Information, above).

Highly recommended hotels in each price category are indicated by a star ★.

Category	Cost*
Very Expensive	over DM 250
Expensive	DM 180–DM 250
Moderate	DM 120–DM 180
Inexpensive	under DM 120

**Prices are for two people in a double room, including tax and service charge.*

Very Expensive **Atlantic Hotel Kempinski.** There are few hotels in Germany more sumptuous than this expensive and gracious Edwardian palace near the main train station and facing the Aussenalster. The mood is one of thick-carpeted, marble-inlaid panache, with modern touches, especially in the lighting. The lobby is positively baronial, with an imposing grand staircase, deep leather armchairs, and a snack bar where you can partake of champagne and caviar. The rooms exude an understated luxury that's typically Hamburgian, the suites are little short of palatial, and the service is hushed and swift. In fine weather guests can lounge in the formal outdoor courtyard, where only the gurgling fountain disturbs the peace. The Atlantic-Restaurant is a stunning example of Post-Modernism, with rich bird's-eye maple details, black columns, and inlaid marble. *An der Alster 72, tel. 040/28880, fax 040/247129. 243 rooms and 13 suites, all with bath. Facilities: 2 restaurants, bar, lobby snack bar, Lufthansa check-in counter, indoor pool, sauna, solarium, masseur, tanning salon, parking garage. AE, DC, MC, V.*

★ **Garden Hotel Pöseldorf.** The location in chic Pöseldorf, a mile from the downtown area, may discourage those who want to be in the thick of things, but this is one of the most appealing hotels in Hamburg, in business since the 18th century and offering classy and chic accommodations. It's very much the insider's choice. There's no restaurant, but light, cold meals are served in the bar and airy winter garden. *Magdalenenstr. 60, tel. 040/414040. 59 rooms with bath. Facilities: garden. AE, DC, MC, V.*

SAS Plaza Hotel. If you value stylishly sleek modernity over Old World charm, this striking black high rise on the edge of the Planten un Blomen will be your choice. The views are good; the service polished. Many rooms are swankily decorated, with dark paneling; public rooms are elegant and large. *Marseillerstr. 2, tel. 040/35020. 563 rooms and suites, all with bath. Facilities: 2 restaurants, 3 bars, sauna, indoor pool, masseur. AE, DC, MC, V.*

★ **Vier Jahreszeiten.** Some claim that this handsome 19th-century town house on the edge of the Binnenalster is the best hotel in Germany, combining the very best of Old World elegance with impeccable service and luxury. If they're right, it's probably because it's still a family-owned concern. The hotel opened in 1897, and it's still owned and run by the Haerlin family. Antiques—the hotel has a set of near-priceless Gobelins tapestries—line the public rooms and stud the stylish bedrooms; forests of flowers stand in massive vases; rare oil paintings hang on the walls; and, of course, all the rooms are individually decorated. Of the four restaurants, the Haerlin is the most formal and features superb nouvelle and classic specialties. If you want a room with a view of the lake, make reservations well in advance. *Neuer Jungfernstieg 9–14, tel. 040/34940. 171 rooms and 12 suites, all with bath. Facilities: 4 restaurants, 2 bars, tearoom, pastry shop, wine shop. AE, DC, MC, V.*

Expensive

Aussen Alster. Only minutes from the train station and just 50 yards from the Alster Lakes, this small, discreet hotel is set in a gracious 19th-century town house. Try for a balcony room with a view of the lake. Bikes and sailboats are available for sports-minded guests; joggers can even borrow tracksuits. *Schmilinskystr. 11–13, tel. 040/241557. 27 rooms with bath. Facilities: restaurant, sauna, solarium. AE, DC, MC, V.*

Hotel Abtei. Located on a quiet, tree-lined street a mile north of the downtown area in Hervestehude, this elegant period hotel offers understated comfort and reliable levels of service. Try for a room with a view of the garden. There's no restaurant. *Abteistr. 14, tel. 040/442–2905. 12 rooms with bath. AE, DC, MC, V.*

Hotel-Garni Mittelweg. With chintz curtains, flowered wallpaper, old-fashioned dressing tables, and a country-house-style dining room that, unfortunately, serves only breakfast, this hotel possesses a small-town charm that seems almost out of place in bustling, big-business Hamburg. A converted turn-of-the-century mansion in up-market Pösseldorf, it's well located on fashionable Mittelweg, a short walk from the Alster Lakes and the city center. *Mittelweg 59, tel. 040/414–1010. 30 rooms with bath or shower. No credit cards.*

Hotel Senator. The Costabel family runs their brand-new hotel with a personal touch and Hamburg flair. Warm brown tones lend a homeyness, too, to the modern, well-equipped rooms. The Senator is well placed between the main railway station and the Aussenalster, and a short walk away from major shopping streets. *Lange Reihe 18–20, tel. 040/241203. 56 rooms with bath. Facilities: restaurant, bar, terrace, underground parking. AE, DC, MC, V.*

Mellingburger Schleuse. If you want off-the-beaten-track lodgings, this hotel is the place for you. Only a 20-minute drive from the downtown area, it is idyllically located in a forest—the Alsterwanderweg hiking trail passes right by the doorstep. The hotel itself is 250 years old, with a thatched roof, peasant-style furnishings, and a restaurant that serves traditional northern German dishes. *Mellingburgredder 1, tel. 040/602–4001. 31 rooms with bath. Facilities: restaurant, terrace café, indoor pool. AE, DC, MC.*

Moderate

Alameda. For no-frills lodging, this is a good bet. Small and basic, the hotel occupies the first two floors of a downtown building. *Colonnaden 45, tel. 040/344–000. 18 rooms, some with bath. AE, DC, MC, V.*

Baseler Hof. Centrally located near the Binnen Alster and the opera house, this hotel offers friendly and efficient service. Rooms are neatly if functionally furnished. *Esplanade 11, tel. 040/359–060. 155 rooms with bath. Facilities: restaurant, café. AE, DC, MC, V.*

Hotel-Pension am Nonnenstieg. The owner, Frau Hedermann, is friendly and helpful and makes this unassuming little hotel homey. Ask for a room with a kitchen alcove if you want to cook for yourself. Extra beds can be put in rooms at no extra charge to accommodate families, and prices are lower for longer stays.

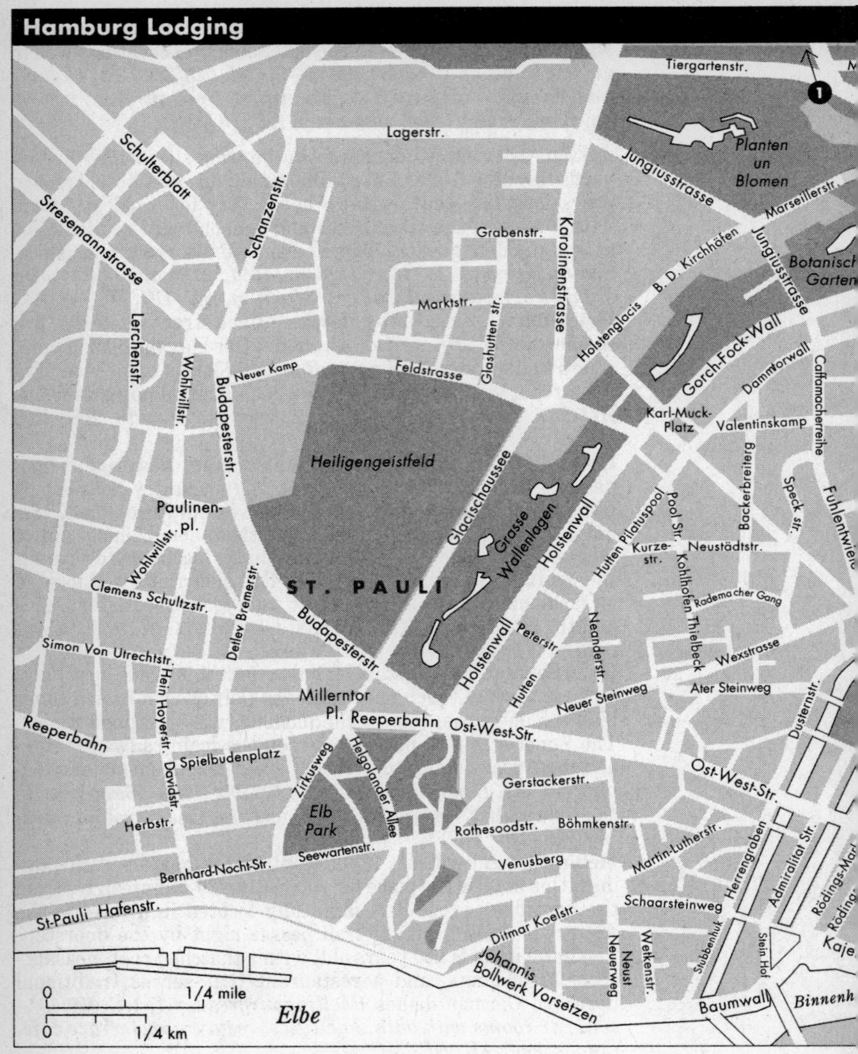

Alameda, **6**
Atlantic Hotel Kempinksi, **10**
Aussen Alster, **14**
Baseler Hof, **7**
Garden Hotel Pöseldorf, **9**
Hotel Abtei, **4**
Hotel-Garni Mittelweg, **5**
Hotel-Pension am Nonnensteig, **1**
Hotel-Pension bei der Esplanade, **6**
Hotel Senator, **13**
Kronprinz, **12**
Mellingburger Schleuse, **3**
Nippon Hotel, **16**
SAS Plaza Hotel, **2**
Steens Hotel, **11**
Vier Jahreszeiten, **8**
Wedina, **15**

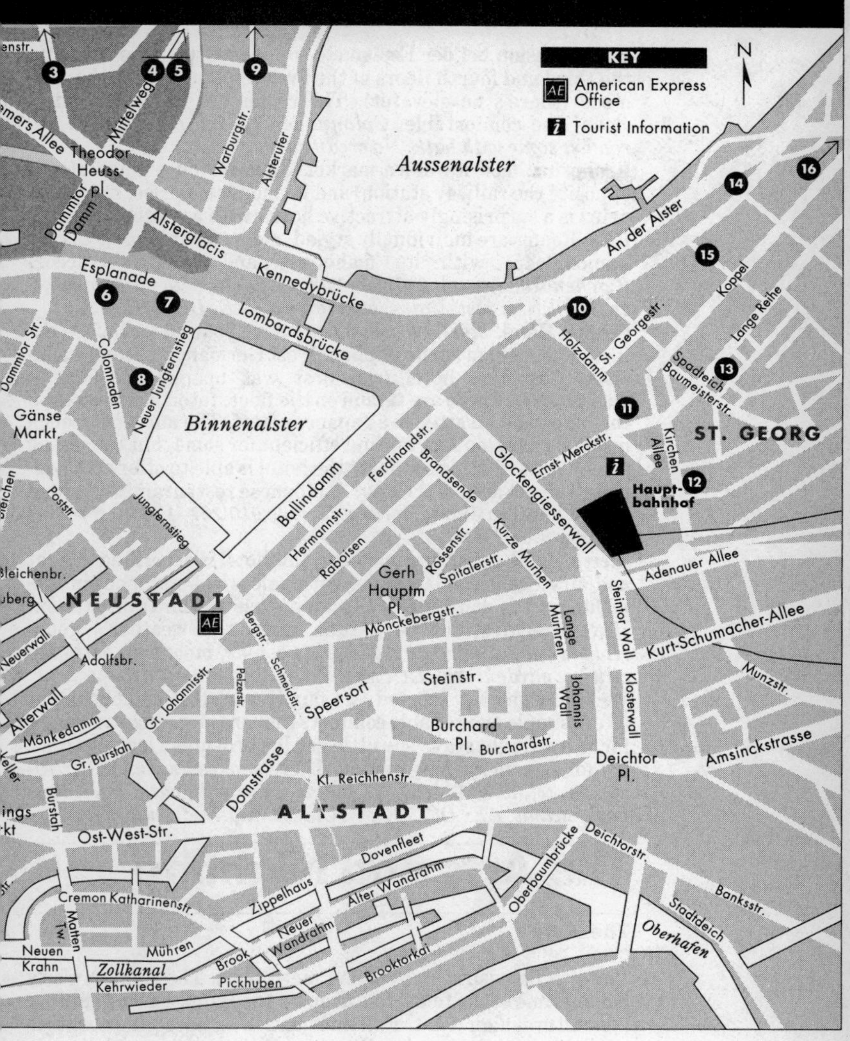
KEY
American Express Office
Tourist Information
N
Aussenalster
Binnenalster
NEUSTADT
ALTSTADT
ST. GEORG
Theodor Heuss-pl.
Mittelweg
Warburgstr.
Alsterufer
Dammtor Damm
Alsterglacis
Esplanade
Kennedybrücke
Lombardsbrücke
An der Alster
Dammtor Str.
Colonnaden
Neuer Jungfernstieg
Gänse Markt.
Jungfernstieg
Ballindamm
Poststr.
Bleichenbr.
Neuerwall
Adolfsbr.
Alterwall
Mönkedamm
Gr. Burstah
Burstah
Gr. Johannisstr.
Bergstr.
Pelzerstr.
Schmiedstr.
Speersort
Domstrasse
Hermannstr.
Raboisen
Ferdinandstr.
Brandsende
Rossenstr.
Gerh Hauptm Pl.
Mönckebergstr.
Spitalerstr.
Kurze Murhen
Lange Murhen
Glockengiesserwall
Ernst-Merckstr.
Holzdamm
St. Georgestr.
Koppel
Lange Reihe
Spadteich
Baumeisterstr.
Kirchen Allee
Haupt-bahnhof
Adenauer Allee
Steintor Wall
Kurt-Schumacher-Allee
Munzstr.
Steinstr.
Johannis Wall
Klosterwall
Burchard Pl.
Burchardstr.
Deichtor Pl.
Amsinckstrasse
Kl. Reichhenstr.
Ost-West-Str.
Dovenfleet
Deichtorstr.
Oberbaumbrücke
Zippelhaus
Alter Wandrahm
Neuer Wandrahm
Cremon
Katharinenstr.
Matten Tw.
Neuen Krahn
Mühren
Brook
Zollkanal
Kehrwieder
Pickhuben
Brooktorkai
Stadtdeich
Banksstr.
Oberhafen

Nonnenstieg 11, tel. 040/473–869. 30 rooms with bath. No credit cards.

Hotel-Pension bei der Esplanade. Bei der Esplanade takes up the third and fourth floors of the building that houses the Alameda (there's no elevator). The rooms are basic but quiet, clean, and comfortable. *Colonnaden 45, tel. 040/342–961. 20 rooms, some with bath. No credit cards.*

Kronprinz. For its down-market position (on a busy street opposite the railway station) and its moderate price, the Kronprinz is a surprisingly attractive hotel, with a whiff of five-star flair. Rooms are individually styled, modern but homey; ask for number 45, with its mahogany and red-plush decor. *Kirchenallee 46, tel. 040/243–258. 69 rooms with bath or shower. Facilities: restaurant, bar, terrace. AE, DC, MC, V.*

Nippon Hotel. You'll be asked to remove your shoes before entering your room at the Nippon, West Germany's second exclusively Japanese hotel (the first was opened recently in Düsseldorf). There are tatami on the floor, futon mattresses on the beds, and an attentive Japanese staff. The authentic touch might be a bit *too* spartan and efficient for some, but by cutting some Western-style comforts the hotel is able to offer good value in a smart area of the city. A Japanese restaurant was added to the hotel in 1990. *Hofweg 75, tel. 040/227–1140. 42 rooms with bath. AE, DC, MC, V.*

Steens Hotel. Small and intimate, this hotel is decorated in light and airy Scandinavian style, with pale wood and modern furnishings. It's conveniently located close to the train station. Have breakfast in the garden when the weather's good. *Holzdamm 43, tel. 040/244–642. 11 rooms, most with bath. Facilities: garden. AE, DC, MC, V.*

Wedina. Centrally located and family-run, this establishment offers simple and reliable comforts that are more than adequate for an overnight stay. The little garden provides a leafy retreat; try for a room opening onto it. There's no restaurant. *Gurlittstr. 23, tel. 040/243–011. 27 rooms, most with bath. Facilities: pool, sauna. AE, DC, MC, V. Closed mid-Dec.–mid-Feb.*

The Arts and Nightlife

The Arts

The arts flourish in this elegant metropolis. The Hamburg city ballet is one of the finest in Europe—the Ballet Festival in July is a cultural high point. Full information on upcoming events is available in the magazine *Hamburger Vorschau*—pick it up in tourist offices and most hotels for DM 2.30—and the magazine *Szene Hamburg*, sold at newsstands throughout the city for DM 4.

A number of travel agencies sell tickets for plays, concerts, and the ballet. Alternatively, try any of the following ticket agencies in the downtown area: **Theaterkasse im Alsterhaus** (Jungfernstieg 16, tel. 040/352664); **Theaterkasse Central** (Gerhart-Hauptmann-Pl., tel. 040/324–312); and the charming boutique **Garlic**, at Grosse-Bleichen 36 (tel. 040/342–742).

Theater The city has a full program of theater year-round, though you'll need to understand German well to get the most of the productions. Leading theaters include: **Deutsches Schauspielhaus** (Kirchenallee 39, tel. 040/248–713), probably the most beautiful theater in the city, lavishly restored to its full 19th-century opulence in the early 1980s and now the most important venue in Hamburg for classical and modern theater; **Thalia-Theater** (Alstertor, tel. 040/322–666), presenting a varied program of plays old and new; the newly reopened Flora Theater, where at press time *Phantom of the Opera* continues in a long run (corner of Alsenstr. and Stresemannstr., tel. 040/2707–5270); and **Ohnsorg-Theater** (Grosse Bleichen 23, tel. 040/350–80321), presenting works in the local dialect, which even those who know German are likely to find largely incomprehensible. The **English Theater** (Lerchenfeld 14, tel. 040/227–7089) may provide the antidote: As the name suggests, all productions are in English.

Concerts The **Musikhalle** (Karl-Muck-Pl., tel. 040/346–920) is Hamburg's most important concert hall; both the Hamburg Philharmonic and the Hamburg Symphony Orchestra appear regularly. Visiting orchestras from overseas are also showcased here. The **Norddeutscher Rundfunk Studio 10** (Oberstr., tel. 040/413–2504) has regular concerts by the symphony orchestra and guest appearances by visiting musicians.

Opera and Ballet The **Hamburgische Staatsoper** (Dammtorstr. 28, tel. 040/351–721) is one of the most beautiful theaters in the country and the leading northern German venue for top-class opera and ballet. The **Operettenhaus** (Spielbudenpl. 1, tel. 040/270–75270) puts on light opera and musicals.

Film The **British Council Film Club** (Rothenbaumchaussee 34, tel. 040/446057) shows films in English.

Nightlife

The Reeperbahn Whether you think it sordid or sexy, the Reeperbahn in the St. Pauli district is as central to the Hamburg scene as are the classy shops along Jungfernstieg. A walk down Herbertstrase (men only, no women or children permitted), just two blocks south of the Reeperbahn, can be quite an eye-opener. Here prostitutes sit displayed in windows as they await customers. Nearby on Grosse Freiheit (an appropriate name: it means Great Freedom) are a number of the better-known sex-show clubs. **Colibri** is at number 34, **Safari** at number 24, and **Salambo** at number 11. They cater to the package-tour trade as much as to those on the prowl by themselves. Prices are high. If you order anything to drink, ask to see the price list first (legally, it has to be on display), and pay as soon as you're served. Don't expect much to happen here before 10 PM.

Jazz Clubs The jazz scene in Hamburg is thriving as never before. There are more than 100 venues and few nights when you won't have a wide selection from which to choose. Among the leading clubs are **Birdland** (Gärtnerstr. 122, tel. 040/405–277), featuring everything from traditional New Orleans sounds to avant-garde electronic noises; **Cotton Club** (Alter Steinweg 10, tel. 040/343878), Hamburg's oldest jazz club; **Fabrik** (Barnerstr. 36, tel. 040/391079), which offers Sunday-morning *Früschoppen* (brunch) concerts at 11 (they're always packed, so get here early); and **Pö'dingsmarkt/Riverkasematten** (Rödingsmarkt/Ost-West-Str., tel. 040/367–963), one of the oldest and biggest jazz cellars in Germany, presenting a wide range of concerts.

Discos **Hans-Albers-Platz** and the surrounding area is the young folks' scene. **Die Insel** (Alsterufer 35, tel. 040/410–6955), a disco and a restaurant in one, is one of the biggest night spots in Hamburg. Prices can be high, but it's always chic. Pricey, too, is **Top of the Town,** an elegant disco night spot on the 26th floor of the SAS Plaza Hotel (Marseillerstr. 2, tel. 040/3502–3210). **Trinity** (Eimbütteler Chaussee 5, tel. 040/439–8094; dress code: jacket, no sneakers) has an amazing laser show at midnight. **Skyy** (Spielbudenpl.) is tiny and plays African music.

Excursions

Tour 1: Ahrensburg

One of Schleswig-Holstein's major attractions is the romantic 16th-century **Schloss Ahrensburg** (Ahrensburg Castle), in the town of Ahrensburg, about 25 kilometers (16 miles) northeast of Hamburg. Ahrensburg itself is mainly a commuter town, home to about 27,000 people. The magnificent castle and nearby **Bredenbecker Teich** lake make it worth a visit—it's an ideal day's excursion.

Getting There **By Car:** Take the A-1 Autobahn for 25 kilometers (15 miles), and get off at the Ahrensburg exit. Alternatively, you can take Bundestrasse B-75.

By Train: Take the S-bahn line S-4 to Ahrensburg or the U-bahn line U-1 to Ahrensburg-Ost.

Exploring Surrounded by lush parkland on the banks of the Hunnau, Schloss Ahrensburg, a whitewashed-brick, moated Renaissance castle, stands much as it did when it was constructed at the end of the 16th century. Originally built by Count Peter Rantzau, it changed hands in 1759 and was remodeled inside by its new owner. The interior was again altered in the mid-19th century and recently underwent renovation.

Inside are period furniture and paintings, fine porcelain, and exquisite crystal. On the grounds stands a simple 16th-century church erected at the same time as the castle, although the west tower was completed later and Baroque alterations were made in the 18th century. The church is nestled between two rows of 12 almshouses, or *Gottesbuden* (God's cottages). *Admission: DM 3. Open Tues.–Sun. 10–12:30 and 1:30–5.*

Tour 2: Altes Land

The marshy **Altes Land** extends 30 kilometers (19 miles) west from Hamburg along the south bank of the Elbe River to the town of Stade. This traditional fruit-growing region is dotted with huge half-timbered farmhouses and crisscrossed by canals. The fertile land is a popular hiking spot, especially in spring, when the apple and cherry trees are in blossom. Some of the prettiest walks take you along the dikes running next to the Rivers Este and Lühe. Much of the territory is best covered on foot, so wear your walking shoes. You may want to bring a picnic lunch as well.

Getting There **By Car:** Take B-73 west from Harburg.

By Ferry: Ferries depart from the Landungsbrücken boat landing in the St. Pauli district of Hamburg every hour between

9 and 5 from May to September. Take the ferry to Cranz or Lühe.

Exploring From the dock at **Cranz,** walk south into the suburb of **Neunfelde** and visit the Baroque St. Pancras Church, with its unusual painted barrel roof. The altar inside was built in 1688, and the organ, dating from the same period, was designed by Arp Schnitger, an organ builder and local farmer.

The village of **Jork** in Lower Saxony lies some 9 kilometers (5 miles) on foot to the west of Neunfelde, just beyond the confluence of the Este and Elbe rivers. Stroll through Jork and take in the early 18th-century church and decorative farmhouses. The old windmill in nearby **Borstel** is worth a short detour.

Lühe is the ferry docking point that's closest to the town of Stade, but be prepared to walk about 13 kilometers (8 miles) to reach it. Stade lies on the west edge of the Altes Land on the River Schwinge and was once a member of the Hanseatic League of trading towns. Four times the size of Jork, with a population of 45,000, Stade is notable for the ruins of a rampart wall around the Altstadt (Old Town); it also contains the obligatory half-timbered houses.

16 Berlin

Including Potsdam and Magdeburg

Introduction

Since autumn 1989 Berlin has been in the headlines as the focal point and touchstone of a reuniting Germany, culminating in the historic vote on June 20, 1991, by the German parliament to make the city once again the seat of the German government. Thus ends one of the great geographic and political anomalies of the 20th century: a city split in two by a 12-foot-high concrete wall, with its larger western half an island of capitalist democracy, surrounded by an East Germany run by hard-line Stalinist Communists. Built in 1961 at the height of the Cold War, the Berlin Wall symbolized the separation of two distinctly different political and economic systems. Ironically, though, it also became a major tourist attraction, where viewing platforms along the western side enabled visitors to see the battlefront-like No Man's Land, guarded by soldiers and peppered with deadly mines and booby traps. The Wall's demolition cast it once more as a symbol: this time, though, a symbol of the change sweeping over former Iron Curtain countries. Two large chunks of the Wall have been left standing as reminders of the grim past.

Berlin actually began as two cities, more than 750 years ago. Museum Island, on the Spree River, was once called Cölln, while the mainland city was always known as Berlin. As early as the 1300s, Berlin prospered from its location at the crossroads of important trade routes, and it became filled with merchants and artisans of every description. After the ravages of the Thirty Years' War (1618–48), Berlin rose to power as the seat of the Brandenburg dynasty, and 200 years later when the Brandenburgian and Prussian realms united under the Hohenzollerns, Berlin was the chosen capital. The 1701 coronation of the enlightened ruler King Friedrich II—also known as Frederick the Great—set off a renaissance in the city, especially in the construction of academic institutions such as the Academy of Arts and the Academy of Sciences.

The Prussian Empire, especially under Count Bismarck in the late 19th century, proved to be the dominant force in unifying the many independent German principalities. Berlin maintained its status as the German capital throughout the German Empire (1871–1918), the post–World War I Weimar Republic (1919–1933), and Hitler's Third Reich (1933–1945). In the 1920s and early '30s the city also served as an important European social and cultural capital, tinged with a reputation for decadence. But during World War II, acting as the Nazi headquarters, it was bombed to smithereens—at the end of hostilities there was more rubble in Berlin than in all other German cities combined. Most of what you see there today has been built, or rebuilt, since 1945.

With the division of Germany after World War II, Berlin also was partitioned, with American, British, and French troops in the districts to the west, the Soviet Union's forces to the east. After the Potsdam Agreement in 1945, the three western zones of occupation gradually merged into one, becoming West Berlin, while the Soviet-controlled eastern zone defiantly remained separate. In 1948, in an attempt to force the Western Allies to relinquish their stake in the city, the U.S.S.R. set up a blockade cutting off all overland supply routes from the West. The Western Allies countered by mounting the Berlin Airlift, during which some 750,000 flights delivering 2 million tons of goods kept Berlin alive for most of a fateful year, until the Soviets finally lifted the blockade. As peace conferences repeatedly failed to resolve the question of Germany's division, in 1949 the Soviet Union established East Berlin as the capital of its new puppet state in East Germany. West Berlin was not technically part of the West Germany Republic, though it was clearly tied to its legal and economic system. The division of the city was emphasized even more in 1961, when the East Germans constructed the infamous Berlin Wall.

With the Wall now on the junk pile of history, access to the eastern part of the city is easy, and visitors can at last appreciate the qualities that mark the city as a whole. Its particular charm has always lay in its spaciousness, its trees and greenery, its racy atmosphere, and the ease with which you could reach the lakes and forests within its perimeter. It is a vast city, laid out on an epic scale—West Berlin alone is four times the size of Paris. Whole towns and villages are inlaid into the countryside beyond the downtown area. The really stunning parts of the prewar capital are in the eastern sector, with its grand boulevards and monumental buildings, the classical Brandenburg Gate, and the stately tree-lined avenue of Unter den Linden.

What really makes Berlin special, however, are the intangibles—the spirit and bounce of the city. Here is life in a pressure cooker, life on the edge—literally and figuratively. Berliners of whatever age are survivors; they have lived with adversity all their lives, and have managed to do so with a mordant wit and cynical acceptance of life as it is rather than the way one hopes it might be.

Berliners are brash, no-nonsense types, who speak German with their own racy dialect. Their high-voltage energy is invariably attributed to the bracing Berlin air, the renowned *Berliner Luft*. Crisis has been a way of life here for as long as anyone can remember. "To survive with a measure of style and humor" could serve as the city's theme.

Essential Information

More than three years after the official unification of the two Germanys, the nuts-and-bolts work of joining up the two halves is by no means complete, and uncertainties still abound. We have given addresses, telephone numbers, and other logistical details based on the best available information, but please understand that changes are taking place at a furious pace in everything from postal codes and telephone numbers to street names. At press time (early summer 1992), callers from West Berlin to East Berlin dial "9" instead of the "02" city code. Callers from East Berlin to West Berlin dial "849" instead of the "030" city code. These procedures apply only to calls within Berlin.

Important Addresses and Numbers

Tourist Information The **Verkehrsamt Berlin** (main tourist office) is located in the heart of the city in the Europa-Center (tel. 030/262–6031). If you want materials on the city before your trip, write **Verkehrsamt Berlin Europa-Center** (D-1000 Berlin 30). For information on the spot, the office is open daily 7:30 AM–10:30 PM. There are also offices at **Tegel Airport** (tel. 030/410–13145; open daily 8 AM–11 PM); **Bahnhof Zoo** train station (tel. 030/313–9063; open daily 8 AM–11 PM); and at the former **Dreilinden** border crossing (tel. 030/803–9057; open daily 8 AM–11 PM). Berlin has an information center especially for women, offering help with accommodations and information on upcoming events. Contact **Fraueninfothek Berlin** (Leibizstr. 57, tel. 030/324–5078; open Tues.–Sat. 9–9, Sun. and public holidays 9–3).

The main office of the **Reisebüro** (the former East German tourist office) is at Alexanderplatz 5, (tel. 030/212–4675 or 030/210–4209; open Mon.–Fri. 8 AM–8 PM, Sat. 9–6). There's another branch at **Schönefeld Airport** (tel. 030/687–8248).

For information on all aspects of the city, pick up a copy of *Berlin Turns On,* free from any tourist office.

Embassies and Consulates **United States Embassy** (Neustädtische Kirchstr. 4–5, tel: 238–5174); **United States Consulate** (Clayallee 170, tel. 030/832–4087); **British Consulate** (Uhlandstr. 7–8, tel. 030/309–5292).

Following the unification of the city, the American and British embassies in former East Berlin have taken on the character of information centers. The **American** office is still at Neustädtische Kirchstrasse 4–5 (tel. 030/220–2741) and the **British** office remains at Unter den Linden 32–34 (tel. 030/220–2431). **Canada** has a Consulate-General at the Europacenter (tel. 030/2611161).

Emergencies **Police** (tel. 030/110). **Ambulance and emergency medical attention** (tel. 030/310–031). **Dentist** (tel. 030/1141 or after 9 PM, tel. 030/892–0379). **Pharmacies** in Berlin offer late-night service on a rotation basis. Every pharmacy displays a notice indicating the location of the nearest shop with evening hours. For emergency pharmaceutical assistance, call 030/1141 or 030/247033.

English-language Bookstores **Marga Schoeller** (Knesebeckstr. 33, tel. 030/881–1112). **Buchhandlung Kiepert** (Hardenbergstr. 4–5, tel. 030/331–0090).

Travel Agencies **American Express Reisebüro** (Kurfürstendamm 11, tel. 030/882–7575). **American Lloyd** (Kurfürstendamm 36, tel. 030/883–7081).

Car Rental **Avis** (Tegel Airport, tel. 030/410–13148); Budapesterstr. 43, Am Europa-Center, tel. 030/261–1881); Haus der Reise, Alexanderplatz 5, tel. 030/2125575.
Europcar (Kurfurstenstr. 101, tel. 030/213–7097).
Hertz (Tegel Airport, tel. 030/410–13315; Budapesterstr. 39, tel. 030/261–1053).

Arriving and Departing by Plane

Airlines flying to West Berlin's **Tegel Airport** from major U.S. and European cities include United, TWA, Air France, British Airways, Lufthansa, Euro-Berlin, and some charter companies. Because of increased air traffic following unification, the former military airfield at Tempelhof is being used increasingly. Despite substantial government subsidies, domestic fares are high. Tegel Airport is only 6 kilometers (4 miles) from the downtown area, and Tempelhof is even closer. For information on arrival and departure times for Tegel, call 030/41011.

East Berlin's **Schönefeld Airport** is about 24 kilometers (15 miles) outside the downtown area. It is used principally by Soviet and Eastern European airlines, although with the increase in flights to Tegel, it's been taking more and more charter traffic. For information on arrival and departure times, call 02/672–4031.

Between the Airport and Downtown Blue airport bus number 109 runs at 10-minute intervals between Tegel and downtown via Kurfürstendamm (the main avenue), Bahnhof Zoologischer (the main train station), and Budapesterstrasse. The total trip takes 30 minutes; fare is DM 3. Expect to pay about DM 20 for the same trip by taxi. If you rent a car at the airport, take the Stadtautobahn (there are signs), the highway into Berlin. The Halensee exit leads to Kurfürstendamm (Ku'damm for short).

From Schönefeld, a shuttle bus leaves every 10–15 minutes for the nearby S-bahn station; S-bahn trains leave every 20 minutes for the Friedrichstrasse station downtown. A regular city bus also leaves every 10 or 15 minutes for the West Berlin Rudow subway station. A taxi ride from the airport takes about 40 minutes. By car, follow the signs for "Stadtzentrum Berlin."

Arriving and Departing by Train, Bus, and Car

By Train There are five major rail routes to Berlin from the western half of the country (from Hamburg, Hannover, Köln, Frankfurt, and Nürnberg), and the network is set to expand to make eastern German territory more accessible. At press time, trains were being run jointly by the former East German Deutsche Reichsbahn (DR) and former West Germany's Deutsche Bundesbahn (DB), and reduced-price DB tickets are accepted. Check out the 10-day "Berlin Saver Ticket," sold at West German stations; it offers reductions of 33%. Trains from western Germany arrive at Berlin's main terminus, Bahnhof Zoologischer Garten (Bahnhof Zoo). The U-bahn (subway) and S-bahn (suburban railroad) stop here, too. East Berlin's chief stations are at Friedrichstrasse or the Ostbanhof. For details, call **Deutsche Bundesbahn Information** (tel. 030/19419) or **Deutsche Reichsbahn** (tel. 030/31102116); **reservations** (tel. 030/311022112).

By Bus Buses are slightly cheaper than trains; Berlin is linked by bus to 170 European cities. The main station is at the corner of Masurenallee and Messedam. Reserve through DER (state), commercial travel agencies, or the station itself. For information, call 030/301–8028.

By Car The "transit corridor" roads linking former West Germany with West Berlin are still there, but the strict restrictions that once confined foreign motorists driving through East Germany have vanished, and today you can travel through the country at will. Expressways link Berlin with the eastern German cities of Magdeburg, Leipzig, Rostock, Dresden, and Frankfurt-Oder. At press time, speed restrictions of 130 kilometers per hour (80 miles per hour) still applied, and you must carry your driver's license, car registration, and insurance documents with you.

Getting Around

By Public Transportation Berlin is too large to be explored on foot. To compensate, the city has one of the most efficient public transportation systems in Europe, a smoothly integrated network of subway (U-bahn) and elevated (S-bahn) train lines, buses, trams (in East Berlin only), and even a ferry (across the Wannsee Lake), making every part of the city easily accessible. There's also an all-night bus service, indicated by the letter "N" next to route numbers. In summer, there are excursion buses linking the downtown area with the most popular recreational areas.

A DM 3 ticket (DM 2 for children) covers the entire system for two hours and allows you to make an unlimited number of changes between trains and buses. The best deal for visitors who plan to travel extensively around the city is the **Berlin Ticket,** valid for 24 hours and good for all trains and buses; it costs DM 12 (DM 6 for children). A six-day pass allowing unlimited travel on all city buses and trains between Monday and Saturday costs DM 28. If you plan to visit the Wannsee Lake, buy the **combined day ticket,** good for the entire network and the excursion boats of the Stern- und Kreisschiffahrt line; it costs DM 18.50 (DM 9.30 for children). If you are just making a short trip, buy a **Kurzstreckentarif.** It allows you to ride six bus stops or three U-bahn or S-bahn stops for DM 2 (DM 1.20 for children). Buy it in packs of five for the best value (DM 7 adults, DM 5 children). Finally, there's a ticket good only for rides along the Ku'damm on buses 119 and 129; it costs DM 1.

All regular tickets are available from vending machines at U-bahn and S-bahn stations. Punch your ticket into the red machine on the platform. The Berlin Ticket and the combined day ticket can only be bought from the main BVG ticket offices at the Bahnhof Zoo station and at the Kleistpark U-bahn station. For information, either call the **BVG** (Berliner Verkehrsbetriebe, tel. 030/216–5088) or go to the information office on Hardenbergplatz, directly in front of the Bahnhof Zoo train station.

The fare structure now covers transportation systems for both parts of Berlin, although cheap, subsidized tickets are still sold to East Berlin residents. Don't be tempted to buy one if you're traveling in East Berlin (it's difficult to do that anyway, because East Berliners normally have to show their identity documents in order to take advantage of the special fare); the fine is hefty if unauthorized travelers are found in possession of subsidized tickets. It doesn't help, either, to plead ignorance as a foreigner. For visitors and West Berlin residents, the fares are the same in both halves of the now-united city.

By Taxi Fares start at DM 3.40 and increase by DM 1.69 per kilometer (DM 2.69 after midnight). There's an additional charge of 50 pfennigs per piece of luggage. Figure on paying around DM 10 for a ride the length of Ku'damm. Hail cabs in the street or order one by calling 030/691–001, 030/6902, 030/216–60, 030/261–026, 030/240024, or 030/240–202, or 030/3646 in East Berlin.

By Bike Bicycling is popular in Berlin. While it's not recommended in the downtown area, it's ideal in outlying areas. Some bike paths have been set up and many stores that rent bikes carry the Berlin biker's atlas to help you find them. Outfits renting bicycles include: **Fahrradbüro** Berlin (Hauptstr. 146, tel. 030/

Berlin Public Transit System

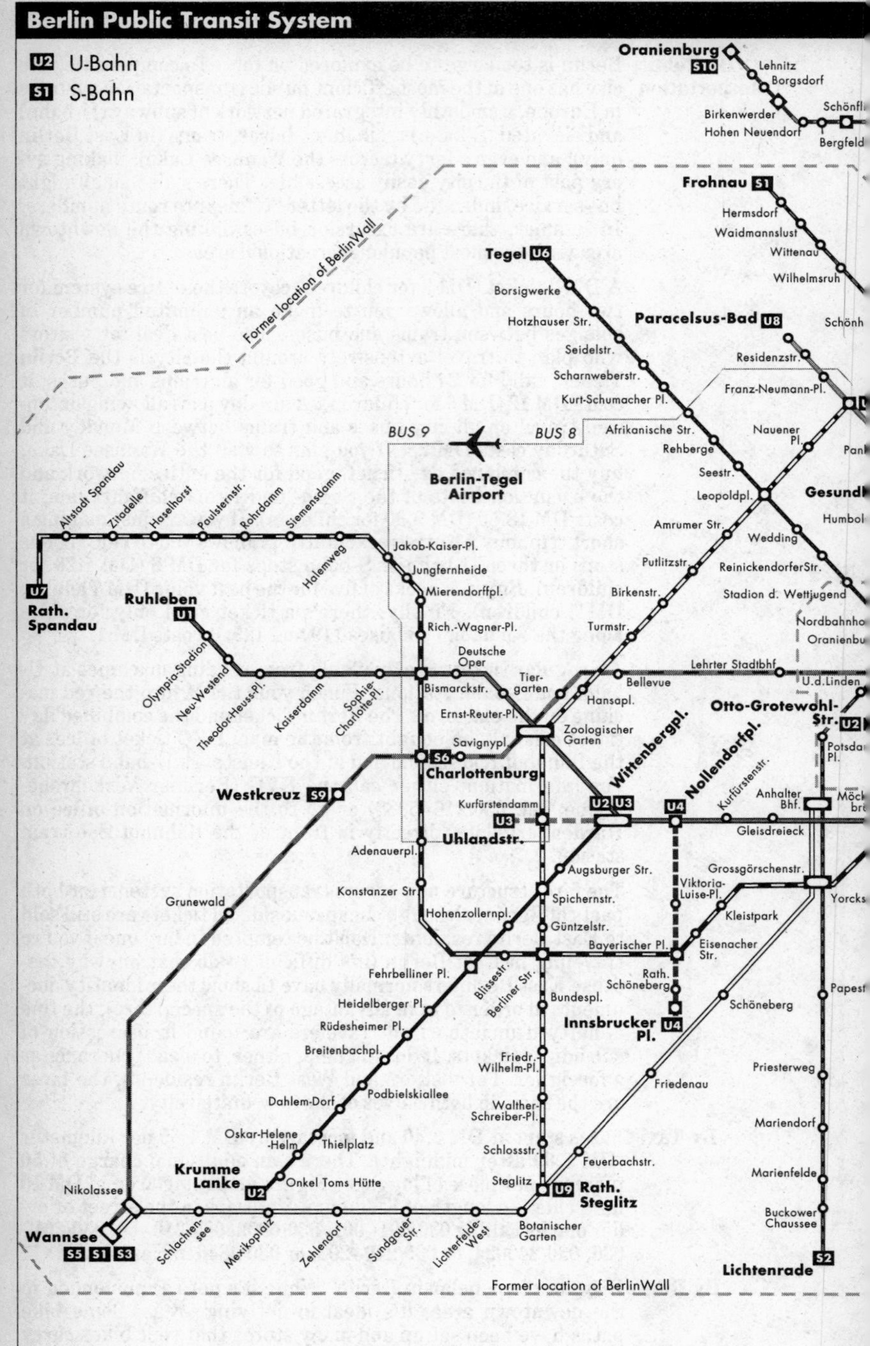

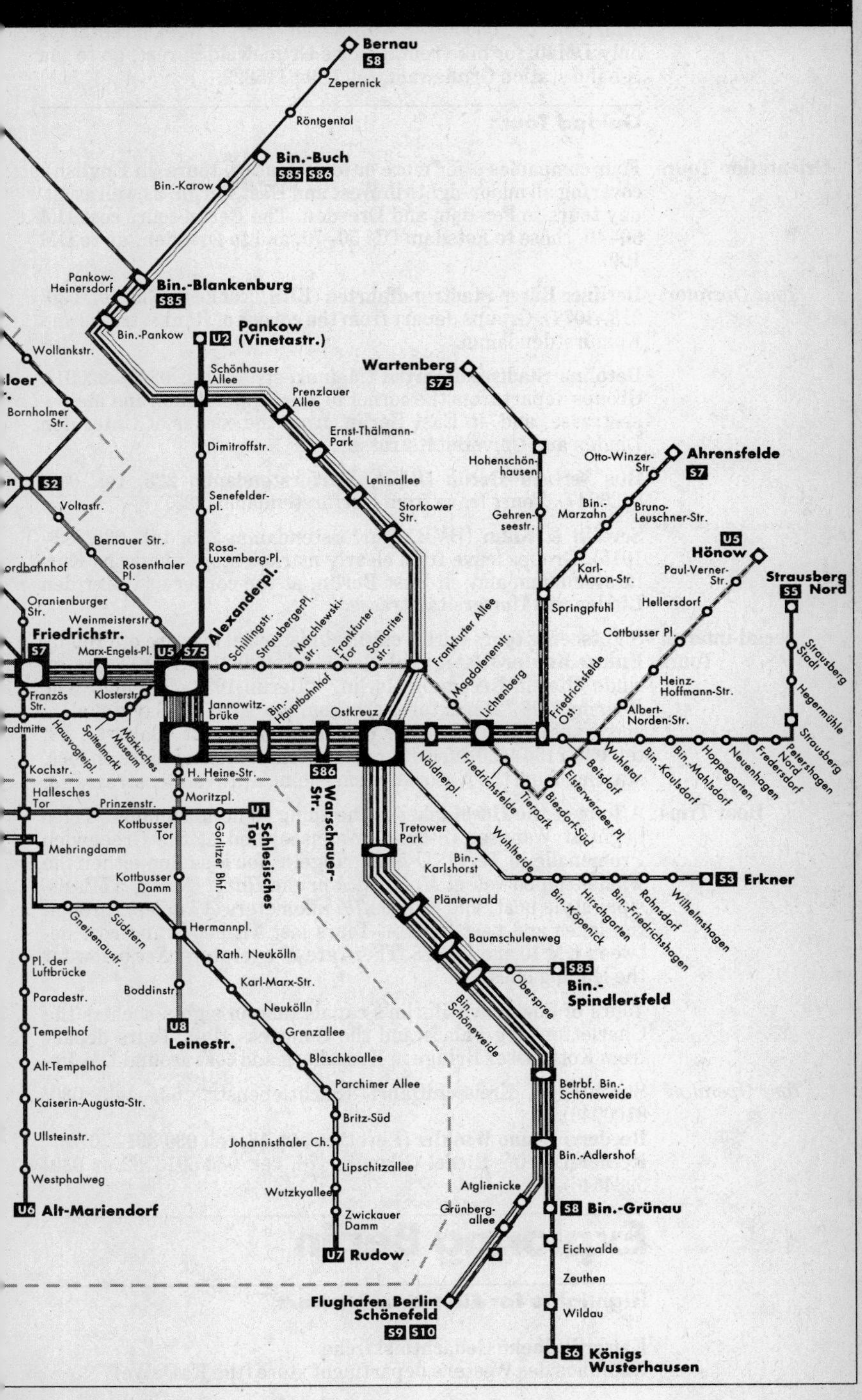
Bernau
S8
Zepernick
Röntgental
Bln.-Buch
S85 S86
Bln.-Karow
Pankow-Heinersdorf
Bln.-Blankenburg
S85
Bln.-Pankow
Pankow (Vinetastr.)
U2
Wollankstr.
Bornholmer Str.
Schönhauser Allee
Prenzlauer Allee
Ernst-Thälmann-Park
Leninallee
Storkower Str.
Dimitroffstr.
Senefelder-pl.
Rosa-Luxemberg-Pl.
Wartenberg
S75
Hohenschön-hausen
Gehren-seestr.
Otto-Winzer-Str.
Ahrensfelde
S7
Bln.-Marzahn
Bruno-Leuschner-Str.
U5
Hönow
Paul-Verner-Str.
Karl-Maron-Str.
Springpfuhl
Hellersdorf
Strausberg Nord
S5
S2
Voltastr.
Bernauer Str.
Rosenthaler Pl.
Oranienburger Str.
Weinmeisterstr.
Friedrichstr.
S7
Marx-Engels-Pl.
U5
S75
Alexanderpl.
Schillingstr.
StrausbergerPl.
Marchlewski-str.
Frankfurter Tor
Samariter str.
Frankfurter Allee
Magdalenenstr.
Lichtenberg
Friedrichsfelde Ost
Cottbusser Pl.
Heinz-Hoffmann-Str.
Albert-Norden-Str.
Strausberg Stadt
Hegermühle
Strausberg
Französ Str.
Klosterstr.
Jannowitz-brüke
Bln.-Hauptbahnhof
Ostkreuz
Hausvogteipl.
Spittelmarkt
Märkisches Museum
H. Heine-Str.
Moritzpl.
S86
Warschauer-Str.
Nöldnerpl.
Friedrichsfelde
Tierpark
Biesdorf-Süd
Elsterwerdeer Pl.
Beisdorf
Wuhletal
Bln.-Kaulsdorf
Bln.-Mahlsdorf
Hoppegarten
Neuenhagen
Fredersdorf
Petershagen Nord
Kochstr.
Hallesches Tor
Prinzenstr.
U1
Schlesisches Tor
Kottbusser Tor
Görlitzer Bhf.
Tretower Park
Bln.-Karlshorst
Wuhlheide
Erkner
S3
Mehringdamm
Kottbusser Damm
Bln.-Köpenick
Hirschgarten
Bln.-Friedrichshagen
Rahnsdorf
Wilhelmshagen
Plänterwald
Gneisenaustr.
Südstern
Hermannpl.
Baumschulenweg
Rath. Neukölln
S85
Bln.-Spindlersfeld
Oberspree
Pl. der Luftbrücke
Karl-Marx-Str.
Paradestr.
Boddinstr.
Neukölln
Tempelhof
U8
Leinestr.
Grenzallee
Bln.-Schöneweide
Alt-Tempelhof
Blaschkoallee
Parchimer Allee
Betrbf. Bln.-Schöneweide
Kaiserin-Augusta-Str.
Britz-Süd
Ullsteinstr.
Johannisthaler Ch.
Bln.-Adlershof
Westphalweg
Lipschitzallee
Atglienicke
U6
Alt-Mariendorf
Wutzkyallee
Grünberg-allee
S8
Bln.-Grünau
Zwickauer Damm
U7
Rudow
Eichwalde
Zeuthen
Flughafen Berlin Schönefeld
Wildau
S9 S10
S6
Königs Wusterhausen

784–5562) and **Räderwerk** (Körtestr. 14, by U-bahn station Südstern, tel. 030/691–8590), which offers a week's rental for only DM40; for bike rental in the Grunewald Forest, go to the S-bahn station Grunewald, tel. 030/8115829.

Guided Tours

Orientation Tours Four companies offer more or less identical tours (in English), covering all major sights in West and East Berlin, as well as all-day tours to Potsdam and Dresden. The Berlin tours cost DM 30–40, those to Potsdam DM 50–70, and to Dresden, up to DM 100.

Tour Operators **Berliner Bären Stadtrundfahrten** (BBS, Rankestr. 35, tel. 030/213–4077). Groups depart from the corner of Rankestrasse and Kurfürstdendamm.

Berolina Stadtrundfahrten (Meinekestr. 3, tel. 030/8822091). Groups depart from the corner of Kurfürstendamm and Meinekestrasse, and, in East Berlin, from the corner of Unter den Linden and Universitätstrasse.

Bus Verkehr Berlin (BVB, Kurfürstendamm 225, tel. 030/8826847). Tours leave from Kurfürstendamm 225.

Severin & Kühn (BVB, Kurfürstendamm 216, tel. 030/883–1015). Groups leave from clearly marked stops along the Kurfürstendamm and, in East Berlin, at the corner of Unter den Linden and Universitätstrasse.

Special-interest Tours Sightseeing tours with a cultural/historical bias are offered by **Kultur Kontor** (Savignypl. 9–10, tel. 030/310–888). Tours include "Berlin Becoming Berlin," "Berlin 1933–45," and "The Roaring '20s." Departures are from the corner of Savignyplatz and Kantstrasse. **Berliner Geschichtswerkstatt** (Goltzstr. 49, tel. 030/215–4450) also offers historical tours and tours on foot, starting from the Naturkundemuseum, at Invalidenstrasse 43.

Boat Trips A tour of the **Havel lakes** is the thing to do in summer. Trips begin at Wannsee (S-bahn: Wannsee) and at the Greenwich Promenade in Tegel (U-bahn: Tegel). You'll sail on either the whale-shaped vessel *Moby Dick* or the *Havel Queen*, a Mississippi-style boat, and cruise 27½ kilometers (17 miles) through the lakes and past forests. Tours last 4½ hours and cost between DM 10 and DM 15. There are 20 operators. *See* below for the leading ones.

Tours of downtown Berlin's **canals** take in sights such as the Charlottenburg Palace and the Congress Hall. Tours depart from Kottbusser Bridge in Kreuzberg and cost around DM 10.

Tour Operators **Stern- und Kreisschiffahrt** (Sachtlebenstr. 60, tel. 030/8100040).
Reederei Bruno Winkler (Levetzowstr. 16, tel. 030/391–7010).
Reederei Heinz Riedel (Planufer 78, tel. 030/6913782 or 030/6934646).

Exploring Berlin

Highlights for First-time Visitors

Kaiser Wilhelm Gedächtniskirche
Kaufhaus des Westens department store (the KaDeWe)

Zoologischer Garten
Haus am Checkpoint Charlie (Wall Museum)
Reichstag
Brandenburger Tor
Pergamon Museum
Gemäldegalerie, Dahlem
Schloss Charlottenburg
Ägyptisches Museum
Alexanderplatz

Tour 1: West Berlin

Numbers in the margin correspond to points of interest on the Berlin map.

Your tour of West Berlin begins on its best-known street, the
1 **Kurfürstendamm.** Berliners (and most visitors as well) refer to it affectionately as the Ku'damm. Its 2-mile length is lined with shops, department stores, art galleries, theaters, movie houses, hotels, and some 100 restaurants, bars, clubs, and sidewalk cafés. It bustles with shoppers and strollers most of the day and fairly far into the night. Traffic can remain heavy into the wee hours of the morning.

This busy thoroughfare was first laid out in the 16th century as the path by which Elector Joachim II of Brandenburg traveled from his palace on the Spree River to his hunting lodge in the Grunewald. The Kurfürstendamm (Elector's Causeway) was developed into a major route in the late 19th century on the initiative of Chancellor Bismarck, the "Iron Chancellor," who was the force behind the original unification of Germany.

The Ku'damm is much more important today than it was to prewar Berlin. It was a busy shopping street, but by no means the city's most elegant one, being fairly far removed from the heart of the city, which was on the opposite side of the Brandenburg Gate in what became East Berlin. The Ku'damm's prewar fame was tied mainly to the rowdy bars and dance halls that studded much of its length and its side streets. Some of these were really low-down dives, scenes of erotic circuses, where kinky sex was the norm.

Similar clubs, along with cabarets and avant-garde theaters, were set on and along side streets of the Friedrichstrasse, in East Berlin. While there's no nighttime action at all on the now dreary Friedrichstrasse, Ku'damm certainly has its share of *Kneipen*, the German term for friendly neighborhood bars.

Along with the rest of Berlin, the Ku'damm suffered severe wartime bombing. Almost half of its 245 late-19th-century buildings were destroyed in the 1940s. The remaining buildings were damaged in varying degrees. What you see today (as in most of Berlin) is either restored or was constructed during the past decades. While the street is frequently described as "glittering" and/or "sophisticated," there are those who are convinced that it has lost whatever real charm and flair it may once have possessed. But it is certainly the liveliest stretch of roadway in Berlin, East or West, and definitely where the action is.

The Ku'damm starts at the western end of the Breitscheidplatz, a large square on which several notable landmarks stand.
2 The ruins of the **Kaiser Wilhelm Gedächtniskirche** (Memorial Church), built between 1891 and 1895, stand as a dramatic re-

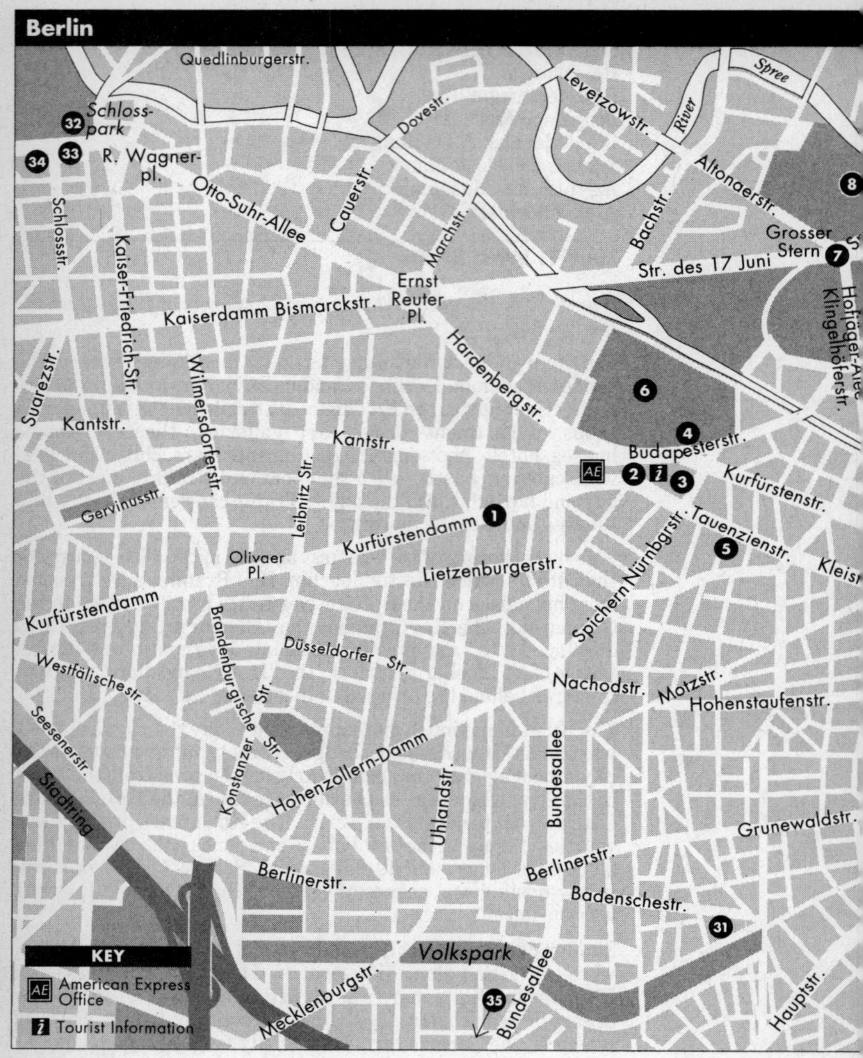

Ägyptisches Museum, **33**
Alexanderplatz, **25**
Altes Kammergericht, **14**
Antikenmuseum, **34**
Berlin Cathedral, **23**
Bertolt Brecht House and Museum, **28**
Brandenburger Tor, **11**
Checkpoint Charlie, **16**
Dahlem Museum Complex, **35**
Deutsche Staatsoper, **19**
Elefantor, **4**
Europa-Center, **3**
Fischerinsel, **26**
Gendarmenmarkt, **17**
Kaiser Wilhelm Gedächtniskirche, **2**
Kaufhaus des Westens, **5**
Kongresshalle, **9**
Kreuzberg, **30**
Kulturforum, **15**
Kurfürstendamm, **1**
Marienkirche, **24**
Märkisches Museum, **27**
Museum für Deutsche Geschichte, **21**
Museumsinsel, **22**
Palais Unter den Linden, **20**
Potsdamerplatz, **13**
Rathaus Schöneberg, **31**
Reichstag, **10**
St. Hedwig's Cathedral, **18**
Schloss Bellevue, **8**
Schloss Charlottenburg, **32**

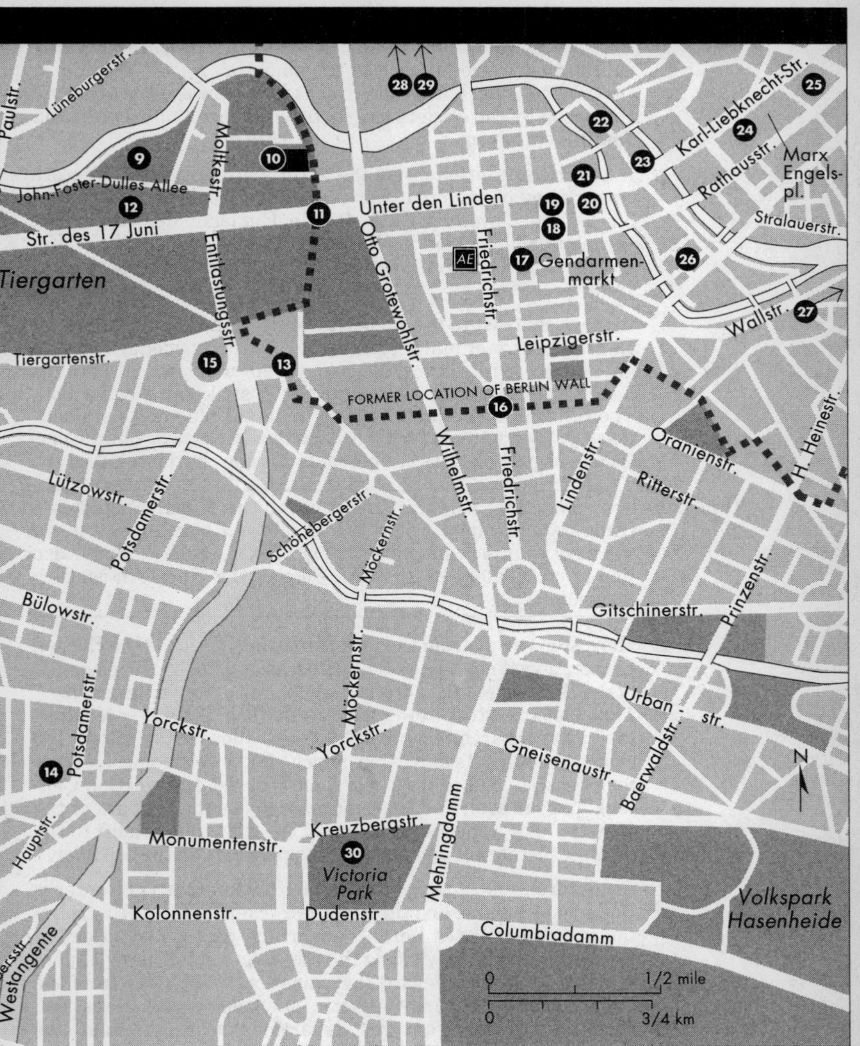

Siegessäule, **7**
Soviet Victory Memorial, **12**
Synagogue, **29**
Zoologischer Garten, **6**

minder of the war's destruction. The bell tower, now known as the "hollow tooth," is all that remains of this once-imposing church that was dedicated to the emperor, Kaiser Wilhelm I. On the hour, you'll hear the chimes in the tower play a melody composed by the emperor's grandson, Prince Louis Ferdinand von Hohenzollern.

A historic exhibition inside the tower features a religious cross constructed of nails that were recovered from the ashes of the burned-out Coventry Cathedral in England, destroyed in a German bombing raid in November 1940. *Kaiser Wilhelm Memorial Church. Admission free. Open Tues.–Sat. 10–6, Sun. 11–6.*

In stark contrast to the old bell tower is the adjoining Memorial Church and tower built in 1959–1961. This ultramodern octagonal church, with its myriad honeycomb windows, is perhaps best described by its nickname: the lipstick and powder box. The interior is dominated by the brilliant blue of its stained-glass windows, imported from Chartres in France. Church music and organ concerts are presented in the church regularly.

Time Out Set some time aside for a coffee at the **Einstein Stadtcafe** (Kurfürstendamm 67, near the Memorial Church), where you can have your pick among a variety of exotic coffees. You'll also find an art gallery on the first floor of this fine 19th-century mansion.

---

3 Mere steps away from the new Memorial Church is the **Europa Center,** a vast shopping and business complex on the east side of the Brietscheidplatz often described as a "city within a city." This 1960s 22-story tower block—dubbed "Pepper's Manhattan" after its architect, K. H. Pepper—houses more than 100 shops, restaurants and cafés, an ice rink, two cinemas, a theater, a casino, and the Verkehrsamt (Tourist Information Center). You can even find thermal baths above the car park at the very top. For a spectacular view of the city, take the lift to the i-Punkt restaurant and observation platform on the top floor.

Across from the entrance to the Tourist Information Center is
4 Budapesterstrasse and the **Elefantor** (Elephant Gate), which is the main entrance to Berlin's aquarium, part of the adjoining zoo complex. Before visiting the zoo, take a stroll along Tauenzienstrasse, the boulevard that runs southeast away from the corner of the Europa-Center. Tauenzienstrasse leads you
5 straight to Germany's largest department store, the **Kaufhaus des Westens** (Department Store of the West), known to Berliners as KaDeWe. An enormous selection of goods can be found on its six floors, but it is most renowned for its food and delicatessen counters, restaurants, champagne bars, and beer bars covering an entire floor. The KaDeWe is currently having an additional three floors added; work was scheduled to be completed by the end of 1992.

Go into the U-bahn station near KaDeWe on Wittenbergplatz. This subway station, Berlin's first, was built in 1913 and has recently been painstakingly restored. Take the train one stop to the Zoologischer Garten. This station, also known as Bahnhof Zoo (Zoo Station), also serves as West Berlin's main railway station.

6 Opposite the station is the entrance to the **Zoologischer Garten** (Zoological Gardens). Dating from 1841, it is the oldest zoo in Germany and is set in the southwestern corner of the 630-acre park called the Tiergarten (Animal Garden). The northern edge of the park is bounded by the Spree River, which flows from East Berlin. Even if you're not a zoo enthusiast, both the park and the very modern zoo offer much of interest.

After being destroyed during the Second World War, the zoo was carefully redesigned to create surroundings as close to the animals' natural environment as possible. The zoo houses more than 11,000 animals, and has been successful at breeding rare species. The zoo boasts the world's largest and most modern birdhouse, a terrarium renowned for its crocodiles, and an aquarium with more than 10,000 fish, reptiles, and amphibians. *Zoologischer Garten. Hardenbergpl. 8. Admission to zoo only: DM 7.50 adults, DM 4 children under 15. Combined tickets to zoo and aquarium: DM 12.50 adults, DM 6 children. Open daily 9–dusk.*

From the zoo, you can set off diagonally through the Tiergarten, which in the 17th century served as the hunting grounds of the Great Elector. The park suffered severe damage from World War II bombing raids. Later Berliners, desperate for fuel during the freezing winter of 1945–1946, cut down much of its ancient forest for firewood. Replanting began in 1949, and today's visitor will see a beautifully laid-out park with some 14 miles of footpaths and 6½ acres of lakes and ponds.

At the center of the park you'll approach the traffic intersection known as the Grosser Stern (Big Star), so called because five roads meet here. This is the park's highest point, and the site of
7 the **Siegessaüle** (Triumphal Column). This 227-foot-high granite, sandstone, and bronze column was originally erected in 1873 to commemorate the successful Prussian military campaigns; it was set up in front of the Reichstag, a ½ mile away. The column came close to being finished off by anarchists in 1921, after the collapse of the empire. Six kilos of explosives were placed in its stairwell, and the fuse was already sizzling when the bomb was discovered. In 1939, as Hitler was having Berlin redesigned according to his megalomaniacal plans, the column was moved to its present site. A climb of 285 steps up through the column to the observation platform affords splendid views across much of Berlin. *Siegessäule at Grosse Stern. Admission: DM 1.20 adults, 70 pf children under 14. Open Mon. 3–5:45, Tues.–Sun. 9–5:45.*

8 Follow the Spreeweg Road from the Grosser Stern to **Schloss Bellevue** (Bellevue Palace). Built on the Spree River in 1775 for Frederick the Great's youngest brother Prince Augustus-Ferdinand, it has served as the West German president's official residence in West Berlin from 1959 to the present, but will be vacated when the federal president moves to the former German Crown Prince's Palace on Unter-den-Linden in a few years. The 50-acre palace grounds have been transformed into a park with an English garden on its western edge. This park-within-a-park was originally dedicated by an English statesman, Anthony Eden, who later became one of Nazi Germany's staunchest political opponents. Berliners often refer to it jokingly as the Garden of Eden. *Schloss Bellevue Park. Open daily 8–dusk. Closed when the president is in residence.*

Leave the Schloss Bellevue and head east along the John-Foster-Dulles Allee, keeping the Spree River in sight on your left.
9 You'll soon arrive at the **Kongresshalle** (Congress Hall), a meeting and conference center that was a feat of engineering in its day. The hall was built in 1957 as the American contribution to the International Building Exhibition, Interbau. Its resemblance to an open oyster shell earned it the title "pregnant oyster." The roof collapsed in 1980 and has been rebuilt.

Rejoin John-Foster-Dulles Allee again and continue east to the
10 **Reichstag** (Parliament Building), which was erected in the late 19th century to house the Prussian parliament and later performed a similar function for the ill-fated Weimar Republic. The Reichstag was burned to a shell under mysterious circumstances on the night of February 28, 1933, an event that provided the Nazis with a convenient pretext for outlawing all opposition parties. After rebuilding, the Reichstag was again badly damaged in 1945 in the last Allied offensive of the war. Today the west wing houses a restaurant and a popular exhibition of German history since 1800. The Bundestag will once again be meeting in the Reichstag, but at press time the timetable had not yet been determined. *Reichstag Exhibition: Questions of German History in the Reichstag. Pl. der Republik. Admission free. Open Tues.–Sun. 10–5.*

Behind the Reichstag is the old line of the Berlin Wall, few traces of which now remain. It was here, at the end of Strasse des 17 Juni (June 17 Street), that visiting Western dignitaries as well as tourists stood on a wooden viewing platform to peek over the 3-foot-thick Wall into the No Man's Land separating the two political halves of Berlin. Crosses still dot the neighborhood and the banks of the Spree River adjoining the Reichstag—grim reminders of lives lost as East Germans tried to escape to the West after the barrier was built.

Just south of the Reichstag, where Strasse des 17 Juni meets Unter den Linden, is another monumental symbol of German
11 unity and of the long division of Berlin—the mighty **Brandenburger Tor** (Brandenburg Gate). Ever since the Wall was built the Brandenburger Tor, once the pride of imperial Berlin, was stranded in the eerie no-man's-land. When the Wall came down, it was the focal point of much celebrating, for this evocative symbol of Berlin was finally restored to all the people of the newly united city. The Brandenburger Tor is the only remaining gate of an original group of 14 built by Carl Langhans in 1788–1791, in virile classical style, as a triumphal arch for King Frederick Wilhelm II. The quadriga, a chariot drawn by four horses and driven by the Goddess of Peace, was added in 1793. The goddess was originally naked, but puritanical protesters persuaded the city fathers to clothe her in a sheath of sheet copper. Troops paraded through the gate after successful campaigns, the last time being in 1945 when victorious Red Army troops took Berlin. The upper part of the gate, together with its chariot and Goddess of Peace, were destroyed in the war, but in 1957 the original molds were discovered in West Berlin and a new quadriga was cast in copper and presented as a gift to the people of East Berlin—a remarkable, rare instance of Cold War–era East-West cooperation.

A short distance west, along Strasse des 17 Juni—a name that commemorates the unsuccessful 1953 uprising of East Berlin
12 workers against the Soviets—you will reach the **Soviet Victory**

Memorial, until 1990 a Russian enclave in the West. Built directly after the end of World War II, before power plays between opposing sides had been set in motion, it was located in the western rather than the eastern sector. Responsibility for the monument was turned over to the German government at reunification in October 1990. Although no longer guarded by Soviet troops, it still serves as a major attraction. The semicircular monument, which shows a bronze statue of a soldier, rests on a marble plinth taken from Hitler's former Berlin headquarters, flanked by what are said to be the first two tanks to have fought their way into Berlin in 1945.

13 Turn south from the memorial and cross the tip of the Tiergarten to **Potsdamerplatz,** a somewhat dull-looking expanse that was once among the busiest squares in prewar Berlin. Potsdamerplatz is the point where the British, American, and Russian sectors met and is often referred to as the three-sector corner. The Wall cut through the center of the square. Not far from the square, on part of the wasteland on the other side of the dividing border, is a little knoll marking one of the entrances to Hitler's reinforced concrete bunker, where he spent his last days. At press time, discussions were under way on what should be done with the site.

14 On nearby Potsdamerstrasse, on Heinrich-von-Kleist-Park, is the former **Altes Kammergericht** (Prussian Court Building) in which many Nazi show trials were held before the infamous Judge Roland Freisler. The building was taken over by the Allies in 1945 and used by the Allied forces until 1991, when it was returned to the Berlin Justice Ministry. It was here that the four-power agreement, which set the rules governing communication between the two halves of the city, was signed in 1971.

15 Several blocks north, in nearby Kemperplatz, lies the **Kulturforum** (Cultural Forum), a large square where you'll find a series of fascinating museums and galleries. Their contents will shift as state collections that were stuck on opposite sides of the Wall are reunited. Two new buildings will join the complex. One, opening in 1993, will house the collection of drawings and prints currently at Dahlem (*see* Tour 3, below). The roof that resembles a great wave belongs to the **Philharmonie** (Philharmonic Hall). Built in 1963, it is home to the renowned Berlin Philharmonic Orchestra. (*see* The Arts and Nightlife, below). *Philharmonie ticket office: Matthäikirchstr. 1. Open weekdays 3:30–6, weekends 11–2.*

The Philharmonie added the **Musikinstrumenten-Museum** (Musical Instruments Museum) to its attractions in 1984. It is well worth a visit for its fascinating collection of keyboard, string, wind, and percussion instruments. *Tiergartenstr. 1, tel. 030/254–810. Admission free. Open Tues.–Fri. 9–5, weekends 10–5. Guided tours on Saturdays at 11 with a noon presentation of the Wurlitzer organ. Tour admission: DM 3.*

Opposite the Philharmonie is the **Kunstgewerbemuseum** (Museum of Decorative Arts). Inside this three-story building you'll find a display of the development of arts and crafts in Europe from the Middle Ages to the present. Among its treasures is the Welfenschatz (Guelph Treasure), a collection of 16th-century gold and silver plate from Nürnberg. The most impressive single piece is a reliquary in the form of a domed Byzantine church. Made in Köln in 1175, it is believed to have held the head of St. Gregory when it was brought back from Constantinople in 1773. Other displays of particular interest are the ceramics and porcelains. *Tiergartenstr. 6, tel. 030/266–2911. Admission free. Open Tues.–Fri. 9–5, weekends 10–5.*

Leave the museum and walk south past the mid-19th-century church of St. Matthaeus to the **Neue Nationalgalerie** (New National Gallery), a modern glass-and-steel building designed by Mies van der Rohe and built in the mid-1960s.

The gallery's collection comprises paintings, sculptures, and drawings from the 19th and 20th centuries, with an accent on works by such Impressionists as Manet, Monet, Renoir, and Pissarro. Other schools represented are German Romantics, Realists, Expressionists, Surrealists, and the Bauhaus. The gallery also has a growing collection of contemporary art from Europe and America. *Potsdamerstr. 50, tel. 030/266–2666. Admission free to downstairs gallery. Open Tues.–Fri. 9–5, weekends 10–5.*

The last stop on the tour of the Cultural Forum is the **Staatsbibliothek** (National Library), opposite the Neue Nationalgalerie. This modern building, housing one of the largest libraries in Europe, with four million volumes, was designed by Hans Scharoun, the architect of the Philharmonie. *Potsdamerstr. 33, tel. 030/2661. Admission free. Open Mon.–Fri. 9–9, Sat. 9–5.*

Tour 2: East Berlin

Much of East Berlin was cleaned and restored in recent years, the idea being that when you crossed from West Berlin you should see a modern, fresh, and above all orderly city. The lower end of the Friedrichstrasse has been rebuilt, and much of the 4-square-mile "Berlin Mitte" district, the center of the city, has been given a thorough face-lift. When you wander off the beaten path, however, you will frequently find the drabness and sameness for which the socialist eastern zone was better known. Massive showcase housing and other communal projects hastily built in the '50s and '60s now show their age and shoddy construction, but newer projects are being planned on a more human scale, with greater effort to incorporate them into their surroundings.

For a sense of déjà vu, enter the eastern part of Berlin at
16 **Checkpoint Charlie,** the most famous crossing point between the two Berlins during the Cold War, and the setting of numerous spy novels and films. On the West Berlin side, visit **Haus am Checkpoint Charlie** (the Wall Museum). The museum reviews the history of the events leading up to the construction of the Wall and displays records and photographs documenting methods used by East Germans to cross over into the West (one of the most ingenious instruments of escape was a miniature submarine). Also displayed are paintings, drawings, and exhibits of Berlin history since the erection of the Wall. *Friedrichstr. 44. DM 5 adults, DM 3.50 children. Open daily 9 AM–10 PM.*

Follow busy, shop-lined Friedrichstrasse north for six blocks to Johann-Dieckmann-Strasse (or ride the U-bahn to Stadtmitte station) and turn right to come to the large square called
17 **Platz der Akadamie,** still one of Europe's finest piazzas. It's the site of the beautifully reconstructed **Schauspielhaus,** built in

1818 and East Berlin's main concert hall, and the rebuilt **German** and **French cathedrals.** The French cathedral contains the **Huguenot Museum,** with exhibits charting the history and the art of the Protestant refugees from France—the Huguenots—expelled at the end of the 17th century by Louis XIV. Their energy and commercial expertise did much to help boost Berlin in the 18th century. *Admission DM 1 adults, 50 pf children. Open Tues., Wed., Sat. 10–5; Thurs. 10–6; Sun. 11:30–5.*

Time Out The **Arkade Café** at the northwest corner of the square is the right spot for light snacks, a cup of coffee, and a beer. The pastries are excellent, too. *Französischstr. 25.*

---

18 Head down Französischestrasse to **St. Hedwig's Cathedral,** a substantial, circular building that's similar to the Pantheon in Rome. Note the tiny street called Hinter der Katholische Kirche; it means "Behind the Catholic Church." When the cathedral was built in 1747, it was the first Catholic church built in resolutely Protestant Berlin since the Reformation in the 16th century.

19 Head north one block and you'll reach the **Deutsche Staatsoper** (State Opera House), lavishly restored in the late '80s. A performance here can be memorable. *Unter den Linden 7. The box office is open weekdays noon–5:45.*

You are now on **Unter den Linden,** the central thoroughfare of old Berlin; its name means simply "under the linden trees." Something of its former cosmopolitan elegance is left, though these days it can hardly claim to rival the Champs Élysées. On the north side is **Humboldt University,** originally built in 1766 as a palace for the brother of Friedrich II of Prussia. It became a university in 1810, and Karl Marx and Friedrich Engels were
20 once among its students. The **Palais Unter den Linden** is also on this boulevard; it's the former crown prince's palace, today used as a government guest house. At the eastern end of Unter den Linden, housed in the onetime arsenal (Zeughaus), is the
21 **Museum für Deutsche Geschichte** (Museum of German History), constructed from 1695 to 1705. This magnificent Baroque building was later used as a hall of fame glorifying Prusso-German militarism. Today it provides a compendium of German history from 1789 to the present. Displays focus on a range of relics, from the hat Napoléon wore at the Battle of Waterloo to relief portrayals of faces of soldiers through the ages. *Unter den Linden 2. Admission: DM 3 adults, DM 1.50 children. Open Mon.–Thurs. 9–6, weekends 10–5.*

Turn left and follow the Spree Canal and you'll come to Museum
22 Island, or **Museumsinsel,** on the site of one of Berlin's two original settlements, Cölln, dating from 1237. Today you'll find a complex of four remarkable museums here. *Admission: Varies from free to DM 3 (extra if you want to take photographs). Wed.–Sun. 10–6. Pergamon Museum: daily 10–6. Check hours before visiting, as they do change occasionally.*

The **Altes Museum** (Old Museum; entrance Lustgarten) is an austere neoclassical building just north of Marx-Engels-Platz that features postwar East German art; its large etching and drawing collection, from the old masters to the present, is a treasure trove. The **Nationalgalerie** (National Gallery, entrance on Bodestrasse) houses an outstanding collection of 18th-, 19th-, and early-20th-century paintings and sculptures and often hosts special temporary exhibits. Works by Cézanne, Rodin, Degas, and one of Germany's most famous portrait artists, Max Liebermann, are part of the permanent exhibition.

Even if you aren't generally inclined toward the ancient world, make an exception for the **Pergamon Museum** (entrance on Am Kupfergraben). It is not only the standout in this complex but it is one of Europe's greatest museums. The museum's name is derived from its principal and best-loved display, the Pergamon altar, a monumental Greek temple found in what's now Turkey and dating from 180 BC. Adorning it are finely carved figures of gods locked in battle against giants. As much as anything, perhaps, this vast structure illustrates the zeal of Germany's 19th-century archaeologists, who had it shipped piece by piece from a mountaintop to Berlin. Equally impressive is the Babylonian Processional Way in the Asia Minor department. As you walk through the museum, you cannot help but wonder how they ever got away with dismantling and exporting these vast treasures.

Last in the complex is the **Bodemuseum** (entrance on Monbijoubrücke), with its superb Egyptian, Byzantine, and early Christian relics, sculpture collections, and coin gallery. The Sphinx of Hatshepsut, from around 1500 BC, is stunning, as are the Burial Cult Room and Papyrus Collection. There is also a representative collection of Italian Renaissance paintings.

From the museum complex, follow the Spree Canal back to Unter den Linden and the enormous, impressive 19th-century
23 **Berlin Cathedral** (Berliner Dom). A small museum in it (entrance on Unter den Linden) records the postwar reconstruction of the building, which was due to be completed by the end of 1991.

The modern building across Unter den Linden is the **Palast der Republik** (Palace of the Republic), a ponderous, postwar monument to socialist progress. It housed a theater, a dance hall, several restaurants, and former East Germany's rubber-stamp parliament. The building was closed in 1990 when it was discovered to be contaminated with asbestos, and at press time a decision still had not been made as to whether to tear down or decontaminate the edifice.

Follow Karl-Liebknechtstrasse to take a look at the 13th-centu-
24 ry **Marienkirche** and its late-Gothic fresco *Den Totentanz* (*Dance of Death*). Obscured for many years, it was restored in 1950, revealing the original in all its macabre allure. Like something out of an Ingmar Bergman movie, Death dances with everyone, from peasant to king. The fresco and the tower were both 15th-century additions. *Alexanderplatz. Open Mon.–Thurs. 10–12 and 1–4, Sat. 12–4. Organ recitals: Sat. 4:30.*

25 The Marienkirche borders **Alexanderplatz,** the square that formed the hub of Berlin city life. It's a bleak sort of place, open and windswept, surrounded by grimly ugly modern buildings, with not so much as a hint of its prewar elegance—a reminder not just of the Allied bombing of Berlin but of the ruthlessness with which what remained of the old buildings was demolished by the East Germans. Finding Alexanderplatz from any other part of the city is no problem; just head toward the **Fernsehturm,** the unmissable TV tower (completed in 1969 and 1,198 feet high) that stands at its center.

In the base of the tower is the Berlin Information Office. Here, you'll be able to get an excellent brochure, listing (in English) every worthwhile sight in the city, along with the clearest of maps and a diagram of the public transportation system.

For DM 3 (DM 1.50 children) you can take the elevator to the viewing platform halfway up the tower, which is open 9 AM–midnight. On a clear day, you will see Berlin extending in all directions. The revolving café is ideal for a coffee break with a view, though the food is not worth the time you'll have waited in line to get up here. The area around the tower offers ample shopping opportunities. The focal point for shopping is the **Kaufhof** department store, which took over the former East German Centrum Warenhaus, next to the Hotel Stadt Berlin at the very top of the plaza.

Time Out If it's a cold day, escape the keen wind that almost always seems to sweep across Alexanderplatz in the winter months and dodge into the **Suppenterrine** for a bowl of steaming-hot, fresh-made soup. Never did plain cabbage soup taste so good. If it's a hot day and Alexanderplatz is roasting in the sun, the Suppenterrine is also a good refuge and source of cold Berlin beer. *Alexanderpl. Open weekdays 10–8, Sat. 9–3.*

Walk across the lower end of the square past the **Rathaus** (Town Hall, also known as the Rotes Rathaus, or Red Town Hall), a marvel of red brick and friezes depicting the city's history. The complex of buildings next to the town hall has been handsomely rebuilt, centering around the remains of the twin-spired, 12th-century **Nikolaikirche** (St. Nicholas's Church), Berlin's oldest parish church. The quarter that has grown around it, the **Nikolai quarter,** is filled with stores, cafés, and restaurants.

Wander back down Rathausstrasse into the area around the Breite Strasse—there's an array of fine old buildings here, some rebuilt, some actually moved to this location from else-
26 where in Berlin—and over to the **Fischerinsel** area. This was the heart of Berlin 750 years ago, and today retains some of its medieval character. It provides a refreshing change, too, from some of the heavy and uninspired postwar architecture, which you may by now feel the need to get away from.

Time Out The **Alt-Cöllner Schankstuben,** right on the Spree Canal, is charming and friendly, with tables outside for you to enjoy the waterside view on pleasant days. West along the canal is the Jungfernbrücke, the oldest bridge in the city. *Friedrichsgracht 50.*

Cross over the Gertraudenstrasse and wander up the south
27 bank of the canal to the redbrick **Märkisches Museum,** the museum of city history. It includes a special section on the city's theatrical past and a fascinating collection of mechanical musical instruments. These are demonstrated on Sunday 11–noon and Wednesday 3–4. Next door to the museum live the (live) bears, Berlin's symbol. *Am Köllnischen Park 5. Admission: DM 2 adults, DM 1 children. Open Wed.–Sun. 9–6.*

The upper Friedrichstrasse is undergoing reconstruction. Among its landmarks are the tall **International Trade Center,** next to the Friedrichstrasse rail station, and, farther up, the **Friedrichstadtpalast,** featuring a nightclub, dancing, and occa-

sional musical shows. Despite the rebuilding, the street still
houses a number of small shops, bookstores, and neighborhood
establishments. Walk up beyond the bend where the street
turns into the Chauseestrasse (or take the U-bahn to Oranien-
28 burgerstr.) to find the **Bertolt Brecht House and Museum** and a
library for Brecht scholars. *Chausseestr. 125. Admission: DM
2 adults, DM 1 children. Open Tues., Wed., Fri. 10–noon,
Thurs. 5–7, Sat. 9:30–noon and 12:30–2.*

Brecht is actually buried next door, along with his wife Helene Weigel and more than 100 other celebrated Berliners, in the **Dorotheer Cemetery.** They include the neoclassical architects Schinkel and Schadow as well as the Berlin printer Litfass, the man who invented those stumpy cylindrical columns you'll find across Europe carrying advertisements and theater schedules.

Head back toward the center and turn left down Oranienburger-
29 strasse to the ruins of the massive city **synagogue,** now being
restored. It's an exotic amalgam of styles, the whole faintly
Middle Eastern, built between 1894 and 1905. It was largely
ruined on the night of November 11, 1938, the infamous "crystal night," when Nazi looters and soldiers rampaged across Germany and Austria, burning synagogues and smashing the few Jewish shops and homes left in the country. It was further ruined during the bombing of the city toward the end of the war. From here, take the U-bahn from Oranienburgertor back to the center of the city.

Time Out Stop for coffee, cake, or an Israeli snack of eggplant and pita bread at the newly opened **Beth Cafe** (Tucholskystr. 40, tel. 030/281–3135), the first new Jewish business to open in the city's former Jewish district. Cafe Beth is small and always full, so be prepared to accept the European custom of sharing a table. Just around the corner from the Oranienburgerstrasse synagogue, the Beth Cafe was opened by Berlin's Adass Jisroel Jewish community.

Tour 3: Outlying Sights and Attractions

30 West Berlin's highest natural hill, the **Kreuzberg** (Hill of the Cross) in Victoria Park (Viktoriapark) can be reached by taking the U-bahn at Kochstrasse, across from Checkpoint Charlie, and traveling two stops on the U-6 line to Mehringdamm station. Leave by the Kreuzbergstrasse exit.

The Kreuzberg is on your left, crowned by an iron cross. The monument was erected in 1821 to commemorate the 1813–15 Wars of Liberation. The view from the top embraces the center of East Berlin to the north and Tempelhof airfield to the south. A vineyard on the sheltered southern slope of the Kreuzberg produces Germany's rarest wine, the Kreuzneroberger. It is produced in such small quantities that it is only served at official Berlin functions.

Leave the park by the western exit on Monumentenstrasse and
continue until you reach the intersection with Potsdamerstrasse on the right. Turn left into Hauptstrasse and continue
south until you reach Dominicus-Strasse. Turn right here and
take the first turning on your left, Elsas-Strasse. It will
31 lead you straight to the **Rathaus Schöneberg** (Schöneberg Town
Hall).

After the division of the two Berlins in 1948, the Rathaus Schöneberg was home to the West Berlin Chamber of Deputies and their Senate. The Rathaus is of special interest to Americans, for it was here, on June 26, 1963, that John F. Kennedy made his memorable "Ich bin ein Berliner" speech just months before his assassination.

Completed in 1914, the Rathaus has a 237-foot-high tower from which a replica of the Liberty Bell is rung each day at noon. The bell was given by the American people as a symbol of their support for the West Berliners' struggle to preserve freedom. A document bears the signatures of 17 million Americans who pledged their solidarity with the people of West Berlin. *Rathaus Schöneberg Bell Tower. John-F.-Kennedy-Platz. Open Wed. and Sun. 10–4.*

From the Rathaus, head north up the Innsbrückestrasse to the
U-bahn station at Bayerischer Platz. Take the U-7 line toward
Rathaus Spandau eight stops and get off at Mierendorffplatz.
32 Head south along Mierendorffstrasse to the **Schloss Charlottenburg** (Charlottenburg Palace).

The Charlottenburg Palace complex can be considered the showplace of West Berlin, the most monumental memento of imperial days in the western sector. This sumptuous palace served as a city residence for the Prussian rulers. It has on occasion been referred to as Berlin's very own Versailles. Indeed, some claim that it was Napoléon, when he invaded Berlin in 1806, who first made the comparison to the Sun King's spectacular château near Paris. The comparison hardly seems appropriate. Charlottenburg is on a smaller, more intimate scale than Versailles. Its proportions and decoration are restrained; formal gardens are not nearly as vast. Nor are you likely to encounter the kind of crowds that flock to Versailles. But you are sure to be suitably impressed.

A full day is not too much time to devote to Charlottenburg. In addition to the apartments of the Prussian nobility, there are the landscaped gardens to be visited, and several excellent museums set within and just inside the grounds.

This gorgeous palace started as a modest royal summer residence in 1695, built on the orders of King Friedrich I for his wife, Queen Sophie-Charlotte. Later, in the 18th century, Friedrich the Great made a number of additions, such as the dome and several wings in the Rococo style. In time the complex evolved into the massive royal domain you see today. The palace was severely damaged during World War II but has been painstakingly restored. Many of the original furnishings and works of art survived the war and are on display today.

Behind heavy iron gates, the Court of Honor—the courtyard in front of the palace—is dominated by a fine Baroque statue, the Reiterstandbild des Grossen Kurfürsten (the equestrian statue of the Great Elector). A 156-foot-high domed tower capped by a gilded statue of Fortune rises above the main entrance to the palace.

Inside, in the main building, the suites of Friedrich I and his wife are furnished in the prevailing style of the era. Paintings include royal portraits by Antoine Pesne, a noted court painter of the 18th century. On the first floor you can visit the Oak Gallery, the early 18th-century Palace Chapel, and the suites of

Friedrich Wilhelm II and Friedrich Wilhelm III, furnished in the Biedermeier style.

Visits to the royal apartments are by guided tour only; tours leave every hour on the hour from 9 to 4. Parks and gardens can be visited for free and offer a pleasant respite from sightseeing.

A gracious staircase leads up to the sumptuous State Dining Room and the 138-foot-long Golden Gallery. West of the staircase are the rooms of Frederick the Great, in which the king's extravagant collection of works by Watteau, Chardin, and Pesne are displayed. In one glass cupboard you'll see the coronation crown, stripped of its jewels by the king, who gave the most valuable gemstones to his wife. Also in the so-called New Wing is the National Gallery's collection of masterpieces from 19th-century German painters such as Caspar David Friedrich, the leading member of the German Romantic school. *Schloss Charlottenburg. Luisenpl., tel. 030/320–911. Admission (includes guided tour): DM 6. Open: Tues., Wed., Fri.–Sun. 10–5, Thurs. 10–8.*

There are several buildings in the park that deserve particular attention, among which are the Belvedere, a teahouse overlooking the lake and Spree River that now houses a collection of Berlin porcelain and the Schinkel Pavilion behind the palace near the river. The pavilion, modeled on a villa in Naples where the king stayed in 1822, was built in 1824–1825 by Karl Friedrich Schinkel, one of 19th-century Berlin's favorite architects. It houses paintings by Caspar David Friedrich and late 18th-century furniture. Also of interest in the park is the mausoleum, which contains the tombs of King Frederick Wilhelm II and Queen Louise.

Just to the south of the palace are a group of small, distinguished museums. The first, across from the palace, is
33 the **Ägyptisches Museum** (Egyptian Museum). The building, once the east guardhouse and residence of the king's bodyguard, is now home to the famous portrait bust of the exquisite Queen Nefertiti. The 3,300-year-old Egyptian queen is the centerpiece of a collection of works that span Egypt's history since 4,000 BC and includes one of the best-preserved mummies outside Cairo. *Schloss Str. 70, tel. 030/320–911. Admission free. Open Mon.–Thurs. 9–5, weekends 10–5.*

Opposite the Ägyptisches Museum in the former west guard-
34 house is the **Antikenmuseum** (Antique Museum). The collection comprises ceramics and bronzes as well as everyday utensils from ancient Greece and Rome, and a number of Greek vases from the 6th to 4th centuries BC. Also on display is a collection of Scythian gold and silverware and jewelry found in the Mediterranean basin. *Schloss Str. 1, tel. 030/320–911. Admission free. Open Mon.–Thurs. 9–5, weekends 10–5.*

The final museum, the **Museum für Vor- und Frügeschichte** (Museum of Pre- and Proto-history), is located in the western extension of the palace opposite Klausener Platz. The museum depicts the stages of the evolution of man from 1,000,000 BC to the Bronze Age. *Spandauer Damm. Admission free. Open Mon–Thurs. 9–5, weekends 10–5.*

Another stop on your tour of West Berlin is also a cluster of mu-
35 seums, the **Dahlem Museum complex.** The best way to get there is by the U-2 subway line, to Dahlem-Dorf station.

The Dahlem complex includes the **Gemäldegalerie** (Picture Gallery), the **Kupferstichkabinett** (Drawings and Prints Collection, currently closed), the **Museum fur Völkerkunde** (Ethnographic Museum) and the **Skulpturengalerie** (Sculpture Gallery).

Begin with the **Gemäldegalerie.** One of Germany's finest art galleries, it houses a broad selection of European paintings from the 13th to 18th centuries. Rembrandt devotees will be particularly pleased to find the world's second-largest Rembrandt collection located on the second floor.

Several rooms on the first floor are reserved for paintings by German masters, among them Dürer, Cranach the Elder, and Holbein. An adjoining gallery houses the works of the Italian masters—Botticelli, Titian, Giotto, Filippo Lippi, and Raphael—and another gallery on the first floor is devoted to paintings by Dutch and Flemish masters of the 15th and 16th centuries: van Eyck, Bosch, Brueghel the Elder, and van der Weyden.

Flemish and Dutch paintings from the 17th century are displayed on the floor above. In the Rembrandt section, where there are 21 paintings by the master, you can see "The Man with the Golden Helmet," a painting formerly attributed to Rembrandt that has since proved by radioactive testing to have been the work of another artist of the same era. *Arnimallee 23–27, tel. 030/83011. Admission free. Open Tues.–Fri. 9–5, weekends 10–5.*

The **Kupferstichkabinett** (Drawings and Prints Collection) includes European woodcuts and engravings from the 15th to 18th centuries, several pen-and-ink drawings by Dürer, and 150 drawings by Rembrandt. There is also a photographic archive. The collection is closed until 1993, when it will reopen in a new building at the Kulturforum. *Entrance: Arnimallee 23. Admission free. Open Tues.–Fri. 9–4, weekends 10–5.*

The **Museum für Völkerkunde** (Ethnographic Museum) is internationally famous for its arts and artifacts from Africa, Asia, the South Seas, and the Americas. American visitors homesick for a taste of their own history should look out for the North American Indian wigwams and the feather cape that once belonged to Hawaii's 18th-century King Kamehameha I. Also of interest is the display of native huts from New Guinea and New Zealand. *Entrance: Lansstr. 8, tel. 030/83011. Admission free. Open Tues.–Fri. 9–5, weekends 10–5.*

The **Skulpturengalerie** (Sculpture Gallery) houses Byzantine and European sculpture from the 3rd to 18th centuries. Included in its collection is Donatello's *Madonna and Child,* sculpted in 1422. *Entrance: Arnimallee 23–27. Admission free. Open Tues.–Fri. 9–5, weekends 10–5.*

Beyond the tour of monuments, museums, and other aspects relating to the Wall and the divided city, no visit to Berlin would be complete without seeing the vast world of lakes and greenery along its western extremities. In no other city has such an expanse of uninterrupted natural surroundings been preserved within city limits.

Along the city's fringe are some 60 lakes, connected by rivers, streams, and canals, in a verdant setting of meadows, woods, and forests. Excursion steamers ply the water wonderland of the Wannsee and Havel. (*See* Guided Tours in Essential Information, above, for details.) You can tramp for hours through the green belt of the Grunewald. On weekends in spring and fall and daily in summer the Berliners are out in force, swimming, sailing their boats, tramping through the woods, riding horseback. To the north, close to the line of the old barbed-wire political boundary, there are still a few working farms. Time and progress seem to have passed right by the rustic village of Lubars.

You can reach Grunewald and the Wannsee on the S-1 or S-3 suburban line from Zoo Station. To reach Lubars, take the U-6 subway to Tegel, then bus number 222 to Lubars.

Shopping

Gift Ideas Berlin is a city of alluring stores and boutiques. Despite its cosmopolitan gloss, prices are generally lower than in cities like Munich and Hamburg.

Fine **porcelain** is still produced at the former Royal Prussian Porcelain Factory, now called **Staatliche Porzellan Manufactur,** or KPM. This delicate, handmade, hand-painted china is sold at KPM's store at Kurfürstendamm 26A (tel. 030/881–1802), but it may be more fun to visit the factory salesroom at Wegelystrasse 1. It also sells seconds at reduced prices. If you long to have the Egyptian Museum's Queen Nefertiti on your mantelpiece at home, try the **Gipsformerei der Staatlichen Museen Preussischer Kulturbesitz** (Sophie-Charlotte-Str. 17, tel. 030/321–7011, open weekdays 9–4). It sells plaster casts of this and other treasures from the city's museums.

Take home a regiment of **tin figures,** painted or to paint yourself, from the **Berliner Zinnfigurenkabinett** (Knesebeckstr. 88).

Antiques On Saturdays and Sundays from 10 to 5, the colorful and lively antiques and handicrafts fair on Strasse des 17 Juni swings into action. Don't expect to pick up many bargains—or to have the place to yourself. Not far from Wittenbergplatz is **Keithstrasse,** a street given over to antiques stores. Eisenacherstrasse, Fuggerstrasse, Kalckreuthstrasse, Motzstrasse, and Nollendorfstrasse—all close to Nollendorfplatz—have many antiques stores of varying quality. Another good street for antiques is **Suarezstrasse,** between Kantstrasse and Bismarckstrasse. The venerable auction house **Christie's** recently opened an outpost at Fasanenstrasse 72 (tel. 030/882–7778), just off the Ku'damm.

In East Berlin, antiques are sold in the Metropol and Palast hotels, in the Nikolai quarter, and in the restored Husemannstrasse. Some private stores along the stretch of Friedrichstrasse north of the Spree Bridge offer old books and prints. **Sotheby's** auction house has set up shop at the Palais am Festungsgraben on Unter den Linden (tel. 030/304–6369).

Shopping Districts The liveliest and most famous shopping area in West Berlin is the **Kurfürstendamm** and its side streets, especially between **Breitscheidplatz** and **Olivaer Platz.** The **Europa-Center** at Breitscheidplatz encompasses more than 100 stores, cafés, and restaurants—this is not a place to bargain-hunt, though! Running east from Breitscheidplatz is **Tauenzienstrasse,** another shopping street. At the end of it is Berlin's most celebrated department store, **KaDeWe.** New and elegant malls include the **Gloria Galerie** (opposite the Wertheim department store on Ku'damm) and the **Uhland-Passage** (connecting Uhlandstrasse and Fasanenstrasse). In both, you'll find leading name stores as well as cafés and restaurants.

For trendier clothes, try the boutiques along **Bleibtreustrasse.** One of the more avant-garde fashion boutiques is **Durchbruch** (Schlutterstr. 54), around the corner. The name means "breakthrough," and the store lives up to its name by selling different designers' outrageous styles. Less trendy and much less expensive is the mall, **Wilmersdorferstrasse,** where price-conscious Berliners do their shopping. It's packed on weekends.

East Berlin's chief shopping areas are along the Friedrichstrasse, Unter den Linden, and in the area around Alexanderplatz. The Palast and Grand hotels have small shopping malls. A number of smaller stores have sprung up in and around the Nikolai quarter; under the Communist regime, all were supplied from the same central sources, but they make fun places to shop for trinkets.

Department Stores

The classiest department store in Berlin is **KaDeWe,** the Kaufhaus des Westens (Department Store of the West, as it's modestly known in English), at Wittenbergplatz. The biggest department store in Europe, the KaDeWe is a grand-scale emporium in modern guise. Be sure to check out the food department, which occupies the whole sixth floor. The other main department store downtown is **Wertheim** on Ku'damm. Neither as big nor as attractive as the KaDeWe, Wertheim nonetheless offers a large selection of fine wares.

East Berlin's former **Centrum** department store, at the north end of Alexanderplatz, has been taken over by the West German Kaufhof department store chain.

Specialty Stores

Men's Clothing

Mientus (Wilmersdorferstr. 73), a large, exclusive men's store, caters to expensive tastes. It offers both conventional/businesswear as well as sporty and modern looks, and carries many top designer labels. Slightly less expensive and exclusive but still up there is **Erdmann** (in the Europa-Center facing Tauenzienstr.). For men's shoes, try **Budapester Schuhe** (Ku'damm 199).

Women's Clothing

For German designer wear, try **Zenker** (Ku'damm 45). It's not cheap, but the styling is classic. If you're looking for international labels, drop by **Kramberg** (Ku'damm 56), then go next door to **Granny's Step,** where you'll find evening wear styled along the lines of bygone times. For modern, Berlin-designed chic, check out **Filato** (Nürnbergstr. 24A). If you're feeling daring, browse through the extraordinary lingerie store **Nouvelle** (Bleibtreustr. 24). Elegant '20s intimate wear made of fine, old-fashioned materials is its specialty.

Jewelry

Fine hand-crafted jewelry can be found at **Wurzbarcher** (Ku'damm 36). **Axel Sedlatzek** (Ku'damm 45) also offers a good selection, but with a twist: He'll custom-design body jewelry for men and women. East Berlin's **Galerie Skarabäus** (Frankfurter Allee 80) and **Galerie "re"** (Finowstr. 2) offer good values.

Sports and Fitness

Bicycling There are bike paths throughout the downtown area and the rest of the city. *See* Getting Around, above, for details of renting bikes.

Golf Berlin's leading club is the **Golf- und Landclub Wannsee** (Stölpchenweg, Wannsee, tel. 030/805–5075).

Jogging The **Tiergarten** is the best place for jogging in the downtown area. Run its length and back and you'll have covered 5 miles. Joggers can also take advantage of the grounds of **Charlottenburg** castle, 2 miles around. For longer runs, anything up to 20 miles, make for **Grunewald.**

Riding Horses are rented out by the **Reitschule Onkel Toms Hütte** (Onkel-Tom-Str. 172, tel. 030/813–2081). Children's ponies are stabled at **Ponyhof Lange** (Buckower Chaussee 82, Marienfelde, tel. 030/721–6008) and the **Ponyhof Wittenau** (Wittenauerstr. 80, tel. 030/402–8535).

Sailing and Windsurfing Boats and boards of all kinds are rented by **Jürgen Schöne** (tel. 030/381–5037) and **Scharfe Lanke** (tel. 030/361–5066).

Swimming The **Wannsee** and **Plötzensee** both have beaches; they get crowded during summer weekends, however. There are public pools throughout the city; there's bound to be at least one near where you're staying. For full listings, ask at the tourist office. The most impressive pool is the **Olympia-Schwimmstadion** at Olympischer Platz (U-bahn: Olympiastadion). The **Blub Padeparadis** lido (Buschkrugallee 64, tel. 030/606–6060) has indoor and outdoor pools, hot tubs, and a solarium (U-bahn: Grenzallee).

Tennis and Squash There are tennis courts and squash centers throughout the city; ask your hotel to direct you to the nearest of these. **Tennis & Squash City** (Brandenburgischestr. 31, Wilmersdorf, tel. 030/879–097) has 7 tennis courts and 11 squash courts. You can even step off the Ku'damm and onto a tennis court, at **"Tennisplätze am Ku'damm"** (Cicerostr. 55A, tel. 030/896–630).

Dining

Dining in Berlin can mean sophisticated nouvelle specialties in upscale restaurants with linen tablecloths and hand-painted porcelain plates, or hearty local specialties in atmospheric and inexpensive inns: The range is as vast as the city. Specialties include *Eisbein mit Sauerkraut,* knuckle of pork with pickled cabbage; *Rouladen,* rolled stuffed beef; *Spanferkel,* suckling pig; *Berliner Schüsselsülze,* potted meat in aspic; *Schlachteplatte,* mixed grill; *Hackepeter,* ground beef; and *Kartoffelpuffer,* fried potato cakes. *Bockwurst* is a chubby frankfurter that's served in a variety of ways and sold in restaurants and at bockwurst stands all over the city. *Schlesisches Himmerlreich* is roast goose or pork served with potato dumplings in rich gravy. *Königsberger Klopse* consists of meatballs, herring, and capers—it tastes much better than it sounds.

East Germany's former ties to the Eastern Bloc persist in restaurants featuring the national cuisine of those other one-time socialist states, although such exotica as Japanese, Chinese, Indonesian, and French food are now appearing.

Highly recommended restaurants are indicated by a star ★.

West Berlin

Very Expensive (over DM 100)

★ **Bamberger Reiter.** One of the city's leading restaurants, this is presided over by Tirolean chef Franz Raneburger. He relies on fresh market produce for his *Neue Deutsche Küche* (new German cuisine), so the menu changes daily. Fresh flowers set off this attractive oak-beamed restaurant. *Regensburgerstr. 7, tel. 030/244–282. Reservations essential. Jacket and tie required. DC, V. Dinner only. Closed Sun., Mon., and Aug. 1–20.*

Frühsammer's Restaurant an der Rehwiese. Here you can watch chef Peter Frühsammer at work in his open kitchen. He's ready with advice on the daily menu: Salmon is always a treat. The restaurant is in the annex of a turn-of-the-century villa in the Zehlendorf district (U-bahn to Krumme Lanke and then bus No. 53 to Rehweise). *Matterhornstr. 101, tel. 030/803–2720. Reservations essential. Jacket and tie required. MC, V. Dinner only. Closed Sun., and 3 weeks during the school summer holidays.*

Rockendorfs. Only fixed-price menus, some up to nine courses, are offered in this elegant restaurant in the north of the city. Exquisitely presented on fine porcelain, the mainly nouvelle specialties are sometimes fused with classic German cuisine. The furnishings are intentionally sparse. *Dusterhauptstr. 1, tel. 030/402–3099. Reservations essential. Jacket and tie required. AE, DC, MC, V. Closed Sun., Mon., 3 weeks in summer, Christmas, and New Year's Day.*

Expensive (DM 75–100)

★ **Alt-Luxembourg.** There are only nine tables at this popular restaurant in the Charlottenburg district, with attentive service enhancing the intimate setting. Chef Kurt Wannebacher produces a divine lobster lasagna. *Pestalozzistr. 70, tel. 030/323–8730. Reservations essential. Jacket and tie required. DC, V. Closed Sun., Mon., 3 weeks in Jan., and 3 weeks in June and July.*

Moderate (DM 50–75)

Alt-Nürnberg. Step into the tavernlike interior and you could be in Füssen or Garmisch in Bavaria: The waitresses even wear dirndls. The Bavarian colors of blue and white are everywhere, and that region's culinary delights, like *Schweinshaxe* (knuckle of pork), dominate the menu. If you prefer to eat Prussian-style, order calves' liver *Berliner Art* (Berlin style). *Europa Centre, tel. 030/261–4397. Reservations advised. Dress: informal. AE, DC, MC, V.*

★ **Conti Fischstuben.** Located in the Hotel Ambassador, this is the best fish restaurant in Berlin. Watery light from the fish tank in the center of the dining room reflects from the dark-paneled walls to create a sophisticated and different atmosphere. *Bayreutherstrasse 43, tel. 030/21902362. Reservations essential. Jacket and tie required. AE, DC, MC, V. Closed lunch and Sun.*

Hecker's Deele. Antique church pews complement the oak-beamed interior of this restaurant that specializes in Westphalian dishes. The *Westfälische Schlachtplatte* (a selection of meats) will set you up for a whole day's sightseeing—the

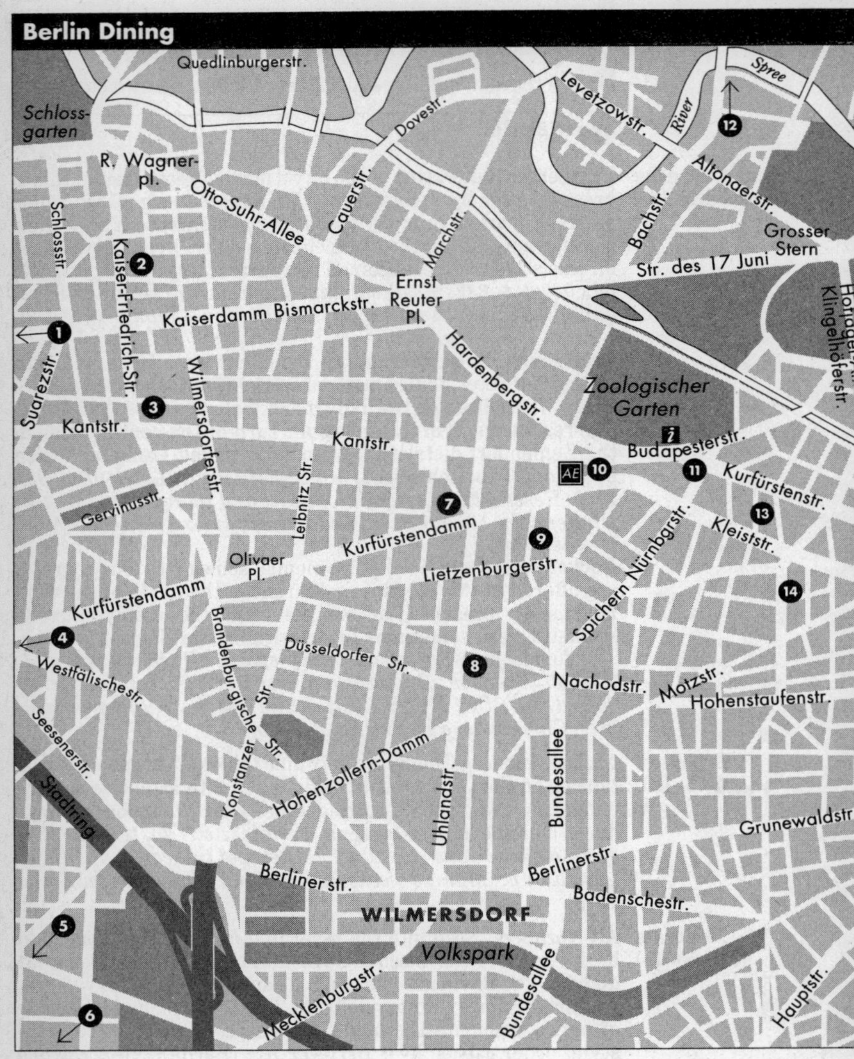

Alt-Berliner Weissbierstube, **19**
Alt-Cöllner Schankstuben, **20**
Alt-Luxembourg, **3**
Alt-Nürnberg, **11**
Arkade, **18**
Bamberger Reiter, **14**
Berlin Esprit, **24**
Blockhaus Nikolskoe, **5**
Cafe Flair, **23**
Conti Fischstuben, **13**
Eierschale, **10**
Ermeler-Haus, **26**
Fioretto, **25**
Frühsammer's Restaurant an der Rehwiese, **4**
Ganymed, **16**
Hardtke, **9**
Hecker's Deele, **7**
Historische Gaststätte auf der Zitadelle, **1**
Moskau, **28**
Mundart Restaurant, **15**
Ponte Vecchio, **2**
Raabe Diele, **27**
Ratskeller, **22**
Rockendorfs, **12**
Schwalbennest, **21**
Wibb's, **8**
Wirtshaus Moorlake, **6**
Zur Goldenen Gans, **17**

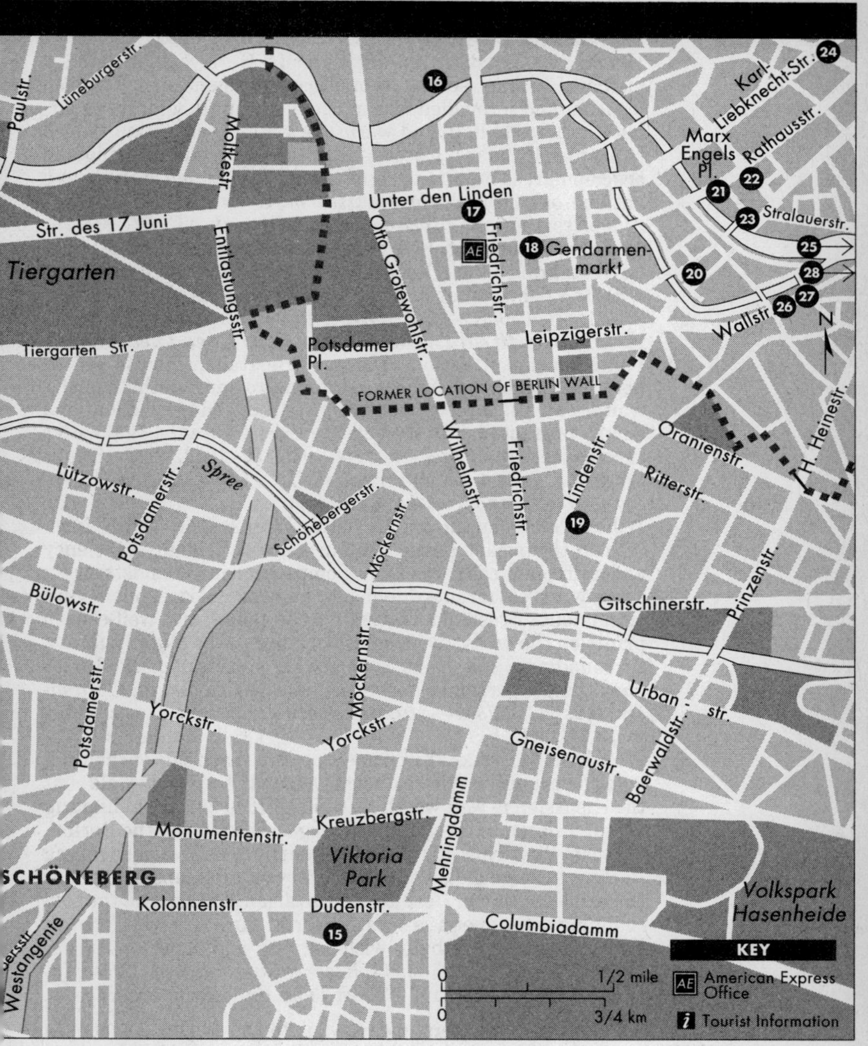
Paulstr.
Lüneburgerstr.
Moltkestr.
16
Karl-Liebknecht-Str.
24
Marx Engels Pl.
Rathausstr.
22
21
Unter den Linden
17
23
Stralauerstr.
Str. des 17 Juni
Entlastungsstr.
Otto Grotewohlstr.
Friedrichstr.
AE
18
Gendarmenmarkt
25
Tiergarten
20
28
27
26
Wallstr.
N
Tiergarten Str.
Potsdamer Pl.
Leipzigerstr.
FORMER LOCATION OF BERLIN WALL
Oranienstr.
H. Heinestr.
Friedrichstr.
Wilhelmstr.
Lindenstr.
Ritterstr.
Lützowstr.
Spree
Potsdamerstr.
Schönebergerstr.
Möckernstr.
19
Prinzenstr.
Bülowstr.
Gitschinerstr.
Potsdamerstr.
Möckernstr.
Urban str.
Yorckstr.
Yorckstr.
Gneisenaustr.
Baerwaldstr.
Mehringdamm
Monumentenstr.
Kreuzbergstr.
Viktoria Park
SCHÖNEBERG
Volkspark Hasenheide
Kolonnenstr.
Dudenstr.
Columbiadamm
15
Westangente
KEY
0
1/2 mile
0
3/4 km
AE American Express Office
Tourist Information

Ku'damm is right outside. *Grolmannstr. 35, tel. 030/88901. No reservations. Dress: informal. AE, DC, MC, V.*

Historische Gaststätte auf der Zitadelle. Here you'll dine like a medieval noble, served a multicourse menu by Prussian wenches and serenaded by a minstrel group. In winter, a roaring fire helps to light and warm the vaulted restaurant, which is part of Spandau's historic Zitadelle. Its medieval banquets are popular, so be sure to reserve your spot at one of the heavy antique oak tables. *Am Juliusturm, Spandau, tel. 030/334–2106. Reservations advised. Dress: informal. AE, DC, MC, V.*

Mundart Restaurant. Five chefs work the kitchen of this popular restaurant in the Kreuzberg district. You can't go wrong with the fish soup or any of the daily specials. *Muskauerstr. 33–34, tel. 030/612–2061. Dress: informal. Reservations advised. No credit cards. Closed lunch, Mon., and Tues.*

★ **Ponte Vecchio.** Delicious Tuscan-style Italian food is served here in a handsome, light-wood dining room. Ask the friendly waiters for their recommendations—the food is excellent and simply presented. Try the delicate *Vitello tonnato*, veal with a tuna sauce. *Spielhagenstr. 3, tel. 030/342–1999. Reservations essential. Jacket and tie required. DC. Closed lunch (except Sun.), Tues., and 4 weeks in summer.*

Wibb's. Gabi, Martin, and Christian Wibbke (the "Wibb" family) run this smart corner restaurant with friendly efficiency and exemplary culinary skills. Competition in Uhlandstrasse is keen, with restaurants dueling for pavement space, but Wibb's stands out. Fresh-cut flowers on the tables and well-chosen prints on the walls give a splash of color to the slightly formal surroundings. The menu is relatively small but packed with good things, particularly the imaginative fish dishes. *Uhlandstr. 142, tel. 030/861–5310. Reservations advised. Dress: informal. AE, MC, V.*

Wirtshaus Moorlake. You'll need a car to reach this enchanting lakeside country-style restaurant, deep in the Grunewald, but the excursion is well worth it. Built in 1840 as a royal hunting lodge, it became an established stagecoach stop on the Berlin–Potsdam run. Now it's a popular destination for weekending Berliners, so go on a weekday; reserve a table upstairs under the exposed beams. Despite the Bavarian character of the surroundings, the menu is mostly Berlin fare. Try the *Königsberger Klopse* (meatballs with herring and capers). *An der Moorlake, tel. 030/805–5809. Reservations advised. Dress: informal. AE, DC, MC, V. Closed Tues. and winter evenings.*

Inexpensive (under DM 50)

Alt-Berliner Weissbierstube. A visit to the Berlin Museum (a permanent historical exhibition on Berlin) must include a stop at the museum's pub-style restaurant. There's a buffet packed with Berlin specialties, and a jazz band plays Sunday morning after 10. *Berlin Museum, Lindenstr. 14, tel. 030/251–0121. No reservations. Dress: informal. No credit cards. Closed Mon.*

Blockhaus Nikolskoe. Prussian King Wilhelm III built this Russian-style wooden lodge for his daughter Charlotte, wife of Russian Czar Nicholas I. Located south of the city on Glienecker Park, it offers open-air riverside dining in the summer. Game dishes are prominently featured. *Nikolskoer Weg, tel. 030/805–2914. Reservations advised. Dress: informal. AE, DC, MC, V.*

Eierschale. Berlin is famous for its breakfast cafés, and this is one of the best—and the best located, on the corner of central Rankestrasse and the Ku'damm. It serves breakfast at all hours, but really gets going in the evenings, when jazz groups perform in a neighboring room. The lunch and supper menus feature filling Berlin fare, but if Mexican-style spareribs are on offer, they're especially to be recommended. Sunday morning is *Frühschoppen* time, when live jazz accompanies the buffet brunch; great fun and an opportunity to witness the highlight of a Berliner's weekend. *Rankestrasse 1, tel. 030/882–5305. Reservations advised. Dress: informal. MC.*

★ **Hardtke.** This is about the most authentic old Berlin restaurant in the city. The decor is simple, with paneled walls and wood floor. The food is similarly traditional and hearty. It's a great place to try *Eisbein.* Wash it down with a large stein of beer. *Meinekestr. 27, tel. 030/881–9827. Reservations advised. Dress: informal. No credit cards.*

East Berlin

Prices in East Berlin have risen rapidly to approximately the same level as in the western part of the city. Our categories, therefore, correspond with those in the West Berlin dining section.

Very Expensive (over DM 100)

★ **Ermeler-Haus.** The Rococo grandeur of this wine restaurant located in a series of upstairs rooms reflects the elegance of the restored patrician home—which dates from the mid-16th century—in which it's housed. The atmosphere is subdued and formal, the wines are imported, and the service and German cuisine are excellent. There's dancing every Saturday evening. *Märkisches Ufer 10–12, tel. 030/2755103. Reservations advised. Jacket and tie required. No credit cards.*

★ **Ganymed.** The atmosphere here is keyed by velvet drapes, oil paintings, and brass chandeliers—as well as by the piano music at night in the front room; it was a favorite of the Brechts! The menu offers a wide range of choices, including cold plates, *cordon bleu* dishes, mixed grills, and even Indonesian cuisine. *Schiffbauerdamm 5, tel. 030/282–9540. Reservations essential. Dress: informal at lunch, jacket and tie required at dinner. No credit cards. Closed Mon.*

Expensive (DM 75–100)

★ **Schwalbennest.** On the edge of the Nikolai quarter, overlooking the Marx-Engels-Forum, this is a fairly new establishment, yet it is already known for its outstanding food and service. There is a wide choice of main dishes and wines. The grilled selections are excellent, but note that the flambéed dishes cost extra, although no additional price is indicated on the menu. *Am Marstall (upstairs), Rathausstr. at Marx-Engels-Forum, tel. 030/212–6919. Reservations essential. Dress: informal at lunch, jacket and tie required at dinner. No credit cards.*

Zur Goldenen Gans. Regional specialties are featured here, particularly game and venison dishes prepared Thüringer Forest style. *Friedrichstr. 158–164, in the Grand Hotel, tel. 030/20920. Reservations advised. Dress: informal. AE, DC, MC, V.*

Moderate (DM 50–75)

★ **Berlin Esprit.** For authentic Berlin specialties you'll probably do no better; the atmosphere is also thoroughly relaxing. *Alexanderpl., in the Hotel Stadt Berlin, tel. 030/2190. Reservations advised. Dress: informal. AE, DC, MC, V.*

★ **Cafe Flair.** This café is immensely popular despite its somewhat limited menu—more intended for snackers than diners—but what there is is good, and no complaints about the service either. There are tables outside for warm-weather sidewalk dining. *Am Marstall (ground floor), Marx-Engels-Forum, tel. 030/212-6919. Reservations advised. Dress: informal. No credit cards.*

Fioretto. The story behind the Fioretto's extraordinary success reads like a fairy tale. Owner and chef Doris Burnelett opened her Italian restaurant in East Berlin's Köpenick in March 1987, but only after the Wall fell was she able to travel to Italy to make sure the recipes she had learned from cookbooks were the real thing. They were—and they earned her a top culinary award in 1991. *Oberspreestr. 176, tel. 030/657-2605. Reservations advised. Dress: informal. No credit cards. Closed lunch (except Sun.) and Mon.*

Moskau. The strong Russian influence shows itself here in its food and drink offerings—superb chicken Kiev and real Russian vodka—but you'll also find a good range of Berlin-style fare from which to choose. Some find the restaurant overpriced, but the Moskau has been a favorite among Berliners for years. It is, however, less central and offers less atmosphere than many other restaurants listed here. *Karl-Marx-Allee 34, tel. 030/279-4052 and 030/279-2869. Reservations essential. Jacket and tie suggested. No credit cards.*

Ratskeller. This is actually two restaurants in one, composed of a wine and a beer cellar, each highly popular, and each with great atmosphere (entrances at opposite corners of the building). Menus are somewhat limited, but include good, solid Berlin fare. The brick-walled beer cellar is guaranteed to be packed during main dining hours, at which time reservations sometimes get ignored; Berliners simply line up to get in. The wine cellar is less crowded, in part because it is slightly more expensive. Among the menu selections are Hungarian goulash soup, chicken, and steaks. *Rathausstr. 15–18 (in the basement of the Rotes Rathaus, or Red Town Hall), tel. 030/212-4464 and 030/212-5301. Reservations advised. Dress: informal. No credit cards.*

Inexpensive (under DM 50)

★ **Alt-Cöllner Schankstuben.** Four tiny restaurants are contained within this charming, historic Berlin house. The section to the side of the canal on the Kleine Gertraudenstrasse, where there are tables set outside, serves as a café. The menu is relatively limited, but quality, like the service, is good. *Friederichsgracht 50, tel. 030/212-5972. No reservations. Dress: informal. No credit cards.*

★ **Arkade.** The Art Deco–style interior is a refreshing change from other East Berlin restaurants, though in good weather you may choose to dine outside. Inside, the front section is more of a café, while the grill counter at the back offers a greater variety. This is a convenient place to grab a snack after a performance at the nearby Komische Oper (Comic Opera). *Französische Str. 25, tel. 030/208-0273. No reservations. Dress: informal. No credit cards.*

★ **Raabe Diele.** The location of this restaurant is the basement of the 16th-century Ermeler-Haus (*see* above). It was largely rebuilt in 1969, meaning that the pine-paneled cellar is new—with canned music—and offers considerably less elegance and atmosphere than the handsome rooms upstairs. On the other hand, the prices are far lower and the menu consists of good Berlin-style cuisine. The service down here is just as attentive as it is upstairs. *Märkisches Ufer 10–12, in Ermeler-Haus, tel.*

030/279–4036. Dress: informal. Reservations advised, particularly at night. AE, DC, MC, V.

Lodging

Berlin lost all of its grand old luxury hotels in the bombing during World War II; though some were rebuilt, today many of the best hotels are modern. While they lack little in service and comfort, you may find some short on atmosphere. For first-class or luxury accommodations, East Berlin is easily as good as West, for the East German government, eager for hard currency, built several elegant hotels—the Grand, Palast, Hilton, and Metropol—which are up to the very best international standards and place in the very top price category. If you're seeking something more moderate, the better choice may be West Berlin, where there are large numbers of good-value pensions and small hotels, many of them in older buildings with some character. In East Berlin, however, the hostels run by the Evangelical church offer outstanding value for your money.

There are no longer any restrictions on who can stay where in East Berlin, as there were in the past. In West Berlin, business conventions year-round and the influx of summer tourists mean that you should make reservations well in advance. If you arrive without reservations, consult the board at Tegel Airport that shows hotels with vacancies, or go to the tourist office at the airport. The main tourist office in the Europa-Centre can also help with reservations (*see* Important Addresses and Numbers in Essential Information, above).

Highly recommended hotels are indicated by a star ★.

Category	Cost*
Very Expensive	over DM 250
Expensive	DM 180–DM 250
Moderate	DM 120–DM 180
Inexpensive	under DM 120

**for two people in a double room, including tax and service*

West Berlin

Very Expensive

★ **Bristol Hotel Kempinski.** Destroyed in the war, rebuilt in 1952, and renovated in 1980, the "Kempi" is a renowned Berlin classic. Located on the Ku'damm in the heart of the city, it has the best shopping at its doorstep plus some fine boutiques of its own within. All rooms and suites are luxuriously decorated and equipped with marble bathrooms, air-conditioning, and cable TV. Children under 12 stay for free if they share their parents' room. *Ku'damm 27, tel. 030/884–340. 315 rooms with bath. Facilities: 3 restaurants, indoor pool, sauna, solarium, masseur, hairdresser, limousine service. AE, DC, MC, V.*

Grand Hotel Esplanade. Opened in 1988, the Grand Hotel Esplanade exudes luxury. Uncompromisingly modern architecture, chicly styled rooms, and works of art by some of Berlin's most acclaimed artists are its outstanding visual aspects. Then there are the superb facilities and impeccable service. The enormous grand suite comes complete with sauna, whirlpool,

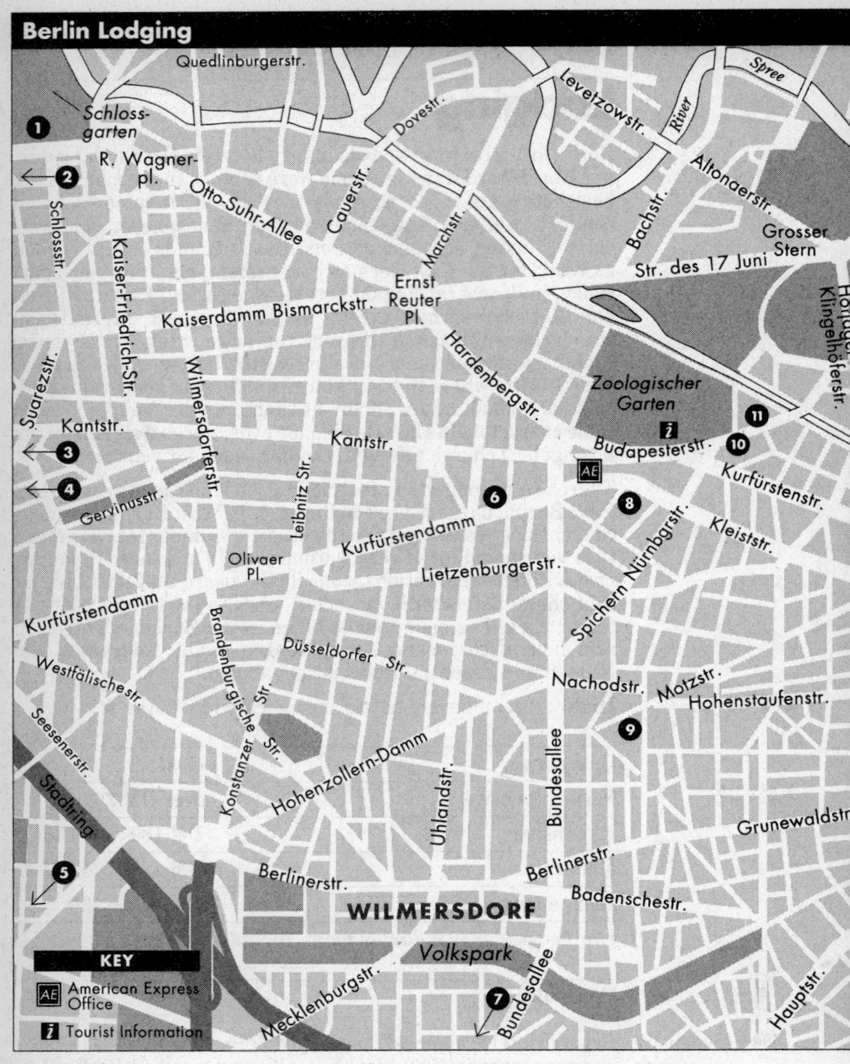

Atrium Hotel, **9**
Berlin Hilton, **24**
Berlin Hilton Krone, **25**
Berolina, **21**
Bristol Hotel Kempinski, **6**
Casino Hotel, **2**
Charlottenhof, **26**
Econtel, **1**
Grand, **22**
Grand Hotel Esplanade, **13**
Herbst, **4**
Hospiz Auguststrasse, **18**
Hospiz am Bahnhof Friedrichstrasse, **17**
Hotel Berlin, **12**
Hotel Müggelsee, **15**
Inter-Continental Berlin, **11**
Landhaus Schlachtensee, **5**
Metropol, **16**
Palast, **19**
Ravenna, **7**
Riehmers Hofgarten, **14**
Schweizerhof Berlin, **10**
Seehof, **3**
Stadt Berlin, **20**
Steigenberger Berlin, **8**
Unter den Linden, **23**

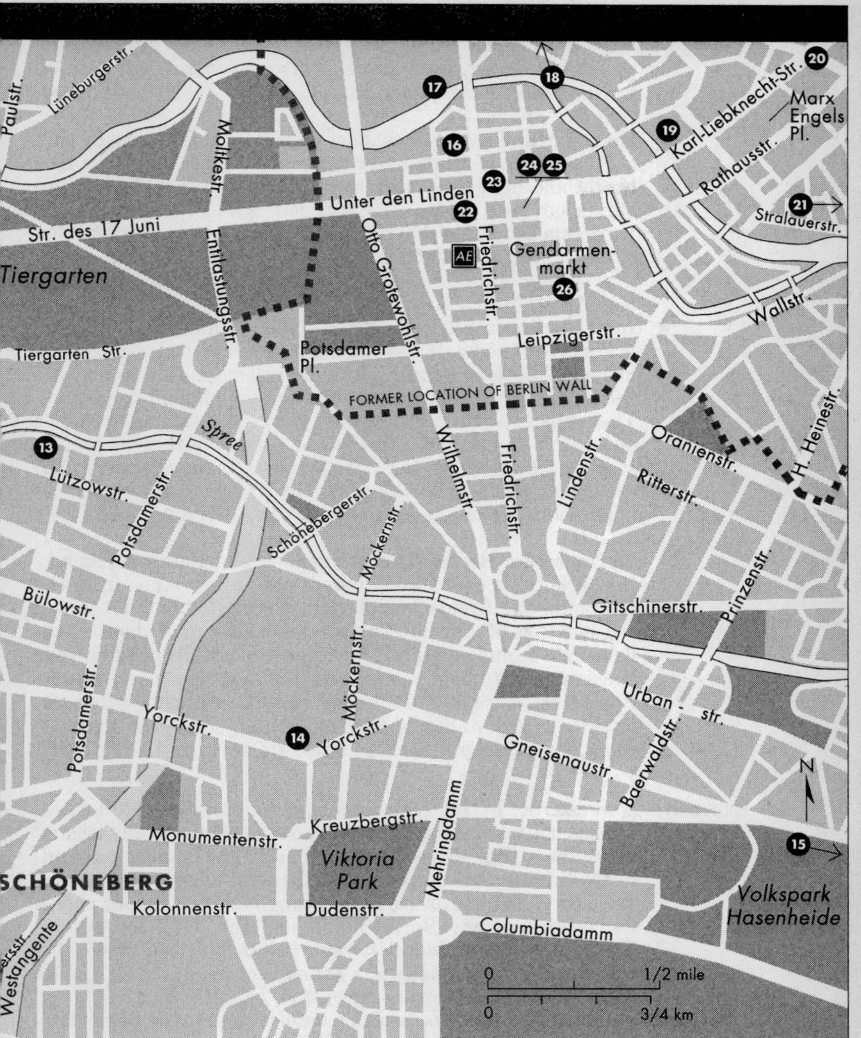
Paulstr.
Lüneburgerstr.
Moltkestr.
17
18
20
Karl-Liebknecht-Str.
Marx Engels Pl.
19
16
24 25
23
Rathausstr.
Unter den Linden
22
21
Stralauerstr.
Str. des 17 Juni
Entlastungsstr.
Otto Grotewohlstr.
Friedrichstr.
AE
Gendarmenmarkt
26
Tiergarten
Wallstr.
Tiergarten Str.
Potsdamer Pl.
Leipzigerstr.
FORMER LOCATION OF BERLIN WALL
Spree
13
Lützowstr.
Potsdamerstr.
Schönebergerstr.
Möckernstr.
Wilhelmstr.
Friedrichstr.
Lindenstr.
Oranienstr.
Ritterstr.
H. Heinestr.
Prinzenstr.
Bülowstr.
Gitschinerstr.
Potsdamerstr.
Möckernstr.
Yorckstr.
14
Yorckstr.
Urban str.
Gneisenaustr.
Baerwaldstr.
N
Kreuzbergstr.
Monumentenstr.
Viktoria Park
Mehringdamm
15
SCHÖNEBERG
Volkspark Hasenheide
Kolonnenstr.
Dudenstr.
Columbiadamm
Westangente
0
1/2 mile
0
3/4 km

and a grand piano for DM 1,200 per night. *Lützowufer 15, tel. 030/261–011. 369 rooms, 33 suites. Facilities: 2 restaurants, pub, poolside bar, pool, sauna, whirlpool, steam bath, solarium, masseur, hairdresser, boutique, medical station, library. AE, DC, MC, V.*

Hotel Berlin. The hotel that bears Berlin's name is actually part of a prominent Scandinavian group, hence the birch-tree bright and light look, modern but furnished in enduring, understated good taste. The location is handy for both the Ku'damm and Unter den Linden. *Lützowplatz 17, tel. 030/260–50. 490 rooms and 21 suites with bath. Facilities: sauna, solarium, beauty center, boutiques, restaurant, beer tavern, piano bar. AE, DC, MC, V.*

★ **Inter Continental Berlin.** The top-billed "Diplomaten Suite" is in a class of its own: It's as large as a suburban house and is furnished in exotic Oriental style. Other rooms and suites may not be so opulently furnished but still show individuality and taste. The lobby is worth a visit even if you're not staying here. It's one-fourth the size of a football field and lavishly decorated; stop by for afternoon tea and pastries. *Budapesterstr. 2, tel. 030/26020. 600 rooms with bath. Facilities: 3 restaurants, indoor pool, sauna, 24-hr room service, boutiques. AE, DC, MC, V.*

Steigenberger Berlin. The Steigenberger group's exemplary Berlin hotel is centrally situated, only a few steps from the Ku'damm and Breidscheidplatz, but remarkably quiet. Small touches that lift the hotel above the usual run of chain establishments include a nightly weather forecast dropped on your bedside table to help you plan for the next day. *Los-Angeles-Platz 1, tel. 030/210–80. 389 rooms and 11 suites, all with bath. Facilities: pool and poolside bar, sauna, solarium, massage room, 2 restaurants, cocktail bar, café, tavern. AE, DC, MC, V.*

Expensive

Schweizerhof Berlin. A newly completed program of refurbishing has not taken away the rustic look in this centrally located hotel; the extras, like room video players and minibars, are up-to-the-minute. Ask for a room in the west wing, where rooms are larger. Standards are high throughout. The indoor pool is the largest of any Berlin hotel, and the hotel is opposite Tiergarten Park. *Budapesterstr. 21–31, tel. 030/26960. 430 rooms with bath. Facilities: sauna, solarium, pool, fitness room, hairdresser, beauty salon. AE, DC, MC, V.*

★ **Seehof.** This handsome lakeside hotel is close to the Berlin fairgrounds and within easy reach of downtown. Most rooms overlook Lietzensee Lake; ask for a balcony room on the second floor. The large indoor pool overlooks the lake, too, and has access to a bar. Dine in the Au Lac restaurant, with its frescoed ceilings and Gobelin tapestries; it specializes in French cuisine and serves a fine six-course gourmet menu. *Lietzensee-Ufer 11, tel. 030/320–020. 77 rooms with bath. Facilities: restaurant, terrace with outdoor bar, indoor pool, sauna, solarium. AE, DC, MC, V.*

Moderate

Casino Hotel. What was once a barracks has been skillfully converted into an appealing hotel with large, comfortable rooms, all tastefully furnished and well equipped—the Prussian soldiers never had it so good! You'll detect the Bavarian owner's influence in the southern German cuisine at the restaurant. The Casino is in the Charlottenburg district. *Königen-*

Elisabeth-Str. 47a, tel. 030/303–090. 24 rooms with bath. Facilities: restaurant, beer garden. AE, DC, MC, V.

★ **Landhaus Schlachtensee.** Opened in 1987, this former villa (built in 1905) is now a cozy bed-and-breakfast hotel. The Landhaus Schlachtensee offers personal and efficient service, well-equipped rooms, and a quiet location in the Zehlendorf district. The nearby Schlachtensee and Krumme Lanke lakes beckon you to swim, boat, or walk along their shores. *Bogotastr. 9, tel. 030/816–0060. 19 rooms with bath. Facilities: breakfast buffet. AE, DC, MC, V.*

Riehmers Hofgarten. A few minutes' walk from the Kreuzberg hill in the heart of the colorful Kreuzberg district and close to Tempelhof airport, the Riehmers Hofgarten is a small hotel housed in a late-19th-century building. The high-ceilinged rooms are comfortable, with crisp linens and firm beds. *Yorckstr. 83, tel. 030/781–011. 21 rooms with bath. AE, DC, MC, V.*

Inexpensive

Atrium Hotel. This little privately run hotel is located within reasonable reach of downtown. The modest rooms are comfortably furnished and clean, the staff efficient and helpful. The only drawback is that there's no restaurant. *Motzstr. 87, tel. 030/218–4057. 22 rooms with bath. MC.*

Econtel. This family-oriented hotel is within walking distance of Charlottenburg Palace. Rooms have a homey feel and are spotlessly clean. *Sommeringstr. 24, tel. 030/346–810. 205 rooms with bath. Facilities: snack bar. MC.*

Herbst. This plain and simple bed-and-breakfast pension is in the Spandau district, where Hitler's mysterious deputy Rudolph Hess spent more than 40 years in jail. There are good connections to downtown by S-bahn. *Moritzstr. 21, tel. 030/333–4032. 22 rooms with bath. AE, DC.*

★ **Ravenna.** A small, friendly hotel in the Steglitz district, Ravenna is near the Botanical Garden and Dahlem museums. All the rooms are well equipped. Suite 111B is a bargain: It includes a large living room and kitchen for only DM 200. *Grunewaldstr. 8–9, tel. 030/792–8031. 45 rooms with bath. AE, DC, MC, V.*

East Berlin

The following price categories reflect hotel prices current at press time (early summer 1992), but with the continuing changes in East Berlin, actual prices quoted may change greatly in 1993.

Very Expensive

Berlin Hilton. Berlin's newest hotel, just opened, overlooks the historic Platz der Akademie, with the German and French cathedrals and the classic *Schaupielhaus* (concert hall). Near Checkpoint Charlie, the location is central to the whole city. All the right touches are here, from heated bathtubs to special rooms for handicapped travelers, nonsmokers, and businesswomen. *Platz der Akademie, tel. 030/23–820. 357 rooms with bath. Facilities: 3 restaurants, cafeteria, pub, wine cellar, bar, discotheque, indoor pool, sauna, solarium, fitness room, bowling, garage. AE, DC, MC, V.*

Grand Hotel. East Berlin's most expensive hotel lives up to its name; opened in 1987, this hotel is grand in every sense of the word. From the moment you step into the air-conditioned atrium lobby, you'll wonder how this example of capitalism at its most elegant ever fitted into a socialist society. From there on in, all is couched in luxury, and really, you could be in any modern, commodious hotel in the world. *Friedrichstr. 158–164, corner Behrenstr., tel. 030/23–270. 315 rooms and 35 suites, all with bath. Facilities: 4 restaurants, winter garden, Bierstube (beer room), bars, concert café, casino, pool, sauna, squash courts, shopping arcade, hairdresser, theater ticket office, car and yacht rental. AE, DC, MC, V.*

★ **Metropol.** This is the choice of businesspeople, not just for its excellent location across from the Friedrichstrasse train station and the International Trade Center. The staff is particularly helpful and friendly. The best rooms are on the front side, facing north. All rooms are well equipped (but note that only public areas are air-conditioned); the hotel's antiques gallery is small but interesting, and the nightclub is an unusually good one, while the restaurants are only fair (except in price!); the exception is the hotel grill-restaurant off the lobby, which is just about the best in East Berlin. *Friedrichstr. 150–153, tel. 030/203–070. 300 rooms with bath. Facilities: 3 restaurants, nightclub, bars, garage, pool, sauna, fitness room, solarium, antiques gallery, shopping mall, car, horse-drawn carriage, and yacht rental available. AE, DC, MC, V.*

Palast. This is a favorite with tour groups because of its proximity to East Berlin's museums—and because it's another of the city's megafacility hotels. The best rooms overlook the Spree River; those on the Alexanderplatz side can be noisy. The shopping mall includes a travel agency, an antiques gallery, and East Berlin's central ticket agency. The restaurants are recommended. *Karl-Liebknecht-Str. 5, tel. 030/23–828. 583 rooms with bath. Facilities: 6 restaurants, 4 bars, garage, Bierstube, nightclub, pool, sauna, fitness room, solarium, bowling, travel office, theater ticket office, antiques gallery, shopping mall, car and yacht rental. AE, DC, MC, V.*

Expensive

Berolina. If being a little way from the city's main tourist attractions is no deterrent, this is a pleasant place to stay near Alexanderplatz. Its roof-garden restaurant (Restaurant Krögel, on the 11th floor) will give you a fine view out over Berlin. *Karl-Marx-Allee 31, tel. 030/210–9541. 344 rooms with bath. Facilities: 3 restaurants, roof garden, souvenir shop, café, bar, sauna, garage. AE, DC, MC, V.*

Hotel Müggelsee. Berlin's biggest and some say most beautiful lake is just beyond your balcony in this establishment, which was once a favorite among East Germany's Communist leaders. The hotel even has its own yacht for the use of its guests. *Am Grossen Müggelsee, tel. 030/660–20. 166 rooms with bath. Facilities: boutiques, tennis court, 2 restaurants, bar, nightclub. AE, DC, M, V.*

Stadt Berlin. With its 40 stories, the Stadt Berlin at the top end of Alexanderplatz competes with the nearby TV tower for the title of premier downtown landmark. The roof dining room features good food and service and stunning views (reservations are essential). As the city's largest hotel, it is understandably less personal. The bar on the 37th floor claims to be the highest in Europe and is open until 5 AM. *Alexanderpl., tel. 030/23–890. 997 rooms with bath or shower. Facilities: 4 restaurants (including roof dining room), 3 bars, garage, shopping, beer garden, Bierstube, sauna. AE, DC, MC, V.*

★ **Unter den Linden.** The class may be missing, but the location on what was once Berlin's most elegant boulevard couldn't be better. The restaurant is drab. *Unter den Linden 14, corner Friedrichstr., tel. 030/220–0311 (tel. 030/220031 for reservations).*

307 rooms with bath or shower. Facilities: restaurant. AE, DC, MC, V.

Moderate

Berlin Hilton Krone. Opened in 1991, the Krone is part of the Hilton Hotel complex, sharing the Hilton's excellent location on East Berlin's beautiful Platz der Akademie, but not its high prices. The facilities offered by the Hilton Krone are correspondingly fewer, but rooms are comfortable and adequately furnished. There's no restaurant, but most of East Berlin's better eating haunts are within a 10-minute walk. *Platz der Akademie, tel. 030/23–820. 148 rooms with bath. Facilities: restaurant, bar. AE, DC, MC, V.*

Charlottenhof. This popular hotel-pension, ideally located on East Berlin's beautiful Platz der Akademie, was taken over by a large West German group in 1991, and by 1992 renovations should be completed. It's to be hoped that room prices remain moderate and that the homey, friendly nature of the original establishment will remain. If that happens, the Charlottenhof will move into the ranks of East Berlin's most recommendable hotels. *Charlottenstrasse 52, tel. 030/392–8426. 86 rooms with bath. Facilities: restaurant, bar. AE, DC, MC, V.*

Inexpensive

★ **Hospiz am Bahnhof Friedrichstrasse.** This Evangelical church-run hostel, both because of price and a convenient location, gets booked up months in advance. It is enormously popular with families, so the public areas are not always particularly restful. The restaurant is cheap and usually busy. Not all rooms have their own bathroom. *Albrechstr. 8, tel. 030/282–5396. 110 rooms, most with bath. Facilities: restaurant. No credit cards.*

Hospiz Auguststrasse. Comfortable rooms and friendly staff make this very low-priced hotel—also run by the Evangelical church—appealing. It is roughly a 10-minute streetcar ride into downtown Berlin. Breakfast is the only meal served here. *Augustr. 82, tel. 030/282–5321. 70 rooms, some with bath. No credit cards.*

The Arts and Nightlife

The Arts

Today's Berlin has a tough task living up to the reputation it gained from the film *Cabaret*, but if nightlife is a little toned down since the '30s, the arts still flourish. In addition to the many hotels that book seats, there are several ticket agencies, including **Theaterkasse Sasse** (Ku'damm 24, tel. 030/882–7360), **Theater-kasse Centrum** (Mienekestr. 25, tel. 030/882–7611). Most of the big stores (Hertie, Wertheim, and Karstadt, for example) also have ticket agencies, while in East Berlin tickets can be obtained from the tourist office in Alexanderplatz, and at ticket offices in the Palast and Grand hotels. Detailed information about what's going on in Berlin can be found in *Berlin Programm*, a monthly guide to Berlin arts (DM 2.50), East Berlin's monthly *Wohin in Berlin?*, and the magazines *Tip* and *Zitty*, which appear every two weeks and provide full arts listings.

Theater

Theater in Berlin is outstanding, but performances are usually in German. The exceptions are operettas and the (nonliterary) cabarets. Of the city's 18 theaters, the most renowned for both its modern and classical productions is the **Schaubühne am**

Lehniner Platz. Also important are the **Schiller-Theater** (Bismarckstr. 110, tel. 030/319–5236), which has an excellent workshop—the **Werkstatt,** specializing in experimental and avant-garde theater; **the Schlosspark-Theater** (Schlossstr. 48, tel. 030/791123); **the Renaissance-Theater** (Hardenbergstr. 6, tel. 030/312–4202); the **Freie Volksbühne** (Schaperstr. 24, tel. 030/8812489). For *Boulevard* plays (fashionable social comedies), there is the **Komödie** (Kurfurstendamm 206, tel. 030/8827893), and at the same address the **Theater am Kurfürstendamm** (tel. 030/8842080), and the **Hansa Theater** (Alt Moabit 48, tel. 030/391–4460). Among the smaller, more experimental theaters is the **Tribune** (Otto-Suhr-Allee 18–20, tel. 030/341–2600), a youthful enterprise.

East Berlin's leading theaters include: the **Berliner Ensemble** (Bertolt–Brecht–Pl., tel. 030/2888155), dedicated to Brecht and works of other international playwrights; **Deutches Theater** (Schumannstr. 13–14, tel. 030/287–1225), for outstanding classical and contemporary German drama; **Friedrichstadtpalais** (Friedrichstr. 107, tel. 030/28360), a glossy showcase for variety revues and historic old Berlin theater pieces; **Kammerspiele** (Schumannstr. 13–14, tel. 030/287–1226), a studio theater attached to the Deutsches Theater; **Maxim-Gorki-Theater** (Am Festungsgraben, tel. 030/2071790), featuring plays by local authors and some contemporary humor; and **Volksbühne** (Rosa-Luxemburg-Pl., tel. 030/2828978), featuring classical and contemporary drama.

Berlin's savage and debunking idiom is particularly suited to social and political satire, a long tradition in cabaret theaters here. The **Stachelschweine** (Europa-Centre, tel. 030/261–4795) and **Die Wühlmäuse** (1/30 Nümbergerstr. 33, tel. 030/213–7047) carry on that tradition with biting wit and style; East Berlin's equivalent is **Distel** (Friedrichstr. 100, tel. 030/287–1226). For children's theater, try **Klecks** (Schinkestr. 8/9, tel. 030/693–7731) or the **Literarisches Figurentheater** (Kleistr. 13–14, Schöneberg); **Puppentheater** (Greifswalderstr. 81–84, tel. 030/436–1343), East Berlin's puppet theater, is nominally for children but can be good entertainment for adults as well.

Concerts Berlin is the home of one of the world's leading orchestras, the **Berliner Philharmonisches Orchester** (Berlin Philharmonic—*see* below) in addition to a number of other major symphony orchestras and orchestral ensembles. The **Berlin Festival Weeks,** held annually from August to October, combine a wide range of concerts, operas, ballet, theater, and art exhibitions. For information and reservations, write **Festspiele GmbH** (Kartenbüro, Budapesterstr. 50, 1000 Berlin 30).

Other concert halls in Berlin include:

Grosser Sendesaal des SFB (Haus des Rundfunks, Masurenallee 8–14, tel. 030/303–11123). Part of the Sender Freies Berlin, one of Berlin's broadcasting stations, the Grosser Sendesaal is the home of the Radio Symphonic Orchestra.

Konzertsaal der Hochschule der Künste (Hardenbergstr 33, tel. 030/31852374). The concert hall of the Academy of Fine Arts is Berlin's second biggest—also known as the "symphony garage."

Philharmonie (Matthaikircherstr. 1, tel. 030/254–880 or 030/261–4383). The Berlin Philharmonic is based here. While the hall undergoes extensive restorations through the summer of

1992, the Philharmonic will play at the Kammermusiksaal, the new chamber music hall within the Philharmonie complex, and at other halls around Berlin, including the Schauspielhaus (*see* below), the Grosser Sendesaal des SFB (*see* above) and Haus des Rundtunks (Masurenallee 8–14, Charlottenburg). Tickets have to be reserved and purchased at the box office; telephone bookings are not accepted. The hall also houses the new Kammermusik-Saal, dedicated to chamber music.

Schauspielhaus (Pl. der Akademie., tel. 030/227–2156). This beautifully restored hall is a prime venue for concerts in East Berlin.

Waldbühne (Am Glockenturm, close to the Olympic Stadium). Modeled along the lines of an ancient Roman theater, this open-air site accommodates nearly 20,000 people. Tickets are available through ticket agencies.

Opera, Ballet, and Musicals

The **Deutsche Oper Berlin** (Bismarckstr. 35, tel. 030/3410249) is one of Germany's leading opera houses and presents outstanding productions year-round. The ballet also performs here. Tickets for both are expensive and sell out quickly. At the **Neuköllner Oper** (Karl-Marx-Str. 131–133, tel. 030/687–6061) you'll find showy, fun performances of long-forgotten operas and humorous musical productions. The skillfully restored **Theater des Westens** (Kantstr. 12, tel. 030/31903193) is the ideal setting for comic operas and musicals like *West Side Story, A Chorus Line,* and *Cabaret.* Experimental ballet and modern dance are presented at the **Tanzfabrik** in Kreuzberg (Möckernstr. 66, tel. 030/786–5861).

East Berlin's main sites for opera, operettas, and dance are the **Deutsche Staatsoper** (Unter den Linden 7, tel. 030/2004762), the **Komische Oper** (Behrenstr. 55–57, tel. 030/2292555), and the **Metropol Theater** (Friedrichstr. 101, tel. 030/2082715).

Film

Berlin has around 90 movie theaters, showing about 100 movies a day. International and German movies are shown in the big theaters around the Ku'damm; the "Off-Ku-damm" theaters show less commercial movies. For (un-dubbed) movies in English, go to the **Odeon** (Hauptstr. 116, tel. 030/781–5667) or the **Arsenal** (Welserstr. 25, tel. 030/246–848). Films from East Germany's state archives are shown Tuesday and Friday at 5:30 and 8 at **Filmtheater Babylon** (Rosa-Luxemburg-Str. 30, tel. 030/212–5076).

In February, Berlin hosts the **Internationale Filmfestspiele,** an internationally famous film festival, conferring "Golden Bear" awards on the best films, directors, and actors. The organizers, under pressure from an increasingly popular film festival that takes place in Munich every June, are considering moving the two-week event to summer. Call 030/254890 for information.

Nightlife

Berlin's nightlife has always been notorious. There are scads of places in West Berlin to seek your nighttime entertainment, and the quality ranges widely from tacky to spectacular. East Berlin's nightlife has not been on a par with the western sector, although that is changing. Dinner-dancing is generally offered at the international-style hotels; some also have nightclubs.

All Berlin tour operators offer **Night Club Tours** (around DM 100, including entrance fees to up to three shows, free drinks, and, in some cases, supper). Most places in West Berlin stay open late; the Western Allies abolished bar closing times as part of the effort to make West Berlin a Western showcase.

Clubs **Chez Nous** (Marburgerstr. 14, tel. 030/213–1810) lives up to Berlin's reputation as the drag-show center of Germany. Empire-style plush is the backdrop for two nightly shows (reservations recommended).

You'll find three more conventional stage shows at **Dollywood** (Kurfürstenstr. 114, tel. 030/248–950) each night, plus a disco. **La Vie en Rose** (Europa Center, tel. 030/323–6006) is a revue theater with spectacular light shows that also showcases international stars (book ahead). If the strip show at the **New Eden** (Ku'damm 71, tel. 030/323–5849) doesn't grab you, maybe the dance music will (two bands nightly). The **New York Bar** (Olivaer Pl. 16, tel. 030/883–6258) is a mellow drinking haven compared to its rowdier neighbors. Despite Mississippi-inspired decor, the **Riverboat** (Hohenzollerndamm 177, tel. 030/878–476) has great Berlin atmosphere. You have a choice at **Zeleste** (Marburgerstr. 2, tel. 030/213–4302): Sit back and listen to jazz or dance the night away in its disco.

Jazz Clubs Berlin's lively music scene is dominated by jazz and rock. For jazz enthusiasts, *the* events of the year are the summer's **Jazz in the Garden** festival and the international autumn **Jazz Fest Berlin.** For information, call the **Berlin Tourist Information Center** (Europa-Center, tel. 030/262–6031).

Traditionally, the best **live jazz** can be found at:

Eierschale (Podbielskiallee 50, tel. 030/832–7097). A variety of jazz groups appear here at the "Egg Shell"; daily from 8:30 PM, admission free.

Flöz (Nassauischestr. 36A, tel. 030/861–1000). The sizzling jazz at this club is sometimes incorporated into theater presentations.

Kunstlerhaus Bethanien (Mariannenpl. 2, tel. 030/614–8010). Jazz and "Free Music" concerts are held at this big venue.

Quartier (Potsdamerstr. 96, tel. 030/2629016). Jazz and rock are both presented.

Discos **Blue Note** (Courbierestr. 13, tel. 030/247–248). For an escape from the usual disco sounds, try the Blue Note; you'll find a tasty mixture of jazz, bebop, and Latin American rhythms. Open until 6 AM.

Dschungel (Nürnbergerstr. 53, tel. 030/246–698). A funky disco, "Jungle," is a current "in" spot. Dance until you drop, or at least until 4 AM. Closed Tuesdays.

Hafenbar (Chauseestr. 20). This is a popular East Berlin disco decorated in '50s style. Closed Wednesdays.

Haifishbar (Unter den Linden 5). This East Berlin disco is part of the Opern Café complex.

Metropol (Nollendorfpl. 5, tel. 030/216–2787). Berlin's largest disco, which stages occasional concerts, is a hot spot for the younger tourist. The black dance floor upstairs is the scene for a magnificent laser light show. The DM 10 cover includes your first drink.

Kneipen Berlin has roughly 5,000 bars and pubs; this includes the dives, too. All come under the heading of *Kneipen*—the place round the corner where you stop in for a beer, snack, conversation, and sometimes to dance.

Bogen 597 (Savignypl., S-bahn passage). Sound effects are provided by the S-bahn—you'll hear and feel the trains passing on the tracks overhead. This is a cozy place that serves a fine selection of wines in addition to the inevitable beer.

Ku'dorf (Joachimstaler-Str. 15). The Ku'dorf makes it easy to go from one Kneipe to another—there are 18 located under one roof here, underground, just off the Ku'damm. Open Monday–Saturday from 8 PM.

Leydicke (Mansteinstr. 4). This historic spot is a must for out-of-towners. The proprietors operate their own distillery and have a superb selection of wines and liqueurs; definitely the right atmosphere in which to enjoy a few glasses.

Sperlingsgasse (Lietzenburgerstr. 82–84). Look for the replica of the Brandenburg Gate on the sidewalk. It'll point you in the direction of the 13 different Kneipen here. All open at 7 PM.

Wilhelm Hoeck (Wilmersdorferstr. 149). Berlin's oldest Kneipe is also its most beautiful. Its superb interior dates back to 1892—all original. Frequented by a colorful cross section of the public, this is a place that's definitely worth a visit.

Wirthaus Wuppke (Schlüterstr. 21). Come here if you're seeking a mellower, quieter atmosphere. It gets as crowded as the others, but it's not so hectic. The food is good and inexpensive.

Yorckschlösschen (Yorckstr. 15). In the summer you can sit in the garden and enjoy a beer and a snack or a hearty meal. If you're lucky, there may be live music.

Zwiebelfisch (Savignypl. 7). Literally translated as the "onion fish," this Kneipe has become the meeting place of literary Bohemians of all ages. It has a good atmosphere for getting to know people. The beer is good, the menu small.

Cafés A leisurely breakfast is one of Berlin's best-loved traditions, and breakfast food is often served as late as 4 PM in cafés throughout the city. The most common menu consists of platters of cheese and cold cuts served with fresh rolls and a side order of yogurt and fresh fruit. Don't forget to order a *Milchkaffee*—a bowl of coffee and warm milk—which Berliners swear is better than the French café au lait.

Rosalinde (Knesebeckstr. 16). This small modern café is decorated all in white with modern art (by local talent) on the walls. It's near Savignyplatz, just a five-minute walk from the Ku'damm. In addition to being a popular breakfast hangout, it's also a good bet for an inexpensive lunch or dinner.

Schwarzes Café (Kantstr. 148). This place is popular with the city's young counterculture crowd. The downstairs is crowded and hot, but upstairs three huge rooms with beautiful plasterwork on the ceilings will tempt breakfasters to linger for hours. It's open nonstop Friday through Sunday.

Casinos West Berlin's leading casino is in the Europa Center. It has 10 roulette tables and three blackjack tables, and is open 3 AM–3 PM. East Berlin's poshest casino is at the Grand Hotel.

Excursions

Tour 1: Potsdam

Getting There Potsdam is virtually a suburb of Berlin, some 20 kilometers (12 miles) southwest of the city center and a half-hour journey by car, train, or bus. City traffic is heavy, however, and a train

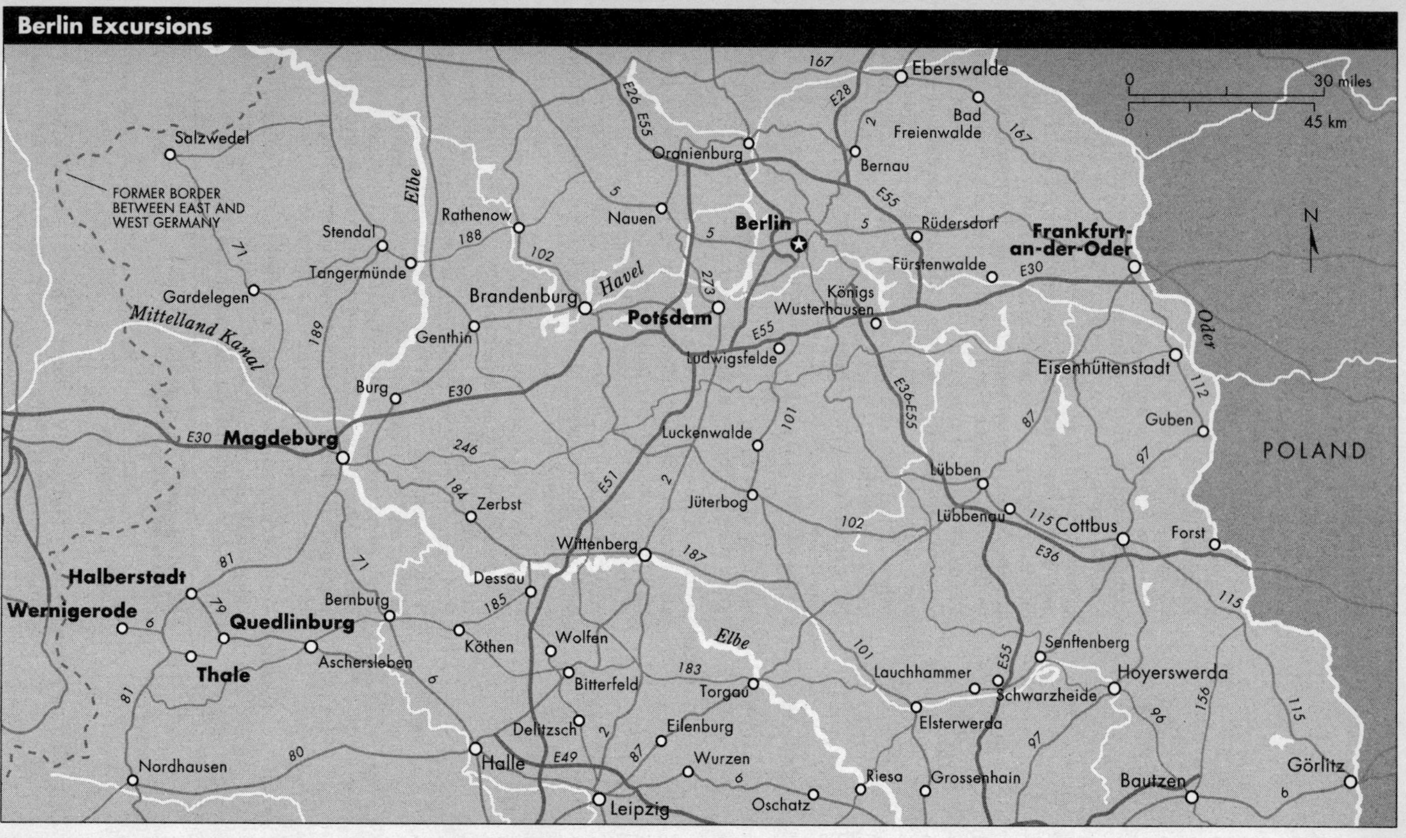

Berlin Excursions
0
30 miles
0
45 km
N
POLAND
Oder
Eberswalde
Bad Freienwalde
Bernau
Frankfurt-an-der-Oder
Rüdersdorf
Fürstenwalde
Eisenhüttenstadt
Guben
Forst
Cottbus
Lübben
Lübbenau
Senftenberg
Hoyerswerda
Schwarzheide
Lauchhammer
Elsterwerda
Grossenhain
Riesa
Oschatz
Bautzen
Görlitz
Königs Wusterhausen
Berlin
Oranienburg
Ludwigsfelde
Potsdam
Nauen
Havel
Brandenburg
Rathenow
Genthin
Luckenwalde
Jüterbog
Wittenberg
Elbe
Torgau
Eilenburg
Wurzen
Leipzig
Bitterfeld
Wolfen
Delitzsch
Dessau
Halle
Köthen
Zerbst
Burg
Magdeburg
Stendal
Tangermünde
Gardelegen
Salzwedel
FORMER BORDER BETWEEN EAST AND WEST GERMANY
Mittelland Kanal
Bernburg
Aschersleben
Quedlinburg
Thale
Halberstadt
Wernigerode
Nordhausen
E26
E55
E28
E30
E36
E36-E55
E51
E49
167
112
115
156
96
97
87
101
102
183
187
188
189
184
185
246
273
71
79
80
81

journey is recommended, even though there are no direct trains. Perhaps the most effortless way to visit Potsdam and its attractions is to book a tour with one of the big Berlin operators (*see* Guided Tours, below).

By Car From Berlin center (Strasse des 17 Juni), take the Postdamerstrasse south until it becomes Route 1 and then follow the signs to Postdam.

By Train Take the S-bahn, either the S–5 or the S–1 line, to Wannsee. Change there for the short rail trip to Potsdam Stadt (for Schloss Sanssouci), Potsdam West (for Schloss Charlottenhof), and Wildpark (for Neues Palais) stations. You also can take bus number 113 from Wannsee to the Bassanplatz bus station. From there you can walk down Brandenburgerstrasse to Platz der Nationen and on to the Green Gate, the main entrance to Sanssouci park, or you can take bus number 695 to the park.

By Bus There is regular bus service from the bus station at the Funkturm, Messedamm 8 (U-1 U-bahn station Kaiserdamm).

By Boat Boats leave hourly from Wannsee landing between 10 AM and 6 PM.

Guided Tours **Severin & Kühn** offers a whole-day tour for DM 89 (including lunch). **Berliner Bären Stadtrundfahrt** conducts an afternoon tour that includes tea in its DM 65 price. Berolina and Bus-Verkehr-Berlin also offer tours of Potsdam from Berlin. (*See* Guided Tours in Essential Information, above.)

Exploring Prussia's most famous king, Friedrich II—Frederick the Great—spent more time at his summer residence in Potsdam than at the official court in Berlin, and it's no wonder. Frederick was an aesthetic ruler, and he clearly fell for the sheer beauty of a sleepy township lost among the hills, meadows, and lakes of this rural corner of mighty Prussia. Frederick's father, Friedrich Wilhelm I, had established the Prussian court at Potsdam, but the royal castle didn't match the demanding tastes of his son and heir, who built a summer palace of his own amid green lawns above the Havel River. He called it "Sanssouci," meaning "without a care" in the French language he cultivated in his own private circle and within the court.

Some experts believe Frederick actually named the palace "Sans, Souci," which they translate as "with and without a care," a more apt name because its construction caused him a lot of trouble and expense and sparked furious rows with his master builder Georg Wenzeslaus von Knobelsdorff (Frederick called him fat and lazy). Growing increasingly restive over the expense, Frederick told von Knobelsdorff he wanted the palace to last only his lifetime, but fortunately the Prussian architect ignored him, and his creation became one of Germany's greatest tourist attractions (5 million visitors a year file through the palace and grounds). In 1993 Potsdam celebrates its 1,000th birthday, so if you plan to visit that year book well in advance.

A double ceremony that took place in 1991 drew big crowds, when Frederick the Great was given the burial he requested in his will but that was denied him by his nephew and successor, Friedrich Wilhelm II. Frederick wanted to be buried beside his hunting dogs on the terrace of his beloved Sanssouci, with no pomp and ceremony; a "philosopher's funeral" was what he decreed. His shocked nephew ordered the body to be laid out in state and then consigned Frederick's remains to the garrison church of Potsdam. The coffin was removed to safety during World War II, after which time it went on a macabre peregrination that ended in the chapel of the Hohenzollern castle in southern Germany. The unification of Germany made it possible to grant Frederick his last wish. On the same day, his father's body was reinterred, on the 250th anniversary of his death, at the so-called Peace Church, also on the Sanssouci grounds.

As you walk through Potsdam's own **Brandenburger Tor,** a victory arch built 25 years after Sanssouci, what you see today of the Hohenzollern palace complex, contained in a beautifully landscaped park and one of the most important European royal residences of its time, is largely re-created. Just weeks before the end of World War II, Potsdam was razed by British bombing, and the battle for Berlin finished it off. The East Germans did a magnificent restoration job. There is no charge to enter the grounds.

The vine-covered terraces on which **Sanssouci** stands are actually an artificial hill, rising in majestic steps from a side stream of the Havel, a few minutes' walk from the center of Potsdam.

Executed according to Frederick's impeccable, French-influenced taste, the palace is extravagantly Rococo, with scarcely a patch of wall left unadorned. Strangely, Frederick occupied only five rooms; his bedroom, study, and circular library (beautifully paneled with cedar wood) can be visited. Five rooms were kept for guests, one exclusively reserved for the French writer and philosopher Voltaire. Johann Sebastian Bach was also a welcome visitor; he and Frederick, a competent musician, performed together in the palace music chamber, considered one of Germany's finest Rococo interiors. To the west of the palace is the **New Chambers** (1747), which housed guests of the king's family; originally it functioned as a greenhouse until it was remodeled in 1771–74. Just east of Sanssouci palace is the **Picture Gallery** (1755–1763), which still displays Frederick's collection of 17th-century Italian and Dutch paintings.

At the end of the long, straight avenue that runs through Sanssouci Park you'll see a much larger and grander palace, the **Neues Palais** (New Palace). Frederick loosened the purse-strings in building this palace after the Seven Years War (1756–63), and it's said he wanted to demonstrate to his subjects that the state coffers hadn't been depleted too severely by the long conflict. Frederick rarely stayed here, however, preferring the relative coziness of Sanssouci. Still, the Neues Palais has much of interest, including an indoor grotto hall, a Jules Verne-like extravaganza of walls and columns set with shells, coral, and other aquatic decoration. There's a fascinating collection of musical instruments, which includes a 900-year-old portable organ; the Upper Gallery, which contains paintings by 17th-century Italian masters; and a bijou court theater in which performances are still given during an annual music festival held in June or July.

After Frederick died in 1786, the ambitious Sanssouci building program ground to a halt and the park fell into neglect. It was 50 years before another Prussian king, Frederick William III, restored Sanssouci's earlier glory. He engaged the great Berlin architect Karl Friedrich Schinkel to build a small palace for the crown prince. The result is the **Schloss Charlottenhof,** set in its own grounds in the southern part of the Sanssouci park. Schinkel gave it a classical, almost Roman appearance, and he let his imagination loose in the interior, too—decorating one of the rooms as a Roman tent, with its walls and ceiling draped in striped canvas.

Just north of the Schloss Charlottenhof, on the path back to Sanssouci, you'll find two other later additions to the park: Friedrich Wilhelm II's **Roman baths** (1836) and a **teahouse** built in 1757 in the Chinese style, which was all the rage at the time. (The teahouse was closed for restoration in 1991 and is expected to reopen in May 1992.) Between the Neues Palais and the Sanssouci is the **Orangerie** (completed in 1860), which, with two massive towers linked by a colonnade, evokes an Italian Renaissance palace. Today it houses 47 copies of paintings by Raphael. Elsewhere in the park, a delicious layer cake **"mosque"** disguises pump works that operated the fountains in the Sanssouci park; the minaret concealed the chimney. The Italianate Peace Church (1845–48) houses a 12th-century Byzantine mosaic taken from an island near Venice.

Time Out Halfway up the park's Drachenberg hill, above the Orangery, stands the curious **Drachenhaus** (Dragon House), modeled in 1770 after the Pagoda at London's Kew Gardens and named for the gargoyles ornamenting the roof corners. When built, it served as the residence of the palace vintner; it now houses a popular café.

The final addition to the Sanssouci park is equally exotic. Resembling a rambling, half-timbered country manor house, the **Schloss Cecilienhof** was built for Crown Prince Wilhelm in 1913 in a newly laid out stretch of the park bordering the Heiliger See, called the New Garden. It was here that the allied leaders Truman, Atlee, and Stalin hammered out the fate of postwar Germany, at the 1945 Potsdam Conference. You can see the round table where they held their meetings; in fact, you can stay the night under the roof where they gathered to make history, for the Cecilienhof is today a very comfortable hotel (*see* Lodging, below). Also in the New Garden is the substantial two-story **Marble Palace,** completed in 1792, using gray-white Silesian marble to ornament the red brickwork. Formerly housing a military museum, it is closed for restoration until 2000. *Information Center, Sanssouci: tel. 0331/22051. Open Apr.–Oct., daily 9–4:30. Schloss Sanssouci admission (guided tours only): DM 6 adults, DM 3 children. Open Apr.–mid-Oct., daily 9–5; mid-Oct.–Jan. 9–3, Feb., and Mar., daily 9–4; closed first and third Mon. of month. New Chambers admission: DM 4 adults, DM 2 children. Open Sat.–Thurs. 9–5. Picture Gallery admission: DM 3 adults, DM 1.50 children. Open mid-May–mid-Oct., daily 9–5, closed fourth Wed. of month. Neues Palais admission with tour: DM 6 adults, DM 3 children; without tour: DM 5 adults, DM 2.50 children. Open Apr.–mid-Oct., daily 9–5; mid-Oct.–Jan., daily 9–3; Feb. and Mar., daily 9–4; closed second and fourth Mon. of month. Schloss Charlottenhof admission (guided tour only) DM 3 adults, DM 2 children. Open mid-May–mid-Oct., daily 9–5; closed fourth Mon. of month. Roman baths admission (additional charge for special exhibitions): DM 2 adults, DM 1 children. Open mid-May–mid-Oct., daily 9–5; closed third Mon. of month. Chinese* *teahouse admission (closed for restoration; reopening May 1992): DM 1. Open mid-May–mid-Oct., daily 9–5; closed one Mon. a month. Orangerie admission (additional charge for special exhibitions): DM 3 adults, DM 1.50 children. Open mid-May–mid-Oct., daily 9–5; closed fourth Thurs. of month. Mosque admission: DM 3. Open mid-May–mid-Oct., daily 9–5; closed fourth Mon. in month. Schloss Cecilienhof admission (nonguests): DM 3, DM 1.50 children. Open daily 9–4:15, closed second and fourth Mon. of month.*

Don't leave Potsdam without looking over the town itself, which still retains the imperial character lent it by the many years during which it served as royal residence and garrison quarters. The central market square, the **Alter Markt,** sums it all up: the stately, domed **Nikolaikirche** (1724), a square Baroque church with classical columns; an **Egyptian obelisk** erected by Sanssouci architect von Knobelsdorff; and the officious facade of the former **city hall** (1755), now the Haus Marchiwitza, with a gilded figure of Atlas atop the tower. Wander around some of the adjacent streets, particularly Wilhelm-Külz-Strasse, to admire the handsome restored burghers' houses.

Three blocks north of the Alter Markt is the **Holländisches Viertel,** built by Friedrich Wilhelm I in 1732 to induce Dutch artisans to settle in a city that needed migrant labor to support its rapid growth. (Few Dutch came, and the gabled, hip-roofed brick houses were used mostly to house staff.) The Dutch government has promised to finance some of the cost of repairing the damage done by more than four decades of Communist administration.

There's a chilling reminder of the Communist years a few steps away from the central shopping street, Brandenburgerstrasse. Turn down Lindenstrasse-Strasse, and at No. 54 you'll find an old guardhouse that served as a prison for victims of the East German State Security Service, the dreaded Stasi. Known as the "Linden Hotel" among East Germans, it's now empty of its political prisoners, and you can step through the outside door and into the tiny exercise yard, overlooked by small barred windows. The new political parties that replaced the Communists have taken over the administrative offices, together with an enterprising Potsdamer who has opened a café there!

Dining **Am Stadttor.** A five-minute walk from the Sanssouci palace and located on Potsdam's main shopping street, the Stadttor is the ideal spot for lunch. The menu isn't exactly imperial Prussian, but the dishes are filling and inexpensive. The soups are particularly wholesome, and the liver Berlin style is as good as any you'll find in the city. The place is popular, so it's advisable to book a table. *Brandenburgerstrasse 1–3, tel. 0331/21729. Reservations advised. Dress: informal. No credit cards. Inexpensive.*

Lodging **Schloss Cecilienhof.** This English country-style mansion is where Truman, Atlee, and Stalin drew up the 1945 Potsdam Agreement. It's here that Truman received the news of the first successful atom bomb test (July 16, 1945). Given the fateful event that took place here, the hotel rooms are somewhat mundane, although comfortable and adequately equipped. The Schloss is set in its own parkland bordering a lake and is a pleasant stroll from Sanssouci and the city center. *Neuer*

Garten, tel. 0331/231–4144, fax: 0331/22–498. 42 rooms with bath or shower. Facilities: sauna, masseur, restaurant. AE, D, MC, V. Moderate.

Tour 2: Magdeburg

Magdeburg's great Gothic cathedral—Germany's oldest and, some say, the country's finest—is worth the trip from Berlin. Much of the city was rebuilt after the 1945 bombing in the dull utilitarian style favored by the Communists, but there are nevertheless corners of the old town where Magdeburg's 1,200-year history still lingers. Apart from the cathedral, the monastery church of Unsere Lieben Frauen contains much of interest. Both are a few strides from the Elbe River, where some fine walks open up through the wooded Kulturpark.

Getting There
By Car
Magdeburg is located just off the E-8 motorway, the old transit road connecting Berlin and Hannover. It's 150 kilometers (90 miles) west of Berlin, a 90-minute drive as long as the motorway is clear. (In summer and at weekends, when the E-8 gets crowded, the two-hour train ride from Berlin might be preferable.) To get to the town center follow the signs for Magdeburg-Stadtmitte.

By Train Trains leave approximately every two hours from Bahnhof Zoo in Berlin; the trip takes about two hours.

By Bus Buses leave from the Funkturm bus station in Berlin.

Guided Tours There are no guided tours of Magdeburg originating in Berlin.

Exploring If you arrive in Magdeburg by train or bus, head east from the main railway station (the bus depot is at beside it) two blocks to the city center, the Alter Markt, which is dominated from the west side by the 17th-century **Rathaus** (City Hall), one of Magdeburg's few remaining Baroque buildings. In front of its arcaded facade is a 1966 bronze copy of Germany's oldest equestrian statue, the **Magdeburger Reiter**, completed by an unknown master around 1240. The sandstone original is now in the nearby **Kulturhistorisches Museum,** where you can also see the simple invention with which the 17th-century scientist Otto von Güricke proved the extraordinary power created by a vacuum. The device consisted of just two iron cups; von Güricke sealed them together by pumping out the air—and then attached the hollow sphere to two teams of eight cart-horses, which were urged to pull the cups apart. The vacuum proved stronger. *Otto-von-Güricke-Strasse 68–73. Admission: DM 3 adults, DM 1.50 children. Open Tues.–Sun. 10–6.*

Time Out If you're hungry after touring the museum, drop in at the **Böthelstube** on the Alter Markt. Local specialties such as *Magdeburger Lose Wurst* and *Kochklops*—a variety of sausage and dumplings—are served with an excellent beer. (Closed Sat. dinner and Sun.)

Head down Breiter Weg (formerly Karl-Marx-Strasse, a name that was one of the first casualties of the fall of East German communism). To your left you'll see the mighty twin towers of Magdeburg's Gothic **Cathedral** of Saints Maurice and Catherine rearing up above the rooftops. Opposite the post office on Breiter Weg turn left into Domplatz, and there is the soaring west front of the cathedral before you. The awesome structure was begun in 1209, making it the oldest Gothic church in Germany; it was completed in 1520. The founder of the Holy Roman Empire, Otto I, lies buried beneath the choir, his tomb overshadowed by graceful columns of Ravenna marble. Study the representations of famous Christian martyrs on the walls of the nave; you'll find them all standing determinedly on the heads of their persecutors (that's Nero under the heel of St. Paul). A more recent memorial is Expressionist artist Ernst Barlach's sculptured group warning of the horrors of war. It was removed by the Nazis in 1933, but it's back with all its original force. *Open Mon.–Sat. 10–noon and 2–4; Sun. 2–4. Guided tours: Mon.–Sat. 10 and 2, Sun. 11:15 and 2.*

Just north of Domplatz and on the way back to the city center is Magdeburg's second great attraction, the Romanesque monastery church and cloisters of **Unser Lieben Frauen.** The church, built in the years 1064–1230, now serves as a concert hall and an art gallery. Gothic sculptures share space with modern East German works in sober surroundings that encourage meditation and reflection—there's also a café for more mundane requirements. *Regierungstr. 4–6, tel. 0391/33741 (concert information). Open Tues.–Sun. 10–6.*

Dining

Haus des Handwerks. The large, echoing restaurant has the atmosphere of an Eastern European railway-station buffet, but the food is substantial and reasonably priced. The cordon bleu steak is always good. It's not central, but it is well worth the 10-minute journey (number 10 tram). *Garaisstr. 10, tel. 0391/51422. Reservations advised. Dress: informal. No credit cards. Moderate.*

Stadt Prag. The "City of Prague" restaurant has a menu that reads like a culinary tour of the former Hapsburg Empire, from chicken Viennese style to Bohemian dumplings by way of Hungarian goulash. *Fritz-Reuter-Allee 10, tel. 0391/51162. Reservations advised. Dress: informal. No credit cards. Moderate.*

Lodging

Hotel International. Magdeburg's leading hotel is typically East German postwar Modern, but it has all the necessary facilities and comforts and is centrally located. Rooms are functional and uninspired in their decoration; if you're looking for space and above-average comfort, reserve a suite apartment (DM 300 or more). *Otto-von-Güricke-Strasse 87, tel. 0391/3840. 331 rooms and 9 suites with bath or shower. Facilities: sauna, garage, 3 restaurants, café, bar, nightclub. AE, DC, MC, V. Expensive.*

Grüner Baum. This is one of the few hotels in East Germany to have remained in private hands throughout the years of Communist state control. The rooms are large, and it's to be hoped they'll stay that way after refurbishing, which will give each room a private bathroom. *Fritz-Reuter-Allee 40, tel. 0391/30862. 35 rooms, none with bath (bathrooms are on each floor). No credit cards. Inexpensive.*

Excursions from Magdeburg

Magdeburg is an ideal center from which to explore the Elbe River countryside between the Harz Mountains and the Brandenburg plains. The Reisebüro (tourist office), near the main railway station (Wilhelm-Pieck-Allee 14), offers bus tours of the region. Ships of the East German shipping line Weisse Flotte (tel. 0391/31907) embark from Magdeburg on day trips and longer cruises on the Elbe.

KD German Rhine Line operates five-day luxury cruises between Magdeburg and Bad Schandau (south of Dresden), with ports of call including Wittenberg, Meissen, and Dresden. For information, contact the company in the United States (tel. 914/948–3600 or 415/392–8817) or in Köln (tel. 0221/20880).

Southwest of Magdeburg is a group of historic old towns easily reached by train or car. From Magdeburg, Route 81 goes 53 kilometers (33 miles) to **Halberstadt,** the gateway to the Harz Mountain area to the south. One of the key commercial and religious centers of the Middle Ages, about 85% of Halberstadt was destroyed in April 1945. Rebuilding has left some remarkable contrasts: Half-timbered 17th-century houses stand alongside stark modern blocks. Dominating the town, the twin-towered **cathedral** is one of the most noteworthy examples of German Gothic, completed in 1491 after 252 years of construction. Inside, note the tapestries and sculptures, the stained-glass windows, and the numerous ancient burial tombs.

Time Out Just south of Halberstadt, the **Jagdschloss Spiegelberger,** a Baroque hunting lodge dating from 1782, now houses a pleasant country restaurant. In the basement is the "great wine cask," a huge wooden barrel constructed in 1594 and holding 132,760 liters (35,080 gallons) of wine.

Heading south on Route 81, look for the turnoff to the right about 9 kilometers (5½ miles), marked for Wernigerode, which is another 14 kilometers (9 miles) along. **Wernigerode** is a colorful small city of half-timbered houses from the Middle Ages, watched over by the castle atop the nearby Agnesberg hill. The castle was last rebuilt in 1862–1885, but parts date from the 1670s and even earlier. Today the Feudalism museum occupies 37 of its rooms. *Open Tues.–Sun. 9–5.*

The 1899 vintage **Harzquerbahn,** a fascinating narrow-gauge railway line mostly using steam power, starts from Wernigerode on its three-hour, 60-kilometer (37½-mile) run through the northern Harz Mountain area to Nordhausen.

From Wernigerode, a scenic drive winds south about 10 kilometers (6 miles) to Elbingerode, then west about 15 kilometers (9 miles) to Blankenburg. Just south of the town, a road cuts east 8 kilometers (5 miles) to **Thale,** site of the renowned **Hexentanzplatz** (Witches' Dancing Place). This rock plateau, with an elevation of 454 meters (1,475 feet), can be reached year-round by a four-minute cable-car ride from the Hubertusbrücke in Bodetal. From the top, there's a splendid view out over the neighboring countryside.

Fifteen kilometers (9 miles) beyond Thale is **Quedlinburg,** known for its picturesque half-timbered houses and detailed carved wood ornamentation. Wander around the town to enjoy the medieval houses, taking special note of the two-story **Rathaus** (City Hall), completed in 1615, its ornate stone front entry dramatically punctuating the Renaissance facade. From 966 to 1802, the castle atop the **Schlossberg** hill was the official residence of the Abbess of Quedlinburg Abbey; adjacent is the 12th-century Romanesque St. Servatius abbey church. The castle today houses a museum of local history.

Return to Berlin via Route 6 to Bernburg and then Route 71/E49 north to Magdeburg, where you can pick up the E30 Autobahn.

Tour 3: Frankfurt an der Oder

Poland is so near Berlin that a day trip to the border is no problem. You can stand on the banks of the famous Oder River, which now marks the eastern limits of reunited Germany, and look across to a Poland that is learning again to coexist with a central European colossus as neighbor. (American citizens no longer require a visa for further travel to Poland.) But where on the border? Frankfurt an der Oder is the obvious choice. Here you'll have an opportunity now missing in Berlin—to feel the chill of visiting the frontier of the old East and West and observe firsthand the new European order at work.

Getting There
By Car

Frankfurt an der Oder is 90 kilometers (55 miles) east of Berlin, about an hour's drive. Head east on East Berlin's Leninallee, joining the E-55 ring-Autobahn and heading south until the Frankfurt/Oder turnoff. Exit at Frankfurt-Stadtmitte.

By Train

Trains depart every two hours from East Berlin's Hauptbahnhof.

By Bus

There's infrequent bus service from East Berlin's Hauptbahnhof.

Exploring

Ninety percent of the historic center of Frankfurt an der Oder was destroyed in May 1945, not by Allied bombing but in a devastating fire that broke out after Germany's capitulation. The fire was sparked by a confrontation between remaining units of the Nazi "Werwolf" resistance and Polish forces from across the Oder River. The flames spread rapidly because the conquered city had no fire brigade. Until then, 80% of the city had survived the war undamaged; the clash between Werwolf fanatics and the Poles left it in smoldering ruins. Today, the strong undercurrent of anti-Polish feeling in Frankfurt an der Oder is palpable, and local police are kept busy smoothing over quarrels between the locals and Poles from across the river, for nowhere is the newly united Germany so close to the East European community with which it now has to live.

Poland virtually overlooks the center of the city, which sits in its faded Prussian glory on the banks of the Oder. The oldest building here is also the most imposing: the City Hall, on Marktplatz, 100 yards west of the Oder. First mentioned in official records in 1348, the building has a 17th-century Baroque facade that now looks out over the hustle and bustle of central Frankfurt. Behind the City Hall, on the banks of the Oder, you'll find another elegant, finely restored Baroque structure, the world's only museum devoted to one of Germany's greatest writers, Heinrich von Kleist (1777–1811). Kleist's birthplace in Frankfurt an der Oder was among the buildings consumed by fire in 1945, but the house containing the **Kleist Gedenk-und Forschungsstätte** does date from the year of the dramatist's birth. Kleist lived only 34 years—he shot himself in a suicide pact with his lover in Berlin in 1811—but his contribution to German literature was monumental. His works—notably the famous history play *Das Kätchen von Heilbronn* (source of one of Carl Orff's greatest compositions) and the comedy *Der Zerbrochene Krug* (premiered by Goethe in Weimar in 1808)—

avoid all attempts at categorization. The original manuscripts of both those plays are to be seen in the museum, which traces Kleist's life and work with exemplary clarity and care. *Fährstr. 7, tel. 030/24520. Open Tues.–Fri. 10–12 and 2–4, weekends 2–5.*

Frankfurt an der Oder is home to the newly reestablished **European University of Viadrina,** scheduled to open in fall 1992. The university, which was closed 180 years ago, will specialize in economics, politics, and business administration and will offer instruction in several European languages.

Dining and Lodging

Stadt Frankfurt. Frankfurt an der Oder is off the tourist track, so its leading hotel falls short of many of the expected facilities and comforts. Rooms are small, but the restaurant can be recommended, particularly its fresh-made *Gemüsetopf* (vegetable stew). *Karl-Marx-Str. 193, tel. 030/3890. 186 rooms and 4 suites with bath or shower. Facilities: restaurant, bar. AE, DC, M, V. Moderate.*

17 Saxony and Thuringia

Including Leipzig, Dresden, and Weimar

Introduction

To those familiar with eastern Germany—the former German Democratic Republic—the name may still conjure up images of dour landscapes and grim industrial cities. This image cannot be changed overnight, even since the collapse of the Communist government. It will take years before the polluted, dying forests in the south can be rejuvenated, and the ancient soot-stained factories replaced. The deteriorating public housing projects of the '50s and '60s cannot be razed any more than the acrid smell of brown coal smoke can be eliminated overnight. But the small towns of eastern Germany—in the new federal states of Saxony and Thuringia—will tell much more about an older Germany than the frenetic lifestyles of Frankfurt, Hamburg, Stuttgart, or Köln. The Communist influence—hard-line as it was—here never penetrated as deeply as did the American impact on West Germany. East Germany clung to its German heritage, proudly preserving connections with such national heroes as Luther, Goethe, Schiller, Bach, Handel, Hungarian-born Liszt, and Wagner. And although bombing raids in World War II devastated most of its cities, the East Germans, over the years, carried out an extensive program of restoring and rebuilding the historic neighborhoods. Meissen porcelain, Frederick the Great's palace at Potsdam, the astounding collections of the Pergamon and Bode museums in Berlin, and those in the Zwinger in Dresden will now be incorporated into the total national heritage.

Traditional tourist sights aside, eastern Germany is also worth visiting precisely because it *is* in transition, poised at a remarkable moment in history. In the wake of ebullient newspaper headlines and photographs of wild parties amid the rubble of the Berlin Wall, it's all too easy to simplify what's going on in the former GDR as a quest for Western-style democracy. The initiative for unification came as much from the west as it did from the east, and East Germans have not been altogether happy with the consequences. Though they enjoyed the highest standard of living of all the Eastern Bloc countries, a number of East Germans still see their western compatriots as the "haves," and themselves as the "have-nots."

These people, bound politically and economically to the Soviet Union for 45 years, are still uncomfortable with their newly acquired freedoms and responsibilities. For most of those years, despite being communism's "Western front," the GDR was isolated from Western ideas, and many now resent the less savory elements of Western society imposed on what was an orderly, if unexciting, way of life. Time has not stood still east of the former border, but it has taken much less of a toll than it has in the West; the rampant commercial overdevelopment that has blighted much of the West German landscape is virtually unknown in the eastern part of the country. As one East Berliner noted following her first visit to the western sector of the city, "The lights are brighter, so you can see the trash more readily."

The main differences for travelers are the absence of a border, no need to change currencies, and—regrettably—higher prices. But the most important change is that visitors now have complete freedom to go wherever they want, to choose their own hotels, and to wander off the "transit corridors" and explore eastern Germany at will.

Essential Information

At press time the former German Democratic Republic—the "new federal states," or "eastern Germany"—was still in a state of flux, particularly in those areas most likely to affect visitors. The transportation and communications systems of the two halves of a country so long divided have to be completely integrated, and that will take time. The former East German tourism ministry and tourist boards are being taken over by West German authorities, and the resultant bureaucratic problems are formidable. Former state-run hotels are passing into private ownership and hundreds of others are being built to accommodate the surge of tourists and business travelers who followed the fall of the Berlin Wall and the opening of the frontiers.

The upheaval reaches down to the smallest concerns of everyday life, with prices rising to match those in the West. Travelers who remember East Germany as a low-budget paradise will be disappointed to find an area nearly as expensive as western Germany and where the cost of comfortable lodgings has gone through the roof. As this process of price adjustment is still under way, it is difficult to accurately predict costs. Museums and art galleries, for instance, were still converting their old admission charges into the new Deutschemark currency. Telephone exchanges in eastern Germany were also being expanded to accommodate the sudden surge in calls from the West, and numbers were being altered at a frustrating rate. It's still a hopelessly difficult task to call eastern Germany from western Germany. One tip: If you are calling long-distance, ask the international operator to book an *Eilgespräch* (urgent call). It costs double, but the wait is less than halved.

We have given addresses, telephone numbers, and other logistical details based on the best available information, but remember that changes are taking place at a furious pace in everything from postal codes to street and even city names. We strongly recommend that you contact the German National Tourist Office (*see* Chapter 1) or your travel agent for the most up-to-date information.

Important Addresses and Numbers

Tourist Information The main office of the **Reisebüro** (the former state tourist office) in East Berlin is at Alexanderplatz 5, tel. 030/212–4675 or 030/210–4209. There's another branch at Schönefeld airport (tel. 030/678–8248).

For tourist information for individual cities, contact:

Chemnitz: Strasse der Nationen 3, tel. 0371/62051.
Dessau: Friedrich-Naumann-Str. 12, tel. 0340/4661.
Dresden: Box 201, Pragerstr. 10/11, tel. 0351/495–5025.
Eisenach: Bahnhofstr. 3–5, tel. 03691/4895 or 6161.
Erfurt: Bahnhofstr. 37, tel. 0361/26267.
Freiburg: Weingasse 9.
Gera: Dr.-Rudolf-Breitscheid-Str. 1, tel. 0365/26432.
Halle: Kleinschmieden 6, tel. 0345/23340.

Leipzig: Sachsenplatz 1, tel. 0341/79590.
Meissen: An der Frauenkirche 3, tel. 03521/4470.
Weimar: Box 647, Marktstr. 4, tel. 03643/2173.

Embassies With the reunification of Germany, the embassies of the United States and the United Kingdom in East Berlin have been downgraded to the rank of consulates or missions. The **Canadian Embassy** in Bonn (Friedrich-Wilhelmstrasse 18, tel. 0228/231061) is responsible for eastern Germany. The **United States** office in East Berlin is at Neustädtische Kirchstr. 4–5, tel. 030/238–5174; the **United Kingdom Consulate** in East Berlin is at Unter den Linden 32–34, tel. 030/220–2431.

Travel Agencies **American Express:** Hotel Bellevue, Köpckestr., Dresden, 15, tel. 0351/56620; Europaisches Reisebüro, Katherinenstrasse, Leipzig, tel. 0341/79210.

Car Rental

Cars can be rented at all major hotels and at airports. Rental cars can be driven into neighboring countries, including Poland and Czechoslovakia. Rental charges correspond with those in western Germany. All the major international car-rental firms are now represented throughout eastern Germany, but don't expect quite the same range of choice in models, and reserve well in advance. All major Western credit cards are accepted.

Avis: Karl-Marx-Strasse 264, tel. 030/685–2093, and Schönefeld airport, tel. 030/672–2441, **East Berlin;** Dresden airport, tel. 0351/583–141, **Dresden;** Leipzig airport, tel. 0341/391-1132, **Leipzig.**

Hertz: Behrens-Str. 23 (opposite Grand Hotel), tel. 030/672-2607, and Herzbergstr, 40–43, tel. 030/255–96164, **East Berlin;** Köpckestr. 15 (in Hotel Bellevue), tel. 0351/584–169, Tiergartenstr. 94, tel. 0351/232–8218, and Dresden airport, tel. 0351/588–348, **Dresden;** Platz der Republik 2 (in Hotel Astoria), tel. 0341/722–470, and Leipzig airport, tel. 0341/243–3026, **Leipzig.**

InterRent-Europcar: Rosa-Luxemburg-Str. 2, tel. 037323/246-3209, Siegfriedstr. 49–60, Lichtenberg, tel. 030/558–9825, and Schönefeld airport, tel. 030/672–2606, **East Berlin;** Liebstadterstr. 5, tel. 0351/232–3399, and Dresden airport, tel. 0351/232–3399, **Dresden;** Johannisplatz 14, tel. 0341/718–9300, and Leipzig airport, 0341/2430–28, **Leipzig.**

Sixt-Budget: Friedrichstrasse 150–153, tel. 030/203–07293, and Schönefeld airport, tel. 030/672–2608, **East Berlin;** An der Frauenkirche 5 (in Hotel Dresdner Hof), tel. 0351/484–1696, Pragerstr. (in Hotel Newa) tel. 0351/496–7112, **Dresden;** Gerberstr. 15 (in Hotel Merkur), tel. 0341/799–1149, and Leipzig airport, tel. 0341/3017, **Leipzig.**

Arriving and Departing by Plane

West Berlin's **Tegel** airport is only 6 kilometers (4 miles) from downtown; East Berlin's **Schönefeld** airport lies about 24 kilometers (15 miles) outside the downtown area. **Dresden Airport** (tel. 0351/589–141) lies about 10 kilometers (6 miles) north of the city. Leipzig's **Schkeuditz** airport is 12 kilometers (8 miles) northwest of the city.

Arriving and Departing by Car and Train

By Car Expressways connect Berlin with Dresden and Leipzig.

By Train International trains stop at Friedrichstrasse or Ostbahnhof stations in East Berlin; from there, there is direct service to Dresden, Leipzig, and most towns covered below. Meissen requires a bus connection from the rail line.

Getting Around

By Car Nearly 1,000 miles of Autobahn and 7,000 miles of secondary roads crisscross eastern Germany. Traffic regulations are strictly enforced, from parking rules to speed limits (130 kph/80 mph on Autobahns, 80 kph/50mph on main roads, and 50 kph/30 mph in towns). The eastern German police have been known to levy fines for the slightest offense, and drinking and driving is particularly forbidden. If not otherwise indicated, cars coming from the right have the right-of-way. On heavily traveled north–south routes, you can avoid some of the trucking by keeping to the roads that run parallel to the Autobahn if you don't feel pressed for time.

Gasoline is available at either **Minol** or **Intertank** filling stations, although now you'll also increasingly find the familiar signs of gasoline brands you know. Diesel fuel may not be available at all stations, and unleaded fuel is sold only on expressways and in main towns. On back roads, filling stations may be scarce, so be careful not to let fuel reserves get too low.

By Train Eastern Germany has three types of trains—Express, the fastest, shown as "IEx" or "Ex" in timetables; fast, shown as "D"; and regular/local services indicated with an "E." The EuroCity and InterCity services of the German Federal Railways, the Bundesbahn, are being progressively incorporated into the eastern German system. The fast categories have varying supplementary fares; local trains do not. Most long- and medium-distance trains have both first- and second-class cars and many have either dining or buffet cars, although these may be joined to the train only from and to specific destinations. First- and second-class sleeping cars and couchettes are available. As rail travel is popular and space is limited, trains are usually full and reservations—make them either via the Reisebüro der DDR or at any major train station—are recommended.

Railway buffs are increasingly welcome, particularly around the narrow-gauge lines in the mountainous south.

By Boat **"White Fleets"** of inland boats, including paddle sidewheelers, ply the inland lakes around Berlin and the Elbe River with their starting point at Dresden, going downstream and on into Czechoslovakia.

The **KD German Rhine Line** is now operating two luxury cruises in both directions on the Elbe River from May to October: a five-day voyage from Bad Schandau (south of Dresden) to Magdeburg, and a seven-day journey from Bad Schandau to Hamburg. Ports of call include Dresden, Meissen, and Wittenberg. From June to September, five-day cruises run between Bad Schandau and Melnik, Czechoslovakia, near Prague. The cruises, aboard new modern power vessels, are in great demand, so reservations should be made several months in advance. For details of the cruises, contact the company in the

United States at 170 Hamilton Avenue, White Plains, New York 10601–1788, tel. 914/948–3600, and at 323 Geary Street, San Francisco, California 94102–1860, tel. 415/392–8817; in Germany contact Köln-Düsseldorfer Deutsche Rheinschiffahrt AG, Frankenwerft 15, 5000–Köln 1, tel. 0221/20880.

By Bus Long-distance bus services linking Frankfurt with Dresden and Leipzig were inaugurated in 1991. Within Saxony and Thuringia, most areas are accessible by bus, but service is infrequent, and mainly serves to connect with rail lines. Check schedules carefully.

Guided Tours

Information on travel and tours to and around eastern Germany is available from most travel agents, but those who specialized in this region before the change in regimes probably will still give you better assistance, particularly during the transition period. Leading agents include:

Berolina Travel (20 Conduit St., London W1R 9TD, tel. 071/629–1664).

Koch (157 E. 86 St., New York, NY 10028, tel. 212/369–3800).

Love Tours (15315 Magnolia Blvd., Suite 110, Sherman Oaks, CA 91403, tel. 800/501–6868).

Maupintour (Box 807, Lawrence, KS 60044, tel. 800/255–4266).

Orbis (342 Madison Ave., Suite 1512, New York, NY 10173, tel. 212/867–5011).

Pecum Tours (2002 Colfax Ave., Minneapolis, MN 55405, tel. 612/871–8171).

Travcoa (2350 SE Bristol, Santa Ana, CA 92707, tel. 800/992–2003).

Exploring Saxony and Thuringia

Highlights for First-time Visitors

Thomaskirche and Nikolaikirche, Leipzig
Buchenwald
Zwinger palace, Dresden
Schiller and Goethe houses, Weimar
Erfurt
Wartburg castle, Eisenach

Dessau to Leipzig

Numbers in the margin correspond to points of interest on the Eastern Germany map.

The southern districts of eastern Germany—Thuringia and Saxony—represent the old Germany of medieval times, and as you travel these regions, you'll see ample evidence of the grandeur of the past, although much has been rebuilt to replace war damages. Alas, you'll also see the ongoing (and just as devastating) damage of a modern industrial society: landscape scarred by coalpits around Leipzig, chemical pollution in the air around Bitterfeld and Wolfen north of Leipzig, and to the southeast thousands of acres of woodland destroyed by that pollution. South of Dresden, as the Elbe River leaves its broad valley, it passes through a region of dramatic narrow channels confined by stone mountains, almost like a miniature Grand Canyon. To the south, the *Erzgebirge,* or ore mountains, form a natural boundary with Czechoslovakia.

Leaving Berlin, go south on the E-51, marked for Leipzig. About 120 kilometers (75 miles) from Berlin, you'll pass ❶ **Dessau,** a name known to every student of modern architecture. Here the architect Walter Gropius in 1925–26 set up his Bauhaus school of design, probably the most widespread influence on 20th-century architecture and decorative arts. Gropius's concept was to simplify design to allow mechanized construction; 316 villas in the Törten section of the city were built in the '20s using his ideas and methods. Stop to view the refurbished Bauhaus building; this was the fountainhead of ideas that has determined the appearance of cities such as New York, Chicago, and San Francisco. Still used as an architecture school, the building can be visited Monday–Friday 10–5, and exhibits are also open Saturday–Sunday 10–12:30 and 2–5.

For a contrast to the no-nonsense Bauhaus architecture, look at Dessau's older buildings, including St. George's church, built in 1712 in Dutch Baroque style, or the 18th-century late-Baroque **Schloss Mosigkau,** 9 kilometers (5½ miles) southwest of Dessau, now a museum.

Try to visit the exquisite mid-18th-century country palace in late afternoon or early evening, when the setting sun lends a warm glow to the biscuit-colored facades of the three wings. Prince Leopold of Anhalt-Dessau commissioned the palace to be built for his favorite daughter, Anna Wilhelmine. She lived at the palace alone, for she never married, and when she died she left the property to an order of nuns. They immediately tore up the formal grounds to make an English-style park, and after a post–World War II attempt to restore the original Baroque appearance, money and enthusiasm ran out. The palace itself, however, was always well maintained, and the present custodians are so concerned about its preservation that you'll be asked to put on felt slippers on your tour of its rooms. Only about one-quarter of the rooms can be visited, but they include one of Germany's very few Baroque picture galleries. Its stucco ceiling is a marvel of Rococo decoration, a swirling composition of pastel-colored motifs. *Tel. 0340/831139. Admission: DM 2 adults, DM 1 children. Open May–Oct., daily 9–6; Nov.–Apr., by appointment only.*

The E-51 Autobahn branches left and right 40 kilometers (25 ❷ miles) south of Dessau: left to Leipzig, right to **Halle.** The temptation is to turn left and ignore Halle, particularly if you're in a hurry. The 1,000-year-old city, built on the salt trade, is one of eastern Germany's worst examples of Communist urban planning, with a hastily built residential area whose name, Halle-Neustadt, has been shortened cynically by the locals to "Hanoi." But if you have the time, Halle is worth a visit, if only to view its fine central market place, the **Markt,** its northern side bristling with five distinctive, sharp-steepled towers. Four of them (two connected by a catwalk bridge) belong to the late-Gothic **Marienkirche** (St. Mary's Church), completed in 1529, where Martin Luther preached and George Frideric Handel learned to play the organ. Handel was born in Halle in 1685, and you'll find several memorials to the great

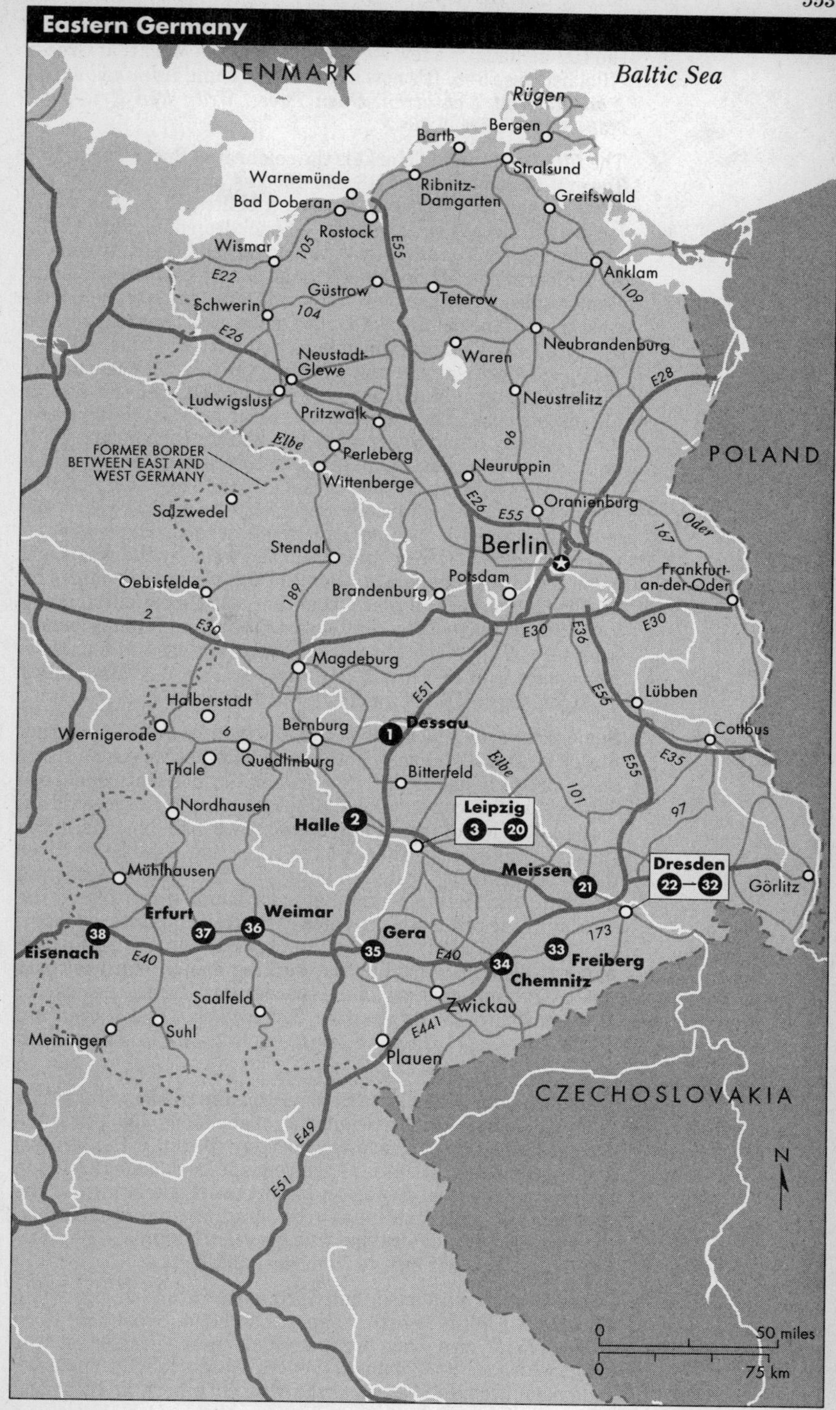
Eastern Germany
DENMARK
Baltic Sea
Rügen
Bergen
Barth
Stralsund
Warnemünde
Ribnitz-Damgarten
Greifswald
Bad Doberan
Rostock
Wismar
105
E55
Anklam
E22
Güstrow
Teterow
109
Schwerin
104
E26
Neubrandenburg
Waren
Neustadt-Glewe
E28
Ludwigslust
Neustrelitz
Pritzwalk
Elbe
96
FORMER BORDER BETWEEN EAST AND WEST GERMANY
Perleberg
POLAND
Neuruppin
Wittenberge
E26
Oranienburg
Salzwedel
E55
167
Oder
Berlin
Stendal
Frankfurt-an-der-Oder
Potsdam
Oebisfelde
Brandenburg
189
2
E30
E30
E36
E30
Magdeburg
E51
Lübben
Halberstadt
E55
Bernburg
Dessau
Cottbus
Wernigerode
6
Quedlinburg
Elbe
E35
Thale
Bitterfeld
E55
101
Nordhausen
Leipzig
3—20
97
Halle
Meissen
Dresden
22—32
Mühlhausen
Görlitz
Erfurt
Weimar
173
Eisenach
Gera
E40
E40
Freiberg
Chemnitz
Saalfeld
Zwickau
Suhl
E441
Meiningen
Plauen
CZECHOSLOVAKIA
E49
N
E51
0
50 miles
0
75 km

composer in and around the city. The house where he was born, the **Händelhaus,** is a few steps away from the Markt, at Grosse Nilolaistrasse 5–6. It's now a Handel museum. *Admission: DM 2 adults, DM 1 children. Open Tues., Wed., and Fri.–Sun. 9:30–5:30; Thurs. 9:30–7.*

The fifth tower on the Markt is the celebrated Roter Turm (Red Tower), built between 1418 and 1506 as an expression of the city's power and wealth; it houses a bell carillon. The tower looks a bit incongruous against the backdrop of modern Halle, like an elaborate sandcastle stranded by the tide. Between the Roter Turm and Marienkirche is the **Marktschlösschen,** a late Renaissance structure now serving as a gallery. On the northwest edge of the old town is a much more traditional expression of Halle's early might (which vanished with the Thirty Years' War), the **Moritzburg,** a castle built in the late-15th century by the archbishop of Magdeburg after he had claimed the city for his archdiocese. The castle is a typical late-Gothic fortress, with a sturdy round tower at each of its four corners and a dry moat. There's a cloisterlike peace in the central courtyard today, quite a contrast to the years when one army of occupation followed another with bloody regularity. In prewar years, the castle contained a leading gallery of German Expressionist paintings, which were ripped from the walls by the Nazis and condemned as "degenerate." Some of the works so disdained by the Nazis are back in place, together with some outstanding late-19th and early 20th-century art. You'll find Rodin's famous sculpture *The Kiss* here. *Staatliche Galerie Moritzburg, Friedemann-Bach-Platz 5. Admission: DM 2 adults, DM 1 children. Open Wed.–Sun. 10–1 and 2–6, Tues. 2–9.*

Some 200 yards southeast of the Moritzburg is Halle's cathedral, the **Dom,** an early Gothic church whose nave and side aisles are of equal height. The nearby former Episcopal residence, the 16th-century **Neue Residenz,** now houses a world-famous collection of fossils dug from brown coal deposits in the Geiseltal Valley near Halle. On the other side of the Saale River (cross the Schiefer bridge to get there) is another interesting museum, the **Halloren- und Salinemuseum,** which traces the history of the salt trade on which early Halle built its prosperity. It includes a full-scale replica of a salt mine, a chilling reminder of the price paid by the working man in centuries past for extracting one of life's necessities from the earth. *Mansfelderstr. 52. Admission: DM 2 adults, DM 1 children. Open Apr.–Sept., Tues.–Sun. 10–5; Oct.–Mar., Tues.–Sun. 10–4.*

From just outside Halle, take the Autobahn 20 kilometers (12½
3 miles) to **Leipzig.** With a population of about 560,000, this is the second-largest city in eastern Germany (Berlin is the largest) and has long been a center of printing and bookselling. Astride major trade routes, it was an important market town in the Middle Ages, and it continues to be a trading center to this day, thanks to the trade fairs that twice a year (March and September) bring together buyers from East and West.

Those familiar with music and German literature will associate Leipzig with the great composer Johann Sebastian Bach (1685–1750), who was organist and choir director at the Thomaskirche (St. Thomas's church); with the 19th-century composer Richard Wagner, who was born here in 1813; and with German Romantic poets Goethe and Schiller, both of whom lived and worked in the area.

In 1813 the Battle of the Nations was fought on the city's outskirts, in which Prussian, Austrian, Russian, and Swedish forces stood ground against Napoléon's troops. This battle (*Völkerschlacht*) was instrumental in leading to the French general's defeat two years later at Waterloo, and thus helped to decide the national boundaries on the map of Europe for the remainder of the century.

Following the devastation of World War II, little is left of old Leipzig. Considerable restoration has been undertaken in the old city, however, and the impression is certainly that of a city with touches of Renaissance character, although some of the newer buildings (notably the university's skyscraper tower) distort the perspective and proportions of the old city. Guided bus tours of Leipzig run daily at 10 and 1:30 (from March to mid-October, there's also a tour at 4); tours leave from the information center downtown at Sachsenplatz 1 (tel. 041/79590).

Numbers in the margin correspond to points of interest on the Leipzig map.

Railroad buffs may want to start their tour of Leipzig at the
4 **Hauptbahnhof,** the main train station. With its 26 platforms, it is the largest in Europe. In 1991 it was expanded to accommodate the anticipated increase in traffic after reunification. But its fin-de-siècle grandness remains, particularly the staircase that leads majestically up to the platforms. As you climb it, take a look at the great arched ceiling high above you; it's unique among German railway stations.

From the station, cross the broad expanse of the Platz der Republik, crowded with nascent capitalists selling everything from shaving soap to Czech Pilsner beer. Better shopping is to be found in the narrow streets opposite you. Behind them is a characterless square, Sachsenplatz, where you'll find Leipzig's main tourist office, Leipzig Information (open Mon.–Fri. 9–7, Sat. 9:30–2). Continue south one block, along Katharinenstrasse, passing the "Fregehaus," No. 11, with its fine oriel and steep roof. In two minutes you'll enter Leipzig's showpiece plaza, the city's old market square, the **Markt,** only slightly smaller than St. Mark's Square in Venice. One side is occupied completely by the recently restored Renaissance city hall, the
5 **Altes Rathaus,** which now houses the municipal museum, where Leipzig's past is well documented. *Markt 1. Admission: DM 3 adults, DM 1.50 children. Open Tues.–Sun. 9–5.*

Starting from all sides of the Markt you'll find small streets that attest to Leipzig's rich trading past, and tucked in among them glass-roofed arcades of surprising beauty and elegance. Invent a headache and step into the Apotheke at Hainstrasse 9, into surroundings that haven't changed for 100 years or more, redolent of powders and perfumes, home cures, and foreign spices. It's spectacularly Jugendstil, with finely etched and stained glass and rich mahogany. Or make for the antiquarian bookshops of the nearby Neumarkt Passage. Around the corner, on Grimmaischestrasse, is Leipzig's finest arcade, the
6 **Mädlerpassage,** where the ghost of Goethe's Faust lurks in every marbled corner. Here you'll find the famous Auerbachs Keller restaurant, at No. 2, where Goethe set a scene in *Faust* (*see* Dining and Lodging, below). A bronze group of characters

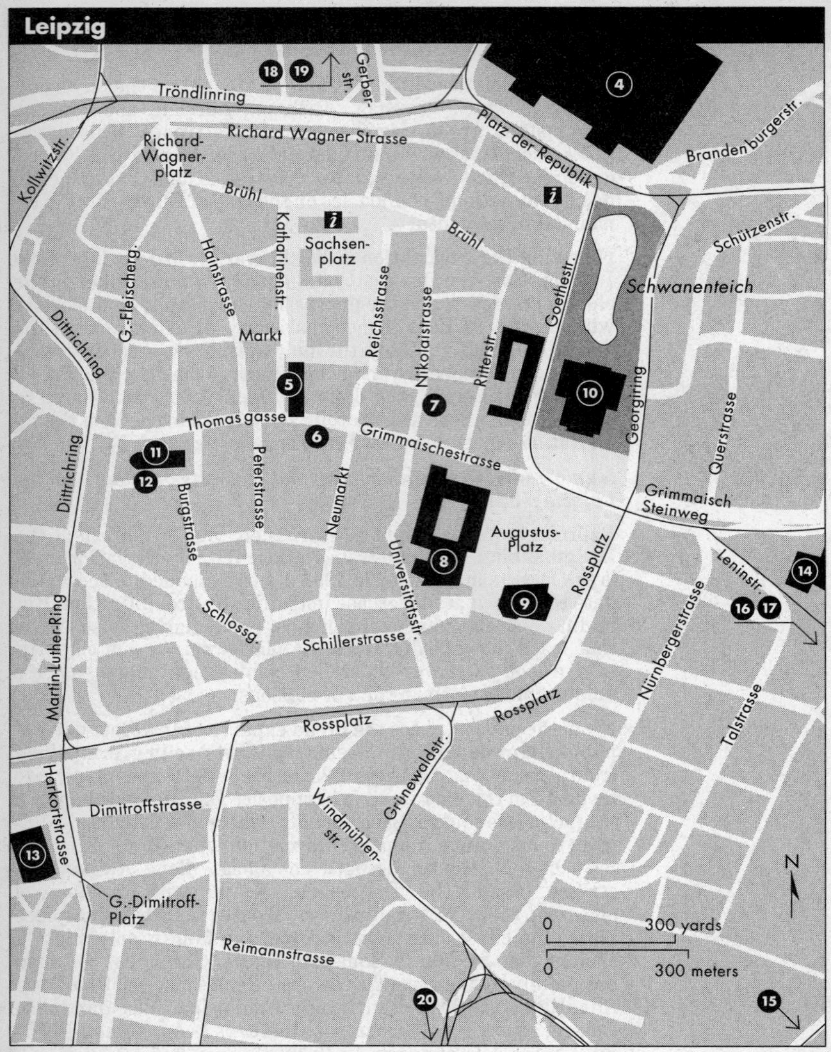

Altes Rathaus, **5**
Bosehaus, **12**
Botanischer Garten, **15**
Exhibition Pavilion, **16**
Gohliser Schlösschen, **18**
Grassimuseum, **14**
Hauptbahnhof, **4**
Leipzig University tower, **8**
Mädlerpassage, **6**
Museum der Bildenden Künste, **13**
Neues Gewandhaus, **9**
Nikolaikirche, **7**
Opera House, **10**
Schiller's House, **19**
Schloss Dölitz, **20**
Thomaskirche, **11**
Völkerschlacht-denkmal, **17**

from the play, sculpted in 1913, beckons you down the stone staircase to the cellar restaurant. A few yards away down the arcade is a delightful Jugendstil coffee shop called Mephisto, decorated in devilish reds and blacks.

Behind Grimmaischestrasse is a church that stands as a symbol of German reunification. It was here, before the undistin-
7 guished facade of the **Nikolaikirche,** that thousands of East Germans demanding reform gathered every Monday in the months before the Communist regime finally collapsed under the weight of popular pressure. "Wir sind das Volk" ("We are the people") was their chant as they defied official attempts to silence their demands for freedom. In the interior of the church, much more impressive than the exterior would lead you to believe, is a soaring Gothic choir and nave with an unusually patterned ceiling supported by classical pillars that end in palm-tree-like flourishes, a curious combination of styles that meld successfully. Luther is said to have preached from the ornate 16th-century pulpit.

Towering over the Nikolaikirche and every other building in
8 the center of the city is the 470-foot-high **Leipzig University tower,** dubbed the "Jagged Tooth" by some of the young wags who study there. They were largely responsible for changing the official name of the university, replacing the postwar title of Karl Marx University with its original one. At press time, however, the vast square spread out below the tower like a space-age campus was still named after Karl Marx. In the shadow of the skyscraper, which houses administrative offices and
9 lecture rooms, is the glass-and-concrete **Neues Gewandhaus,** the modernistic home of the eponymous orchestra, one of Germany's greatest. (Its popular director, Kurt Masur, recently added to his duties the directorship of the New York Philharmonic Orchestra.) In the foyer you can see one of Europe's largest ceiling paintings, a staggering allegorical work devoted to the muse of music by Sighard Gilles, who employed 716 square meters to monumental effect. The statue of Beethoven that stands in the foyer won first prize for sculptor Max Klinger at the World Art Exhibition in Vienna in 1912. The acoustics of the Gewandhaus, by the way, are world-renowned, enhancing the resonance of every tone by a full two seconds.

Opposite the Gewandhaus, on the north side of the Augustus-
10 Platz, is the modern, boxy **Opera House,** the first postwar theater to be built in communist East Germany.

Time Out You'll find several cafés lining Grimmaischestrasse, leading out of the square, but why not buy an ice cream from one of the ubiquitous stands there. The eastern Germans are in love with *Eis* and consume it all year round. The Italian-style ice cream is quite authentic.

Continue west on Grimmaischestrasse to Thomasgasse and the
11 **Thomaskirche,** the Gothic church where Bach was choirmaster for 27 years and where Martin Luther preached on Whit Sunday, 1539, signaling the arrival of Protestantism in Leipzig. Originally the center of a 13th-century monastery that was rebuilt in the 15th century, the tall church now stands by itself, but the names of adjacent streets recall the cloisters that once surrounded it. Bach wrote most of his cantatas for the church's famous boys' choir, the Thomasknabenchor, which was found-

ed in the 13th century; the church continues as the choir's home as well as a center of Bach tradition. In the Middle Ages, the choir was assembled to sing at every public function—from the installation of bishops to the execution of criminals. Its ranks thinned rapidly when the boys were engaged to sing while plague victims were carted to graves outside the city walls.

Bach's 12 children and the infant Richard Wagner were baptized in the church's early 17th-century font; Karl Marx and Friedrich Engels also stood before this same font, godfathers to Karl Liebknecht, who grew up to be a revolutionary, too!

The great music Bach wrote in his Leipzig years commanded little attention in his lifetime, and when he died he was given a simple grave, without a headstone, in the city's Johannisfriedhof cemetery. It wasn't until 1894 that an effort was made to find where the great composer lay buried, and after a thorough, macabre search his coffin was removed to the cemetery church, the Johanniskirche. The church was destroyed by Allied bombs in December 1943, and Bach found his final resting place in the church he would have selected: the Thomaskirche. It's now a place of pilgrimage for music lovers from all over the world, and his gravestone below the high altar is never without a floral tribute. Fresh flowers also constantly decorate the statue of Bach that stands before the church. *Thomaskirchhof. Admission free. Open daily 9–6.*

12 The Bach family home, the **Bosehaus,** still stands, opposite the church, and is now a museum devoted to the life and work of the composer. (The exhibits are in German only; a guide to the museum in English can be purchased in the shop.) Of particular interest is the display of musical instruments dating from Bach's time. *Thomaskirchhof 16. Admission: DM 2 adults, DM 1 children. Open Tues. and Thurs.–Sun. 9–5, Wed. 1–9.*

Time Out Teatime? On the corner of Thomaskirchhof, opposite the church, is the charming **Teehaus** café, offering more varieties of tea than you'd think it was possible to find in eastern Germany. Etched and beveled Jugendstil glass, brass, and dark wood paneling are the perfect complement to the delicate teas, which are served by an enthusiastic staff. *Open daily 10–6.*

From the Thomaskirche, follow Burgstrasse southward, past the 19th-century neo-Gothic monstrosity that now serves as Leipzig's city hall, and you'll come to the city's most outstand-
13 ing museum, the **Museum der Bildenden Kunste,** an art gallery of international standard. The art collection occupies the ground floor of the former Reichsgericht, the court where the Nazis held a show trial against the Bulgarian communist Georgi Dimitroff on a trumped-up charge of masterminding a plot to burn down the Reichstag in 1933. *Georgi-Dimitroff-Platz 1. Admission: DM 3 adults, DM 1.50 children. Open Tues. and Thurs.–Sun. 9–5, Wed. 1–9:30.*

Head across the Martin Luther-Ring up the short Grimmaisch
14 Steinweg to reach the **Grassimuseum** complex (Johannespl. 5–11. Admission: DM 3.05 adults, DM 1.55 children). It includes the **Museum of Arts and Crafts** (open Tues.–Fri. 9:30–6, Sat. 10–4, Sun. 9–1), the **Geographical Museum** (open Tues.–Fri. 10–3, Sun. 9–1), and the **Musical Instruments Museum** (enter from Täubchenweg 2; open Tues.–Thurs. 3–6, Fri. and Sun. 10–1, Sat. 10–3).

15 The **Botanischer Garten** (Botanical Gardens) is a set of splendid open-air gardens and greenhouses. *Linnestr. 1. Admission: DM 2. Open weekdays 9–4, Sun. 10–4; greenhouses Sun. 10–12:30 and 2–4.*

Still farther out, via streetcar numbers 15, 20, 21, or 25, is the
16 **Exhibition Pavilion** at Leninstrasse 210. Its main feature is a vast diorama portraying the Battle of the Nations of 1813 (open Tues.–Sun. 9–4). Slightly farther on Leninstrasse is the mas-
17 sive **Völkerschlachtdenkmal,** a memorial in the formal park; it, too, commemorates the battle (open daily 9–4). Rising out of suburban Leipzig like some great Egyptian tomb, the somber, grey pile of granite and concrete is more than 300 feet high. Despite its ugliness, it's well worth a visit if only to wonder at the lengths—and heights—to which the Prussians went to celebrate their military victories, and to take in the view from a windy platform near the top (provided you can also climb the 500 steps to get there). The Prussians did make one concession to Napoléon in designing the monument: A stone marks the spot where he stood during the battle.

Outside of the center of Leipzig but reachable by public transportation (streetcar numbers 20 and 24, then walk left up Poetenweg, or streetcar number 6 to Menckestr.) is the delightfully
18 Rococo **Gohliser Schlösschen** (Gohliser House), the site of frequent concerts. *Menckestr. 23. Open Mon. and Fri. 1–5, Tues., Thurs., and Sat. 9–1, Wed. 1–8.*

19 Beyond that is **Schiller's House,** for a time the home of the German poet and dramatist Friedrich Schiller. *Menckestr. 21. Admission: DM 2 adults, DM 1 children. Open Tues., Wed., Fri., and Sat. 11–5.*

20 **Schloss Dölitz** (streetcar number 22 or 24, walk up Helenstrasse) contains an exhibition of *Zinnfiguren*, historical tin soldiers. *Torhaus, Schloss Dölitz, Helenstr. 24. Admission: DM 3. Open Sun. 9–1.*

Meissen and Dresden

Numbers in the margin correspond to points of interest on the Eastern Germany map.

21 Route 6 out of Leipzig will take you to **Meissen,** about 80 kilometers (50 miles) away. This romantic city on the Elbe River is known the world over for its porcelain, bearing the trademark crossed blue swords. The first European porcelain was made in this area in 1708, and in 1710 the royal porcelain manufacturer was established in Meissen, close to the local raw materials.

The story of how porcelain came to be produced in Meissen reads like a German fairy tale: Saxony ruler free-spending August the Strong (ruled 1697–1704, 1710–1733) urged alchemists at his court to search for the secret of making gold, which he badly needed to refill a Saxon state treasury depleted by his expensive building projects and extravagant lifestyle. The alchemists failed to produce gold, but one of them, Johann Friedrich Böttger, discovered a method for making something almost as precious: fine hard-paste porcelain. Prince August consigned Böttger and a team of craftsmen to a hilltop castle outside Dresden—Albrechtsburg in Meissen—and set them to work. August hoped to keep their recipe a state secret, but within a few years fine porcelain was being produced by Böttger's method in many parts of Europe.

The porcelain works outgrew their castle workshop in the mid-19th century, and you'll find them today in the town at the foot of the castle mount at Leninstrasse 9. There you can see demonstrations of pieces being prepared. In the same building, a museum displays Meissen porcelain, a collection that rivals that of the Porcelain Museum in Dresden. *Tel. 03521/541. Open Apr.–Oct., Tues.–Sun. 8:30–4:30.*

Meissen porcelain is to be found in one form or another all over town. A set of porcelain bells at the late-Gothic **Frauenkirche,** on the central market square, the **Marktplatz,** was the first of its kind anywhere when installed in 1929. The largest set of porcelain figures ever crafted, can be found in another Meissen church, the **Nikolaikirche,** which also houses remains of early Gothic frescoes. Also of interest in the town center is the 1569 Old Brewery, graced by a Renaissance gable; St. Francis, now housing a city museum; and St. Martins, with its late-Gothic altar.

Time Out Snuggling up to the Frauenkirche is one of Meissen's oldest wine taverns, the **Weinschenke Vinzenz Richter** (Marktplatz 3). Meissen has some of Europe's northernmost and smallest vineyards, producing an excellent white wine. This is the place to try it. *Closed Mon. and Tues.*

It's a bit of a climb up Burgstrasse and Amtsstrasse to the **Albrechtsburg castle,** where the story of Meissen porcelain really began, but the effort is worthwhile. The 15th-century Albrechtsburg is Germany's first truly "residential" castle, a complete break with the earlier style of fortified bastion. It fell into disuse and neglect as nearby Dresden rose to local prominence, but it's still an imposing collection of late-Gothic and Renaissance buildings. In the central courtyard, a typical Gothic *Schutzhof* protected on three sides by high rough-stone walls, is an exterior spiral staircase, **the Wendelstein,** hewn from one massive stone block in 1525, a masterpiece of early masonry. Ceilings of the halls of the castle are richly decorated, although many date only from a restoration in 1870. Adjacent to the castle is a towered early Gothic cathedral.

22 Another 20 kilometers (12 miles) southeast on Route 6 will take you to **Dresden.** Splendidly situated on a bend in the Elbe River, Dresden is a compact city that is easy to explore. In its rococo yellows and greens, it is enormously appealing, and the effect is even more overwhelming when you compare what you see today—or what Canaletto paintings reflect of a Dresden centuries earlier—with the photographs of Dresden in 1945, after a British bombing raid almost destroyed it overnight. It was one of the architectural and cultural treasures of the civilized world, and the fact that despite lack of funds and an often uncooperative Communist bureacracy, the people of Dresden succeeded in rebuilding it is an enormous tribute to their skills and dedication.

Their efforts restored at least the riverside panorama to the appearance Canaletto would have recognized, but some of the other parts of the city center look halfway between construction and demolition. In the coming years the city will look more like a building site than ever as 20 new hotels are added to provide the accommodations the city so desperately needs. Don't think of visiting Dresden without reserving a hotel room well in advance.

Dresden was the capital of Saxony as early as the 15th century, although most of its architectural masterpieces date from the 18th century, when the enlightened Saxon ruler August the Strong and his son, Frederick Augustus II, brought leading Italian and Bavarian architects and designers up from the south. The predominantly Italianate influence is evident today in gloriously overblown Rococo architecture. *Streetcar tours leave from Postplatz Tues.–Sun. at 9, 11, and 1:30; bus tours, leaving from Dr.–Kulz–Ring, run on Tues., Wed., and Thurs., at 11 (call 051/495–5025 for details).*

Numbers in the margin correspond to points of interest on the Dresden map.

The best introduction to Dresden is to arrive by ship (*see* Getting Around by Boat in Essential Information, above), but for motorists or train passengers, the starting point of a Dresden tour will be the main railway station (which has adequate parking). To reach the old part of the city and its treasures you'll first have to cross a featureless expanse surrounded by postwar high rises, leading into the pedestrians-only Pragerstrasse (the tourist information office is at No. 8). Cross busy Dr.-Külz-Ring and you'll enter a far different scene, the broad
23 **Altmarkt,** whose colonnaded beauty has managed to survive the disfiguring efforts of city planners to turn it into a huge outdoor parking lot. The church on your right, the Kreuzkirche, is an interesting combination of Baroque and Jugendstil architecture and decoration. A church stood here in the 13th century, but the present structure dates from the late 18th century. The rebuilt Rathaus is on your left, as is the yellow-stucco, 18th-century Landhaus, which contains the Museum für Geschichte der Stadt Dresden (City Historical Museum). *Ernst-Thälmann-Str. 2. Admission: DM 2 adults, DM 1 children. Open Mon.–Thurs. and Sat. 10–6, Sun. 10–4.*

At the northern end of the Altmarkt, cross Ernst-Thälmann-Strasse (or pause for a window-shopping break on this broad boulevard) into the **Neumarkt** (New Market), which is, despite its name, the historic heart of old Dresden. The ruins on your right are all that remain of Germany's greatest Protestant church after the bombing raid of February 1945. These jagged, precariously tilting walls were once the mighty Baroque
24 **Frauenkirche,** so sturdily built that it withstood a three-day bombardment during the Seven Years' War only to fall victim to the flames that followed the World War II raid. Like the Gedächtniskirche in Berlin, the Frauenkirche has been kept in its ruined state as a war memorial, although plans were announced in 1991 to rebuild it as a European cultural center.

The large, imperial-style building looming behind the Frauen-
25 kirche is the famous **Albertinum,** Dresden's leading art museum. It is named after Saxony's King Albert, who between 1884 and 1887 converted a royal arsenal into a suitable setting for the treasures he and his forebears had collected. The upper story of the Albertinum, accessible from the Brühlsche Terrasse, houses the Gemäldegalerie Alte und Neue Meister (Gallery of old and modern masters), temporarily displaying the highlights of the Sempergalerie while it is being restored (*see* be-

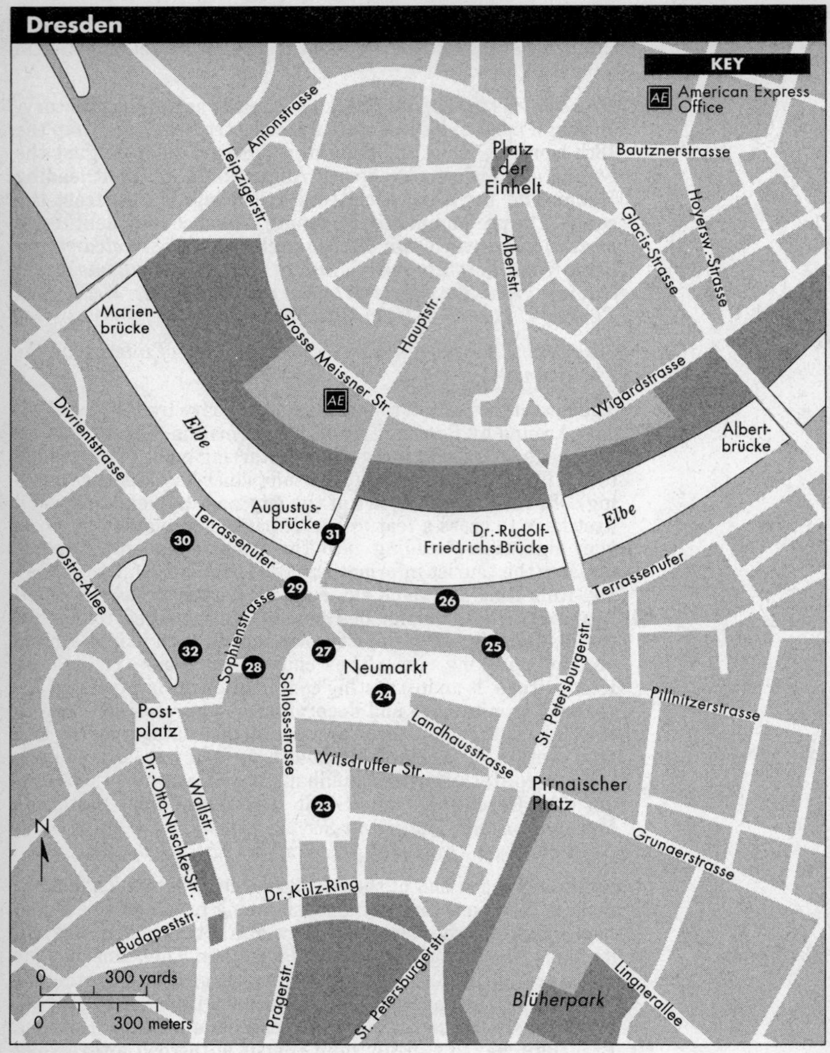

Albertinum, **25**
Altmarkt, **23**
Augustusbrücke, **31**
Brühlsche Terrasse, **26**
Frauenkirche, **24**
Johanneum, **27**
Katholische Hofkirche, **29**
Residenzschloss, **28**
Semperoper, **30**
Zwinger, **32**

low). Permanent exhibits include outstanding work by German masters of the 19th and 20th century (Caspar David Friedrich's haunting *Das Kreuz im Gebirge* is here) and French Impressionists and Post-Impressionists.

Impressive as the art gallery is, it's the Grüne Gewölbe (Green Vault) that draws the most attention. Named after a green room in the palace of August the Strong, this part of the Albertinum (entered from Georg-Treu-Platz) contains an exquisite collection of unique objets d'art fashioned from gold, silver, ivory, amber, and other precious and semiprecious materials. Among the crown jewels is the world's largest "green" diamond, 41 carats in weight, and a dazzling group of tiny gem-studded figures entitled *Hofstaat zu Delhi am Geburtstag des Grossmoguls Aureng-Zeb*. The name gives a false idea of the size of the work, dating from 1708, which represents a birthday gathering at the court of an Indian mogul; some parts of the tableau are so small that they can only be admired through a magnifying glass. Somewhat larger and less delicate is the drinking bowl of Ivan the Terrible, perhaps the most sensational of the treasures to be found in this extraordinary museum. Next door is the Skulpturensammlung (Sculpture Collection) that includes ancient Egyptian and classical works and examples by Giovanni da Bologna and Adriaen de Vries. *Am Neumarkt. Gemäldegalerie Alte und Neue Meister admission: DM 5 adults, DM 2.50 children. Open Tues. and Thurs.–Sun. 9–5, Wed. 9–6. Grünes Gewölbe and Skulpturensammlung admission: DM 5 adults, DM 2.50 children. Open Fri.–Tues. 9–5, Wed. 9–6.*

26 If you leave the Albertinum by the **Brühlsche Terrasse** exit you'll find yourself on what was once known as the "Balcony of Europe," a terrace high above the Elbe, carved from a 16th-century stretch of the city fortifications; from the terrace a breathtaking vista of the Elbe and the Dresden skyline opens up. The southern exit of the Albertinum brings you back to the Neumarkt and to another former royal building that now serves
27 as a museum, the 16th-century **Johanneum,** once the regal stables. Instead of horses, the Johanneum now houses the Vekehrsmuseum, a collection of historical vehicles, including vintage automobiles and engines. *Am Neumarkt. Admission: DM 4 adults, DM 2 children. Open Wed.–Sun. 9–5, Tues. 9–6.*

Walk behind the Johanneum and into the former stable exercise yard, enclosed by elegant Renaissance arcades and used in the 16th century as an open-air festival ground. To spare the royalty on horseback the trouble of dismounting before ascending to the upper-story to watch the jousting and jollities in the yard below, a ramp was built to accommodate both two- and four-legged guests. You'll find the scene today much as it was centuries ago, complete with jousting markings in the ground. More popular than even than jousting in those days was *Ringelstechen*, a risky pursuit in which riders at full gallop had to catch small rings on their lances. Horses and riders often came to grief in the narrow confines of the stable yard.

On the outside wall of the Johanneum is a remarkable example of Meissen porcelain art: a painting on Meissen tiles of a royal procession, 336 feet long. More than 100 members of the royal Saxon house of Wettin, half of them on horseback, are represented on the giant jigsaw made up of 25,000 porcelain tiles, painted in 1904–1907 after a design by Wilhelm Walther. Fol-

low this unusual procession to the end and you will come to the
28 former royal palace, the **Residenzschloss**, where restoration work is under way behind the fine Renaissance facade. Although the work is expected to last well into the 1990s, some of the finished rooms are hosting historical exhibitions. The main gate of the palace, the Georgentor, has acquired its original appearance, complete with an enormous statue of the fully armed Saxon Count George, guarding the portal that carries his name. The palace housed August the Strong's Grünes Gewölbe before it was moved in its entirety to the Albertinum. *Sophienstrasse. Admission: DM 5 adults, DM 2.50 children. Open Mon., Tues., and Thurs.–Sun. 9–5.*

Next to the Herzogschloss is the largest church in Saxony, the
29 **Katholische Hofkirche,** also known as the Cathedral of St. Trinitas. The son of August the Strong, Frederick Augustus II (ruled 1733–1763), brought architects and builders from Italy to construct a Catholic church in a city that had been the first large center of Lutheran Protestantism. They worked away by stealth, so the story goes, and Dresden's Protestant burgers were presented with a fait accompli when the church was finally consecrated in 1754. Seventy-eight historical and biblical figures decorate the Italian High Baroque facade; inside, the treasures include a beautiful stone pulpit by the royal sculptor Balthasar Permoser and a 250-year-old church organ said to be one of the finest ever to come from the mountain workshops of the famous Silbermann family. In the cathedral's crypt are the tombs of 49 Saxon rulers and a precious vessel containing the heart of August the Strong.

Opposite the cathedral on the Theaterplatz is the restored
30 **Semperoper** (Semper Opera house), justifiably one of Germany's best-known and most popular theaters. Richard Wagner's *Rienzi, Der Fliegende Hollander,* and *Tannhäuser,* and Richard Strauss's *Salome, Elektra* and *Der Rosenkavalier* all premiered here. The masterful Dresden architect Gottfried Semper built the opera house in 1838–1841, in Italian Renaissance style, and then saw his work razed in a fire caused by a careless candle-lighter. Semper had to flee Dresden because of his participation in a democratic uprising, so his son Manfred rebuilt the theater, in the neo-Renaissance style you see today. Even Manfred Semper's version had to be rebuilt, after the devastating bombing raid of February 1945. On the 40th anniversary of that raid—February 13, 1985—the rebuilt Semperoper reopened with a performance of *Der Freischutz* by Carl Maria von Weber, another composer who did so much to make Dresden a leading center of German music and culture. The demand to experience the Semper Opera again in all its glory is enormous, and tickets are difficult to obtain in advance. If you're lucky enough to get in, however, an overwhelming experience awaits you. Even if you're no opera buff, the Semper's lavish interior, predominantly crimson, white, and gold, can't fail to impress. Marble, velvet, and brocade create an atmosphere of intimate luxury (it seats 1,323), and the uninterrupted views and flawless acoustics are renowned.

Time Out On the river-bank side of the Theaterplatz you'll see the pavilionlike **Italienisches Dörfchen,** constructed in 1911–1913 on the site of housing for the Italian workers who erected the nearby Hofkirche. The café is a perfect spot for taking a break over a glass of local beer or a pot of coffee.

---

31 The impressive bridge behind the cathedral, the **Augustusbrücke,** is a rebuilt version of an historic 17th-century bridge blown up by the SS shortly before the end of World War II. Renamed for Georgi Dimitroff, the Bulgarian Communist accused by the Nazis of instigating the Reichstag fire, the restored bridge, after the fall of communism, has gotten its original name back honoring August the Strong. You'll find this process of curing the unpleasant hiccups of Communist rule still underway throughout eastern Germany.

Back on the Theaterplatz, in the center of the square directly in front of the opera house, you'll see a proud equestrian statue of King Johann, who ruled Saxony when Gottfried Semper was at work. Don't be misled by Johann's confident pose in the saddle—he was terrified of horses and never learned to ride.

The southwestern side of the square is taken up by another
Gottfried Semper creation, the Sempergalerie, part of the
32 largely 18th-century **Zwinger** palace complex. Built by the
great architect to house parts of the art collections of the Saxon royal house, it contains the world-renowned Gemäldegalerie Alte Meister (Gallery of Old Masters). The Zwinger is being restored and is scheduled to reopen in October 1992. Until then, the Sempergalerie paintings are temporarily on display at the Albertinum (*see* above). The porcelain collection, zoological museum, and Mathematisch-Physikalischer Salon (displaying old scientific instruments) remain open at the palace (*see* below). Call the Zwinger (tel. 051/48420) for the latest information on when the collections will reopen at the palace complex.

Among the priceless paintings in the Sempergalerie collection are examples by Dürer, Holbein, Jan van Eyck, Rembrandt, Rubens, van Dyck, Hals, Vermeer, Raphael (The Sistine Madonna), Titian, Giorgione, Veronese, Velázquez, Murillo, Canaletto, and Watteau. On the wall of the entrance archway you'll see an inscription in Russian, one of the few amusing reminders of World War II in Dresden. It reads, in rhyme: "Museum checked. No mines. Chanutin did the checking." Chanutin, presumably, was the Russian soldier responsible for checking one of Germany's greatest art galleries for anything more explosive than a Rubens nude.

The Sempergalerie forms one side of the fabulous Zwinger, the pride of Dresden and perhaps one of the greatest examples of Baroque architecture. There are two entrances to the Zwinger; the Kronentor (Crown Gate), off of Ostra-Allee, is the one through which August the Strong and his royal retinue once paraded. August hired a small army of artists and artisans to create a "pleasure ground" worthy of the Saxon court, building it on a section of the original city fortifications (the "Zwinger"). They were placed under the general direction of the architect Matthaus Daniel Pöppelmann, who was called reluctantly out of retirement to design what came to be his greatest work, started in 1707 and completed in 1728. Completely enclosing a central courtyard, filled with lawns and pools, the complex comprises six linked pavilions, one of which boasts a carillon of Meissen, hence its name: Glockenspielpavillon. It's an extraordinary scene, a riot of garlands, nymphs, and other Baroque ornamentation and sculpture on the edge of an urban landscape etched in somber gray. The contrast would have been much greater if Semper had not closed in one side of the Zwinger, which was originally open to the riverbank. Stand in the center of this quiet oasis, where the city's roar is kept at bay by the palatial wings that form the outer framework of the Zwinger, and imagine the scene on summer evenings when August the Strong invited his favored guests to celebrate with him—the wedding, for instance, of his son, Prince Friedrich August, to Maria Joseph, Archduchess of Austria. The ornate carriage-style lamps shone, the fountains splashed in the shallow pools, and wide staircases beckoned to galleried walks and the romantic Nymphenbad, a coyly hidden courtyard where nude female statues are protected in alcoves from a fountain that spits unexpectedly at unwary visitors.

The Porcelain Museum, stretching from the curved gallery adjoining the Glockenspielpavillon to the long gallery on the east side, is considered one of the best of its kind in the world. The focus, naturally, is on Dresden and Meissen china, but there are also outstanding examples of Japanese, Chinese, and Korean porcelain. *Porcelain Museum admission: DM 5 adults, DM 2 children. Open Sat.–Thurs. 9–4:30. Zoological Museum, Mathematisch-Physikalischer Salon admission: DM 3 adults, DM 1.50 children. Open Fri.–Wed. 9–4.*

Other less central curiosities in Dresden include the **Armeemuseum** (Military Museum), which covers military history predating the German Democratic Republic (Dr.-Karl-Fischer-Pl., admission DM 3, open Tues.–Sun. 9–5); the **Buch Museum** (Book Museum), which traces the history of books from the Middle Ages to the present (Marienallee 12, admission free, open Mon.–Sat. 9–5); and the **Deutsches Hygene-Museum** (German Museum of Health), with historical displays of medical equipment and a unique glass anatomical figure (Lingnerpl. 1, admission DM 3 adults, DM 1.50 children, open Sat.–Thurs. 9–5).

Numbers in the margin correspond to points of interest on the Eastern Germany map.

From Dresden, you can either take the E-40 Autobahn or, if
33 you have the time, the more scenic road via Freital to **Freiberg.** Once a prosperous silver-mining community, Freiberg is highlighted by two picturesque Gothic town squares, the Upper and Lower Markets. The late Gothic cathedral, with its Golden Gate of 1230, has a richly decorated interior and a Silbermann organ dating from 1711.

34 Route 173 continues on via Oederan and Flöha to **Chemnitz** (on older maps, Karl-Marx-Stadt), about 65 kilometers (41 miles) down the E-40 from Dresden. In recognition of the labor movement, East German officials renamed the city in 1953 to honor Karl Marx; in 1990 the population, now free to express a choice, overwhelmingly voted to revert to the original name. Badly damaged during World War II, Chemnitz has revived as a center of heavy industry, but it never had the architectural attractions of others in the area. Stop to see the rebuilt 12th-century **Red Tower** in the center of the city; the **Altes Rathaus** (Old City Hall), dating from 1496–1498, now incorporating a variety of styles following many reconstructions; and the 250-million-year-old petrified tree trunks, unique in Europe, alongside the city museum. Look, too—assuming it's still there—at the mas-

sive stylized head of a meditative Karl Marx, sculpted by the Soviet artist Lew Kerbel, in front of the district council building in the new city center. Behind it is the motto, "Working Men of All Countries, Unite!"—in German, Russian, French, and English.

35 Take E-40 out of Chemnitz to **Gera,** about 65 kilometers (41 miles) away. Once a princely residence and center of a thriving textile industry, the city has been largely rebuilt after the heavy damage sustained in World War II. Gera has often been compared with old Vienna, although today you have to search long and hard—and even then exercise some imagination—to discover any striking similarities between the German provincial town and the Habsburg capital. After the combined destruction of a world war and more than four decades of Communist mismanagement, some ornate, albeit crumbling house facades, however, do betray Gera's rich past, although the palace in which prince-electors once held court was destroyed in the final weeks of the war and never rebuilt. The palace's 16th-century **Orangerie,** though, does still stand, in the former Küchengarten in the suburb of Untermhaus. An imposing semicircular Baroque pavilion, it now houses an art gallery and a separate collection of works by Gera's most famous son, the satirical Expressionist painter Otto Dix (1891–1969). The Dix gallery was renovated in 1991 for the centenary of the painter's birth, and by 1992 it is hoped that some of Dix's works that vanished in the Nazi purge in the 1930s of "decadent" art will have been added to the collection. *Dimitroffallee 4. Admission: DM 1.05 adults, 55 pf children. Open Mon.–Thurs. 10–5, Sat.–Sun. 10–6.*

Don't leave Gera without lingering in the central town square, the Marktplatz, its Renaissance buildings restored with rare (for eastern Germany) care. The 16th-century city hall, the Rathaus, has a vividly decorated entrance. Note the weird angles of the lower-floor windows; they follow the incline of the staircase that winding up the interior of the building's picturesque 185-foot-high tower.

Time Out At the city hall's vaulted cellar restaurant, the **Ratskeller,** Gera's medieval past crowds in on you from all sides, with painted scenes on glass partitions and on the gnarled walls themselves. The restaurant is open daily from midmorning until midnight, so it's an ideal place for coffee, lunch, or dinner.

Close by is the Baroque **Regierungsgebäude** (government building), incorporating pieces from an earlier 16th-century building.

36 Take the E-40 another 53 kilometers (33 miles) to **Weimar.** Sitting prettily on the Ilm River between the Ettersberg and Vogtland hills, Weimar has a place in German political and cultural history out of all proportion to its size (population: 63,000). It's not even a particularly old city by German standards, with a civic history starting as late as 1410. But by the early 19th century it had become one of Europe's most important cultural centers, where poets Goethe and Schiller were neighbors, Johann Sebastian Bach played the organ for his royal Saxon patrons, Carl Maria von Weber wrote some of his best music, and Liszt was director of music, presenting the first performance of *Lohengrin.* Walter Gropius founded his Staat-

liche Bauhaus here in 1919, and behind the classical pillars of the National Theater the German National Assembly in 1919–1920 drew up the constitution of the Weimar Republic. After the collapse of the ill-fated Weimar government, Hitler chose the unsuspecting little city as the site for the first national congress of his new Nazi Party. On the outskirts of Weimar, the Nazis built—or forced prisoners to build it for them—the infamous Buchenwald concentration camp.

Weimar owes much of its greatness to a woman, the widowed Countess Anna Amalia, who went talent-hunting in the late 18th century for cultural figures to decorate the glittering court that her Saxon forebears had set up in the town. Goethe was among them, and he served the countess as a counselor, advising on financial matters and town design. Schiller followed, and the two became valued visitors to the countess's home. Today their statues stand before the **National Theater,** on Theaterplatz, two blocks west of the Markt, the central market square. The famous pair—Goethe with a patronizing hand on the shoulder of the younger Schiller—should be gleaming, having just been restored. The theater, sadly, isn't the one in which Goethe and Schiller produced some of their leading works; the Baroque building became too small to admit the increasing number of visitors to Weimar, and it was demolished in 1907 and replaced by a larger one with better technical facilities. That theater was bombed in World War II and rebuilt in its present form in 1948. It reopened with a performance of Goethe's *Faust,* which was written in Weimar.

Adjacent to the National Theater is the surprisingly modest home of Countess Anna Amalia, the **Wittumspalais.** Within this exquisite Baroque house you can see the drawing room in which her soirées were held, complete with the original cherry-wood table at which the company sat. The east wing of the house contains a small museum that is a fascinating memorial to those cultural gatherings. *Admission free. Open Wed.–Sun. 9–12 and 1–5.*

Goethe spent 57 years in Weimar, 47 years in the house that has since become a shrine for millions of visitors. **Goethehaus** is at the entrance of the street called Frauenplan, two blocks south of Theaterplatz. It's now a museum containing a collection of writings that illustrate not only the great man's literary might but his interest in the sciences, particularly medicine, and his administrative skills (and frustrations) as Weimar's exchequer. You'll see the desk at which Goethe stood to write (he liked to work standing up) and the modest bed in which he died. The rooms are dark and often cramped, but an almost palpable intellectual intensity seems to illuminate them. *Frauenplan 1. Admission: DM 5 adults, DM 3 children. Open Tues.–Sun. 9–5.*

Around the corner from Goethe's house, on a tree-shaded square, is Schiller's sturdy, green-shuttered home, in which he and his family spent a happy, all-too-brief three years (Schiller died there in 1805). Schiller's study was tucked up underneath the mansard roof, a cozy room dominated by his desk, where he probably completed *William Tell.* Much of the remaining furniture and the collection of books were added later, although they all date from around Schiller's time. *Neugasse. Admission: DM 5 adults, DM 3 children. Open Wed.–Sun. 9–5.*

On the nearby central town square, **Marktplatz,** you'll find another historic Weimar house, the home of the painter Lucas Cranach the Elder, who lived their during his last years, 1552–1553. Its wide, imposing facade is richly decorated and bears the coat of arms of the Cranach family. It now houses a modern art gallery.

Around the corner to the left is Weimar's 16th-century castle, with its restored classical staircase, festival hall, and falcon gallery. The tower on the southwest projection dates from the Middle Ages, but got its Baroque overlay circa 1730. The castle houses eastern Germany's third-largest art collection, including several works by Cranach the Elder and many early 20th-century pieces by such artists as Böcklin, Liebermann, and Beckmann. *Admission: DM 4.05 adults, DM 2 children. Open Tues.–Sun. 10–6.*

As in so many eastern German towns, Weimar's old town center has been reconstructed. Stop by the late Gothic **Herderkirche,** with its large winged altar started by Lucas Cranach the Elder and finished by his son in 1555. Nearby in Jakobstrasse you'll spot the Baroque facade of the **Kirms-Krackow** house, currently closed for restoration. Take time to visit the small garden with the teahouse, and the classically furnished residential rooms. *Jakobstr. 10. Admission DM 1. Open 9–noon, 1–5. Closed Mon.*

A short walk south, past Goethe Haus and across Wieland Platz, will take you to the cemetery where Goethe and Schiller are buried, the **Historischer Friedhof** (Historic Cemetery). Their tombs are in the vault of the classical-style chapel of the leafy cemetery, where virtually every gravestone commemorates a famous citizen of Weimar. The Goethe-Schiller vault can be visited daily (except Tues.) 9–1 and 2–5.

On the other side of the Ilm, amid meadowlike parkland, you'll find Goethe's beloved **Gartenhaus** (Garden House), where he spent many happy hours and wrote much poetry and began his masterpiece *Iphigenie* (admission DM 3 adults, DM 2 children; open daily 9–12 and 1–5). Goethe is said to have felt very close to nature here, and you can soak up the same rural atmosphere today on footpaths along the peaceful little river, where time seems to have stood still. Just across the river from the Gartenhaus is a generous German tribute to another literary giant, William Shakespeare, a 1904 statue showing him jauntily at ease on a marble plinth and looking remarkably at home in his foreign surroundings.

Just south of the city, the lovely 18th-century yellow **Belvedere Palace** once served as a hunting and pleasure castle; today you'll find a Baroque museum inside. The formal gardens were in part laid out according to Goethe's concepts. At press time, the palace was closed for restoration.

In the Ettersberg hills just north of Weimar is a blighted patch of land that contrasts cruelly with the verdant countryside that so inspired Goethe: **Buchenwald.** This was one of the most infamous Nazi concentration camps, where 65,000 men, women and children from 35 countries met their deaths through forced labor, starvation, disease, and gruesome medical experiments. Each is commemorated today by a small stone placed on the outlines of the barracks, which have long since disappeared from the site, and by a massive memorial tower built in a style that some critics find reminiscent of the Nazi megalomania it seeks to condemn. The tower stands on the highest point of Buchenwald, approached by a broad, long flight of steps and sheltering at its base a sculpted group representing the victims of Buchenwald. *Campsite admission: free. Open Tues.–Sun. 9:45–4:30. Bus tours to the site are organized by Weimar's tourist office, Weimar-Information, Marktstr. 4 (tel. 0621/2173).*

Twenty-five kilometers (15 miles) west of Weimar (take the B-7 route, running parallel to the Autobahn) lies one of the most picturesque and best-preserved cities of Thuringia: the "flow-
37 ers and towers" city of **Erfurt.** Erfurt emerged from World War II relatively unscathed, most of its innumerable towers intact (although restored in the early 1970s). Flowers? Erfurt is the center of the eastern German horticultural trade and Europe's largest producer of flower and vegetable seeds, a tradition begun by a local botanist, Christian Reichart, who pioneered seed research. The city outskirts are smothered in greenhouses and plantations, and one of Germany's biggest horticultural shows, the Internationale Gartenbauaustellung, takes place here every year from the end of March through September.

With its highly decorative and colorful facades, this is a fascinating city to discover on foot, and a photographer's delight. Erfurt is dominated by its magnificent cathedral, the 14th-century Gothic **Dom,** reached by a broad staircase from the expansive cathedral square. The Romanesque origins of the cathedral (Romanesque foundations can still be seen in the crypt) are best preserved in the choir, where you'll find glorious stained-glass windows and some of the most beautifully carved choir stalls in all Germany. They have a worldly theme, tracing the vintner's trade back through the centuries. Nearby, look for a remarkable group of free-standing figures: a man flanked by two women. The man is the 13th-century Count von Gleichen. But the two women? There are two stories: one, the respectable version, has it that the women are the count's wives, one of whom he married after the death of the other. The other, possibly older story claims that one of the women is the count's wife, the other his mistress, a Saracen beauty who saved his life under mysterious circumstances during a crusade. The cathedral's biggest bell, the Gloriosa, is the largest free-swinging bell in the world. Cast in 1497, it took three years to install, in the tallest of the three sharply pointed towers, painstakingly lifted inch by inch with wooden wedges. No chances are taken with such a heavy treasure; the bell is rung only on special occasions. *Dom open May–Oct., weekdays 9–11:30 and 12:30–5, Sat. 9–11:30 and 12:30–4:30, Sun. 2–4; Nov.–Apr., Mon–Sat. 10–11:30 and 12:30–4, Sun. 2–4.*

Next to the cathedral and linked to it by a 70-step open staircase is the Gothic church of **St. Severus.** Step inside, if only to admire the extraordinary font, a masterpiece of intricately carved sandstone that reaches practically to the roof of the church.

The cathedral square is bordered by attractive old houses dating from the 16th century. Behind the predominantly neo-Gothic city hall, the **Rathaus,** you'll find Erfurt's outstanding attraction, the **Krämerbrücke** (Shopkeepers' Bridge), spanning the Gera River. You'd have to travel to Florence in Italy to find anything else like this, a Renaissance bridge incorporating shops and homes. Built in 1325 and restored in 1967–1973, the bridge served for centuries, as an important trading center, where goldsmiths, artisans, and merchants plied their wares. Today, antiques shops are a majority of the timber-framed houses that are incorporated into the bridge, some dating from the 16th century. The area around the bridge is criss-crossed with ancient streets lined with picturesque and often crumbling homes. The area is known as **Klein Venedig** (Little Venice), not because of any real resemblance to the lagoon city but for the recurrent flooding caused by the nearby river.

On the way back to the center of town from the Krämerbrucke, follow Gotthardstrasse and you'll pass the **St. Augustine cloisters,** where the young Martin Luther spent his formative years. Today it's a seminary. In nearby Leninstrasse you'll find Erfurt's interesting local-history museum, housed in a late-Renaissance house, **Zum Stockfisch.** *Leninstr. 169. Admission DM 1.05 adults, 55 pf children. Open Sun.–Thurs. 10–6.*

Leninstrasse brings you to the pedestrian-zoned **Anger,** an old street lined with restored Renaissance houses. The **Bartholomäusturm,** base of a 12th-century tower, holds a 60-bell carillon.

Just outside of the center is the **International Garden Exhibition** (open daily 10–7). Slightly farther afield is **Schloss Molsdorf,** one of the most stunning Rococo castles in Thuringia, set in a lovely park in the village of Molsdorf. The complex dates from 1736–1745, but has been considerably renovated since. *Grounds open daily, castle open Wed.–Sun. 2–5. Tours are give hourly.*

38 **Eisenach,** 58 kilometers (36 miles) west on either the main B-7 highway or the E-63 Autobahn (or an hour's journey by rail), is a historic old city that has managed to retain its medieval atmosphere better than most others in eastern Germany. Standing in its ancient market square, ringed by half-timbered houses, it's difficult to imagine that this town was an important center of the eastern German automobile industry, home of the now-shunned Wartburg. The solid, noisy staple of the East Germany auto trade was named after the famous castle that broods over Eisenach, high atop one of the foothills of the Thuringian Forest.

Begun in 1067 (and added to throughout the centuries), **Wartburg** castle hosted the German minstrels Walter von der Vogelweide and Wolfram von Eschenbach, Martin Luther, Richard Wagner, and Goethe. Johann Sebastian Bach was born in Eisenach in 1685 and must have climbed the hill to the castle often. Legend has it that von der Vogelweide, Germany's most famous minstrel, won a celebrated song contest here, the "contest of the Minnesingers" immortalized by the Romantic writer Novalis and in Wagner's *Tannhäuser*. Luther sought shelter within its stout walls from papal proscription, and from May 1521 until March 1522 translated the New Testament from Greek into German, an act that paved the way for the Protestant Reformation. The study in which Luther worked can be visited; it's basically the same room that he used, although the walls have been scarred by souvenir-hunters who, over the centuries, scratched away the plaster and much of the wood paneling. Luther's original desk was vandalized, and the massive table before you is a later addition, although a former possession of the Luther family.

There's much else of interest in this fascinating castle, including a portrait of Luther and his wife by Cranach the Elder, and a very moving sculpture, the *Kneeling Angel*, by the great 15th-century artist Tilman Riemenschneider. The 13th-century great hall is breathtaking; it's here that the minstrels are said to have sung for courtly favors. Don't leave without climbing the belvedere for a panoramic view of the distant hills of the Harz Mountains and the Thuringian Forest, and soak in the medieval atmosphere of the half-timbered, cottage-style interior courtyards of the castle. *Admission DM 3 adults, DM 1.50 children. Open Nov.–Feb., daily 9–5, Mar.–Oct., daily 8:30–5:30.*

The castle, accessible only from the north bridge, is an easy stroll from the center of town, along Friedrich-Engels-Strasse and Reuterweg. On the way, you'll pass the **Reuter-Wagner Museum,** at Reuterweg 2, which has a comprehensive exhibition on Wagner's life and work (DM 1.05 adults, 55 pf children; open Mon.–Fri. 9–12:30 and 2–5, Sun. 9–4). The town also has two museums devoted to Luther and Bach: the **Lutherhaus,** Lutherplatz 8 (open Mon.–Sat. 9–1 and 2–5, Sun. 2–5) and the **Bachhaus,** Frauenplan 21, which is devoted to the whole Bach family, and includes a collection of historical musical instruments (open Mon., Tues., Thurs., and Fri. 9–5; weekends 9–12:30 and 1–5). At Johannesplatz 9, look for what is allegedly the narrowest house in East Germany, built in 1890; the width is just over 6 feet, 8 inches, the height 24½ feet, and the depth 34 feet.

Our tour of the southern part of eastern Germany ends here. You can continue west on E-40 into western Germany, which leads into Route 5 to Frankfurt-am-Main. To return to Berlin, the fastest route is east on E-40 and north on E-51. For a change of scenery, turn off E-40 onto Route 4 north to Nordhausen, where you pick up Route 81 to Magdeburg (*see* Excursions in Chapter 4), and from there the E-30 Autobahn back into Berlin.

What to See and Do with Children

In **Dresden,** the penguin house at the zoo is particularly appealing; the zoo houses about 2,000 animals of some 500 species. *Open summer 8–5:30, winter 8–4:30.*

In Eisenach, at the Wartburg castle, kids can ride donkeys from the *Eselstation* at the start of the pathway to the castle.

Off the Beaten Track

Hellerau, 10 kilometers west of Dresden, on the Elbe River is the site of one of Europe's first experiments in William Morris-style "garden towns." It was founded in 1910 by Walt Dohrn, but the experiment (a furniture factory employing "happy, fullfilled workers" housed in idyllic rural cottages) foundered with his death in a Swiss skiing accident in 1914. Hellerau took off again between the two world wars, but since the end of World War II, the premises that made it famous—an avant-garde theater and an international boarding school—have been a Red Army barracks. The Russians are preparing to move out and there are plans to turn Hellerau into a European Cultural Center.

The **Feengrotte** (Fairy Grotto) at **Saalfeld,** near Gera, is a unique underground lake, transformed into a spectacular fairyland of colored stalactites as you travel through by boat.

Shopping

Souvenirs to buy in Saxony and Thuringia include wooden carvings, old books and prints, and glass Christmas ornaments. You can look for porcelain, but most of the good Meissen is exported; what the shops offer is mainly Dresden or Thuringen china. None of it—if it's good—is inexpensive.

In **Leipzig,** shop on Grimmaischestrasse and the arcades along Sachsenplatz and Markt. You'll find an excellent bookstore run by the Evangelical church opposite the entrance to Leipzig's St. Thomas' church. **Dresden's** shopping districts include Ernst-Thälmann-Strasse, the nearby Neumarkt, and Strasse der Befreiung.

Sports and Fitness

Biking Cycling is not as yet a well-developed recreation in eastern Germany, but trails will unquestionably spring up quickly with the political changes. Bicycle rentals will most certainly be among the early private undertakings to open in the eastern districts. If you're taking your own bicycle, be sure to bring essential spare parts with you. There's good cycling in Dresden along both sides of the Elbe River. Only the really fit should consider the upland Sächsische Schweiz, which is recommended for hikers and climbers.

Fishing The Elbe river tributaries south of Magdeburg offer excellent fishing; also try the rivers and streams around Erfurt and Eisenach. Conditions should improve as the polluted waters are cleaned up.

Hiking From Eisenach, hike into the nearby nature preserve area to the southeast.

Skiing The region south of Erfurt, centering around Oberhof, is a popular winter-sports area, with comfortable hotels and full sports facilities.

Water Sports The Gera and Saale rivers provide opportunities for canoeing; contact the tourist offices at Gera and Halle for rental information.

Winter Sports The upland, heavily forested Thüringer Wald is eastern Germany's second-favorite holiday destination, in summer and winter. Its center is Suhl, administrative center of an area where every 10th town and village is a spa or mountain resort. Suhl's tourist office, Suhl Information, is at Steinweg 1, tel. 066/20052.

Dining and Lodging

Dining

Many of the best restaurants are in the larger hotels. Regional specialties include *Thüringer Sauerbraten mit Klössen* (roast corned beef with dumplings), *Bärenschinken* (cured ham), and *Harzer Köhlerteller mit Röstkartoffeln* (charcoal-grilled meat with roast potatoes). Seafood is plentiful in the lake areas.

Highly recommended restaurants in each price category are indicated with a star ★.

Category	Cost*
Very Expensive	over DM 40
Expensive	DM 25–DM 40
Moderate	DM 15–DM 25
Inexpensive	under DM 15

**per person for a three-course meal and a beer or glass of wine*

Lodging

The choice of hotels in Saxony and Thuringia remains limited, and although private householders may now rent rooms, these are also hard to come by, as the demand is far greater than the supply. Choices in the Dresden area are especially scarce, so if you're planning to travel in high season, it's essential to book in advance. Contact the local tourist information offices for names of bed-and-breakfasts.

Note that during the Leipzig fair—early March and early September—all Leipzig hotels increase their prices.

Highly recommended hotels are indicated by a star ★.

Category	Cost*
Very Expensive	over DM 230
Expensive	DM 190–DM 230
Moderate	DM 130–DM 190
Inexpensive	under DM 130

**Prices are for two people in a double room.*

Chemnitz *Lodging*

Chemnitzer Hof. Look carefully at this older hotel (built in 1930, now on the national register) and you'll spot its origins in the early Bauhaus style, in which ornamentation was discarded in favor of abstract design. Inside, rooms are attractive and service friendly. You'll be in the heart of the city; you might enjoy the sense of living in another era. *Theaterplatz 4, tel. 0371/6840. 106 rooms with bath. Facilities: 2 restaurants, Bierstube, bar, nightclub, sauna, garage. AE, DC, MC, V. Very Expensive.*

Kongress. This modern 26-story skyscraper close to the town center stands in dramatic contrast to the rest of the city, but you'll find comfortable rooms in friendly surroundings here.

Preferred rooms are on the upper floors, overlooking the city. The restaurants, at least under the old regime, leaned heavily toward Russian cuisine. *Karl-Marx-Allee, tel. 0371/6830. 369 rooms with bath. Facilities: 4 restaurants, café, bar, nightclub, sauna, solarium, fitness room, garage. AE, DC, MC, V. Very Expensive.*

Moskau. Accommodations in this modern but plain blocklike structure near the town center are not particularly fancy, but you'll find everything you need. The outdoor cafés in summer are particularly relaxing. *Strasse der Nationen, tel. 0371/6810. 111 rooms with bath. Facilities: restaurant, cafés, nightclub, sauna, garage. AE, DC, MC, V. Moderate.*

Dresden
Dining

Sekundogenitur. This is one of the city's more famous wine restaurants, now connected to the Dresdner Hof hotel complex (*see* below), situated on the riverbank with a view of the river. There is outside dining as well, weather permitting. *Brühlsche Terrasse, tel. 0351/495–1435. Reservations advised. Dress: informal. No credit cards. Closed Mon. Moderate.*

Kügelnhaus. The complex here includes a grill, coffee bar, restaurant, and historic beer cellar, all justifiably popular, so go early or book ahead. *Strasse der Befreiung, tel. 0351/52791. Reservations advised. Dress: informal. No credit cards. Inexpensive.*

Lodging

Bellevue. Across the river from the Zwinger Palace, opera, and main museums, this fairly new hotel cleverly incorporates an old restored town house. Rooms are luxurious and service is good, lagging only when the tour groups arrive and depart. *Köpeckestr., 8060 Dresden, tel. 0351/56–620. 328 rooms with bath. Facilities: 4 restaurants, bar, café, indoor pool, sauna, solarium, fitness room, bowling, jogging course, boutiques. AE, DC, MC, V. Very Expensive.*

Dresdner Hof. The city's newest hotel fits snugly into a corner of the old city and is only a short distance from the Zwinger palace, Albertinum, and other major sights. Housing a wine cellar, several bars, a bistro, and smart restaurants, it offers every possible comfort. The lobby is a stunning black-and-white evocation of Jugendstil. *An der Frauenkirche 5, tel. 0351/48–410. 340 rooms with bath. Facilities: 8 restaurants, café, Bierclub, nightclub, indoor pool, sauna, solarium, fitness room, spa, garage. AE, DC, MC, V. Very Expensive.*

Newa. This modern monolith offers less charm but is close to the main train station. In keeping with the name, the restaurants emphasize Russian cuisine; the main specialty restaurant enjoys a fairly good reputation. *St.-Petersburger-Str. 34, tel. 0351/496–7112. 314 rooms with bath. Facilities: 2 restaurants, bar, café, sauna, garage. AE, DC, MC, V. Expensive.*

Interhotel Prager Strasse. This modern complex of two hotels in tandem, the **Königstein** and **Lilienstein,** is named for the two promontories overlooking the Elbe river south of the city. The hotels are side by side on a pedestrian street between the train station and the city center. Rooms are modern if unexciting; the favored rooms (for the view) overlook the Prager Strasse, although the back rooms are slightly quieter. *Prager Str., tel. 0351/48–460 and 0351/48–560. 300 rooms each. Facilities: 3 restaurants, sauna, garage. AE, DC, MC, V. Moderate.*

Parkhotel Weisser Hirsch. You'll be a considerable distance from the city center here (if driving, take Bautzenerstrasse from Platz der Einheit) in pleasant country surroundings. Facilities are simple, but the parklike setting makes up for the lack of luxury. *Bautzner Landstr. 7, tel. 0351/36–851. 54 rooms, none with full bath. Facilities: restaurant, café (dancing in evenings). No credit cards. Inexpensive.*

Eisenach
Dining

Gastmahl des Meeres. You're always well served at this popular fish restaurant chain in eastern Germany, and Eisenach's version is among the best. It's a large, friendly place, smothered in flowers as fresh as the fish that's caught from the restaurant's tanks. *Auf der Esplanade, tel. 03691/3885. No reservations. Dress: informal. MC. Closed weekends. Moderate.*

Waldschanke. This charming old restaurant is difficult to find, hidden away in a wood on the outskirts of town, but the hunt is well worth it (follow the Wartburgallee for about a mile and then watch for the signs to Prinzenteich). You'll eat lakeside in a former hunting lodge, and if you're lucky, fresh-caught fish or in-season venison will be on the menu. *Johannistal 57, tel. 03691/4465. Reservations advised. Dress: informal. No credit cards. Closed Thurs. and Fri. Moderate.*

Lodging

Auf der Wartburg. In this historic castle, where Martin Luther, Johann Sebastian Bach, and Richard Wagner were also guests, you'll get a splendid view over the town and surrounding countryside. The standard of comfort is above average, and antiques and Oriental rugs mix with modern, moderately stylish furnishings. The hotel runs a shuttle bus service to the rail station. *Wartburg, tel. 03691/5111. 30 rooms, most with bath. Facilities: restaurant. No credit cards. Moderate.*

Hospiz "Glockenhof-Sophienhof." At the base of the Wartburg castle, this hostel, run by the Evangelical church, occupies a half-timbered brick-roofed house that radiates personality fitting to the town. Facilities are modest, but rooms are pleasant. *Grimmelgasse 4, tel. 03691/3562. 23 rooms, most with bath. Facilities: restaurant. No credit cards. Inexpensive.*

Erfurt
Dining

Hohe Lilie. Sweden's King Gustav Adolph established his court in the Renaissance building housing this first-class restaurant. The atmosphere is aptly regal—and so are the prices. But the menu offers good value for money, and some of the dishes—the steak "Erfurtas" for instance—are, by eastern German standards, quite exceptional. *Domplatz 31, tel. 0361/22578. Reservations necessary. Jacket and tie required. AE, DC, MC, V. Expensive.*

Vital. If the Hohe Lilie is too expensive, or booked up, try the nearby Vital. Good portions of typical Thuringian fare (lots of local sausage) are served in simple but pleasant surroundings. Even after German unification it was possible to eat well here for less than DM 20, but prices are bound to rise. *Domplatz 3, tel. 0361/24317. Reservations advised. Dress: informal. No credit cards. Inexpensive.*

Dining and Lodging

Erfurter Hof. This inviting house in a traditional elegant style is under historic preservation, but the interior has been fully renovated to bring it up to modern standards. You're right at the train station and an easy stroll from the town center. The restaurant features cuisine of the Thuringen region, with an emphasis on fish and grilled meats. *Am Bahnhofsvorplatz 1–2, tel. 0361/51–151. 197 rooms, all with bath. Facilities: 2 restaurants, café, wine cellar, bar, nightclub, sauna, garage. AE, DC, MC, V. Very Expensive.*

Kosmos. This recent multistory intruder from outer space is out of place in this town, but you'll be halfway between the train station and the town center. At least the views are splendid; ask for a room on an upper floor overlooking the old city. The prices at Orbis restaurant and Galaxie café are not as far out as the names would imply. *Juri-Gagarin-Ring 126–127, tel. 0361/5510. 320 rooms, all with bath. Facilities: restaurant, café, bar, sauna, garage. AE, DC, MC, V. Moderate–Expensive.*

Gera
Lodging

Gera. The rooms inside this centrally located modern monolith are fortunately far more inviting than the nondescript facade suggests. The specialty restaurants—Ganymed (French), Lotos (East Asian), Elsertal (German), and Bierhöler (local Thüringen cuisine)—have good reputations. Guest rooms are standard but comfortable. Book ahead around Leipzig fair time. *Strasse der Republik, tel. 0365/22–991. 330 rooms with bath. Facilities: 3 restaurants, Bierstube, café, sauna, solarium, garage. AE, DC, MC, V. Very Expensive.*

Halle
Lodging

Stadt Halle. Inside, this central hotel is considerably more appealing than the rather cold facade would lead you to believe. Rooms offer the standard comforts, but several of the public rooms such as the Ufa restaurant (Russian specialties, and from the central Russian republic of Bashkir at that) and the Messe Club bar are quite attractive. Halle also takes overflow from Leipzig at Fair time, so plan and book accordingly. *Ernst-Thälmann-Pl., tel. 0345/25050. 345 rooms with bath. Facilities: 2 restaurants, café, bar, nightclub, garage. AE, DC, MC, V. Very Expensive.*

Leipzig
Dining

Altes Kloster. Game is featured in this fascinating, Old World restaurant, once part of a cloister. *Klostergasse 5, tel. 0341/282–252. Reservations advised. Jacket and tie required. No credit cards. Moderate.*

★ **Auerbachs Keller.** This historic restaurant (built 1530) in the city center is immortalized in Goethe's *Faust*. The menu features regional dishes from Saxony, often with Faustian names. There is a good wine list. Both a visit and reservations are a must. *Grimmaische Str. 2–4, tel. 0341/209–131. Reservations required. Jacket and tie required. AE, DC, MC, V. Moderate.*

Paulaner. Intimate, attractive, and quiet, this small place offers a limited selection of good local food. *Klostergasse 3, tel. 0341/281–985. Reservations advised. Dress: informal. No credit cards. Inexpensive.*

Lodging

Astoria. Many prefer this older hotel for its solid comfort and atmosphere in the grand style, as well as for its central location by the main train station. There's considerable traffic in the area, so you'll do best with a quieter room on the side rather than the front. The Galerie restaurant literally puts you into an art museum for lunch or dinner. *Platz der Republik 2, tel. 0341/71–710. 309 rooms with bath. Facilities: 2 restaurants, bar, dance café, nightclub, sauna, garage. AE, DC, MC, V. Very Expensive.*

Merkur. The city's newest and by far most luxurious hotel is imposing for its high-rise profile as well as its Japanese features (restaurant and garden). Rooms in this Japanese-built hotel offer every luxury, including full air-conditioning, and you'll be close to the main train station. *Gerberstr. 15, tel. 0341/7990. 440 rooms with bath. Facilities: 4 restaurants, 2 bars, coffee bar, nightclub, indoor pool, sauna, solarium, spa, bowling, shops, parking. AE, DC, MC, V. Very Expensive.*

Stadt Leipzig. Set back from the Ring, this postwar modern monolith from the '60s is surprisingly quiet, considering its central location close by the main train station. Public rooms are attractive: dark wood paneling in the Vignette restaurant sets the tone for a quiet meal. *Richard-Wagner-Str. 1–6, tel. 0341/288–814. 340 rooms with bath. Facilities: 3 restaurants, café, bar, nightclub, sauna, garage. AE, DC, MC, V. Expensive.*

International. This traditional hotel offers appropriate charm and friendly personnel. You're within steps of the heart of the city, and not far from the train station either. The spacious rooms offer old-fashioned comfort but with modern facilities. The sidewalk café is popular. *Tröndlinring 8, tel. 0341/71–880. 108 rooms with bath. Facilities: restaurant, Bierstube, bar, café, garage. AE, DC, MC, V. Moderate.*

Zum Löwen. This is another of the postwar modern hotels built to handle Leipzig Fair traffic, but in this case, the house is personable and cheerful, if not opulent. Around the corner from the Astoria, you'll be close to the train station and within an easy stroll of the city center. *Rudolf-Breitscheid-Str., tel. 0341/7751. 108 rooms with bath. Facilities: restaurant. AE, DC, MC, V. Moderate.*

Parkhotel. The location directly across from the train station could hardly be better, but the accommodations are simple if not downright spartan—virtually none of the rooms have baths. *Richard-Wagner-Str. 7, tel. 0341/7821. 174 rooms. Facilities: restaurant, parking. No credit cards. Inexpensive.*

Meissen
Dining and Lodging

Bahnhofshotel. This small hotel is directly at the train station and convenient to the center of town. Rooms have a dated modern decor but are attractive, with satisfactory baths. The restaurants remind one a bit of the train station, which is only appropriate. *Grossenhainer Str. 2, tel. 03521/3320. 18 rooms with bath. Facilities: restaurant, parking. AE, DC, MC, V. Moderate.*

Weimar
Dining

Weisser Schwan. This historic restaurant in the center of town, right by the Goethe house (*see* Meissen and Dresden in Exploring Saxony and Thuringia, above), dates from 1500. Its various rooms, including the library, offer international and Thuringian specialties, particularly fish and grilled meats. *Frauenstorstr. 23, tel. 03643/61715. Reservations essential. Jacket and tie advised. AE, DC, MC, V. Closed last Mon. of month. Expensive.*

Elephantenkeller. In the ancient vaulted cellar restaurant of the Elephant hotel (*see* below), you'll eat well on traditional Thuringian cuisine in surroundings that haven't changed much since Goethe's day. Only the functional 1950s style of some of the furnishings disturb the overall atmosphere reinforced by the well-worn flagstones of the floor and the squat sandstone pillars behind which many lunchtime deals are being sealed in postreunification Germany. Try the *Weimarer Zwiebelmarkt* soup, an onion soup made with pork-knuckle stock. *Markt 19, tel. 03643/61471. Reservations advised. Dress: informal. No credit cards. Moderate.*

Lodging

Belvedere. Opened in 1990, this luxurious hotel is about 1½ kilometers (1 mile) outside of the town center, across from a gorgeous wooded park—Goethe helped plan the layout—which is worth a stroll even if you're not staying at the Belvedere. Rooms in the hotel are, if anything, overcomplete; you'll lack nothing, except possibly to be closer to the center. *Belvedere Allee, tel. 03643/2429. 300 rooms with bath. Facilities: 2 restau-*

rants, café, Bierclub, 3 bars, indoor pool, sauna, solarium, fitness room, spa, bowling, garage. AE, DC, MC, V. Very Expensive.

Elephant. This hotel, dating from 1696, is one of the Germany's most famous; you'll follow the choice of Goethe, Schiller, Herder, Liszt—and Hitler—all of whom have been guests here. Behind the sparkling white facade are comfortable modern rooms, thanks to recent renovations, but a feeling for the historic past is ever-present. Book well ahead. *Am Markt 19, tel. 03643/61–471. 116 rooms with bath. Facilities: 4 restaurants, bar, nightclub, sauna, garage. AE, DC, MC, V. Expensive.*

Hospiz. This hostel run by the Evangelical church is only steps away from Goethe's house. Rooms are modest, but so is the price; the public rooms are attractively furnished with antiques. In 1991 bathrooms were being added to the rooms and old furniture replaced, so rates will have risen accordingly. *Amalienstr. 2, tel. 03643/2711. 21 rooms, 12 with bath. Facilities: restaurant, parking. No credit cards. Moderate.*

The Arts and Nightlife

The Arts

Opera The opera in **Dresden** has regained its international reputation since the house, which was almost totally destroyed in World War II, was reopened in 1985 following an eight-year reconstruction. Just to see the magnificent house alone is worth the trip; a performance is that much better. Tickets are reasonably priced but also hard to get; they're often included in package tours. Try your luck at the evening box office (the *Abendkasse*, left of the main entrance) about a half hour before the performance; there are usually a few dozen tickets available.

Several smaller cities, notably **Chemnitz,** also have opera houses that turn out interesting performances, occasionally of relatively little known or contemporary works.

Music The Neues Gewandhaus in **Leipzig,** a controversial piece of architecture, is home to a splendid orchestra. Tickets to concerts are very difficult to obtain unless you reserve well in advance and in writing only (Gewandhaus zu Leipzig, Karl-Marx-Platz, Leipzig 7010). Sometimes spare tickets are available at the box office a half hour before the evening performance. Of the music festivals in the area, the best known are the Handel festival in **Halle** (June) and the Music Days in **Leipzig** (June), as well as the International Bach Festival held every four years during September and October. **Dresden** organizes an international Dixieland festival each May.

Nightlife

Leipzig comes to life particularly during Fair time, although in the past this was as much to extract hard currency from the visitors as it was to entertain them. In most cities the leading hotels run nightclubs year-round (*see* Dining and Lodging, above), and many of these are not bad at all. In **Leipzig,** try the Merkur, Kongress, Chemnitzer Hof, and Moskau; in **Dresden,** the Dresdner Hof; in **Gera,** the Gera; in **Erfurt,** the Erfurter Hof; and in **Weimar,** the Belvedere and Elephant hotels.

18 The Baltic Coast

Including Lübeck

Introduction

The Baltic Coast is Germany's half-forgotten eastern shoreline, as unfamiliar to most postwar Germans as it is to foreigners. It's a region of white, sandy beaches (340 kilometers [210 miles] of them), coves, chalk cliffs, ancient ports, and fishing villages where time and custom seem to have stood still. Until World War II some of the beach resorts had been popular holiday destinations since the mid-19th century, when sunbathing and sea swimming first became fashionable. But the entire 1,130-kilometer (706-mile) weaving coastline—from the Trave River estuary, above Lübeck, to Swinemünde, at the Polish border—was plunged into isolation when the Iron Curtain came down just east of Lübeck. On the island of Rügen, for example, the clock appears to have stopped in the 1920s and 1930s; the architecture, the pace of life, even the trains—they are steam powered—are caught in a time warp.

The tour threads a route through five leading Hanseatic League ports, whose medieval merchants became rich monopolizing trade across the Baltic Sea between the 12th and 16th centuries. Much of their wealth was invested in buildings; some of the finest examples of north German Gothic and Renaissance redbrick architecture, with its tall stepped gables, are to be found here. Except for the cities of Schwerin and Rostock (the latter was former East Germany's chief port and shipbuilding center), the Baltic Coast is a rural region, but one in which the sea has long played a pivotal role. Indeed, many of the locals are tough seafaring folk, traders and fishermen since these shores were settled.

The route takes us east from Lübeck to Usedom Island, parallel to the coast, but slightly inland. If you see an interesting-looking road that wanders off to the north, it's likely to lead to the coast and could be worth a detour.

Essential Information

Important Addresses and Numbers

Tourist Information The principal regional tourist office for the Baltic Coast is **Ostsee Tourist**, Hermann-Duncker-Platz 3, 2500 Rostock 1, tel. 0381/380208.

There are local tourist information offices in the following towns and cities:

Bad Doberan: Kurverwaltung, Am Markt 5, tel. 038203/3001.
Greifswald: Informationsbüro, Strasse der Freundschaft 102, 2200 Greifswald, tel. 03834/3460.
Lübeck: Verkehrsverein, Beckergrube 95, 2400 Lübeck, tel. 0451/1228109.
Rostock: Touristbüro, Schnickmannstr. 13, 2500 Rostock, tel. 0381/22619.
Rügen Island: Hauptstr. 9, 2337 Binz, tel. 038393/2241.
Schwerin: Tourist-Information, Am Markt 11, 2750 Schwerin, tel. 0385/864509.
Stralsund: Touristbüro, Alter Markt 15, 2300 Stralsund, tel. 03831/2439.
Usedom Island: Kurverwaltung, Dünenstr. 45, 2252 Ahlbeck, tel. Ahlbeck 039775 (operator assistance only).

Wismar: Touristbüro, Bohrstr. 5a, 2400 Wismar, tel. 03841/2958.

Car Rental **Avis:** Schmiedestr. 17, tel. 0451/72008, **Lübeck;** Hermann-Duncke-Platz 2, tel. 0381/380243, **Rostock.**
Hertz: Wahlhalb Insel 1–5, tel. 0451/71747, **Lübeck;** Stralsunde Chausee, tel. 0381/71747) **Rostock.**

Arriving and Departing by Plane

The nearest international airport to the start of the tour is in Hamburg, just half an hour southwest of Lübeck by train or car. Berlin, with two international airports (Tegel and Schönefeld), is 280 kilometers (175 miles) south.

Arriving and Departing by Car and Train

Lübeck is linked to the Intercity train network, with hourly connections with Hamburg. There is also train service from Berlin to Lübeck, but service across the territory of former East Germany is generally much slower because of poor track conditions. Lübeck is 56 kilometers (35 miles) from Hamburg via Autobahn A1 (E-22).

Getting Around

By Car With the exception of high summer (July and August), roads along the coast are not overcrowded. Route 105 covers much of the journey. Road surfaces in eastern Germany generally are not good, although major improvements are under way. There is a maximum speed limit of 130 kph (80 mph) on motorways in eastern Germany, and 80 kph (48 mph) on other main out-of-town roads.

By Train A north–south train line links Berlin with Schwerin and Rostock. An east-west route connects Hamburg, Lübeck, and Rostock, and some trains continue through to Stralsund and Sassnitz on Rügen Island. At press time, train service offered by the Bundesbahn and Reichsbahn was merging. Contact major train stations or tourist offices for schedule changes.

By Bus Local buses link the main train stations with outlying towns and villages, especially the coastal resorts. Buses operate throughout Rügen and Usedom islands.

By Boat The **Weisse Flotte** (White Fleet) line operates a number of ferries linking the Baltic ports, as well as short harbor and coastal cruises. Boats depart from Warnemünde (Am Strom 124, tel. 081/52624), Wismar (call Wismar tourist office for schedule: tel. 03841/2958), Stralsund (Pavillon am Hafen, tel. 03831/692473), and Sassnitz (call Rügen Island tourist office for schedule: tel. 038393/2241). For the latest service information contact the Rostock tourist office (tel. 0381/22619). Harbor and coastal cruises also operate from Lübeck; contact the Lübeck tourist office for details. In addition, ferries run between Rostock, Warnemünde, Stralsund, and Sassnitz and Sweden and Denmark.

Guided Tours

A number of half-day and full-day tours of the coastal region, taking in many of the attractions discussed below, are organized by the **Rostock** tourist office. For the latest schedules, contact Ostsee Tourist, Hermann-Duncker-Platz 3 (tel. 0381/380208). Guided tours of **old Lübeck** depart daily from the Lübeck tourist office, Markt (tel. 0451/1228106) between mid-April and mid-October, and on weekends only from mid-October to mid-April.

Exploring the Baltic Coast

Highlights for First-time Visitors

Schloss Schwerin
Markplatz, Wismar
The medieval seaport of Stralsund
Rügen Island
A ride on the steam train "Molli"
High-Gothic cloister church, Bad Doberan

Lübeck to Rostock

Numbers in the margin correspond to points of interest on the Baltic Coast map.

The starting point of this 525-kilometer (328-mile) tour is a historic and pretty port just west of the now-departed Iron Cur-
1 tain. The ancient core of **Lübeck,** dating from the 12th century, is surrounded by canals fed by the Trave River and was one of the chief strongholds of the Hanseatic merchant princes who controlled trade on the Baltic. But it was the roving King Henry the Lion (Heinrich der Löwe) who established the town and, in 1173, laid the foundation stone of the redbrick Gothic cathedral.

Today Lübeck is close to every German's heart or, more precisely, his hip pocket: The town's famous landmark, the **Holstentor** gate, is pictured on Germany's DM 50 note. The ancient gate on Holstentor Platz, built between 1464 and 1478, is flanked by two round, squat towers—solid symbols of Lübeck's prosperity as a trading center. A short walk along Holtenstrasse brings you to one of Europe's most striking medieval market squares, which looks like a Hollywood backdrop for a tournament of jousting knights. Among the buildings lining the arcaded **Marktplatz,** the **Rathaus** (Town Hall), dating from 1240, is particularly noteworthy, having been subjected to several architectural face-lifts that have added Romanesque arches, Gothic windows, and a Renaissance roof. From the square, turn left into Breitestrasse, where you'll pass the 18th-century Baroque Buddenbrookhaus, made famous by novelist Thomas Mann's saga *Buddenbrooks*. Mann's family once lived in the house, which is still privately owned and not open to the public. Continue on along Breitestrasse and turn right into Koberg. Here you will find one of the oldest and most beautiful hospitals in the world. Built in the 14th century by the town's rich merchants, the Gothic **Heiligen-Geist-Hospital** (Holy Ghost Hospital) is still caring for the infirmed. At the other end of the old town you'll find the oldest building in Lübeck, the **Dom,** or cathedral, its foundation stone laid in 1173 by that gaddabout royal Henry the Lion. The Gothic Dom, incorporating late-Romanesque and Renaissance features, was severely damaged in World War II but rebuilt in 1958–1977.

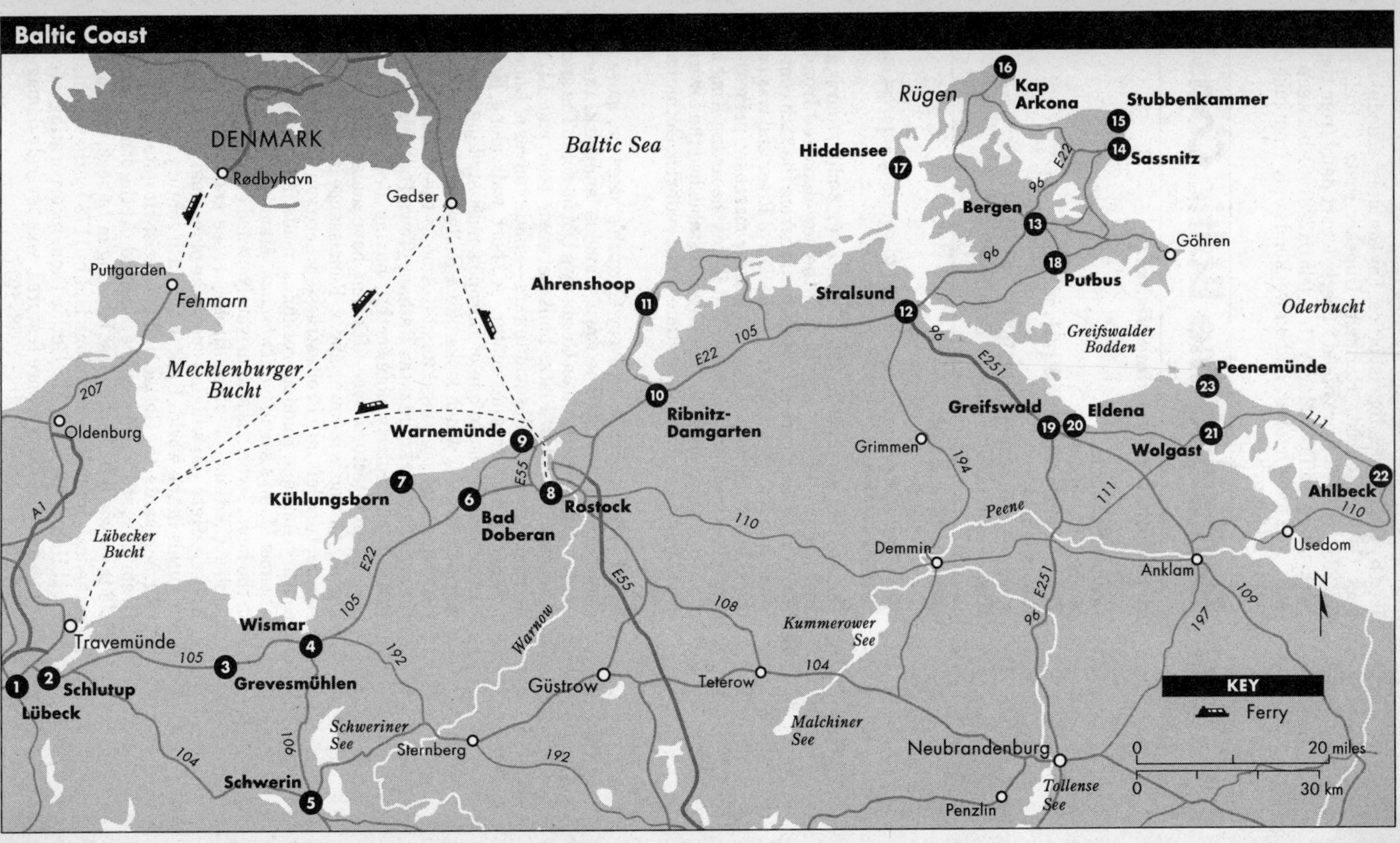
Baltic Coast
DENMARK
Rødbyhavn
Gedser
Baltic Sea
Rügen
Kap Arkona
Stubbenkammer
Sassnitz
Hiddensee
Bergen
Göhren
Putbus
Puttgarden
Fehmarn
Ahrenshoop
Stralsund
Oderbucht
Greifswalder Bodden
Mecklenburger Bucht
207
Oldenburg
Ribnitz-Damgarten
Peenemünde
Greifswald
Eldena
Wolgast
Warnemünde
Grimmen
Kühlungsborn
Bad Doberan
Rostock
Ahlbeck
A1
Lübecker Bucht
Peene
Demmin
Usedom
Anklam
E22
E55
E251
105
96
110
194
111
108
109
197
Warnow
Kummerower See
Wismar
Travemünde
Grevesmühlen
192
104
Schlutup
Lübeck
Güstrow
Teterow
KEY
Ferry
106
Schweriner See
Sternberg
Malchiner See
Neubrandenburg
Schwerin
Penzlin
Tollense See
N
0
20 miles
30 km

Leave Lübeck on the B-104 and after crossing the Trave into
2 **Schlutup** see if you can still spot vestiges of the no-man's-land between East and West Germany, a flat, empty 100-yard-wide corridor once lined with barbed-wire fences punctuated by heavily armed watchtowers. At Selmsdorf, take Route 105, which until recently was the most northerly transit corridor road for foreigners traveling across East Germany between
3 West Germany and Poland. Stop at **Grevesmühlen** to view the Gothic St. Nikolai parish church and a pretty Renaissance town hall. A couple of miles east of the town is one of the highest hills in the region, the Iserberg; from here on a clear day you can view the coastline and the island of Poel. This region has been buffeted by more than stiff sea storms; over the centuries the armies of Sweden, Denmark, Prussia, and France fought here for control of the coast. A grim reminder of a more recent conflict can be found in nearby Tannenberg, site of a memorial cemetery for some of the 8,000 Nazi concentration camp victims who drowned when four ships that were transporting them were mistakenly attacked by Allied planes and sunk in Lübeck Bay only days before the war ended.

Back on Route 105, another 22 kilometers (14 miles) will take
4 you to **Wismar,** a picturesque port that was one of the original three sea-trading towns that banded together in 1259 to combat Baltic pirates (the other two were Lübeck and Rostock). From this mutual defense pact grew the great and powerful private trading block that dominated the Baltic for centuries: the Hanseatic League. The Thirty Years' War was particularly devastating for this region—the prewar population was halved—and the power of the Hanseatics was broken. Wismar became the victim of regular military tussles and finally fell to Sweden. The town was mortgaged to a German Mecklenburg duke in 1803 on a 100-year lease, and it was only when this expired in 1903 that Wismar legally rejoined Germany.

Despite its checkered history, the wealth originally generated by the Hanseatic merchants can still be seen in Wismar's rich and ornate architecture, particularly in the patrician gabled houses that frame the **Marktplatz,** the main square, one of the largest and most colorful in northern Germany. The style of buildings on the square ranges from redbrick late-Gothic through Dutch Renaissance to 19th-century neoclassical. Of particular interest is the **Wasserkunst,** the ornate pumping station in Dutch Renaissance style built in 1602 by the Dutch master Philipp Brandin. Not only was it a work of art, it supplied the town with water until the mid-19th century.

Time Out The oldest building on the Marktplatz (1308) is also a colorful seaman's tavern, the **Alter Schwede,** with a gabled redbrick facade dating from 1380. Traditional regional dishes are served, including the hearty potato-and-bacon casserole called *Griebenroller. Am Markt 16, tel. 03841/3552.*

Walk west to reach the 250-foot-high tower of the ruined **Marienkirche** church, bombed in World War II, just behind the Marktplatz. At noon, 3 PM, and 5 PM, listen for one of 14 hymns played on its clarion bells. Next to it stands the **Fürstenhof,** home of the former dukes of Mecklenburg, an early 16th-century Italian Renaissance structure with touches of late-Gothic. The facade is a series of fussy friezes depicting scenes from the Trojan War. Another victim of the war is adjacent to the Fürstenhof, the **Georgenkirche,** the cathedral of St. George. Today it's the biggest Gothic religious ruin in Europe.

Backtrack through the Marktplatz and along Krämerstrasse to reach the **Nikolaikirche,** a late-Gothic church with a 120-foot-high nave. Important architectural relics rescued from the bombed ruins of other Wismar churches are displayed here, notably the Gothic high altar from the Georgenkirche. Across the street the Dutch Renaissance **Schabbelthaus** houses a fascinating museum of local history. *Schweinsbrücke 8. Admission: DM 2 adults, DM 1 children. Open May–Sept., Tues.–Sun., 10–4; Oct.–Apr., Tues.–Sat. 10–4.*

If you've got an hour to spare, wander among the jetties and quays of the port, a mix of the medieval and modern.

From Wismar, you can continue on along Route 105 to Bad Doberan, 36 kilometers (23 miles) away. But if time permits,
5 make a 32-kilometer detour south on the B-106 to **Schwerin,** the second-largest town in the region (the largest is Rostock) and capital of the new state of Mecklenburg-Vorpommern. It's worth the side trip just to visit the giant **Schloss Schwerin** (Schwerin Palace) of the Mecklenburg royal family, built in 1857 on an island in the vast Schweriner See Lake close to the old town. A pastiche of historical styles, the palace, surmounted by 15 turrets large and small, is reminiscent of a French château, and, indeed, was modeled on Chambord in the Loire Valley. Surprisingly, the Communist government restored and maintained the fantastic opulence of this rambling 80-room reminder of an absolutist monarch system. Antique furniture, objets, silk tapestries, and paintings are sprinkled throughout the salons (the Throne Room is particularly extravagant), but of special interest are the ornately patterned and highly burnished inlaid wooden floors and wall panels. The palace stands on the site of an earlier Renaissance castle, of which only the chapel, built in 1560, survives, and is surrounded by parkland laid out in the 18th century and containing many beautiful species of trees. *Lennestr. Admission: DM 3, adults, DM 1.50 children. Palace and gardens open Tues–Sun 10–5.*

Time Out The King's Hall of the palace is today Schwerin's most picturesque coffee shop, which also makes its own ice cream. Concerts are held here daily, usually in the afternoons (tel. 0385/865001 for schedule).

Schwerin's showpiece square, the **Alte Garten,** opposite the entrance to the palace island, was the scene of military parades during the years of Communist rule. It is dominated by two buildings, the ornate neo-Renaissance state theater, 1883–1886, and the Staatliche Galerie (admission free; open Tues.–Sun. 9–4), which houses an interesting collection of paintings by 19th-century German artists such as Max Liebermann and Lovis Corinth, plus an exhibition of Meissen porcelain. Another noteworthy sight in Schwerin's old town is the Gothic cathedral, or Dom. The bronze baptismal font dates from the 14th century; the altar was built in 1440. Religious scenes painted on the walls of the adjoining Marienkapelle (Chapel of Maria) date from the Middle Ages. Sweeping views of the old town and lake await those with the energy to climb the 219 steps to the top of the 320-foot-high cathedral tower. *Buschstr. Tower open Mon.–Sat. 11–12, 2:30–4:30, Sun. 2:30–4:30.*

6 Return to Wismar and pick up the B-105 again to **Bad Doberan,** whose finely preserved redbrick cloister church is one of the finest of its kind in the region. It was built by Cistercian monks between 1294 and 1368 in the northern German Gothic style, with a central nave and transept. The main altar dates from the early 14th century and features a 45-foot-tall cross. Many of the monastic buildings have been preserved; the former corn granary has been turned into a school. *Admission: DM 2 adults, 50 pf children. Guided tours: Sept.–June, Tues.–Sat. 9, 10, 2, and 3, Sun. 2, 3; July–Aug., Mon.–Sat. 9, 10, 2, and 3, Sun. 2, 3.*

No visit to this part of the world would be complete without a ride on "Molli," a quaint little steam train that has been chugging up and down a 10-mile-long narrow-gauge track between Bad Doberan and the nearby beach resorts of Heiligendamm
7 and **Kühlungsborn** since 1886. The train acquired its nickname after a little local dog of the same name that barked its approval every time the smoking iron horse passed by. At the start of the 40-minute journey the engine and its old wooden carriages make their way through the center of Bad Doberan's cobbled streets. "Molli" runs 13 times daily in both directions between Bad Doberan and Kühlungsborn, from 5 AM until 10 PM. The fare is DM 4.50 adults, DM 2.50 children.

Horse-racing fans may be interested to know that the first race course in Europe outside Britain was established in Bad Doberan in 1807. The site is still remembered in the name of one of Molli's station halts, Rennbahn, which is German for race course.

From Bad Doberan, resume your journey east along the B-105 an-
8 other 14 kilometers (9 miles) to **Rostock,** the biggest port and shipbuilding center of former East Germany. Once-thriving Rostock suffered from the dissolution of the Hanseatic Pact in 1669, as the area was fought over and trade declined. While Hamburg, Kiel to the west, and Stettin to the east (now Poland) became leading port cities, Rostock languished until the late 1940s, when the newly formed German Democratic Republic found that it needed a sea outlet and Rostock was reestablished as a major port.

The city suffered severe damage in World War II bombings, but much of the old town's core has been rebuilt, including large segments of the medieval old town wall and the facades of the late-Gothic and Renaissance houses of the rich *Hanse* merchants. (One of the best views of old Rostock is from a boat in the harbor; *see* Getting Around in Essential Information, above.) The finest examples are to be found along the main street, the pedestrian-only **Kröpelinerstrasse,** which begins at the old western gate, the Kröpeliner Tor, and leads into the town square (Markt/Ernst-Thälmann-Platz). You'll immediately notice the architectural potpurri that is the **Rathaus** (Town Hall). Basically 13th-century Gothic with a Baroque facade, the building spouts seven slender, decorative towers, looking like candles on a peculiar birthday cake. The square is surrounded by historic gabled houses. Head north on Langestrasse out of the square to reach the four-centuries-old **Marienkirche** (St. Mary's Church), the architectural gem of Rostock. The Gothic structure boasts a bronze baptismal font from 1290, and some interesting Baroque features, notably the oak altar (1720) and organ (1770). The unique attraction, however, is the huge astronomical clock dating from 1472; it has a calendar extending to the year 2017. At the rear of Marienkirche in Am Ziegenmarkt is Rostock's former mint, the **Münze.** The town started producing its own coins in 1361, and only the relinquished this right in 1864. The Münze has a fine Renaissance arched entrance and a stone relief depicting coin makers going about their work.

Just beyond the city walls, through the Steintor, you'll come to the **Schiffahrtmuseum,** at August-Babel-Strasse 1, which traces the history of shipping on the Baltic and displays models of ships throughout the ages. *Admission: DM 1.50 adults, 50 pf children. Open daily May–Sept. 9:30–4:30, Oct.–Apr., Tues.–Fri. 9:30–4:30.*

9 The nearby seaside resort-cum-fishing village of **Warnemünde,** at the mouth of the Warnow River, is now virtually a suburb of Rostock, a 14-kilometer (9-mile) ride north on Route 103. For years it has been a popular summer holiday destination for East German families, drawn by a 2-mile-long sandy beach, a giant heated saltwater pool with artificial waves as high as 4 feet, among other attractions. Children will also enjoy climbing to the top of the town landmark, a 115-foot-high **lighthouse,** which on clear days offers views of the coast and Rostock Harbor. *Am Strom. Admission: 50 pf. Open daily.*

Time Out Next door to the lighthouse, the **Teepott** occupies a converted flying-boat hangar. It's an unusual setting for relaxing over a beer or coffee and cake while watching the water traffic in the mouth of the Warnow. *Am Leuchtturm. Open daily.*

Return to Rostock and pick up Route 105, traveling east for 30
10 kilometers (19 miles) to **Ribnitz-Damgarten.** The town is the center of the amber (in German, *Bernstein*) business, unique to the Baltic Coast. You can see a fascinating exhibition of how the precious "Baltic gold" is collected from the sea and refined to make jewelry and objets d'art in the **Bernsteinmuseum,** which adjoins the main factory. (You can buy amber at the factory, which is open the same hours as the museum; *see* below.) The museum has examples of amber dating back 4,000 years. The biggest lump of raw amber ever harvested from the sea weighed more than 23 pounds—enough to make 30 necklaces. But the piece has never been cut; it is on exhibition today in the Naturkundemseum in Berlin. *Im Kloster 1–2, tel. 03821/2931. Admission free. Open June–Sept., Tues.–Sat., 9:30–5, Sun. 2–4; Oct.–May, Tues.–Sat. 9:30–4.*

At Ribnitz, you can continue directly along Route 105 the 40 kilometers (25 miles) to the medieval port of Stralsund, the crossing point for Rügen Island, or take a circular back route (35 kilometers [22 miles] longer) by striking out for Wustrow on the coast and the narrow isthmus that leads to what the Germans call the half-island of **Darss.** This half-moon-shaped finger of land was once three separate islands that have filled into one over centuries of shifting sand. Much of Darss has been a nature reserve since 1966, partly to protect the ancient forest of beech, holly, and juniper, but also because of the area's topographical uniqueness. The area contains many rare plants and provides shelter for a huge variety of sea birds. Darss is also noted for its old fisherman's cottages with reed-thatched roofs.

11 The village of **Ahrenshoop** is a especially picturesque, the site
of an art colony that started in the late 19th century and
brought together painters from across Germany and beyond.

Follow signs to Barth to get off the "island" over a causeway
12 and rejoin Route 105 to reach **Stralsund,** Germany's main producer of fishing boats. In 1815 the Congress of Vienna awarded
the city to the Prussians after having been under Swedish control. Although it was rapidly industrialized, this jewel of the
Baltic features a historic city center painstakingly rebuilt and
restored.

Following an attack by the Lübeck fleet in 1249, a defensive wall was built around Stralsund, parts of which you'll see on your left as you come into the old town. The old market square, the **Alter Markt,** boasts the best local architecture, ranging from Gothic through Renaissance to Baroque. Most of the buildings were rich merchants' homes, notably the late-Gothic **Wulflamhaus,** with 17 ornate, steeply stepped gables. Stralsund's architectural masterpiece, however, is the 13th-century **Rathaus** (Town Hall), considered by many to be the finest secular example of redbrick Gothic in northern Germany. Note the coats of arms of the main towns that formed the exclusive membership of the Hanseatic League. The 13th-century Gothic **Nikolaikirche** (Church of St. Nicholas) also faces onto the square. Its treasures include a 15-foot-high crucifix from the 14th century and a Baroque altar. Walk down the pedestrian street Ossenreyerstrasse and along through the Apollonienmarkt to the Katherinenkloster, a former cloister, on Monchstrasse. Forty rooms of the cloister now house a series of museums related to the sea, including an aquarium.

Stralsund is also the departure point for the island of Rügen
13 and its administrative capital, **Bergen.** (White Fleet boats will
also take you from Stralsund to various towns on Rügen.) The
island has been joined to the mainland since 1936 by a causeway
that carries road and train traffic. The main road over the
causeway from Stralsund (Route 96) cuts straight across the
island southwest to northeast, a distance of 51 kilometers
(32 miles). The route runs between the Grosser Jasmunder
Bodden, a giant sea inlet, and a smaller expanse of water—the
14 Kleiner Jasmunder Bodden Lake—to the port of **Sassnitz,**
where ferries run to Sweden.

What Rügen lacks in architectural interest it makes up for in
15 natural beauty. From the chalk cliffs of the **Stubbenkammer**
headland on the east coast of the island, through the blustery
16 sand dunes of **Kap Arkona** in the north (its lighthouse marks the
northernmost point in eastern Germany, and you can see the
Danish island of Moen from a restored watchtower next door),
to the quiet waters and coves of the Grosser Jasmunder Bodden
in the center, this is a nature lover's paradise. Off the northwest corner of Rügen is a smaller island, the sticklike
17 **Hiddensee.** Motorized transport is banned on Hiddensee,
which adds to its tranquillity. A ferry will take you there from
the village of Schaprode.

Rügen first became popular as a holiday destination with the development of the railways in the mid-19th century, and many of the grand mansions and villas on the island date from this period. Despite its continuing popularity during the Communist years, little new development has taken place since the

mid-1930s, leaving the entire island in a kind of time warp. For example, dances—all the rage in the 1920s and 1930s—continue on Rügen with afternoon coffee dances at cafés and dinner dances at hotels, and the island still retains its own regular steam-train service, the Rasender Roland (Racing Roland),
18 which runs 24½ kilometers (15 miles) from **Putbus** to the southeast corner of the island. Near Binz, climb the 125-foot-high lookout tower by Jagdschloss Granitz for a splendid view in all directions.

Retrace your route back across the Stralsund causeway and head south along Route 96 for 32 kilometers (20 miles) to
19 **Greifswald,** the last in the string of Hanseatic ports on this tour. The town was a busy sea trading center in the Middle Ages but became a backwater in the 19th century, when ships became too large to negotiate the shallow Ryck River leading to the sea. Today's visitors have German army commander Colonel Rudolf Petershagen to thank for being able to see many of its original buildings. In charge of Greifswald in early 1945, he surrendered the town to the approaching Soviet forces rather than see it destroyed. Ironically, lack of funds for restoration over the next 40 years left some historic buildings in desperate need of repair.

Stroll along the Strasse der Freundschaft to the **Platz der Freundschaft,** presided over by a medieval **Rathaus,** rebuilt in 1738–1750 following a fire, modified in the 19th century and again in 1936. The square is surrounded by splendid old houses in redbrick Gothic styles. Three churches shape the silhouette of the city: the 13th-century **Dom St. Nikolai** (St. Nicholas' Cathedral) at the start of Martin-Luther-Strasse, a Gothic church from whose 300-foot-high tower one can get an impressive view; the 14th-century **Marienkirche** (St. Mary's Church), on the corner of Brüggstrasse and Friedrich-Loeffler-Strasse, the oldest surviving church in Greifswald, and noted for its remarkable 60-foot-high arches and a striking four-cornered tower; and the 13th-century **St. Jacob's,** later rebuilt to a three-nave design.

Time Out After admiring the Renaissance facade of the Rathaus in the market square, descend into its vaulted cellars for a cool glass of wine from a surprisingly good selection (there's even a tasting bar). The **Ratsweinkeller** is closed on Sunday.

---

20 Just outside Greifswald, in what is now the suburb of **Eldena,** stand the ruins of a 12th-century Cistercian monastery made famous in a painting by Caspar David Friedrich (now at the Gallery of Romantic Painting in Berlin), who was born in Greifswald, in 1774. The monastery, which led to the founding of Greifswald, was plundered by rampaging Swedish soldiers early in the Thirty Years' War and abandoned. The Gothic structure was further cannibalized by townsfolk over the next two centuries until it was made a protected national monument, a result of the publicity it gained from the celebrated Friedrich painting.

Still heading south, take Route 109, then Route 111 off to the
21 left, for the fastest journey to **Wolgast** (34 kilometers [21 miles]) and the causeway crossing to Germany's other main Baltic island of Usedom. Wolgast's chief attraction is the old town square, **Karl-Liebknecht-Platz,** where the pretty mid-17th-century half-timbered house known locally as the **Kaf-**

feemühle and a Baroque **town hall** are situated. The Kaffeemühle, far from serving coffee, is the local history museum, the **Kreismuseum,** which tells the life story of another locally born artist of the Romantic era, Philipp Otto Runge. The museum also has an exhibition detailing the development of Germany's V2 rocket during World War II, spearheaded by scientist Werner von Braun (who later developed the U.S. space program). *Admission free. Open Tues.–Fri. 9–5, weekends 9–4.*

On its seaboard side, 25-mile-long Usedom Island has almost 20 miles of sandy shoreline and a string of resorts. The best of
22 them and the island's main town is **Ahlbeck,** which features an unusual 19th-century wooden pier with four towers. Ahlbeck's promenade is lined with turn-of-the-century villas, some of which are now small but as yet unsophisticated hotels. Much of the island is a nature reserve that provides refuge for a number of rare birds, including the giant sea eagle, which has a wing span of up to 8 feet. Most of Usedom is German territory, except for the easternmost corner, which belongs to Poland. If you stroll along the beach to the right of Ahlbeck's pier you'll come to the border. (U.S. citizens can now enter Poland without a visa.) Just west of Ahlbeck, you'll come to Heringsdorf, the oldest resort on the island, and the place chosen by Russian playwright Maxim Gorky for a quiet sojourn during 1922. He stayed in the villa called Irmgard, now a protected monument.

23 At the northern end of Usedom is **Peenemünde,** the launch site of the world's first jet rockets, the V1 and V2, developed by Germany toward the end of World War II and fired at London (*see* above).

Usedom is the end of this tour. If you are traveling by car you can leave the island by another causeway at the southwest corner, reached from the town of Usedom and emerging on the mainland at Anklam. From Anklam you can take Route 109 all the way to Berlin (162 kilometers, or 101 miles). If you are traveling on to Poland, follow Route 109 and turn left at Pasewalk into Route 104. From there it is 85 kilometers (53 miles) to the border and the Polish town of Szczecin, still called Stettin by the Germans.

What to See and Do with Children

The **Zoologischer Garten** at Rostock has one of the biggest collections of exotic animals and birds in northern Germany. This zoo is particularly noted for its polar bears, some of which were bred in Rostock. *Tiergartenallee 10, tel. 0381/37171. Admission: DM 3.50 adults, DM 2 children. Open May–Sept., daily 7:30 AM–8 PM; Oct.–Apr., daily 7:30–5:30.*

In Stralsund, an **aquarium** of Baltic Sea life is part of the maritime museum the Meeresmuseum, which also displays the skeleton of a giant whale and a 25-foot-high chunk of coral. *Katharinenberg 14a. Admission: DM 2.50 adults, DM 1 children. Open May–Oct., daily 10–5; Nov.–Apr., Wed.–Sun. 10–5.*

Along the Warnow River 5 kilometers (3 miles) north of the center of Rostock, you'll find a museum of shipbuilding on board the old freighter *Frieden.* The museum is in the hold of the 10,000-ton ship, built in 1952, which also houses a youth hostel and a small restaurant. The *Frieden* is moored to the riverbank on the right-hand side of the road. *Schiffbaumuseum. Schmarl 22. Admission: DM3 adults, DM1.50 children. Open Sept.–June, Tues.–Sun. 8:30–4:30; July–Aug. daily 8:30–4:30.*

If the weather is too bad for outdoor swimming, children will be just as pleased to splash in the heated seawater pool at Warnemünde. *Seepromenadestr. Admission: DM 3.50 adults, DM 2 children. Open May–Sept., daily 9–7.*

After a sea storm, head for a beach and join the locals in the perennial quest for amber stone washed up among the seaweed. Your children may also stumble upon a little pebble with a hole worn in the middle. Prevalent on this coast, they are called *Hühnergötter* (chicken gods) by the locals, who believe they bring good luck.

Shopping

The choice of goods, as well as the number of shops, has improved considerably in eastern Germany since 1989, but the retail industry is still very much in flux. However, antiques and bric-a-brac that have languished in cellars and attics since World War II are still surfacing, and the occasional bargain can be found. The best places to look are **Schwerin** (on and around Schmiedestrasse and Schloss-strasse and **Rostock** (along Kröpellingerstrasse and side streets.) You can buy amber baubles at the state-owned jewelry factory adjacent to the Bernsteinmuseum in **Ribnitz-Damgarten.** The Spring Markets held during April and May in **Stralsund** include a multitude of flea-market stalls.

Sports and Fitness

Biking The coastal region is ideally flat for cycling, a fact that numerous entrepreneurs have been quick to note. So now, not only do the bigger hotels provide bicycles for guests, but lots of shops are beginning to rent them on a daily or weekly basis at modest rates. However, train stations in this region are not yet renting bicycles. Escorted tours are being organized by the tourist offices; contact the regional tourist office in **Rostock** for more information.

Camping There are 150 campsites scattered along the coast. Contact the local tourist offices for a list of locations and facilities offered.

Fishing Fishing is another rapidly expanding leisure industry. Every port along the coast now has small boats for hire, and some boatmen will lead you to the shoals. There's freshwater angling in season in the rivers and in **Schweriner See** lake, but equipment may sometimes be in short supply. For information on equipment availability, contact the Rostock tourist office (tel. 0381/22619) for Warnemünde harbor and the Schwerin tourist office (tel. 0385/864509) for the Schweriner See.

Water Sports As private enterprise revives, a wide range of water-based activities is becoming available: windsurfing, sailing, surfing (although, to be realistic, the waves here are modest), and pedalboat riding. Equipment is available for hire at the beach resorts. If you have difficulty locating what you want, contact the local tourist offices. The best protected area along the coast for sailing is **Grosser Jasmunder Bodden,** a huge bay on Rügen Island. Boats for the bay can be hired at **Lietzow** and **Ralswiek. Warnemünde** has an international sailing regatta in July.

Beaches

Good beaches exist all along the Baltic coast. Virtually all the sandy beaches are clean and safe, sloping gently into the water. At the height of the season (July–August), the seaside resort beaches, with food services and toilets, are packed. The busiest are at **Bansin** (Usedom Island), **Binz** (Rügen Island), **Ostseebad Kühlungsborn,** and **Warnemünde.** More remote and quieter beaches can be found at **Timmendorf** on **Poel Island,** where the water quality is particularly good (you can drive there from Wismar, or take a White Fleet boat); **Kap Arkona** (reachable on foot only); and **Hiddensee Island,** off Rügen. The prettiest coves and beaches are located at **Ahrenshoop** on the Darss peninsula, **Nienhagen** (near Warnemünde), and the **Grosser Jasmunder Bodden** on Rügen Island to the west of Lietzow.

Some beaches allow nude bathing; in German it's known as *Freikörperkultur* (literally, "free body culture"), FKK for short. The most popular of these bare-all beaches are at Nienhagen and Prerow (on Darss).

Dining and Lodging

Dining

As in all other areas of former East Germany the number and variety of eating places are far more limited than in the western half of Germany. The situation is quickly changing, however, heralding both a return of traditional regional dishes and the first-time appearance of upmarket international cuisine. For the moment, the bigger towns and cities offer the best choice, but it is also increasingly possible to stumble across a new, out-of-the-way restaurant or an old pub with a new menu. Potatoes and fish remain the two main staples in the area. Among the local specialties to look out for are *Mecklenburger Griebenroller,* a custardy casserole of grated potatoes, eggs, herbs, and chopped bacon; *Mecklenburger Fischsuppe,* a hearty fish soup with vegetables, tomatoes, and sour cream; and *Pannfisch,* the region's own fish patty. A delicacy that originated during the time of Sweden's influence is *Grützwurst,* an oatmeal-based liver sausage sweetened with raisins. A favorite local nightcap since the 17th century is *Eierbier* (egg beer), a concoction of egg whites, beer, ginger, cinnamon, sugar, and water stirred vigorously and served warm. It's said to soothe the stomach, and it's guaranteed to give you a sound night's sleep.

Highly recommended restaurants in each price category are indicated with a star ★.

Category	Cost*
Very Expensive	over DM 50
Expensive	DM 40–50

Moderate	DM 25–40
Inexpensive	under DM 25

** per person for a three-course meal, excluding drinks*

Lodging

The choice of hotels in this area remains limited. The bigger, more expensive modern hotels established under the former regime provide the best facilities, albeit rather functional and unfashionable. Smaller hotels and pensions range from the charming but basic to the charmless and basic. In high season all accommodations, especially along the coast, are in great demand. Try to book well in advance, but if this is not possible, throw yourself at the mercy of the local tourist office, which will probably be able to find you simple, inexpensive bed-and-breakfast accommodations in a private home. Highly recommended hotels are indicated with a star ★.

Category	Cost*
Very Expensive	over DM 180
Expensive	DM 120–180
Moderate	DM 70–120
Inexpensive	under DM 70

** All prices are for a standard double room for two, including tax and service charge.*

Bad Doberan
Dining
★ **Weisser Pavilion.** A Chinese pagodalike structure built in the 19th century in an English-style park is an exotic setting for lunch or high tea (the café closes at 8 PM). Specialties are cheese and beef fondue and a fiery dessert drink with the intimidating name of *Feuerzangenbowle*, a mélange of fruits flambéed with pear schnapps. *Am Kamp, tel. 038203/2326. Reservations advised. Dress: informal. No credit cards. Closed Sat. Moderate.*

Lodging **Hotel Kurhaus.** This late-18th-century half-timbered building has been accommodating visitors for more than 125 years. It was completely renovated in 1986 to raise it to international standards. Rooms are plainly but comfortably furnished. *August-Bebelstr. 2, tel. 038203/3036. 37 rooms, most with bath or shower. Facilities: restaurant. AE. Moderate.*

Greifswald
Dining **Ratsweinkeller.** Down in the dimly lit vaulted cellars of the medieval town hall, the kitchen offers an international menu. The game dishes, in season, are particularly mouth-watering; order the rabbit in green-pepper sauce if it's available. The *Griebenroller* is also exceptionally good. *Platz der Freundschaft 2, tel. 03834/3285. Reservations advised. Dress: informal. No credit cards. Moderate.*

Lodging **Boddenhus.** A nondescript apartment-block-style building reflects the rooms within: drab furnishings and plain carpets and walls. The hotel's facilities, however, are generally excellent, from the tennis courts to the sauna bar. *Karl-Liebknecht-Ring 1, tel. 03834/5241. 75 rooms, most with bath, and 9 suites with bath. Facilities: restaurant, café, 2 bars, sauna, solarium, beauty salon, tennis courts. AE, DC, MC, V. Closed Jan. 2–15. Moderate.*

Kühlungsborn
Dining and Lodging
★ **Arendsee.** This new low-rise hotel has been tastefully designed to blend in with the adjoining turn-of-the-century villas. Rooms are exceptionally well decorated in pastel colors and furnished with light, patterned easy chairs, as well as TV and minibar. The Arendsee caters to families with young children, who need connecting rooms or extra beds. The restaurant offers a mix of regional and international dishes. *Strandstr. 46, tel. 038293/691. 66 rooms and 6 suites with bath. Facilities: restaurant, indoor saltwater pool, sauna, solarium, sun terrace. AE, DC, MC, V. Expensive.*

Lübeck
Dining and Lodging
Mövenpick Hotel Lysia. The location of this ultramodern member of the Swiss-owned chain is perfect—a two-minute walk from the famous Holsten Gate and the old town, and five minutes from the main train station. If you fancy an Old World atmosphere, the Mövenpick is not for you. Rattan furniture, lots of brass details, and vividly colored contemporary paintings create a bright, breezy look throughout, although the built-in furniture in the guest rooms smacks of motel decor. The menu in the sprawling, too brightly lit restaurant is daunting in its variety—from Swiss specialties such as *Rösti* to venison with lingonberries and other local seasonal fare—and the chef succeeds beyond all expectations. Save room for the dizzying array of gooey ice-cream concoctions. *Bein Holstentor, tel. 0451/1504–0, fax 0451/1504111. 197 rooms with bath. Facilities: restaurant, pub, shop, Hertz reservation desk, fitness center, sauna, indoor and outdoor parking. AE, DC, MC, V. Very Expensive.*

Dining
★ **Wullenwever.** Culinary experts say this restaurant has set a new standard of dining sophistication for Lübeck. It is certainly one of the most attractive places to eat in the town, with nursery-blue furniture, chandeliers, and oil paintings hanging on pale pastel walls. In summer tables are set in a quiet flower-strewn courtyard. Try the homemade pasta in truffle cream, or the baked pike-perch fillets with red-wine sauce. *Beckergrube 71, tel. 0451/704333. Reservations necessary. Jacket and tie required. AE, DC, MC, V. Expensive.*

Lodging
★ **Kaiserhof.** The most attractive hotel in Lübeck consists of two early 19th-century merchant's houses linked together, tastefully renovated and retaining many of the original architectural features. It's located just outside the moated old-town center—a five-minute walk from the cathedral—and although the hotel lacks a full restaurant, it offers many other facilities in short supply elsewhere in the region. *Kronsforder Allee 13, tel. 0451/791011. 67 rooms and 6 suites with bath. Facilities: café, bar, indoor pool, sauna, solarium, fitness room, garden terrace. AE, DC, MC, V. Expensive–Very Expensive.*

Jensen. Only a stone's throw from the Holstentor, this very comfortable and long-established, family-run hotel is ideally situated for viewing all the main attractions, and faces the "moat" that surrounds the old town. *An der Obertrave 4, tel. 0451/71646. 44 rooms and 2 suites with bath. Facilities: restaurant, wine bar. AE, DC, MC, V. Expensive.*

★ **Altstadt.** Behind the landmark old facade stands a hotel that opened in 1984. The Altstadt offers modern but not luxurious comforts. The studios, fitted with small kitchens, are a particularly good value if you plan to stay a few days. There is no restaurant. *Fischergrube 52, tel. 0451/72083. 19 rooms and 9 studios with bath. AE, MC. Moderate.*

Rostock
Dining

Riga. This modern, comfortable redbrick and oak-paneled restaurant in the Hotel Warnow (*see* below) specializes in Latvian cuisine. Fish figures prominently. Ask for the baked Baltic cod (*Kabeljau*) and the *Pilzrahmsuppe*, wild mushroom soup with ham. *Hermann-Duncker-Platz 4, tel. 0381/37381. Reservations advised. Jacket and tie required. AE, DC, MC, V. Expensive.*

Fünf Giebel Haus. This modern but rustic-style wine tavern with burnished redwood paneling and chunky wood tables serves regional fare that includes creamed button-mushroom soup with fresh herbs, and pork fillets in pepper sauce with almond-potato cakes. *Breitstr. 21, tel. 0381/22660. Reservations advised. Dress: informal. No credit cards. Moderate.*

★ **Zur Kogge.** Looking like the cabin of some ancient sailing vessel, this old sailors' beer tavern serves mostly fish. Order the Mecklenburger Fischsuppe if it's on the menu; Pannfisch is also a popular choice. *Wokrenterstr. 27, tel. 0381/34493. Reservations essential in evening. Dress: informal. No credit cards. Inexpensive.*

Lodging

Warnow. This modern eight-story building is decorated in a clumsy mixture of styles, from a pale pinewood cellar bar to the mock-Louis XV Salon Granitz; the reception area looks like a bank foyer. Rooms are cozy but dated, also eclectically furnished. The Warnow does have its strong points: a central location and much-sought-after modern comforts. Warning: More than half of the rooms are singles. *Hermann-Duncker-Platz 4, tel. 0381/37381. 312 rooms with bath. Facilities: 2 restaurants, café, 2 bars, beer garden. AE, DC, MC, V. Expensive.*

Congress. True to its name, this hotel caters to by-the-sea conferences. Most facilities of the hotel, which resembles a '60s-era university building, are geared to the business traveler. Rooms are bright but plain and cheaply furnished. *Leningraderstr. 45, tel. 0381/7030. 250 rooms, most with bath or shower. Facilities: restaurant, bars. AE, DC. Moderate–Expensive.*

Rügen Island
Dining

Gastmahl des Meeres. The decor is faded, but the fish is fresh at this lively and popular restaurant in Sassnitz. Regional dishes such as Pannfisch and Mecklenburger Fischsuppe are served, but go for the house specialty: *Zander* (pike-perch) in an herb-cream sauce. *Strandpromenade 2, tel. 038393/22320. Reservations advised for dinner. Dress: informal. No credit cards. Closed Mon. Moderate.*

Dining and Lodging

★ **Cliff-Hotel Rügen.** There are enough distractions at this all-in-one seaside resort in Sellin to keep the whole family entertained. Rooms are painted in bright pastel shades, with simple, colorfully patterned chairs; most have sea views. Guests can take short sea trips aboard the hotel yacht, complete with sun deck. The Seeterrassen restaurant serves a mix of international and local dishes. *An der Küste 1, Sellin, tel. 038393/80. 162 rooms and 6 suites with bath. Facilities: café, bar, indoor pool, sauna, beauty salon, tennis court, bowling alley, sun terrace. AE, V. Very Expensive.*

Mitropa-Rügen-Hotel. Many of the rooms here provide views of the busy little port of Sassnitz, where ferries to Sweden (Trelleborg) operate. Among the attractions of this well-established but modern hotel is a dance hall where locals and summer visitors congregate. The best of the two restaurants is the rustically decorated Rügenklause, where you can select from a menu that ranges from steak and french fries to such local specialties as *Griebenroller. Seestr. 1, Sassnitz, tel. 038393/32090. 147 rooms and 2 suites with bath. Facilities: café, bars, indoor pool, sauna, solarium, sun terrace, hairdresser. No credit cards. Expensive.*

★ **Nordperd.** This modern, four-story hotel is located on the southeast tip of the island at the seaside resort village of Göhren. The decor is white and bright, with cheerful patterned upholstery and curtains. One of the better-equipped hotels on the island—all rooms have a TV, phone, and minibar (some have coastal views)—it has a cheerful restaurant serving regional dishes. Look for *Rügenwild*, a pot roast made with game. *Nordperd-str. 10, Göhren, tel. 038393/381. 51 rooms with bath. Facilities: restaurant, bar, fitness room, sauna, sun terrace. AE, DC, MC, V. Expensive.*

Schwerin
Dining

★ **Weinhaus Uhle.** One of the best eating places in Schwerin, it's named after the wine merchant who opened the restaurant back in 1740. You can dine on regional specialties served in a colorful, unspoiled setting, accompanied by a small band that plays nightly. *Schusterstr. 13–15, tel. 0385/864455. Reservations advised. Dress: informal. No credit cards. Moderate–Expensive.*

Waldburg. This cozy restaurant set on the banks of the Schweriner See specializes in game. Be on the lookout for *geräucherten Gans* (smoked goose). *Schlossgartenallee 70, tel. 0385/812552. Reservations advised. Dress: informal. No credit cards. Moderate.*

Lodging

★ **Stadt Schwerin.** This modern hotel will put you right in the center of town. Rooms are pleasant but not luxurious. The hotel operates its own cruises on Schwerin's giant lake. *Grunthalplatz 5–7, tel. 0385/812498. 162 rooms and 4 suites with bath. Facilities: restaurant, bar, indoor pool, sauna, nightclub. AE, DC, MC, V. Expensive–Very Expensive.*

Niederländischer Hof. The facilities at this small, comfortable, established hotel in the center of the old town are above average for the Baltic Coast. The restaurant specializes in Mecklenburg dishes. *Karl-Marx-Str. 12, tel. 0385/83727. 32 rooms, most with bath. Facilities: restaurant, bar. No credit cards. Moderate.*

Stralsund
Dining

★ **Scheelehaus.** A high, beamed ceiling and half-timbered walls of red brick give this centuries-old restaurant the air of a baronial hall. The 10-foot-high windows still have the original thick, bull's-eye panes. House specialties include onion soup, and pork with peaches and *Kartoffelbällchen*—potato balls filled with an almond, apple, and cinnamon mixture. *Fährstr. 23, tel. 03831/2987. Reservations advised for dinner. Dress: informal. No credit cards. Moderate.*

Lodging

Baltic. The friendliness of the staff makes up for the lack of luxury in this simply furnished old hotel in the historic heart of town. It is often fully booked, especially in high summer. If you dine in the restaurant, try the spicy Hungarian goulash or the *Kasslerbraten*, smoked pork coated in honey. *Frankendamm 17, tel. 03831/5381. 21 rooms, 2 with bath, and 3 suites with bath. Facilities: restaurant, bar, disco. No credit cards. Moderate–Expensive.*

Usedom Island
Dining

★ **Cafe Asgard.** A visit here is a step back into the 1920s, which is when this restaurant with dancing first opened its doors. You'll dine amid silk wallpaper, potted plants, crisp white napery, and fresh flowers. The specialty is *Feuertopf Göttergarten*, a spicy fondue. The Asgard is open all day, so if you stop by between meal times, settle for a homemade pastry. If you're in a foot-tapping mood, visit the Golden Twenties dance hall above the restaurant. *Strandpromenade 13, Bansin, tel. Bansin 558 (operator only). Reservations advised for dinner in July and Aug. Dress: informal. No credit cards. Moderate.*

★ **Seebrücke.** Perched on pilings over the Baltic, the "Sea Bridge" is the historic center of Ahlbeck. Built in Scandinavian Romantic style in the 19th century, this structure is punctuated by four towers and wrapped with a promenade. Run by a Boston businessman, the Seebrücke serves moderately priced lunch and dinner, and as you might expect, the emphasis is on seafood. If you don't want a full meal, stop in to enjoy the building and the view, over coffee and a piece of one of the delectable cakes. *Dünenstr, tel. Seebrücke 8320 (operator only). Reservations recommended for dinner. Dress: informal. AE, MC, V. Moderate.*

Dining and Lodging

★ **Ostseehotel.** Generations of vacationing families have stayed at this snug, if slightly dated, hotel in a 19th-century villa on Ahlbeck's promenade. Most of the airy but spartan rooms have sea views; few have private bathrooms. The restaurant serves mainly hearty local pork and potato dishes, but the goulash soup is exceptional; also look for fresh pike-perch in season. Dances are held several times a week during the summer. *Dünenstr. 41, Ahlbeck, tel. Ahlbeck 8132 (operator only). 37 rooms, most without bath. No credit cards. Moderate.*

Hotel Stadt Berlin. This turn-of-the-century villa turned hotel in Heringsdorf has been accommodating summer visitors since the 1920s. Its facilities are rather well-worn and some of the furnishings threadbare and dated, but there is a friendly holiday atmosphere. The bright little restaurant serves solid but predictable local fare. During the summer there are lively dances several times a week. *Ernt-Thälmann-str. 38, Heringsdorf, tel. Heringsdorf 413 (operator only). 26 rooms, none with bath. No credit cards. Closed Jan. Inexpensive.*

Warnemünde

Dining

★ **Neptun Spezialitätenrestaurants.** The six restaurants at Neptun Hotel (*see* below) are the best places to eat in the Warnemünde/Rostock area, both for variety and quality. Each restaurant specializes in a national cuisine: German (northern cuisine); Swedish (particularly fish; try the crab Malmo); Russian (the *Tschaika*—steak with rice—is recommended); Hungarian (the *Siebenbürger Schweinelende*—pork in a spicy sauce, Transylvania style—is particularly good), Cuban (*Kubanische Bodega*, specially processed raw fish with mussels and onions). The sixth restaurant serves a wide selection of Asian food, from Malaysian to Vietnamese. *Schillerstr. 14, tel. 0381/5381. Reservations advised, and necessary on summer weekends. Dress: informal. AE, DC, MC, V. Expensive.*

Lodging

★ **Neptun.** One of the few postwar hotels on the coast, the 19-story concrete-and-glass Neptun is an eyesore on the outside, but inside has many redeeming qualities often lacking elsewhere in this region. Every one of the neat and plain standardized rooms has a sea view. *Seestr. 19, tel. 0381/5371. 348 rooms with bath. Facilities: 6 restaurants, bars, outdoor and indoor pools, tennis courts, sauna, solarium, therapeutic baths, supervised children's playroom, beauty salon, disco. AE, DC, MC, V. Very Expensive.*

Promenadenhotel. The gray exterior of this small hotel belies the bright and friendly interior, which wears a 1960s look. Some of the rooms overlook the sea promenade. The in-house dance hall is a popular venue on weekends. *Seestr. 5, tel. 0381/52782. 23 rooms, most without bath, and 1 suite with bath. Facilities: restaurant, bar, dance hall. No credit cards. Inexpensive.*

Wismar
Dining

★ **Alte Schwede.** Regarded as one of the most attractive, authentic taverns on the Baltic—and correspondingly busy—the eatery has a cooking staff intent on reviving Mecklenburg's traditional cuisine, which features both game and fish dishes. *Am Markt 20, tel. 03841/3520. Reservations advised for dinner. Dress: informal. No credit cards. Moderate.*

Weinberg. An old wood-beamed wine tavern near the market square has the well-worn look to be expected of a place that has been in business since 1575. The furniture is a bit threadbare and the menu unspectacular, but there is an excellent wine list. *Lübschestr. 31, tel. 03841/3550. Reservations necessary on Fri. and Sat. evenings when dances are held. Dress: informal. No credit cards. Closed Mon. Moderate.*

Gastmahl des Meeres. This small, no-frills fish restaurant is favored by locals as well as visitors. Ask for the rich fish-and-vegetable soup. *Altböterstr. 6, tel. 03841/2134. No reservations. Dress: informal. No credit cards. Inexpensive.*

Lodging

★ **Hotel Wismar.** Wismar's only hotel, it's handily located in the old-town center a few strides from the market square and other attractions. It's small and well-worn but clean, with a reasonably priced restaurant serving regional dishes. *Breitstr. 10, tel. 03841/2498. 18 rooms, none with bath. No credit cards. Moderate.*

Mecklenburger Hof. This simple pension, clean and plainly furnished, stands in the old-town center just a few minutes' walk from the old market square. *Gerberstr. 16, tel. 03841/2706. 10 rooms, none with bath. No credit cards. Inexpensive.*

The Arts and Nightlife

The Arts

A resurgence of traditional *Volksfeste*—popular festivals—is following in the wake of 1989, in particular *Fischerfeste* (fishermen's festivals) in the ports and coastal towns. For a schedule of events contact the local tourist offices.

Rostock and **Schwerin** have the biggest variety of entertainment to offer, including classical music concerts. Rostock's Volkstheater (Doberanerstr. 134, tel. 0381/244253) performs plays (German only) and concerts. Plays (German only) and operas are performed regularly at **Schwerin's** Mecklenburger Staatstheater (Am Alten Garten, tel. 0385/83993). Concerts occasionally take place at **Wismar's** Stadttheater (Philipp-Müller-str. 5). Contact the local tourist offices for the latest information on performances.

The summer season brings with it a plethora of special concerts, the highlights being the "Music in May" concerts at **Rostock** and **Stralsund; Greifwald's** Bach Week in June, including open-air concerts at the ruins of the Eldena cloister; **Schwerin** Summerfest on the Lankowersee lake, also in June; an international brass band competition in **Rostock** in July; and a series of concerts in **Bad Doberan** in August.

Nightlife

Rostock, Schwerin, and **Warnemünde** have the most to offer night owls. Nearly all the seaside resorts, even the smallest, have almost nightly dances during the summer months. The biggest hotels are the places to head for in search of fun.

In **Rostock,** the Warnow Hotel's Newa Bar has nightly dancing and cabaret; the Sky Bar on the 19th floor of the Neptun Hotel offers the chance to sit under the stars (the roof opens up) and watch the ship lights twinkling on the sea until 4 AM. Discos worth trying are the Trocadero in **Wismar** (Wismarerstr. 6), and the Kurhaus in **Warnemünde** (Seestr.) In **Schwerin** there's the Achteck, a big disco in a new octagonal building (Neumühlerstr. 20), and the Lesecafe am Pfaffenteich (Wilhelm-Pieck-str. 16), which attracts a very young coffee and cola crowd. Disco dances are held in the Strandpavillon (Am Strand 15) Friday–Sunday until 4 AM. **Stralsund's** Baltic Hotel (Frankendamm 22) has dancing in the main bar. Dancing and cabaret are to be found at the Störtebeker Keller (Ossenreyerstr. 40).

German Vocabulary

Words and Phrases

	English	German	Pronunciation
Basics	Yes/no	Ja/nein	yah/nine
	Please	Bitte	**bit**-uh
	Thank you (very much)	Danke (vielen Dank)	**dahn**-kuh (**fee**-lun dahnk)
	Excuse me	Entschuldigen Sie	ent-**shool**-de-gen zee
	I'm sorry	Es tut mir leid.	es toot meer lite
	Good day	Guten Tag	**goo**-ten tahk
	Good bye	Auf Wiedersehen	auf **vee**-der-zane
	Mr./Mrs.	Herr/Frau	hair/frau
	Miss	Fräulein	**froy**-line
	Pleased to meet you.	Sehr erfreut.	zair air-**froit**
	How are you?	Wie geht es Ihnen?	vee **gate** es **ee**-nen?
	Very well, thanks.	Sehr gut, danke.	zair goot **dahn**-kuh
	And you?	Und Ihnen?	oont **ee**-nen

Numbers	1 eins	eints	6 sechs	zex
	2 zwei	tsvai	7 sieben	**zee**-ben
	3 drei	dry	8 acht	ahkt
	4 vier	fear	9 neun	noyn
	5 fünf	fumph	10 zehn	tsane

Days of the Week	Sunday	Sonntag	**zone**-tahk
	Monday	Montag	**moan**-tahk
	Tuesday	Dienstag	**deens**-tahk
	Wednesday	Mittwoch	**mit**-voah
	Thursday	Donnerstag	**doe**-ners-tahk
	Friday	Freitag	**fry**-tahk
	Saturday	Samstag	**zahm**-stahk

Useful Phrases	Do you speak English?	Sprechen Sie Englisch?	**shprek**-hun zee **eng**-glish?
	I don't speak German.	Ich spreche kein Deutsch.	ich **shprek**-uh kine doych
	Please speak slowly.	Bitte sprechen Sie langsam.	**bit**-uh **shprek**-en zee **lahng**-zahm
	I am American/British	Ich bin Amerikaner(in)/ Engländer(in)	ich bin a-mer-i-**kahn**-er(in) **eng**-glan-der(in)
	My name is . . .	Ich heiße . . .	ich **hi**-suh
	Yes please/No, thank you	Ja, bitte/Nein, danke	yah **bi**-tuh/**nine** dahng-kuh
	Where are the restrooms?	Wo ist die Toilette?	vo ist dee twah-**let**-uh
	Left/right	Links/rechts	links/rechts

Open/closed	Offen/geschlossen	O-fen/geh-**shloss**-en
Where is . . .	Wo ist . . .	**vo** ist
the train station?	der Bahnhof?	dare **bahn**-hof
the bus stop?	die Bushaltestelle?	dee **booss**-hahlt-uh-**shtel**-uh
the subway station?	die U-Bahn-Station?	dee OO-bahn-**staht**-sion
the airport?	der Flugplatz?	dare **floog**-plats
the post office?	die Post?	dee **post**
the bank?	die Bank?	dee **banhk**
the police station?	die Polizeistation?	dee po-lee-**tsai**-staht-sion
the American/ British consulate?	das amerikanische/ britische Konsulat?	dahs a-mare-i-**kahn**-ishuh/**brit**-ish-uh cone-tso-**laht**
the Hospital?	das Krankenhaus?	dahs **krahnk**-en-house
the telephone	das Telefon	dahs te-le-**fone**
I'd like to have . . .	Ich hätte gerne . . .	ich **het**-uh gairn
a room	ein Zimmer	I-nuh **tsim**-er
the key	den Schlüssel	den **shluh**-sul
a map	eine Karte	I-nuh **cart**-uh
How much is it?	Wieviel kostet das?	**vee**-feel **cost**-et dahs?
I am ill/sick	Ich bin krank	ich bin krahnk
I need . . .	Ich brauche . . .	ich **brow**-khuh
a doctor	einen Arzt	I-nen artst
the police	die Polizei	dee po-li-**tsai**
help	Hilfe	**hilf**-uh
Stop!	Halt!	hahlt
Fire!	Feuer!	**foy**-er
Caution/Look out!	Achtung!/Vorsicht!	**ahk**-tung/**for**-zicht

Dining Out

A bottle of . . .	eine Flasche . . .	I-nuh **flash**-uh
A cup of . . .	eine Tasse . . .	I-nuh **tahs**-uh
A glass of . . .	ein Glas . . .	ein glahss
Ashtray	der Aschenbecher	dare Ahsh-en-bekh-er
Bill/check	die Rechnung	dee **rekh**-nung
Do you have . . . ?	Haben Sie . . . ?	**hah**-ben zee

Food	Essen	**es**-en
I am a diabetic.	Ich bin Diabetiker.	ich bin dee-ah-**bet**-ik-er
I am on a diet.	Ich halte Diät.	ich **hahl**-tuh dee-**et**
I am a vegetarian.	Ich bin Vegetarier.	ich bin ve-guh-**tah**-re-er
I cannot eat . . .	Ich kann . . . nicht essen	ich kan . . . nicht **es**-en
I'd like to order	Ich möchte bestellen . . .	ich **mohr**-shtuh buh-shtel-en
Is the service included?	Ist die Bedienung inbegriffen?	ist dee beh-**dee**-nung **in**-beh-grig-en
Menu	die Speisekarte	dee **shpie**-zeh-car-tuh
Napkin	die Serviette	dee zair-vee-**eh**-tuh
Separate/all together	Getrennt/alles zusammen	ge-**trent/ah**-les tsu-**zah**-men

Menu Guide

English	*German*
Made to order	Auf Bestellung
Side dishes	Beilagen
Extra charge	Extraaufschlag
When available	Falls verfügbar
Entrées	Hauptspeisen
Homemade	Hausgemacht
. . . (not) included	. . . (nicht) inbegriffen
Depending on the season	je nach Saison
Local specialties	Lokalspezialitäten
Set menu	Menü
Lunch menu	Mittagskarte
Desserts	Nachspeisen
. . . style	. . . nach . . . Art
. . . at your choice	. . . nach Wahl
. . . at your request	. . . nach Wunsch
Prices are . . .	Preise sind . . .
Service included	*inklusive Bedienung*
Value added tax included	*inklusive Mehrwertsteuer (Mwst.)*
Specialty of the house	Spezialität des Hauses
Soup of the day	Tagessuppe
Appetizers	Vorspeisen
Is served from . . . to . . .	Wird von . . . bis . . . serviert

Breakfast

Bread	Brot
Roll(s)	Brötchen
Butter	Butter
Eggs	Eier
Hot	heiß
Cold	kalt
Decaffeinated	koffeinfrei
Jam	Konfitüre
Milk	Milch
Orange juice	Orangensaft
Scrambled eggs	Rühreier
Bacon	Speck
Fried eggs	Spiegeleier
White bread	Weißbrot
Lemon	Zitrone
Sugar	Zucker

Appetizers

Oysters	Austern
Frog legs	Froschschenkel
Goose liver paté	Gänseleberpastete
Lobster	Hummer
Shrimp	Krabben
Crawfish	Krebs
Salmon	Lachs
Mussels	Muscheln
Prosciutto with melon	Parmaschinken mit Melone

Mushrooms	Pilze
Smoked . . .	Räucher . . .
Ham	Schinken
Snails	Schnecken
Asparagus	Spargel

Soups

Stew	Eintopf
Semolina dumpling soup	Grießnockerlsuppe
Goulash soup	Gulaschsuppe
Chicken soup	Hühnersuppe
Potato soup	Kartoffelsuppe
Liver dumpling soup	Leberknödelsuppe
Oxtail soup	Ochsenschwanzsuppe
Tomato soup	Tomatensuppe
Onion soup	Zwiebelsuppe

Methods of Preparation

Blue (boiled in salt and vinegar)	Blau
Baked	Gebacken
Fried	Gebraten
Steamed	Gedämpft
Grilled (broiled)	Gegrillt
Boiled	Gekocht
Sauteed	In Butter geschwenkt
Breaded	Paniert
Raw	Roh

When ordering steak, the English words "rare, medium, (well) done" are used and understood in German.

Fish and Seafood

Eel	Aal
Oysters	Austern
Trout	Forelle
Flounder	Flunder
Prawns	Garnelen
Halibut	Heilbutt
Lobster	Hummer
Scallops	Jakobsmuscheln
Cod	Kabeljau
Crawfish	Krebs
Salmon	Lachs
Spiny lobster	Languste
Mackerel	Makrele
Herring	Matjes
Mussels	Muscheln
Red sea bass	Rotbarsch
Sole	Seezunge
Squid	Tintenfisch
Tuna	Thunfisch

Meats

Mutton	Hammel
Veal	Kalb(s)
Lamb	Lamm

Beef	Rind(er)
Pork	Schwein(e)

Cuts of Meat

Example: For “Lammkeule” see “Lamm” (above) + “. . . keule” (below)

breast	. . . brust
scallopini	. . . geschnetzeltes
knuckle	. . . haxe
leg	. . . keule
liver	. . . leber
tenderloin	. . . lende
kidney	. . . niere
rib	. . . rippe
Meat patty	Frikadelle
Meat loaf	Hackbraten
Cured pork ribs	Kasseler Rippchen
Liver meatloaf	Leberkäse
Ham	Schinken
Sausage and cold cut platter	Schlachtplatte
Brawn	Sülze
Cooked beef with horseradish and cream sauce	Tafelspitz

Game and Poultry

Duck	Ente
Pheasant	Fasan
Goose	Gans
Chicken	Hähnchen (Huhn)
Hare	Hase
Deer	Hirsch
Rabbit	Kaninchen
Capon	Kapaun
Venison	Reh
Pigeon	Taube
Turkey	Truthahn
Quail	Wachtel

Vegetables

Eggplant	Aubergine
Red cabbage	Rotkohl
Cauliflower	Blumenkohl
Beans	Bohnen
green	*grüne*
white	*weiße*
Button mushrooms	Champignons
Peas	Erbsen
Cucumber	Gurke
Cabbage	Kohl
Lettuce	Kopfsalat
Leek	Lauch
Asparagus, peas and carrots	Leipziger Allerlei
Corn	Mais
Carrots	Mohrrüben
Peppers	Paprika
Chanterelle mushrooms	Pfifferlinge
Mushrooms	Pilze
Brussels sprouts	Rosenkohl

Red beets	Rote Beete
Celery	Sellerie
Asparagus (tips)	Spargel(spitzen)
Tomatoes	Tomaten
Cabbage	Weißkohl
Onions	Zwiebeln
Spring onions	Frühlingszwiebeln

Side dishes

Potato(s)	Kartoffel(n)
fried	*Brat . . .*
boiled in their jackets	*Pell . . .*
with parsley	*Petersilien . . .*
fried	*Röst . . .*
boiled in saltwater	*Salz . . .*
mashed	*. . . brei*
dumplings	*. . . klöße (knödel)*
pancakes	*. . . puffer*
salad	*. . . salat*
Pasta	Nudeln
French fries	Pommes Frittes
Rice	Reis
buttered	*Butter . . .*
steamed	*gedämpfter . . .*
Potato pancakes	Kartoffelpuffer

Condiments

Basil	Basilikum
Vinegar	Essig
Spice	Gewürz
Garlic	Knoblauch
Herbs	Kräuter
Caraway	Kümmel
Bay leaf	Lorbeer
Horseradish	Meerettich
Nutmeg	Muskatnuß
Oil	Öl
Parsley	Petersilie
Saffron	Safran
Sage	Salbei
Chives	Schnittlauch
Mustard	Senf
Artificial sweetener	Süßstoff
Cinnamon	Zimt
Sugar	Zucker
Salt	Salz
Horseradish	Meerrettich

Cheese

Mild:	Allgäuer Käse, Altenburger (goat cheese), Appenzeller, Greyerzer, Hüttenkäse (cottage cheese), Kümmelkäse (with carraway seeds), Quark, Räucherkäse (smoked cheese), Sahnekäse (creamy), Tilsiter, Ziegekäse (goat cheese).
Sharp:	Handkäse, Harzer Käse, Limburger.

curd	frisch
hard	hart
mild	mild
ripe	reif
sharp	scharf
soft	weich

Fruits

Apple	Apfel
Orange	Apfelsine
Apricot	Aprikose
Blueberry	Blaubeere
Blackberry	Brombeere
Strawberry	Erdbeere
Raspberry	Himbeere
Cherry	Kirsche
Grapefruit	Pampelmuse
Cranberry	Preiselbeere
Raisin	Rosine
Grape	Weintraube
Banana	Banane
Pear	Birne
Kiwi	Kiwi

Nuts

Peanuts	Erdnüsse
Hazelnuts	Haselnüsse
Coconut	Kokosnuß
Almonds	Mandeln
Chestnuts	Maronen

Desserts

. . . soufflé	. . . auflauf
. . . ice cream	. . . eis
. . . cake	. . . kuchen
Honey-almond cake	Bienenstich
Fruit cocktail	Obstsalat
Whipped cream	(Schlag)sahne
Black Forest cake	Schwarzwälder Kirschtorte

Drinks

chilled	eiskalt
with/without ice	mit/ohne Eis
with/without water	mit/ohne Wasser
straight	pur
room temperature	Zimmertemperatur
. . . brandy	. . . geist
. . . distilled liquor	. . . korn
. . . liqueur	. . . likör
. . . schnapps	. . . schnaps
Egg liquor	Eierlikör
Mulled claret	Glühwein
Caraway-flavored liquor	Kümmel
Fruit brandy	Obstler
Vermouth	Wermut

When ordering a Martini, you have to specify "gin (vodka) and vermouth", otherwise you will be given a vermouth (Martini & Rossi).

Beers

nonalcoholic	Alkoholfrei
A dark beer	Ein Dunkles
A light beer	Ein Helles
A mug (one quart)	Eine Maß
Draught	Vom Faß
Dark, bitter, high hops content	Altbier
Strong, high alcohol content	Bockbier (Doppelbock, Märzen)
Wheat beer with yeast	Hefeweizen
Light beer, strong hops aroma	Pils(ener)
Wheat beer	Weizen(bier)
Light beer and lemonade	Radlermaß
Wines	Wein
Red wine	Rotwein
White wine and mineral water	Schorle
Sparkling wine	Sekt
White wine	Weißwein
dry	herb
light	leicht
sweet	süß
dry	trocken
full-bodied	vollmundig

Nonalcoholic Drinks

Coffee	Kaffee
decaffeinated	*koffeinfrei*
with cream/sugar	*mit Milch/Zucker*
with artificial sweetener	*mit Süßstoff*
black	*schwarz*
Lemonade	Limonade
orange	*Orangen . . .*
lemon	*Zitronen . . .*
Milk	Milch
Mineral water	Mineralwasser
carbonated/non-carbonated	*mit/ohne Kohlensäure*
. . . juice	. . . saft
(hot) Chocolate	(heiße) Schokolade
Tea	Tee
iced tea	*Eistee*
herb tea	*Kräutertee*
with cream/lemon	*mit Milch/Zitrone*

Index

Personal Itinerary

Departure *Date*

Time

Transportation

Arrival *Date* *Time*

Departure *Date* *Time*

Transportation

Accommodations

Arrival *Date* *Time*

Departure *Date* *Time*

Transportation

Accommodations

Arrival *Date* *Time*

Departure *Date* *Time*

Transportation

Accommodations

Addresses

Name

Address

Telephone

Name

Address

Telephone

Name

Address

Telephone

Name

Address

Telephone

Name

Address

Telephone

Name

Address

Telephone

Name

Address

Telephone

Name

Address

Telephone

Name

Address

Telephone

Name

Address

Telephone

Name

Address

Telephone

Name

Address

Telephone

Name

Address

Telephone

Name

Address

Telephone

Name

Address

Telephone

Name

Address

Telephone

Fodor's Travel Guides

U.S. Guides

Alaska
Arizona
Boston
California
Cape Cod, Martha's Vineyard, Nantucket
The Carolinas & the Georgia Coast
Chicago
Disney World & the Orlando Area
Florida
Hawaii
Las Vegas, Reno, Tahoe
Los Angeles
Maine, Vermont, New Hampshire
Maui
Miami & the Keys
New England
New Orleans
New York City
Pacific North Coast
Philadelphia & the Pennsylvania Dutch Country
San Diego
San Francisco
Santa Fe, Taos, Albuquerque
Seattle & Vancouver
The South
The U.S. & British Virgin Islands
The Upper Great Lakes Region
USA
Vacations in New York State
Vacations on the Jersey Shore
Virginia & Maryland
Waikiki
Washington, D.C.

Foreign Guides

Acapulco, Ixtapa, Zihuatanejo
Australia & New Zealand
Austria
The Bahamas
Baja & Mexico's Pacific Coast Resorts
Barbados
Berlin
Bermuda
Brazil
Budapest
Budget Europe
Canada
Cancun, Cozumel, Yucatan Penisula
Caribbean
Central America
China
Costa Rica, Belize, Guatemala
Czechoslovakia
Eastern Europe
Egypt
Euro Disney
Europe
Europe's Great Cities
France
Germany
Great Britain
Greece
The Himalayan Countries
Hong Kong
India
Ireland
Israel
Italy
Italy's Great Cities
Japan
Kenya & Tanzania
Korea
London
Madrid & Barcelona
Mexico
Montreal & Quebec City
Morocco
The Netherlands Belgium & Luxembourg
New Zealand
Norway
Nova Scotia, Prince Edward Island & New Brunswick
Paris
Portugal
Rome
Russia & the Baltic Countries
Scandinavia
Scotland
Singapore
South America
Southeast Asia
South Pacific
Spain
Sweden
Switzerland
Thailand
Tokyo
Toronto
Turkey
Vienna & the Danube Valley
Yugoslavia

Fodor's Travel Guides

Special Series

Fodor's Affordables

Affordable Europe

Affordable France

Affordable Germany

Affordable Great Britain

Affordable Italy

Fodor's Bed & Breakfast and Country Inns Guides

California

Mid-Atlantic Region

New England

The Pacific Northwest

The South

The West Coast

The Upper Great Lakes Region

Canada's Great Country Inns

Cottages, B&Bs and Country Inns of England and Wales

The Berkeley Guides

On the Loose in California

On the Loose in Eastern Europe

On the Loose in Mexico

On the Loose in the Pacific Northwest & Alaska

Fodor's Exploring Guides

Exploring California

Exploring Florida

Exploring France

Exploring Germany

Exploring Paris

Exploring Rome

Exploring Spain

Exploring Thailand

Fodor's Flashmaps

New York

Washington, D.C.

Fodor's Pocket Guides

Pocket Bahamas

Pocket Jamaica

Pocket London

Pocket New York City

Pocket Paris

Pocket Puerto Rico

Pocket San Francisco

Pocket Washington, D.C.

Fodor's Sports

Cycling

Hiking

Running

Sailing

The Insider's Guide to the Best Canadian Skiing

Fodor's Three-In-Ones (guidebook, language cassette, and phrase book)

France

Germany

Italy

Mexico

Spain

Fodor's Special-Interest Guides

Cruises and Ports of Call

Disney World & the Orlando Area

Euro Disney

Healthy Escapes

London Companion

Skiing in the USA & Canada

Sunday in New York

Fodor's Touring Guides

Touring Europe

Touring USA: Eastern Edition

Touring USA: Western Edition

Fodor's Vacation Planners

Great American Vacations

National Parks of the West

The Wall Street Journal Guides to Business Travel

Europe

International Cities

Pacific Rim

USA & Canada